ECONOMICS

ECONOMICS
Australian Edition

ROGER WAUD
University of North Carolina, Chapel Hill

ANTHONY HOCKING
University of Tasmania

PHILIP MAXWELL
Curtin University of Technology

JOSEF BONNICI
Deakin University

HarperEducational

A Division of HarperCollinsPublishers

Adapted with permission from
Waud, Roger N. *Economics* (3rd edition)
Published by arrangement with Harper & Row Publishers, Inc.
New York, New York, USA

Copyright 1986 by Roger N. Waud

First Published February 1989, reprinted November 1989, December 1990
Harper Educational *Publishers*
a Division of Harper Collins *Publishers*
PO Box 226, Artarmon, NSW 2064, Australia.

Economics.

  Includes index.
  ISBN 0 06 312109 3

  1. Economics. 2. Waud, Roger N., 1938 –
  Economics.

330

Typeset by Saba Graphics, Christchurch, New Zealand
Printed in Australia by Macarthur Press

Brief Contents

Detailed Contents

3   The Nature of the Mixed Economy   51

4   Demand, Supply, and Price Determination   73

TWO
Aggregate Income, Employment, Fiscal Policy and International Trade   101

APPENDIX Indifference Curves and Consumer Demand 525

21 Applications of Demand and Supply   535

22 The Firm and its Costs of Production   559

SIX
Market Structure, Pricing and
Government Regulation   591

23 Perfect Competition and Price Takers   593

24 Monopoly and Monopoly Power   633

SEVEN
Price Determination of Economic Resources 735

Preface

The primary purpose of this book is to demonstrate how the principles of economics are used to analyse real-world events and problems. Waud's *Economics* which is now in its Fourth US edition has always had this aim. This first Australian edition maintains and develops this thrust in an Australian context.

As users of the previous US editions will know, Waud's *Economics* endeavours to provide an integrated learning package for students. It places emphasis on explaining key concepts and illustrating them with practical and familiar examples. Each chapter contains a number of pedagogical features to facilitate student understanding.

On Explaining Things

It may seem an odd pitch to make about a textbook, but this book places an emphasis on explanation. In recent years many economics principles texts seem to put a premium on being terse — even to the point of being 'slick'. But there is a trade-off between brevity and explanation. Given the need to explain, the ideal is to be as brief as possible but not briefer than necessary. As a practical matter, books typically and unavoidably end up somewhat to one side or the other of the ideal.

Every effort has been taken to make the book as understandable as possible. Numerous examples are provided to give concreteness to difficult concepts.

Checkpoints

Checkpoints appear in every chapter, generally at the ends of major sections. At each Checkpoint the student is signalled to stop and answer a series of questions about concepts just presented — to stop and check on his or her progress and grasp of the material. Questions and problems placed at the ends of chapters are too often easily ignored, like so much litter at the back of a closet that one is rarely forced to face. The Checkpoints are intended to surmount this problem by helping the student reconsider what has just been read — to assure the student's understanding of concepts as they are encountered. Answers to the Checkpoints appear at the back of the book to provide immediate feedback.

Learning Objectives

Learning objectives are listed and set off from the major text at the beginning of each chapter. They outline a plan of study for the chapter, as well as provide an overview of what's to be done. After completing the chapter, the student can also use the list of learning objectives as a quick check to see whether he or she has mastered the material in the chapter.

Policy Perspectives

One important feature of the book is the inclusion of 'Policy Perspectives'. These are a series of discussions of contemporary economic questions. Each chapter contains a number of policy perspectives which relate chapter content material to real world problems and provide students with the opportunity to grapple with those problems. Ultimately, a basic education in economics should attempt to develop a facility, indeed a habit, for disentangling and making sense of the important economic issues encountered daily in the popular press and on television. The policy perspectives provide effective vehicles for showing the beginning student why the study of economics is useful.

Economic Thinkers

Economic Thinkers essays are not so much personal biographies as studies in the history of economic thought. Their major purpose is to highlight the development of economic thinking on major problems and concerns while indicating the significant role that particular individuals have played in this development.

Key Terms and Concepts

Terminology is unavoidably abundant in economics. In addition, words that have several meanings in common everyday usage often have a more precise meaning when used in economics. Such words, along with other important economic terms, appear in boldface type when they are first introduced and defined in the text. The 'Key Terms and Concepts' list at the end of each chapter highlights the new terminology presented in the chapter. These terms and concepts are defined again in the glossary at the back of the book.

Summaries

The summaries at the end of each chapter are fairly comprehensive. They tie together the main concepts developed in the chapter as well as alert the student to areas that may require re-reading.

Questions and Problems

Questions and problems are also located at the end of each chapter. They are generally more complex and extended than the questions found in the Checkpoints. Some are almost case studies. Many may be readily used for class discussion. Answers to all end-of-chapter questions and problems are provided in the Instructor's Manual. The Checkpoints together with the end-of-chapter questions and problems and Policy Perspective questions provide significantly more in-text questions and problems than are offered by most other economic principles texts currently available.

Figures, Graphs, and Tables

Liberal use of real-world data is made in tables and figures throughout the book. Quite often, tables containing hypothetical data are used to illustrate particularly difficult concepts. The captions describing each graph and figure generally begin with a brief summary statement followed by a reasonably complete description of what is portrayed.

SUPPLEMENTS AND TEACHING AIDS

The text is supplemented by the following learning and teaching aids; two student study guides, and instructor's manual, transparency masters, and an expanded computerised test bank adapted from the comprehensive test bank provided for US students.

Study Guides

The *Microeconomics* Study Guide has been prepared by Sarah Male and Rosalie Viney of the Economics Department at the University of Tasmania. The *Macroeconomics* Study Guide has been compiled by Clive Reynoldson and Yvonne Melotte of the Western Australian College of Advanced Education. At the beginning of each study guide chapter there is a summary of the corresponding chapter in the textbook. Then a set of basic problems follows, with at least one problem for each basic concept developed in the textbook chapter. The problems are aimed at helping the student use the economic principles developed in the text to quantitatively analyse a specific issue. The basic problem set is followed by a set of multiple-choice questions, a set of true-false questions, and a set of problems, questions, and exercises on matching terms. Each of the sets of problems, questions and exercises is designed to give complete coverage to each major concept developed in the textbook chapter. The answers to all problems, questions, and exercises are given at the back of the study guide.

Instructor's Manual

Three suggested outlines for a one-semester course appear at the beginning of the Instructor's Manual. Each chapter of the manual first gives a summary of the corresponding textbook chapter along with a discussion of important chapter concepts and learning objectives. The manual contains answers to all end-of-chapter textbook questions and problems, and to Policy Perspectives questions. Multiple choice quizzes are also included for lecturer and tutor use.

Test Bank

The Computerized Test Bank has been adapted by Clive Reynoldson and Yvonne Melotte of the Western Australian CAE. The material has been thoroughly class-tested and integrated with the Australian *Economics*.

Transparency Masters

All important graphs, roughly 90 in number, are available to adopters as a set of transparency masters.

ACKNOWLEDGMENTS

Many people have made helpful comments and contributions to this book at various stages of its development. We owe an enormous amount to the many American academics who have assisted Roger in the preparation of the various American editions of this text. Others have given unstintingly towards the production of the Australian adaptation so that it reflects the quite different institutional background and different policy issues we face.

At the University of Tasmania, colleagues, including Sarah Male, Rosalie Viney, Mike Kidd, Peter Earl and Bob Rutherford have advised and persuaded, usually with success.

In preparing this edition we owe a particular debt of gratitude to our excellent secretarial assistance. At Curtin University, Pat Kendall, Debbie Peirce and Marlene Green have done a wonderful job. At Deakin, Margaret Agnew, Jenny Foot, Jan-Maree McIntyre, Yvonne Watts and June Gerrard must be similarly commended. At University of Tasmania, Julie Waldon must be singled out for special thanks in carrying out what amounts to a complex editorial task with great skill and forbearance. Without them this Australian edition would never have materialised.

For Harper and Row, Alex Macleod and Lawrie Grigg were the inspiration behind the project. Alex brought to it the necessary, but sometimes missing, quality of a determination to find out what the users of this book needed in a foundation text rather than what was felt to be good for them. He remains the link man for much of Australia between authors and users and we appreciate his presence. Lynne Segal, as with earlier projects, has done a highly professional job as production editor.

Tony Hocking, Philip Maxwell, Joe Bonnici and Roger Waud

POSTSCRIPT:
The response to the first printing of *Economics: Australian Edition* has been very pleasing. A number of users have passed on constructive comments and corrections which have been incorporated into this second printing. We wish to thank particularly Bill Junor, Trevor Stegman and Neil Warren from the University of New South Wales, David Spiers from Ballarat CAE, Stuart Hosking from Warrnambool IAE, Sarah Male, Michael Kidd and Julie Waldon from the University of Tasmania, Shirley Richardson from Gippsland IAE, and Dianne Thomson from Victoria College. I also must thank my students in the Economics 550 class at Curtin during the first semester in 1989, for their assistance. Ms Pan Xiao Gi has been particularly helpful with her commentary.

It would be remiss as well to overlook the co-ordinating roles of Pip Moran at Harper and Row, Robin Voigt, the earlier work of Anita Ray and to thank again Alex Macleod for his great work with the package.

Philip Maxwell
October, 1989

ONE

Introduction

1

Economics and Economic Issues

AFTER READING THIS CHAPTER YOU WILL BE ABLE TO:

1. Define the terms *economy* and *economics*.

2. List and define the basic economic terms used most often in economic discussions.

3. Distinguish between and give examples of positive and normative statements.

4. Identify the basic elements that make up any economic theory.

5. Construct a simple graph from data given in a table.

6. Define the terms *macroeconomics* and *microeconomics*.

7. Define and give examples of the three major fallacies that may be found in statements of economic theory or analysis.

8. Explain the role of economic theory and analysis in economic policymaking.

It has been said that there are three kinds of people: those who make things happen, those who watch things happen, and those who wonder what happened. If you sometimes find yourself among the last group, the study of economics is for you.

How can the study of economics help you? Most importantly, a knowledge of economics will help you to analyse economic issues that are reported daily in newspapers and on television. Although the laws of economics may not be as absolute as the law of gravity, they will help you deal with facts and opinions about economic issues. As a result, you will be able to come to intelligent, informed conclusions when faced with both day-to-day problems and questions of national policy.

ECONOMY AND ECONOMICS

The word **economy** typically brings to mind ideas of efficiency, thrift, and the avoidance of waste by careful planning and use of resources. We might say that some job was done with an 'economy of motion', meaning that there was no unnecessary effort expended. The word comes from the Greek *oikonemia*, which means the management of a household or state. In this sense, we often speak of the Australian or the US economy of a capitalist, socialist, free-market, or planned economy; or of industrialised and underdeveloped economies. We use the term in this last sense when we refer to *a particular system of organization for the production, distribution, and consumption of all things people use to achieve a certain standard of living.*

The term **economics**, on the other hand, is not so simple. It covers such a broad range of meaning that any brief definition is likely to leave out some important aspect of the subject. Most economists would agree, however, that economics is a social science concerned with the study of economies and the relationships among them. *Economics is the study of how people and society choose to employ scarce productive resources to produce goods and services and distribute them among various persons and groups in society.* This definition touches upon several important concepts — choice, scarcity, resources, production and distribution — with which we will be concerned both in this chapter and throughout the book.

Before reading any further you should understand that, whatever it is, economics is not primarily a vocational subject such as accounting, marketing, or management. Nor is it primarily intended to teach you how to make money, though it may help. Economics studies problems from society's point of view rather than from the individual's. Nevertheless, it is likely you will find the study of economics helpful in whatever career you choose. Moreover, it should make you a more knowledgeable and able citizen.

THE LANGUAGE OF ECONOMICS

As is the case with many subjects, the words used in economics often seem strange to the beginner. Physicists talk about neutrons, quarks, and hysteresis; soccer coaches talk about running off the ball, closing down space, and off-side traps. To make sense of a typical news item about economic issues you must be familiar with the language of economics. Economists frequently use common words to mean something more precise than is generally expected in everyday conversation. For instance, when you say someone has a lot of money, common usage suggests that you mean a person who owns a lot of things such as cars, houses, buildings, bonds, shares, cash and so on. In economics, however, we generally accept that 'money' means one's holdings of currency and demand deposits at a bank. When we mean something else, we always spell out exactly what other items we mean to include in our definition of money. Certain basic terms, such as money, will come up again and again throughout this book. The following definitions will help you to understand and use them correctly.

Economic Goods

An economic good is any item that is desired and scarce. In general, economic goods may be classified as either commodities or services. Commodities are tangible items such as food or clothing. (*Tangible* means, quite literally, able to be touched.) Commodities do not have to be consumed when they are produced; that is, they may be stored. Services are intangibles (that is, nontouchables) such as shoeshines or haircuts. They cannot be stored or transferred. For example, I cannot give you my haircut (a service), but I can give you my coat (a commodity). Such distinctions are not always clear-cut. For example, the economic good electricity might be called a service by some who say it is intangible and a commodity by those who note that it can be stored in a battery. Most often, an economic good is simply referred to as a good. You may have heard of the output of the economy referred to as 'goods and services.' This is done largely to remind us of the existence of services.

Whether they are commodities or services, all economic goods share the quality of being **scarce**. That is, there is not enough of them to supply everyone's needs and desires. As a result, people have to pay to obtain them. What they have to pay is called the **price** of the good. As we will see in Chapter 4, price is determined to a large extent by the number of people who desire and are able to pay for a particular good, together with what it costs producers to provide it.

People desire economic goods because these goods provide some form of satisfaction. A refrigerator provides satisfaction by keeping food cold. A stereo system provides satisfaction by giving us entertainment. Because an economic good gives us satisfaction, we say that it is useful to us. As a result, economists sometimes refer to the satisfaction a good yields as its utility. The creation of goods that have utility is called production. Production is carried out through the use of economic resources.

Economic Resources

Economic resources, also called the factors of production, are all the natural, man-made, and human resources that are used in the production of goods. These resources may be broken down into two broad categories, nonhuman resources (capital and land) and human resources (labour).

Capital

Capital is an example of a term that is used to mean one thing in everyday conversation and another in economics. We often speak of capital when referring to money, especially when we are talking about the purchase of equipment, machinery, and other productive facilities. It is more accurate to call the money used to make the purchase financial capital. An economist would refer to this purchase as investment. An economist uses the term capital to mean all the man-made aids used in production. Sometimes called investment goods, capital consists of machinery, tools, buildings, transportation and distribution facilities, and inventories of unfinished goods. A basic characteristic of capital goods is that they are used to produce other goods. For example, electricity is produced with capital goods consisting of boilers, turbines, fuel storage facilities, poles, and kilometres of wire. Capital is scarce relative to the desire for the output of goods and services made with the use of capital.

Land

To an economist, *land* is all natural resources that are used in production. Such resources include water, forests, oil, gas, mineral deposits, and so forth. These resources are scarce and, in many cases, are rapidly becoming more scarce.

Labour

Labour is a very broad term that covers all the different capabilities and skills possessed by human beings. Labour is scarce relative to the desire for the output of goods and services made with the help of labour. Labour consists of welders, carpenters, masons, hod carriers, dentists, scientists, teachers, managers, and so forth. The term *manager* embraces a host of skills related to the planning, administration, and coordination of production. A manager may also be an entrepreneur (or enterpriser). This is the person who

comes up with the ideas and takes the risks that are necessary to start a successful business. The founders of companies are entrepreneurs, while those running them are more accurately called managers.

The Firm

These economic resources of land, capital, and labour are brought together in a production unit that is referred to as a business or a *firm*. The firm uses these resources to produce goods, which are then sold. The money obtained from the sale of these goods is used to pay for the economic resources. Payments to those providing labour services are called wages. Payments to those providing buildings, land, and equipment leased to the firm are called rent. Payments to those providing financial capital (those who own shares and bonds) are called dividends and interest.

Gross Domestic Product

The total dollar value of all the final goods (as distinguished from goods still in the process of production) produced by all the firms in the economy is called the *gross domestic product* (GDP). In order to make meaningful comparisons of the GDP for various years, economists often use real GDP — GDP adjusted so that it only reflects changes in quantity of output, not changes in prices. When the real GDP goes down, we say the economy is in a state of recession. A severe recession is called a depression, although there is no general agreement as to how to decide exactly when a recession becomes a depression.

Inflation and Unemployment

The economic health of the nation, of which GDP is one measure, is directly affected by two other important factors, *inflation* and *unemployment*. Inflation is an ongoing general rise in prices. The steeper this rise, the faster the decline of a dollar's purchasing power. The unemployment rate measures the percentage of the total number of workers in the labour force who are actively seeking employment but are unable to find jobs. The higher the unemployment rate, the more the economy is wasting labour resources by allowing them to stand idle. However, it is generally believed that a decrease in the unemployment rate will lead to an increase in inflation, all other things remaining the same. ('All other things remaining the same' is an important phrase in economics that we will look into later in this chapter.)

Positive and Normative Statements

Intelligent discussion of economic issues requires that we distinguish between positive and normative statements. In the previous paragraph we made the statement that 'a decrease in the unemployment rate will lead to an increase in inflation'. This is a statement that may be supported or refuted by examining data. As such, we can say it is a **positive statement**. *Positive statements tell us what is, what was, or what will be. Any disputes about a positive statement can be settled by looking at the facts.* 'It rained last Thursday' and 'the sun will rise in the east tomorrow' are positive statements.

But now let's change our statement about inflation and unemployment slightly. Let's say 'it is *better* to decrease unemployment and live with the resulting increase in inflation than to allow a large number of people to go without jobs'. This is a **normative statement** — *an opinion or value judgment*. Those of you who are looking for jobs would probably tend to agree with this statement. But your grandparents who are retired and living on fixed incomes would be likely to disagree. Since they are not seeking employment, an increase in the number of jobs available would in no way compensate them for a rise in prices. As far as they are concerned, it would probably be better to slow the rise in prices. This, of course, would lead to an increase in unemployment, which would make all job-seekers very unhappy. The dispute between these two groups cannot be settled by facts alone.

Normative statements tell us what should be (*normative* means establishing a norm or standard). *Although normative statements often have their origin in positive statements, they cannot be proved true or false by referring to objective data.* For example, I may make the normative statement, 'You shouldn't drink and drive'. This statement has its origin in the positive statement, 'Drinking alcoholic beverages slows down one's ability to

---

CHECKPOINT * 1.1

Pick out a short news item in today's paper and make a list of all the positive statements and a list of all the normative statements. Examine the normative statements and try to determine what kinds of positive statements they may be based on.

*Answers to all Checkpoints can be found at the back of the text.

react'. We could disagree forever over the first statement, but statistical studies could be brought to bear on any dispute over the second.

In any discussion about economic issues, as soon as voices rise you can almost be certain that the discussion has shifted from logic and fact to value judgment and opinion. However, don't forget that value judgments and opinion often parade in the clothes of logic and fact.

ECONOMIC REALITY AND ECONOMIC THEORY

Economic reality — making a living, paying the rent, shopping for food, paying taxes, and so forth — forces us to deal with a large and confusing swarm of facts, figures, and events. The activities of households, firms, and federal, state, and local governments all have a direct effect on our economic lives. In order to make some sense out of the world around us we have all formulated some economic theories, even without being aware of doing so.

How to hold down inflation is a topic about which practically everyone has a theory. One individual, having just filled out an income tax return, might say, 'If we don't curb all this government spending, inflation will get worse'. The owner of a small business, on the other hand, feels that 'if something isn't done to control trade unions and big business, we'll never bring inflation under control'. Based on observations of the way certain groups, organisations, and institutions function, each individual has focused on the relationship that appears to be most relevant to an explanation of inflation. From these examples, we can say that *an*

economic theory *is an attempt to describe reality by abstracting and generalising its basic characteristics. Economists often refer to an economic theory as a law, principle, or model.* Each of these terms may be taken to mean the same thing.

Observations and Predictions: The Scientific Method

The inflation-control theories of the individuals above share two common features: (1) each is based on observation of facts or events, and (2) each makes a prediction about the consequences of certain events. We can now add to our definition of an economic theory by saying that *an economic theory provides an explanation of observed phenomena that may be judged by its ability to predict the consequences of certain events.*

Although economics is not a science like chemistry or physics, it does make use of the **scientific method** in arriving at and testing theories. The aspects of the scientific method that we are most concerned with here are induction and deduction. **Induction** *is the process of formulating a theory from a set of observations.* **Deduction** *is the process of predicting future events by means of a theory.* The predictions made by deduction are then tested by once again observing facts or events to see if what was predicted actually takes place. If not, the theory will have to be changed to conform to reality, and the whole process begins again. For example, suppose there is an increase in government spending, the crucial event in the first individual's theory, but we do not observe the predicted increase in inflation. Following the scientific method, we must either modify or discard the theory because of its failure to predict correctly. The process of induction and deduction is never-ending, since all theories must be continually retested in light of new facts and events.

Constructing a Theory

Our income-tax payer and our small-business owner, needless to say, did not really use the scientific method in drawing up their theories. But now let's see how an economist would go about formulating a theory. As an example, we will analyse the law of demand, a theory that will be referred to many times throughout this book.

Elements of Economic Theory

Every formal statement of a theory has four basic elements:

1. a statement of specific variables;
2. a set of assumptions about other variables that may be relevant;
3. a hypothesis about the way the specific variables are related;
4. one or more predictions.

The law of demand states that the quantity of a good demanded per unit of time will increase as the price of the good decreases, all other things remaining the same. Let's break this statement down into the four elements listed above.

Variables. The law of demand is concerned with two variables, price and quantity demanded. We call these variables because they can vary, that is, they are subject to change. As we noted in our discussion of the language of economics, price is the amount that must be paid to obtain a good. Quantity demanded is the amount of that good that people want and can pay for per unit of time.

Assumptions. The law of demand makes the assumption that, except for price, all other variables that might influence demand will remain the same. This assumption, which is a feature of all economic theories, is often referred to as **ceteris paribus**. Logically enough, that's Latin for 'all other things remaining the same'. This assumption is important when we come to the point of testing our theory. Real-world events may not turn out as the theory says they should. We must be sure to find out whether this is because the theory is wrong or because something other than just price has changed, thus violating the *ceteris paribus* assumption.

Hypothesis. A hypothesis is a statement of the way we think the variables in question relate to each other. Our hypothesis in the law of demand is that as price decreases, quantity demanded will increase. This is known as an **inverse relationship**, since the variables are changing in opposite ways. If the variables change in the same way (an increase in one leads to an increase in the other), we say they have a **direct relationship**.

Prediction. Here we move directly into the realm of the real world. Armed with our theory, what can we say will likely happen if the manager of our local clothing store reduces the price of Australian woollen sweaters from $45 to $35? While customers might not break down the doors to get in, our theory tells us that we can safely bet that the number of sweaters they want to buy will increase. Historically, the development of the automobile is a good example of the validity of the law of demand. The original cars, which were made on an individual basis, were so expensive that only the rich could afford them. Then Henry Ford developed the assembly-line method of production, which made cars less costly to produce. As a result of using this method, he was able to reduce prices. The quantity demanded soared.

How Exact Is Economic Theory?

Since economic theory tries to explain and predict human behaviour, you probably wonder how it is possible to be very exact. Economic theory cannot be as exact as Newton's three laws of motion. But economic behaviour is on average more predictable than the behaviour of many subatomic particles currently studied in high energy physics. If economic behaviour weren't predictable, stores wouldn't hold sales, banks wouldn't need vaults and security guards, and parking tickets wouldn't carry fines. If you don't think economic behaviour is predictable, drop a bucket of coins in a public swimming pool some summer afternoon. Make a practice of this and see if you notice a predictable pattern of behaviour.

The law of demand is a good predictor because people's behaviour on average is such that they will buy more of a good the lower its price is. True, there is the occasional person who will buy more of a good the higher its price because of 'snob appeal'. But this is unusual. When we look at the behaviour of a large group of individuals, the on-average similarity of the behaviour of the majority of them dominates the unusual behaviour of the few.

CHECKPOINT 1.2
During petrol tanker driver strikes, people often wait in long queues to fill their cars' petrol tanks. What does the law of demand suggest to you about a way in which those queues could be shortened?

Theories into Graphs

So far, we have been using words to explain how the law of demand works. But when we come to the point of relating the theory to data obtained through research, it is time to use pictures. In economics, the pictures we use take the form of graphs. Let's construct a graph from data about electricity use.

FIGURE 1.1
Basic Elements of a Graph

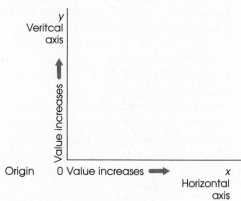

Every graph starts out with two lines. One is called the vertical (or y) axis. The other is called the horizontal (or x) axis. The point at which they meet is called the origin and has a value of 0. The value of the variable being measured on each axis increases as you move farther away from the origin. This means moving up along the vertical axis and to the right along the horizontal axis.

Basic Elements of a Graph

An ordinary graph starts out with two lines, which are called axes. One of the lines is drawn vertically, the other horizontally. The point at which they meet is called the origin and has a value of zero (see Figure 1.1). The value along each axis increases as we move away from the origin. This means moving up along the vertical axis and to the right along the horizontal axis.

In the case of the law of demand, we noted that we would be looking at two variables, price and quantity demanded. In economics, it is customary to use the vertical axis to measure price. Quantity demanded, therefore, is measured along the horizontal axis. What does this mean in terms of our investigation into the demand for electricity? We now have to find out what numbers to use on each axis. In other words, we must determine how much electricity is demanded at various prices. Let's suppose that our research into electricity demand in one city comes up with the data given in Table 1.1.

Constructing a Graph

Returning to our graph, we can now label the vertical axis 'Price per kilowatt-hour' and the horizontal axis 'Kilowatt-hours demanded (in millions per month)', as shown in Figure 1.2. (These labels correspond to the column headings in Table 1.1.) We divide the vertical axis evenly into units representing $.01 increases in price. We divide the horizontal axis evenly into units representing 10-million kilowatt-hour increases in quantity demanded. Our next task is to find the points on the graph corresponding to the quantity demanded per hour figure and the price per kilowatt-hour figure for each of the six pairs of numbers given in Table 1.1. (We have labelled these pairs of numbers a, b, c, d, e, and f in our table.)

For combination a, we first move right along the horizontal axis to a point equal to 15 million kilowatt-hours. We then move directly upward from that point until we are opposite the point on the vertical axis that represents a price of $.06. We label the point at which we have arrived a, since it corresponds to combination a on our table. We use the same procedure to locate points b, c, d, e, and f. Our graph now looks like Figure 1.2.

If we draw a line connecting points a through f we have what is called a demand curve. Our graph now looks like Figure 1.3. In this case, we see that the demand curve slopes downward and to the right. This tells us that as price decreases (moves down along the vertical axis), quantity demanded increases (moves right along the horizontal axis).

Thinking back to our discussion of the elements of a theory (p. 9), you will re-

TABLE 1.1
Demand for Electricity at Different Prices
(Hypothetical Data)

	Price per Kilowatt-Hour	Kilowatt-Hours Demanded (in Millions per Month)
(a)	$.06	15
(b)	.05	17
(c)	.04	20
(d)	.03	25
(e)	.02	35
(f)	.01	50

This table tells us how much electricity will be demanded per month at various prices. If the price is $.06 per kilowatt-hour, the quantity demanded will be 15 million kilowatt-hours per month (combination a). If the price is $.03 per kilowatt-hour, the quantity demanded will be 25 million kilowatt-hours (combination d).

remember that we called this type of relationship between two variables an inverse relationship. All inverse relationships (one variable increasing while the other is decreasing) produce this type of downward, rightward-sloping curve. It is one of the major purposes of a graph to show us, without our even having to read the specific numbers involved, what the relationship between the variables is. When we compare the picture of demand provided by our graph with our theory, we see that the theory is consistent with the facts. The downward, rightward slope

of the demand curve shows us that as price decreases, quantity demanded increases.

Finally, it should be emphasised that an economic theory can be (1) stated in words, (2) represented in a table (Table 1.1), and (3) illustrated in the form of a graph (Figure 1.3).

CHECKPOINT 1.3

Suppose that the State Electricity Commission says it is finding it difficult to produce all the electricity its customers are demanding. Keeping in mind the graph in Figure 1.3, let us suppose we

FIGURE 1.2
Demand for Electricity at Various Prices

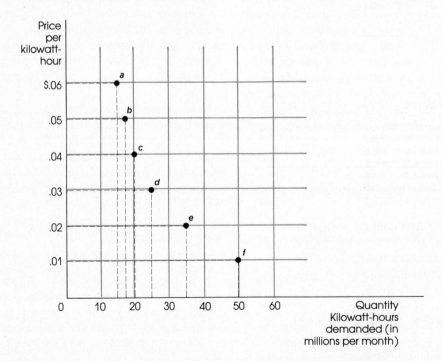

Using the data obtained from Table 1.1, we are able to locate points on the graph that represent the various price-quantity demanded combinations for electricity. To locate combination c, for example, we move right along the horizontal axis until we come to 20 million kilowatt-hours. We then move directly upward from this point until we are opposite the $.04 mark on the vertical axis. The same procedure is used to find the other combinations listed in Table 1.1.

FIGURE 1.3
Demand Curve for Electricity

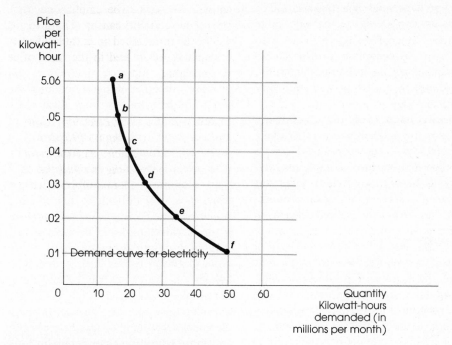

After we have located all the points that correspond to the price-quantity demanded combinations in Table 1.1, we draw a line connecting them. This line is called the demand curve. In this case, because the relationship between price and quantity demanded is an inverse relationship, the curve slopes downward and to the right.

were able to obtain information on electricity demand in another state. In this case, let us suppose that the data indicate that the demand in this other state is less sensitive to changes in price than the demand in the state we've been looking at so far. What sort of shape do you think the demand curve for electricity would have compared with the one shown in Figure 1.3? In which state would an increase in price most relieve the strain on the supplying authority? Why?

MACROECONOMICS VERSUS MICROECONOMICS

Economists often use the terms *macroeconomics* and *microeconomics* to distinguish between different levels of economic analysis.

In **macroeconomics** we are concerned with the workings of the whole economy or large sectors of it. These sectors include government, business and households. For the purposes of analysis, the smaller groups that make up these large sectors are often lumped together and treated as one unit. For example, the consumer sector may be treated as though it were one large household. The business sector might be considered to be one large business. Macroeconomics deals with such issues as economic growth, unemployment, recession, inflation, stagflation, the balance of payments, and monetary and fiscal policy.

Microeconomics, on the other hand, focuses on the individual units that make up the whole of the economy. Here we are interested in how households and businesses behave as individual units, not as parts of a larger whole. Microeconomics studies how a household spends its money. It also studies the way in which a business determines how much of a product to produce, how to make best use of the factors of production, what pricing strategy to use, and so on. Microeconomics also studies how individual markets and industries are organised, what patterns of competition they follow, and how these patterns affect economic efficiency and welfare.

ECONOMIC REASONING: COMMON PITFALLS

In order to analyse an economic issue or problem correctly, we must avoid certain common pitfalls of economic reasoning. One of the most common fallacies arises from the difficulty of distinguishing between cause and effect. Another is commonly known as the fallacy of composition.

Cause and Effect

As we have seen in our analysis of the law of demand, a key interest of economics is to determine how events in the real world can be explained and even predicted. In other words, we are looking for causes. We want to be able to say with reasonable certainty that if A happens, B will be the result. Having analysed the law of demand, we are able to say that if price is decreased, quantity demanded will increase, all other things remaining the same. Unfortunately, it is not always easy to tell if some event was the cause of another event or if it just preceded it in time. The situation is especially tricky when event B regularly follows event A.

In economics there are many times when it is very difficult to tell whether A caused B or B caused A. Perhaps there is no causal relationship between B and A at all, but both occur together because event C always causes both A and B to happen. A fire causes smoke and light, but smoke doesn't cause light and light doesn't cause smoke. People in high income brackets tend to have better health and more education than people in low-income brackets. Possibly they were born with a hardier constitution and more than the average amount of energy. These factors would enable such people to attend school more regularly and have a greater capacity for work. If so, it is possible that high income and education are no more causally related than smoke and light, but that being born with a hardy constitution causes both. On the other hand, it may be that higher education causes higher income, which makes it possible to afford a better diet and better medical care.

The rather common fallacy of concluding that A caused B simply because A occurred before B is known as the **fallacy of false cause**.

Fallacy of Composition

Common sense will tell you that if you

ECONOMIC THINKERS

Adam Smith — 1723–1790

Adam Smith is often thought of as the father of modern economics, although his great work, *An Inquiry into the Nature and Causes of the Wealth of Nations* (1776), would not look very much like a modern economics textbook to today's reader.

One of Smith's most significant contributions to economic thought was his explanation of the importance of the division of labour and its relationship to the development of the economy. In his famous description of operations in a pin factory, Smith shows how output can be greatly increased by dividing tasks into small segments, each performed by specialists who require little training.

Smith's central theme was the value of enlightened self-interest, and he preached the doctrine of laissez faire. In Smith's view, the role of government should be minimised, in contrast with the power governments had exercised over all types of commerce in the past. Beyond maintaining national security, preserving internal order, and undertaking a few tasks such as public education, government was, according to Smith, to exercise little power. An advocate of economic freedom, Smith generally accepted the idea of 'natural order' taught by a fellow Scot, philosopher Francis Hutcheson, which implied the removal of restrictions of all kinds. Such a theory well suited the rising commercial class in Western Europe, particularly in England, which found government regulations irksome. Freedom allowed the natural instincts provided by a wise providence (in other words, self-interest) to prevail and provide the drive to turn the wheels of trade and commerce.

As Smith saw it, it would be foolish to assume that people satisfy the needs of others simply as a result of feelings of altruism. On the contrary, the baker, the brewer and the candlestick maker each undertakes to satisfy the needs of others as a means of satisfying his or her own needs. By seeking to fulfil personal needs, each individual is helping to increase the wealth of society:

He generally, indeed, neither intends to promote the public interest nor knows how much he is promoting it. By preferring the support of domestic to that of foreign industry, he intends only his own security; and by directing that industry in such a manner as its produce may be of the greatest value, he intends only his own gain; and he is in this, as in many other cases, led by an invisible hand to promote an end which was no part of his intention.

FOR FURTHER READING

Clark, John J., and others. *Adam Smith 1776-1926*. University of Chicago Press, 1928.
Smith, Adam, *An Inquiry into the Nature and Causes of the Wealth of Nations*. Edwin Cannan ed. London: Methuen 1904.

find yourself in a burning building, you should get out as fast as you can. However, if the burning building is a crowded film theatre and each individual in it tries to get through the door at the same time, the results are likely to be tragic. What is good advice for you as an individual is not good advice for the group as a whole. *The false assumption that what is true for a particular part of the whole is also true for the whole itself is called the* **fallacy of composition**. (The whole is made up, or composed, of two or more individual parts.)

We can see how this fallacy works on an economic level if we consider the following example. If you are unemployed and have a mortgage on your house, you might be wise to sell the house. You can use the money obtained from the sale to pay off the mortgage and buy a cheaper house. In this way you can eliminate the burden of monthly mortgage payments. But if everyone on your block decides to do the same thing, the glut of houses on the market may drive prices down so low that you may not be able to get enough money to pay off the mortgage and buy a new house. What makes good economic sense for the individual does not necessarily make good economic sense for the whole economy. We will see other examples in this book where what is true at the microeconomic level is not necessarily true at the macroeconomic level.

In judging what is true for the whole of society, we must not go to the opposite extreme and assume that what is true for the whole is also true for the individual parts. Such an assumption is known as the **fallacy of division**. For example, while it is true that society as a whole may benefit from a highly competitive marketplace, some individual firms with weak management skills may go bankrupt.

CHECKPOINT 1.4
Think of some examples where confusions about cause and effect might arise. Can you think of a fallacy of composition that frequently occurs when a crowd watches a football game?

ECONOMIC POLICY

Economic theories have by and large evolved as responses to problems. In other words, necessity has been the mother of invention. But theory is only a tool, a way of looking at economic reality. It does not provide ready-made solutions to problems. John Maynard Keynes, a highly regarded policymaker as well as theorist, put it this way:

> The theory of economics does not furnish a body of settled conclusions immediately applicable to policy. It is a method rather than a doctrine, an apparatus of the mind, a technique of thinking, which helps its possessor to draw correct conclusions.

Economic policy *is concerned with finding solutions to economic problems.* While policymakers use economic theory to help them, they must go beyond it as well. They must consider the cultural, social, legal and political aspects of an issue if they are to formulate a successful policy. In the end, making economic policy involves making value judgments such as those we explored when we looked at the conflict between unemployment and inflation. And an economist has no special claim over anybody else to making these judgments.

Economic Analysis and Economic Policymaking

While economic theory and analysis may

not always be able to tell policymakers what they should do, it can usually tell them what they shouldn't do. An understanding of economic principles can keep us from both pursuing unwise policies and chasing conflicting goals. A few examples will illustrate how this is so.

An Unwise Policy

The printing of money by a government in order to finance its expenditures has long been considered by economists to be an unwise move. Despite their warnings, however, history is a graveyard of fallen governments that have yielded to this temptation. Somehow it always seems easier to turn on the printing press than to raise taxes. After World War I, the German government printed such quantities of money that the rate of inflation reached several thousand per cent per week! At this point the deutschmark ceased to have any value at all as a medium of exchange. No one would accept it in payment for goods or services. Faith in the government's ability to manage was seriously shaken. The resulting political instability probably contributed in some degree to the rise of Adolf Hitler and the Nazi party.

Conflicting Goals

In the conflicting goals category, an election year is often marked by talk of reducing unemployment and reducing inflation — both at the same time. Full employment today is often defined as an unemployment rate of roughly 6 per cent. Almost everyone would agree that a 3 per cent rate of inflation is low. But almost any economist will tell you that these two goals conflict with each other. A 6 per cent unemployment rate goal is probably

not compatible with a 3 per cent inflation rate goal. Research findings, while not final or always clear-cut, might indicate that a 6 per cent unemployment rate is possible only if we are willing to accept a 12 per cent inflation rate. On the other hand, in order to cut inflation to 3 per cent, we might have to live with an unemployment rate of 11 per cent. This serves to remind us that an economy's behaviour can only be modified within limits. (You can't expect a large bus to take corners like a sports car, or a sports car to carry 50 passengers.) Economic analysis can help us to form realistic policy objectives that don't conflict with one another.

The conflict between goals can be illustrated further by looking at the case of a retail clothing store. Suppose the owner stocked a large number of winter coats — the goal, to make money from their sale. But suppose the winter season is drawing to a close and the owner still has a large number of winter coats on hand. The owner has another goal — to make room for new spring fashions. Economic analysis, in particular the law of demand, tells the owner to lower prices, in other words, to have a sale. But this may mean that the coats will have to be sold for less than their wholesale cost. As a policymaker, the owner has to choose between making money on winter coats and making room for the new fashions.

Economic Policy, Special Interests, and the Role of the Economist

Making economic policy forces us to choose among alternatives that have different consequences for different groups. Each of us is a member of one or more special interest groups. As students and educators, we might find it in our interest to pay special attention to any proposed legislation that affects education and institutions of learning. Similarly, trade unions are concerned about legislation on compulsory unionism and the powers and rights of unions to help one another enforce strikes and deal with strikebreakers. Business interests are also concerned with labour legislation, but their stands on such matters are usually opposed to those of unions. Farmers and consumers are both concerned with agricultural policy, but once again their interests are often in conflict. Resolution of these conflicts typically involves choices such as those we have discussed in connection with the inflation-unemployment trade-off. That is, we must make choices that are matters of value judgment. As we have noted, economists have no special calling to make subjective judgments as to what particular group should gain at another's expense. Economists probably do their greatest service to policymaking when they take the goals of all parties concerned as given and confine themselves to exploring and explaining which goals are compatible and which conflict, and what economic consequences will result from different policy actions.

Major Economic Policy Goals in Australia

A list of economic policy goals that most economists, policymakers, and citizens feel are important in Australia would probably look like this:

1. *Price stability*: in recent years this has meant checking inflation.
2. *Full employment*: in recent years many economists would take this to mean keeping the unemployment rate down to perhaps 6 per cent.
3. *Economic growth*: continued growth in the standard of living for the average citizen.
4. *Environmental standards*: more control over the pollution and wastes that our production processes produce and impose on the environment.
5. *External balance*: this refers to maintaining balance between a country's receipts from, and payments to, the rest of the world.
6. *An equitable tax burden*: people, especially the middle-income groups, have shown increasing concern that our tax system favours those, typically in higher income brackets, who are in a position to take advantage of various loopholes in our tax laws to avoid or greatly reduce their 'fair share' of the tax burden.
7. *Economic freedom*: the idea that businesses, consumers, and workers should be given much freedom in their economic activities.
8. *An equitable income distribution*: the national income should be shared fairly so that no one lives in poverty while some enjoy excessive wealth.

We have already pointed out how economic experience has suggested that goals 1 and 2 may not be compatible, and that there seems to be a trade-off between the achievement of one at the expense of the other. The same may be true of goals 3 and 4 and of goals 4 and 7. Goals 2, 3, and 8 all seem compatible in the sense that if we achieve 2 and 3, we will very likely ensure an equitable income distribution, goal 8. With respect to goal 6, some would argue that certain of the so-called loopholes are important as a spur to risky business ventures and that without

POLICY PERSPECTIVE

Why Economists Disagree — The Role of Ideology

Put two economists in the same room and what do you get? An argument, or so it would seem to most people. Why do economists seem to disagree so much? How can the Nobel prize be awarded in economics, and how can economics be regarded as a science if different economists can come up with such dissimilar answers when confronted with the same policy issue? The problem is that economics, unlike chemistry and physics for example, deals with human beings, the societies they live in and the questions of who shall get what and how. Such questions invariably raise issues of value judgment about what is a 'good' and 'just' society, that is, issues of political ideology. The way different economists view an issue and the nature of their policy recommendations are usually coloured by their particular ideological orientation.

In the context of current Australian debate it is useful to identify four broad political ideologies which provide different positions on many key economic issues. These may be termed the traditional Conservative position, the traditional Labor position, the Socialist left position and the New Right position.

The Traditional Conservative Position

These views are usually espoused by economists who support Liberal and National parties. They generally favour free enterprise and the encouragement of competition within the economy. In this context they support reducing the size of public sector activities, or at least maintaining them at present levels. Following from this they favour reduced income taxation, supported perhaps by the introduction of widespread consumption taxes. They support deregulation in a number of areas, as well as privatisation of a significant number of public enterprises — holding the view that the private sector will provide such services more efficiently and effectively. In the incomes policy area they advocate decentralised wage fixation as most desirable. When in government they have tended to focus attention on low inflation as the major goal and balancing budgets as desirable. They tend to favour significant defence spending, and holding current spending levels on social welfare and education rather than letting them increase.

The Traditional Labor Position

As represented by the Australian Labor Party supporters of this view traditionally favour government intervention in the Australian economy as a way of ensuring equal opportunity and a more equitable income for all citizens. While accepting that the private sector has a role to play in the economy, they believe that the public sector should be actively involved in modifying market outcomes which are not in the community interest. In achieving this such economists endorse progressive income taxation and deficit budgeting to achieve a society where full employment is possible and income and wealth are more equally distributed. In reaching this position they generally support centralised wage fixation. With the accession to office by the Hawke government in 1983 certain parts of the traditional Labor position have changed. In embracing deregulation of the financial sector, floating the dollar, endeavouring to contain public sector growth and introducing tax reform the Australian Labor Party adopted certain policy positions which had previously been the preserve of conservative forces. By following a so-called 'corporatist' model of government they partially abandoned the socialist goals with which they had earlier been associated.

The Socialist Position

To understand the representative socialist position it is necessary to recognise the central role played by Marxist analysis. It is impossible to do justice to the Marxist critique of capitalism in this short space, but in brief, Marx essentially viewed capitalism essentially as a system by which those who own the means of production, the capitalist class, are able to dominate and exploit the working class. According to Marx, the dominant capitalist class shaped private values, religion, the family, the educational system, and political structures, all for the purpose of production for private profit. Marxist analysis does not separate economics from politics and society's value system. The bourgeois democracies of the Western world are viewed as simply the tools for the dominant capitalist interests. For a Marxist, the problem with the capitalist system is the system itself, and no resolution of the problem is possible without changing the system. Coupled with this Marxist heritage, the socialist left are motivated by what they see as the failings of present-day liberalism. Recent government policies for general social improvement are viewed as attempts to protect only some interest groups. And those who *really* benefit under such programs are seen as being those who have always gained. Corporate power continues to grow and the same elitist groups rule who have always ruled. Furthermore, goals to improve the national well-being are also perceived as contributing to the exploitation of less-developed nations, continuing the cold war, and increasing the militarisation of the economy.

The 'New Right' Position

The ideology of the so-called New Right in Australia shares much in common with right wing conservatism in the US. It is rooted in two basic propositions. First, individual rights and the freedom of consenting parties to enter into private contracts (such as between buyer and seller) must be preserved to the greatest extent possible. Second, a competitive market system is central to the proper organisation of society. Proponents oppose any 'unnatural' interference in the marketplace, and view the growth of big government as a major threat to economic progress and individual freedom. The government's proper role is: to maintain law and order; to define and preserve property rights; to see that contracts are enforced; to provide a legal system to settle disputes; to promote competition by preventing the growth of monopoly power; to provide services not naturally provided by the market, such as national defence; to deal with problems not naturally solved by markets alone, such as environmental pollution; and to supplement private charity and the family, to aid children and others handicapped for reasons beyond their control. In short, the 'New Right' believe that government, the ultimate monopoly, should not do for people what they are capable of doing for themselves. Where government goes beyond these bounds, not only is individual freedom theatened, but otherwise well-intended government policies can cause or worsen economic problems. For example, proponents argue that a government-enforced minimum wage, higher than that otherwise determined by the market, provides greater income for some workers but reduces the quantity demanded of those workers who are poorest, typically the unskilled and disadvantaged. Certain elements of the 'traditional conservative' economic position are common with those of the 'New Right'. The emphasis of the 'New Right' on the key role of the market and small government differentiates them from less radically minded economists. .

When considering any economist's analysis of an economic issue it is always helpful to know his or her idological orientation — to know 'where he or she is coming from'.

Questions

1. What do you think a socialist would say about the New Right view that wages should be determined in a market environment, without interference from either government or the trade unions?

2. Among the eight major economic policy goals we have listed, how do you think traditional conservatives and Labor views differ on the relative importance which they attach to achieving those goals that we argued tend to conflict with one another?

this there would be less of the sort of enterprising activity essential to economic growth and full employment, goals 2 and 3. They would contend that goal 6, therefore, may not be compatible with goals 2 and 3.

Economic Analysis and the Economist

The examples we have considered illustrate why economic analysis is useful in formulating economic policy. In sum, economic analysis (1) helps to predict what the consequences of any policy action are likely to be, (2) indicates from among several ways to achieve a given goal which ones are most efficient in that their side effects are least detrimental, or possibly even helpful, to the achievement of other goals, (3) suggests which goals are compatible with one another and which

are not, and (4) indicates what the likely trade-offs are between goals that are not mutually compatible.

If economic analysis does nothing else but keep policymakers from pursuing foolhardy policies, this alone is justification for its use as a policy tool. When economists go beyond the exercise of economic analysis summarised by points 1 to 4, they join the ranks of the various parties to any policy dispute. Their opinions and programs are then properly treated as those of a special interest group. Since economists, just like everyone else, usually do have opinions on matters of value judgment, they often use their economic expertise in support of a cause. In the end, therefore, the burden of separating objective economic analysis from value judgment must rest with you, the citizen. This fact alone should justify the time you devote to the study of economics.

SUMMARY

1. Economics is a social science concerned with the study of how society chooses to use its scarce resources to satisfy its unlimited wants. Economics studies the many issues and problems associated with this process from an overall point of view.

2. Goods are produced by using economic resources. Economic resources are of two basic kinds — human resources (labour) and nonhuman resources (capital and land). Economic resources are also referred to as the factors of production.

3. Discussions of economic issues make use of two kinds of statements. Positive statements are statements of fact. Normative statements, which may be based on positive statements, are statements of opinion.

4. In an effort to explain 'how things work', economic analysis makes use of the scientific method. This method uses induction to formulate a theory from observation of facts and events. The theory is then used to predict future events (deduction).

5. Every economic theory has four basic elements: (1) a statement of variables, (2) a set of assumptions, (3) a hypothesis, and (4) one or more predictions about future happenings. Economic theories may also be called economic laws, principles, or models. Economic theory is exact to the extent that economic behaviour is predictable.

6. Economic theories, such as the law of demand, may be represented graphically.

7. Economic analysis has been divided into two broad areas. Macroeconomics is concerned with the functioning of the whole economy or large sectors within it.

Microeconomics focuses on individual units such as households and firms.

8. In economics, it is important to determine whether one event is the cause of another event or if it simply preceded it in time.

9. The assumption that what is true of the parts is true of the whole is known as the fallacy of composition. The assumption that what is true of the whole is true of the parts is known as the fallacy of division.

10. Economic policymakers use economic theory and analysis to help them formulate ways in which to solve the problems posed by economic reality. In most cases, the solution to these problems involves resolving a conflict between special interest groups. Such a resolution usually depends upon value judgments, and economists are no more qualified than anyone else to make such judgments. Economic analysis is most useful in determining the possible consequences of various policies.

KEY TERMS AND CONCEPTS

ceteris paribus
deduction
direct relationship
economic policy
economics
economic theory
economy
fallacy of composition
fallacy of division
fallacy of false cause
induction
inverse relationship
macroeconomics
microeconomics
normative statement
positive statement

price
scarce
scientific method

QUESTIONS AND PROBLEMS

1. Why is economics called a social science instead of a social study?

2. Why is it that economists, who supposedly use scientific methods when analysing economic issues, are so often in disagreement?

3. Pick out a story from the financial and business section of today's newspaper and find instances in which a concept or subject is mentioned or discussed that is related to one or more of the economic terms introduced in this chapter.

4. Open today's newspaper at the financial and business section. Pick a story at random and calculate the ratio of positive statements to the total number of statements in the story. Now go to the financial and business *editorial* section and do the same.

5. *Think* about the following experiment. Suppose you were to run an ad in your local paper this week stating that you own a vacant one hectare block and that somewhere on the block is buried a metal box containing $10. You state that any and all are welcome to come and dig for it and that you will give the $10 to whomever finds it during the coming week. How many people do you think will show up to dig? Suppose, instead, you had said the box contained $30 instead of $10. How many diggers do you think would show up during the same week? Estimate how many would show up during the same week if the reward were $60, $120, or $150. Now construct a graph that measures dollars of reward on the vertical axis and number of diggers on the horizontal axis. Find the points representing each combination of dollars and diggers and draw a line connecting them.

a. Is the relationship you observe between the size of the dollar reward and the number of diggers an inverse relationship or a direct relationship?

b. What led you to hypothesise the relationship you did between the size of the dollar reward and the number of diggers?

c. If you actually ran the ads over the course of a year and tabulated the number of diggers who showed up for each reward, plotted the results, and found a relationship opposite to the one you had predicted, what would you conclude about your theory? Might the season of the year during which you ran each ad have had something to do with the difference between your theory and what actually happened? Suppose when you ran the $150 reward ad it rained for the whole week the offer was good. Suppose when you ran the $120 reward ad it was sunny the first day of the week and rained the next six. Suppose for the $90 reward ad it was sunny for the first two days and rained the next five. Suppose for the $60 reward ad it was sunny for the first three days and rained the next four. Suppose for the $30 reward ad it was sunny the first five days and rained the next two. Finally, for the $10 reward ad suppose it was sunny the whole week. How do you think the curve obtained by plotting the combinations of dollar reward and number of diggers might look now? Looking back at the first curve you drew, how important do you think your 'other things remaining the same' assumption was?

d. Suppose your original curve was based on the assumption that it was always sunny. If instead it was always raining, where would the curve be — to the left or to the right of the original curve?

e. What would you predict would happen if you raised the amount of the reward money to $1,000?

f. Can you, as my economic policy adviser, recommend how I might clear off and dig up a one hectare block that I own in town?

g. Can you, as my economic policy adviser, tell me how to deal with the social tensions that might arise between the people who show up to dig on my block?

h. Do you think people respond to economic incentives?

i. Do you think human behaviour is predictable?

2

Scarcity, Choice and the Economic Problem

AFTER READING THIS CHAPTER YOU WILL BE ABLE TO:

1. Explain why the combination of scarce resources and unlimited wants makes choice necessary.

2. Define the term economic efficiency and distinguish between unemployment and underemployment of resources.

3. Explain the concept of the production possibilities frontier and show why when an economy is on the frontier, it can have more of one good only by giving up some of another.

4. Demonstrate why the selection of an output combination on today's production possibilities frontier affects the location of tomorrow's frontier.

5. Formulate the basic questions posed by the fundamental economic problem that every economy must answer.

6. Distinguish among pure market economies and command economies.

In this chapter we will focus on the basic economic problem that has always confronted human beings and the fundamental questions it poses. Then we will look into the ways economies may be organised to answer these questions. The answers are related to the fundamental issues of how well people live, how hard they work, and how choices about these matters are to be made.

THE ECONOMIC PROBLEM

The basic **economic problem** *that underlies all economic issues is the combined existence of scarce resources and unlimited wants.* Benjamin Franklin, one of the founding fathers of the United States, put it neatly. 'The poor have little — beggars none; the rich too much — enough not one.' As we noted in Chapter 1, the economic resources of land, labour, and capital exist only in limited amounts. Consequently, there is a limit to the quantity of economic goods that can be produced with these scarce resources. But unfortunately, people's desires for goods are really unlimited for all intents and purposes of economic analysis. While in theory it may be possible to attain a level of abundance that would satisfy everybody's appetites for all things, no such state has ever existed. And at this time, the prospects of achieving such a state seem remote to nonexistent. One has only to consider living standards in a comparatively rich country like Australia to realise the truth of this. There is hardly a person who couldn't draw up a list of wanted goods that far exceeds his or her means to obtain them. Ask yourself, or anyone else, what you would do with an additional hundred dollars. If you felt completely without want, you might say that you

would give it to a charity. But why does charity exist? Because some other group or person has unsatisfied wants.

Opportunity Cost and Choice: A Simple Example

Scarcity and unlimited wants force us to make choices. Let's consider a simple example. Suppose an early settler decided to live alone in the High Country on the New South Wales–Victoria border. He produces only two goods: potatoes (food) and wood (for heat). His scarce resource is the time he has to grow potatoes and cut wood. This coupled with his strength and degree of the skill he has will determine how much he can produce. This settler Paddy will make sure that he doesn't waste these resources.

The Production Possibilities Frontier

Paddy has an economic problem and we can see that clearly, if we make use of a production possibilities frontier. *A production possibilities frontier, or just production frontier is a line or a curve representing the maximum possible output combinations of goods that can be produced with a fixed amount of resources.*

Suppose Paddy's production possibilities frontier is the downward-sloping straight line shown in Figure 2.1. It shows the *maximum possible* combinations of potatoes and wood that Paddy can *choose* to produce in a year if he uses his time in the most efficient manner. The points on the line are *alternatives* but we will come to that later. For the moment, it is important to see the production possibilities frontier as a boundary which Paddy cannot step over.

For example, he cannot choose to

produce a combination of 27 sacks of potatoes and 17 tonnes of wood (point *f* on Figure 2.1). He simple doesn't have the time and energy to devote to potato growing and harvesting and wood cutting. On the other hand, Paddy can produce

---

FIGURE 2.1
Paddy's Production Possibilities Frontier

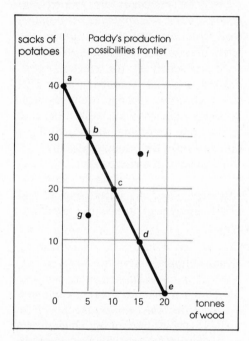

Paddy's production possibilities frontier is represented by the downward-sloping straight line *ae*. Each point on the frontier represents some maximum-output combination of sacks of potatoes and tonnes of wood that Paddy can choose to produce annually if he fully utilises his fixed resources as efficiently as possible.

Paddy cannot produce any combinations represented by points to the right or above the frontier, such as *f*. He simple doesn't have enough resources, time, stamina and ability to grow potatoes and chop wood. Paddy can produce any combination represented by points to the left or below the frontier, such as *g*. But he wouldn't want to because that would entail an inefficient utilisation of his resources.

---

any combination lying along the frontier *a* to *e*, or of course combinations represented by points inside the frontier, such as *g*. Given that he has already decided to spend his time growing potatoes and cutting wood it is hard to see why he would want to produce at point *g*. To do so would represent an inefficient use of his limited resources.

Opportunity Cost

Paddy will always choose to produce a combination of goods represented by a point on his production possibilities frontier. (Later we will see that the frontier may not be a straight line.) Five of these possible combinations are indicated by points *a, b, c, d* and *e*. For example, if Paddy chooses combination *b*, he will grow 30 sacks of potatoes and chop 5 tonnes of wood during the coming year. Alternatively, he may choose combination *c*, consisting of 20 sacks of potatoes and 10 tonnes of wood. All he has to do is devote less of his fixed resources to potato growing and use the resources released from that activity to chop more wood. If Paddy chooses to produce combination *c* instead of *b*, he has to give up 10 sacks of potatoes (the difference between 30 and 20). However, he gains 5 tonnes of wood (the difference between 10 and 5). Conversely, if he chooses combination *b* instead of *c*, he gives up 5 tonnes of wood and gains 10 sacks of potatoes.

In general, if Paddy wants to produce more of one kind of good, he must of necessity produce less of the other. We say he must pay an **opportunity cost**. *The opportunity cost equals the amount of one good that must be given up in order to have more of another.* We see from Paddy's production possibilities frontier in Figure 2.1 that he has to *give up* 2 sacks of potatotes in order to get an additional tonne of wood (a move downward along his production possibilities frontier). Conversely, he has to *give up* half a tonne of wood in order to get an additional sack of potatoes (a move upward along his production possibilities frontier). Hence the opportunity cost of a tonne of wood is 2 sacks of potatoes. The opportunity cost of a sack of potatotes is half a tonne of wood.

TABLE 2.1
Paddy's Opportunity Cost of Growing Potatoes and Cutting Wood

To produce	Will cost Paddy the opportunity to produce
1 extra sack of potatoes	0.5 tonnes of wood
1 extra tonne of wood	2 sacks of potatoes

Choice

When Paddy uses his fixed resources efficiently, he can choose to produce any output combination on his production possibilities frontier. Whenever he considers the choice between one combination and another along the frontier, however, he is always forced to choose between a combination with more wood and less potatoes and a combination with less wood and more potatoes. If he could have more of both or more of one without having to sacrifice any of the other, there would be no 'hard' choice because nothing would have to be given up. Unfortunately, Paddy's limited or scarce resources always force him to give up something — to pay an opportunity cost — whenever he makes a choice. A choice requires that one opportunity be given up to gain another.

The concept of a production possibilities frontier, the existence of opportunity costs, and the need for choice are just as relevant for an entire economy as they are for Paddy. Let's see why.

Scarcity, Production and Efficiency

Given that resources are limited and people's wants are unlimited the problem that faces any economy is how to use scarce resources and organise production so as to satisfy to the greatest extent possible society's unlimited wants. This means that the available resources must be used as efficiently as possible. In other words, the maximum output must be obtained from the resources at hand.

There are two major problems that can prevent a society from achieving **economic efficiency**. These are **unemployment and underemployment**, or **resource misallocation**.

Unemployment

Maximum economic efficiency cannot be achieved if available resources are not fully used. This holds true for both human and nonhuman resources. As long as there are workers looking for work and unable to find it, or if plant capacity remains unused, maximum economic efficiency cannot be achieved. Notice that we stress that in order to have economic efficiency all *available* resources must be employed. Some parts of the population may not seek employment. By custom and law some people, such as children and the aged, may be prevented from working. Certain kinds of land are prohibited by law from use for certain types of productive activity. However, whenever there are available resources standing idle, there are fewer inputs into the economy's productive process. As a result, there is a lower output of goods to satisfy society's wants.

Underemployment, or Resource Misallocation

If certain available resources are used to do jobs for which other available resources are better suited there is underemployment, or misallocation of resources. For example, if cabinetmakers were employed to make dresses and dressmakers were employed to make cabinets, the total amount of cabinets and dresses produced would be less than if each group were employed in the activity for which it was trained. Similarly, if it was decided to grow Australia's sugar cane in South Australia and wheat on the sub tropical, wet, humid Queensland coast, the same total land area would produce far less than it yields at the moment. Resource underemployment also results whenever the best available technology is not used in a production process. A house painter painting with a toothbrush and a farmer harvesting wheat with a pocketknife are both underemployed. A 10 tonne bulldozer is underemployed if it is only used to clear scrub or put in a new dam two or three times a year. Solutions to the underemployment of resources are not easy. It is often suggested we do not make the fullest use of schools and tertiary institutions. It is said they should be used more at night, at weekends and in summer vacations. But it is not just a question of using resources for their own sake. To be employed productively they must result in something that people want. Unfortunately, not enough teachers and students are prepared to work like nurses from midnight to 8.00 a.m. to make this a productive use of the idle resources. *Nevertheless whenever there is resource underemployment, or misallocation, a reallocation of resources to productive activities for which they are better suited will result in a larger output of some or all goods and no reduction in the output of any.*

Production Possibilities Trade-off

When an economy's available resources are fully employed (that is, there is no unemployment or underemployment), we say that economy is producing its maximum possible output of goods. Given that resources are limited, the maximum possible output level is, of course, limited too. Therefore, as in Paddy's world, producing more of one kind of good will of necessity mean producing less of another. Again, the amount of reduction in the production of one good that is necessary in order to produce more of another is called *opportunity cost*.

Let us illustrate this concept by focusing on the issue of the cost of cleaning up environmental pollution. Suppose that the output of an economy may be divided into two categories — scrubbers and bundles of all other goods. (A scrubber is an antipollution device that removes pollutants from factory smokestack emissions.) One bundle will contain one of each and every good produced in the economy *except* a scrubber. A bundle may be thought of as a good — the composite good. The issue to be illustrated here is of more than academic interest. If we are to have a cleaner environment, we will need to use scrubbers in many production processes that cause pollution. How do we measure the cost to society of providing these devices?

Production and Choice

In answering this question we will make certain assumptions:

1. The existing state of technology will remain unchanged for the period in which we are examining this issue.

2. The total available supply of resources (land, labour, and capital) will remain the same. However, these resources may be shifted from producing scrubbers to producing bundles of all other goods and vice versa.

3. All available resources are fully employed (there is no unemployment or underemployment in the economy).

Given the existing supply of resources and level of technology, society must make choices. Should its fully employed resources be devoted entirely to the production of bundles of all other goods? Or should it reduce its output of bundles and use the factors of production released from that activity to produce scrubbers? If so, what combinations of bundles and scrubbers can it produce, given that its resources are fully employed? Clearly, the more scrubbers the economy produces, the more resources will have to be devoted to their production. Fewer resources will then be available for the production of bundles. Given that resources are fully employed, whatever combination of bundles and scrubbers the economy might think of producing, any other combination will necessarily contain more of one and less of the other. If the economy wants to produce more scrubbers, it will have to give up a certain number of bundles. If it wants to produce more bundles, it will have to give up a certain number of scrubbers.

Just as in Paddy's world, something must be given up in order to gain something. In short, you can't get something for nothing. You have to pay an opportunity cost.

Choices for Pollution Control

Some of the possible combinations of bundles and scrubbers that the economy we have been considering can produce per year when all resources are fully employed are listed in Table 2.2. If this economy were to devote all of its resources to producing bundles of all other goods, it would be able to produce 80 million bundles per year and no scrubbers (combination A). Although it seems very unrealistic and highly unlikely, the economy could devote all of its fully employed resources to producing scrubbers and go without all other goods (combination E). Such a choice would certainly carry environmental considerations to the extreme, in the sense that the cost would amount to giving up the production of all other goods. However, at the other extreme, combination A would probably not be very desirable either. With this combination, the economy would not be doing anything at all about pollution. If it were deemed desirable to do something about pollution, the economy could be moved away from point A toward point E. *To do this, resources would have to be shifted out of the production of bundles and into the production of scrubbers.* How much of a shift in this direction society chooses to make will depend upon the degree of concern about pollution. A cleaner environment will cost something. Suppose society's concern is such that it chooses to produce combination B instead of combination A. The cost of the 50,000 scrubbers it will now have is the 20 million bundles of all other goods it must give up to achieve this combination. If society has an even greater concern about pollution, combination C or even combination D could be chosen. However, to have the greater quantities of scrubbers associated with combination *C* or combination *D* requires that society forgo the production of more bundles of all other goods.

TABLE 2.2
Possible Combinations of Scrubbers and Bundles of All Other Goods That May Be Produced in a Full-Employment Economy (Hypothetical Data)

Product	Production Possibilities (Output per Year)				
	A	B	C	D	E
Scrubbers (in thousands)	0	50	80	100	110
Bundles of all other goods (in millions)	80	60	40	20	0

The Opportunity Cost of Choice

In summary, because economic resources are scarce, a full-employment economy cannot have more of both bundles and scrubbers. To have more of one, it must give up some of the other. The cost of having more of one is the opportunity cost, or the amount of the other, that must be given up. By choosing combination *B* in Table 2.2 instead of combination *A*, society must forgo the opportunity of having 20 million bundles of all other goods (the difference between 80 million and 60 million). The opportunity cost of the 50,000 scrubbers is therefore 20 million bundles. The opportunity cost of choosing combination *C* instead of combination *B*, or the opportunity cost of having an additional 30,000 scrubbers, is another 20 million bundles. The opportunity cost of choosing *C* instead of *A*, or the opportunity cost of having 80,000 scrubbers, is 40 million bundles, the difference between the number of bundles associated with combination *A* and the number associated

with combination *C*.

Whenever scarcity forces us to make a choice, we must pay an opportunity cost. This cost is measured in terms of forgone alternatives. All costs are opportunity costs (often simply referred to as costs). If you buy a note pad for a dollar, you forego the opportunity of spending that dollar on something else. Since the pad cost you a dollar, you now have a dollar less to spend on all other goods, unless you have an infinite supply of money, which is impossible. There is no free lunch.

---

*CHECKPOINT * 2.1*
What is the opportunity cost to Paddy of choosing combination d instead of combination c in Figure 2.1? Of choosing combination b instead of combination d? Of choosing combination d instead of combination b?

*Answers to all Checkpoints can be found at the back of the text.

The Economy's Production Possibilities Frontier

To derive our hypothetical economy's production possibilities frontier, let's plot the data from Table 2.2 on a graph. On the horizontal axis we measure the number of scrubbers. On the vertical axis we measure the number of bundles. As we did in Chapter 1, we now locate all the points on the graph that represent the possible scrubbers-bundles combinations listed in our table. If we draw a line connecting the points, the result looks like Figure 2.2. The curve slopes downward because when the available resources are fully employed, more scrubbers can be produced only by producing fewer bundles.

FIGURE 2.2
The Production Possibilities Frontier

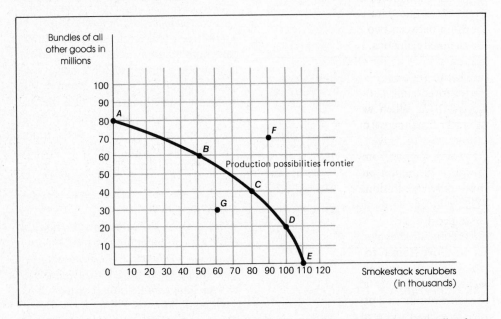

Each point on the downward-sloping curve represents some maximum-output combination for an economy whose available resources are fully employed. In this case, the output consists of scrubbers and bundles. Because no combination to the right or above the curve is possible, it is called the production possibilities frontier.

Point G represents a combination of scrubbers and bundles produced when the economy is operating inefficiently. Unemployment or underemployment of economic resources has resulted in a smaller output than is actually possible. Point F, on the other hand, represents a combination that cannot be produced given available resources and technology. This point can only be achieved if the production possibilities curve shifts outward as a result of economic growth.

On and Off the Frontier

The curve we have drawn by connecting all the points on the graph is our hypothetical economy's production possibilities frontier. *Each point on a production possibilities frontier represents a maximum output combination for an economy whose available resources are fully employed.* The term *frontier* is used because it is not possible for the economy to produce any combination of scrubbers and bundles represented by a point above or to the right of the curve. For example,

a combination of quantities of scrubbers and bundles represented by the point F in Figure 2.2 is not possible.

What if the economy's available resources are not being used efficiently (they are either unemployed or underemployed)? Then the economy cannot produce any combination of scrubbers and bundles represented by any point on its production possibilities frontier. It will only be able to produce output combinations represented by points inside the frontier, such as point G.

The Law of Increasing Costs

Figure 2.2 illustrates how graphs plotted from economic data can make the relationship between two economic variables immediately obvious. In Figure 2.2 we are struck at once by the change in the trade-off between bundles and scrubbers as we move from combination A to B to C and so on to E. When we move from A to B, a sacrifice (or cost) of 20 million bundles allows us to have 50,000 scrubbers. However, a move from B to C, which costs another 20 million bundles, allows us to have only an additional 30,000 scrubbers. The additional quantity of scrubbers obtained for each succeeding sacrifice of 20 million bundles continues to get smaller as we move from C to D to E. The reason for the deteriorating trade-off is that economic resources are more adaptable to some production processes than others. As more and more resources are shifted from the production of bundles into the production of scrubbers, we are forced to use factors of production whose productivity at making scrubbers is lower and lower relative to their productivity at making bundles. For example, when we move from A to B, a large number of engineers and scientists might be moved from bundle production to the highly technical production of scrubbers. As we continue moving from B to E, it becomes harder and harder to find labour resources of this nature. When moving from D to E, only the labour least suited for producing scrubbers will be left — poets, bricklayers, and so forth.

The decrease in the number of additional scrubbers obtained for each additional sacrifice of 20 million bundles as we move from A to E is a common economic phenomenon. It is sometimes called the **law of increasing costs**. To illustrate this law more clearly, divide the number of bundles that must be sacrificed by the additional number of scrubbers obtained by moving from one combination to the next. In the move from A to B, it costs 20 million bundles to obtain 50,000 scrubbers, or 400 bundles per scrubber. In the move from B to C, it costs 20 million bundles to obtain 30,000 scrubbers, or 666.6 bundles per scrubber. The move from C to D costs 1,000 bundles per scrubber. The move from D to E costs 2,000 bundles per scrubber. We are accustomed to measuring costs in dollars — so many dollars per unit of some good. Since dollars merely stand for the amounts of other goods they can buy, we have simply represented the cost of scrubbers in terms of bundles of other goods. *The law of increasing costs says that when moving along the production possibilities frontier, the cost per additional good obtained measured in terms of the good sacrificed rises due to the difference in productivity of resources when used in different production processes.*

Economic Growth

The production possibilities frontier in Figure 2.2 is based on a given state of technology and a fixed quantity of resources (land, labour, and capital). What happens if there is a change in technology or in the quantity of resources? The potential total output of the economy will change. Hence the production possibilities frontier will shift position.

The economy's population and labour force tend to grow over time. So too does its stock of capital — the quantities of machines, buildings, highways, factories, and so forth. In addition there are advances in the state of technology. *The growth in the economy's resources and improvements in technological know-how cause* **economic growth**, *an increase in the* *economy's ability to produce output.* This shifts the economy's production possibilities frontier outward (up and to the right) as shown in Figure 2.3. As a result the economy can produce more of both scrubbers and bundles when its available resources are fully employed.

Ecology's Price Tag

Some people are wondering whether the cost of protecting the environment is outrunning the benefits of doing so. The production possibilities frontier shows us the nature of the choices and the associated costs that must be considered when answering this question. The economist can objectively say that society would be making an inefficient use of resources if it decided to produce a combination of goods inside the frontier. Similarly, an economist can objectively say that a combination above or to the right of the frontier is not possible. But the following also needs to be said. In an economy such as that summarised in Table 2.2, it must

---

FIGURE 2.3
Economic Growth Means That the Production Possibilities Frontier Shifts Outward

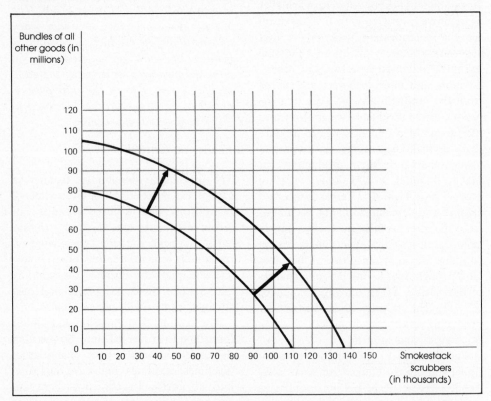

Growth in the economy's available resources and technolgical know-how shifts the production possibilities frontier outward. This allows the economy to produce more of both scrubbers and bundles — to have economic growth.

---

be pointed out to those who would like to produce 80,000 scrubbers that they cannot produce 80 million bundles as well. Almost everyone is for God, mother, and country — and environmental protection. The question is, How much are we willing to pay for it, *in terms of other goods and services not produced*?

Choice of Product Combination: Present Versus Future

We are all aware that choices made today are an important determinant of the choices available to us tomorrow. Therefore it should not surprise us that *an economy's present choice of a point on its production possibilities frontier influences the future location of that frontier.*

To demonstrate why this is so, suppose we divide the total output of an economy into two categories — consumption goods and capital goods. Consumption goods are such things as food, clothing, movies, tennis balls, records, and so forth. Capital goods are such things as machinery, tools, and factories; they enable us to produce other goods, including machinery, tools, and factories. An increase in the quantity

FIGURE 2.4
Present Choices Affect Future Production Possibilities Frontiers

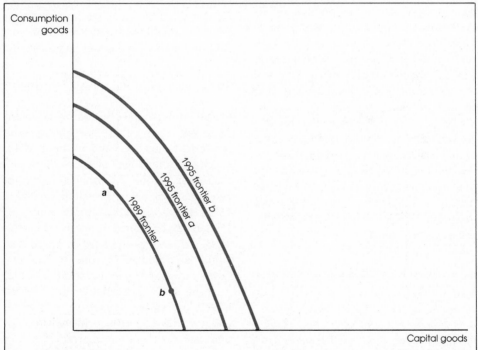

If the economy chooses point *a* on its 1989 frontier, it emphasises consumption goods production; if it chooses point *b*, it favours capital goods production. Therefore choice *a* gives rise to less economic growth or a smaller outward shift in the frontier (to 1995 frontier *a*) than does choice *b* (to 1995 frontier *b*).

and quality of capital goods contributes to economic growth, the expansion of the economy's capacity to produce all goods. Suppose the production possibilities frontier for our economy in 1989 is as shown in Figure 2.4 — capital goods are measured on the horizontal axis, consumption goods are measured on the vertical axis.

If the economy chooses point *a* on its 1989 frontier, it will produce an output combination consisting mostly of consumption goods. Alternatively, if it chooses point *b* on the frontier, the economy will produce a combination predominantly made up of capital goods. All other things remaining the same, we can expect the economy's future (1995) production possibilities frontier to be farther out if it chooses point *b* on its 1989 frontier than if it chooses point *a*. That is, the choice of point *a* on the 1989 frontier will give rise to 1995 frontier *a*, whereas choosing point *b* will give rise to 1995 frontier *b*. The reason is that choice *b* produces more capital goods, the kind of goods that contribute to economic growth, whereas choice *a* produces fewer of such goods. We hasten to add, however, that this does not mean *b* is a better choice than *a*. After all, remember that choice *b* means having fewer consumption goods to enjoy in 1989 relative to the number resulting from choice *a*.

CHECKPOINT 2.2
In Table 2.2 what is the opportunity cost of choosing combination C instead of D; B instead of C; or A instead of D? Consider the movement from E to A in Figure 2.2 and represent the law of increasing cost measured in terms of scrubbers.

BASIC PROBLEMS FOR ANY ECONOMY

Given an economy's available resources and technology, we have seen how the production possibilities from which it may choose can be characterised by a production possibilities frontier. A frontier can be determined for any economy, whatever its form of government. A knowledge of what is possible is necessary in order to answer a number of important questions or problems that any economy, be it that of the Soviet Union or Australia or Pakistan, must solve. These questions confront socialist, communist, and capitalist countries, developed and underdeveloped economies alike. These questions are:
(1) What and how much to produce?
(2) How should production be organised?
(3) For whom should goods be produced?

What and How Much to Produce

We could draw up an incredibly large list of goods that could be produced in Australia from apples and automobiles to zucchini, zoom lenses and zips. Some of the goods on the list, while possible to produce, might not be desired by anybody. Other goods, such as various kinds of food, might be desired by nearly everyone. If we were to draw up a list of goods that could be produced by one of the less developed countries in the world, it would probably be considerably shorter. Nevertheless, given its respective list, each country would have to decide what goods and how much of each to produce.

In the economy summarised in Table 2.1, the answer to the question, 'What to produce?' was scrubbers and bundles of all other goods. The question, 'How much?' really asks what point on the production possibilities frontier would be selected. The answer to this question must be decided by society's tastes and priorities. The answer is thus a value judgment. As we noted in Chapter 1, an economist's value judgment has no superior claim over anyone else's. It may be that a relatively underdeveloped country seeking rapid economic growth and industrialisation would feel little concern about the environmental impact of these processes. It might not want to divert resources to producing scrubbers. However, a country such as the United States, having experienced growth and industrialisation, might be more aware of their adverse environmental impact. It therefore might be more willing to divert a larger share of resources to producing scrubbers. Whether the cost of protecting the environment is outrunning the benefits will depend on who is assessing the benefits.

Who makes the decisions about what and how much to produce? The answer to this question varies greatly from one economy to another. In countries such as the Soviet Union or Communist China, these decisions are made by a central planning bureau of the government. In Australia and New Zealand, North America and Western Europe many of the decisions about resource allocation are made by the pricing system, or market mechanism. However, government also intervenes in this process to a significant extent. The prices of some important products are effectively determined by state governments. For example government established dairy authorities operate in most states and require government approval before increasing milk prices. State electricity commissions require government approval before they raise power charges. Public metropolitan

transport systems also need to have fare increases approved for buses, trams and trains. Air fares by private carriers have been subject to approval by the independent air fares tribunal appointed by the Commonwealth Government.

Government also affects the allocation of resources in our economy by restricting the freedom of businesses or individuals to produce what they want. Controls exist on pollution, environmental damage and shop trading hours in most Australian states. Similarly safety standards and building regulations prevent the economy from operating in a completely free fashion. Such controls exist because our society, through its elected leaders, has decided the market mechanism does not produce entirely satisfactory or optimal results if left without such checks.

There is considerable debate about how much regulation of the market mechanism there should be in Australia. The debate about when markets should be regulated and how they can best be regulated will be considered in more detail. The role of government in our system is an important subject in both macroeconomics and microeconomics.

How Should Production Be Organised?

In discussing the production possibilities frontier, we emphasised that to be on the frontier it is necessary to use economic resources in the most efficient way. Once society has determined what goods to produce, the amount of each of those goods it will be able to produce will depend on how available resources are allocated to various productive activities. Earlier we said it would be pretty stupid to try and grow our sugar cane in South Australia and wheat on the sub tropical

Queensland coast. It would be equally silly if we didn't choose the appropriate technology. Cutting cane by hand is no longer the best way of doing things in Australia (though it still may be so in poorer countries or on difficult land). Similarly no one attempts to harvest wheat in broad hectares using a scythe. Ideally, *society should allocate available resources to productive activities and use known productive techniques in such a way that no reallocation of resources or change of technique could yield more of any good without yielding less of another. This is true of any combination of goods represented by any point on the production possibilities frontier.*

This ideal is easy enough to understand and describe. But it may have struck you by now as a little like being told that the way to make money on the stock market is to buy low and sell high. You can understand that perfectly and wouldn't disagree a bit. But only a moment's reflection will lead you to ask the inevitable question: 'Yes, but how do I *know* when a stock is at its low and when it is at its high?' The stock market crash has provided plenty of evidence that very few people *do know* when prices are going to rise and precisely when they are going to fall. Similarly, an economy doesn't have a big television screen up in the sky with a picture of its production possibilities frontier and a white dot that can be moved around by turning knobs until society has got itself right at the desired spot on the frontier. Society can't 'see' the economy's production possibilities frontier, nor is it a simple matter of turning a few control knobs to 'move' onto it. So how should an economy go about organising its available resources in order to use them most efficiently? How will the most efficient production techniques be deter-

mined? What regulating mechanisms or management techniques can be used to ensure that the appropriate kinds and necessary amounts of resources will be directed to industries producing desired goods? Any economy, be it centrally planned or completely market oriented, wants to be on its production possibilities frontier. The question is, How does it get there?

For Whom to Produce

For whom should the output of the economy be produced? Put another way, how should the economy's total output be distributed among the individual members of the economy? Should it be distributed to individuals according to their productive contribution to the making of that output? Or should we take from each according to his or her ability and give to each according to his or her need? If people receive strictly according to their productive contribution, it's clear some people are going to be terribly poor. On the other hand, if there is no relationship between an individual's productive contribution and the reward received for it, what will be the incentive for hard work? If the able and productive members of society do not have incentives to work hard, the total output of the economy will not be as large. If the total pie is smaller, there simply will be less to go around. All societies must wrestle with this problem. They must decide how to distribute output in such a way as to encourage the productive members to work up to their ability and at the same time try to maintain a minimum standard of living for all. In short, they must decide what degree of income inequality can be tolerated given these conflicting goals. The range of opinion on this is wide indeed and can fire the most heated debates. It is a matter of politics, cultural values, and moral issues.

In addition to solving this problem, all economies must decide how much of the total output should go to government, how much to business, and how much to households. This, of course, raises questions about how taxes should be levied and who should pay them. It raises questions about how much of the decision-making process for allocation of resources should be in the hands of the government rather than of the private sector (households and businesses). In wartime, any society is likely to give to the government whatever portion of output it needs to ensure survival. In peacetime, without the pressure of such a common goal, decisions about how to distribute total output are not usually made with such a consensus.

Full Utilisation of Resources

In our discussion of economic efficiency and the problem of how to organise production, we emphasised that *an economy can fall short of its production possibilities frontier of resources are misallocated or if the best-known production techniques are not used. Another kind of economic inefficiency, also noted earlier occurs whenever available resources are allowed to stand idle. This kind of inefficiency will also keep an economy from operating on its production possibilities frontier*.

In twentieth-century capitalist economies, such as that of the United States, there have been frequent periods of recession, which means that significant amounts of labour and other available resources have been idle, or unemployed. During the depression of the 1930s, the measured unemployment rate was around

25 per cent. Economists estimate that the actual rate of unemployment may have been considerably higher than this. (The reason is that some of the unemployed were not reported.) In capitalist economies we often refer to the recurring pattern of increasing and decreasing unemployment associated with decreasing and increasing output as **business fluctuations** or **business cycles**. Centrally planned economies such as those of the Soviet Union, Communist China, and the Eastern European nations are not free from the problem of fluctuations in their production of output. The underlying reasons why they have these difficulties are different, and for ideological reasons they describe the problem differently. An economist visiting the United States from the central planning bureau of an Eastern European country was asked if they experienced anything like our business fluctuations. He said, 'Oh, no.' The question was then rephrased, 'Well, don't you ever experience fluctuations in production?' He responded, 'Oh, you mean "technical cycles"!'

In the industrialised economies of the Western world, the problem of eliminating or reducing unemployment of labour and other available resources is a high priority of economic policy. Australia has long identified full employment as one of its major economic objectives together with price stability. In the 1960s we believed that we could achieve reasonable price stability with an unemployment rate of about two per cent of the labour force. Since the inflation of the 1970s we no longer believe such a target is attainable. The reduction of unemployment is still an important objective for Australian governments, but with unemployment and inflation running at 7 to 10 per cent achieving a 5 per cent level would be a big improvement.

Unemployment of economic resources is similar in its effects to the underemployment of economic resources that results from their misallocation to inappropriate activities or when the best-known techniques of production are not used. Both unemployment and underemployment cause the economy to produce at a point inside its production possibility frontier. However, the appropriate ways to deal with these two problems are quite different. *The underemployment problem requires an answer to the question of how to organise production.* When it is argued that allowing new firms to set up in an industry or the removal of government controls on shopping hours will lead to unemployment this is usually an indication that underemployment exists. Fewer people could do the same job and the goods would be produced more cheaply if the controls were removed. These kinds of problems are generally studied in microeconomics.

Remedies for the unemployment problem generally take the form of ensuring that there is enough demand for goods and services to require the full utilisation of all available resources to meet that demand. You might think it strange that resources could be idle at all, and that it could be due to a low demand for goods. After all, don't people work in order to earn income to buy goods? Unfortunately, in a money-using economy producing many kinds of goods, a person's offer of labour services in one place is quite removed from his or her desired purchase of goods in another. A line of unemployed job-seekers at a steel mill's gate does not mean that each wants to work in direct exchange for a tonne of cold rolled steel to be carried home at the end of the day. The mill manager's plans to produce steel and hire workers are affected quite differently by a line of job-seeking, unemployed steelworkers than they are by a line of customers wanting to place orders. It is not obvious that if workers were employed in the back, customers would materialise out front to purchase their output. This is true even though the workers would most likely use their earned money to buy a multitude of items requiring steel. All firms in the economy producing all kinds of goods are in the same situation as the steel mill. Clearly when there are unemployed labourers and other resources in the whole economy, it is a result of the totality of these situations. The remedies for this sort of problem are studied in macroeconomics.

Change, Stability and Growth

All economies are subject to change. The underlying causes of change are sometimes quite predictable. Population growth and the increase of technological know-how are a main impetus to economic growth. These kinds of change are fairly steady and ongoing. Population growth in underdeveloped countries is typically higher than in more industrialised countries. It is so high, in fact, that it poses a problem for those economies. Namely, it makes it very difficult to increase the standard of living. The growth in the number of people to be fed makes it difficult to divert resources from agricultural production to the capital formation needed for industrialisation. This applies not just to the formation of physical capital but to the investment in human capital needed to provide the level of literacy and know-how required of the labour force in an industrialised economy. Australia's immigration policy after the Second World War was designed to bring large numbers of settlers partly because

---

POLICY PERSPECTIVE

Choice of an Economic System

Societies choose not only what combination of goods and services to produce, but also the way in which they will produce them. A completely unregulated laissez faire system or a pure command economy are unknown — national economies mix to varying degree the market and government decision making. One measure of the range is illustrated in the following table. It expresses government expenditure as a percentage of the value of production in various countries. It gives an indication of how great the variation can be even in economies we do not normally think of as planned economies.

TABLE P2.1
Government Outlays as a Percentage of the Gross Value of Production in Various Countries 1984

Country	Government share of value of production
France	48
Greece	35
India	20
Italy	44
Japan	30
Korea (South)	21
Sweden	60
USA	32

Source; *United Nations Accounts Statistics, 1986*

As many of the planned economies use a different method of calculating the value of production it is not possible to make a direct comparison. An indication of the difference is provided by the fact that only about 5 per cent of Hungary's value of material production in 1984 was attributed to the private sector. Expenditure is not the only indication of how an economic system operates. A government may regulate an economy without engaging directly in production or being a heavy spender. The extent to which societies depend on the market place and government planning changes. Sometimes this change is gradual and sometimes it occurs as a sudden policy shift — perhaps revolution. In many western countries the government sector is larger than it was 20 years ago. Yet in some command economies there is recognition that market forces have a role to play in economic decision making. Yugoslavia, Hungary, China and even the USSR itself show increasing signs of recognising market mechanisms can help society make the right choices and operate in a more efficient manner. Table P2.2 shows how the relative importance of the government sector has changed in Australia in recent years.

TABLE P2.2
The Government Sector in Australia 1975 to 1985

Year	Federal Government	Government outlays as a share of the value of production (per cent)
1965	Liberal/CP	30
1970	Liberal/CP	32
1975	ALP	37
1980	Liberal/NCP	38
1985	ALP	43

Questions

1. Study the two tables. What do they indicate about the importance of government in the Australian economy? What influence, if any, does the political party in power in Canberra appear to have had on the size of the government sector?
2. What reasons might there be for some people expressing concern about the size of the government sector in Australia? Which of the following do you think are affected by the size of the government sector:
   (a) the position on our production possibilities frontier,
   (b) Australia's capacity to reach its production possibilities frontier,
   (c) our ability to push the frontier outwards.

it was considered that a faster rate of population growth was necessary for faster economic growth and partly because it was thought that a larger population would make Australia a less tempting prey for potential enemies. Immigration and population policy has undergone many changes in the 40 years since that policy was formulated. Great attention has been given to Australia's capacity to absorb immigrants and the criteria for admitting people have changed considerably. A more mature outlook has meant that the old 'White Australia Policy' has been replaced by one based on merit, Australia's labour force needs and humanitarian and social considerations.

The relationship between population and economic well-being is a complex one. In China and India, the need is to restrict the rate of growth of the population and

birth control measures are of paramount importance. In much of Africa the ever present fear of starvation is a constant reminder that the global economic system cannot provide sufficient food to provide the barest essentials in some countries in contrast to great wealth in others.

Often, drastic institutional and political changes, even when well intended, can cause severe economic problems for an economy. After the Communists took over in China in 1949, they instituted a new agricultural and industrialisation program. This program increased grain production from 108 million tons in 1949 to 182 million tons in 1956 and steel production from 360,000 tons in 1950 to 3.32 million tons by 1956. Then in 1958 the Chinese leadership attempted to institute what they called the Great Leap Forward. They constructed backyard steel furnaces throughout the country, mandated 18-hour workdays, and transferred half a billion peasants into giant communes. All this, combined with three years of bad weather, proved to be too much change for the economy to adapt to. In some places, there was near starvation for the first time since the Communist takeover. Production dropped sharply and economic progress may have been set back by as much as a decade.

A major cause of instability in industrialised Western economies in recent years has been increases in the general levels of prices that we commented on earlier. This phenomenon is more commonly referred to as inflation. Since World War II, the general direction of prices has been continually upward. But during the 1970s the rate of increase of prices rose considerably. Perhaps of equal concern from the standpoint of stability has been the variation in the rate of increase. In Australia, the annual rate of inflation, measured by the consumer price index, rose very sharply, from an average of under 5 per cent from 1969/70 to 1972/73 to over 13 per cent in 1973/74 and more than 18 per cent the following year. It remained at over 12 per cent for the next two years before gradually coming down to levels around 8 per cent in the mid 1980s. This sort of variation caused considerable uncertainty among consumers and business. Businesses became more reluctant to undertake investment in new plant and equipment essential for economic growth. Wage bargaining was accompanied by friction as the Arbitration Commission tried methods of fixing wage rates to maintain workers' real wages and unions attempted to anticipate how high inflation would be in the future. Consumers were confused, and it must be said

so too was the Commonwealth Government. Economists, who a few years earlier had been so confident were unable to agree about the advice they could give to government. Inflation was accompanied by business recession. One thing economists are agreed upon is that severe price inflation is a most undesirable source of change in an economy.

Every economy has to contend with various kinds of change at one time or another. Some are thought to be desirable, such as the growth in technological knowledge. In industrialised economies of the West, change in consumer tastes and an economy's ability to adapt to meet those changes is generally considered desirable. Other kinds of change, including inflation, recession, and external shocks to the economy, such as that caused by the Arab oil embargo, are on everybody's bad list. About some forms of change we have mixed feelings. A typical conflict we face continuously in Australia is between the need to develop industries that use our natural resources and the desire to preserve the environment. Recently, in Queensland and Tasmania forest-based industries and forest workers have claimed they are threatened by conservationist policies of the Commonwealth Government. The sense of conflict is heightened because of the failure of Australians to agree about how much development there should be and how much conservation. Who do you think is right? Why?

A major problem to be solved by an economy is how to adapt to various kinds of change so as to maximise the benefits derived from the desirable aspects of change and minimise the losses caused by the undesirable.

CHECKPOINT 2.3
Do you think the questions of what to produce and for whom to produce it are of a normative or a positive nature? Why?

THE VARIETY OF ECONOMIC SYSTEMS

There is a wide variety of ways of organising an economy to answer the basic questions we have discussed in this chapter. How an economy deals with the basic problem of scarcity — the questions it poses — is also an expression of its vision of the relationship between the individual and society. The way in which a society chooses to organise its economy is therefore to a large extent a reflection of its cultural values and political **ideology**. It was in recognition of this fact that the subject of economics was originally called political economy. Almost any debate over the relative merits of various types of economic systems cannot avoid dealing with the different political ideologies on which they are based. In this section we will consider two basic types of economic systems without dwelling at any length on their political and ideological implications. Nonetheless, it should be kept in mind that these implications are usually regarded as matters of considerable importance.

Pure Market Economy, Laissez Faire Capitalism

Laissez faire is a French expression that means 'let [people] do [as they choose].' Especially in matters of economics, it means allowing people to do as they please without governmental regulations and controls. *The ideological basis of such an economic system is the belief that if each economic unit is allowed to make free choices in pursuit of its own best interests, the interests of all will be best served.*

What are the main features of a **pure market economy** based on laissez faire **capitalism**? The means of production are privately owned by private citizens and private institutions. Private property is the rule. Government ownership is generally limited to public buildings and other facilities needed by the government in order to provide such things as national defence, a judicial system, police and fire protection, and public schools and roads. There is freedom of choice for consumers, businesses, and all resource suppliers. Consumers may purchase what they want subject to the limits of their money incomes — there is consumer sovereignty. Businesses are free to purchase and utilise resources to produce whatever products they desire and sell them in markets of their choice — there is free enterprise. Suppliers of resources such as labour, land, and financial capital are likewise free to sell them in whatever markets they please. The major constraint on businesses and resource suppliers is imposed by the marketplace, where consumer sovereignty decides what goods and services can and cannot be produced and sold profitably. Freedom of choice and all market activities are subject to the broadest legal limits consistent with maintaining law and order and with enforcing contracts freely entered into by consenting parties.

The Market Mechanism

The mechanism that serves to coordinate the activities of consumers, businesses, and all suppliers of resources is the market.

A **market** is defined as an area within which buyers and sellers of a particular good are in such close communication that the price of that good tends to be the same everywhere in the area. The answers to the questions of what and how much to produce are determined by the signals communicated between buyers and sellers via the interacting network of markets and prices. The potential buyers of a good make contact with the sellers or suppliers in the market. Then a price must be determined such that suppliers will provide just the quantity of the good that buyers wish to purchase. On the buyers' (demand) side of the market, the level of the price determines who will buy the good and how much will be bought. On the suppliers' side of the market, the price level determines who will supply the good and how much will be supplied. If buyers want more than is being supplied at the prevailing price, they will signal their desires for more by bidding up the price. Suppliers will then respond by providing more of the good. If at the prevailing price sellers are providing a larger quantity of the good than buyers demand, prices will be bid down. This will be a signal to sellers to reduce the quantity of the good they supply to the market. In this way prices serve as the communicating link between buyers and sellers in a market economy.

Markets Determine What, How, for Whom

The markets for different goods are interrelated because the alternative to using one good is to use another. If the price of beef were felt to be too high, one alternative would be to buy poultry. And if the price of poultry were likewise thought to be too high, another alternative might be to buy ham. Hence the amounts of these goods buyers will demand will depend on the price of beef relative to the price of poultry and ham. Similarly, suppliers will be induced to supply those goods that are selling for the highest prices relative to the prices of other goods. Changes in the price in one market will set up a chain reaction of adjustments in quantities demanded and supplied in related markets. For example, other things being equal, an increase in demand for new housing will cause an increase in the price (wages) of architects, bricklayers, carpenters, furniture sales personnel, and so on. This will induce labour resources to move from other activities into those that now appear relatively more rewarding. All markets in the economy are interrelated with one another to varying extents in this way. It is the 'invisible hand' of the marketplace that determines the allocation of resources, *what* goods will be produced, and *how much* of each.

Competition among suppliers of goods and labour services will ensure that the most efficient and productive will charge the lowest price for any good and thus make the sale to shopping buyers. Hence the forces of the marketplace will cause labour and other resources to flow into those occupations and uses for which they are best suited. This is the way a market economy determines *how production should be organised.*

For whom are goods produced in a market economy? Obviously, for whomever is able to pay the price for them. And who are these people? Those who are able to sell their labour services and any other resources they own that can be used in the production of other goods. The emphasis is on competition and a reward structure oriented toward the most efficient and productive. The vision of the individual's relation to society that underlies pure market, laissez faire capitalism has sometimes been characterised as an ideology of the survival of the fittest. All are free to go into any line of work or business they choose, to take any risks at making as much or losing as much money as they care to. The individual is entitled to all the rewards of good decisions and must bear the full consequences of bad ones.

Resource Utilisation

How fully do pure market systems utilise their available resources? This is difficult to evaluate, because history provides few, if any, examples of a pure market economy without any form of government intervention. However, many of the industrialised economies of the Western world have a significant portion of their economic decisions determined by market forces. This was even more so in the nineteenth century and the twentieth century prior to World War II. The Great Depression, which afflicted these nations during the 1930s, together with the record of previous decades, suggests that pure market economies have difficulty keeping their available resources fully employed all the time.

Change, Stability and Growth

As to change, stability and growth, economies that most closely approximate pure market, laissez faire capitalism have achieved some of the highest standards of living in the world. Such systems seem particularly well suited to responding to the changing tastes of consumers. They are also able to develop new products and bring new technologies to the everyday use of the masses. From the standpoint of stability, fluctuations in economic activity as measured by GDP, employ-

ment, and the behaviour of prices have always been a source of concern in such economies.

Obviously, one would be hard pressed to find a pure form of this type of economy today. In the late eighteenth century at the beginning of the Industrial Revolution, England and the United States came pretty close. Nonetheless, there are still many economies today where markets play a dominant role. Moreover, *the concept of pure market, laissez faire capitalism may be viewed as one extreme on a spectrum of ways of organizing an economy.*

The Command Economy

In the **command economy**, also called the planned economy, the government answers the questions of how to organise production, what and how much to produce, and for whom. These answers take the form of plans that may extend for as far as 10 to 20 years into the future. In such a planned economy, the government literally commands that these plans be carried out.

Government Domination

Typically, the government owns the means of production, as in the Soviet Union or Communist China, but this is not always so. In Nazi Germany the government controlled and planned the economy, but ownership remained largely in private hands. *In economies where planning is the most centralised and complete, the government must be very authoritarian. Therefore, it is often a totalitarian regime — ideologically committed to communism or to fascism.* Even in these economies the government may allow markets to operate in certain areas of the economy if it is consistent with, or helpful to, the achievement of other planning objectives. The Soviet Union allows this to some extent in its agricultural sector, for example. In a command economy all forms of labour, including management, are essentially government employees. The state is the company store, the only company.

Planning What, How and for Whom

The underlying rationale for a command economy is that the government knows best what is most beneficial for the entire economy and for its individual parts. In a command economy there are differences between what consumers may want and what the planners have decided to produce. If planners do not want to devote resources to television sets, consumers simply will go without. Once the plan for the entire economy has been drawn up, each producing unit in the economy is told what and how much it must produce of various goods to fulfill its part of the plan. This determines each unit's need for labour, capital equipment, and other inputs. Obviously it is not easy to centrally coordinate all the component parts of the plan to ensure that the right kinds and amounts of labour, capital, and other inputs are available to each producing unit so that each may satisfy its individual plan. *How to organise production* is quite a task for central planners overseeing the economy of an entire nation. Managing BHP, Elders IXL or TNT pales by comparison.

For *whom* is output produced? Centrally planned economies typically provide for all citizens regardless of their productive contribution to the output of the economy. However, planners cannot avoid the fact that human nature does respond to material incentives. As a result, government-determined wage scales vary from one occupation or profession to the next, depending on where planners feel there are shortages or surpluses of needed labour skills. This, of course, depends on how authoritarian the government wants to be in allowing people to pick and choose their occupation or profession. For example, it appears that Communist China is more authoritarian in this regard than some of the Eastern European countries.

Resource Utilisation

Full utilisation of available resources presumably does not pose a problem in a command economy. Remember that by full utilisation we mean that there are no available resources standing idle. This is a different issue from whether or not resources may be underemployed due to poor planning. In the Soviet Union planners seem to have continual difficulty in meeting their agricultural goals. If they think their goals are reasonable, their relatively frequent shortfalls from these goals suggest that the resources devoted to agriculture may not be as efficiently employed as possible, even allowing for setbacks caused by bad weather.

Change, Stability and Growth

How do planned economies deal with *change* and *growth*? Obviously, in a planned economy growth and many kinds of change can be engineered by the central planning bureau to a large extent. If the government wants more economic growth, the central planning agency will draw up plans devoting a larger share of the economy's resources to the production of capital goods. On the other hand, critics argue that authoritarian control, large bureaucratic structure, and centrally dictated goals put a damper on individual initiative and innovation. Because of this it is argued that technological discovery and change are inhibited. This is considered a major factor in economic growth, a factor that critics feel is weak in planned economies. The *stability* of planned economies depends on how well the government is able to set realistic goals and structure the appropriate plans to attain them. If goals are too ambitious, and if the amount of reorganisation in the economy is too great for the time allowed, the loss of economic stability can be severe. This was the case with Communist China's ill-fated Great Leap Forward discussed earlier.

Summing Up

The planned or command economy may be viewed as representing the other extreme on the spectrum of economic organisation from that of pure market, laissez faire capitalism. No two economies in the world are exactly alike, but each may be thought of as lying somewhere on the spectrum between the two extremes we have described. Most fall under the very broad category of the **mixed economy**, which represents all the in-betweens. All economies have to grapple with the economic problem posed by scarcity, unlimited wants, and the consequent need for choice. In the next chapter we will examine the nature of the mixed economy.

CHECKPOINT 2.4
Describe the likely process of selecting a point on the production possibilities frontier of Figure 2.2 (that is, the combination of scrubbers and bundles) for a pure market economy and a planned, or command, economy. For each of these

two kinds of economies, what difference do you think it makes, in terms of the point chosen on the frontier, if they are industrially underdeveloped as compared to the likely outcome if they are industrially advanced?

SUMMARY

1. While available economic resources are limited, human wants are virtually unlimited. This creates the fundamental problem of scarcity, which makes it necessary to make choices.

2. Economic efficiency requires that there be no unemployment or underemployment of resources. Unemployment exists whenever some available resources are idle. Underemployment (or resource misallocation) exists if certain available resources are employed to do jobs for which other available resources are better suited. It also exists whenever the best available technology is not used in a production process.

3. When there is no unemployment or underemployment of available resources, an economy is able to produce the maximum amount of goods possible. When producing this maximum, the economy is said to be on its production possibilities frontier. This frontier is a curve connecting the maximum possible output combinations of goods for a fully employed economy. In this situation, the production of more of one kind of good is possible only if the economy produces less of another. The cost of having more of one good is the amount of the other that must be given up. This cost is often called the opportunity cost of a good.

4. Economic growth occurs when an economy's available supply of resources is increased or when there is an increase in technological know-how. As a result, the production possibilities frontier expands outward. The output combination chosen on today's frontier affects the amount of capital goods that will be available tomorrow. Therefore, today's choice will affect the location of tomorrow's production possibilities frontier.

5. Any economy, whatever its political ideology, must answer certain questions that arise because of the basic economic problem of scarcity. Every economy must decide what goods to produce, how much to produce, how to organise production, and for whom output is to be produced. The answer to the question of what to produce determines the nature and location of the production possibilities frontier. The answer to the question of how much to produce determines the point chosen on the frontier. How to organise production determines whether the chosen point on the frontier will be reached. For whom to produce is largely determined by ideological orientation as to the proper mix of free markets, government regulation, and central planning.

6. Every economy must concern itself with maintaining full employment of its resources (avoiding unemployment). This has frequently been a problem for the industrialised economies of the West. Every economy must also deal with change. The stability of an economy depends very much on how well it is able to adjust to change. An important kind of change is economic growth, and economies are often judged on how well they promote economic growth.

7. There are two basic kinds of economies, or ways of organising the process of deciding what and how much, how, and for whom to produce. Each kind presumes a particular relationship between the individual and the state. They are basically distinguished by the amount of government intervention they permit in the decision-making process of the economy.

   a. *Pure market, laissez faire capitalism.* Individual economic units are given free choice in all economic decisions, which are completely decentralised. There is no interference by government in the form of regulations or controls. Markets and prices are the sole coordinating mechanisms for allocating resources and organising production.

   b. *Command or planned economy.* An authoritarian government decides what and how much, how, and for whom to produce. Government typically owns the means of production, plans economic activities, and commands that these plans be carried out. The underlying rationale is that the government knows best what is most beneficial for the entire economy and its individual parts.

KEY TERMS AND CONCEPTS

business cycles
business fluctuations
capitalism
command economy
economic efficiency
economic growth
economic problem
ideology
laissez faire
law of increasing costs
market
mixed economy

opportunity cost
production possibilities frontier
pure market economy
resource misallocation
trade-off
underemployment
unemployment

QUESTIONS AND PROBLEMS

1. What is the opportunity cost to you of continuing studies at college? How would you estimate it? What elements should you include in your calculation? How might the opportunity cost of attending college or university differ for a part-time and a full-time student? If the government were to increase the student administration fee to $1,000 would this affect the opportunity cost of attending college?

2. The following is a production possibilities table for computers and jet aeroplanes:

| Product | Production Possibilities | | | | |
	A	B	C	D	E
Computers (in thousands)	0	25	40	50	55
Jet aeroplanes (in thousands)	40	30	20	10	0

a. Plot the production possibilities frontier for the economy characterised by this table.

b. Demonstrate the law of increasing costs using the data in this table.

c. Suppose technological progress doubles the productivity of the process for making computers and also of that for making jet aeroplanes. What would the numbers in the production possibilities table look like in that case? Plot the new production possibilities frontier.

d. Suppose technological progress doubles the productivity of the process for making computers but there is no change in the process for making jet aeroplanes. What would the numbers in the production possibilities table be now? Plot the new production possibilities frontier.

e. Suppose technological progress doubles the productivity of the process for making jet aeroplanes but there is no change in the process for making computers. What would the numbers in the production possibilities frontier be now? Plot the new production possibilities frontier. Why is it that, despite the fact that there is no change in the productivity of producing computers, it is now possible at any given level of production of jet aeroplanes to have more computers?

3. Consider a production possibilities frontier for consumer goods and capital goods. How would the choice of a point on that frontier affect the position of tomorrow's frontier? Choose three different points on today's production possibilities frontier and indicate the possible location of tomorrow's frontier that is associated with each.

4. Construct your own production possibilities frontier by putting a grade point scale on the vertical axis to measure a grade in your economics course and the number of waking hours in a typical day (say 16) on the horizontal axis. Out of those 16 hours per day, how many do you think you would have to give up to get a *D*? a *C*? a *B*? an *A*? Plot the frontier determined by these combinations.

5. Compare and contrast the ways in which the two types of economies we have discussed deal with the five basic questions or problems any economy faces.

3

The Nature of
the Mixed Economy

AFTER READING THIS CHAPTER YOU WILL BE ABLE TO:

1. Explain why markets exist.

2. Explain how money makes trading much easier and therefore
    promotes specialisation and trade.

3. Define *normal profit*.

4. Define the role of profit in the creation and allocation of capital.

5. State the nature and rationale of government intervention in a
    mixed economy.

In a mixed economy the answers to the questions what and how much to produce, how to organise production, and for whom to produce are determined by a mixture of government intervention, regulation and control in some areas of the economy, coupled with private enterprise and a reliance on markets in other areas.

In some mixed economies, government intervention extends to the ownership of certain industries — such industries are called **nationalised industries**. In Australia, for example, the railways, postal system, telephones, electricity, gas and water supply are all publicly owned. The public by and large felt that these industries would operate better under complete government control than under private ownership subject to varying degrees of government regulation, as is the case with the railways and airlines in the United States. Hence, *a mixed economy may involve not only a mixture of private and public decision making but a mixture of private and public ownership as well.*

The role of government varies from one mixed economy to the next, reflecting the varying opinions on this issue in different countries. Nonetheless, there are certain characteristics common to all. They all have markets where the exchange of goods and services takes place using money as the medium of exchange. They all have had a strong tradition of capitalism stemming from their history of economic development, particularly the fact that they experienced the Industrial Revolution.[1] They all have felt the need to modify

[1]Countries that most commonly come to mind are Australia, the United States, Great Britain, Canada, the Scandinavian countries, France, West Germany, Italy, New Zealand, and Japan.

capitalism and the workings of free markets through government intervention.

In this chapter we will get a brief overview of some of the main characteristics of mixed economies like our own. Much of the analysis in the rest of this book will focus on mixed economies. This chapter will also briefly explore the role of markets, money, profits, and government in such an economic system. Of course a good deal of what we say about each of these subjects is true whether or not we are speaking of a mixed economy.

MARKETS AND MONEY

Specialisation gives rise to the need for trade, and trade creates markets. Money makes trade easier and therefore encourages specialisation and a more extensive development of markets. Let's consider the truth of each of these statements in turn.

Specialisation and Markets

Why do markets exist in the first place? Why are goods traded? What is it that leads people to go to market? The answer lies in the fact that each of us is better at doing some things than at doing others. We tend to specialise in that thing we are best at. We 'trade on it'. Have you ever heard it said of film stars that 'they trade on their good looks'?

When each of us specialises in that particular thing he or she is best at, the whole economy is able to produce more of everything than if each of us tries to be self-sufficient. Of course when each specialises in producing one thing, each is dependent on others for the production of everything else. *With specialisation most of what one produces is a surplus that must be traded for the other things that one wants. Hence the more* **specialisation of labour** *there is in an economy, the greater is the need for trade.* And as trade becomes more important to the functioning of an economy, markets in all kinds of goods and services become more commonplace.

The Role of Money

A prominent characteristic of markets with which you are familiar is that goods are traded for money. *In a* **barter economy** *goods are traded for goods.* The more an economy is characterised by specialisation of labour, the less likely it is that we will observe goods being traded directly for goods. What led people to start using money in the first place? The fundamental reason for the invention and existence of money is that it makes specialisation and trade much easier. This is most obvious if we consider the difficulties of trade in a barter economy.

Trade in a Barter Economy

Suppose you are a member of an economy in which each individual specialises in the production of a particular good. Like everyone else, you produce more of your particular good than you need for yourself and trade the surplus for other goods. Suppose you specialise in chopping wood and today you decide to go shopping for a pair of sandals. Lugging your wood on your back, you go in search of a sandal maker. Finding one at last, you are disappointed to find that the sandal maker has no need for chopped wood. No trade takes place, and so with aching back and

sore feet you continue on your quest. Your problem is twofold. You must first find someone who has sandals to trade. Second, while you may encounter several such people, you must find among them one who wants to acquire chopped wood. In other words, you are looking for an individual who coincidentally has sandals to trade and also wants chopped wood. In order to have a trade, it is necessary to have a coincidence of wants.

At this point you might ask, is it not possible that someone who has sandals to trade, but no need for chopped wood, might accept the wood and then trade it for something he or she does want? Yes, it is possible, but very inconvenient. If that person accepts the wood, the problem of finding a coincidence of wants has really just been transferred from you to him or her.

In sum, *the difficulties involved in finding a coincidence of wants tend to discourage specialisation and trade in a barter economy.* Given the effort and time that must be spent just to find a coincidence of wants, many individuals in a barter economy would find it easier to be more self-sufficient and produce more items for their own consumption. To this extent, the gains from specialisation and trade cannot be fully realised.

Money as a Medium of Exchange

How does the use of money allow us to get around these difficulties? *Money eliminates the need for the coincidence of wants.* If the economy uses money to carry on trade, you can sell your chopped wood to whoever wants it and accept money in exchange. Whether the purchaser makes something you want is now irrelevant. As long as you can use the money received to buy what you want you are satisfied. You can use the money to buy a pair of sandals or anything else. Similarly, the sandal maker will accept your money even though he or she may have no need for your chopped wood. We say money serves as the medium of exchange.

At different times and in different societies, the medium of exchange used as money has taken many forms — from hounds' teeth to precious stones to gold coin to currency and cheques. Whatever its form, *money's common characteristic is that it must be acceptable to people because they know they can use it as buyers. Because money eliminates the need for coincidence of wants, it promotes specialisation and trade and thereby makes possible the gains that stem from specialisation and trade. The incentive for societies to use money in exchange derives from these gains. The introduction of money into a barter economy essentially causes that economy's production possibilities frontier to be shifted outward.*

=====

*CHECKPOINT * 3.1*

Suppose there are three people, A, B, and C, and that A specialises in growing corn, B in catching fish, and C in growing wheat. A has a surplus of corn, B a surplus of fish, and C a surplus of wheat. Suppose A would like to get some wheat from C, but C doesn't have any desire for A's corn. Suppose that C would like to get some fish from B, but B doesn't want any of C's wheat. And suppose that B would like to get some corn from A, but A doesn't want any of B's fish. Each wants something from one of the others, but has nothing to offer in exchange. What is lacking here? Further, suppose each lives alone on an island 20 kilometres from each of the others and that each has a boat. Describe how trade would have to be carried on under a bar-ter system, if it were carried on at all. By comparison, describe how trade would be carried on if A, B, and C used money.

*Answers to all Checkpoints can be found at the back of the text.

=====

MARKETS AND PROFITS

A money-using economy with extensive markets fosters specialisation among workers and in the methods of production. This specialisation leads to the development of more sophisticated production processes, which typically require large amounts of investment in capital goods. In a capitalistic economy where the productive units or firms are privately owned either by those who run them or by shareholders, sizeable amounts of funds, or financial capital, must be raised by the owners in order to acquire the capital goods. Whether or not it is worthwhile to commit funds to such investments depends on that controversial thing called profit. And the amount of profit is determined by the markets where the goods produced by the capital goods are sold. Another key role played by profit in a capitalistic economy is to provide an incentive for entrepreneurial activity. The entrepreneur described in Chapter 1 is a key factor in the creation and organising of new production techniques and the founding of firms that employ these techniques to satisfy the demands of new and continually changing markets.

What Is a Normal Profit?

Profit is one of the most controversial and least understood concepts in economics.

For some people the mere mention of the word conjures up images of exploitation and robber barons carving out their pound of flesh from the downtrodden. But what is a 'reasonable' profit, or what economists call a normal profit? When we say that a firm is earning a normal profit, what must be the relationship between its total sales revenue and its total costs?

In order to answer these questions, recall that we emphasised in the previous chapter that all costs are opportunity costs due to the fact that resources are scarce and have alternative uses. Our discussion of the production possibilities frontier indicated that if resources are used to produce one good, they are not available to produce other goods. The cost of the one good is thus the alternative goods that must be forgone in order to produce it. This notion of cost is directly applicable to the individual firm. All the resources, including financial capital and entrepreneurial skills, that a firm needs in order to produce its product have alternative uses in the production of other products by other firms. Hence *the costs of production for a firm are all those payments it must make to all resource suppliers in order to bid resources away from use in the production of alternative goods. When the firm's total sales revenue is just sufficient to cover these costs, all resources employed by the firm are just earning their opportunity costs.* In particular, *the financial capital and the entrepreneurial skills used by the firm are being compensated just enough to keep them from leaving and going into some other line of productive activity. That amount of compensation is called a normal profit.*

Profit and the Allocation of Resources

Changes in the level of profits that are earned in different markets play an important role in the efficient allocation of resources in a dynamic, changing economy. Suppose that a market for a new product develops or that there is a sudden increase in demand for an existing product. Firms already in the market or those first to enter will find they can earn more than normal profits or above-normal profits. This happens because demand so exceeds the existing capacity to meet it that prices considerably in excess of cost can be charged. Above-normal profits serve as a signal to entrepreneurial skills and financial capital in other areas of the economy that they can earn more by moving into the new and expanding markets. Resources will continue to move into these areas so long as above-normal profits exist. Eventually, enough resources will have moved into these markets and increased capacity sufficiently that above-normal profits will no longer exist. In this way *above-normal profits serve to allocate resources to those areas of the economy where they are most in demand. Similarly, of course, below-normal profits in one area of the economy will cause entrepreneurial skills and financial capital to move out of that line of productive activity and into those where they can earn their opportunity cost.*

Controversy About the Role of Profit

Whenever you read something or hear a discussion about profit, you should ask yourself how the term is being used. There is a good deal of misunderstanding about the nature of profit in mixed economies.

Early Views on Profit

Suspicion of profit is an ancient theme

in Western culture. A sixteenth-century French thinker, Michel de Montaigne, wrote an essay entitled 'The Profit of One Man is the Damage of Another'. His thesis was that 'man should condemn all manner of gain'. However, with the dawn of the era of capitalism two centuries ago, the profit motive found an able defender in Adam Smith — the renowned author of *The Wealth of Nations*. In this book, published in 1776, Smith argued that profits are the legitimate return for risk and effort. He put forward the notion that the 'invisible hand' of market forces turns private greed into productive activity, which provides goods for the benefit of all. A century later, Karl Marx argued the opposite view. He maintained that labour, not capital, was the ingredient that added value to goods or raw materials in the production process. He asserted that profit was the 'surplus value' that the capitalist unjustifiably added on to the real worth of the product.

In the early part of the twentieth century, the Fabian socialists argued that profits should be 'taxed into oblivion' to create a new socialist order. If they meant above-normal profit, they might have a good case in certain circumstances. Suppose the Fabians' expressed desire to tax profits into oblivion were meant to apply to normal profits. This would effectively remove any return to financial capital and entrepreneurial skill. It would, therefore, remove the incentive for anybody to provide the financial capital necessary for the creation of physical capital goods or the innovative effort necessary to create new technology and supply new markets. When an economy ceases to build capital goods, the growth in its capacity to produce other goods stops. If the Fabians meant by profits normal profits, taxing profits out of

existence would certainly be an extreme position. There would definitely be a new social order.

The taxation of profits will undoubtedly always be a much debated issue in mixed capitalistic economies. Unfortunately, much of the debate is often the result of misunderstanding over the meaning or meanings of the word profit.

Profit in Today's Economy

Today the average individual directly or indirectly owns a sizeable portion of the shares of companies listed on the Stock Exchange. The dividends paid on these shares derive directly from the profits of these companies. Nearly half of all corporate shares, measured in dollar value, are owned by institutions such as superannuation funds, insurance companies, university or school endowments, and churches. Hence, for many Australians such things as the assurance of a retirement income, and the soundness of an insurance policy are heavily dependent on the continued profitability of these companies. When profits go down or turn into losses, the average person in the street

---

CHECKPOINT 3.2
Samuel Gompers (1850-1924) was an American trade union leader. He was the first president of the American Federation of Labor — the equivalent of the ACTU — a position he held from 1886 until his death (except for one year, 1895). He once said, 'The worst crime against working people is a company which fails to operate at a profit'. What do you suppose he meant by this? Like Gompers, Marx championed the working class. How do their views on profit seem to differ?

---

often has as much cause for concern as the corporate board of directors. It should be said, however, that above-normal profits derived from situations where competition in the marketplace is nonexistent or inhibited are generally considered not to be in the economy's best interest.

GOVERNMENT'S ROLE IN THE MIXED ECONOMY

As with profits, there is always a good deal of controversy over the appropriate role of government versus that of markets in determining what, how, and for whom to produce. 'Be thankful you don't get all the government you pay for' say some who are sceptical of what government does and how efficiently it does it. A critic of the market system once said, 'Competition in the marketplace brings out the best in products and the worst in people'.

Government, whether it is local, state or federal, performs four main functions in a mixed economy: (1) it provides the legal and institutional structure in which markets operate; (2) it intervenes in the allocation of resources in areas of the economy where public policy deems it beneficial to do so; (3) it redistributes income; and (4) it seeks to provide stability in prices, economic growth, and economic conditions generally. Of course, government actions in any one of these spheres almost invariably have implications for the others.

Legal and Institutional Structure for Markets

Even in pure market, laissez faire capitalism, the government must provide for legal definition and enforcement of contracts, property rights, and ownership.

It must also establish the legal status of different forms of business organisations, from the owner-operated small business to the large company. It must provide a judicial system so that disputed claims between parties arising in the course of business can be settled. Government also provides for the supply and regulation of the money supply, the maintenance of a system of measurement standards, and the maintenance of a police force to keep order and protect property.

You will find little disagreement anywhere as to the need for government to provide this basic legal and institutional structure. Since the turn of the century, however, the legal sanctions and constraints on the functioning of markets and the economic relationships between business, trade unions, and consumers have become more complex. In Australia the government has taken an active role in trying to maintain competition in markets. In several industries where market size and the technology of production preclude more than one efficient producer, state or federal governments own and operate the industry. As noted already, the organisations responsible for railways, postal system, telephones, electricity, gas and water supply in Australia are government owned and controlled. They should operate, therefore, in the public interest.

In attempting to maintain competitive conditions in other markets the Australian Federal Parliament passed the Australian Industries Preservation Act in 1906. This legislation was based on the Sherman Act in the USA, which sought to prohibit the restraint of trade and outlawed the practice of monopolisation. The Australian legislation ran into constitutional difficulties and, after 1913 was not used. In the ensuing fifty years many Australian businesses used restrictive trade practices widely. During the early 1960s the federal government decided that further legislation outlawing restrictive trade practices was necessary. In 1965 the Federal Parliament passed the Trade Practices Act. This prohibited collusive bidding and collusive tendering, and made certain other practices such as price discrimination and monopolisation examinable. Although invalidated by constitutional challenge in 1971, subsequent federal governments have legislated on trade practices on a number of occasions since. The Whitlam Labor government introduced a new Trade Practices Act in 1974. The Fraser coalition government introduced the Trade Practices Amendment Act in 1977, and in 1986 the Hawke Labor Government made further amendments to the 1974 act. Current trade practices legislation in Australia covers horizontal agreements between competing firms, misuse of market power, exclusive dealing, resale price maintenance, price discrimination and mergers.

In addition to the operation of public enterprises in 'natural monopoly' situations, and trade practices legislation to maintain competition, governments in Australia also intervene in the operation of the economy in other areas. These include environmental protection legislation, marketing schemes and subsidies for primary producers, tax concessions and development restraints in mining, tariff and quota protection in manufacturing and legislation regulating the operation of the financial sector.

Government intervention in the marketplace through creation and change of certain aspects of the legal and institutional structure has often proved beneficial. In other instances, it has not. Recent activity in deregulating the activities of the finance sector in Australia — following the Campbell Inquiry's final report in 1981 — suggests that government regulations had become outdated and burdensome. A rather more celebrated example of disastrous government intervention relates to the Volstead Act passed by the US Congress in 1919. It prohibited the production and sale of alcoholic beverages. The act became so unpopular that Congress repealed it in 1933. Many observers feel that it provided a tremendous economic windfall to the underworld, which did a thriving business in the illicit production and sale of the liquor that a thirsty public would not do without. This is felt to have laid the foundation for modern organised crime as a big business in the United States.

Resource Allocation

Government affects resource allocation in our economy through its spending activities, its tax policies, and its own production of certain goods and services.

Government Spending

In Australia over 60 per cent of all output is produced and sold in markets. The quantity and variety of goods and services represented by this major part of total output is the result of decisions made by numerous firms and consumers — the private sector of our economy. The rest of the economy's output is the result of government (public sector) expenditure decisions. This includes all levels of government — state, federal, and local. Though some of this output of goods and services is produced by private businesses, it is done under government contract and reflects government decisions about what

---

POLICY PERSPECTIVE

Should Profit Be the Only Objective of Business?

Do businesses have obligations to society beyond making profit? There is considerable disagreement over the appropriate answer to this question. On one side of the issue it is argued that the *only* responsibility of business is to make profits because by pursuing that goal alone society's interests are best served. Alternatively, the other side of the issue holds that businesses should act according to higher moral principles to prevent damage to society that might otherwise result from a single-minded pursuit of profit. In the extreme, this view holds that it amounts to 'murder for profit' when businesses produce and advertise cigarettes, sell cars that are not 'adequately crashproof', and dump toxic wastes in rivers. Are there not moral principles that should inhibit such behaviour even at the cost of forgone profit opportunities?

The 'Only Profits' View

The view that profit should be the sole objective of business points out that corporate managers in today's world are responsible to the company's shareholders (the owners) who expect them to do everything within the law to earn the owners a maximum return (profit) on their investment. The 'only profits' view argues that if a corporate executive takes an action that the executive feels is 'socially responsible' and that action reduces profit, then the executive has spent (in effect, stolen) the owners' money. This violates a fundamental tenet of our political economic system that no individual shall be deprived of property without his or her permission. Corporate executives who want to take socially responsible actions should use their own money, supporting special interest groups, charities, or political parties and causes that promote the social actions they desire. However, to the extent that executives sacrifice profit to such actions, they effectively deprive shareholders of the right to spend the sacrificed higher profits (which otherwise belong to shareholders) on social actions of the shareholders' choosing, and on anything else for that matter. If company executives and shareholders choose to spend their own money to support (in whatever way) social actions to regulate business behaviour, so be it.

The 'Profits Plus Other Concerns' View

The point of view that business should not pursue profit to the complete exclusion of other social concerns argues that the sole pursuit of profit tends to give rise to immoral, if not illegal, business behaviour. According to this view business firms do have a moral responsibility not to design products or engage in behaviour (for example, deceptive advertising) that they have reason to believe will seriously injure or possibly kill people. Business's willingness to do what is clearly immoral for the sake of profit conflicts with an old moral precept (going back at least to Aristotle) that money is a means to an end, in itself not the sort of end that justifies acting immorally to get it. The 'profits plus other concerns' view also argues that if profit is the sole objective of business then the associated abuses and immoral behaviour that result will lead the public to impose greater government regulation on business activity. Increased government intrusion in the private sector will cause economic inefficiency as well as pose potential threats to individual freedoms. Therefore, it is argued, it is in the long run in the best interest of business (and all of us) to pay heed to moral principles while pursuing profit. Otherwise society will increasingly use the government and political processes to correct perceived abuses.

How Do You Get Socially Responsible Business Behaviour?

Is it really possible for firms to be 'socially responsible' and survive in a competitive market? Firms that incur additional costs to make a safer product or avoid polluting the environment, say, may put themselves at a competitive disadvantage vis-a-vis less socially responsible rival firms. Will the more socially responsible firms not be driven out of business, leaving only those motivated solely by profit, thus making the greater government regulation predicted by the 'profits plus other concerns' view inevitable? It depends on the nature of the socially responsible behaviour firms engage in. Firms that make products that get a reputation for being unsafe, for example, will lose sales to the safer products of rivals — they will be disciplined by the market while the more socially responsible firms will be rewarded.

On the other hand, socially responsible firms that voluntarily incur costs to prevent environmental pollution are likely to lose out to less socially responsible rivals because pollution control efforts don't show up in product quality where they will be rewarded by the market. Therefore government regulation to protect the environment may be the only solution to pollution control problems, while the discipline of the market may be a more reliable and efficient way to enforce product safety. Even on the issue of product safety however, the question is 'how many injuries and lost lives does it take for the market to react against an unsafe product?' Where the public has answered 'too many', government regulation has been called for, giving rise to such regulatory bodies as the Bureau of Air Safety Investigation.

The Role of Human Nature

What if human nature is such that it is only realistic to expect that the main objective of business is profit, as Adam Smith believed (see Adam Smith, p. 14)? Then the relevant questions are: (1) What kinds of socially irresponsible business behaviour will be curbed by the discipline of the market, and what kinds will not? (2) Where market discipline is of questionable effectiveness, are the costs of government regulation (in terms of increased threat to individual freedom as well as increased tax cost) less than the costs (such as injury and loss of life) that trigger market discipline?

Some perspective on answers to the last question is provided by the following examples. Despite the fact that lower speed limits are known to reduce highway fatalities, there is no public outcry for lower speed limits. The public values reduced travel time more than reduced fatalities. (People do put a price on life!) Similarly, there is a limit to what people will pay for a 'crash-proof' car. A business that tried to produce them, out of a sense of social responsibility, would probably go bankrupt because only a few people would be willing to pay a price that would cover the cost of making them.

If the public is unwilling to pay for such a level of product safety, it would hardly seem justifiable to many citizens for the government to impose it by subsidising production of such cars with taxpayers' money. It would also be misleading to assume the absence of such cars is due to car manufacturers' lack of social conscience and singular pursuit of profit.

Questions

1. In all Australian states motorcyclists are required to wear crash helmets. Why might you expect a helmet manufacturer to differ from a motorcycle company on the two views about profit in this case?

2. In Australia it is legal to sell alcoholic beverages but not marijuana. How *might* this distinction be justified?

---

to produce and for whom — roads for motorists, schools, and hospitals are just a few examples.

Taxation

Another way in which the government affects the allocation of resources is through its power to levy taxes. For example, we have already noted how changes in profit affect the incentive to create new capital goods. From our discussion of the production possibilities frontier in the previous chapter, we know that there is a trade-off between producing capital goods and producing goods for present consumption. In order to produce more of one kind of good, it is necessary to obtain the resources to do so by cutting back on production of the other. That is, it is necessary to reallocate resources from one line of productive activity to another. By changing the rate of taxation of profit, the government changes the incentive to produce capital goods relative to the incentive to produce goods for current consumption. For instance, suppose the government increased taxes on profits. This would discourage the production of capital goods relative to consumer goods. Some resources would therefore be

reallocated from capital goods production to consumer goods production. This is but one example of the way in which the government can affect the allocation of resources through tax policy.

Government Production of Goods and Services

Another way that the government affects resource allocation is by producing goods and services itself. There are certain kinds of goods and services that would not be produced at all if the choice were left up to the market mechanism, even though it might be acknowledged by everybody that such goods provide benefits for all. Such goods are **public goods**.

An essential feature of a public good is that it cannot be provided to one person without providing it to others. If the government provides a dam to protect your property from floods, the benefits accrue to your neighbour as well. Public goods are not subject to the so-called **exclusion principle**. *Any good whose benefits accrue only to those who purchase it is said to be subject to the exclusion principle.* Those who do not buy the good are excluded from its benefits. The exclusion principle almost invariably applies to goods produced and sold in a market economy. When producers cannot prevent those who don't pay for the good from having it, the exclusion principle does not hold for that good. If one can have a good without paying for it, then there is no way for producers to charge and receive a price to cover the costs of producing it. Hence there will be no incentive for firms to produce it in a market economy. If I build a lighthouse, there is no way I can exclude any ship at sea from benefiting from its beacon. Hence there is no way I can charge ships at sea for its service. So I won't build it, despite the fact that shipping companies all agree that it cuts down their economic losses due to shipwrecks. Similarly, it is difficult to privately produce and sell the services of a dam, national defence, cloud seeding, and clean air.

Another feature of a public good is that once it is provided for one citizen, there is no additional cost to providing it for others. This is really just another aspect of the fact that when a public good provides benefits to one, it unavoidably provides them to others. It costs no more to protect one ship at sea than to protect several with the same lighthouse.

Of course, there are many goods that are not by nature public goods that the government provides anyway. Examples of goods and services that can be privately produced and sold in markets but are provided by state, local, or federal government are education, police and fire protection, certain kinds of preventive medical treatment, sewage treatment, garbage collection, bridges, toll roads, and air shows financed by the government through the Royal Australian Air Force. In most of these cases, it is usually argued that there are substantial social benefits, and that if their provision were left strictly to private producers and markets, less of these goods would be produced than is desirable.

Income Redistribution

In virtually all modern, industrialised, mixed economies there are specific government policies aimed at alleviating the hardships of poverty. If people cannot earn some minimal standard of living in the marketplace, it is generally agreed that they should be given economic assistance in some form. Whatever form it takes, this assistance makes it necessary to redistribute income from those judged to have enough to those who do not. One obvious way to do this is for the government simply to levy heavier income taxes on people in higher income brackets and transfer the money collected to those in lower brackets.

Many government transfers of income and wealth between citizens do not necessarily redistribute from the rich to the poor. For example, family allowance payments by the Australian government, financed from general tax revenue were, until late 1987, given to families without any income means test. The level of payment depended on the number of children in a family. The poor, the middle classes and the rich all received the same range of benefits under this program, regardless of need.

Government has played a growing role in income redistribution since World War II. This is illustrated in Figure 3.1, which shows that an increased share of federal government outlays takes the form of payments to individuals. The payments to individuals are transfer payments in the form of old age pensions, invalid pensions, unemployment benefits, student living allowances and a variety of other payments. The payments to individuals are sometimes referred to as income mainte-nance programs because they effectively maintain minimum income levels for the recipients. They represent an income redistribution from taxpayers to those receiving the payments. The share of total federal government outlays accounted for by payments to individuals grew from 17.3 per cent in 1949-50 to 25.1 per cent in 1983-84.

A good deal of the transfer of income and wealth among citizens takes the form of government provision of goods and services at zero or below cost to the citizens who use them. These are not included in 'payments to individuals'. The costs of providing such goods and services are covered by tax revenue, much of which is collected from citizens who may not themselves use these governmentally provided goods and services. Public education, parks and recreation areas, public libraries, and a partially subsidised public health system are but a few examples. Again, a wealthy person might choose to use these facilities while someone with a much lower income might use them little or not at all, even though he or she pays taxes used to subsidise the government provision of such goods and services. An often quoted example in this area is university education.

Another way in which the government affects income distribution is by direct intervention in the marketplace. Well-known examples of this are price stabilisation programs for key agricultural commodities, as well as subsidies assisting in their production. Federal government support for a centralised wage fixing system which ensures that all wages move in accordance with National Wage Case recommendations is another notable example in this area. Employers often claim that, by keeping wages artificially high, such a system aggravates unemployment. Another notable example of direct government intervention in the market place relates to the imposition of tariffs and quotas of manufacturing, for example, textiles, clothing, footwear and motor vehicle manufacture have been notable in Australia in recent decades. Critics argue that consumers suffer because they are unable to purchase the cheapest product. Supporters suggest that high tariff walls are necessary to establish a viable manufacturing base.

Economic Stabilisation

In the previous chapter we noted the difficulties that market-oriented economies have avoiding recessions in economic activity, fluctuations in employment and GDP, and unacceptable levels of inflation. In most capitalistic, mixed economies, we observed that a good deal of responsibility for avoiding these difficulties has been vested in the government — witness the Australian government's 1945 White Paper which laid down that 'Governments should accept the responsibility for stimulating spending on goods and services to the extent necessary to sustain full employment'. It advocated this in the context that it should 'at the same time

FIGURE 3.1
Shares of Major Components of Commonwealth Budget Outlays

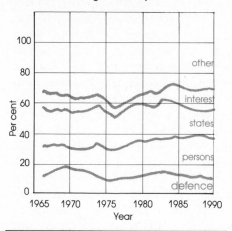

POLICY PERSPECTIVE

Who Benefits from Government Polices?

It is a common misconception that the public finance system primarily redistributes income between those whose incomes are derived from wages, salaries and profits to benefits which support the aged, the unemployed, single parents and other disadvantaged groups. In Australia, government outlays are important as well in reallocating resources in areas such as education, health and housing. In a notable recent study, based on data from the national Household Expenditure Survey 1984, the Australian Bureau of Statistics (ABS) has estimated the effects of government benefits and taxes on household income. In particular it estimates the way that benefits from education, health, housing and social security and welfare outlays flow to households classified

- by age of household head, and
- by gross income decile.

Computing average weekly tax per household the authors also estimate the net effects (benefits minus taxes) of government activity in each of these household groups.

The Benefits

Education benefits were highest for households whose head was aged between 35 and 44 years. Health benefits rose gradually as households aged. Housing government benefits were highest for young households and then fell away. Social security and welfare

---

FIGURE P3.1
Weekly Benefits per Household by Age of
Household Head

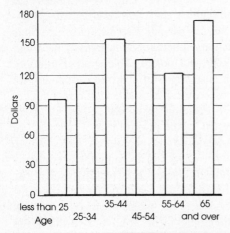

benefits averaged about $40 per week for young and middle aged family heads (up to 54 years of age), rose to more than $60 for households with heads between 55 and 64 years, and to more than $120 for households whose heads were over 65 years. As can be seen from Figure P3.1, the distribution of *total* government benefits to households is highest for those whose heads were aged between 35 and 44 years, and over 65 years.

As households become more affluent education benefits rise. Health benefits tend to be lowest for the poorest 10 per cent of households and highest for the next 20 per cent, and the richest 10 per cent. Social security and welfare benefits are highest for the bottom 30 per cent of income earners and then decline. The *total* of government benefits is highest for households whose incomes fall in the second and third deciles. In 1984 households in both groups received an average of more than $180 per week in benefits. In all other decile ranges, households received around $120 per week.

The Incidence of Taxes

Using income and expenditure data from the Household Expenditure Survey, the ABS estimated that average direct tax payments per household were $91.60 per week and those indirect taxes which could be allocated were $37.74 per week.

Average weekly tax payments per household increase as the age of household head rises — up to the 45-54 year age group. They then decline rather dramatically for the 55-64 year and 65 year and over groups (see Figure P3.2). As might be expected average weekly tax paid rises as income rises with those households in the eighth, ninth and tenth deciles contributing more than half of the total.

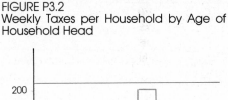

FIGURE P3.2
Weekly Taxes per Household by Age of
Household Head

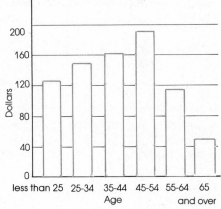

Benefits Less Taxes

The net effects on households of government benefits and taxes are summarised in

Figure P3.3. When classified by age we see that older households, particularly those with heads over 65 years, received positive net benefits. Younger households received negative benefits. When classified by Gross Income Decile we see that households receiving the lowest 50 per cent of income tended to receive positive net benefits from Government. Households in the sixth decile broke even and those in the seventh to tenth deciles all had negative benefits.

FIGURE P3.3
Net Weekly Benefits by Age of Household Head

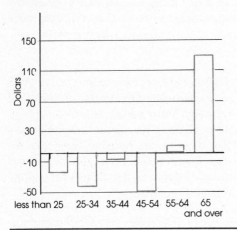

Questions

1. In which major areas is it possible to measure the redistribution of incomes by government in Australia?

2. Which household groups benefit most from government redistribution of income in Australia? Which benefit least?

---

avoid inflationary pressure on prices' and that external viability i.e. the maintenance of an adequate level of internal reserves, should always be attained. Fiscal policy — government expenditure and tax changes aimed at smoothing out fluctuations in economic activity — unavoidably affects resource allocation, income distribution, and even the competitive market structure of industries in which the government buys goods and lets contracts for public projects. By changing the levels of interest rates, monetary policy has similar effects on resource allocation and income distribution.

Controversy About the Role of Government

In recent years there has been a growing scepticism about the ability of government to provide services to the public, direction to the economy, and solutions to a number of social problems. This has led to a critical examination of how government functions in our economy, a search for the reasons why once-optimistic expectations about the government's role have often not been fulfilled.

Efficiency in Government

Some critics point out that government bureaucracies by their very nature do not have the built-in incentives for efficiency that exist in the typical business firm. The reward of profit and the threat of loss are absent. Moreover, it is typically difficult to measure either output or performance. It is often impossible for a public servant to show how and where he or she has saved the taxpayer's money. How can one tell how efficiently the Department of the Treasury, the local library, or a state school system is being operated? If efficient performance is hard to demonstrate, it is likely to be unrecognised and unrewarded, so why try so hard? Similarly, an inefficient performance is equally hard to detect. Neither the carrot nor the stick is much in evidence under these circumstances. In short, because the relationship between taxpayer dollars and benefits produced is hard to establish, the incentives for efficiency are weak.

Special Interest Legislation

Special interest groups often push hard for legislation that provides special benefits for them and possibly little or no benefit for anyone else. Special interest groups often get their way even when it may not serve the broader public interest. Why?

Suppose some special interest group presses for a program that will cost each individual taxpayer only a dollar. The total cost of the program may be tens of millions of dollars. But as far as the individual taxpayer is concerned the extra dollar of taxes will hardly be noticed. For the individual taxpayer it is scarcely worth the effort to become informed about the program. However, those in the special interest group may stand to benefit substantially, so that they have very strong feelings about whether the program is approved or not. Consequently a political party which doesn't vote for the special interest group's program stands to lose the group's vote in the next election and quite likely a helpful financial contribution to its campaign as well. On the other hand, voting for the program will probably cost the party few if any votes among the other largely uninformed voters. Consequently the party votes for the special interest group's program, even though it may not be in the broader public interest.

For example, you are a Federal member of parliament for the Government party, in a state where a large company wishes to mine uranium in an area adjoining a national park. The state stands to gain major revenues from a tax on the mine's output, and the mine will bring employment to the region. Business interests in your state support the new mine. There is a risk however, that radioactive waste may leak from the proposed on-site processing plant. This would endanger flora and fauna in the national park, and might be a health hazard for tourists visiting the park. Citizens in your state and throughout Australia are ill informed about these potential problems. The National environmental lobby, which has only minor support in your state, decides to press the national government to extend the boundaries of the national park so that mining cannot proceed. The Cabinet agrees to sponsor the legislation but with other government colleagues from the state you cross the floor of parliament to defeat the bill. This outcome is not in the nation's long term interest.

Consumer Preferences and the Bundle Problem

When you buy goods in the marketplace, you shop for them on an item-by-item basis. You are able to be very selective. Your selection of governmentally provided goods and services is much more limited because you must select them through an intermediary, the political party for which you vote. Each party really represents a bundle of public goods and services, the ones which it will support and vote for if elected. Your choice of bundles is limited by the number of parties represented by candidates in your electorate. Each candidate may have certain goods and services in his or her party's bundle that you want and others that you don't want. You vote for the candidate whose bundle most closely matches your preferences. Even then you are forced to take some public goods and services you don't want in order to get those that you do want.

For example, you choose to vote for candidate A because his party supports the construction of a dam that you want very much. The party may also be in favour of price supports for dairy products, which you don't want, but you don't feel as concerned about price supports as you do about the dam. Candidate B's party is against the price supports but does not favour the dam either. You vote for A instead of B. Even though A's bundle of goods and services doesn't match your preferences perfectly, it comes closer than the alternative bundle represented by B.

Bias Toward Current Benefit, Hidden Cost Projects

Because politicians must worry about getting reelected, there is a natural tendency for them to favour projects and programs that have immediate, highly visible benefits and less visible costs. An objective economic analysis of project A might show it to be more worthwhile than a number of other projects. But suppose project A's benefits are spread over a distant future, while tax increases will be required to cover its immediate costs. Project A is therefore likely to lack support, while other economically less worthwhile projects that have more immediate benefits and less visible costs will be pushed forward.

It should be emphasised that none of these criticisms of the way government functions to provide goods and services is a criticism of politicians and government bureaucrats. They respond to rewards and incentives just like people in other walks of life. Given that, these criticisms are directed at the ways in which the reward and incentive structures of our political and governmental institutions are not always geared to provide goods and services in the most economically efficient manner.

Resource Utilisation

How good are mixed economies at maintaining a *full utilisation of their available resources?* The Depression of the 1930s, which plagued the industrialised economies of the West, led these countries to call for more government intervention in the future. In this way, these economies hoped to avoid another episode of such dramatic underemployment of resources. The ideas put forward at that time by the English economist John Maynard Keynes provided a rationale for how government intervention could prevent such a calamity. Income tax reductions and stepped-up government expenditures to offset the fall in expenditures by businesses and consumers were among the recommended measures to be used. Most economists today are of the opinion that such government intervention would be appropriate and effective in averting another Great Depression. However, there is considerable debate among economists as to whether such intervention has been either practicable or effective in alleviating the recessions that have occurred in the Australian economy since 1970.

Change, Stability and Growth

Mixed economies justify government intervention, at least in part, as a means of promoting stability and growth and those kinds of change that are considered desirable. How well mixed economies have succeeded is a matter of continual debate among economists.

In Australia some economists think that the recent antitrust activities of the government on the whole have helped to prevent the growth of monopoly and thereby promoted competition in some areas of the economy. It is felt that more competition better serves changing consumer tastes and leads to more innovation in products, which is a spur to economic growth. On the other hand, the government has intervened to assist large corporations, as in the case of BHP with the steel plan. Some critics feel that this interferes with the beneficial working of the marketplace, which serves to weed out inefficient producers, a form of change felt to be desirable. Furthermore, they ask, why should the government prop up certain large failing corporations when

many smaller businesses fail every day because they are unable to meet the rigours of the marketplace?

With regard to economic growth and stability, many economists argue that in Australia greater growth and stability have been promoted by government intervention. Others say, not so, that the increasing growth of government has stifled the private sector with heavy personal income and company profits taxes. In addition, they argue that government policies have been a major cause of inflation. The reply to these criticisms is often 'Well, even if there is some truth to that, at least we have not had another Depression'. Debates over the pros and cons of mixed economies and the appropriateness or folly of government intervention in different areas of the economy are unending. We will encounter these issues again and again throughout this book.

CHECKPOINT 3.3
Explain how the government's power to enforce contracts contributes to the development of markets. Is the postal service a public good or not? Why or why not? Was conscription into the armed forces a form of government transfer of income or wealth? Why or why not? It appears that sometimes when a government agency isn't working very efficiently, its budget is increased. What happens when a private business doesn't operate very efficiently?

SUMMARY

1. Individuals have different abilities for performing different tasks. Because of this, individuals have an incentive to specialise in production and to trade the

surplus of their output in excess of their own need for the other goods they want but don't produce themselves. This incentive stems from the fact that specialisation and trade make possible a larger output of goods and services than is possible if each individual tries to be self-sufficient — that is, if there is no specialisation and trade.

2. There is an incentive to use money as a medium of exchange because it eliminates the need for the coincidence of wants, which is necessary for trade to take place in a barter economy. Because of this, money promotes specialisation and trade and hence makes possible a larger output of goods and services than is possible within the context of a barter system of trade.

3. A firm's costs are all those payments it must make to all resource suppliers in order to bid resources away from use in alternative lines of production of goods. Among the resources used by the firm are financial capital and entrepreneurial skills. When they are being compensated just enough to keep them from leaving and going into some other line of productive activity, we say they are earning a normal profit.

4. Above-normal profits will draw resources to those areas of the economy where they are most in demand. Below-normal profits in one area of the economy will cause entrepreneurial skills and financial capital to move out of that line of productive activity and into those where they can earn their opportunity cost.

5. At minimum in any economy, government typically has basic responsibility for maintaining law and order, providing for the nation's money supply, its national defence, the judicial system, and a uniform standard of time, weight, and measurement. In mixed economies government: reallocates resources in instances where it is felt the market mechanism gives unacceptable or undesirable outcomes; often strives to maintain competitive conditions in markets not naturally conducive to them; redistributes income in accordance with some norm of equity and concern for those who can't work or earn a minimally adequate income; and attempts to maintain economic stability with reasonably full employment of resources.

6. There are several reasons why the government is not a very efficient producer of goods and services. Government bureaucracies have a weak incentive structure due to the difficulty of measuring their output and judging their performance. Politicians often support special interest legislation because it wins them votes from special interest groups without losing the votes of an often ill-informed public. A voting citizen must choose from a limited number of parties, each representing a particular bundle of goods and services that typically does not accurately match the voter's preferences. Politicians are subject to an incentive structure biased toward the adoption of projects and programs with highly visible immediate benefits and well-hidden costs.

7. Government policies are likely to be effective in preventing another Depression. There is less agreement as to how effective government policies are at avoiding the periodic bouts of unemployment associated with post-World War II recessions. Controversy also surrounds the government's intervention in the marketplace, which is sometimes intended to promote competition through antitrust policy and occasionally to protect large corporations from outside competition. There is also ongoing debate about the government's effect on economic growth and inflation.

KEY TERMS AND CONCEPTS

barter economy
coincidence of wants
exclusion principle
nationalised industries
normal profit
public goods
specialisation of labour

QUESTIONS AND PROBLEMS

1. We have discussed specialisation in terms of its economic advantages. From the labourer's standpoint, what are some of the disadvantages of specialisation often heard about in the modern industrialised world?

2. We have noted that it might be possible that someone who has sandals to trade, but no need for chopped wood, might nonetheless accept the chopped wood and trade it for something else. In a situation such as this, where there is a lack of coincidence of wants, do you think the sandal maker would be more, or less, willing to accept strawberries than chopped wood (given that the sandal maker wants neither and must trade them for something he or she does want)? Why? Compared to a situation where there is a coincidence of wants between woodchopper and sandal maker, how do you think the terms of the exchange (the amount of wood needed to purchase a pair of sandals) would be different if the woodchopper wanted sandals but the sandal maker didn't want chopped wood?

3. Elaborate on the following statement: 'Profits can, of course, be immoral — if they are exploitive, for example, or result from price-fixing schemes or monopolies. But most profits . . . are an essential and beneficial ingredient in the workings of a free-market economy'.

4. Describe the nature of the role of profit that the author of the following statement must have in mind. 'Today profits, far from being too high, are still too low to ensure the nation's continued economic health. Among the top 20 industrialised countries, Australia in recent years has fared badly in terms of new industrial investment per capita. . . .'

5. A perhaps overly cynical view of government is that the function of government is to distribute money, that the effectiveness of government is measured by the sums dispensed, and that the worth of politicians is weighted by how much they are able to get the government to spend in their electorates. It is illegal for a politician to slip a derelict $5 for a vote, but a politician may buy office by legislating billions of dollars. As a result of this situation, some critics of government claim there is much more government spending than can be justified on objective economic grounds.

One way of dealing with this problem is to require that the government establish some sort of total spending ceiling at the beginning of each new term. The Hawke government's Economic Trilogy in the mid-1980s contained elements of this approach.

a. Why might this force members of the government party to make more economic choices?

b. Why might this curb the 'you vote for my pet project and I'll vote for yours' type of logrolling among members of the government?

4

Demand, Supply, and Price Determination

AFTER READING THIS CHAPTER YOU WILL BE ABLE TO:

1. Formulate and explain the law of demand and construct its graphical representation, the demand curve.

2. Enumerate the determinants of demand.

3. Demonstrate the significance of, and recognise the difference between, shifts in the position of a demand curve and movements along a fixed demand curve.

4. Formulate and explain the law of supply and construct its graphical representation, the supply curve.

5. Enumerate the determinants of supply.

6. Show how demand and supply interact to mutually determine equilibrium price and quantity (also called market equilibrium).

7. Demonstrate how changes in the determinants of demand and supply disturb the existing market equilibrium and result in the establishment of a new market equilibrium.

In this chapter we will focus on the laws of demand and supply. We will examine in some detail the notion of the demand curve and the supply curve. And we will consider how demand and supply interact to determine the equilibrium price at which the quantity of a good or resource supplied is just sufficient to satisfy demand for it. We will see how all of this is necessary for a better understanding of how markets work and how prices function to allocate resources.

DEMAND AND DEMAND CURVES

You have already met the notion of demand and its graphical representation called the demand curve in Chapter 1. There it was presented as an example of an economic theory or law. Here we want to examine in more detail the law of demand and how the demand curve is determined. We will see how individual demand curves can be combined to give the demand curve representing the entire market demand for a particular product, resource or service. Finally, we will examine the very important distinction between shifts in the position of a demand curve and movements along it.

Law of Demand

As we saw in Chapter 1, the **law of demand** is a theory about the relationship between the amount of a good a buyer both desires and is able to purchase per unit of time and the price charged for it. Notice that we emphasise the ability to pay for the good as well as the desire to have it. Your ability to pay is as important as your desire for the good, because in economics we are interested in explaining and predicting actual behaviour in the marketplace. Your *unlimited* desires for goods can never be observed in the marketplace because you can't buy more than you are *able* to pay for. At a given price for a good, we are only interested in the buyer's demand for that good which can effectively be backed by a purchase.

The law of demand hypothesised that the lower the price charged for a product, resource or service, the larger will be the quantity demanded per unit of time. Conversely, the higher the price charged the smaller will be the quantity demanded per unit of time — all other things remaining the same. For example, the law of demand predicts that the lower the price of steak, the more steak you will desire and be able to purchase per year — all other things remaining the same. As we noted in Chapter 1, the law of demand is confirmed again and again by observed behaviour in the marketplace. Businesses have sales (cut prices) and the amount of goods they sell per period increases. If the price of steak goes up the amount purchased per unit of time decreases. Why is this? For most goods there are other goods that may be used to satisfy very nearly the same desires. When the price of steak goes up, if the prices of pork chops, lamb chops and hamburgers remain unchanged, then all these kinds of meats are now relatively cheaper compared with steak. Hence buyers will purchase more of them and less of steak. These kinds of meats are *substitutes* for steak. Although not exactly the same as steak they are another kind of meat that will do.

Individual Demand

The inverse relationship between the price of a good and the quantity of the good demanded per unit of time can be depicted graphically as we demonstrated in Chapter 1. Suppose we consider an individual's demand for cheese. Table 4.1 shows the number of kilos of cheese that the individual will demand per month at each of several different prices. Note that the higher the price the smaller the quantity demanded per month. Conversely, the lower the price the greater the quantity that will be demanded per month. Why? Again, because the higher the price of cheese, the greater the incentive to cut back on consumption of it and eat other kinds of food instead — assuming their prices and all other things remain the same. *Relative* to cheese, other kinds of protein simply become cheaper to eat as the price of cheese rises. Conversely, more cheese will be demanded when successively lower prices are charged for it because it will become less and less expensive relative to other kinds of foods.

TABLE 4.1
An Individual's Demand for Cheese
(Hypothetical Data)

Price per kilo	Quantity Demanded (Number of kilos per Month)
$10	1.0
8	2.0
6	3.0
4	4.5
2	6.5

If we plot the price and quantity combinations listed in Table 4.1 on a graph, we obtain the **demand curve** DD shown in Figure 4.1. (If you need to brush up on how to plot data on a graph, refer back to p. 11.) Economists almost always represent the demand for a good, resource or service by use of a demand curve.

Verbal descriptions or tabular descriptions such as Table 4.1, while useful, are not typically as readily understood. This is an instance where a picture is worth a thousand words.

Demand Determinants: The Other Things That Remain the Same

When we draw a demand curve such as that in Figure 4.1, we emphasise the way in which the price charged for a good determines the quantity of it demanded. The price of the good is thereby singled out as the determining factor and all other things are said to be equal or remain the same. (If you prefer Latin, you may say *ceteris paribus*.) The important point is that *movement along the demand curve means that only the price of the good and the quantity of it demanded change. All other things are assumed to be constant or unchanged.* What are these other things? They are (1) the prices of all other goods, (2) the individual's income, (3) the individual's expectations about the future and (4) the individual's tastes. A change in one or more of these other things will change the data in Table 4.1. Therefore the position of the demand curve in Figure 4.1 will be shifted. Such a shift in the demand curve is called a *change in demand*. A movement along a fixed demand curve is referred to as a *change in the quantity demanded*. To avoid serious confusion it is essential to use each of these economic terms precisely.

Prices of All Other Goods

We may classify all other goods according to their relationship to the good for which the demand curve is drawn, say good X. Other goods are either substitutes for X,

FIGURE 4.1
An Individual's Demand Curve for Cheese

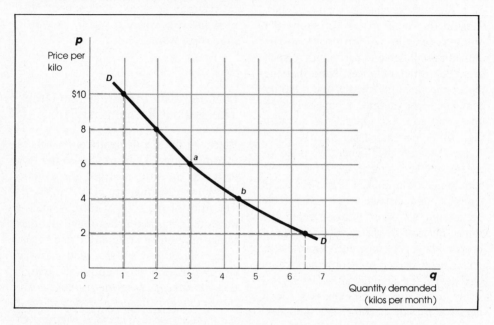

The individual's demand curve for cheese is plotted here using the data from Table 4.1. It slopes downward from left to right reflecting the inverse relationship between the quantity demanded and the price of the good. It illustrates the law of demand, which says that individuals will demand more of a good the lower is its price. A change in the price of the good causes a change in the quantity demanded and is represented by a movement along the demand curve. For example, if price changes from $6 per kilo to $4 per kilo, the quantity demanded increases from 3 to 4.5 kilos per month. This is represented by the movement from a to b along the demand curve *DD*.

complements of X or basically unrelated to X.

Substitute good: *A good is a substitute for X to the extent that it can satisfy similar needs or desires as X.* Different substitute goods will, of course, vary in the extent to which they satisfy the needs or desires that X does. T-bone steak is a closer substitute for rumpsteak than are lamb chops, although both T-bone steak and lamb chops typically would be regarded as substitutes for rumpsteak. *When the price of a substitute good for good X rises, the demand curve for good X will shift rightward.* This is so because

when the price of the substitute *rises*, it becomes cheaper to use X instead of the substitute good.

For example, suppose initially the demand curve for cheese is *DD* in Figure 4.2. Now suppose the price of a substitute, ham, rises. This will cause the individual's demand curve to shift rightward from *DD* to $D_1 D_1$. This means that at *any* given price of cheese (measured on the vertical axis of Figure 4.2), the quantity of cheese demanded (measured on the horizontal axis) will now be larger as a result of the increase in the price of ham.

The opposite of the above is also true

A change in demand results from a change in one or more of the five determinants of demand.

CHECKPOINT * 4.1
1. If there was an increase in the price of bananas what effect would this be likely to have on the demand for oranges? Why?
2. As the price of personal computers falls what effect would you expect this to have on the demand for software programs?
3. A sharp increase in the prices of petroleum products in the 1970s was followed by an increase in demand for 4 cylinder cars. As cars and petrol are considered to be complementary goods how can this result be explained?
4. What effect would you expect the announcement of a failure of the Brazilian coffee crop to have on demand for instant coffee in Australia?

* Answers to all checkpoints can be found at the end of the text.

SUPPLY AND SUPPLY CURVES

Given that there are demands for goods, what is the nature of the process that determines how those demands will be met? To answer this question we must have an understanding of the law of supply and the concept of a supply curve and its determinants.

Law of Supply

The law of supply is a statement about the relationship between the amount of a good a supplier is willing and able to supply and offer for sale per unit of time and each of the different possible prices at which that good might be sold. That is, if we said to the supplier, 'Suppose the good can be sold at a price of such and such dollars per unit. How many units of the good would you be willing and able to produce and offer for sale per unit of time?' We write down the answer along with the price we quoted to the supplier. Then we repeat the question exactly *except* that now we quote a somewhat higher price. We often observe that the higher the price, the larger the quantity the supplier is willing and able to supply for sale per unit of time. And, of course, the lower the price, the smaller the quantity that is offered. This observed relationship is the **law of supply** which *says that suppliers will supply larger quantities of a good at higher prices than at lower prices.*

The Supply Curve

Suppose the supplier whom we have been questioning is a cheese manufacturer. Table 4.3 lists some of the answers that the supplier gave in response to our questions. If we plot the data of Table 4.3 on a graph, we obtain this supplier's supply curve. As in Figure 4.1, we measure the price per unit (a kilo) on the vertical axis and the number of units (kilos) on the horizontal axis. The resulting curve SS is shown in Figure 4.4. We have plotted only the five price-quantity combinations. At all the possible prices in between, we presumably could have filled in the whole curve as shown by the solid line connecting the five plotted points. You may view the **supply curve** in different ways. *It indicates the maximum amount of the good the supplier is willing to provide per unit of time at different possible prices.* Or alternatively, you may say *it shows what prices are necessary in order to give the supplier the incentive to provide various quantities of the good per unit of time.*

The shape of the supply curve clearly shows that as the price of the good rises the supplier supplies more of the good; as the price falls the supplier supplies less of the good. Why is this? Just as with a demand curve, *such movement along a supply curve always assumes that all other things will remain the same.* Among other things, the prices of all other resources and goods are assumed to remain the same, including the prices of the inputs used by the supplier. Thus the profit that can be earned from producing a good will almost certainly increase as the price of the good rises. The supplier has a greater incentive to produce more of the good. This is one basic reason why a supply curve slopes upward to the right. Another is the fact that beyond some point most production processes run into increasing production costs per unit of output. This is because certain inputs such as plant and equipment cannot be increased in a short period of time. Hence as the producer increases output by using more of the readily variable inputs, such as labour and materials, fixed plant and equipment capacity causes congestion and bottlenecks. Productive efficiency drops and the cost of additional units of output rises. Therefore producers must receive a higher price to produce these additional units.

Consider the individual manufacturer's supply curve for cheese shown in Figure 4.4. Assuming the prices of all other resources and goods are constant, if the price per kilo is raised from $2 to $4, it becomes relatively more profitable to produce cheese. In this instance, the price increase is just sufficient to make it

worthwhile to employ the additional resources necessary to increase production from 200 kilos per month to 600 kilos per month. This is indicated by the move from point *a* to point *b* on the supply curve. Similarly, successively higher prices make it even more profitable to produce cheese, and the supply of cheese will be even larger.

TABLE 4.3
An Individual Producer's Supply of
Cheese (Hypothetical Data)

Price per Kilo	Quantity Supplied (Number of Kilos per Month)
$10	1,200
8	1,100
6	900
4	600
2	200

Suppose that there are 100 cheese manufacturers each of whom has a supply curve identical to that of Figure 4.4. At each price per kilo listed in Table 4.3, the quantity of cheese supplied by the sum of all producers is simply 100 times the amount supplied by one producer. Using these data, Figure 4.5 shows the market or industry supply curve *SS* for cheese. Note that the units on the horizontal axis of Figure 4.5 are a hundred times larger than those on the horizontal axis of Figure 4.4.

Supply Determinants: The Other Things That Remain the Same

When we draw a supply curve such as *SS* in Figure 4.5, we emphasise the way in which the price of the good determines the quantity of it supplied. As with a demand curve, the price of the good is

FIGURE 4.4
An Individual Producer's Supply of Cheese

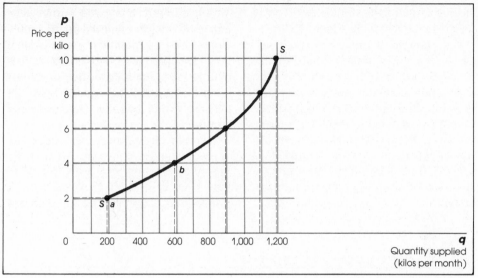

An individual producer's supply curve for cheese is plotted here using the data from Table 4.3. It slopes upward from left to right reflecting a direct relationship between the quantity of the good supplied and the price of the good. It illustrates the law of supply, which says that suppliers will supply more of a good the higher is its price. A change in the price of the good causes a change in the quantity supplied and is represented by a movement along the supply curve. For example, if price changes from $2 per kilo to $4 per kilo, the quantity supplied increases from 200 kilos per month to 600 kilos per month. This is represented by the movement from *a* to *b* along the supply curve *SS*.

singled out as the determining factor and all other things are assumed to be unchanging. These other things are (1) the prices of resources and other factors of production, (2) technology, (3) the prices of other goods, (4) the number of suppliers, and (5) the suppliers' expectations. If one or more of these things change, the supply curve will shift.

1. Prices of Resources

As we saw in Chapter 1, all production processes require inputs, such as labour services, raw materials, fuels and other resources and goods. These inputs to a production process are frequently referred to as the **factors of production**. The supplier of a good has to purchase these factors in order to produce the good.

Suppose now that the price of one or more of the factors of production should fall — that is, one or more of the input prices that were assumed to be constant when we drew *SS* now changes to a lower level. Hence at each possible price of the good suppliers will find it profitable to produce a larger amount of the good than they were previously willing to supply. The supply curve will therefore shift rightward to a position such as S_1S_1 in Figure 4.5. Conversely, if one or more of the input prices should rise, the cost of production will now be higher and producers will not be willing to supply as much at each possible price of the good. The supply curve will therefore shift leftward to a position such as S_2S_2 in Figure 4.5.

For example, if producers could sell cheese for $4 per kilo they would be willing to supply 60,000 kilos per month. This price-supply combination is represented by point a on the market supply curve SS in Figure 4.5. Suppose that the price of one or more inputs falls so that the market supply curve shifts rightward to S_1S_1. Now a price of $3 per kilo is sufficient to induce suppliers to produce 60,000 kilos of cheese per month, as

indicated by point d on S_1S_1. Because they are receiving $4 per kilo, however, they are encouraged to expand output even more until they have moved up the supply curve S_1S_1, from point d to point b. Here they are producing 80,000 kilos per month. At point b, the price of $4 per kilo is just sufficient to induce producers to supply this quantity of cheese per month.

Alternatively, suppose the price of one or more inputs should rise so that the supply curve shifts leftward from SS to S_2S_2. Now a price of $5.60 per kilo is sufficient to induce suppliers to produce

---

FIGURE 4.5
Shifts in the Market Supply Curve for Cheese

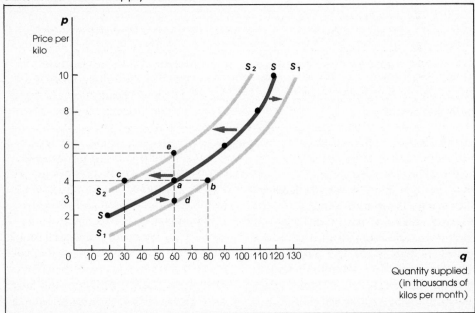

The position of the supply curve is established by the determinants of supply. These are the prices of factors of production, technology, the prices of other goods, the number of suppliers and the suppliers' expectations about the future. Changes in any of these will cause a change in supply, which is represented by a rightward or leftward shift in the supply curve. A rightward shift represents an increase in supply. A leftward shift represents a decrease in supply. *Warning:* Do not confuse the concept of a *change in supply*, represented by a shift in the supply curve, with the concept of a *change in the quantity supplied*, represented by movement along a fixed supply curve such as that described by the movement from *a* to *b* in Figure 4.4.

60,000 kilos of cheese per month, as indicated by point e on S_2S_2. However, if they are receiving only $4 per kilo, they will reduce output until they have moved back down the supply curve S_2S_2 from point e to point c, where they will produce 30,000 kilos per month. Once again, at point c the price of $4 per kilo is just sufficient to induce suppliers to produce this level of output and no more.

2. Prices of Other Goods

Along a fixed supply curve, it is also assumed that the prices of other goods are unchanged. Why do we distinguish between the prices of other goods and the prices of factors of production? The prices of factors of production refer only to the goods used in the production of the good for which the supply curve is drawn. The prices of other goods we now refer to are all the other goods not used in the production of the good for which the supply curve is drawn.

Factors of production are attracted to those production activities where they are paid the highest prices. The higher the price the producer gets for the good produced with those inputs, the greater his or her willingness to pay high prices for those factors. Hence, if the price of beef rises relative to the price of milk, farmers will use less of their pastureland for dairy cattle in order to make it available for grazing beef cattle. The opportunity cost of using pasture to produce the milk used in cheesemaking has effectively risen because the value of that pasture in its alternative use of producing beef has risen. Factors must be paid their opportunity cost if they are to be used in a particular productive activity. That is, the price that must be paid a factor input must be at least as high as what

it could earn in an alternative activity. Since the price of pastureland will go up because of its increased value in beef production, the cost of using it in dairying production will rise. The supply curve for cheese will then shift leftward, such as from SS to S_2S_2 in Figure 4.5. To induce cheese manufacturers to supply any given quantity of cheese, the price of a kilo of cheese will have to be higher. Why? To cover the increased cost of pastureland, which is now more expensive to use because of its increased value in beef production due to the rise in the price of beef. Again we are reminded that the economic problem is how to allocate scarce resources to alternative uses.

3. Technology

Any production process uses some form of technology, whether it involves making butter and cheese in Burnie, Tasmania, making clothes with sewing machines in Melbourne or using giant earth moving equipment for iron-ore mining in the Pilbara. The term **technology** *refers to the production methods used to combine resources of all kinds, including labour, to produce goods and services.* The history of the human race is in no small way a history of the advancement of technology.

This advancement has been characterised by an increase in the ability of humans to produce goods and services — that is, by an increase in productivity. Often productivity is measured as output produced per labour hour used in the production process. Increases in productivity are then taken to mean increases in output per labour hour. *Because technological advance increases productivity, it lowers the cost of producing goods.* Suppose, for example, that there is a technological advance in the technique used to produce, process and mature cheese. This lowers the cost of manufacturing cheese. Suppose the position of the supply curve in Figure 4.5 is at SS before the technological advance. The advance will cause the supply curve to shift rightward to a position such as S_1S_1. At every level of output the price necessary to induce suppliers to produce that output level will now be lower because costs will be lower.

Circumstances that reduce productivity can arise as well. A drought will reduce the productivity of land and cause crop yields to be less. Such adverse developments essentially require the application of additional production techniques if output levels are to be maintained — fruit orchards, or market gardens may require additional irrigation and power charges for pumping water from farm dams are increased. Such increases in production costs cause the supply curve to move to the left. Drought can affect rural production in other ways. In the drier parts of Australia, wheat production and the carrying capacity of the land for sheep and cattle is determined by rainfall. Irrigation does not normally exist as a backup. When crops are lighter or flocks and herds are reduced the supply curve also moves to the left. Falling supply then is reflected in rising flour and meat prices.

Remember that whenever we speak of movement along a fixed supply curve, the state of technology is assumed to be unchanged.

4. Number of Suppliers

When we constructed the market or industry supply curve SS in Figure 4.5, we did it by assuming there were a hundred identical individual suppliers, each with a supply curve like that shown in Figure 4.4. Summing the individual supply curves horizontally gave us the market supply curve SS. If there had been more suppliers, the market supply curve would have been further to the right at a position such as S_1S_1. It follows from these observations that when more suppliers enter the industry, the market supply curve will shift to the right. When suppliers leave the industry, it will shift to the left. When we speak of movement along a market supply curve, it is assumed that the number of suppliers does not change.

5. Suppliers' Expectations

This term refers to the expectations suppliers have about anything that they think affects their economic situation. For example, in 1986 fear that the Commonwealth Government might intervene to restrict logging in Tasmania's Lemonthyme and Southern forests led to a rapid acceleration in tree felling so that stocks could be received before the ban came into force. Conservationists claimed that trees that would normally have taken months to fell and remove were dropped in a matter of days, to be removed later. Similarly when airline operators fear a strike they may schedule extra flights before it begins in order to minimise the effects on their business and their passengers. In each case the supply curve moves temporarily to the right. Changes in expectations can cause the supply curve to shift in either direction depending on the particular situation. However, for any movement along a supply curve, expectations are assumed to remain unchanged.

In sum, the other things that are assumed to remain unchanged when we move along a supply curve are (1) the prices of resources and other factors of production, (2) the prices of other goods, (3) technology, (4) the number of suppliers, and (5) the suppliers' expectations.

When one or more of these things change, the supply curve shifts.

Changes in Quantity Supplied Versus Shifts in Supply

Warning: Along with our earlier warning about the demand curve, another common confusion in economics concerns the distinction between movement along a supply curve versus shifts in the supply curve.

Movement along a supply curve represents a change in the price of the good under consideration and the associated change in the quantity of the good supplied. All other things are assumed to be unchanged. By convention, when we simply refer to *a change in the quantity of a good supplied*, we mean *a movement along a fixed supply curve*, such as that from *d* to *b* in Figure 4.5, unless we say otherwise.

A change in one or more of the five determinants of supply discussed above will cause the supply curve to shift in the manner shown in Figure 4.5. By contrast, movement along a fixed supply curve always assumes these five things remain unchanged. By convention, when we simply refer to *a change in supply* we mean *a shift in the position of the supply curve*, unless we say otherwise. *When the supply curve for a good shifts rightward more of that good will be supplied at every price. When the supply curve shifts leftward less of that good will be supplied at every price. A change in supply results from a change in one or more of the five determinants of supply.*

CHECKPOINT 4.2
1. If wages go up what effect will this have on the supply curve in Figure 4.5?

2. An artificial insemination program leads to an increase in the milk yield of Friesian cows. What effect will this have on the supply curve of cheese manufacturers?
3. Suppose the price of butter was to rise. What effect would you expect this to have on cheese manufacture? Would we refer to those effects as a change in the supply of cheese, or a change in the quantity supplied, or perhaps something else?
4. Explain the economic process by which farmland used to produce cattle might become converted into a factory property that produces pet foods, or a butter and cheese factory.

====

MARKET EQUILIBRIUM: INTERACTION OF SUPPLY AND DEMAND

As any armchair economist knows, supply and demand are what economics is all about. Like the blades of a scissors, supply and demand interact to determine the terms of trade between buyers and sellers. That is, supply and demand mutually determine the price at which sellers are willing to supply just the amount of a good that buyers want to buy. The market for every good has a demand curve and a supply curve that determine this price and quantity. When this price and quantity are established, the market is said to be in equilibrium. In equilibrium there is no tendency for price and quantity to change.

Equilibrium Price and Quantity

In order to see how equilibrium price and quantity are determined in a market, consider again our hypothetical example of the market demand and supply for cheese. Table 4.4 contains the market supply data (usually called the market **supply schedule**) on which the market supply curve *SS* of Figure 4.5 is based. It also contains the market demand data (usually called the market **demand schedule**) that determine the market demand curve for cheese. In this case, the market demand schedule has been obtained by supposing that there are 20,000 individual buyers in the market. Each of these buyers is assumed to have an individual demand schedule like that given in Table 4.1. (That table contained the data for the individual demand curve of Figure 4.1.) The market quantity demand data of Table 4.4 thus equals 20,000 times the individual quantity demand data given in Table 4.1.

Market Adjustment When Price Is Above the Equilibrium Price

Observe in Table 4.4 that at a price of $10 per kilo suppliers would supply the market 120,000 kilos of cheese per month (column 2). Buyers, however, would only demand 20,000 kilos per month (column 3). At this price, there is an excess of supply over demand, or a *surplus* of 100,000 kilos of cheese (column 4). A price of $10 per kilo serves as a relatively strong incentive to suppliers on the one hand, and a relatively high barrier to buyers on the other. If suppliers should produce the 120,000 kilos, they will find they can sell only 20,000. They will be stuck with 100,000 kilos. This surplus will serve notice to suppliers that $10 per kilo is too high a price to charge. They will realise that the price must be lowered if they want to sell more cheese (column 5), as the law of demand would predict. If they continue to produce 120,000 kilos per month in the belief that they can sell that much for $10 per kilo, unwanted inventories will grow due to the continuing surplus. Competition among suppliers will cause the price to be bid down as each tries to underprice the others in order to sell their individual surpluses.

TABLE 4.4
Market Supply and Demand for Cheese (Hypothetical Data)

(1)	(2)	–	(3)	=	(4)	(5)
Price per Kilo	Total Number of Kilos Supplied per Month		Total Number of Kilos Demanded per Month		Surplus (+) or Shortage (-)	Price Change Required to Establish Equilibrium
$10.00	120,000	–	20,000	=	+ 100,000	decrease
8.00	110,000	–	40,000	=	+ 70,000	decrease
6.00	90,000	–	60,000	=	+ 30,000	decrease
5.00	78,000	–	78,000	=	0	no change
4.00	60,000	–	90,000	=	– 30,000	increase
2.00	20,000	–	130,000	=	– 110,000	increase

As a result of suppliers' attempts to correct this undesirable situation through competitive price cutting, the price eventually falls to $8 per kilo. Now suppliers will produce a lower total quantity of cheese, 110,000 kilos per month (column 2), and buyers will increase quantity demanded to 40,000 kilos per month (column 3). At this price, the quantity supplied will still exceed the quantity demanded, however. Though smaller, the surplus amounts to 70,000 kilos of cheese per month (column 4). Again, if suppliers continue to produce 110,000 kilos per month in the belief that they can sell that much for $8 per kilo, unwanted inventories will continue to grow due to the continuing surplus. This situation will cause individual suppliers to continue to try to underprice one another in their competitive attempts to get rid of their individual surpluses. The price in the market will therefore continue to fall (column 5).

At $6 per kilo, the quantity supplied will still exceed the quantity demanded, but the surplus that cannot be sold will have fallen to 30,000 kilos of cheese (column 4). Nonetheless, this will still signal that price must fall further (column 5). Only when price has been reduced to $5 per kilo by the competition among suppliers will they be induced to produce and supply a quantity that is just equal to the quantity that will be demanded at that price, 78,000 kilos per month (columns 2 and 3). No unsold surplus will be produced (column 4) and there will be no incentive to change price any further (column 5). Market equilibrium will prevail. **Market equilibrium** *is established at the price where the quantity of the good buyers demand and purchase is just equal to the quantity suppliers supply and sell. The price and quantity at which this occurs are called the* **equilibrium price** *and* **equilibrium quantity**. In equilibrium the forces of supply and demand are in balance and market clears itself. Price and quantity will have no tendency to change. They are at rest.

The process just described and the equilibrium achieved are readily visualised with the aid of a market demand curve and a market supply curve. Using the supply and demand schedule data given in Table 4.4, the market supply curve and demand curve for cheese are constructed in Figure 4.6. This is done in exactly the same manner used to obtain the demand and supply curves drawn in the previous figures in this chapter. Indeed the supply curve SS in Figure 4.6 is the same one shown in Figure 4.5 as SS. Both the quantity demanded and the quantity supplied are measured on the horizontal axis in Figure 4.6. Equilibrium occurs at the point where the market demand and supply curves intersect. The equilibrium point corresponds to the equilibrium price of $5 and the equilibrium quantity of 78,000 kilos of cheese bought and sold per month. It is readily apparent from the diagram that at prices above $5 supply exceeds demand. Competition among suppliers attempting to underprice one another in order to get rid of their surpluses will cause the price to be bid down. This price cutting will cease when the equilibrium price is reached — the price at which quantity demanded equals quantity supplied.

Market Adjustment When Price Is Below the Equilibrium Price

Suppose that we consider an initial price below the equilibrium price, say $2 per kilo. The situation in the market for cheese is now reversed. The price inducement for suppliers to manufacture cheese is relatively low and so they produce relatively little. Because the price barrier to buyers is relatively low the quantity demanded is relatively high. From Table 4.4 the total quantity supplied is 20,000 kilos per month (column 2), while the total quantity demanded is 130,000 kilos per month (column 3).

FIGURE 4.6
The Market Demand and Supply Determine the Equilibrium Price and Quantity
for Cheese

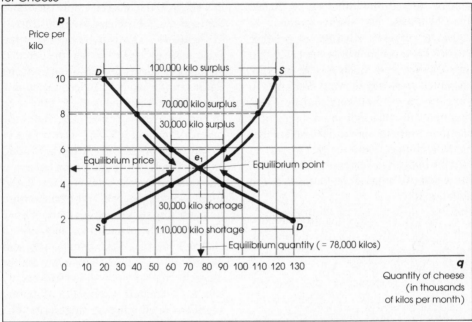

The determination of the equilibrium price and quantity is indicated by the intersection of the
market demand curve DD and the market supply curve SS at e_1. The equilibrium price is $5 per
kilo and the equilibrium quantity is 78,000 kilos. At prices above the equilibrium price, there will
be surpluses as indicated. These surpluses will cause a competitive bidding down of price, thereby reducing the quantity supplied and increasing the quantity demanded until they are equal
and equilibrium is achieved. At prices below the equilibrium price, there will be shortages as indicated. These shortages will cause a competitive bidding up of price, thereby increasing the
quantity supplied and decreasing the quantity demanded until they are equal and equilibrium
is achieved.

Hence there is now an excess demand for cheese. Buyers cannot purchase as much as they want at this price. The shortage amounts to 110,000 kilos (column 4).

There is not enough cheese 'to go around' at $2 per kilo. Buyers begin to bid up price (column 5) as they compete with one another by letting suppliers know they are willing to pay more to get the inadequate supply increased. The cheese manufacturers soon get the message that buyers will pay more because the available

supplies quickly disappear from the shelves of stores and supermarkets. As the price of cheese is bid up, suppliers are encouraged to devote more resources to its production in accordance with the law of supply. At the same time, as price rises, buyers will begin to reduce the quantity of cheese that they demand, in accordance with the law of demand. When price has risen to $4 per kilo, suppliers will be encouraged to increase production to 60,000 kilos per month (column 2). The quantity demanded will be reduced to

90,000 kilos per month (column 3). The quantity demanded still exceeds the quantity supplied, but the shortage has been reduced considerably — to 30,000 kilos (column 4). Nonetheless, there is still a shortage. Buyers will continue to bid price up (column 5) as they compete with one another for a supply of output inadequate to satisfy demand. Only when price has been bid up to $5 per kilo will the quantity demanded be equal to the quantity supplied — 78,000 kilos per month (columns 2 and 3). Market equilibrium will prevail. The shortage has been eliminated. All buyers who demand cheese at $5 per kilo will be able to get it. All suppliers who are willing to supply it at $5 per kilo will find they can sell exactly the quantity they desire to supply. There will be no further incentive for price to be changed.

This process of adjustment to equilibrium is illustrated in Figure 4.6. At prices below $5 per kilo, quantity demanded clearly exceeds quantity supplied and a shortage will exist. Competitive bidding by buyers attempting to secure some of the inadequate supply will cause price to rise. As price rises suppliers are induced to buy more inputs and produce more cheese. The quantity demanded, on the other hand, will fall as buyers are increasingly discouraged from purchasing cheese as the price rises. Again, this process will eventually lead to the equilibrium point where the demand and supply curves intersect to determine the equilibrium price and quantity.

The Nature of Market Equilibrium

Whether price is initially above or below the equilibrium level, market forces operate to cause adjustment to the same equilibrium point. If the process starts from above the equilibrium price level, we may imagine buyers moving down the demand curve DD and suppliers moving down the supply curve SS as adjustment takes place. If the process starts from below the equilibrium price level, buyers move up DD and suppliers up SS. There is only one price at which the quantity supplied is equal to the quantity demanded. At that price every buyer will be able to buy exactly the quantity each demands, and every supplier will be able to sell exactly the quantity each desires to supply. *At the equilibrium price the demand intentions of buyers are consistent with the supply intentions of suppliers.* When these intentions are actually carried out in the form of buyers' bids to purchase and suppliers' offers to sell, they mesh perfectly. *In equilibrium, the decisions of buyers are not frustrated by shortages and the decisions of sellers are not frustrated by surpluses.* Since shortages lead to price rises and surpluses to price reductions *the absence of shortage or surplus will mean price will neither rise nor fall.* The market is in equilibrium.

Changes in Supply and Demand

Suppose the market for cheese is initially in the equilibrium position depicted by the intersection of the demand and supply curves shown in Figure 4.6. These curves are reproduced as DD and SS in Figure 4.7. We know from our discussion of the determinants of supply and demand that any change in one or more of these determinants will cause either the supply curve or the demand curve or both to shift. Such a shift will undo the existing market equilibrium at e_1 and establish a new equilibrium position in the market.

A Change in Demand

Consider first the effect of an expected decrease in milk production. Such an expectation would very likely cause people to change their expectations about the future price and availability of cheese. In particular, people are now likely to expect that the future price of cheese will be higher. Therefore, they will want to buy more cheese now and 'stock up' on it in order to avoid paying a higher price for it later. Hence the market demand curve for cheese will shift rightward to D_1D_1 as shown in Figure 4.7. At every possible price the quantity demanded is now larger.

In particular, at the initial equilibrium price of $5 per kilo the quantity demanded

will increase from 78,000 to 120,000 kilos per month. At this price the quantity demanded will now exceed the quantity suppliers are willing to provide. Specifically, there is now a shortage amounting to 42,000 kilos of cheese. This shortage is the difference between point a on D_1D_1 and the initial equilibrium point e_1 on the supply curve SS in Figure 4.7. As a result of this shortage, buyers will tell sellers they are willing to pay a higher price for cheese in order to get some. When price is eventually bid up high enough, equilibrium will once again be established. Now equilibrium is found at point e_2 where the demand curve D_1D_1 intersects the supply curve SS. The new equilibrium price is $6.60 per kilo, and the new equilibrium

FIGURE 4.7
An Increase in Demand for Cheese

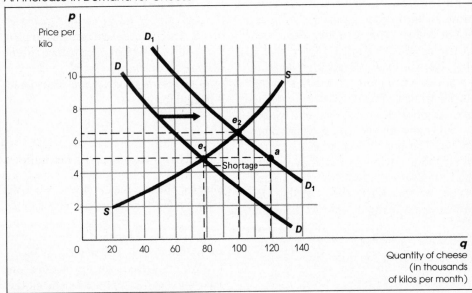

The market is initially in equilibrium where market demand curve DD intersects market supply curve SS at e_1. At this point, the equilibrium price is $5 per kilo and the equilibrium quantity is 78,000 kilos. The increase in demand is indicated by the rightward shift of the market demand curve from DD to D₁D₁. This initially gives rise to the shortage of 42,000 kilos indicated. Competitive bidding among frustrated buyers pushes the price up until market equilibrium is established at e_2. The new equilibrium price is $6.60 per kilo and the new equilibrium quantity is 100,000 kilos.

FIGURE 4.8
A Decrease in the Supply of Cheese

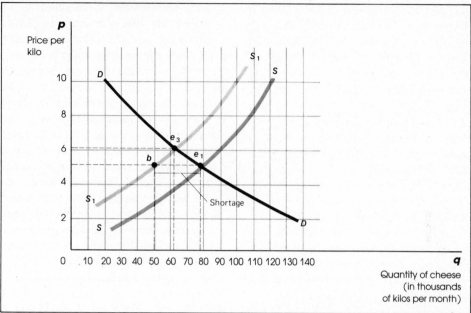

The market is initially in equilibrium where market demand curve *DD* intersects market supply curve *SS* at e_1. This gives an equilibrium price of $5 per kilo and an equilibrium quantity of 78,000 kilos. The decrease in supply is indicated by the leftward shift of the market supply curve from *SS* to S_1S_1. This initially gives rise to the indicated shortage of 28,000 kilos, represented by the distance between points *b* and e_1. Competitive bidding among frustrated buyers pushes the price up until market equilibrium is established at e_3. The new equilibrium price is $6 per kilo, and the new equilibrium quantity is 62,000 kilos per month.

quantity bought and sold is 100,000 kilos per month. Hence *an increase in demand represented by a rightward shift in the demand curve will increase both price and quantity assuming other things remain the same*. (Supply is one of the things that remain unchanged, as represented by the unchanged position of the supply curve.)

It is interesting to note that the expectation of an increase in the price of cheese is in fact sufficient to cause an actual price increase. Eventually price rises enough to ration or cut back the quantity demanded (a movement from *a* to e_2 along D_1D_1) while at the same time causing an increase in the quantity supplied (a

movement from e_1 to e_2 along *SS*). This increase in quantity supplied is sufficient to restore equilibrium in the market and eliminate the shortage.

A Change in Supply

For the moment set aside the effect of a change in expectations on the market. In our discussion of the determinants of the supply curve we noted that adverse weather conditions cause the supply curve to shift leftward. In addition, we know from our earlier discussions that increases in the prices of inputs will also cause the supply curve to shift leftward. Again consider the initial equilibrium as shown in Figure 4.8. (The demand curve DD and the supply curve SS are in exactly the same position as DD and SS in Figure 4.7.) Suppose both a poor season and a rise in farmers' costs conspire to reduce supply or shift the market supply curve leftward from SS to S_lS_l. At every possible price, suppliers will now reduce the quantity of cheese they are willing to supply. In particular, at the initial equilibrium price of $5 per kilo, they are now only willing to supply 50,000 kilos of cheese per month. At this price buyers will continue to demand 78,000 kilos per month, however. The quantity demanded therefore exceeds the quantity supplied and there is now a shortage amounting to 28,000 kilos, represented by the distance between points b and e_l. Again this causes the price to be bid up. When the price reaches $6 per kilo, the quantity demanded will again equal the quantity supplied. Equilibrium in the market will once more be restored. The equilibrium point is now at the intersection of DD and S_lS_l indicated by e_3. At the new equilibrium price of $6 per kilo, the equilibrium quantity bought and sold is 62,000 kilos per month. Hence *a decrease in supply, represented by a leftward shift in the supply curve, will increase price and decrease quantity assuming other things remain the same.* (Demand is one of the things that remain the same, as represented by the unchanged position of the demand curve.)

Both Supply and Demand Change

Suppose that in fact the expectations affecting cheese demand and the events affecting cheese supply have all occurred at about the same time. To analyse the consequences for the market for cheese we must consider the rightward shift in the demand curve of Figure 4.7 together with the leftward shift in the supply curve of Figure 4.8. This combination of shifts is shown in Figure 4.9. Again the market supply curve SS and the market demand curve DD are the same as shown in Figures 4.7 and 4.8, and the initial equilibrium point determined by their intersection is again shown as e_l. The rightward shift in the demand curve from DD to D_lD_l caused by the changed expectations is exactly the same as that shown in Figure 4.7. The leftward shift in the supply curve from SS to S_lS_l caused by a poor season and rising farmers' costs is exactly the same as that shown in Figure 4.8. At the initial equilibrium price of $5 per kilo, the quantity demanded increases from 78,000 to 120,000 kilos per month. At the same time, the quantity suppliers are willing to supply falls from 78,000 to 50,000 kilos per month. The shortage now is equal to the sum of the shortages shown in Figures 4.7 and 4.8. Specifically, there is now a shortage amounting to 70,000 kilos per month, the difference between point a on D_lD_l and point b on S_lS_l. To restore equilibrium, price will have to be bid up until the quantity of cheese demanded once again equals the quantity suppliers are willing to provide. This occurs where the demand curve D_lD_l intersects the supply curve S_lS_l at e_4. The new equilibrium price is $7.60 per kilo, and the equilibrium quantity bought and sold is now 80,000 kilos of cheese per month.

Note that when the leftward shift of the supply curve is considered together with the rightward shift of the demand curve in Figure 4.9, the resulting rise in price is greater than when either shift is considered alone, as in Figures 4.7 and 4.8. This is readily apparent from Figure

4.9. When only the demand shift was considered, the new equilibrium point was e_2. When just the supply shift was considered, the new equilibrium point was e_3. When the effect of both shifts is considered, the new equilibrium point is e_4, which occurs at a higher price than at either e_2 or e_3.

When demand increases and supply decreases, as in Figure 4.9, it is possible for the new equilibrium quantity bought and sold to be either larger or smaller than that of the initial equilibrium position. Whether it is larger or smaller depends on the relative size of the shifts in the two curves. In the hypothetical example cf Figure 4.9, the relative sizes of these shifts are such that the new equilibrium quantity associated with e_4 is slightly larger than the initial equilibrium quantity associated with e_1. If the leftward shift of the supply curve had been somewhat larger, or the

---

FIGURE 4.9
Combined Effects of an Increase in Demand and a Decrease in Supply for Cheese

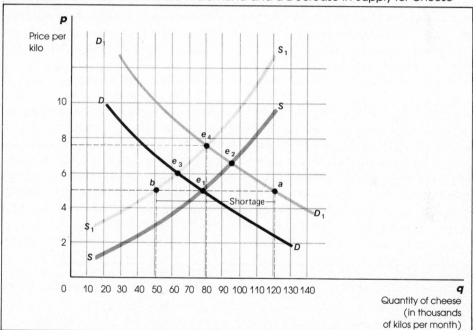

The combined effects of the increase in demand in Figure 4.7 and the decrease in supply in Figure 4.8 are shown here. Starting from the initial equilibrium determined by the intersection of DD and SS at e_1, the market demand curve shifts rightward to D_1D_1 while the market supply curve shifts leftward to S_1S_1. The initial shortage amounts to 70,000 kilos, the sum of the initial shortages indicated in Figures 4.7 and 4.8. Competitive bidding among frustrated buyers pushes the price up until market equilibrium is established at e_4. At that point, the new equilibrium price is $7.60 per kilo, and the new equilibrium quantity is 80,000 kilos per month. Notice that the new equilibrium price is higher than that established when either the increase in demand or decrease in supply is considered separately, as in Figures 4.7 and 4.8. The new equilibrium quantity is larger given the relative sizes of the demand and supply curve shifts shown here. Had the leftward shift of the supply curve been larger or the rightward shift of the demand curve been smaller, or both, the new equilibrium quantity could have been smaller than the initial equilibrium quantity at e_1.

POLICY PERSPECTIVE

Accounting Lecturers in Short Supply

There is a strong demand for accountants by business in Australia today. Graduates earn in excess of $20,000 in their first year and can expect considerably more after a few years in a job. The general level of salaries in the accounting profession has caused problems for universities and colleges that train accounting graduates. It is difficult to obtain accounting teachers of a sufficiently high calibre because the opportunity cost of working in universities is so high. Universities have to pay lecturers in accounting the same rate they pay to other university teaching staff.

Figures P4.1(a) and P4.1(b) depict the Australian markets for accounting lecturers and new accounting graduates respectively. In Figure P4.1(a) the market for lecturers is not in balance — the number of teachers falls short of the number required. In Figure P4.1(b) demand and supply for young graduates are in equilibrium at an annual salary of $22,000. Of course, these are quite different markets; the new graduate would not be able to do the lecturer's job. However, as we shall see, there are important links between the two markets.

In practice universities and colleges face a choice of either finding some way of paying accounting lecturing staff more (perhaps by a backdoor method such as accelerated promotion), restricting enrolments, or asking teaching staff to work longer hours. The last two alternatives do nothing to solve the basic problem. Suppose universities were to pay higher salaries. What effect do you think this would have on the market for accounting graduates? How would the supply of graduates and graduate salaries be affected? Another possible solution, with little prospect of being accepted in the immediate future in Australia, would be to charge accounting students a special fee and to use the revenue to pay accounting lecturers higher salaries. How would this solution affect the market for new graduate accountants?

FIGURE P4.1(a)
The Market for Accounting Lecturers

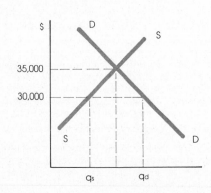

FIGURE P4.1(b)
The Market for New Accounting Graduates

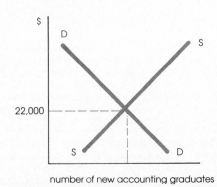

number of new accounting graduates

rightward shift of the demand curve somewhat smaller, or both, the new equilibrium quantity might have been somewhat less than the initial equilibrium quantity.

CHECKPOINT 4.3

1. A sharp fall in the number of new cars being registered in Australia each month in 1987 was followed by dealers' offers to reduce prices to buyers if they acted immediately. How would you depict this situation using demand and supply curves?

2. Migration to Australia of European settlers has brought people with a love of cheese and has also brought skilled cheese makers. How would you expect these influences to affect the demand and supply of cheese, the price and the quantity sold?

3. If the price of electricity, council rates and government sales taxes all rise what do you predict would be the effect on the equilibrium price of cheese and the quantity sold?

4. Suppose you were told that consumers' incomes were increasing, but the quantity of shoes sold had fallen. What possible explanations of this fall in sales could you give? Assume that shoes are a normal good.

SUMMARY

1. The law of demand asserts that the lower (higher) the price charged for a good, the larger (smaller) will be the quantity demanded — all other things remaining the same. This law may be represented graphically by a demand curve that slopes downward left to right on a graph with price measured on the vertical axis and quantity measured on the horizontal. Any point on a demand curve tells us the quantity of a good buyer's desire to purchase per some specified unit of time at the price associated with that point.

2. In addition to the price of the good for which the market demand curve is drawn, the other determinants of market demand are (1) the prices of all other goods (2) money income (3) expectations (4) tastes and (5) the number of buyers in the market. A change in one or more of these determinants will cause the market demand curve to shift either rightward (an increase in demand) or leftward (a decrease in demand). A shift in the demand curve is referred to as a change in demand. It is to be distinguished from a change in the quantity demanded, which refers to a movement along a fixed demand curve. The latter can only occur because of a change in the price of the good for which the demand curve is drawn.

3. The law of supply asserts that suppliers will supply larger quantities of a good at higher prices for that good than at lower prices — all other things remaining the same. This law may be represented graphically by a supply curve that slopes upward left to right on a graph with price measured on the vertical axis and quantity measured on the horizontal axis. Any point on a supply curve tells us the quantity of a good suppliers are willing to produce and desire to sell per some specified unit of time at the price associated with that point.

4. Along with the price of the good for which the supply curve is drawn, the other determinants of supply are (1) the prices of resources and other factors of production (2) the prices of other goods (3) technology (4) the number of suppliers and (5) the suppliers' expectations. A change in any of these determinants will cause the supply curve to shift either rightward (an increase in supply) or leftward (a decrease in supply). Such a change is called a change in supply. It is to be distinguished from a change in the quantity supplied which is a movement along a fixed supply curve due to a change in the price of the good for which the supply curve is drawn.

5. Supply and demand interact to adjust price until that price is found where the quantity of the good demanded is just equal to the quantity supplied. This is the equilibrium price and quantity, which is determined by the intersection of the supply and demand curves. When this point of intersection is established we have market equilibrium.

6. Changes in supply and demand, represented by shifts in the supply and demand curves, will upset equilibrium and cause either shortages or surpluses. This will set in motion competitive price bidding among buyers and sellers that will ultimately restore market equilibrium, most typically at new levels of equilibrium price and quantity.

7. An increase (decrease) in demand will lead to an increase (decrease) in equilibrium price and quantity — other things remaining the same. An increase (decrease) in supply will lead to a decrease (increase) in equilibrium price and an increase (decrease) in equilibrium quantity — other things remaining the same. When both supply and demand change, the effect on equilibrium price and quantity depends on the particular case.

KEY TERMS AND CONCEPTS

complementary good
demand curve
demand schedule
equilibrium price
equilibrium quantity
factors of production
inferior good
law of demand
law of supply
market demand curve
market equilibrium
normal good
substitute good
supply curve
supply schedule
technology

QUESTIONS AND PROBLEMS

1. Classify each of the following goods according to whether *in your opinion* it is a normal or inferior good: shoes, beer, life insurance, potato chips, auto insurance, stereo equipment, retread tyres, Australian champagne.

2. Classify each of the following pairs of goods according to whether you think they are substitutes, complements, or basically unrelated to each other: ham and eggs, meat and potatoes, Fords and Toyotas, ice skates and swimsuits, coffee and tea, butter and margarine, apples and oranges, knives and forks, newspapers and hats.

3. Suppose today's weather forecast states that chances are 9 out of 10 there will be rain during all the coming week. What effect do you think this will have on the demand curve for each of the following: umbrellas, football tickets, electricity, taxi rides, parking space in shopping centres, camping equipment, books, and aspirin?

4. What do you predict would happen to the market demand curve for orange juice in Australia as a result of the following:

a. a rise in average income;

b. an increase in the birthrate;

c. an intensive advertising campaign that convinces most people of the importance of a daily quota of natural vitamin C;

d. a fall in the price of fresh oranges;

e. a fall in the price of grapefruit juice?

5. What will happen to the supply of cars if each of the following should occur? Explain your answers.

a. an increase in the price of trucks;

b. a fall in the price of steel;

c. introduction of a better assembly-line technique;

d. an increase in the desire of vehicle manufacturers to improve their public image rather than to earn as much money as possible;

e. an increase in the price of cars?

6. If goods are expensive because they are scarce, why aren't rotten eggs high priced?

7. What do you think would be the effect on building activity of an increase in the price of cement? What would be the effect on the supply curve of cement of an upsurge in public sector building programs?

8. What effect do you think an advertising campaign for coffee would have on each of the following — other things remaining the same: the price of coffee, the price of tea, the quantity of sugar bought and sold, the price of doughnuts, the quantity of sleeping pills bought and sold, the price of television advertising time on the late show?

9. Suppose you read in the paper that the price of petrol is rising along with increased sales of petrol. Does this contradict the law of demand or not? Explain.

10. Suppose there is a strike in the steel industry. Other things remaining the same, what do you predict will happen to the price of steel, the price of automobiles, the quantity sold and the price of aluminium, the price of aluminium wire, the price and quantity of copper wire sold, and the price of electricity? At each step of this chain spell out your answer in terms of the relevant shift in a demand or supply curve. What do you think of the characterisation of the economy as a chain of interconnected markets?

11. There has been a considerable fall in the price of video recorders since they first came out. Is the fall consistent with an increase in demand, supply, neither, or both?

12. On occasions when there has been a petrol shortage in New South Wales, the State Government has limited sales one day to cars with odd numbered registration plates and the next to cars with even numbers. Why did they do this?

TWO

Aggregate Income, Employment, Fiscal Policy and International Trade

5
Macroeconomic Concepts

AFTER READING THIS CHAPTER YOU WILL BE ABLE TO:

1. Explain the interconnecting economic relationships between households, businesses, government and other countries as characterised in flow diagrams.

2. Define the concept of GDP and list the kinds of economic transactions that are and are not included in this measure.

3. Explain the difference between current dollar or money GDP and constant dollar or real GDP.

4. State some of the deficiencies of GDP as a measure of the economy's welfare.

5. Define aggregate demand and supply and explain how they determine the economy's equilibrium price and total output levels.

This chapter begins our study of macro-economics. Recall from Chapter 1 that macroeconomics is concerned with the performance of the economy as a whole or with large sectors of it, such as government, business, and households. Macroeconomics attempts to explain why the economy's total output of goods and services fluctuates over time, giving rise to the business cycle with its accompanying upward and downward movements in the unemployment rate and the rate of inflation. Macroeconomics is concerned with the potentially helpful as well as possibly harmful role that government plays in these events, including such issues as the government's ability to control inflation, the effectiveness of government policies aimed at smoothing the business cycle, and the size and effects of government budget deficits, an issue of much concern in recent years.

We will use flow diagrams in this chapter to develop a descriptive overview of the ways in which the major sectors of a capitalistic, mixed economy like that of Australia are linked together. We will then examine the important concept of gross domestic product, or GDP, the most commonly used measure of the economy's total output of goods and services. In Chapter 6 we will examine the historical record of the Australian economy in order to gain perspective and a feel for the way the economy behaves, the nature of the business cycle, and the closely related problems of inflation and unemployment. Chapter 7 will present the basics of national income accounting, the way we go about keeping track of the economy's performance. Chapters 8, 9, 10, 11 and 12 will focus on explaining how the economy's total level of output is determined, the reasons why the economy does not always operate at full capacity (full employment), and the nature of public

policies aimed at correcting this recurrent problem.

THE CIRCULAR FLOW OF GOODS AND MONEY

In a capitalistic, mixed economy like that of Australia money is used by households, businesses, and government to buy and sell goods and resources in markets, to pay and collect taxes, and to borrow and lend in financial markets. The flow of goods and resources in exchange for money, the flow of money to fulfil tax obligations to government and to redistribute income from one group to another, the flow of money from lenders to borrowers in exchange for borrowers' IOUs, and the expenditure of the borrowed funds on goods can all be envisioned schematically in a flow diagram.

The Exchange Flow Between Households and Businesses

Consider first a flow diagram representing an economy in which there is no government intervention in economic activities. For the moment, we will also ignore the existence of financial markets and simply assume that businesses and households are the only two groups of decision makers. The relationship between these two groups is shown in Figure 5.1. The upper channel represents the flow of economic resources (land, labour, and financial capital) owned by households and supplied to businesses. The direction of this flow is indicated by the anticlockwise arrow running from households to businesses. In exchange for these services, businesses make money payments in the form of wages, rents, interest, and the distribution of profits.

FIGURE 5.1
The Exchange Flow Between Businesses and Households

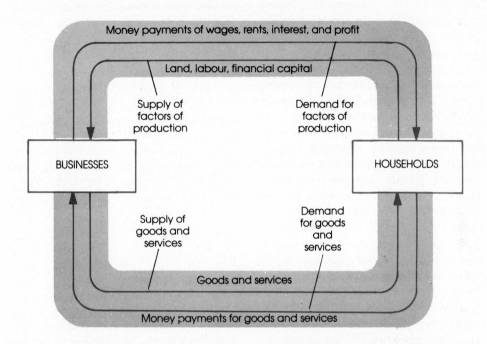

In a money-using economy, businesses obtain the resources (land, labour, and financial capital) necessary for production from households in exchange for money payments (wages, rents, interest, and profit) as indicated in the upper flow channel. These payments are income to the households, which spend it on goods and services produced by businesses. This is indicated by the money payments made to businesses in exchange for goods and services in the lower flow channel. Businesses use the money proceeds from sales to purchase the resources in the upper flow channel, thus completing the loop.

These payments constitute business demand for factors of production. The direction of this flow is indicated by the clockwise arrow running from businesses to households. All these exchanges take place at mutually agreeable money rates of exchange (or prices), determined by the functioning of markets for production inputs. *Wages* go to labour, *rents* to landowners, *interest* and *profits* to those supplying financial capital and entrepreneurial skills (a particular kind of labour service). All these money payments received by households constitute income.

The lower channel represents the flow of goods and services produced and supplied by businesses using all the inputs provided by the upper flow channel. This flow of goods and services in the lower channel runs from businesses to households, as indicated by the anticlockwise arrow. The goods and services are demanded and purchased by the households with the money receipts (or income) obtained by selling the services of their resources, as indicated in the upper channel. The money payments made to businesses in exchange for goods and services are indicated in the lower channel by the arrow running clockwise from households to businesses. These exchanges also take place at mutually agreeable prices determined by the functioning of markets.

The money payments made by businesses in the upper channel are viewed as costs by them, while their receipt by households is viewed as income. The money payments received by businesses in the lower channel are viewed by them as sales revenue. For households these payments are the expenditures of the income they receive for supplying the resources that were used to produce the goods and services. Hence, in this money-using, pure market economy we have a clockwise flow of money payments made against an anticlockwise flow of resources, goods, and services. The clockwise circular flow of money expenditures may be thought of as the demand for the anti-clockwise circular supply flow of resources, goods, and services, although both flows take place at the same time. These simultaneous flows reflect the ongoing and repetitive exchanges between buyers and sellers in the many markets of the economy.

The Exchange Flows with Financial Markets

The exchange flows shown in Figure 5.1 are oversimplified in several respects. For one thing, businesses produce and sell goods to one another — capital equipment, for example. Similarly households buy from and sell labour services to one another, for example domestic services such as babysitting.

Households and Businesses Save

We also know that households do not

typically spend all their income on goods and services, nor do businesses pay out all their sales revenue for the current use of land, labour, and financial capital. *Households save part of their income, usually by putting it in banks and other financial institutions. Similarly, businesses save part of their sales revenue. Some of this saving takes the form of* **depreciation allowances.** *These allowances are funds that are set aside for the replacement of capital equipment when it wears out. The rest of their saving usually takes the form of* **retained earnings.** Like households, businesses put savings in banks and other financial institutions. Often they use their savings to purchase bonds and other forms of IOUs issued by parties that want to borrow money. Banks and other financial institutions perform the function of taking the savings of households and businesses and lending this money to borrowers who in turn use it to buy goods and services. When businesses, and sometimes households, use their savings to buy bonds and IOUs directly without the assistance of the intermediary role played by banks and other financial institutions, the effect is the same — savings are lent to borrowers.

The Role of Financial Markets

The markets that perform the function of taking the funds of savers and lending them to borrowers are called **financial markets.** The households and businesses that lend their savings to borrowers through these financial markets receive compensation in the form of interest payments. Financial markets serve the function of taking the funds from the saving flows of businesses and households and lending them to borrowers at interest rates mutually agreeable to both lenders and borrowers. Who are the borrowers?

FIGURE 5.2
Exchange flows with Savings and Financial Markets

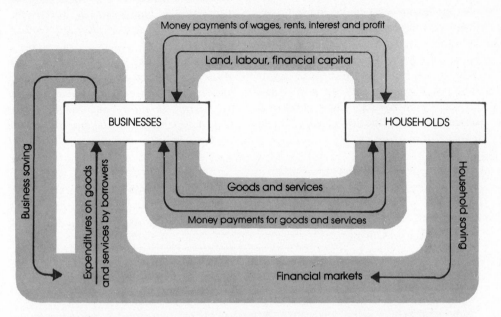

This diagram elaborates on Figure 5.1 by adding the savings flows from households and businesses. These feed into the financial markets, where they are loaned to borrowers at some mutually acceptable rate of interest. The borrowers then spend the funds on goods and services produced by businesses. The financial markets thus serve to redirect the savings money flows, otherwise diverted from expenditure on goods and services, back into the hands of those who will spend them on goods and services. Figure 5.2 may be viewed as representing a pure market, laissez faire capitalist economy.

Other businesses and households. What do they do with the borrowed funds? Spend them on goods and services. *In effect, financial markets take the savings, or the flow of funds provided by those businesses and households that do not want to.spend them on goods and services, and put them in the hands of those that do want to spend them on goods and services.*

Flow Diagram with Financial Markets and Savings

The role of financial markets can be represented in diagram form by making some changes in Figure 5.1. Figure 5.2 reproduces Figure 5.1 with the addition of savings flows and financial markets. Note now that not all of the sales revenue

of businesses is immediately paid out in wages, rents, interest, and profit. Some is retained and saved, and it flows from businesses into the financial markets as indicated by the anticlockwise arrow labeled 'Business saving'. (It should be emphasised that these savings are still owned by the shareholders of the businesses who have provided financial capital.) Similarly, households do not spend all of their income on goods and services. That which is not spent is saved and flows into financial markets as indicated by the clockwise arrow labelled 'Household saving'.

The financial markets in the lower part of the diagram lend out the savings of businesses and households to other businesses and households that want to borrow funds. These borrowers do not borrow money and make interest payments on their loans just for the privilege of holding the money. They use it to buy goods and services from businesses, as indicated by the upward-directed arrow labelled 'Expenditures on goods and services by borrowers'. These goods and services are part of the flow labelled 'Goods

and services', indicated by the anticlockwise arrow running from businesses to households. The business borrowers purchase goods and services from other businesses.

The main point is this: *The flow of money which is diverted away from further expenditure on goods and services by saving is redirected through the financial markets into the hands of those*

FIGURE 5.3
Exchange Flows with Savings and Financial Markets and Government

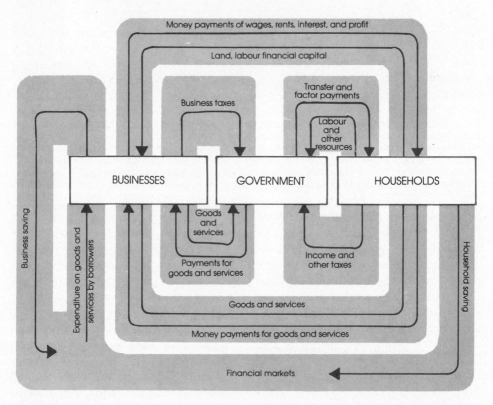

This diagram elaborates on Figure 5.2 by adding government, which is financed by taxes from businesses and households. Government uses tax proceeds to make transfer payments to households as well as to hire labour and purchase other resources from households. Government also uses tax revenue to purchase goods and services from businesses. In this way government reallocates resources and redistributes income. Also, by varying tax rates and the level of its expenditures, government can affect the size of the flows in the flow channels — that is, the level of economic activity. Figure 5.3 may be viewed as representing a capitalistic, mixed economy.

who will spend it on goods and services. In performing this function financial markets play a crucial role in capitalistic, market-oriented economies. Because there is no government economic intervention indicated in Figure 5.2, it may be interpreted as representing an economic system of pure market, laissez faire capitalism.

The Exchange Flows Between Businesses, Households, and Government

In order to characterise a capitalistic, mixed economy in a flow diagram it is necessary to bring government into the picture. This has been done in Figure 5.3. (The term *government* as used here includes federal, state, and local government.)

Government Expenditures, Taxes, and Transfers

In order to carry out its functions, government must hire labour and other resources owned by households. This is indicated by the anticlockwise arrow running from households to government labelled 'Labour and other resources'. The money payments by government for these resources are indicated by the clockwise arrow running from government to households labelled 'Transfer and factor payments'. The factor payments are made to cover wage, rent, and interest payments to households in exchange for labour services, buildings and land rented to the government, and the financial capital provided through household holdings of government bonds. These factor payments are viewed as expenditures by the government and as income by the households. Transfer payments represent government

payment to households of pensions, other social security benefits, and other payments such as unemployment benefits. Transfers also include tax refunds. Transfer payments are viewed as income by the households receiving them.

In order to help finance its operations, the government must collect taxes from households in the form of income taxes, property rates, and sales taxes. These tax payments by households to government are represented by the clockwise arrow running from households to government labelled 'Income and other taxes'. The government also collects taxes from businesses in the form of company taxes, rates, payroll taxes and sales taxes. These tax payments to government are represented by the clockwise arrow running from businesses to government labelled 'Business taxes'. There is yet one other way in which government can finance its operations. That is by issuing and selling new government bonds in the financial markets. The money proceeds from these sales can be used in the same ways as tax proceeds. (The flow channel between government and the financial markets is not shown in Figure 5.3.)

The government uses receipts from bond sales along with the tax receipts from businesses and households in part to make the transfer and factor payments to households already mentioned. The government also uses these receipts to purchase goods and services from businesses. These include anything from paper clips and staples to sophisticated defence equipment, and the construction of dams, highways, and buildings by private contractors. The payments for these items are represented by the clockwise arrow running from government to businesses labelled 'Payments for goods and services'. The provision of goods and services in exchange for these payments is indicated by the anticlockwise arrow running from businesses to government labelled 'Goods and services'.

Government Affects Resource Allocation and Income Distribution

The taxes paid by businesses must come out of their sales revenue, while those paid by households must come out of their income. By increasing or decreasing the amount of these taxes, government can divert a larger or smaller share of the sales revenue of businesses and the income receipts of households into activities determined by government expenditures, as opposed to the market activities determined by business and household expenditures. This is an obvious way in which government affects resource allocation. Similarly, it can be seen how the government affects income distribution through the redistribution of tax proceeds to households in the form of transfer payments.

Government Affects the Level of Economic Activity

By changing its expenditure and tax policies, government can affect the level of overall economic activity as represented by the flows in Figure 5.3. Consider two extreme examples.

Suppose government increases income taxes on households but does not spend the increased tax proceeds. This obviously takes income from households that would otherwise have been spent on goods and services or saved and put in the financial markets, where it could have ultimately been used by some borrower to buy goods and services. Hence, the volume in the lower two flow channels of Figure 5.3 would be reduced. This would lead to a drop in sales by businesses and a con-

sequent drop in some or all of the categories of business saving, business taxes, and income earned by households, as measured by businesses' money payments of wages, rent, interest, and profit in the upper flow channel of Figure 5.3.

Alternatively, suppose government increased expenditures on goods and services but did not raise taxes to finance these expenditures. Suppose, instead, that it financed them by simply printing money. The result would be that businesses would experience an increase in the dollar volume of sales. This would lead to an increase in some or all of the categories — business saving, business taxes, and income earned by households.

Changes in the expenditure plans of businesses and households can also lead to changes in economic activity as represented by the flows in Figure 5.3. Government stabilisation policy is aimed at changing all or some combination of government expenditures, tax rates, and the money supply in such a way as to offset undesirable changes in the level of economic activity that may result from changes in business and household expenditure plans.

The flow diagrams are very simplified pictures of the economy. Much detail is omitted. Nonetheless, they give some idea of how the mixed economy's various decisionmaking units — business, households, and government — are linked together to form an interlocking, interdependent system.

Exchange Flows with Other Countries

In the discussion so far we have overlooked economic transactions between our economy and the rest of the world. As you shall see in later chapters international trade plays a significant part in the determination of living standards in a country like Australia.

Superimposing the international sector onto Figure 5.3 is a complex task. It is sufficient for us here to note the major links which exist. The first of these occurs through the exports of goods and services to other countries by the home economy's businesses and public enterprises. As a result of such activities there is an injection of funds from foreign countries into our economy's circular flow.

Offsetting export activities are the imports of households, government and the business sector from other countries. The payments for imported goods and services represent a leakage of funds from the economy's circular flow.

The final link between any economy and the outside world takes place through international financial markets where borrowing and lending takes place. Transactions in these capital markets allow a nation to adjust its balance of payments position.

CHECKPOINT * 5.1

How would the flow diagram in Figure 5.3 have to be changed for the Australian economy to reflect the operations of public enterprises such as Qantas, Telecom and the Commonwealth Bank?

*Answers to all Checkpoints can be found at the back of the text.

WHAT IS GROSS DOMESTIC PRODUCT (GDP)?

Probably the most cited measure of the economy's overall performance is its **gross domestic product (GDP).** In short, *GDP is the market value of all final goods and services produced in the economy during a year.* GDP has several important characteristics. First, it is a flow concept. Second, it is measured in money terms. Third, it only includes goods and services bought for final use, not unfinished goods in the intermediate stages of production that are purchased for further processing and resale. Fourth, GDP has two sides — it may be viewed from the income side or from the expenditure side.

GDP Is a Flow

A **flow** *is a quantity per unit of time,* such as so many litres of water running through a pipe per minute. By contrast, a stock is a quantity measured without respect to time, such as the number of litres of water in a tub. GDP is a flow measured as the quantity of final goods and services produced by the economy per year. It is a flow that is measured at an annual rate.

We could measure GDP by giving a complete listing of all final goods and services produced per year — the number of cars, haircuts, toothbrushes, car washes, and so forth. (We couldn't add the quantities of these different goods together to get one number — you can't add apples and shirts.) This obviously would be a rather cumbersome list, probably about the size of a large city's telephone directory, depending on how fine a breakdown of product description is desired. It is far easier and less awkward to simply summarise all this information by adding up the dollar values of all these goods. Hence the dollar value of GDP is given as the sum of the price of a car times the number of cars per year plus the price of a haircut times the number of haircuts per year plus the price of a toothbrush times the number of toothbrushes per year plus the price of a car wash times the number of car washes per year plus . . . , and so forth. *GDP may be viewed either as a flow of numbers of units of final goods and services produced per year or as a flow of the dollar value of these final goods and services produced per year.*

The importance of distinguishing between final goods and services produced this year and those produced in other years cannot be overemphasised. Only those produced this year are to be counted in this year's GDP. Those produced in other years are counted in GDP for the years in which they were produced.

The measurement of GDP requires that we add up all the market transactions representing the purchase and sale of final goods and services. Such transactions measure the dollar value of productive activity that actually went into the production of final goods and services this year. However, there are many market transactions in our economy that do not involve the purchase and sale of final goods and services produced this year. For the purpose of measuring GDP, these are nonproductive transactions, and care must be taken not to include them in the measurement of GDP. In addition, it should be recognised that some productive activities that should be included in GDP do not always show up as market transactions.

Productive Versus Nonproductive Transactions

Many market transactions that occur in our economy do not represent the production of a good. Therefore, we don't want to count them in GDP.

The purchase and sale of *used goods* is an example of such a transaction. If A buys B's 2-year-old stereo set for $300, this transaction does not involve the purchase of a final good produced *this year*. When the set was purchased new 2 years ago, its purchase price was included in GDP for that year. What about a set produced and purchased in February of this year and then resold by the initial buyer a month later? The purchase of the set by the *initial* buyer would be included in GDP for this year because it was produced this year. However, it would not be correct to include the resale transaction in GDP because this would amount to counting the production of the set more than once. *The resale of a used good is a transaction that merely represents the transfer of ownership of a previously produced good — it does not represent the production of a new good.* Always remember that GDP is a measure of productive activity. You and I could buy and sell the same car back and forth daily, but we have not produced any new cars.

There are also certain types of *financial transactions* in our economy that do not represent any productive activity that adds to the output of final goods and services. Therefore, they are not included in GDP. Such transactions include (1) the trading of shares, bonds, and other kinds of securities in financial markets; and (2) private and public transfer payments.

1. The trading in shares and bonds in financial markets amounts to several tens of billions of dollars per year. None of this is counted in GDP, however, because it only represents the trading of paper assets. True, businesses and government often issue new stocks and bonds to raise funds to spend on currently produced final goods and services. But this only amounts to a minute fraction of the total yearly purchases and sales of securities. Funds raised and used to purchase final goods and services are included in GDP when

they appear in business firms' accounts recording such sales.

2. Private and public **transfer payments** are transactions in which the recipient is neither expected nor required to make any contribution to GDP in return. The transfer of funds from one individual to another, either as a gift, a bequest, or a charitable donation, constitutes a private transfer payment not included in GDP. Also included under private transfer payments are payments out of private superannuation funds. Public transfer payments are made to some groups in the economy by the government. Such payments include unemployment benefits, age, invalid and war service pensions. While these payments are not included in GDP, the national income accounts do keep a record of them, as we shall see.

Productive Nonmarket Transactions

If GDP is to measure the economy's production of final goods and services, it is necessary to recognise that not all productive activities show up as market transactions on the business accounting statements used to construct an estimate of GDP. Therefore, it is necessary to impute a dollar value to productive activities not represented by a market transaction and to include this dollar value in the calculation of GDP.

For example, people who live in their own home do not write themselves a rent cheque every month. However, those who do not own their home must make such an explicit rent payment. Both groups receive a currently produced service — the shelter provided by their dwellings — yet only the payments made by renters to landlords show up as a market transaction. The rent on owner-occupied homes must be imputed as the rent payments the owners would have to make if they rented

their homes from landlords. These payments could also be looked at as the amount of rent owners could receive if they were to rent their home to somebody else. Such an imputed rent on owner-occupied homes is included in GDP, along with the rent payments made to landlords. Similarly, the value of the food that farm families produce and consume themselves must be imputed and included in GDP.

However, there are a number of productive nonmarket transactions that are not included in GDP. The productive services of homemakers — cooking, laundering, house cleaning — are not included despite the fact that this constitutes a sizeable amount of productive activity. (If you're not convinced; just check the want ads to see what it would cost you to hire a cook and a housekeeper.) Many people repair and remodel their own homes, cars, and a host of other items. Yet the productive services of the do-it-yourselfers are not included in GDP, largely because it is so difficult to estimate and keep track of the total value of such activities in our economy.

Value Added: Don't Double Count

We have stressed that GDP only includes goods and services bought for final use. It does not include the unfinished goods in the intermediate stages of production that are purchased by one firm from another for further processing and resale. The market value of a final good is the full value of the good in that it already includes the **value added** at each stage of the production process. If we also counted the purchases of the component parts of the good each time they were sold by a firm at one stage of the production process to a firm at the next stage, we would end up counting the market value of the final good more than once. For example, we don't want to count the sale of Dunlop tyres to the Ford Motor Company because the cost of the tyres will be included in the price of the cars that Ford sells to final customers. If we did include the sale of tyres from Dunlop to Ford, the tyres would be double counted in GDP.

These points are illustrated by the example in Table 5.1. Suppose it costs you $.50 to buy a writing pad in your local retail store. This pad is a final product since you intend to use the paper yourself, not to transform it into another product and resell it. The market value of the final product, $.50, equals the sum of the values added at each stage of the production process.

How does this work? Firm 5, the retail store that sells the pad of paper to you, must pay $.45 of the $.50 it receives (columns 3 and 4) to Firm 4, the paper manufacturer that provides Firm 5 with the paper. Firm 5 pays out the remaining $.05 in wages, rent, interest, and profit to the factors of production used by Firm 5 to provide the retailing service. This $.05 constitutes the value added (column 5) to the final product by Firm 5 through its provision of these services. Firm 4 must pay $.30 of the $.45 received from Firm 5 to Firm 3, the pulpwood mill, for the pulpwood Firm 4 processes into writing pad. Firm 4 pays out the remaining $.15 in wages, rent, interest, and profit to the factors of production it uses to process pulpwood into paper. This $.15 is the value added to the final product by the paper manufacturer. Proceeding back through each stage of production, the pulpwood mill adds value to the final product by processing the logs it buys from the logging company. And the logging company adds value to the final product by making logs out of the trees it buys from the tree farm.

The value added to the final product at each stage of production is the

TABLE 5.1
Sale Receipts, Cost of Intermediate Products, and Value Added at Each Stage of Production of Writing Pads (Cents per Pad of Paper)

	(1)	(2)	(3)	(4)	(5)
	Production Stage	Product	Sale Price of Product	Cost of Intermediate Product	Value Added (Wages, Interest, Rent, and Profit)
Firm 1	Tree farm	Trees	$.15	— $.00	= $.15
Firm 2	Timber logging company	Logs	.20	— .15	= .05
Firm 3	Pulpwood mill	Pulpwood	.30	— .20	= .10
Firm 4	Paper manufacturer	Writing Pad	.45	— .30	= .15
Firm 5	Retail store	Retailing service	.50	— .45	= .05
Final Sale					$.50 (Final sale price = sum of value added)

difference between what the firm sells its product for and what it pays for the intermediate materials or good it processes at that production stage. This difference is paid out in wages, interest, rent, and profit to all the factors of production that provide the productive services which add value to the product at that stage of production. The sum of the values added at each stage of production equals the sale price of the final good or service.

In the example of Table 5.1, the $.50 sale price of the final good, a writing pad, equals the sum of the value-added figures of column 5. If, instead, we added up the sales figures in column 3 we would get $1.60. This figure overstates the value of the final good because it counts the value added by Firm 1 five times, that by Firm 2 four times, Firm 3 three times, and Firm 4 two times. In order to avoid this double, or multiple, counting, it is necessary to subtract the purchase price of intermediate products to be processed at each stage of production, as indicated by the arrows. This leaves the value added figures of column 5, the sum of which equals the correct value of the final product. For this reason that is the only figure we want to include in GDP. We do not add in the sales transactions between the first four firms.

CHECKPOINT 5.2

While the purchase and sale of used cars are not included in GDP, the sales commissions earned by used-car dealers are. Similarly, the purchase and sale of shares on the Australian Stock Exchange are not included in GDP, but the sales commissions earned by stockbrokers are. Why are the sales commissions generated from these activities included in GDP while the sales themselves are not? During the last 30 years or so the proportion of working wives in the labour force has increased considerably. What effect does this have on GDP? Construct a hypothetical value-added table like Table 5.1 for the production and sale of a loaf of bread.

MONEY GDP VERSUS REAL GDP

Money GDP is the economy's gross domestic product measured in terms of the prices at which final goods and services actually sell. Real GDP is money GDP adjusted to remove the effects of inflation. It is important to understand what this means.

Adjusting GDP for Price Change: A Simple Example

Suppose, for simplicity, that the entire economy produced only one kind of good. Say that good is widgets. In any given year the economy's money GDP equals the current price of a widget multiplied by the number of widgets produced during the year. Any change in money GDP from one year to the next could therefore be due to a change in price or a change in quantity or both. However, we typically are only interested in GDP to the extent that it measures the quantity of output produced.

For instance, suppose the economy has a dollar GDP of $1,000 in 1988, which results from the production of 1,000 widgets that sell at a price of $1 per widget. It will be no better or worse off in 1998 with a dollar GDP of $2,000 if that GDP again results from the production and sale of 1,000 widgets, at a price of $2 per widget. When prices rise over time in this way we have **inflation** — a decrease in the purchasing power of a dollar. It takes $2 to buy one widget in 1998 that could have been purchased for $1 in 1988. Similarly, if prices decline over time we have **deflation,** an increase in the purchasing power of a dollar. The task is to somehow adjust the dollar GDP figure so that it only reflects changes in quantity of output produced and not price changes — not inflation or deflation.

Table 5.2 illustrates the way in which national income accountants would make this adjustment for our simple widget economy. Suppose that over a 5-year period the current price p of widgets rises, as shown in column 2. Suppose also that the quantity Q of widgets produced each year is increasing at a rate of 10 percent per year, as shown in column 3. The money GDP for each year equals the current price p times Q, as shown in column 4. Clearly the increase in money GDP (or GDP in current prices) from year to year is much greater than the yearly increase in the physical quantity of widgets produced, due to the increases in the current price of widgets. Since these money GDP figures are inflated over time

by the rising current price of widgets (column 2), it is necessary to adjust them so that they only reflect changes in quantities of output produced, and not price changes.

This adjustment is made by constructing a **price index.** A price index expresses the current price of widgets in each year as a ratio relative to the current price in some base, or benchmark, year. This base year may be chosen arbitrarily. In Table 5.2, the base year is the third year. The price index constructed in this way is shown in column 5. For example, the price of a widget in year 1 is two-fifths, or 40 percent, of the price of a widget in year 3 ($2 ÷ $5). Hence, if we want to adjust the money GDP of year 1 (column 4) to obtain output in terms of year 3 prices, we must multiply the money GDP of year 1 by 5/2 or, equivalently, divide it by .40, the value of the price index in year 1. Year 1 GDP expressed in year 3 prices is $5,000 (column 6). By the same procedure the money GDP of each of the other 4 years may be expressed in terms of year 3 prices to give real GDP, or GDP in constant dollars or prices (column 6). The GDP figures in column 6 are 'real' in the sense that the year-to-year change

TABLE 5.2
Adjusting Money GDP for Price Level Changes to Obtain Real GDP: A Simple Example

(1)	(2)	(3)	(4)	(5)	(6)
Year	Price per Widget (p)	Number of Units (Widgets) of Output per Year (Q)	Money GDP or GDP in Current Prices	Price Index	Real GDP or GDP in Constant Prices or Dollars
			$p \times Q = (2) \times (3)$	(2) ÷ Price in year 3	(4) ÷ (5)
1	$ 2	1,000	$ 2,000	2/5 = .40, or 40 per cent	$5,000
2	3	1,100	3,300	3/5 = .60, or 60 per cent	5,500
3 = base year	5	1,210	6,050	5/5 = 1.00, or 100 per cent	6,050
4	7	1,331	9,317	7/5 = 1.40, or 140 per cent	6,655
5	10	1,464	14,640	10/5 = 2.00, or 200 per cent	7,320

accurately reflects the year-to-year change in the quantity of widgets produced in the economy (column 3). The figures in both columns increase at a rate of 10 percent per year. It also may be said that the GDP figures of column 6 are stated in constant dollars or prices in the sense that they are all expressed in terms of the year price of widgets.

In sum, **money GDP,** *or GDP in current prices or dollars, measures the dollar value of final goods and services produced in a given year at the prices at which they actually sold in that year.* **Real GDP,** *or GDP in constant prices or dollars, measures the dollar value of final goods and services sold in a given year in terms of the prices at which those goods sold in some base, or benchmark year.*

Money and Real GDP in Australia

Our widget economy example greatly over-simplifies the problem of transforming money GDP into real GDP, yet the basic principle of adjustment carries over to the real world. The essential difference, of course, is that a real world economy typically produces a multitude of different goods, not just widgets. This means there are many different prices that may change over time, so that the price index used must be constructed as an average (usually a weighted average) of all these prices.

Such a price index (called the GDP deflator) for the Australian economy is shown for selected years in column 3 of Table 5.3. The base year is 1979-80. This column tells us, among other things, that the general level of prices rose 64.5 per cent from 1980 to 1986, that the general level of prices in 1970 was 36.6 per cent of that prevailing in 1980, and that prices more than quadrupled between 1970 and 1986. Money GDP — GDP in current

prices or dollars — is shown in column 2. Using exactly the same procedure as in Table 5.2, the money GDP figures in column 2 of Table 5.3 are divided by the price index for the corresponding year in column 3 to give real GDP in column 4. This real GDP is thus expressed in constant 1979-80 prices or dollars. The behaviour of real GDP in column 4 indicates that the *quantity* of final goods and services produced by the economy increased by about three quarters between 1970 and 1986. Column 2 indicates that money GDP, the quantity of final goods and services evaluated in current prices, increased almost eightfold over this period. Clearly if we want a more accurate measure of the economy's productive performance we must use real GDP — GDP measured in constant dollars (column 4).

The difference in the behaviour of money GDP (GDP in current dollars) and real GDP for the years since 1969-70 is shown graphically in Figure 5.4. While GDP in current dollars rises continuously throughout these years, largely reflecting the inflation in prices during this period, GDP in constant (1979-80) dollars generally grows more slowly. In one financial year — 1982-83 — real GDP declined in Australia by 0.6 per cent. Figure 5.4 shows that whenever we talk, read, or write about GDP it is important to be clear whether it is money GDP or real GDP that is referred to. There is obviously a difference.

CHECKPOINT 5.3
Using Table 5.2 calculate real GDP in terms of constant year 2 dollars. It is sometimes said that calculating real GDP 'inflates' the money GDP data for years before the base year. In what sense is that so?

TABLE 5.3
Money GDP and Real GDP in Australia, Selected Years (in $000 million)

(1)	(2)	(3)	(4)
Year ending 30 June	Money GDP (Current Dollars)	Price Index[a] Base Year 1979-80	Real GDP (Constant 1979-80 Dollars)
		(as a percentage)	(2) ÷ (3)
1970	30.6	36.6	83.5
1972	37.8	40.7	92.7
1974	51.6	51.2	100.8
1976	73.2	69.7	105.0
1978	90.9	83.4	109.0
1980	116.4	100.0	116.4
1982	150.3	121.6	123.6
1984	192.4	144.8	132.7
1986	238.9	164.5	145.2

[a]GDP deflator
Source: Australian Bureau of Statistics

FIGURE 5.4
Australian Gross Domestic Product (GDP) in Current and Constant 1979-80 Dollars —
1969-70 to 1985-86

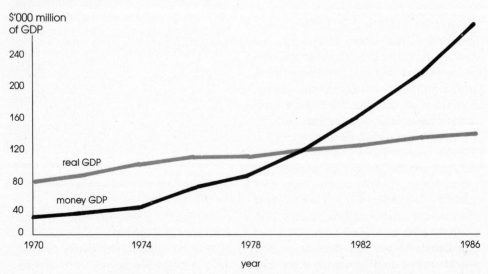

Since 1970, GDP in current dollars (money GDP) has grown continuously. However, GDP in constant 1979-80 dollars (real GDP) reveals that growth in the Australian economy's production of final goods and services has not been as rapid or continuous. The difference between these graphs reflects the influence of inflation.

POLICY PERSPECTIVE

What GDP Does Not Measure

It is easy, and tempting, to look at GDP as a measure of society's well-being. Yet it was never intended to be a measure of social welfare. It is simply an accounting measure of economic activity. While there is certainly reason to believe that an economy is 'better off' if it has a large real GDP — more goods and services for all — this is not necessarily so. On the other hand, a society may become better off in ways that GDP simply does not measure. Let's consider some of the 'goods' and 'bads' that GDP does not measure.

Product Quality

A generation ago, even a multimillionaire couldn't buy the kinds of medicines commonly available to the person of average means today. Yesteryear's cars didn't have four-wheel brakes, automatic transmissions, and a host of safety features commonly built into today's cars. Suppose you were given a catalogue from Myer for 1950 and a copy of a recent Myer catalogue with the prices in each listed in the same constant dollars. From which one would you rather buy kitchen appliances, sports equipment, TV sets, adding machines (calculators), and air conditioners? *Because GDP is a quantitative rather than a qualitative measure, it does not measure product improvement and the development of new kinds of goods.* The GDP in 1950 did not include the kinds of goods that are included in today's GDP. But when their value is measured in dollars alone, yesterday's products are indistinguishable from today's.

Costs Not Measured: Pollution

GDP does not measure many of the byproducts associated with producing the goods and services that are measured by GDP. And many of these by-products are 'bads' — smoke, noise, polluted rivers and lakes, garbage dumps, and tips. The costs of health problems (both physical and mental) caused by such environmental blight are either not measured at all or do not show up until years after the production of the GDP that caused them. These undesirable by-products tend to increase right along with growth in GDP. If the costs of these bads were subtracted from GDP, the resulting GDP would not appear as large or grow as fast. It would also be a more accurate measure of society's true well-being.

Leisure and GDP

For most people a certain amount of leisure is desirable. When people take more of it, less working time is devoted to producing goods and services. This means GDP will be smaller than it otherwise might be. However, this increase in leisure must add to people's sense of wellbeing more than enough to offset the forgone output, or else people wouldn't have chosen to take it. Therefore it would be completely misleading to interpret the reduction in GDP that results from increased leisure as a reduction in society's well-being. For example, the length of the average workweek has been roughly cut in half over the last century. Workers have chosen to take more leisure, and as a result GDP is not as large as it would be if workers put in as many work hours as they typically did a hundred years ago. However, it would be erroneous to conclude that society is worse off because GDP is not as large as it could be. Why? Because more leisure has been chosen in *preference* to the additional output.

Per Capita GDP and the Distribution of Output

If we divide up a side of beef among five people, each individual will certainly be better off than if we have to divide it up among ten people. Similarly in order to assess how well off a nation is, we need to know more than just the size of its annual output, its real GDP. We also need to know how that output is divided among its citizens. If it were divided equally among them, then we would simply divide the nation's GDP by its population. This gives **per capita GDP.**

Figure P5.1 shows how real per capita GDP (in 1979-80 dollars) has grown since 1949-50 in Australia.

While there is in fact no economy where GDP is distributed equally among its citizens, per capita GDP gives a simple measure of how well off an economy would be if its GDP were divided up in this fashion. For example, in 1973 the GDP of Bangladesh was approximately $11.4 billion, while that of Chile was about $11.3 billion. However, Bangladesh had a population roughly eight times as large as Chile's. Consequently, per capita GDP in Bangladesh was about $150, while in Chile it was $1156. Hence, despite the fact that both nations had about the same level of GDP, Chilean citizens would appear to be much better off than those of Bangladesh.

Because an economy's GDP is typically distributed unequally among its citizens, it is necessary to study this distribution in more detail in order to get a more accurate assessment than that provided by per capita GDP.

FIGURE P 5.1
Real Per Capita GDP in Australia (1979-80 Dollars)

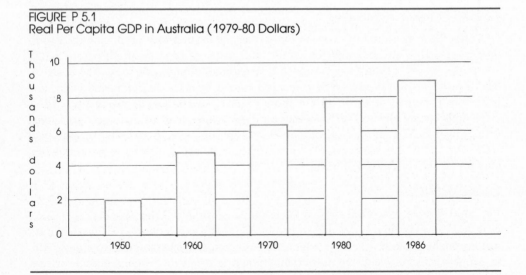

Composition of GDP

The kinds of goods produced by an economy are completely hidden from view by a GDP figure. One economy could have a $100 billion GDP composed entirely of weapons for war, and another could have a $100 billion GDP composed entirely of sports cars, steak dinners, and fine clothes. These economies would clearly have different kinds of living standards, though you could never tell it from GDP data. GDP alone tells nothing about the composition of the economy's output. The composition of GDP in countries such as Australia has shifted more toward the production of services and away from production of non-durable goods in the past fifty years. Durable goods production and expenditure on construction have tended to maintain their relative percentage contributions.

Questions

1. Suppose the portion of an economy's GDP spent on health care increases over time. What considerations would be important in deciding whether this represented an increase in society's well-being or not?
2. How do coffee breaks and sick leaves affect GDP? Which sort of time loss affects GDP in the same direction as societal well-being?

FIGURE 5.5
Aggregate Demand and Supply Determine the Economy's Equilibrium Price Level and Real GDP

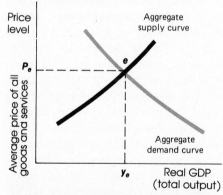

The aggregate demand curve is negatively sloped indicating that the lower the economy's price level the larger is the quantity of total output (real GDP) demanded. The economy's aggregate supply curve is positively sloped indicating that the economy's businesses will produce a larger quantity of total output (real GDP) the higher the economy's price level. The interaction of the aggregate demand and supply curves at point e determines the economy's equilibrium price level p_e and total output y_e.

INTRODUCTION TO AGGREGATE DEMAND AND AGGREGATE SUPPLY

Chapter 4 showed how demand and supply interact to determine price and output for a particular good or service. In a similar fashion we can envision an aggregate demand curve and an aggregate supply curve interacting to determine the economy's price level and its level of total output. The price level is a price index such as the GDP deflator and the economy's total output is represented by real GDP. Here we will introduce the basic elements of aggregate demand and supply which will be used and developed more fully in later chapters.

The Aggregate Demand Curve

The **aggregate demand curve** *(AD) shows the relationship between the economy's total demand for output and the price level of that output.* The aggregate demand curve slopes downward left to right (is negatively sloped) as shown in Figure 5.5. Its shape indicates that *the lower the price level the larger the quantity of total output demanded, and the higher the price level the smaller the quantity demanded.*

Difference Between AD Curve and Individual Demand Curve

Though the shape of the AD curve looks like that of a market demand curve for an individual good, such as wheat or petrol, the reasons for its shape are not the same. Recall that movement along a market demand curve for a particular good corresponds to a change in the price of that good, the prices of all other goods assumed constant. The price of the particular good therefore changes *relative* to the prices of all other goods. The particular good becomes either cheaper or more expensive relative to all other goods, depending on the direction of its price change. By contrast, movement along the *AD curve* corresponds to a change in *the economy's price level,* an average of the prices of *all* the goods and services that make up total output. So the reasons why the *AD* curve slopes downward left to right are different.

Slope of the AD Curve

There are several reasons why the *AD* curve has a negative slope. For our purposes it is sufficient to focus on one, the effect of changes in the price level on consumer wealth. Much consumer wealth consists of fixed-dollar assets — assets whose values are fixed in terms of dollars. The most obvious example is money itself. Others are corporate and government bonds and savings accounts. Whenever the price level rises the real value or purchasing power of these fixed-dollar assets declines; that is, the amount of goods and services that can be purchased with them goes down. (For example, the quantity of goods that a 10-dollar bill will buy declines roughly 20 per cent if there is a 20 per cent increase in the price level.) Conversely, whenever the price level falls the purchasing power of fixed dollar assets goes up.

Therefore, the aggregate demand curve has a negative slope because a higher price level, by reducing the purchasing power of consumer wealth causes consumers to cut back on the quantity of goods and services they demand. A lower price level increases the purchasing power of consumer wealth and causes them to increase the quantity of goods and services they demand.

The Aggregate Supply Curve

*The **aggregate supply curve** (AS) shows the amount of total output that the economy businesses will supply at different price levels.* The aggregate supply curve shown in Figure 5.5 is upward sloping left to right (positively sloped). In later chapters we will examine conditions that give rise to a vertical aggregate supply curve, as well as conditions that can cause the aggregate supply curve to be horizontal.

The positively sloped *AS* curve in Figure 5.5 reflects short-run conditions. In the short run, when the economy's price level (the average of all prices) rises the prices of firms' products tend to rise faster than firms' costs. Therefore firms' profits rise, encouraging them to expand output. Hence in the short run the higher the economy's price level the larger the quantity of total output supplied. We will examine the *AS* curve in greater detail in subsequent chapters.

The Interaction of Aggregate Demand and Supply

The intersection of the aggregate demand and aggregate supply curves at point *e* in Figure 5.5 determines the economy's equilibrium price level p_e and its equilibrium level of total output y_e. Again it should be emphasised that the economy's price level is an index or average of the prices of all the individual goods and services produced in the economy, an index such as the GDP deflator for example. The economy's total output is its real GDP — its GDP measured in constant dollars. If the economy were the simple one-good, widget economy of our earlier example, then its equilibrium real GDP or total output y_e would be the total number of widgets produced and sold. Its equilibrium price level p_e would be the price per widget.

In later chapters we will study why aggregate demand and supply curves shift, and how these shifts affect the economy's output, employment, and price level. We will find that there are different views on these matters and hence different schools of thought on how to deal with the problems of economic fluctuations (the business cycle), unemployment, and inflation — problems which will be described in the next chapter.

CHECKPOINT 5.4

Explain why the economy's aggregate demand curve is fundamentally different from a demand curve for a single good. Why is the aggregate demand curve negatively sloped?

SUMMARY

1. A mixed economy and the basic economic links between its three groups of decision-making units — businesses, households, and government — can be given a skeletal representation in a flow diagram. Such a diagram can show the flow of resources and of goods and services in exchange for money; flows of savings into the financial markets, where they are loaned to borrowers and spent

on goods and services; and the flows of taxes, transfers, and expenditures linking the government to businesses and households; and flows of goods, service and money between our economy and other economies — the rest of the world.

2. Gross domestic product (GDP) is the market value of the economy's total output of final goods and services produced during a year.

3. GDP does not include so-called nonproductive transactions, such as the purchase and sale of used goods, the trading of shares and bonds in financial markets, and private and public transfer payments. Certain productive nonmarket activities are included, such as the imputed rent on owner-occupied housing and the value of food produced and consumed by farm families. However, other activities are not included, such as the services performed by homemakers and the myriad of tasks performed by do-it-yourselfers.

4. Money GDP, or GDP in current prices or dollars, measures the dollar value of GDP in a given year in terms of the prices at which final goods and services actually were sold in that year. Real GDP, or GDP in constant prices or dollars, measures the dollar value of GDP in a given year in terms of the prices at which final goods and services sold for in some base, or benchmark, year.

5. When calculating GDP, care must be taken to avoid double, or multiple, counting of intermediate goods.

6. GDP is an accounting measure and was never intended to be a welfare measure. GDP does not reflect changes in product quality or in the composition of output, nor does it take account of the costs of pollution or the benefits of leisure. Per capita GDP is a better indicator of an economy's welfare than GDP alone, but neither really tells us anything about the true distribution of any economy's output among its citizens.

7. The aggregate demand curve is negatively sloped and indicates that the economy's total demand for output is larger the lower the price level. The aggregate supply curve is positively sloped in the short run indicating that the economy's businesses will produce a larger quantity of total output the higher the price level. The intersection of the aggregate demand and supply curves determines the economy's equilibrium total output and price level.

KEY TERMS AND CONCEPTS

    aggregate demand curve
    aggregate supply curve
    deflation
    depreciation allowance
    financial markets
    flow
    gross domestic product (GDP)
    inflation
    money GDP
    per capita GDP
    price index
    real GDP
    retained earnings
    transfer payments
    value added

QUESTIONS AND PROBLEMS

1. 'Despite general agreement about the need for tremendous amounts of new capital, there is no consensus about how the money should be raised. Some economists generally favour more generous individual tax cuts . . . to stimulate

consumer buying, which, in turn, creates heightened economic activity. Other economists . . . would prefer federal policies that would enable companies to keep more of their earnings either through higher depreciation allowances for the purchase of new equipment or a further lowering of the company tax rate'.

In Figure 5.3, where would the first group's policies affect the flow diagram as contrasted with those of the second group?

2. Why is GDP a flow and inventory not a flow?

3. When we measure GDP, why is the problem of productive versus nonproductive transactions never an issue in the case of services (as distinct from goods)?

4. How is a transfer payment different from the purchase of a final good? Why is Christmas so 'good for business' if gifts are merely private transfer payments?

5. Home milk delivery service used to be more common a generation ago than it is today, yet milk consumption per capita has not changed all that much in the meantime. What effect do you think the gradual decrease in home milk delivery has had on GDP and why?

6. For a number of years during the last third of the nineteenth century in the Australia the general level of prices fell. Suppose you were told that GDP in current prices tripled over this period of time.

a. What would you be able to conjecture about the change in real GDP? (We do not in fact have GDP figures and price indices for this period that are of the quality of those constructed for the years since 1948-49.)

b. In 1870 the population of Australia was

roughly 1.65 million, and by 1900 it was approximately 3.77 million. What would you be able to conjecture about the change in per capita real GDP over this period of time?

7. When measuring GDP, what similarity do you see between the problem of double, or multiple, counting and the problem of nonproductive market transactions?

8. It has been argued that the production of goods often gives rise to bad by-products, such as polluted rivers and air, whose costs to society are not included in the price of the final good. Suppose the average price of a car is $12,000.

Suppose it would cost $1,000 to clean up the air and water pollution associated with the production of a car but that neither the car manufacturer nor the buyer of the car has to pay the cost — the 'mess' is simply not cleaned up. If the company were forced to clean up the mess, what would be the effect on money GDP? What would be the effect on real GDP? What do you think of the contention that GDP is such a 'silly' measure that if allowance were made for the cost of bads, GDP actually would go up?

9. Indicate in Figure 5.3 where the various flows that constitute the economy's total demand for goods and services appear.

6

Economic Fluctuations, Unemployment and Inflation

AFTER READING THIS CHAPTER YOU WILL BE ABLE TO:

1. Describe the way the economy moves over time.

2. Explain how the structure of the economy affects the business cycle.

3. Define the concepts of frictional, structural, and cyclical unemployment and the concept of full employment.

4. Describe Australia's recent experience with inflation.

5. Distinguish between anticipated and unanticipated inflation and explain who gains and who loses when inflation is unanticipated.

Economic fluctuations have been a major problem for economics throughout its history, and unemployment and inflation are major costs associated with that problem. In this chapter we will concern ourselves with the nature of business cycles and the interrelated problems of unemployment and inflation. Much of our discussion in the following chapters will focus on trying to understand the causes of economic fluctuations, unemployment, and inflation. We will also look at various policies aimed at eliminating or at least reducing these problems.

HOW THE ECONOMY MOVES

Even the most casual observer of our economy is aware that it seems to move by 'fits and starts'. Periods of rapid growth alternate with periods of slower growth or even contraction. These economic fluctuations, often referred to as business cycles, are most commonly recognised by their effects on unemployment, sales, and the behaviour of prices — in particular the rate of inflation. Of course the business cycle is reflected in many other measures of economic activity as well.

Growth and Fluctuations

Some idea of the way the economy moves is conveyed in part a of Figure 6.1 by the graph of real GDP (1966/67 dollars) since 1929-30. Two things are obvious. The economy grows over time, but there are irregular fluctuations in its rate of growth from one year to the next. The size of these fluctuations is further illustrated by the graph of the annual percentage changes in real GDP over this period of time, part b of Figure 6.1. Since

World War II these fluctuations have been less violent than those of the 1930s or the 1940s. The size of the fluctuations during the 1930s was a reflection of unstable conditions resulting from the Depression. Those of the 1940s came about when the economy was converted to wartime during the first half of the decade and then reconverted to peacetime during the second half. It is easy to see from part a of Figure 6.1 why one might describe the economy as 'climbing a cliff and then resting on a plateau before climbing another cliff'.

The Business Cycle

The fluctuations in real GDP that are so clearly shown in part b of Figure 6.1 are often called **business cycles.** Comparing parts a and b of Figure 6.1, we can see that business cycles are a phenomenon quite separate from the growth trend in this aggregate measure of economic activity. The growth trend (of roughly three per cent over this period) is represented by the horizontal unbroken line in the bottom graph. The business cycles during this period are represented by the irregular but recurrent up-and-down movement of the saw-toothed solid line about this trend. In general, *business cycles are irregular but recurrent patterns of fluctuations in economic activity. They are apparent in aggregate measures of sales, output, income, employment, and a host of other measures over a period of years, quite apart from any long-run trends in these series.*

Phases of the Business Cycle

A hypothetical, idealised version of the business cycle, measured in terms of real GDP, is shown in Figure 6.2. The cycle

FIGURE 6.1
Real GDP Fluctuates About a Long-Term Growth Trend

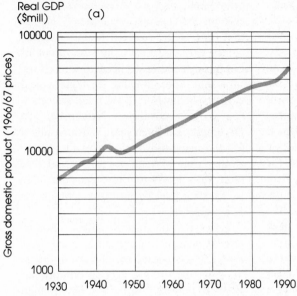

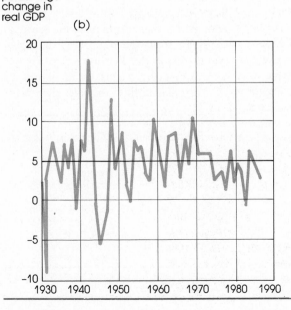

Part a shows real GDP (1966-67 dollars) since 1929. It fluctuates about a long-term growth trend.

Note that the vertical axis in part a is a logarithmic, or ratio, scale on which equal distances represent equal percentage changes. (Convince yourself by measuring that the distance from 1000 to 10000 equals that from 10000 to 100000.) If real GDP were plotted on an ordinary arithmetic scale, its plot would curve sharply upward because a given percentage change in a small number would be represented by a smaller distance than the same percentage change in a larger number.

The plot of the annual percentage changes in real GDP shown in part b gives a more vivid picture of the fluctuations in real GDP. These fluctuations are the so-called business cycles with their peaks and troughs. These fluctuations have been milder since the early 1950s by comparison with the 1930s and the turbulent war and postwar years of the 1940s.

may be viewed as having four phases: a peak, a recession, a trough, and an expansion. The recession phase corresponds to the contraction, or slowing down, of economic activity. During this phase unemployment rises while sales, income, and investment all fall. An unusually severe recession is sometimes called a **depression,** such as the Great Depression of the 1930s, which is so noticeable in Figure 6.1. The lower turning point of the business cycle is often called the **trough.** At this point economic conditions are at a low ebb. This is followed by an upturn in economic activity, or the **expansion** phase of the cycle. During this phase unemployment falls and sales, income, output, and capital formation all rise. This phase and the subsequent upper turning point or **peak** phase of the cycle are sometimes referred to as a 'boom'. Output, income, sales, and capital formation reach their highest levels while unemployment falls to its lowest level. Business and consumer optimism about the future typically rise throughout the expansion phase of the cycle and fall during the recession phase.

Comparison of the real world of Figure 6.1 with the hypothetical one of Figure 6.2 indicates that actual business cycles are not nearly as regular or periodic as the idealised picture presented in Figure 6.2. This is the reason real-world business cycles are often more accurately called business fluctuations — no two are ever quite alike. Furthermore it is not always very clear when the economy is passing into another phase of the business cycle.

Seasonal Variation

To get a clearer picture of business cycles, we have seen that it is helpful to abstract from any long-run trend that may be in the data. This is essentially what we did in part b of Figure 6.1. In addition, it is also helpful to adjust the data for **seasonal variation.** For example, general retail sales are typically high in December because of the Christmas holidays. On the other hand, sales of a particular good, slow combustion heaters, are typically low at that time of the year but high during the winter months. From the standpoint of the business cycle we need to know how sales look after allowing for their typical seasonal behaviour. 'Raw' retail sales data typically rise from November to December in a given year. When we allow for the usual seasonal rise in these data at that time of year, we might find that retail sales have risen less than normally — for example, because the economy is in a recession.

How do statisticians adjust data to remove seasonal variation? Suppose past monthly sales data for air conditioners indicate that, on average, air conditioner sales in February are 1.9 times as high as average monthly sales over the course of a year. Similarly, suppose air conditioner sales in August are only .7 times as large as average monthly sales over the course of a year. To remove the seasonal variation from the data, the statistician would divide the February sales figures by 1.9 and the August sales figures by .7. In similar fashion the sales figures for

TABLE 6.1
The Timing of Business Cycles in Australia
1950 to 1983

Peak	Trough
April, 1951	November, 1952
August, 1955	January, 1958
August, 1960	September, 1961
April, 1965	January, 1968
May, 1970	March, 1972
February, 1974	October, 1977
June, 1981	May, 1983

Source: Boehm & Moore *The Australian Economic Review* (4, 1984) p.45.

each month would be adjusted by such seasonal adjustment factors. The resulting sales figures are said to be *seasonally adjusted*.

One of the difficulties with seasonal adjustment is that seasonal variation patterns often change over time. Given that the seasonal adjustment factors are necessarily derived from past data, they are not able to account for these changes in the most recent data. Thus seasonal adjustment may not accurately remove the seasonal variation from these data.

Duration of Cycles

The ups and downs of the Australian economy have been traced by a number of economists for the period between 1950 and the early 1980s. Boehm and Moore (*Australian Economic Review*, 1984) recognise seven cycles over this period. The timing of these cycles is reported in Table 6.1. Measured from trough to trough the average duration was 61 months. The average length of the expansion phase was 36.3 months, and the average length of the recession phase was 24.7 months. The longest cycle was 76 months, while the shortest was only 44 months.

CHECKPOINT* 6.1

When we look at the graph in part a of Figure 6.1, it appears that the expansion phase of business cycles is a great deal longer than the recession phase. Would you agree with this assessment? Why or why not? What do you think the monthly seasonal adjustment factors

FIGURE 6.2
Phases of the Business Cycle

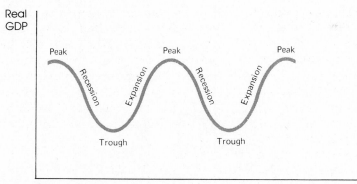

The two hypothetical business cycles shown here (measured in terms of real GDP) are idealisations. Actual business fluctuations are never quite this regular or periodic, and no two are ever quite this similar to each other.

The recession phase of the cycle corresponds to the contraction, or slowing down, of economic activity. During this phase unemployment rises while sales, income, output, and investment all fall, along with business and consumer optimism. The lower turning point is the trough of the cycle. Here economic activity is at its lowest ebb. In the ensuing expansion phase of the cycle sales, income, output, and investment all rise while unemployment falls. Business and consumer optimism are also on the rise throughout this phase. Finally the expansion loses steam at the upper turning point, or peak, and the cycle then repeats itself.

POLICY PERSPECTIVE

Dating Business Cycle Peaks and Troughs — When Do They Occur?

How do we know when the expansion phase of a business cycle is over and a recession has begun, or when a recession is over and an expansion has begun? Such turning points in the business cycle become easier to recognise the more time passes after their occurrence. However there is an unavoidable arbitrariness in designating the dates of turning points because economic theory provides no hard and fast criteria.

Many economists and public servants are sympathetic to designations of turning points that focus on the behaviour of real GDP. For example, a business cycle peak might be said to have occurred and the economy to be in a recession if real GDP does not grow for at least two quarters in a row. One might well ask why the criterion is not one quarter, or three out of four, all of which points out the element of arbitrariness in any definition. Other important factors that economists often take into consideration are the behaviour of the unemployment rate, the rate of investment spending on new

FIGURE P6.1
Real GDP and Designated Peaks and Troughs in Business Cycles in Australia 1973 — 1987

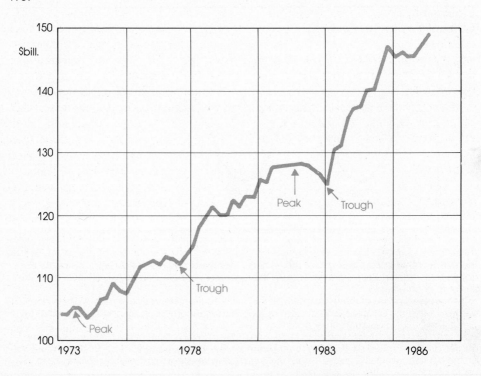

plant and equipment, and the rate of capacity utilisation in the manufacturing sector (that is, the degree to which the available stock of capital equipment is being used in production).

Using the peak and trough analysis reported in Table 6.1, it is an interesting exercise to plot movements in real GDP over time. This appears in Figure P6.1.

Questions

1. Some observers say that the recessions of the early 1980s indicated in Figure P6.1 could really be viewed as just one larger recession. On the basis of the evidence in Figure P6.1 how would you defend this interpretation?

2. Consider the designated peaks and troughs in Figure P6.1. Does the location of any of them suggest that considerations other than the behaviour of real GDP may have played prominently in making the designation? Why?

---

for textbook sales would look like over the course of a year?

*Answers to all Checkpoints can be found at the back of the text.

Determinants of the Business Cycle

The characteristics of the business cycles of an economy will depend on the shocks that hit it and the way it is 'put together' — the nature of its products, the structure of its markets, and the interconnecting relationships between its industries and the way it is influenced by other economies.

Product Characteristics — Durables and Nondurables

Industries that produce durable goods — steel, machinery, motor vehicles, construction, consumer appliances, and so forth — experience much larger fluctuations in employment, production, and sales over the course of the business cycle than do industries that produce nondurable goods — clothing, food products, agricultural commodities, and so forth. The major reason for this lies precisely in the difference in the nature of durable and nondurable goods.

When the economy goes into a recession, unemployment rises. Businesses find themselves with idle productive capacity in the face of lagging sales as consumer and business optimism about the future declines. Consumers tend to make the old car or refrigerator last another year, particularly if they are unemployed or faced with increasing job uncertainty. Similarly, businesses make do with existing plant and equipment, especially since some of it is made idle by the slowdown in sales and the accompanying buildup of unsold inventories. In short, when times are bad and a cloud of uncertainty shrouds the future, durable goods purchases will tend to be postponed. This is possible precisely because durable goods are durable. This, of course, means that a recession hits the durable goods industries especially hard.

By contrast, nondurable goods purchases cannot be put off nearly as long. People can't postpone eating, brushing their teeth, being sick, or heating their homes. They also seem very reluctant to cut back on smoking, drinking and other personal consumption habits. As a result history shows that during recessions nondurable goods industries do not experience nearly as severe a decline in employment, production, and sales as do the durable goods industries.

On the other hand, during business cycle expansions, durable goods purchases previously postponed are now carried out. Rising sales put increasing demands on productive capacity and businesses have a greater incentive to buy new equipment and expand plant size. Similarly, consumers have more job certainty, employment and pay cheques rise, and more households are willing to replace the old car and refrigerator with new ones. As a result, durable goods purchases pick up at a faster rate than purchases of nondurables.

Market Structure

Markets in which there are numerous firms competing with one another in the production and sale of a product tend to reduce prices more sharply in the face of declining demand than do markets dominated by a few large firms that have monopoly-type power. On the other hand, monopoly-type markets tend to reduce output and employment more sharply than do markets with numerous competing firms. In short, over the course of the business cycle, monopoly-type markets adjust to changing demand largely by changing production rather than by changing price. Highly competitive markets with numerous firms adjust largely by changing price rather than by changing output.

Monopoly-type market structures tend to prevail in durable goods industries such as steel, oil, electrical machinery, appliances, and motor vehicles. On the other hand, competitive market structures tend to prevail in nondurable goods industries such as agriculture and wearing apparel. There are literally tens of thousands of farmers, for example.

Causes of Business Cycles

We have briefly examined a few of the important aspects of the economy's internal, or endogenous, structure that determine how it moves when it is subjected to external shocks. The nature of its products (durable versus nondurable), the structure of its markets (competitive versus monopolistic), and the interconnecting relationships between its industries are all important internal determinants of the economy's motion. In subsequent chapters we will examine other characteristics of the economy's internal structure that are also important determinants of the way it moves. These determinants affect the economy just as weight, size, and centre of gravity affect the way a rocking horse moves when given a push.

Now we will briefly describe a few frequently cited explanatory factors underlying business cycles that are generally regarded as external, or exogenous, causes, like the push applied to a rocking horse. Among these factors are changes in population growth rates and migration trends; new inventions and technological developments; the discovery of new mineral deposits and energy sources; the opening up of new land frontiers; and political events and social upheavals, like wars.

Most of these factors are thought of as external to the workings of the economy — like the push given to the rocking horse. But it is sometimes difficult to make a clear-cut distinction on this score. For example, increases in the population growth rate seem to be encouraged by economic expansion and dampened by recessions. However, this is a two-way street. Increases in the population growth rate tend to stimulate economic expansion, while decreases tend to slow down the growth of demand for goods and services. The same sort of two-way influences may exist for many of the so-called external factors listed above. Unstable economic conditions in post-World War I Germany may have contributed to the rise of Hitler and the advent of World War II, which in turn pulled many Western economies including Australia out of the depression years of the 1930s. On the other hand, the fourfold increase in oil prices by the Arab oil-exporting countries in 1973-1974 is viewed by most economists as an external shock to the western economies which helped trigger the major recession of the middle and late seventies.

Finally, the ebb and tide of optimism or confidence about the future — what John Maynard Keynes called 'animal spirits' — is often cited as a crucial factor in the business cycle. For example, it is sometimes argued that optimism lost touch with reality in the late 1920s. This allegedly led to excessive speculation in land and stocks and to overinvestment in plant, equipment, and property far beyond what demand warranted. When sober judgment finally set in, most western economies were plunged into the deepest and longest depression in the modern era, and a mood of deep pessimism prevailed. At its depth in 1932 US President Franklin Roosevelt may have measured the main problem very well when he said, 'The only thing we have to fear is fear itself'.

CHECKPOINT 6.2
The American economist, Gardner Means did a study of the percentage drop in product price and the percentage drop in production in each of 10 industries during the onset and downturn of the Depression of the 1930s. These Industries were textile products, agricultural implements, agricultural commodities, petroleum, motor vehicles, leather, cement, food products, iron and steel, and automobile tyres. How do you think they ranked (1) in terms of the degree of price reduction he observed in each of them, and (2) in terms of the degree of output reduction?

UNEMPLOYMENT AND EMPLOYMENT

The economy's **labour force** *includes all persons over the age of 15 who are employed plus all those who are unemployed but actively looking for work.* The labour force in our economy amounts to more than half of the population over 15. While the labour force includes people in the military, unemployment is a problem that only afflicts the civilian labour force. Our discussion of unemployment and employment therefore focuses on the civilian labour force. In the discussion that follows, we will consider such questions as, Are there different types of unemployment? Is there such a thing as a normal level of unemployment, or what is full employment? What are the costs of unemployment?

Types of Unemployment

A worker may become unemployed in basically three different ways. (1) The worker may leave his or her current job to look for a better job, giving rise to what is called *frictional unemployment*. (2) The worker's current job may be permanently eliminated — the plight of blacksmiths at the turn of the century — possibly causing so-called *structural unemployment*. (3) The worker's current job may be temporarily eliminated by a recession, thus giving rise to *cyclical unemployment*. Let's look more closely at each of these types of unemployment.

Frictional Unemployment

Many times, workers quit jobs to look for ones that pay better or are more attractive in some other way. In the meantime they are often unemployed for short periods of time while they are between jobs. Suppose, for example, that each worker in the labour force changed jobs once a year and was unemployed for a 2-week period while in transition. Suppose also that the number of workers changing jobs at any one time is spread evenly over the year. At any time during the year 2/52, or 3.8 per cent, of the labour force is thus unemployed, if there are no other causes of unemployment. If only half of the labour force switched jobs in this manner, the unemployment rate would be 1.9 per cent.

Other forms of frictional unemployment are due to seasonal layoffs, such as those that affect farm workers and those in the tourist industry. New entrants into the labour force with marketable job skills are also frequently unemployed for a brief period of time before finding a job.

Structural Unemployment

As the term structural implies, this kind of unemployment is due to fundamental changes in the structure of labour demand — specifically, the kinds of jobs that the economy offers. Technological change, the development of new industries and the demise of old ones, and the changing economic role of different regions in the country all mean that new kinds of jobs need to be done and that many old ones cease to exist. The new jobs often require different skills and educational backgrounds than the old ones and are frequently located in different geographic regions.

Workers often find themselves displaced by these structural changes. They may lack the required skills and training needed to gain employment in other areas of the economy. Often they are dismayed by the prospect of having to move away from old friends and familiar neighbourhoods. As a result, they end up among the ranks of the long-term and hard-core unemployed. This is a particular problem among older workers, unskilled workers in declining economic regions. A notable recent example of structural unemployment has occurred among mature management and technical personnel in companies taken over by so-called 'corporate raiders'. As takeovers or mergers proceed the jobs of many experienced executives have been eliminated. Often aged over forty, these people face major retraining to regain employment, usually at levels far below those which they held previously. In general, *the basic characteristic of the structurally unemployed is their lack of marketable skills.*

Cyclical Unemployment

Cyclical unemployment is caused by the business cycle. When the economy's total demand for goods and services rises during the expansion phase of the cycle, employment rises and unemployment falls. During the recession phase of the cycle, total demand for goods and services falls, causing unemployment to rise and employment to fall. Cyclical unemployment looms large in the movement of the unemployment rate.

Natural Rate of Unemployment — Or, What Is Full Employment?

It is clear from our discussion of frictional unemployment that full employment cannot mean that there is a zero rate of unemployment. *The general view among economists is that the existence of frictional unemployment and a certain amount of structural unemployment constitutes a natural rate of unemployment towards which the economy automatically gravitates in the absence of other disturbances.* Full employment is the level of employment associated with the natural rate of unemployment. In the early 1960s economists generally felt that full employment roughly corresponded to a 1.5 per cent unemployment rate — what might he called the natural unemployment rate. Since that time the level of the natural unemployment rate has been revised upward. In recent years a number of economists have come to think that it may be somewhat more than 6 per cent. Why is this? Should we be concerned? How we measure unemployment and the nature of the relationship between population growth and labour force growth have a lot to do with the answers to these questions.

Measuring Unemployment

The most commonly used definition of **unemployment** *states that to be considered unemployed you must be out of work, looking for a job, and available to take one immediately.*

Some think this definition is too broad because it doesn't distinguish between those who need jobs to support themselves and their families and those who don't. Hence critics say this measure overstates unemployment distress. They point out that a full-time student seeking part-time work or a job-seeking teenager living at home with two working parents counts just as much in this measure of unemployment as does a jobless head of household out of work for weeks. However, others argue that this measure understates unemployment because it doesn't include 'discouraged' workers who have dropped out of the labour force after a prolonged, unsuccessful search for a job, nor does it include part-time workers who are looking for a full-time job.

Population and Labour Force Growth

Longer-run changes in the size of the labour force relative to the size of the total population have implications for the unemployment rate and the percentage of the working-age population employed. So do longer-run changes in the age and sex makeup of the labour force.

If the size of the total population grows faster than the size of the labour force, the number of people demanding goods and services will grow faster than the number of people who want jobs. Other things remaining the same, this should tend to lower the unemployment rate. On the other hand, if the size of the labour force grows more rapidly than the size of the total population, the number of people wanting jobs increases faster than the number demanding goods and services. This will tend to increase the unemployment rate, other things remaining the same.

From the latter half of the 1960s up to the present, the Australian economy has had to cope with a labour force that has grown faster than the total population — the labour force as a percentage of the total population has increased, as shown in Figure 6.3. In part this has been due to the maturing of the post-World War II 'baby boom' generation, which has swelled the working-age population during these years. In addition, the proportion of working-age women who have moved into the labour force has increased dramatically. Whereas only about 30 per cent of the country's population of adult females were in the labour force in the early years after World War II, somewhat more than 45 per cent now work or are seeking work. Despite this, the economy has done quite well in providing jobs for these people. In the decade from 1976 to 1986 total employment in Australia increased by 17.7 per

cent while population rose by 14.1 per cent. In other words, total employment grew faster than the total population. Job creation during the 1976-86 decade resulted in a growth in employment of nearly 1,045,000 in Australia. This compared with growth of 1,050,000 between 1956 and 1966, and of 1,070,000 between 1966 and 1976. Employment increased by 27.7 per cent from 1956 to 1966, by 22.3 per cent from 1966 to 1976, and by 17.7 per cent from 1976 to 1986.

On the negative side, many economists argue that the more rapid rate of growth of the labour force relative to that of the total population has contributed to a rise in the level of what should be considered the natural unemployment rate (the rate that corresponds to so-called full employment). They believe that the unusually large increase in the number of new job-

FIGURE 6.3
Labour Force as Percentage of Australia's Total Population

The labour force as a percentage of the total population has increased since the early 1960's. This reflects the maturing 'baby boom' generation entering the labour force, and the decline of the birth rate since that time.

FIGURE 6.4
The GDP Gap, the Unemployment Rate, and the Changing General Price Level in
Australia since 1958

Per cent   (a)

Annual percentage change in
price index (GDP deflator)

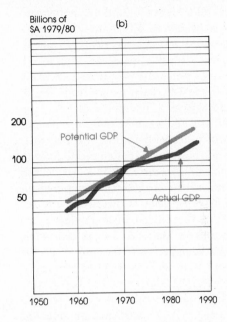

Billions of
$A 1979/80   (b)

Potential GDP

Actual GDP

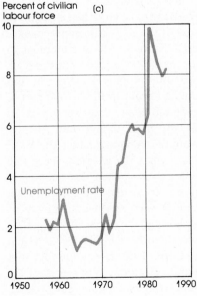

Percent of civilian   (c)
labour force

Unemployment rate

The difference between potential and actual GDP
since 1958 is the GDP gap shown in part b,
expressed in constant 1979-80 dollars. Comparison of
the behaviour of the unemployment rate with that of
the GDP gap indicates how the unemployment rate
rises when the GDP gap widens and falls when the
GDP gap narrows. From 1966 through 1969, the
Vietnam War years, the unemployment rate was at
its lowest levels and actual GDP exceeded potential
GDP (the GDP gap was negative). This reflects the
fact that the potential GDP does not represent the
maximum GDP the economy can produce but that
which it can produce at some natural rate of
unemployment.

Up through 1971 the annual percentage rise in
the general price level (the GDP deflator), part a,
tended to be larger when the GDP gap narrowed
and the unemployment rate fell and smaller when
the GDP gap widened and the unemployment rate
rose. By contrast there was a dramatic jump in the
percentage rise in the general price level in the mid
1970s, accompanied by an unprecedented
widening in the GDP gap. The pre-1971 pattern has
since reemerged.

seekers relative to the growth in the population pushes the level of frictional unemployment higher. Another possible factor in a higher natural unemployment rate is the increased flow into the public's pockets of transfer payments — unemployment benefits, pensions, and so on. This may well cause people who are really not trying very hard to get employed to list themselves as unemployed.

What is the meaning of all this for our interpretation of the unemployment rate? It is often assumed that an economy with an unemployment rate of 3 per cent is healthier than one with an unemployment rate of 6 per cent. Is this necessarily so? In 1956 the official unemployment rate in Australia was only 2.1 per cent while the participation rate (the ratio of people in the labour force to the population aged 15 years and above) was 57.8 per cent. In 1986 the unemployment rate was 8.3 per cent, but the participation rate was 61.9 per cent. When the participation rate is considered along with the unemployment rate, the difference in the health of our economy (at least from the standpoint of jobs) between these two periods does not appear as great as when we compare the unemployment rates alone.

The Costs of Unemployment

Labour is an essential factor of production in our economy. Consequently, the greater the total demand for goods and services, the higher is the level of employment and the lower the level of unemployment, given the available labour supply. Recall from Chapter 2 that unemployment exists whenever any available factors of production are idle. The term *available* is important. *Unemployment exists whenever there are labourers who make themselves available for work by actively looking for a job but are unable to find one.* For society as a whole, unemployment means fewer goods and services are produced, and a smaller pie means there is less available for all. This is the economic cost of unemployment. As a matter of public policy, unemployment is of particular concern because it also represents hardship for those unemployed. How might we measure these costs and hardships?

Economic Cost: The GDP Gap

How can we measure the economic cost of unemployment to society? First we might estimate the economy's *potential GDP,* or what GDP would be if the economy were 'fully' employed. We would then subtract actual GDP from potential GDP to get the GDP gap. **The GDP gap** is the dollar value of final goods and services not produced because there is unemployment. The GDP gap is therefore a measure of the cost of unemployment.

Several economists have attempted to measure the GDP gap for Australia. A recent set of estimates by Nguyen and Siriwardana appear in Figure 6.4, part b. The unemployment rate is shown in Figure 6.4, part c. We can see by comparing the two graphs how the GDP gap widens when the unemployment rate rises and narrows when the unemployment rate falls. In the late 1960s during the Vietnam war period unemployment was very low and the actual GDP equalled or exceeded potential GDP (the GDP gap was negative). This reflects the fact that the potential GDP does not represent the maximum GDP the economy can produce but rather that which it can produce at what is considered the normal level of unemployment. At the normal level of unemployment, the economy is considered to be operating at full employment. When the economy produces above its potential level, productive facilities are being utilised beyond their most efficient capacity levels and there is much overtime employment. The unemployment rate is squeezed below what is considered its normal level.

The GDP gap for the years in which the economy operated below its potential is indicated by the shaded areas in Figure 6.4, part b. These areas represent the economic costs of unemployment, measured in constant 1979-80 dollars.

Other Costs of Unemployment

The burden of unemployment is obviously more severe if you happen to be one of the unemployed than if you are among the employed. And different groups in the labour force tend to have a higher incidence of unemployment than others. For example, in March 1983, when our economy experienced its highest rate of unemployment since World War II, the overall unemployment rate for the civilian labour force was 10.4 per cent. Yet among males it stood at 9.9 per cent while among females it was 11.2 per cent. Among adults (persons aged 25 years and over) it was 7.3 per cent, while among teenagers, the newest entrants to the labour force, it was about 25 per cent.

Aside from those aspects of unemployment that can be quantified, there is a social pathology associated with unemployment that is more difficult to measure. The unemployed worker often suffers a loss of self-esteem. Medical researchers have reported findings suggesting that anxiety among unemployed workers leads to health problems and family squabbles. Severely prolonged unemployment of

family breadwinners often leads to broken homes and desertion. History suggests that high unemployment rates tend to spawn political and social unrest, and that more than one social order has been upset for want of jobs. The high unemployment rates among teenagers in our cities has had a lot to do with the sense of hopelessness, desperation, and anger that leads to high crime rates.

CHECKPOINT 6.3
Comparing parts b and c of Figure 6.4, what appears to be the level of the natural unemployment rate on which the estimate of potential GDP, the full employment level of GDP, is based?

PRICE CHANGE AND INFLATION

The burden of unemployment falls most heavily and obviously on those who are unemployed. Inflation, while often more subtle, affects virtually everybody. This happens because **inflation** *is a pervasive rise in the general level of prices of all goods and services. Inflation therefore, reduces the purchasing power of money.* The term inflation is not used when the prices of just a few goods rise. Rather, inflation refers to a situation in which the average of all prices rises. (Deflation is just the opposite of inflation — the average of all prices falls.) When we discussed the difference between money GDP and real GDP in the previous chapter, we saw that inflation means a dollar will purchase fewer goods tomorrow than it does today.

Recent Experience with Inflation

The annual percentage change in a measure of the general price level (the GDP deflator) for the years since 1958 is shown in Figure 6.4, part a. Note that the general price level has gone up, though at different rates, in almost every year over this period.

It is interesting to compare the size of these percentage increases with the changes in the size of the GDP gap, Figure 6.4, part b, and the unemployment rate, Figure 6.4, part c. Roughly speaking, up through 1971 the percentage rise in the general price level tended to be smaller when the GDP gap widened and the unemployment rate rose — when the economy had more excess capacity. This has long been regarded as the conventional pattern in the relationship between inflation, the GDP gap, and the unemployment rate.

However, the dramatic jump in the percentage rise in the general price level in the mid seventies was accompanied by an unprecedented degree of widening in the GDP gap. In other words, the economy experienced a severe period of inflation during a deep recession. This unconventional combination of events has given rise to the term *stagflation,* which means the occurrence of economic stagnation combined with high rates of inflation. Since the late 1970s the conventional relationship between inflation and the GDP gap appears to hold again. In subsequent chapters we will examine explanations of the conventional pattern of the relationship between inflation and unemployment, as well as explanations of the pattern known as stagflation.

Anticipated Versus Unanticipated Inflation

Inflation is sometimes said to be the most effective, continuously operating thief. It steals the purchasing power of your money whether you hold it in your hand, your wallet, your cheque account, or even in the vault of a bank. People have an incentive to protect themselves from inflation just as they have an incentive to protect themselves from theft of any kind. And they will attempt to do so if they anticipate or expect inflation. It is when they fail to anticipate inflation that they are most often hurt by it.

Anticipated Inflation and Contracts: Indexing

The terms of a great many economic transactions are stated in dollars and are spelled out in a contract to which all parties to the transaction agree. Trade unions and management agree to working conditions which stipulate the hourly wage rate to be paid, along with other conditions of employment — length of workweek, amount of vacation, and so on. Loan contracts set out the terms of loans mutually agreed to by borrowers and lenders. These terms include the amount of a loan, the interest rate to be paid by the borrower, and the rights of each party in the event of default. Superannuation schemes, insurance policies, rent leases, construction contracts, and contracts to produce and deliver goods to a customer by a certain date at a certain price are all examples of such contracts.

When one or both parties anticipate inflation, they will attempt to account for it explicitly in the terms of the contract. The Prices and Incomes Accord between the Hawke Labor government and the

Australian Council of Trade Unions in 1983 is a good example of such an agreement. Set in the context of a nationally centralised wage fixation system it sought to ensure the maintenance of real wages for all Australian workers. This was to be achieved by indexing wages to movements in the Consumer Price Index.

Suppose instead that unions had failed to anticipate inflation and agreed to wage increases of say 5 per cent, which did not keep pace with an inflation rate of 10 per cent. If average hourly wage rates were initially $10, the real wage rate would fall to $9.55 by the end of the year. That is, the average money wage of $10.50 after one year would only have 95.5 per cent of the purchasing power it had at the beginning of the year. With full wage indexation, average money wages after a year would have been $11 per hour. The real wage would remain at $10 — 10 constant dollars.

In sum, *it is not only money (cash and cheque accounts) that is robbed of purchasing power by inflation, but any contract that is stated in terms of dollars. If the inflation is anticipated, the terms of the contract can be set to protect its real value from the erosion of inflation.*

Gainers and Losers from Unanticipated Inflation

We can see that if inflation is correctly anticipated, people can try to take steps to protect themselves against it. Unfortunately, the world is an uncertain place. What is anticipated is often different from what occurs. *The amount of inflation that occurs that is unexpected is* **unanticipated inflation.** *Whenever there is unanticipated inflation, there are both gainers and losers.* Who are they?

1. *Creditors versus debtors.* Suppose A, the creditor or lender, lends $100 to B, the debtor or borrower, at a 10 per cent rate of interest for 1 year. We will assume that A entered into this loan agreement anticipating that there would be no inflation over the year. This means that A, the creditor, was induced to lend $100 of purchasing power by the prospect of getting back $110 of purchasing power 1 year from now. Conversely, B, the debtor, is willing to agree to pay A $110 of purchasing power 1 year from now in order to get $100 of purchasing power today.

Suppose that over the course of the year there actually is a 20 per cent rise in the general price level — a 20 per cent rate of inflation — that was completely unanticipated by A. Now when B pays $110 at the end of the year, as stipulated by the loan agreement, this $110 has only about 90 per cent of the purchasing power of the original $100 that A lent B. The 20 per cent rate of inflation more than offsets the 10 per cent rate of interest on the loan. As it turns out, A has given up more purchasing power than A actually gets back. Due to unanticipated inflation, A has suffered a loss. B, on the other hand, ends up paying back less purchasing power than was originally received. Because of unanticipated inflation, B has gained. B's gain in purchasing power is just equal to A's loss. A would never have entered into the loan agreement with B had A known that this was going to be the outcome. B in effect has ended up getting a loan on much more favourable terms than would have been possible had A correctly anticipated the inflation.

Whenever there is unanticipated inflation, there is a redistribution of wealth from creditors to debtors that would not have occurred if the inflation had been anticipated.

2. *Fixed-income groups.* We have noted how trade unions anticipating inflation would like to get a cost-of-living clause in the wages of their members. Indeed, all those anticipating inflation would want to ensure that their real income would not be reduced by inflation. For example, many retired people have found that their superannuation schemes do not have a provision for this. The dollar incomes they receive do not rise with inflation and their real incomes therefore fall. The same thing can happen to any group of individuals in our economy who fail to anticipate inflation or who fail to anticipate it sufficiently. People with fixed-dollar incomes lose ground relative to those whose dollar incomes rise right along with any increase in the general price level. The fixed-dollar income group's claim on a share of the economy's total pie falls relative to those whose dollar incomes keep pace with inflation.

3. *Fixed-dollar versus variable-dollar assets.* We have seen that if you lend out money (enter into a loan contract) but fail to anticipate a rise in the general price level, you can end up getting back a smaller amount of purchasing power than you initially bargained for. There are a number of assets that have fixed-dollar values that give them this property.

If you put $100 into a savings account at your local bank, you can subsequently withdraw the $100 plus the initially stipulated rate of interest at any time. If in the meantime there is an unanticipated rate of inflation, you will not get back the amount of purchasing power you had counted on. There are several kinds of **fixed-dollar assets** — money, bonds, bank loans to businesses and consumers, and in general *any kind of asset that guarantees a repayment of the initial dollar amount invested plus some stipulated rate of interest* (zero in the case of money). Parties who make these kinds of investments without anticipating inflation end up recovering an amount of purchasing power less than they had bargained for.

On the other hand, there are many assets, **variable-dollar assets,** that *do not guarantee, the owner any fixed-dollar value that may be recovered.* Such assets are also frequently called real assets. If you buy a piece of land, you can get rid of it any time, but only at what you can sell it for. The same is true of a share in a corporation (an indirect ownership of a real asset), a painting, a car, a house, or an antique. When there is an inflation, these assets can frequently (but not always) be sold at prices that are higher than their original purchase price by an amount that reflects the increase in the general price level. People owning these kinds of assets do not necessarily lose purchasing power as do those holding fixed-dollar assets such as money, savings accounts, and bonds. Consequently *an unanticipated inflation will result in a loss of wealth on holdings of fixed-dollar assets and often in little or no loss of wealth on variable-dollar assets.* Fixed-dollar asset holders may thus lose relative to variable-dollar asset holders. Since many people own some of each kind, whether they are net gainers or losers will depend largely on the relative proportions of the total assets they hold in each.

Unanticipated Inflation and Uncertainty

It is often argued that inflation isn't necessarily bad provided it occurs at a constant rate that everyone comes to anticipate. Then all parties can make their plans and enter into economic transactions on terms that fully take account of the inflation. There will be no gainers and

POLICY PERSPECTIVE

The Consumer Price Index —
Does it Measure the Cost of Living or What?

Probably the most commonly used and widely publicised measure of the general level of prices in the economy is the **consumer price index** (CPI) compiled by the Australian Bureau of Statistics (ABS). The rate of inflation is often measured as the percentage rate of change in the CPI. Very often the press, politicians, and people in general interpret the CPI as a measure of the 'cost-of-living,' and changes in the CPI as changes in the cost of living. However, examination of the way the CPI is constructed reveals that change in the CPI may be a misleading measure of the actual change in the cost of living.

The Market Basket

The CPI is a weighted average of the prices of a market basket of goods and services purchased by a typical metropolitan area worker's family. The weights are calculated as equal to the proportions of a typical worker's expenditures made on food, clothing, housing, medical care, and so on, based on an ABS survey of the estimated pattern of household expenditure in 1984-85.

One problem with viewing changes in the CPI as changes in the cost of living is immediately obvious. While construction of the CPI for any subsequent year (after 1984-85) uses the subsequent year's prices for each expenditure category, the weights used are still those for 1984-85. However, we know that expenditure patterns change over time, a fact that the CPI ignores. How does this bias the CPI as a tool for measuring changes in the cost of living? When the prices of different goods change relative to one another consumers tend to spend more on goods that have become relatively cheaper, less on those now relatively more expensive and, as shown in Figure P6.2, differences in the amount of price change between different kinds of goods and services have been substantial. By not changing the weights in the CPI to reflect this fact, over time the CPI increasingly overstates the importance of the relatively higher priced goods. Therefore the CPI, and change in the CPI, is biased upward.

Changing Composition and Quality of Market Basket

Another problem with the CPI is due to the fact that some items consumers buy today were not available in 1984-85 and are therefore not represented at all in the calculation of today's CPI. A somewhat similar problem arises from the fact that the CPI does not take account of changes in the quality of goods and services. Typically, higher-quality items cost more. For example, a jet plane capable of carrying 120 passengers costs more than yesteryear's propeller-driven aircraft of the same capacity, though the jet aircraft may cut travel time in half. Hence, the price per constant-quality unit of a 120-passenger aircraft has not gone up nearly as much as the price of such a plane. Similarly today's medical care is much better than in the past (some drugs and cures weren't even available), and much more expensive as well. But again,

FIGURE P6.2
Percentage Increase in Prices of Major Expenditure Classes of the CPI 1984-1987

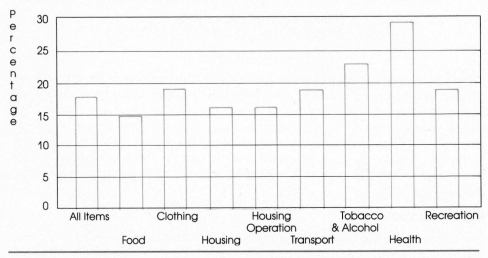

the price per constant-quality unit of medical care has not gone up nearly as much (if at all) as the quality unadjusted price of medical care used in the CPI. The lack of adjustment for quality improvement in the goods and services represented in the CPI is another source of upward bias in that price index.

Because of the above considerations it is important that the CPI basket is revised regularly to avoid overstating the rate of inflation. In Australia the ABS conducts such an exercise about every five years. The last revision which they made was in 1987.

Questions

1. On the basis of the evidence in Figure P6.2 which expenditure class's price increase probably causes the CPI to *overstate* the cost of living in Queensland and the Northern Territory relative to the rest of Australia.

2. On the basis of the evidence in Figure P6.2 which expenditure class's price behaviour was such as to most likely lead to an *understatement* of the importance of those goods in the basket between June 1985 and June 1987.

losers, no unplanned redistributions of income and wealth such as occur when there is unanticipated inflation.

When there is uncertainty about what the rate of inflation may be, fear of the consequences of unanticipated inflation make it harder for businesses and consumers to make plans. This puts a damper on the economy's ability to operate at a full-employment level — to close the GDP gap. Thus, one of the major goals of economic policy is price stability.

In sum, *price stability is one of the major goals of economic policy because (1) it is necessary in order to avoid the arbitrary redistribution of wealth that results from unanticipated inflation, and (2) by reducing uncertainty about inflation it enhances the economy's ability to operate at its full-employment potential.*

CHECKPOINT 6.4

Deflation is the opposite of inflation. Explain how an unanticipated deflation would affect the distribution of wealth between creditors and debtors, and between fixed-income groups and nonfixed-income groups. If inflation 'steals' money, what does deflation do? When you look at parts a and b of Figure 6.4 for the years 1972-78, can you think of a possible reason for the severity of the mid-1970s recession based on inflationary considerations?

WHERE DO WE GO FROM HERE?

We noted at the outset that the business cycle, unemployment, and inflation are all more or less interrelated problems. In the following chapters, we will examine how modern economics attempts to analyse their causes. This will require that we become more familiar with the institutional structure of the economy as well as with some tools of economic analysis. Ultimately, we want to grapple with the following sorts of issues: How do government deficits affect the economy? Can monetary and fiscal policy effectively put a damper on business fluctuations? Is there a trade-off between inflation and unemployment? (That is, can we reduce the amount of one of them only if we are willing to have more of the other?) Why is it that during the 1970s our economy was plagued with recessions and their accompanying high unemployment while suffering from inflation at the same time — the so-called problem of stagflation (the simultaneous existence of stagnation and inflation)?

SUMMARY

1. The economy grows through time but exhibits fluctuations about its growth trend called business cycles. The four phases of the business cycle — recession, trough, expansion, peak — may vary considerably in magnitude and duration from one cycle to the next, and no two cycles are ever exactly alike.

2. The business cycle affects different industries and segments of the economy in varying degrees. Durable goods industries tend to experience larger fluctuations than nondurable goods industries. These are usually industries with a few large, dominant (monopoly-type) firms that tend to have larger fluctuations in output and employment than in product price. Industries with many small competitive firms tend to show larger fluctuations in product price than in output and employment — typically these are nondurable goods industries.

3. While many determinants of the business cycle reflect the internal structure of the economy, others are considered exogenous (external). The distinction is not always clear-cut, however.

4. Three basic types of unemployment may be identified: frictional, structural, and cyclical. There are several measures of unemployment along with considerable controversy over which is the most appropriate one. There is reason to believe that the economy's so-called natural rate of unemployment has risen since World War II.

5. The greater the economy's total demand for goods and services, the greater the total demand for labour needed to produce them. As a result, the level of employment is higher and the level of unemployment is lower. One measure of the cost of unemployment is the GDP gap, the dollar value of the goods and services not produced when there is idle labour. Though often hard to measure, there are also psychological and social costs associated with unemployment. Moreover, the burden of unemployment is quite unevenly distributed among different groups in our economy.

6. Inflation is a rise in the general level of prices of all goods and services. Inflation reduces the purchasing power of money. The effects of anticipated inflation will be accounted for in the terms of economic contracts of all kinds.

7. Unanticipated inflation will result in a loss of purchasing power (wealth and income) among creditors, fixed-dollar income groups, and fixed-dollar asset holders. It results in an arbitrary redistribution of income and wealth. Uncertainty about inflation breeds a fear of these consequences of unanticipated inflation, and this inhibits the economy's ability to perform at its full-employment potential. For these reasons price stability is a major goal of economic policy.

8. The consumer price index (CPI) is a measure of the general level of prices in the economy, and as such is often interpreted as a measure of the 'cost of living'. The CPI most likely overstates the rate of inflation because the market basket weights are changed infrequently, new products are not included, and there is no allowance for the changing quality of the goods included in the market basket.

KEY TERMS AND CONCEPTS

business cycles
consumer price index (CPI)
depression
expansion
fixed-dollar assets
GDP gap
indexing
inflation
labour force
peak
potential GDP
recession
seasonal variation
trough
unanticipated inflation
unemployment
variable-dollar asset

QUESTIONS AND PROBLEMS

1. Can you give reasons why the average length of business cycle expansions should be longer than the average length of recessions, as indicated in Table 6.1?

2. How would you expect changes in the size of the armed forces to affect potential GDP? How would failure to take account of this manifest itself in Figure 6.4, part b?

3. Suppose you are an interviewer in the Commonwealth Employment Service. As a practical matter, how would you distinguish the frictionally unemployed from the cyclically unemployed from the structurally unemployed?

4. Since the early 1960s the growth rate of the total population has been considerably lower than it was during the 1950s and late 1940s — the years of the so-called baby boom. Assuming that the population growth rate remains constant at its present lower level, what are the implications for unemployment in the early part of the twenty-first century?

5. In the event of an unanticipated inflation, which of the following assets would you prefer to own: a stamp collection, Aussie-bonds, cash, a collection of old English coins, stocks and shares, a fast-food restaurant, a contract to deliver towels and linen to a hotel chain, a deposit in a savings bank, a mortgage on your neighbour's house?

6. How does inflation affect fixed-dollar income groups? What does it do to their share of real GDP?

APPENDIX

The Accelerator Principle

THE ACCELERATOR PRINCIPLE: AN INSIGHT

We have argued that one reason durable goods industries experience more severe fluctuations than nondurable goods industries is that durable goods purchases can be put off more easily than nondurable goods purchases. The so-called accelerator principle provides yet another insight into the causes of this greater variability in durable goods industries.

An Example

The way the accelerator principle works is perhaps best illustrated by an example. Suppose we consider the relationship between shoe sales by the shoe industry (a nondurable or semidurable goods industry) and the sale of shoemaking machines by the shoe machinery industry (a durable goods industry). We will assume that in order to produce $1,000 worth of shoes the shoe industry needs to have roughly $2,000 worth of shoe machinery. In other words, the production of $1 worth of the nondurable good requires the aid of approximately $2 worth of the durable good. What does this say about the relationship between changes in the year-to-year level of shoe sales and

changes in the year-to-year level of the sales of shoe machines?

An answer to this question is given by the data in Table A6.1. In year 1, retail shoe sales are $10 million (column 1). The shoe industry uses $20 million worth of shoe machinery (column 2) to produce this quantity of shoes. We will assume that it has this stock of shoe machinery on hand at the beginning of year 1, so that it does not need to add to its capital stock of shoe machines during year 1. Net investment in shoe machinery is therefore zero (column 3). Suppose, however, that $2 million worth of shoe machines wear out every year. The shoe industry must therefore buy $2 million of shoe machines from the shoe machine industry for replacement (column 4). Hence in year 1, shoe industry output and sales are $10 million (column 1), while the shoe machine industry's output and sales are $2 million (column 4).

Now suppose that in year 2 annual retail shoe sales increase by 30 per cent to $13 million (column 1). The shoe industry now needs $26 million worth of shoe machines (column 2) to produce this amount of shoes. Hence the additional $3 million of shoe production means the industry must add $6 million worth of new shoe machinery (column 3) to its stock of shoe machines. This plus the annual replace-

TABLE A6.1
The Accelerator Principle: Retail Shoe Sales and Shoe Machine Sales (Hypothetical Data in Millions of Dollars)

	Shoe Industry			Shoe Machine Industry
	(1)	(2)	(3)	(4)
	Annual Retail Shoe Sales	Stock of Capital: Shoe Machines*	NI = Net Investment in Shoe Machines	Sale of Shoe Machines = NI + Replacement
Year 1	$10	$20	$ 0	$ 0 + $2 = $ 2
Year 2	13	26	6	6 + 2 = 8
Year 3	20	40	14	14 + 2 = 16
Year 4	27	54	14	14 + 2 = 16
Year 5	31	62	8	8 + 2 = 10
Year 6	31	62	0	0 + 2 = 2

*Assumes that $2 worth of shoe machinery is needed to produce every $1 worth of shoes.

ment of $2 million worth of shoe machinery brings total shoe machine sales to $8 million (column 4). The upshot is that a 30 per cent increase in shoe industry sales between years 1 and 2 causes a 300 per cent increase in the sales of the shoe machine industry. In other words, there is an accelerator effect.

When shoe sales rise by 54 per cent to $20 million in year 3 (column 1), the shoe industry needs $40 million worth of shoe machinery (column 2). Therefore net investment in shoe machinery rises to $14 million (column 3). This plus replacement expenditures causes total shoe machine sales to rise to $16 million (column 4). Hence a $7 million, or 54 per cent, increase in shoe sales between years 2 and 3 (column 1) causes an $8 million, or 100 per cent, increase in shoe machine sales (column 4). Again we see an accelerator effect.

But now suppose the increase in shoe sales between years 3 and 4 is again $7 million, the same as it was between years 2 and 3 (column 1). The shoe industry now needs $54 million worth of shoe machines (column 2). Net investment in shoe machines is once again $14 million (column 3). This plus the annual $2 million replacement expenditure means that shoe

machine sales (column 4) are once again $16 million. The startling conclusion is that shoe sales must keep growing at $7 million per year if shoe machine sales are just to stay the same!

When shoe sales increase by only $4 million between years 4 and 5 to $31 million (column 1), the shoe industry's net investment in shoe machines declines to $8 million (column 3). This plus the annual $2 million for replacement means that total shoe machine sales are now only $10 million (column 4), down from the $16 million of the previous year — this despite the fact that annual shoe sales still increased! Suppose that in year 6 shoe sales don't increase at all (column 1). There is now no need for the shoe industry to increase its stock of shoe machines (column 2), so net investment in shoe machines falls to zero (column 3). The shoe machine industry's total sales fall to $2 million (column 4), the annual replacement requirement of the shoe industry. If shoe sales fall in subsequent years, the shoe industry might even cut back on these replacement expenditures.

The annual shoe sales (column 1) and the annual shoe machine sales (column 4) are plotted in Figure A6.1 to give a graphic illustration of the accelerator principle. In general, *the accelerator principle says that ever larger increases in the level of retail sales are needed in order for net investment in capital or durable goods to rise. For net investment to remain constant, retail sales must increase by a constant amount every year. When the expansion of retail sales begins to slow down, the level of net investment will actually fall.* Table A6.1 and Figure A6.1 clearly show that due to the accelerator principle the mere expansion and subsequent levelling off of retail shoe sales caused an expansion, a peak, and a recession in the sale of shoe machinery — a complete business cycle in the shoe machinery industry.

Qualifications and Extensions

Capital goods — goods used to produce other goods — make up a large part of the output of the economy's durable goods industries. (Consumer durables, such as passenger cars, also account for a sizeable portion.) While other factors also affect investment in capital goods, the accelerator principle would seem to provide a key insight into the relatively large fluctuations in the behaviour of capital investment in our economy. However, two qualifications on the way the accelerator principle works should be noted. First, if the economy is in the early stages of an expansion, there may be excess capacity in nondurable goods industries, so that expansion can occur with no increase in capital goods. Second, in the later stages of an expansion, there may be no excess capacity in capital goods industries, so that nondurable goods industries cannot get more capital.

The accelerator principle is also relevant to inventory investment, both in durable and nondurable goods. For example,

suppose that for every $1 worth of sales of canned goods, grocers want to keep $2 worth of canned goods in inventory. Table A6.1 and Figure A6.1 could then represent canned goods sales (column 1); the desired inventory of canned goods (column 2); net inventory investment in canned goods (column 3); and gross inventory investment in canned goods, which would include the replacement expenditure that is due to damaged canned goods (column 4).

FIGURE A6.1
The Accelerator Principle: Retail Shoe Sales and Shoe Machine Sales (Hypothetical Data)

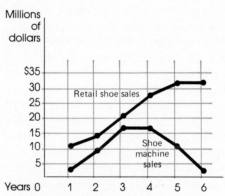

The graph of retail shoe sales is plotted from the data in column 1 of Table A6.1 and the graph for shoe machine sales is plotted from the data in column 4.

The ever larger increases in shoe sales between years 1 and 2 and between years 2 and 3 cause an even more pronounced rise in the sale of shoe machines over this time span. This is known as the accelerator effect. When the rise in shoe sales between years 3 and 4 is the same as that between years 2 and 3, shoe machine sales flatten out. When the expansion of shoe sales slows down between years 4 and 5, shoe machine sales actually decline — a downward accelerator effect. When the sale of shoes flattens out between years 5 and 6, the resulting decline in shoe machine sales is even greater. Hence the expansion and subsequent flattening out of shoe sales results in an expansion, a peak, and a recession in shoe machine sales — a complete business cycle in the shoe machine industry. This is an example of the accelerator principle in action.

QUESTIONS AND PROBLEMS

1. Using the same sales figures in column 1 of Table A6.1, suppose the shoe industry needed roughly $3 worth of shoe machinery for each $1 of shoes produced and sold. How would this affect the behaviour of shoe machine sales in column 4? What insight does this give you into the role of capital intensity (the amount of capital required to produce a dollar's worth of output) as a factor in the behaviour of business cycles?

2. Would you expect the effect of the accelerator principle on investment expenditures to be the same during the expansion phase of the business cycle as during the recession phase? Why or why not?

7

Measuring National Income and Product

AFTER READING THIS CHAPTER YOU WILL BE ABLE TO:

1. Explain how, for purposes of national income accounting, GDP may be viewed from two sides — the expenditure side and the income side.

2. Appreciate the relationship between gross domestic product and other key national accounting concepts.

In this chapter we will focus on national income accounting. National income accounting provides us with aggregate measures of what is happening in the economy. It is the way we measure the various flows depicted in the flow diagrams of Chapter 5.

WHY IS NATIONAL INCOME ACCOUNTING IMPORTANT?

When you drive your car, you usually keep an eye on the speedometer to see how fast you are going. You check the fuel gauge before starting out to make sure you have enough petrol to reach your destination. The temperature gauge warns you about engine overheating before serious damage is done (the radiator boils over or the radiator hose breaks). Without the information these gauges provide, you could find yourself in a dangerous situation. The same is true with respect to the performance of our economy.

When our economy plunged into the Depression of the 1930s, the general lack of any timely, systematic measurements of what was happening became painfully apparent. This experience spurred the government to develop today's national income accounting procedures. Armed with relatively recent statistical measurements of the economy's performance, businesses, households, and government policymakers are better informed about what has been happening in the economy and where it appears to be headed. Businesses and households are therefore in a better position to make economic plans. Government policymakers need this kind of information to assess the economy's performance in order to implement timely policies to improve that performance. Shy of this lofty ambition, policymakers need such information at least to avoid policy actions that may harm the economy's performance.

The Two Sides of GDP

Envision a sales counter in any store or business. On one side stands the customer paying out money in exchange for the good or service that the store provides. On the other side stands the proprietor, giving the customer the good or service in exchange for the customer's money. Corresponding to every purchase there is a sale, since there are always two sides to every transaction. We know from our discussion of value added in Chapter 5 that all the money received on the seller's side of the counter ultimately is paid out in wages, rent, interest, and profit as compensation to the owners of the factors of production used to produce and distribute the product. Therefore all the money received on the seller's side of the counter is income to all the owners of the factors of production — land, labour, and capital.

We may think of all such counters in the economy across which all final goods and services flow as one big sales counter. The total of all the money flowing across the counter in exchange for all the final goods and services produced in a year is the money GDP. When we view GDP from the buyer's side of the counter, where expenditures are made and goods are taken off the counter, we are viewing GDP from the expenditure, or output, side. This viewpoint is often referred to as the *expenditure, or output, approach* to GDP. On the other hand, if we look at GDP from the seller's side of the counter, where all the income is received and ultimately distributed to the owners of productive factors, we are viewing GDP from the income, or earnings, or allocations side — often called the *income approach* to GDP. These two sides of GDP may be summarised by the following equation, which is *always* valid:

$$\left.\begin{array}{l}\text{total}\\\text{expenditures}\\\text{on final}\\\text{goods and}\\\text{services}\end{array}\right\} = \text{GDP} = \left\{\begin{array}{l}\text{total income}\\\text{from}\\\text{production}\\\text{and}\\\text{distribution}\\\text{of final}\\\text{output}\end{array}\right.$$

The left side of this equation may be thought of as representing the lower flow channel in Figure 5.2 of Chapter 5, and the right side as representing the upper flow channel.

To understand the elements that go into national income accounting and the basic concepts used in much macroeconomic analysis, we need to look at both ways of viewing GDP in more detail. In fact, this is necessary even if you only want to make some sense out of an everyday news item about the state of the economy.

THE EXPENDITURE SIDE OF GDP

The economy can be divided into four distinct sectors: household, business, government, and foreign. Total expenditure on GDP can be divided up according to which of these sectors makes the expenditure. Private final consumption expenditures are made by households; private domestic investment expenditures by businesses; government expenditures by state, local, and federal government; net exports reflect our trade with foreigners.

Private Final Consumption Expenditure (*C*)

Private final consumption expenditures by households are often simply termed *consumption,* or designated *C.* These are household expenditures on consumer durables such as cars and household appliances, on consumer nondurables such as food and clothing, and on services such as medical care, shelter, haircuts, and dry cleaning. Also included are imputed household expenditures, such as the value of food that farm families produce and consume themselves.

Gross Private Investment (*I*)

Recall the distinction we made in Chapter 1 between the common usage of the term *investment* and that used by economists. In common usage people often speak of investing money in stocks and bonds, for example. However, these are only financial transactions representing the purchase of titles of ownership. When economists and national income accountants use the term **investment,** they are referring primarily to business firms' expenditures on new capital goods — goods that are used to produce other goods and services.

The term *private* means we are referring to expenditures by private business firms, as opposed to government agencies. The term *gross* will be explained below. **Gross private investment,** often designated *I,* includes all final purchases of new tools and machines by business firms, all construction (residential as well as business), and changes in inventories. Several clarifying remarks are in order.

1. Only *new* tools and machines are included because, as we have already stressed, purchases of secondhand goods are not included in GDP.

2. Residential construction of owner-occupied dwellings is included along with factories and home units. These dwellings are income-producing assets in the sense that they produce a service, shelter, that could be rented out — just like flats or other commercial structures. (You might wonder why cars and furniture, which can also be rented, are included in consumption, since the line of reasoning we've been using suggests that they could be included in investment. The fact that they are included under consumption simply illustrates that there is a certain arbitrariness in national income accounting conventions.)

3. Why are changes in business inventories included in gross private investment? First of all, inventories are included in investment because they are a necessary part of the productive process just like any other capital good. Inventories consist of stocks of raw materials and other inputs, goods in various stages of completion, and finished goods not yet sold. The firm has money invested in inventories just as it has money invested in other capital goods. The basic reason for taking account of inventory changes is that GDP is supposed to measure the economy's output of goods and services during a year. But what do inventory changes have to do with this?

Suppose that the economy's production of output for the year exceeds the quantity of output actually sold during the year. The amount of output not sold must go into **inventories,** stocks of unsold goods. Inventories at the beginning of the year consist of goods produced in previous years (and therefore not included in this year's GDP). Therefore, inventories at the end of the year will be larger by the amount of output produced but not sold this year. Therefore, in order to correctly

measure this year's total output, or GDP, we must add this increase in inventories to *this year's* sales of final goods and services.

Alternatively, suppose the quantity of output sold during the year exceeds the quantity of output produced by the economy. Since this excess of sales over production can only occur by selling goods out of inventories, inventories will be lower at the end of the year than at the beginning. Since inventories at the beginning of the year consist of goods produced in previous years, the sale of those goods should not be included in this year's GDP. Hence, the decrease in inventories must be subtracted from this year's total sales of final goods and services in order to correctly measure *this year's* total output, or GDP.

Gross Versus Net Investment: Depreciation

Capital goods wear out and get 'used up' during the course of producing other goods — they are subject to **capital depreciation.** Machines, tools, and equipment need to be repaired or replaced. Factories and buildings require maintenance. That part of gross private investment expenditures that goes toward these replacement activities simply maintains the economy's existing stock of capital. What is left over represents a net addition to the economy's capital stock and is therefore called **net private investment.** *Gross private investment* equals replacement investment plus net private investment.

For example, in 1985-86 gross private fixed capital expenditure in Australia was about $38 billion. Of this amount about $27 billion was replacement investment, or what national income accountants now call consumption of fixed capital. This means that there was roughly $11 billion ($38 billion minus $27 billion) worth of net additions to private capital stock in Australia in 1985-86.

Investment and Capital Formation

To a large extent, the economy's ability to produce goods and services depends on its stock of capital goods. (Land and labour are its other important factors of production.) Growth in the economy's capital stock is therefore important because it contributes to growth in the economy's GDP. When gross investment is greater than replacement investment, net investment is positive and there is growth in the capital stock. When gross investment equals replacement investment, net investment is zero and there is no growth in the capital stock. If gross investment is less than replacement investment, net investment is negative and the economy's capital stock is wearing out faster than it is being replaced.

The relationship between gross investment, replacement investment, and net investment since 1966/67 is summarised in Figure 7.1, which plots the ratio of gross investment to replacement investment. When this ratio is greater than 1, gross investment is greater than replacement investment. This means that net investment is positive and the capital stock is growing. Figure 7.1 shows that this has been the case every year in Australia since 1966/67 when the current data series was first collected by the ABS. During the Depression of the 1930s and also during several years of World War II the ratio fell below unity. During both of these periods net investment was negative and the economy's capital stock was actually declining. What is notable in Figure 7.1

is the general fall in the ratio of Gross Fixed Capital spending to the consumption of capital between 1966/67 and 1986/87.

Government Spending (G)

Government spending, often designated G, includes spending on final goods and services by government at all levels — federal, state, and local. Expenditures on services include wages paid to all government employees, civilian and military. We have already noted that government transfer payments are not included in GDP because they are not purchases of current production. These payments are not included in government expenditures for the same reason they are not included in GDP.

Net Exports (X)

The total expenditures on final goods and services in our economy include those made by foreigners on our output as well as those made by our own citizens on foreign goods and services. Foreign purchases of our output are **exports.** Our purchases of foreign output are **imports.** Since GDP is supposed to be a measure of productive activity in our economy, it should only measure the output actually produced domestically. Imports are already counted in C, I, and G. Imports must therefore be subtracted from total expenditures on final goods and services when measuring GDP. Exports are not included in C, I, and G. Since exports represent goods produced domestically they must be added in. National income accountants do this by simply adding in exports and subtracting out imports. That is, they add in the difference between exports and imports, or **net exports,** which are designated X.

X = net exports = (exports — imports)

Net exports can be either positive or negative depending on whether exports are larger or smaller than imports.

Summary of the Expenditure Side of GDP

When GDP is viewed from the expenditure side, it is equal to the sum of personal consumption expenditures C, gross private investment I, government expenditures G, and net exports X. In brief, from the expenditure side:

$$GDP = C + I + G + X$$

*CHECKPOINT * 7.1*

Consider the following statement by an economic commentator about GDP growth: '. . . though the June quarter's growth rate probably will not exceed that in the March quarter, the composition will be better as more growth will come from personal consumption and less from inventory accumulation'.

Why do you think she felt that this particular composition of growth in the fourth quarter of the financial year would be better than that of the third quarter?

*Answers to all Checkpoints can be found at the back of the text.

FIGURE 7.1
The Ratio of Gross Fixed Capital Expenditure to Consumption of Fixed Capital in Australia 1966-1987.

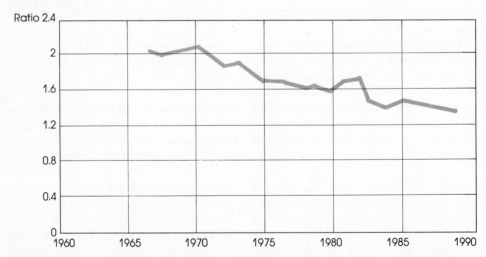

When the ratio of gross investment to replacement investment is greater than 1, net investment is positive and the economy's capital stock is growing. When the ratio equals 1, net investment is zero and the capital stock remains unchanged. When the rate of gross investment to replacement investment is less than 1, net investment is negative. This means that the capital stock is wearing out or being used up faster than it is being replaced. This was true during the Great Depression of the 1930s and for several years during World War II. As can be seen on the above graph net investment has been positive in every year between 1966 and 1987.

THE INCOME SIDE OF GDP

Now let's consider GDP from the seller's side of the counter. Viewed from this vantage point, GDP is distributed as payments or income to the owners of all the inputs that contribute to its production. These payments consist of wages, interest, rent, and profit. The Australian Bureau of Statistics (ABS) records income payments as wages, salaries and supplements to workers, and as gross operating surpluses for six different enterprise groups. These six groups are companies, unincorporated enterprises, dwellings owned by persons, public enterprises, general government and financial enterprises. Gross operating surpluses include payments to rent, interest and profits as well as a residual to the wages of executives. In reporting these surpluses the ABS also includes an item subtracting imputed bank service charges. It is a charge which would reduce the reported gross operating surpluses, but the ABS finds it difficult to allocate this charge accurately among bank customers.

The only other item computed in the incomes approach are indirect taxes less subsidies. This appears because factors of production must pay indirect taxes (and receive subsidies) before income is distributed to them. Indirect taxes include sales tax, excise taxes, business property taxes, licence fees, customs duties and other non-income taxes. Subsidies are payments to producers to undertake production of particular commodities.

Since indirect business taxes are paid to the government, they are not a payment or earned income to a factor directly used by the firm to produce a product, as is the case for wages, interest, rent, and profit. Nonetheless, indirect business taxes must be paid out of the sales price of the product. For example, suppose a business firm must receive $10 per unit of a good to cover the costs of all the factors used to produce it. If the government levies a 7 per cent sales tax, the firm must charge a price of $10.70 to cover both its factor costs and the $.70 it owes the government. Since $10.70 is what must be spent to get a unit of the product (the expenditure side of GDP), the $.70 indirect business tax must be included on the income side of GDP if the two sides are to be equal. This

TABLE 7.1
The Expenditure Side and Income Side of GDP: Australia 1986-87 ($bill)

Expenditure Side of GDP				Income Side of GDP	
Private Final Consumption Expenditure (C)	$156.4			Wages, Salaries and Supplements	$131.3
Gross Private Investment (I)	40.6			Gross Operating Surplus Companies	35.4
Government Spending (G)	67.7	GDP = $264.4 =	Unincorporated	29.3
				Dwellings owned by persons	28.5
Exports (X)	42.6			Public Enterprises	9.8
less Imports (M)	-47.4			General Government	5.8
				Financial Enterprises	0.0
Statistical Discrepancy	4.4			less Imputed Bank Service Charge	-6.5
				Indirect Taxes less Subsidies	30.8

Source: Australian Bureau of Statistics

is necessary even though the sales tax is not an item of earned income for any factor of production. Subsidies are payments to producers encouraging them to continue or increase production.

Summary of the Two Sides of GDP

Table 7.1 summarises our discussion of the two sides of GDP. The items on the expenditure or output side are on the left, and the items on the income or allocation side are on the right. Data for the Australian economy for 1986-87 are given to illustrate how the sum of the expenditure items on the lefthand side of the table add up to the sum of the income items on the righthand side of the table. Each side, of course, sums up to GDP.

So that the expenditures and income approach to computing GDP balance in practice, the Australian Statistician includes a Statistical Discrepancy item on the expenditures side of the ledger. The Statistical Discrepancy may be positive or negative. It is included on the expenditures side by convention and does not necessarily imply that the incomes method of computation is more accurate.

===

CHECKPOINT 7.2

Until the Federal Government in Australia Introduced the dividend imputation technique in its 1985-86 Budget, it was often argued that shareholders' dividends were treated unfairly by tax laws. As well as companies being taxed on their profits, shareholders were also subject to income tax — double taxation. How does double taxation most likely affect the size of retained earnings relative to the size of dividend payments?

===

RELATED NATIONAL INCOME ACCOUNTING CONCEPTS

There are several other important and related national income accounting concepts needed for a complete picture of the basics of national income accounting. These are national turnover of goods and services, gross domestic product at factor cost, domestic factor incomes, national income, national disposable income and gross national expenditure. Another important concept which the ABS does not report directly is net domestic product. The relationship between most of these measures and GDP is shown diagrammatically in Figure 7.2. Australia's national accounting system is in close accord with the framework suggested by the United Nations in 1968.

Gross National Expenditure (GNE)

This consists of the sum of private final consumption spending (*C*), gross private Investment (*I*) and government spending (*G*). As can be seen from Table 7.1 above this amounted to $269.2 billion for Australia during the 1986/87 financial year.

National Turnover of Goods and Services

This refers to the total annual flow of goods and services in the economy, free of duplication. One can compute the measure either by considering the supply of goods and services or the demand for goods and services. From the **supply side** perspective, national turnover is the sum of payments to factors of production and

POLICY PERSPECTIVE

When is a recession not a recession?

One rule of thumb which economic commentators often use in assessing economic performance relates to movements in quarterly estimates of real Gross Domestic Product. When real GDP falls in *three successive quarters* they judge that an economy is in recession. But GDP estimates are themselves subject to continuing revision, the majority of which occurs in the two years following their initial publication. In 1985 the Australian statistician noted that:

> Estimates of national income and expenditure have been prepared from a wide range of statistical sources, some of which are available quickly and some only with a delay of several years. Therefore, estimates for recent years may be subject to considerable revision as firmer data come to hand.

Notable components of the national accounts which are revised include income from companies, income from unincorporated enterprises, and consumption of fixed capital (i.e. depreciation). This occurs because income tax statistics do not become available for about two years after the end of the financial year.

In the light of these comments, consider movements in estimated real GDP in Australia for the 1985/86 financial year. During that year real GDP seems to have fallen in at least two quarters. As revisions to GDP estimates have appeared, it is unclear, however, whether real GDP fell in three consecutive quarters. The relevant percentage change estimates are as follows:

Date of Estimate	Percentage Real GDP Change on Previous Quarter (seasonally adjusted Data)			
	Sept.85	Dec. 85	Mar. 86	June 86
August, 1986	+ 2.2	– 0.7	+ 0.3	– 0.9
November, 1986	+ 2.4	– 0.7	– 0.1	– 0.3
March, 1987	+ 2.4	– 1.1	+ 0.3	– 0.5
June, 1987	+ 1.6	– 0.5	– 0.2	– 0.1
August, 1987	+ 1.5	– 0.4	+ 0.3	– 0.4

These are plotted in Figure P7.1

The November, 1986 and June, 1987 data estimates each suggest a recession during the latter part of the 1985/86 financial year. The August, 1986, March, 1987 and August, 1987 estimates do not satisfy the rule of thumb. The message in this case is that since GDP estimates are imperfect and subject to considerable revision, it is advisable to be wary in placing too much emphasis on arbitrary rules of thumb in commenting on their movement.

FIGURE P7.1
Changing Estimates of Real GDP Growth — Australia 1985/1986

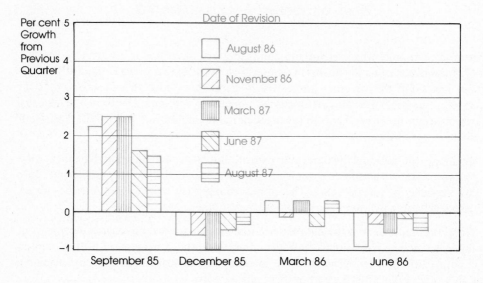

Furthermore, even if the percentage changes in real GDP reported in March, 1987 and August, 1987 were positive, they are so small that one should be wary in placing much weight on them. Though technically there was no recession the economy was certainly in a sluggish phase.

Questions

1. Use the data from the above table to estimate the annual percentage change in Australia's real GDP during the 1985-86 financial year. How much variation is there in the five estimates you have made?

2. How is it possible to explain considerable variation in estimates of a country's GDP growth during a specific year?

for imports, i.e.

National turnover = GDP + M.

In 1986-87 Australia's National Turnover of goods and services was $311.8 billion (i.e. $264.4 billion (GDP) plus $47.4 billion (imports)).

From the **demand side** perspective, national turnover is the sum of goods and services purchased and exports i.e. GNE plus Exports. For 1986–87 this was $311.8

billion (i.e. $269.2 billion (GNE) plus $42.6 billion (Exports)).

Gross Domestic Product at Factor Cost

We have seen already that not all of the market value of goods and services is received by factors of production. Some is paid to government in indirect taxes. This is offset partially when the government pays subsidies to some producers. As the return in a period to factors of production GDP at factor cost is equal to Gross Domestic Product less indirect taxes plus subsidies. The ABS estimated this to be $233.6 billion in 1986-87 (i.e. $264.4 bill (GDP) *minus* $34.7 billion (indirect taxes) plus $3.9 billion (subsidies)).

Domestic Factor Incomes (*DFI*)

When we subtract depreciation allowances from GDP at factor cost, we obtain the estimate of Domestic Factor Incomes. The ABS describes this aggregate as 'that part of the value added by factors of production which accrues as income to their suppliers after allowing for consumption of fixed capital'. The initial ABS estimate of Domestic Factor Incomes (DFI) for the 1986-87 financial year was $189.9 billion (i.e. $233.6 billion (GDP at Factor Cost) *minus* $43.7 billion (depreciation)).

National Income (*NI*)

Whereas Gross Domestic Product refers to output produced within the geographical boundaries of a country, **national income** is concerned with the income received by a country's residents. Some income generated domestically is paid to overseas residents while some income generated in other countries is paid to our residents. The concept of national income is estimated by subtracting net income paid overseas, and depreciation allowances, from GDP. For 1986-87 National Income has been estimated to be $210.5 billion, i.e. $264.4 billion (GDP) less $43.7

billion (depreciation) less $10.2 billion (net income paid overseas).

National Disposable Income (*NDI*)

This is simply National Income less net transfers to overseas. In 1986/87 such net transfers for Australia were initially estimated to amount to a deficit of $1,348 million. Hence National Disposable Income was estimated to be $211.8 billion.

Household Income (*HI*)

Although not referred to in Figure 7.2 this is another important national aggregate. It is the total income which normal residents receive in a given period. It consists of wages, salaries and supplements, income from unincorporated enterprises, personal transfer payments and some transfers from overseas. For 1986-87 it is estimated to be $216.9 billion.

Household Disposable Income (*HDI*)

We arrive at this aggregate after subtracting direct taxes, fees, fines, consumer debt interest and unrequited transfers to overseas from household income. The initial ABS estimate for 1986-87 was $172.5 billion.

Net Domestic Product (*NDP*): GDP Minus Depreciation

If you wear out 2 hammers while producing 10 hammers, you are 8 hammers 'better off', not 10. True, 10 hammers were produced and that quantity is a measure of total productive activity over some

FIGURE 7.2
Relationships Between Main Identities in Australia's National Accounting Framework

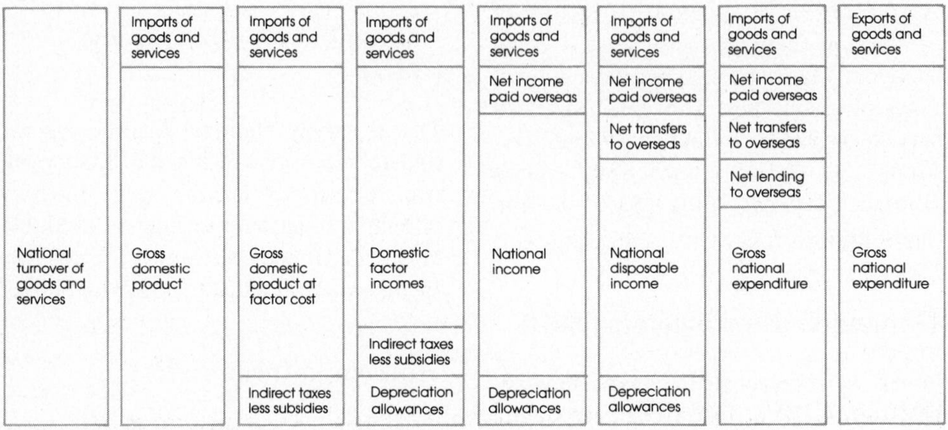

	Imports of goods and services	Imports of goods and services	Imports of goods and services	Imports of goods and services	Imports of goods and services	Imports of goods and services	Exports of goods and services
				Net income paid overseas	Net income paid overseas	Net income paid overseas	
					Net transfers to overseas	Net transfers to overseas	
						Net lending to overseas	
National turnover of goods and services	Gross domestic product	Gross domestic product at factor cost	Domestic factor incomes	National income	National disposable income	Gross national expenditure	Gross national expenditure
			Indirect taxes less subsidies				
		Indirect taxes less subsidies	Depreciation allowances	Depreciation allowances	Depreciation allowances		

period of time. But in order to assess what that productive activity has actually provided, it is necessary to deduct the 2 hammers used up to get the *net* product of our efforts.

Similarly, GDP is a measure of the economy's total productive activity. But it makes no adjustment to account for the quantity of the year's output that must be used to replace the goods used up in producing this year's output. To do so we *subtract the annual depreciation of the economy's capital stock, or capital consumption allowance, from GDP to get the economy's* **net domestic product (NDP)**. *Net domestic product measures the dollar value of the economy's annual output of final goods and services after adjustment is made for the quantity of the year's output needed to replace goods used up in producing that output.*

Net domestic product may be obtained by deducting the consumption of fixed capital from the current estimate of GDP. Using 1986-87 ABS data, estimated consumption of fixed capital amounted

to $43.7 billion. Hence Net Domestic Product was $220.7 billion.

CHECKPOINT 7.3

You have been given the following data from the Australian National Accounts for the 1983/84 financial year.

	$Mill
Gross Domestic Product	*192,276*
Imports	*30,764*
Exports	*28,010*
Consumption of Fixed Capital	*30,653*
Indirect Taxes	*25,660*
Subsidies	*3,247*

With the assistance of Figure 7.2 estimate
(a) National turnover of goods and services.
(b) Gross domestic product at factor cost.
(c) Domestic factor incomes.
(d) Gross national expenditure.

for the 1983-84 financial year.

SUMMARY

1. When GDP is viewed from the expenditure, or output, side it equals the sum of personal consumption expenditures, made by households; gross private investment expenditures, made by business firms; government expenditures, made by federal, state, and local governments; and net exports, the difference between foreign purchases of our goods and our purchases of foreign goods.

2. From the income side, GDP consists of payments to the factors of production i.e. wages to labour, interest to capital, rent to land, and profit to entrepreneurial activity. In practice it is recorded as wages, salaries and supplements payable to labour and gross operating surpluses as payments to the other factors of production. Additionally, a certain amount goes to pay indirect business taxes less subsidies.

3. In addition to GDP there are several other important and interrelated national income accounting concepts. They include (1) National turnover of goods and services, (2) Gross national expenditure, (3) GDP at factor cost, (4) Domestic factor incomes, (5) National income, (6) National disposable income, (7) Household income, (8) Household disposable income and (9) Net domestic product.

KEY TERMS AND CONCEPTS

capital depreciation
domestic factor incomes
exports
gross private investment
gross domestic product at factor cost
gross national expenditure
imports
indirect taxes

inventory
investment
national income
national disposable income
national turnover of goods and services
net exports
net domestic product (NDP)
private final consumption expenditure
subsidies

QUESTIONS AND PROBLEMS

1. GDP is supposed to measure the economy's output of final goods and services. But in what way and to what extent could it also be said to be a measure of the value of the services of productive factors?

2. Gross National Product (GNP) is the key national accounting aggregate in the USA. It refers to the market value of final goods and services produced by an economy's residents during a year.

How does it compare with GDP? Identify some countries where you would expect GDP to be significantly less than GNP.

3. In periods of deep recession a nation's capital stock will decline because net investment is negative e.g. during the early 1930s. How is it possible to explain the completion of a major investment project such as the Sydney Harbour Bridge during this period?

4. Given the following national income accounting data for Australia in 1985/86 compute estimates of wages, salaries and supplements, the statistical discrepancy, gross national expenditure and the national turnover of goods and services.

	$Mill
Private Final Consumption Spending (C)	141,919
Gross Private Investment (I)	42,501

Government Spending (G)	62,960
Exports	38,075
Imports	45,386
Gross Domestic Product	240,136
Total Gross Operating Surpluses	96,968
Indirect Taxes	13,108
Subsidies	1,499
Imputed Bank Service Charge	5,391

8

Aggregate Demand and Supply: The Income-Expenditure View

AFTER READING THIS CHAPTER YOU WILL BE ABLE TO:

1. State the reasons why classical economists thought a capitalistic, laissez faire economy would automatically tend to operate at a full employment equilibrium.

2. Distinguish between the classical view and the Keynesian analysis in terms of aggregate demand and aggregate supply.

3. Explain the concepts of the consumption function and the saving function and the determinants of consumption and saving.

4. Explain the nature of investment expenditures and their determinants.

5. Explain how the equilibrium level of total income is determined according to the income-expenditure approach.

Chapter 6 introduced some of the characteristics of the economy's performance, along with two problem areas of major concern — unemployment and inflation. And in Chapter 7 we saw how we keep tabs on the economy's performance by the use of national income accounting. However, in order to better understand aggregate economic activity in general, we need to become familiar with the way aggregate demand and aggregate supply interact to determine total income, output, employment, and the economy's price level, a subject briefly introduced in Chapter 5.

Our journey begins in this chapter. First we will examine why many economists from Adam Smith's time up through the 1930s believed that capitalistic, market-oriented economies naturally tended to operate at full employment — a view that essentially assumes the aggregate supply curve is vertical. Then we will see why and how the Depression of the 1930s forced a major rethinking on this issue — the Keynesian revolution. This gave rise to the income-expenditure theory, an approach that assumes the economy's price level is inflexible so that the aggregate supply curve is horizontal and the equilibrium level of total income, output, and employment is determined solely by aggregate demand. We will examine this approach here and in the next chapter. Government expenditure and taxation will be introduced into this framework in Chapter 10. Then in Chapter 11 we will allow the price level to vary with changes in total income, output, and employment, and will see more generally how aggregate demand and supply jointly determine the economy's price level and its total income, output, and employment levels.

THE CLASSICAL VIEW OF INCOME AND EMPLOYMENT

Classical economists subscribed to the notion that capitalistic, market-oriented economies naturally tended to operate at a full-employment output level. The classical economist's faith in this point of view was based on Say's Law,[1] an appealing yet deceptive argument.

Say's Law

Simply put, **Say's Law** *states that supply creates its own demand.* According to Say's Law, people only work to produce and supply goods and services because they want to acquire the income to buy goods and services. A level of total dollar spending insufficient to purchase the full-employment output of goods and services was considered impossible because the total income earned from the production of the economy's total full-employment output would be spent to purchase that output.

Classical economists subscribed to two fundamental assumptions about how the economy worked — *two assumptions essential to a belief in Say's Law. First, prices and wages always adjust quickly to clear markets. Second, the interest rate always adjusts to equate saving and investment.*

Prices and Wages Adjust to Clear Markets

The classical economists argued that if the economy's aggregate demand for goods and services declined, flexible prices and wages would quickly adjust downward

[1]Initially put forth by the French economist Jean Baptiste Say (1767-1832).

until the total quantity of goods and services demanded was once again restored to the initial full-employment total output level. Let's briefly examine their argument.

A decline in the economy's aggregate demand is reflected in leftward shifts in the demand curves in each of the economy's many product markets. Product prices fall in response, and workers quickly and willingly accept lower wages in order to keep their jobs. This adjustment occurs in every product market in the economy so that each continues to produce and sell the same quantity of output and employ the same amount of labour as before the initial decrease in demand. Therefore the economy continues to produce the full-employment total output level that it did before the downward adjustment of all prices and wages.

Saving and the Income-Expenditure Flow

Our examination of the circular-flow diagrams of the economy in Chapter 5, and our discussion in Chapter 7 of how GDP may be viewed either from the expenditure side or the income side, both indicated that:

$$\left.\begin{array}{l}\text{total expenditure} \\ \text{on final goods} \\ \text{and services}\end{array}\right\} = \left\{\begin{array}{l}\text{total income from} \\ \text{the production and} \\ \text{sale of final output}\end{array}\right.$$

For the purpose of simplifying our discussion of this relationship, we will assume there is no government expenditure or taxation.

Consideration of the total-expenditure-equals-total-income relationship immediately suggests a possible problem for a believer in Say's Law. *While it is unde-niably true that every dollar of expenditure on goods and services creates a dollar of income, it does not follow that the person receiving the income necessarily spends all of it.* What happens when households save some of their income? As long as there is a saving leakage from total dollar income, won't total dollar expenditure and total dollar output and income continue to get smaller and smaller? The answer is yes. The continuing fall in total demand that results when households do not spend all their income means wages and prices would have to fall continually to maintain full employment — hardly a realistic state of affairs!

The Interest Rate Equates Saving and Investment

But classical economists had an answer to the problem posed by the saving leakage from the income-expenditure flow. *If that part of total income that is saved is just matched by an equivalent amount of investment expenditure by businesses,* then the leakage from the income-expenditure flow that results from saving is offset by the injection of investment into that flow.

But what assures that the amount of investment expenditures businesses intend to make will be equal to the amount of saving that households intend to do? Classical economists contended that in a capitalist economy the **interest rate** would always adjust — like the price in any other market — to ensure that total intended investment in the economy would equal total intended saving. If the interest rate is viewed as the price of borrowing, businesses will demand more borrowed funds for investment at low interest rates than at high rates. Therefore, the investment curve for the economy must slope downward (like any demand curve), as shown in Figure 8.1. Saving out of income involves a sacrifice by households — the forgone consumption they could have enjoyed. Therefore, it is necessary to pay households a higher interest rate to induce them to save more. Hence, the saving curve for the economy — the supply of dollars available to be loaned out of total income — is upward sloping (like any supply curve), as shown in Figure 8.1.

FIGURE 8.1
Classical Economists Argued That the Interest Rate Would Make Saving and Investment Equal

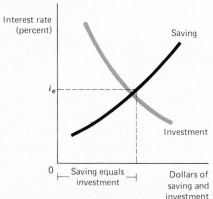

For businesses, the interest rate is the price of borrowing. Consequently, they will demand more borrowed funds for investment at low interest rates than at high rates. Thus the investment curve slopes downward.

Classical economists contended that saving out of income by households is a sacrifice in the form of forgone consumption. Therefore households can be induced to save more only by paying them a higher interest rate. Hence, the saving curve slopes upward.

The equilibrium interest rate, i_e, equates the quantity of dollars demanded for investment by businesses with the quantity of dollars households are willing to save. According to classical economists, this equality ensured that the economy would operate at full employment.

The intersection of the saving and investment curves in Figure 8.1 corresponds to the equilibrium level of the interest rate, i_e. As in any other market,

if the price (interest rate) is above this level, the supply of dollars to loan (saving) exceeds the demand for dollars to invest (investment) and price will be bid down to i_e. Similarly, if the price (interest rate) is below this level, demand exceeds supply, and price will be bid up to i_e. Because of the market adjustment of the interest rate, classical economists argued that the savings plans of households would always be equal to the investment plans of businesses.

Therefore, classical economists maintained that the economy would operate at its full-employment output level without the need for continually falling wages and prices. *Say's Law assumed that the unfettered forces of free markets and laissez faire capitalism would guarantee full employment with price stability. If there were disturbances that caused investment or saving curves to shift, or shifts in demand and supply curves in any other market, adjustments in wages, prices, and the interest rate would always return the economy to a position of full-employment equilibrium.*

The classical view of the economy can be represented in terms of the *aggregate demand (AD)* and *aggregate supply (AS)* curves (introduced in Chapter 5) shown in Figure 8.2. The aggregate supply curve AS is vertical at the full-employment total output level y_f (horizontal axis), reflecting the classical view that prices, wages, and the interest rate will always adjust quickly to any shift in aggregate demand to keep the economy operating at y_f. Suppose the AD curve is initially AD_1 so that the economy's price level is p_1, corresponding to the intersection of AD_1 and AS at e_1. If aggregate demand declines as represented by a leftward shift in the AD curve from AD_1 to AD_2, then the economy's price level (the average of all prices including wages) falls to P_2, corresponding to the intersection of AD_2 with AS at e_2. The equilibrium output level is still y_f.

AGGREGATE DEMAND AND EMPLOYMENT: THE INCOME-EXPENDITURE APPROACH

Classical economists had always acknowledged that capitalistic, market-oriented economies might experience occasional, temporary bouts of unemployment, possibly caused by rapid shifts in the composition of demand or by such things as wars and crop failures. But then came the 1930s. A prolonged depression — the Great Depression — gripped the capitalist, market-oriented economies of the world. The gap between classical theory and fact was now too great to ignore.

In Australia, the official rate of unemployment was almost 30 per cent in 1933. Between 1930 and 1937 it was never below 10 per cent. Over this same period money GDP declined dramatically and gross private capital spending fell by considerably more than 50 per cent.

The Keynesian Revolution

A group of Cambridge University economists led by John Maynard Keynes offered an explanation that went beyond the bounds of the classical framework and sparked what has come to be called the Keynesian revolution. In 1936 Keynes

FIGURE 8.2
Aggregate Demand and Supply in the Classical View

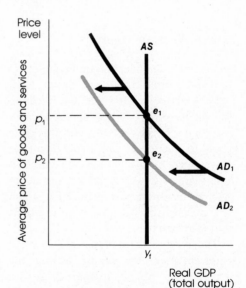

The aggregate supply curve AS in the classical view is vertical at the full-employment level of total output y_f because prices, wages, and the interest rate always adjust quickly to maintain full employment in response to any change in aggregate demand. For example, if the AD curve shifts leftward from AD_1 to AD_2 the economy's equilibrium price level would fall from p_1 to P_2 while total output would remain at y_f.

published his analysis — *The General Theory of Employment, Interest, and Money* — which argued that the inevitability of full-employment equilibrium was an unlikely proposition at best and simply wrong in general. Keynes argued that it is irrelevant whether complete wage and price flexibility would ensure full-employment if *in fact* wages and prices are slow to adjust in the real world. During the Great Depression economists noted that this was true in a number of markets and that wages were particularly slow to adjust downward. Keynes also argued that disposable income — not the interest rate — is the main determinant of saving. Given this, Keynes questioned the ability of the interest rate to equate saving and intended investment as required by Say's Law.

The Keynesian Analysis

In the classical model the equilibrium level of total output (constant dollar total income or real GDP) is determined on the supply side by virtue of Say's Law's assertion that the economy automatically tends to operate at full employment, as represented by the vertical AS curve at y_f in Figure 8.2. Aggregate demand serves only to determine the price level which is assumed to adjust quickly to any shift in the AD curve.

The Keynesian analysis switches the emphasis from the supply side to the demand side. *Keynesian analysis focuses on how the equilibrium level of total income, output, and employment is determined in an economy that operates at less than full employment and where the price level is not flexible.* The equilibrium level of total output and employment is completely determined by aggregate demand, as shown in Figure 8.3.

The aggregate supply curve AS is horizontal at the fixed (inflexible) price level p_0. If the AD curve is AD_1 then the equilibrium level of total output is y_1 (horizontal axis), corresponding to the intersection of AD_1 and AS at e_1, a level less than the full-employment output level y_f. Suppose aggregate demand falls as represented by a shift from AD_1 to AD_2. Now total output declines (but not the price level, as in the classical model) from y_1 to y_2 and the associated level of employment falls as well (it takes less labour to produce less output). In sum,

FIGURE 8.3
Aggregate Demand and Supply in the Keynesian Analysis

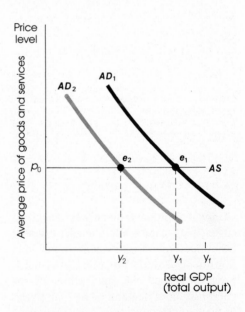

When the price level is not flexible the aggregate supply curve AS is horizontal at the fixed price level, indicated here as p_0 (vertical axis). Shifts in the aggregate demand curve, such as from AD_1 to AD_2, cause total output and employment to change. Total output, income, and employment are completely demand determined.

the level of total income, output, and employment vary directly with aggregate demand and are completely demand determined.

The Income-Expenditure Approach: Determining Aggregate Demand

The upshot of the Keynesian analysis is straightforward. In an economy that operates at less than full employment and where the price level is not flexible, an explanation of the determination of total output, income, and employment requires an explanation of the determination of aggregate demand — why is the AD curve where it is and why does it shift? An analysis known as the income-expenditure approach provides an answer to this question. It boils down to an explanation of the behaviour of the four main expenditure categories — consumption C, investment I, government G, and the net exports X — that constitute the expenditure side of GDP (discussed in the previous chapter), the left side of the relationship:

$$\left.\begin{array}{l}\text{total expenditure}\\ \text{on final goods}\\ \text{and services}\end{array}\right\} = \left\{\begin{array}{l}\text{total income from}\\ \text{the production and}\\ \text{sale of final output}\end{array}\right.$$

In the next section we will examine consumption and investment spending, two of the key components of total expenditure. Then we will see how consumption and investment combine to determine the equilibrium level of total income, output, and employment according to the income-expenditure approach, under the simplifying assumption that government spending and net exports are zero. Throughout our discussion it will be assumed that the price level is unchang-

ing. Ultimately we will want to examine what causes the price and output levels to change at the same time, a more complicated issue that will be taken up in Chapter 11 and subsequent chapters.

CHECKPOINT 8.2

How would you describe the way saving and investment plans were matched for Robinson Crusoe in his one-man island economy? Could he have an unemployment problem? How well would Say's Law describe the way his economy worked? What is it about modern industrialised economies, as compared to Robinson Crusoe's, that leads to difficulties for Say's Law?

THE CONSUMPTION AND SAVING FUNCTIONS

Consumption is the portion of their disposable income that households spend on goods and services. Personal saving is the remaining part, the portion of disposable income that households refrain from spending. Therefore, whatever explains consumption behaviour must also explain personal saving behaviour.

Consumption and Saving Depend on Income

Keynes contended that the single most important determinant of consumption expenditure and personal saving is the household's disposable income. Statistical studies tend to bear out that claim.

Using hypothetical data, Table 8.1 shows the total amount of consumption (column 2) that the economy's households would plan to do at different levels of

FIGURE 8.4
The Consumption Function and the Saving Function

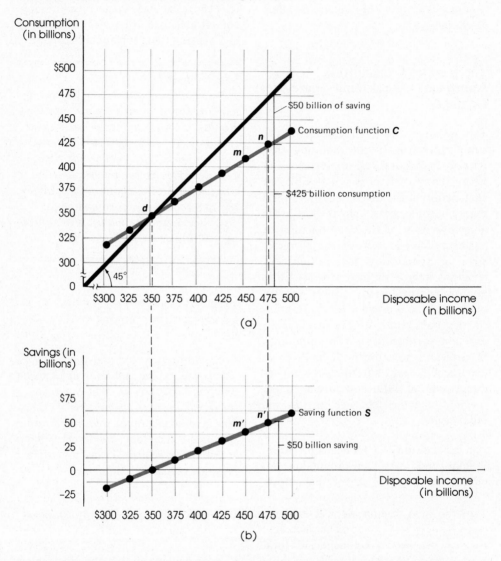

(a)

(b)

The consumption function *C* in part a is plotted from the data in columns 1 and 2 of Table 8.1. Note that as disposable income increases, consumption also increases, but by a smaller amount. Movement along the consumption function is caused by a change in disposable income, while all other things that affect consumption are assumed to remain unchanged.

The amount of saving at any disposable income level is represented by the vertical distance between the consumption function and the 45° line in part a. In other words, what households don't consume they save.

Using the data from columns 1 and 3 in Table 8.1, saving also may be plotted against disposable income (part b) to give the saving function *S*. The saving function slopes upward, reflecting the fact that the level of planned saving rises as disposable income rises.

disposable income (column 1). The difference between disposable income and consumption is the amount of saving (column 3). This is the amount that households refrain from spending at each level of disposable income. Note that as income increases so do both consumption and saving. All other factors that affect consumption are assumed to be given — that is, fixed and unchanging.

TABLE 8.1
The Consumption and Saving Schedules
(Hypothetical Data in Billions of Dollars)

(1)	(2)	(3)
Disposable Income (DI)	Consumption (C)	Saving (S)
		S=(1)-(2)
300	320	-20
325	335	-10
350	350	0
375	365	10
400	380	20
425	395	30
450	410	40
475	425	50
500	440	60

The Consumption Function: Graphical Representation

The income-consumption relationship may be represented graphically by measuring consumption expenditures on the vertical axis and disposable income on the horizontal axis. In Figure 8.4, part a, both axes are measured in the same units, billions of dollars. The consumption data from column 2 of Table 8.1 and the disposable income data from column 1 are plotted in Figure 8.4, part a, to give the consumption curve C. When actual levels of the economy's consumption expenditures are plotted against the associated levels of the economy's disposable income, economists have found a

relationship that looks very much like the consumption curve C shown in part a.

Note the 45° line that bisects the 90° angle formed by the horizontal and vertical axes of the diagram. Any point on the 45° line corresponds to the same dollar magnitude on either axis. This line serves as a very useful reference for interpreting the relationship between disposable income, consumption, and saving. At any given level of disposable income, the vertical distance between the corresponding point on the consumption curve C and the 45° line represents the amount of saving, or the amount of that disposable income households refrain from spending. For example, at a disposable income level of $475 billion (horizontal axis) the vertical distance to the corresponding point on the consumption curve (point n) measures the $425 billion of consumption spending (vertical axis) that takes place at that disposable income level. The vertical distance from that point on the consumption curve up to the 45° line measures the $50 billion of saving that takes place when disposable income is $475 billion.

At point d, where the consumption curve intersects the 45° line, the entire $350 billion of disposable income goes into consumption expenditure — saving is zero. At disposable income levels greater than $350 billion, saving is positive and is equal to the vertical distance between the 45° line and the consumption curve.

At disposable income levels less than $350 billion, the consumption curve lies above the 45° line and the economy's households spend more than the amount of disposable income. Households are able to spend more than disposable income either by drawing on wealth accumulated in the past or by borrowing. This amounts to negative saving, or what may be called dissaving.

The relationship between the level of disposable income and the level of consumption, represented by the consumption curve *C,* is called the **consumption function.** The term *function* is used here because the level of consumption expenditure is determined by (is a function of) the level of disposable income. *The consumption function shows that as disposable income increases, consumption also increases, but by a smaller amount. Movement along the consumption function is caused by a change in disposable income, while all other things that affect consumption are assumed to remain unchanged.*

The Saving Function: Graphical Representation

What households don't consume out of income they save. When income increases, consumption increases, by a smaller amount because part of any increase in income goes into saving. And saving obviously gets larger as income increases.

Another very useful representation of the relationship between disposable income and saving is shown in part b of Figure 8.4. The axes are drawn to exactly the same scale as those in part a of Figure 8.4, except that saving is measured on the vertical axis. The saving function *S* is plotted from the data in columns 1 and 3 of Table 8.1.

The vertical distance between the saving function and the horizontal axis represents the amount of saving that the economy's households would desire to do at each income level. At any given income level the vertical distance between the saving function and the horizontal axis in part b is the same as the vertical distance between the consumption function and the

45° line in part a. This correspondence is pointed out at the $475 billion disposable income level, for example, and is also obvious at the break-even point.

The **saving function** *shows the relationship between the economy's level of disposable income and the level of desired or planned saving. It slopes upward reflecting the fact that the level of planned saving rises as income rises.*

Movements Versus Shifts in Consumption and Saving

In Chapter 4 we discussed the difference between movement along a good's demand curve and shifts in the position of its demand curve. A similar distinction must be made between movement along a consumption function or a saving function and shifts in these functions.

Movements Along the Consumption and Saving Functions

Movement along a consumption function can only be caused by a change in disposable income, all other things affecting consumption assumed to be unchanged. Of course, for any movement along a consumption function, there is a corresponding movement along the associated saving function. For example, in Figure 8.4, part a, if disposable income rises from $450 to $475 billion, there is a movement along the consumption function from point *m* to point *n* and a corresponding movement along the saving function in Figure 8.4, part b, from point *m'* to point *n'*.

Shifts in the Consumption and Saving Functions

When any of the other things (besides

disposable income) that affect consumption changes, there is a shift in the consumption and saving functions. For example, suppose the consumption function is initially in the position C_0, as shown in part a of Figure 8.5. The associated saving function is S_0, as shown in part b. If the consumption function shifts downward from C_0 to C_1, the saving function then shifts upward from S_0 to S_1. At any given disposable income level, households now consume less and save more. On the other hand, if the consumption function shifts upward from C_0 to C_2, the saving function then shifts downward from S_0 to S_2. In this case households now consume more and save less at any given disposable income level.

Other Determinants of Consumption and Saving

What are the 'other things' that can change and thereby cause shifts in the consumption and saving functions? Some are the following.

1. Credit conditions

The easier it is for consumers to obtain credit and the lower the interest rate they pay for it, the more likely they are to borrow from banks and other financial institutions to buy cars, household appliances, and other goods on credit. This would tend to shift the consumption function upward and the saving function downward. Tougher credit conditions and a higher interest rate have the opposite effect.

2. Wealth

The size and composition of the stocks of assets (bank accounts, cash, bonds, stocks, houses, etc.) owned by consumers is an important determinant of consumer spending. Disposable income is not the only source of funds consumers have. Consumption spending can also be financed by withdrawals from bank accounts or by cashing in other forms of wealth. An increase in wealth would tend to shift the consumption function upward and the saving function downward — a decrease would have the opposite effect.

3. Expectations about employment, prices, and income

Consumer expectations about the course of the economy play a crucial role in their willingness to spend. For example, if consumers begin to expect lower levels of employment and income, they might try to save more for possible rainy days ahead. The result would be a downward shift in the consumption function and an upward shift in the saving function. Changes in expectations about inflation also affect consumption and saving, but the direction of the shift is not as clear.

CHECKPOINT 8.3

Suppose a news item reports that 'most forecasters still look for somewhat lower interest rates and expect consumer outlays to remain strong'. If the forecasters are right, how will the consumption function shift and why? How will the saving function shift?

INVESTMENT AND ITS DETERMINANTS

Of the three major categories on the expenditure side of GDP — consumption, investment, and government — invest-

FIGURE 8.5
The Consumption and Saving Functions Shift When the 'Other Things' Change

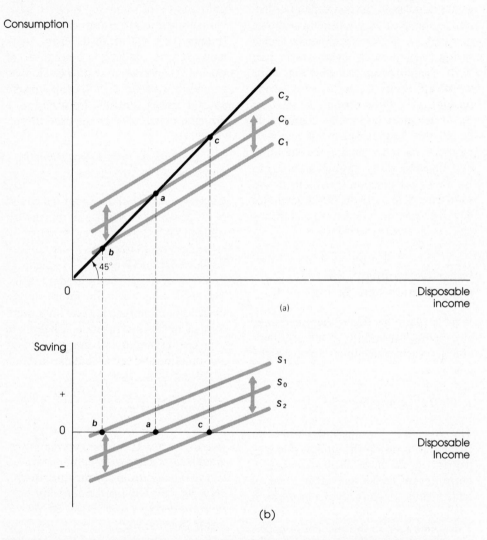

(a)

(b)

Movement along the consumption function or the saving function is due to changes in disposable income. All other things that affect consumption are assumed to be unchanged. When any of these other things change, they cause a shift in the consumption and saving functions.

Suppose the consumption function is initially C_0 (part a) and the associated saving function is S_0 (part b). If the consumption function shifts downward from C_0 to C_1, the saving function then shifts upward from S_0 to S_1. At any given income level, households now consume less and save more. Similarly, if the consumption function shifts upward from C_0 to C_2, the saving function then shifts downward from S_0 to S_2. Households consume more and save less at any given disposable income level.

ment expenditures vary the most. This is evident from the graphic representation of these three categories for the Australian economy in Figure 8.6 between 1972 and 1987. As long as members of households are employed and have a steady source of income, consumption varies very little, growing rather steadily through time with the growth of the economy. Government expenditure, while not quite as steady as consumption, has certainly been less variable than investment. What are the main determinants of investment expenditure, and what accounts for its variable behaviour?

Investment and Profit

If businesses anticipate that revenue from the sale of goods and services produced with the aid of capital goods will more than cover all costs of production, so that

---

FIGURE 8.6
Investment Varies More than Consumption and Government Expenditures

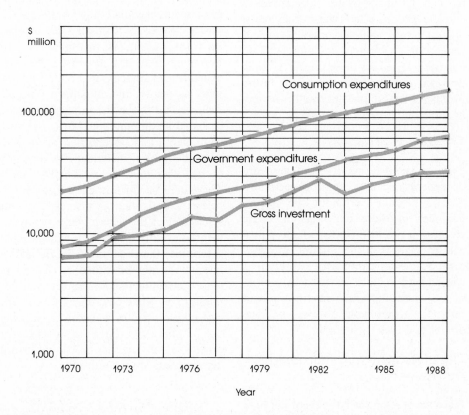

Shown here are consumption, gross investment and government expenditures over the 1972–1987 period. (Note that the vertical axis is a logarithmic, or ratio, scale on which equal distances represent equal percentage changes.) Investment expenditures have been the most variable of these major components of the expenditure side of GDP during this period.

there is a profit, they will invest in the capital goods. Otherwise they won't. A major underlying reason why investment is so variable (as illustrated in Figure 8.6) is the fact that the decision whether or not to invest in capital goods depends on business expectations about future profits.

Forecasting Future Profit

Put yourself in the shoes of an investment decision maker. In order to forecast prospective profits in any meaningful way, you have to forecast the magnitudes of all of the ingredients that will enter into the calculation of profit: sales revenues and the level of costs (wage rates, rents, interest rates, materials prices, land and water rates, various taxes and tax rate changes). Based on these forecasts, come up with your 'best' forecast of the future profits (or losses) likely to result from any investment currently undertaken.

Changing Expectations

Quite obviously profit forecasts are dependent on the current expectations held by businesses about the future. Changes in these expectations cause changes in profit forecasts, which in turn lead to changes in the amount of investment businesses want to do. Expectations can be very volatile, buffeted by continually changing information about markets, government policies, political events, and even the weather.

The Investment Schedule and Its Determinants

When we develop the basic theory of how the economy's level of total income and employment are determined according to the income-expenditure approach, we will need to add the consumption plans of households to the investment plans of businesses to get the economy's total intended or planned expenditure on goods and services. In order to do this we will need to relate the level of businesses' investment spending plans to income, just as consumption spending plans are related to income by the consumption function. To simplify the ensuing discussion we will assume government taxes are zero and make no distinction between GDP, DFI, NI, NDI, HI, HDI and NDP because we will ignore all those things that differentiate these measures from one another.

The relationship between income and planned investment is represented by the investment schedule I shown in Figure 8.7, part a. The economy's total dollar income, or total output, is measured on the horizontal axis, and its gross investment expenditures are measured on the vertical axis. As drawn, the investment schedule I shows that businesses in aggregate plan to spend an amount equal to I_0 on plant, equipment, and inventories no matter what the level of income in the economy — *all other things remaining the same.* Therefore, the investment schedule I is perfectly horizontal at the level I_0. Our discussion of the determinants of investment, the 'other things', will indicate what determines the position of the I schedule and how it may be shifted by changes in these determinants. Remember that the question of what determines investment expenditure in our economy is basically one of what determines the prospects for profit. Some of the more important determinants are the following.

1. Variation in Total Income

It seems reasonable to believe that the higher the level of current economic activity as measured by the level of total income, the more optimistic businesses will be about prospects for future profits. This optimism may well encourage them to invest more at higher income levels. If so, the investment schedule *I* may slope upward as shown in Figure 8.7, part b.

2. *The Interest Rate*

The funds that businesses use to make investment expenditures on capital goods either must be borrowed from outside the firm or must be generated internally in the form of the firm's business saving (also called retained earnings). If they are borrowed from outside the firm, the cost of borrowing is the interest rate that must be paid to the lender. If they are generated internally, the cost to the firm is the forgone interest the firm could have earned if it had lent the funds to someone else. In either case the interest rate is the cost of the funds invested in capital goods. The higher the interest rate, the more this cost cuts into profit and reduces the incentive to invest in capital goods. Conversely, the lower the interest rate, the larger the profit and the greater the incentive to make investment expenditures.

Since the interest rate is among the 'other things' assumed unchanged for any *movement along* the investment schedule, a change in the interest rate will cause the *I* schedule to shift, as shown in Figure 8.8. In sum, *increases in the interest rate shift the investment schedule downward and decreases in the interest rate shift it upward.*

3. *Technological Change and New Products*

Technological change often makes existing capital equipment obsolete. Firms that

fail to invest in capital goods that feature the latest technological breakthrough will find themselves at a competitive disadvantage relative to those that do. Those that acquire the latest capital first will get a competitive jump on rivals. Given these

FIGURE 8.7
The Investment Schedule

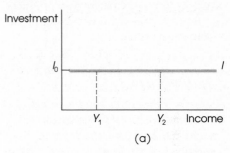

(a)

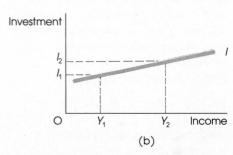

(b)

In these diagrams the amount of investment expenditure in the economy is measured on the vertical axis and the economy's total income on the horizontal axis. The investment schedule *I* shows the total amount of investment businesses desire to make at each level of the economy's total income, all other things remaining the same.

The investment schedule in part a is perfectly horizontal. This means that desired investment expenditure in the economy equals I_0 no matter what the level of total income.

The investment schedule in part b slopes upward on the assumption that businesses will be more optimistic about profit prospects the higher is the current level of economic activity as measured by total income. Therefore, desired investment will be larger at higher income levels. For example, desired investment will equal I_1 at income level Y_1, and the larger amount I_2 at the higher income level Y_2.

carrot-and-stick incentives, technological change often results in an upward shift in the investment schedule, such as from I_0 to I_2 in figure 8.8.

The development of new products opens up new markets. Lured by the resulting profit opportunities, firms will want to invest in the capital goods necessary to produce these new products. This too will cause an upward shift in the investment schedule.

CHECKPOINT 8.4

How would an increase in the prices of new capital goods affect the investment schedule? How do you think the investment schedule would be affected if trade unions and management in major industries throughout the country successfully negotiated new wage contracts without resorting to strikes?

FIGURE 8.8
Shifts in the Investment Schedule

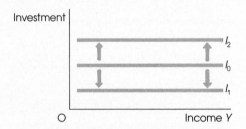

The Investment schedule shows the total amount of investment businesses desire to do at each level of income, all other things that affect Investment remaining the same. If one or more of these other things should change, it will cause the investment schedule to shift, either upward from I_0 to a position such as I_2, or downward to a position such as I_1. Among the other things that can cause such shifts are changes in the interest rate, technology, expectations about prospective profits, and the development of new products.

TOTAL EXPENDITURE AND TOTAL INCOME: DETERMINING EQUILIBRIUM

Now we will see how the consumption function and the investment schedule combine to determine the economy's equilibrium level of total income, output, and employment. We will continue to make no distinction between NI, NDI, HI and HDI because we assume there is no government expenditure or taxation, that all saving is personal saving, and that capital depreciation is zero. We also continue to assume that net exports are zero and that the price level is fixed.

*The **equilibrium income level** is the one income level, among all possible income levels, at which the dollar value of the economy's total expenditure on output is just equal to the dollar value of total output that the firms in the economy produce. The equilibrium income level is also the level of total income that will be sustained once it is achieved.* Let's see how the equilibrium income level is determined.

Total Expenditure Equals Consumption Plus Intended Investment

We have examined how the level of consumption expenditure and intended investment expenditure can be shown in a graph with the income level measured on the horizontal axis and desired consumption expenditures (Figure 8.4, part a) or intended investment expenditures (Figure 8.7) measured on the vertical axis. We may now combine these two components to form the economy's total spending or *total expenditure schedule.* We assume that the only components of total expenditure are consumption and investment.[2]

The hypothetical example of Table 8.2, which is shown graphically in Figure 8.9, shows how this is done. At each level of total income, column 1 of Table 8.2, the economy's households wish to spend an amount given by the associated level of consumption expenditures *C* shown in column 2. Column 3 of Table 8.2 shows the level of intended or planned investment expenditures *I* for the entire economy associated with each level of total income in column 1. Our example assumes that the amount of intended investment is the same ($30 billion) no matter what the level of total income. (This pattern of investment could be represented by a horizontal investment schedule like that shown in Figure 8.7, part a.) The total expenditure level, column 4 of Table 8.2, is obtained by adding the level of consumption expenditures (column 2) to

[2] Government expenditures will be introduced in Chapter 10 and net exports will be ignored until we discuss international trade in a later chapter.

the intended investment expenditures (column 3). It is represented in Figure 8.9 as the economy's *total expenditure schedule E.*

The economy's total expenditure schedule represents the amount of total spending on final goods and services that the economy's households and businesses desire to do at each possible level of total income.

Total Income Equals Expected Total Spending

Total income is the sum of all payments received by the suppliers of all productive factors — land, labour, capital, and all other inputs — used in the production of the economy's total output. Therefore total income is the dollar value of this total output. The economy's firms produce this total output because they *expect* to sell it. That is, the dollar value of this total output (which equals total income) equals the level of *expected total spending* on final goods and services — the level of total *sales expected by the economy's businesses* which they therefore produce to meet.

TABLE 8.2
Total Expenditure Equals Consumption Plus Intended Investment (Hypothetical Data in Billions of Dollars)

(1)	(2)		(3)		(4)
Total Income	Consumption Expenditure (C)		Intended Investment (I)		Total Expenditure (E)
					E = (2) + (3)
$ 200	$ 300	+	$300	=	$ 600
400	400	+	300	=	700
600	500	+	300	=	800
800	600	+	300	=	900
1,000	700	+	300	=	1,000
1,200	800	+	300	=	1,100
1,400	900	+	300	=	1,200
1,600	1,000	+	300	=	1,300
1,800	1,100	+	300	=	1,400

This concept is also represented graphically in Figure 8.9. Expected total spending is measured on the vertical axis and total income on the horizontal axis. Since total income (horizontal axis) is always equal to expected total spending (vertical axis), this relationship may be represented by the already familiar 45° line. Why? Because any point on this line corresponds to a dollar magnitude on either axis that is exactly equal to the corresponding dollar magnitude on the other axis.

For example, suppose the economy's business firms expect total spending to be $100 billion (vertical axis), which corresponds to point e on the 45° line. They will then proceed to produce $100 billion of total output, an amount just sufficient to satisfy expected total spending. Since this $100 billion is the total of all payments for the factors used to produce the total

FIGURE 8.9
Determining the Equilibrium Level of Total Income

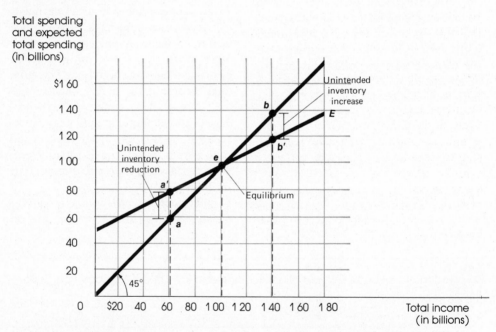

The economy's total expenditure schedule E combines with the 45° line to determine the equilibrium level of total income, which equals $100 billion, corresponding to the intersection at point e. This level of total income gives rise to a level of total spending that just buys up the total output the economy's businesses produce. Thus, there are no changes in inventories.

At total income levels lower than the equilibrium level, total expenditure is greater than total output. Therefore, unintended inventory reduction is necessary in order to satisfy the excess of total spending over total output. This will lead the economy's businesses to increase total output, causing total income to rise toward the equilibrium level.

At total income levels greater than the equilibrium level, total expenditure is less than total output. There are unintended inventory increases equal to the excess of total output over total spending. Therefore, the economy's businesses will decrease total output, causing total income to fall toward the equilibrium level.

The data on which Figure 8.9 is based are shown in Table 8.3.

output, it is the level of total income in the economy. Measured on the horizontal axis, a total income level of $100 billion also corresponds to point e on the 45° line.

Determining the Equilibrium Level of Total Income

We can now see how the economy's equilibrium level of total income is determined. This is the level of total income that will be sustained once it is achieved. To do this we combine the economy's total expenditure schedule E with the 45° line that represents the relationship between expected total spending and total income. This combination in Figure 8.9 is based on the hypothetical data of Table 8.3. First we will consider two possible nonequilibrium levels of total income. It will then be readily apparent why the equilibrium level of total income occurs where the total expenditure schedule E intersects the 45° line at point e.

Unintended Inventory Reduction

Let us suppose that the economy's business firms *expect* total spending (vertical axis) to be $60 billion. This corresponds to point a on the 45° line of Figure 8.9. Acting on the basis of this expectation, they produce $60 billion worth of total output. Since this represents $60 billion of payments to all the factors used to produce this total output, the economy's total income level (horizontal axis) is $60 billion, which also corresponds to point a on the 45° line. However, with a total income level of $60 billion, the *actual* level of total spending in the economy will turn out to be $80 billion,

corresponding to point a' on the economy's total expenditure schedule E. But the economy only produced $60 billion worth of total output during the period. Consequently, the only way the total spending of $80 billion can be satisfied is for businesses to sell $20 billion of goods from inventories, stocks of goods produced and accumulated during *past* periods. The amount of this *unintended inventory reduction* is represented by the vertical distance between point a' on the economy's total expenditure schedule E and point a on the 45° line. It is *unintended* because the economy's business firms underestimated what the level of total spending in the economy was going to be.

The fact that the economy's business firms have to sell from inventories tells them that they underestimated total spending. If they were to continue doing this, unintended inventory reduction would also continue. Eventually, perhaps quickly, this would cause them to revise their expectations of total spending upward. The dollar value of total output produced, and hence the level of the economy's total income, would rise accordingly. This adjustment process will continue as long as there is any unintended reduction of inventories.

When and where will the adjustment stop? When unintended inventory reduction ceases — at the income level at which the level of total spending is just equal to that expected. In Figure 8.9 this occurs at a total income of $100 billion, corresponding to the intersection of the total expenditure schedule E with the 45° line at point e. It is therefore the equilibrium level of total income.

Starting from any level of expected total spending — and hence total income — less than $100 billion, total income will tend to rise until the equilibrium level is reached and there is no longer any unintended reduction of inventories. This is illustrated in Table 8.3. You should check the numbers shown there and relate them to Figure 8.9.

Unintended Inventory Increase

Consider what happens at total income levels greater than the equilibrium level. Suppose the economy's business firms expect total spending (vertical axis) to be $140 billion, corresponding to point *b* on the 45° line in Figure 8.9. Therefore, they produce that amount of total output and the economy's total income (horizontal axis) is $140 billion. But at that total income level, actual total spending (vertical axis) will turn out to be only $120 billion, point *b'* on the economy's total expenditure schedule *E*. This means that $20 billion of the economy's total output will go unsold and therefore end up as an unintended inventory increase. This increase is represented by the vertical distance between points *b* and *b'* in Figure 8.9.

The $140 billion level of total income will not be sustained. Why? Business firms will not go on producing more output than they can sell, thereby increasing their

unsold inventory. Instead, they will revise their expectations of total spending downward and produce less. As a result, total income will fall to the equilibrium total income level of $100 billion, which corresponds to the intersection of the economy's total expenditure schedule *E* and the 45° line at point *e* in Figure 8.9. We can now see that, starting from any level of total income greater than the equilibrium level, total income will tend to fall to the equilibrium level. Again this is illustrated in Table 8.3. You should check the numbers in this table and relate them to Figure 8.9.

In sum, *the economy's equilibrium level of total income gives rise to a level of total spending that just purchases the total output that the economy's businesses desire to produce. In equilibrium there is no change in inventories because total spending just matches the dollar value of total output.*

Equilibrium Without Full Employment

Recall that we are assuming the economy's price level is fixed. Therefore if total spending and total income change, the entire change is due to a change in the

TABLE 8.3
How the Economy's Equilibrium Total Income Level Is Determined (Hypothetical Data in Billions of Dollars)

(1)	(2)	(3)	(4)	(5)
Expected Total Spending	Total Income	Total Expenditure (*E*)	Change in Inventories	Total Income Will Tend to
$ 20	$ 20	$ 60	$-40	rise
40	40	70	-30	rise
60	60	80	-20	rise
80	80	90	-10	rise
100	100	100	0	equilibrium
120	120	110	+10	fall
140	140	120	+20	fall
160	160	130	+30	fall
180	180	140	+40	fall

number of actual physical units of output produced by the economy. And this requires a change in the amount of labour used in production. Consequently, every level of total income on the horizontal axis of Figure 8.9 corresponds to a different level of total employment.

These considerations suggest that *a major implication of the income-expenditure approach is that the level of employment associated with the equilibrium level of total income need not correspond to full employment, and typically will not.* For example, suppose that the labour force will be fully employed only when the economy produces the level of total output associated with a total income level equal to $140 billion. However, we have already seen that if the economy's total expenditure schedule is *E* (Figure 8.9), total spending is not sufficient to sustain this level of total income. Consequently, some of the labour force will be unemployed. In general, the lower the equilibrium level of total income, the higher the unemployment rate.

SUMMARY

1. Classical economists argued that a capitalistic, laissez faire economy would automatically tend to operate at a full-employment equilibrium. This contention was based on Say's Law, which states that supply creates its own demand.

2. The classical argument held that if wages and prices were perfectly flexible, a drop in total demand would result in a downward adjustment in wages and prices sufficient to reestablish a full-employment level of total output. In addition, the leakage from the income-expenditure flow due to saving would create no problem because the interest rate

would adjust to ensure that saving plans always equalled investment plans.

3. The Depression of the 1930s led to a critical reexamination of the classical position. It became obvious that in a number of markets, prices and particularly wages were sticky, or slow to adjust downward. The notion that saving and investment plans could be equated by interest rate adjustments alone was brought into question.

4. The Keynesian revolution led to the development of income-expenditure theory and its basic building blocks — the consumption function, the saving function, and the investment schedule. The consumption function shows the amount households want to consume (spend) and the saving function the amount they want to save (not spend) at each disposable income level. The investment schedule shows the amount businesses want to invest at each income level.

5. Movements along the consumption and saving functions are caused by changes in disposable income, all other things that influence consumption and saving remaining the same. Changes in one or more of the other things will cause shifts in the consumption and saving functions. Important among these other things are credit conditions, consumer wealth, and consumer expectations about unemployment, prices, and income.

6. Investment expenditures are more variable than the other two major components of the expenditure side of GDP, consumption and government expenditures. The expectation of profit is what determines the level of desired investment expenditure. The variability of investment expenditure results from the difficulty and complexity of forecasting prospective

---

POLICY PERSPECTIVE

The Great Depression — Attempts to Explain a Paradox

One of the most frightening things about the Great Depression is that no one, especially economists, seemed to have an adequate explanation that might suggest a policy for dealing with it.

In almost any city, long lines of unemployed workers could be seen seeking a free meal or some sort of assistance for their impoverished families. Somehow it all seemed a paradox. Why was it that able-bodied workers, who wanted nothing so much as a job in order to buy badly needed food and other goods, could not find work producing these products? Wouldn't the income they earned give rise to the demand that would justify the production that would give them employment? Couldn't failing businesses see the connection between the lack of customers at the front door and the long line of unemployed workers seeking jobs at the back door? How could this situation go on for so long? These riddles led to a growing fear. Had Karl Marx been right all along — would capitalism fall by its own weight? What was the matter?

Wage and Price Flexibility

Many economists of the day, schooled in the classical tradition, argued that the problem lay in a number of markets where wages and prices were 'sticky'. They contended that in some product markets large monopoly-type firms were not willing to lower product prices as rapidly as was necessary in the face of declining product demand. Similarly, they argued that many unemployed workers were too reluctant to accept lower, or low enough, wages to gain employment. Hence, these economists concluded that classical wage and price flexibility was not allowed to work to bring the economy back to a full-employment equilibrium. Even though wages and prices did fall during the Great Depression, see Figure P8.1 showing movements in prices, they contended that the decline was not far enough or fast enough. However the evidence in Figure P8.1 certainly provides room for debate on this issue. Some of these same economists, and others as well, also argued that government interference in banking and financial markets was keeping the interest rate from adjusting properly to equate saving and investment plans.

Can the Interest Rate Match Saving and Investment Plans?

Perhaps the weakest link in the classical argument was the idea that interest rate adjustment would ensure the equality of saving and investment plans.

Many Things Affect Saving

The classical economists' argument that households are induced to save more at high interest rates than at low rates raises some questions. Even if the assertion is true, it may take large changes in interest rates to really affect the level of saving much at all, other things remaining the same. Indeed, many of the 'other things' may be much more important determinants of saving plans than the interest rate is.

For example, much household saving is directed toward accumulating the funds needed to make some future purchase — a house, an automobile, a college education, a vacation, and so forth. Saving may also be aimed at providing a 'nest egg' for unforeseen emergencies such as job loss, illness, or simply a general sense of security. Saving can also provide for retirement years. Some people may simply want to accumulate enough wealth to be able to live off the interest it can earn. The last motive has an interesting implication. The higher the interest rate, the less wealth it takes to earn a given level of income. If the interest rate is 5 per cent, it takes $10,000 to earn $500 per year. At an interest rate of 10 per cent, it takes half that amount, or $5,000, to earn $500 per year. Therefore, if people save in order to accumulate just enough wealth to be able to earn a certain income level from it, the higher the interest rate the less will be the amount of saving necessary to achieve their goal. Of course, this

FIGURE P8.1
Price Levels in Australia During the Great Depression

Level of
Price Index

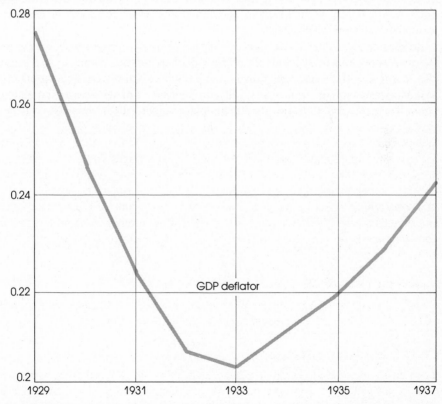

Source: N.G. Butlin *Australian National Accounts 1788-1983*

is just the opposite of the classical proposition that saving will increase when the interest rate increases.

Investment — How Important Is the Interest Rate?

During the Great Depression capital consumption, or depreciation of the economy's capital stock, was actually larger than the amount of gross investment in some years. In other words, net investment was negative. Many economists question whether interest rates lower than those that actually prevailed would have substantially increased investment expenditures in those years. A host of other factors are generally considered to be more important determinants of the level of investment.

For example, our discussion of the accelerator principle in the appendix of Chapter 6 indicated that the behaviour of retail or final sales is extremely important. Since total income is just the receipts from total sales of the economy's total output of final goods and services, the accelerator principle suggests that the economy's total investment will be strongly affected by the behaviour of total income. The fact that money GDP in Australia fell more than a quarter between 1929 and 1932 would seem to have some bearing on the fact that gross investment fell by over 50 per cent during this same period of time. No matter how low the rate of interest, dramatically falling sales would hardly seem likely to encourage businesses to invest in new plant and equipment or more inventories.

Regarding the interest rate, Keynes argued that there might well be a lower limit (above zero) to how far it could fall. Without getting into the complexity of his argument, this meant that the interest rate might not be able to fall low enough to match saving and investment plans and ensure full employment. Keynes also noted that even if the interest rate fell to zero, investment plans might still be less than saving plans,

---

FIGURE P8.2
Even at a Zero Interest Rate Saving May Not Equal Investment

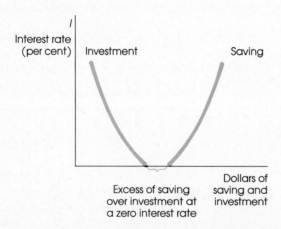

Here intended saving, represented by the saving curve, exceeds intended investment, represented by the investment curve, even when the interest rate is zero.

as shown in Figure P8.2. The leakage from saving would then lead to a continuing fall in aggregate demand for goods and services.

Questions

1. Could you envision the paradox described here occurring in Robinson Crusoe's world (one person living alone on an island)? Why or why not?

2. How might a decline in the total income level affect the saving curve S in Figure P8.2?

profits combined with the sensitivity of expectations to changes in the economic environment.

7. The investment schedule represents the relationships between the level of planned investment and the level of total income. Several important determinants of profit prospects that can cause shifts in the investment schedule are interest rate changes, technological change, and the development of new products.

8. According to the income-expenditure approach the equilibrium level of total income, output, and employment occurs where the total expenditure schedule intersects the 45° line. At equilibrium the total income earned from production of the economy's total output corresponds to a level of total spending just sufficient to purchase that total output.

9. At levels of total income less than the equilibrium level, total spending is greater than total output and there is unintended inventory reduction. This leads the economy's business firms to increase total output, so that total income and employment rise toward the equilibrium level. At levels of total income greater than the equilibrium level, total spending is less than total output and there are unintended increases in inventories. The economy's business firms then reduce total output, so that total income and employment tend to fall toward the equilibrium level.

CHECKPOINT 8.5

Give the explanation of what happens in the economy starting at any level of expected total spending and proceeding from column 1 to 2 to 3 to 4 to 5 in Table 8.3.

KEY TERMS AND CONCEPTS

consumption function
equilibrium income level
interest rate
saving function
Say's Law

QUESTIONS AND PROBLEMS

1. According to Say's Law, supply creates demand. Why couldn't this law be stated the other way around, namely, that demand creates supply?

2. Suppose you were a completely self-sufficient farmer and hunter living in the wilderness. What would be the relationship between your saving and investment decisions? What would be the significance of the notion of involuntary unemployment?

3. Explain why wage and price flexibility are not sufficient to restore a full-employment equilibrium subsequent to a fall in total demand.

4. Using a diagram like Figure 8.1, illustrate what would happen if there were no positive level of the interest rate that would equate saving and investment plans. Describe what would be happening in the economy in this situation.

5. How do you think the following would affect the consumption and saving functions and why?

a. Employer-subsidised superannuation schemes for employees are set up throughout the economy.

b. There is a decline in the stock market.

c. The government announces that petrol will be rationed to consumers starting 3 months from now.

d. Households anticipate that the rate of inflation is going to rise from 5 per cent per year to 15 per cent per year during the next 6 months.

e. Households begin to doubt the future of the old age pension, causing concern about the level of future payments which the government will be able to make to them.

6. What do you think would be the effect on prospective profit of each of the following and how would the investment schedule shift as a result?

a. Unions demand that employers make larger contributions to employee superannuation schemes.

b. New sources of natural gas are discovered.

c. Federal Parliament passes a law allowing larger tax write-offs for research and development costs.

d. Federal Parliament passes a law outlining stiffer controls on industrial disposal waste.

e. War breaks out in the Middle East, threatening the destruction of oil fields in the area.

f. The Prime Minister calls for price ceilings on final products and an increase in income taxes.

7. Compare and contrast the way businesses decide to invest with the way households decide how much to consume, and explain why investment is more variable than consumption.

8. How do you think the position of the total expenditure schedule E in Figure 8.9 would be affected by each of the following?

a. a decline in the expected profitability of business;

b. a rise in the interest rate;

c. an increase in the wealth of households;

d. an increase in consumer indebtedness.

9. Why does total income equal expected total spending? In what sense are inventories a buffer against mistakes in forecasting?

10. In Table 8.3, suppose the economy's level of total expenditure (column 3) is higher by $10 billion at every level of total income (column 2). What would be the new equilibrium level of total income, and how would columns 4 and 5 be changed? Can you sketch this change in Figure 8.9?

11. Why is it that the unintended inventory increase represented by the vertical distance between b and b' in Figure 8.9 is included in total income, while the unintended inventory reduction equal to the vertical distance between a' and a is not?

9

Total Expenditure and the Multiplier in Income Determination

AFTER READING THIS CHAPTER YOU WILL BE ABLE TO:

1. Distinguish between realised and intended investment and explain their relationship to saving and equilibrium.

2. Describe and explain the paradox of thrift.

3. Define and explain the marginal and average propensities to consume and to save.

4. Define the multiplier and illustrate why autonomous changes in the components of total expenditure have multiplier effects.

In this chapter we will examine more closely the Keynesian view of how the economy's equilibrium level of total income, output, and employment is determined. First, we will focus on the relationship between investment and saving in the determination of equilibrium. Then we will examine the so-called paradox of thrift. Finally we will define and explain the marginal propensity to consume and the marginal propensity to save. We will use these concepts to explain the important Keynesian concept of the multiplier, which tells us how total income will change in response to a change in total expenditure.

We will continue to make no distinction between GDP, NDP, NI, HI and DI because for the time being, we will assume there is no government expenditure or taxation, that all saving is personal saving, and that capital depreciation is zero. We also continue to assume that net exports are zero. Throughout this chapter we will also assume that wages and prices are unchanging, an assumption that simplifies the analysis without interfering with the learning objectives in any way. The concepts developed in this chapter will prove very useful to us in the next chapter, where we introduce government expenditure and taxation into this framework.

EQUILIBRIUM AND REALISED VERSUS INTENDED INVESTMENT

So far, our discussion of how the equilibrium level of total income is determined has focused on the total expenditure schedule E and its relationship to the 45° line. Now let's look at this relationship more closely. First, we will explicitly recognise that the total expenditure

schedule E is equal to the sum of consumption and the level of intended or desired investment, as was shown in Table 8.2. Then we will explicitly recognise the relationship between total income and consumption (the consumption function) and total income and saving (the saving function). These relationships were shown in Figure 8.4 of Chapter 8.

Continuing with our hypothetical example, the data from Tables 8.2 and 8.3 are shown again in columns 1, 2, 4, 5, and 6 of Table 9.1. Also shown is the level of saving (column 3), which is equal to the difference between total income and consumption (column 1 minus column 2). Realised investment, which is equal to the sum of columns 4 and 6, is shown in column 7. These relationships are shown in Figure 9.1, part a, which is the same as Figure 8.9 except that the consumption function has been added. This function is the level of consumption expenditure C (column 2) associated with each level of total income (column 1). We will use Figure 9.1 to help us define the concept of realised investment and its relationship to intended investment. We will then examine the relationship between these two types of investment and saving, both when the economy is at its equilibrium income level and when it is not.

Realised Investment Always Equals Saving

In Chapter 7 gross private investment was defined as including all final purchases of new tools and machines by business firms, all construction expenditures, *and all changes in inventories*.

At Total Income Levels Below Equilibrium Level

We have seen that when the economy is

at a below-equilibrium level of total income, there is an unintended inventory change. This change is an inventory reduction, which is represented by the vertical distance between the total expenditure schedule E and the 45° line. For example, when total income is $60 billion (Figure 9.1, part a), there is an unintended inventory reduction of $20 billion, which is represented by the vertical distance between a' and a. The amount of intended investment, or the investment that business firms *desire* to do, is $30 billion, which is represented by the vertical distance a' to a'' between the total expenditure schedule E and the consumption function C. However, this $30 billion investment expenditure, when combined with the $50 billion of consumption expenditure (a sum equal to $80 billion), exceeds the $60 billion of total output produced during the period, correspond-

ing to point a on the 45° line, by $20 billion. Hence, $20 billion of goods has to be sold from inventory to satisfy this excess of total spending over total production. The $20 billion decrease, or *negative change,* in inventories is an offset to the $30 billion of intended investment. It is often called a disinvestment. Actual investment, or **realised investment,** therefore amounts to only $10 billion, which is represented by the vertical distance between point a on the 45° line and point a'' on the consumption function C.

Note that this vertical distance between point a on the 45° line and point a″ on the consumption function also represents the amount of saving that households do out of the $60 billion total income. Therefore, it follows that *realised investment is equal to saving.* At any total income level less than the equilibrium level of total income (which is equal to $100

TABLE 9.1
Determination of the Equilibrium Level of Total Income, and the Relationship Between Intended Investment, Realised Investment, and Saving (Hypothetical Data in Billions of Dollars)

(1)	(2)	(3)	(4)	(5)	(6)	(7)
Total Income and Output	Con-sumption Expenditure (C)	Saving (S)	Intended Investment (I)	Total Expenditure (E) or Total Spending	Unintended Inventory Change Equals Total Output Minus Total Expenditure	Realised Investment Equals Intended Investment Plus Unintended Inventory Change
		S = (1) − (2)		E = (2) + (4)	(1) − (5)	(4) + (6)
$ 20	$ 30	$-10	$30	$ 60	$-40	$-10
40	40	0	30	70	-30	0
60	50	10	30	80	-20	10
80	60	20	30	90	-10	20
100	70	30	30	100	0	30
120	80	40	30	110	10	40
140	90	50	30	120	20	50
160	100	60	30	130	30	60
180	110	70	30	140	40	70

billion in our example), intended invest-ment is always greater than realised investment. A comparison of columns 4 and 7 of Table 9.1 for the total income levels (column 1) less than the equilibrium level bears this out. At any of these total income levels, it is also always true that realised investment equals saving (com-pare columns 3 and 7). You should relate these numbers to Figure 9.1.

At Total Income Levels Above Equilibrium Level

At total income levels greater than the equilibrium level, we observed that there are unintended inventory increases repres-ented by the vertical distance between the total expenditure schedule E and the 45° line. For instance, at a total income level of $140 billion (Figure 9.1, part a), we see a $20 billion unintended inventory increase. This increase is equal to the vertical distance between b and b'. Once again the amount of intended investment that the economy's business firms desire to do equals $30 billion. This desired investment is represented by the vertical distance between point b' on the total expenditure schedule E and point b'' on the consumption function C. This amount of investment expenditure plus the $90 billion of consumption expenditure gives a total spending level of $120 billion. But this level is $20 billion lower than the $140 billion level of total output produced during the period (point b on the 45° line). As a result, $20 billion of unsold goods remain on shelves and in warehouses as inventory. This $20 billion increase or positive change in inventories is unin-tended investment, an unplanned addition to the $30 billion of intended investment. Therefore, *actual or realised investment* amounts to $50 billion, which is equal to the vertical distance between point b on

the 45° line and point b'' on the consump-tion function C.

Again this vertical distance represents the amount of saving, equal to $50 billion, that takes place when the total income level is $140 billion. Once more we see that *realised investment is equal to saving*. Indeed, this is true at any total income level greater than the equilibrium level. For example, in Table 9.1 compare columns 3 and 7 for each of the total income levels in column 1 greater than the $100 billion equilibrium level. It is also true that at any total income level greater than the equilibrium level, realised investment is always greater than intended investment, as we can see by comparing columns 4 and 7. Again, you should relate these numbers to Figure 9.1.

Equilibrium Level of Total Income

Now consider the equilibrium level of total income, which is $100 billion. It is only here that the level of intended investment is equal to the level of realised investment, in this case $30 billion, which is repres-ented by the vertical distance from e to e' in Figure 9.1, part a. This reflects the fact that there is no unintended change in inventory because the $100 billion level of total spending just equals the $100 billion of total output produced. Again observe that realised investment equals saving, just as at all other levels of total income. But only at equilibrium is it also true that intended investment equals saving.

By way of summary, we can say that:

1. Actual or realised investment always equals saving no matter what the level of total income.
2. Intended investment equals saving only at the equilibrium level of total income.
3. Realised investment and intended

investment are equal only at the equilibrium level of total income. At all other levels of total income, they differ by the amount of unintended inventory change.

Leakages-and-Injections Interpretation of Equilibrium

In Figure 8.4 of Chapter 8, we examined the correspondence between the consumption function and the saving function. The saving function S in Figure 9.1, part b, corresponds to the consumption function C in Figure 9.1, part a, in exactly the same manner. The saving function is based on the data from columns 1 and 3 of Table 9.1. Figure 8.7, part a, of Chapter 8 showed us that when the level of intended investment is the same at all income levels, it may be represented by a horizontal investment schedule. Hence, the $30 billion level of intended investment represented by the vertical distance between the consumption function C and the total expenditure schedule E in Figure 9.1, part a, also can be represented by the investment schedule I in Figure 9.1, part b. This investment schedule is based on the data from columns 1 and 4 of Table 9.1.

The combination of the saving function S and the investment schedule I in Figure 9.1, part b, is an alternative but completely equivalent way to that shown in part a for representing how the equilibrium level of total income is determined. The points corresponding to a, e, b, and so forth in part a are similarly labeled in part b. The vertical distances between these points have exactly the same meaning in part b that they have in part a. However, the combination of the saving function S and the investment schedule I in part b suggests another interesting interpretation

of the determination of the equilibrium level of total income. This is the leakages-and-injections interpretation.

The Circular Flow

We anticipated this interpretation in Chapter 8. There we noted that the circular-flow nature of the total-spending-equals-total-income relationship suggests that saving is like a leakage from the ongoing flow, while investment is like an injection to that flow. Investment spending by businesses acts as an offset to the saving by households (their refraining from spending out of income) and can prevent a sharp drop in the ongoing level of total spending. This is so because not all of the economy's output is sold to consumers. Some of it is sold to businesses in the form of capital goods; thus, investment spending takes a portion of total output off the market.

What will be the equilibrium, or unchanging, level of the total-spending-equals-total income circular flow? It will be that level of total income at which the associated amount of leakage due to saving is just exactly offset by the amount of injection due to intended investment — the level of total income at which intended investment equals saving. This level is represented in Figure 9.1, part b, by the intersection of the saving function S and the investment schedule I at point e, which corresponds to a total income level of $100 billion.

At Total Income Levels Above Equilibrium Level

At total income levels greater than the equilibrium level, the leakage from saving will be larger than the injection from intended investment. This can be seen by

FIGURE 9.1
Determinations of the Equilibrium Level of Total Income, and the Relationship Between
Intended Investment, Realised Investment and Saving

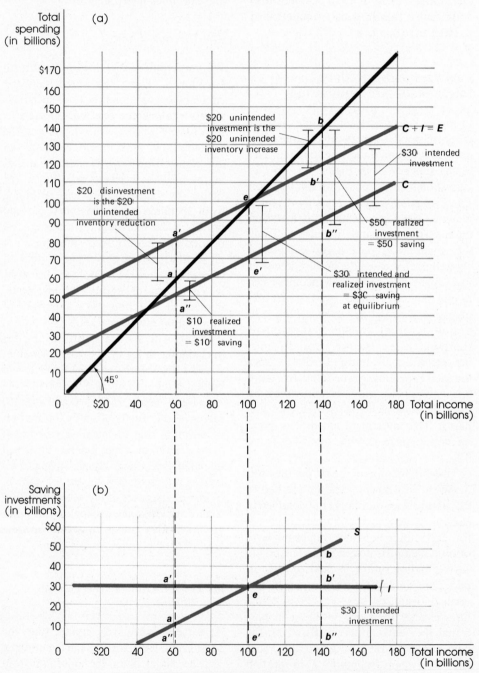

comparing columns 3 and 4 of Table 9.1, and it is also represented by the fact that the saving function S lies above the investment schedule I to the right of point e. For example, at a total income level of $140 billion, point b'', the leakage from total income due to saving equals $50 billion, which is represented by the vertical distance from b'' to b. However, the injection due to intended investment is only $30 billion, the vertical distance from b'' to b'. This means that of the $50 billion of total output *not* purchased by consumers only $30 billion is taken off the market through intended investment spending by businesses. The rest, amounting to $20 billion and represented by the vertical distance from b' to b, is left unsold on shelves and in warehouses as an unintended addition to inventory. This addition to inventory will lead the economy's businesses to reduce production of total output and thereby cause the level of total income to fall, as we discussed earlier in looking at Figure 9.1, part a. Total income will continue to fall until the amount of total output consumers refrain from purchasing — the amount consumers save — equals the amount

businesses purchase — their intended investment spending. This equality occurs only at the equilibrium total income level of $100 billion, the level at which intended investment and saving both equal $30 billion, as represented by the vertical distance between point e' and e in Figure 9.1, part b.

At Total Income Levels Below Equilibrium Level

At total income levels less than the equilibrium level, the leakage from saving will be less than the injection from intended investment. This may be seen by comparing columns 3 and 4 of Table 9.1. It is also represented by the fact that the saving function lies below the investment schedule to the left of point e in Figure 9.1, part b. For instance, at a total income level of $60 billion, point a'', the leakage from total income due to saving is only $10 billion, represented by the vertical distance from a'' to a. But the injection from intended investment amounts to $30 billion, which is equal to the distance from a'' to a'. The difference, amounting to $20 billion, is the excess of total demand or

---

The diagram in part a is the same as that in Figure 8.9 except that the components that make up total expenditure E, consumption C, and intended investment I are explicitly shown along with the level of saving (which is equal to the difference between consumption C and the 45° line). At total income levels larger than the equilibrium level of $100 billion, realised investment exceeds intended investment by the amount of unintended inventory increase. At total income levels less than the equilibrium level, intended investment is greater than realised investment by the amount of unintended inventory reduction. Realised investment always equals saving, no matter what the level of total income. But intended investment equals saving, hence realised investment, only at the equilibrium level of total income.

The diagram in part b shows an alternative but completely equivalent way to represent the determination of the equilibrium level of total income. It combines the saving function S, corresponding to the consumption function in part a, with the investment schedule I, which shows the level of intended investment; the investment schedule I is the same as the vertical distance between the total expenditure schedule E and the consumption function C in part a. The points corresponding to a, e, b, and so forth in part a are similarly labelled in part b. The vertical distances between these points have exactly the same interpretation in part b as in part a. The equilibrium level of total income is determined by the intersection of the saving function S and the investment schedule I at point e.

ECONOMIC THINKERS

John Maynard Keynes — 1883-1946

John Maynard Keynes, the great British scholar, was doubtless the most influential economist of the first half of the twentieth century. In 1936 he published *The General Theory of Employment, Interest, and Money,* a book that had about the same impact on affairs as had Adam Smith's *The Wealth of Nations.*

Up to this point Keynes had generally accepted the elements of neoclassical economics as espoused by such great economists as Alfred Marshall, who had been his teacher at Cambridge. Neoclassical economics assumed that Say's Law of markets was valid, that full employment was the natural case when the economy was in equilibrium. Prices and interest rates would be flexible, varying with demand and supply. Free competition would be the normal case. If unemployment occurred, there would be a tendency toward the restoration of full employment. There would at all times be sufficient demand to take the goods produced off the market. Any deviations from this norm would be brief (of course there might be hard times, the business cycle, etc.) but these would be abnormal and largely self-correcting.

Keynes objected to these concepts in whole or in part. He contended that the economy might well be in equilibrium and at the same time at a position of less than full employment. That is, aggregate demand for goods and services might be inadequate to support full employment. Of course there was increasing evidence that prices and wages were often rigid due to monopolistic elements in the economy, unions, price fixing, non-price competition, and other factors. US economists especially argued that this was in fact most often the case.

However, Keynes's theory did not rest merely on the existence of rigid prices and wage rates. In his view the volume of employment was determined by the level of 'effective demand'. Even if wages were flexible, the same problem might exist due to the possible rigidity of interest rates.

Keynes suggested increased government expenditures to supplement private expenditures for consumption and investment in the event that these expenditures were inadequate to provide full employment, which was often the case.

During the 1930s there were few economists in the Australian Public Service, and their influence on policy making was slight. With Labor party leadership and a Labor Treasurer during World War II, the situation changed. The Treasurer, Ben Chifley, understood and supported Keynesian doctrine. By 1944 there also existed in the bureaucracy a number of influential young economists who were Keynesians. By the 1950s Keynesian economics had become well integrated into basic theory and policy making in Australia and most other Western economies.

FOR FURTHER READING

Harrod, R.F. *The Life of John Maynard Keynes.* London: Macmillan, 1951.

Petridis, A. 'Australia: economists in a federal system' in Coats, A.W. *Economists in Government: An international comparative study,* Durham: Duke University Press, 1981.

spending over total output, which is represented by the vertical distance between *a* and *a'*. In order to satisfy this excess demand, producers must sell goods from inventories. But this reduction in inventories will lead the economy's businesses to increase the production of total output. Consequently the economy's total income will rise, as we discussed earlier in connection with part a of Figure 9.1. Total income will continue to rise, and the amount of leakage due to saving will continue to increase until it equals the amount of injection into the circular flow due to intended investment. Again, this equality occurs only at the equilibrium total income level of $100 billion, the level at which the saving function *S* intersects the investment schedule *I* at point *e* in Figure 9.1, part b.

Equilibrium Level of Total Income

The equilibrium level of total income, corresponding to the intersection of the saving function S and the investment schedule I, is the only level where the total of the saving plans of the economy's households just matches the total of the investment plans of the economy's businesses. At any other level there will be a discrepancy between the plans of these two groups.

CHECKPOINT * 9.1

Explain why realised investment is always equal to saving. Explain why it is sometimes said that 'this is obvious because the part of total output that is not consumed must go someplace'.

*Answers to all Checkpoints can be found at the back of the text.

THE PARADOX OF THRIFT

You have probably heard the old saying, attributed to Benjamin Franklin, the American scholar. 'A penny saved is a penny earned'. It seems like good advice for a household. But it may not be good for the economy if all households do so. It is a case of the fallacy of composition — what is true of the part is not necessarily true of the whole.

Suppose the equilibrium level of total income and output in the economy is $140 billion. This level is determined by the intersection of the saving function S_0 with the investment schedule I at point e_0 in Figure 9.2, part a. The level of saving and investment (vertical axis) is $40 billion. Now suppose the economy's households follow Benjamin Franklin's advice. They decide to save more at every level of total income. The result would be an upward shift in the saving function from S_0 to S_1. But look what happens! The equilibrium level of total income and output falls from $140 billion to $100 billion, as determined by the intersection of S_1 and I at e_1. Furthermore, the amount of saving that actually takes place remains unchanged at $40 billion. A penny saved is not a penny earned. Quite the contrary, the *attempt* to save more results in no increase in saving and, worse yet, leads to an actual decline in the total income earned!

This **paradox of thrift** is even more pronounced if the level of intended investment varies with the level of total income, so that the investment schedule I slopes upward as shown in Figure 9.2, part b. Then the same upward shift in the saving function from S_0 to S_1 results in an even greater fall in total income and output, from $140 billion to $80 billion, as determined by the intersection of S_1

POLICY PERSPECTIVE

A Common Misconception About the Saving-Investment Process — The Role of Banks

The Australian banking system survived the crisis of the Great Depression because senior bankers followed rigidly the maintenance of cash reserve ratios, and advance to deposit ratios. This was a legacy of the bank failures of the 1890s but it did little to assist recovery. What was not well understood then was the exact nature of the crucial role that banks play in an economy's savings-investment process. Because of this, inappropriate bank policies can cause disruptions in the saving-investment process, and hence in the economy's income-expenditure flow, thereby contributing to, or even causing, a severe economic downturn.

Before the time of Keynes the extent of the role of banks in maintaining the income-expenditure flow was often not fully appreciated because of a common misconception, namely, the idea that dollars from saving must somehow flow from the hands of savers into the hands of investors in order for investment expenditures to be able to occur. But in fact households may bury their unspent dollars in the backyard if they wish. In a modern economy the banking system is able to create money (we shall see how in a later chapter) and lend it to businesses that want to invest in plant, equipment, and inventories. As long as the amount of money banks lend to businesses in this way is equal to the amount households desire to save, investment plans will continue to equal saving plans and there need be no interruption in the income-expenditure flow.

The fact that dollars do not literally have to flow from the hands of savers into those of investors illustrates how much the motives and decisions of savers may be disconnected from those of investors. It also highlights an important point. If households put their savings in sugar bowls and mattresses or bury them in the backyard, investment will have to be financed by the banking system. Widespread bank failures, or inappropriate lending policies remove this source of financing and cause intended investment spending to fall, thereby reducing the economy's equilibrium level of total income, output, and employment as well.

Questions

1. We have noted that if households put their savings in sugar bowls and mattresses or bury them in the backyard, investment will have to be financed by the banking system. What bearing does this have on the fact that total spending is always greater than total income at levels of total income less than the equilibrium level?

2. What effect do you think widespread bank failures would have on the consumption function?

and I at e_1. Moreover, the amount of saving that actually takes place is now smaller! The attempt by the economy's households to save more leads to the paradoxical result that they end up saving less.

What explains the paradox of thrift? The answer is that the attempt to save more results in a larger leakage from total income. At the initial equilibrium level of total income, $140 billion in our example, the leakage exceeds the amount of intended investment spending. Consequently, the level of total income falls as the economy's businesses cut back the production of total output in order to

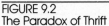

FIGURE 9.2
The Paradox of Thrift

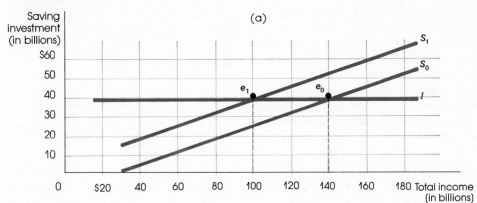

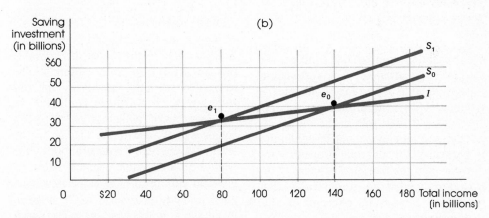

It may well be good advice for a household to try to save more, but bad for the economy if all households attempt to do so.

Suppose the economy's equilibrium level of total income is initially $140 billion, as determined by the intersection of the saving function S_0 and investment schedule I at point e_0. If the economy's households attempt to save more, the saving function will shift up to the position S_1. Given the investment schedule I in part a, total income and output will fall to $100 billion and the amount of saving will in fact remain unchanged at $40 billion. If the level of intended investment varies with the level of total income and output, as shown in part b, the attempt to save more actually causes the amount saved to fall!

avoid unintended inventory increases. This fall in total output and income continues until the level of saving, or leakage, is once again brought into equality with the level of intended investment, or injection. At this point there is no unintended inventory accumulated and the economy is once again at equilibrium.

CHECKPOINT 9.2

Explain the paradox of thrift in terms of what happens if the economy's households attempt to save less. To do so, use Figure 9.2, parts a and b. Suppose a news item suggests that consumers may attempt to rebuild 'their savings' that have 'dwindled'. What do you as an 'analyst' think about this? What are the possible implications for car workers and steelworkers?

MARGINAL AND AVERAGE PROPENSITIES TO CONSUME AND TO SAVE

Students often confuse the concepts of marginal and average. The distinction between them is important to our understanding of the consumption and saving functions and their role in the theory of income and employment determination. In particular, the marginal propensity to consume and the marginal propensity to save are needed to understand the important Keynesian concept of the multiplier, as we shall see.

Marginal Propensity to Consume and to Save

The **marginal propensity to consume (MPC)** is the fraction or proportion of

any change in disposable income that is consumed:

$$MPC = \frac{\text{change in consumption}}{\text{change in disposable income}}$$

The term *marginal* refers to the fact that we are interested *only* in the *change* in the level of consumption brought about by a *change* in the level of disposable income. Similarly, the **marginal propensity to save (MPS)** is the fraction or proportion of any *change* in disposable income that is saved:

$$MPS = \frac{\text{change in saving}}{\text{change in disposable income}}$$

These concepts are shown in Table 9.2. As we move from one level of disposable income to the next in column 1, the *change* (Δ) in the level of disposable income, ΔDI, is given in column 2. The associated *change* in the level of consumption, ΔC, brought about by the *change* in disposable income, ΔDI, is given in column 4. The associated marginal propensity to consume, *MPC*, is shown in column 7. In this case, *MPC* (which is $\Delta C \div \Delta DI$) equals .60. Similarly, the change in the level of saving, ΔS, brought about by the *change* in disposable income, ΔDI, is given in column 6. The associated marginal propensity to save, *MPS*, is given in column 8. In this case, the *MPS* (which is $\Delta S \div \Delta DI$) equals .40.

Suppose, for example, that disposable income rises from $450 billion to $475 billion, an increase of $25 billion (column 2). What do households do with this increase? According to Table 9.2, they consume .60 of it which is $15 billion (column 4), and save .40 of it, which is $10 billion (column 6). These are the only two things households can do with the increase — consume part of it and save the rest. By definition, then, the fraction of the increase in disposable income consumed, *MPC,* plus the fraction saved, *MPS,* when added together are equal to the whole increase in disposable income. Therefore, *the sum of MPC and MPS must always equal 1:*

$$MPC + MPS = 1$$

The data in Table 9.2 show us that this is true, since

$$.60 + .40 = 1$$

The marginal propensity to consume is represented graphically by the slope of the consumption function, as shown in Figure 9.3, part a. (Figure 9.3 is the same as Figure 8.4.) The slope of any line is the ratio of the amount of vertical change in the line to the associated amount of horizontal change. For the consumption function, the vertical change ΔC is associated with the horizontal change ΔDI. Similarly, *the marginal propensity to save is represented graphically by the slope of the saving function* as shown in Figure 9.3, part b.

If the consumption function is a straight line, then so is the saving function. When the consumption function is a straight line, its slope (*MPC*) has the same value at every point along the line. The same is

TABLE 9.2
The Consumption and Saving Schedules, the Marginal Propensity to Consume, and the Marginal Propensity to Save (Hypothetical Data in Billions of Dollars)

(1)	(2)	(3)	(4)	(5)	(6)	(7)	(8)
Disposable Income (DI)	Change in DI (ΔDI)	Con-sumption (C)	Change in C (ΔC)	Saving (S)	Change in S (ΔS)	Marginal Propensity to Consume (MPC)	Marginal Propensity to Save (MPS)
				$S=(1)-(3)$		$MPC = \dfrac{(4)}{(2)}$	$MPS = \dfrac{(6)}{(2)}$
300		320		− 20			
	25		15		10	.60	40
325		335		− 10			
	25		15		10	.60	.40
350		350		0			
	25		15		10	.60	.40
375		365		10			
	25		15		10	.60·	.40
400		380		20			
	25		15		10	.60	.40
425		395		30			
	25		15		10	.60	.40
450		410		40			
	25		15		10	.60	.40
475		425		50			
	25		15		10	.60	.40
500		440		60			

FIGURE 9.3
The Marginal Propensity to Consume and the Marginal Propensity to Save

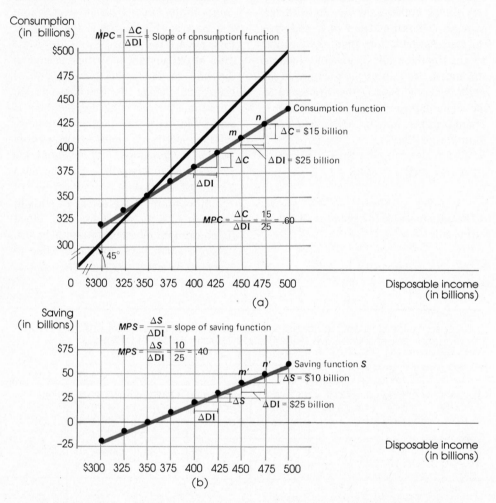

(a)

(b)

The slope of a line is the ratio of the amount of vertical change in the line to the associated amount of horizontal change.

For the consumption function, the vertical change ΔC is associated with the horizontal change ΔDI, as shown in part a. Hence, the slope of the consumption function is $\Delta C \div \Delta DI$, which is the marginal propensity to consume, MPC. Similarly, the slope of the saving function is $\Delta S \div \Delta DI$, which is the marginal propensity to save, MPS, as shown in part b.

Both of these functions are straight lines. Therefore, the marginal propensity to consume is the same no matter where it is measured along the consumption function. The same is true of the marginal propensity to save measured anywhere along the saving function. In the examples shown here, which are based on the data in Table 9.2, the MPC equals .60 and the MPS equals .40.

true of the slope (*MPS*) of the straight-line saving function. The consumption and saving functions of Figure 9.3 are both straight lines. If, however, the consumption function were a curve that was less steeply sloped at higher disposable income levels, then the saving function would be a curve that gets more steeply sloped at higher disposable income levels. In that case the *MPC* would be smaller at higher income levels and the *MPS* would be larger. Draw such consumption and saving functions and illustrate these characteristics.

Average Propensity to Consume and to Save

The **average propensity to consume (APC)** is the fraction or proportion of *total* disposable income that is consumed:

$$APC = \frac{\text{consumption}}{\text{disposable income}}$$

Note that whereas the *MPC* is the ratio of the *change* in consumption to the *change* in disposable income, the *APC* is the ratio of the *level* of consumption to the *level* of disposable income. The *APC* and the *MPC* are therefore two distinctly different concepts.

Table 9.3 shows the same data in columns 1, 2, and 3 for DI, *C,* and *S* as in columns 1, 3, and 5 of Table 9.2. The average propensity to consume for each level of disposable income (column 1), and its associated level of consumption (column 2), is shown in column 4. *APC* equals $C \div DI$, which is the consumption data in column 2 divided by the disposable income data in column 1. Note that unlike the *MPC* (column 7 of Table 9.2), the *APC* (column 4 of Table 9.3) declines as disposable income increases.

The **average propensity to save *(APS)*** is the fraction or proportion of *total* disposable income that is saved:

$$APS = \frac{\text{saving}}{\text{disposable income}}$$

Again, the *APS* and the *MPS* are distinctly different concepts. While the

TABLE 9.3
The Consumption and Saving Schedules, the Average Propensity to Consume, and the Average Propensity to Save (Hypothetical Data in Billions of Dollars)

(1)	(2)	(3)	(4)	(5)
Disposable Income (DI)	Consumption (C)	Saving (S)	Average Propensity to Consume (APC)	Average Propensity to Save (APS)
		$S = (1) - (2)$	$APC = \frac{(2)}{(1)}$	$APS = \frac{(3)}{(1)}$
300	320	-20	1.07	-.07
325	335	-10	1.03	-.03
350	350	0	1.00	.00
375	365	10	.97	.03
400	380	20	.95	.05
425	395	30	.93	.07
450	410	40	.91	.09
475	425	50	.89	.11
500	440	60	.88	.12

TABLE 9.4
Multiplier Effect of an Expenditure Increase, Round by Round
(Hypothetical Data in Billions of Dollars)

Expenditure Round	(1) Change in Income and Output	(2) Change in Consumption MPC = ⅔	(3) Change in Saving MPS = ⅓
First round	$20.00 ⟶	$13.34	$6.66
Second round	13.34 ⟵	8.90	4.44
Third round	8.90 ⟵	5.94	2.96
Fourth round	5.94 ⟵	3.96	1.98
Fifth round	3.96 ⟵	2.64	1.32
Rest of the rounds	7.86 ⟵	5.22	2.64
Totals	$60.00	$40.00	$20.00

MPS is the ratio of the *change* in saving to the *change* in disposable income, the *APS* is the ratio of the *level* of saving to the *level* of disposable income.

The *APS* of our example is shown in column 5 of Table 9.3. Note that while *APC* (column 4) falls as disposable income increases, the *APS* (column 5) increases. In other words, if the fraction of total disposable income consumed gets smaller at higher disposable income levels, it follows that the fraction of total disposable income saved must get larger. Since all disposable income is either consumed or saved, it also follows that

$$APC + APS = 1$$

═══════════════════════════

CHECKPOINT 9.3

Show graphically how the consumption function would have to look if its MPC and APC are always equal to each other, no matter what the disposable income level. What would be true of the relationship between the MPS and the APS of the saving function in this case, and what

would the saving function look like? How would the consumption function have to shift for the APC to increase and the MPC to remain unchanged? Show what would happen to the saving function in this case.

═══════════════════════════

AUTONOMOUS EXPENDITURE CHANGE AND THE MULTIPLIER EFFECT

Our examination of the business cycle in Chapter 6 indicated that total income, output, and employment are always 'on the move'. One of the main reasons for this movement is that total expenditure frequently shifts. In the simple economy we are considering in this chapter, where government expenditure and taxation are ignored, shifts in total expenditure can be caused by shifts in either or both of its components — consumption and intended investment. Such shifts are represented by changes in the position of the total expenditure schedule that are reflected in changes in the equilibrium levels of total income, output, and employment.

Shifts in the consumption and saving functions, the investment schedule, and hence the total expenditure schedule, are due to causes *other* than changes in the level of total income. Changes in the level of total income cause *movement along* these curves. Changes in all other things — expectations, wealth, interest rates, and so forth — cause *shifts or changes in the position* of these curves. In order to keep this extremely important distinction in mind, changes in expenditure which cause the total expenditure schedule to shift are often referred to as *exogenous,* or *autonomous,* expenditure changes.

Shifts in total expenditure, whatever the underlying cause, give rise to even larger changes in total income and output. This is referred to as the multiplier effect. Given the dollar amount of the shift in total expenditure, the resulting change in total income and output will be several times larger, or some multiple of this amount. This multiple is called the **multiplier.** For instance, if intended investment rises by $10 billion and the resulting change in total income amounts to $30 billion, the multiplier is 3. If the rise in total income is $40 billion, the multiplier is 4. Let's see why there is a multiplier effect and what determines the size of the multiplier.

Graphical Interpretation of the Multiplier Effect

Suppose the economy's business firms believe that sales are going to pick up in the coming year and that they are going to need more productive capacity to meet this increase. Let's suppose that investment spending increases from $20 billion to $40 billion.

The effect of this increase on total income and output is shown in Figure 9.4. In this figure the economy is initially in equilibrium at a total income level of $80 billion. This is the level at which the total expenditure schedule E_0 (which equals C_0 + I_0) and the 45° line intersect, point *a* in part a. Equivalently, it is the point at which the investment schedule I_0 and the saving function S intersect, point *a* in part b. A $20 billion autonomous increase in investment from I_0 to I_1 causes the total expenditure schedule in part a to shift upward from E_0 (which equals C_0 + I_0) to E_1 (which equals C_0 + I_1). Equivalently, this is represented in part b by the upward shift in the investment schedule from I_0 to I_1. Each of the diagrams shows that the equilibrium level of total income rises from $80 billion to $140 billion — given by the intersection of E_1 and the 45° line at point *b* in part a and by the intersection of S and I_1 at point *b* in part b. In other words, the $20 billion increase in investment causes a $60 billion increase in total income and output. This is the multiplier effect. The value of the multiplier is 3 in this hypothetical example.

The multiplier effect also applies for any autonomous decrease in the level of investment spending. For example, suppose that the economy is now at the equilibrium total income level of $140 billion. Then suppose the economy's business firms' expectations about future sales turn pessimistic, and investment spending shifts downward $20 billion from I_1 to I_0. This is represented in Figure 9.4, part a, by a downward shift in the total expenditure schedule from E_1 (which equals C_0 + I_1) to E_0 (which equals C_0 + I_0). Equivalently, it is represented in part b by a $20 billion downward shift in the investment schedule from I_1 to I_0. In either diagram we can see that total income and output fall by $60 billion, from $140

FIGURE 9.4
Shifts in Total Expenditure Have a Multiplier Effect on Total Income and Output

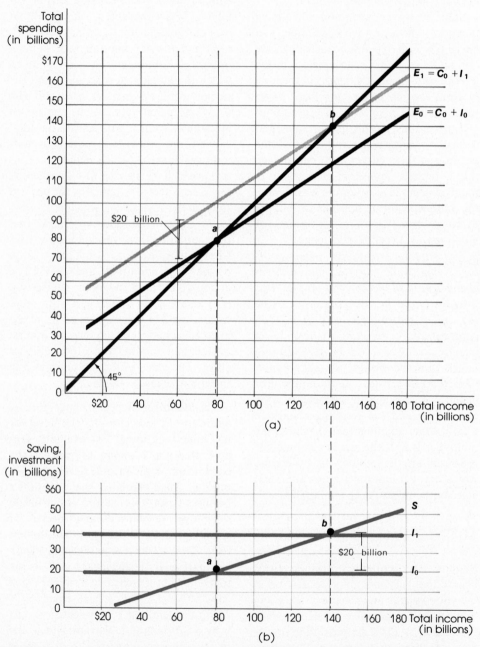

(a)

(b)

The total expenditure schedule in part a will be shifted by a shift in either or both of its components, the consumption function (hence the saving function) and the investment schedule. If the investment schedule shifts upward by $20 billion from I_0 to I_1, the total expenditure schedule billion to $80 billion. Once again, the multiplier effect is at work, and the value of the multiplier is 3.

A Numerical Interpretation of the Multiplier Effect

We can also provide a numerical interpretation of the example of the multiplier effect that is illustrated in Figure 9.4. In this example, the marginal propensity to consume MPC, which is the slope of the consumption function, is $2/3$. Hence, the marginal propensity to save MPS, the slope of the saving function, is $1/3$. We will see how the MPC and the MPS play a crucial role in the multiplier effect and in the determination of the size of the multiplier.

To do so, let's consider the data in Table 9.4. Again, we will assume that the economy is initially in equilibrium at a total income level of $80 billion. The table shows how an autonomous increase in investment expenditure of $20 billion has a chain-reaction effect on the economy. The autonomous expenditure increase causes an increase in income. Part of this income increase is spent, causing a further increase in income, part of which is spent, and so on, round after round. At the first round firms react to the increase in total expenditure by increasing total output by $20 billion. This increased output, of course, is received as increased income (column 1) in the form of wages, rents, interest, and profit by the households who

own the factors of production used to produce the increased output. Given an MPC of $2/3$, households will spend $13.34 billion of this income increase (column 2) and save $6.66 billion (column 3).

At the second round firms react to this $13.34 billion increase in total expenditure by increasing total output an equivalent amount. This gives rise to another increase in payments to factors of production and a further rise in total income of $13.34 billion (column 1). In turn, $2/3$ of this, or $8.90 billion, is spent (column 2), and $4.44 billion is saved (column 3).

At the third round, the $8.90 billion increase in total expenditure again causes a like increase in total output, factor payments, and hence income (column 1). Then $2/3$, or $5.94 billion, of this increase is spent at the fourth round, $3.96 billion is spent at the fifth round, and so forth until the additions to total income ultimately become so small they are insignificant. Adding up all the round-by-round increases in total income in column 1, the total increase in total income and output is $60 billion. This is the same result we saw in Figure 9.4.

Why does the expansion in total income end here? The reason is that the $60 billion increase in total income gives rise to a $20 billion increase in the amount of saving, or leakage (column 3), that is just enough to offset the initial $20 billion increase in investment, or injection. At this point the economy is once again in equilibrium. Total income has increased

will shift upward from E_0 (which equals $C_0 + I_0$) to E_1 ($C_0 + I_1$). Consequently, the equilibrium level of total income and output will rise from $80 billion to $140 billion, or by three times the amount of the investment spending increase. This is the multiplier effect. The multiplier equals 3 in this example.

Part b shows an equivalent representation of this shift in terms of the investment schedule and the saving function. This diagram indicates clearly why there is $60 billion increase in total income in response to the $20 billion increase in investment spending. The $60 billion increase in total income gives rise to a $20 billion increase in saving, or leakage, that is just enough to offset the initial $20 billion increase in investment, or injection.

by three times the initial increase in investment because the economy's households save $1/3$ of any increase in income. The multiplier is 3, just as it was in Figure 9.4.

The Multiplier and the *MPS* and *MPC*

Our example of the multiplier effect, illustrated in Figure 9.4 and Table 9.4, suggests that the size of the multiplier depends on the size of the *MPS* or its complement, the *MPC*. (Remember that *MPS* + *MPC* = 1, always in this model).

Recall that the *MPS* is represented by the slope of the saving function (see Figure 9.3, part b). The *MPS*, or slope of the saving function *S*, in Figure 9.4, part b, is $1/3$. This means that every $1 increase in saving (vertical movement) corresponds to a $3 increase in total income (horizontal movement). Consequently, when the investment schedule shifts upward by $20 billion from I_0 to I_1, saving likewise rises by $20 billion (vertical axis) and total income rises by $60 billion (horizontal axis). Every $1 of increase in investment spending gives rise to a $3 increase in total income. The multiplier is therefore 3. But this is just the reciprocal of the *MPS* — the value of the *MPS*, which is equal to $1/3$, turned upside down.

When we look at the numerical illustration of our example in Table 9.4, the same conclusion emerges. When the *MPS* equals $1/3$, every $1 of increased investment ultimately results in $3 of increased total income — the $20 billion increase in investment spending ultimately results in a $60 billion increase in total income. The multiplier is 3. If the *MPS* had been $1/2$, the ultimate increase would have been $40 billion — the multiplier is 2. If the *MPS* had been $1/4$, the increase would

have been $80 billion — the multiplier is 4.

In sum, for the simple economy of this chapter (no net exports, no government expenditures, no taxation), *the multiplier is equal to the reciprocal of the MPS:*

$$\text{the multiplier} = \frac{1}{MPS}$$

If *MPS* equals $1/3$, for example, then

$$\text{the multiplier} = \frac{1}{1/3} = 3$$

Note that because *MPC* + *MPS* = 1, it is true that *MPS* = 1 — *MPC*, and so we can also say

$$\text{the multiplier} = \frac{1}{1 - MPC}$$

Also note that *the smaller the MPS, and therefore the larger the MPC, the larger the multiplier. Conversely, the larger the MPS, and hence the smaller the MPC, the smaller the multiplier.* (Convince yourself of this by computing the multiplier first when *MPS* = $1/2$, hence *MPC* = $1/2$; and second when *MPS* = $1/4$, hence *MPC* = $3/4$.)

Two Important Points

Finally, two important points should be made about our discussion of the multiplier effect and the multiplier. First, our example assumed that the multiplier effect was triggered by an autonomous shift in investment spending. Exactly the same results would have followed if the trigger had instead been an autonomous shift in consumption spending, as represented by a shift in the consumption and saving functions. Second, the multiplier effect and the multiplier are just as applicable to downward shifts in investment or consumption spending as they are to upward shifts.

CHECKPOINT 9.4

Suppose that the total expenditure and investment schedules are E_0 and I_0 in parts a and b respectively in Figure 9.4. Show what the effect would be in both parts a and b if there were a $20 billion upward shift in the consumption function. Suppose the MPS is $^1/_5$. Show what the effect of a $10 billion downward *shift in consumption would be in a table like Table 9.4. Also, illustrate this effect graphically, using a figure like Figure 9.4, parts a and b. Suppose a news item notes that 'consumers have spent so heavily in recent months that their savings have dwindled. . . .' In what sense is the word* savings used? *Suppose the news item seems to be talking about both movements along and shifts in the consumption function. Illustrate what is being said in terms of a diagram like Figure 9.4.*

SUMMARY

1. Realised investment is always equal to saving. Intended investment equals saving only at the equilibrium level of total income. Therefore, intended investment and realised investment are equal at the equilibrium level of total income but differ from each other by the amount of unintended inventory change at all other levels of total income.

2. Intended investment may be viewed as an injection into the circular flow of spending and income, while saving may be viewed as a leakage from that flow. At the equilibrium level of total income, the injection of intended investment is equal to the leakage due to saving. Graphically, this corresponds to the point at which the investment schedule intersects the saving function. At levels of total income greater than the equilibrium level, the leakage due to saving exceeds the injection due to intended investment, and total income will tend to fall toward the equilibrium level. At less than equilibrium levels of total income the leakage due to saving is less than the injection from intended investment. This inequality causes total income to rise toward the equilibrium level.

3. If households try to save more, the economy's total income will fall and the level of saving will be no higher than it was initially, or it may even be lower. This is the paradox of thrift.

4. The marginal propensity to consume (*MPC*) is the fraction of any change in disposable income that is consumed — represented graphically by the slope of the consumption function. The marginal propensity to save (*MPS*) is the fraction of any change in disposable income that is saved — represented graphically by the slope of the saving function. The sum of the *MPS* and the *MPC* always equals 1.

5. The average propensity to consume (*APC*) is the fraction of disposable income that is consumed, and the average propensity to save (*APS*) is the fraction of disposable income that is saved. The sum of the *APC* and the *APS* always equals 1.

6. Autonomous spending changes represented by shifts in the total expenditure schedule cause changes in total income that are several times the size of the initial spending change. This multiplier effect may be triggered by changes in either or both of the components of total expenditure — the consumption function (and therefore the saving function) and the investment schedule. In the simple economy of this chapter, the multiplier equals the reciprocal of the marginal propensity to save.

KEY TERMS AND CONCEPTS

average propensity to consume (*APC*)
average propensity to save (*APS*)
marginal propensity to consume (*MPC*)
marginal propensity to save (*MPS*)
multiplier
paradox of thrift
realised investment

QUESTIONS AND PROBLEMS

1. Why does realised investment always equal saving? When realised investment and intended investment are not equal, why does the level of total income, output, and employment tend to change?

2. When injections exceed leakages, what happens to the economy's level of total income? What is the relationship between intended investment and realised investment in this situation? If the level of total income is falling, what must be the relationship between saving and intended investment? If the level of total income is rising, what must be the relationship between realised investment and saving?

3. Explain the paradox of thrift in terms of Figure 9.1, part a. Suppose the marginal propensity to consume *MPC* decreases because households want to save more out of income so they won't be so hard-pressed for funds when Christmas shopping time rolls around. What do you predict this decrease in *MPC* will do to ease their budget problems come Christmas?

4. Show what happens to the consumption and saving functions as a result of the following:

a. The *MPS* decreases.

b The *APC* increases.

c. The *APC* decreases and the *MPS* increases.

d. The *APS* and the *MPS* decrease.

e. The *APC* and the *MPC* increase.

f. The *APC* decreases and the *MPC* increases.

5. If the saving function shifts downward, what must happen to the investment schedule in order for the total demand schedule to remain unchanged? What will happen to the level of employment in this instance? Why will this happen?

6. What happens to the value of the multiplier if the consumption function becomes steeper? What happens to the value of the multiplier if the saving function shifts downward to a position parallel to its initial position? What is the effect on the level of total income in this case?

10

Government Spending, Taxation, and Fiscal Policy

AFTER READING THIS CHAPTER YOU WILL BE ABLE TO:

1. Explain how government spending and taxation affect total expenditure and the equilibrium level of GDP.

2. Explain the practical limitations of discretionary fiscal policy.

3. Describe how automatic stabilisers work to moderate the cyclical swings in our economy.

4. Outline the major views of budget policy and be able to explain the concept of the cyclically adjusted budget deficit.

5. Explain the financing effects of budget surpluses and deficits.

6. Describe the differences between public and private debt and the nature of the possible burdens of the government debt.

We are now familiar with the basic explanation of why the equilibrium level of total income may be less than the full-employment level. This chapter brings the role of government into the analysis and shows how **fiscal policy** — government's management of its spending, taxing, and debt-issuing authority — affects the equilibrium level of total income, output, and employment. One of the primary objectives of present-day fiscal policy is to smooth out the ever present fluctuations in economic activity and prod the economy closer to full-employment without inflation. While fiscal policy cannot be expected to accomplish such a task alone, it must play a key role.

In this chapter we will continue to assume that wages and prices are inflexible so that the economy's general price level is fixed. We will relax this assumption in the next chapter and allow the price level to vary with changes in total income, output, and employment, as determined by the interaction of aggregate demand and supply.

THE GOVERNMENT BUDGET

Like any budget, *the federal* government's budget *is an itemised account of expenditures and revenues over some period of time.* In this case, the time period is the fiscal year beginning 1 July and ending 30 June of the following year. The expenditure, or outlay, side of the budget consists of several major categories of expenditure. These include social security and welfare, payments to the states, health, defence, education, interest on government debt, and some other areas as well (we considered movements over time in most of these categories in Figure 3.1, Chapter 3). The estimates presented

by the Australian Treasurer in his 1987–88 Budget documents are shown in Figure 10.1. Revenues to cover these outlays come largely from individual and company income taxes. Also important are excise duties. These are taxes levied on the sale of certain products such as alcohol and tobacco. Sales taxes charged on other products, and customs duties levied on certain internationally traded goods also provide some revenue. The respective percentages in each of these classes also appear in Figure 10.1 for the 1987–88 financial year.

Unlike the United States where about one third of Federal spending is on defence, the Australian government spends only about one tenth of its outlays in this area. Like the US, however, about one third of the Australian government's budget goes to social security and welfare. Another major part of Australian government spending goes in payments to the states. This occurs because the States have, by agreement with the Commonwealth, given up the practice of levying income taxes in exchange for an annual distribution of funds to them.

An important observation from part a of Figure 10.1 is that such a significant part of Federal receipts come from pay-as-you-earn (PAYE) taxpayers. This percentage has grown over the years. The growth has been possible because individual tax payers moved up into higher marginal tax brackets. Critics argue that such high tax rates reduce the population's incentive to work.

An examination of state government budgets shows the largest proportion of outlays going to education and health. Large amounts are also spent on police, the judicial system, transport and economic development. Apart from payments from the Commonwealth government, states obtain their revenues from non-income taxes such as payroll tax, stamp duty, gambling taxes and duties payable by financial institutions. Local government generates its revenues largely from property rates.

In Australia total government outlays as a percentage of GDP have exceeded 40 per cent since the early 1980s. This compares with a level of around 30 per cent in the early 1970s. Commonwealth spending has traditionally accounted for about half of total government outlays in Australia.

FIGURE 10.1
Estimated Receipts and Outlays at 1987/88 Australian Federal Budget (percentage contributions of major groupings)

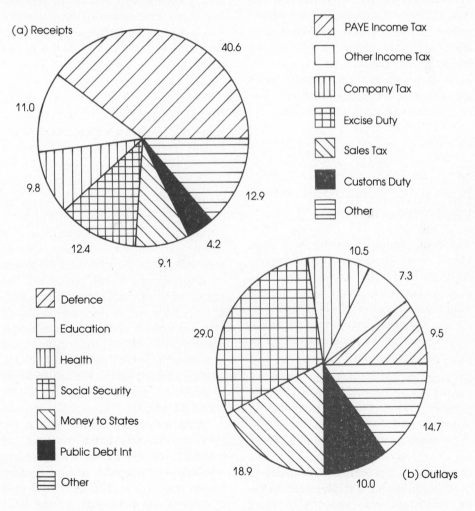

Deficits and Surpluses

A government has a **balanced budget** if total expenditures equal total tax revenues. It has a **budget surplus** if expenditures are less than tax revenues. It has a **budget deficit** if expenditures are greater than tax revenues. The Federal Budget in Australia was in deficit every year since 1953–54 and has shown very few surpluses since the years of the Great Depression. Only on ten occasions during this time was the deficit less than one per cent of GDP. The planned deficit of $27 million in 1987–88 was the lowest since 1970–71. In this chapter we will see why budget deficits generally tend to stimulate income, output and employment, while surpluses have the opposite effect.

Fiscal Policy and the Full Employment Objective

The Great Depression of the 1930s made people in Western-style economies like Australia fearful that another depression might occur when peacetime conditions returned at the end of World War II. This led the Australian government to issue a White Paper on the matter in 1945. This document argued that:

> Governments should accept the responsibility for stimulating spending on goods and services to the extent necessary to sustain full employment.

It advocated, however, that the achievement of full (or high) employment should be consistent with reasonable price stability and the economy's external viability. Recent developments in economic theory, due to Keynes and his followers, suggested that the consumption and investment decisions of individual households and businesses could give rise to either too little or too much aggregate demand. The collective effect of private decisions based on self-interest could result in either excessive unemployment or excessive inflation. By contrast, Keynesian theory suggested that government acting for society as a whole could manage its spending and taxing activities to prevent these unwanted developments. This is the spirit of Keynesian fiscal policy. Let's see how it works both in theory and in practice.

PRINCIPLES OF DISCRETIONARY FISCAL POLICY

Discretionary fiscal policy is the government's deliberate regulation of its spending and taxing activities to attempt to smooth out business fluctuations and ensure maximum employment with as little inflation as possible. Our discussion of discretionary fiscal policy will be simplified by assuming that the only kind of taxes collected by the government are personal income taxes. This means that household income, HI, now differs from household disposable income, DI, by the amount of these taxes. We will continue to make no distinction between GDP, NDP, NI, and HI. They are all the same — what we called total income in the previous chapter. From now on we generally will use the term GDP when referring to total income. In our simplified world, then, GDP differs from DI only by the amount of personal income taxes T.

Government Expenditure and Total Expenditure

Suppose initially that government spending and taxation are zero. Assume that the equilibrium level of GDP is $120 billion as determined by the intersection of the total expenditure schedule $C + I$ and the 45° line in Figure 10.2, part a. This intersection corresponds to the intersection of the saving function S and the investment schedule I in Figure 10.2, part b. If the full-employment level of GDP is $160 billion, the economy is plagued by a considerable amount of unemployment when GDP is only $120 billion.

The economy can be pushed to full employment if the government spends $20 billion on goods and services. This amount of government spending G then adds another layer onto the total expenditure schedule, pushing it vertically upward by $20 billion to the position $C + I + G$ in Figure 10.2, part a. Given that the MPC is assumed to equal ½ (hence the MPS equals ½), the multiplier is 2. Therefore, GDP increases by $40 billion from $120 billion to $160 billion, corresponding to the intersection of the total expenditure schedule $C + I + G$ with the 45° line.

This also may be shown in terms of Figure 10.2, part b. Here the $20 billion of government spending G adds another layer onto the investment schedule I to give the schedule $I + G$. The intersection of $I + G$ with the saving function S is the point at which the leakage from saving, equal to $60 billion, is just offset by the sum of the injections from intended investment I, equal to $40 billion, and government spending, equal to $20 billion. When we bring government spending into the picture, we see that it is no longer necessary for intended investment to equal saving at equilibrium. What is important

is that the leakages from income equal the injections into it, or that $S = I + G$, in this case. (Note that government expenditures do not have to be financed by taxes, although they can be, as we shall see below.)

Of course, a decline in G will cause the total expenditure schedule (part a) and the $I + G$ schedule (part b) to shift downward and the equilibrium level of GDP to fall. In sum, *increases in the level of government spending will cause increases in the level of GDP, just like upward shifts in the level of intended investment and consumption. Decreases in government spending will cause decreases in GDP.*

Taxation and Total Expenditure

Government spending is one side of fiscal policy. Taxation is the other. Suppose the government decides to finance its $20 billion expenditure by levying a lump-sum tax of $20 billion. This is a lump-sum tax in the sense that government will collect $20 billion in taxes no matter what the level of GDP. How will this affect the equilibrium level of GDP?

Figure 10.3 demonstrates what will happen. The equilibrium of Figure 10.2, part a, determined by the total expenditure schedule $C + I + G$, is shown again in this figure. Initially GDP equals DI. When the government imposes the lump-sum tax, a wedge equal to $20 billion will be driven between GDP and household and disposable income DI at every level of GDP. Since part of every dollar of DI is consumed and the rest saved, it follows that the reduction in DI will be reflected partly in a reduction in consumption and partly in a reduction in saving. The degree of reduction in each category is determined by the size of the MPC and the MPS. The MPC and MPS are each equal

FIGURE 10.2
Effect of Government Spending on Equilibrium GDP

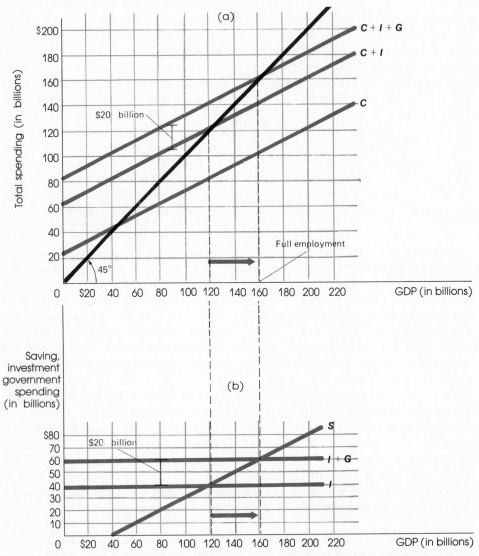

Government spending of $20 billion causes the total expenditure schedule to shift upward from
C + I to C + I + G in part a. The equilibrium level of GDP is thereby increased from $120 billion, cor-
responding to the intersection of C + I and the 45° line, to $160 billion, corresponding to the inter-
section of C + I + G and the 45° line.

This can be shown equivalently in terms of leakages and injections in part b. The $20 billion of
government expenditure adds another layer G onto the investment schedule I to give the I + G
schedule. The new equilibrium level of GDP at $160 billion corresponds to the intersection of the
saving function S and the I + G schedule. Here the $60 billion leakage from saving is exactly
offset by the injections which equal the sum of the $40 billion of intended investment I and the
$20 billion of government spending G.

to ½ in this case. Therefore, the $20 billion tax will cause a $10 billion reduction in consumption and a $10 billion reduction in saving at every level of GDP. The consumption function is the only component of the total expenditure schedule affected by the tax. It is shifted down by $10 billion from C to C_1, at every level of GDP. Consequently, the total expenditure schedule is shifted downward by $10 billion from $C + I + G$ to $C_1 + I + G$, as shown in Figure 10.3, part a. The equilibrium level of GDP therefore declines from $160 billion, the full-employment level, to $140 billion. This $20 billion change is the result of the multiplier effect.

We get the same result if we take the leakages-injections point of view. The equilibrium of Figure 10.2, part b, determined by the intersection of the saving function S and the $I + G$ schedule, is shown again in Figure 10.3, part b. When the $20 billion lump sum tax is imposed, DI is reduced by this amount at every level of GDP. With an MPS of ½ this means that saving is reduced by $10 billion at every level of GDP, so that the saving function shifts downward from S to S_1. In addition to the leakage from GDP due to saving, now there is also a $20 billion leakage due to taxes at every level of GDP. Adding this to the saving function gives us the total leakage function $S_1 + T$. The equilibrium level of GDP is now $140 billion, determined by the intersection of $S_1 + T$ and $I + G$ in Figure 10.3, part b. Here the sum of the leakages from GDP, which is equal to saving plus taxes, is just offset by the sum of the injections, which is equal to intended investment plus government spending. At equilibrium, $S_1 + T = I + G$.

Whether we look at it from the total expenditure schedule vantage point of part a or from the leakages-injection vantage point of part b, we see that imposing a tax will cause the equilibrium level of GDP to fall. Similarly, removing the tax would cause the total expenditure schedule to rise or, equivalently, the $S + T$ function to fall, so that the equilibrium level of GDP would increase. In sum, *increases in taxes will cause decreases in GDP. Decreases in taxes will cause increases in GDP.*

The Balanced Budget Multiplier

Note that the $20 billion of government spending alone *increases* the equilibrium level of GDP from $120 billion to $160 billion (Figure 10.2). However, the $20 billion lump-sum tax collected to finance the spending *decreases* the equilibrium level of GDP from $160 billion to $140 billion (Figure 10.3). The net increase in the equilibrium level of GDP — from $120 billion to $140 billion — is therefore $20 billion. In short, a $20 billion increase in government spending, financed by a $20 billion increase in taxes, results in a $20 billion increase in GDP.

This illustrates the **balanced budget multiplier:** *a government expenditure increase balanced by an equivalent increase in taxes will result in an increase in GDP of exactly the same size. The balanced budget multiplier equals 1.* The increase in GDP is equal to 1 times the amount of the government expenditure increase, or 1 times the amount of the government tax increase. Similarly, a government expenditure decrease balanced by an equivalent decrease in taxes will result in a decrease in GDP of exactly the same size. The balanced budget multiplier equals 1 no matter what the size of MPS and MPC.

What explains the operation of the

FIGURE 10.3
Effect of Government Taxation on Equilibrium GDP

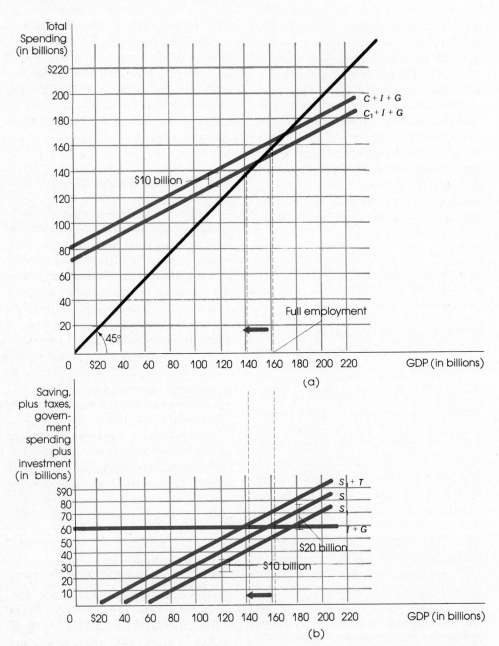

(a)

(b)

balanced budget multiplier? Consider our example again. The government expenditure increase of $20 billion is in part offset by the $20 billion increase in taxes. Why? Because with an *MPC* of ½, and therefore an *MPS* of ½, the tax increase causes a $10 billion decrease in consumption spending. The net result is an increase in total spending of $10 billion — the difference between the $20 billion increase in government spending and the $10 billion reduction in consumption spending. This is only the initial effect, however. The $10 billion net increase in total spending times the multiplier 2 ultimately gives a net increase in GDP of $20 billion.

In the example shown in Figures 10.2 and 10.3, GDP must equal $160 billion if there is to be full employment. Starting from a GDP level of $120 billion, the balanced budget multiplier tells us that a $20 billion increase in government spending, financed by a $20 billion increase in taxes, will only increase GDP to $140 billion. This is what we found in Figure 10.3. Assuming that we want a balanced government budget, how much would government spending and taxes have to be increased in order to raise GDP from $120 billion to $160 billion? According to the balanced budget multiplier, both government spending and taxes would have to be raised by $40 billion.

Discretionary Fiscal Policy in Practice

Our analysis of the effects of government expenditure and taxation on the equilibrium level of GDP indicates how discretionary fiscal policy might be used to combat recessions and overheated, inflationary booms.

Reductions in government expenditures, increases in taxes, or both may be used to reduce the level of total expenditure when economic expansions create excessive inflationary pressures. If the government budget is in deficit to begin with, a reduction in the deficit or possibly its replacement with a surplus will be required to reduce total expenditure. If the budget is balanced to begin with, the creation of a budget surplus will be required to reduce total expenditure. If a surplus exists initially, an even larger surplus will be required.

When the economy is slipping into a recession, increases in government expenditures, reductions in taxes, or both may be used to increase total expenditure. If the government budget is initially in deficit, these actions will give rise to an even larger deficit. If the budget is balanced to begin with, a deficit will result. And if a surplus exists initially, the surplus will be reduced or replaced by a deficit.

Suppose the government imposes a lump-sum tax of $20 billion. This means that DI will be $20 billion less at every level of GDP.

Assuming that the *MPC* equals ½, and therefore that the *MPS* is also ½, consumption will be $10 billion less at every level of GDP. The consumption function will be shifted downward by this amount. The total expenditure schedule will therefore shift downward by this amount, from $C + I + G$ to $C_1 + I + G$ in part a. The equilibrium level of GDP will fall from $160 billion to $140 billion.

In terms of the leakages-injections approach of part b, with an *MPS* of ½, the $20 billion reduction in DI will cause saving to be $10 billion less at every level of GDP. Hence, the saving function will be shifted downward by this amount, from S to S_1. The $20 billion tax leakage must be added to the saving leakage at every level of GDP to give the total leakage function $S_1 + T$. The new equilibrium level of GDP is $140 billion, determined by the intersection of the $I + G$ schedule and the $S_1 + T$ function. At this level the leakage, which equals saving plus taxes, is just offset by the injections, which equal intended investment plus government spending. At this level $S_1 + T = I + G$.

These prescriptions for the ideal exercise of discretionary fiscal policy are not so easy to carry out in practice. Let's see why.

Politics and Priorities

Federal government expenditure and tax programs are ultimately formulated and passed by Federal parliament. This political process is affected by many different special interest groups and lobbies, each with a list of priorities that often conflicts with the goals of discretionary fiscal policy. For example, suppose prudent fiscal policy calls for a reduction in government expenditures to reduce inflationary pressures. But no member of Federal Parliament wants government expenditures that affect his or her region to be cut back. The other alternative is to increase taxes. But which taxes, and who shall pay them? Neither the public nor politicians ever like increasing taxes (at least in an explicit way).

The politics of working out compromises between different interest groups within the government takes time. This process usually occurs in Australia, federally, on an annual basis with the planning of the Federal Budget. As most readers will know the Federal Treasurer normally delivers the budget statement on the third Tuesday of August each year. In some years as well, the Government will present legislation to parliament which changes its budgetary position, e.g. in so called 'mini-budget' statements. In any event there remains a question of whether the government can implement its fiscal policy in time to counteract either inflationary pressures or a recession.

Forecasting, Recognition, and Timing

The sluggishness of the democratic political process is not the only thing that can throw off the timing of fiscal actions. This problem aside, it is necessary to be able to forecast the future course of the economy fairly accurately. Otherwise, it is not possible to take appropriately timed fiscal actions to head off expected recessions or curb inflationary booms. Forecasting is still more an art than a science, despite the development of large economic (that is, statistical or econometric) models of the economy. The record of economic forecasters, both in government and out, is mixed at best.

It is not only difficult to forecast where the economy is going. Often it is almost as hard to recognise where the economy is. Frequently the economy has been in a recession for several months before economists, policymakers, and other observers have recognised and agreed that this is the case. Part of the problem is the fact that many important measurements of the economy's performance are only available sometime after the events that they measure have occurred. For instance, statistics on GDP become available every quarter year. The first measurement of GDP for the third quarter of the year (July through September) may not be available until sometime in November, for example. In general, what is the result of this recognition lag? It is that discretionary fiscal policy tends to be more of a reaction to past developments in the economy than an anticipation of those to come.

In practice, the forecasting and recognition problems combine with political considerations and the sluggishness of democratic decision making to create serious timing problems for discretionary fiscal policy. In addition, even when a change in government spending or taxes finally takes place, there is often a considerable time lag before its full effect on the economy is realised. Given all these considerations, it is not hard to see how a government spending increase — or a tax cut — intended to offset a recession might be badly timed. Such actions could end up taking place in the expansion phase of the business cycle, *after* the trough of the recession has passed. Rather than reducing the depth of the recession, these actions would simply add inflationary pressures to the expansion phase of the cycle that follows. Similarly, a government spending decrease — or a tax increase — intended to offset inflationary pressures during a boom in the economy could end up taking place after the boom has passed. Such actions could actually cause or worsen the next recession. To this extent, *the timing problems associated with discretionary fiscal policy can make economic fluctuations worse.*

State and Local Governments

Discretionary fiscal policy might be more effective if it represented a coordinated effort of federal, state, and local government. If anything, state and local governments tend to conduct their fiscal activities in ways that contribute to, rather than smooth out, the fluctuations of the business cycle. This happens largely because state and local governments, are under more pressure to balance their budgets than is the federal government. Their ability to tax and raise money to finance expenditures rises and falls with the business cycle. Therefore, they tend to spend more heavily on postponable projects such as schools and highways during periods of general economic prosperity than during recessions.

*CHECKPOINT * 10.1*

Consider again the example of Figures 10.2 and 10.3, and suppose that the MPS is ¼ and the MPC is ¾. Explain how the total expenditure schedule is now affected by a $10 billion increase in government expenditures financed entirely by a $10 billion increase in lump-sum taxes. Give an explanation in terms of the leakages-injections approach. Explain why the balanced budget multiplier equals 1 no matter what the value of MPC and MPS.

*Answers to all Checkpoints can be found at the back of the text.

AUTOMATIC STABILISERS: NONDISCRETIONARY FISCAL POLICY

Discretionary fiscal policy requires deliberate action by the Government in Parliament. However, our economy also contains automatic stabilisers. **Automatic stabilisers** *are built-in features of the economy that operate continuously without human intervention to smooth out the peaks and troughs of business cycles.* They are comparable to the automatic pilot that keeps an aeroplane on course. Like an automatic pilot, the economy's automatic stabilisers don't necessarily eliminate the need for deliberate action. But they do reduce it. Two of the most important automatic stabilisers operating in the Australian economy are the income tax system and unemployment benefits. Let's look at each of these to see how they work.

POLICY PERSPECTIVE

The Variety of Taxes and Their Effects on Spending

There are a variety of different taxes — income taxes, sales taxes, company profit taxes, property rates, and so forth. All of them have one thing in common. They take spending power away from those taxed. However, beyond this, these taxes differ in the burden each places on different groups in the economy.

Roughly speaking, a particular tax is said to be *progressive* if it takes a larger percentage out of a high income than it takes out of a low income. The personal income tax is an example of a progressive tax. (We will define this term in more detail shortly.) A sales tax on Rolls Royces is another progressive tax because typically only people with high incomes buy them. A particular tax is said to be a **regressive tax** if it takes a smaller percentage out of a high income than it takes out of a low income. For example, a sales tax on food is considered regressive because the percentage of income spent on food by a low-income household is usually larger than that spent by a high-income household. Therefore, the amount of food sales tax paid by the low-income household, measured as a percentage of its income, is larger than the corresponding percentage for a high-income household.

A given amount of tax revenue could be collected by using progressive taxes or regressive taxes or some combination of both. However, it is not clear in general whether progressive or regressive taxes have a more depressing effect on total income and expenditures. Some economists argue that progressive taxes on personal and business income reduce the incentive to work and depress investment spending. Therefore, they feel progressive taxes depress total spending more than regressive taxes. Other economists claim that regressive taxes depress total spending more because of their effect on consumption. They argue that low-income groups consume more of their income than high-income groups. Since regressive taxes fall heaviest on low-income groups, these economists contend that consumption spending is more depressed by regressive taxes.

Such considerations indicate that raising or lowering taxes to bring about a *given size change in GDP* is far more difficult than was suggested by our discussion of Figure 10.3. In the real world government has to decide which of a wide variety of taxes to change. Often there is only the vaguest idea of what the effects on GDP will be.

A notable recent exercise in attempted tax reform in Australia occurred with the publication of a White Paper by the Hawke Labor Government in June 1985. Seeking to reduce tax avoidance and tax evasion, this document advocated the introduction of a broad-based consumption tax, and reduction in the levels of personal and company income taxes. After an inconclusive Taxation Summit in July 1985, the Federal Treasurer, Mr Keating, introduced a revised policy package to Federal Parliament in September 1985. While reducing individual personal income tax rates, it introduced the taxation of fringe benefits and a capital gains tax. It increased company income tax rates but also abolished the double taxation of share dividends. Together with these and some other minor measures, the Australian economy began experiencing the impact of the tax changes during 1986.

Questions

1. The levying of the lump-sum tax illustrated in Figure 10.3 amounts to collecting a fixed sum of money from every adult in the economy. Would you regard this as a progressive or a regressive tax?

2. Name some special interest groups in our economy and indicate how you think they would stand on the issue of progressive versus regressive taxes.

Tax Structure

Up to now we have used only lump-sum taxes in our analysis, so that the amount of tax revenue is the same no matter what the level of GDP. In reality, the tax structure of the Australian and other Western economies is such that the amount of tax revenue rises when GDP increases and falls when GDP declines. The significance of this for economic stability is illustrated in Figure 10.4. There it is assumed that the level of government and intended investment expenditures is the same at all levels of GDP — the $I + G$ schedule is flat.

Part a of Figure 10.4 shows the lump-sum tax case with which we are already familiar. Suppose that the sum of investment and government expenditure is initially $30 billion, as represented by the $I_0 + G$ schedule. The equilibrium level of GDP is $120 billion, determined by the intersection of $S + T$ and $I_0 + G$. If investment spending increases by $10 billion from I_0 to I_1, the $I_0 + G$ schedule shifts up to $I_1 + G$ and the equilibrium level of GDP increases by $40 billion, from $120 billion to $160 billion. If at this point investment were to decrease by $10 billion, the $I_1 + G$ schedule would shift back down to $I_0 + G$. GDP would decrease by $40 billion, from $160 billion to $120 billion,

in response to a $10 billion fluctuation in investment.

Proportional Taxes

Now consider the effect of the same fluctuation in investment, given the same saving function S, when the economy's tax structure is such that tax revenues rise and fall *proportionally* with GDP. This situation is shown in part b of Figure 10.4. The tax revenue at each level of GDP is represented by the vertical distance between the saving function S and the saving plus tax function $S + T$. This distance gets proportionally larger as GDP increases. *With a* **proportional tax,** *an X per cent rise (or fall) in GDP always results in an X per cent rise (or fall) in tax revenues.* For example, suppose the proportional tax rate is .2. If GDP increases by 10 per cent, from $100 billion to $110 billion, tax revenues will increase by $2 billion from $20 billion (.2 × $100 billion) to $22 billion (.2 × $110 billion). That is, tax revenues also increase by 10 per cent. Given the position of the saving function S, the larger (smaller) is the proportional tax rate, the steeper (less steep) will be the $S + T$ function in part b.

When the $I + G$ schedule is in the position $I_0 + G$, the equilibrium level of

GDP is $130 billion. When the $10 billion increase in investment shifts the schedule up to $I_1 + G$, the equilibrium level of GDP increases by $20 billion to $150 billion. Similarly, a $10 billion fall in investment pushing the $I + G$ schedule down from $I_1 + G$ to $I_0 + G$ would cause a $20 billion fall in GDP from $150 billion to $130 billion. In short, the same $10 billion fluctuation in investment causes a smaller fluctuation in GDP under a proportional tax structure than under a lump-sum tax structure — a $20 billion versus a $40 billion GDP fluctuation. Why is this?

Recall that taxes, like saving, are a leakage that drains off potential spending on goods and services. With a lump-sum tax the tax leakage does not change with changes in GDP. But with a proportional tax the leakage increases as GDP increases and has an *ever greater* braking effect on further rises in GDP. Hence, a rise in injections due to increased investment or government spending or both is more quickly offset by an increase in leakages under a proportional tax structure than under a lump-sum tax structure. Similarly, a fall in the level of injections results in a more rapid decline in leakages under a proportional tax structure. Therefore, GDP does not have to decline as far to reestablish the equality between injections and leakages.

The stabilising effect of the proportional tax structure is greater the larger is the proportional tax rate or the per cent of GDP that is collected in taxes. An increase in the proportional tax rate makes the $S + T$ function in part b steeper. This means that the shift in the $I_0 + G$ schedule to $I_1 + G$, or from $I_1 + G$ to $I_0 + G$, will cause an even smaller change in GDP. Hence, the economy is more stable in that it is less sensitive to such a disturbance.

Progressive Taxes

In reality, tax revenues in our economy tend to rise and fall more than proportionally with increases and decreases in GDP. This happens largely because personal and business income is subject to a progressive tax. *A* **progressive tax** *on income imposes successively higher tax rates on additional dollars of income as income rises.* For example, the first $10,000 of an individual's income might be subject to a 20 per cent tax rate, the second $10,000 to a 30 per cent rate, the third to a 40 per cent rate, and so forth. This means that the fraction of total income taxed away gets larger as total income rises. If the individual in our example makes $10,000, then 20 per cent, or one-fifth, of it goes to taxes; if the individual's income is $20,000, then 25 per cent (equal to the average of 20 per cent and 30 per cent), or one quarter, of it goes to taxes, and so forth. By contrast, with a proportional tax rate the fraction

---

Proportional taxes and progressive taxes act as automatic stabilisers because they increase leakages when GDP rises and decrease leakages when GDP falls.

The leakages-injections diagrams of parts a, b, and c all have the same saving function and the same $10 billion $I + G$ schedule shifts. The only difference between the diagrams is that they each assume different tax structures. When taxes are lump sum (part a), the leakage due to taxes is the same no matter what the level of GDP. A $10 billion shift in the $I + G$ schedule, from $I_0 + G$ to $I_1 + G$ or vice versa, causes a $40 billion change in GDP. By comparison, the same shifts in the $I + G$ schedule under a proportional tax structure (part b) cause a smaller change (equal to $20 billion) in GDP. The same shifts under a progressive tax structure result in a still smaller change (equal to $10 billion) in GDP.

FIGURE 10.4
The Tax Structure as an Automatic Stabiliser

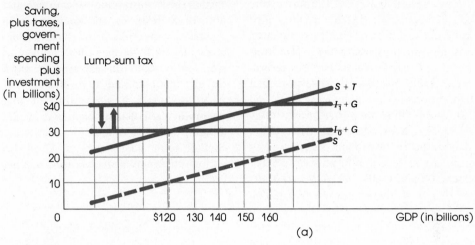

(a)

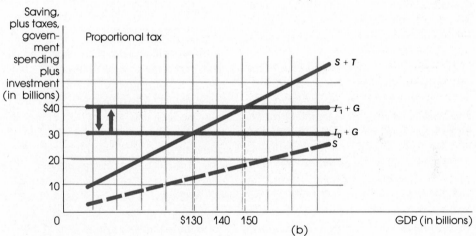

(b)

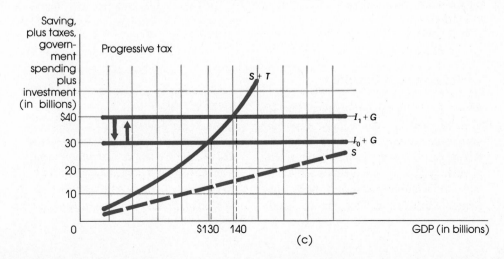

(c)

of total income taxed away is the same no matter what the level of total income.

The effect of a progressive tax structure on the economy's stability is illustrated in Figure 10.4, part c. The saving function S is the same as in parts a and b. However, the $S + T$ function now curves upward, reflecting the fact that taxes rise more than proportionally with increases in GDP and fall more than proportionally with decreases. Now the same $10 billion fluctuation in investment considered in parts a and b results in an even smaller fluctuation in GDP. When $I_0 + G$ shifts up to $I_1 + G$, there is only a $10 billion increase in GDP from $130 billion to $140 billion. By comparison, under the proportional tax rate of part b, this shift resulted in a $20 billion increase in GDP. With the lump-sum tax of part a, there was a $40 billion increase.

In general, *the progressive nature of the Australian economy's tax structure acts as a built-in stabiliser by automatically increasing tax leakages more than proportionally as GDP rises and by reducing such leakages more than proportionally as GDP falls. This is generally desirable because increasing leakages during an inflationary expansion will have a dampening effect on the economy. Conversely, decreasing leakages during a recession will tend to buoy up spending.*

Unemployment Benefits

Since the 1930s **unemployment benefits** have become an increasingly important automatic stabiliser in our economy. Recessions swell the ranks of the unemployed. Without some form of assistance, laid off workers must cut back their spending drastically. This only makes the recession worse. Paying laid off workers unemployment benefits enables them to sustain their consumption spending better and thus cushions the downturn. In Australia unemployment benefits are available to both men and women of working age who are searching for work but are unable to find it. At the 1986/87 Federal Budget it was estimated that unemployment benefit payments would amount to $3,558 million — nearly 5 per cent of total federal outlays. Over this period unemployment averaged 8.3 per cent.

Automatic Stabilisers Are a Double-Edged Sword

The same characteristics of automatic stabilisers that make them desirable can also make them very undesirable under certain circumstances. For example, the tendency of Australia's tax structure to increase leakages when GDP rises helps to curb inflationary pressures when the economy is near full employment. However, if the economy is coming out of the depths of a recession, the same tendency for leakages to rise acts as a drag on economic recovery. This phenomeon is commonly known as *fiscal drag*. To offset its impact governments will have to undertake discretionary increases in G or cut tax rates.

=====

CHECKPOINT 10.2
Suppose the government spending component of the I + G schedules in Figure 10.4 is always equal to $20 billion, whatever the level of GDP. For each of the cases shown in parts a, b, and c of Figure 10.4, explain how the government budget

POLICY PERSPECTIVE

Discretionary Versus Nondiscretionary Expenditures

While automatic stabilisers tend to smooth out the peaks and troughs of business cycles, they do not eliminate them entirely. Research on the matter suggests that the amplitude of business cycles (the difference in GDP from trough to peak) may be reduced by anywhere from one fifth to one half as a result of the presence of automatic stabilisers. This means there is still a role for well-timed discretionary fiscal policy in eliminating that part of the business cycle not smoothed out by the automatic stabilisers.

Discretionary fiscal policy expenditures usually have a different impact on the economy than do the expenditures arising from nondiscretionary fiscal policy. Discretionary government expenditures are typically for goods and services — roads, buildings, trucks, research grants, and so forth. Nondiscretionary government spending usually takes the form of transfer payments, such as unemployment benefits, pensions, and interest on the government debt. Hidden behind a given dollar figure for government expenditure is a variety of decisions about the role of government in our economy.

Viewed only in terms of the expansionary impact on the economy, however, most economists regard government spending on goods and services as more expansionary than transfer payments. For example, suppose that the multiplier equals 2 and that the economy is not operating at full employment. Government spending of $20 billion on goods and services will cause the economy to produce $40 billion of additional output — $20 billion to meet government purchases and $20 billion to meet increased consumer spending as a consequence of the multiplier effect. Alternatively, if the government paid out the $20 billion in unemployment compensation benefits, no increase in output would be needed to satisfy government purchase orders. The government would simply hand unemployed workers $20 billion. The unemployed will spend half of this on goods and services (because a multiplier of 2 implies an *MPC* of ½), or $10 billion. The operation of the multiplier effect on this $10 billion expenditure means that the economy's total output increases by $20 billion. In sum, a $20 billion government expenditure on goods and services causes the economy's total output to increase by $40 billion. But a $20 billion transfer payment causes total output to rise by only $20 billion.

Questions

1. In 1970 federal transfer payments in Australia were equal to roughly 8 per cent of GDP. By the mid-1980s they had risen to about 12 per cent of GDP. Over the same period of time federal government purchases of goods and services as a share of GDP fell from 6.4 per cent to the equivalent of about 5.8 per cent. What implications about fiscal policy might you draw from these trends over this time period?

2. If the trends reported in question 1 had been just the opposite how do you think the GDP gap would have been affected compared to the way it actually behaved?

234 TWO: AGGREGATE INCOME, EMPLOYMENT AND FISCAL POLICY

changes as a result of the $10 billion change in investment, both when it represents an increase from I_0 to I_1 and when it represents a decrease from I_1 to I_0. That is, for each case, does the budget remain balanced, go from surplus to deficit or from deficit to surplus, or what? In light of your findings, how might you state the way the automatic stabilisation effect works in terms of the government budget?

BUDGET POLICY

Government budget policy is the joint result of government spending and tax policy. Budget policymakers have to consider such questions as: When and how often should the budget be balanced? When should it be in surplus, when in deficit? How should deficits be financed — by printing money or issuing bonds? And what should be done with surpluses? These questions have always provoked controversy.

Different Views on Budget Policy

The following represent three of the most often heard views on budget policy. Now that we are familiar with how government spending and taxation can affect the economy, we can consider the economic implications of each of them.

Classical View:
Balance the Budget Annually

The classical economists generally believed that government expenditures

should be matched by government tax revenues every fiscal year — that is, that the budget should be balanced annually. As a result of the Depression of the 1930s and the loss of faith in the classical theory of full employment, few economists subscribe to this view today. Yet, there are still politicians and others who believe that the government budget should be balanced annually. Generally, they view the government budget in the same way as the budget of a household or business firm. Households and businesses that have budget deficits often go bankrupt.

However, if the government budget is balanced every year, the income-expenditure view argues that fiscal policy will add to economic instability rather than reduce it. For example, suppose the economy is in the expansionary phase of a business cycle. As GDP rises tax revenues rise even faster because of a progressive tax structure. Given the level of government expenditures, the increase in tax revenues may well give rise to a budget surplus. In order to keep the budget balanced, the government will have to cut taxes or increase government expenditures or both. However, we have seen that increases in government expenditure, as well as reductions in taxes, push up total expenditure. This will add to the economic expansion.

On the other hand, suppose the economy is entering a recession. As GDP declines, tax revenues will fall. Given the level of government expenditure, this may result in a budget deficit. In order to keep the budget balanced, the government will have to increase taxes or reduce government spending or both. But such actions will reduce total expenditure even further and make the recession worse.

Thus, the annually balanced budget would make the expansion phase of the business cycle larger and the recession phase deeper. Business cycles would be more severe.

Balance the Budget Cyclically

Another point of view argues that the budget should be balanced over the course of the business cycle. That is, the budget should be balanced over whatever period of time it takes for a complete business cycle, measured from either trough to trough or peak to peak. Those who favour this approach contend that balancing the budget in this way will at the same time permit the exercise of a stabilising fiscal policy. During a recession the government would run a budget deficit by increasing spending and reducing taxes to stimulate the economy. During the expansion and boom phase of the cycle, the government would run a surplus by cutting back its spending and increasing taxes in order to curb inflationary pressures. Ideally, the size of the deficit that occurs in the recession is just matched by the size of the surplus during the boom. The budget is therefore balanced over the business cycle.

In reality, it is very difficult to do this because recessions and expansions typically differ from one another in length and magnitude. Therefore, the size of the deficit incurred while fighting the recession is not likely to be the same as the size of the surplus generated by attempts to curb an inflationary expansion.

Functional Finance

The functional finance point of view contends that the goals of economic stabilisation and full employment without inflation should come ahead of any concern about balancing the budget. This means that the budget may have to run in deficit over a period of several years in order to keep employment high or run in surplus to curb inflation. Proponents of functional finance argue that any difficulties associated with ongoing deficits or surpluses are far outweighed by the benefits of high employment without inflation.

Critics of the functional finance approach argue that it throws away the fiscal discipline imposed by a balanced budget objective. Generally, the critics do not argue for slavish pursuit of a balanced budget. Rather, they believe that it should be a rough guideline used to keep inflationary deficit spending under control.

The Cyclically Adjusted Budget

Each of the viewpoints on budget policy we have just mentioned has obvious drawbacks. The annually balanced budget is destabilising. Balancing the budget over the business cycle is very difficult if not impossible. Functional finance seems to lack any standard for evaluating budget policy performance. Another budget concept — the cyclically adjusted budget — has gained popularity among economists and policymakers because it provides a way of judging to what extent fiscal policy is pushing the economy toward a high-employment level of GDP. (A high-employment level might be deemed to be a level of GDP where the unemployment rate is 6 per cent, for example.)

The Actual Budget and the Cyclically Adjusted Budget

The *actual* government budget surplus or deficit is equal to the difference between *actual* government expenditures and *actual* tax revenues. Suppose actual GDP is less than the high-employment level of GDP. Given that the tax structure is progressive, the actual tax revenues are less than the amount that would be collected at the high-employment GDP level. The actual government budget might well show a deficit, as prudent fiscal policy would say it should during a recession. Injections from government spending exceed tax leakages (there is a net injection). But is this actual budget deficit large enough to combat the recession? How can we tell?

Suppose we compare this actual level of government spending with the amount of tax revenue that would be collected *if* GDP were at the high-employment level. It might turn out that the high-employment level of tax revenue would exceed actual government spending. In other words, if the economy were at the high-employment level of GDP, there would be a budget surplus. And this means that actual fiscal policy would be a force tending to push GDP down and away from the high-employment level! Clearly, the *actual* budget deficit is not as large as it should be if fiscal policy is to be oriented toward pushing GDP up to the high-employment level.

We conclude that *compared to the actual budget deficit or surplus, a more meaningful measure of the impact of fiscal policy is the difference between the actual level of government spending and the level of tax revenue that would be collected if the economy were operating at a high-employment level of GDP. This is the* **cyclically adjusted budget.** If actual GDP is below the high-employment level of GDP and there is a cyclically adjusted budget deficit, fiscal policy may be viewed as a force favourable to the achievement of a high-employment level of GDP. On the other hand, if under these same circumstances there is a cyclically adjusted budget surplus, fiscal policy may be viewed as not sufficiently expansionary for the purpose of achieving a high-employment level of GDP. If actual GDP is above the high-employment level of GDP, the existence of a cyclically adjusted budget deficit would suggest that fiscal policy is overly expansionary and is contributing to inflationary pressures. However, if under these same circumstances there is a cyclically adjusted budget surplus, fiscal policy may be viewed as a force favourable to curbing excessive expansion.

Finally, note carefully the following point. Even if the cyclically adjusted budget (deficit or surplus) indicates that the current stance of fiscal policy is favourable to the achievement of a high-employment level of GDP, it is no guarantee that this goal will be realised. Consumption and investment spending may be either so expansionary or so contractionary that a high-employment equilibrium level of GDP cannot be reached or maintained. Put another way, even though the cyclically adjusted budget may be favourable to the achievement of a high-employment level of GDP, the *size* of the cyclically adjusted budget (deficit or surplus) may not be large enough given the existing level of consumption and investment spending.

Recent Public Sector Deficit Experience

Figure 10.5 compares the difference between the public sector's actual deficit and the cyclically adjusted budget deficit in Australia from 1970–71 to 1982–83. The public sector's actual deficit in Australia is known officially as the *public sector borrowing requirement* (PSBR). The estimates of the cyclically adjusted budget deficit are those of John Nevile.[1] Observe that throughout the period Australia's public sector ran an actual deficit but there was a cyclically adjusted surplus between 1970-71 and 1974-75 and between 1981-82 and 1982-83. Budgetary policy was obviously contractionary during these periods. The cyclically adjusted budget deficit between 1975-76 and 1979-80 indicates a period of expansionary fiscal policy. Fiscal stance was relatively more expansionary in 1972-73, and from 1974-75 to 1978-79 than in the immediately preceding years. By contrast there was a notable tightening in 1979-80.

Effects of Deficit Financing on the Economy

By definition, a budget deficit means that tax revenues are less than government expenditures. How and where does the government get the funds to finance the difference? There are two ways in which the government can obtain the needed funds: (1) it can borrow the money from the public by selling government bonds, or (2) it can issue new money to its creditors. It can also do some combination of both. The expansionary effect on the economy of a budget deficit varies, depending on which method is used to finance the deficit.

[1]Nevile, J.W. 'Budget Deficits and Fiscal Policy in Australia', CAER Working Paper No. 68, University of New South Wales, Sydney, August, 1984. Nevile refers to the term 'structural deficit' and the estimates we report are for his pessimistic assumption about economic activity and with adjustment for an 'inflation tax' on holders of public debt.

Bond Financing

Like any other bond, a government bond is a contract whereby the borrower (the government) agrees to pay back the lender (the buyer of the bond) the amount lent plus some rate of interest after some specified period of time. For example, consider a $1,000 government bond that pays a 5 per cent rate of interest and promises to pay back the lender after 1 year. At the end of 1 year the lender, or bond buyer, gets back $1,050 (the original $1,000 plus 5 per cent of $1,000, or $50) from the government, the bond seller. As with any bond, the only way the government can sell the bond (borrow the $1,000) is by paying a high enough rate of interest to induce people to buy it (lend the $1,000).

The government must sell its bonds in the bond market, in competition with bonds sold by businesses that are trying to borrow funds to finance their investment spending. In order to induce the public to buy these government bonds instead of those issued by the business sector, the government will have to pay an interest rate high enough to make their bonds relatively more attractive. This competition between the financing needs of the government and those of the business sector will push up the rate of interest. We know from our discussion in Chapter 8 (see Figure 8.8) that this interest rate rise will cause the level of investment spending to fall, as represented by a downward shift in the investment schedule. Therefore, *when a government deficit is financed by selling government bonds, the expansionary effect of the deficit on the economy is somewhat offset by a downward shift in investment spending.*

Creating Money

The other way in which the government can finance the deficit is to create the needed money. We will be able to describe the way this is done in a modern economy after we have studied how the banking system works in Chapters 13 through 15. For the moment, we can simply assume that the government cranks money out with a printing press. In practice the same result can be achieved in Australia by the Federal Treasury borrowing from the

---

FIGURE 10.5
Public Sector Budget Position
Australia 1970-71 to 1982-83

Per cent
of GDP

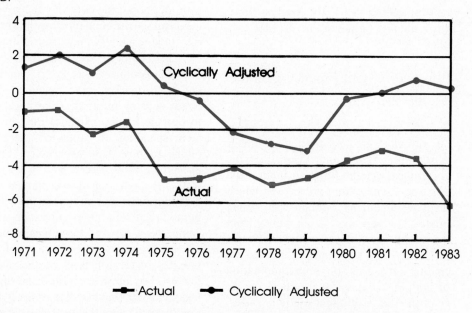

—■— Actual   —●— Cyclically Adjusted

Between 1970-71 and 1974-75 and between 1981-82 and 1982-83 there was a cyclically adjusted surplus. Fiscal policy was contractionary. It was clearly expansionary between 1975-76 and 1979-80 when there was a cyclically adjusted deficit. Notice also that fiscal policy became more expansionary than in the previous year in 1972-73 and from 1974-75 to 1978-79. It tightened dramatically in 1979-80.

Reserve Bank. By writing cheques against these loans, the Treasury sets in train a process where people receiving these cheques deposit them in their accounts with trading banks. As a result of this the money supply increases. Using this method means that there is no longer a need to issue bonds and, hence, there is no rise in the interest rate that depresses investment spending. It follows that *when the government finances a deficit by creating new money, the expansionary effect of the deficit on the economy will be greater than when the deficit is financed by borrowing (issuing bonds).*

What to Do with a Budget Surplus

The government may collect more tax revenue than it spends (have a budget surplus) in the boom phase of an expansion. (Note, however, that budget surpluses have been rare.) The budget surplus is desirable at this phase of the business cycle because it is anti-inflationary, meaning that it dampens inflationary pressures. But the extent of this dampening effect depends on what the government does with the surplus. There are two possibilities. The government can use the surplus to retire some of the outstanding government debt by paying back bondholders. Alternatively, the government can simply hold on to the surplus as idle funds. This amounts to withdrawing the money from the economy.

Suppose the surplus is used to retire outstanding debt. Think of the surplus as the net leakage — the excess of the leakage due to taxes over the injections of government spending. Returning the surplus to the economy by retiring debt offsets this net leakage to the extent that it puts money back into the hands of the

public, who then spend it. Debt retirement thereby reduces the anti-inflationary effect of the budget surplus. However, if the government simply holds the surplus as idle funds, there is no offset to reduce this net leakage. We conclude that the *anti-inflationary effect of a government budget surplus is greater when the surplus funds are held idle than when they are used to retire government debt.*[2]

CHECKPOINT 10.3
Compare Figure 10.5 with Figure 6.4, part b, and describe how well fiscal policy has performed in view of the behaviour of the GDP gap between 1970–71 and 1982–83. What are the implications for the cyclically adjusted budget concept of the fact that the expansionary impact of a deficit depends on how it is financed? Similarly, what are the implications for this concept of the different ways of disposing of a surplus?

THE PUBLIC DEBT

The public debt is a subject of controversy and a source of concern to many people. Should we be concerned about it? Who owes what to whom? How can we tell whether the debt is too big or not? What are the burdens of the debt? Almost every citizen worries about these questions from time to time.

[2]Note that retiring government debt removes government bonds from the bond market and thus reduces competition with private bonds. This tends to reduce the interest rate and thereby stimulate investment spending. This is another source of stimulus to the economy that occurs when there is debt retirement.

POLICY PERSPECTIVE

The Deficit Problem — Crowding Out Capital Formation

In recent times there has been increasing concern about the size of federal government budget deficits in a number of countries; i.e. government spending in excess of tax revenue. During the mid-1970s and in the early 1980s federal government deficits in Australia approached 4 per cent of GDP. These percentages were much smaller in the late 1960s, the late 1970s and in the middle 1980s as respective governments have sought to approach balanced budgets.

A critical concern often expressed about federal deficits is that they absorb resources that would otherwise be available to build up the economy's capital stock. It is therefore often said that deficits 'crowd out' investment, or capital formation. The argument may be illustrated in terms of the leakages-injections relationship for a closed economy which says that the sum of the injections, investment (I) plus government spending (G), must equal the sum of the leakages, saving (S) plus taxes (T), or $I + G = S + T$. When there is a deficit government spending G is larger than tax revenue T, which means S is larger than I. Part of the economy's saving S must go to finance the deficit leaving the rest to finance investment I. If part of saving did not have to finance the deficit it would be available to finance a larger level of investment spending, or capital formation.

For example, suppose I and G each equals $50 billion and that S equals $60 billion while T equals $40 billion. Then $I + G = S + T$ is (in billions) $50 + $50 = $60 + $40, and the government budget deficit equals $G - T = $50 - $40 = $10. Since tax revenue ($T = $40) is not sufficient to finance all of government spending ($G = $50), $10 of saving ($S = $60) must go to finance the deficit, leaving $50 of saving to finance investment ($I = $50). In other words, part of the economy's saving S must be used to finance the deficit and the other part is used to finance investment I. What if government spending were larger, say, $G = $90 instead of $50? Then the deficit would be larger, $G - T = $90 - $40 = $50. This $50 excess of government spending over tax revenue would have to be financed out of saving, leaving only $100 of the total saving ($S = $60) to finance investment. Now $I + G = S + T$ would be $10 + $90 = $60 + $40. Investment I is now only $10. The larger deficit has crowded out investment, reducing it from $50 to $10! Our example illustrates how growing deficits can cause the economy's rate of capital formation to decline due to crowding out.

Questions

1. In our initial example what would have to happen to investment if taxes were cut to $10?

2. In our initial example how would balancing the budget by raising taxes affect the rate of capital formation?

What Is the Public Debt?

Since the beginning of World War II the public sector in Australia has traditionally been in deficit. Financing these deficits by selling government bonds has resulted in a large increase in the stock of bonds outstanding — the size of the government debt. As can be seen from Figure 10.6 there has been a large increase in the size of Australia's public debt since the early 1970s.

Public Versus Private Debt

Most of us are accustomed to thinking in terms of private debt, the personal debt people incur when they borrow money to buy a car, a house, to pay their children's school fees. The chief fear is that of not being able to pay the debt off as repayments come due. If you can't, your assets — the car, the house, the furniture — may be seized by those who have lent you money. They may even be able to put a lien on your pay cheque. This is a legal claim that allows them to take a part of every pay cheque (direct from your employer) until they have been paid back the amount originally lent to you. In short, a private debt is what one party, the debtor, owes another, the creditor. Failure by the debtor to repay the creditor on time can result in severe hardship and loss for the debtor. Of course, the creditor is made poorer as well, possibly losing all that was originally loaned.

The government, or public, debt is different from a private debt in certain important respects, though it is similar in others. Consider the following hypothetical example. Suppose that the government's debt is held entirely by its own citizens, and that each citizen owns the same number of government bonds as every other citizen. Since it is the citizens'

government, the public debt is the citizens' debt, or what the citizens owe themselves! Suppose the government decided to pay off the entire debt by levying and collecting a tax of the same size from each citizen. The amount of taxes that each citizen would pay the government would be just equal to the amount of money each would receive from the government for the government bonds that each holds. It is the same as if each citizen were to take X dollars out of his or her left pocket and put the X dollars back into the right pocket.

What about interest payments on a government's debt held entirely by and distributed equally among its own citizens? Again, suppose the government levies and collects a tax of the same size from every citizen to pay the interest on the debt. Each citizen would then pay an amount of taxes exactly equal to the interest payments received on the government bond he or she holds. Again, what each citizen takes out of the left pocket matches what is put back into the right pocket.

Obviously, in our hypothetical example the existence and size of the government debt is of no consequence whatsoever. The example shows how different a government, or public, debt can be from a private debt.

The Burden of the Government Debt

Our hypothetical example serves another important purpose. It suggests that any cause for concern about the government debt lies in the fact that certain of the example's assumptions don't hold in reality. Because of this, the government debt imposes certain burdens similar to those of a private debt.

FIGURE 10.6
Public Debt in Australia 1952–53 to 1985–86 ($A bill).

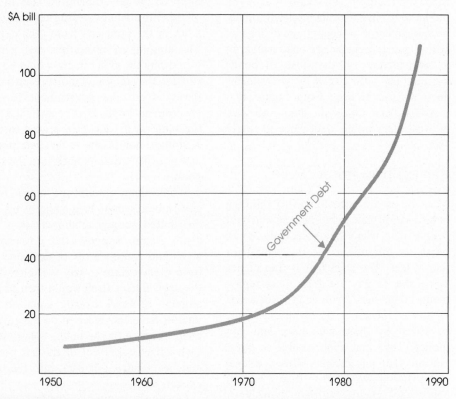

Between 1952–53 and 1985–86 government debt in Australia grew more than tenfold reflecting the fact that government has consistently budgeted for deficits. The increase has been concentrated particularly in the years since 1970.

Distribution Effects

First of all, government bonds outstanding are not distributed equally among the nation's citizens. Some people hold none and others own a great number. However, any attempt to retire some or all of the debt would have to be financed out of taxes that are paid by all citizens (except those who somehow avoid paying taxes). This large transfer payment would result in a redistribution of income. Some citizens would end up paying out an amount of taxes larger than their holdings of government bonds. These citizens would be net losers since they would pay out more than they would get back. Others would be net gainers in this transfer. Their tax payment toward the debt retirement effort would be less than their holdings of government bonds.[3]

[3]Many government bonds are held by trust funds, banks, insurance companies, and other businesses. A multitude of citizens either own or have claims on these institutions and therefore own government bonds indirectly. This makes no difference to our argument.

Interest payments on the public debt have the same distribution effects. These interest payments are transfer payments, financed by taxes on the general population and paid to those holding government bonds. A citizen is a net gainer if the amount received in interest payments exceeds his or her share of the tax payments used to pay interest on the debt. Otherwise the citizen is a net loser in this transfer.

In sum, the issue of public debt burden may be viewed in terms of the distribution effects of the transfer payments used to retire the debt or pay interest on it. It is a burden to those citizens who are net losers in this transfer. *For them the burden is similar to that of a private debt.*

Relative Size of Public Debt and GDP

It is difficult to give an accurate statistical measure of the burden created by redis-

FIGURE 10.7
Ratio of GDP to Public Debt in Australia: A Measure of the Debt Burden

One measure of the burden of public debt is its size relative to that of GDP, shown here as the ratio of GDP to public debt. As a result of spending during World War II the debt of government in Australia exceeded annual GDP levels until the mid-1950s. By the mid-1970s GDP was almost two and a half times our public debt. To the extent that GDP represents the tax capacity to pay off the debt as well as to pay interest on it, the burden of the debt on the Australian economy has declined since 1945. In recent years the ratio has begun to fall, however, suggesting that the debt burden is increasing.

tribution effects. Whatever they are, the economy's ability either to retire the public debt or to pay interest on it is all relative to the economy's capacity to pay taxes. A reasonable measure of this ability is the size of the GDP relative to the size of the debt and to the amount of the interest payments that must be paid on it.

Figure 10.7 indicates that since the early 1950s in Australia, GDP has become much larger relative to the size of the government debt. Immediately after World War II, Australia's public debt was larger than GDP. This continued until the mid-1950s. Since the late 1940s, however, GDP has usually grown at a faster rate than government debt. By the mid-1970s GDP was almost two and a half times the size of our public debt. Using this criterion the burden of the public debt declined steadily between the late 1940s and 1975-76. Since then, and particularly in recent years the ratio of GDP to the size of the debt has declined, suggesting that the debt burden is increasing.

What about the level of interest payments on the public debt relative to the size of GDP? Between 1945 and the mid-1970s this consistently declined to a low figure of 3 per cent. With greater borrowing and higher interest rates this figure then began to rise again. It currently is more than 5 per cent. Though this still seems a small fraction of Australia's total GDP, the increase is cause for concern if it continues.

External Versus Internal Debt

Government debt (bonds) held by Australian citizens is what these citizens collectively owe to themselves. The redistribution effects associated with taxation and transfer payments only redistribute the economy's total output

domestically. As a nation there is no loss in total output. That part of government debt held by foreigners is another matter. Interest payments on such debt, as well as the retirement of that debt, amounts to a transfer of purchasing power from a nation's citizens to foreigners. In other words, a part of the nation's output must be given up to another nation. It is like private debt in that one party loses purchasing power by virtue of the obligation to pay another.

In Australia the portion of government debt held by foreigners has increased in recent years. In the mid-1970s foreigners held about 5 per cent of Australia's total government debt. By the mid-1980s this figure exceeded 20 per cent. While this is still a small portion of the total debt, the increase is somewhat disturbing. Some say it reflects the fact that political turmoil abroad has caused foreign investors in general to seek the relatively safe haven provided by Australian government bonds.

Is the Debt a Burden on Future Generations?

It is sometimes argued that government debt creation imposes a burden on future generations. Is this true? Yes and no.

Debt creation does saddle future generations with the redistribution effects associated with the taxes and transfer payments needed to make ongoing interest payments on the debt. To the extent that taxpayers and bondholders are not necessarily the same people, this redistribution of income will be a burden to some members of future generations.

The creation of public debt during times when the economy is operating at full employment *may* represent a burden to future generations, but not necessarily.

POLICY PERSPECTIVE

Deficits and the Growing Government Debt — Facing Up to a Problem

Whatever the size of a government budget deficit, financing that deficit results in the creation of an equivalent amount of new government debt. One of the major concerns about the large deficits of recent years is that they have caused an increase in the rate of growth of the government debt.

Debt Growing Faster than GDP

In contrast to most of the postwar period, since the mid-1970s in Australia the rate of growth of government debt has generally exceeded the rate of growth of GDP, resulting in a decline in the ratio of GDP to government debt, as can be seen from Figure 10.7. Given the rate of interest that must be paid on government debt, total interest payments on the debt tend to become an ever larger factor in the government's budget as long as the debt grows at a faster rate than GDP. While interest payments on the debt represented 4.4 per cent of the Commonwealth budget in 1975–76, by 1986–87 they represented 10.66 per cent. (See Figure 3.1, Chapter 3).

Obviously the rate of growth of government debt cannot exceed the rate of growth of GDP indefinitely. Eventually the interest payments on the debt would take up the whole government budget, crowding out all other government expenditure categories (education, defence, social security payments, and so forth), until finally the government would simply be forced to repudiate the debt — the government would literally be bankrupt. No doubt political pressures would build up to reduce deficits and curb growth of the government debt long before this point were reached.

Limiting Growth of Deficits

What kind of limit on the size of government deficits is necessary if the growth rate of the government debt is not to exceed the growth rate of GDP? The answer is that the dollar size of the deficit must not exceed the growth rate of nominal GDP multiplied by the dollar size of the government debt. For example, if the debt equals $1 billion and nominal GDP is growing at 5 per cent per year, then the deficit should not exceed $50 million. A $50 million deficit would require the government to issue (sell) $50 million of new government bonds, thus increasing the debt by another $50 million (to $1.05 billion), or at a 5 per cent annual rate. Actual Federal Budget deficits were so large in Australia between 1974–75 and 1978–79, and again between 1982–83 and 1985–86 that Federal public debt grew at an average rate of about 15 per cent per year during these periods. Nominal GDP grew only at about 10 per cent per annum. Efforts by the Fraser government in the late 1970s and early 1980s and by the Hawke government in the mid-1980s to reduce government deficits reflect a general concern in the Australian economy about the importance of reducing the size of the public debt.

Questions

1. How might changes in the level of interest rates affect the urgency of the need to bring down the growth rate of the public debt?

2. How does the distribution of holdings of government debt among citizens bear on the urgency to bring down the growth rate of government debt?

New government bonds may 'crowd out' bonds being issued by businesses when the economy is producing at maximum capacity. To this extent business may have to cut back on capital expansion for lack of funds. The government gets the funds and uses the resources that would otherwise go to businesses for something else. Suppose the government spends the funds from its bond sales inefficiently or on something society doesn't want — fighter planes that don't fly or fancy bicentennial parties. Present and future generations are *burdened* because of the forgone capital that would have allowed the economy to produce more now and tomorrow. Note, however, that the government might have raised taxes instead of selling bonds to get the funds for those foolish expenditures. *Only* when selling bonds is easier than raising taxes (due to political considerations, say) is it true that creating government debt is a cause of the burden. Even then the real cause is poor fiscal policy.

Creation of public debt can be a blessing under certain conditions. Suppose the economy is in a recession. Prudent fiscal policy would call for increased government spending and reduced taxes — in short, a deficit. And creating this deficit requires the creation of more government debt.[4] If the government didn't take these

actions, the economy would have a longer and deeper recession than otherwise. Goods and services, including capital goods, that otherwise could be produced would not be. This year's forgone production would be forever lost to society. Society would be saddled with *the burden of doing without goods it could have had* — now and in the future.

CHECKPOINT 10.4

Suppose that half of the nation's citizens each hold an equal share of the public debt and that all citizens each pay an equal share of the taxes used to pay interest on the debt. Given this situation, how large do you think the total debt could be in relation to GDP before serious unrest might develop? What would government bankruptcy mean in this case?

SUMMARY

1. The government budget is an itemised account of government expenditures and revenues over the course of a year. The budget is said to be balanced, in surplus, or in deficit depending, respectively, on whether government spending equals, is less than, or is greater than government tax revenues. The Australian Federal

[4]Even if the government financed the deficit by creating more money ('printing' it), it would be necessary to create more bonds under

modern central banking arrangements, the subject of Chapters 13 through 15.

government frames its budget aiming to maintain high employment, price stability and external viability for the economy.

2. The equilibrium GDP can be raised by increasing government expenditures or by lowering taxes or by doing both. Conversely, the equilibrium GDP can be lowered by decreasing government expenditures or by raising taxes or by doing both. According to the balanced budget multiplier, a simultaneous increase in government expenditures and taxes of a matched, or balanced, amount will result in an increase in GDP equal to the increase in government spending. The converse is true of a decrease.

3. During a recession a suitable discretionary fiscal policy calls for government deliberately to increase government spending and reduce taxes. An inflationary expansion would call for a decrease in government spending and an increase in taxes. In practice, discretionary fiscal policy is hampered by the difficulty of forecasting the future; timing problems due to the politics and sluggishness of democratic processes and to lags in recognising the current state of the economy; the tendency of fiscal actions by state and local government to accentuate contractions and expansions; and the variety of taxes that government may change, each having a quantitative impact that is difficult to assess.

4. Nondiscretionary fiscal policy relies on the economy's built-in automatic stabilisers. Chief among these are a progressive tax structure and unemployment benefit payments, which cause tax revenues to vary more than proportionally with changes in GDP. These automatically tend to generate expansionary budget deficits during recessions and budget surpluses that dampen inflationary pressures during expansions. Automatic stabilisers reduce but do not eliminate the need for discretionary fiscal policy. Sometimes they pose a problem, for they can slow down the recovery from a recession and, to this extent, hinder rather than help the economy.

5. Annually balanced budgets tend to accentuate the business cycle. A cyclically balanced budget policy is difficult to follow because the expansion phase of a business cycle typically differs in length and magnitude from the recession phase. Consequently, functional finance is the budget policy most often followed.

6. Given the actual level of government spending, the cyclically adjusted budget measures what the budget deficit or surplus would be if GDP were continually at a high employment level. The cyclically adjusted budget deficit or surplus is a more accurate measure of the impact of fiscal policy than is the actual budget deficit or surplus.

7. A budget deficit has a more expansionary impact on the economy if it is financed by creating new money than if it is financed by borrowing. A budget surplus has less of a contractionary impact on the economy if the surplus is used to retire debt outstanding than if it is simply left to accumulate in the government treasury.

8. The public debt, or the stock of government bonds outstanding, was larger than GDP in the immediate post-World War II years. Up through 1975–76 GDP grew faster than the debt until it was roughly two and a half times the size of the debt. By this criterion the debt became less of a burden over time. In some recent years the ratio of GDP to government debt has declined, suggesting that the debt burden is increasing.

9. The government debt may be a burden to the extent that the taxes and transfer payments needed to make interest payments on the debt cause a redistribution of income among citizens, to the extent that the debt is held by foreigners, and to the extent that debt creation allows the financing of unproductive or unnecessary government spending.

KEY TERMS AND CONCEPTS

automatic stabilisers
balanced budget
balanced budget multiplier
budget deficit
budget surplus
cyclically adjusted budget
fiscal drag
fiscal policy
government budget
progressive tax
proportional tax
public debt
public sector borrowing requirement
public sector deficit
regressive tax
unemployment benefits

QUESTIONS AND PROBLEMS

1. Suppose that the government budget is balanced and that the economy is experiencing an inflationary boom. Assuming the economy's *MPC* is 4/5, compare and contrast each of the following discretionary fiscal actions in terms of their effectiveness in dealing with this situation:

a. increase lump-sum taxes by $10 million;

b. decrease government spending by $10 million;

c. decrease both government spending and lump-sum taxes by $10 million;

d. decrease government spending by $16 million and lump-sum taxes by $20 million.

2. Between 1929–30 and 1936–37 in Australia the unemployment rate did not fall below 10 per cent, yet the public sector had deficits in every one of those years. If deficits are expansionary, what were the possible problems? Use a leakages-injections diagram to illustrate your answer. (Any of the diagrams from Figure 10.4, parts a, b, or c will do, but show both the government spending schedule and the investment schedule separately, as well as their sum.)

3. Assume a $100 million downward shift in consumption spending. Using the diagrams in parts a and b of Figure 10.4, what would be the difference in the discretionary change in government spending required to keep the equilibrium GDP from changing, comparing the lump-sum tax case with the proportional tax case? What does this illustrate about the relationship between the role of automatic stabilisers and the need for discretionary fiscal action?

4. A number of economists have argued that discretionary fiscal policy is not well suited to deal with the relatively brief recessions that economies such as Australia have experienced since World War II. They contend that it is necessary to rely more on the built-in stabilisers to deal with such recessions. On the other hand, they argue that the relative importance of discretionary versus nondiscretionary fiscal policy is just the reverse in a depression like that of the 1930s. Explain why you would agree or disagree with these economists.

5. It has been argued by some economists that financing government deficits by borrowing may actually result in completely offsetting the expansionary effect of the deficit. What must they be assuming about the degree of difficulty of inducing the public to buy government bonds and the degree of sensitivity of investment spending to interest rate changes? These economists would refer to this as a situation of 'complete crowding out', where the real issue is one of *who* will decide how resources are to be used — the government or the private market. Explain.

6. Relative to other views on budget policy, it has been said that 'functional finance isn't so much a deliberate budget policy as a rationalisation for what actually happens'. Considering all the difficulties associated with discretionary fiscal policy, as well as the difficulties of pursuing the other budget policies, give an assessment of this statement.

7. In what sense is the public debt 'what we owe ourselves'? In what sense, and why, might this not be true from the standpoint of an individual taxpayer? Why do foreign holdings of our nation's government debt put us in a position like that of an individual who is in debt?

11

Aggregate Demand and Supply: Inflation and Supply-Side Economics

AFTER READING THIS CHAPTER YOU WILL BE ABLE TO:

1. Derive the aggregate demand curve from the total expenditure schedule, and explain why and how the aggregate demand curve shifts.

2. Explain the shape of the aggregate supply curve, and why and how the curve shifts.

3. Use the aggregate demand and supply curves to describe the difference between demand-pull and cost-push inflation and to explain stagflation.

4. Describe supply-side economics and explain its implications for fiscal policy.

In a money-using, market-oriented economy such as that of Australia, total output and the general price level are jointly determined by the interaction of aggregate demand and aggregate supply. So far our analysis of the determination of total income, output, and employment has assumed that prices and wages, hence the general price level, are fixed. In sum, we have assumed that the aggregate supply curve is perfectly horizontal at the unchanging general price level, as shown in Figure 8.3 in Chapter 8. This means that any change in the dollar value of total income and output is due entirely to a change in the quantity of real output — so many bushels of wheat, pairs of shoes, tonnes of steel, and so forth. Now we want to allow for the real-world situations in which *both* the general price level and total output change at the same time.

In this chapter we will examine in greater detail the way in which aggregate demand and aggregate supply interact to jointly determine total income, output, employment, and the economy's price level. Our analysis will allow us to distinguish between demand-pull and cost-push inflation and the closely related problem of stagflation. It also will provide a framework for examining supply-side economics and some of the policies of the Reagan administration in the USA, often referred to as Reaganomics, and the New Right movement in Australia.

THE AGGREGATE DEMAND CURVE

When we introduced the aggregate demand curve (*AD*) in Chapter 5 we saw that it shows the relationship between the economy's total demand for real GDP, or total output, and the economy's price level. It was argued that the *AD* curve has a negative slope because a higher price level, by reducing the purchasing power of consumer wealth, causes consumers to cut back on the quantity of goods and services they demand. Now we can use the income-expenditure approach developed in the last three chapters to see more clearly why this is true, and also to examine the causes of shifts in the *AD* curve.

The Price Level and Total Expenditure

In Chapter 8 we noted that an increase in consumer wealth would tend to shift the consumption function upward, while a decrease in wealth would tend to shift it downward. Much consumer wealth consists of fixed-dollar assets such as money, corporate and government bonds, and saving accounts. We pointed out in Chapter 5 that when the price level rises the real value or purchasing power of fixed-dollar assets declines, and that when the price level falls their purchasing power increases. Hence an increase in the price level reduces consumers' real wealth (the purchasing power of a given dollar amount of wealth), while a fall in the price level increases it. Therefore an increase in the price level, by reducing real wealth, will shift the consumption function downward. Conversely, a fall in the price level, by increasing real wealth, will shift the consumption function upward.

Since the consumption function is a major component of the total expenditure schedule (as shown in Figure 10.1), any shift in the consumption function will cause the total expenditure schedule to shift and thus cause the equilibrium level of real GDP to change. Therefore, *a fall in the price level, by shifting the consump-*

tion function upward causes the aggregate expenditure schedule to shift upward and the equilibrium level of real GDP to increase. A rise in the price level has the opposite effect, causing the total expenditure schedule to shift downward and the equilibrium level of real GDP to decrease.

Derivation of the AD Curve

Figure 11.1, part a, shows the determination of the equilibrium level of real GDP by the total expenditure schedule for three different possible price levels. The total expenditure schedule E_1 associated with the lowest of the three price levels, p_1, determines an equilibrium level of real GDP equal to $200 billion, corresponding to the interaction of E_1 with the 45° line at point e_1. For a higher price level p_2 the associated total expenditure schedule is E_2 and equilibrium real GDP is lower, equal to $140 billion. And for a yet higher price level p_3 the associated expenditure schedule E_3 and equilibrium real GDP of $80 billion are even lower.

Each combination of equilibrium real GDP and its associated price level in part a determines a point on the aggregate demand curve AD in part b of Figure 11.1. Points e_1, e_2, and e_3 on the AD curve in part b correspond respectively to the points e_1, e_2, and e_3 in part a. The negative slope of the AD curve reflects the fact that increases in the price level cause equilibrium real GDP to fall while decreases cause it to rise.

Changes in the price level cause shifts in the total expenditure schedule that change equilibrium real GDP, and correspond to movements along the AD curve. Therefore movement along the AD curve shows the response of equilibrium real GDP to changes in the price level.

Shifts in the AD Curve

In Chapters 9 and 10 we saw that any autonomous, or exogenous, change in consumption and investment spending, in government spending and tax rates, or in net export expenditure will cause the total expenditure schedule to shift and equilibrium real GDP to change.[1] We shall now show that such exogenous changes also cause the AD curve to shift.

We have seen that any change in the price level will cause the total expenditure schedule to shift and give rise to *movement along* the AD curve, as illustrated in Figure 11.1. But for a given price level we know that any exogenous expenditure or tax rate change will also cause the total expenditure schedule to shift and equilibrium real GDP to change. (These were the only kinds of cases considered in Chapters 9 and 10.) Since the price level is given, or unchanged, such a change in real GDP certainly can't be represented by movement along an AD curve. Therefore it must be represented by a shift in the AD curve.

This is illustrated in Figure 11.2. Suppose the price level is given as p_0 and the total expenditure schedule is E_0 in part a of Figure 11.2. The equilibrium real GDP is $100 billion and the point corresponding to e_0 in part a is e_0 on the AD curve in part b. Suppose there is an exogenous expenditure increase (an increase in government spending, say) that shifts the total expenditure schedule up from E_0 to E_1 and increases equilibrium real GDP to $200 billion, corresponding to point e_1 in part a. Given the price level

[1]In Chapters 9 and 10 we largely ignored net exports. Recognising such expenditure simply adds one more layer to the consumption, investment, and government spending that add up to give the total expenditure schedule, as shown in Figure 10.2 for example.

FIGURE 11.1
The Relationship Between Total Expenditure and the Aggregate Demand Curve

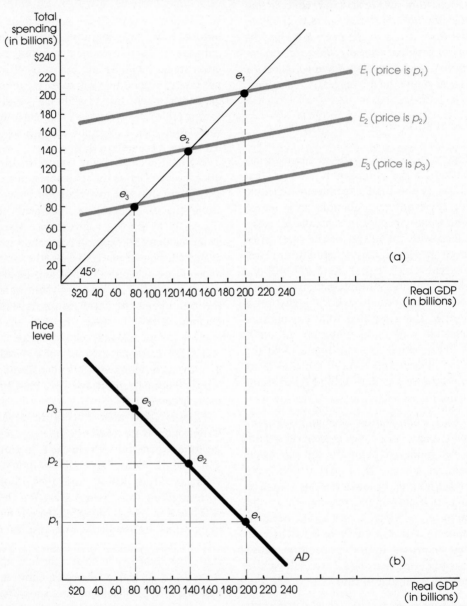

Increases in the economy's price level from p_1 to p_2 to p_3 cause the total expenditure schedule to shift downward from E_1 to E_2 to E_3 and the equilibrium level of real GDP to decline from $200 billion to $140 billion to $80 billion as shown in part a. In part b we plot these price levels and their associated levels of equilibrium real GDP to get the points e_1, e_2, and e_3 on the aggregate demand curve AD, corresponding to the points e_1, e_2, and e_3 in part a. Note that changes in the price level cause *shifts* in the total expenditure schedule that correspond to movements along the AD curve.

p_0, the AD_0 curve in part b is shifted rightward to AD_1 and the equilibrium point e_1 on AD_1 corresponds to point e_1 in part a.

The conclusions of Chapters 9 and 10 about the effects of exogenous expenditure and tax rate changes on the total expenditure schedule can now be stated in terms of their effects on the AD curve.

1. *An exogenous increase in consumption, investment, government or net export expenditure will shift the AD curve rightward. An exogenous decrease in any of these expenditures will shift the AD curve leftward.*

2. *A tax rate increase will shift the AD curve leftward. A tax rate decrease will shift the AD curve rightward.*

=====

*CHECKPOINT * 11.1*

Explain why changes in the price level cause movement along the AD curve and why exogenous expenditure changes cause the AD curve to shift. What would be the effect on the AD curve of a $10 billion increase in government expenditures financed by a $10 billion increase in lump-sum taxes?

Answers to all Checkpoints can be found at the back of the text.

=====

THE AGGREGATE SUPPLY CURVE

When we introduced the aggregate supply curve (AS) in Chapter 5 we saw that it shows the amounts of total output, or real GDP, that the economy's business will supply at different price levels. Now we will examine the shape of the AS curve in greater detail as well as consider how and why it can shift.

Shape of the AS Curve

A typical aggregate supply curve (AS) is shown in Figure 11.3. Three distinctly different ranges of the curve are readily apparent. It is horizontal to the left of point a. It increases at an increasing rate between points a and c, and then becomes vertical above point c.

Horizontal Range — Only Output Changes

When the economy's firms produce any level of real GDP less than y_a, corresponding to point a on the AS curve, they have a great deal of unused capacity. In fact, there is so much unemployed labour and idle plant and equipment to the left of a on the AS curve that firms would produce and sell more at prevailing prices if there were only more buyers. Therefore *real GDP can be increased along the horizontal range of the* AS *curve without any change in the economy's price level* p_0 *because there is so much excess capacity in the economy.* Over this 'Keynesian' range of the AS curve any change in aggregate demand changes real GDP but has no effect on the economy's price level, as illustrated earlier in Figure 8.3 (Chapter 8).

Intermediate Range — Both Price and Output Change

The AS curve slopes upward over the range from a to c indicating that as the price level rises the economy's firms produce more output, or real GDP, *other things remaining the same.* When we introduced the AS curve in Chapter 5 we

FIGURE 11.2
The Relationship Between Shifts in the Total Expenditure Schedule and Shifts in the *AD* Curve

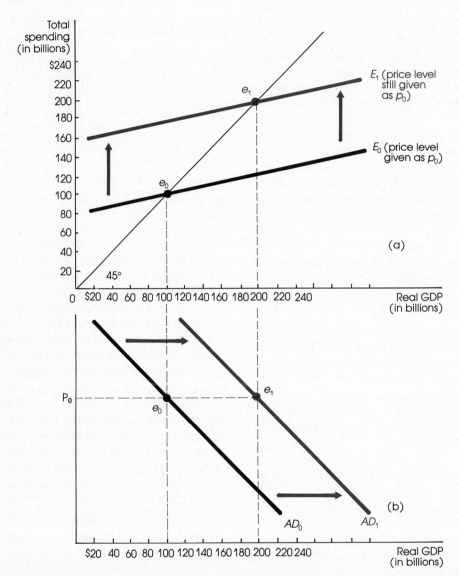

Assume a given, or unchanging, price level p_0. Then an exogenous increase in consumption, investment, government, or net export expenditure, or a reduction in tax rates, shifts the total expenditure schedule upward from E_0 to E_1, part a. This shift increases equilibrium real GNP from the level associated with point e_0 to that associated with point e_1. Corresponding to the shift from E_0 to E_1, part a, the aggregate demand curve shifts rightward from AD_0 to AD_1, bart b. Given the price p_0, the points e_0 and e_1 on AD_0 and AD_1 correspond to points e_0 and e_1 in part a and the associated equilibrium levels of real GNP. An exogenous reduction in consumption, investment, government, or net export expenditure, or an increase in tax rates, shifts the total expenditure schedule downward and the aggregate demand curve leftward, giving the price level p_0.

noted that the positive slope reflects short-run conditions. In particular, in the short run when the price level (the average of all prices) rises over the range from *a* to *c*, the prices of firms' products tend to rise while the prices of firms' inputs are assumed to remain unchanged, or 'the same'. Hence firms' profits rise along the positively sloped range of the *AS* curve from *a* to *c* and they respond by increasing output — real GDP increases.

The critical assumption here is of course that input prices remain unchanged in the short run. There are a number of reasons

why the prices of several inputs are often essentially fixed in the short run. For example, purchasing contracts between firms and suppliers are often entered into at pre-arranged prices that are re-negotiated after completion of the contract, which may take a considerable length of time. Similarly, plant and equipment leasing agreements as well as building rental contracts can fix the prices of such inputs for up to several years. However, in Australia the price of one of the most important inputs — labour — may not be as fixed in the short run as in the case of other countries. Due to the centralised wage fixing system and the acceptance that wages should keep pace with prices, the cost of labour tends to be much more flexible upwards than in other countries. For example, in the USA labour contracts between firms and workers often set money wages up to three years in advance. In contrast, in Australia under full wage indexation between 1983 and 1986, wages were increased an average of twice a year. This suggests that the short run in Australia is much shorter than that in other countries — probably six months or less. We will shortly examine the effect changes in input prices have on the *AS* curve.

FIGURE 11.3
The Aggregate Supply Curve

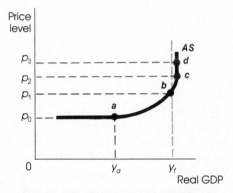

The aggregate supply curve *AS* is horizontal over the 'Keynesian' range up to point *a* because there is so much unemployment and idle capacity that the economy's firms will increase output (real GDP) at the existing price level if there is demand for it. The *AS* curve rises over the intermediate range from *a* to *c* because as the economy's price level rises product prices rise relative to fixed input prices in the short run and firms are induced by rising profits to increase output. On the vertical or 'classical' range of the *AS* curve above point *c* the economy is up against the limits of its capacity to produce output so that changes in the price level cause no change in output. This capacity constrained level of real GDP is larger than the real GDP level y_f — the 'full-employment' level associated with a so-called natural rate of unemployment.

Another important characteristic of the *AS* curve over the range from *a* to *c* is that the slope increases *at an increasing rate*. This reflects the fact that as firms expand output in the short run and operate closer to full capacity production becomes less efficient. Consequently *increasingly* larger amounts of labour and other inputs are required per additional unit of output produced. Therefore, even though wages and other input prices remain unchanged, the cost per additional unit produced increases at an increasing rate. Hence to keep profits rising, and induce firms to supply more output, increasingly higher product prices must be received by firms to cover their increasingly higher per unit production costs. For this reason the economy's price level rises at an increasing rate per additional unit of total output, or real GDP, over the range from *a* to *c* along the *AS* curve.

In sum:

The AS curve rises over the intermediate range because while input prices remain unchanged in the short run, product prices (hence the economy's price level) can rise, thereby increasing profits and inducing the economy's firms to increase output. The AS curve rises at an increasing rate over the intermediate range because per unit production costs rise at an increasing rate and product prices (hence the economy's price level) must do likewise if profits are to rise and induce further increases in output.

The Vertical Range — Only Price Changes

When the economy's price level has risen to p_2, corresponding to point c, the *AS* curve becomes vertical. The economy has reached the absolute limit of its productive capacity. Over this range increases in the price level, such as from p_2 to p_3, corresponding to movement from c to d along *AS*, will not result in any increase in real GDP — nothing more can be produced. Shifts in aggregate demand over the vertical or 'classical' range of the *AS* curve only change the price level and cause no changes in real GDP, as illustrated earlier in Figure 8.2.

Finally it should be emphasised that when the economy is up against its productive capacity limit it produces a level of real GDP greater than the economy's potential real GDP level y_f

associated with a so-called natural level of unemployment (discussed in Chapter 6), or what might be termed the 'full-employment' level of real GDP. This is indicated in Figure 11.3 by the fact that the vertical range of the *AS* curve lies to the right of y_f which corresponds to point *b* on the *AS* curve at price level p_1.

Shifts in the *AS* Curve

There are a number of reasons why the *AS* curve can shift. Among the most important are changes in input prices, productivity changes, and changes in the size of the economy's labour force and its capital stock.

Changes in Input Prices

We have emphasised that in the short run input prices are assumed to remain unchanged. They are among the other things assumed to remain the same when there is *movement along* the *AS* curve. Recalling our discussion of market demand and supply curves in Chapter 4 immediately suggests that any change in any of those 'other things', such as input prices, will cause a shift in the *AS* curve.

One particularly important input price is the money wage rate. Given the prices firms are receiving for their products, if workers demand and get higher money wages, firms will find their profits reduced or possibly even eliminated. Consequently whatever their current output levels, firms will only be willing to continue producing at those levels if they receive higher prices. Therefore whatever the real GDP, the associated price level will have to be higher if the economy's firms are to continue to produce that level of real GDP. Thus the *AS* curve will shift up, such as from AS_0

to AS_1 in Figure 11.4.

For example, suppose the economy's firms had been willing to produce the real GDP y_0 at price level p_0 prior to the increase in money wages, corresponding to point a on AS_0. After the money wage increase they will be willing to produce y_0 only if the price level is p_1, corresponding to point b on AS_1 in Figure 11.4. Equivalently, prior to the money wage increase the economy's firms were willing to produce a real GDP level y_1 at price level p_1, corresponding to point c on AS_0. After the increase they are only willing to produce a smaller real GDP level y_0 at the price level p_1, corresponding to point b on AS_1. In sum:

An increase in money wages or any other input price will cause an upward shift in the AS curve. A decrease in money wages or any other input price will shift the AS curve downward.

Changes in Productivity

Another important item assumed to remain the same along the AS curve is technology — the state of scientific and managerial knowledge. Improvements in technology increase labour productivity which means each worker can produce more. Given money wage rates and the prices of other inputs this means that production costs per unit of output go down. The economy's firms are therefore willing and able to produce and sell their products at lower prices. Moreover, given the size of the labour force and the quantity of the economy's other resources, the maximum amount of output the economy can produce is increased. Consequently the AS curve shifts down

FIGURE 11.5
Increased Productivity Shifts the AS Curve
Downward and Rightward

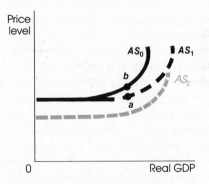

Given money wage rates and the prices of other inputs, an increase in productivity causes production costs per unit of output to go down so that the economy's firms are willing and able to sell their products at lower prices. In addition, the maximum amount of output the economy can produce is increased. Therefore a productivity increase shifts the AS curve downward and to the right, such as from AS_0 to AS_2.

Given money wage rates and input prices, an increase in the size of the economy's labour force and its capital stock shifts the AS curve rightward, such as from AS_0 to AS_1.

FIGURE 11.4
Increases in Input Prices Shift the AS
Curve Upward

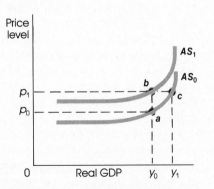

At any given level of real GDP an increase in money wages or any other input price will reduce or eliminate firms' profits. Therefore they will only continue to produce their current levels of output if they receive higher product prices. This means that whatever the level of real GDP, the economy's associated price level will have to be higher as represented by an upward shift in the AS curve, such as from AS_0 to AS_1.

and to the right, such as from AS_0 to AS_2 in Figure 11.5.

An increase in productivity shifts the AS curve downward and to the right, reflecting the fact that the economy's firms are now willing to produce any level of real GDP at a lower price level, and that the maximum real GDP the economy can produce is increased.

Changes in Labour Force and Capital Stock

If the size of the economy's labour force and its stock of capital increase, there will be an increase in the maximum level of real GDP that the economy can produce. This will cause the AS curve to shift rightward, such as from AS_0 to AS_1 in Figure 11.5.

Note that for any level of real GDP over the intermediate ranges of AS_0 and AS_1, the corresponding point on AS_0 is higher than the corresponding point on AS_1 — point b is higher than point a, for example. This is explained by recalling that when output is increased over the intermediate range of the AS curve production becomes less efficient as the economy gets closer to full capacity. With a larger labour force and capital stock these inefficiencies do not become as severe along AS_1 as along AS_0 until higher levels of real GDP are reached.

CHECKPOINT 11.2

Explain how a decline in the price of imported oil would affect the AS curve.

INTERACTION OF AGGREGATE DEMAND AND SUPPLY

Our analysis of the determination of total income, output, and employment in

Chapters 8, 9, and 10 assumed the AS curve was horizontal. Therefore the price level remained unchanged whenever the AD curve shifted, as in Figure 8.3 in Chapter 8. Now we will examine the way in which that analysis is modified when the price level can vary with output because of the existence of the upward sloping intermediate and vertical ranges along the AS curve, such as shown in Figure 11.3. In addition, we will examine the distinction between demand-pull and cost-push inflation, and gain some understanding of the problem of stagflation.

Modification of the Analysis When the Price Level Changes

Figure 11.2 showed the change in real GDP at a given price level in response to an exogenous, or autonomous, expenditure increase (in consumption, investment, government, or net export spending), or a tax rate reduction, which shifts the total expenditure schedule upward and the AD curve rightward. Such a shift is repeated again in Figure 11.6, but now allowing for the price level to change along the upward sloping intermediate range of the AS curve. The adjustment can be broken into two steps.

Step 1. The total expenditure schedule E shifts upward from E_0 to E_1' in part a of Figure 11.6, causing the AD curve to shift rightward from AD_0 to AD_1, as shown in part b. *If* the economy's firms were willing to increase output at *the price level p_0* in response to the increase in aggregate demand, real GDP would increase from y_0 to y_1', corresponding to a move from point e_0 to point e_1'. The adjustment would be exactly the same as that already described in Figure 11.2. The increase in real GDP from y_0 to y_1' would be equal to the multiplier effect discussed in Chapters 9 and 10. Now, however, because the AS curve is upward sloping, the economy's firms are not willing to produce a real GDP greater than y_0 at the price level p_0. Therefore at p_0 there is an excess demand for total output equal to the distance between point e_0 and e_1'.

Step 2. The excess demand causes the economy's price level to rise. The increase in the price level will cause the total expenditure schedule to shift downward to E_1 in part a, which gives rise to movement up along the AD_1 curve, part b, as previously shown in Figure 11.1. The adjustment is complete once the total expenditure schedule has shifted down to E_1, part a, and the price level has risen to p_1 corresponding to the intersection of AD_1 and AS at point e_1 in part b. Compared to the increase in real GDP that occurs when the price level remains unchanged (from y_0 to y_1'), real GDP now increases by a smaller amount (from y_0 to y_1) because some of the increase in aggregate demand is absorbed by a rise in the price level. In sum:

When the economy is operating along the intermediate range of the AS curve, an exogenous expenditure change, or an exogenous tax rate change, will have a smaller multiplier effect on real GDP than when the economy is operating along the horizontal range of the AS curve.

Finally, note that along the vertical range of the AS curve the multiplier effect on real GDP equals zero. Any exogenous expenditure or tax rate change will only cause a change in the price level along the vertical range.

Demand-Pull Inflation: Shifts in the AD Curve

Suppose the AD curve is initially in the position AD_0 in Figure 11.7 so that the

FIGURE 11.6
Change in Real GDP and the Price Level Due to Exogenous Expenditure Change

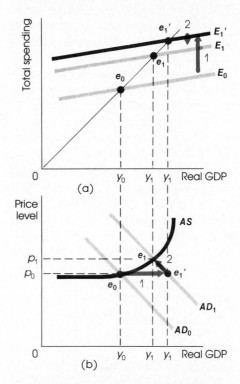

Initially equilibrium real GDP is y_0 and the equilibrium price level is p_0 at point e_0 in both part a and part b. An exogenous expenditure increase shifts the total expenditure schedule upward from E_0 to E_1' (arrow 1, part a) and the AD curve rightward from AD_0 to AD_1. If the economy's firms were willing to increase output in response to the increase in aggregate demand at price level p_0, real GDP would increase from y_0 to y_1' (arrow 1, part b), an amount equal to the simple multiplier effect. However, because the AS curve is upward sloping there is instead an excess aggregate demand at P_0. Therefore the price level rises causing the total expenditure schedule to shift downward to E_1 (arrow 2, part a) and movement up along the AD_1 curve (arrow 2, part b), restoring equilibrium at point e_1 (parts a and b), at real GDP level y_1, and price level p_1. The multiplier effect on real GDP (equals the increase from y_0 to y_1) is smaller when the price level rises compared with the effect (y_0 to y_1') when the price level remains unchanged.

equilibrium price level and real GDP are p_0 and y_0 respectively, corresponding to point e_0 on the AS curve. An exogenous expenditure increase, or tax rate reduction, which shifts the AD curve rightward from AD_0 to AD_0' increases equilibrium real GDP from y_0 to y_0'. However, along this horizontal, or Keynesian, range of AS from point e_0 to e_0' there is so much excess capacity and unemployment that firms are willing to increase output at existing prices in response to increased demand — the price level remains unchanged at p_0.

Further increases in aggregate demand, such as represented by shifts from AD_0' to AD_1 to AD_2, along the intermediate range of the AS curve between points e_0' and e_2 cause the price level to rise. Moreover, the rise in the price level becomes ever larger relative to the increase in real GDP as the economy moves closer and closer to its full-employment real GDP level y_f, and then beyond to its capacity level y_c where the price level rises to p_2, corresponding to point e_2. Further increases in aggregate demand, such as from AD_2 to AD_3, move the economy up along the vertical, or classical, range of the AS curve and pull the price level up from p_2 to p_3 while real GDP remains unchanged at y_c.

The increase in the price level which is caused by increases in aggregate demand along the intermediate and vertical ranges of the AS curve is often referred to as demand-pull inflation. **Demand-pull inflation** *originates on the demand side of the economy's markets for goods and services and is caused by increases in aggregate demand.*

Cost-Push Inflation: The Stagflation Problem

We have seen how an increase in money wages or any other input price will cause

the AS curve to shift upward, as shown in Figure 11.4 for example. Such upward shifts give rise to **cost-push inflation.**

Cost-Push Inflation

Cost-push inflation may originate in the labour market where powerful unions coerce firms to pay higher wages under the threat of labour walkout or strike. The resulting rise in per unit costs of production is then likely to cause these firms to charge higher product prices. Similarly, a few large firms in key industries might use their market power to try to raise

FIGURE 11.7
Demand-Pull Inflation

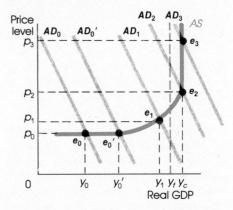

The rise in the price level caused by increased aggregate demand is called demand-pull inflation.

When aggregate demand increases from AD_0 to AD_0' over the horizontal, or Keynesian, range of the AS curve real GDP increases from y_0 to y_0' while the price level remains unchanged at p_0. Increases in aggregate demand over the intermediate range, such as from AD_0' to AD_1 to AD_2, pull up the price level to an ever greater extent (from p_0 to p_1 to p_2) relative to the increase in real GDP (from y_0' to y_1 to y_c). Increases in aggregate demand, such as from AD_2 to AD_3, over the vertical or classical range of the AS curve pull up the price level (from p_2 to p_3) without increasing real GDP at all.

profits by charging higher prices for their products. Cost-push can also originate with an increase in the price of any vital resource needed to produce a variety of products. The sharp rise in the price of imported oil in 1973–1974 and again in 1979 drove up the cost of energy, a necessary ingredient to any production process. The resulting rise in per unit production costs pushed up the prices of almost all products, as was reflected in the dramatic rise in the general price level.

Stagflation

During these cost-push episodes of the 1970s the unemployment rate rose at the same time that the inflation rate increased, a phenomenon often referred to as **stagflation** (from a combination of the word stagnation, meaning high unemployment, and inflation, a rising price level). We will examine stagflation more extensively in Chapter 17. However, we can begin to get some insight into the problem by examining the relationship between cost-push inflation and unemployment at this point.

Suppose the economy's aggregate supply curve is initially AS_0 in Figure 11.8, intersecting the aggregate demand curve AD_0 at e_0 to give a full-employment equilibrium level of real GDP y_f and price level p_f. Now suppose the economy experiences some sort of cost-push — for example, an increase in the price of imported oil. This will push up costs of production and business firms will now charge higher prices to cover their higher costs. To induce the economy's firms to produce any given level of real GDP, the general price level will have to be higher than previously. This is represented by an upward shift in the aggregate supply curve from AS_0 to AS_1. The economy's equil-

ibrium price level will *rise* from p_f to p_1 while its equilibrium level of real GDP will *decline* from y_f to y_1, corresponding to the intersection of AS_1 and AD_0 at point e_1. Since the equilibrium level of real GDP is now less than the full-employment level, employment is reduced and unemployment increased. In sum, *cost-push inflation originates on the supply side of the economy. A cost-push results in a rise in both the general price level and the unemployment rate, a phenomenon known as stagflation.*

FIGURE 11.8
Cost-Push Inflation and Stagflation

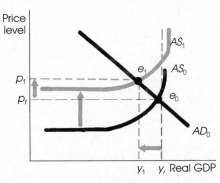

An increase in input prices shifts the AS curve upward from AS_0 to AS_1 along the AD curve AD_0 pushing up the price level from p_f to p_1 — a process known as cost-push inflation. The associated fall in real GDP from y_f to y_1 raises the unemployment rate. The simultaneous increase in the price level and the unemployment rate is often referred to as stagflation.

CHECKPOINT 11.3

Suppose the AS curve to the right of point e_0 in part b of Figure 11.6 were more steeply sloped. Given the same AD_0 and AD_1 curves, how would the total expenditure adjustment in part a now be different? Suppose a demand-pull and a cost-push inflation occurred simultaneously and in such a way that *there was no change in real GDP. Construct a diagram showing how the AS and AD curves would have to shift to give rise to such an occurrence.*

SUPPLY-SIDE ECONOMICS: IMPLICATIONS FOR FISCAL POLICY

Our discussion in Chapter 10 of the effects of government spending, taxation, and budget policy on the economy presented a strictly Keynesian point of view. In particular, according to the Keynesian view, taxes only affect the demand side of the economy. By causing a deficit (or surplus) in the government's budget, tax changes increase (or decrease) aggregate demand, thus increasing (or decreasing) total income, output, and employment. Moreover, we have seen that according to the Keynesian analysis, a dollar of government expenditure has a more expansionary impact on the economy than a dollar of tax cuts because the government spends the whole dollar, whereas taxpayers save part of any tax cut.

In recent years a number of economists, journalists, and politicians have been challenging the Keynesian view that tax cuts affect the economy only by affecting aggregate demand. Indeed, the views of these 'supply-siders' have become an integral part of the Reagan administration's economic policy program in the US and the New Right movement in Australia. Basically, supply-siders argue that lower tax *rates* give rise to higher after-tax rewards or greater incentives to work, save, and invest. As people respond to these incentives the economy's capacity to produce and supply goods and services is increased. Two basic supply-side

propositions follow from this.

1. The resulting increase in the economy's supply of total output, or real GDP, will put downward pressure on prices and hence help fight inflation.
2. The increase in total income and output may well give rise to an increase in tax *revenue* despite the reduction in tax *rates*. This view is just the opposite of the Keynesian view that a reduction in tax rates will always result in a reduction in tax revenue. In other words, supply-siders argue that a reduction in tax rates can reduce a government budget deficit or increase a budget surplus — just the opposite of the Keynesian view. Let's examine the supply-side reasoning underlying each of these propositions.

Tax Rates and Incentives

Supply-side economics stresses cutting income tax *rates*. (Remember, tax rates are not the same thing as tax *revenues*, the amount of money collected from taxpayers.) In particular, supply-siders argue that marginal tax rates are what must be reduced. The **marginal tax rate** is defined as follows:

$$\text{marginal tax rate} = \frac{\text{change in tax liability}}{\text{change in income}}$$

The marginal tax rate indicates how much of an additional dollar of one's income, the marginal or last dollar earned must be paid in taxes. For example, if the marginal tax rate is .3, 30 cents of an *additional* dollar of income must be given to the government, leaving the individual with 70 cents of after-tax income.

The marginal tax rate of a proportional income tax is constant because the same percentage of every additional dollar of income is taxed away, regardless of the amount of income earned. If the proportional tax rate is .2, for example, then an individual earning an additional dollar will have to give 20 cents of it to the tax collector whether the individual's income is $10,000, $100,000, or $1,000,000.

The marginal tax rate of a progressive income tax rises as income increases. For example, suppose the progressive income tax structure is such that the first $10,000 of an individual's income is subject to a 20 per cent rate, the second $10,000 to a 30 per cent rate, the third to a 40 per cent rate, and so forth. Then for income levels less than $10,000 the marginal tax rate on an additional dollar of income is .2, for income levels between $10,000 and $20,000 it is .3, for income levels between $20,000 and $30,000 it is .4, and so forth.

Supply-siders argue that a reduction of marginal tax will increase work effort, encourage more saving and investment, improve resource allocation, and reduce the amount of resources devoted to tax-avoidance activities. Each of these effects of reduced marginal tax rates will tend to increase the economy's aggregate supply of goods and services. Let's consider why.

Tax Rate Effects on Work Effort

When an individual considers whether or not to work harder or longer, the relevant question is, What will be the additional after-tax income, or take-home pay, resulting from the additional effort? The larger the marginal tax rate, the smaller the after-tax reward and therefore the less the incentive to work harder or longer. This consideration is relevant not only to people contemplating the merits of additional work effort in their currently

held job (more overtime, for example) but also to those contemplating promotion possibilities, career choices, new business ventures, and other forms of innovative work effort. For example, suppose the marginal tax rate on additional income above $30,000 were .95. Few people would want to put in the additional time and effort, acquire the additional training and education, or take on the additional responsibility and risks necessary to earn an income greater than $30,000. In sum, supply-siders argue that higher marginal tax rates encourage people to take more leisure time and work less. This can occur in many ways: a reduction in overtime; earlier retirement; more absenteeism; fewer second breadwinners in households; lower labour productivity; and greater reluctance to take more responsible (and higher paying) jobs, to pursue more demanding (and higher paying) careers, or to undertake other innovative, often risky and demanding, forms of work effort. Therefore, *supply-siders argue that reducing marginal tax rates will stimulate work effort and thereby increase the economy's aggregate supply of output.*

Tax Rate Effects on Saving and Investment

As we have discussed before, one of the determinants of the amount of saving is the rate of return that can be earned on savings. If the rate of interest is 10 per cent, an individual would receive $10 on $100 of saving after 1 year, a rate of return of 10 per cent. But this is $10 of income and would be taxed just like any other form of income. Hence the higher the marginal tax rate on income, the smaller the fraction of the $10 that the individual could keep. For example, if the marginal tax rate were .3, the individual could keep only $7 after tax. The after-tax rate of return would be 7 per cent. It is the after-tax rate of return that is important to the individual who is deciding how much to save. The higher the marginal tax rate, the lower the after-tax rate of return and the smaller the incentive to save. Saving is necessary for capital formation, which increases the economy's capacity to produce goods. Therefore, *supply-siders argue that the increase in saving caused by a reduction of marginal tax rates tends to increase the economy's aggregate supply of output.*

Business willingness to invest in capital goods also depends on the after-tax rate of return on the dollars invested in capital goods. *Supply-siders argue that reduction of marginal tax rates stimulates investment spending, increasing capital formation and thereby aggregate supply.*

Tax Rate Effects on Resource Allocation

High marginal tax rates encourage the creation and use of loopholes in the tax law, the legal ways in which payment of taxes at going marginal tax rates can be avoided. These loopholes encourage workers, savers, and investors to direct resources into activities where after-tax rates of return are relatively high only because of special tax exemptions and advantages created by the loopholes. Such tax advantages are available to those investing in real estate, for example. As a result, it is possible that the economy devotes too many resources to residential and commercial construction at the expense of other productive activities not offering tax advantages. *Supply-siders argue that reductions in marginal tax rates would reduce the 'payoff' from loopholes and therefore lead to a more efficient*

allocation of resources, hence increasing the economy's capacity to supply goods.

Tax Rates and Tax Avoidance

Seeking out and taking advantage of often complicated tax loopholes typically requires the use of trained lawyers and accountants. Higher marginal tax rates make it more worthwhile for taxpayers to employ such services in order to avoid taxes. It is estimated that millions of dollars' worth of highly skilled and educated labour is employed annually in this fashion — labour that otherwise could be employed in producing goods and services more useful from society's viewpoint. Therefore, *supply-siders argue that a reduction of marginal tax rates would increase the economy's capacity to supply goods and services by reducing the use of resources for tax-avoidance activities.*

Inflation and Tax Rate Reduction

Supply-siders argue that the increase in the economy's supply of total output resulting from reductions in marginal tax rates will put downward pressure on prices and hence help fight inflation, the first of the two supply-side propositions noted before. This proposition can be illustrated in terms of the economy's aggregate supply curve.

Suppose the economy initially has an equilibrium level of real GDP y_0 and price level p_0, determined by the intersection of AD_0 and AS_0 at point a in Figure 11.9.

Effect of Tax Rate Reduction on the Aggregate Supply Curve

Suppose there is a reduction in marginal tax rates. For the moment let's focus only on the effect on the aggregate supply curve. Since marginal tax rates are now lower, workers, other resource suppliers, and firms will get to keep a larger fraction of the dollars they earn from the sale of the goods and services they produce. Suppliers can supply the same quantity of goods as before, but they can now sell the goods at a lower price and still receive the same after-tax income. Hence the reduction of marginal tax rates shifts the aggregate supply curve AS_0 down to the position AS_1.

FIGURE 11.9
Demand-Side and Supply-Side Effects of Reduction in Marginal Tax Rates

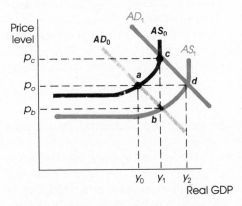

A reduction in marginal tax rates causes the economy's aggregate demand curve to shift rightward, according to the Keynesian, or demand-side, view, and the aggregate supply curve to shift downward and to the right, according to the supply-side view. When the AD curve shifts rightward from AD_0 to AD_1, real GDP increases from y_0 to y_1, and the price level rises from p_0 to p_c if supply-side shifts are ignored. Allowing for the supply-side effects of the tax rate reduction, the AS curve also shifts, such as from AS_0 to AS_1. In the example shown here, the result of both shifts is that real GDP increases from y_0 to y_2 while the price level remains unchanged at p_0. Hence supply-siders argue that tax rate reductions increase real GDP more and the general price level less than is suggested by a strictly Keynesian, or demand-side point of view.

Notice also, however, that the aggregate supply curve is shifted rightward as well. This reflects the increase in the economy's capacity to supply goods caused by the reduction in marginal tax rates, an increase due to increased work effort, increased capital formation, more efficient resource allocation — all the effects of marginal tax rate reductions just discussed. The economy's full capacity output level, corresponding to the vertical segment of the aggregate supply curve, has increased — the vertical segment of AS_1 lies to the right of that for AS_0.

As a consequence of the shift in the AS curve from AS_0 to AS_1, the economy's equilibrium level of real GDP increases from y_0 to y_1 while its equilibrium price level falls from p_0 to p_b, corresponding to the intersection of AD_0 and AS_1 at point b. We see now why supply-siders argue that reducing marginal tax rates puts downward pressure on prices and helps fight inflation.

Supply-Side and Demand-Side Views Combined

Let's now combine the demand-side effects of a reduction in marginal tax rates, as illustrated in Figure 11.2, with the supply-side effects. On the demand side, a reduction in marginal tax rates will cause the aggregate demand curve in Figure 11.9 to shift rightward — from AD_0 to AD_1, say. Now if we ignore any supply-side effects of the tax rate reduction, as is customary in the Keynesian view, we simply move up along the aggregate supply curve AS_0 from point a to point c. Real GDP increases from y_0 to y_1 and the price level rises from p_0 to p_c.

However, suppose we also take into account the shift in the aggregate supply curve from AS_0 to AS_1, the supply-side

---

POLICY PERSPECTIVE

Indexing Income Taxes — Putting the Brakes on Rising Tax Rates

Our income tax structure suffers from *bracket creep* — a process whereby inflation automatically increases taxes paid even though the government doesn't legislate higher tax rates. The effect of bracket creep has been quite dramatic: while in 1958 only one-in-40 taxpayers were hit by rates over 40 per cent, in 1987 one-in-two fell within this category.

Personal income in Australia is subject to a progressive tax. Recall that a progressive tax on income imposes successively higher tax rates on additional dollars of income as income rises. This is shown in Table 11.1 which gives the various marginal tax rates applicable in Australia over three recent years. Thus, for example, a person earning $19,500 in 1985 would pay no tax on the first $4595, 26.67 cents in the dollar on the next $7905 (i.e. $12,500 — 4595) of income, and 30 cents in the dollar on the final $7000 (i.e. $19,500–$12,500). Hence the total tax payable is:
$0 + $7905 (.2667) + $7000 (.30) = $0 + $2108 + $2100 = $4208.
This shows that as one's total income rises, the fraction of that total income that is taxed away gets larger; if the individual earns $12,500, then $2108 or 16.9 per cent of it goes in taxes; if the income is $19,500, then $4208 or 21.6 per cent is taxed away.

Inflation and the Progressive Tax Structure

The problem with our progressive tax structure is that it is calculated on the basis of fixed-dollar amounts that don't allow for changes in the purchasing power of the dollar resulting from inflation. In other words, the thresholds are not indexed to the rate of inflation. This implies that even if your dollar income rises at the same rate as the general price level, the quantity of goods you could purchase after paying taxes declines. To correct in part for this defect, the marginal tax rates have, as shown in Table 11.1, been reduced. However, this reduction has not been sufficient to eliminate

---

TABLE P11.1
Changing Marginal Income Tax Rates in Australia. 1985–87

Income range (per year) $	Marginal tax rate (cents per dollar)		
	June 85	June 86	July 87
0 to 4,595	0.00	0.00	0.00
4,596 to 5,100	26.67	25.00	0.00
5,101 to 12,500	26.67	25.00	24.00
12,501 to 12,600	30.00	30.00	24.00
12,601 to 19,500	30.00	30.00	29.00
19,501 to 28,000	46.00	46.00	40.00
28,001 to 35,000	47.33	48.00	40.00
35,001 to 35,787	55.00	60.00	49.00
37,788 and over	60.00	60.00	49.00

Source: OECD Economic Survey, Australia 1986/87, p.77.

bracket creep with the result that the average income earner ended up paying a bigger proportion of income under the July 1987 rates than under the June 1985 rates. To see this, consider once more the income of $19,500 in 1985. (This income level is close to average earnings in that year.) In 1986, inflation was 8.3 per cent. If we maintain the same real income as in 1985, we get $19,500 × 1.083 = $21,118.50 as the equivalent income in 1986. The tax payable on this income in 1986 is as follows:

Income Range $	Tax in 1986
0 to 4,595	$ 0.00
4,596 to 12,500 (i.e. 7,905 × .25)	$1,976.25
12,501 to 19,500 (i.e. 7,000 × .30)	$2,100.00
19,501 to 21,118 (i.e. 1,618.0 × .46)	$ 744.28
Total Tax payable	$4,820.46

So, the total tax payable in 1986 would be $4820 or 22.82 per cent of total earnings. In 1985, this same person would have paid 21.60 per cent of their earnings as tax. Thus purely due to bracket creep, and despite the lower marginal rates, this average earner's tax burden has increased by 1.22 per cent of earnings.

In July 1987, the Hawke Government introduced dramatically revised marginal tax rates. Let's see how these rates fare, and whether bracket creep has been eliminated. Inflation in 1987 was 9.8 per cent and in 1988 an estimated 5.5 per cent. Thus the average income of $21,118.5 in 1986 would have to be increased to $23,188.11 in 1987 (i.e. 21,118.5 × 1.098) and to $24,463.46 in 1988 (i.e. 23,188.11 × 1.055). The tax payable on this income in 1988 is as follows:

Income Range $	Tax in 1988
0 to 5,100	0
5,101 to 12,600 (i.e. 7,500 × 0.24)	$1,800.00
12,601 to 19,500 (i.e. 6,900 × 0.29)	$2,001.00
19,501 to 24,463 (i.e. 4,963 × 0.40)	$1,985.20
Total Tax payable	$5,786.20

Here, the tax payable as a proportion of income is 5786.27/24,463 = 23.65 per cent. Hence, the proportion of income taxed has increased by a further 0.83 per cent over 1987, despite the so-called dramatic tax changes of July 1987.

How Indexing Income Taxes Works

It has often been pointed out that this loss of purchasing power amounts to an unlegislated tax rise, literally 'taxation without representation'. In January 1985, the Reagan administration in the USA introduced indexation of income tax brackets to the rate of inflation precisely to avoid this problem of taxation without representation. In Australia, however, politicians have shied away from indexation. Only for a brief period in 1976 was partial tax indexation introduced. This was quickly dropped, perhaps because giving tax reductions is more likely to attract votes than to have the effect of inflation neutralised due to the automatic rises in tax brackets.

As an example of how tax indexation would work, let us adjust the 1985 tax brackets for the effect of inflation. This is shown in Table 11.2 below where we have calculated the indexed ranges for 1986, 1987 and 1988. The last column shows the 1985 marginal tax rate regime.

TABLE P11.2
Income tax ranges under indexation

1985	1986 (1985 indexed at 8.3%)	1987 (1986 indexed at 9.8%)	1988 (1987 indexed at 5.5%)	1985 Marginal tax rate
0 — 4,595	0 — 4,976	0 — 5,464	0 — 5,764	0
4,596 — 5,100	4,977 — 5,523	5,465 — 6,065	5,765 — 6,398	26.67
5,101 — 12,500	5,524 — 13,538	6,066 — 14,864	6,399 — 15,682	26.67
12,501 — 12,600	13,539 — 13,646	14,865 — 14,983	15,683 — 15,807	30.00
12,601 — 19,500	13,647 — 21,119	14,984 — 23,188	15,808 — 24,463	30.00
19,501 — 28,000	21,120 — 30,324	23,189 — 33,296	24,464 — 35,127	46.00
28,001 — 35,000	30,325 — 37,905	33,297 — 41,620	35,128 — 43,909	47.33
35,001 — 35,787	37,906 — 38,757	41,621 — 42,555	43,910 — 44,895	55.00
35,788 and over	38,758 and over	42,556 and over	44,986 and over	60.00

Questions

1. Using the upper income threshold for 1988 in Table 11.2, (i.e. 5764, 6398, 15,682 etc.) plus in addition $50,000 and $60,000 income levels, calculate the percentage of income taxed using the 1985 marginal tax rate regime.

2. Using the same upper income thresholds as in question (a) calculate the percentage of income taxed under the 1987 marginal tax regime (given in Table 11.1).

3. From the results in questions (a) and (b) what conclusions can be drawn regarding the burden of taxation on different income groups under the 1987 marginal tax regime as compared with an indexed 1985 marginal tax system?

view of the effects of the reduction in marginal tax rates. Then the equilibrium level of real GDP is increased to y_2 while the price level remains unchanged at p_0, corresponding to the intersection of AD_1 and AS_1 at point d.

In conclusion, our example suggests that *when supply-side effects are taken into account, marginal tax rate reductions are likely to be less inflationary and lead to larger increases in output than is suggested by a strictly demand-side, or Keynesian, point of view.*

Tax Rate Reduction and Tax Revenues — The Laffer Curve

While a reduction in marginal tax rates may cause an expansion in the economy's capacity to produce goods and services, won't it also lead to larger budget deficits due to a decline in tax revenues? Some supply-siders, such as Arthur Laffer, say no. This brings us to the second supply-side proposition: *supply-siders argue that the increase in total income and output (real GDP) resulting from a reduction in marginal tax rates may well give rise to an increase in tax revenue despite the reduction in tax rates.* This proposition may be characterised in terms of the popularly known **Laffer curve** shown in Figure 11.10.

FIGURE 11.10
The Laffer Curve

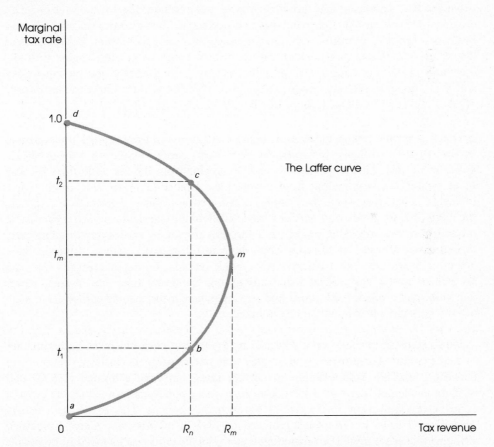

The Laffer curve suggests that tax revenue (horizontal axis) rises as the marginal tax rate is increased up to some rate t_m, corresponding to point m on the curve, where the maximum possible tax revenue is R_m. Tax rates higher than t_m discourage productive efforts so much that total income falls, causing tax revenue to decline. The curve implies that if the marginal tax rate *is above t_m rate reduction will give rise to increased tax revenue. It also implies that for every marginal tax rate above t_m there exists a lower rate that would generate the same tax revenue.*

POLICY PERSPECTIVE

Tax Evasion and the Underground Economy — Another Source of Deficit Growth

Tax avoidance, the *legal* use of tax loopholes, has long been a common practice made possible by our complicated tax laws which offer a myriad of exceptions, write-offs, special deductions, and exemptions to this or that particular group in our society. However in recent years a number of industrialised countries, including Australia, have experienced a significant and growing loss of tax revenue due to tax evasion. Tax evasion is *illegal*, unlike tax avoidance, and refers to income taxes individuals and businesses should pay but do not, encompassing income earned from both legal and illegal activity. Higher tax rates encourage people to go to greater lengths to 'hide' income from the tax collector, despite the risks of getting caught and having to pay stiff fines, possibly even serving a prison term. Higher tax rates increase the rewards of 'cheating' and thus make it more worthwhile to take these risks.

One way people engage in tax evasion is to participate in the so-called 'underground economy'. It is difficult, for example, for wage earners employed by businesses, government, and other organisations to hide income from the tax authorities because of automatic tax withholding from paycheques. Higher tax rates encourage people to engage in activities where the income earned is easier to hide. Such activities include the bartering of goods and services, and 'cash only' transactions. For example, a moonlighting car mechanic might fix a farmer's tractor in exchange for a few kilos of bacon and a bushel of corn, or simply be paid off in cash. In such instances, there are no cheques that can be traced from bank records, or payroll records that can be audited by tax authorities. The underground economy refers to all such barter and cash-only exchanges of goods and services wherein the income earned from such activity goes unreported and thereby untaxed.

How much tax revenue is not collected by the federal government as a consequence of tax evasion? A recent study estimates that tax evasion in Australia amounts to between 2 and 3½ billion dollars at current rates, imposing a burden of $200 and $350 on the 'honest' taxpayer.[2] Furthermore, a major policy concern is that tax evasion contributes significantly to the size of government's deficits. This is the main reason behind the Hawke government's proposal in 1987 of an Australia Card. Combined with an efficient computerised matching system, such a card was intended to tie people to their financial transactions such as share dealings and real estate sales. The mere presence of such a system, it was claimed, would have been enough to discourage some tax evasion and return into government coffers hundreds of millions of dollars. The Australian Taxation Office estimated that in the first year of operation alone, the Australia Card would have helped collect an extra $725 million in unpaid taxes.

Questions

1. In Sweden, which has very high marginal tax rates, it is reported that the average worker is absent from his or her job one day a week due to 'illness'. Can you offer an explanation for this amazingly high rate of absenteeism in a country known for its generally high health standards?

2. If loopholes in our present tax laws were greatly reduced or eliminated, what effect do you think this would have on tax evasion activity?

[1]For an excellent discussion on the underground economy, see Carter, M. (1984), 'Issues in the Hidden Economy — A Survey', *Economic Record*, Vol. 60, No. 170, September, pp.209–21.
[2]Norman, N.R. (1982), 'The Economics of Tax Evasion', paper presented at the 11th Conference of Economists, Adelaide.

The Laffer curve shows the relationship between the marginal tax rate (vertical axis) and the amount of tax revenue the government receives (horizontal axis). It is easy to establish the two points where the Laffer curve meets the vertical axis. Clearly if the marginal tax rate is zero, the government will receive no tax revenue, which corresponds to point *a* at the origin of the graph. At the other extreme, if the marginal tax rate is 1, so that every dollar of income is confiscated by the government, people will have no incentive to work and again tax revenue will be zero, corresponding to point *d*. If the marginal tax rate is t_1 (roughly .2, say), government tax revenue would equal R_n, corresponding to point *b* on the Laffer curve. If the rate is increased to t_m, tax revenue rises to R_m, corresponding to point *m* on the curve. Notice, however, that any further increase in the rate will actually cause the level of tax revenue to decline. At t_2, for instance tax revenue falls back to the level R_n, corresponding to point *c*. Why? Above some marginal tax rate, such as t_m, the after-tax rewards for working and capital formation become so low that these productive activities are

reduced. The resulting decline in total income is so great that tax revenues decline despite the increased marginal tax rate. For example, suppose that the economy has a proportional tax structure and the marginal tax rate is increased from .5 to .6. If total income declines from $250 billion to $200 billion, tax revenues decline from $125 billion to $120 billion.

Increasing Tax Revenue by Tax Reduction

Some supply-siders contend that current marginal tax rates in Australia are high enough that we are at a point such as *c* on the Laffer curve. They argue that by lowering the marginal tax rate and moving down the curve, tax revenue would increase. For instance, moving from point *c* down to point *m* would increase tax revenue from R_n to R_m in Figure 11.10. Moreover, if the supply-siders are right, a lower marginal tax rate would yield the same level of tax revenue currently realised. For example, in Figure 11.10 the rate t_1 will yield the same tax revenue, R_n, as the rate t_2.

POLICY PERSPECTIVE

Where Are We on the Laffer Curve?

Scepticism about the supply-siders' argument that lowering marginal tax rates will lead to increased tax revenues is fairly widespread. Many economists and policymakers agree that the proposition may be true in the long run, after sufficient economic growth. As to the short run, however, many critics argue that the decrease in tax rates would not have a sufficient impact on the economy's supply side to expand income enough to actually increase tax revenues. Furthermore, many economists seriously question whether we are on the upper portion of the Laffer curve. Empirical studies of this question for the United States suggest that the USA is not.[1] A similar study for Sweden, which has much higher tax rates than Australia, concludes that Sweden is on the upper portion of its Laffer curve.[2]

To examine this issue for Australia requires much more empirical evidence than is currently available. We really don't know at what level of tax rates the economy's tax revenue would begin to decline. However, it is interesting to note that in the Liberal tax policy released for the 1987 Federal election, the proposed $5 billion tax cut as a result of lowering marginal tax rates was estimated to give rise to $900 million extra tax flowing from 'positive incentive effects of the lower taxes'. Thus, it appears that the Liberal Party believes Australia is on the lower portion of the curve so that a cut in taxes would result in a net decrease in tax revenue.

[1]Bruce Bender, 'An Analysis of the Laffer Curve', *Economic Inquiry,* July 1984, pp.414–420. Also see Don Fullerton, 'On the Possibility of an Inverse Relationship Between Tax Rates and Government Revenues', *Journal of Public Economics,* October 1982, pp. 3–22.
[2]Charles E. Stuart, 'Swedish Tax Rates, Labour Supply, and Tax Revenues', *Journal of Political Economy,* October 1981, pp. 1020–1038.

CHECKPOINT 11.4

How would a strictly demand-side, or Keynesian, point of view regarding the effects of an increase in marginal tax rates be modified when supply-side effects are taken into account? How do you think closing all tax loopholes would affect the position of the Laffer curve in Figure 11.10?

POLICY PERSPECTIVE

How Australians Fare in the Income Tax League

Table 11.3 provides a comparison of how Australians fare in the income taxation league. The first column shows the marginal tax rate for an average production worker in 1986 in 22 of the 24 countries which belong to the Organisation for Economic Cooperation and Development (OECD). For the average Australian worker the marginal tax rate is seen to be 47.3. This means that out of each additional dollar of income, 47.3 cents are taxed away by the government. From the standpoint of the individual this rate appears rather high. Furthermore, even if we allow for the tax changes in 1987–88, almost half of all taxpayers will still face a marginal tax rate of 40 per cent. In contrast, fewer than 28 per cent were in this category in 1983/84 and as low as three per cent of taxpayers in the mid-1950s. No wonder there has been general dissatisfaction with our high rate of income taxation. Bracket creep — a process whereby inflation pushes taxpayers into higher tax brackets — is mostly to blame for this drastic change.

In July 1985, the Hawke Government convened a National Taxation Summit[1] with participants from the major interest groups such as unions, employers, farmers and even consumer organisations. The objective of the tax summit was to reform the Australian taxation system, with the government proposing to reduce the emphasis on income taxation in favour of a more broadly based tax on goods and services. With such a motley group of participants, consensus could not be reached on this or any other proposal. In late 1985, the government did introduce a tax reform package. Although by historical standards it is a major reform, it did not go as far as the government's preferred option at the tax summit. The result has been that income taxation, especially for lower income groups, has remained relatively high.[2]

While Australians might think they are the most highly taxed people on earth, Table 11.3 shows that Australia is nowhere near the top in the taxation league. If we rank the 22 countries with one being most taxed and 22 least taxed, then Australia comes in at thirteen, almost in the middle of the league. There are successful economies ranked higher e.g. Sweden and West Germany. However, important trading nations ranked below Australia include Japan, the United States and the United Kingdom. Such international comparisons dispel the claim that Australia is one of the most highly taxed countries in the world.

However, being ranked middle in the taxation league does not mean necessarily that we have the optimal method and rate of taxation. In determining such issues there are important factors that a country must decide on. First, the appropriate rate of taxation depends on the benefits that one wants to have available for the unemployed and pensioners, for health and education etc. It would make little sense to argue for Japan's taxation rates but to want to maintain Sweden's level of benefits.

Second, there is the method of taxation. Australia relies heavily on personal income taxation. In 1986/87, 45 per cent of total government revenue was derived from personal income tax. This was one of the highest ratios among OECD members. Such a situation

TABLE P11.3
Recent and proposed changes in personal taxation systems

	Overall taxation	Income tax		
	Marginal tax rates on average wages under present tax systems	Top marginal rate		
		Previous	Present	Proposed
Australia	47.3	60.0	55.0	49.0
Austria	54.5		62.0	
Belgium	62.7		86.7	
Canada	33.7	63.6	51.3	
Denmark	62.4	73.0	68.0	
Finland	53.2		68.5	
France	51.2	65.0	58.0	50.0
Germany	62.7		56.0	53.0
Greece	40.1	60.0	63.0	
Iceland	n.a.		55.6	
Ireland	61.3	65.0	58.0	
Italy	57.8	76.0	65.0	56.0
Japan	31.5	88.0	76.5	65.0
Luxembourg	53.6	57.0	56.0	
Netherlands	61.9	60.0	72.0	
New Zealand	30.0	66.0	48.0	
Norway	60.1	71.0	57.6	
Portugal	35.9	84.4	68.8	
Spain	52.8	68.5	66.0	
Sweden	62.0	87.7	77.4	
Switzerland	39.4		45.8	
Turkey	n.a.	78.0	50.0	
United Kingdom	43.9	83.0	60.0	
United States	40.9	75.0	38.0	

Notes: Overall marginal tax rate for an average (unmarried) production worker, allowing for direct taxes at all levels of government, social security contributions by both employers and employees, and relevant tax concessions. The major data source is OECD (1986), *The Tax/Benefit Position of Production Workers 1981–1985*. The figures shown are estimates for 1986.
Global effective rate (excluding social security contributions) but allowing for deductibility of taxes paid to lower levels of government.

Source: OECD Economic Outlook, Vol.41, June 1987, p.22.

makes the government's finance sensitive to tax avoidance and evasion. Because of this there have been continuing calls for a broad-based consumption tax as a trade off for lowering income tax. With a consumption tax there is less scope for tax evasion since the tax is collected when an individual spends income. While such a consumption tax has many appealing features, it suffers from one major drawback, namely that it is regressive — that is people on lower incomes tend to be hit more heavily than people on higher incomes. This is the major reason why consensus on a consumption tax could not be reached at the 1985 Taxation Summit.

Finally there is the effect of high marginal rates on incentives. The argument here is similar to the supply sider's argument that high marginal rates may deter people from working harder. This is a tricky issue to resolve — one loaded with value judgements but little empirical evidence. It is interesting to note from Table 11.3 that most of the OECD countries have opted for lower top marginal rates. This suggests that most countries seem to believe that very high marginal tax rates may be counter-productive to the economy. Australia is in good company here in reducing its top marginal rates. What is surprising is that it took a Labor government to move to lower top marginal rates. Recall however that this was done as a trade off for the Fringe Benefits tax which aimed at stopping income from being transformed into a non-income benefit so as to avoid income taxation.

[1]For further discussion of the Tax Summit and the reforms that the government eventually adopted, see *State of Play 3*, Chapter 7, pp.126–147.
[2]For a critical view of the structure of the Australian Taxation system, see *Spending and Taxing* by Freebairn, Porter and Walsh, chapter 12, pp.197–222.

SUMMARY

1. An increase in the economy's price level causes the total expenditure schedule to shift downward and the equilibrium level of real GDP to decrease, while a decrease in the price level shifts the total expenditure schedule upward and increases equilibrium real GDP. The aggregate demand curve (AD) plots this relationship between the price level and the equilibrium level of real GDP. Movement along the AD curve thus shows the response of equilibrium real GDP to changes in the price level.

2. An exogenous increase in expenditure or a tax reduction will shift the AD curve rightward. An exogenous decrease in expenditure or a tax rate increase will shift the AD curve leftward.

3. The aggregate supply curve (AS) shows the amounts of total output, or real GDP, that the economy's businesses will supply at different price levels. Over the horizontal range of the AS curve there is so much excess capacity that real GDP can be increased without any change in the price level. The AS curve rises over the intermediate range because input prices

remain unchanged in the short run while product prices (hence the economy's price level) can increase thereby raising profits and inducing the economy's firms to increase output. Over the vertical range of the AS curve the economy has reached its production capacity limit and increases in the price level will not induce any increase in real GDP.

4. Changes in input prices, in productivity, in the size of the labour force, or in the capital stock will cause the AS curve to shift.

5. The AD and the AS curves jointly determine the equilibrium price level and the equilibrium level of real GDP. An exogenous expenditure change, or an exogenous tax rate change, will have a smaller multiplier effect on real GDP along the intermediate range of the AS curve than along the horizontal range. The multiplier effect is zero along the vertical range.

6. Given the position of the AS curve, rightward shifts in the AD curve along the intermediate and vertical ranges of the AS curve give rise to demand-pull inflation. Upward shifts in the AS curve give rise to cost-push inflation. Given the position of the AD curve, an upward shift in the AS curve increases both the general price level and the unemployment rate, a phenomenon known as stagflation.

7. Supply-side economics takes issue with the demand-side, or Keynesian, view that tax cuts only affect aggregate demand. Supply–siders argue that lower marginal tax rates increase the economy's capacity to supply output by providing higher after-tax rewards, which encourage work effort and other productive activities.

8. Two basic propositions follow from the supply-side view of the effects of lower marginal tax rates: (1) the resulting increase in total output, or real GDP, will help to fight inflation; and (2) total income may increase to such an extent that tax revenue rises despite the reduction in tax rates, a proposition that is characterised by the Laffer curve.

KEY TERMS AND CONCEPTS

bracket creep
cost-push inflation
demand-pull inflation
Laffer curve
marginal tax rate
stagflation

QUESTIONS AND PROBLEMS

1. Explain the derivation of the AD curve from the total expenditure schedule. Explain how each of the following would affect the AD curve: an exogenous increase in consumption expenditure; an exogenous reduction in tax rates; a decrease in the price level; an exogenous increase in government spending; an exogenous decrease in net export spending; an exogenous increase in investment spending.

2. Explain the concept of the AS curve and its shape. Explain how and why it is affected by changes in technology.

3. Explain how and why the multiplier effect varies over the three different ranges of the AS curve.

4. Suppose trade unions begin to demand higher wages in order to keep up with a rising cost of living (a rising general price level) caused by rightward shifts in the AD curve. Using the AD and AS curves explain how this could give rise to stagflation.

5. Suppose marginal tax rates on income are reduced. Rank the following as either 'much' or 'little' in terms of the effect the reduction would have on work effort: self-employed house painter, mail carriers, building contractor, police officer, senator, shoeshine person, barber, mayor, automobile company executive, librarian, real estate salesperson, owner of machine-tool shop.

6. Suppose that the economy's total income equals $200 billion and that income is subject to a proportional tax rate of .5. If the proportional tax rate is reduced to .4, how much would total income have to rise in order for total tax revenue to increase?

12

International Trade and the National Economy

AFTER READING THIS CHAPTER YOU WILL BE ABLE TO:

1. Describe present-day world trade flows and the pattern of Australian trade.

2. Assess the relative importance of international trade to the Australian economy.

3. Explain how trade affects total income, output and employment.

Virtually every nation finds it advantageous to trade with other nations. To varying degrees all are linked to one another by trade flows and financial networks that circle the globe. In this chapter we describe the nature of world trade and consider how it affects the Australian economy. Recognising that exports provide a major injection into an economy's circular flow, and that imports are a substantial leakage, we then consider how such trade flows affect the total income level.

THE IMPORTANCE OF INTERNATIONAL TRADE

International trade plays a significant role in the determination of living standards throughout the world. Since 1945 the level of international trade has risen dramatically and has influenced in differing degrees the prosperity of all countries. For nations such as Australia international trade plays a very important role. From sales of our exports such as agricultural commodities and minerals, we are able to purchase imports of foreign manufactured goods and services which enrich our living standards. To appreciate Australia's position in the scheme of things let's first look briefly at some of the quantitative dimensions of international trade. Then we will consider how foreign trade affects an economy's total income, output and employment.

TABLE 12.1
World Trade Exports, 1984

	Value (in Billions of Dollars)		Percentage of Total Exports	
Developed Countries	1,496.5		64.3	
United States		253.1		10.9
Canada		104.0		4.5
Japan		196.0		8.4
France		116.2		5.0
West Germany		197.5		8.5
Italy		84.4		3.6
United Kingdom		107.6		4.6
Australia		30.5		1.3
Other Developed Countries[1]		198.2		8.5
Developing Countries	546.4		23.5	
OPEC[2]		215.0		9.2
Other		331.3		14.2
Communist Countries	284.0		12.2	
USSR		108.6		4.7
Eastern Europe		116.1		5.0
China		30.9		1.3
Total	2,326.8		100.0	

[1]Includes other OECD countries, South Africa, and non-OECD Europe (OECD: Organization for Economic Cooperation and Development).
[2]Organization of Petroleum Exporting Countries.

Source: International Monetary Fund, Organization for Economic Cooperation and Development, and Council of Economic Advisers, Australian Bureau of Statistics.

The Size of World Trade Flows

Table 12.1 provides an overall view of the magnitude of world trade, measured in Australian dollars. The table shows the total dollar value of exports of goods by the nations of the world in 1984 — that is, the dollar values of goods produced by each nation and then sold abroad.

Some perspective on the total value of world exports is provided by comparing these figures with the total GDP of Australia, a middle sized economic power by world standards. For the calendar year 1984 Australia's GDP was $204.4 billion. This means the total US exports of $253.1 billion were significantly larger than Australia's GDP, and the exports of Japan and West Germany were almost as large as Australia's GDP. Total world exports were about eleven times the size of Australia's total production.

To gain a further perspective it is also interesting to note that some economies are much more dependent on international trade than others. This is illustrated in Figure 12.1 which shows the value of exports of selected countries as a percentage of their respective GDP in 1985. In that year exports from Australia amounted to 14.6 per cent of GDP. Australia's degree of openness is significant but considerably smaller than that of most member nations of the European Economic Community. It is also smaller than for New Zealand, Sweden and Canada. High index values for France, West Germany, Italy and the United Kingdom arise simply from their close trading ties as members of the European Common Market. Canada's high index value occurs because of its substantial trade with the United States. Sweden has the highest percentage of the ten countries selected. This reflects how trade has helped

Sweden achieve a high level of economic development. The low indicator values for the USA and Japan may first appear surprising, since in dollar terms the US ranked first and Japan a close third in total value of exports for all countries. Both are, however, relatively closed economies with most trade occurring between their regions rather than with other countries. Differences among countries, then, largely reflect differences in size, the extent of development of internal markets, and the quantity and diversity of their supply of resources.

The Pattern of Australian Trade

The pattern of Australia's trade with the rest of the world is illustrated by the export and import data in Table 12.2 and Figure 12.2. As can be seen from Table 12.2 the total dollar value of Australia's imports in 1985–86 ($34.691 billion), the goods purchased abroad, was somewhat larger than the total dollar value of our exports ($32.818 billion). The majority of our *exports* went to Asia with Japan taking more than half of this total. China and the newly industrialised countries of Asia i.e. South Korea, Taiwan, Malaysia, Singapore, Indonesia etc., also were significant buyers of our goods. The United States bought nearly 10 per cent of Australian exports while Europe accounted for over 19 per cent, the oil producing nations of the Middle East about 7 per cent, and our near neighbour New Zealand 4.6 per cent.

On the *import* side, Asian nations again made up the greatest percentage with 37.3 per cent. Almost a quarter of our imports came from Japan. The two other major sources of Australian imports were the USA and the nations of the European Economic Community (which of course

FIGURE 12.1
Exports as a Percentage of GDP.
Selected Countires 1985

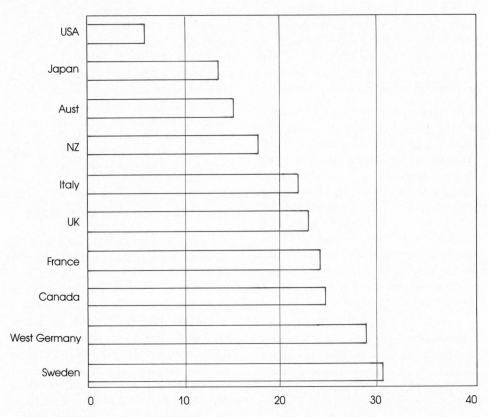

Australia's level of exports as a percentage of GDP is larger than the USA and Japan but smaller than many other Western economies.

includes our traditional trading partner Britain and other major economies such as West Germany, France and Italy). Just over 4 per cent of our imports came from New Zealand and 3.4 per cent came from the Middle East.

One point of interest is the notable imbalances between export and import volumes when different countries and regions are compared. Even though total export and import values differed it is clear that Australia ran considerable surpluses

with most of its Asian trading partners and also with the Middle East. There were significant trading deficits with the United States, Canada and the European Economic Community. The reasons for these imbalances will become apparent in the next section when we discuss the commodity composition of Australian trade.

Before we do that it is interesting to reflect on how Australia's trading patterns have been changing. Up until the 1950s Britain was Australia's main trading partner. In 1950 more than 30 per cent of our exports and nearly 50 per cent of our imports came from the United Kingdom. With Britain joining the European Economic Community in the early 1970s, the strong economic growth in Japan and other Asian economies and Australia's continuing development, our trading patterns with other countries have changed.

As can be seen from Figure 12.2 Japan and other Asian nations almost doubled their share of our *exports* between 1960–61 and 1985–86. The percentage shares of other traditional partners — the US, Canada and New Zealand — remained

relatively constant, as did the share of other European nations. Within this latter figure our exports (mainly agricultural commodities and minerals) to the EEC declined but increased with the countries of Eastern Europe, particularly the USSR. Reflecting their new-found wealth as oil exporters the countries of the Middle East also emerged as much more significant buyers of Australian exports — especially of our wheat and of live sheep.

We have seen already that Japan was the main source of Australian *imports* in the mid-1980s with almost a quarter of the total. This share had increased by a factor of four since 1960. It reflected in

FIGURE 12.2
The Changing Pattern of Australian Exports and Imports

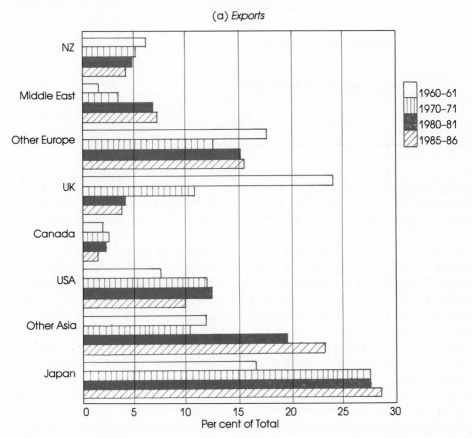

(a) *Exports*

1960–61
1970–71
1980–81
1985–86

(b) *Imports*

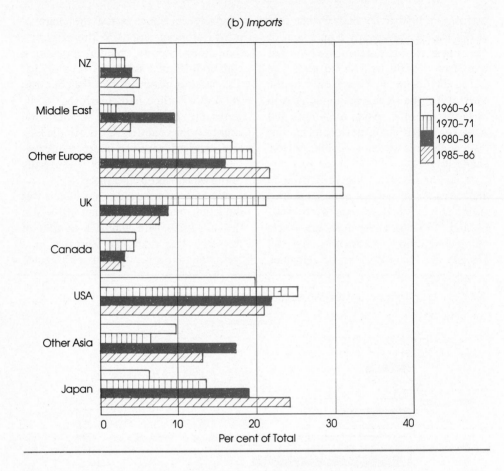

our increasing consumption of Japanese manufactures. By contrast the import share of the United States remained relatively stable between 1960 and 1985. Our imports from Europe fell from about 48 per cent of the total in 1960–61 to 24 per cent in 1980–81. During the 1980s this figure has again risen. Also of note is the growing share of Australian markets for New Zealand producers (reflecting our Closer Economic Relations agreement) and the variable percentage shares of the countries of the Middle East. This latter situation reflects the impact of wide variations in the price of oil on world markets in the light of the activities of member countries of OPEC (the Organization of Petroleum Exporting Nations).

CHECKPOINT * 12.1
Outline significant changes which have occurred in the direction of Australia's international trade since the early 1960s. Who now takes the majority of our exports? Why do you think Britain's position as a destination for Australia's exports has declined so dramatically?

*Answers to all checkpoints can be found at the back of the text.

TABLE 12.2
Australian Merchandise Exports and Imports by Area 1985–86

Area	Exports	Per cent of Total	Imports	
Asia	51.1		37.3	
Japan		28.4		23.8
China		4.6		1.3
ASEAN		6.5		4.6
South Korea		4.0		1.6
Taiwan		3.2		3.3
Other		4.4		2.7
North America	11.6		23.2	
USA		9.9		21.0
Canada		1.4		2.0
Other		0.3		0.2
Europe	19.2		29.0	
EEC		14.1		24.2
Other		5.1		4.8
Middle East	6.9		3.4	
New Zealand	4.6		4.2	
Other Countries	6.1		2.9	
Total	100.0		100.0	
	Value of Exports ($b)		Value of Imports ($b)	
	32.818		34.691	

Source: Australian Bureau of Statistics

The Commodity Composition of Australian Trade

The composition of Australian exports and imports by type of good is illustrated in Figure 12.3.

Machinery and transport equipment accounted for almost 44 per cent of Australia's total import bill in 1985–86. Next in importance were imports of other manufactured goods. These two groups represented 73.3 per cent of total merchandise imports. Chemicals (8.7 per cent) and mineral fuels and related materials (5.6 per cent) were the only other broad commodity groups with any significant contribution to imports. Reflecting

Australia's status as an exporter of agricultural commodities and minerals three broad groups — food and live animals, crude materials except fuel, and mineral fuels and related materials — made up nearly 80 per cent of Australia's exports in 1985–86. The manufacturing sectors contributed only 16.9 per cent of the total. Even though Australia built up its secondary industry in the 1950s and 1960s it clearly still faces great difficulty in competing internationally.

CHECKPOINT 12.2
Consider your own purchasing patterns. In a typical trip to the supermarket how

FIGURE 12.3
Australian Exports and Imports by Broad Commodity Group 1985-86

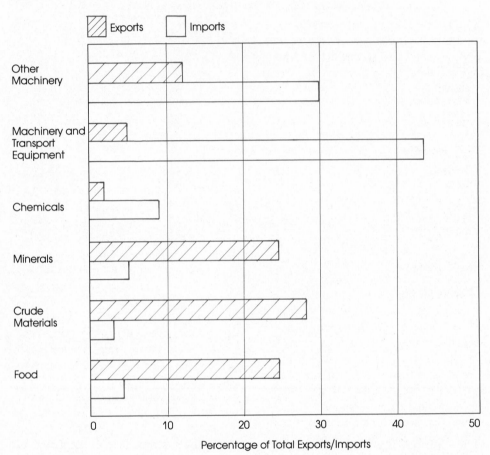

Percentage of Total Exports/Imports

Australian imports consist mainly of manufactures while our exports are dominated by food, other agricultural commodities and minerals.

much Australian produce do you buy? What imported foodstuffs do you purchase? Contrast this with the electrical appliances which you use. How many of these were made in Australia? Overseas? Finally consider the major resources and mining developments in the state where you presently live. How much of these are devoted to domestic consumption? To exports?

TRADE AFFECTS TOTAL INCOME, OUTPUT, AND EMPLOYMENT

Until now, our analysis of the determination of total income, output, and employment has assumed that the economy is isolated from international trade — that it is a **closed economy.** In reality, as we have just seen, Australia is an **open economy** — one that trades with other nations. World trade affects the economy's aggregate demand for goods and services and, hence, the levels of total income, output, and employment. Let's see how exports and imports can be incorporated into the analysis of income determination that we initially developed in Chapters 8, 9, and 10.

Exports, Imports, and Net Exports

Total expenditures on final goods and services in our economy include those arising from **exports,** the purchases of domestic output by foreigners. Hence, exports increase domestic production, incomes, and employment. They may be viewed as an injection into the economy's income stream, just like investment and government spending. **Imports,** on the other hand, represent expenditures by a country's citizens on output produced abroad. Such expenditures are a leakage from our economy's total income, just like saving. That is, imports also may be viewed as income *not* spent on domestically produced goods and services. As such, unlike exports, imports decrease domestic production, incomes, and employment. Therefore, the net effect of trade on a country's total income, output, and employment depends on whether the injections from exports are greater or less than the leakages due to imports. Recalling from Chapter 7 that net exports X equals exports minus imports, we may say that the net effect depends on whether net exports X is positive or negative. Exactly how does this difference affect the total income level?

Determinants of Exports and Imports

To answer this question, we must first consider what determines the volume of a country's exports and imports. Certainly, differences between countries in terms of resource endowments, levels of industrial development, consumption patterns, and size are significant determinants. The extent and nature of barriers to trade are also important. We will examine the role of these considerations in Chapter 20. In Chapter 21 we will see that exchange rates and differences in rates of inflation between nations also play an important role.

However, given all these factors, the volume of a country's exports will depend mainly on income levels in other countries. For example, if Japan is in the expansion phase of a business cycle, the volume of Australian exports to it will generally rise. Conversely, a recession in Japan will tend to lower its demand for Australian exports. On the other hand, the volume of a country's exports typically will depend very little, if at all, on its own total income level. What about the volume of a country's imports? Like consumption spending, a country's imports generally vary directly with its total income level. As a country's total income rises, its purchases of foreign products tend to increase right along with purchases of domestically produced goods.

Trade and the Equilibrium Level of GDP

We can now examine exactly how trade affects the economy's total income level, or its level of GDP. We will use the leakages-injection approach that we developed in Chapters 9 and 10. Initially, suppose that there are no exports or imports, that the economy is a closed economy. Suppose that the sum of saving S and taxes T, the total leakages, varies with the level of GDP as shown by the

FIGURE 12.4
Trade Affects the Equilibrium Level of GDP

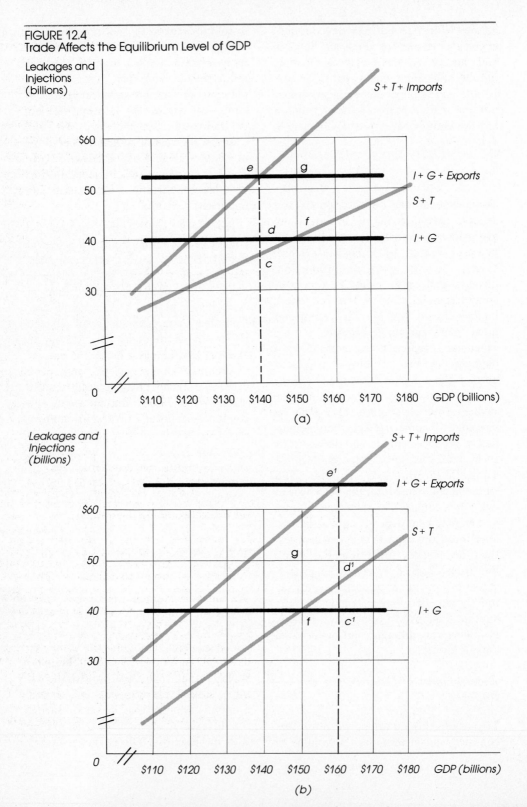

upward-sloping $S + T$ function in Figure 12.4, part a. The sum of investment spending I and government spending G, the total injections, is represented by the $I + G$ schedule. The equilibrium level of GDP is $150 billion, corresponding to point f, at which the $I + G$ schedule and $S + T$ function intersect. At this level of GDP, the injections from government and investment spending are just equal to the leakages due to saving and taxes. In this case, $I + G = S + T = 40 billion.

Now consider what happens when there are exports and imports — that is, when the economy is an open economy. At every possible level of GDP, the leakages due to imports must be added to those due to saving and taxes. Total leakages at each GDP level are therefore represented by the $S + T + Imports$ function shown in Figure 12.4, part a. The vertical distance between the $S + T$ function and the $S + T + Imports$ function represents the volume of imports at each level of GDP. Note that this vertical distance is greater at higher levels of GDP. This reflects the

fact that the volume of imports varies directly with GDP, so that the leakage from imports is greater at higher levels of GDP.

Now consider exports. At every possible level of GDP the injections due to exports must be added to those due to investment and government spending. Total injections at each GDP level are represented by the $I + G + Exports$ schedule in Figure 12.4, part a. The vertical distance between the $I + G$ schedule and the $I + G + Exports$ schedule represents the volume of exports at each level of GDP. This vertical distance is the same at every level of GDP, a reflection of the fact that spending by foreigners on domestic output, or exports, is independent of the level of GDP. In part a, exports equal $12 billion.

Net Exports Negative. The equilibrium level of GDP is now $140 billion, corresponding to the intersection of the $S + T + Imports$ function and the $I + G + Exports$ schedule at point e. At this level of GDP, the sum of the injections due to investment, government, and export

---

Exports, the purchase of domestic output by foreigners, are an injection into the economy's income stream just like investment and government spending. Imports, purchased by a country's citizens of output produced abroad, are a leakage from the economy's income stream just like saving and taxes. In an open economy equilibrium occurs at that level of GDP where the sum of the injections due to investment I, government G, and export spending is just equal to the sum of the leakages from savings S, taxes T, and imports.

If the economy is a closed economy (it neither exports nor imports), the equilibrium level of GDP would be $150 billion, corresponding to the intersection of the $I + G$ schedule and the $S + T$ function at point f, as shown in parts a and b. In equilibrium, $I + G = S + T = 40 billion.

If the economy is an open economy (it exports and imports) with exports of $12 billion (part a), the equilibrium level of GDP is $140 billion, corresponding to the intersection of the $I + G + Exports$ schedule with the $S + T + Imports$ function at point e. In equilibrium $I + G + Exports = S + T + Imports = $52 billion. The equilibrium level of imports, which is equal to $16 billion (the vertical distance between c and e), is larger than the $12 billion of exports (the vertical distance between d and e). Net exports X, therefore, are negative, or minus $4 billion (the vertical distance between c and d).

If exports were $26 billion, the equilibrium level of GDP would be $160 billion, corresponding to the intersection of the $I + G + Exports$ schedule and the $S + T + Imports$ function at point e' in part b. In equilibrium, $I + G + Exports = S + T + Imports = $66 billion. The equilibrium level of imports, which is equal to $22 billion (the vertical distance between d' and e') is less than the $26 billion of exports (the vertical distance between c' and e'). Net exports X are positive, or $4 billion (the vertical distance between c' and d').

Positive net exports have an expansionary effect, and negative net exports have a contractionary effect on GDP.

spending is just equal to the sum of the leakages from saving, taxes, and imports. In this case, *I + G + Exports = S + T + Imports* = \$52 billion. Note that the volume of exports, represented by the vertical distance between points *d* and *e*, is less than the volume of imports, represented by the vertical distance between points *c* and *e*. The difference, which is equal to the vertical distance between points *c* and *d*, equals net exports *X* (exports minus imports). In this case net exports are negative, minus \$4 billion. The leakages due to imports are greater than the injections due to exports. Hence, when net exports are negative in an open economy, the equilibrium level of GDP (\$140 billion) is lower than the closed economy equilibrium level of GDP (\$150 billion).

Net Exports Positive. Alternatively, suppose the volume of exports were larger, or \$26 billion, as shown in Figure 12.4, part b. Now the *I + G + Exports* schedule intersects the *S + T + Imports* function at point *e'*. The equilibrium level of GDP corresponding to this point is \$160 billion. In this case, *I + G + Exports = S + T + Imports* = \$66 billion. The volume of exports (\$26 billion), represented by the vertical distance between points *c'* and *e'*, now exceeds the volume of imports (\$22 billion), represented by the vertical distance between points *d'* and *e'*. Net exports *X* are therefore positive, represented by the vertical distance between *c'* and *d'* (\$4 billion). The injections due to exports exceed the leakages due to imports. When net exports are positive in an open economy, the equilibrium level of GDP (\$160 billion) is greater than the closed economy equilibrium level of GDP (\$150 billion).

Net Exports Zero. Finally, suppose that the level of exports were such that the *I + G + Exports* schedule intersected the *S + T + Imports* function at point *g* in parts a and b of Figure 12.4. Then exports would equal imports, as represented by the vertical distance between points *f* and *g*. Net exports would be zero. The equilibrium level of GDP would be \$150 billion, the same as the equilibrium level for the closed economy.

Summary of the Effects of Trade

In sum, when the net exports of an open economy are negative, the equilibrium level of GDP is lower than the equilibrium level that would prevail if the economy were closed. Conversely, when net exports are positive, the equilibrium level of GDP is greater than the closed economy level. When net exports are zero, the open economy and the closed economy level of GDP are the same. Hence, *the effects of trade on an economy's total income, output, and employment are expansionary when net exports are positive and contractionary when net exports are negative.*

The Effects of Trade on Aggregate Demand and Aggregate Supply

Aggregate Demand

Early in Chapter 11 we noted that changes in expenditure will shift the *AD* curve. An exogenous increase in aggregate expenditure will shift the *AD* curve to the right. An exogenous decrease in aggregate expenditure will shift the *AD* curve to the left. This effect was illustrated in Figure 11.2.

The level of net exports is an important part of aggregate expenditure. If a country's net exports increase then its *AD* curve moves to the right. If net exports decrease its *AD* curve shifts to the left.

It is interesting to consider how an 'exogenous' change in aggregate expenditure might be generated from international trading transactions. One typical cause is a change in a country's terms of trade. The terms of trade refer to the ratio of prices between export goods and import goods.

The movement in Australia's terms of trade since the early 1950s is shown in Table 12.3.

TABLE 12.3
Australia's Terms of Trade (1975 = 100)
1953–1987

Year	Terms of Trade
1953	174.3
1957	142.1
1960	115.4
1965	117.1
1970	106.8
1975	100.0
1980	81.0
1985	77.0
1987	66.7

Source: Australian Bureau of Statistics

The rather dramatic decline reflects our export dependence on primary commodities whose prices have risen at a much slower rate than our imports which are dominated by manufactured goods. In discussing Australia's terms of trade, Fred Gruen noted that since 1970 our terms of trade decline meant on average that it required 3 per cent more exports each year to pay for the same value of imports. Achieving this growth has not always been possible and net exports have often been decreased as a result. As we have just discussed this means that aggregate demand decreases and the *AD* curve moves to the left.

Aggregate Supply

Much of Australia's manufacturing depends on the use of imported inputs.

Just think of the motor vehicle industry as an example. Our falling terms of trade reflect rising import prices, and rises in input prices. If import prices rise quickly, and this can happen for a number of reasons, a supply-side shock occurs in the economy. As we saw in Figure 11.4 the AS curve will shift upwards as a result.

CHECKPOINT 12.3

Suppose that the economy's citizens decide to reduce the volume of goods and services they buy from abroad, no matter what the level of GDP. Show how this would affect the equilibrium level of GDP in Figure 12.4, part a. At the $140 billion equilibrium level of GDP in Figure 12.4, part a, the leakages from imports exceed the injections from exports. How then can this be the equilibrium level of GDP? How is the effect of net exports (positive or negative) on the economy similar to the effect of a government budget deficit or surplus?

SUMMARY

1. In 1984 the volume of world trade was roughly about eleven times Australia's GDP. Total exports for the USA — the world's largest trading nation — were greater than Australia's GDP by about $50 billion. The exports of Japan and West Germany were about the same size as our GDP.

2. For many countries exports present a sizeable proportion of their GDP — for some as much as half or more. In 1985 the value of Australia's exports was 14.6 per cent of GDP. This compared with higher percentages for members of the

EEC, New Zealand, Sweden and Canada and lower percentages for Japan and the USA.

3. The pattern of Australia's overseas trade has changed noticeably since 1950 when Britain received about a third of our exports and provided nearly half of our imports. Japan is now our major trading partner. More than half of our exports went to Asian countries in 1985–86. Japan, the United States, and Europe each account for more than 20 per cent of our imports.

4. Nearly three quarters of Australia's imports in 1985–86 were manufactured goods. Our major exports were agricultural commodities and minerals which made up nearly 80 per cent of the total. Manufactures were only 16.9 per cent of total exports.

5. Exports may be viewed as an injection into an economy's income stream, just like investment and government spending. Imports are a leakage from the economy's income stream. The effects of trade on a nation's GDP are expansionary when net exports (exports minus imports) are positive, and contractionary when net exports are negative.

KEY TERMS AND CONCEPTS

commodity composition of trade
closed economy
exports
imports
open economy
pattern of trade
terms of trade

QUESTIONS AND PROBLEMS

1. Identify some historical examples of totally closed economies. Why do you think that the USA and Japanese economies are relatively more closed than many others in the world today? How can you explain this with the knowledge that the USA, and Japan are the two largest internationally trading nations?

2. Is it possible that the value of a country's exports in a given year could be greater than its GDP? Explain your answer. Identify examples of countries with very high export to GDP ratios.

3. Which factors are significant determinants of a country's level of exports? Why then do textbooks such as this one assume the value of exports are constant in developing simple models of an open economy?

4. Suppose that the level of a nation's exports fluctuates from year to year. Using a diagram like Figure 12.4, can you explain why the resulting fluctuations in the nation's GDP might be smaller if it imports goods than if it doesn't import? How might the composition of imports — whether the nation imports mostly consumption goods or mostly capital goods — affect your answer?

THREE

Money, Banking and Monetary Policy

13

The Nature and Functions of Money and Banking

AFTER READING THIS CHAPTER YOU WILL BE ABLE TO:

1. Explain the nature and functions of money.

2. Describe the differences between commodity money, fiat money, bank money or chequeable deposits, and near money.

3. State the nature of the relationship between the supply of money, prices, and the value of money.

4. Explain how banks evolved from a mere safekeeping function to a fractional reserve banking operation, creating money through their lending activities.

5. Describe the purposes, organisation, and functions of the Reserve Bank of Australia.

6. Describe the role of depository institutions as creators of money and as financial intermediaries.

It has been said that money is 'the oil that lubricates the wheels of trade'. When the economy's monetary system is functioning well, this seems an apt analogy. However, history shows that money and the closely related activity of banking are often the source of economic instability, inflation, and unemployment. Indeed, monetary problems have frequently plagued our economy throughout its history.

This chapter focuses on the basic nature and functions of money and banking. In addition, we will see how and why the Reserve Bank of Australia has developed to provide the basic structure for money and banking in our economy. Chapter 14 will study in detail the way our banking system affects the size of the economy's money supply. Chapter 15 will focus on how the money supply affects the level of aggregate demand for goods and services and on the role that money plays in determining the economy's equilibrium level of total output and employment.

THE NATURE OF MONEY

What does money do? What are the different kinds of money? What determines the value of money?

What Money Does

Essentially, money does three things. It functions as a medium of exchange, a unit of account, and a store of value.

Money as a Medium of Exchange

Without money people would have to carry on trade by *barter* — the swapping of goods for goods. In Chapter 3 we saw that for trade to take place in a barter economy there must be a *coincidence of wants* between individuals. If I have good X to trade and I want to get good Y, I must find someone who not only wants to get good X but also coincidentally has good Y to give in exchange. The difficulties involved in finding a coincidence of wants tend to discourage and inhibit specialisation and trade in a barter economy (recall the discussion in Chapter 3). Because of this, the gains from specialisation and trade cannot be fully realised and therefore the total output of the economy is less than it otherwise might be. However, if money is used to carry on trade, I can sell good X to whomever wants it and accept money in exchange. Whether the purchaser has the good Y that I want is now irrelevant. I can use the money to buy good Y from whomever has it, regardless of whether or not they want good X. Trade is now easier because **money** *is something that is generally acceptable to everyone as payment for anything.*

The existence of money eliminates the need for a coincidence of wants. Therefore when goods are bought and sold using money as the medium of exchange, the economy is able to be more productive. Its production possibilities frontier is shifted outward.

Money as a Unit of Account

In a barter economy, comparing the relative values of different goods and services is much more complicated than in a money-using economy. For example, to get an idea of the cost of an orange in a barter economy would require a knowledge of the rate at which oranges exchange for apples, shoes, tea, bread, haircuts, and so forth. A shopping trip would entail numerous cross comparisons of the exchange rates between widely different goods and services. 'Let's see, if 3 oranges will buy 8 apples and 5 apples will buy 2 pears, that must mean . . . ah . . . 15 oranges will buy 16 pears'. There is no need for such complex calculations if everything is valued in terms of the same unit of account, money. Then in the above example the price of an orange is $.16, of an apple $.06, and of a pear $.15.

Money provides a common unit of account for expressing the market values of widely different goods and services. The existence of this common unit of account greatly reduces the time and effort needed to make intelligent economic decisions. As a result, more time and effort are available for use in other productive activities. This is another reason why money shifts the economy's production possibilities frontier outward.

Money as a Store of Value

You can hold wealth in many forms: houses, yachts, stocks, bonds, jewellery, and so on. But *no form of wealth is as readily convertible into other goods and services as money is. This ready convertibility, or* **liquidity,** *makes money an attractive store of value, or source of purchasing power.*

If you had to sell your new wristwatch within the next 5 minutes to get money to make purchases, you would probably only get a fraction of what you paid for it. If you had paid $50 for it, you might only be able to get $20 — a loss of $30. If instead you had $50, you could easily make $50 worth of purchases within 5 minutes. In general, you can rank assets on a scale from the most liquid to the least liquid according to the amount of loss, including **transaction costs** (such as brokerage fees, advertising costs, and time

and effort searching for a buyer), that would result if they had to be converted into money *within a short period of time.* Money of course heads the list. A car, a house, a painting, or a piece of land might be at or near the bottom.

Kinds of Money

Throughout history money has taken many forms. Many of the oldest kinds of money are still used today, while new kinds continue to be developed. In order of their historical evolution, the principal kinds of money are commodity money, coins, paper money, and demand deposits. All these different kinds of money share one common characteristic that is the essence of 'moneyness'. Namely, *money is something that is generally acceptable to everyone as payment for anything.*

Commodity Money

The earliest forms of money were commodities that often had other uses besides serving as money. Hides, furs, rum, jewellery, precious stones and metals, and livestock are but a few examples. Even today these items often serve as money in some economically underdeveloped regions of the world. When the German deutschemark became worthless as a result of the German hyperinflation in the early 1920s, Germans used cognac and cigarettes as money.

Some commodities are better suited for use as money than others. The ideal commodity money does not suffer from handling and time — it wears well. Eggs and other perishables won't do. It should be valuable enough that small amounts, easily carried, are sufficient to buy a week's groceries. Anything requiring a wheelbarrow instead of a purse is out. The ideal commodity money is easily divisible for making change and small purchases. Diamonds, the most durable commodity, are too difficult to split. Finally, the market rate of exchange of the commodity money with other goods should be relatively stable.

Historically the precious metals, gold and silver, have been the most continuously used forms of commodity money. Small amounts are quite valuable, so that as a commodity money they are easy to carry. Both are attractive metals and interact little with other substances, though silver does tarnish and gold is soft.

Coins

Coins were a natural outgrowth of the use of precious metals as commodity money. Using gold dust in bulk form meant that every merchant needed a scale to carry on business. Every transaction, however small, required careful and time-consuming weighing. The first coins were made by kings or rulers who weighed out an amount of precious metal and made a coin out of it. The coin had the amount of precious metal it contained stamped on it (its 'face value') along with the ruler's seal as a guarantee of the weight. This made trading easier as long as the ruler was honest and the citizens didn't tinker with the coins to 'clip' or remove precious metal from them. Monarchs and those they ruled being human (despite the monarchs' frequent claim to the contrary), the debasement of the coin of the realm was common.

Another problem with coins is that they often disappear from circulation whenever the market value of the precious metal they contain exceeds the amount of the face value stamped on them. Suppose a 20-cent piece contains $.30 worth of silver. Eventually circulation will bring the 20-cent pieces into the hands of someone who will melt them down for the $.30 worth of silver rather than use each coin for purchasing $.20 worth of goods, the face value stamped on the coin.

To avoid this problem governments now issue **token coins** — *coins that contain an amount of metal that is worth much less than the face value of the coin.* Such coins are **fiat money** — *money that the government declares by law to be legal tender for the settlement of debts.* This means that if you owe somebody $.20 and you offer them a 20 cent coin to pay off the debt, they must accept it. If they don't, they no longer have a legal claim on you. This illustrates an important characteristic of fiat money. *Fiat money is money that is not backed by or convertible into gold or any other precious metal. It is acceptable because the government declares it to be acceptable, not because of the value of the materials contained in it. It is acceptable not as a commodity itself but rather because people know that it can be used to buy goods and services.*

Paper Money

Paper money, the bills in your wallet, is also money in today's economy. It too illustrates that money is acceptable because it will buy goods. The value of the bills themselves as a commodity is next to nothing. Indeed, the materials needed to make a $1 bill, or a $10,000 bill, cost but a tiny fraction of a cent. Today all paper money in Australia is issued by the Reserve Bank of Australia (which we shall look at shortly) in the form of Australian dollars.

Demand (or Current) Deposits

If you place currency (coins and paper money) in a **demand deposit** at a trading bank, the bank is legally obligated to give that money back to you the moment you ask for it — that is, on demand. Demand deposits are also called cheque accounts because you can write cheques against them.

A cheque is nothing more than a slip of paper, a standardised form, on which you write the bank an order to withdraw funds from your cheque account and pay them either to someone else or to yourself. The cheque is a convenience that makes it unnecessary for you to go to your bank and withdraw currency from your demand deposit every time you need money to make a purchase or pay a bill. The receiving party (an individual, business, or other institution) has only to sign, or endorse, the cheque to receive the funds from your bank out of your demand deposit. Often the party receiving the cheque will simply endorse and deposit it in his or her own cheque account, frequently in a different bank. The banks conveniently handle the transfer of funds from your cheque account to that of the receiving party.

Demand deposits function as money by virtue of the cheque-writing privilege. Compared to currency they have several advantages. Lost or stolen currency is almost impossible to recover. Lost or stolen cheques are much more difficult for another party to use, so that a demand deposit is relatively secure from such mishaps. Cheques may be sent through the mail much more readily and safely than currency. Cheques therefore make trade possible between parties separated by great distances. They also provide a convenient record of completed transac-tions. Given these advantages, it is not surprising that in terms of dollar value, cheques account for by far the largest amount of transactions in our economy. One disadvantage of demand deposits is that banks either pay no interest or a very low rate of return on them.

Today almost all economists regard demand deposits as money because they can be converted into currency on demand and because cheques are such a widely used medium of exchange.

This has given rise to the 'narrow' definition of money, termed M1:

$$M1 = currency + deposits\ in\ cheque\ accounts$$

This is called the narrow definition of money because it is possible to define broader measures of money — the topic of the next section.

Near Money

Currency and demand deposits are regarded as money because they seem to perform all three functions of money (as a medium of exchange, a unit of account, and a store of value) better than any other asset. But there are several other kinds of assets that fulfil the unit of account and store of value functions at least as well. In addition, they can be converted rather easily into currency or current deposits. These assets are often called **near money** — they are like money except that they are not usually regarded as a medium of exchange.

The most important forms of near money are the various non-chequeable deposits with trading banks, savings banks and other financial institutions such as building societies and credit unions.

If we add to M1 the fixed deposits with

trading banks we get M2, a broader measure of money i.e.:

M2 = M1 + all other deposits with trading banks

Similarly, if we add to M2 deposits with savings banks we get M3, ie.

M3 = M2 + deposits with savings banks.

Trading banks and savings banks generally operate jointly and, to the casual observer, are virtually indistinguishable from each other. Indeed, most savings banks are subsidiaries of trading banks. One of the major differences between savings and trading banks is that only the latter are allowed to issue cheque accounts. This means that trading banks administer the domestic and international payments systems. In contrast, the primary function of savings banks is to provide loans to individuals for housing construction or purchase.

Despite this difference in the function of the two types of banks, their interest bearing deposits are very similar. Thus it would make little sense to include the interest bearing deposits of trading banks and exclude those of savings banks in any broader measure of the money supply. For this reason, M2 has fallen into disuse so that throughout the 1970s and early 1980s, M3 was predominantly used as 'the' measure of money. Furthermore, the Reserve Bank no longer lists M1 and M2 as separate measures of the money supply.

Table 13.1 provides an idea of the sizes of M1, M2 and M3, along with the relative

TABLE 13.1
Measures of Money in Australia: M1, M2, M3 and Broad Money (Seasonally Adjusted, Millions of Australian Dollars, June 1987)

		Percentages of			
		M1	M2	M3	Broad Money
Currency	$9,655	35.6	15.1	8.3	5.2
Plus: Current deposits with trading banks	$17,463	64.4	27.2	15.1	9.4
Equals: M1	$27,117	100.0			
Plus: Other deposits with trading banks	$36,989		57.7	31.9	19.9
Equals: M2	$64,106		100.0		
Plus: Deposits with savings banks	$51,882			44.7	27.9
Equals: M3	$115,988			100.0	
Plus: Borrowings from the private sector of the non-bank financial institutions	$70,117				37.6
Equals: Broad Money	$186,105				100.0

Source: Reserve Bank of Australia *Bulletin*

importance of the various components that make up each of these definitions of money. Table 13.1 also shows an additional measure called 'Broad Money'. This is a relatively recent measure defined as:

Broad Money = M3 + all borrowings of the non-bank financial institutions

One of the problems with M3 is that it only measures currency plus money deposited with banks. As you will know, there are many other non-bank financial institutions (NBFIs) which accept deposits similarly to those of trading and savings banks. Ignoring such deposits risks getting an incomplete measure of money supply, especially if there occur shifts from, say, the NBFIs to banks.

You might well ask at this stage — why all this diversity in financial institutions? Part of the reason relates to the functions they perform — as we have seen, savings banks concentrate more in the housing sector while trading banks are more commercially oriented. However, a major part of this diversity of institutions relates to the different regulations imposed by the government. Traditionally, banks have borne the brunt of government regulations, largely due to their unique ability to create money — regulations we will examine later. Thus, for example, the interest rate banks could pay to their depositors has often been controlled by the government. In contrast, the interest paid by say, building societies has been much less controlled and thus tended to be higher than that of banks. This spurred considerable growth in the NBFIs in the 1960s and 1970s, partly at the expense of banks.

In recent years, the emphasis on financial deregulation has meant that the government has moved away from using direct controls and more toward a market-oriented approach to the monetary sector. This deregulation has resulted in considerable change, such as the formation of new banks by previous NBFIs and the ability of banks to compete on a more equal footing in being able to offer market interest rates to depositors. Deregulation of the financial market has resulted in more funds being attracted into the banking sector and thus a considerable expansion of the money supply as measured by M3. In such an environment, excluding the borrowings from the household sector of the NBFIs from our measure of money becomes less desirable. Indeed, including the borrowings of the NBFIs is one way to offset in part the expansion of the money supply that otherwise would show up in M3. Consequently, in recent years, 'Broad Money' is most often used to measure the money supply in Australia.

Credit Cards and Trade Credit

A near money is often just as good a store of value as currency and demand deposits. But a near money is not a medium of exchange, though it can be readily converted to one. Credit cards and trade credit have very much the opposite properties of near money. They cannot serve as a store of value, but they are a medium of exchange.

If a business will sell you goods and services without requiring your immediate payment in the form of cash or a cheque, we say the business has extended you credit. If you carry a recognised credit card, many businesses will sell goods and services to you on the spot in exchange for nothing more than your signature on a credit slip bearing your credit card

---

POLICY PERSPECTIVE

The Issue of Australian Currency[1]

The Reserve Bank is the sole issuing authority for Australian currency notes. The Reserve Bank Act provides for the issue, re-issue and cancellation of Australian notes to be effected through the Reserve Bank's Note Issue Department.

The cost of producing and maintaining the note issue is met by earnings from investment of funds which are the counterpart of the notes on issue; net profits are paid to the Commonwealth Government. The value of notes on issue depends on the community's demand, and fluctuates substantially as a result of seasonal and other factors.

The present series of Australian notes dates from the introduction of decimal currency in 1966 when $1, $2, $10 and $20 notes were first issued. Subsequently $5, $50 and $100 notes have been added to this series. No new issues of the $1 have been made since the introduction in May 1984 of the $1 coin. The Treasurer announced in March 1987 that a $2 coin will be introduced in 1988. The $2 note will then be progressively withdrawn.

TABLE P13.1
Australian notes on issue ($ million)

At end June	$1	$2	$5	$10	$20	$50	$100	Total
1970	40	117	72	466	501	—	—	1196
1975	52	129	110	672	1181	401	—	2545
1980	68	144	142	563	1888	1744	—	4549
1985	45	179	194	522	2312	3430	1552	8234
1986	42	174	204	525	2282	3442	2246	8915
1987	40	173	213	525	2274	3539	2978	9742

Although the growth in the total amount on issue was substantial over the period shown in Table P13.1, the number of notes in circulation has grown less rapidly because of greater public use of higher denomination notes. While there was a tendency for the life of notes (i.e. average period between issues and withdrawal) to rise over the period to about 1984, enhanced efforts by the Reserve Bank to improve the quality of currency in circulation have since led to a reversal in this trend. There are significant differences in the average life of the various note denominations. High usage denominations such as $2 and $5 notes have an average life of about 7 months, only about one fifth of that of the $100 note.

Australian notes are printed at the Reserve Bank's Note Printing Branch at Craigieburn, Victoria. The Note Printing Branch also assists in the design of notes and conducts research pertinent to note printing (including security aspects).

Notes are distributed from the Note Printing Branch to the Reserve Bank's other branches. These are located in Canberra, Darwin, and each of the state capital cities (as well as London and New York). From those points, some are issued directly to the Reserve Bank's customers and the public as a result of the encashment of cheques and similar transactions; the bulk is issued to commercial banks. The Reserve Bank plays a coordinating role in distribution of notes and coins to individual branches of these banks. Certain country branches of the Commonwealth Bank of Australia operate note issue agencies on behalf of the Reserve Bank. Costs of transporting notes to distributing centres are met by the Reserve Bank; the banks bear the cost of transport and insurance between these centres and their branches. Cash that is surplus to banks' requirements, and notes that are no longer fit to remain in circulation are returned to the Reserve Bank.

When notes are returned to the Reserve Bank, high speed electronic currency verification, counting and sorting machines (CVCS) are used to count and check them for authenticity, sort them according to fitness for re-issue, bundle notes for re-issue and shred unfit notes.

A summary of the Reserve Bank's note issue transactions with the public is shown in Table P13.2.

TABLE P13.2:
Note issue transactions (millions of pieces)

Year ended Last Wedn. in	Notes Issued			Notes Received	Increase (Decrease) in notes on issue
	New	Re-issue	Total		
1974/75	298	682	980	930	50
1979/80	342	887	1229	1208	20
1980/81	356	957	1313	1286	27
1981/82	367	1042	1409	1383	25
1982/83	341	1102	1443	1426	16
1983/84	349	1104	1453	1460	(7)
1984/85	414	967	1381	1374	7
1985/86	479	1010	1489	1479	10
1986/87	450	1137	1587	1574	13

Most note printing is devoted to maintaining the stock of notes in circulation by replacing notes that have become unfit for circulation. As can be seen from Table P13.2, a relatively small proportion of new note production is required to accommodate increases in the number on issue.

Occasionally, notes may be accidentally mutilated or partly destroyed. In such cases, the public may seek replacement at any branch of the Reserve Bank or through another bank. Such claims may be met wholly or in part. The Bank assesses claims only against clear evidence concerning the quantity and denomination of notes involved.

Coins are produced by the Royal Australian Mint in Canberra. The Mint sells the coins to the bank at face value. Any profit on the manufacture of coin thus accrues immediately to the Mint and is paid to the Commonwealth Government. The Mint arranges delivery of new coins to the Reserve Bank which in turn issues it to banks under arrangements similar to those for notes.

[1]Much of this policy perspective is quoted directly from: Reserve Bank of Australia, *Functions and Operations,* Sydney, 1987, pp.23–4.

number. This allows you to defer payment by cash or cheque for some period of time. The credit card essentially serves as a short-term medium of exchange, a substitute for a cheque or cash. It is short term because the business ultimately expects to receive either currency or a cheque.

Businesses often extend credit to other businesses that are regular customers — a wholesaler supplying a retailer, for example. Such credit is called **trade credit.** It allows one business to buy goods from another without making immediate full payment by cheque or with currency. Trade credit is usually extended on the basis of past dealings that have convinced the seller that the buyer is financially sound and reliable — that the buyer will ultimately 'pay up' with currency or a cheque. Like the credit card, trade credit serves as a short-term medium of exchange even though it is not a store of value.

Credit cards and trade credit reduce the need for currency and chequeable deposits as mediums of exchange. They cannot replace currency and chequeable deposits, however, because such credit is not a store of value.

What Determines the Value of Money or What Backs Money?

Money in our economy today is neither backed by nor convertible into gold or any other precious metal. Coins contain an amount of metal that is worth much less than their face value. Paper money is just that — pieces of paper. Both coins and paper money are money because the government declares it so — they are fiat money. Chequeable deposits are just bookkeeping entries. Indeed, the government has not even declared chequeable

deposits to be money, which only shows that general acceptability in exchange is more important than a government declaration. If coins, currency, and chequeable deposits are not backed by gold or any other precious metal, and if they have no value in and of themselves, then what determines their purchasing power or real value? The value of money is determined by supply and demand, just like the value of anything else. Let's see why.

Money Demand and Supply

Money's value derives from its scarcity relative to its usefulness in providing a unique service. The unique service lies in the fact that money can be readily exchanged for goods and services. The economy's demand for money derives from its demand for this service. Therefore, the economy's demand for money is largely determined by the total dollar volume of its current transactions as well as its desire to hold money for possible future transactions.

What determines the supply of money? In the next chapter we will see how our economy's depository institutions as a whole can create money in the form of chequeable deposits. We will also see how the government, through the Reserve Bank, can promote or limit this kind of money creation. Therefore, not only is the government in a position to control the supply of fiat money (coins and paper money), it is also able to regulate the supply of money more broadly defined.

Money Demand and Supply Determine Money's Value

The value of a unit of money (such as a dollar) is its purchasing power, or the

POLICY PERSPECTIVE

Money and Prices — Two Cases of Hyperinflation

There are interesting historical illustrations of the relationship between the amount of money supplied to the economy, the price level, and the value of a unit of money.

During the Revolutionary War in the USA, it was very difficult for the government to raise sufficient revenue through taxation to finance military operations. Consequently, both the states and the Continental Congress resorted to printing money to pay for supplies, weapons, and troops. As a result, the supply of paper money in the economy increased by an enormous amount between 1774 and 1781. This increase in the supply of paper money greatly exceeded the growth in the economy's capacity to produce goods and services. Hence, the growth in the money supply was much larger than the growth in the quantity of transactions involving the purchase and sale of goods and services. As a result, the prices at which these transactions took place rose rapidly, and the purchasing power of a unit of paper currency fell accordingly. State laws passed in an effort to control the rapid rise in the price level and the deteriorating value of the dollar were fruitless because they attacked the symptom, the hyperinflation, rather than the cause of the problem, the tremendous increase in the money supply. Public jawboning, private threat, ostracism, boycotts, fines — all proved useless against the flood of paper money.

A more recent example of hyperinflation occurred in Germany between 1921 and 1923. The German government increased the supply of currency to such an extent that the wholesale price index rose to a level in November 1923 that was 30 billion times higher than it was in January 1921! By this point the deutschemark's value as money had been destroyed. An item purchased for a mark in 1921 cost 30 billion marks in 1923. Cases of hyperinflation like this one are relatively rare. But many governments, particularly in underdeveloped countries, regularly print fiat money to finance their expenditures. Inflation rates of the order of 50 to 200 per cent per year are not uncommon in these countries.

amount of goods and services that it will buy. The higher the economy's price level, the smaller the quantity of goods and services that a unit of money will buy. Conversely, the lower the price level, the larger the quantity of goods and services a unit of money will buy.

If you are going to the grocery store to buy four loaves of bread and the price of bread is $.50 per loaf, then you will need $2 of money to exchange for the bread. However, if the price of a loaf of bread is $1 per loaf, you will need $4 of money. There is obviously a relationship between the total quantity of such transactions in the economy, the prices at which they take place, and the economy's demand (need) for money. Oversimplifying somewhat, the following tends to be true. Given the economy's total quantity of transactions (such as the number of bread loaves purchased) and its demand for money needed to execute these transactions, the greater the supply

FIGURE 13.1
Money and Consumer Prices in Australia Since 1950

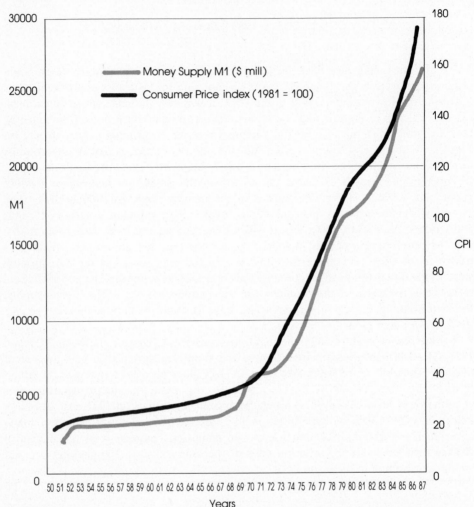

The general level of consumer prices and the money supply tend to move together. This is illustrated by the behaviour of the Consumer Price Index (CPI) and the money supply, defined as M1. Note that M1 is plotted on the left vertical axis, and that the CPI is plotted on the right vertical axis.

of money, the higher the price level at which these transactions will tend to take place. Conversely, the smaller the supply of money, the lower the price level at which these transactions will tend to take place. Thus, the supply of money and the demand for it play an important role in determining the price level in the economy. Therefore, it follows that the supply and demand for money play an important role in determining the purchasing power, or value, of a unit of money.

In sum, *given the demand for money, the larger the supply of money, the higher the price level will tend to be and, hence, the less the purchasing power, or value, of a unit of money. Conversely, the smaller the supply of money, the lower the price level will tend to be and hence the greater the purchasing power, or value, of a unit of money.*

The tendency for the general level of prices and the money supply to move together is illustrated in Figure 13.1. In this figure, money, defined as M1, is plotted along with the Consumer Price Index (CPI) for the years since 1950.

CHECKPOINT * 13.1

What would you rather use for money, $10 worth of aluminium or $10 worth of steel? Why? Rank the following in terms of their liquidity: a savings deposit, a $10 bill, a 90-day Treasury bill, a stamp collection, a $100 bill, a demand deposit, a Master Card credit card, a block of land in the suburbs. Rank each of the above items as a store of value, given that there is a 10 per cent rate of inflation. Explain this quote: 'Money is acceptable because it is acceptable'. Using the information in Figure 13.1, evaluate how a dollar bill has served as a store of value over the period since 1950.

*Answers to all Checkpoints can be found at the back of the text.

THE DEVELOPMENT OF BANKING

An examination of the nature and development of early banking practices will enable us to better understand how modern banks function. It will also reveal why it was felt necessary to create the Reserve Bank of Australia in order to put commercial banking on a sounder footing. In addition, we will gain further insight into the nature of money and how it functions.

Primary Functions of Banks

Modern banks have three primary functions: (1) they provide safekeeping services for all kinds of assets, not just money; (2) they make loans; and (3) as a group they create money. Originally the provision of safekeeping services was their only function. The functions of lending and money creation developed later, although today these functions represent by far the most important role of banks in our economy.

Safekeeping — The Oldest Banking Function

Goldsmiths were the forerunners of early banks. They had to have strong safes in order to protect and keep gold. Aware of this, people would often bring their own gold to the goldsmith for deposit in the safe. Usually the goldsmith received a fee for this safekeeping service. The depositor received a receipt designating the amount of gold deposited and attesting to the depositor's right to withdraw the gold on demand upon presentation of the receipt. When gold depositors needed their gold to purchase goods and services, they simply presented their receipts to the goldsmith, who then gave them back their gold. Perhaps the closest counterpart of the goldsmith's safe in a modern bank is the safe-deposit box you rent from the bank for an annual fee.

Lending — The First Commercial Banks

We might think of early commercial banking as evolving from the original safekeeping activities of goldsmiths. Suppose such a bank opens and accepts 1,000 ounces of gold from depositors. The depositors in turn receive receipts — their legal claim to the gold. The bank's balance sheet is shown in Table 13.2. Like any balance sheet, the left-hand side shows the assets of the bank, or what it has in its possession. In this case, the bank's assets consist of the 1,000 ounces of gold. The right-hand side shows the bank's liabilities — the claims on the bank's assets, or who owns them. In this case the liabilities consist of the depositor's receipts, which are their proof of legal ownership, or claim to the gold. Like all balance sheets, total assets must equal total liabilities — assets amounting to 1,000 ounces of gold are balanced by liabilities or receipts laying claim to 1,000 ounces of gold.

On a typical day the quantity of receipts turned in at the bank's deposit window by depositors wishing to withdraw their gold amounts to only a small fraction of the total 1,000 ounces of gold. Moreover, these withdrawals are often approximately offset by new deposits of gold with the bank. As a consequence, our early banker observes that there is usually a sizeable amount of gold standing idle in the safe. It occurs to the banker that in addition to the fees earned for providing safekeeping services, there is another possible moneymaking activity. Why not lend out some of this idle gold to people who are willing to pay the banker interest to borrow it? As long as the banker keeps enough gold in the safe to meet withdrawal demands of depositors, the depositors never even need to know that some of their gold is being lent to other people. Even if they do know, they won't care as long as they can always get their gold back on demand.[2]

Suppose the banker observes that depositors never withdraw more than 15 percent of the gold in the safe on any one day. The banker therefore decides it is safe to loan out about 80 percent, or 800 ounces, of the gold. This leaves 20 percent, or 200 ounces, in the safe as a reserve to satisfy depositors' withdrawal demands, somewhat more than the banker's experience suggests is necessary. The banker receives an IOU from each party that borrows gold. This note, a contract signed by the borrower, states the amount of gold owed to the bank, the date it must be paid back, and the interest rate that the borrower must pay the banker for the loan. The bank's balance sheet now appears as shown in Table 13.3. Comparing this balance sheet with that in Table 13.2, we see that for assets the bank now has 200 ounces of gold plus a number of pieces of paper, the IOUs, stating that various borrowers owe the bank 800 ounces of gold. For liabilities the bank still has obligations to give depositors 1,000 ounces of gold on demand, represented by paper gold receipts in the hands of depositors.

[2] One ounce of gold is indistinguishable from any other. Depositors are therefore only concerned about being able to get back the number of ounces of gold deposited, not the exact same particles of gold they deposited.

TABLE 13.2
Balance Sheet of an Early Commercial Bank

Assets			Liabilities	
Ounces of gold	1,000		Ounces of gold receipts	1,000
Ounces of total assets	1,000	=	Ounces of total liabilities	1,000

The bank will have no difficulties as long as the depositor's demands for withdrawal do not exceed 200 ounces of gold in any one day. Should this happen, the bank would be unable to honour its commitment to give depositors their gold on demand.

Money Creation and the Early Commercial Banks

Now that we have looked at the principle behind the way in which early banks evolved to combine safekeeping and lending functions, it is not difficult to see how they became creators of money as well.

It takes time and effort for depositors to go to the bank to withdraw gold every time they need it to make purchases of goods and services. In the community in which our early bank operates, suppose that the merchants know their customers fairly well and that the bank has a sound reputation. Merchants are therefore willing to sell goods in exchange for customers' gold receipts. The customer simply signs the paper gold receipt and specifies that its ownership has been transferred to the merchant. The merchant can either take the receipt to the bank to claim gold or use it to make purchases from someone else, transferring its ownership once again in the same manner. The receipt itself is now used as money. It is acceptable in trade because people know it can be redeemed for gold on demand at the bank. It is used as money because it eliminates the need for frequent trips to the bank. And receipts are also easier to carry.

Expanding the Bank's Lending Activities. Once the gold receipts are being used as money, the banker sees a way to expand the bank's lending activity. At present the banker has to keep only a fraction of the gold as reserves — the rest is loaned out. Specifically, 200 ounces is kept in the safe and 800 ounces leaves the bank on loan. But if gold receipts are now acceptable as money, why not just give borrowers paper gold receipts rather than actual gold in exchange for their IOUs? The borrower can use the receipts just as readily as the gold to make purchases. The banker previously felt that it was necessary to keep only 200 ounces of actual gold on hand (asset side of Table 13.3) when there were gold receipts outstanding amounting to claims on 1,000 ounces (liability side of Table 13.3). If this was workable, wouldn't 1,000 ounces of gold in the safe be adequate if there were gold receipts outstanding amounting to claims on 5,000 ounces? There would still be gold receipt claims on 5 ounces for every 1 ounce of actual gold, just as before.

As a consequence of the fact that gold receipts are acceptable as money, the banker can now keep all 1,000 ounces of deposited gold in the safe and print up and loan out gold receipts amounting to claims on 4,000 ounces of gold. Now the banker can earn interest on 5 times as many IOUs, generated by the lending of 4,000 ounces of gold as represented by

TABLE 13.3
Early Commercial Bank's Balance Sheet After Loaning Out 800 Ounces of Gold

Assets		Liabilities	
Ounces of gold (reserves)	200		
Ounces of gold in IOUs	800	Ounces of gold receipts	1,000
Ounces of total assets	1,000 =	Ounces of total liabilities	1,000

TABLE 13.4
Early Commercial Bank's Balance Sheet After Loaning Out Gold Receipts for 4,000
Ounces of Gold

Assets		Liabilities	
Ounces of gold (reserves)	1,000		
Ounces of gold in IOUs	4,000	Ounces of gold receipts	5,000
Ounces of total assets	5,000 =	Ounces of total liabilities	5,000

the gold receipts given to borrowers (previously the banker earned interest on IOUs for 800 ounces of gold). These receipts will have the same claim on the gold in the safe as the receipts received by the original gold depositors. Our early commercial bank's balance sheet now looks as shown in Table 13.4. All 5,000 ounces' worth of gold receipts are now circulating in the economy as money. Note, however, that there are only 1,000 ounces of actual gold.

As in the case depicted by Table 13.3, it is also true here that if all holders of these gold receipts brought them into the bank at one time and demanded gold, they could not be satisfied. The bank would not be able to honour its commitments to give out gold on demand. However, as long as no more than 20 per cent of the gold receipts are presented for payment at one time, there is no problem.

Bank Notes and Fractional Reserve Banking

It is now easy to see how banks got into the business of issuing paper money in the form of **bank notes.** The gold receipts of our hypothetical early commercial bank are but a short step removed from the status of these notes. To take this short step all the bank has to do is give a gold depositor bank notes instead of a receipt with the depositor's name on it.

Suppose the bank decides to print up

a bank note that says 'one dollar' across the front of it and, in smaller letters below this, 'this note is redeemable for one ounce of gold on demand.' Now the note could just as well have been called 'one Kanga', 'one Royal', 'one Roo', or 'one Mark'. The dollar[3] was chosen fairly recently as the basic unit of account in Australia with the introduction of decimal currency in 1966. Before that date, the unit of account was based on sterling (with pounds, shillings and pence) since 1825 (see the Historical Perspective on p. 313 for a description of Australia's early monetary experience). As far as the money-using public was concerned, the important thing was that the bank note could be converted into gold or other equally acceptable foreign currency at the bank on demand. Our hypothetical early commercial bank's balance sheet now appears as shown in Table 13.5. Compare this with Table 13.4.

During much of the nineteenth century, each bank in Australia could issue its own uniquely engraved bank note or currency. Through their lending activity such banks typically ended up issuing an amount of bank notes considerably larger than the amount of gold they had to back up the notes. That is, the bank notes had only

[3] The name derives from the old German word *thal*, meaning 'valley.' Its early origin stems from coins used in the valley of Saint Joachim in Bohemia as early as 1519. These coins were called *Joachimsthaler* and then *thaler*, which in English became 'dollar.'

TABLE 13.5
Early Commercial Bank's Balance Sheet After One-Pound Bank Notes Replace Gold Receipts (Hypothetically £1 = 1 Ounce of Gold)

Assets		Liabilities	
Gold reserves (1,000 ounces)	£1,000	Bank notes	£5,000
IOUs	4,000		
Total assets	£5,000 =	Total liabilities	£5,000

fractional backing, thus giving rise to the term **fractional reserve banking.** There was usually nothing wrong with this if a bank used good judgment and didn't issue 'too many' bank notes. But the main difficulty with a system that combined fractional reserve banking with a convertible currency (convertible into gold) was that even a well-managed bank could get caught short. Banks frequently found themselves confronted with demands to exchange gold for their bank notes that exceeded the amount of gold in their safes. When this happened a bank would be forced to close its doors. People left holding that bank's currency were really holding only worthless pieces of paper.

Fractional reserve banking of this kind typified banking in Australia from 1851 to 1910. Many note-issuing private banks came into existence during this time. In 1910, the Commonwealth Bank — a government owned bank — assumed responsibility for the issue of a national currency.

Bank Panics and Economic Instability

The adoption of a national currency did not put an end to the nation's monetary and banking problems. Just as the banks had created bank notes when they made loans, they could also create demand deposits. When they granted a loan and received an IOU, they simply credited the amount of the loan to a demand deposit in the borrower's name. Banks now came to use national currency as reserves, either keeping them in their own safe or possibly on deposit at another bank. Again the reserves typically amounted to only a fraction of the amount of their demand deposit liabilities. As an example, the asset side of the balance sheet in Table 13.5 would now have £1,000 of national currency as reserves and, as before, the £4,000 of IOUs. The liability side would have £5,000 of demand deposits.

The Nature of Bank Panics

The problem, as before, was that if too many depositors attempted to withdraw currency from their demand deposits, the bank might not have enough reserves to satisfy their demands. Because of this, bank panics and financial crises were still frequent. Even a rumour that a bank had made some bad loans (an IOU that some borrower wasn't meeting interest payments on or couldn't pay off) could cause people holding deposits at the bank to panic. There would then be a 'run on the bank' as depositors rushed to withdraw currency from their accounts — 'to get their money out'. Even if the rumour was false, the bank might be forced to close because the sudden increase in demand for deposit withdrawals could exceed the amount of currency in its safe. Paradox: the rumour of possible bankruptcy could cause bankruptcy.

In general, bank failures caused by runs on banks could be triggered by an adverse turn of events anywhere in the economy. Once banks started to fail, a chain reaction could set in, causing a recession throughout the economy. One of the most common causes of these financial crises was the growth of the economy itself as Australia developed into a fully fledged economy in the last third of the nineteenth century and early part of the twentieth. Let's see why.

Limits to Money Supply Expansion

Commercial banks themselves could not increase the total amount of the national currency available in the economy. They could of course provide credit (make loans) to feed economic expansion. The increase in deposits created by this loan expansion meant that the amount of demand deposits would get ever larger relative to the amount of currency available for bank reserves. Compounding the problem was the fact that more currency was also needed to serve as a medium of exchange in an expanding economy. The result was that bank reserves would become an ever smaller fraction of deposit liabilities, and banks would become more susceptible to a sudden surge of deposit withdrawals. The bank caught short might scramble to withdraw currency from its deposit at another bank, setting off a chain of bank failures and a general financial crisis. Consumers and businesses who dealt with these banks would suffer financial losses. This would cause a general decline in consumption and investment expenditures — that is, a decline in aggregate demand. GDP would fall, unemployment would rise, and the economy would be plunged into recession.

It was clear that the nation's monetary system, its money-creating mechanism, was not responsive enough to the economy's ever growing need for money — the money supply mechanism was not 'elastic' enough. The money supply could not readily 'stretch out' to meet the increasing demand for money caused by economic expansion. This occurred so often that recessions were typically referred to as financial crises or panics. After the financial crisis of the early 1930s, a Royal Commission was set up in 1935 under the chairmanship of Mr Justice Napier, to enquire into the monetary and banking system in Australia.

CHECKPOINT 13.2

Why might a bank note be said to be like an IOU? When currency is convertible into gold, how does the amount of gold in the economy put a limit on the amount of money in the economy? Describe how you think people's opinions about the soundness of banks at any particular time would affect the upper limit to the amount of the economy's money, defined as currency plus demand deposits. If bankers were to become cautious about the business outlook, how do you think this would affect the amount of IOUs on their balance sheets, and why and how would this affect the amount of money in the economy? How do you think this would affect total demand for goods and services?

HISTORICAL PERSPECTIVE

The Country has no Treasury[4]

The stores of the First Fleet did not include money. This was a natural omission since the new colony was intended to be populated by convicts who would prove self-supporting once these initial stores were exhausted. Thus the colony was to be a special kind of prison, and prisons do not require a monetary system.

Unfortunately for Captain Arthur Phillip and a succession of governors, the lack of a monetary system was to bedevil the development of the local economy. The government store which initially came to be the chief market for colonial produce paid for its local supplies with store receipts. These quickly became a kind of generally circulating government note issue — their attraction being that they were regularly withdrawn in exchange for bills on the British Treasury which were exchangeable for sterling in England. These early Treasury Bills (which earned no interest) were the sole kind of money with which imports could be bought. This system was aided by barter and payment in kind — for example, wages being paid in rum or with claims on merchants. However, as the role of the gaol in the economy receded and was overtaken by commercial activities, there emerged private note issue. The following 1810 statement by Governor Macquarie demonstrates the problems this raised;

> The people have been in some degree forced on the expedient of issuing and receiving notes of hand to supply the place of real money, and this *petty banking* has thrown open a door to frauds and impositions of a most grievous nature to the country at large. The persons principally concerned in this nefarious practice are to be found amongst the lower orders of society, and not infrequently among the convicts themselves, such being the credulity of the people that the notes of hand issued by these wretches are taken and passed into as free a circulation as if guaranteed by the best securities. When a considerable quantity has been thus disposed of, the issuers either become actually insolvent, or declare themselves so, in order to defraud their unwary creditors. Injurious, however, as this system is to the public, it cannot be totally laid aside until some other and better is substituted in its stead; at present the agricultural and commercial pursuits of the territory are much impeded and obstructed by the want of some adequately-secured circulating medium.[5]

The first bank in Australia was the Bank of New South Wales, set up in 1816–17 through the urging of Governor Macquarie. Quantitatively its operation and note issue were small, as were those of the 10 or so banks that started operations between 1820 and 1830. (Most of these banks failed during the slump of the 1830s.) Indeed the lack of a domestic currency was so critical that in 1822 there was a large-scale importation of spanish dollars (around $400,000), with the result that the country moved towards a dollar standard. This did not last as in 1825 the British government imposed on its empire a sterling exchange standard, with British units of monetary accounting and the circulation of British coins. This changeover took a long time to take effect completely, and it wasn't until 1849 that British coins were the only ones in circulation.

In 1851, the discovery of gold provided the initial impetus to a huge surge of economic activity. It is only in the latter half of the nineteenth century that banks came into their own as they were the principal purchasers of gold. The banks participated fully in the spread of population and wealth, opening many branches in new business centres. Between 1853 and 1888 some 28 colonial banks were set up throughout Australia. Bank money expanded considerably during this prosperous period, stimulated by speculative capital inflows from the UK, especially in the late 1880s. However, as the capital flows reversed in 1890 due to financial difficulties in the UK, about 40 banks suspended payment in both Sydney and Melbourne. The recovery of the economy from this bank crash was long and protracted with the result that the only new bank established up to the outbreak of World War I was the government owned Commonwealth Bank. In 1910, the Commonwealth Bank assumed responsibility for note issue by levying an annual tax of 10 per cent on private bank notes in circulation. This soon dried up private bank issue and gave the Commonwealth Bank a monopoly of issue — one of its first central banking functions.

[4]For further discussion of Australia's early monetary experiences see *Foundations of the Australian Monetary System 1788–1851* by S.J. Butlin, Sydney University Press, 1953.
[5]Macquarie to Castlereagh, 30 April 1810, Historical Records of Australia, Series I, Vol. VII, pp.264–5.

THE RESERVE BANK OF AUSTRALIA: FUNCTIONS AND OPERATIONS

The Napier Commission reported in 1937 and recommended Commonwealth legislation requiring trading banks to be licensed and subject to general supervision of the central bank. It also recommended that each bank should maintain a certain percentage of its Australian deposits with the central bank, which was to be empowered to take control of any bank in difficulties so as to protect the depositors. While this report was being debated, World War II broke out, and the government introduced the recommendations by regulation. Additionally, it controlled interest rates and the direction of investments. These regulations were mostly incorporated in the Banking Act of 1945 which firmly established the Commonwealth Bank of Australia as Australia's central bank. As well it was empowered to conduct ordinary banking business. In 1953 the Commonwealth Bank of Aus-

tralia was divided into two bodies namely, the Commonwealth Trading Bank, which took over the commercial banking functions, and the Commonwealth Bank which assumed the role of Australia's central bank. However, the two banks were still closely linked, with provision for sharing premises and exchanging staff. It was only in 1960 that a complete separation took place with the establishment of the Reserve Bank to take over the Commonwealth Bank and to become Australia's central bank with its own Board, Governor and staff.

The Reserve Bank Act 1959 establishes that:

It is the duty of the Board, within the limits of its powers, to ensure that the monetary and banking policy of the Bank is directed to the greatest advantage of the people of Australia and that the powers of the Bank under this Act are exercised in such a manner as, in the opinion of the Board, will best contribute to:

a. the stability of the currency in

Australia;

b. the maintenance of full employment in Australia, and

c. the economic prosperity and welfare of the people of Australia.

Although the avoidance of inflation is not specifically mentioned, the Reserve Bank interprets objectives a, b and c above as implying that 'the broad objective of monetary policy is sustainable and hence, non-inflationary growth of the economy'.[6]

The policy of the Reserve Bank is determined by its Board, which consists of a maximum of ten members. There are three official members — the Governor of the Bank (who is also Chairman of the Board), the Deputy Governor (Deputy Chairman of the Board) and the Secretary to the Treasury. The remaining seven members are appointed by the Governor-General for a term of five years. They are eligible for reappointment. Of these seven members, at least five must be persons who are not officers of the Bank or of the Commonwealth Public Service. Over recent years, members of the Board have come from the rural sector, manufacturing, mining, retailing, the trade union movement and the universities.

The Governor and Deputy Governor of the Reserve Bank are appointed by the Governor-General for periods not exceeding seven years, although they also are eligible for reappointment. Subject to the policy of the board, the governor (or in his absence, the deputy governor) is responsible for the management of the bank.

This structure of the Reserve Bank gives it a certain degree of autonomy. Furthermore, it is quite possible for a government to find it has to deal with a board set-up by a previous administration. The Reserve Bank Act lays down the procedures which are to be followed if there is a difference of opinion between the government and the board of the Reserve Bank. Basically, the government has the final say on the policy to be adopted. However, an order determining the policy to be implemented by the Reserve Bank has to be laid before each House of Parliament, including a statement by the government on the matter on which opinions had differed. So while the government of the day has the right to determine monetary policy, any strong disagreements by the Reserve Bank will be made public and thus may expose the government to some embarrassment. To date, recourse to this procedure has not been taken.

Debt Management

Debt management involves the financing of the Commonwealth Government's budget deficit as well as refinancing its maturing debt. The Reserve Bank, in association with the Treasury, advises the Commonwealth Government on its loan-raising program. This involves not only cost considerations, but also maintaining an appropriate maturity structure of debt on issue. The Reserve Bank conducts tenders for Treasury Notes and Treasury Bonds. It also processes applications for subscriptions to and redemptions of Australian Savings bonds. Let us take a closer look at each of these various Commonwealth Government securities.

Treasury Notes

The primary aim of any bank or other depository institution is to make a profit,

[6] Reserve Bank of Australia, *Functions and Operations*, 1987, p.8.

usually by accepting deposits at a lower interest rate than they charge on their loans. This profit is used to meet the running costs of the bank, to provide a return to the shareholders of the bank and also to provide the funds for the bank for future growth. Most of the investments or loans of banks and other depository institutions are medium to long-term, taking years before they fully mature. However, banks and other depository institutions also have a demand for short-term investments which they can quickly turn into cash as the need arises. Obviously it costs money to leave cash unnecessarily lying in the tills. Even if the cash is going to be used say, within a few weeks, the bank or depository institution is losing money since it has to pay an interest cost to its depositors. This is where Treasury Notes fulfil a useful function.

Treasury Notes are Commonwealth Government securities with terms to maturity of 13 or 26 weeks. They are sold regularly, usually weekly, and the Reserve Bank stands ready to rediscount (i.e. to buy) Treasury Notes which are within 90 days to maturity. The rediscount rate (which determines the buying price) is varied by the Reserve Bank from time to time. Thus if an unexpected shortage of cash (i.e. tight liquidity) occurs which the Reserve Bank wants to ease, it will rediscount or buy back Treasury Notes at an attractive rediscount rate.

This facility makes Treasury Notes very attractive to banks and other depository institutions since they provide them with a return, while in case of need they can always be sold back to the Reserve Bank, albeit at a small cost. The Reserve Bank uses Treasury Notes to iron out seasonal fluctuations in liquidity. For example, in the months preceding the traditionally tight June quarter when tax payments

drain cash from the economy, the Reserve Bank increases its sales of Treasury Notes. This is done so that the banks or other depository institutions would have Notes on hand to sell back to the Reserve Bank as the tax payments increase the demand for money. In this way the Reserve Bank avoids a financial crunch occurring each time tax payments become due.

Treasury Notes are sold by competitive tender. That is, the Reserve Bank announces on a Friday afternoon whether a tender is to be held the following Wednesday, and, if so, how many Notes will be offered and in what maturities. Bids are then lodged with the Bank by noon on Wednesday and Notes allotted according to the highest bidder. In this way the price of Treasury Notes is competitively established by the market.

Treasury Bonds

Treasury (or Commonwealth) Bonds differ from Treasury Notes in that they are Commonwealth Government Securities with longer terms to maturity, ranging from 1 year to over 15 years — the average years to maturity over recent years has been around 8 years. Quantitatively, Treasury Bonds are much more important than Treasury Notes: at the end of June 1987, Treasury Notes outstanding totalled around $8 billion while Treasury Bonds outstanding totalled approximately $40 billion. Bonds are the major source of financing the government deficit and are an important instrument of monetary policy — as we will examine later. Bonds are sold in a similar way to Notes, that is by competitive tenders, so that their price is market determined.

Australian Savings Bonds

Australian Savings Bonds are normally issued for seven to eight years and are designed to meet the needs of the smaller private investor. In fact there is a $200,000 limit on an individual's holding of Savings Bonds. In contrast, both Treasury Notes and Bonds are largely bought by banks and other financial institutions.

Savings Bonds also differ in one important characteristic. They can be redeemed for their face value at any time on one month's notice, with some interest penalty if they are redeemed before they have been held for 6 months. Bonds cannot be redeemed before they mature, so that if the holder needs to cash them he/she must sell them on the market, with the possibility of a capital loss if the price of new bonds has fallen. This difference is important and will be explored in the next chapter.

Lender of Last Resort

Until a few years ago, under the so-called Liquid Assets and Government Securities (LGS) convention negotiated between the Reserve Bank and the major trading banks in 1956, the Reserve Bank provided a lender of last resort facility to trading banks. This involved the undertaking that should the ratio of liquid assets (such as cash) and other government securities to total deposits of a trading bank fall below 18 per cent, then the Reserve Bank would have to lend money to the trading bank concerned at some penalty rate. This convention provided an unlimited source of funds to trading banks in case they needed it. It earned trading banks the reputation that they could never fail since there was always the Reserve Bank to back them. This privileged position amongst depository institutions that trading banks used to enjoy has been lost with the abandonment of the LGS convention in 1984. Instead, the Reserve Bank has provided two 'safety valves' to reduce the prospect of money market conditions tightening more sharply than intended. First, as we have already seen, holders of Treasury Notes may rediscount them (i.e. sell them) at the Reserve Bank. Second, there are two facilities available to the authorised dealers in the short-term money market. As the name suggests, this market is concerned with short-term money and short-term financial assets. The dealers authorised or licensed to operate in this market borrow money from those who want to keep it at call or on very short term, and invest it in short term assets. It is similar to a banking operation, with assets and liabilities both very short. However, the authorised dealers enjoy a special relationship with the Reserve Bank. They have the lender of last resort facility where they can borrow money by putting up as security Treasury Notes and Bonds. They can also enter into repurchase agreements with the Reserve Bank whereby they undertake to buy or sell a given volume of Treasury Bonds and Notes, subject to the transaction later being reversed at a specified date and price.

Both these facilities to the authorised short-term money market dealers carry a price. However, they provide an important function whereby not only banks but also other depository institutions can get access to funds lent by the Reserve Bank. In essence any depository institution can borrow indirectly from the Reserve Bank.

How the Reserve Bank Affects the Money Supply

We have seen how a bank or any depository institution can make a loan by accepting the debt instrument, or IOU, of an individual or business and crediting a demand deposit or a chequeable deposit in the borrower's name for the amount of the loan. The asset side of the bank's balance sheet is increased by the dollar amount of the IOU, and the liability side is increased by the same amount in the form of a chequeable or demand deposit held in the name of the borrower. The borrower is now treated as a depositor so that money may be withdrawn or cheques written on his or her account. *Hence, banks or any depository institution can create money by extending credit in the form of loans to businesses and households.* We will investigate this process in more detail in the next chapter.

The amount of money supplied to the economy through deposit creation is limited only by the amount of reserves that depository institutions have. The Reserve Bank can control the amount of reserves available in a number of ways. First, it can conduct open market operations, that is sell or buy Treasury Notes and Bonds. If, for example, the Reserve Bank sells Treasury Bonds, it takes in money and reduces the amount of cash in the system. This will affect the amount of money available in the economy which in turn affects the reserves that depository institutions can get hold of. Second, the Reserve Bank can set the legal reserve requirements for banks. (The reserve requirements of non bank depository institutions fall under State legislation.) By varying the reserve requirements, the ability of depository institutions to make loans is directly affected — a higher reserve requirement will mean that less funds are available for loans. Third, as we have already seen, the Reserve Bank can affect the amount of money in the system through its lender of last resort facility and repurchase agreements with the authorised money market dealers. In principle this is an important privilege. In

the nineteenth and early twentieth centuries many banks were forced to close because of a lack of reserves to satisfy depositors' withdrawal demands. This borrowing privilege is intended to make it possible for a bank with otherwise sound assets to borrow whatever reserves are needed to meet a sudden surge of deposit withdrawals. In practice, many economists feel that this borrowing privilege has not always been granted when it should have been, citing especially experiences during the Great Depression.

In sum, *it is the control over depository institution reserves that gives the Reserve Bank the ability to influence the size of the economy's money supply and thereby affect the level of total demand for goods and services in the economy. It is through this mechanism that the Board of the Reserve Bank must try to implement monetary policy.* We will examine this process in more detail in the next three chapters.

Depository Institutions as Financial Intermediaries

A financial intermediary *is a business that acts as a middleman (intermediary) by taking the funds of lenders and making them available to borrowers. A financial intermediary tries to cover its costs and make a profit on the difference between the interest it charges borrowers and the interest it must pay to attract the funds of lenders.* When a financial intermediary accepts a lender's funds, it issues an obligation against itself, a liability, to pay the lender back. When the intermediary in turn lends these funds to a borrower, it takes on an asset in the form of the borrower's IOU, or obligation, to pay the funds back.

The liabilities that a trading bank issues are in the form of demand, savings, and time deposits. Savings deposits might be in the form of passbook savings accounts, tailored to small depositors. Time deposits might be in the form of large negotiable certificates of deposit (CDs) that are usually issued in denominations of $100,000. CDs are much like short-term bonds and are tailored to the needs of large businesses and other institutions seeking to earn interest on the large amounts of funds they have at their disposal from time to time. In addition to creating chequeable deposits through their lending activities, trading banks also receive funds deposited in demand, savings, and time deposits, which they can then lend out.

Merchant banks, savings banks, building societies and credit unions issue liabilities against themselves that are much like the savings and time deposits of trading banks. Merchant banks make loans and accept deposits mostly to businesses. Savings banks and building societies make loans mostly to people buying homes and other real estate, thereby acquiring mortgages as assets. Credit unions acquire assets in the form of claims against people to whom they make consumer loans. Though they are not depository institutions, insurance companies are also financial intermediaries. Insurance companies issue liabilities in the form of insurance policies. The premiums they collect from policyholders are used to acquire assets such as mortgages, various kinds of bonds, and corporate securities.

The Role of Financial Intermediaries

What special services and advantages do financial intermediaries provide for our economy? Basically, there are three.

1. *Financial intermediaries have expertise as credit analysts. They have the ability and experience to evaluate and compare the risk and return, or credit worthiness, of different kinds of loan opportunities.* Imagine trying to prudently loan out your money by doing this in your spare time, after performing a day's work as a carpenter or doctor or whatever. Credit analysts do this full time for a living, just as carpenters and doctors work full time. Credit analysis is just another area of specialisation in a modern, industrialised economy.

2. *Financial intermediaries take the many different-sized amounts of funds that households, businesses, and other institutions want to lend and package them into the typically different-sized amounts that individual borrowers want to borrow.* For example, many small depositors at a commercial bank can indirectly make a $50,000 loan to a business.

3. *Financial intermediaries provide an opportunity for small lenders with small amounts of money to participate in risk-reducing diversification.* By depositing a small amount of money in a financial intermediary, a depositor in effect takes a proportional share of every loan the intermediary makes. Simply stated, the depositor has not put all of his or her eggs in one basket. The likelihood of loss is therefore reduced.

Additional Functions of the Reserve Bank

The Reserve Bank's most important and most difficult task is to attempt to manage the economy's money supply in a manner that avoids inflation while at the same time promoting the achievement and maintenance of a high-employment level of GDP. However, in addition to this and its other functions already mentioned, there are several other important functions that are indispensable to the smooth operation of our monetary system.

1. *The Reserve Bank serves as banker to banks.* Banks maintain Exchange Settlement Accounts with the Reserve Bank. These accounts are used to settle balances between banks arising from clearances of cheques. They are also used to settle transactions between the bank and the Reserve Bank due to purchases and sales of government securities, foreign exchange and Australian notes and coin. Interest is not paid on the accounts of trading banks and they must be maintained in credit. Savings banks are offered interest-bearing fixed deposit facilities.

2. *The Reserve Bank acts as banker to governments.* Through its branches, the Reserve Bank provides a comprehensive range of banking services to the Commonwealth government, four state governments and a number of Commonwealth and State instrumentalities. In addition, should the Commonwealth's budget be in deficit and not financed by the sale of government securities to the private sector then it may be required to finance this deficit. This is done basically by the Reserve Bank creating deposit liabilities on itself (i.e. printing money) in exchange for government securities issued by the Treasury. In this way the government can finance its deficit by printing money — in other words, the government would be borrowing from itself! In the next three chapters we will take a closer look at the use (and possible abuse) of this function.

3. *The Reserve Bank manages Australia's foreign reserves.* Australia's official reserves of gold and foreign currencies are held by the Reserve Bank. The holdings of foreign currencies are invested abroad in short-term marketable securities issued by overseas governments. The return on these assets contributes to the Reserve Bank's profit, most of which is passed on to the Commonwealth government to supplement its revenue. The Reserve Bank also buys and sells foreign currencies in the market for a number of reasons such as; to smooth out exchange rate fluctuations, to manage the foreign reserves and to meet the requirements of the Commonwealth government and its instrumentalities, such as when aircraft are bought from overseas by the Defence Department, Qantas and Australian Airlines.

4. *The Reserve Bank exercises prudential supervision of banks and monitors other financial intermediaries.* In order to maintain an adequate stock of liquid assets, banks have to hold a certain percentage of their total deposits in the form of Prime Assets. This Prime Assets Ratio (PAR) is set at 12 per cent for trading banks and 13 per cent for savings banks. Furthermore, there are a number of other requirements that banks must observe relating to: ownership, capital adequacy, exposure and associations with non-banks. The Reserve Bank also monitors closely the operation of other financial intermediaries and, under the Financial Corporations Act of 1974, has the power to regulate the operations of non-bank financial institutions. In recent years the emphasis of the Reserve Bank has moved away from relying on regulations and instead shifted the responsibility of prudential management on to the institutions themselves. This approach is in line with its more market oriented approach to the monetary system that it has adopted in recent years.

Where Do We Go from Here?

In the next chapter, we will examine in more detail the nature of the modern bank and how it works. We will also study how the whole banking system functions to create money and how this process is influenced by the Reserve Bank. In Chapter 15, we will examine how the money supply affects the level of aggregate demand for goods and services, and the role that money plays in determining the economy's equilibrium level of total output and employment.

CHECKPOINT 13.3
How does the Reserve Bank give elasticity to the money supply? Why do you suppose the Reserve Bank is sometimes referred to as the 'lender of last resort'?

SUMMARY

1. Money is anything that functions as a medium of exchange, a store of value, and a unit of account. Money is the most liquid of all assets.

2. The basic kinds of money are commodity money, currency (fiat money consisting of coin and paper money), demand deposits (chequing accounts), and other chequeable deposits. A near money can function as a unit of account and store of value like money, but not as a medium of exchange — though it is readily convertible into money.

3. Money in our economy is neither backed by nor convertible into gold. It has value because of the goods and services it will buy due to its acceptability in trade. The purchasing power of money depends on the price level. And this in turn depends on the government's management of the money supply.

4. Banks evolved from the safekeeping service provided by goldsmiths to become lenders as well. After gold receipts began circulating as money, banks were able to create money (bank notes) through the expansion of their lending activities. This eventually gave rise to present-day fractional reserve banking, with demand deposits and other chequeable deposits serving as money by virtue of the cheque-writing privilege.

5. The Reserve Bank was established to provide the economy with a more elastic money supply so that the bank panics and financial crises that plagued Australia in the nineteenth and early twentieth centuries might be avoided. The major purpose of the Reserve Bank is the formulation and implementation of monetary and banking policy in order to ensure: (a) the stability of the currency of Australia, (b) the maintenance of full employment and (c) the economic prosperity and welfare of the people of Australia. The Reserve Bank is principal banker to the Australian government, some statutory bodies and State governments; it is banker to banks and certain other financial institutions; it prints and manages the note issue. As agent for the Commonwealth, the Reserve Bank distributes coins and manages the Commonwealth's domestic borrowing programs through the sale or purchase of government securities. In the international sphere, the Reserve Bank oversees Australia's foreign exchange market, and holds and manages Australia's official reserves of gold and foreign exchange.

6. The economy's depository institutions function as financial intermediaries, accepting deposits and making loans. Depository institutions can create money by creating chequeable deposits through their lending activities. Because of the

Reserve Bank's control over the reserves of depository institutions, the Reserve Bank has the ability to influence the size of the economy's money supply and hence the level of total demand for goods and services in the economy.

7. The Reserve Bank also serves as a banker to banks and the government, provides the economy's paper money, and supervises and regulates the banking practices of member banks and other financial intermediaries.

KEY TERMS AND CONCEPTS

authorised dealers
Australian Savings Bonds
automatic transfer service (ATS)
bank note
broad money
building societies
certificate of deposit (CD)
credit union
demand deposit
depository institution
fiat money
financial intermediary
fractional reserve banking
lender of last resort
liquidity
M1
M2
M3
merchant bank
money
near money
savings bank
time deposit
token coins
trade credit
trading bank
transactions costs
Treasury Notes
Treasury Bonds

QUESTIONS AND PROBLEMS

1. What are the differences between inflation and deflation in terms of their effects on the three basic functions of money?

2. Compare and rank the different definitions of money — M1, M2, M3 and Broad Money — in terms of their relative merits (1) as mediums of exchange and (2) as stores of value. What difference would it make to your answer to (2) if (a) there was an inflation, (b) there was a deflation, or (c) there was neither inflation nor deflation?

3. Our money is no longer backed by nor convertible into gold or any other precious metal. Why is it still valuable?

4. Why might fractional reserve banking be described as the 'swapping of one debt obligation for another?'

5. The Australian economy was largely agricultural in the nineteenth century. In the spring, banks would make many loans to farmers, who needed money to plant crops. It was anticipated that once the crops were harvested and sold, the farmers would be able to pay off their loans to the banks in the late summer and early autumn. Describe the likely chain of events resulting from a drought. Suppose you were the banker in a farm community, and in the middle of the summer farmers came to you requesting loans so that they could construct irrigation ditches in their fields. What would you do? Why? What role might rumour play in all of this, depending on the *likely* outcome of your decision on these loan requests?

6. Why and how might central banking (the existence of the Reserve Bank) have greatly reduced bank panics in the nineteenth and early twentieth centuries?

Why might deposit insurance also have helped?

7. Describe how the basic functions of the Reserve Bank are supposed to contribute to economic stability.

8. Why and how is financial intermediation important to our economy?

14

Banks, Money Creation, and the Role of the Reserve Bank of Australia

---

AFTER READING THIS CHAPTER YOU WILL BE ABLE TO:

1. Explain the nature of the balance sheet of a bank.

2. Describe the conflict between the bank's desire to make profits and its need for liquidity and security.

3. Characterise the differences and similarities between the operation of an individual bank in a system of many banks and the operation of the banking system considered as a whole.

4. Describe how deposit expansion and money creation takes place in our banking system.

5. Explain and describe the main tools used by the Reserve Bank of Australia to affect the economy's money supply.

6. Define the major determinants of the demand for money.

7. Explain how money demand and money supply interact to determine the equilibrium level of the interest rate in the money market.

How do the Reserve Bank's actions affect our banking system, the money supply, and the level of economic activity in general? To answer this question we must first look more closely at the way banks operate. We will then examine the process by which our banking system as a whole is able to expand and contract the total amount of demand or current deposits a principal component of the money supply. We will also examine the tools and methods that the Reserve Bank uses to control this process and thereby pursue its monetary policy objectives. Finally, we will consider the major determinants of the demand for money and see how money demand and supply interact to determine the equilibrium level of the interest rate in the money market.

THE BANKS

The previous chapter described the origins and basic nature of banks and the way they function. We saw that a bank is a business seeking to make a profit, just like any other kind of business. We also saw that banks create money in the process of extending credit through their loan-making activity, their principal source of earnings.

Our discussion was aided by the use of a highly simplified version of a bank's balance sheet. In order to better understand how modern banks operate, we need to look at the bank balance sheet in more detail. We also need to consider the distinction between actual, excess, and required reserves in order to understand the deposit expansion (or contraction) process by which our banking system increases (or decreases) the economy's money supply. The bank's need for liquidity on the one hand and its desire to make a profit on the other bear closely

on how this deposit expansion (or contraction) process works. With this in mind, we will also consider how banks juggle the often conflicting goals of liquidity and profitability.

Our discussion could be conducted in terms of any one of the different types of non-bank financial institutions (NBFIs) such as Building Societies and Credit Unions. While such NBFIs were disadvantaged compared to banks in that they were not allowed to issue cheque accounts directly, in practice this limitation was easily overcome. NBFIs have offered their customers cheque drawing facilities using agency arrangements with banks. For example, customers of NBFIs are allowed to draw cheques on an account which these institutions maintain with a bank. Their cheques are eventually met by equivalent transfers of funds from the accounts of the customers. Furthermore, under the Cheques and Payment Orders Act of November 1986, provision has been made for NBFIs to issue payment orders similar in all respects to cheques. The effect of this Act once it becomes operational, will be to blur further the distinction between banks and NBFIs. However, we will focus on banks because their deposits make up the largest share: in September 1987 banks' deposits from the general public totalled over $109 billion, and comprised 61 per cent of total borrowings from the general public by all financial intermediaries. The basic principle of deposit expansion and money creation illustrated by banks, as well as the problem of balancing liquidity against profitability, apply in similar fashion to NBFIs.

The Balance Sheet: Assets and Liabilities

Our discussion of how a bank gets started

and the way in which it manages its assets and liabilities will be conducted in terms of the bank's balance sheet.

Starting a Bank

Suppose a group of people decide to start a bank, calling it Citizens' Bank. Say they put $100,000 of their own money into the business and receive in exchange shares of capital stock — paper certificates indicating their ownership of the bank. The owners' $100,000 of capital stock is the equity, or net worth, of the bank. The $100,000 is used to buy a building and other equipment needed to operate a bank. At this point Citizens' Bank's balance sheet is as shown in Table 14.1. The left, or asset, side of the balance sheet shows what the bank owns. The right, or liability and equity, side of the balance sheet shows the claims against the bank. The bank's total assets equal its total liabilities and equity, of course, because everything the bank possesses is claimed by someone.

The Bank Opens Its Doors

The bank is now ready for business. When its doors open suppose that customers deposit $1,000,000 in currency. The bank now adds $1,000,000 in demand or current deposits to the liability and equity side of its balance sheet and $1,000,000 cash to the asset side. Its balance sheet now appears as shown in Table 14.2. Those who have claims on the bank, represented on the liability and equity side of the balance sheet, are divided into two groups — the owners of the bank and the nonowners. The claims of the owners represent the bank's equity, or net *worth*, amounting to $100,000 (the value of the stock certificates issued by Citizens' Bank). The claims of the nonowners are represented by the $1,000,000 of current deposits. The nonowners' claims constitute the bank's liabilities. Hence, **equity** (*or* **net worth**) *equals the difference between total assets and total liabilities.*

Required Reserves, Actual Reserves, and Excess Reserves

Suppose the legal **required reserves** imposed by the Reserve Bank on banks is 20 per cent. This means that a bank is required by law to hold an amount of reserves equal to 20 per cent of the total amount of its demand deposits. *The ratio of required reserves to the total amount of demand deposits is the* **required reserve ratio.** *The law defines* **reserves** *as the cash held in the bank's vault and the deposits of the bank held with the Reserve Bank.* Since Citizens' Bank has $1,000,000 of current deposits, it must hold at least $200,000 (20 per cent of $1,000,000) in the form of reserves. Suppose it deposits $200,000 of its $1,000,000 of cash in its account at the Reserve Bank. Citizens' Bank's balance sheet now appears as shown in Table 14.3. While its legally

TABLE 14.1
Balance Sheet of Citizens' Bank

Assets		Liabilities and Equity	
Building and equipment	$100,000	Equity (stock certificates of Citizens' Bank)	$100,000
Total assets	$100,000 =	Total liabilities and equity	$100,000

required reserves amount to $200,000, its total reserves actually amount to $1,000,000 — $200,000 on deposit at Reserve Bank and $800,000 in the form of cash in its vault. Citizens' Bank's total reserves now exceed its required reserves by $800,000. This amount is called its **excess reserves.**

In sum, *total (or actual) reserves are equal to required reserves plus excess reserves.* Required reserves are the reserves that a bank is legally required to hold against current deposits. Required reserves are equal to the amount of current deposits multiplied by the required reserve ratio. Excess reserves are the reserves held above and beyond the amount needed for required reserves. Excess reserves are equal to total reserves minus required reserves.

Loaning Out Excess Reserves

At this point Citizens' Bank has excess reserves of $800,000. A bank's largest potential source of earnings is the interest it can earn by making loans and buying and holding various kinds of bonds and securities. Citizens' Bank therefore will want to put these excess reserves to work rather than hold 'idle' cash which earns no interest at all.

Suppose it loans out $300,000 to consumers who want to buy cars, household appliances, and perhaps bonds and stocks. Suppose $200,000 is loaned to businesses that need money to stock inventories of goods and raw materials and to buy equipment. The bank holds IOUs from these consumers and businesses in the form of notes (typically the IOUs of consumers and small businesses) and commercial paper (the IOUs of large corporations). Suppose the bank also purchases $100,000 worth of Commonwealth Government securities and $100,000 of other securities, such as corporate bonds and local government securities. As a precautionary measure,

TABLE 14.2
Balance Sheet of Citizens' Bank

Assets		Liabilities and Equity	
Cash	$1,000,000	Current deposits	$1,000,000
Building and equipment	$100,000	Equity (stock certificates of Citizens' Bank)	$100,000
Total assets	$1,100,000 =	Total liabilities and equity	$1,100,000

TABLE 14.3
Balance Sheet of Citizens' Bank

Assets		Liabilities and Equity	

Reserves
  On deposit at
  Reserve Bank
  Cash
	$1,000,000
	200,000
	
	800,000
		Current deposits	$1,000,000

Building and equipment	100,000	Equity (stock certificates of Citizens' Bank)	$100,000
Total assets	$1,100,000 =	Total liabilities and equity	$1,100,000

TABLE 14.4
Balance Sheet of Citizens' Bank After Loaning Out Excess Reserves

Assets		Liabilities and Equity	
Reserves	$ 300,000	Current deposits	$1,000,000
On deposit at Reserve Bank	200,000		
Cash	100,000		
Consumer loans	300,000		
Business loans	200,000		
Government securities	100,000		
Other securities	100,000		
Building and equipment	100,000	Equity (stock certificates of Citizens' Bank)	100,000
Total assets	$1,100,000	= Total liabilities and equity	$1,100,000

Citizens' Bank elects to keep $100,000 of its cash as excess reserves — to meet sudden withdrawal demands by depositors or to be able to provide credit to a regular loan customer on short notice. Citizens' Bank's balance sheet now appears as shown in Table 14.4.

Real-World Bank Balance Sheet

The stages of development of our hypothetical Citizens' Bank, illustrated in Tables 14.1 through 14.4, are like those of a real-world bank. The Citizens' Bank balance sheet shown in Table 14.4 is now very similar to the balance sheet of a typical trading bank in our economy. You will recall from the previous chapter that there are also savings banks (mostly concerned with housing loans) and merchant banks (basically banks for the business sector). However in the rest of this chapter we will focus on trading banks primarily for ease of exposition.

Consider, for example, the consolidated balance sheet of all trading banks in Australia shown in Table 14.5. This consolidated balance sheet is obtained by adding together the assets and liabilities of all the individual trading banks in the economy. The distribution of assets and

liabilities in Table 14.5 is fairly representative of that of a typical trading bank. We can see that the asset side of the balance sheet of our hypothetical Citizens' Bank in Table 14.4 is similar to the asset side of this consolidated balance sheet.

A comparison of the liability and equity sides of these two balance sheets reveals a number of important items we didn't introduce in our Citizens' Bank example — namely, fixed deposits and certificates of deposits. Fixed or term deposits are funds left with the banks for agreed periods of time (for example 3, 12, 18 months). The interest rates paid on them vary with the term of the deposit and prior to 1980 were subject to ceilings set by the Reserve Bank. Currently there are no controls on the rates paid on these deposits. We have already come across certificates of deposits in the previous chapter. Basically they are large denomination deposits which have a specific date to maturity but have the advantage that they can be transferred to other holders. As far as the banks are concerned they are fixed deposits, but they have greater liquidity to holders than traditional fixed deposits because of their marketability. The minimum denomination for a certificate of deposit is currently $50,000, while maturity restrictions and controls on interest rates paid have been completely removed. The Reserve Bank imposes legal reserve requirements on all deposits, including fixed deposits and certificates of deposit. Note from Table 14.5 that the total amount of fixed deposits and certificates of deposits is more than twice the amount of current deposits.

Liquidity and Security Versus Profit: Bank Portfolio Management

As a financial intermediary, a trading bank primarily engages in making short- to medium-term loans to businesses and households, as well as purchasing and holding bonds and other securities. *The bank's income-earning assets — its loans, bonds, and securities — together with its excess reserves constitute the bank's portfolio.* A bank manages its portfolio by adjusting the relative proportions of the different income-earning assets it holds in such a way as to satisfy two often conflicting objectives: (1) the maintenance of liquidity and security and (2) the realisation of profit.

Maintenance of Liquidity and Security

In the previous chapter, we saw how banks could fail if they didn't have adequate reserves to meet depositors' demands to withdraw their funds. It is clear from Table 14.5 that modern banks hold an amount of reserves equal to only a fraction of their deposit liabilities. Moreover, the largest part of a bank's reserves typically are held to satisfy the legal reserve requirement, and the bank can't really use these to satisfy depositors' withdrawals. (We shall see shortly that the main purpose of

required reserves is to give the Reserve Bank control over the banking system's money creation process.) Hence, in practice a bank will have to use its excess reserves to meet any sudden surge of deposit withdrawals. And if these excess reserves are not adequate, it will then have to liquidate some of its income-earning assets — that is, convert them into funds that can be used to meet deposit withdrawals.

A bank therefore needs to restrict itself to holding income-earning assets that are relatively liquid and secure. As we saw in the previous chapter, *the more liquid an asset is, the easier it is to convert into money without loss. The security of an asset refers to the degree of likelihood that the contracted obligations of the asset will be met.* For example, a bond is a contract stipulating that the borrower, the bond issuer, will pay the lender, or bondholder, a certain amount of interest on specified dates and return the amount of money borrowed (the principal) on the maturity date of the bond. Commonwealth bonds are the most secure asset a bank can hold. Loans made to consumers and households are less secure and, of course, the degree of security will vary from one consumer or business to the next.

It is important to recognise that liquidity and security, though related, are not the same thing. For example, a Treasury Note that matures in 13 weeks is for all intents and purposes just as secure as a Treasury bond that matures in 5 years. Yet the market value or price of the 5-year Treasury Bond will tend to fluctuate more on a day-to-day basis than that of the 13 week Treasury Note. The Treasury Note is, therefore, considered more liquid. (A simple, but not complete, explanation is that a Treasury Note is typically closer to its maturity date — the date when its price is guaranteed.) This is true in general of shorter-term bonds as compared to longer-term bonds.

In the case of loans to consumers and businesses, represented by financial paper and notes (IOUs of businesses and consumers), and in the case of bonds issued by corporations and local governments, the shorter the term to maturity, the greater the degree of security generally associated with such assets. This is so because there is more certainty about the likely financial situation of the borrowers in the short run than in the long run. In general, a bank restricts its holdings of earning assets to shorter-term loans, bonds, and securities because of the relatively higher degree of liquidity and security associated with these assets. This restriction is dictated by the large amount of deposit liabilities subject to withdrawal on demand.

Balancing Profit Against Liquidity and Security

A bank is like any other business in that it wants to maximise the profits realised by its owners, the stockholders. First and foremost, however, the bank is obliged to meet deposit withdrawals on demand. Whenever it is unable to do this, the bank is out of business.

Obviously, if a bank held nothing in its portfolio but vault cash, it would maximise liquidity and security. It would never have any problem satisfying demands for deposit withdrawal. But without any earning assets in its portfolio the bank wouldn't be very profitable either. At the other extreme, if a bank holds no excess reserves and tries to hold only those earning assets that yield the highest return, it may earn large profits. But the bank will run a high risk that

TABLE 14.5
Consolidated Balance Sheet of All Trading Banks in Australia, June 1985 (in Millions of Dollars)

Assets	$	Liabilities and Equity	$
Reserves: cash assets including Statutory Reserve Deposits and other deposits with the Reserve Bank	3589	Current deposits not bearing interest	$11570
		Current deposits bearing interest	3499
Loans	42882	Fixed deposits	26332
Commonwealth, local and semi-government securities	8199	Owners equity	9046
Other Securities	7477	Bills payable and other liabilities	26248
Fixed Assets	1315		
Bills receivable and all other assets	19111		
Total assets	82573	Total liabilities	$82573

Source: **Reserve Bank Bulletin,** November 1987. Reserve Bank Bulletin Supplement, June 1986.

it will not be able to meet a sudden surge of deposit withdrawals. Clearly, *there is a conflict between the maintenance of liquidity and security on the one hand and the realisation of profit on the other. The main task of bank portfolio management is to strike a balance between these conflicting objectives.*

Borrowers whose ability to repay loans is questionable typically must pay higher interest rates to obtain loans. Similarly, the lower the probability that the contractual obligations of a bond or security will be met, the higher is the interest it must yield to get a lender to buy it. In short, the less security an earning asset offers, the greater the return that can usually be realised from holding it. The higher return is compensation for the higher probability that the asset holder, or lender, may suffer a sizeable loss if the asset does not meet its contractual obligations (the borrower fails to make interest payments or pay the loan, or principal, back or both). Obviously, there is a temptation to acquire earning assets that offer less security but higher returns in order to increase bank profits, hoping of course to avoid the possible losses.

It is also tempting for a bank to hold longer-term bonds because their market value fluctuates more than that of short-term bonds. Consequently, if the portfolio manager can purchase a long-term bond when its market value is low and sell it when its value rises, sizeable profits can be realised. Of course, if the bank needs money to meet a sudden surge of deposit withdrawals on a given day, it might be forced to sell some of its long-term bonds for considerably less than it paid for them. In short, the greater profits that can possibly be realised on long-term bonds must be weighed against the fact that they are less liquid than short-term bonds.

The balance between the need for liquidity and security and the desire for profit is reflected in the consolidated balance sheet for all trading banks, Table 14.5:

1. The banks' reserves are of course their most liquid and secure assets. However, reserves (vault cash and deposits at the Reserve Bank) either earn no interest or a very low rate of return.

2. Among the income-earning assets, holdings of *Commonwealth Government securities* are highly liquid and just as secure as vault cash or deposits at the Reserve Bank.

3. *Loans to businesses and consumers* represent by far the largest portion of the income-earning assets. Their degree of security is considerably less than that of reserves and Commonwealth securities but they yield much higher rates of return and are the main source of trading bank earnings. The loans are predominantly short term, some for periods less than a month but few for a period longer than 5 to 10 years. The loans are represented by notes (typically the IOUs of consumers and small businesses) and commercial paper (the IOUs of large corporations) of varying degrees of liquidity.

4. Other securities consist mostly of Ordinary and Preference shares in associated and subsidiary companies such as savings banks and finance companies.

The relative proportions of these four categories of assets in trading bank portfolios reflect each individual bank's choice of balance between liquidity, security, and profitability. However, these proportions also reflect certain legal requirements that trading banks subject to the Banking Act are required to observe. In Australia, there are two main requirements; namely the Statutory

Reserve Deposit (SRD) ratio and the Prime Assets Ratio (PAR).

Statutory Reserve Deposits

Each trading bank has to maintain a Statutory Reserve Deposit (SRD) account with the Reserve Bank. A certain percentage of a trading bank's Australian deposits must be lodged in its SRD account. This proportion is called the SRD ratio and at the time of writing (early 1988) it stands at 7 per cent. The purpose of this SRD ratio is primarily to limit the ability of the banking system to lend and thus limit its ability to create money. If the Reserve Bank increases the SRD ratio to, say 10 per cent, then banks have to put a higher percentage of their total deposits in its SRD account, thereby reducing the amount it can loan out. Since 1981, the SRD ratio has not been changed from 7 per cent, although prior to that date it was changed on a number of occasions. One of the problems in using this method of affecting the money supply is that it is a very blunt instrument. For example, increasing the SRD ratio forces the banks to increase the percentage of reserves they hold not only of new deposits but also of existing deposits. Short of recalling their loans, banks will have to restrict any new lending drastically so as to comply with the higher reserve requirements. This could have a destabilising effect on the economy — by freezing any new bank loans it could cause some companies to default on their payments and hence set in motion the seeds of a recession. As a result of the bluntness of this instrument of Monetary Policy, the Reserve Bank has in recent years moved away from trying to affect the money supply through changes in the SRD ratio. This policy shift is quite in line with the Reserve Bank's overall policy change of

moving away from direct regulation to affect the supply of money. Instead, it has tended to rely more on market oriented policies such as open market operations — i.e. the buying and selling of government securities on the market in order to influence the level of the money supply. We will examine how open market operations affect the money supply shortly.

In addition to limiting the amount a bank can lend, SRD deposits carry a further cost, namely they earn a very low rate of return — at present 5 per cent. As may be seen from Table 14.5 out of $47,279 million deposits in 1985, $35,709 million or over 75 per cent of deposits were interest bearing deposits. With interest rates that banks pay much higher than 5 per cent, it is understandable that banks would not be keen on keeping a higher deposit than necessary in their SRD accounts. As far as the banks are concerned, their SRD deposits carry a cost to them. Being profit seeking institutions, they try to minimise this cost by not having more than is absolutely necessary in their SRD accounts.

Prime Assets Ratio

In May 1985, the Reserve Bank introduced the Prime Assets Ratio (PAR) under which each trading bank maintains at all times specified liquid assets (such as cash and loans to authorised dealers in the short-term money market) and Commonwealth government securities equivalent to 12 per cent of its assets in Australian currency within Australia. Currently 3 per cent of their total deposits held in SRD accounts also count as Prime Assets. The purpose of the PAR ratio is to ensure that trading banks maintain an adequate cushion of high quality liquid assets. Should the ratio of Prime Assets to total assets fall below the set level, then the trading bank concerned is obliged to, in the first instance, borrow the shortfall from the authorised money market dealers who have access to the lender of last resort facility within the Reserve Bank. This sets alarm bells ringing as far as the Reserve Bank is concerned. Under the Banking Act the Reserve Bank has extensive powers from merely obtaining information relating to the financial stability of a bank to the actual takeover of the bank's business in the interests of the depositors. While the Reserve Bank has such extensive powers, it does not see its role as that of policing banks. Rather, it sees its function as exercising *prudential supervision* over the operations of banks subject to the Banking Act, and ensuring that they follow *prudential principles and standards* in their operations. The word prudential, meaning exercising caution and wise judgment, is used extensively in Reserve Bank publications relating to its relationship with banks. The Reserve Bank uses prudential to describe its role in the sense of not being too intrusive and regulatory in its supervision of banks. In fact it states that 'the prime responsibility for the prudential management of a bank lies with the bank itself'. However, its prudential supervisory role also presumes prudential behaviour of banks. In other words, it expects banks to follow wise and judicious management practices. To strengthen its supervisory role, the Treasurer announced in May 1987, the Government's intention to introduce amendments to the Banking Act which would make more explicit the Reserve Bank's powers in relation to the prudential supervision of banks.

Prior to the establishment of PAR, there was a similar arrangement called the Liquid Assets and (other) Government Securities (LGS) convention whereby trading banks agreed to maintain 18 per cent of their total deposits in the form of liquid assets such as cash and other government securities. The LGS ratio was set at 18 per cent of deposits, with the requirement that banks borrow directly from the Reserve Bank, on penalty terms, should their liquid assets fall below 18 per cent of deposits. This convention was abandoned with the establishment of the PAR in 1985. The PAR is similar in many respects to the LGS convention, although it refers to total assets rather than total deposits of banks. The scope of the PAR requirement is as a prudential ratio rather than a tool of monetary policy. In other words, the Reserve Bank does not expect the PAR to be varied in order to influence the lending ability of banks.

---

*CHECKPOINT * 14.1*

From 1933 through 1940 trading banks kept a considerably larger portion of their assets in the form of excess reserves than is the case today. Why do you suppose they did this?

*Answers to all Checkpoints can be found at the back of the text.

DEPOSIT EXPANSION AND THE BANKING SYSTEM

In the previous chapter we saw how a bank can make a loan by accepting the IOU of an individual or business and crediting a demand deposit in the borrower's name for the amount of the loan. The asset side of the bank's balance sheet is increased by the amount of the IOU, and the liability

TABLE 14.6a Balance Sheet of Citizens' Bank

Assets		Liabilities and Equity	
Reserves	$1,000,000	Current deposits	$1,000,000
Required reserves	200,000		
Excess reserves	800,000		
Building and equipment	100,000	Equity	100,000
Total assets	$1,100,000 =	Total liabilities and equity	$1,100,000

side is increased by the same amount in the form of a demand deposit held in the name of the borrower. The borrower may then write cheques against this demand deposit and the bank is obliged to honour these cheques. We will now examine how the banking system as a whole, consisting of many such banks, creates money through this process. Again we will focus on trading banks. It should be emphasised, however, that the process of money creation described applies to all depository institutions and that the banking system as a whole includes all of these institutions.

First we will consider the position of an individual bank in a system of many banks. We will then examine the process of money creation when there are many banks in the economy.

The Individual Bank in a System of Many Banks

Consider once again the Citizens' Bank when it is in the position shown by its balance sheet in Table 14.3, reproduced here as Table 14.6a. In the rest of this chapter we will use required reserves to refer to both SRD and Prime Assets that banks are required to hold. Furthermore, at the time of writing banks are required to hold 12 per cent of their total assets in Prime Assets and 7 per cent of deposits in their SRD account, 3 per cent of which counts as part of their Prime Assets. Since this is rather complicated to calculate we will not use these actual reserve require-

ments but rather will maintain our previous assumption that the required reserve ratio is 20 per cent of deposits. As may be seen from Table 14.6a, this assumption leaves Citizens' Bank with $800,000 excess reserves and thus in a position to make loans by creating demand deposits.

What amount of loans and, hence, current deposits will the Citizens' Bank create? It cannot create more than $800,000 worth. At this stage Citizens' Bank's balance sheet appears as in Table 14.6b. The bank cannot lend out more than $800,000 because borrowers will most likely immediately spend these funds by writing cheques against the $800,000 of current deposits that the bank has credited to them. Since Citizens' Bank is just one among many banks in the banking system, it is likely that these cheques will be made payable to parties who deposit their money in these other banks. Therefore, when all of these cheques are presented to the Citizens' Bank for collection of payment, Citizens' Bank will have to pay out its $800,000 of excess reserves to satisfy the cheques, which are orders to withdraw the $800,000 of deposits on demand. Assume that this happens. Citizens' Bank's balance sheet will now appear as in Table 14.7.

Note that the bank is now 'fully loaned up'. It has just the amount of reserves on hand to meet the legal reserve requirement — $200,000 of reserves held against $1,000,000 of demand deposits. There are

TABLE 14.6b
Balance Sheet of Citizens' Bank After Making Loans of $800,000 But Before Cheques Are Written Against Bank

Assets		Liabilities and Equity	
Reserves	$1,000,000	Current deposits	$1,800,000
IOUs: loans to businesses, to consumers	800,000		
Building and equipment	100,000	Equity	100,000
Total assets	$1,900,000 =	Total liabilities and equity	$1,900,000

no excess reserves. While the Citizens' Bank now has the same amount of demand deposits it had in the beginning, it has created $800,000 more money in the economy. That money is now deposited in other banks. Although unlikely, it could have happened that all of the cheques written against the $800,000 of demand deposits created by Citizens' Bank in Table 14.6b were paid to parties who redeposited them at Citizens' Bank. The deposits of those who wrote the cheques would then be reduced by $800,000, while the deposits of those who received the cheques would be increased by $800,000. The total amount of demand deposit liabilities at Citizens' Bank would remain unchanged at $1,800,000. Also unlikely, but possible, the $800,000 of demand deposits created in Table 14.6b might be withdrawn by the borrowers in the form of currency, so that the final position of the bank would be as shown in Table 14.7.

In general, *a single bank in a banking system composed of many banks cannot lend more than the amount of its excess reserves. This is so because borrowers will most likely write cheques against the deposits that will cause the bank to lose these excess reserves, along with the deposits, to other banks.* This means that a single bank cannot permanently increase the amount of its demand deposit liabilities (by making loans) beyond the amount it had to begin with.

A Banking System of Many Banks

We will now see that a banking system made up of many banks can make loans and create current deposits equal to several times the amount of total excess reserves in the system.

Why is this so? Recall that a single bank in a banking system of many banks cannot permanently increase the amount of its current deposits because the current deposits it creates by lending are transferred by cheque writing borrowers to other banks. As a result, the current deposits of other banks are increased.

TABLE 14.7
Balance Sheet of Citizens' Bank After Cheques For $800,000 Are Written Against Bank

Assets		Liabilities and Equity	
Reserves	$ 200,000	Current deposits	$1,000,000
IOUs: loans to businesses and consumers	800,000		
Building and equipment	100,000	Equity	100,000
Total assets	$1,100,000 =	Total liabilities and equity	$1,100,000

Therefore, the amount of current deposits in the *whole* banking system is increased. Reserves and deposits cannot be lost to other banks outside the banking system because there are no banks outside the system. Let's now explore in more detail lending and deposit creation in a banking system consisting of many banks. We will see why the amount of money created is some multiple of the total amount of excess reserves.

Money Creation in a Banking System of Many Banks

Suppose somebody deposits $1,000 of currency in a current account at Bank A. Assume now that the legally required reserve ratio is 10 per cent, or .10, and that the bank was fully loaned up prior to the time of the $1,000 deposit. Bank A now has $1,000 more current deposits as liabilities and $1,000 more reserves as assets, of which $100 are required reserves and $900 are excess reserves. (In the discussion to follow, we will ignore all items on the bank's balance sheet but those that change as a result of deposit expansion.) Bank A's balance sheet changes as follows:

BANK A

(Bank A receives $1,000 in current deposits.)

Assets		Liabilities	
Reserves	+ $1,000	Current deposits	+ $1,000
Required reserves	+ 100		
Excess reserves	+ 900		
Assets	+ $1,000	Liabilities	+ $1,000

Bank A, as an individual bank, can now lend out $900 by creating $900 of new current deposits, an amount equal to its excess reserves. At this point Bank A's balance sheet changes like this:

BANK A

(Bank A makes $900 of loans, increasing current deposits by $900.)

Assets		Liabilities	
Reserves	$1,000	Current deposits	$1,000
Loans	+ 900	Current deposits	+ 900
Assets	+ $1,900	Liabilities	+ $1,900

Presumably, the party borrowing the $900, in whose name Bank A creates the $900 demand deposit, will soon spend that $900 by writing a cheque against the deposit for that amount. That is, the borrower will use the money to pay for some good or service. Suppose the recipient of that cheque deposits the cheque in another bank, Bank B. Since the cheque is drawn against Bank A, $900 of reserves will be transferred from Bank A to Bank B. After all this, the change in Bank A's balance sheet is the following:

BANK A

(Bank A loses $900 of reserves and deposits after cheque is written against it.)

Assets		Liabilities	
Reserves (1,000 − $900)	+ $ 100	Current deposits ($1,900 − $900)	+ $1,000
Loans	+ 900		
Assets	+ $1,000	Liabilities	+ $1,000

Bank A is now fully loaned up. It has $1,000 of demand deposits and holds $100 of reserves, just the amount required by law, given that the required reserve ratio is .10. It has no excess reserves.

When the $900 cheque drawn on Bank A is deposited in Bank B, and $900 of reserves are transferred from Bank A to Bank B, the following changes are made in Bank B's balance sheet:

BANK B

(Bank B receives $900 deposit from Bank A, and $900 of reserves are transferred to Bank B.)

Assets		Liabilities	
Reserves	+ $900	Current deposits	+ $900
Required reserves	+ 90		
Excess reserves	+ 810		
Assets	+ $900	Liabilities	+ $900

Bank B's current deposits and reserves are each increased by $900. With a required reserve ratio of .10, the increase in the amount of its legally required reserves amounts to $90, while the increase in its excess reserves amounts to $810.

Suppose that Bank B now creates demand deposits by lending out $810, an amount equal to its excess reserves. Bank B's balance sheet will now change as follows:

BANK B

(Bank B makes $810 of loans, increasing current deposits by $810.)

Assets		Liabilities	
Reserves	$ 900	Current deposits	$ 900
Loans	+ 810	Current deposits	+ 810
Assets	+ $1,710	Liabilities	+ $1,710

Now suppose the borrower writes a cheque for $810 against this newly created demand deposit. If the recipient of the cheque deposits it in another bank, Bank C, $810 of reserves will then be transferred from Bank B to Bank C. The change in Bank B's balance sheet appears as follows:

BANK B

(Bank B loses $810 of reserves and deposits after cheque is written against it.)

Assets		Liabilities	
Reserves $900 — $810)	+ $ 90	Current deposits $1,710 — $810)	+ $900
Loans	+ 810		
Assets	+ $900	Liabilities	+ $900

Now Bank B has $900 of current deposits and $90 of reserves. The reserves are equal to 10 per cent of the amount of current deposits, just the amount it is legally required to hold. Bank B is fully loaned up — it has no excess reserves.

The Pattern of Lending and Deposit Creation. There is a pattern to this process of lending and deposit creation. Bank A's excess reserves allow it to make loans and create new current deposits equal to the amount of its excess reserves, which are then transferred by cheque-writing borrowers to Bank B. Bank B acquires all of Bank A's excess reserves in this process. Bank B is required to hold a fraction (equal to the legally required reserve ratio) of these new reserves against its newly acquired current deposits. The remainder are excess reserves that allow B to make loans and create new current deposits, which are in turn transferred by cheque-writing borrowers to Bank C, and so on. After borrowers write cheques transferring Bank C's newly created current deposits, along with its excess reserves, to Bank D, the change in Bank C's balance sheet will be as follows:

BANK C

Assets		Liabilities	
Reserves	+ $ 81	Current deposits	+ $810
Loans	+ 729		
Assets	+ $810	Liabilities	+ $810

And repeating the same pattern another step further, the change in Bank D's balance sheet would appear as follows:

BANK D

Assets		Liabilities	
Reserves	+ $ 73	Current deposits	+ $729
Loans	+ 656		
Assets	+ $729	Liabilities	+ $729

And similarly, for Bank E the change is:

BANK E

Assets		Liabilities	
Reserves	+ $ 66	Current deposits	+ $656
Loans	+ 590		
Assets	+ $656	Liabilities	+ $656

The complete process of current deposit expansion throughout the banking system is summarised in Table 14.8. Starting with the initial current deposit of $1,000 at Bank A (column 1), follow the arrows and notice that the successive increases in current deposits at Banks B, C, D, and so on become smaller and smaller. This reflects the fact that when a bank receives current deposits and reserves from another bank, only a portion of these reserves, the excess reserves (column 2), can be passed on to yet another bank through lending and the creation of new current deposits.

The other portion must be kept as required reserves (column 3). If we want to know the total amount of new current deposits that this process creates — the total amount of money creation — we must add up all the deposit increases throughout the banking system, as shown in column 1.

The Process of Deposit Creation Completed. When the entire process of deposit expansion is complete, all banks in the banking system are fully loaned up — there are no excess reserves anywhere in the banking system. The initial $1,000 increase in reserves is totally tied up as required reserves (column 3). Including the initial increase in current deposits of $1,000 at Bank A, the total increase in current deposits and, therefore, money for the whole banking system amounts to $10,000. That is, the total increase in current deposits (column 1) is 10 times the initial $1,000 increase in reserves at Bank A. This multiple of 10 is the reciprocal of the required reserve ratio of .10. Similarly, viewed in terms of the initial increase in excess reserves of $900 at Bank A, the total amount of new money created by the expansion process is $9,000 (column 2). Again, the multiple is 10.

In sum, *a single bank in a banking system cannot permanently increase the amount of its current deposits by lending out its excess reserves. But when each individual bank in the system lends out its excess reserves, the banking system considered as a whole can. That is, the total expansion in demand deposits throughout the entire banking system is equal to a multiple of any increase in reserves. The multiple is equal to the reciprocal of the required reserve ratio.*

Deposit Contraction: Destruction of Money by the Banking System

The deposit expansion or money creation process is also reversible. Suppose the banking system is fully loaned up and a depositor at Bank A decides to withdraw $1,000 of currency. In essence this leads to a reversal of the process summarised in Table 14.8 — think of the direction of the arrows as now being reversed.

Initially Bank A loses $1,000 of reserves in the form of cash (column 1). Since it has $1,000 less current deposits, it no longer needs to hold the $100 in required reserves (column 3) against these deposits. But since Bank A was fully loaned up to begin with, it is now short $900 of the amount of required reserves it must hold against its remaining deposits. Consequently, Bank A will have to get rid of $900 of other assets in its portfolio (column 2) to replenish its reserves. Suppose it does this by selling $900 of government bonds to someone who holds current deposits in Bank B. This party writes a cheque against Bank B for $900 (column 1) payable to Bank A. Bank A deposits this $900 cheque in its account at the Reserve bank. Since deposits at the Reserve Bank count as reserves, Bank A now has just the amount of reserves needed to satisfy its legal reserve requirement.

However, when Bank A's account at the Reserve Bank is marked up, or credited, $900, Bank B's account at the Reserve Bank is drawn down, or debited, $900. While Bank B no longer needs to hold $90 of required reserves (column 3) because it has lost $900 of current deposits (column 1), it is now short $810 of the amount of required reserves it must hold against its remaining deposits. Therefore, Bank B sells $810 of government bonds to someone who holds current deposits in Bank C. This party writes a cheque against Bank C for $810 (column 1) payable to Bank B. Bank C then loses deposits and finds itself short of required reserves, and the whole contraction process is repeated over and over with respect to Banks D, E, F, and so forth. In the end, the total reduction in current deposits for the whole banking system amounts to $10,000 (column 1). Hence, the initial decrease in current deposits and, therefore, reserves of $1,000 results in a total reduction in the amount of current deposits that is 10 times greater. Note again that this multiple is the reciprocal of the required reserve ratio $1/10$, or .10.

In sum, *the process of multiple contraction of current deposits is just the reverse of the process of multiple expansion of deposits.*

Determining the Deposit Multiplier

We have seen that any initial increase in reserves can result in an increase in the total amount of current deposits, or new money, that is equal to a multiple of the amount of increase in reserves. This was true for the banking system consisting of many banks, provided they were fully loaned up. The multiple equals the reciprocal of the required reserve ratio r or $1/r$. This reciprocal is often called the **deposit multiplier:**

$$\text{deposit multiplier} = \frac{1}{r}$$

If the required reserve ratio is 20 per cent, or .20, the deposit multiplier $1/r$ equals $1/.20$, or 5. If the required reserve ratio were 10 per cent, or .10, then the deposit multiplier would equal $1/.10$, or 10. In this case, for example, the maximum increase in the dollar amount of new current deposits resulting from a $10 increase in reserves would be $100. We can express this through the following equation:

$$\$10 \times \frac{1}{r} = \$10 \times 10 = \$100$$

In general, if E is the change in reserves and D is the maximum increase in current deposits, then

$$D = E \times \frac{1}{r}$$

Of course, the deposit multiplier is applicable to a decrease in reserves as well as to an increase. That is, if reserves are removed from the banking system when it is fully loaned up, there will be a contraction in the amount of current deposits in the system that is equal to the amount of reserves removed multiplied by the deposit multiplier $1/r$. For example, in our discussion of multiple deposit contraction, the legally required reserve ratio was .10. The deposit multiplier was therefore 10. Assuming that the banking system was fully loaned up, we saw that an initial $1,000 reduction in reserves resulted in a total loss of current deposits amounting to $10,000 for the whole banking system ($1,000 × 10).

Other Determinants of the Size of the Deposit Multiplier

By now you have probably been struck by the similarity between the deposit multiplier and the income or expenditure multiplier discussed in Chapter 9. Indeed, the deposit expansion process of Table 14.8 looks very similar to the income expansion process of Table 9.4. Just as the deposit expansion multiplier is equal to the reciprocal of the required reserve ratio, the expenditure multiplier is equal to the reciprocal of the marginal propensity to save. Just as the expenditure multiplier reflects the fact that expenditure by one party is income for another, the deposit multiplier reflects the fact that reserves and deposits lost by one bank are reserves and deposits gained by another. The size of the expenditure multiplier is determined by the amount of leakage into saving at each round of expenditure, as determined by the size of the MPS. Similarly, the size of the deposit multiplier is determined by the amount of leakage of reserves into required reserves at each round of the deposit expansion process.

The similarity between the two multipliers ends here, however. This is so because the expenditure multiplier deals with a flow, income, while the deposit multiplier deals with a stock, the money supply. Moreover, money and income are completely different concepts. Nonetheless, the leakage concept is very useful to our understanding of the other determinants of the size of the deposit multiplier.

Leakages into Excess Reserves

Up to this point in our discussion of the deposit multiplier, we have assumed that leakage into required reserves is the *only* type of leakage from the deposit expansion process. In other words, we have assumed that banks are always fully loaned up. In reality, this is not always the case.

For example, as part of their portfolio management policy banks may want to keep a certain amount of excess reserves on hand for liquidity purposes. This constitutes another source of leakage from the deposit expansion process in addition to the leakage into required reserves. This

TABLE 14.8
Expansion of the Money Supply by Lending and Deposit Creation by the Banking System (Legally Required Reserve Ratio Is .10)

Bank	(1) New Reserves and Current Deposits	(2) Excess Reserves Equal to the Amount Bank Can Lend, Equal to New Money Created (1) − (3)	(3) Required Reserves (1) × required reserve ratio of .10
A	$ 1,000	$ 900	$ 100
B	900	810	90
C	810	729	81
D	729	656	73
E	656	590	66
F	590	531	59
G	531	478	53
H	478	430	48
All remaining banks	4,306	3,876	430
Total	$10,000	$9,000	$1,000

means that a greater portion of the reserves one bank receives from another is set aside at each round of deposit expansion — part to satisfy legal reserve requirements and part to be held as excess reserves to satisfy the liquidity objectives of a bank's self-imposed portfolio management policy. In short, a smaller amount of reserves is now passed on from one bank to the next and, therefore, the full amount of deposit expansion will be less. This makes the deposit multiplier smaller. For example, if the legal reserve requirement is 10 per cent and in addition banks set aside as excess reserves another 10 per cent of any reserves received, the deposit multiplier is equal to 1 ÷ .20 (the sum of .10 and .10), or 5.

Similarly, the deposit multiplier for the deposit contraction process will be smaller if banks choose to keep excess reserves on hand for liquidity purposes. Why? Each bank will be able to meet deposit withdrawals out of excess reserves before it needs to start selling off assets, which would lead to further deposit withdrawals at other banks, in the manner we have already described.

Leakages Due to Cash Withdrawal

Another source of leakage from the deposit expansion process is cash withdrawal. In our discussion it was assumed that when a cheque was written against a deposit at one bank, the recipient deposited the entire amount in another bank. In reality, the recipient may deposit only part of the amount of the cheque and hold the rest in cash. Since cash in banks constitutes reserves, this means that a smaller amount of reserves ends up being transferred from one bank to the next, and the full amount of the deposit expansion process is reduced accordingly. For example, suppose that in addition to the 10 per cent leakage into excess reserves, there is another 10 per cent leakage due to cash withdrawals by the public at each step of the deposit expansion process. The deposit expansion multiplier will now be equal to $1 \div .30$ (the sum of .10, .10, and .10), or 3.3.

Variation in Willingness to Lend and Borrow

Finally, the willingness of banks to lend and the eagerness of businesses and consumers to borrow tends to vary with economic conditions. At one extreme, if there is no lending and borrowing, there will be no deposit expansion at all. At the other extreme, when banks are fully loaned up there is the maximum possible amount of deposit expansion. The amount of deposit expansion usually lies somewhere between these two extremes, depending on the banks' willingness to lend and the demand for loans by borrowers. Generally, banks are more cautious and eager borrowers less numerous when the economy is in the contraction phase of a business cycle. Obviously, therefore, the amount of excess reserves banks hold will tend to vary over the course of the business cycle. Consequently, so will the size of the deposit multiplier.

In sum, *the theoretical deposit multiplier calculated as the reciprocal of the required reserve ratio assumes that banks are fully loaned up. It tells us the maximum amount of deposit expansion or contraction that can take place in response to a change in excess reserves. In reality, banks are not always fully* loaned up and there are also leakages due to cash withdrawal by the public. Consequently, the size of the actual deposit multiplier is typically variable as well as smaller than the theoretical deposit multiplier.

CHECKPOINT 14.2

Change the required reserve ratio in Table 14.8 to .25 and show how the deposit expansion process will look as a result. How might the actions of one bank or one depositor put a stop to this expansion process? Suppose bankers' willingness to lend increases. Describe how and why this will affect the economy's money supply. With a required reserve ratio of .25, what will be the maximum possible effect on the economy's money supply if you decide to withdraw $100 in cash from your bank? Under what conditions will your withdrawal have the least possible effect on the money supply? (Define the money supply as current deposits plus currency held outside of banks.)

THE ROLE OF THE RESERVE BANK OF AUSTRALIA

The Board of the Reserve Bank, is responsible for the conduct of *monetary policy* in our economy. *Monetary policy is deliberate action taken to affect the size of the economy's money supply for the purpose of promoting economic stability and maximum output and employment with a minimum of inflation.*

The Reserve Bank is able to affect the size of the economy's money supply by controlling the quantity of reserves in the banking system. If the Reserve Bank increases the quantity of reserves, money creation takes place through the process of deposit expansion. If the Reserve Bank decreases the quantity of reserves, the amount of money in the economy is reduced through the process of deposit contraction. In this section we will examine the tools the Reserve Bank actually uses to conduct monetary policy.

The Two Major Tools of Monetary Policy

There are two major tools that the Reserve Bank can use to conduct monetary policy: (1) open market operations, and (2) setting reserve requirements for trading banks and other depository institutions. We will consider each of these tools in turn.

Again we will illustrate our discussion in terms of trading banks. However, again we emphasise that the discussion also applies to other depository institutions and that the banking system includes all such institutions.

Open Market Operations

The Reserve Bank can directly affect the amount of bank reserves by buying or selling government securities, such as Treasury Notes, in the open market where these securities are traded. Such transactions are called **open market operations.** Open market operations are the Reserve Bank's most important tool for carrying out monetary policy. *When the Reserve Bank conducts open market purchases, it buys government bonds and puts reserves into the banking system, causing an expansion of deposits and hence an increase in the economy's money supply. When the Reserve Bank conducts open market sales, it sells government bonds and takes reserves out of the banking system, causing a contraction of deposits*

and hence a decrease in the economy's money supply. Let's consider how each of these operations works in more detail.

1. *Open Market Purchases.* Suppose the Reserve Bank buys $100,000 of Treasury Notes in the open market and the seller is a trading bank. (We will focus only on those items in the Reserve Bank's and the trading bank's balance sheet that are affected by this transaction.) The Reserve Bank pays the trading bank by increasing (crediting) the trading bank's reserve account at the Reserve Bank by the amount of the purchase, or $100,000. Hence, the Reserve Bank has $100,000 more assets in the form of Treasury Notes and $100,000 more liabilities in the form of trading bank reserve deposits at the Reserve Bank. The changes in the Reserve Bank's balance sheet look like this:

RESERVE BANK

Assets		Liabilities	
Treasury Notes	+ $100,000	Trading bank reserve deposits	+ $100,000

The trading bank now has lost $100,000 of assets in the form of Treasury Notes sold to the Reserve Bank, but it has gained $100,000 of assets in the form of reserves — deposits at the Reserve Bank. The changes in the trading bank's balance sheet therefore look like this:

TRADING BANK

Assets	
Reserves: deposits at the Reserve Bank	+ $100,000
Treasury Notes	− $100,000

Note that while the total amount of the trading bank's assets have not changed, the trading bank now has more reserves. If the trading bank previously was fully loaned up, it now has $100,000 of excess reserves. It is now in a position to make new loans by creating current deposits if it wishes. We have seen how this can lead to deposit expansion, or money creation, throughout the banking system.

Suppose that the Reserve Bank buys $100,000 of Treasury Notes in the open market, but the seller is one individual or a business other than a bank. The Reserve Bank simply makes out a cheque for $100,000 drawn against itself and payable to the seller of the Treasury Notes. Suppose the seller deposits the cheque in a trading bank. The trading bank then presents the cheque in its account at the Reserve Bank and hence, its reserves increase by $100,000. The changes in the Reserve Bank's balance sheet are as follows:

RESERVE BANK

Assets		Liabilities	
Treasury Notes	+ 100,000	Trading bank reserve deposits	+ $100,000

Again, the Reserve Bank has $100,000 more assets in the form of Treasury Notes and $100,000 more liabilities in the form of trading bank reserve deposits.

The trading bank now has $100,000 more liabilities in the form of current deposits and $100,000 more assets in the form of reserves represented by deposits at the Reserve Bank. These changes in the trading bank's balance sheet look like this:

TRADING BANK

Assets		Liabilities	
Reserves: deposits at the Reserve Bank	+ $100,000	Current deposits	+ $100,000

Again, we see that trading bank reserves are increased by the amount of the open market purchase. Assuming that the trading bank was initially loaned up, it now has excess reserves because it is only required to hold a fraction of its new reserves against its newly acquired $100,000 of current deposits. Deposit expansion and money creation can take place just as before.

In sum, *trading bank reserves are increased by the amount of Reserve Bank open market purchases no matter whether the seller of the securities is a bank or a nonbank.*

2. Open Market Sales. Suppose the Reserve Bank sells $100,000 of Treasury Notes in the open market and the buyer is a trading bank. The Reserve Bank takes payment from the trading bank by reducing the trading bank's reserve deposit with it by $100,000. In other words, the Reserve Bank's liability to the trading bank is reduced by $100,000, while its assets are reduced to the extent of the $100,000 of Treasury Notes it sells. The changes in the Reserve Bank's balance sheet look like this:

RESERVE BANK

Assets		Liabilities	
Treasury Notes	— $100,000	Trading bank reserve deposits	— $100,000

The trading bank has gained $100,000 of assets in Treasury Notes purchased from the Reserve Bank. But it also has had to give up $100,000 of its reserve deposits at the Reserve Bank to pay for them. The changes in the trading bank's balance sheet look like this:

TRADING BANK

Assets	
Reserves: deposits at the Reserve Bank	− $100,000
Treasury Notes	+ $100,000

While the total amount of the trading bank's assets has not been changed by these transactions, the trading bank now has less reserves. This can set in motion the deposit contraction process, or reduction in the money supply, we have already discussed.

What if the buyer of the $100,000 of Treasury Notes sold by the Reserve Bank is an individual or business other than a bank? Suppose payment is made to the Reserve Bank with a cheque drawn against the buyer's deposit at a trading bank. When the Reserve Bank receives the cheque, it decreases (or debits) the trading bank's reserve deposits at the Reserve Bank by $100,000. Once again, payment to the Reserve Bank is represented by a reduction of the Reserve Bank's liability to a trading bank. The change in the Reserve Bank's balance sheet looks like this:

The trading bank's current deposit liabilities are reduced by $100,000 because of the cheque written by its depositor, the

RESERVE BANK

Assets		Liabilities	
Treasury Notes	− $100,000	Trading bank reserve deposits	− $100,000

buyer of the Treasury Notes. The trading bank's assets are likewise reduced $100,000 by the reduction in its reserve deposits at the Reserve Bank that takes place when its depositor's cheque clears. The trading bank's balance sheet is changed as follows:

TRADING BANK

Assets		Liabilities	
Reserves: deposits at the Reserve Bank	− $100,000	Current deposits	− $100,000

Again, we see that $100,000 of trading bank reserves are removed from the banking system by the Reserve Bank's open market sale of $100,000 of Treasury Notes.

In sum, *bank reserves are decreased by the amount of the Reserve Bank's open market sales, regardless of whether the buyer is a bank or a nonbank.*

Legal Reserve Requirements

A news item reports that the Reserve Bank 'may have to dig deeper into its bag of credit-tightening tricks to stem the sharp rise in the nation's money supply'. It suggests that the Reserve Bank may resort to an increase in legal reserve requirements such as in the SRD ratio because 'stiffer reserve requirements normally will temper the banking system's lending ability'. Let's see why this is so.

Suppose that all banks in the banking system are fully loaned up and that the required reserve ratio is .10. None of the banks has any excess reserves. The balance sheet of a typical bank would look like this (only its reserves and current deposits are shown):

TYPICAL BANK

Assets		Liabilities	
Reserves	$100,000	Current deposits	$1,000,000

The bank has $100,000 of reserves, which is just equal to 10 per cent of its current deposit liabilities of $1,000,000.

Increase in the Legal Reserve Requirement. Suppose that the Reserve Bank wants to tighten up the economy's money supply, or bring about a 'credit tightening', as it is put in the news item. This means that the Reserve Bank wants to force the banks in the banking system to reduce their lending activity or their holdings of other earning assets. This will cause a deposit contraction throughout the banking system and hence a reduction in the money supply.

To bring this about, suppose the Reserve Bank increases the legal reserve requirement from 10 per cent to 12 per cent. Our typical bank is now required to hold $120,000 of reserves against its $1,000,000 of current deposits (.12 × $1,000,000). Since it only has $100,000 of reserves, it is $20,000 short. In order to make up this deficiency, the bank must reduce its loans or sell off $20,000 of its other earning assets (or do some combination of both totalling $20,000). This will set in motion the deposit contraction

process, or the reduction in the money supply, we have discussed before.

Decrease in the Legal Reserve Requirement. On the other hand, if the Reserve Bank wants to ease up on credit, or increase the money supply, it can reduce the reserve requirement. Suppose, for example, that it reduces the required reserve ratio from .10 to .08 (from a 10 per cent reserve requirement to an 8 per cent reserve requirement). Our typical bank is now required to hold only $80,000 of reserves against its $1,000,000 of current deposits. Therefore, it has $20,000 of excess reserves. If it loans this out, deposit expansion, or money creation, can take place throughout the banking system in the manner we have already discussed.

In sum, *an increase in the required reserve ratio such as in the SRD ratio will force a deposit contraction, or money supply reduction, if banks are fully loaned up. This contraction will be less pronounced to the extent that banks have excess reserves. A decrease in the required reserve ratio increases the amount of excess reserves, encouraging banks to increase lending and deposit expansion, thereby increasing the money supply.*

In practice the Reserve Bank does not change reserve requirements very often. This is so largely because as we have seen before, reserve requirement changes of even a half of a point (from 7 per cent to 7.5 per cent, for example) can require quite an abrupt adjustment throughout the banking system.

Other Tools of Monetary Policy

In addition to the two major tools of monetary policy we have discussed, the Reserve Bank has three other tools it currently uses: setting the Treasury Note rediscount rate; entering the foreign exchange market; and moral suasion. Let us have a look at each of these tools in turn.

Treasury Note Rediscount Rate

Recall that one of the 'safety valves' the Reserve Bank provides to the money market is the option of selling back or rediscounting Treasury Notes. This facility is intended to provide an outlet for banks or other financial institutions where they can convert Treasury Notes into cash without selling them on the market. While a single holder can sell Treasury Notes on the market, usually at a small cost, if there are many sellers trying to unload Treasury Notes at the same time, the price of the Notes may tumble, thereby resulting in considerable financial losses to the sellers. By providing the rediscount facility, the Reserve Bank is in effect setting a floor to any possible price fall of Treasury Notes. The rediscount rate does normally involve a penalty price which indirectly affects the interest rate. For example if the Reserve Bank raises the rediscount rate, then the cost of selling notes rises, putting downward pressure on the price of bonds and hence upward pressure on interest rates.

In addition to providing a rediscount facility for Treasury Notes, the Reserve Bank may also enter repurchase agreements (repos) for both Treasury Notes and Bonds. As we have already seen, a repurchase agreement is an undertaking to buy or sell a given volume of securities, subject to the transaction later being reversed at a specified date. Repos are carried out between the Bank and authorised money market dealers and have made a significant contribution to smooth out the ups and downs in liquidity and thus interest rates.

Foreign Exchange

On 9 December 1983, the Treasurer announced that the Australian dollar was being allowed to float — that is its value in terms of foreign currency would be determined by the foreign exchange market. This market involves both buyers and sellers of Australian dollars. For example importers would want to sell Australian dollars in exchange for foreign currency which they need to pay their overseas suppliers. Conversely, exporters have foreign currency which they want to exchange for Australian dollars so as to enable them to pay their various suppliers and workers in Australia. There are also other participants in the foreign exchange market, such as those who want to borrow from overseas or invest in Australia. We will take a more detailed look at the foreign exchange market in the chapter on the Balance of Payments (Chapter 21). However, for our immediate purposes it is sufficient to make the point that the value of the Australian dollar on the foreign exchange market depends on the supply and demand of Australian dollars. The Reserve Bank, being the holder of Australia's foreign exchange reserves, can enter the foreign exchange market and buy or sell the Australian dollar so as to affect its price, i.e. the exchange rate. In many ways the operation is similar to open market operations in government securities. Selling foreign exchange (from the reserves) implies that the Reserve Bank is accumulating Australian dollars, thereby reducing the money supply. This will tend to reduce liquidity and increase interest rates. Conversely, buying foreign exchange injects Australian dollars into the system affecting both the exchange rate and the interest rate. Thus, the Reserve Bank, through its foreign

HISTORICAL PERSPECTIVE

Monetary Milestones: 1937–1987[1]

August 1937

The **Royal Commission into Banking** reported.
   The Commission's recommendations provided a framework for the regulation of the banking system; some aspects of this framework are still in existence. A major part of the recommendations concerned the development of the Commonwealth Bank as the Central Bank. One specific recommendation was that the Central Bank publish a monthly statistical bulletin.

November 1937

Statistical Bulletin first published.
   Statistics included a series on 'Volume of Money' — equivalent to the current M3.

September 1939

The outbreak of **World War II** led to certain **wartime banking regulations.**
   Exchange control was introduced at the outbreak of War, replacing the Exchange Mobilisation Agreement of the early 1930s. Controls were extended in 1941/42 to cover interest rates, bank lending and profitability.

August 1945

The **Commonwealth Bank Act 1945** and the **Banking Act 1945** came into operation.
   The Acts, extending the 1937 Royal Commission's recommendations, provided the framework for much of the post-War regulation of the banking system. The Commonwealth Bank, as Central Bank, retained control over interest rates, banks' lending policies and various other aspects of banking.

July 1951

The **Commonwealth Bank Act 1951** took effect.
   This Act reconstituted the Bank's Board, which had been dissolved in the 1945 Act. The new Board held its inaugural meeting in September 1951.

April 1953

The **Commonwealth Bank Act 1953** came into operation.
   The General Banking Division of the Commonwealth Bank was reconstituted as the Commonwealth Trading Bank.

February 1956

The **Liquid Assets and Government Securities (LGS) Convention** for trading banks established.

February 1959

The first **Authorised Short-Term Money Market dealers** commenced operations.
  This marked the establishment of what has since been known as the official short-term money market.

November 1959

Seasonal securities were issued for the first time.
  These securities helped in the management of the seasonal liquidity flows arising mainly from the pattern of Commonwealth Government payments and receipts.

January 1960

The **Reserve Bank Act 1959** and the **Banking Act 1959** came into operation.
  This legislation established a separate Commonwealth Banking Corporation, and vested the central banking functions in the Reserve Bank of Australia.

July 1962

Treasury notes were first issued to replace seasonal securities.

February 1966

Decimal currency was introduced.
  The dollar replaced the pound, at the ratio of £1 = $2. The dollar was pegged to Sterling at $2.50 = £Stg1.

November 1967

Sterling depreciated against the US$ but the $A did not follow.
  This was the first change in the exchange rate of the $A against Sterling since the 1930s.

August 1971

The United States **suspended convertibility of the US$** into gold.
  Foreign exchange markets abroad closed temporarily. The Reserve Bank withdrew temporarily the banks' authorities to deal in foreign exchange. Disturbances to international markets continued, with trading interrupted on several occasions during 1971 and 1972.

December 1971

The **Australian dollar** was fixed to the US$.
  This broke the long-standing link to Sterling, which later floated against the US$, as did a number of major currencies.

August 1974

The **Financial Corporations Act** became operative.
  The Act governs some aspects of non-bank financial corporations and provides for the collection of statistics from these corporations. Part IV of the Act, which

provides for the Reserve Bank to exercise direct control over various aspects of the operations of these intermediaries, has not been proclaimed.

September 1974

The fixed link of the **Australian dollar to the US$** was discontinued.
The dollar was thereafter maintained at a constant value against a trade-weighted basket of currencies.

February 1976

The Government announced a **monetary projection,** based on the aggregate M3, for the year 1976/77.
The projection provided for growth of M3 of 10–12 per cent in the year to June 1977. Projections were in operation every year until 1984/85, during that year they were discontinued.

November 1976

The fixed link of the **Australian dollar to the trade-weighted basket of currencies** was discontinued.
Following a devaluation of 17 ½ per cent, a flexible link was introduced. The exchange rate was kept under constant review and adjusted frequently.

January 1979

The **Committee of Inquiry into the Australian Financial System** was established.
The 'Campbell Committee' issued its Interim Report in May 1980, and its Final Report in September 1981. The Committee's findings provided a major impetus to the deregulation of the financial system which occurred in the 1980s.

December 1979
Treasury notes were offered at tender for the first time.

December 1980

Ceilings on **interest rates paid on bank deposits** were removed.
While movement on the direction of freer markets had been under way for a number of years, this was one of the first big steps in the deregulatory process which took place in the first half of the 1980s.

June 1982

The Loan Council agreed to the introduction of **a tender system for Treasury bonds.**
The first tender was announced in July 1982. This, together with the tender arrangements for Treasury notes, improved the processes of debt and liquidity management.

May 1983

The **Review Group on the Australian Financial System** was commissioned by the Treasurer.

The 'Martin Review Group' reported on the recommendations of the Committee of Inquiry into the Australian Financial System, the Government's economic and social objectives, and the need to improve the efficiency of the financial system. The Report was published in December 1983.

December 1983

The **Australian dollar floated. Most exchange controls** were abolished.
These were major steps in the process of deregulation of the financial system. The float of the dollar improved control over domestic liquidity. The removal of exchange controls allowed much freer flows of capital into and out of Australia.

August 1984

The Reserve Bank established a separate **Supervision Unit.**
This provided a focal point for discussions with banks on prudential matters. The broad principles of prudential supervision policy were subsequently set out in a series of papers published by the Bank.

Maturity restrictions on bank deposits were removed.
This enabled banks to offer interest on call deposits and short-term fixed deposits.

January 1985

Conditional projections for M3 were discontinued.
The Treasurer announced that because of the effects of deregulation, M3 was considered an unreliable indicator of monetary conditions. The practice of announcing a projection for M3 at the time of the Commonwealth budget was discontinued. Following this, monetary policy was set with reference to the 'checklist' of economic indicators.

February 1985

The Treasurer announced that sixteen **foreign banks** would be invited to establish operations in Australia.
Discussions between the potential new banks, the Reserve Bank, and the Treasury followed, and the first bank with significant foreign ownership commenced business later that year.

April 1985

Further **deregulation of banks.**
The remaining ceilings on lending rates (other than for loans for owner-occupied housing of amounts less than $100,000) were removed. The ceiling on new loans for housing was removed in April 1986.

May 1985

The **LGS convention abandoned** and **PAR** (Prime Assets Ratio) **introduced**.

November 1986

The Cheques and Payment Orders Act was passed by Parliament.

This Act extends to non-bank financial institutions and customers certain legal protections regarding cheques. It also provides for new cheque-like instruments called payment orders.

May 1987

Announcement of **proposed amendments to the Banking Act 1959.**

The Government foreshadowed amendments to the Banking Act which would make more explicit the Reserve Bank's supervisory powers.

[1]Adopted from *Bulletin* Reserve Bank of Australia, November 1987

---

exchange operations, can influence domestic liquidity.

The stated aim of the Reserve Bank is not to try and fix the exchange rate at a particular level. This was the system that operated prior to the floating of the Australian dollar — called a fixed exchange rate regime. Rather, the Reserve Bank seeks to smooth out what it considers as sharp fluctuations in the short term which tend to be counterproductive since they increase the uncertainty and cost to those dealing in the foreign exchange market. Note that this section has introduced an important topic, namely the close link between the (domestic) money market and the foreign exchange market. We will explore further this important topic in later chapters.

Moral Suasion

Moral suasion refers to the ability of the Reserve Bank to influence the behaviour of financial intermediaries through informal discussion. The Reserve Bank attaches considerable importance to its direct contacts with financial intermediaries and states that these have broadened in recent years. Furthermore, moral suasion is more in line with its perceived role of prudential supervision of the financial system rather than relying on direct regulation.

Prior to deregulation of the financial system and the floating of the exchange rate, the Reserve Bank used many controls to 'manage' the financial system. These included interest rate controls, foreign exchange controls and even directions to financial intermediaries as to whom and how much to lend. Most, if not all, of these controls have been dismantled in the belief that a deregulated financial market operates more efficiently and is better able to cope with Australia's increasing integration in the international financial markets.

MONEY DEMAND AND SUPPLY AND THE INTEREST RATE

The demand for money interacts with the supply of money to determine the rate of interest in what is often referred to as the *money market.* We have seen how the Reserve Bank regulates the supply of money. Now let's examine the determinants of the demand for money. We will then put these pieces — demand and supply — together and examine the nature of equilibrium in the money market.

Transactions and Precautionary Demands for Money

Part of the demand for money stems from the service it provides as a medium of exchange. In short, money is needed to transact the purchase and sale of goods and services. This need is referred to as the **transactions demand** for money. What determines the size of this demand? The amount of transactions taking place in the economy, of course. One rough measure of the amount of such transactions is the level of total income, as represented by the level of money GDP for example. *When total income rises, the transactions demand for money increases, and when total income declines, the transactions demand decreases.*

Money is also needed for precautionary purposes. Hence, there is a **precautionary demand** for money. Unforeseen events or emergencies often require immediate expenditures. Money is the most liquid asset and, therefore, ideally suited to meet such contingencies. For this reason most of us carry a little more currency with us than is needed to cover anticipated transactions for such things as lunch and bus fare. Some people even keep sizeable amounts of currency in safes and safe-deposit boxes just in case some of their other assets cannot be readily liquidated. It is probably generally true that the precautionary demand for money in the economy varies with the level of total income, as does the transactions demand.

Money Demand and the Interest Rate

The level of total income is an important determinant of money demand primarily because of its relationship to the transactions and precautionary motives for holding money. The interest rate is also regarded as an important influence on the demand for money.

The Interest Rate: An Opportunity Cost

It has been said that 'money is barren'. Money in the form of currency is barren because it does not earn interest. Money in the form of current deposits is barren to the extent that either it earns no interest or a very low rate of return. Those who hold current accounts must forgo the opportunity to earn the higher rates of return available on other assets, such as stocks and bonds. Therefore the opportunity cost of holding money (whether for transactions, precautionary, or any other purposes) is the forgone interest that could be earned on other assets.

In a simplified world where the only two assets are barren money and interest-earning bonds the interest rate may be thought of as the price of holding money. As with any good or service, people will demand less money when its price is high than when it is low, all other things remaining the same. That is, the higher the interest rate, the lower the quantity of money demanded; and the lower the interest rate, the greater the quantity demanded. This inverse relationship between the demand for money and the interest rate is illustrated by the demand curve for money L shown in Figure 14.1. (The letter L is used to designate the demand curve for money simply as a reminder that money is the most liquid asset — the demand for money is the demand for liquidity.)

The Interest Rate and Bonds

The interest rate is an important determinant of the demand for money because people also desire to hold money for speculative purposes (in addition to the desire to hold money for transactions and precautionary purposes). However, before considering the speculative demand for money, it is necessary to understand why interest rates and bond prices always move in opposite directions.

A bond is a promissory certificate issued by borrowers (typically businesses and governments) in exchange for funds provided to them by lenders. The bond represents the borrower's promise to pay back to the lender (the bondholder) the amount of money borrowed (the principal) at the end of a certain number of years (the maturity date). The bond also promises that the borrower will make payments (coupon payments) of a set number of dollars to the lender at regular intervals (annually, for example). The coupon payments represent the rate of return, or the interest rate, that induces the lender to loan money to the borrower.

Consider a bond that promises to make coupon payments of $10 per year, year in and year out, forever. (Such bonds, called consols, are issued by the British government, for example.) If you purchased (invested in) such a bond for $100, you would earn a 10 per cent rate of interest — the $10 coupon payment divided by the $100 purchase price, expressed as a percentage. If you paid $200 for the bond, you would earn a 5 per cent rate of interest — $10 divided by $200, expressed as a percentage. Obviously, the higher the price you pay for the bond, the lower the interest rate you receive. Conversely, the lower the price paid, the higher the interest rate. Calculation of the interest rate earned on a bond with a set maturity date is more complicated, but the link between the interest rate realised on the bond and the price of the bond

is the same. *The price of a bond and its interest rate always move in opposite directions.*

FIGURE 14.1
The Demand for Money Is Inversely Related to the Interest Rate

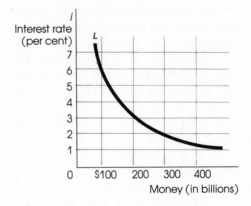

The demand curve for money slopes downward from left to right for two reasons.

First, the interest rate represents the opportunity cost of holding money. Therefore, a smaller quantity of money is demanded at a high than at a low interest rate.

Second, the nature of the speculative demand for money suggests that people will desire to hold more money and fewer bonds when the interest rate is below what is considered its normal level. This is so because bond prices are then above their normal levels, and it is thought likely that they will once again decline to those levels, resulting in losses to bondholders. On the other hand, if the interest rate is above its normal level, bond prices are below their normal levels. People will desire to hold less money and more bonds because it will be thought likely that bond prices will rise to their normal levels and bondholders will realise gains. In sum, the speculative demand for money also suggests that a smaller quantity of money is demanded at a high than at a low interest rate.

The Speculative Demand for Money

Suppose people believe that there is some average, or 'normal', level for the interest rate, a level determined by their observation of the interest rate in the past. Because bond prices and the interest rate are linked, this means there is also some normal level of bond prices.

If the interest rate is currently above what people consider to be its normal level, bond prices will be below their normal level. People will tend to believe that the interest rate is likely to fall and, therefore, that bond prices will rise. People will therefore prefer to hold more bonds and less money because of the gains they will realise if the likely rise in bond prices occurs. On the other hand, if the interest rate is currently below its normal level, bond prices will be above their normal level. People will tend to believe that the interest rate is likely to rise and that bond prices are likely to fall. They will want to hold more money and fewer bonds because of the losses on bonds that would result if the likely fall in bond prices occurs. Thus, the **speculative demand** for money provides another reason why less money is demanded at a high than at a low interest rate.

The demand curve for money in Figure 14.1 slopes downward left to right not only because of the opportunity cost of holding money, represented by the interest rate, but also because of the speculative demand for money arising from the fact that interest rates and bond prices fluctuate.

Changes in the Demand for Money

A change in the quantity of money demanded is represented by movement along the money demand curve of Figure 14.1. This movement occurs when the interest rate changes, all other things remaining the same. A change in the demand for money is represented by a shift in the position of the money demand curve. Such a change occurs when one or more of the other things changes. (Recall the distinction made in Chapter 4 between a change in quantity demanded and a change in demand.)

Among the other things that can change, the economy's total money income (or money GDP) is a particularly important determinant of the transactions demand for money. It also influences the demand for money for precautionary purposes. (Recall the distinction between money GDP and real GDP made in Chapter 5. Hereafter, the term total income is always taken to mean total money income or money GDP.) If total income increases, both the transactions and the precautionary demand for money rise. A decline in total income has the opposite effect. Therefore, a rise in total income will increase the demand for money and cause the demand curve for money to shift rightward, such as from L_0 to L_1 in Figure 14.2. A decline in total income would cause a leftward shift, such as from L_1 to L_0.

The Money Supply

Through its control over bank reserves and the setting of reserve requirements, we have seen how the Reserve Bank affects the deposit expansion or contraction process and the creation or destruction of money. In short, we have seen how the Reserve Bank controls the economy's money supply.

At any given time, the supply or stock of money available to satisfy the demand for money is fixed. The fixed supply of money may be represented by a vertical supply curve such as M_0 in Figure 14.3. (The vertical supply curve means that the money supply is unresponsive to the interest rate.) M_0 represents a stock of money equal to $20 billion. If the Reserve Bank were to increase the money supply by $10 billion, the money supply curve would be shifted rightward from M_0 to M_1, as shown in Figure 14.3. A decrease in the money supply would be represented by a leftward shift in the money supply curve.

FIGURE 14.2
Changes in the Demand for Money:
Shifts in the Money Demand Curve

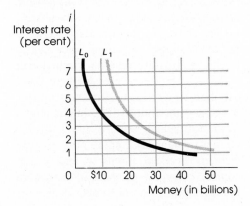

Money (in billions)

Changes in the demand for money are represented by shifts in the money demand curve, such as from L_0 to L_1. Shifts are caused by changes in one or more of the other things assumed constant when we move along a demand curve. Among these other things, the economy's total income is particularly important because when total income rises, it increases the transactions demand and the precautionary demand for money; when total income declines, it has the opposite effect. Therefore, an increase in total income shifts the demand curve for money rightward, such as from L_0 to L_1. A decline in total income would shift it leftward, such as from L_1 to L_0.
Changes in the quantity of money demanded are represented by movement along a fixed money demand curve. Such movement occurs when the interest rate changes, all other things remaining the same.

FIGURE 14.3
The Money Supply Curve

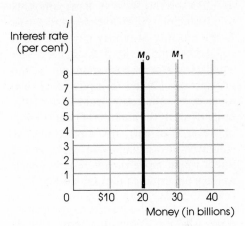

Money (in billions)

The fixed supply or stock of money available to satisfy demand may be represented by a vertical supply curve. (The fact that the supply curve is vertical means that the money supply is unresponsive to the interest rate.)
For example, M_0 represents a stock of money equal to $20 billion. If the Reserve Bank were to increase the money supply by $10 billion, the money supply curve would be shifted rightward from M_0 to M_1. A decrease in the money supply would be represented by a leftward shift in the money supply curve, such as from M_1 to M_0.

The Money Market: The Interaction of Supply and Demand

Now we are ready to bring money demand and money supply together to form the money market. At the outset we should remind ourselves that the supply of money and the demand for money are measured as stocks, not flows.

Equilibrium and Disequilibrium

Suppose that money demand and supply are represented by the demand curve L

and supply curve *M* shown in Figure 14.4. The supply or stock of money made available by the Reserve Bank amounts to $30 billion. Given the demand curve *L,* the quantity of money demanded will equal $30 billion only if the interest rate equals 6 per cent, corresponding to the intersection of *L* and *M* at point *e.* Hence, 6 per cent is the equilibrium level of the interest rate. If the interest rate were higher or lower than this, the money market would be in disequilibrium, and market forces would move the interest rate back to the 6 per cent equilibrium level.

Interest Rate Below the Equilibrium Level. For example, if the interest rate were 4 per cent, the quantity of money demanded would equal $50 billion, represented by point *d* on the demand curve. At this interest rate, there would be an excess demand for money of $20 billion (equal to the $50 billion demanded minus the $30 billion supplied). This excess demand is represented by the distance between *c* and *d* in Figure 14.4. In their attempts to obtain more money people try to convert other assets, such as bonds, into money by selling them. While each individual thinks he or she will be able to get more money in this way, obviously society as a whole cannot increase the amount of money it has. A seller of securities gains the money balances that the buyer of the securities loses, and so the total money supply is unaltered. The total amount of money available is fixed at $30 billion, and every bit of this is always held by somebody.

Consequently, as people try to sell bonds for money, they only succeed in pushing bond prices down. This means that the interest rate will rise. When the interest rate rises, the quantity of money demanded declines (as represented by the movement up along the demand curve away from point *d*), and the amount by which money demand exceeds money supply gets smaller. When will this process stop? When bond prices have fallen far enough to raise the interest rate level to 6 percent. At this point people will demand, or be satisfied to hold, just that quantity of money that is supplied (as represented by the intersection at point *e* of the money demand curve *L* and the money supply curve *M*).

Interest Rate Above the Equilibrium Level. Alternatively, what if the interest rate is above the equilibrium level of 6 per cent? Suppose it is 9 per cent. At this level, the quantity of money demanded equals $10 billion (represented by point *a* in Figure 14.4). There is an excess supply of money amounting to $20 billion (equal to the $30 billion supplied minus the $10 billion demanded), represented by the distance between points *a* and *b*. Of course, every bit of the $30 billion of money supplied would be held by people. But at an interest rate of 9 per cent, this is more than people desire to hold. Consequently, people will try to convert their excess money holdings into other assets, such as bonds. The attempts to buy bonds will cause bond prices to rise and the interest rate to fall. As the interest rate falls, the quantity of money demanded increases (represented by the movement down along the demand curve away from point *a*), and the excess supply of money gets smaller. Finally, when bond prices have risen far enough to lower the interest rate level to 6 per cent, the money market will be in equilibrium. At a 6 per cent interest rate, the $30 billion money supply is just the amount people desire to hold.

FIGURE 14.4
The Money Market: Equilibrium and Disequilibrium

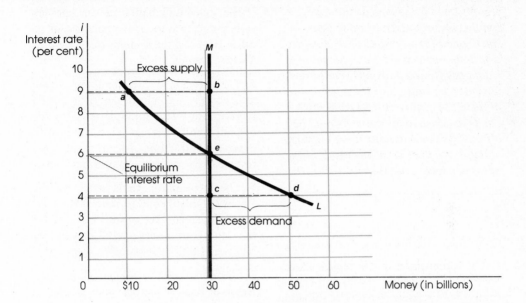

Money market equilibrium occurs at that interest rate at which the money demand curve L
intersects the money supply curve M at point e, corresponding to a 6 per cent interest rate in this
case.

At interest rates below the equilibrium level, there is an excess demand for money. For
example, at a 4 per cent interest rate the excess demand for money amounts to $20 billion,
which is represented by the distance between c and d. In their attempts to get more money
people will try to sell bonds, pushing bond prices down and the interest rate up until it reaches
the 6 per cent equilibrium level.

At interest rates above the equilibrium level, there is an excess supply of money. For example,
at a 9 per cent interest rate the excess supply of money amounts to $20 billion which is
represented by the distance between a and b. In their attempts to reduce their holdings of
money people will try to buy bonds, pushing bond prices up and the interest rate down until it
reaches 6 per cent, the equilibrium level.

Summary: Money Demand and Supply and the Interest Rate

In sum, *there are three basic sources of money demand: the transactions demand, the precautionary demand, and the speculative demand. These three combined make up the demand for money as represented by the demand curve for money. The money supply is determined by the Reserve Bank of Australia. The demand for money and the supply of money jointly determine the equilibrium rate of interest in the money market.*

CHECKPOINT 14.3

Which of the following would have the greatest effect on the interest rate: (1) an increase in money demand accompanied by an increase in money supply, (2) an increase in money demand alone, and (3) an increase in money demand accompanied by a decrease in money supply? Illustrate each of these cases — (1), (2), and (3) — graphically. How do you think the demand curve for money would be affected if people were to revise upward their notions of the normal level of the interest rate? How do you think the demand curve for money would be affected if people became more uncertain about their jobs, say, as the result of the onset of a recession? Why?

SUMMARY

1. The composition of the typical bank's portfolio of earning assets reflects a compromise between two often conflicting objectives; (a) the maintenance of liquidity and security and (b) the realisation of profit.

2. A trading bank generally restricts its holdings of earning assets to short-term loans, bonds, and securities because of their relatively high degree of liquidity and security. This restriction is dictated by the large amount of trading bank deposit liabilities that are subject to withdrawal on demand.

3. In general, the amount of current deposits, or money, that a single bank can create through lending cannot exceed the amount of its excess reserves. This is so because borrowers will most likely write cheques against these newly created deposits that the cheque recipients will deposit in other banks.

4. By contrast, when each individual bank in the banking system lends out its excess reserves, the banking system as a whole can create an amount of current deposits, or money, that is a multiple of the total amount of excess reserves in the system. While individual banks in the banking system can lose reserves and deposits to other banks in the system, the system as a whole cannot.

5. The multiple for the banking system as a whole is the reciprocal of the required reserve ratio. This multiple is called the deposit multiplier. It also applies to deposit contraction, which is just the reverse of the deposit expansion process.

6. The two major tools used by the Reserve Bank to conduct monetary policy are (a) open market operations, and (b) the setting of reserve requirements for banks and other depository institutions.

7. Open market operations refer to the Reserve Bank's buying and selling of government securities in the open market. When the Reserve Bank buys government securities, it puts reserves into the banking system, causing an expansion of current deposits and hence an increase in the economy's money supply. When the Reserve Bank sells government bonds, it takes reserves out of the banking system, causing a contraction of current deposits and hence a decrease in the economy's money supply.

8. An increase in the required reserve ratio as for example in the SRD ratio, will force a deposit contraction, or money supply reduction. The extent of reduction will depend on the amount of excess reserves in the banking system. A decrease in the required reserve ratio increases the amount of excess reserves, encouraging banks to increase lending and deposit expansion, thereby increasing the money supply.

9. Other tools that the Reserve Bank uses

include the setting of the Treasury Note rediscount rate, entering the foreign exchange market and moral suasion.

10. There are three basic components of the demand for money: the transactions demand, the precautionary demand, and the speculative demand. The transactions and precautionary demands for money vary directly with the level of total income. The speculative demand for money varies inversely (negatively) with the level of the interest rate.

11. Both because of the speculative demand for money and the fact that the interest rate is the opportunity cost of holding money, the money demand curve slopes downward. Because of the transactions and precautionary demands for money, the money demand curve is shifted rightward by an increase in total money income and leftward by a decrease.

12. The money supply curve is vertical, representing the assumption that the Reserve Bank of Australia controls the money supply. The money supply and demand curves jointly determine the equilibrium interest rate in the money market. An increase in the money supply lowers the equilibrium interest rate, a decrease raises it.

KEY TERMS AND CONCEPTS

    deposit multiplier
    equity
    excess reserves
    Liquid Assets and Government Securities (LGS) Convention
    LGS ratio
    margin requirement
    net worth
    open market operations
    precautionary demand

    Prime Assets Ratio (PAR)
    required reserve ratio
    required reserves
    reserves
    Statutory Reserve Deposits (SRD)
    SRD ratio
    speculative demand
    transactions demand

QUESTIONS AND PROBLEMS

1. Consider the balance sheet of the following individual bank, Bank X, in a banking system of many banks:

BANK X			
Assets		Liabilities and Equity	
Reserves	$ 220,000	Current	$ 950,000
Loans,	780,000	deposits	
securities		Equity	50,000
and other			
assets			
Total assets	$1,000,000 =	Total liabilities and equity	$1,000,000

Assume the required reserve ratio is 20 per cent (.20).

a. How much excess reserves does Bank X have?

b. Suppose Bank X creates an amount of current deposits through lending that equals the amount of its excess reserves multiplied by the deposit multiplier. What will be the amount of the new loans it has created? What will Bank X's balance sheet look like before any cheques have been written against the new deposits?

c. Given your answer to part b, suppose now that borrowers write cheques against the newly created current deposits and that the recipients of these cheques deposit them in other banks. What will happen to the level of reserves in Bank X? What now will be the level of excess reserves in Bank X?

d. Given your answers to part c, describe what Bank X must do to get its house in order. Once it has done so, how will its balance sheet look?

e. What does this example tell us about the difference between an individual bank and the banking system as a whole?

f. Starting again with the answer to part a, if you were running Bank X, describe what you would do at this point. How would Bank X's balance sheet now look after your management strategy had been carried out?

2. It is sometimes said that there is a 'trade-off' between bank profits on the one hand and liquidity and security on the other. Describe what is meant by this and why it is so. How does the trade-off affect the size of the deposit multiplier?

3. Suppose Bank A's balance sheet looks as follows and that the required reserve ratio is 15 per cent (.15):

BANK A

Assets		Liabilities and Equity	
Reserves	$ 200,000	Current deposits	$ 900,000
Loans, securities and other assets	800,000	Equity	100,000
Total assets	$1,000,000 =	Total liabilities and equity	$1,000,000

a. What would be the maximum amount of cash that depositors could withdraw before Bank A would be forced to do something about the amount of loans, securities, and other assets it holds?

b. Suppose Bank A decides to make loans by creating current deposits. Assume that Bank A and all other banks in the banking system expect that 5 per cent of any loans they make will be withdrawn immediately in the form of cash. What will be the maximum amount of deposit expansion, or money creation, that will take place throughout the banking system as a whole?

c. Show the deposit expansion process of part b in a table like Table 14.8.

4. What is the effect on the size of the actual deposit multiplier of increases and decreases in the public's desire to hold currency? If the public's desire to hold currency rises during recessions and falls during the expansionary phase of the business cycle, over the course of the business cycle how does this affect the Reserve Bank's ability to change the money supply per dollar of any open market purchase or sale?

5. It has been said that the Reserve Bank can be much more effective when it wants to contract the money supply than when it wants to expand the supply. Why might this be so? Explain in terms of each of the two main tools of monetary policy.

6. How can it be that when there is an excess supply of money, people hold more than they want, yet when equilibrium is restored, they are content to hold the same amount? Where did the excess go? If there is an excess demand for money, what must be true of people's desired holdings of bonds?

7. How would the money demand curve change if people's demand for money became more sensitive to changes in the interest rate? Show how this would affect the money demand curve L passing through point *e* in Figure 14.4. Would a money supply increase now have a larger or smaller effect on the equilibrium level of the interest rate? If the money demand curve shifts rightward by an amount equal to $20 billion from point *e,* would the rise in the interest rate be greater or less than would have been the case before the demand for money became more sensitive to changes in the interest rate?

15

The Role of Money in Income Determination

AFTER READING THIS CHAPTER YOU WILL BE ABLE TO:

1. Explain why the interest rate is a determinant of the level of investment spending.

2. Describe and explain the Keynesian view of how money affects aggregate demand.

3. Describe and explain the equation of exchange and the monetarist view of how money affects economic activity.

4. Compare and contrast the monetarist and Keynesian views on the stability of velocity in the equation of exchange.

5. Describe the evidence on the behaviour of velocity in Australia.

In the last chapter we examined how the Reserve Bank is able to change the level of bank reserves and thereby cause the economy's money supply to expand or contract. But how and why do changes in the economy's money supply affect the general level of economic activity? In this chapter we will focus on this question.

We should note at the outset that economists are not in complete agreement on just how and to what extent money affects the economy. In this chapter we will focus first on the Keynesian view by introducing money into the Keynesian analysis of income determination we developed in Chapters 8 and 9. Then we will examine the monetarist point of view and compare it with the Keynesian interpretation.

ROLE OF THE MONEY MARKET IN INCOME DETERMINATION: KEYNESIAN VIEW

We will now combine our understanding of the workings of the money market, developed in the previous chapter, with the Keynesian analysis of income determination that we developed in Chapters 8 and 9. We will then be able to examine the role of money in the determination of total income, output, employment, and the price level from the Keynesian viewpoint.

Our first step in putting the pieces together is to show the relationship between the money market, the interest rate, and the level of investment expenditures in the economy. We will then be able to examine the relationship between the money market and the economy's aggregate demand for goods and services and, hence, the relationship between the

money supply provided by the Reserve Bank and total income, output, employment and the price level.

Money, Interest, and Investment

What is the relationship between the money market and investment expenditures? To answer this we first recall the relationship between the interest rate and investment expenditures discussed in Chapter 8. We will then see how the interest rate serves to link the money market and the level of investment expenditures.

Investment and the Interest Rate

In Chapter 8 we argued that the interest rate is the cost to a firm of funds invested in capital goods. If such funds are borrowed from outside the firm, the cost of borrowing is the interest rate that must be paid to lenders. If the funds are generated internally, the cost is the forgone interest the firm could have earned by lending the funds to someone else.

Interest Rate Versus Expected Rate of Return. When a firm considers whether or not to purchase or invest in a capital good, it must compare its expected rate of return on the capital good with the interest rate. If the firm is going to use its own funds, the two relevant choices are either to lend the funds to some other party or to invest them in the capital good. If the expected rate of return is higher than the interest rate, the firm can earn more by investing internally generated funds in the capital good than by lending them out. The firm will earn the difference between the expected rate of return on the capital good and the interest rate. Similarly, if the firm borrows outside funds to invest in the capital good, it will earn exactly the same difference — the difference between the expected rate of return on the capital good and the interest rate that must be paid on the borrowed funds. However, if the expected rate of return on the capital good is less than the interest rate, it will not pay to invest in the capital good.

Expected Rate of Return on a Capital Good. What is the expected rate of return? The **expected rate of return** *is the amount of money a firm expects to earn per year on funds invested in a capital good expressed as a per cent of the funds invested.*

What determines the expected rate of return on a capital good? Profit, or the anticipation of profit — as noted in Chapter 8. For example, suppose that the annual revenue anticipated from the sale of goods and services produced with the aid of a capital good amounts to $500. Suppose that the anticipated annual costs of production, *excluding* the interest rate cost of the funds invested in the capital good, equals $400. The difference, in this case $100, is the amount of money the firm expects to earn per year on the funds invested in the capital good. If the price of the capital good is $1,000, the expected rate of return on the $1,000 investment in the capital good is 10 per cent — $100 ÷ $1,000, expressed as a percentage.

If the interest rate is 9 per cent, the firm could borrow the $1,000 at a cost of $90 per year. Alternatively, $1,000 of internal funds could earn $90 per year if lent out at 9 per cent. Either way the firm will come out ahead $10 per year if it invests in the capital good. The capital good is therefore a profitable investment,

and the firm should buy it. If on the other hand the interest rate is 11 per cent, the same calculations show that the firm will lose $10 per year if it invests $1,000 in the capital good. The good will not be a profitable investment, and the firm should not buy it. In sum, *a firm will invest in a capital good if its expected rate of return is higher than the interest rate. It will not invest if the expected rate of return is less than the interest rate.*

Inverse Relationship Between Interest Rate and Investment Spending. At any given time a typical firm has a number of investment projects it could undertake — build new plant, buy a new fleet of trucks, build a new loading dock, and so on. The firm forms an expectation of what the rate of return would be for each of these projects. The lower the interest rate, the larger is the number of these projects having expected rates of return higher than the interest rate. Hence, the lower the interest rate, the greater the amount of investment expenditure by the firm. Of course, the higher the interest rate, the smaller the number of projects with expected rates of return above the interest rate — therefore, the smaller the amount of investment expenditure by the firm.

If we consider all the firms in the economy, the total amount of investment spending will increase as the interest rate decreases. This inverse, or negative, relationship between the interest rate and investment is illustrated by the downward-sloping investment demand curve I_d in Figure 15.1. *The investment demand curve shows the total dollar amount of investment projects, or capital goods formation, that the economy's firms will demand or desire to do at each interest rate.* The investment demand curve is just another way of representing the relationship between the interest rate and investment spending that we discussed in Chapter 8 (Figure 8.8).

The Money Market and the Level of Investment

Now we can see how the money market and the level of investment spending in the economy are related. The connecting link between them is the interest rate. This is illustrated in Figure 15.2, where the money market is shown in part a and the investment demand curve is shown in part b.

Suppose initially that the money supply provided by the Reserve Bank amounts to roughly $21.5 billion, represented by the money supply curve M_0 in part a. Given the money demand curve L, the equilibrium interest rate in the money market is 7 per cent, determined by the intersection of M_0 and L at point a. The number of investment projects with expected rates of return greater than 7 per cent is such that there will be $30 billion of investment spending when the interest rate is at that level, corresponding to point a' on the investment demand curve I_d in part b.

FIGURE 15.1
The Investment Demand Curve: Investment Spending Varies Inversely with the Interest Rate

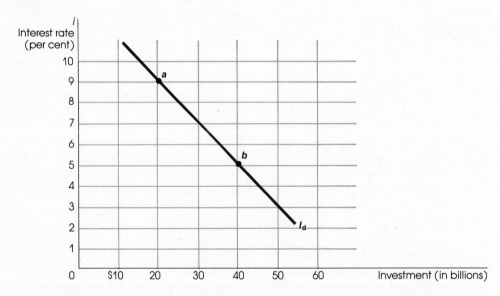

The investment demand curve I_d downward sloping, reflecting the inverse, or negative, relationship between the level of the interest rate and the amount of investment expenditure in the economy. For instance, if the interest rate were 9 per cent, there would be $20 billion of investment spending, corresponding to point a on the investment demand curve I_d. At a lower interest rate, such as 5 per cent, the amount of investment spending would be larger, equal to $40 billion, corresponding to point b.

The reason for the inverse relationship between the interest rate and investment is that the lower the interest rate, the larger the number of investment projects that have an expected rate of return greater than the interest rate. The economy's firms will invest in all those projects that are profitable, as represented by the fact that their expected rates of return are higher than the interest rate.

Suppose the Reserve Bank increases the money supply (say by open market purchases) from $21.5 billion to $30 billion. This increase is represented by the rightward shift in the money supply curve from M_0 to M_1 in part a. At the original 7 per cent interest rate, there is now an excess supply of money. As people attempt to convert this excess into other assets such as bonds, bond prices rise and the interest rate falls to 6 per cent. This is the new equilibrium interest rate represented by the intersection of M_1 and L at point b. The drop in the interest rate

from 7 to 6 per cent increases the amount of investment spending in the economy by $5 billion to $35 billion, corresponding to point b' on the investment demand curve I_d. This happens because investment projects with expected rates of return between 6 and 7 per cent now become profitable. Therefore, they are undertaken in addition to all those having expected rates of return greater than 7 per cent.

In sum, *the Reserve Bank can influence the amount of investment spending in the economy through its control over the money supply.* Increases in the money supply

FIGURE 15.2
The Money Market and Investment Spending Are Linked by the interest Rate

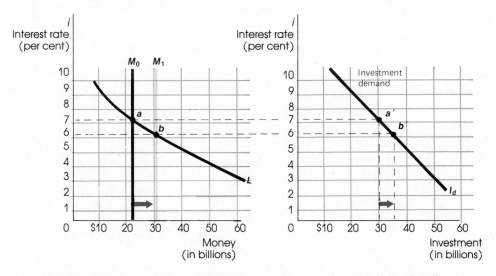

The intersection of the money demand and money supply curves in part a determines the equilibrium level of the interest rate. Given the investment demand curve I_d, this interest rate determines the amount of investment spending in part b.

Suppose the money supply provided by the Reserve Bank amounts to $21.5 billion, represented by the money supply curve M_0 in part a. The equilibrium interest rate is then 7 per cent, determined by the intersection of the money demand curve L and the money supply curve M_0 at point a. The 7 per cent interest rate will give rise to $30 billion of investment spending, corresponding to point d on the investment demand curve I_d in part b.

Suppose the Reserve Bank increases the money supply from $21.5 billion to $30 billion, represented by the rightward shift in the money supply curve from M_0 to M_1 in part a. The interest rate will then fall to a new equilibrium level of 6 per cent, determined by the intersection of the money demand curve L and the money supply curve M_1 at point b. This drop in the interest rate will cause an increase in investment spending to $35 billion corresponding to point b' on the investment demand curve I_d in part b.

lower the interest rate and cause investment spending to increase. Decreases in the money supply raise the interest rate and cause investment spending to decrease.

Money, Real GDP, and the Price Level

We know from our discussion in Chapters 8 and 9 that investment spending is an

FIGURE 15.3
Money Supply Change: Partial Versus General Equilibrium Analysis

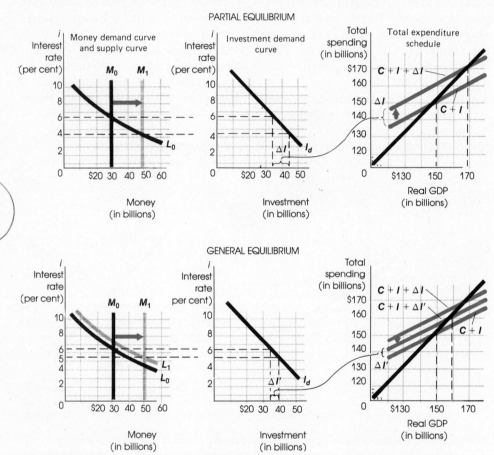

The top half of the figure shows the partial equilibrium analysis of the effects of a $20 billion increase in the money supply. The interest rate falls from 6 per cent to 4 per cent, causing a rise in investment ΔI of $10 billion, which in turn causes the total expenditure schedule to shift upward from $C + I$ to $C + I + \Delta I$. This upward shift in turn causes real GDP to rise from $150 billion to $170 billion. This analysis is partial because it doesn't allow for the effect of the rise in real GDP on money demand and hence on the interest rate.

The bottom half of the figure shows the general equilibrium analysis of the effects of the same $20 billion money supply increase. Now the interest rate falls a smaller amount, from 6 per cent to 5 per cent, because of allowance for the fact that the rise in real GDP causes the money demand curve to shift rightward from L_0 to L_1. Because of this, the rise in investment $\Delta I'$ of $5 billion is smaller. Hence, the total expenditure schedule shifts upward a smaller amount, from $C + I$ to $C + I + \Delta I'$, and therefore the rise in real GDP is less, from $150 billion to $160 billion.

important part of total spending in the economy. We saw that it plays a crucial role in determining the level of the total expenditure schedule, which in turn determines the equilibrium level of real GDP, as in part a of Figure 11.2. We are now in a position to introduce the money market into that analysis.

The Interconnecting Links Between the Money Market, Investment, and Real GDP

Consider the upper half of Figure 15.3. Suppose initially that the money supply curve M_0 (representing a money supply of $30 billion) and money demand curve L_0 (corresponding to a total income of $150 billion) determine a 6 per cent interest rate. Given the position of the investment demand curve, this interest rate in turn gives rise to a level of investment of $35 billion. This amount of investment spending determines the position of the total expenditure schedule $C + I$, which in turn determines the equilibrium level of real GDP of $150 billion. This level of real GDP determines the position of the money demand curve L_0 (because the transactions and precautionary demand for money are influenced by the level of real GDP), which together with M_0 determines the 6 per cent interest rate.

Partial Equilibrium Analysis. Now suppose the Reserve Bank increases the money supply by $20 billion (from $30 billion to $50 billion), represented by the rightward shift in the money supply curve from M_0 to M_1, the upper half of Figure 15.3. At the initial interest rate of 6 per cent, there would now be an excess supply of money. This excess causes the interest rate to fall from 6 per cent to 4 per cent, determined by the intersection of M_1 and L_0. The decline in the interest rate from 6 per cent to 4 per cent means that there

would be an increase in the number of investment projects having expected rates of return greater than the interest rate. The resulting increase in investment spending ΔI (change in I) would amount to $10 billion (a rise from $35 billion to $45 billion). This increase would cause the total expenditure schedule to rise from $C + I$ to $C + I + \Delta I$ and real GDP to increase from $150 billion to $170 billion.

This is only a partial equilibrium analysis, however. *In **partial equilibrium analysis** we focus on a change in one market and its consequences for that market and possibly a few others. All other markets are assumed to be unchanged. In **general equilibrium analysis** we consider the adjustments that a change in one market may cause in each and every other market.*

Our analysis of the consequences of a money supply change in the upper half of Figure 15.3 is a partial equilibrium analysis because it does not take into account the effect the rise in real GDP will have on the money demand curve and hence on the interest rate. A general equilibrium analysis of the consequences of the $20 billion increase in the money supply from M_0 to M_1 must take account of this effect.

General Equilibrium Analysis. The general equilibrium analysis is shown in the lower half of Figure 15.3. As the interest rate falls and increased investment causes a rise in real GDP, the rise in real GDP causes the money demand curve to shift rightward at the same time. This shift in the money demand curve keeps the interest rate from falling as far as it does when the shift is ignored, as in the partial equilibrium analysis in the upper half of Figure 15.3. Consequently the rise in investment $\Delta I'$ is now less, amounting to only $5 billion. The resulting upward shift in the total expenditure schedule is now smaller — from $C + I$ to $C + I + \Delta I'$. The rise in real GDP is therefore smaller — from \$150 billion to \$160 billion. The position of the money demand curve at L_1 corresponds to (is determined by) the \$160 billion real GDP level. In the general equilibrium analysis, the level of the interest rate falls to 5 per cent, a higher level than the 4 per cent of the partial equilibrium analysis.

In conclusion, our analysis indicates that *an increase in the money supply causes a decrease in the interest rate and an increase in the level of real GDP. A decrease in the money supply will have the opposite effect, causing an increase in the interest rate and a decrease in the level of real GDP.*

Easy Money Versus Tight Money. When the Reserve Bank increases the money supply, it is often said to be following an easy-money policy, or to be 'easing credit'. This manner of speaking reflects the fact that the fall in the interest rate makes it cheaper to borrow, or to get credit. An easy-money policy stimulates the economy because it leads to a rise in real GDP. On the other hand, a tight-money policy, or a policy of 'credit tightening', refers to the opposite situation — a reduction in the money supply leading to a rise in the interest rate and a decline in real GDP.

The Link Between Money and the AD Curve

In Chapter 11, Figure 11.6, we saw how a shift in the total expenditure schedule due to an exogenous expenditure change will cause the aggregate demand curve (AD) to shift. Similarly, the shift in the total expenditure schedule caused by the money supply change shown in Figure 15.3 will also cause the AD curve to shift. This is illustrated in Figure 15.4. The increase in the money supply causes the increase in investment spending $\Delta I'$ which in turn shifts the total expenditure schedule upward from E_0 to E_1 in part a of Figure 15.4. This corresponds to the upward shift in the total expenditure schedule by the amount $\Delta I'$ in the general equilibrium in Figure 15.3. Corresponding to the upward shift in the total expenditure schedule, the AD curve in part b shifts rightward from AD_0 to AD_1. In sum:

According to the Keynesian view, an increase in the money supply lowers the interest rate, thereby causing an increase in investment spending which shifts the total expenditure schedule upward and the AD curve rightward. A decrease in the money supply raises the interest rate which decreases investment spending, thereby shifting the total expenditure schedule downward and the AD curve leftward.

The Link Between Money and the Price Level

Thus far we have shown that an increase in the money supply shifts the AD curve rightward so that there is an increase in the quantity of total output (real GDP) demanded *at any given price level.* But what actually happens to the price level? We are now on familiar ground which we already explored in Chapter 11. There we saw that to determine the price level it was necessary to bring the aggregate supply curve (AS) into the picture.

When we take account of the interaction of the AS curve with the AD curve in part b of Figure 15.4 we see that the price level was initially p_0, determined by the intersection of AD_0 and AS at point e_0. The increase in the money supply that shifts the AD curve rightward from AD_0 to AD_1 causes the price level to rise to

p_1, corresponding to the intersection of AD_1 and AS at point e_1.

Recall our discussion of general equilibrium, the lower half of Figure 15.3. There the money demand curve was shifted rightward from L_0 to L_1 by the increase in real GDP. Recall however from the previous chapter (Figure 14.2) that a change in total income, or money GDP, causes the money demand curve to shift. Money GDP can be thought of as equal to the product of the price level and total output (in a simple widget economy the price per widget times number of widgets), where real GDP is a measure of total output. Therefore a shift in the money demand curve caused by a change in money GDP can be due to a change in either real GDP or the price level, or

both. Since the rightward shift in the AD curve in part b of Figure 15.4 causes both real GDP and the price level to increase, we see now that in the general equilibrium determined by the intersection of AD_1 and AS the rightward shift in the money demand curve in the lower half of Figure 15.3 is due to an increase in *both* real GDP and the price level — the increase in money GDP, or total income.

In general, the response of the price level to an increase in the money supply is determined by the slope of the AS curve along the range over which the AD curve shifts. If the AD curve shifts along the horizontal range of the AS curve, where the economy has a great deal of excess capacity and unemployment, there will be no increase in the price level. If the shift

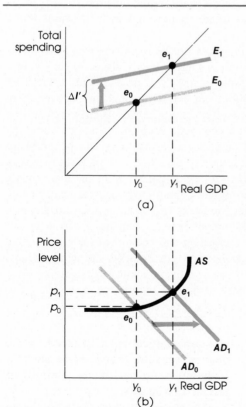

(a)

(b)

FIGURE 15.4
Changes in the the Money Supply Affect Real GDP and the Price Level

An increase in the money supply increases investment spending by $\Delta I'$ thereby shifting the total expenditure schedule upward from E_0 to E_1, part a, and the aggregate demand curve rightward from AD_0 to AD_1, part b.

Real GDP increases from y_0 to y_1 and the price level rises from p_0 to p_1, part b, as the economy moves from its initial equilibrium position, corresponding to point e_1 in parts a and b, to its new equilibrium, corresponding to point e_0. The amount of change in the price level relative to that in real GDP depends on the state of the economy, as reflected in the slope of the AS curve over the range where the shift in the AD curve occurs.

POLICY PERSPECTIVE

Ideological Differences Between Keynesians and Monetarists

Before beginning our discussion of monetarism, it should be recognised that monetarists and modern-day Keynesians (sometimes called neo-Keynesians) typically have differing political views and opinions on the proper role and size of government in our economy. Monetarists tend to favour a more laissez faire or free-market economy, with government intervening mainly to restrain monopoly and other forms of anticompetitive market practices. They believe that the market system generally does a good job of efficiently allocating resources to answer the basic economic questions of what to produce, how to produce it, and for whom. Those who adhere more to the Keynesian point of view tend to be less satisfied with the results provided by the market mechanism in a number of areas of the economy. They believe that the government can and should play a more effective and active role in correcting the shortcomings of the market mechanism. Monetarists, on the other hand, tend to view government as generally inefficient, bureaucratically cumbersome, and prone to making large mistakes when dealing with problems. Moreover, they generally fear the political implications of increasing government's control over the economy's decision-making process. They argue that increased government control poses a threat to personal freedoms and puts a damper on individual initiative.

   In view of these ideological differences, it should not be surprising that monetarists are leery of fiscal policy as a stabilization tool. We have already discussed (in Chapter 10) the timing problems associated with discretionary fiscal policy. Quite aside from this, however, monetarists fear that fiscal policy gives rise to too much direct government intervention in the economy. On the other hand, Keynesians feel government intervention is needed to solve other kinds of social and economic problems. So, why shouldn't the government also use its spending and taxation authority to attack the problems of economic instability, unemployment, and inflation? Besides, Keynesians see the Great Depression of the 1930s as evidence that the self-regulating forces of the marketplace are not sufficient to ensure that the economy will continuously operate near its full-employment capacity. They also argue that monetary policy alone was incapable of coping with such a depression. In contrast, monetarists see regulation of the money supply as a much more powerful tool for affecting the economy. They argue that the Great Depression was so severe largely because governments did a particularly bad job of managing monetary policy. Moreover, monetarists feel comfortable using monetary policy to regulate economic activity. It doesn't require the same direct and potentially extensive government intervention in the economy as fiscal policy.

---

is over the immediate range, as in part b of Figure 15.4, where the economy is operating ever closer to its capacity limit, then both real GDP and the price level increase. Rightward shifts of the *AD* curve along the vertical range of the *AS* curve only increase the price level because the economy is up against the limit of its productive capacity.

Summary of the Keynesian View on How Money Affects the Economy

According to the Keynesian view, a change in the money supply changes the interest rate, thereby causing a change in investment spending, which in turn shifts the total expenditure schedule and hence the AD curve. The resulting change in real GDP and the price level depends on the amount of excess capacity and unemployment in the economy, as reflected in the slope of the AS curve along the range over which the AD curve shifts.

CHECKPOINT * 15.1

Suppose the investment demand curve in Figure 15.2, part b, is pivoted clockwise about point a' so that it is now steeper. Given the increase in the money supply from M_0 to M_1 shown in Figure 15.2, part a, will the resulting increase in investment spending in part b now be larger or smaller than before? Suppose the money demand curve L in part a is pivoted clockwise about point a so that it is steeper. Given the money supply increase from M_0 to M_1, will the resulting increase in investment spending (given the original investment demand curve I_d shown in part b) now be larger or smaller than before? In the lower half of Figure 15.3, if money demand were more sensitive to a change in total income (that is, if the change in the transactions and precautionary demand for money is greater per dollar of change in total income), would the increase in total income resulting from the increase in the money supply from M_0 to M_1 be larger or smaller than before?

*Answers to all Checkpoints can be found at the back of the text.

MONETARIST VIEW ON THE ROLE OF MONEY

The Keynesian view of how money affects economic activity went largely unchallenged up until the 1960s when a school of thought known as **monetarism** began to assert itself. The monetarists, largely led by Milton Friedman (winner of the 1976 Nobel Prize in Economics), argue that money plays a much more important role in determining the level of economic activity than is granted to it by the Keynesian view. We will now examine the monetarist view and also consider some of the main differences between it and the Keynesian view. We will begin by examining the equation of exchange, a notion that goes back to the classical economists.

Monetarism and the Equation of Exchange

The dollar value of the purchases of final goods and services produced by the economy during a year is the economy's money GDP — the GDP expressed in terms of the prices at which the goods are actually purchased. (Recall the distinction between real GDP and money GDP made in Chapter 5.) Each purchase typically requires the buyer to give money in exchange for the good or service provided by the seller. The economy's money supply, its total stock of money, is used to transact all these exchanges during the course of a year.

Money GDP, a flow, is usually several times larger than the economy's money stock. This means that the money stock must be used several times during the year to carry out all the transactions represented by the money GDP. In effect, the money stock must go around the circular flow of money exchanged for goods (discussed in Chapter 5) several times during the course of a year. This idea is given expression by the **equation of exchange**, which is written

$$M \times V = p \times Q$$

In this equation $p \times Q$, price times quantity, is money GDP. For example, if the economy produces nothing but widgets, p would be the price per widget and Q the quantity of widgets produced per year. More realistically, for an economy that produces many kinds of goods, Q may be thought of as real GDP and p as an index of current prices (the prices at which goods are currently bought and sold). M is the economy's money supply. V is the number of times the money stock must 'turn over' during a year in order to transact all the purchases of final goods and services that add up to money GDP. In other words, V is the number of times a typical dollar of the money stock must go around the circular flow of money exchanged for final goods and services during a year. For this reason V is called the velocity of circulation of money, or simply the **velocity** of money.

For example, if the economy's money supply M is $30 billion and its money GDP is $150 billion, the equation of exchange would be

$$\begin{array}{ccc} M & V & \text{GDP} \\ \$30 \times & 5 & = \$150 \end{array}$$

The velocity of money V is therefore 5. This means that the money stock must turn over five times per year. A dollar of the money stock typically would be used five times per year in the purchase of final goods and services.

The Equation of Exchange as Definition

The equation of exchange as it stands is true simply by definition. If you know the size of the money supply and the level of the money GDP, you can calculate the value of V. By definition V has to take on whatever value is necessary to maintain the equality between the two sides of the equation $M \times V = p \times Q$. However, suppose you took annual money GDP data and money stock data for a series of years in an economy and calculated the value of velocity for each of those years. If the calculated values of velocity didn't change much from year to year and from the earlier to the later years, your curiosity should be aroused. You should be even more curious if the same calculations for different economies revealed the same kind of regularity for V.

Regularity in any phenomenon is the watchword of science. When Galileo dropped objects of unequal weight from the same height on the Leaning Tower of Pisa, he discovered that they always reached the ground at the same time. No matter how different the weights, he always found this to be true. He thus discovered the law of falling bodies. Had he found no regularity in the relationship between the time taken for objects of different weights to reach the ground, his experiments would have been of little interest. It is regularity that leads to the formulation of theories — and often to controversy. Galileo's experiments and his formulation of the law of falling bodies went against the then prevailing opinion that heavier bodies fall faster than light ones. This opinion was so strong that he was forced to resign from his position as professor of mathematics at the University of Pisa.

The story of Galileo gives us some perspective on the depth of feeling that often characterises the clash between monetarist and Keynesian viewpoints about the role of money. Here, too, regularity is a large part of the issue. *Monetarists argue that velocity V in the equation of exchange is fairly stable or regular.* Those leaning toward the Keynesian point of view dispute this contention. You might well ask why not settle the argument by an appeal to facts — the calculations of velocity already mentioned. As in Galileo's time, facts aren't always convincing. Moreover, the facts about velocity are not as clearcut as those about falling bodies, as we shall see later.

The Equation of Exchange as Theory: The Quantity Theory of Money

What does it mean to say that velocity V is stable? It means that V is more than just a symbol that takes on whatever value is necessary to ensure equality between the left- and right-hand sides of the equation of exchange. The classical economists contended that V was reasonably stable because it reflected the institutional characteristics of the economy. These characteristics include the frequency with which people are paid, the organization of banking, and the level of development of the transportation and communications systems. They argued that these determinants of the economy's payments mechanism were slow to change and that therefore V was stable. This view of the equation of exchange became known as the **quantity theory of money**.

With the assumption that V is stable, the equation of exchange passes from the realm of definition to that of theory because it enables us to predict the consequences of an event, namely a change in the money supply. (You might want to review the discussion of the characteristics of a theory in Chapter 1.) If the money supply is increased by a certain per cent, then money GDP will increase by a like per cent. In the previous example where M equals \$30 billion, V equals 5, and the money GDP equals \$150 billion, suppose the money supply M is increased from \$30 billion to \$40 billion — a 33 per cent increase. If V is stable at a value of 5, money GDP will increase 33 per cent, from \$150 billion to \$200 billion.

Monetarist View of the Money Transmission Mechanism

Monetarism may be viewed as a sophisticated version of the quantity theory of money. Monetarists contend that the effects of money supply changes on the economy are transmitted through a host of channels, not just via the interest rate route, which is so strongly emphasised in the Keynesian point of view. In particular, monetarists argue that an increase in the economy's money supply initially increases the money holdings of consumers and businesses. That is, there is an excess supply of money. The excess money holdings are then spent on goods and services, directly pushing up aggregate demand and money GDP (equal $p \times Q$). Conversely, a decrease in the economy's money supply creates an excess demand for money. In an attempt to increase their money holdings, consumers and businesses cut back on their spending. This causes aggregate demand for goods and services to fall and money GDP to decrease.

In sum, *monetarists tend to believe that the cause-effect transmission from changes in the money supply to changes*

ECONOMIC THINKERS

Milton Friedman — 1912–

Milton Friedman, who has spent most of his career at the University of Chicago, was awarded the Nobel Prize for Economics in 1976.

Friedman is perhaps best known for his 'monetarist' views, which put emphasis on the importance of the money supply in the economy, and for his view that the role of government should be severely limited. Fiscal (Keynesian) policy is, in his view, less effective than monetary policy for affecting economic activity.

Friedman maintains that the general prosperity since World War II has not been due to 'fine tuning' by the Government, or to various counter-cyclical devices, but to the fact that the great economic errors of the interwar period were largely avoided, especially severe reductions in the supply of money. Friedman holds that neither monetary nor fiscal policy will eliminate minor business fluctuations. Consequently, an automatic policy designed to increase the money supply by some given figure each year would be far superior to actions of the Reserve Bank or to policies devised by the Treasury. This automatic policy would work much more effectively if accompanied by meaningful efforts to reduce price rigidity stemming from monopolistic elements in the economy. Furthermore, he believes, a modest but steady increase in the money supply is the best way to try to maintain aggregate demand at the level of full employment.

Friedman's other claim to fame is his frequent questioning of most governmental policies designed to stimulate or regulate economic activity. Friedman would largely confine the government to the role of rule maker and umpire. Friedman sees these 'rules' as having to do largely with property rights, contracts, and the provision of the money supply. The role of umpire is played by the police, the courts, and the monetary authorities.

FOR FURTHER READING

Among Friedman's major works are *Price Theory: A Provisional Text* (1962); *A Monetary History of the United States* (coauthored with Anna J. Schwartz, 1963); *The Optimum Quantity of Money and Other Essays* (1969); *A Theory of the Consumption Function* (1957); *Essays in Positive Economics* (1953); *Freedom and Capitalism* (1962); and *Free to Choose* (1980).

---

in money GDP are reasonably direct and tight. That is, in terms of the equation of exchange, monetarists believe that V, the velocity of money, is quite stable. Hence, they argue that changes in the money supply have a fairly direct effect on money GDP.

An extreme version of monetarism would assume that velocity is an unchanging constant — as in the hypothetical example above where velocity was assumed always to equal 5. If this crude version of monetarism were true, monetary policy would indeed be a powerful and reliable tool for affecting the level of money GDP, or total income. The Reserve

Bank would know that it could change money GDP by any percentage amount it desired simply by changing the economy's money supply by that percentage amount. However, not even the most ardent monetarists subscribe to the view that velocity is constant.

Monetarist Versus Keynesian Views of the Equation of Exchange

The Keynesian view of the equation of exchange holds that V the velocity of money, is much less stable than the monetarists contend. Moreover, the Keynesian view argues that velocity V may in fact move in the opposite direction from changes in the money supply M. Hence, attempts to affect the level of money GDP by changing the money supply are largely thwarted by offsetting changes in velocity.

To illustrate the differences between the monetarist and Keynesian views of velocity it is helpful to interpret the equation of exchange in terms of the Keynesian transmission mechanism. As already pointed out, monetarists argue that money supply changes affect the economy through other channels in addition to the interest rate channel. The monetarist view which we now present pertains only to the interest rate channel.

The Keynesian view that velocity is not very stable is consistent with a particular view of the Keynesian transmission mechanism, namely, that money demand is quite sensitive to changes in the interest rate while investment demand is not. The monetarist view that velocity is stable is consistent with a view that investment demand is quite sensitive to changes in the interest rate while money demand is not. The implications of these views are

illustrated in Figure 15.5. (Note that this figure is similar to Figure 15.3.)

Effects of a Money Supply Change on Money GDP

In the ensuing discussion we assume for simplicity that the price level is fixed. Therefore money GDP and real GDP are the same and we call them total income.

The top half of Figure 15.5 corresponds more closely to the Keynesian view of the interest rate sensitivity of investment demand and money demand than does the bottom half, or monetarist view. For instance, the money demand curve L_1 is less steeply sloped than the money demand curve L_2. Hence, money demand as represented by L_1 is more sensitive to a change in the interest rate (the Keynesian view) than is money demand as represented by L_2 (the monetarist view). For example, a drop in the interest rate from 8 per cent to 7 per cent would result in a $10 billion increase in money demand along L_1. But the interest rate would have to drop from 8 per cent to 6 per cent for there to be a $10 billion increase in money demand along L_2. The investment demand curve I_1 is more steeply sloped than the investment demand curve I_2. Investment demand as represented by I_2 is, therefore, more sensitive to a change in the interest rate (the monetarist view) than is investment demand as represented by I_1 (the Keynesian view). For example, a drop in the interest rate from 8 per cent to 7 per cent would result in an increase in investment of $5 billion along I_1. Along I_2 such a drop in the interest rate would result in an increase in investment of $10 billion.

Suppose the Reserve Bank increases the money supply by $10 billion, represented by the rightward shift in the money supply

FIGURE 15.5
Differing Views on the Impact of a Change in the Money Supply

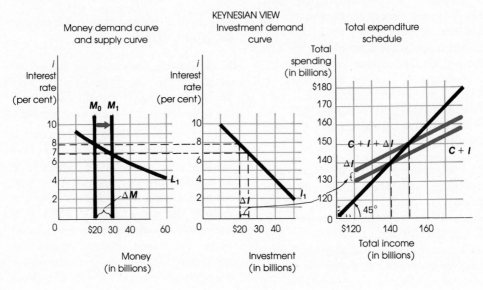

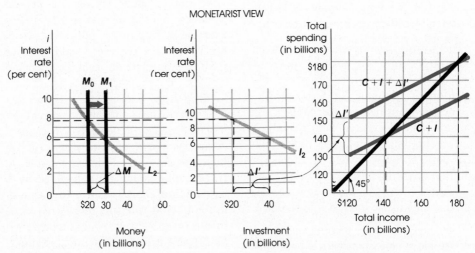

An increase in the money supply causes less of a change in total income according to the Keynesian view (top half of figure) than it does according to the monetarist view (bottom half of figure). This difference is due to the fact that money demand is more sensitive to interest rate changes in the Keynesian view than in the monetarist view, while investment demand is less sensitive to interest rate changes in the Keynesian view than in the monetarist view. Comparing the money demand curves, this means that L_1 is less steeply sloped than L_2, while for the investment demand curves I_1 is more steeply sloped than I_2. Consequently, in the monetarist view the increase ΔM in the money supply from M_0 to M_1 results in a larger reduction in the interest rate, a larger increase in investment, and hence a larger increase in the total expenditure schedule and total income than occurs in the Keynesian view.

curve from M_0 to M_1. Let's compare the difference in the effects on total expenditure and total income that result from the difference between L_1 and L_2 and between I_1 and I_2. (We will ignore the effects of the total income change on the money demand curve because it only complicates our analysis without affecting our comparison of the different points of view.) In the upper half of Figure 15.5 (the Keynesian view), the money supply increase causes the interest rate to fall from 8 per cent (the intersection of M_0 and L_1) to 7 per cent (the intersection of M_1 and L_1). In the lower half of Figure 15.5 (the monetarist view), the same money supply increase results in a larger drop in the interest rate, from 8 per cent to 6 per cent, because the money demand curve L_2 is steeper than L_1.

The larger drop in the interest rate, combined with the fact that I_2 is not as steep as I_1, results in a larger increase in investment spending in the lower half of Figure 15.5 than in the upper half. The increase in investment spending ΔI, in the upper half of the figure, amounts to $5 billion. This increase in investment shifts the total expenditure schedule upward by $5 billion from $C + I$ to $C + I + \Delta I$, resulting in a $10 billion increase in total income from $140 billion to $150 billion in the upper half of Figure 15.5. In the lower half of the figure, the $20 billion increase in investment shifts the total expenditure schedule upwards by $20 billion from $C + I$ to $C + I + \Delta I'$, causing a $40 billion increase in total income from $140 billion to $180 billion. Clearly, a $10 billion increase in the money supply would cause one to predict a greater effect on total expenditure and income if one takes the monetarist rather than the Keynesian point of view.

Changes in Velocity

What do the two points of view expressed in Figure 15.5 imply about the stability of velocity? At the initial equilibrium position in both the upper and lower halves of Figure 15.5, the money supply is $20 billion and total income (or money GDP) is $140 billion. In both cases the equation of exchange is

$$\$20 \times V = \$140$$

In the initial equilibrium position velocity V therefore equals 7. After the $10 billion increase in the money supply, the equation of exchange at the new equilibrium in the upper half of Figure 15.5 (the Keynesian view) is now

$$\$30 \times V = \$150$$

Therefore velocity must now equal 5. In the Keynesian view velocity has fallen from 7 to 5.

At the new equilibrium in the lower half of Figure 15.5 (the monetarist view), the equation of exchange is now

$$\$30 \times V = \$180$$

Velocity must now equal 6. In the monetarist view velocity has fallen from 7 to 6. Therefore, velocity changes by less in the monetarist view (from 7 to 6) than in the Keynesian view (from 7 to 5).

In sum, we can now see why *Keynesians argue that the effects of a money supply increase can be largely offset by a movement in velocity in the opposite direction, and why monetarists believe such offsetting effects are relatively weak.*

Velocity in the Real World

What do real-world data show about the relationship between the money supply and money GDP? How does velocity actually behave?

The Money Supply and Money GDP

Figure 15.6 illustrates the behaviour of the money supply (M1, defined as currency plus current deposits and money GDP in Australia for the years since 1950. Monetarists contend that the almost parallel movement shown by the money supply and money GDP reflects a causal relationship running from the money supply to money GDP. However, Keynesians reply that the observed relationship is equally supportive of their point of view. They argue that the causality can also run in the other direction — from money GDP to the money supply. They point out that the economy's total expenditure schedule

$C + I + G$ can shift upward for a host of reasons that have nothing to do with money supply changes. Technological change, changes in profit expectations, and the development of new products can cause investment I to rise. Changes in consumer tastes, an increase in consumer optimism, population growth, and so forth can cause the consumption function C to shift upward. Government expenditures G may increase for reasons of national defence or to build more highways, schools, and so forth. Keynesians argue that these autonomous increases in total spending in the economy lead to an increase in the demand for loans from banks as businesses and consumers borrow to finance their spending. Banks *respond* by lending out excess reserves and thereby create money through the deposit

FIGURE 15.6
Money Supply and Money GDP in Australia 1949-50 and 1986-87

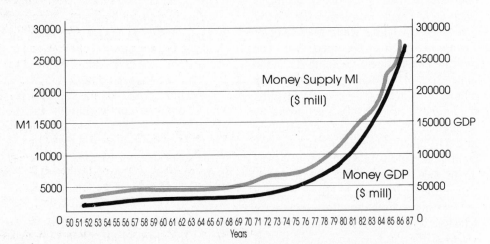

There is a striking parallel in the movements of the money supply and money GDP. Monetarists cite this as evidence to support their claim that the money supply is an important causal determinant of money GDP. Keynesians claim that this parallel movement is equally supportive of the view that causation runs in the opposite direction — from money GDP to the money supply. They argue that total expenditure $C + I + G$ can shift upward for reasons unrelated to money. As total expenditure shifts upward, consumers and business increase their demand for loans from banks in order to carry out their plans for increased spending. As a result, banks increase loans through the deposit expansion process that gives rise to an increase in the money supply.

expansion process we studied in the previous chapter. Growth in the money supply is, therefore, caused by the increase in the total expenditure on goods and services rather than the other way around.

The ongoing debate between monetarists and Keynesians finds both sides enlisting the data of Figure 15.6 as support for their point of view.

The Evidence on Velocity

Velocity can be calculated from the money supply and money GDP data given in Figure 15.6. We can do this simply by recognising that the equation of exchange $M \times V = p \times Q$ may also be expressed as

$$V = \frac{p \times Q}{M}$$

Dividing money GDP ($p \times Q$) by money supply data (M) gives us velocity in Australia since 1950, plotted in Figure 15.7, part b. This figure shows us that velocity has climbed steadily upward from a value of about 2 to around 10. In addition to this long-run trend, velocity has varied on a year-to-year basis. This variation is illustrated in Figure 15.7, part c, which shows the year-to-year percentage change in the velocity data plotted in part b.

Monetarists believe that the growth in velocity has been reasonably slow and predictable. They suggest that the long-run upward trend in velocity since 1950 reflects the increased use of credit cards and the increased availability of short-term credit for consumer purchases. Both of these developments make it possible for individuals or businesses to transact any given amount of purchases of final goods and services with a smaller balance of money on hand. Hence, the economy's money supply turns over more often, or goes around the circular income-expenditure flow more times, during the course of a year — velocity increases.

Keynesians acknowledge the impact of these same developments on velocity. But they also note that the long-run rise in velocity has been accompanied by a long-run rise in the interest rate, shown in part a of Figure 15.7. We have already discussed the fact that Keynesians believe both that money demand is quite sensitive and investment demand relatively insensitive to interest rate changes. And we saw how this implied that velocity is more unstable in the Keynesian view as compared to the monetarist view in which money demand is less sensitive and investment demand more sensitive to interest rate changes — our discussion of Figure 15.5. In particular, while the interest rate went from 8 per cent to 7 per cent, velocity changed from 7 to 5 in the Keynesian view (top half of Figure 15.5). By comparison, in the monetarist view (bottom half of Figure 15.5), while the interest rate went from 8 per cent to 6 per cent, velocity only changed from 7 to 6, despite the fact that change in the interest rate was larger. Hence, Keynesians believe velocity is quite sensitive to interest rate changes. And Keynesians claim the long-run rise in the interest rate (Figure 15.7, part a) that accompanies the long-run rise in velocity (Figure 15.7, part b) is consistent with their point of view.

A Constant Money Growth Rate

Monetarists believe there is a fairly stable relationship between the money supply and money GDP — in other words, a fairly stable V. But they do not advocate attempts to offset recessions and curb excessive economic expansions by alter-

FIGURE 15.7
The Behaviour of Velocity and the Interest Rate in Australia

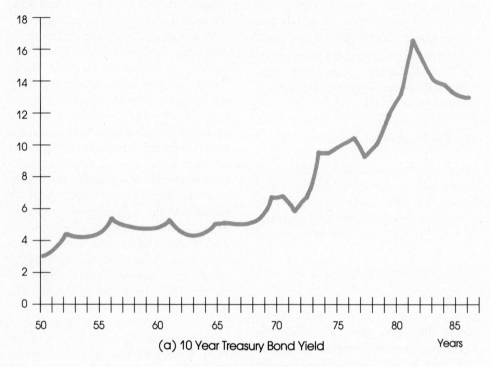

(a) 10 Year Treasury Bond Yield

Velocity of Circulation

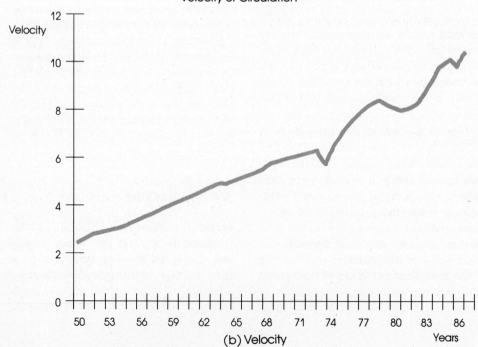

(b) Velocity

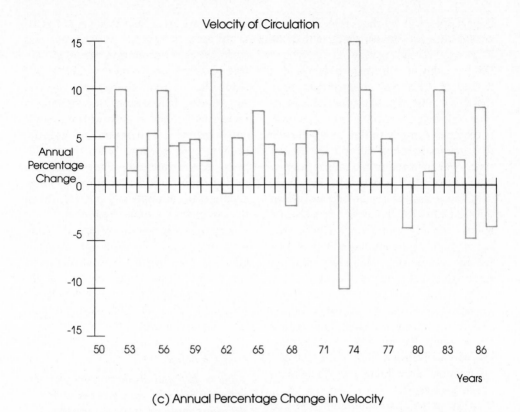

(c) Annual Percentage Change in Velocity

Velocity, plotted in part b, is calculated by dividing money GDP by the money supply (M1). It shows a long-run rising trend since 1950. The short-run stability of velocity is more easily judged from the year-to-year percentage changes in velocity plotted in part c.

Monetarists believe that the evidence in parts b and c covering the period since the early 1950s shows that velocity is reasonably stable. The more variable behaviour of velocity from 1977 seems less supportive of this view. It is argued that the long-run rising trend in velocity since 1950 is due to the increased use of credit cards and availability of short-term credit.

Keynesians take special note of the way that the interest rate in part a moves in a parallel manner to velocity in part b. This is consistent with their view that money demand is sensitive to the interest rate. Our discussion of velocity in connection with Figure 14.5 showed how this view implies that velocity is sensitive to the interest rate rising when the interest rate rises and falling when the interest rate falls.

nately expanding and contracting the money supply. They generally argue that such a discretionary monetary policy is more likely to aggravate economic fluctuations than to minimise them. Why?

Time Lags in Monetary Policy

Monetarists contend that changes in the money supply affect the level of economic

activity over a long and variable period of time. Yes, a change in the money supply will definitely affect the level of money GDP. But there is a time lag between the point when the money supply change occurs and the point when its effect on money GDP is fully realised. Moreover, monetarists claim that the length of this time lag is quite variable and difficult to predict. Research by the foremost monetarist, Milton Friedman, suggests that the length of this time lag may vary anywhere from roughly a half year to two and a half years. As a result, monetarists argue that it is almost impossible for policymakers to schedule expansions or contractions in the money supply so that they will have their impact on the economy at the desired time. An expansion of the money supply, intended to offset a recession, may have its greatest impact a year or more down the road, after the economy has recovered and is already expanding. Hence, the money supply increase may end up adding fuel to a potentially inflationary situation rather than offsetting a recession. Similarly, a contraction of the money supply, intended to curb an overheated economy, may end up having its greatest impact after the economy has already begun to slow down. As a result, the money supply contraction may actually contribute to an ensuing recession.

Most monetarists contend that the historical record suggests that discretionary monetary policy has in fact tended to destabilise rather than stabilise the economy. Therefore, monetarists claim that monetary policy mismanagement must bear some of the blame for economic instability.

Implications for Monetary Policy

What is the upshot of the monetarist contentions? Some prominent monetarists, such as Milton Friedman, argue that the most appropriate monetary policy is to avoid discretionary decisions to expand or contract the rate of growth of the money supply. Instead, they recommend *a constant money growth rate rule*, whereby the Reserve Bank concentrates on expanding the money supply at a constant rate, year-in and year-out.

Monetarists argue that this will automatically tend to smooth out the business cycle. When the economy's rate of growth (the growth rate of money GDP) falls below the constant money supply growth rate, during a recession, the continually increasing money supply will automatically provide a stimulus to get the economy going again. When the economy's growth rate rises above this rate, during a boom, the slower growing money supply will automatically put a curb on the excessive economic expansion.

Keynesians generally regard the constant money growth rule as unnecessarily cautious. They feel that there are definitely times when discretionary changes in the rate of growth of the money supply are obviously called for. This issue continues to be hotly debated by the two camps.

===

CHECKPOINT 15.2

What is the main distinction between the equation of exchange viewed as a definition and as a theory? Consider again the money supply increase discussed in Figure 15.5. Keynesians have argued that the money demand curve becomes flatter at lower interest rate levels. At some very low interest rate, they argue, the curve may become perfectly flat. If the money supply is increased enough to push the interest rate down to this level, Keynesians argue that further increases in the money supply will be completely offset by decreases in velocity V. Can you explain why in terms of a diagram like Figure 15.5?

===

POLICY PERSPECTIVE

The Operation of Monetary Policy

The operational focus of monetary policy in Australia has tended to change over time. In the 1920s and 1930s, monetary policy was completely directed at fixing the exchange rate (i.e. the rate at which the Australian dollar exchanges for, say, US dollars). How monetary policy can do this will be examined in the chapter dealing with the balance of payments and the exchange rate (Chapter 21). After World War II, the focus shifted primarily to the stability of interest rates. Thus, for example, money supply was allowed to expand if there were upward pressures on the interest rate. The main tools used at this period were direct controls over the banking system, such as the changing of reserve requirements and interest rate controls. These earlier ways of operating monetary policy were found to be rather inadequate — introducing all sorts of distortions in the financial system as a result of regulations. More recently, the focus has been the containment of the growth in monetary aggregates. Following a period of considerable economic and financial instability in the early 1970s, the government started issuing targets or, as they preferred to call them, 'conditional projections' for the growth in M3. The Treasurer specified these monetary targets in terms of a percentage growth range for the coming financial year.

Figure P15.1 graphs the actual growth rate for M3 as well as the target growth rates, the range indicated by boxes between 1976 and 1985. Thus, for example, the first target for the year 1976/77 was set at 10-12 per cent. The actual growth rate turned out to be 11 per cent, well within target. Similarly for 1977/78, the target range was 8-10 per cent while the actual growth for M3 was 8 per cent. This initial success, however, was not maintained. The monetarist prescription at the time was to decrease the targets, year by year, till the money supply stops growing at 'excessive' rates. Thus, as may be seen from the graph, the target for 1978/79 was set at 6-8 per cent, but the actual turned out to be 11.8 per cent. In fact, after the first two years, targets were exceeded in every year until 1983/84 when the projection was achieved after a mid-term upward review of the target range. In 1985, this method of conducting monetary policy by announcing targets and trying to rein in the money supply increase to meet the targets, was discontinued. This was done mainly on the grounds that it was becoming harder and harder to determine an appropriate target. In turn, this was due to the effect financial deregulation was having on the conventional measures of money such as M3. With the entrance of new banks and increased competition in the banking sector, there was a predictable increase in lending activity by banks which translated itself into rather high growth rates in M3 — as for example a growth rate of 17.4 per cent in 1985. While historically this appeared high — especially in light of the previous monetary targets set — deregulation was producing a different relationship between M3 and output. In other words, velocity was undergoing considerable changes, largely due to institutional change. In this environment, historical relationships between money and output became irrelevant as far as setting current monetary target rates for M3. Thus targeting the growth rate of M3 was discontinued, and the Reserve Bank adopted what it calls a 'check-list' of factors it looks at in determining its monetary policy. This 'check-list' includes the growth rates of M3 and Broad Money, interest rates and exchange rates as well as trends in the economy generally.

FIGURE P15.1
Growth of Money

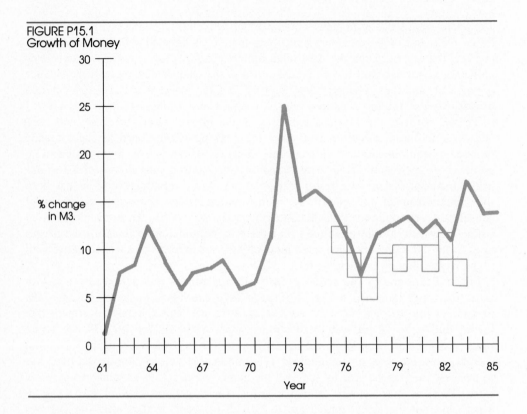

Other countries where rapid changes in the financial system have been taking place have also experienced problems with monetary targeting. For example, in the USA (see the following International Policy Perspective) and UK, a wider set of indicators are being used rather than relying on monetary targets, while Canada has abandoned monetary targeting altogether.

Financial deregulation in Australia has caused a considerable level of activity of the non-bank financial sector (NBFI) to be transferred to the banking sector. In response to this a number of NBFIs such as building societies have formed new banks, so that their lending now constitutes part of M3 while previously it did not. As a result of such changes the Reserve Bank started publishing a broader measure of money in 1984. As we saw in Chapter 14, this includes the liabilities of the NBFIs as well. Figure P15.2 charts the growth rates of both M3 and Broad Money. Note that until 1984, Broad Money tended to grow faster than M3, in part due to regulations inhibiting the competitiveness of the banking system. However, after 1984, there has been a switching around in the growth rates, with M3 growing faster than Broad Money. While it is likely that Broad Money has become a more relevant measure to look at since it is less affected by deregulation, it is unlikely that targeting Broad Money will be substituted for targeting M3 in the near future. Not only is financial deregulation affecting Broad Money as well through increased intermediation by financial institutions, but also there is the problem of uncertain lags in the control of Broad Money and in the relationship between Broad Money and GDP.

FIGURE P15.2
Monetary Aggregates

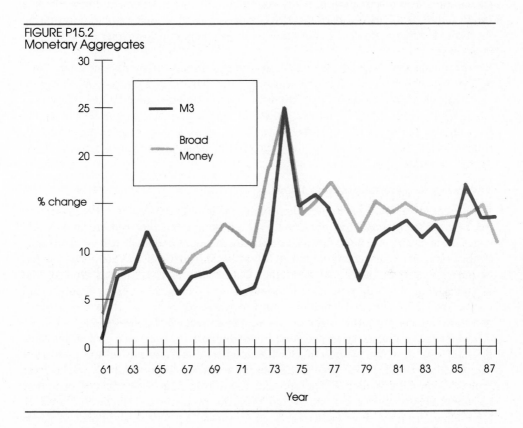

Questions

1. A monetarist looking at Figure P15.1 would argue that it provides clear evidence that monetary targeting worked. He would simply point to the fact that the period of the early 1970s (before monetary targeting was introduced) was characterised by excessive increases in M3. In contrast, the period of monetary targeting was characterised by much lower growth rates in M3. How would a Keynesian respond to this monetarist way of looking at Figure P15.1?

INTERNATIONAL POLICY PERSPECTIVE

A US Monetarist Experiment? How the Federal Reserve Under Volcker Slowed Inflation

The monetarist idea that the government should concentrate more on controlling the growth rate of the money supply and less on stabilising interest rates at targeted levels gained more serious attention in many countries as inflation worsened during the late 1960s and early 1970s. In 1975 the US Congress passed a joint resolution requiring the Federal Reserve Bank (Fed) to state its money supply growth rate targets a year in advance.

Monetarists say the Fed responded by using a variety of money measures (M1, M2, M3, and so on), emphasising whichever one was most consistent at any given time with its continued desire to concentrate on controlling interest rates. Moreover, whenever the Fed missed its money growth target for a particular quarter during the latter half of the 1970s it simply started anew to try to achieve it in the next quarter, rather than trying to correct for the overly rapid or sluggish money growth of the previous quarter.

The Switch to Controlling Money Growth

In October 1979, amid panic over the rapidly rising inflation rate (see Figure P15.3), the Fed, led by its new chairman Paul Volcker, announced that henceforth it would concentrate much more on hitting its money growth targets and much less on controlling interest rates. Mr. Volcker and other Fed officials said from the outset that they wouldn't be pure monetarists, but would take other factors such as interest rates into account when deciding how tightly to control money growth. Nonetheless, from October 1979 to October 1982 the Fed made its most determined effort to follow monetarist prescriptions, sharply cutting back money supply growth (see Figure P15.3).

The Reagan administration provided broad support for the Fed's goal of reducing inflation with slow money growth. But the administration also pushed through major tax cuts that would, it was argued, enable the economy to grow rapidly at the same time inflation was declining. This supply-side line of reasoning argued that the economic incentives created by the tax cuts would stimulate production so much that, even in a booming economy, price increases would be slowed by huge new supplies of goods and services as well as by the tight monetary policy.

What Happened

The tax cuts were phased in over a 2-year period beginning in October 1981 while the Fed slowed money growth with a vengeance during the latter half of 1981 (see Figure P15.3). Inflation declined rapidly and unemployment soared to over 10 per cent by late 1982 as the economy plunged into a deep recession (Figures P15.3 and P15.4). Some economists warned of a possible depression. The supply-side contention that inflation would be cured painlessly without the throes of a recession wasn't accurate. Most economists said the main reason was that the Fed's slowing of the money growth rate simply overwhelmed the stimulus of the tax cut.

By July of 1982 the Fed, alarmed by the severity of the recession and under increasing pressure from Congress, wanted to give the economy more breathing room. Finally, at the Federal Open Market Committee (FOMC) meeting in October 1982, the FOMC accepted Chairman Volcker's argument that it was time to suspend the policy of focusing so heavily on controlling money supply growth, and adopt a broader, more flexible approach. The Fed eased credit and suspended pursuit of its money growth rate targets for the second half of 1982. Since then it has based its actions on a variety of factors, including interest rates, the behaviour of prices, and economic growth.

FIGURE P15.3
Money Growth Rate and Inflation

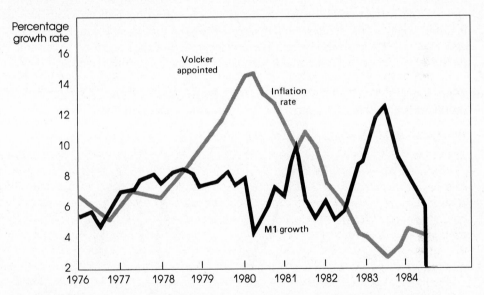

Percentage growth of the money supply (M1) and consumer prices, by quarter, from a year earlier.

Before 1979, the trend of money supply increases and inflation was steadily upward. Under Chairman Volcker, the Fed adopted the monetarist goal of slowing money growth, and inflation fell. But M1 growth became more erratic, not smoother as the monetarists wanted.

SOURCE: Morgan, Stanley & Co.

An Assessment of the 'Monetarist' Experiment

The Fed's policy during the 1979–1982 period helped bring about a drastic reduction in inflation in the US with the rate of consumer price increases tumbling from 13.3 per cent in 1979 to 3.9 per cent in 1982. At the same time, however, money growth was extremely erratic (see Figure P15.3), not slow and steady as monetarists advocated.

Monetarists contend that the volatility of money growth means that monetarism was never really followed as prescribed. Anna Schwartz, who collaborated with Milton

Friedman in research on the relation between money supply movements and the economy, believes the Fed espoused monetarist principles as a smokescreen for raising interest rates (Figure P15.5). Even a Fed governor has conceded that setting money growth rate targets helped shield the Fed against criticism that would be associated with a policy of setting interest rates high enough to curb inflation. Schwartz contends that the high interest rate policy's side effects (high unemployment and a deep recession) have been unfairly attributed to monetarism whose prescription for slow but *steady* money growth was never really followed.[1]

What Has Monetarism Accomplished?

The cause of monetarism has not always been served well even by its truest believers. In late 1983 Milton Friedman predicted a recession for the first half of 1984 and a resurgence of inflation by the second half. The sharp slowdown in M1 growth in late 1983 (see Figure P15.5) was the basis for the recession forecast. And he said inflation would surge because of the rapid growth of the money supply from mid-1982 to mid-1983. He was wrong. The economy experienced a strong expansion in the first half, and there was no major resurgence of inflation in the second half.

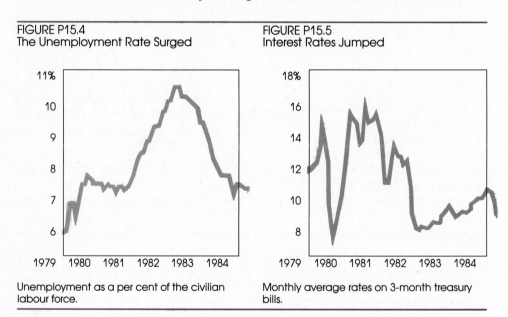

FIGURE P15.4
The Unemployment Rate Surged

Unemployment as a per cent of the civilian labour force.

FIGURE P15.5
Interest Rates Jumped

Monthly average rates on 3-month treasury bills.

Monetarism's clout has declined since 1979 when the Fed first seemed to embrace it. Overall however, many economists contend that in future years inflation rates are likely to be lower than they would have been before monetarism focused so much attention on the importance of controlling money supply growth.

Questions

1. Monetarists argue for a slow steady growth in the money supply because they claim no one understands the economy well enough to adjust the rate of money growth appropriately for any given time. Given this assertion, it could be said that it was inconsistent for Milton Friedman to predict the course of the economy in 1984 on the basis of the behaviour of money growth in 1982. Why?

2. What evidence do you see in Figure P15.5 that the Fed relaxed its focus on controlling money supply growth and 'broadened' its focus to include other factors?

[1]'Money's Role,' *Wall Street Journal* Dec. 10, 1984, p. 16.

SUMMARY

1. Businesses will invest in those capital goods having an expected rate of return greater than the interest rate. The lower the interest rate, the larger the amount of investment spending that is profitable by this criterion. Hence, the investment demand curve slopes downward because more investment spending will take place at low than at high interest rates.

2. According to the Keynesian view the money market is linked to the level of investment spending by the interest rate. The level of investment spending determines the level of the total expenditure schedule and hence the level of real GDP. The level of real GDP in turn determines the position of the money demand curve in the money market.

3. An increase in the money supply lowers the interest rate. According to the Keynesian view this increases investment spending, which pushes up the total expenditure schedule, raising the level of real GDP. The rise in real GDP pushes the money demand curve rightward, causing the interest rate to rise, though not enough to offset the full effects of the initial decrease in the interest rate. A partial equilibrium analysis would ignore the effect on the money demand curve of the rise in real GDP.

4. According to the Keynesian view increasing the money supply lowers the interest rate and raises the real GDP level — this is often referred to as an easy-money policy. Decreasing the money supply raises the interest rate and lowers the real GDP level — this is often called a tight-money policy.

5. An increase in the money supply causes the aggregate demand curve (AD) to shift rightward, while a decrease in the money supply causes it to shift leftward. The AD curve and the aggregate supply curve determine the price level.

6. Keynesians tend to favour government intervention in the economy because they see shortcomings in the way the market system answers the economic questions of what to produce, how, and for whom. They are also doubtful that markets have the self-regulating ability to ensure economic stability and full employment without the aid of an active fiscal policy. Monetarists tend to see government intervention as an unnecessary and harmful interference with the market system, a threat to individual freedom, and a dampener on individual initiative.

7. The equation of exchange, $M \times V = p \times Q$ is a definitional relationship between the economy's money stock M and the economy's total money income, or money

GDP, which is equal to the price level p times the quantity of real output Q. V is the velocity of circulation of money. When V is regarded as stable — a reflection of institutional characteristics of the economy — the equation of exchange becomes the expression for the quantity theory of money.

8. Monetarism may be regarded as a sophisticated version of the quantity theory of money. Monetarists argue that the cause-effect transmission from changes in the money supply to changes in money GDP are reasonably direct and tight. They argue that the effects of a money supply change are transmitted through a host of channels, not just the interest rate channel so strongly emphasised by the Keynesian view. While monetarists regard velocity as stable, Keynesians believe the velocity of money is unstable, consistent with their view that money demand is sensitive and investment demand relatively insensitive to interest rate changes.

9. Keynesians favour discretionary monetary policy. Monetarists argue that such a policy is likely to aggravate the business cycle rather than diminish it. Therefore, some prominent monetarists argue for a constant money growth rate rule.

KEY TERMS AND CONCEPTS

equation of exchange
expected rate of return
general equilibrium analysis
monetarism
partial equilibrium analysis
quantity theory of money
velocity

QUESTIONS AND PROBLEMS

1. Using a partial equilibrium analysis, start with the initial equilibrium position in the top half of Figure 15.3 (money supply M_0 equal to $30 billion) and trace through the likely effects of each of the following (indicate the direction of changes where it is not possible to measure the precise magnitudes of changes):

a. The Reserve Bank reduces the required reserve ratio.

b. The Reserve Bank makes an open market sale of bonds.

c. The Reserve Bank reduces the money supply by $7.5 billion.

2. How would your answers to question 1 be affected if full adjustment in all markets is taken into account — that is, how would the answers in each case be different if a general equilibrium analysis were carried out instead of a partial equilibrium analysis?

3. In Figure 15.3, how would the slopes of the money demand curve L_0 and the investment demand curve I_d have to be different for the $20 billion increase in the money supply to have a larger impact on real GDP? What implications do the slopes of the money demand and investment demand curves have for the effectiveness of monetary policy?

4. Link up the analysis in the top half of Figure 15.3 with the analysis in Figure 15.4, and describe how monetary policy affects the level of real GDP and the price level p. Do the same thing using the bottom half of Figure 15.4 and explain how the effect on real GDP and the price level would be different.

5. Suppose the Reserve Bank is prone to making mistakes in its exercise of discretionary monetary policy. According to which view, Keynesian or monetarist, would the resulting fluctuations in money GDP be the greatest? Why? What bearing does this have on the Keynesian view versus the monetarist view about discretionary monetary policy?

6. Assume the Reserve Bank decides to implement monetary policy by always keeping the interest rate at the same target level. For instance, if the interest rate falls below the target level, the Reserve Bank conducts open market sales to push it back up, while if the interest rate rises above the target level, the Reserve Bank conducts open market purchases to push it back down. Suppose there are autonomous changes in spending, reflected in shifts in the total expenditure schedule. Do you think the Reserve Bank constant interest rate policy would tend to stabilise or destabilise the economy? Why?

7. What problems does discretionary monetary policy share with discretionary fiscal policy? (Recall the discussion of discretionary fiscal policy in Chapter 10.) In what ways would the exercise of discretionary monetary policy differ from the exercise of discretionary fiscal policy?

FOUR

Inflation, Unemployment, Economic Stability and Growth

16
Monetary and Fiscal Policy and Budget Deficits

AFTER READING THIS CHAPTER YOU WILL BE ABLE TO:

1. Explain the differences between Keynesian and monetarist views on the extent to which fiscal policy actions affect real GDP and the price level.

2. Explain the different effects on the economy of pure fiscal policy actions as distinguished from those accomplished by money supply changes.

3. Give reasons and explain why it is often difficult to coordinate monetary and fiscal policy.

4. Describe how monetary policy and government deficits can combine to give the economy an inflationary bias.

5. Describe the difference between the money interest rate and the real interest rate, and explain how this difference complicates the conduct of monetary and fiscal policy.

The basic question to be addressed in this and the next chapter is: To what extent can monetary and fiscal policy smooth out economic fluctuations (the so-called business cycle) and prod the economy closer to full employment without excessive inflation? In this chapter we will first focus on why Keynesians and monetarists hold differing opinions on the effectiveness of fiscal policy. Then we will examine why fiscal actions that cause government budget deficits have monetary implications that make it difficult to distinguish purely fiscal from purely monetary effects. We will then see how budget deficits can give rise to conflicts between monetary and fiscal policy.

FISCAL POLICY: KEYNESIAN VERSUS MONETARIST VIEWS

Aside from the ideological differences discussed in the last chapter, why do Keynesians have more faith than monetarists in the ability of fiscal policy to smooth out the business cycle, foster full employment, and curb inflation? How can fiscal policies which cause deficits have monetary effects? Are fiscal and monetary policies well coordinated or do they frequently work at cross-purposes with each other? Let's now consider each of these questions in turn.

Pure Fiscal Policy and Crowding Out

The basic differences between the Keynesian and monetarist views on the effectiveness of fiscal policy are perhaps most clearly illustrated in terms of pure fiscal policy. *Pure fiscal policy* consists of changes in government expenditure,

taxation, or both that do not change the money supply.

Monetarists argue that pure fiscal policy causes very little change in total income and employment. For example, the monetarist view holds that an increase in government expenditure leads to the **crowding out** of private sector expenditure, particularly investment spending. Hence, any expansionary effect on aggregate demand caused by an increase in government spending is largely offset by an accompanying decline in investment spending. In contrast, Keynesians argue that crowding out is not that significant.

Why There Is Crowding Out

What is the explanation for the crowding-out effect and the difference in opinion between Keynesians and monetarists regarding its size? The answer hinges on the effect of a rise in total income on money demand, the interest rate, and investment spending.

Recall the increases in the economy's total income cause the money demand curve to shift rightward, as illustrated in Figure 14.2, Chapter 14. Our discussion of general equilibrium (Figure 15.3 in Chapter 15) showed us how this rightward shift in the money demand curve would tend to dampen an expansion in total expenditure and real GDP, and therefore the amount of rightward shift in the AD curve Figure 15.4.

Consider now Figure 16.1 where the differences in slope between the investment demand curves, I_1 and I_2, and the money demand curves, L_1 and L_2, reflect the differences between the Keynesian and monetarist views discussed earlier in Figure 15.5. For a *given* increase in total income, there will be a certain amount of rightward shift in the money demand

FIGURE 16.1
Keynesian View Versus Monetarist View of the Effects of an Increase in Total Income on
Investment

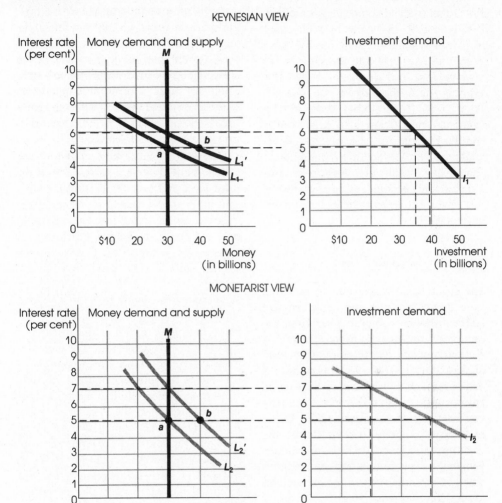

A given increase in total income will shift the money demand curve rightward, from L_1 to L_1' in the
Keynesian view and from L_2 to L_2' in the monetarist view. At the initial equilibrium interest rate of 5
per cent, the amount of this rightward shift equals the distance from a to b. The money demand
curve is more steeply sloped in the monetarist than in the Keynesian view. Therefore, the interest
rate rises further in the monetarist view (from 5 to 7 per cent) than in the Keynesian view (from 5
to 6 per cent). Combined with the fact that the investment demand curve I_2 is less steeply
sloped than I_1, this means that investment spending is reduced more in the monetarist than in
the Keynesian view.

curve as shown in Figure 16.1. L_1 shifts to L_1' (Keynesian view), and L_2 shifts to L_2' (monetarist view). The amount of this shift, equal to the distance between a and b, is of course the same in both cases because both shifts are caused by the same given increase in total income. Note, however, that in the monetarist view the resulting rise in the interest rate is larger (from 5 to 7 per cent) than in the Keynesian view (from 5 to 6 per cent). The larger rise in the interest rate, combined with the fact that I_2 has a flatter slope than I_1, results in a larger reduction in investment spending, or more crowding out, in the monetarist view than in the Keynesian.

The Crowding-Out Effect

The effect of crowding out on the total expenditure schedule and hence on real GDP is shown in Figure 16.2. Here the economy's total expenditure schedule is E_1, which means that the equilibrium level of real GDP is GDP_0, as shown in both the upper and lower half of the figure. Now suppose government spending increases by the amount ΔG. If we momentarily ignore the effects of the resulting rise in real GDP on money demand, the economy's total expenditure schedule is shifted up to E_2 (upper and lower half of Figure 16.2). However, if we allow for the effects of the real GDP rise on money demand, the interest rate, and the level of investment spending, as shown in Figure 16.1, the total expenditure schedule cannot rise to the position E_2 in Figure 16.2. Why? Because the effect of the rise in government spending will be offset in part by the reduction, or crowding out, of investment spending that results from the rise in the interest rate. According to the Keynesian view (upper

half of Figure 16.2), the crowding out of investment will equal $-\Delta I$, so that the total expenditure schedule is shifted up to E_3 — or by an amount equal to $\Delta G - \Delta I$. Equilibrium real GDP rises from GDP_0 to GDP_k. According to the monetarist view (lower half of Figure 16.2), the crowding out of investment will be larger, equal to $-\Delta I'$. The total expenditure schedule is shifted up by a smaller amount, equal to $\Delta G - \Delta I'$, to E_3', and real GDP rises only from GDP_0 to GDP_m.

Figure 16.3 shows how crowding out affects the AD curve and hence both the price level and real GDP. Recall that a shift in the total expenditure schedule due to an exogenous expenditure change shifts the AD curve, as shown previously in Figure 11.6, Chapter 11. Corresponding to the shift in the total expenditure schedule from E_1 to E_3 according to the Keynesian view, Figure 16.2, the AD curve shifts from AD_1 and AD_3 along the AS curve in Figure 16.3 and the price level rises from p_1 to p_3 as real GDP increases from GDP_0 to GDP_k. Corresponding to the shift in the total expenditure schedule from E_1 to E_3' according to the monetarist view, Figure 16.2, the AD curve shifts from AD_1 to AD_3' along the AS curve in Figure 16.3 and the price level rises from p_1 to p_3' as real GDP increases from GDP_0 to GDP_m. Clearly the increase in the price level and real GDP is smaller according to the monetarist view.

Crowding Out and Taxation

Our illustration of the crowding-out effect has assumed that the fiscal action taken was an increase in government spending. But a tax reduction also shifts the total expenditure schedule upward and the AD curve rightward, as we saw in Chapters 10 and 11, and results in the same type of crowding-out effect. Similarly, an increase in government expenditures matched by an increase in taxes (a balanced budget increase) shifts the total expenditure schedule upward (discussed Chapter 10) and the AD curve rightward, giving rise to the crowding-out effect.

In sum, *monetarists believe fiscal policy actions have very little effect on real GDP, the price level, and employment because of the offsetting crowding-out effect. The Keynesian view holds that fiscal policy has a sizeable effect because the offsetting crowding-out effect is not that significant.*

Fiscal and Monetary Effects Combined: Financing Budget Deficits

Fiscal policy has monetary effects whenever a fiscal action is accompanied by a change in the money supply. This may happen whenever a change in government expenditure, taxation, or both gives rise to a government budget deficit or surplus.

Financing Budget Deficits Without a Money Supply Change

Recall our discussion of the financing of

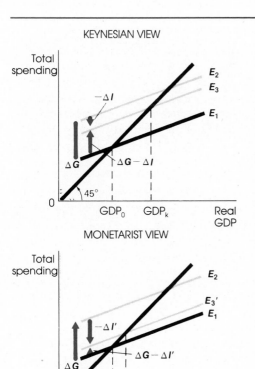

FIGURE 16.2
The Crowding-Out Effect of Fiscal Policy

An increase in government expenditure ΔG pushes the total expenditure schedule from E_1 up to E_2 if we momentarily ignore the effects of the rise in real GDP on money demand, the interest rate, and investment. Taking account of such effects (as illustrated in Figure 16.1), the rise in real GDP increases the demand for money, which pushes up the interest rate and causes a reduction, or crowding out, of investment spending.

This crowding out of investment spending is larger according to the monetarist view (bottom half of Figure 16.1) than according to the Keynesian view (top half of Figure 16.1). Consequently, there is a greater offsetting change in investment in the monetarist view, equal to $-\Delta I'$, than in the Keynesian view, equal to $-\Delta I$. As a result, the total expenditure schedule only rises from E_1 to E_3' increasing GDP from GDP_0 to GDP_m in the monetarist view. By comparison the exact same increase in government spending, ΔG, increases the total expenditure schedule from E_1 to E_3 and GDP from GDP_0 to GDP_k in the Keynesian view.

government budget deficits in Chapter 10. There we noted that whenever government expenditure exceeds tax revenues the government must finance the difference by issuing government bonds. If the public (businesses, individuals, and private institutions) buys the bonds, they typically write cheques against their current deposits. These cheques are made payable to the Reserve Bank for the amount of government bonds purchased. The government then spends this money, putting it right back into the hands of the public. There is no change in the supply of money in the economy when the government deficit is financed in this fashion. Hence, the only question is how much the expansionary effect of the government expenditure increase, tax reduction, or both is offset by the crowding-out effect — the same issue we discussed in connection with Figures 16.2 and 16.3.

Financing Budget Deficits with a Money Supply Change: Monetising the Government Debt

In Chapter 10 we observed that if the government chooses not to finance its

---

FIGURE 16.3
Crowding-Out Effect on Aggregate Demand

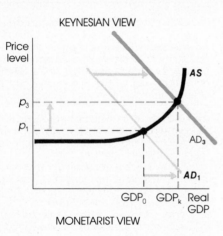

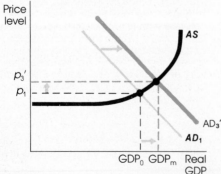

An exogenous government expenditure increase, or an exogenous tax reduction, causes less crowding out of investment spending and therefore gives rise to a larger rightward shift of the *AD* curve according to the Keynesian view than according to the monetarist view. Consequently the Keynesian view holds that such fiscal policy actions cause larger increases in real GDP and the price level than is the case according to the monetarist view.

POLICY PERSPECTIVE

The Choice Between Fiscal and Monetary Policy

In principle, the goals of monetary and fiscal policy are the same — to smooth out economic fluctuations, to promote full employment, and to curb inflation. Ideally, therefore, those who advocate the use of discretionary, or 'activist', policies would argue that policymakers should coordinate monetary and fiscal actions to achieve these ends. For example, during a recession appropriate fiscal policy should give rise to a deficit, while appropriate monetary policy should increase the rate of expansion of the money supply. On the other hand, if the economy is operating close to full employment and inflationary pressures are increasing, prudent fiscal policy should generate a budget surplus, and monetary policy should reduce the rate of expansion of the money supply. In practice, choosing the appropriate monetary and fiscal policies as well as coordinating them is not an easy task.

The Political Process

A major reason coordination is difficult is that the size and timing of government expenditure and tax programs are influenced by other considerations in addition to those of economic stabilisation. Expenditure and tax programs are a product of the political processes of both houses of parliament and reflect the objectives and priorities of many different special interest groups and regions of the country. There is often little regard for the fiscal policy implications of expenditure and tax programs conceived under these conditions.

After its election to office in 1983, the Hawke government failed to control the Senate with the result that it often had to negotiate with the Australian Democrats in order to ensure the timely passage of important bills. Furthermore, while the Commonwealth government is in a better position to have a broader perspective on fiscal policy, it often needs the cooperation of state governments — for example, in the Commonwealth government's attempts in recent years to reduce the borrowing requirements of all levels of government. This often involves protracted negotiations, sometimes with hostile State premiers belonging to a different party than that of the Commonwealth government. Even if the State and Commonwealth governments are of the same party, the different timing of State and Commonwealth elections is sufficient to create considerable friction between the two levels of government.

A typical member of parliament finds it difficult, if not politically unrewarding, to consider actions taken on behalf of constituents in terms of their impact on the overall government budget. For example, a member of the House of Representatives or senator who votes for closing down army bases in his or her electorate because the army no longer needs them risks defeat at the polls. It may be true that the base closings will help trim the Commonwealth government's budget and relieve inflationary pressures in the economy. But local voters will be more concerned about the adverse impact of the base closings on the local economy.

The question is not whether or not to have fiscal policy. Whenever decisions are made about government spending and taxation, for whatever reasons, the resulting government expenditure and tax actions unavoidably affect total income, output, employment, and the level of prices. All such actions amount to a fiscal policy, even when they are taken primarily in pursuit of other objectives unrelated to maintaining economic stability, reasonably full employment, and a rein on inflation. A basic difficulty with fiscal policy as a stabilisation tool is that there are so many other objectives that often take precedence in the determination of government spending and tax policy. It is largely for this reason that fiscal policy often conflicts with monetary policy.

Unlike fiscal policy, monetary policy is made by a relatively small group of people — the Board of the Reserve Bank. The public does not have direct ballot box control or influence over the Board, and monetary policy does not have to be approved by both houses of parliament. This leaves monetary policy relatively more free to pursue economic stabilisation objectives as compared to fiscal policy.

Lags of Policies

A further problem in adopting appropriate fiscal and monetary policies is the problem of lags in the actual operation of a policy. Of interest here is the time it takes from when the government decides that a certain impact must hit the economy as quickly as possible to the instant when the policy hits the economy with its full force. We may divide this lag into two parts. There is the time taken to implement the policy (the 'inside' lag) and the time taken by the policy itself, once implemented, to hit the economy (the outside lag). For monetary policy, the inside lag is short, since only the Reserve Bank Board is involved in the decision process. In contrast the inside lag for fiscal policy can be quite long, not only because it often requires parliamentary approval, but also because it may take time to actually draw up the plans, especially if a major public works project is involved. For example, in December 1982 the Fraser Government introduced a wages pause as a result of spiralling unemployment experienced in that year. The money saved from the government's wages bill as a result of this wages pause was to be used to set up a training and temporary employment scheme for the unemployed. Twelve months after the introduction of the wages pause, the money was still sitting in the government coffers mostly unspent and waiting for the programs to be set up.

While the inside lag for fiscal policy may be long, the outside lag is usually short. For example, in the wages pause case, once the training and employment scheme was set up, the impact on the economy was immediate — the extra income earned by the participants in the scheme had an immediate effect on the economy. In the case of monetary policy, the outside lag can be quite long, anywhere between six months and a year. The reason for this is that, for example, a drop in the interest rate causes investors to revise their investment upwards but it will take time for them to make this decision, arrange for financing and spend the money. Thus, in summary, it appears that monetary and fiscal policy have reversed lags — monetary policy having short inside lags and long outside lags while fiscal policy has the opposite, long inside and short outside lags.

Interest Rate Effects

Expansionary fiscal policy financed by selling bonds tends to increase the interest rate.

This may prove unpopular with voters, especially if it affects the politically sensitive mortgage interest rates. Expansionary monetary policy has the opposite effect on interest rates, thereby encouraging the government to adopt a combination of monetary and fiscal policies that restrain the rise in interest rates. For contractionary purposes, however, the influence of fiscal and monetary policies on the interest rate is reversed. Thus, an appropriate policy mix might be required if the government is to slow down the economy without too large a rise in the interest rate.

The preceding discussion suggests that the impact of a policy is equal in magnitude but opposite in direction if the government adopts a contractionary policy rather than an expansionary one. However, in the case of monetary policy this may not be the case. Expansionary monetary policy is usually applied during a recession when there is excess capacity and profits are down. In this environment, a fall in the interest rate may not affect investment spending by much so that monetary policy in these circumstances may be weak. Keynesians love to use this argument to point out the weakness of monetary policy — they often use the analogy that though you can bring a horse to the trough you can't force it to drink. For contractionary purposes, however, monetary policy does not suffer from such problems. For example, as a policy to fight inflation — by forcing up the interest rate and thus slowing down demand for goods and services — monetary policy is believed to be much more useful.

Size of Government

Expansionary fiscal policy such as an increase in government spending, implies that the government gains more control over the total output of the economy, allowing it to increase its influence on the allocation and distribution of goods and services within the economy. This would be considered an advantage by those leaning towards the socialist philosophy. Those believing in the efficacy of the free market and the capitalist system are against this form of fiscal policy. They favour the use of monetary or tax policy, arguing that any reallocation of resources is done more efficiently by changes in the interest rate or income in the hands of individuals.

Finally there are those who argue that monetary policy, through its effect on the interest rate, affects the whole economy (the interest rate rises for everybody). In contrast, fiscal policy is more flexible since it can be targeted where needed, say to a region with unusually high unemployment rates. For those believing in the wisdom of government in wielding discretionary power, this is a distinct advantage of fiscal policy.

Questions

1. Even if it were possible to coordinate monetary and fiscal policy *initiatives*, what other problems might cause the *results* of such efforts to be uncoordinated?

2. What do you think a monetarist would say about the idea of coordinating monetary and fiscal policy?

---

deficit by selling bonds to the public, it can 'print the money' it needs. Now that we've seen how the Reserve Bank can create money (Chapters 13 and 14), we can see exactly how this is done.

Rather than sell the deficit-financing

government bonds to the public, suppose the Treasury simply sells them directly to the Reserve Bank. How can the Reserve Bank pay for the bonds? Since the Reserve Bank is the government's banker, suppose it simply credits or adds to the Treasury's account at the Reserve Bank (the government's cheque account) the amount of funds necessary to cover the purchase of the bonds. Then the government writes cheques against this account when it purchases goods and services in the economy. The cheque recipients, who provide the goods and services, deposit the cheques in their banks and the economy's money supply is increased by this amount. In sum, one arm of the government, the Reserve Bank creates money for another arm of the government, the Treasury. The Treasury spends this money, thereby increasing the entire economy's money supply.

When the Reserve Bank finances government deficit spending in this way, it is said to be *monetising the government debt* — turning newly issued government bonds directly into newly created money. That is, the Reserve Bank is 'printing money'. The Reserve Bank may purchase an amount of bonds equal only to a portion of the bonds sold by the Treasury to finance the budget deficit. In that case, only that portion of the deficit spending is financed by 'printing money'.

When deficit spending is financed by monetising the government debt, the money supply is increased. And we know that such an increase will cause a rightward shift in the economy's *AD* curve and a rise in real GDP and the price level (Figure 15.4). This shift is an addition to the rightward shift in the *AD* curve and the rise in the price level that results from the increase in government spending, reduction in taxes, or both (Figure 16.3).

In sum, *deficit spending financed by the creation of money — monetising the government debt — is more expansionary than deficit spending financed only by selling bonds to the public — that is, without the creation of money.*

Keynesian View Versus Monetarist View on Deficit Financing

Monetarists argue that deficit spending has a pronounced expansionary effect on the economy only to the extent that it is financed by the creation of money. This position is dictated by the monetarist view that money supply increases are very expansionary (bottom half of Figure 15.5), while government expenditure increases, tax reductions, or both are largely offset by crowding out (bottom halves of Figure 16.2 and Figure 16.3). The Keynesian view doesn't see money supply increases as nearly so expansionary (top half of Figure 15.5) or the crowding-out effect as nearly so large (top halves of Figures 16.2 and Figure 16.3). Consequently, the Keynesian view holds that deficit spending is expansionary largely because of the direct effects of government expenditure, tax reduction, or both on the economy's aggregate demand curve for goods and services. Keynesians would agree that deficit spending is more expansionary if it is financed by money creation than by the sale of bonds to the public without money creation. However, they don't think the method of financing makes nearly as much difference as the monetarists do.

---

*CHECKPOINT * 16.1*

Is having a high multiplier good or bad for the economy? Explain, giving both sides of the argument.

*Answers to all Checkpoints can be found at the back of the text.

MONETARY POLICY AND GOVERNMENT DEFICITS

In the preceding Policy Perspective we discussed some of the difficulties of coordinating monetary and fiscal policy. We will now focus more specifically on the role that the interest rate plays in the conflict between government deficit financing and the objectives of monetary policy.

Autonomous increases in consumption and investment spending and increases in government spending, reductions in taxes, or both, cause the total expenditure schedule to shift upward and the AD curve rightward. However, the resulting rise in total income, or money GDP, will lead to an increase in the demand for money. This in turn will cause the interest rate to rise. The result is a cutback in investment spending that tends to dampen the rise in aggregate demand, with the extent of the cutback depending on the interest rate sensitivity of investment demand and money demand. (Recall the Keynesian view versus the monetarist view on this issue.) The only way to avoid this interest rate rise is for the Reserve Bank to increase the money supply. Of course, if the economy is already operating at or close to full employment, such a monetary expansion will result in a rise in the price level as the AD curve shifts rightward along the upward-sloping aggregate supply (AS) curve.

Interest Rate Stability and Deficit Spending

Over the years critics of the Reserve Bank have frequently claimed that it is overly concerned with maintaining interest rate stability. As a result, such critics allege, the Reserve Bank often expands the money supply to keep the interest rate from rising when the rise itself is caused by an inflationary increase in aggregate demand. It would be wiser for the Reserve Bank to refrain from increasing the money supply and, thus, allow the interest rate rise to check the expansion of aggregate demand, thereby dampening inflationary pressures. Instead, when the Reserve Bank expands the money supply in such a situation, it adds further fuel to the inflationary increase in aggregate demand.

Critics go on to argue that these inflationary implications of the Reserve Bank preoccupation with interest rate stability are of even more concern in the presence of government deficit spending. Why?

Interest Rate and Aggregate Demand

Recall our discussion of government deficit spending. There we observed that a government deficit must be financed by issuing new government bonds. Recall that when these bonds are sold to the public, there is no change in the economy's money supply as long as the Reserve Bank doesn't engage in open market purchases (monetise the debt). The money that the public gives to the Treasury in exchange for the new bonds is returned to the economy when the government spends it. This government spending shifts the AD curve rightward, increasing real GDP and the price level, and thus the demand for money. *The interest rate rises* and cuts back investment spending (the crowding-out effect), which tends to dampen the rightward shift in the AD curve.

However, if the Reserve Bank does not

want the interest rate to rise, it must engage in open market purchases. That is, as soon as the interest rate begins to rise, the Reserve Bank will carry out open market purchases to keep it down. But this amounts to financing the government deficit by printing money, or monetising the government debt. The money supply is increased. Government deficit spending financed in this way causes the economy's *AD* curve to shift rightward, both because of the spending increase and because of the increase in the money supply. Clearly, if the Reserve Bank does not want the interest rate to rise, the curb on the rise in aggregate demand due to the crowding-out effect is absent and inflationary pressures are greater.

An Inflationary Bias

This is the reason that critics of the Reserve Bank contend that a preoccupation with interest rate stability gives monetary policy an inflationary bias that is accentuated by government deficit spending. They claim that this bias was of particular concern in the early 1970s. More alarming, however, has been the behaviour of the cyclically adjusted budget, which economists generally regard as a more accurate measure of the expansionary impact of fiscal policy (see Chapter 10). Critics of the Reserve Bank note that the government ran a cyclically adjusted budget deficit since the early 1970s - fiscal policy has been predominantly expansionary (see Chapter 10, Figure 10.5). To the extent that the Reserve Bank has been preoccupied with interest rate stabilisation, critics argue that monetary policy and fiscal policy jointly contributed to the inflationary pressures that plagued the economy throughout the 1970s and early 1980s.

Inflation and the Interest Rate: Real Versus Money Interest Rate

There is another important consideration that bears on the issue of interest rate stability and monetary policy: the relationship between inflation and the interest rate. Whenever there is inflation, it is necessary to recognise the existence of two distinct measures of the interest rate: the real interest rate and the money interest rate.

The Real Interest Rate

The **real interest rate** *is the interest rate calculated in terms of its purchasing power over goods and services.* Suppose I agree to lend you $100 for 1 year at an interest rate of 10 per cent. At the end of 1 year you will pay me back the $100 plus $10, or $110. If there is *no change in the general price level* in the meantime, I give up $100 of purchasing power over goods today in exchange for $110 of purchasing power over goods a year from now. In 1 year I will get back 10 per cent more purchasing power than I originally gave up. Hence, in this example the real interest rate equals 10 per cent. The real interest rate is the rate that we would actually see in the market when the general price level is stable — that is, when there is no inflation (or deflation).

The Money Interest Rate

The **money interest rate** *(sometimes called the nominal or market rate) is the interest rate calculated in terms of units of money, not purchasing power over goods.* Only when the general price level is expected to be stable is it true that the money interest rate equals the real interest rate. This is so because under these circumstances the purchasing power of a unit of money remains unchanged. Whenever there is anticipated inflation (or deflation), the money interest rate and the real interest rate will differ from each other by the amount of the anticipated inflation (or deflation). This is so because when there is a change in the general price level, the purchasing power of a unit of money changes.

Anticipated Rate of Inflation

The anticipated rate of inflation is the difference between real and money interest rates. To illustrate the difference between the real interest rate and the money interest rate, consider our $100 loan example again. To be willing to lend you $100, I again insist on getting back 10 per cent more purchasing power in 1 year than I originally gave up. But now suppose both you and I *expect* a 5 per cent rate of inflation. This means we both expect the purchasing power of a unit of money, a dollar, to decline by 5 per cent over the next year. Therefore, I must charge you an additional 5 per cent just to compensate myself for the anticipated loss in purchasing power on each unit of money, or dollar, that I lend you. Hence, I lend you $100 at a money rate of interest of 15 per cent. The 15 per cent money rate of interest equals the 10 per cent real rate of interest plus the anticipated rate of inflation of 5 per cent. This additional 5 per cent may be thought of as an inflation premium that is added on to the real rate of interest. You will be willing to pay the 15 per cent money rate of interest to borrow the $100 from me. Why? Because you will recognise that you are going to pay me back dollars that have lost 5 per cent of their purchasing power due to inflation.

In short, the 15 per cent money rate of interest means that I lend you $100 of money now, and in 1 year you repay me $115 of money. The 10 per cent real rate of interest means that I lend you $100 of purchasing power *now*, and in 1 year you repay me the equivalent amount of purchasing power *plus* another 10 per cent of purchasing power.

In summary:

$$\text{money interest rate} = \text{real interest rate} + \text{anticipated rate of inflation}$$

If the anticipated rate of inflation is zero, then the money interest rate and the real interest rate are the same. The money interest rate is the one we actually observe in the market for loans and bonds. The real interest rate is unobservable unless the anticipated rate of inflation is zero. In everyday life, the 'interest rate' that people talk about is the money interest rate.

Now let's consider the implications of the distinction between the money and the real interest rate for the interest rate stabilisation issue.

Interest Rate Stability and Anticipated Inflation

Critics who claim that the Reserve Bank is too preoccupied with interest rate stability are referring to the money interest rate, since it is the rate observed in the market. The alleged inflationary bias of such a policy seems even more likely when this fact is recognised.

For example, assume the economy is operating close to full employment, somewhere along the steeply sloped range of the *AS* curve. Now suppose there is an increase in aggregate demand (possibly due to an increase in government deficit

---

POLICY PERSPECTIVE

Why Have Real Interest Rates Been So High?

The persistently high level of real interest rates since the early 1980s has been a major concern of policy makers, the business community, and any person who borrows money. Since only nominal or money rates of interest are directly observable, it is necessary to subtract an estimate of the anticipated inflation rate from a nominal interest rate to obtain a measure of the real interest rate (recall that the nominal interest rate equals the real interest rate plus the anticipated rate of inflation). This is how the real interest rate was obtained from the nominal interest rate shown in Figure P16.1. We used the yield on ten year Treasury Bonds for the nominal interest rate and the percentage change in the consumer price index as a measure of anticipated inflation.

Two main points are worth noting about Figure P16.1. First, the real interest rate was negative from 1951 to 1953, and for most of the period between 1972 and 1978. What this means is that lenders were not even being compensated for the effect of inflation. In this situation, it would pay to borrow to the hilt — not only do borrowers get the use of the funds but when they repay back the principal and interest, they end up paying less in real terms than they had borrowed! Such periods of negative real interest rates are somewhat destabilising to the economy, causing savers to 'flee' from financial investments into assets such as real estate which at least keep up with the rate of inflation. This higher demand for real estate in turn pushes up its price, causing those who are still holding financial assets to further lose out, since if they want to invest in real estate now, they have to pay higher prices. Thus, a self-fulfilling chain reaction is set in motion which may do considerable damage to the financial system, leading investors to hedge against inflation by investing in perhaps less productive investments. That high inflation is the main cause of negative real interest rates may be seen from Figure P16.2. In 1952, during the first of the negative interest rate periods, inflation is seen to have reached 23 per cent. This was largely due to the effect of the Korean War on prices — the increased demand for commodities as a result of the war caused large increases in commodity prices and thus a 'boom' in Australia.

The second period of negative interest rates 1972–1978 is seen to coincide with the inflation bulge during this period in Figure P16.2. The inflation during this period was largely due to a wages explosion in conjunction with a tripling in the price of oil. Both these factors resulted in a persistently high inflation rate. We will have more to say about this in the next chapter. It is worth noting that negative real interest rates during this period also occurred in other countries. For example, the USA had real rates averaging around –2 per cent during this period. This observation introduces an important point in our discussion of the determinants of the interest rate. Because Australia is a relatively small, open, economy the interest rate is affected by the general level of interest rates overseas. The way this influence operates is largely a topic of the international chapter (Chapter 21). However, briefly we can say at this stage that if Australia has a lower interest rate than the rest of the world, money in Australia

FIGURE P16.1
Nominal and Real Interest Rates

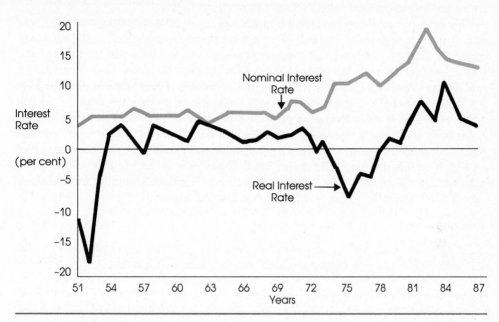

FIGURE P16.2
Inflation

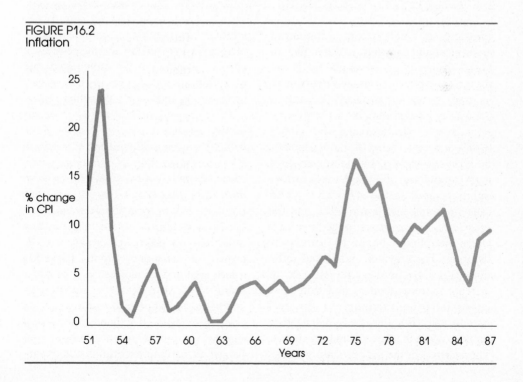

will tend to flow overseas in search of the higher real rate of return while foreign investment will be discouraged. Thus, for Australia to remain attractive it must maintain a competitive real interest rate in relation to other countries.

This leads us to the second point regarding Figure P16.1, namely the high real rate of interest from 1981 onwards. This again proved quite a shock to the economy, especially after the negative real rates experienced in the 1970s and an average real rate of around 2.5 per cent from 1954 to 1970. In contrast, from 1981 onwards, the real interest rate averaged around 6 per cent, reaching a previously unseen peak of 9.2 per cent in 1985. Such high real rates were also in evidence overseas — in the USA, real interest rates reached a peak of 8 per cent in 1981-82. This reinforces the point mentioned above that real interest rates in Australia are affected from overseas rates and hence explains, in part, why Australia was faced with unprecedented high real rates of interest since the early 1980s. Other reasons which also contribute to high real interest rates — for example, the decline in Australia's earnings from overseas due to low commodity prices — will be examined in Chapter 21.

Questions

1. In the 1980s Australia experienced a dramatic fall in Investment expenditures. From Figure P16.1, can you suggest a reason why this occurred? Explain.

2. As a result of the negative real rates of return in the 1970s, there was a huge increase in investment in residential construction. In what way is this good for the economy? In what way could this be bad for the economy? Explain.

---

spending, an increase in autonomous investment and consumption spending, or both). The resulting rise in real GDP and the price level causes money demand to increase, which in turn leads to a rise in the money interest rate. Now the Reserve Bank reacts by increasing the money supply in order to bring the money interest rate back down (say, by making an open market purchase). But this causes a further rightward shift in the *AD* curve, which causes another increase in GDP and the price level. The increases in the price level cause people to begin to anticipate inflation. The onset of anticipated inflation causes the money interest rate to increase more as lenders now add on a larger inflation premium to the real interest rate. But this leads the Reserve Bank to again increase the money supply. The increase in the money supply causes

another increase in aggregate demand, a further rise in real GDP and the price level, another increase in the anticipated rate of inflation and hence in the money interest rate, and so on for another round.

By trying to stabilise the level of the money interest rate, the Reserve Bank actually triggers self-defeating increases in the anticipated rate of inflation, which cause the money interest rate to rise even more as inflation gets worse! At some point in this process the Reserve Bank becomes alarmed at the accelerating inflation and slams the brakes on the growth of the money supply, triggering a recession and an increase in unemployment. Now the Reserve Bank feels compelled to fight the recession above all else. Once again it expands the money supply. The process repeats itself, accompanied by periodic recessions and expansions with fluctuations in the inflation rate and unemployment. The Reserve Bank's alternation between fighting inflation and unemployment has been tagged the 'stop-go policy' by critics.

Implications for Fiscal and Monetary Policy

A pattern of conflict among policy goals seems to be a major contributing factor to the inflation-unemployment process. The Reserve Bank would like to stabilise interest rates, but this goal conflicts with its desire to curb inflation. And its desire to curb inflation conflicts with its desire to avoid recession and unemployment. When the fiscal policy stance is one of almost continual budget deficits, particularly cyclically adjusted budget deficits, the inflationary bias of a monetary policy oriented toward interest rate stabilisation is accentuated by the inflationary bias of fiscal policy.

Many critics of fiscal and monetary policy make the following recommendations. (1) The Reserve Bank should worry less about interest rate stabilisation. These critics contend that this would help reduce the Reserve Bank contribution to the inflationary bias jointly shared by fiscal and monetary policy. They claim that if the Reserve Bank focused less on interest rate stabilisation, it could more effectively restrain demand-pull inflation. This in turn would go far to eliminate the periodic need to tighten the money supply in an attempt to curb an acceleration of inflation, efforts that often bring on recession and unemployment. (2) The Government must act more responsibly to curb excessive deficit spending, particularly during those times when the economy is experiencing inflationary expansion. At such times, a reduction or

elimination of the cyclically adjusted budget deficit would in turn make it easier for the Reserve Bank to control inflation without causing a recession.

CHECKPOINT 16.2

If the general price level declined over a long period of time so that people came to expect deflation, would the money interest rate be above or below the real interest rate? Why? Starting with the mid 1950s, compare the behaviour of the money interest rate shown in Figure P 16.1, with the annual percentage rate of change of the price level shown in Figure P 16.2. How might you explain the relationship between these two measures?

SUMMARY

1. Keynesians argue that fiscal policy is a more powerful economic stabilisation tool than monetary policy. Disagreeing, monetarists claim that pure fiscal policy actions have little effect on total income and employment because of offsetting crowding-out effects on private spending, particularly investment. Keynesians, on the other hand, do not believe the crowding-out effect is that significant. Monetarists argue that deficit spending stimulates the economy only to the extent it is financed by money creation.

2. It is often difficult to coordinate fiscal and monetary policy in order to achieve economic stability and reasonably full employment with a minimum amount of inflation. A major reason is that many other considerations and political pressures affect government expenditure and tax programs, and these often take priority over economic stabilisation objectives. By contrast, the monetary policymaking process is more organised, relatively more sheltered from political pressure, and, therefore, more easily and continuously focused on economic stabilisation goals.

3. A monetary policy that is preoccupied with interest rate stability tends to have an inflationary bias, particularly in the presence of government deficit spending. This bias is accentuated by the onset of anticipated inflation, which causes the money interest rate to be greater than the real interest rate. Critics of such a policy argue that the inflation-unemployment problem would be lessened if monetary policymakers worried less about interest rate stability and fiscal policymakers avoided high-employment budget deficits during periods of inflationary economic expansion.

4. The high levels of real interest rates since the early 1980s are unprecedented in the post-World War II years. It has been argued that the cause is largely due to high overseas interest rates.

KEY TERMS AND CONCEPTS

> crowding out
> inside lags
> money interest rate
> outside lags
> real interest rate

QUESTIONS AND PROBLEMS

1. It is often said that the extent of the crowding-out effect that results from a pure fiscal policy action is different when the economy is in a recession than when it is operating close to full-employment capacity. Explain why this might be so. Suppose a deficit is financed entirely by money creation. Can there still be a crowding out? Explain.

2. Suppose the economy is in a deep depression like the Great Depression of the 1930s. Suppose also that the money demand curve becomes very flat at a low level of the interest rate, and suppose that the equilibrium interest rate is at this low level. Would a pure fiscal policy action, such as a balanced budget government expenditure and tax increase, have a crowding-out effect? Under these conditions, would it make any difference whether the government resorts to a pure fiscal policy action as opposed to deficit spending financed by money creation?

3. Consider the interest rate that your local bank is currently paying on savings or time deposits. Using the currently reported rate of inflation, calculate what you think is the real rate of interest earned on such deposits. Remember that the money interest rate you earn is taxable income. Taking this into account, what do you think of the real rate of interest you earn on such deposits?

4. A number of economists claim that the Reserve Bank can push the money interest rate down in the short run. That is, they say that open market purchases have the initial effect of pushing it down but that these same purchases 'sow the seeds' leading to a later rise in the interest rate. Explain how and why this might be so.

17

The Inflation-Unemployment Trade-off: Supply-Side, Accelerationist, and New Classical Views

AFTER READING THIS CHAPTER YOU WILL BE ABLE TO:

1. Explain the concept of the Phillips curve.

2. Explain why cost-push inflation or stagflation can cause the inflation rate and the unemployment rate to increase at the same time, contrary to the Phillips curve.

3. Explain the accelerationist view of the inflation-unemployment trade-off.

4. Explain the new classical view and its implications for monetary and fiscal policy.

5. Describe how the changing nature of the labour force can affect the aggregate supply curve and worsen the inflation-unemployment trade-off.

It is conventional to associate a rising rate of inflation with a declining unemployment rate during the expansion phase of the business cycle. The behaviour of inflation and unemployment during the 1960s certainly seemed to exhibit such a relationship. Until recent years it was also conventional to expect a declining rate of inflation along with a rising unemployment rate during recessions. However during the 1970s and until the recession of 1983, inflation declined little, if at all, during periods of rising unemployment. These experiences have bled the public and sent perplexed economists scrambling for explanations.

In this chapter we will look at the recent behaviour of inflation and unemployment in Australia. We will begin by asking whether there is an inflation-unemployment trade-off, as suggested by a concept known as the Phillips curve. While there has been much controversy over the possible existence of such a curve, that debate has given rise to some interesting new explanations of inflation and unemployment that go beyond the Keynesian and monetarist analyses considered in previous chapters. We will examine these new developments in economic thinking as well as their implications for monetary and fiscal policy. We will also look at the changing nature of the unemployment problem and its implications for inflation.

IS THERE AN INFLATION-UNEMPLOYMENT TRADE-OFF?

Ever since the late 1950s, economists, policymakers, and politicians have speculated and argued about the existence of a trade-off between inflation and unemployment. Many have claimed that it is possible to reduce unemployment if we are willing to tolerate higher rates of inflation. Conversely it is often claimed that inflation can be reduced only by incurring higher rates of unemployment. The implication is that there exists a trade-off — we can have less unemployment for more inflation, or less inflation for more unemployment.

The graphical representation of this trade-off is known as the **Phillips curve,** after the British economist A. W. Phillips, who in 1958 put forward empirical evidence of such a trade-off for the British economy over the period 1862–1957. Economists have subsequently devoted considerable effort to investigating the possible existence of Phillips curve trade-offs in industrialised countries for the postwar period. The experience with inflation and unemployment during the 1960s, 1970s, and the early 1980s suggests that such a trade-off is not so simple or straightforward. Indeed, the experience of recent years has raised serious questions about whether such a trade-off even exists.

The Phillips Curve

Recall our discussion of the upward-sloping range of the aggregate supply curve in Figures 11.3 and 11.7 in Chapter 11. There we saw that increases in aggregate demand cause output and employment to increase, unemployment to fall, and the economy to move closer to full employment and beyond to full utilisation of its productive capacity. However, over this range of the AS curve increases in aggregate demand result in ever larger increases in the general price level and ever smaller increases in employment and the quantity of output, or real GDP. Similarly, the ever larger increases in the general price level are accompanied by ever smaller reductions in the unemployment rate. This description characterises the onset of demand-pull inflation as the economy approaches full employment. It suggests that we can only have a lower unemployment rate if we are willing to have a higher rate of inflation. This is the essence of the logic underlying the Phillips curve concept.

FIGURE 17.1
The Phillips Curve: The Inflation-Unemployment Trade-Off (Hypothetical Example)

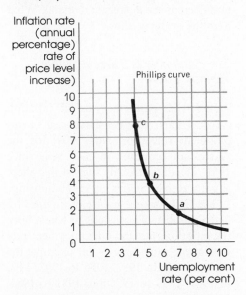

The Phillips curve is downward sloping left to right, suggesting that there is a trade-off between inflation (vertical axis) and unemployment (horizontal axis). The curve implies that the economy typically will experience both inflation and unemployment at the same time and that price stability and full employment are not compatible goals of fiscal and monetary policy. Most economists agree that increases in aggregate demand will lead to higher rates of inflation and lower unemployment rates, a movement up along the curve. However, today most would question whether this process is reversible — namely, whether the economy could move back down the *same* curve if there is a decrease in aggregate demand.

Graphical Representation of the Phillips Curve: A Menu of Choices

A hypothetical Phillips curve is shown in Figure 17.1. The annual percentage rate of increase in the price level, the rate of inflation, is measured on the vertical axis, and the unemployment rate is measured on the horizontal axis. The curve slopes downward left to right, a reflection of the fact that a lower unemployment rate can only be achieved by having a higher rate of inflation, and vice versa.

The Phillips curve represents a menu of choices for monetary and fiscal policy. For example, the hypothetical Phillips curve of Figure 17.1 suggests that if policymakers want to keep the rate of inflation at 2 per cent or less, they must be willing to settle for an unemployment rate of 7 per cent or more, as represented by point *a* on the Phillips curve. On the other hand, if policymakers are willing to tolerate a 4 per cent inflation rate, the unemployment rate can be reduced to 5 per cent, point *b* on the Phillips curve. The trade-off between inflation and unemployment, represented by the slope of the curve between points *a* and *b*, is a reduction of 2 percentage points in the unemployment rate in exchange for a 2 percentage point increase in the inflation rate. However, the trade-off worsens between points *b* and *c*. If policymakers want to reduce the unemployment rate from 5 per cent to 4 per cent, they must be willing to settle for an increase in the inflation rate from 4 per cent to 8 per cent.

The lower right-hand portion of the Phillips curve suggests that to achieve a zero rate of inflation would require an unacceptably high rate of unemployment. Conversely, the upper left-hand portion suggests that a reduction of the unemployment rate below 4 per cent would give rise to prohibitively high rates of inflation. The Phillips curve reminds us that economics is a study of choices, and that every choice has an associated cost. For example, choosing point *b* instead of point *a* means choosing a 5 per cent instead of a 7 per cent unemployment rate, a reduction in unemployment that is considered desirable. However, the cost of this choice is an additional 2 percentage points of inflation, from a rate of 2 per cent at point *a* to 4 per cent at point *b* — a move that is undesirable but necessary in order to achieve the lower unemployment rate.

It should be emphasised that the Phillips curve shown in Figure 17.1 is strictly a hypothetical example. The curve could lie to the left or right of the position shown. It might conceivably intersect the horizontal axis at a 10 per cent unemployment rate. This would suggest that if we were willing to settle for a 10 per cent unemployment rate, we could have a zero rate of inflation.

Implications of the Phillips Curve: The Reversibility Issue

One important implication of the Phillips curve is that the economy typically will experience both inflation and unemployment at the same time. In other words, price stability and full employment are not compatible goals of fiscal and monetary policy. Another implication is that the economy can move up along the Phillips curve, reducing the unemployment rate and increasing the rate of inflation. However, the Phillips curve also implies that this process is reversible — that the economy can move back down the curve, as from point *c* to point *b* to point *a*, reducing the rate of inflation and increasing the unemployment rate. This impli-

cation is far more questionable and controversial than the others. Why?

It appears to most observers of the Australian economy that the rate of inflation rises more readily than it falls. Almost all economists would agree that an increase in aggregate demand is likely to lead to an increase in the rate of inflation and a reduction in the unemployment rate, a movement up the Phillips curve. But few would argue that the economy is likely to follow the same path back down the Phillips curve in response to a decrease in aggregate demand. What does the evidence show?

The Evidence: Is There a Stable Phillips Curve?

Figure 17.2 plots the rate of inflation (vertical axis) and the associated unemployment rate (horizontal axis) for the Australian economy in each year since 1951. The data strongly suggest that there is not a stable Phillips curve relationship.

The first striking feature of Figure 17.2 is the number of occasions in which both the inflation rate and unemployment rate rose at the same time — for example the periods 1951 to 1952, 1955 to 1957, 1960 to 1961, 1973 to 1975 and 1981 to 1983. These movements are completely contrary to the alleged shape of the Phillips curve. The data in Figure 17.2 suggest that the economy has experienced an upward spiralling inflation rate associated with a cyclical unemployment rate. Furthermore, on average, the unemployment rate seems to have increased during the 1970s and early 1980s.

Rather than following an inflation-unemployment tradeoff, Figure 17.2 suggests that the economy tends to follow irregular cyclical loops as far as the inflation and unemployment rates are concerned. For example, the first loop appears from 1951 to 1956. A second, clearer loop occurs from 1960 to 1964. This is followed by a tighter loop from 1965 to 1970. From 1971 to 1980 there is a much wider loop. Again, another loop occurs from 1981 to 1987. Note that these loops seem to have shifted further and further to the right, giving rise to higher average levels of inflation and unemployment. Much of the rest of this chapter is concerned with possible explanations for the phenomena shown in Figure 17.2.

Supply-Side Shocks and Stagflation

The concept of the Phillips curve really derives from the notion that increases in aggregate demand tend to increase inflation and reduce unemployment, while decreases in aggregate demand tend to

FIGURE 17.2
The Relationship Between Inflation and Unemployment

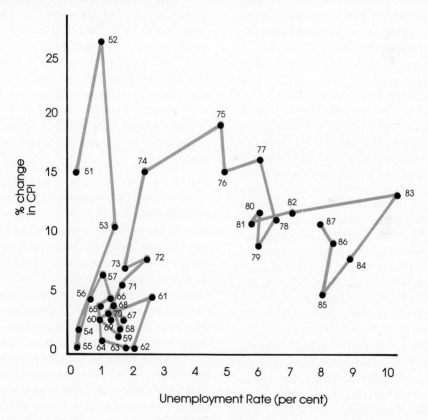

The relationship between the inflation rate (vertical axis) and the unemployment rate (horizontal axis) in the Australian economy suggests that the Phillips curve is not stable. Periods of increasing rates of inflation are accompanied by higher unemployment rates – as for example the periods 1951 to 1952, 1955 to 1957, 1960 to 1961, 1973 to 1975, and 1981 to 1983. The data suggests that the economy has experienced an upward spiralling inflation rate associated with a cyclical unemployment rate.

reduce inflation and increase unemployment. However, during the 1970s the Australian economy suffered a number of severe shocks on the supply side — large increases in the price of oil and other fuels, intermittent worldwide food and raw materials shortages as well as a wages explosion in 1973 and 1974. With both food prices and overall inflation rising rapidly in 1973, a series of wage agreements were struck which left inflation far behind and culminated in average weekly wages rising by 28 per cent in 1974. These shocks have led economists to focus more attention on the role of aggregate supply and its interaction with aggregate demand as an explanatory factor underlying the behaviour of inflation and unemployment.

Recall our discussion in Chapter 11 of cost-push inflation and the way it might be represented in terms of the aggregate supply curve, as illustrated in Figure 11.8. (You may want to reread that discussion at this point.) There we noted that a cost-push inflation could occur in a number of ways. It might come about because powerful unions force firms to pay higher wages by threatening to strike. These firms then pass on the resulting rise in per unit costs, at least in part, in the form of higher product prices. Cost-push inflation may also result because a few large firms in key industries exercise their market power to raise profits by increasing the prices they charge for their products. Another source of cost-push inflation, which was common during the 1970s, is increases in the prices of vital resources, such as energy and imported materials. Again, such increases cause increases in per unit production costs that push up the prices of almost all goods and services, as reflected by a rise in the general price level. In Figure 11.8 we saw how cost-push inflation is represented by an upward shift

of the aggregate supply curve. For example, the aggregate supply curve AS_0 in Figure 11.8, shifted upward to AS_1.

Given a cost-push, the economy can experience an increase in both the rate of inflation and the unemployment rate at the same time — the phenomenon termed stagflation, discussed previously in Chapter 11 and illustrated in Figure 11.8. Note that this is contrary to the conventional Phillips curve trade-off. Note also, however, that it does provide a possible explanation for the simultaneous increases in the rate of inflation and the unemployment rate incurred from 1951 to 1952, from 1955 to 1957, from 1960 to 1961 and certainly for the periods 1973 to 1975, and from 1981 to 1983, as shown in Figure 17.2. The 1973 to 1975 and 1981 to 1983 episodes in particular were clearly the consequence of supply shocks, resulting in each instance from dramatic increases in the price of oil and an explosion in wages.

CHECKPOINT * 17.1

Suppose the Phillips curve in Figure 17.1 shifts in such a way that unemployment can be reduced with a smaller increase in the rate of inflation. Sketch how the new Phillips curve might look. Suppose the Phillips curve in Figure 17.1 shifts so that the economy can have a zero per cent rate of inflation when it has a 9 per cent unemployment rate, and yet require larger increases in the inflation rate for each percentage point of reduction in the unemployment rate. Sketch how such a Phillips curve might look. If the Phillips curve represents a menu of choices, is the policymaker's selection of a point on the curve a normative or a positive issue? Why?

---

*Answers to all Checkpoints can be found at the back of the text.

FIGURE 17.3
The Accelerationist View

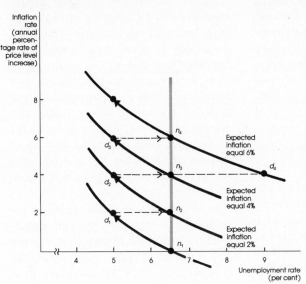

The accelerationist view holds that in the long run the economy tends to operate at its natural rate of unemployment, here hypothetically assumed to be 6.5 per cent. An increase in aggregate demand increases profit and hence output and employment in the short run, thereby temporarily reducing the unemployment rate below the natural rate while increasing the inflation rate (n_1 to d_1). However workers, recognising the decline in their real wages, then demand higher money wages which reduce profits causing production to fall and unemployment to return to its natural rate (d_1 to n_2). Repetition of this process causes the inflation rate to accelerate and the short-run Phillips curve to shift upward. Hence there is no stable long-run Phillips curve trade-off.

ACCELERATIONIST AND NEW CLASSICAL VIEWS

While the simultaneous increase in the inflation and unemployment rates of 1973–1975 and 1981–1983 were caused by supply-side shocks, the factors underlying the inflation-unemployment rate pattern for other years shown in Figure 17.2 are less clear. Only the years 1962–1965 and 1975–1979 bear a resemblance to the hypothetical Phillips curve of Figure 17.1, and even these years suggest that the Phillips curve has shifted over time.

Attempts to explain the data of Figure 17.2 have contributed to the development of the accelerationist view of the inflation-unemployment trade-off. This view essentially holds that the Phillips curve shifts upward as workers increase their expected rate of inflation. Milton Friedman, in his Nobel prize address, has added to this view

the notion that increasing variability of the inflation rate increases the average level of the unemployment rate. Finally, probably the most controversial and dramatic development in macroeconomic thinking in recent years has been the emergence of the new classical view which is based on the theory of rational expectations. The new classical view concludes that *systematic* monetary and fiscal policy is essentially unable to affect unemployment and the level of total output in the economy! We will consider each of these views in turn.

The Accelerationist View and the Natural Rate

The **accelerationist view** contends that in the long run a downward-sloping Phillips curve (such as that in Figure 17.1) does not exist. Instead it is argued that in the long run the economy tends to operate at its **natural rate of unemployment,** described earlier in Chapter 6. Basically *the accelerationist view holds that expansionary monetary and fiscal policies aimed at reducing the unemployment rate below the natural rate will result in an ever increasing, or accelerating, rate of inflation.* Let's see why.

Adjustment to the Natural Rate: The Short-Run Trade-Off

Assume, for example, that the natural rate of unemployment is 6.5 per cent, corresponding to point n_1 in Figure 17.3. However suppose policymakers and politicians think that a 6.5 per cent unemployment rate is too high — that disgruntled voters will turn on them if something isn't done to reduce it. Consequently expansionary monetary and fiscal policies are initiated thereby increasing aggregate demand which in turn pulls up the price level. *Given the level of money wages,* firms will realise increased profits and therefore expand output and hire more labour. As a result, in the short run the economy moves from point n_1 to point d_1 in Figure 17.3. The unemployment rate has been reduced to 5 per cent but the inflation rate has risen from zero per cent to 2 per cent. Thus there is a Phillips curve type trade-off, at least in the short run, according to the accelerationist view.

However the position d_1 cannot be maintained in the longer run. Why? Because while the general price level of final goods and services has risen, the money wages of workers have remained unchanged.[1]

This means that a worker's real wage, which equals the money wage divided by the general price level, has fallen. A worker gets paid the same number of dollars but these dollars buy less. Correctly perceiving themselves as worse off, the labour force demands and receives a higher money wage in order to 'catch up' with the rise in the general price level. However when the money wage has risen to restore the real wage level that initially existed at n_1, firms' profits will be reduced back to their initial level. Firms therefore reduce output back to its initial level. Hence the unemployment rate returns again to the natural rate level of 6.5 per cent. Now however the inflation rate is 2 per cent, so that the economy is at point n_2 in Figure 17.3.

Note that at the initial point n_1 the inflation rate was zero per cent and so workers had come to *expect* a zero per cent rate of inflation. Only *after* the economy has made the short-run move to point d_1 do workers become aware that their expectation of a zero rate of inflation is no longer valid, that the inflation rate is in fact 2 per cent. Along with the catch-up increase in their money wage which moves the economy to point n_2 workers revise their expected rate of inflation upwards to 2 per cent. Hence according to the accelerationist view there is a short-run Phillips curve passing through points n_1 and d_1 that is stable as long as workers expect a zero rate of inflation. When they revise their expected inflation rate upwards to 2 per cent, the short-run Phillips curve shifts upwards until it passes through point n_2.

[1] When total demand increases, businesses are the first to become aware of it. They notice that goods are moving off shelves faster, that inventories are becoming more rapidly depleted, and that there is an increase in their backlogs of unfilled orders. Only *after* firms have increased prices do workers in general begin to become aware of the price increases — for example, during the course of shopping around for various goods and services.

We can modify the accelerationist view to account for Friedman's view of the natural rate as shown in Figure 17.4. The line through u_1, u_2, u_3, and u_4 representing the long-run relationship between the inflation rate and the natural rate of unemployment is now positively sloped — the natural rate is larger the higher the inflation rate. For example (using hypothetical data), when the inflation rate is zero per cent the natural rate of unemployment is 6.5 per cent (point u_1), for a 2 per cent inflation rate the natural rate is 6.8 per cent (point u_2), and for a 4 per cent inflation rate it is 7.1 per cent (point u_3). Instead of the adjustment path (Figure 17.3) n_1 to d_1 to n_2 to d_2, and so forth, the adjustment path (Figure 17.4) is now u_1 to b_1 to u_2 to b_2, and so on.

In sum, *combining the accelerationist view with Friedman's view of the natural rate it follows that persistent attempts by policymakers to stimulate aggregate demand to reduce the unemployment rate below the natural rate will cause an ever increasing rate of inflation as well as an increasing natural rate of unemployment.*

The Evidence. The data points in Figure 17.2 do suggest that the variability of the inflation rate has increased over time. That is, the magnitude of the up and down movements in the inflation rate (measured on the vertical axis) appears to have increased during the 1970s and early 1980s. Also, it appears that the level of the inflation rate has on-average increased along with the rise in inflation variability, as Friedman has observed. And along with these increases the average level of the unemployment rate seems to have increased as well, consistent with Friedman's view that there exists a long-run relationship wherein the natural rate of unemployment tends to increase with the level of the inflation rate.

How well does the accelerationist view combined with Friedman's view of the natural rate conform to the evidence in the data? A suggestive interpretation comparing the facts of Figure 17.2 with the theory as represented in Figure 17.4 is shown in Figure 17.5. Examining Figure 17.5 one should remember that, like beauty, the degree of apparent conformity

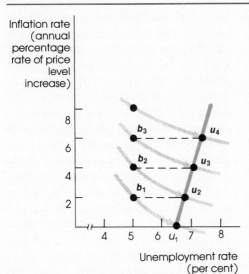

Inflation rate (annual percentage rate of price level increase)

Unemployment rate (per cent)

FIGURE 17.4
Accelerationist View When Natural Rate Rises With Inflation Rate

According to Milton Friedman's view of the natural rate, increased variability of the inflation rate reduces the efficiency with which market prices guide economic activity, thereby reducing the economy's natural rate of output and hence increasing its natural rate of unemployment. Since greater inflation rate *variability* appears to be associated with higher *levels* of the inflation rate, the natural rate of unemployment tends to rise with the level of the inflation rate, as indicated by the points u_1, u_2, u_3, u_4. Combining this view of the natural rate with the accelerationist view of the short-run Phillips curve, the implication is that persistent policy attempts to reduce unemployment below the natural rate will cause ever increasing inflation along with a rising natural rate of unemployment (u_1 to b_1 to u_2 to b_2 and so forth).

between fact and theory is all in the eye of the beholder.

The New Classical View

According to the accelerationist view policymakers can keep the unemployment rate below the natural rate, though the benefits to society of a higher level of employment can be achieved only at the cost of an ever increasing rate of inflation. By contrast, *the **new classical view** argues that policymaker attempts to reduce the unemployment rate below the natural rate cannot succeed and, worse yet, they still impose the costs of an ever increasing inflation rate on society.* In brief, while the accelerationist view offers the prospect of a trade-off between the benefit of lower unemployment and the cost of ever increasing inflation, the new classical view argues there will be only the cost and no benefit. The linchpin of the new classical view is the theory of rational expectations.

Rational Expectations

*The **theory of rational expectations** holds that people form their expectations about the future course of economic activity (wages, prices, employment, and so forth) on the basis of their knowledge, experience, and understanding of how the economy works, including the effects of monetary and fiscal policy. Furthermore they make use of all relevant, available economic data and information when they form their expectations.* The theory of rational expectations implies that people do not persist in making the same mistakes (that is, systematic mistakes) over and over when predicting future events. Rather, they become aware of their systematic errors and alter their behaviour to eliminate them. In short, the theory of

rational expectations asserts that people go about forming their expectations in a reasonable, or rational, way.

The Policy Ineffectiveness Argument

Consider now how the theory of rational expectations would change the accelerationist scenario described in Figure 17.3. Recall that there an increase in aggregate demand, caused by an increase in the money supply, say, led to an increase in the price level. Given the *unchanged* level of many wages in the short run, profits rose, stimulating output and employment and thereby reducing the unemployment rate below the natural rate (n_1 to d_1). In the long run workers realised that the price level had risen, hence that their real wages had fallen, and demanded and received money wage increases that restored real wages to their initial level. Thus profits fell to their initial level and unemployment rose back to the natural rate (d_1 to n_2). The process could be repeated over and over again.

Note that in this scenario it was the fact that workers' *expectation* of the inflation rate was lower than the actual inflation rate during each expansion phase (n_1 to d_1, n_2 to d_2 and so forth) which made the short-run unemployment rate reduction possible. Workers incorrectly perceived that their real wage was higher because while they were immediately aware of the increase in their money wage, they were not immediately aware of the *actual* rate of increase in the price level. For example, along the short-run Phillips curve n_1 to d_1 (Figure 17.3) workers expected a zero rate of inflation, but in fact the price level rose at a 2 per cent rate. Along the short-run Phillips curve from n_2 to d_2 they expected a 2 per cent rate of inflation, but the price level actually rose at a 4 per cent rate.

According to rational expectations theory workers will not keep making this same (systematic) mistake over and over. They will know the way the system works and form their expectations on the basis of that knowledge. In particular, they will know that the inflation rate increases whenever the monetary authority expands the money supply in an attempt to reduce the unemployment rate below the natural rate. They will immediately expect the higher inflation rate and immediately realise that they must push up their money wage simply to maintain the level of their real wage. Hence firms' profits will not increase in response to the increase in aggregate demand because the increase in

the price level will be offset immediately by increases in money wages. Consequently there will be no reduction in the unemployment rate below the natural rate. Monetary policy attempts to lower the unemployment rate will only succeed in causing an ever increasing rate of inflation. The economy will move directly from n_1 to n_2 to n_3, and so on, in Figure 17.3. There is not even a short-run Phillips curve trade-off. Hence, *according to the new classical view, systematic policymaker attempts to affect real variables in the economy, such as total output (real GDP) and the unemployment rate, will be ineffective. Thus the new classical view implies that systematic monetary and fiscal policy efforts to smooth out the*

FIGURE 17.5
Combined Accelerationist-Friedman Natural Rate Views: Theory Versus Facts

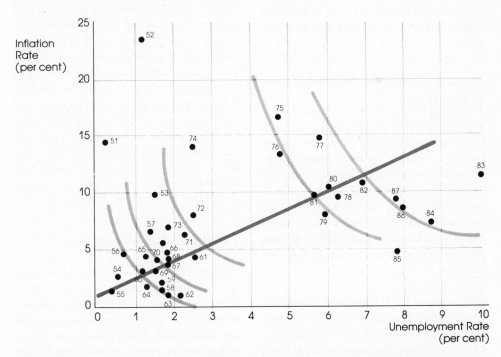

Combining the data of Figure 17.2 with the theory represented in Figure 17.4 suggests that there may be a 'rough' correspondence between theory and fact. There is obviously considerable room for interpretation and disagreement on this issue however.

business cycle will be ineffective.

Note that the new classical view emphasises that it is *systematic* policy efforts that have no effect on real variables. Systematic policy actions are those that are predictable because, according to rational expectations theory, people understand both how the economy works (from experience) and how government policymakers react to the economy's performance — for example, by slowing money supply growth during business cycle expansions and increasing it during recessions. The only kind of policy actions that will affect real variables are those that are unpredictable. They come as 'surprises' — they are random events. But as the new classical view points out, monetary and fiscal actions that are random must be totally unrelated to the economy's performance except by chance. Such actions can hardly be said to constitute a meaningful policy.

Reasons Why Policy Is Still Effective

The new classical view's conclusion that systematic monetary and fiscal policy will not affect the economy's real variables is certainly contrary to what most economists and policymakers believe. Even the most ardent supporters of the new classical view would likely agree that there are considerations that suggest why systematic monetary and fiscal policy actions are still able to affect the economy's real variables.

Learning and Lags. The theory of rational expectations (the backbone of the new classical view) assumes that people form expectations on the basis of what they have learned about the economy through experience and information gathering. If we envision a world where there is no change in technology, institutions, laws, customs, and tastes, then it would seem that one could become fairly well informed about how the economy works. In the real world all of these things are subject to ongoing change in varying degrees. Therefore learning about 'how the system works' is more difficult. Learning about change is subject to time lags, and new knowledge is already in the process of becoming obsolete.

Policymakers and politicians come and go so that predicting policymaker behaviour and knowing policymaker objectives (what they will do versus what they say they will do) is not easy. Just as history shows that no two business cycles are ever exactly alike, policymaker response to such cycles (the mix of monetary and fiscal action, its magnitude, duration, and timing) is also bound to differ from one cycle to the next. To this extent there is always a certain amount of unpredictability and surprise in any 'systematic' policy action. Returning to Figure 17.3, for example, workers must be able to perfectly predict the amount of monetary expansion and its effect on the price level. Having done so, they must then increase their money wages in unison with the price level if firms are not to experience any increase in profits which would cause them to increase employment and output.

Flexibility of Prices and Wages

The new classical view's policy ineffectiveness argument implicitly assumes prices and money wages are perfectly flexible. Indeed it is as if there is an invisible auctioneer who raises prices and wages in the face of excess demand and lowers prices and wages in the face of excess supply. However, in the real world such an auctioneer is not only invisible but also

---

POLICY PERSPECTIVE

Restrictionists and Expansionists

In Australia, the debate between Monetarists and Keynesians often manifests itself in terms of two distinct policy prescriptions — restrictionist policies versus expansionist policies.

Restrictionists

Restrictionists are, broadly speaking, monetarists whose top priority is controlling inflation. Lately, this camp has also been emphasising the balance of payments crises. As the name suggests, restrictionists see the solution of these two major problems in terms of restricting the rate of growth of the economy. In the case of inflation, for example, they feel that excess demand is one of the main contributing factors which needs to be controlled. They normally advocate lower government spending, lower budget deficits and a tighter monetary policy with the aim of putting a dampener on excess demand. Even though the economy has not been close to full employment since the early 1970s, they feel that excess demand is a problem. Restrictionists point to the structure of Australia's highly unionised labour market with its history of centralised wage fixing as the main culprit in adopting such a pessimistic policy of continuously dampening excess demand. They basically believe that unions have too much monopoly power so that at the slightest whiff of an economic upturn, an inflationary spiral will be set in motion, with wage rises followed by price increases and validated or financed by a loose monetary policy. Restrictionists suggest that the labour market needs to be deregulated and made more competitive so that wages can more accurately reflect the productivity of labour and the profitability of business. However, so long as the labour market remains in its present highly inflexible form with excessive union power, any economic recovery will be aborted before it starts.

This view has been reinforced by Australia's recent balance of payments problems. Restrictionists fear that our inflexible labour market won't allow a cut in living standards that is required as a result of Australia's lower export earnings. Furthermore, any economic recovery may well worsen the situation by encouraging more imports and thus aggravating our balance of payments problems (we will take a closer look at how this works and at Australia's balance of payments problems in Chapter 33). Thus, again the policy prescription is to dampen the economy so as to avoid a balance of payments crisis.

Growth in GDP

Before examining the expansionist position let us look briefly at Australia's recent growth performance shown in Figure P17.1. The period between mid-1974 and mid-1983 is widely regarded as a period of dismal economic performance, punctuated by brief, unfulfilled periods of recovery. During this period, unemployment climbed from 2.4 per cent to almost 10 per cent, despite the fact that output grew at an annual average rate of growth of 2.3 per cent. The Indecs Economic Special Report[1] estimates that Australia needs about 3.25 to 3.75 per cent annual growth of real GDP to keep unemployment from rising. This growth rate in output is required not only because the labour force is growing from year to year, but also because technological change is displacing a certain number of workers. Thus, for Australia to stabilise its unemployment rate, output should grow between 3.25 and 3.75 per cent — anything less causes the unemployment rate to worsen. No wonder then that unemployment went up so drastically between 1974 and 1983. The economy was growing too slowly to absorb the growth of the labour force and absorb the displaced workers. By contrast between mid-1983 and mid-1987 output grew by an average of 4.3 per cent, thereby allowing unemployment to fall from a peak of almost 10 per cent to around 7.8 per cent. Note, however, that in 1987 output growth declined once more to around the 2 per cent mark (probably as a result of Australia's lower export earnings due to lower commodity prices). If this lower growth rate is maintained it could herald once more some increase in unemployment, with the major difference from 1974 being that the unemployment rate would start to rise from a much higher base (7.8 per cent as compared to 2.4 per cent in 1974 — see Figure P17.2).

Both restrictionists and expansionists use Figure P17.1 to support their respective positions. On the one hand restrictionists point out that the period 1974 to 1983 was

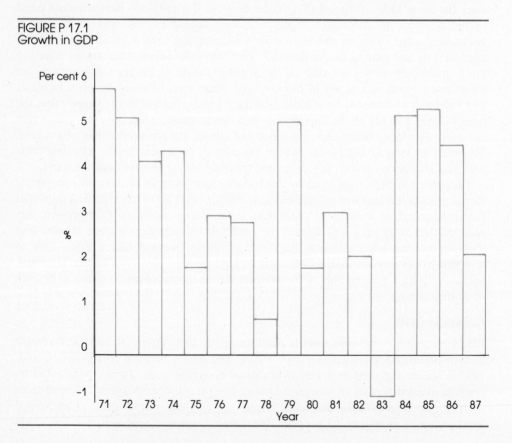

FIGURE P 17.1
Growth in GDP

one of the worst inflationary periods in Australia's history (see Figure P17.2) despite the fact that the unemployment rate was rising. In other words, if inflation got so bad despite the increase in the unemployment rate, how much worse would inflation have been if output was growing more strongly. This is the main source of their pessimism and their policy prescription to keep the growth of output restrained.

FIGURE P17.2
Unemployment

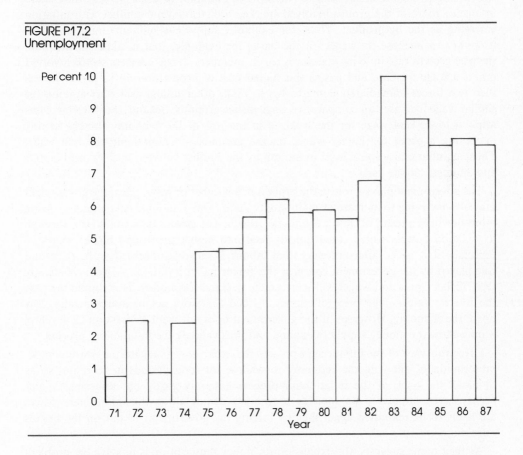

The expansionists (broadly speaking, Keynesians), on the other hand see the period 1974 to 1983 as a failed monetarist experiment since during most of that period restrictionist policies were in force. They see the increase in the unemployment rate as a huge waste which could be avoided with alternative macroeconomic policies. Indeed they point out that the period 1984 to 1987 — a period when expansionists' policy was in operation — saw one of the longest growth spurts for the Australian economy since the early 1970s.

The Expansionists

The major departing point of expansionists concerns what they believe is the main driving mechanism behind the inflationary process. For them, inflation is the result of a conflict over the distribution of the national cake or GDP between principally business and labour, and to a lesser extent, government. So long as GDP had been growing strongly in the 1960s and early 1970s, the problem tended to be solved by having the shares of all three main groups growing strongly. However, as soon as an economic slow-down occurred in the mid-1970s, none of the three major groups was willing to take a smaller share. Attempts to maintain or even increase their share by one or more of the groups involved sparked a distributional conflict with inflation emerging as the by-product. Thus, for example, suppose a militant union exercises its power to increase its wages on the basis, for example, that it wants to maintain the past growth rate in living standards for its members. If the business sector involved grants a wage increase and passes this higher cost of production on to higher prices, then two forces immediately come to work. First, other unions will start arguing for similar wage increases on comparative wage justice grounds. Second, the price increases imply a lower real wage for the workers in the rest of the economy thereby setting in motion a claim for higher wages on the grounds of maintaining the real wage. Thus, an inflationary spiral is set in motion by the conflict between business and labour and amongst labour itself.

The government plays a role in the process in a number of ways. First, the government may also be trying to increase or maintain its share from a national cake that is growing more slowly as a result of slower economic growth. The government can do this through its taxation powers which could quickly feed into higher prices and higher wages — especially if it is the after-tax wage that labour is mostly concerned with. A second role played by the government concerns the 'financing' of inflation. As we have already seen, higher prices and wages will increase the demand for money. This should increase the interest rate — the price of money — and therefore act to automatically slow down the economy. However, if the government does not want a recession to develop, it may allow the money supply to expand and thus validate the inflationary process.

Given this view of the inflationary process the expansionists regard the restrictionists' prescription of allowing the economy to wallow for long periods in recession so as to break the back of the inflationary process not only costly but unnecessary and perhaps even impotent. As soon as a recovery comes along the inflationary forces are likely to be rekindled again thereby forcing the government to put on the brakes once more.

As their name suggests, the expansionists' policy prescription is to solve the problem by encouraging output to expand faster so as to diffuse the distributional conflict. Furthermore, to prevent the re-emergence of the distributional conflict as soon as output starts to grow faster, expansionists propose the use of an incomes policy, such as the Prices and Incomes Accord of 1983 between the ACTU and the government which established full wage indexation for consumer prices. The purpose of the agreement was largely twofold; first to control the overall rate of increase of wages, and second, to prevent any leapfrogging amongst labour groups themselves.

It was perhaps inevitable that the Hawke Government should embrace an incomes policy given the apparent lack of success of the fight inflation first policy of the Fraser Government. We will take a closer look at the topic of incomes policy in the next chapter. However, it is relevant to note at this stage the two main objections of the restrictionists to the Hawke Government's approach. First, they point out that the kind of wage indexation system adopted in Australia tends to perpetuate whatever the starting rate of inflation happens to be. Second, one of the main problems that restrictionists see is the structure of Australia's labour market, in particular at not providing any flexibility for wages to adjust according to profitability in the various sectors. Restrictionists see the kind of deal that the Hawke Government has worked out with the unions as perpetuating such inflexibility of the labour market, rather than trying to change it. Mindful of its critics, the Hawke Government has gone some way to meet their criticisms by trying to tie wage increases to productivity increases rather than to just increases in prices. This so called two-tier wages system will also be discussed in the next chapter.

Questions

1. How would an expansionist respond to the abovementioned criticism by the restrictionists regarding the tendency for the wage indexation system to perpetuate whatever the starting rates of inflation happen to be?

2. Explain why the policies of the expansionists are, broadly speaking, Keynesian?

3. Apart from emphasising the costs of inflation first, identify the other major common beliefs between the restrictionists and monetarists.

[1] *State of Play 4,* Indecs Economics Special Report, Chapter 4

FURTHER READING
Indecs, *State of Play 4 – An Indecs Economic Special Report,* Allen & Unwin, 1986, pp. 7-24.

non-existent in most markets. It is the actual participant who must evaluate not only current market conditions but also predicts and discounts the future effects of government policy. Obviously, this is not an easy task and could involve considerable losses if the participants err in changing prices or wages. Because of this problem, firms and labour react slowly to a disequilibrium situation. For example, instead of cutting prices in the face of a deficient demand, firms tend to be quantity adjusters in the short-run — cutting output and hence creating unemployment. Similarly, in the face of excess demand, firms may proceed cautiously in raising prices. Not only are there costs in increasing prices immediately such as, for

example, losing customer goodwill, remarking costs and losing out to competitors who do not increase prices at the same time, but also most firms use their inventories as a buffer and utilise FIFO (first-in, first-out) accounting procedures, leading them to price according to the cost of producing old rather than new inventory. In the case of wages, the recent Australian experience under centralised wage fixing has tended to dampen wide wage movement. In fact, not only have wages tended to respond with a considerable lag to prices, but the Hawke Government has even managed to trade-off lower wage increases for lower taxation.

All the above arguments cast doubts

on the relevance in the real world of the assumption of perfect flexibility in prices and wages on which the new classical results on policy ineffectiveness crucially depend.

Conflicting evidence

Experience has also dealt a damaging blow to the new classical position. One implication of rational expectations is that if an economy wants to reduce its high inflation rate, then all it needs is for the government to adopt restrictive policies, especially limiting the growth of the money supply. The economy will then immediately lower its expected rate of inflation, moving down the long run Phillips curve, for example from n_3 to n_2 or n_1 in Figure 17.3. Thus because of rational expectations, the economy will not have to suffer higher unemployment than the natural rate and can move quickly and painlessly to lower levels of inflation.

Unfortunately, the experience of most countries during the application of restrictive policies in the late 1970s and early 1980s has involved a considerable increase in unemployment. In Australia, for example, a fight inflation first strategy was adopted by the newly elected Fraser Government in 1975. During the following years of restrictive policy, unemployment jumped up from 4.6 per cent in 1975 to 9.9 per cent in 1983. (See Figure P17.2). Thus either the participants involved were slow learners or else they did not believe the government would really pursue restrictive policies and hence discounted them. In any case, the evidence so far both in Australia and overseas is not supportive of the new classical views. It is interesting to note that Milton Friedman has also not supported the new classical position, even though one may interpret this

position to be a logical extension of his theories.

CHECKPOINT 17.2
Explain why it is, or is not, reasonable to believe that short-run Phillips curves are shaped such as those in Figure 17.4 for example.

INFLATION AND THE CHANGING NATURE OF EMPLOYMENT

What level of the unemployment rate corresponds to 'full employment'? This is the level that is regarded as the acceptable, or the normal or natural, unemployment rate. Recall our discussion of this question in Chapter 6. (You may want to reread that discussion.) There we observed that many economists believe that since the mid-1960s there has been a definite rise in the *level* of the unemployment rate that corresponds to the natural unemployment rate. What are the implications of this rise for efforts by policymakers to deal with the problems of inflation and unemployment?

Aggregate Supply and Inflation: Policy Implications

The changing nature of unemployment has implications for the aggregate supply curve and the relationship between inflation and unemployment. These implications are illustrated in the hypothetical example of Figure 17.6. The aggregate supply curve corresponding to the situation *before* the change in the nature of unemployment just described is AS_1, and AS_2 is the aggregate supply curve *after* these changes.

Assume that these changes make no difference in the economy's ability to produce any real GDP up to y_a, corresponding to point a on the aggregate supply curves. However, beyond point a AS_2 lies above AS_1. This reflects the fact that along AS_2 beyond point a, as compared to AS_1, it is harder for the economy's producers to obtain and efficiently use the additional labour needed to increase output because the 'all other' portion of the labour force described above is much larger for AS_2 than for AS_1. (Remember that money

wages and other input prices are fixed for any movement along an AS curve — AS_2 doesn't rise more rapidly than AS_1 because of any change in money wages or input prices.) Hence for increases in real GDP beyond y_a *per unit production costs rise more rapidly along AS_2* because of production inefficiencies associated with using labour that is less well trained and less committed to continuous employment. This, in turn, causes a more rapid rise in the prices firms charge for their products. Therefore, for any given increase in real GDP beyond point a, the economy's price level rises more along AS_2 than along AS_1.

Implications for Fiscal and Monetary Policy

Consider the implications of this for fiscal and monetary policy. Assume the economy's AD curve is initially at AD_0 in Figure 17.6, so that real GDP is y_a and the price level is p_0. Suppose policymakers want to reduce unemployment by stimulating aggregate demand enough to increase real GDP to y_0 where the associated unemployment rate is 6 per cent. This is done by either increasing the money supply or government expenditures, reducing taxes, or some combination of these.

If the aggregate supply curve is AS_1 the price level doesn't begin to rise until the economy reaches point b on the aggregate supply curve. The policymakers' goal is achieved once the AD curve has been shifted to AD_1 where it intersects AS_1 at point c on AS_1. The economy's price level rises from p_0 to p_1. By comparison, suppose instead the economy's AS curve is AS_2, reflecting the changes in the nature of the labour force described above. Now in order for policymakers to achieve their

---

FIGURE 17.6
The Changing Nature of the Labour Force Affects the Aggregate Supply Curve

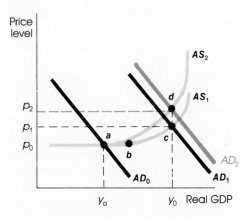

The changing nature of the labour force has caused price level increases to be larger when the economy approaches full employment.

Such change causes the aggregate supply curve to change shape from AS_1 to AS_2. As a result, if monetary or fiscal policy attempts to reduce unemployment by increasing real GDP from y_a to y_0, for example, the AD curve must be shifted rightward from AD_0 to AD_2 along AS_2, a larger amount than the shift to AD_1 required along AS_1. Consequently the increase in the price level from p_0 to p_2 along AS_1 is greater than that from p_0 to p_1 along AS_1. Thus the changing nature of the labour force tends to worsen the short-run inflation-unemployment trade-off along the Phillips curves in Figures 17.6 and 17.4.

goal the AD curve must be shifted further to the right to the position AD_2. The economy's price level rises more, from p_0 to p_2 corresponding to point d on AS_2.

Summary of Implications of the Changing Nature of Unemployment

In sum, as a result of the changing nature of the labour force, the economy has to incur a larger rise in the price level in order to reduce the unemployment rate. Policymakers' attempts to reduce the official unemployment rate to levels considered natural or 'acceptable' in the past now seem to generate higher rates of inflation. This is why policymakers and economists over the past 2 decades have tended to move the 'full-employment' benchmark for the official unemployment rate upward from around 1 to 2 per cent, to 5 to 6 per cent. It is argued that this helps avoid excessively expansionary fiscal and monetary policy. Taking account of the effect on the aggregate supply curve of the changing nature of the labour force only worsens the short-run inflation-unemployment trade-off along the Phillips curves shown in Figures 17.3 and 17.4.

CHECKPOINT 17.3
Look at the data in Figure 17.2 again. Do you see any pattern in these data that might, at least in part, be attributable to the changing nature of the labour force?

SUMMARY

1. Economists have speculated that there is a trade-off between inflation and unemployment. The trade-off may be represented by the Phillips curve, which indicates that lowering the unemployment rate means accepting more inflation, and that reducing inflation means accepting more unemployment. However, evidence suggests that movements up the Phillips curve (increasing inflation and reducing unemployment) cannot be followed by movements back down the same curve (reducing inflation while increasing unemployment). Data show that the economy has experienced an upward-spiralling inflation rate associated with a cyclical unemployment rate.

2. Increases in the price of inputs to production that are initiated on the supply side of the economy raise production costs and give rise to cost-push inflation. This is represented by an upward shift of the aggregate supply curve. Given the position of the AD curve, the price level rises, output declines, and the rate of unemployment increases. Such a process underlies stagflation wherein the economy experiences an increase in both the inflation and unemployment rates at the same time.

3. The accelerationist view of the possibility of an inflation-unemployment trade-off holds that in the long run a downward sloping Phillips curve does not exist. In the short run the accelerationist view argues that there is a trade-off. However, in the long run policymaker actions that move the economy up along short-run Phillips curve will cause the curve to shift upward as workers increase their expectation of the rate of inflation to match the actual rise in the inflation rate. Therefore expansionary monetary and fiscal policies intended to reduce the unemployment rate below the natural rate will cause an ever increasing, or accelerating, rate of inflation. Milton Friedman has argued that the natural rate itself is not fixed, but rather tends to increase with the level of the inflation rate.

4. In Australia the debate between Keynesians and Monetarists is often couched in terms of expansionist policies and restrictionist policies. Restrictionists are, broadly speaking, monetarists who put top priority on fighting inflation first. Their policy prescription is to restrain growth so as to dampen excessive wage demands and reduce the demand for imports, thereby alleviating Australia's balance of payments problems. Expansionists, who are, broadly speaking, Keynesians, see the cause of inflation as due to a conflict regarding the distribution of the national cake in association with lower economic growth. Their policy prescription is to encourage economic growth in association with an incomes policy.

5. The new classical view is based on the theory of rational expectations which holds that people form their expectations about the future course of economic activity on the basis of all relevant economic knowledge, experience, and data, and in such a way that they do not make repeated, or systematic, mistakes. Because of rational expectations, the new classical view holds that there is not even a short-run trade-off between inflation and unemployment, and that policymakers' attempts to reduce the unemployment rate, below the natural rate will *only* cause an ever increasing rate of inflation.

6. In general, the new classical view argues that monetary and fiscal policy are ineffective influences on real variables in the economy, such as output and the unemployment rate. However critics of this view point out that lags in learning about a changing economy and 'how the system' works, coupled with the fact that policymakers are never perfectly predic-

table or systematic, make it highly unlikely that firms and workers can anticipate policy actions so well as to render them ineffective. Furthermore, the empirical evidence both in Australia and overseas is not supportive of the new classical views.

7. Many economists argue that due to the changing composition of the labour force such as the increased participation rate of women, the natural rate of unemployment has been increased. This has caused the aggregate supply curve to rise more sharply as real GDP is increased. Consequently, policymakers' attempts to reduce the official unemployment rate to levels considered 'acceptable' in the past now cause sharper rises in the general price level, or more inflation. Therefore, a number of economists and policymakers advise that the 'full-employment' benchmark of the official unemployment rate should be moved upward in order to avoid excessively inflationary fiscal and monetary policy. The changing nature of the labour force worsens the short-run inflation-unemployment trade-off along the Phillips curve.

KEY TERMS AND CONCEPTS

accelerationist view
expansionists
natural rate of unemployment
new classical view
Phillips curve
rational expectations theory
restrictionists

QUESTIONS AND PROBLEMS

1. Which years in Figure 17.2 most strongly suggest the possible existence of a Phillips curve?

2. Classify each of the following changes according to whether you think they affect the economy's aggregate demand curve, the economy's aggregate supply curve, or both. Explain your answer in each case.

a. an increase in personal income taxes;

b. an increase in employers' legally required contribution to employee social security taxes;

c. a worldwide strike by dockworkers;

d. an increase in employee absenteeism;

e. the outbreak of war;

f. a major discovery of oil within Australia;

g. a stock market crash;

h. an announced upward revision of the forecast of GDP growth in the coming year.

3. According to the new classical view an anticipated (expected) increase in the money supply will affect *nominal* GDP. Why is it that the adjustment of expectations that offsets any real effects of such an increase does not offset the nominal effects also?

4. You read about the classical view of income and employment in Chapter 8. How is the new classical view similar to the (old) classical view? How are they different?

5. How do you think each of the following would affect the shape of the aggregate supply curve and why?

a. increasing unemployment benefits and relaxing the requirements for eligibility;

b. setting up job-market clearinghouses that provide extensive information about job openings across the country;

c. increasing the age at which people become eligible for retirement benefits.

18
Incomes Policies

AFTER READING THIS CHAPTER YOU WILL BE ABLE TO:

1. Describe how a supply-side shock can set in motion an inflationary spiral.

2. Explain what incomes policies are and how they affect the economy.

3. Describe the effect of the Prices and Incomes Accord and outline its impact on the economy.

4. Outline the evolution of the wage fixing system in Australia.

5. Summarise the different views of the restrictionists and expansionists regarding the Prices and Incomes Accord.

In our discussion of restrictionists and expansionists in the Policy Perspective of the previous chapter, we pointed out that expansionists identify the source of inflation as due to a distributional conflict over the division of the economic cake. Furthermore, most expansionists argue that expansionary policies should go hand-in-hand with incomes policies — that is policies which are directed at overcoming the conflict over the distribution of income, or 'who gets what from the national cake?' In this chapter we will take a closer look at incomes policies, with particular emphasis on the Australian experience in recent years with the Prices and Incomes Accord negotiated initially between the Labor Party and the Australian Council of Trade Unions (ACTU) in 1983. But first, let us examine how a shock to the economy can lead to a distributional conflict and an inflationary spiral.

SUPPLY SIDE SHOCKS AND INFLATION

External Shocks

Suppose the Australian economy suffers an external shock such as a fall in export earnings. This actually happened to Australia in the mid-1980s. In newspaper commentary, this fall in export earnings was often discussed under the heading of a fall in Australia's terms of trade. The terms of trade refer to the ratio of two price indices — the exports price index divided by the imports price index. So a fall in the terms of trade really means that the price of Australia's exports declines relative to the price of Australia's imports. The fall in the price of exports in the mid-1980s was due to a number of factors: lower demand for Australia's primary products due to slower world growth; a smaller appetite by the world economy for raw materials due to technological innovation; and an increase in the supply of many of Australia's exports by competitor countries.

The fall in Australia's earnings from overseas will obviously imply a fall in the rate of growth of GDP. Furthermore it is likely to lead to a depreciation of the Australian dollar — that is the value of the Australian dollar in terms of foreign currency falls as a result of Australia's lower earnings of foreign currency from overseas. We will examine this effect more fully in Chapter 33 when we take a closer look at the determination of the exchange rate. At this stage, it is sufficient to note that this fall in the value of the Australian dollar makes imports more expensive. Since a percentage of imports is used to produce most goods, for example in car production, the costs of production will increase shifting the AS curve from AS_0 to AS_1 in Figure 18.1. This is the supply-side shock to the economy. There is also a demand-side shock due to the fall in exports. This is captured in Figure 18.1 by a shift to the left in the AD curve, from AD_0 to AD_1. Thus the net result of such an external shock is for the economy to move back to a lower level of output (from y_0 to y_1) and a higher price level (from p_0 to p_1). Note that in Figure 18.1 we have shifted the AS curve by more than the AD curve. This results in a higher price level at e_1 than at e_0 and assumes that the supply-side effect dominates. In contrast, had we assumed that the demand-side effect dominates, then we would have shifted the AD curve more than the AS curve, leading to an overall price fall. (You might want to try out this case yourself on a new diagram). As we will see later, the fall in Australia's terms of trade in the mid-1980s led to a considerable acceleration in the rate of inflation suggesting that the supply side effects dominated. Thus most economic commentators tended to identify the fall in the terms of trade with a supply side shock.

FIGURE 18.1
A Fall in Australia's Terms of Trade

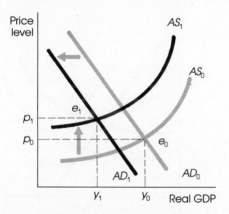

A fall in Australia's terms of trade leads to lower export earnings, shifting the AD_0 curve left to AD_1. The lower export earnings will also cause the value of the Australian dollar to fall or depreciate. This makes imports more expensive, leading to higher costs of production and thus a shift upwards in the AS_0 curve to AS_1. The economy settles initially at e_1, with a lower level of output and a higher price level.

Unions React

Whether the economy remains at point e_1 depends, to a large extent, on the reaction of labour. Two factors are at work at this stage. First, the fall in output from y_0 to y_1 increases unemployment and thus dampens wage demands. However,

since the price level has increased from p_0 to p_1, the real wage labour gets, that is the money wage (w) divided by the price level (p) has fallen from w/p_0 to w/p_1. In the highly unionised labour market of Australia, it is not unreasonable to assume that unions will react to this loss in purchasing power by demanding a compensatory wage increase. However, higher wages are a cost to industry — on the average it has been estimated that some 60 per cent of the price of a final product is due to labour costs. Thus, as the cost of production increases, we get a further shift in the AS curve from AS_1 to AS_2 in Figure 18.2. The economy now moves to e_2, with a lower level of output (y_2) and a higher price level (p_2). This higher price level may induce further wage increases, although note that unemployment is getting worse with each upward shift in the AS curve. In Figure 18.2, real

FIGURE 18.2
Wages Increase

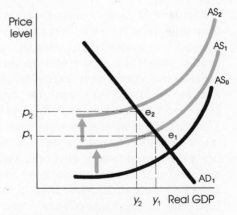

Unions react to the loss in purchasing power as result of the higher prices and demand compensatory wage increases. This increases costs to industry and hence shifts the AS curve upwards from AS_1 to AS_2. The economy now moves to e_2 with a lower level of output (y_2) and a higher price level (p_2).

GDP has fallen from y_1 to y_2 as the economy moves from e_1 to e_2. Thus, with higher unemployment, the bargaining power of unions may not be as strong so that wages may not respond fully to the higher prices. In other words, the inflation may burn itself out — this is the main point of the restrictionists in advocating restrictive economic policies as a cure for inflation.

Expansionists also agree that inflation should peter out eventually. However, they argue that the process is long, involving considerable waste of resources as the economy goes through a long period of low growth or even a continuous recession. Furthermore, they point out that as soon as recovery comes along, the distributional conflict is likely to be activated once again.

An important factor which may give rise to an inflation is the reaction of governments, often committed to a policy of full employment. In particular, note that in the movement of the economy from e_1 to e_2 in Figure 18.2, a credit squeeze is developing.

This is what causes output to decline from y_1 to y_2: as the price level rises, the demand for money rises, pushing up interest rates which reduce consumption expenditures, investment expenditures, and so on. It is very hard for any government to stand by and allow such a credit squeeze to develop and create a major recession, especially in the Australian environment where elections have been held at an average of once every two years over the past 15 years. Even in the last year of the restrictionist Fraser government in 1982–83, the policy stance swung into an expansionary mode as a result of the severe increase in unemployment.

The policy response to such a credit squeeze has tended to be to loosen monetary policy — allowing the money supply to rise sufficiently to reduce pressures on the interest rate and alleviate unemployment. Such an increase in the money supply is shown in Figure 18.3 where the AD curve is shifted from AD_1 to AD_2 so that output does not fall by much (y_1 to y_3 as compared to the do nothing policy with output falling from y_1 to y_2).

FIGURE 18.3
The Government Increases the Money Supply

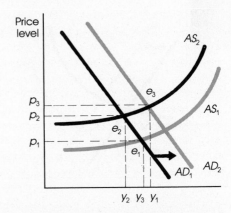

The government reacts to the higher unemployment by increasing the money supply, shifting the AD curve to the right from AD_1 to AD_2 so that output does not fall by as much (y_1 to y_3 as compared to y_1 to y_2 in Figure 18.2), and prices rising further to p_3.

Now the price level is even higher, at p_3 so that not only has the price increase from p_1 to p_2 been validated but a further stimulus is given to prices. Here we have the seeds of inflation, with the three major groups, labour, business and the government, all playing their part in maintaining the inflation. Restrictionists tend to blame both unions and government for such an inflationary spiral, arguing that the labour market needs to be made more responsive to Australia's fortunes while the government should take a tougher line in its monetary policy. Expansionists, rather than putting the blame on a specific group, tend to be more pragmatic and argue for the use of some mechanism such as income policies to diffuse what they see as a distributional conflict.

WAGES AND INCOMES POLICIES

There are many types of incomes policies, from mandatory wage and price controls to merely guidelines for prices and wages to adhere to set increases. Over the past 25 years, many countries have tried some form of wage-price controls. Examples of such countries are Canada, the USA, Finland, Ireland, Italy, Denmark, Norway, Sweden and the UK. The results from these controls have been disappointing. Often they have been followed by catch-up increases once the controls are relaxed or removed. Furthermore, as discussed in the next section, there are considerable undesirable effects of wage-price controls.

Effect of Controls on Resource Allocation

In a market-oriented economy, prices provide the signals that determine what to produce, how to produce it, and for whom. Critics argue that wage-price controls (and guidelines as well) interfere with this crucial function, and that as a result, they give rise to the misallocation of resources (land, labour and capital). In a dynamic economy there are a multitude of different markets in which supply and demand are continually shifting due to

changes in technology, consumer tastes, and a host of other factors. If wages and prices are not free to change to reflect these shifts in supply and demand, there are no effective signals to redirect the use of resources in response to these changes. For example, suppose the demand for a particular product increases. If price controls prevent the price of the product from rising, there will be no signal indicating to suppliers society's desire that more resources be devoted to the production of this product. As a result there will be a shortage of the product, such as that shown in Figure 18.4.

In a changing economy with extensive wage-price controls that are effectively enforced, shortages and bottlenecks will occur in many markets as time passes. Buyers will not be able to buy all they want at the controlled price. With controls, markets simply cannot function to equate supply and demand. For example, in a typical market, such as that shown in Figure 18.4, there is a shortage at the controlled price p_c equal to the quantity demanded q_d minus the quantity supplied q_s. Since all buyers cannot be satisfied, who will decide which buyers get the quantity q_s of the product and which do not?

One way is simply to sell to those first in line — first come, first served. In many markets, however, sellers will take care of their friends first. The trouble with either of these possibilities is that some buyers get all they want while the rest get none. To many this seems a most unfair and undesirable aspect of a price control program. One way around the problem is for the government to issue ration coupons to all who want the product. The total amount of these coupons will be just enough to lay claim to the total quantity of the product supplied, which in Figure 18.4 is q_s. Since each buyer who wants the product at price *p* will be given some of the coupons, all will be assured of getting some of the product. Obviously, some buyers will not be able to get all they would have liked, but this seems more equitable than a situation in which some get none at all. Such a ration coupon system was used during World War II in Australia, and in many other countries.

A similar argument can be developed regarding wage controls and the undesirable effect that these could have in not allowing the wage rate to fluctuate according to demand. Most economists agree that wage and price controls have considerable consequences leading to resource misallocation. However, the

problem remains as to how to tackle the inflationary spiral identified earlier.

CHECKPOINT * 18.1

Some critics of wage-price controls argue that such regulations control wages and prices artificially, and that as a result when controls are removed, there is a 'price explosion'. What do you think these critics mean, and how might you explain their position in terms of Figure 18.1?

*Answers to all Checkpoints can be found at the back of the text.

THE PRICES AND INCOMES ACCORD

The Hawke Government's answer has been the Prices and Incomes Accord, initially negotiated between the Labor party and the ACTU in 1983, and later ratified at a National Economic Summit which included a number of employer groups. The Hawke Government has seized on an important issue in developing the Accord — consensus. Overseas experience has shown that one of the most important factors in the success of incomes policies has been the degree of consensus that can be established between the main parties involved. The consensus in turn depends on the extent to which there is common agreement on the economic situation and the willingness to exercise restraint in market power. Considerable scepticism was initially expressed from many quarters regarding the viability of such an Accord. However, after five years, many commentators have been surprised by its apparent success. As we will see later, the Accord appears to have achieved

---

FIGURE 18.4
Price Controls Cause Shortages

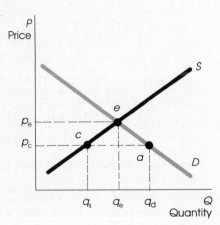

The intersection of the demand curve *D* and supply curve *S* at point *e* determines the equilibrium price p_e and quantity q_e in a freely functioning market. If price controls forbid suppliers to sell their product at a price higher than p_c they will supply quantity q_s to the market, corresponding to point *c* on *S*. But buyers will demand the larger quantity q_d, corresponding to point *a* on *D*. Therefore there will be a persistent shortage equal to q_d minus q_s.

both real wage moderation and a greatly reduced level of industrial disruption.

The Details

In December 1982, the Fraser Government instituted a wages pause in its attempt to control an inflation rate which had climbed to 12 per cent, despite a record 10 per cent rate of unemployment. In March 1983 the Hawke Government was elected and thus found itself in a very harsh economic environment, with both inflation and unemployment at unacceptably high levels. The Hawke Government designated its Prices and Incomes Accord as the centrepiece of its economic policy which would allow the government to pursue expansionary policies to counter unemployment, while dampening inflationary pressures by containing wage growth.

The Accord established the following points of agreement:

- a return to centralised wage fixing,
- an end to the Fraser Government's wages pause,
- the introduction of full wage indexation to the Consumer Price Index to be awarded at six-monthly intervals,
- increases in wages in relation to national productivity growth to be granted from 1985 onwards,
- each union must sign an agreement not to make wage claims outside the wage indexation system.

The prices aspect of the Accord was covered by the establishment of the Prices Surveillance Authority (PSA) in early 1984. The PSA's brief was to monitor prices rather than control them, and investigate industries where price rises appeared excessive. However, it had no power on prices, its function being merely to publicise cases of excessive price increases. Thus the Hawke Government shied away from what would have been an administrative nightmare to control the thousands of prices involved in the CPI. Not only were the direct costs judged to be too high, but also the indirect costs due to resource misallocation were deemed to be unwarranted and against a more efficient running of the economy.

An interesting feature of the Accord which underlies the consensus achieved relates to the concept of a 'social wage'. The Statement of Accord between the ACTU and the Labor Party sees the social wage as 'expenditure by governments that affect the living standards of the people by direct income transfers or provision of services' (Advisory Committee on Prices and Incomes, 1984, p.125). Such services include health insurance, education, housing and social welfare. In other words the aim of the Accord is to improve the living standards of the average Australian and not merely to protect real wages. Furthermore the effect of taxation policy on income was explicitly recognised, thereby focusing attention on take-home pay rather than gross income. As we will see below, this more realistic approach of concentrating on the after-tax pay made it possible to introduce policy flexibility by trading some wage increases for lower income tax rates.

The principal result of the Accord over its first two years was the slow down in the rate of growth of real wages despite the full indexation clause. This was due, in part, to no catch-up claim being granted once the wages pause was lifted. The second reason for a slow down in wages growth was due to the so called 'Medicare fiddle'. The ACTU was in favour of comprehensive medical cover provided by the government for all Australians, and supported the government when it introduced Medicare in 1984, funded by an increase in the marginal tax rate of just over one per cent. However, this transferred the expenditure for health cover from being a voluntary expense whose cost is captured in the CPI, to a mandatory tax payment where cost does not form part of the CPI. As a result, the CPI increase for the second half of 1984 was affected. Officially prices did not increase and hence no wage increases were granted even though the average taxpayer was still paying for health cover through the tax system. Many commentators where surprised that the ACTU accepted the use of such a discounted CPI. This example shows the commitment to the social wage concept: the union movement regarded the provision of Medicare as a desirable social service and was prepared to offset this service with lower wage claims than otherwise would have been the case.

The Accord Mark II

The initial Accord ran for two years and expired in October 1985. During 1985 Australia experienced a considerable fall in her terms of trade leading to a major depreciation of the Australian currency. At this time there was considerable discussion as to whether the Accord would hold in the face of such a depreciation. The issue was whether a wages offset could be negotiated as a result of the inflationary impact of the depreciation. As we will see in Chapter 33, a depreciation allows the price of Australia's exports to decline and the price of imports to increase — making both the export and import competing sectors more competitive. This sets in motion the corrective mechanism necessary to overcome the balance of payment problems — that is exports and the import

competing sector should be stimulated whilst imports should decline. However, if the effect of higher import prices flows through to higher wages as a result of full wage indexation to the CPI, then the competitive advantage from a depreciation is, in large part, nullified.

In September 1985, a further two year agreement, known as the Accord Mark II, was signed. Under this new Accord it was agreed that:

- Full wage indexation to the CPI was to be continued, except for discounting the April 1986 increase by two per cent to help offset the impact of the depreciation. As compensation for the discount, the government agreed to introduce an income tax cut from September 1986.
- The productivity claim which, under the previous Accord, was due to be heard in July 1985, would be deferred for a further year until July 1986 when it was to be taken in the form of 3 per cent of wages to set up new or extend superannuation benefits phased in over two years.
- Unions would make no extra claims outside the wages system.

The Accord Mark II drew some criticism on the grounds that the discount for the depreciation of the dollar was not sufficient. The Government and the ACTU rebutted these criticisms by pointing out that the Accord Mark II provided real wage certainty while minimising as much as possible the inflationary impact of the depreciation.

The Two-Tier System

Before the Accord Mark II had taken effect, the terms of trade deteriorated further with the result that the dollar depreciated again markedly in November 1985. This caused the April 1986 wage hearing to be dragged on for several months — perhaps to emphasise the extent of the balance of payments crisis. The Treasurer, Mr Keating, made his infamous remark about the possibility of Australia becoming a 'banana republic' unless steps were taken for Australia to become more competitive. In June 1986 the Prime Minister, Mr Hawke, addressed the nation, announcing the government's intention to argue that the subsequent national wage rise be delayed until January 1987, as well as the phased implementation of the 3 per cent wage increase in the productivity/superannuation award. In its subsequent decision, the Arbitration Commission supported the government's view and delayed the next wage case till January 1987.

The January 1987 wage case culminated in the March 1987 announcement of the two-tiered system of wage determination, or what some commentators preferred to call, the Accord Mark III. This system was intended to give a more flexible wage fixing criteria and shared union-management responsibility for lifting the economic performance and stability of the economy.

Under the first tier, Australia's 6.5 million wage and salary earners got a flat $10 per week increase with a possible 1.5 per cent increase in October 1987. This latter payment was eventually deferred until February 1988 due to the October 1987 stock market crash. Under the second tier, workers were granted the right to negotiate extra increases of up to 4 per cent of wages. These second-tier increases were subject to certain criteria such as increased efficiency and removal of obsolete work practices so as to speed up the restructuring of industry and the

economy. Superannuation claims up to 3 per cent of wages could be negotiated immediately between the parties involved. In case of disagreement on both second-tier increases and superannuation claims, the Arbitration Commission would arbitrate and award, in the case of the second tier, a maximum of 2 per cent not before September 1988, and another maximum of 2 per cent not before July 1988. In the case of superannuation, the Commission would award a maximum of 1.5 per cent no earlier than January 1988 with the remaining 1.5 per cent payable not before January 1989.

This two-tiered system has, to a certain extent, broken new ground from full wage indexation to the CPI. It is estimated that even after all the increases are granted (i.e. a flat $10 plus 1.5 per cent under the first tier and four per cent under the second tier), the average worker would still experience some fall in real wages. Furthermore, more than half of the increase was to be linked to factors other than the CPI — factors which are meant to improve the efficiency of the system. Whether this system will operate as intended is too early to tell at the time of writing. However, it is worth noting that this system is, at least, a start in breaking the traditional nexus of wages to the CPI and bringing in issues of productivity and work practices into the picture.

The Effects

What effect has the Accord had on containing wage growth, improving the competitiveness of the Australian economy and diffusing competing income claims? To attempt an answer to these questions let us examine the behaviour of several relevant measures shown in Table 18.1.

Wages Drift

The first column in Table 18.1 shows the percentage change in award rates. From 1983–84 onwards, there appears to have been a marked decline in the rate of increase in awards. Of more significance, however, is the fact that once the effect of inflation is taken into account, there has been a sustained *decline* in real awards, totalling 11.6 per cent from 1983–84 to 1986–87. This is an impressive result, clearly indicating that the centralised wage fixing system has been delivering considerable restraint on wage awards.

At this point, critics of the Accord raise the question of the extent of adherence to the wage indexation guidelines — that is the growth in over-award payments or what is called *wages drift*, a phrase originating from Sweden to denote the excess of wages paid over award rates.

Unfortunately, our official statistics on wage rates for individual occupations do not allow us to get a detailed measure of wages drift. Instead, we have to rely on aggregate statistics, resulting in a rather imperfect measure and an inability to resolve conclusively the extent of wages drift. The most common measure of wages drift has been the excess growth of average weekly ordinary-time earnings (i.e. excluding overtime payments) over the award rate. This is shown in column 5 in Table 18.1 and is derived by deducting column (1), the nominal award rates, from column (3), the nominal average weekly ordinary time earnings. As can be seen from column (5) wages drift appeared to be on the decline from 1982–83 to 1985–86, but showed a small increase in 1986–87. The 1987–88 Budget Papers attribute this increase, in part, to the 'cashing-out' of fringe benefits. Recall that with the introduction of the fringe benefits tax, companies started being taxed on fringe benefits that they provided to their employees. This meant that the scope for fringe benefits (as a means of avoiding income tax) declined and therefore there was a move to 'cash' these benefits through direct payment. The point here is that under our measure of wages drift, this appears in a similar way as an increase in over-award payments, even though the benefits were always there (but not included in the wages series).

A second problem with attributing all the wages drift to overaward payments concerns compositional changes in employment. The average weekly ordinary time earnings is simply the aggregate wage bill divided by the number employed. If there is a relative increase in the number of highly paid employees covered in the survey, then this would inflate the average wage paid and according to our measure appear as an increase in wages drift even though there may have been no increase in over-award payments.

Problems such as the two above-mentioned ones make it difficult to estimate accurately the degree of over-award payments. Overall, however, it does appear that wages drift has not been offsetting completely the substantially lower growth rates in award rates. As already noted, from 1982–83 to 1985–86, wages drift appeared to be declining while the slight increase in 1986–87 may be due to some special circumstances such as cashing-out of fringe benefits tax and compositional changes in employment.

Real Labour Costs

While restrictionists tend to concentrate

TABLE 18.1
Award Rates of Pay and Earnings

	Award rates of pay: Adult wage & salary earners[a]		Average weekly earnings (survey basis)[a]		Wages drift
			Full-time adults: ordinary time earnings		(3–1)
	Nominal (1)	Real[b] (2)	Nominal (3)	Real[b] (4)	(5)
Year-					
1981–82	12.3	2.5	13.4	3.6	1.1
1982–83	11.1	–0.3	14.2	2.6	3.1
1983–84	5.3	–2.3	7.8	–0.1	2.5
1984–85	5.4	–1.0	7.6	1.1	2.2
1985–86	4.6	–3.7	6.2	–2.3	1.6
1986–87	4.7	–4.6	7.2	–2.3	2.5

Source: Budget Statement No. 2, 1987–88, p.26.
[a] percentage change on previous period.
[b] Deflated by the implicit price deflator for private final consumption expenditure.

TABLE 18.2
Earnings and Costs

	Average earnings growth (national accounts basis)[a]		Index of real unit labour costs[b] (Non-form sector) (3)	Profit share[d] (4)
	Nominal (1)	Real Income (2)		
Year-				
1981–82	14.4	4.4	107.3	11.5
1982–83	12.8	1.3	107.2	10.9
1983–84	5.0	–2.7	102.0	12.7
1984–85	7.3	0.8	100.1	13.0
1985–86	6.2	–2.2	98.4	13.1
1986–87	6.6	–2.9	97.9	12.9

Source: Budget Statement No. 2, 1987–88, p.26–8.
[a] Percentage change on previous period.
[b] Deflated by the implicit price deflator for private final expenditure.
[c] Base: average 1966–67 to 1972–73 = 100.0.
[d] The ratio of the gross operating surplus of trading companies and financial enterprises to gross non-farm products at factory costs.

on wages drift in the debate on the impact of the Accord, expansionists focus on a different set of figures relating primarily to real labour costs.

Table 18.2 gives the average earnings measured on a national accounts basis. This differs from the average earnings level in Table 18.1 (based on survey data) in that it covers the majority of direct labour costs, including on costs such as super-annuation payments by employers and workers' compensation claims incurred.

FIGURE 18.5
Index of Real Unit Labour Costs (1966–67 to 1972–73 = 100.0)

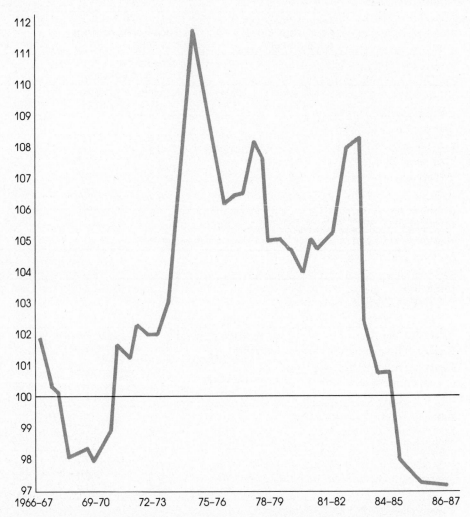

The index of real unit labour costs clearly shows the 'bulge' that occurred in unit labour costs between the 1970–71 and 1982–83. It also shows that by 1986–87, real unit labour costs stood lower than in 1969–70.

Source: 'The Round-up', The Treasury, various issues.

The earnings on a national account basis shown in Table 18.2 provide a measure of earnings viewed as costs. Column 1 shows a considerable deceleration from 1983–84 onwards in the nominal increase of these earnings as compared to the very high rates achieved between 1981 and 1983. In column (2) these earnings are deflated for the effect of inflation, with the result that the cumulative fall from 1983–84 onwards has been 7.0 per cent. To put this fall in a better historical perspective, the Treasury publishes an index of real unit labour costs shown in column (3) of Table 18.2. The base for this index (100) is the average of 1966–67 to 1972–73, a period when unit labour costs were considered at an appropriate level. This index should also provide a measure of what is called the 'real wage overhang' which refers to the extent that real wages have grown at a faster rate than the increase in labour productivity. This occurred consistently throughout the 1970s and early 1980s. However, as shown in column (3) of Table 18.2, the index has taken a nose-dive from 1983–84 onwards and by 1986–87 had reached 97.9, a level not seen since 1968–69 as Figure 18.5 clearly demonstrates.

This is perhaps the best measure of the success of the Accord and lies behind the Hawke Government's often repeated statement that it has been instrumental in reducing the real unit labour cost to the lowest level since the late 1960s. Finally, Table 18.2, column (4) gives the profits share as a percentage of non-farm GDP. This has averaged around 13 per cent from 1983–84 onwards — a marked improvement on the 1981–83 period. This is attributable in part to the economic recovery since 1983–84. However, it also reflects the decline in real unit labour costs — thereby increasing profits and their share of the national cake.

CHECKPOINT 18.2

The index of real unit labour costs is obtained by dividing the growth in labour costs from some base data (the average of 1966–67 to 1972-7) by the increase in productivity (measured as a per hour worked basis). The resulting division is then deflated by an index of the inflation of business prices. Explain the logic of this index of real unit labour costs. Compare the movements in this index with the rise in unemployment shown in Figure P17.2. What conclusions, if any, can be drawn? Explain.

FIGURE 18.6
Working Days Lost Due to Industrial Disputes[a]

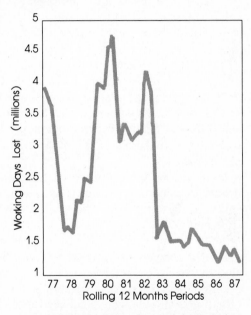

The number of working days lost due to industrial disputes declined dramatically from 1983 onwards. Under the Accord, Australia appears to have enjoyed one of the longest periods of industrial calm in recent history.

Source: Industrial Relations Digest, August 1987, p.56.

Industrial Disputes

One other major measure that is relevant in assessing the effect of the Accord is the number of working days lost due to

HISTORICAL PERSPECTIVE

The Australian Arbitration Commission

In the early 1890s, the world was hit by a financial crash which led to withdrawals of a large share of deposits from Australian financial institutions by overseas holders. This precipitated a financial crisis in Australia, which, at its height, led to 13 banks closing their doors between April and May 1893. The financial crisis affected the Australian economy very severely: interest rates soared, prices for agricultural produce fell by 50 per cent, public works stopped as well as private construction. Attempts by employers to reduce rates of pay led to considerable industrial strife which brought to a virtual halt the pastoral and mining industries. When pastoralists employed non-union shearers, waterside workers in Melbourne and Sydney refused to load their cargo. At the same time, marine officers demanded improved conditions. However, their employers refused to negotiate while the marine officers were members of the trade union movement, on the grounds that discipline would not be maintained if officers and men were members of a union. This dispute spread, with waterside workers and coal miners going on strike in support of the marine officers. The situation culminated in armed clashes verging on civil war. At one stage the Riot Act was read in Sydney and there was fighting between union and non-union labourers in most states. Never before had there been such industrial strife in Australia which spread throughout most of the country.

Many unions were unprepared for such a lengthy conflict with the result that, financially exhausted, their members had to return to work. However, these disruptive strikes of the early 1890s affected the course of development of industrial relations. It became clear that the system of voluntary conciliation and arbitration which existed in limited form at the time, was not sufficient. It was widely recognised that some system of compulsory conciliation and arbitration was necessary. As a result, in the constitution signed by Queen Victoria in July 1900, Federal Parliament had the power to make laws relating to conciliation and arbitration for the prevention and settlement of industrial disputes extending beyond the limits of any one state. This did not mean that Federal Parliament had the power to regulate industrial matters by legislation. Rather, it only had the power to set up the machinery for conciliation and arbitration — only this structure could deal with interstate industrial disputes. In 1904, Federal Parliament passed the Commonwealth Conciliation and Arbitration Act, providing for the establishment of the Commonwealth Court of Conciliation and Arbitration (which in 1956 was renamed the Conciliation and Arbitration Commission).

The Basic Wage

The main function of the Arbitration Court, as it quickly became known, was to be that of conciliation. If this failed and no agreement was possible, the president of the court was to arbitrate on a dispute and then give a decision. In reaching such a decision, the president had to act according to 'equity, good conscience and the substantial merits of the case'. This criterion still applies today. The court's decision was to be in the form of an award which was binding to both employers and the trade unions involved.

The first major decision delivered by the Arbitration Court, the Harvester Judgement of 1907, established what later became known as the 'basic wage'. Interestingly, this case did not follow from an industrial dispute but rather from the operation of the Excise Tariff Act 1906. The act was intended to protect Australian manufacturers from overseas competition by levying duties on imported goods. In order to pass some of the benefits of protection to the employees concerned, the Act specified that unless a 'fair and reasonable wage' was paid, manufacturers would be liable to a tax which would effectively eliminate tariff protection. To avoid the tax, employers had to produce a certificate stating that they had paid fair and reasonable wages. The Arbitration Court was one of the authorities empowered to issue these certificates so that many employers applied to the Court for such certificates. Thus the Court found itself having to establish what is a fair and reasonable wage since the Act left this phrase undefined.

Mr Justice Higgins, who was appointed President of the Arbitration Court in 1907, went to great lengths to establish the costs of 'the normal needs of the average employee regarded as a human being in a civilised society'. Lacking any statistical data regarding the cost of living he had to establish himself what the basic necessities were and how much they cost. He determined that a fair and reasonable wage was 42 shillings per 6 day working week for unskilled workers. Justice Higgins also established a schedule of 'fair and reasonable' payment for skilled workers. He thus effectively established a dual wages system by dividing wages into a component needed for living, and a component to compensate for skills and other factors. This type of system survived until 1967, when the total wages concept was introduced. Under this total wages system, the Commission decides on the total wage at one sitting rather than, as before, in two separate sittings (i.e. one for the basic wage and the other for the skills margin). This change arose on the grounds that from the overall economic point of view it is the total wage that matters. Note that this approach introduces another important element in wage determination, namely the capacity to pay. Over the years, the Arbitration Commission has often fluctuated between the 'needs' approach to wage setting and the capacity to pay criterion. In some periods, as for example during the height of the Great Depression between 1930 and 1934, the capacity to pay criterion clearly dominated — wages were cut by 10 per cent due to the dire economic circumstances of the Australian economy. In other periods, as for example in the early years of the Arbitration Court, the needs criterion was the most influential in the Court's deliberations.

Wage Indexation

After establishing the dual wage system, the next landmark decision was the introduction of automatic quarterly adjustments in the basic wage for price increases. However, this did not take place until 1921 when the newly established Commonwealth Bureau of Census and Statistics started producing a more comprehensive index of price movements. This system of wage indexation continued until 1953. It was discontinued in that year as a result of the very high inflation rate of around 25 per cent in 1951 due to the Korean War boom. It was felt that with such high inflation rates, automatic wage indexation could easily lead to a serious wage-price spiral. This argument was to be echoed in the 1970s and 1980s when wage indexation was twice introduced. It is interesting to note the counter case where, after the wages explosion of 1974, wage indexation in 1975 was introduced as a means of controlling or limiting wage increases which were, for a time, running at a higher rate of increase than prices. Thus, the effect of wage indexation on inflation depends on the starting point — that is whether wages are increasing faster than prices or prices rising faster than wages. In the former case, the effect would clearly be to reduce inflationary pressures, while in the latter case it would tend to maintain the wage-price spiral.

During the 1950s and 1960s, the Arbitration Commission started losing some of its influence in wage fixation. It was becoming increasingly common for unions and employers to agree on over-award rates. The Arbitration Commission was then put in the position where it had to grant similar increases to other, perhaps weaker, unions on comparative wage justice grounds. This perhaps explains the major reason why, under the Prices and Incomes Accord, the Arbitration Commission sought and got a commitment that unions would not seek increases outside the wage fixation system.

Questions

1. What is the function of the Arbitration Commission? Explain.

2. Should the Arbitration Commission be abolished? Discuss.

FURTHER READING

Healey, B. *Federal Arbitration, in Australia, An Historical Outline* — Georgian House, 1971.
Deery, S. and Plowman, D. *Australian Industrial Relations,* (2nd edition), McGraw-Hill, 1985, Chapter 11.
Indecs, *State of Play 4 An Indecs Economics Special Report,* Allen & Unwin, 1986, Chapter 3.

industrial disputes. Figure 18.6 graphs this statistic from 1977 to 1987. Clearly, from 1983 onwards, there has been a marked fall in working days lost due to industrial disputes. Thus it seems that despite the fall in real wages, the distributional conflict has been diffused. Under the Accord, Australia appears to have enjoyed one of the longest periods of industrial calm in recent history.

Critics use a variety of arguments to counteract the above results. They point out that the period 1982–83 was one of the worst recessionary experiences in Australia since World War II. This may have shocked the unions into accepting whatever they could get. Some critics even claim that the Accord has prevented real wages from falling further given the high levels of unemployment experienced. They argue, Australia would have been much better served with a deregulated labour market and collective bargaining rather than centralised wage fixing. This would not only have provided even lower overall real unit labour costs but also would have provided greater efficiency in the economy.

Despite these arguments it is hard to reject the evidence so far about the effect of the Accord. Not only has Australia had substantially lower real wage costs than in the past, but this has been achieved with the minimum of industrial disruption. Furthermore, supporters of the Accord are quick to point out that the two most recent periods of wages explosion in 1973–74 and 1981–82 took place under collective bargaining — the system which is supposed to provide better results than the Accord. This is perhaps why many critics of the Accord emphasise the need to deregulate the labour market — in other words reduce the muscle of unions. Whether this is a feasible proposal or not is hard to say. Certainly in a country like Australia with high unionisation there is likely to be considerable resistance to such substantial changes, with the possibility of a protracted and costly conflict. Supporters of the Accord point out that it would be madness to enter such a world when the Accord appears to be functioning properly in restraining (real) wages growth and limiting industrial disruption. So long as the Accord holds, the critics are likely to find themselves on weak ground. How long the Accord lasts is anybody's guess. However, from overseas experience, it is clear that such consensus does occasionally break down. If or when this happens there may well be an attempt at deregulating the labour market.

SUMMARY

1. Incomes policies are policies directed at overcoming the conflict over the distribution of national income. The term 'incomes' implies that non-wage sources of income such as profits, dividends, rents and interest rates are included in incomes policies. However, in practice, most incomes policies have focused on wages and prices.

2. An external shock to the Australian economy, such as the fall in the terms of trade in the mid-1980s, causes the aggregate supply curve to shift upwards. This is due to the resulting depreciation of the Australian dollar and hence the consequent rise in the price of imports. The net effect of such a supply-side shock is a fall in real output and a rise in prices. Should unions react to this increase in prices by demanding compensatory wage increases, then the cost of production will rise further so that the aggregate supply curve shifts further upwards and prices rise once more. This second rise in prices may lead to more wage claims so that the whole process repeats itself. It is unlikely that the economy moves to an endless wage-price spiral — the resulting increase in unemployment each time wages rise is likely to, eventually, dampen wage demands. However, the government faced with a worsening recession, may loosen monetary policy and allow the money supply to increase so as to stimulate the economy. This shifts the AD curve to the right, giving rise to higher output than otherwise would be the case. Prices also increase so that an inflationary wage-price spiral may be set in motion, with the government perhaps unwittingly financing or validating the inflationary process.

3. Expansionists argue that the government should use incomes policies to diffuse the distributional conflict. In contrast, restrictionists believe that the rising unemployment and a firm monetary policy should cure the wages-prices spiral. Expansionists, although agreeing with the end result of such a policy, claim that this process takes too long and the conflict is likely to re-emerge once the economy starts to recover.

4. The Hawke Government's answer to this problem has been the Prices and Incomes Accord. The Accord has gone through three versions already, and although initially viewed with scepticism, has surprised most critics at not only lasting so long but also at the considerable wage moderation and industrial peace achieved.

5. Under the Accord, award rates declined by 11.6 per cent from 1983–84 to 1986–87. Wages drift, that is the growth in over-award payments, appears to have been minimal. Looking at average earnings from a costs basis (i.e. including on costs such as superannuation payments by employers and workers' compensation claims incurred) real average earnings declined by 7 per cent between 1983–84 and 1986–87. Furthermore, the Treasury's index of real unit labour costs stands at its lowest level since the late 1960s.

6. The Australian Arbitration Commission has played a central role in wage determination this century. From its early days, it set the pace of wage increases under the dual wages system. This included a basic wage to cover necessities of life, and a margin for skill. For a long time, from 1921 to 1953, the basic wage was adjusted quarterly to increases in the Consumer Price Index. This was discontinued in 1953 as a result of high inflation due to the Korean War boom and the fear of creating a wages-prices spiral. Wage indexation was introduced in 1975 for the opposite reasons, namely to contain wage increases following a wages explosion in 1974. This system lasted till 1981 when it broke down and culminated in a second wages explosion in 1981–82. The Prices and Incomes Accord introduced wage indexation in 1983 and gave the Arbitration Commission once more a central role to play in wage determination in Australia.

KEY TERMS AND CONCEPTS

award rates of pay
basic wages
fringe benefits tax
terms of trade
total wage
wages drift
wage-price spiral

QUESTIONS AND PROBLEMS

1. The Arbitration Commission has often been confronted with two issues in its deliberations: the capacity to pay argument as against maintaining real wages. Explain what these issues involve and why they are often in conflict.

2. Suppose the government institutes a wage-price guidelines policy. If you are running a business, what would determine your willingness to comply with the guidelines?

3. It has been said that because controls affect resource allocation, inflation actually takes place even though prices are not allowed to rise. Explain the logic underlying this view.

4. 'Controls can affect expectations in a variety of ways, some tending to curb and others to aggravate inflation'. Elaborate on this statement.

5. It has been argued that if all wages and salaries as well as all fixed-dollar assets were indexed, the slightest bit of excessive fiscal or monetary expansion would create an inflation that would feed on itself, getting worse and worse, eventually turning into hyperinflation. Explain why you agree or disagree with this point of view.

6. While job-training programs are aimed at reducing unemployment, they each have implications for inflation as well. What are the inflationary implications?

19

Economic Growth

AFTER READING THIS CHAPTER YOU WILL BE ABLE TO:

1. Define the concept of economic growth.

2. Describe the ways in which economic growth and its major components are measured.

3. Explain the classical view of economic growth.

4. Summarise the sources of economic growth.

5. Describe the problems underlying the slowdown of economic growth in Australia during the 1970s, and the apparent recovery from those difficulties in the 1980s.

6. Explain the controversy over the benefits and costs of economic growth and the concern about possible limits to economic growth.

Our discussion in preceding chapters has dealt mostly with the analysis of income and employment determination in the short run. We have focused on the problem of how to smooth out economic fluctuations and at the same time keep the economy operating close to full employment without generating excessive inflation. The framework of income and employment analysis that we have used throughout implicitly assumes that there is a given, unchanging quantity of resources and a given state of technology. That assumption is what makes it a short-run analysis. In the short run, there is a given amount of labour, capital, and land to employ, a given state of technological know-how, and a given population to clothe, house, and feed.

Economic growth takes place because in the long run the quantity of available resources, the state of technology, and the size of the population all change. It is necessary to study economic growth in order to understand how and why the economy's capacity to produce goods and services changes in the long run. Economic growth (or the absence of it) also has important implications for how well we can handle many of the problems that confront our economy in the short run. Emphasising the importance of the short run, Keynes once remarked that 'in the long run we are all dead'. Nonetheless, the long-run phenomenon of economic growth has important consequences for how well we live in the short run.

Our first concern in this chapter will be the definition and measurement of economic growth. Then we will examine the major past and present explanations of why there is economic growth. Finally, we will consider the apparent slowdown in Australia's economic growth, the issue of the benefits and costs of economic

growth, and the increasing concern about the possible limits to economic growth.

DEFINING AND MEASURING ECONOMIC GROWTH

We can define economic growth in several different, but related, ways. Moreover, how we define economic growth largely determines how we measure it. Definition and measurement are closely related issues.

Defining Economic Growth

Defined quite generally, **economic growth** *is the expansion of an economy's capacity to produce goods and services that takes place over prolonged periods of time, year in and year out, from decade to decade, from one generation to the next, or even over the course of centuries.*

The Expanding Production Possibilities Frontier

Recall our discussion of the economy's production possibilities frontier in Chapter 2. Suppose the economy produces two kinds of goods — consumer goods and capital goods. The production possibilities frontier *AA* in Figure 19.1 shows the different maximum possible combinations of quantities of capital and consumer goods that the economy can produce if it fully employs all its available resources of labour, capital, and land, given the existing state of technological know-how. If there is an increase in the quantity or quality of any of these resources or if there is improvement in the state of technological know-how, the economy's production possibility frontier will shift outward to a position such as *BB*. As a result, the economy can produce more of both kinds of goods. This gives us an insight into the nature and causes of economic growth. Economic growth may be viewed as the continual shifting outward of the production possibilities frontier caused by growth in the quantity or quality, or both, of the economy's available resources, by ongoing improvement in the state of technological know-how, or by some combination of both.

Staying on the Frontier

When the economy's production possibilities frontier shifts outward, the economy's *capacity* to produce increases. But the economy will not realise the full benefits of this capacity increase unless it is always on its production possibilities frontier. In Chapter 2 we saw that there are two reasons why the economy may operate inside its production possibilities frontier.

First, the economy will not operate on its production possibilities frontier if any of its resources are unemployed. Whenever part of the labour force is unemployed or whenever there is unused plant capacity, the economy operates inside its production possibilities frontier. In order to remain on the frontier, the economy's aggregate demand for goods and services must grow at a rate sufficient to utilise fully the increased productive capacity provided by economic growth.

Second, the economy will not operate on its production possibilities frontier if any of its resources are underemployed — that is, if there is not efficient resource allocation. Efficient resource allocation requires that resources be employed in those activities for which they are best suited. Only then will the economy be able to realise the maximum possible output with its available resources.

In sum, if the economy is to stay on its expanding production possibilities frontier and realise the gains from economic growth, it must avoid both unemployment and underemployment. While it is not possible to eliminate unemployment completely, fiscal and monetary policy must see to it that aggregate demand expands fast enough to utilise the increased productive capacity provided by economic growth. And, in order to minimise underemployment, markets must operate efficiently to allocate resources to those productive activities in which the value of their

FIGURE 19.1
Economic Growth Shifts the Production Possibilities Frontier Outward

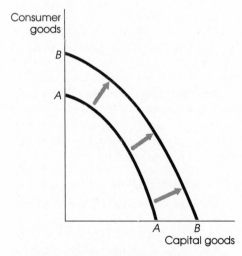

Economic growth may be represented by an outward shift of the production possibilities frontier, such as from *AA* to *BB*. The shift is caused by growth in the quantity or quality, or both, of the economy's available resources, by ongoing improvement in the state of technological know-how, or by a combination of both. To realise the full benefits of economic growth, the economy must maintain full employment and avoid inefficient allocation of its resources.

contribution to total output will be greatest.

The Interdependence of Demand and Economic Growth

The rate of increase of aggregate demand for goods and services and the rate of economic growth are interrelated. If aggregate demand doesn't expand fast enough to keep the economy operating on its production possibilities frontier, the resulting unemployment will mean that a certain amount of capital goods that could be produced will not be. Capital goods not produced today will not be available to produce other goods tomorrow. Consequently, the outward expansion of the economy's production possibilities frontier will not be as great. There will be less economic growth than otherwise would have been possible had aggregate demand expanded fast enough to keep the economy continually operating on its production possibilities frontier.

For example, during the Great Depression aggregate demand declined so much that the nation's firms actually allowed their capital stock to wear out faster than they replaced it — net investment was negative. This meant that the economy's capital stock actually declined. One of the major costs of the Great Depression was the enormous quantity of capital goods that the economy never produced. This lack of capital goods production resulted in a severe decline in the rate of expansion of the economy's productive capacity, and hence in its rate of economic growth.

Measuring Economic Growth

If economic growth is represented by an outward expansion of the economy's production possibilities frontier, then *one*

measure of economic growth is the rate of growth of the economy's full-employment level of total output. This is the level of total output the economy can produce when it is on its production possibilities frontier. The money value of full-employment total output can change because of a change in prices. Since we are only interested in measurements of growth that represent an increase in the output of actual goods and services, economic growth rates must be calculated using constant-dollar, or real, measures of full-employment total output. An example of such a measure is potential, or full-employment, real GDP measured in constant 1979–80 dollars, as was shown in Figure 6.4, part b.

Full Employment Real GDP

The rate of growth of full-employment real GDP is a measure of the growth in the economy's overall capacity to produce goods and services. But it tells us little about how the economy's standard of living is changing over time. One measure of the economy's standard of living is output per capita, the economy's full-employment total output level divided by the size of its population.

We can express this as

full-employment real GDP per capita

$$= \frac{\text{full-employment real GDP}}{\text{population}}$$

It is obvious from this expression that growth in full-employment real GDP does not necessarily mean an increase in the standard of living as measured by full-employment real GDP per capita. If full-employment real GDP (the numerator) grows faster than population (the denominator), full-employment real GDP per capita will grow and the economy's standard of living will increase. However, if full-employment real GDP grows at a slower rate than population, full-employment real GDP per capita declines and the standard of living goes down. Remember, however, that full-employment real GDP per capita is an average and, thus, a very rough measure of living standards. Few economists consider it an ideal measure of the economy's standard of living. For example, it doesn't tell us anything about the actual distribution of income in the economy. (At this point you should reread the discussions in Chapter 5 of what GDP does not measure.) *Nonetheless, the rate of growth of output per capita is a measure of economic growth that provides a rough indication of change in the standard of living.*

Output per Labour Hour

Another important measure closely linked to economic growth is output per labour hour (often referred to as output per man hour). Output per labour hour is the conventional way of measuring **productivity.** It gives us some indication of how efficiently each labour hour combines with the capital stock and the existing state of technology to produce output. Output per labour hour is an appealing measure of productivity because it is a combined reflection of the quality of labour (education, technical skill, motivation), the quantity and quality of capital that labour uses, and the degree of sophistication of the state of technology. *The greater the rate of growth of output per labour hour, the larger the rate of growth of productivity, and this obviously contributes to the rate of economic growth.*

Components of Full Employment Total Output

The economy's full-employment total output Q may be viewed as having four components. The size of the economy's population N (the number of people) is the first component. The second is the fraction of the population that makes up the labour force. This fraction is equal to the number of labourers L divided by the size of the population N. Note that the number of labourers L may be computed as the population N multiplied by the fraction of the population in the labour force (the participation rate):

$$L = N \times \frac{L}{N}$$

The third component is the average number of hours H that each labourer actually works. The total number of labour hours actually worked by the entire labour force therefore equals L multiplied by H. Note that the total number of labour hours $L \times H$ may be expressed as

$$L \times H = N \times \frac{L}{N} \times H$$

The fourth component is productivity, or output per labour hour, which is equal to full employment total output Q divided by the total number of labour hours $L \times H$:

$$\frac{Q}{L \times H}$$

The economy's full-employment total output Q is equal to the total number of labour hours $L \times H$ multiplied by output per labour hour $Q/(L \times H)$:

$$Q = L \times H \times \frac{Q}{L \times H}$$

Since

$$L \times H = N \times \frac{L}{N} \times H$$

the economy's full-employment total output Q may also be expressed as

$$Q = N \times \frac{L}{N} \times H \times \frac{Q}{L \times H} \qquad (1)$$

Equation 1 shows that the economy's full-employment total output Q may be viewed as being equal to the product of the four components: the size of the population N multiplied by the fraction of the population in the labour force L/N multiplied by the average number of hours each labourer actually works H multiplied by output per labour hour $Q/(L \times H)$. Clearly the growth of the economy's full-employment total output Q will depend on the way each of these four components in Equation 1 changes over time. (Note that the N, L, and H in the numerator of Equation 1 may be cancelled out by the N, L, and H in the denominator of Equation 1 to give $Q = Q$ which is true by definition.)

The total output of the Australian economy, as measured by real GDP (in constant 1966–67 dollars), is shown in part a of Figure 19.2. Since 1950 real GDP has increased roughly fourfold. Let's examine the role that each of the four components has played in this growth.

Role of the Components of Total Output in Economic Growth

1. *Population — P.* Population growth contributes to economic growth from both the demand side and the supply side. A growing population means a growing demand for all kinds of goods and services. On the supply side, an increasing population provides the ever larger pool of labour needed to produce the larger quantity of output required to satisfy growing demand.

Throughout its history of European settlement Australia has experienced steady population growth due to a high birthrate, a declining death rate, and at times substantial immigration. The white Australian population increased from approximately 5658 persons in 1800 to approximately 3.8 million in 1900 (of course it must be remembered that the population of aboriginal people may have been as high as 750,000). By 1987 it had increased to about 16.2 million. In recent years the birthrate has declined somewhat, reflecting a trend toward smaller families. (This trend may be due in part to the increasing participation of women in the labour force.) Population experts project the population will grow to somewhere between 18.9 million and 19.5 million by the year 2001, the range reflecting the difference between assuming a low or a high rate of immigration and fertility. At the end of June 1987, the annual increase in the population was 230,486, with net immigration contributing 103,659 persons and natural increases 126,827 persons. The Australian Bureau of Statistics estimates that by the year 2021, 48.3 per cent of the increase in population will be due to net overseas migration. The growth in the postwar Australian population since 1950 is illustrated in part f of Figure 19.2. Clearly, population growth has been a contributing factor to the growth in real GDP shown in part a.

2. *Labour force participation rate — L/P.* While the population provides the source of the labour pool, it is the proportion or fraction of the population that actually joins the labour force, L/P, that determines the size of the labour pool. This fraction is called the participation rate — the larger this rate the larger the labour force provided by a given sized population and hence the greater the productive capacity of the economy.

FIGURE 19.2
The Components of Economic Growth in the Australian Economy Since 1950

(a)

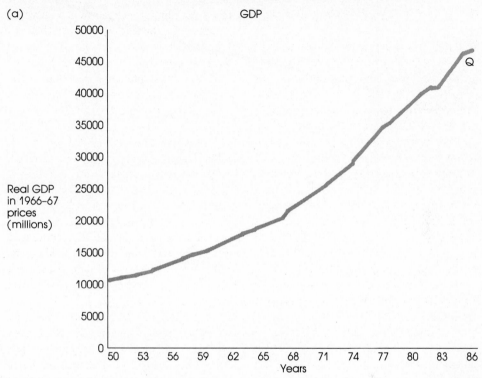

(b)

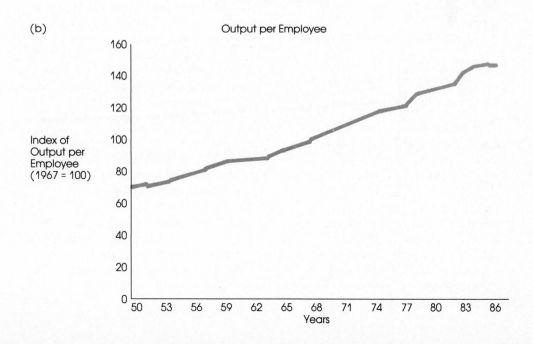

(c)

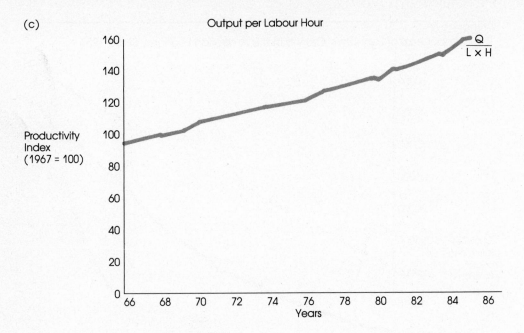

(d)

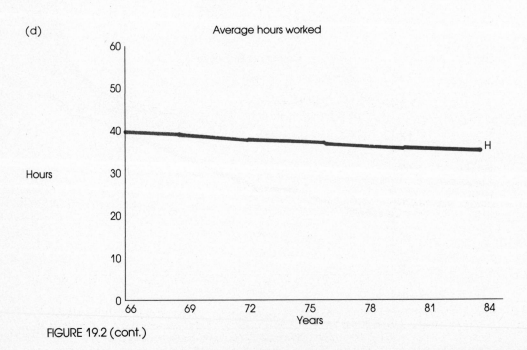

FIGURE 19.2 (cont.)

FIGURE 19.2 (cont.)

(e)

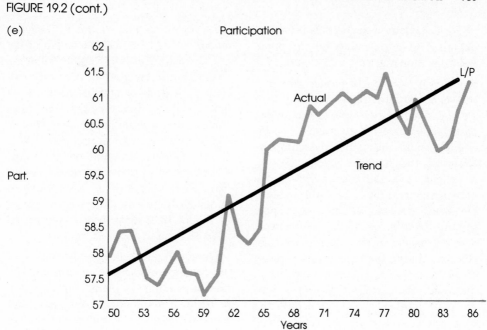

Participation

Part.

Years

(f)

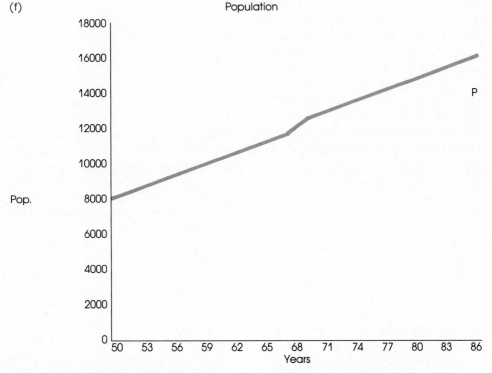

Population

Pop.

Years

The growth of total output Q measured by real GDP (part a), is the product of change in four components: population, P; the fraction of the population in the labour-force, L/P; the average hours worked per labourer, H; and productivity, or output per labour hour, Q/(L x H).

The behaviour of the participation rate, expressed as a percentage of the population, is shown in part e of Figure 19.2. Since 1950, the participation rate has shown an upward trend — also shown on the diagram. However, the actual participation rate has fluctuated considerably around this trend, reflecting the effect of the business cycle. During recessions, as for example in 1982–83, the participation rate falls. This is due to fewer jobs being available, leading some people to stop looking for a job — effectively withdrawing from the labour market. In contrast, during the expansionary phase of the business cycle there tends to be an increase in the participation rate — jobs are more available, thereby encouraging some people to re-enter the labour force or perhaps to enter earlier than otherwise would be the case. Note from the diagram that during the latest period of economic recovery from 1984 to 1987 the participation rate has steadily climbed, reaching a record of 62 per cent. This augurs well for the economy since the higher the participation rate the more productive the capacity of the economy. However, a higher participation rate has also meant smaller falls in the unemployment rate.

This is because the extra jobs created end up being 'neutralised' by more people entering the labour force, thereby leaving the unemployment rate higher than otherwise would be the case. An important implication from this discussion is that in comparing the unemployment rate over time or between countries, one must make an allowance for different rates of participation. In other words, a country with low unemployment and participation rates may be not much better off than another country with a higher unemployment rate offset in part by a higher participation rate.

3. *Hours, average hours worked per labourer — H.* In 1890 the length of the average workweek was roughly 60 hours. During the early part of the twentieth century, it declined steadily to about 43 hours in 1930. Since then the decline has continued at a more gradual pace (interrupted by an increase during World War II). From 1948 to around 1966 the average workweek only declined by about 1 hour, from about 40 hours per week down to about 39 hours, as illustrated in part c of Figure 18.2, since then, it appears to have declined to about 35 hours.

Obviously, a decline in the length of the average workweek tends to reduce the rate of economic growth. However, the reduction in hours worked reminds us that economic growth is certainly not the be-all and end-all of the 'good life.' Most economists argue that the steady decline in the average workweek reflects a preference for more leisure, one of the fruits made possible by the higher standard of living provided by economic growth.

4. *Output per labour hour — $Q/(L \times H)$.* Growth in productivity, or output per labour hour, is the principal component in economic growth. In all countries that have experienced sustained increases in their standard of living, productivity growth has been the wellspring. Productivity growth results from increases in the educational and skill levels of the labour force, growth in the quantity and quality of capital, and the steady advancement of the state of technological know-how. As shown in Figure 19.2 b, output per employee more than doubled in Australia from 1950 to 1987. While this gives an indication of the increase in productivity that has taken place, it does not take into account the fact that the working week has been getting shorter over this period.

Unfortunately, data on average hours worked in Australia are only available from 1966 onwards. Thus we could not calculate the output per labour hour from 1950. Instead we have provided in Figure 19.2 c an index of output per labour hour from 1966. But even over this shorter period we find that output per labour hour has doubled — clearly demonstrating that part b of Figure 19.2 is giving a conservative estimate of the increase in productivity per employee.

Comparing parts b, c, d, e and f of Figure 19.2, we can see that productivity growth (parts b and c) has been one of the most important contributors to the growth in real GDP (part a). Population growth (part f), which doubled over the period, and the increased participation rate have also had a major influence on growth. In contrast, the decline in average hours worked per week (part d) has tended to hold back growth in real GDP. But it should be stressed that if the shorter work week represents a choice of more leisure in exchange for less growth in the output of goods, it signifies an increase in well being.

The Significance of Growth Rates — The 'Rule of 72'

What difference does it make whether an economy grows at 3 per cent, or 4 per cent, or 5 per cent? A great deal! A rule-of-thumb calculation known as the 'rule of 72' readily shows why. For any growth rate in real GDP, the rule of 72 says that the number of years it will take for real GDP to double in size is roughly equal to 72 divided by the growth rate. For example, if the economy's real GDP grows at a rate of 2 per cent, it will take approximately 36 years (72 ÷ 2) for real GDP to double. If it grows at a 3 per cent rate, it will take 24 years to double (72 ÷ 3). A 6 per cent growth rate would mean real GDP would double in only 12 years (72 ÷ 6)!

Consider the implications of different growth rates for our economy. Economists tend to agree that in the 1960s the economy could grow 4 per cent each year without setting off demand-pull inflation. However, because of the slowdown in productivity growth during the 1970s and early 1980s, this figure may be more like 3, or even 2, per cent. According to the rule of 72, at a 4 per cent growth rate real GDP would double in roughly 18 years (72 ÷ 4). Starting from the year 1984, this doubling would occur in the year 2002. However, if the 'safe growth' rate needed to avoid excessive inflation is 3 per cent, real GDP would not double until approximately the year 2008, which is 24 years from 1984. If the safe growth rate is 2 per cent, real GDP would not double until the year 2020.

Suppose we start with the actual level of real GDP in 1980 and project these two different growth paths into the future, as shown in Figure 19.3. Clearly, the farther into the future we go on these two different paths, the greater the difference in the possible levels of real GDP. In 1990 the difference amounts to roughly $1.5 billion. By 1995 real GDP on the 4 per cent growth path is about $64.3 billion, while on the 3 per cent growth path it is about $59.4 billion, a difference of $4.9 billion. By the year 2001 the difference amounts to about $10.4 billion!

---

*CHECKPOINT * 19.1*

From 1966 to 1987 productivity in the Australian economy roughly doubled (Figure 19.2, part c). What does the rule of 72 tell us about the rate of growth of productivity during this time period?

Suppose it is projected that productivity growth in Australia may average no more than 1.5 per cent per year in coming years. What does this imply about the projected behaviour of the other three components of economic growth, given a 'safe growth' rate of 3 per cent per year?

* Answers to all Checkpoints can he found at the back of the text.

EXPLAINING ECONOMIC GROWTH

It has been difficult for economists to come up with a single, comprehensive theory that explains economic growth. How does a country that has experienced a low and unchanging standard of living for centuries transform itself into one that realises a sustained, decade-by-decade increase in productivity and real GDP per capita? Part of the difficulty economists have with this question is that a good deal of the answer no doubt requires an explanation of the political, cultural, and sociological processes that underlie such a transformation. The classical economists, such as David Ricardo and Thomas Malthus, painted a rather gloomy picture of the prospects for economic growth. Subsequent generations of economists have had the benefit of observing economic growth on a scale that the classical economists had not anticipated. Present-day explanations of economic growth place a great deal of emphasis on such things as capital formation, technological change, and saving.

FIGURE 19.3
The Difference Between a Real GDP Growth Rate of 4 Per Cent and a Rate of 3 Per Cent

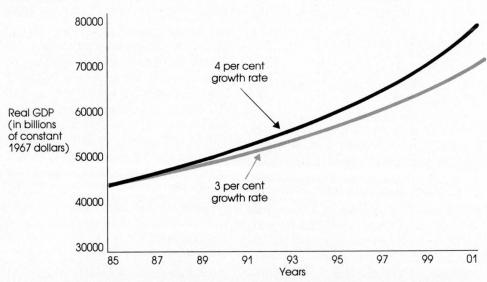

Starting from the actual level of real GDP in 1987, the difference between growing at a 3 per cent and a 4 per cent rate becomes more pronounced as we proceed into the future. In 1950 the difference amounts to $1.5 billion. But by the year 2001 it will amount to about $10.4 billion.

The Classical View of Economic Growth

During the late eighteenth and early nineteenth centuries the Industrial Revolution in England was just getting under way. Much of the rest of Western Europe remained untouched by this development. Observing the world around them, it is little wonder that classical economists, such as Malthus and Ricardo, argued that a nation's economic growth would inevitably lead to stagnation and a subsistence standard of living. In its simplest form, their argument rested on two basic premises. The first was the law of diminishing returns. The second was the proposition that the population would expand to the point where the economy's limited resources would only provide a subsistence living.

Production and the Law of Diminishing Returns

The law of diminishing returns is a proposition about the way total output changes when the quantity of one input to a production process is increased while the quantities of all other inputs are held constant. Classical economists applied this law to economic growth. *Given the state*

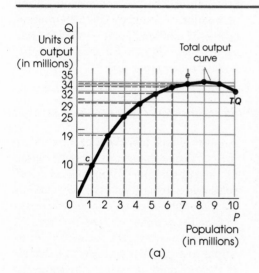

(a)

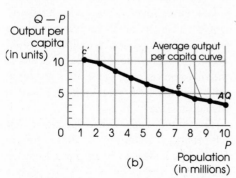

(b)

FIGURE 19.4
Total Output, Average Output per Capita, and the Law of Diminishing Returns

Given an unchanging state of technology, when a larger and larger population P works with a fixed quantity of land and other resources, total output Q (vertical axis, part a) increases by successively smaller amounts, a reflection of the law of diminishing returns. Thus the TQ curve (part a), which represents the relationship between population size and total output, rises less and less steeply as population size increases. The average output per capita (vertical axis, part b) for each population size is calculated by dividing total output Q by population P. Again reflecting the law of diminishing returns, the average output per capita curve AQ declines as population increases.

of technological knowhow, classical economists argued that as a larger and larger population works with a fixed amount of land and other resources, the increase in total output becomes less and less. In other words, there are diminishing returns in the form of successively smaller additions to total output. As a consequence the average output per capita declines as the population grows.

The law of diminishing returns is illustrated in Figure 19.4 for a hypothetical country. In part a, population P is measured on the horizontal axis and total output Q on the vertical axis. The total output curve TQ shows the relationship between the size of the country's population and the quantity of total output that population can produce, assuming a fixed quantity of resources and a given state of technological know-how. With a population of 1 million the economy is able to produce a total output of 10 million units. If the population increases by 1 million, to a total of 2 million, the level of total output rises by 9 million units to a total of 19 million units. A population increase to 3 million results in an increase in total output from 19 million to 25 million units, or a rise of 6 million units, and so forth. Note that each successive 1 million person increase in the population results in a smaller increase in total output. The successively smaller increases in total output associated with each 1 million person increase in population reflect the law of diminishing returns. Once the population reaches 8 million, further increases in population actually cause total output to fall. That is, the TQ curve bends over and begins to decline beyond a population of 8 million.

The consequences of diminishing returns for average output per capita are shown in Figure 19.4, part b. Average

output per capita (vertical axis) is calculated for each population level P (horizontal axis) by dividing the total output Q (from part a) by P. For example, when the population size is 1 million and total output equals 10 million units, corresponding to point c on TQ (part a), average output per capita is 10 units, corresponding to point c' (part b). The average output per capita is calculated and plotted in a similar fashion for each population size to give the average output per capita curve AQ. Notice that because of the law of diminishing returns, average output per capita decreases as the population size increases, as indicated by the declining AQ curve. For instance, when population is 7 million and total output equals 35 million, point e on TQ (part a), average output per capita is 5 units, point e' on AQ (part b).

The Subsistence Living Level

Another crucial ingredient of the classical theory of economic growth was the notion of a subsistence living level. *The* **subsistence living level** *may be viewed as the minimum standard of living necessary to keep the population from declining.* At the subsistence level the number of births would just equal the number of deaths. If the standard of living fell below the subsistence level, economic hardship would cause the death rate to rise above the birthrate and the population would decline. If the standard of living rose above the subsistence level, the death rate would fall below the birthrate and the population would increase.

The subsistence living level for our hypothetical economy is illustrated in Figure 19.5. The axes in parts a and b are exactly the same as those in parts a and b of Figure 19.4. Given any population size (horizontal axis), the subsistence total output curve SQ in part a indicates the minimum total output (vertical axis) necessary to maintain that population — that is, to keep it from declining. For example, the subsistence total output level necessary to sustain a population of 1 million is 5 million units of output, corresponding to point d on SQ. Similarly, the SQ curve indicates that it would take 10 million units of output to sustain a population of 2 million, 15 million units to sustain a population of 3 million, and so forth.

The subsistence living level may also be expressed in per capita terms. The average per capita subsistence level for any size population may be obtained by dividing the corresponding subsistence total output level by the population size. For example, for a population of 1 million requiring a subsistence total output of 5 million units (corresponding to point d on SQ), the average per capita subsistence level is 5 units of output per person. Alternatively, observe from the SQ curve that every additional population of 1 million requires another 5 million units of total output to maintain a subsistence level of living. Hence, whatever the population size, the average per capita subsistence living level in our hypothetical economy is 5 units of output per person, represented by the horizontal line L in part b.

Population Growth and Diminishing Returns

The classical view of economic growth combined the law of diminishing returns with the notion of the subsistence living level. Figure 19.6 illustrates the classical view by combining the TQ and AQ curves of Figure 19.4 with the SQ and L curves of Figure 19.5.

Suppose the population is initially 1 million. Given the fixed quantity of resources and the state of technological know-how, the economy will be able to produce a total output of 10 million units, corresponding to point c on total output curve TQ (part a). However, the subsistence total output level needed for a population of 1 million is only 5 million units, point d on the subsistence total output curve SQ (part a). In terms of total output, the economy's standard of living exceeds the subsistence level by 5 million units, represented by the vertical distance between points c and d in part a. In per capita terms, the average output per capita of 10 units (point c' in part b) exceeds the per capita subsistence living level of 5 units (point d' in part b) by 5 units. Consequently, the death rate will be lower than the birthrate and the population will increase. Suppose the population increases to 2 million. The economy will produce a larger total output of 19 million units (point f in part a), which again exceeds the subsistence total output level of 10 million units (point g in part a), this time by 9 million units. In per capita terms, the average output per capita of 9.5 units (point f' in part b) again exceeds the per capita subsistence living level of 5 units (point g' in part b). Hence, the population will continue to increase.

According to the classical view, population and output will continue to grow as long as the economy's standard of living exceeds the subsistence living level. That is, population and total output grow as long as the total output curve TQ lies above the subsistence total output curve SQ (part a). Putting it in per capita terms, they will continue to grow as long as the average output per capita curve AQ lies above the per capita subsistence living level curve L (part b). Once the population reaches 7 million, total output produced will be 35 million units (part a), which is just equal to the subsistence level of total output needed to sustain a population of 7 million. This level corresponds to the intersection of the SQ and TQ curves at point e in part a. In per capita terms, at a population of 7 million average output produced per capita is 5 units, which is just equal to the per capita subsistence living level, corresponding to the intersection of AQ and L at point e' (part b). At this point population and output will cease to grow. Economic growth stops. The economy has reached

a static, or unchanging, equilibrium position.

What a dismal equilibrium it is, characterised by stagnation and a subsistence standard of living. If the population were to rise above 7 million, total output produced would be less than the subsistence total output level required to sustain the larger population (to the right of point e in part a, the TQ curve lies below the SQ curve). Average output per capita would be less than the per capita subsistence living level (to the right of point e' in part b, the AQ curve lies below L). Consequently, famine and disease would cause the death rate to rise above the

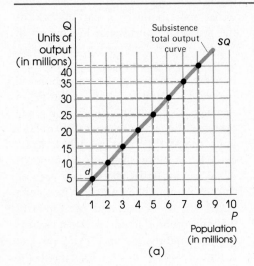

(a)

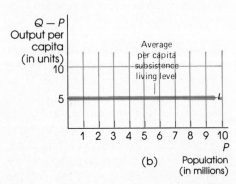

(b)

FIGURE 19.5
The Subsistence Living Level

The subsistence total output curve in part a shows the subsistence level of total output (vertical axis) associated with any given size population (horizontal axis) in a hypothetical economy. The subsistence level of total output for any given size population is that which provides a standard of living just sufficient to keep the total population from declining (the number of births just equals the number of deaths). The average per capita subsistence living level is equal to the subsistence level of total output for any given size population divided by the population. For the hypothetical economy shown here, the average per capita subsistence living level is 5 units of output per person, represented by the horizontal line L in part b.

birthrate and the population would tend to fall back to the 7 million level. On the other hand, if the population were to fall below the 7 million level, total output would exceed the subsistence total output required to sustain the smaller population (the *TQ* curve lies above the *SQ* curve to the left of point *e* in part a). Living standards would rise since the average output per capita would be above the per capita subsistence living level (the *AQ* curve lies above *L* to the left of point *e'* in part b). Unfortunately, according to the classical view, this would cause the birthrate to exceed the death rate. The population would tend to increase to 7 million again, and the standard of living would once again decline to the subsistence level.

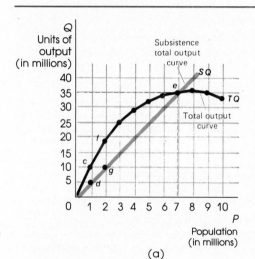

(a)

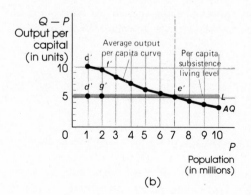

(b)

FIGURE 19.6
The Classical View of Economic Growth

At any population size less than 7 million the total output curve *TQ* lies above the subsistence total output curve *SQ* in part a. Because the quantity of total output produced (vertical axis) exceeds the subsistence total output level, the classical view argued that the birthrate would be higher than the death rate. Hence, both the population (horizontal axis) and total output would grow. At any population size greater than 7 million the total output curve *TQ* lies below the subsistence total output curve *SQ*. Since the total output produced is less than the subsistence total output level, the death rate would exceed the birthrate. Hence, both the population and total output would decline. Long-run equilibrium occurs at the intersection of *TQ* and *SQ*, point *e*, where the total output level produced is just sufficient to support a population of 7 million at a subsistence living level.

The argument may also be represented in per capita terms, part b. Consider any population size less than 7 million. Average output per capita, given by the *AQ* curve, is greater than the per capita subsistence living level of 5 units of output per person, given by the horizontal line *L*. Hence population rises, causing average output per capita to fall toward the per capita subsistence living level. Now consider any population level greater than 7 million. Average output per capita is less than the per capita subsistence level — the *AQ* curve lies below *L*. Hence, population declines and average output per capita rises toward the per capita subsistence level. The longrun equilibrium occurs at a population size of 7 million, where average output per capita just equals the per capita subsistence level, corresponding to the intersection of *AQ* and *L* at *e'*.

ECONOMIC THINKERS

Thomas R. Malthus — 1766–1835

Thomas Malthus, a clergyman by training, was in many ways the epitome of the gentleman English scholar. Taking his A.B. degree from Jesus College, Cambridge, in 1788, he was appointed vicar at Albury near the family home and lived a quiet scholarly life. The economic views of Malthus fall into two broad categories: one, devoted to population problems, for which he is best known; and, two, his work on the inadequacy of aggregate demand, in which he was a forerunner of the great economist J. M. Keynes. His views on population were embodied in his famous work, *An Essay on the Principle of Population As It Affects the Future Improvement of Society* (1798), and his broader views were put forth in his book, *Principles of Political Economy,* published in 1820.

Malthus did not quarrel with the mildly cheerful view of Adam Smith relative to the future of humankind, but as he saw the future, it was a far cry from the optimistic picture drawn by his contemporaries Godwin, Condorcet, and their followers. Malthus forecast that the future was likely to be grim. He began with two postulates:

1. Food is necessary to people's existence.
2. The passion between the sexes is necessary and is likely to continue.

Following these basic postulates, he argued that 'the power of the population is infinitely greater than the power of the earth to produce subsistence for man'. That is, population would outstrip the ability of people to produce adequate food.

Since the science of keeping vital statistics was in its infancy and data relating to agricultural output were for all practical purposes nonexistent, the quantification of the theory was at best a theoretical approximation. This fact in no way inhibited Malthus, although later he did some empirical research to answer critical comment. His research may be summed up as follows:

Year	1	25	50	75	100	125	150	175	200	225
Population	1	2	4	8	16	32	64	128	256	512
Subsistence	1	2	3	4	5	6	7	8	9	10

That is, population, if unchecked, would increase 512 times after 225 years, the food supply only 10 times.

If the means are available, population will naturally increase. There are, however, two kinds of checks on population. These checks are either 'preventive', reducing birthrates, or 'positive', affecting the mortality rate. Among the lower classes the positive check is more common, since they suffer high rates of infant mortality and more often die from poor nutrition and general ill health resulting from lack of resources. On the other hand, those in the upper classes are more influenced by the preventive check since they tend to marry later and have fewer children, wishing to preserve their living standards. The poor have little to lose, so there is no reason to defer marriage.

As a further consequence, such policies as public relief (the 'poor laws') defeat their own purpose, resulting only in an upsurge of population. Generally, Malthus favoured the preventive check over the positive. All this was, to be sure, unfortunate, for 'to prevent the recurrence of misery is alas, beyond the power of man'. For a man of the cloth to take such a dim view of the arrangements of Providence may seem to pose a bit of a problem, and Malthus tried to answer this seeming contradiction in the last two chapters of his Essay, which attempt to mesh the principle of population with a view of a providentially ordered universe.

FOR FURTHER READING

Bonar, James. *Malthus and His Work*. New York: Macmillan, 1924.

The 'Dismal Science'

If economic growth tended to lead society to such a dismal long-run equilibrium position, the prospects for ever improving economic well-being would seem dim indeed. It is this implication of the classical view of economic growth that earned economics its designation as the 'dismal science'. The classical view is still relevant today in the so-called underdeveloped countries of the world. The near subsistence living standards and the high rates of population growth that plague those countries do suggest a rush toward the dismal long-run classical equilibrium. But the classical view bears little resemblance to the spectacular rise in living standards and the sustained economic growth experienced by the present-day industrialised, or developed, countries.

Sources of Growth and Rising Living Standards

How can the long-run classical equilibrium and a subsistence living level be avoided? One way is for the total output curve, hence the average output per capita curve, to shift upward fast enough to stay ahead of population growth. Obviously, it would also help if population growth didn't increase every time output per capita rose above the subsistence living level.

Economic growth with rising living standards is depicted in Figure 19.7. Suppose the population is initially P_1. Total output corresponding to point b on total output curve TQ exceeds the subsistence total output level corresponding to point a on the subsistence output curve SQ (part a). Hence, average output per capita corresponding to point b' on the average output per capita curve AQ exceeds the per capita subsistence level L by an amount represented by the vertical distance between b' and a' (part b). Assume this above-subsistence standard of living causes the population to rise to P_2 in the manner suggested by the classical view. However, in the meantime suppose the total output curve shifts up to TQ' and hence that the AQ curve shifts up to the position AQ'. Now, even though the population grows to P_2, the standard of living is not driven down to the subsistence level corresponding to points c and c'. Instead, total output rises to point d on TQ' and average output per capita rises to point d' on AQ'. The standard of living has actually increased, as represented by the fact that the vertical distance between c' and d' is greater than that between a and b'.

What would cause economic growth to take place in this fashion, rather than along the lines suggested by the classical view? In particular, what causes the increase in productivity that allows any given size population to produce more, as represented by the upward shift in TQ and AQ? And what factors might inhibit the tendency for population growth to be so responsive to increases in the standard of living? While there is no hard and fast blueprint, most economists now agree that any list of the key elements in economic growth should include capital deepening,

technological change and innovation, education or investment in human capital, rising aspirations for a better standard of living, and saving and investment.

Capital Deepening

Capital deepening *is an increase in the stock of capital (machines, tools, buildings, highways, dams, and so forth) relative to the quantities of all other resources, including labour.* Capital deepening makes it possible for any given size population to produce a larger total output, so that average output per capita is increased. This, of course, is reflected in upward shifts of the TQ and AQ curves, such as those shown in Figure 19.7. Given the size of the population, the state of

---

FIGURE 19.7
Economic Growth with Rising Living Standards

When the total output curve TQ and hence the average output per capita curve AQ shift upward rapidly enough, economic growth will be accompanied by rising average output per capita.

Suppose the total output and average output per capita curves are in the positions TQ and AQ respectively, and population is P_1. The standard of living exceeds the subsistence living level. Therefore, economic growth will tend toward the classical long-run equilibrium with population P_2 existing at a subsistence living level, corresponding to points c and c'. However, if in the meantime TQ and AQ shift up to TQ' and AQ' average output per capita will rise, as represented by the fact that the vertical distance between c' and d' is greater than that between a and b'.

Upward shifts in AQ and TQ are caused by capital deepening, technological change and innovation, and an increase in the quality of the labour force caused by investment in human capital.

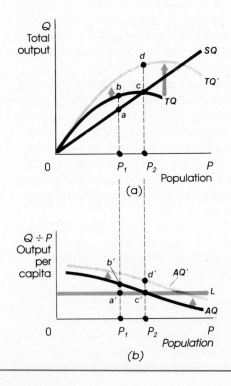

technology, and the quantities of all other resources, there are diminishing returns to capital deepening just as there are to increases in the population. Increases in the quantities of the *same kinds* of machines, tools, buildings, highways, and dams beyond a certain point (that is, more of the same capital goods labour is already using) obviously will not yield further increases in total and per capita output. Why? Because there will not be enough population and quantities of other resources with which to combine them in productive activities. The emphasis on 'same kinds' of capital brings us to the role of technological change and innovation.

Technological Change and Innovation

Invention and scientific discovery lead to technological change and innovation in production techniques. Even the most casual observer of economic life is struck by the changes that take place over time in the kinds of capital and procedures used to produce goods and services. When existing capital wears out, it is often replaced with *new kinds* of capital incorporating the new technology. Perfectly usable capital is often simply made obsolete by the development of new kinds of capital. As a result, even if the economy did not increase the quantity of resources devoted yearly to the replacement of worn-out or obsolescent capital, the productive capacity of the economy would grow. Hence, for any given size, population, and quantity of all other resources, total output would be larger. Again, this would be reflected in the upward shift of the TQ and AQ curves, such as that shown in Figure 19.7.

Some kinds of technological change are the result of changes in the form of a capital good, so-called **embodied technical change**. This is the kind of technological change that most often comes to mind. The diesel locomotive replaced the steam locomotive. Jet airliners have largely replaced the propeller variety. The electronic pocket calculator has made the slide rule obsolete. The list goes on and on.

Other kinds of technological change take the form of new procedures or techniques for producing goods and services, so-called **disembodied technical change**. Examples are the use of contour ploughing to prevent soil erosion on farms, the development of new management techniques in business, and the pasteurisation of milk. Such technological changes are not embodied in the form of a capital good. Of course, many types of embodied technical change make disembodied technical changes possible and vice versa. The electronic computer has made many new kinds of managerial procedures possible. And these procedures in turn make it possible to use new kinds of capital goods, or embodied technical changes. For example, computers enable airlines to use sophisticated procedures for scheduling and controlling the flow of passengers between airports more efficiently. This efficiency makes it practical to use certain kinds of jet aircraft.

Education and Investment in Human Capital

Just as investment in capital goods increases productive capacity, so too does investment in human beings in the form of education, job training, and general experience. It is no accident that literacy rates and average years of schooling per capita tend to be higher in developed countries than in underdeveloped countries. Improvements in the quality of the labour force shift the *TQ* and *AQ* curves upward, as in Figure 19.7, in the same way that embodied and disembodied technical changes do.

Improvements in sanitation, disease prevention, nutrition, and the general health of the population are also forms of investment in human capital. A healthier population is more capable of learning and generally gives rise to a more productive labour force less prone to absenteeism and accidents. In addition, increases in the average life span make it possible to develop a more experienced labour force and to provide the larger pool of able managers and leaders needed to fill administrative positions.

Rising Aspirations and Population Growth

If a society is to realise both economic growth and a rising standard of living, population growth must somehow be kept from literally 'eating up' every increase in output per capita above the subsistence living level, as in the classical view. Countries that have experienced an industrial revolution and the progression from underdeveloped to developed status have somehow managed to escape from the drag of excessive population growth. One explanation is that once an economy realises a rise in the standard of living above the subsistence level, the actual experience instils a taste for the 'good life', or at least a better life. More and better food, clothing, and housing breeds a keen awareness that living *can be* more comfortable. People aspire to a better standard of living and become more aware of the relationship between curbing family size, and hence population growth, and the

ability to realise these aspirations.

The effect of a rise in the aspiration level, measured in terms of average output per capita, on population size is shown in Figure 19.8. Suppose the aspiration level rises to *AL*. That is, people desire a standard of living, measured in terms of average output per capita, that exceeds the subsistence level by an amount equal to the vertical distance between *AL* and *L*. The population will not get larger than P_a, corresponding to the intersection of *AL* with the average output per capita curve *AQ* at point *a*. The long-run equilibrium average output per capita at point *a* is higher than that corresponding to the classical view at point *b*, where the larger population P_b exists at a subsistence living level. Now when capital deepening, technological change, and investment in human capital cause the *AQ* curve to shift upward, economic growth will cause

FIGURE 19.8
The Effect of a Rising Aspiration Level on Population

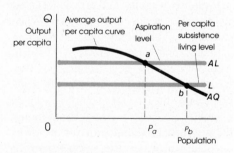

Suppose the aspiration level, measured in terms of average output per capita, is *AL*. The population will not get larger than P_a, corresponding to the intersection of *AL* with the average output per capita curve *AQ* at point *a*. The long-run equilibrium average output per capita at point *a* is higher than that corresponding to the classical view at point *b*, where a larger population P_b exists at a subsistence living level.

population and output per capita to tend toward equilibrium positions corresponding to the intersection of the rising AQ curve with AL.

Another explanation of the decline in the population growth rate that tends to accompany economic development is that this decline is in part due to a change in the role of children. Such a change is brought about by the nature of economic development. The populations of under-developed countries are largely involved in agricultural activities, eking out a meagre living with primitive tools. It is argued that under such circumstances children are viewed as 'another pair of hands', useful for the work they can perform starting at a relatively early age. In addition, they are insurance that there will be somebody to look after aging parents. As economic development progresses, an ever larger portion of the population becomes employed in the economy's expanding industrial sector. Families earning livelihoods in factories, stores, and trades servicing a more urbanised population no longer view children as contributors to the family's economic well-being. Rather a child is primarily a dependent to be fed, clothed, and housed until he or she enters the labour force as a self-sufficient young adult. In short, in an industrial and urban setting, children are more of an economic burden on the family. The incentive to have large families that exists in a rural, agricultural setting is greatly reduced. It is therefore argued that as an increasing portion of the population moves into the industrial sector the birthrate, and hence population growth, tends to decline.

The Role of Saving and Investment

In previous chapters we saw how saving, the refraining from consumption, makes it possible for investment to take place. Investment expenditures create new capital goods, which replace capital stock that is worn out or obsolescent, as well as increase the size of the economy's capital stock. Saving and investment are thus crucial to the capital formation and technological change that make possible economic growth and increasing output per capita.

Consider Figure 19.7 once again. The upward shift of TQ to TQ', and hence of AQ to AQ', requires saving and investment. When the population is P_1 and the total output curve is TQ, there is an excess of output above that required for subsistence. This excess is represented by the vertical distance between points a and b (part a). In order for capital formation to shift TQ up to TQ', the population must refrain from consuming all the excess output that the economy is able to produce. That is, some of it must be saved. What is not consumed is available for investment or the formation of the capital goods that increase the economy's productive capacity, as represented by the upward shift of the total output curve from TQ to TQ'.

Other Factors in Economic Growth

A distinguishing characteristic of developing economies is a growing *specialisation of labour accompanied by increases in the scale of production*. In the early stages of economic development, a worker is typically engaged in many different tasks. For example, at the beginning of the Industrial Revolution in England (in the latter half of the eighteenth century), production was typically organised along the lines of the so-called cottage industry. A family occupying a cottage on a modest parcel of land would raise a small number of farm animals, tend a few crops, and engage in crafts such as spinning, weaving, and tanning. The family supplied much of its own food and made a good deal of its own clothing. An individual worker typically performed many different tasks. With the advent of the Industrial Revolution and the advancement of production technology, greater specialisation and increases in the scale of production took place, thereby reducing per unit (of output) costs of production. Lower-priced, mass-produced goods led to the expansion of markets, an integral part of the economic growth process.

Another important ingredient of economic growth is the *development of extensive capital markets*, that is, markets where savers lend funds to borrowers who make the investment expenditures that give rise to capital formation. The growth of banking and other financial institutions that pool the savings of a large number of small savers and lend them out to investors plays a crucial role in the development of capital markets. Some economists even suggest that the state of development of a country's financial institutions provides the single most revealing indication of a country's state of economic development.

Economic growth requires a *favourable cultural social and political environment*. Legal institutions are needed to provide law and order and to enforce contracts between parties to economic transactions. Cultural attitudes toward work and material advancement are an important determinant of the incentives for economic growth. A social structure that allows reasonably fluid upward and downward mobility based on performance and merit is more conducive to economic growth than a rigid social structure that puts a

premium on the station of one's birth. Finally, economic growth rarely takes place in societies racked by political instability.

CHECKPOINT 19.2

Do you think the law of diminishing returns is applicable to technological change and investment in human capital? Why or why not? What are the implications of your answer for economic growth?

ISSUES IN ECONOMIC GROWTH

Recent Problems with Economic Growth

What are the aspects of economic growth that are currently of most concern to Australia? Figure 19.9 graphs the percentage change in output per labour hour since 1967. This Figure is derived from the data in Figure 19.2 part c and shows the rate of productivity growth from year to year of the Australian economy. Let us try to interpret this figure which, at first glance, appears to have no obvious pattern.

Productivity growth tends to be highly affected by the business cycle. When output growth accelerates, so normally does productivity growth so that output per labour hour rises. Conversely, when output growth slows down, productivity growth drops or even becomes zero or negative. For example, in the recession year of 1978, productivity growth was almost zero, at 0.02 per cent. Again in the recession of 1983, productivity growth slackened considerably to 0.49 per cent. Several factors contribute to this result including variations in the pace of work according to pressures of demand (i.e. during periods of low demand the workforce may work at a slower pace, thereby reducing productivity per labour hour); a tendency by employers to hold on to their experienced workforce even during periods of low demand so that they can 'bounce' back with higher production levels as soon as demand picks up; the relatively fixed nature of some types of indirect labour such as administration and factory cleaning staff, the costs of which do not vary directly with the level of production; and some clear cases of economies of scale whereby the production process becomes more efficient as production levels rise.

While this discussion provides a useful explanation of some of the ups and downs of the bars in Figure 19.4, there is a more long-term effect which is important to recognise. If we average the percentage change in output per labour hour from 1967 to 1974, (a period which coincides with relatively high economic growth), we find that the average rate is 3.6 per cent. In contrast, the period 1975 to 1987 yields a rate of growth of 1.9 per cent. Thus, apparently there has been a considerable slowdown in the growth of productivity. This is not a phenomenon confined to Australia but also matches the experience of most OECD countries. The reasons are closely tied to the lower economic growth experienced by most developed countries since the mid-1970s and have already been discussed in the previous chapter where we noted the different reasons given by restrictionists and expansionists and their respective policy prescriptions. (At this stage you might want to revise the Policy Perspective on restrictionists and expansionists of the previous chapter.)

One argument mentioned only briefly in a previous chapter concerns the effect of the increase in the price of oil which

FIGURE 19.9
Percentage Change in Output per Labour Hour

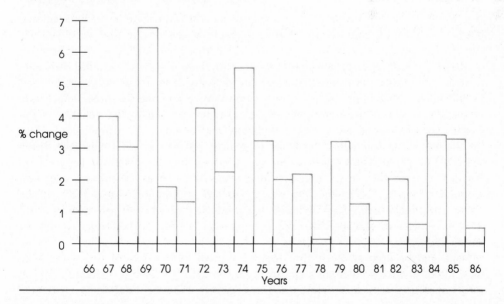

POLICY PERSPECTIVE

How Serious Are the Limits to Growth?

Predictions of an end to economic growth are certainly not new. Indeed, the dismal classical view, nearly 200 years old, seems very relevant in many of today's underdeveloped countries, a fact sometimes easily forgotten by those living in the industrialised or developed countries of the world. But in recent years the hard facts of pollution, energy shortages, urban sprawl, and traffic congestion have served as increasingly insistent reminders that there may well be limits to economic growth.

Resource Limitations

As we have already seen, the classical view of economic growth envisioned an inevitable tendency for countries to reach a point where both population and total output would cease to grow — a dismal long-run equilibrium of stagnation and misery. Due to the law of diminishing returns, output per capita would decline continuously until a subsistence standard of living was reached. However, capital deepening, technological change, investment in human capital, a rising aspiration level, and a favourable cultural, social, and political environment have all conspired to put off such a doomsday in the world's developed countries. But there are those who emphasise 'put off'. Put off for how long? It is undeniable that the earth's resources are limited. Therefore, these analysts argue that it is certainly not possible to beat the law of diminishing returns indefinitely. As the earth's resources are used up and population increases, the law of diminishing returns inevitably points to a declining per capita output.

Doomsday Predictions

Among the doomsday predictions, a group known as the Club of Rome (an international business association composed of business people, academicians, and scientists) has constructed an elaborate computerised model of world economic growth.[1] The Club of Rome model assumes that population and production grow at certain historically realistic percentage rates and that there are definite limits to world resources and technological capabilities. Given these assumptions, a computer is used to generate predictions of the future trends of industrial output per capita, the quantity of the world's resources, food per capita, population, and pollution. The predictions reach the alarming conclusion that the limits to growth will be reached somewhere in the years 2050 to 2100. The Club of Rome says that this conclusion follows largely from the depletion of the earth's nonrenewable resources — coal, petroleum, iron ore, aluminium, and so forth. Once the limit is reached, it is predicted that there will be an uncontrollable decline in population and productive capacity. If resource depletion does not trigger the collapse, then the precipitating factors will be famine, pollution, and disease.

What can be done to avert this doomsday prediction? Many of those who take the Club of Rome's predictions seriously argue that efforts should be made to establish zero population growth and zero economic growth. That is, establish a no-growth equilibrium. The Club of Rome suggests that by using appropriate technology, it may be possible to cut pollution, hold population growth in check, and reduce the amount of resources used per unit of output. In addition, investment in capital should be limited to the replacement of worn-out or obsolescent capital. Moreover, resources should be shifted away from the production of industrial products and toward the provision of more food and services.

Perspective on Growth and Doomsday

Many find such doomsday predictions quite unconvincing. They observe that modern-day doomsday predictions sound very similar to the classical view of economic growth. The economic growth of the countries of Western Europe, the United States, Canada, Japan, the USSR, New Zealand, and Australia is completely at odds with the classical view. This is so largely because the classical view did not foresee the tremendous advance of technology that has taken place over the last century or more. Critics of the 'doomsdayers' argue that current doomsday predictions again vastly underestimate the potentials of science, innovation, and technological change.

This criticism may be well taken. One wonders what the classical economists of the early 1800s would have thought if one of their number had predicted that in the twentieth century people would fly to the moon, jet aircraft carrying 450 passengers would cross continents in the time it takes a stagecoach to go 25 uncomfortable miles, in a split second an electronic computer would do calculations that would take a thousand clerks years, electronic communication would allow people to watch and hear a live event on the other side of the world, or most of the populous areas of the world could be obliterated in a few seconds by nuclear explosions. The list goes on and on. Imagine how farfetched such a list would seem to someone living in 1900, let alone the classical economists of the early 1800s. This puts a perspective on the pitfalls of making predictions about economic growth in the twenty-first century.

Questions

1. Of all the resources at our disposal, which seems the most abundant?

2. Would the steps suggested to avert the doomsday predictions seem to imply more, or less, government intervention in the economy?

[1]Dennis L. Meadows and others, *The Limits to Growth,* Washington, D.C.: Potomac Associates, 1972.

occurred in the mid-1970s, and the impact this could have had on labour productivity. In particular, some economists contend that the resulting rise in energy costs increased the cost of using labour-saving machinery and fostered the use of more labour intensive, and less productive technologies. Whether these effects will be reversed as a result of the collapse in oil prices in the mid-1980s is hard to tell at this stage.

Costs and Benefits of Growth

The benefits of economic growth have always seemed quite obvious. The basic economic problem is to satisfy humanity's unlimited wants in the face of ever present scarcity. Economic growth eases this problem by reducing scarcity. Without growth the only way one person can be made better off is by taking something away from another. With economic growth there can be more for everyone — the lot of all can be improved. However, it has become increasingly apparent in the more industrialised countries, where economic growth has been most spectacular, that there are also costs to economic growth. Among these are pollution and a possible decline in the quality of life.

Pollution and the Environment

When the economy produces 'goods', it also produces by-products that are 'bads' — smoke, garbage, junkyards, stench, noise, traffic jams, urban and suburban congestion, polluted water, ugly landscapes, and other things that detract from the general quality of life. In fact *all* output, both goods and bads, *eventually* returns to the environment in the form of waste. The more we experience economic growth, the more obvious this fact becomes. Many people are justifiably concerned about the undesirable effects of growth on the environment and the balance of the world's ecological system. There is concern about disappearing species of wildlife and about the rising incidence of cancer related to synthetic products. There is concern about the destruction of the earth's ozone layer by the use of aerosol spray cans. Scientists also allege that the large-scale burning of fossil fuels has increased the carbon dioxide content of our atmosphere to such an extent that the earth's average temperature has increased a few degrees. The list of such worrisome by-products of economic growth goes on and on.

Critics of economic growth argue that some curbs on growth are necessary if these increasingly undesirable aspects of industrialisation are to be controlled. Others caution that we must be careful not to confuse the control of growth with the control of pollution. They argue that the additional productive capacity made possible by growth could at least in part be devoted to pollution control efforts and the correction of past environmental damage. They point out that pollution control and a clean environment cost something, just like any other good, and that economic growth and increased productive capacity make it easier for society to incur that cost. (Recall our discussion of the production possibilities frontier and the production of scrubbers in Chapter 2.)

The Quality of Life — Progress Versus Contentment

Economic growth implies change. Change is often what is most desired and needed by an impoverished population in an underdeveloped country. But many question whether continual change is as obviously beneficial in developed economies such as Australia. Technological change, if anything, seems to have accelerated in the last half century. As a result, skills and training acquired in youth become obsolete more rapidly. There is more pressure to 'keep current', to 'retool', and to 'update' one's skills. Fail to do so and you may be demoted or even out of a job. Such pressure creates anxiety and a sense of insecurity.

POLICY PERSPECTIVE

How We Keep Running Out of Energy — The Role of the Market

At various times it has appeared that we were about to run out of energy sources, important ingredients for economic growth. The alarm about an energy crisis during the 1970s and early 1980s was not the first. In the past, the dire predictions of exhausted energy reserves have always proved wrong. Why? Usually because those predictions failed to take account of the effects of rising energy prices, which encouraged people to seek out cheaper forms of energy and to develop more energy-efficient technology.

For example, prior to the Industrial Revolution in the late 1700s wood was the main source of fuel. People used so much wood it was feared that the forest would soon be exhausted, resulting in energy shortages and widespread hardship. But as the forests around towns and cities were used up, the price of wood rose and coal was gradually substituted for wood. The growing demand for coal led to the development of more efficient (less costly) mining methods, and coal soon replaced wood as the primary source of energy.

During the early 1800s lamps burning sperm-whale oil were commonly used to light houses. Population growth and an expanding economy increased the demand for whale oil so much that people became concerned about the possible extinction of whales. The price of whale oil rose about 600 per cent over a period of about 35 years. This price rise led domestic and commercial users of whale oil to seek substitute fuels such as lard oil, distilled vegetable oil, and coal gas. Eventually, by the early 1850s, kerosene made from coal oil became the dominant fuel for lighting. The whale oil crisis had passed. The discovery of petroleum in the late 1850s provided an even cheaper way to make kerosene, and petroleum replaced coal oil as the major source of kerosene.

The important point to note about the wood and whale-oil 'crises' is that the forces of demand and supply operated to encourage energy conservation as well as the development of alternative energy sources. For example, as the price of whale oil rose, consumers were motivated to conserve on its use (don't leave whale oil lamps burning when they're not needed for reading or sewing, and get by with less light in hallways and porches). At the same time, consumer demand for substitute fuels increased, causing their prices to rise. The rising prices of substitute fuels made them more profitable to produce, which encouraged enterprising firms and individuals to increase the supply of these fuels. Consumer demand turned from a fuel that was becoming scarce to fuels that were becoming more plentiful. All this occurred in the absence of a national energy policy or any other form of government intervention — a stark contrast to the way we have dealt with our own energy problems in recent years.

Questions

1. How does the market mechanism work to expand the potential for economic growth?

2. How would you explain the large increase in the number of compact cars on the road over the past 15 years?

We have noted that an above-subsistence aspiration level may be necessary to avoid the tendency toward the long-run equilibrium of stagnation envisioned by the classical view. But some growth critics worry that aspiration levels in growth-oriented, industrialised countries are geared toward a 'keep up with the Joneses' mentality. Goods may be valued more for the status they confer on the owner than the creature comforts they provide. ('I'd better get a new car this year or I may not look like I belong in this neighbourhood'.) Consequently, people work harder, produce more, enjoy it less, and complain about smog, traffic congestion, and the rat race. What there is of contentment, or peace of mind, may come largely from the sense that you're 'making it', or better yet, that you've 'arrived'.

Since the beginning of the Industrial Revolution, many critics have argued that industrialisation forces labour into dehumanising jobs, requiring the performance of monotonous, mind-numbing tasks. Mass production, assembly-line jobs may provide bread for the table but little food for the soul. However, it has been said that those who make this criticism are not familiar with living conditions in countries where there is no industrialisation.

SUMMARY

1. Economic growth is the expansion of an economy's capacity to produce goods and services that takes place over prolonged periods of time. It may be viewed as a continual shifting outward of the economy's production possibilities frontier caused by growth in the quantity and quality of the economy's available resources (land, labour and capital) and by ongoing improvement in the state of technological know-how.

2. The full benefits of growth will be realised only if there is an adequate expansion of aggregate demand and an allocation of resources to those productive activities where the value of their contribution to total output is greatest.

3. The rate of growth of full-employment real GDP provides a measure of the growth in the economy's overall capacity to produce goods and services. The rate of growth of output per capita provides a rough measure of growth in the economy's standard of living. The rate of growth of output per labour hour provides a measure of the growth in the economy's productivity — the efficiency with which each labour hour combines with the capital stock and the existing state of technology to produce output.

4. Growth in the economy's full-employment total output may be viewed as the product of change in each of the following four components: (1) population, (2) the fraction of the population that participates in the labour force, (3) the average hours worked per labourer, and (4) output per labour hour. The cumulative effects of seemingly small differences in growth rates become ever larger as time passes.

5. The classical economists' view of economic growth held that a nation's economic growth naturally tended toward stagnation and a subsistence standard of living. Citing the law of diminishing returns, they argued that as a larger and larger population works with a fixed amount of land and other resources the increase in total output becomes less and less, given the state of technological know-how. Consequently, average output per

capita declines as population grows. Both output and population growth cease once output per capita has fallen to the subsistence level.

6. The drag on economic growth imposed by the law of diminishing returns and population growth can be overcome by capital deepening, technological change and innovation, and education and other forms of investment in human capital. The drag on rising living standards imposed by excessive population growth can be overcome by rising aspiration levels that tend to curb family size and hence population growth.

7. Saving and investment play an important role in economic growth because they are crucial to the process of capital formation and technological change that gives rise to sustained economic growth and increasing output per capita. Other important sources of economic growth are the increased specialisation of labour, increases in the scale of production, the development of extensive capital markets, and the existence of a favourable cultural, social, and political environment.

8. From the mid-1970s onwards there was a decline in productivity growth as well as a decline in economic growth. This phenomenon occurred in many countries and may be due to the rise in energy prices. We also looked at the changes in productivity from year to year, and how these are affected by the stage of the business cycle. That is, during periods of economic expansion, productivity tends to rise while during periods of economic recession, productivity growth tends to slow down.

9. Economic growth is beneficial in that it reduces the burden of scarcity by increasing output. However, in recent years developed countries have become increasingly aware of some of the undesirable by-products of growth — pollution, congestion, uncertain effects on the ecological system, and the sense of anxiety, insecurity, and lack of contentment that may afflict citizens in a growth-oriented society.

10. Doomsday predictors argue that the limits of economic growth are likely to be reached sometime in the latter half of the next century, largely as a result of depletion of the earth's nonrenewable resources. Critics of these predictions contend that such a forecast is most likely wrong because it grossly underestimates the advance of science, technology, and innovation, which has always been a major source of economic growth.

KEY TERMS AND CONCEPTS

capital deepening
disembodied technical change
economic growth
embodied technical change
productivity
subsistence living level

QUESTIONS AND PROBLEMS

1. The rate of growth of real GDP is frequently used as a measure of economic growth. If we view economic growth as an outward expansion of the production possibilities frontier, what shortcomings does this suggest are associated with the use of real GDP to measure economic growth?

2. It is technologically possible to produce the *same* quantity of total output with different combinations of quantities of capital and labour. More capital may be used and less labour, or more labour and less capital. For example, a rise in the price of capital relative to the price (wage) of labour will typically cause firms to use more of the now relatively cheaper labour and less capital. Conversely, an increase in the price of labour relative to the price of capital would typically cause firms to use more of the now relatively cheaper capital and less labour. What are the implications of these possibilities for the use of output per labour hour as a measure of productivity? What bearing do these possibilities have on the apparent slow-down of Australian productivity growth during the 1970s, given that energy prices increased dramatically during these years?

3. Population growth can be both a blessing and a curse for economic growth. Explain.

4. It is sometimes argued that in the short run, low productivity growth can create jobs because more workers will be required to satisfy rising demand. But it is then said that in the long run, low productivity growth means a slower growth of total output, which 'hurts employment'. Explain why you agree or disagree with this argument. What does a comparison of parts a, b, c, and d of Figure 19.2 suggest about the validity of this argument?

5. Can you explain why it might be possible for rising aspirations to cause the growth in total output to be *negative* and the growth in average per capita output to be *positive*, while at the same time there is technological progress? What are the implications of such a situation for population growth?

6. The classical view of economic growth envisioned a long-run equilibrium in which output per capita was just equal to the subsistence living level. However, if we consider the role played by saving and investment, is it really possible for long-run equilibrium to occur at such a position? Why or why not?

FIVE

The Price System and the Organisation of Economic Activity

20

Elasticity of Demand and Supply and Further Topics in Demand Theory

AFTER READING THIS CHAPTER YOU WILL BE ABLE TO:

1. Define the concept of elasticity and show how it is measured.

2. Explain the relationship between total revenue and elasticity along a demand curve.

3. List the determinants of the elasticity of demand.

4. List the determinants of the elasticity of supply.

5. Explain the theory of utility and show how it explains the existence of a downward-sloping demand curve based on the law of diminishing marginal utility.

In this chapter we will examine the important concept of elasticity, which helps us to measure the responsiveness of quantity to price change in demand and supply analysis. We will then build on the tools of supply and demand analysis that we first developed in Chapter 4 in order to analyse some familiar but controversial economic issues.

BRIEF REVIEW OF SUPPLY AND DEMAND

Before beginning our discussion of elasticity, let's briefly review the basics of demand and supply developed in Chapter 4. The *law of demand* says that in general people will demand a larger quantity of a good at a lower price than at a higher price. The law of demand is represented graphically by a downward-sloping demand curve, such as D_0 in Figure 20.1, part a. The *law of supply* says that in general a larger quantity of a good will be supplied at a higher price than at a lower price. The law of supply is represented graphically by an upward-sloping supply curve such as S_0 in Figure 20.1, part a.

The intersection of the market demand curve D_0 and market supply curve S_0, part a of Figure 20.1, determines the equilibrium price p_e and quantity q_e. At the equilibrium price the market is said to be in equilibrium because the quantity demanded is exactly equal to the quantity supplied. At any price above the equilibrium price, the quantity supplied exceeds the quantity demanded so that there is a market surplus. This surplus will push the market price down to the equilibrium level. At any price below the equilibrium level, the quantity demanded exceeds the quantity supplied and there is a market shortage.

The shortage will push the market price back up to the equilibrium level.

Movement along a demand curve means that only the price of the good and the quantity of it demanded change. All other things are assumed to be constant, or unchanged. Among these other things are (1) the prices of all other goods, (2) income, (3) expectations, (4) tastes, and (5) the number of buyers in the market. A movement along a demand curve is referred to as a *change in the quantity demanded*. If one or more of the other things change, then the demand curve will shift in the manner shown in part b of Figure 20.1. Such a shift in the demand curve is called a *change in demand*. Note that when demand increases, the demand curve shifts rightward, such as to D_1, thereby increasing both the equilibrium price and quantity. When demand decreases, such as to D_2, both equilibrium price and quantity decrease.

As with a demand curve, movement along a supply curve means that only the price of the good and the quantity of it supplied change. Among all other things assumed to be constant, or unchanged, are (1) the prices of resources and other factors of production, (2) technology, (3) the prices of other goods, (4) number of suppliers, and (5) expectations. Movement along a supply curve is referred to as a *change in the quantity supplied*. If one or more of the other things change, the supply curve will shift as shown in part c of Figure 20.1. This is referred to as a *change in supply*. An increase in supply is represented by a rightward shift in the supply curve, such as to S_1, thereby reducing equilibrium price while increasing equilibrium quantity. When supply decreases, such as to S_2, equilibrium price rises while equilibrium quantity decreases.

FIGURE 20.1
Demand and Supply Determine Equilibrium Price and Quantity in the Market

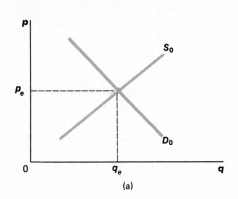

(a)

The intersection of the supply and demand curves S_0 and D_0 respectively, determine the equilibrium price p_e and quantity q_e in the market, part a.

A rightward shift of the demand curve to D_1, part b, increases both the equilibrium price and quantity. A leftward shift to D_2 decreases equilibrium price and quantity.

A rightward shift of the supply curve to S_1, part c, reduces equilibrium price and increases equilibrium quantity. A leftward shift of the supply curve to S_2, reduces equilibrium quantity and increases equilibrium price.

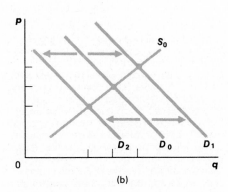

(b)

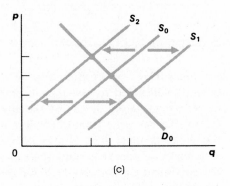

(c)

ELASTICITY — THE RESPONSIVENESS OF QUANTITY TO PRICE CHANGE

What does it mean when someone says that 'the public has demonstrated that it's very responsive to price changes'? In other words, how responsive is 'very' responsive? In economic analysis, we find it helpful to use a specific quantitative measure of the degree of responsiveness of quantity demanded to a change in price. We call this measure the **elasticity of demand**. Similarly, the **elasticity of supply** is used to measure the degree of responsiveness of quantity supplied to a change in price.

The elasticity of demand, or supply, is measured as the ratio of the percentage change in quantity demanded, or supplied, to the percentage change in price. Elasticity therefore measures the percentage change in quantity (demanded or supplied) per 1 per cent change in price.

ELASTICITY OF DEMAND

The responsiveness of the quantity of a good demanded to a change in its price is reflected in its demand curve. This is illustrated in Figure 20.2. At a price of p_1 the quantity demanded is q_1. Suppose the price is lowered from p_1 to p_2. If the demand curve looks like d_e, the quantity demanded increases from q_1 to q_e On the other hand, if the demand curve looks like d_i, the quantity demanded only increases from q_1 to q_i. For the exact same change in price the change in quantity demanded is greater for the demand curve d_e than it is for d_i. The reason is that for this price change the demand curve d_e is more 'stretched out' than the demand curve d_i. Hence for this price change we say that the demand curve d_e is more 'elastic' than the demand curve d_i. Our graphical example of Figure 20.2 gives us a feel for the origin of the term elasticity. But a precise measure of elasticity cannot be obtained by looking at a demand curve or a supply curve. Indeed, we shall see that the appearance of such curves is not a reliable indicator of the elasticity of demand or supply.

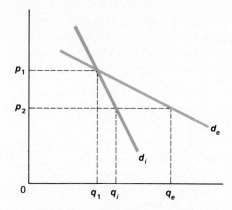

FIGURE 20.2
Change in Quantity Demanded in Response to a Price Change

Suppose the price of a good is initially p_1 and the quantity demanded is q_1. If the demand curve is d_e, the quantity demanded increases from q_1 to q_e in response to a fall in price from p_1 to p_2. However, if the demand curve is d_i, the quantity demanded increases by a smaller amount, from q_1 to q_i. For the exact same change in price the change in quantity demanded is greater for the demand curve d_e, than it is for d_i. This reflects the fact that the demand curve d_e is more 'stretched out' than the demand curve d_i. For this price change we say that the demand curve d_e is more elastic than the demand curve d_i.

Coefficient of Elasticity

By measuring the responsiveness of quantity demanded to a change in price in percentage terms, we avoid the confusion that can arise from differences in the choice of units. The number arrived at as a result of these calculations is called the **coefficient of elasticity** (e_d). We can obtain this number with the formula:

$$e_d = \frac{\text{percentage change in quantity demanded}}{\text{percentage change in price}}$$

The sign of the coefficient of elasticity

of demand is negative because the sign of the change in price is opposite to the sign of the associated change in quantity along a demand curve. (This is so, remember, because price and quantity demanded are inversely related according to the law of demand.) By convention the minus sign is usually ignored.

Armed with the coefficient of elasticity, we may now give a much more precise meaning to the concept of elasticity by defining the terms elastic and inelastic. **Elastic demand** *exists when the coefficient of elasticity (e_d) is greater than 1.* Put another way, we can say that *demand is elastic if a given percentage change in price results in a larger percentage change in quantity demanded.* Conversely, **inelastic demand** *exists when the coefficient of elasticity is less than 1. We can also say demand is inelastic if a given percentage change in price results in a smaller percentage change in quantity demanded.* Suppose the price of salt per kilo increased from $1.00 to $1.20 and the quantity demanded decreased from 500 kilos per month to 450 kilos per month. The coefficient of elasticity would be .5. A 20 per cent increase in price resulted in only a 10 per cent decrease in quantity demanded. In the special in-between case where the percentage change in price results in an equal percentage change in quantity demanded, we say that demand is **unit elastic** or of *unitary elasticity.* In this case the coefficient of elasticity equals 1. Put another way, if the price of a good falls by 1 per cent and the quantity demanded increases by 1 per cent, demand for that good is unit elastic.

The elasticity of demand for most goods falls between two extremes. At one extreme, the quantity of a good demanded does not change at all in response to a change in price. In this case we say demand

is **perfectly inelastic**, and the demand curve for the good is perfectly vertical. At the other extreme is a good for which demand is zero when price is above a certain level, but unlimited when price is at or below that level. We then say the demand for that good is **perfectly elastic**, and the demand curve is perfectly horizontal at that price level.

Calculating Elasticity

Suppose we wanted to calculate the elasticity of demand for tickets to the Grand Final. The demand curve for tickets is shown in Figure 20.3. Let's begin by computing the elasticity for the price change between points *a* and *b* on the demand curve. At point *a* the price of $12 per ticket has an associated quantity demand of 50,000 tickets. We will use this as our base point. At point *b*, the price of $10 per ticket has an associated quantity demand of 60,000 tickets. We must therefore compute the percentage change corresponding to a $2 change in the price of a ticket and the percentage change corresponding to the associated 10,000 ticket change in the quantity of tickets demanded. Using the formula for the coefficient of elasticity, our calculations for the elasticity of demand would be

$$e_d = \cfrac{\cfrac{10,000}{50,000}}{\cfrac{2}{12}} = 1.2$$

Alternatively, suppose we use point b as our reference point. Ten dollars per ticket and 60,000 tickets would be the base price and quantity from which we would compute the percentage change corresponding to a $2 change in the price of a ticket and the percentage change

FIGURE 20.3
Demand for Tickets to the Grand Final

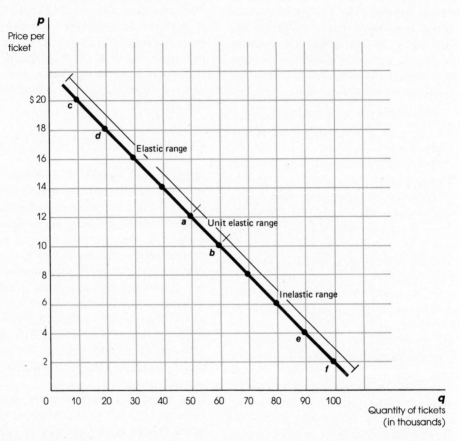

The *elasticity of a demand curve is typically different over different ranges.* For this hypothetical demand curve for tickets to the Grand Final, the coefficient of elasticity is 6.33 over the range *c* to *d* and gets progressively smaller as we move down the curve from left to right. It is unit elastic over the range *a* to *b* and becomes progressively more inelastic below this range. The coefficient of elasticity over the range *e* to *f* is .16.

Note, however, that the *slope* of this demand curve is the same over all ranges, because the curve is linear (a straight line). From this example, we can see why the slope of the curve over any range is not a good indicator of the elasticity over that range.

corresponding to the associated 10,000 ticket change in the quantity of tickets demanded. Our calculations for the elasticity of demand would now be

$$e_d = \frac{\dfrac{10{,}000}{60{,}000}}{\dfrac{2}{10}} = .83$$

These two calculations result in considerably different values of the elasticity of demand despite the fact that they are based on the same change along the same demand curve. Moreover, in this particular instance, the first calculation indicates that demand is elastic, while the second indicates it is inelastic. This conflict is clearly an unsatisfactory state of affairs. How can we resolve it?

The Arc Elasticity

The conventional way around this difficulty is to use the averages of the two quantities and the two prices as base points when computing the percentage changes in quantity and price used to calculate the coefficient of elasticity. The average of the two quantities associated with points a and b is $(50,000 + 60,000)/2$, which equals 55,000. The average of the two prices is $(12 + 10)/2$, which equals 11. The percentage change in quantity is therefore $(10,000/55,000) \times 100$, or 18.2. The percentage change in price is $(2/11) \times 100$, or 18.2. The calculation of the coefficient of elasticity is now

$$e_d = \frac{\dfrac{10,000}{55,000}}{\dfrac{2}{11}} = \frac{18.2}{18.2} = 1$$

In general then, we may restate our formula for the coefficient of elasticity so that it reads

$$e_d = \frac{\dfrac{\text{change in quantity}}{\dfrac{\text{sum of quantities}}{2}}}{\dfrac{\text{change in price}}{\dfrac{\text{sum of prices}}{2}}}$$

This new formula is sometimes called the **arc elasticity** along a demand curve. It is also sometimes called the midpoint formula.

Variation in Elasticity Along a Demand Curve

At this point you should be warned against thinking that the elasticity of demand is the same over all ranges of a demand curve. Although it is possible to construct demand curves where the coefficient of elasticity is the same over all ranges, such curves are not typical.

Consider again the demand curve in Figure 20.3, which is fairly typical. Using the arc elasticity formula we can determine the coefficient of elasticity for the range c to d by making the following calculations:

$$e_d = \frac{\dfrac{10,000}{\dfrac{30,000}{2}}}{\dfrac{2}{\dfrac{38}{2}}} = 6.33$$

We have already seen that for the range a to b, e_d has a value of 1. The value of e_d over the range e to f is

$$e_d = \frac{\dfrac{10,000}{\dfrac{190,000}{2}}}{\dfrac{2}{\dfrac{6}{2}}} = .16$$

It is apparent that the demand curve is very elastic at the highest price levels and becomes less and less elastic as we move to lower price levels. At price levels below the a to b range, the demand curve is inelastic and becomes more so as we move to yet lower price levels. Elasticity is higher in the upper-left part of the demand curve because the base quantity level from which the percentage change in quantity is computed is small. On the other hand, the base price from which the percentage change in price is computed is large. When we compute the coefficient of elasticity, a relatively large percentage change in quantity is divided by a relatively small percentage change in price. This gives an elastic demand over this range. In the lower-right part of the demand curve, the situation is just the opposite. The base quantity level from which the percentage change in quantity is computed is large, while the base price level from which the percentage change in price is computed is small. When we compute the coefficient of elasticity, a relatively small percentage change in quantity is divided by a relatively large percentage change in price to give a coefficient of elasticity less than 1. This indicates an inelastic demand.

Slope and Elasticity

Obviously the elasticity of demand typically will be different at different parts of the demand curve. It is easy for beginning students of economics to confuse the slope of a demand curve over some range with the elasticity of demand over that range. Slope and elasticity are different concepts. *The* **slope of the demand curve** *over some range is defined as the change in price over that range divided by the associated change in quantity demanded.* This is obviously not the same as the coefficient of elasticity.

For a straight-line demand curve, such as that in Figure 20.3, the slope is the same over its entire length. For every $2 change in price, the associated change in quantity of seats demanded is always 10,000. We have already seen, however, that the elasticity is decidedly different between the ranges *c* to *d*, *a* to *b*, and *e* to *f* for example. This illustrates how misleading it can be to judge the elasticity of demand by looking at the slope. While the slope of the demand curve can be readily observed from the appearance of the demand curve over any range, the elasticity cannot. Consider the demand curve in Figure 20.4. The slope over the range *a* to *b* is clearly

steeper than that over the range *c* to *d*. The slopes over both of these ranges are clearly steeper than the slope over the range *e* to *f*. Yet this demand curve has been constructed so that it is unit elastic throughout its length. The coefficient of elasticity is always equal to 1, whether it is calculated for the range *a* to *b*, *b* to *c*, *c* to *d*, *d* to *e*, or *e* to *f*.

Elasticity and Total Revenue

The **total revenue** *received from the sales of a good is equal to the quantity of the good sold multiplied by the price per unit.* There is a definite relationship between total revenue and the elasticity of demand. The way total revenue changes as we move along a demand curve tells us how elasticity changes along the demand curve. And conversely, the way elasticity changes along a demand curve tells us how total revenue changes.

Consider again the demand curve in Figure 20.3, reproduced in Figure 20.5. At point *c*, total revenue is equal to the price per ticket of $20 multiplied by the 10,000 tickets demanded at that price, or $200,000. At point *d*, total revenue is equal to $18 per ticket times 20,000 seats, or $360,000. Hence if price is lowered from $20 to $18 per ticket, total revenue increases. We have already observed that demand is elastic over this range, which means that the percentage change in quantity is greater than the percentage change in price. In other words, when the price of tickets is lowered from $20 to $18, the loss in revenue due to the reduction in price is more than offset by the gain in revenue due to the increase in the quantity of tickets sold. Conversely, if the price per ticket is raised from $18 to $20, total revenue falls because the gain in revenue due to the increase in price is more than offset by the loss in revenue due to the reduction in the number of seats sold. Hence, *in the elastic portion of a demand curve, a change in price, up or down, results in a change in total revenue in the opposite direction.*

Now consider the behaviour of total revenue over the range *e* to *f* on the demand curve of Figure 20.5. At point *e* total revenue is equal to the price per ticket of $4 multiplied by the 90,000 tickets demanded at that price, or $360,000. At point f total revenue is equal to $1 per ticket times 100,000 tickets, or $100,000. Therefore, if price is lowered from $4 to $2 per seat, total revenue decreases. Recall that demand is inelastic over this range, which means that the percentage change in quantity is less than the percentage change in price. Hence when the price is

lowered from $4 to $2 per ticket, the loss in revenue due to the reduction in price is larger than the gain in revenue due to the increase in the quantity of tickets sold. Conversely, if the price per ticket is raised from $2 to $4, total revenue rises from $200,000 to $360,000 because the gain in revenue due to the increase in price more than offsets the loss in revenue due to the decrease in the number of tickets sold.

Therefore, *in the inelastic portion of a demand curve, a change in price, up or down, results in a change in total revenue in the same direction.*

Over the range *a* to *b* the demand curve of Figure 20.5 is unit elastic. At point *a* total revenue is $600,000, which is determined by a price of $12 per ticket multiplied by 50,000 tickets. Total revenue is also $600,000 at point *b*, where the price of $10 per ticket is multiplied by 60,000 tickets. Thus, whether price is lowered from $12 to $10 or raised from $10 to $12, total revenue remains unchanged. This is so because the percentage change in price in one direction is exactly the same as the percentage change in quantity in the other. The change in revenue due to the change in the price per seat is exactly offset by the change in revenue due to the change in the opposite direction of the quantity of seats sold. *In that portion of a demand curve that is unit elastic a change in price, up or down, has no effect on total revenue.* Because the demand curve of Figure 20.4 is unit elastic throughout its length, total revenue remains the same no matter what price is charged.

Usually the easiest way to estimate whether a demand curve is elastic, inelastic, or unit elastic over a certain range is to examine the change in total revenue as price and quantity vary over that range. Always remember that *along the elastic portion of a demand curve, total*

FIGURE 20.4
Unit Elastic Demand Curve

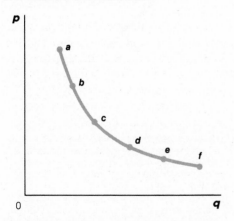

This demand curve is unit elastic (the coefficient of elasticity equals 1) throughout its length. However, the slope varies throughout its length. The slope is very steep over ranges along the upper-left portion of the curve, such as *a* to *b*, and becomes progressively flatter as we move down along the demand curve from left to right. This again illustrates why it is misleading to judge the elasticity of a demand curve over any range by its slope over that range.

FIGURE 20.5
Relation Between Elasticity of Demand and Total Revenue

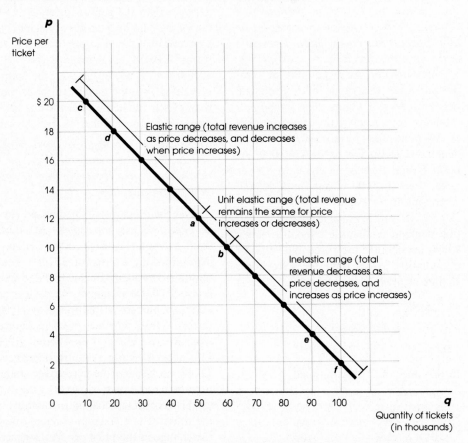

Total revenue (equals price per ticket times the number of tickets demanded at that price) gets progressively larger as we move down the demand curve from left to right over the elastic range. Total revenue reaches its maximum over the unit elastic range and gets progressively smaller as we move down the demand curve over the inelastic range. As we move up the demand curve from right to left, total revenue rises to a maximum at the unit elastic range and then falls continuously thereafter.

Use the numbers in the diagram to convince yourself of the validity of these statements. Also note in Figure 20.4 that because the demand curve has the same elasticity throughout its length, total revenue is the same at all points on it.

revenue and price move in the opposite direction. Along the inelastic portion of a demand curve, total revenue and price move in the same direction. This rule is summarised in Table 20.1. With these rules in mind, in Figure 20.5 you should be able to convince yourself that total revenue from Grand Final ticket sales is at a maximum when tickets are priced at either $10 or $12. Note that in this hypothetical example the Melbourne Cricket Ground would be only about half full while the Sydney Cricket Ground would be bursting at the seams.

TABLE 20.1
Revenue Effects of Price Changes

Price Movement / Elasticity	Elastic	Unity	Inelastic
Increase	Revenue Falls	Revenue Constant	Revenue Increases
Fall	Revenue Increases	Revenue Constant	Revenue Falls

What Determines Elasticity of Demand?

There are three main determinants of the elasticity of demand for a good: (1) the degree of substitutability with other goods, (2) the size of the portion of buyer's income typically devoted to expenditure on the good, and (3) the length of time over which demand conditions are considered.

1. Degree of Substitutability

In Chapter 4 it was argued that the demand curve for a good typically slopes downward from left to right because there are other goods that to varying degrees can be used as substitutes for the good. Hence, if the price of a good goes up, it becomes more expensive relative to its substitutes. Therefore, less of that good and more of the substitute goods will be demanded. Conversely, if the price of a good goes down, it becomes less expensive relative to its substitutes. In this case, more of that good and less of its substitutes will be demanded. The demand curve for a good will be flatter the more close substitutes it has and the more perfect is their degree of substitutability for that good. Conversely, the demand curve for a good will be steeper the fewer close substitutes it has and the less perfect is their degree of substitutability for that

good. How is the degree of substitutability related to the elasticity of demand?

Before answering this question we should first be clear about the terminology commonly used to describe the degree of steepness, or slope, of a demand curve. Recall that you cannot judge whether a demand curve is elastic or inelastic over a certain range simply by looking at it. However, when *comparing* slopes of demand curves (those shown in Figure 20.2, for example), it is common practice to say that the steeper demand curve is 'less elastic' than the flatter demand curve. Or alternatively, we can say the flatter demand curve is 'more elastic' than the steeper demand curve. The terminology 'more', or 'less', 'elastic' is often used even when comparing two demand curves over a price range where they are both inelastic. The use of this terminology is accurate as long as it is understood to mean that the 'more elastic', or flatter, demand curve has a higher coefficient of elasticity than the 'less elastic', or steeper, demand curve over the same price range. This means that the comparison is only valid for a change in price away from a point of intersection of the demand curves. For example, for the price change from p_1 to p_2 in Figure 20.2, demand curve d_e is more elastic than d_i.

In sum, abiding by these conventions of usage, the following statements can be made about the appearance of demand

POLICY PERSPECTIVE

Sales Tax Revenue from Motor Vehicles

In March 1987 the Australian Government announced that the Automotive Chamber of Commerce had asked it to halve the sales tax on motor vehicles. The sales tax on vehicles valued at up to $30,000 was twenty per cent and the tax on vehicles over $30,000 was thirty per cent. Such tax cuts would substantially reduce the price of cars at a time when new motor vehicle registrations were the lowest for a number of years. The argument put to the government was that the increase in the number of vehicles sold as a result in the drop in price would more than compensate the government for the lost revenue on each individual vehicle.

What can one conclude about the estimated price elasticity of demand for motor vehicles in Australia? How large would the percentage increase in unit sales have to be for the government not to lose revenue from the tax cut?

To answer this question it is important to distinguish between the revenue consequences for the automotive industry and the consequences for the Government.

Before Tax Cut	Luxury Vehicle		
	$		$
Price of Car	20,000		30,000
+ tax 20%	4,000	+ tax 30%	9,000
	24,000		39,000
After Tax Cut			
Price of Car	20,000		30,000
+ tax 10%	2,000	+ tax 15%	4,500
	22,000		34,500
Overall Price Reduction	2,000		4,500
% price reduction	8.33		11.54
% Government tax reduction	50.0		50.0

For the government to maintain sales revenue there needs to be a doubling of motor vehicle sales. For this to occur in either category on the values chosen this would mean the demand for cars was highly elastic (around 10) since the percentage price fall to the consumer is between 8 and 12 per cent, but there needs to be a 100 per cent increase in sales. Within a matter of hours the Ministry for Trade and Industry put out a press statement emphatically rejecting the idea of a cut in sales tax. The reason — massive and immediate cancellations of existing orders for new cars were occurring. Why? How can we reconcile these events with the demand and supply analysis in the previous chapter? To what extent did the fall in sales orders invalidate the original idea behind the sales cut suggestion or suggest the price elasticity estimations were incorrect?

curves. We can say that the flatter a demand curve is over any given price range, the more elastic is demand over that range. Conversely, the steeper a demand curve is over any given price range, the less elastic is demand over that range. It follows that *the more close substitutes a good has and the more perfect is their degree of substitutability for that good the greater is the elasticity of demand for that good. Conversely, the fewer close substitutes a good has and the less perfect is their degree of substitutability for that good, the smaller is the elasticity of demand for that good.*

In the Policy Perspective doubt was expressed about the likelihood of there being the high elasticity of demand for cars required to make a sales cut attractive to the Commonwealth Government. There are only limited substitutes for motor vehicles and these do not service everyone's requirements. However, when we come down to makes and models of cars it is an entirely different story. The Ford Laser, Mitsubishi Magna and Nissan Skyline, for example, each face fierce competition from rivals. A price change in one is likely to lead to a significant increase or fall in its sales if its rivals' prices are unchanged.

Similarly close substitutability of different makes of red wine gives them, as individual labels a much higher price elasticity of demand than has red wine measured as a general category. There are plenty of substitutes for red wine, but they are not as close as the substitutes within the red wines themselves. By contrast, there are few, if any, substitutes for an artificial heart valve. Therefore, demand for artificial heart valves is probably quite inelastic.

2. Size of Expenditure

If you went to the store to buy a number of things, chances are the number of books of matches you might purchase would be little affected by whether they cost 2 or 3 cents a book. If they were 3 cents and you were pretty sure they could be had elsewhere for 2 cents, you probably wouldn't feel it was worth the hassle and cost (the opportunity cost of your time, for example) to make a special trip just to buy a few books of matches for 2 cents apiece instead of 3 cents. This is probably true even though the latter price is 50 per cent higher than the former. For this reason your demand for matches is probably fairly inelastic. On the other hand, if you were shopping for a new car a price difference of a few hundred dollars among similar models would probably send you shopping all over town, even though such differences might amount to less than 10 per cent of the purchase price. Therefore your demand for a particular model and make of car is almost certainly much more elastic than your demand for matches. What this illustrates is that *in general the demand for a good will tend to be more elastic the larger is the portion of your income required to purchase that good.*

3. Time

It is costly and time consuming for buyers to gather information about the prices and types of different goods and the degree to which they may serve as substitutes for one another. As a result, it takes time for buyers to adjust their consumption habits in response to price changes that alter the relative expensiveness of different goods. For example, if the price of one brand of toothpaste is lowered significantly

FIGURE 20.6
Effect of Time on the Elasticity of
Demand

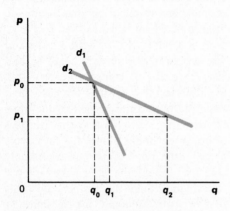

When the price of a good changes, it takes time for all buyers to become aware of the change (time to shop around, for example) and to adjust their consumption habits. The demand curve d_1 for a particular good holds for a shorter period of time, say a week, than the demand curve d_2, which holds over a longer period of time, say a month. The demand curve d_2 is more elastic than d_1. When price falls from p_0 to p_1, the quantity of the good demanded increases from q_0 to q_1 after a week according to the demand curve d_1, but by the larger amount from q_0 to q_2 after a month according to the demand curve d_2.

relative to that of other brands, there may be little switching away from other brands to the cheaper brand the first day after this price change. However, as time passes and knowledge of the new price difference spreads among buyers the quantity demanded at the new lower price of the cheaper toothpaste will increase. Hence the demand curve for this toothpaste will be flatter in the long run than in the short run. This means that the long-run demand curve will be more elastic throughout its length than the short-run demand curve.

Suppose that d_1 in Figure 20.6 represents the demand curve for a good that holds for a week and d_2 represents the demand curve that holds for a month. It is obvious that a fall in price from p_0 to p_1 results in a larger increase in the quantity demanded after a month (q_0 to q_2) than after a week (q_0 to q_1). In general, *the elasticity of demand for a good is greater in the long run than in the short run because buyers have more time to adjust to a change in price.*

CHECKPOINT* 20.1
We have already calculated the coefficient of elasticity for the ranges c to d, a to b, and e to f along the demand curve in Figure 20.3. When the price of a ticket is $18 the number sold is 20,000. When the price falls to $16 the number sold increases to 30,000. Use the arc elasticity formula to calculate the coefficient of elasticity for this range. What do you observe about the elasticity of demand as we move down the demand curve from left to right? The VFL Grand Final game is usually 'sold out.' Let's assume that total revenue is at its maximum. Where do you think the demand curve actually is — to the right or left of the hypothetical demand curve shown in Figure 20.2? Could the elasticity of the demand curve in the range lying directly above the 100,000-seat point on the horizontal axis be inelastic? Why or why not?

* Answers to all Checkpoints can be found at the back of the text.

ELASTICITY OF SUPPLY

The notion of elasticity is also applicable to supply. The arc formula used to

POLICY PERSPECTIVE

Oil Demand Adjustment to Price Change

The price of oil rose nearly twentyfold between 1973, when the OPEC (Organisation of Petroleum Exporting Countries) imposed its embargo, and 1980. We might expect such a large price increase to reduce the quantity of petroleum products demanded substantially. But how much time does it take?

Prior to 1973, 2 decades of falling real prices (prices in terms of other goods) for oil and petroleum products led firms and consumers to acquire large stocks of energy-using durable goods — houses, factories, commercial buildings, motor vehicles, and machinery and equipment. Western society developed an oil-dependent technology extending to electricity generation. The large increase in the price of oil in 1973 and 1974 suddenly made existing stocks of housing and building much more costly to heat and stocks of motor vehicles and machinery and equipment much more expensive to operate. However, firms and consumers were stuck with these durable goods in the short run and indeed a system that literally ran on oil. No matter what the price of the oil it was essential for the industrial world's continued operation. *In the short run the demand for oil is quite inelastic.* Many countries such as Italy and Yugoslavia with no domestic oil supplies found themselves with immediate and intractable balance of payments problems as their foreign oil payment bills rose. It took years to complete the adjustment to substitute sources of energy and to replace existing durable goods with more energy-efficient durable goods.

The elasticity of demand for oil, like that of other goods, is larger in the long run than in the short run. Over the long run, oil consumers have more time to seek out alternative energy sources, develop and build more energy-efficient durable goods, and generally change their energy consumption habits. Hence, as illustrated in Figure P5.1, the short-run demand curve for oil D_s is less elastic than the long-run demand curve D_l. Therefore, if OPEC raises the price of oil from p_e to p_o for example, the quantity of oil demanded falls from Q_e to Q_s, a short-run adjustment corresponding to a move from point *a* to point *b* on D_s. *However, as time passes and buyers are able to make all the oilsaving adjustments to the higher price p_{oz}* the demand curve shifts from D_s to D_l and the quantity of oil demand falls from Q_s to Q_b corresponding to point *c* to D_l.

There is some evidence on how long the adjustment process might take. In the United States it has been estimated that the 1 year elasticity of demand for petrol lies between .2 and .4. That is a 10 per cent rise in the real price of petrol causes a 2 to 4 per cent reduction in consumption after 1 year — perhaps due mainly to such factors as increased car pooling and shorter vacation trips. The estimated 5-year elasticities are higher, ranging between .6 and .8. Over a 5-year period, consumers appear to adjust by buying more fuel-efficient cars, moving closer to work and generally changing fuel consumption habits. The result is that a 10 per cent petrol price rise reduces consumption about 6 to 8 per cent. Note however, that even the 5-year elasticity of demand is still inelastic. This suggests that the ultimate adjustment to OPEC oil price increases may take considerably longer, perhaps a decade or more.

One feature of the 1980s has been a decline in world oil prices though they remain well above the 1973 levels. The fall in prices came because of the failure of the OPEC countries to maintain a common pricing policy and to agree on the production cuts needed to maintain prices at desired levels. Production cuts were made necessary because of the successful long term adjustment by oil-consuming countries which resulted in a fall in oil consumption from the oil-guzzling 1960s and early 1970s. Refusal of some oil-producing countries to join OPEC or agree to its policies compounded their problems. In Australia oil prices have not fallen and as a result it has not been possible to observe responses to price falls as distinct from increases. They have not fallen because the Australian Government's oil pricing policy developed in the 1970s provided it with an important source of revenue from local producers when oil prices were rising. It has not been able to do without that revenue and allow oil prices in Australia to reflect the fall in the world price.

Questions

1. What do the elasticity estimates for petrol demand imply about the behaviour of petrol sales revenue when petrol prices increase?

2. Do you think the demand for oil would be more or less elastic for an oil price decrease compared to the response for an oil price increase? Why?

FIGURE P20.1
The Elasticity of demand for Oil Increases with Passage of Time

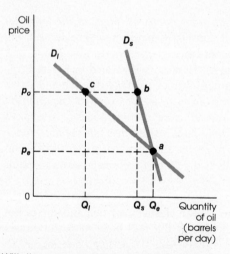

With the passage of time the elasticity of oil demand increases and the demand curve shifts from the short-run position D_s to the long-run position D_l. Therefore, when the price of oil is increased from p_e to p_o, demand for oil decreases from Q_e to Q_s in the short run but by a larger amount from Q_s to Q_l in the long run.

calculate the elasticity of demand may also be used to determine the elasticity of supply. Thus the formula for elasticity of supply may be expressed as

$$e_s = \frac{\text{percentage change in quantity supplied}}{\text{percentage change in price}}$$

and the arc elasticity of supply as

$$e_s \text{ ARC} = \frac{\dfrac{\text{the change in quantity supplied}}{\dfrac{\text{the sum of quantities}}{2}}}{} \div \frac{\dfrac{\text{the change in price}}{\dfrac{\text{the sum of prices}}{2}}}{}$$

Supply is more elastic the larger is the change in the quantity of output produced by suppliers in response to a change in price. Figure 20.7 shows an inelastic supply curve S_i and an elastic supply curve S_e. Consider a change in price from p_0 to p_1.

FIGURE 20.7
Elasticity of Supply

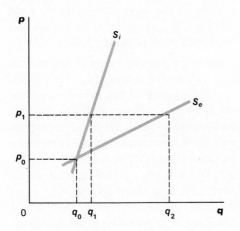

The greater the elasticity of supply, the larger the quantity-change response to a change in price. If price increases from p_0 to p_1, the increase in quantity supplied will be from q_0 to q_1 for the inelastic supply curve S_i. The same price increase will result in a larger increase in supply, from q_0 to q_2, for the elastic supply curve S_e.

The increase in quantity supplied would be from q_0 to q_1 for the inelastic supply curve S_i, a smaller increase than from q_0 to q_2 for the elastic supply curve S_e. **Elastic supply** *exists when the coefficient of elasticity is greater than 1.* **Inelastic supply** *exists when the coefficient of elasticity is less than 1. It is unit elastic if the coefficient equals 1.*

What Determines Elasticity of Supply?

There are two main determinants of the elasticity of supply of a good: (1) the degree of substitutability of factors of production among different productive activities and (2) time.

1. Degree of Substitutability

When the price of a good rises, it becomes profitable to produce more of it. We examined the reasons why this is so when we discussed the law of supply and the nature of the supply curve in Chapter 4. The increase in the quantity of a good that can be supplied in response to an increase in its price depends, in part, on the ease with which needed factors of production can be induced away from other uses. And this in turn will depend on how readily factors may be adapted from use in other lines of production to production of the good in question.

For example, land that can be used equally well to produce oats or wheat will be easily converted from wheat to oats production if there is an increase in the price of oats (assuming the price of wheat remains unchanged, of course). The greater the degree of substitutability of land between wheat and oats production, the larger will be the increase in the quantity of oats supplied in response to any given increase in its price. Consequently, the supply curve for oats will be flatter, or more elastic. Similarly, if the price of oats should fall, land will be readily taken out of oats production and converted to wheat production. The quantity of oats supplied will be noticeably reduced. On the other hand, if the price of handcrafted artwork were to rise, the quantity produced might increase very little because of the difficulty of finding additional craftspersons. The substitutability of labour between other activities and this one is low. Similarly, a fall in the price of artwork might lead to little reduction in the quantity supplied because the craftspersons like their work so much they are willing to take a considerable cut in wages rather than do something else. The supply curve for handcrafted artwork might therefore be quite steep, or inelastic. In general, *the greater the degree of substitutability of factors of production between the production process of one good and the production processes of other goods, the greater the elasticity of supply of that good.*

2. Time

The relationship between time and the elasticity of supply is closely related to the degree of substitutability. The more time there is, the more factors of production can be shifted from one productive activity to another. In the oats-wheat example, if the price of oats rises, it will not be possible to increase the quantity of oats supplied during the first week. After the price rise, time will be needed to convert the land to growing oats. As time passes, it will be possible to convert more and more land and other resources to oats production.

In general, in economics we distinguish between the **short run** and the **long run**. *In the short run the quantities of at least some of the factors of production available for the production of a good are given, or fixed.* Hence the short run is a period of time that is not long enough to allow the quantities of all factors of production to be changed. *A short run during which none of the factors of production can be changed is sometimes called a* **market period**. At the other extreme *in the long run there is sufficient time to change the quantities of all factors of production.*

Since none of the factors of production can be changed during a market period, it is not possible in this period to change the quantity of output supplied in response to a change in price. Therefore the supply of a good for a market period is perfectly inelastic. The vertical supply curve of a good in a market period appears as S_m in Figure 20.8. In the short run, some factors of production can be changed, and therefore it is possible, to some extent, to change the quantity of output supplied in response to a price change. Supply may still be inelastic, but it is not perfectly inelastic as in the market period. The supply curve for a good in the short run appears as S_s in Figure 20.8. In the long run, all factors of production may be changed. Thus, the change in quantity of

POLICY PERSPECTIVE

The J Curve

There was a massive depreciation of the Australian dollar in 1985 and a further depreciation in 1986. Table P20.1 shows the trade weighted index of the dollar's value in terms of other currencies for the period from January 1985 to December 1986.

TABLE P20.1
Australia's Exchange Rate and Balance of Merchandise Trade 1985-1986

	Exchange Rate Trade Weighted Index	Quarter Ending	Exports A$m	Imports A$m	Balance of Merchandise Trade A$m
Jan. 85	80.8	Mar. 85	6821	6963	-142
April 85	64.2	June 85	8696	8387	305
July 85	68.5	Sept. 85	8477	9297	-820
Oct. 85	63.4	Dec. 85	7979	9150	-1171
Jan. 86	62.7	Mar. 86	8151	8611	460
April 86	61.4	June 86	7647	8588	-911
July 86	49.3	Sept. 86	8214	9628	-1414
Oct. 86	54.0	Dec. 86	9141	9616	-475

Sources: Reserve Bank of Australia, *Bulletin*, December 1986
          Australian Bureau of Statistics, *Balance of Payments Quarterly*, Ref. 5302, Canberra

The table also shows the value of exports, the value of imports and the balance of merchandise trade. It was hoped that the depreciation of the dollar would lead to a restoration of the competitiveness of Australian producers on local and overseas markets and help to overcome the fundamental balance of payments disequilibrium.

However, the figures show that notwithstanding the devaluation the trade deficit (one of the key elements in the balance of payments) continued, and, for a time got worse. Exports rose but imports rose a lot more. This led some commentators to conclude that the depreciation wasn't working to help the Australian external policies. Yet there are good reasons why the balance of trade can be expected to get worse before it gets better. It has frequently been observed that short-run demand and supply is less elastic than are the long-run responses. The anticipated result, an initial deterioration in the balance of trade followed by a subsequent improvement, has been expressed pictorially as a J curve.

Depreciation makes the Australian dollar worth fewer units than any foreign currency. This affects both the cost (supply) of imports to Australia and the prices Australian exports receive on world markets. Figures P20.2 and P20.3 show the effects on imports and exports respectively.

In Figure P20.2 the effects of the depreciation on imports are analysed. Before depreciation the foreign supply curve SS intersects demand at E and q_0 imports are purchased at A$$p_0$. The depreciation shifts the foreign supply curve (expressed in A$) upwards and to the left by the percentage of the devaluation. Foreign suppliers still require the same amount of their local currency to induce them to supply any given quantity to Australia but a given amount of foreign currency now requires *more* Australian currency.

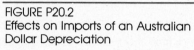

FIGURE P20.2
Effects on Imports of an Australian
Dollar Depreciation

FIGURE P20.3
Effects on Exports of an Australian
Dollar Depreciation

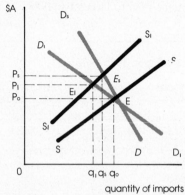

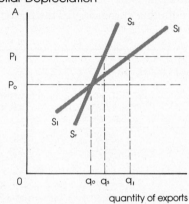

quantity of imports

quantity of exports

In the short run Australian demand for imports is relatively inelastic (D_sD_s). Australian importers are locked into contracts or have no alternative source of supply. Hence although the quantity imported falls to q_s the price of imports rises sharply to A$$p_s$. If demand is absolutely inelastic the result is an increase in import payments as occurred in 1985. In the longer term we expect local industries to compete more successfully with the imports. In consequence the demand for imports becomes more elastic — there is a further fall in the quantity of imports to q_s and a fall in the price of imports to A$$p_l$. If demand for imports is absolutely elastic in the long term the result will be a reduction in Australia's import bill.

A slightly different picture emerges when we look at the effect on exports, shown in Figure P20.3. Generally speaking Australia is a price taker on world markets — the quantity it sells does not affect international prices. As an Australian dollar is now worth less in terms of foreign currencies and internationally determined prices, the depreciation can be represented as an increase in the price of Australian exports — from A$$p_o$ to A$$p_l$ in Figure P20.3.

The result of the depreciation is likely to be an increase in export receipts, but less in the short run than the long run. In the short run exporters are unable to mobilise resources to respond to higher prices and the supply curve is represented by S_sS_s — quantity exported rises from q_o to q_s. In the longer term the full response is shown by the more elastic supply curve S_lS_l and the export quantity increases further to q_2.

Question

The alarm expressed in Australia in 1986 was due to the apparent slowness of the long term effects to work themselves through coupled with the fear that the competitive benefits of depreciation might be eroded by continuing inflation. Study Table P20.1. To what extent does the information it contains support the J curve theory and the reasoning given in Figures P20.2 and P20.3? What possible reasons would there be for the balance of trade to continue to get worse?

---

the good supplied in response to a price change can be much greater than in the short run. Supply is more elastic and the supply curve appears as S_l in Figure 20.8. In sum, if price rose from p_0 to p_l in Figure 20.8, the quantity of the good supplied

---

FIGURE 20.8
The Effect of Time on the Elasticity of Supply

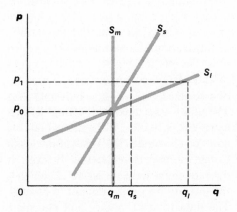

The more time suppliers have to respond to a change in price, the greater will be the change in the quantity of output they supply. Suppose price rises from p_0 to p_1. In the very short run, or market period, all factors of production are fixed and it is therefore not possible to change the quantity produced and supplied. Hence, the supply curve is perfectly inelastic, or vertical, like S_m. In the short run, some factors of production, such as plant and equipment, are fixed. But some, such as labour, may be changed. Therefore, the supply curve is more elastic, like S_s, and the quantity of output supplied can be increased from q_m to q_s. In the long run, all factors of production can be changed and the supply curve is even more elastic, like S_l, and the quantity of output supplied can be increased an even larger amount from q_m to q_l.

---

would remain at q_m in the market period, would increase from q_m to q_s in the short run, and would increase from q_m to q_l in the long run.

CHECKPOINT 20.2
When we calculate the coefficient of elasticity for the change in quantity supplied that results from a change in price, we automatically get a positive number. Hence we don't need to adopt a convention of ignoring the minus sign as we do when we calculate the coefficient of elasticity for demand. Why is there this difference between the coefficient of elasticity for supply and that for demand?

CONSUMER UTILITY AND DEMAND THEORY[1]

Up to now we have based our assumption that demand curves slope downward from left to right on simple common sense and casual observation of the economic world around us. If pushed further, we might reason that if the price of a good is reduced, it will now take a smaller portion of our money income to buy the same quantity of it. This means that more of our money income is now available to purchase more of other goods, as well as more of the good whose price has fallen. In this sense, a price reduction has the same effect on demand for the good as an increase in real income (purchasing power). This demand-increasing aspect of a price reduction is termed the **income**

[1]This section may be skipped without disturbing the continuity of the text.

effect. In addition to this effect, we would also expect demand for the good whose price has fallen to increase because that good is now cheaper relative to all other goods. Hence consumers would substitute more of that good for others. This demand-increasing aspect of a price reduction is termed the **substitution effect**.

In general, any change in the price of a good (up or down) may be said to have a substitution effect and an income effect on the demand for that good — all other things, such as the consumer's tastes and money income, remaining the same. The substitution and income effects of a change in price on the demand for a particular good provide a somewhat fuller explanation of why the demand curve for a good slopes downward from left to right.

Yet another explanation for the shape of a demand curve is based on the concept of utility.

The Concept of Utility

In Chapter 1 we noted that people desire goods because they provide some sort of satisfaction or service. A movie provides entertainment, which gives satisfaction. An apple or a glass of milk provides not only satisfaction but nourishment, which serves to sustain life. The service or satisfaction a good yields is often referred to as the **utility** that the consumer gets from the good. Utility is not to be confused with 'usefulness.' A record may not be considered as 'useful' as a screwdriver, but one may feel there is more utility in the form of satisfaction associated with the former than with the latter.

It is not possible to compare the utility I get from eating a muesli bar with the utility you get from eating one. The issue of how much more you enjoy a muesli bar than I do is not something that can be settled by objective measurement, as

is the case in a dispute over which one of us is taller, for example. However, the concept of utility has been used by economists to provide an explanation for the shape of a consumer's demand curve for a good. This can be done because it is possible to imagine an individual consumer making comparisons of the different levels of utility that he or she associates with different kinds and quantities of goods.

Total Utility

Suppose we consider the utility that a particular (hypothetical) individual gets from eating chocolates over some given period of time, say a day. This is known as total utility. Assume that this utility, or satisfaction, is measured in units called utils. The relationship between the amount of chocolates consumed and the amount of associated utility is shown in Table 20.2. The utility associated with eating the first chocolate is 10 utils. If the individual eats another chocolate, the total utility from eating the two chocolates is 19 utils. If the individual were to eat 10 chocolates, the total utility would amount to 55 utils. The data for total utility and chocolate consumption from Table 20.2 are plotted in Figure 20.9, part a. This graph clearly shows that total utility increases as the number of chocolates eaten increases. However, total utility reaches a maximum at 10 chocolates. If the individual eats 11 chocolates, the total utility doesn't change. The last chocolate neither adds to nor subtracts from satisfaction. If a twelfth chocolate is consumed, the individual starts to feel sick and total utility decreases to 54 utils.

Marginal Utility

A more useful consideration from an economist's point of view is the way total utility changes with the consumption of each additional chocolate. *The change in total utility that occurs with the consumption of an additional unit of a good is the* **marginal utility**. It refers to the increment, or addition, to total utility associated with the additional, or marginal, unit of the good consumed. The marginal utility associated with chocolate eating for our hypothetical individual is shown in the third column of Table 20.2. For example, if the individual has had one chocolate already, the additional, or marginal, utility associated with eating a second is 9 utils. This brings the total utility to 19 utils. The additional, or marginal, utility of a third chocolate is 8 utils, which brings the total to 27 utils, and so forth. Observe that as the consumer

eats more chocolates, the marginal utility associated with eating one more chocolate gets smaller and smaller. This is clearly seen in the graph of the marginal utility in Figure 20.9, part b.

Law of Diminishing Marginal Utility

The important thing to note about marginal utility is that it decreases as more of the good is consumed over a given period of time. It is, of course, possible that the second or third unit of a good consumed may add more to total utility than the first. (For some chocolate eaters this may be true.) But for almost any good one can think of, marginal utility will eventually begin to fall as more and more of the good is consumed over a given period of time and one's appetite for that good becomes satiated. Even the marginal utility associated with the consumption of salted peanuts eventually begins to fall.

Economists believe this observation about the behaviour of marginal utility to be so universal that they call it the **law of diminishing marginal utility**. *This law states that, given the consumer's tastes, the marginal utility associated with the consumption of any good over a given period of time will eventually begin to fall as more and more of the good is consumed.* This law is demonstrated by the downward-sloping marginal utility curve in Figure 20.9, part b, for example. The law simply reflects the widely observed fact that the more a person has of a good, the less satisfaction or utility is derived from having one more unit of the good.

How the Consumer Allocates Expenditures Among Goods

No consumer has an unlimited budget. Therefore it is necessary to make choices — more of one good can be obtained only

TABLE 20.2
One Individual's Total Utility and Marginal Utility from Eating Chocolates During a Day (Hypothetical Data)

Number of Chocolates per Day	Total Utility (Utils)	Marginal Utility (Change in Utility per Additional Chocolate)
1	10	
		9
2	19	
		8
3	27	
		7
4	34	
		6
5	40	
		5
6	45	
		4
7	49	
		3
8	52	
		2
9	54	
		1
10	55	
		0
11	55	
		-1
12	54	

FIGURE 20.9
Total Utility and Marginal Utility

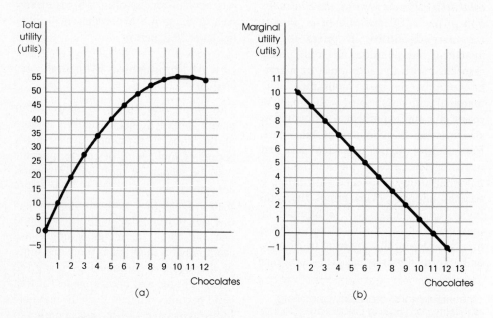

(a)

(b)

The data on total utility associated with the individual's daily consumption of chocolates from Table 20.2 are graphed in part a. Part b is a graph of the data on marginal utility from the same table. Total utility clearly rises as the individual eats more chocolates, but at a diminishing rate. The slowdown is clearly shown by the graph of the additional, or marginal, utility (part b) that the individual realises from each additional chocolate eaten. The fact that it slopes downward from left to right illustrates the *law of diminishing marginal utility*. This law states that the marginal utility associated with the consumption of any good over a given period of time will eventually begin to fall as more and more of the good is consumed. It reflects the widely observed fact that typically the more a person has of a good, the less satisfaction, or utility, is derived from having one more unit of the good.

by purchasing less of another. Given a limited budget, the individual consumer's problem is how to allocate expenditure of that budget among goods so as to make total satisfaction, or total utility, as large as possible. Given a limited budget, how does a consumer determine what combination of goods should be purchased in order to realise the greatest possible satisfaction? A simple example will help us to understand the answer to this question.

Determining the Utility-Maximising Combination of Goods: A Simple Example

Let's consider a consumer who has a total daily income of $11. Suppose there are only two goods, X and Z. (We could consider many goods, but exactly the same principles apply as in the simpler case of two goods.) The utility that our consumer gets from the two goods is shown in Table 20.3. Column 2 gives the total utility obtained from the consumption of the quantity of good X indicated in column 1. Column 3 shows the marginal, or additional, utility derived from the consumption of each successive unit of good X. Similarly, columns 5 and 6 show the total and marginal utility, respectively, derived from the consumption of good Z. For each good the law of diminishing marginal utility is reflected in the fact that marginal utility declines (columns 3 and 6) as more of the good is consumed.

The consumer's preferences or feelings about goods X and Z, as reflected in the utility data of Table 20.3, combined with the prices of the two goods, will determine the combination of X and Z that maximises the consumer's total utility, given a fixed budget of $11 per day. In order to see how the consumer chooses this combination, the marginal utility data of columns 3 and 6 must be expressed as marginal utility per dollar spent. This makes it easier to compare the additional utility obtainable by spending a dollar on one of the goods with the additional utility obtainable by spending that dollar on the other good. Suppose the price of a unit of X is $1, while that of a unit of Z is $2. The marginal utility per dollar spent on X, column 4, is found by dividing the marginal utility data in column 3 by $1. Similarly the marginal utility per dollar spent on Z, column 7, is found by dividing the data in column 6 by $2.

We can now see how our consumer will go about spending a daily income of $11 on X and Z. Remember, the consumer's objective is to allocate expenditures on X and Z in such a way as to achieve the highest possible level of utility. Comparing columns 4 and 7, the consumer should first purchase 1 unit of good Z because its marginal utility of 11 utils per dollar is higher than X's. The consumer still has

$9 to spend. At this point the consumer could get the same marginal utility per dollar, 10 utils, from 1 unit of X or 1 unit of Z. So the consumer buys both of them. The consumer now has 1 unit of X, 2 units of Z, and $6 yet to spend. Comparing columns 4 and 7 again, the consumer next should buy a second unit of X since its marginal utility per dollar is greater than that of a third unit of Z. Having done this, observe that the marginal utility per dollar of a third unit of Z exceeds that of a third unit of X. Hence a third unit of Z is purchased. Now the consumer has 2 units of X, 3 units of Z, and $3 left to spend. The consumer is indifferent as to the choice between a third unit of X and a fourth unit of Z since each yields 6 utils per dollar spent. However, the consumer has just enough money left to buy each of them.

The consumer has now spent the whole daily income of $11 to obtain a combination consisting of 3 units of X and 4 units of Z. Note that this combination is such that the marginal utility derived from the last dollar spent on each good is the same. This combination gives the consumer the highest total utility possible, given a budget of $11. Total utility equals 95 utils, the sum of the 25 utils derived from the 3 units of X, column 2, plus the 70 utils derived from the 4 units of Z, column 5. There is no other combination that can be purchased for $11 that will give the consumer as much total utility. For example, $11 could purchase a combination consisting of 1 unit of X and 5 units of Z — total utility equals 88 utils. Or $11 could buy 5 units of X and 3 units of Z, giving a total utility of 89 utils. Notice that for either of these combinations it is not true that the marginal utility derived from the last dollar spent on each good is the same.

TABLE 20.3
Utility, Marginal Utility, and Marginal Utility per Dollar Obtained from Goods X and Z[a]
(Hypothetical Data)

(1) Quantity of Good	Good X: Price = $1			Good Z: Price = $2		
	(2) Total Utility from X (Utils)	(3) Marginal Utility (Utils)	(4) Marginal Utility per Dollar (*MU*/Price)	(5) Total Utility from Z (Utils)	(6) Marginal Utility (Utils)	(7) Marginal Utility per Dollar (*MU*/Price)
1	10	10	10	22	22	11
2	19	9	9	42	20	10
3	25	6	6	58	16	8
4	29	4	4	70	12	6
5	31	2	2	78	8	4
6	30	1	1	80	2	1

[a]It is assumed that the marginal utility of either good is unaffected by the quantity of the other good consumed.

The rule that emerges from our example of picking the combination of goods that maximises total utility is: *To maximise total utility the consumer should spend a given money income to buy that combination of goods such that the marginal utility derived from the last dollar spent on each good is the same.*

Why the Rule Works

We can get additional insight into why the rule works by restating it more concisely. The marginal utility (*MU*) per dollar spent on X is equal to the *MU* of good X divided by the price of X, column 4 of Table 20.3. The marginal utility (*MU*) per dollar spent on Z is equal to the *MU* of good Z divided by the price of Z, column 7 of Table 20.3. The utility-maximising rule says that the consumer should spend a given money income to buy that combination of X and Z that makes the marginal utility of the last dollar spent on X equal to the marginal utility of the last dollar spent on Z or, more concisely,

$$\frac{MU \text{ of good } X}{\text{price of } X} = \frac{MU \text{ of good } Z}{\text{price of } Z}$$

For the optimum combination of 3 units of X and 4 units of Z in Table 20.3, obtained by spending the $11 of money income, this equality is met:

$$\frac{6 \text{ utils}}{\$1} = \frac{12 \text{ utils}}{\$2}$$

If this equality is not satisfied, it is always possible to increase total utility by buying less of the good having the lower marginal utility per dollar and buying more of the good with the higher marginal utility per dollar.

For instance, suppose our consumer in Table 20.3 spent the $11 money income to buy a combination consisting of 5 units of good X and 3 units of good Z. Then the marginal utility derived from the last dollar spent on X is 2 utils (column 4 of Table 20.3), which is less than the marginal utility of 8 utils (column 7 of Table 20.3) derived from the last dollar spent on Z. The equality is not satisfied:

$$\frac{2 \text{ utils}}{\$1} \neq \frac{16 \text{ utils}}{\$2}$$

The consumer's total utility could be increased if he or she purchased a smaller amount of X and a larger amount of Z. To see why, suppose the consumer reallocates expenditures by taking $2 away from expenditure on X and instead spending that $2 on more Z. This reduces consumption of X by 2 units (from 5 units to 3 units) and the utility derived from X by 6 utils, the sum of 2 utils plus 4 utils in column 3 of Table 20.3. The additional $2 of spending on Z increases consumption of Z by 1 unit (from 3 units to 4 units), and the utility derived from consumption of Z rises by 12 utils, column 6 of Table 20.3. The net gain in total utility resulting from this reallocation of expenditures is 6 utils — total utility increases from 89 utils (equal to 31 utils, column 2, plus 58 utils, column 5) to 95 utils (equal to 25 utils, column 2, plus 70 utils, column 5).

The utility-maximising rule works because whenever the marginal utility derived from the last dollar spent on good Z is greater than that derived from the last dollar spent on X, the increase in utility obtained by consuming more Z is greater than the decrease in utility that results from consuming less X. The marginal utility per dollar spent on Z declines as the consumer moves down Z's diminishing marginal utility curve, and the marginal utility per dollar spent on X increases as the consumer moves up the diminishing marginal utility curve of X. As the consumer continues to reallocate expenditures from X to Z, at some point the marginal utility of the last dollar spent on X is brought into equality with the marginal utility of the last dollar spent on Z. The rule is satisfied. At this point

total utility cannot be increased more by any further reallocation of expenditure.

Why a Demand Curve Slopes Downward

We are now in a position to see how utility theory explains why a demand curve slopes downward, from left to right.

Recall that movement along a fixed demand curve means that only two things change — the price of the good and the quantity of the good demanded. All other things remain unchanged, including the consumer's income and all other prices. Assume that the consumer whose preferences are reflected in the utility data of Table 20.3 is maximising the total utility obtainable from a daily income of $11 by purchasing 3 units of X and 4 units of Z. Hence we already have one point on the consumer's demand curve for Z: given an income of $11 and a price of $1 per unit of the other good X, the quantity of Z demanded at a price of $2 is 4 units.

Suppose now that the price of Z is lowered to $1 per unit, all other things remaining unchanged. This means that the data for the marginal utility per dollar in column 7 will double. In fact these data will be identical to the data in column 6. The combination of 3 units of X and 4 units of Z no longer gives the consumer the largest possible total utility. Applying the utility-maximising rule, the consumer will now purchase the combination consisting of 5 units of X and 6 units of Z. Here the marginal utility derived from the last dollar spent on X will equal the marginal utility derived from the last dollar spent on Z, 2 utils per dollar. Lowering the price of Z from $2 per unit to $1 per unit has caused the quantity of Z demanded to increase from 4 units to 6 units.

This analysis based on utility theory gives the basic proposition of the law of demand. *A decrease in the price of a good will result in an increase in the quantity of that good demanded by the consumer given that the consumer's budget and the prices of all other goods are held constant.* If this is true for each consumer, it will also be true for all of them taken together. Hence the market demand curve will slope downward, from left to right.

CHECKPOINT 20.3
Suppose that

$$\frac{MU \; of \; X}{price \; of \; X} > \frac{MU \; of \; Z}{price \; of \; Z}$$

Explain why and how the consumer's expenditures out of a fixed budget will be reallocated until

$$\frac{MU \; of \; X}{price \; of \; X} = \frac{MU \; of \; Z}{price \; of \; Z}$$

Why can we expect the demand curve for X to slope downward?

---

1. Elasticity of demand is the degree of responsiveness of the quantity of a good demanded to a change in its price. It is measured by the coefficient of elasticity, which is the percentage change in quantity divided by the percentage change in price.

2. When the coefficient of elasticity is greater than 1, demand is said to be elastic. When the coefficient is less than 1, demand is said to be inelastic. The quantity demanded is less responsive to price change when demand is inelastic than when it is elastic.

3. The elasticity of demand is typically different over different parts of a demand curve. Therefore it can be very misleading to judge the elasticity of demand along a certain part of a demand curve by the slope, or flatness or steepness, of the demand curve along that part.

4. Whether a demand curve is elastic or inelastic along a certain part can be determined by observing how total revenue changes along that part as price changes. If total revenue moves in the opposite direction to price, demand is elastic; if total revenue moves in the same direction as price, demand is inelastic.

5. The main determinants of the elasticity of demand for a good are the degree of substitutability with other goods, the size of the portion of a buyer's income that must be devoted to expenditure on the good, and the length of time over which demand conditions are considered. Demand will usually be more elastic the greater is the degree of substitutability with other goods, the larger is the portion of a buyer's income that must be devoted to expenditure on the good, and the longer the length of time over which demand conditions are considered.

6. The concept of elasticity is also applicable to supply. Supply is more elastic the larger is the change in the quantity of output produced by suppliers in response to a change in price. The greater the degree of substitutability of factors of production among different productive activities and the longer the time period over which supply is considered, the more elastic is supply.

7. Income and substitution effects of price changes provide explanations for the law of demand. By the income effect, when the price of a good declines, the consumer's money income can buy more of the good whose price has fallen, as well as more of all other goods. By the substitution effect, we would also expect demand for the good whose price has fallen to increase because that good is now cheaper relative to all others. The income and substitution effects of a price increase cause the demand for the good whose price has risen to fall.

8. Another explanation for the law of demand is provided by the theory of utility. This theory assumes that the amount of utility a consumer gets from a good can be measured. This measurement is the basis for the law of diminishing marginal utility, which says that the more of a good a consumer has, the smaller the addition to total utility provided by an additional unit of the good.

9. The law of diminishing marginal utility can be used to show how the consumer's total utility is maximised when the consumer spends a given size budget in such a way that the marginal utility derived from the last dollar spent for each good is the same. Assuming that the consumer's budget is spent in accordance with this principle, it is possible to derive a downward-sloping demand curve for each good.

KEY TERMS AND CONCEPTS

arc elasticity
coefficient of elasticity
elastic demand
elasticity of demand
elasticity of supply
elastic supply
income effect
inelastic demand
inelastic supply
law of diminishing marginal utility
long run
marginal utility
market period
perfectly elastic
perfectly inelastic
short run
slope of the demand curve
substitution effect
total revenue
unit elastic
utility

QUESTIONS AND PROBLEMS

1. Classify the following goods and services according to whether you think the demand for them over a period of a year is elastic or inelastic: petrol, margarine, kidney machines, Swan Lager, haircuts, electricity, chocolate ice cream, appendectomies, garbage, fire insurance, funeral services, medical doctors and postal services.

2. Classify the following goods and services according to whether you think the supply of them over a period of a year is elastic or inelastic: Rembrandt paintings, advice, soft drinks, suspension bridges, medical doctors, car salespersons, corn, ivory, matches, cactus plants, 5-year-old wine and oil tankers.

3. Suppose you own a lake in the Central Highlands of Tasmania, which has been well stocked with Brown Trout. You are now about to develop a tourist attraction by offering a fishing accommodation package but need to decide how much to charge for such a unique experience. Suppose also, as a result of market research, you discover that the price elasticity of demand for your fishing holiday is unity. What conclusions would this be likely to lead you to about the price you should charge: a high price with few takers or a lower one with more tourists?

After completing the research and making a tentative decision on a pricing policy for your venture you learn that a second landowner is also going to open a fishing lodge. What effect do you think his decision is likely to have on the elasticity of demand for your project? Is it likely to affect your charges?

4. Suppose the demand curve for a good shifts rightward while the supply curve shifts leftward. Rank the following sets of conditions according to the size of the change in price you would predict as a result of the shifts: demand curve elastic and supply curve inelastic, demand curve inelastic and supply curve inelastic, and demand curve elastic and supply curve elastic.

5. Suppose the demand curve for a good shifts rightward and the supply curve remains fixed. Rank the following sets of conditions according to the size of the change in quantity you would predict as a result of the shift: supply curve inelastic and demand curve inelastic, supply curve elastic and demand curve inelastic, and supply curve inelastic and demand curve elastic.

6. Suppose the supply curve for a good shifts leftward and the demand curve remains fixed. Rank the following sets of conditions according to the size of the change in quantity you would predict as a result of the shift: supply curve elastic and demand curve inelastic, supply curve inelastic and demand curve elastic, and supply curve inelastic and demand curve inelastic.

7. I buy caviar each month at a price of $2 per 50 grams and pay monthly for water at a price of $.01 per 100 litres. I get 2,000 utils from the last 50 grams of caviar I eat and 50 utils from the last 100 litre bath I take. Am I maximising my utility or should I change the combination of caviar and water I consume per month? If so, how should I reallocate my expenditures between these two goods?

8. Suppose a consumer gets the following utility shown in the table, from drinking beer and eating peanuts:

Cans of beer	Total Utility	Bags of nuts	Total Utility
1	20	1	10
2	36	2	19
3	48	3	27
4	56	4	34
5	60	5	40
6	60	6	45
7	56	7	49
8	48	8	52
9	36	9	54
10	20	10	55

a. What are the marginal utilities associated with drinking beer and eating peanuts?

b. Suppose the consumer has $7.50 to spend just on beer and nuts and plans to spend it all on them. If the price of beer is $1 per can and peanuts are 50 cents a bag, show that he will maximise utility if he follows the rule $MUb/Pb = MUn/Pn$ where MUb and MUn are the marginal utility of a can of beer and nuts respectively. Pb and Pn are the prices of beer and nuts. Remember the consumer must spend the entire $7.50. *Hint*: if you find this difficult take any combination of beer and nuts that uses all the money and keep switching dollars from one good to the other until total utility is at its greatest.

c. Suppose the price of beer doubles and the amount available for spending goes up to $10. What combination of beer and nuts will now maximise utility?

APPENDIX

Indifference Curves and Consumer Demand

There is an objection to using the law of diminishing marginal utility to explain the existence of downward-sloping demand curves. It is the fact that utility can't be measured in the way we measure distance, weight and temperature. An alternative explanation of demand curves that doesn't require measurement of this nature is based on the concept of a consumer's indifference curves. Despite the misgivings about the measurement of utility the concept is still widely used when attempting to measure the benefits and costs to consumers of events that lead to price changes and changes in the quantity consumed. The use of this measure will be discussed in Chapter 21.

THE CONCEPT OF AN INDIFFERENCE CURVE

Suppose there are two goods, A and B, and we want to find out how a particular consumer feels about consuming various combinations of these two goods. We might begin by saying to the consumer, 'Suppose you have 10 of B and 2 of A. Tell us what other combinations of B and A would give you exactly the same satisfaction'. Another way of putting this would be to say, 'What other combinations of B and A would leave you feeling no better off and no worse off than you do when you have 10 of B and 2 of A?' Yet another way of saying exactly the same thing would be, 'Tell us those combinations of B and A about which you would feel *indifferent* as to whether you have one of them or the combination consisting of 10 of B and 2 of A'.

In response, suppose this particular consumer gives us five other combinations of B and A. These combinations together with the combination of 10 of B and 2 of A are listed in Table A20.1. They are also plotted as the points *a, b, c, d, e,* and *f* in Figure A20.1. The consumer could list many more combinations until there is a continuum of points forming the curve connecting points *a* to *f*. This curve is called an **indifference curve**. The list of all the combinations represented by the points on this curve is called an **indifference schedule**. Table A20.1 lists six of the combinations from this schedule. The essential characteristic of an indifference schedule is that the consumer feels indifferent as to which particular combination of B and A is consumed. This is because the consumer gets exactly the same satisfaction from any one combination as from any other. Correspondingly, *the consumer gets equal satisfaction at any point along an indifference curve.*

Marginal Rate of Substitution

There is a particularly important point to note about the indifference schedule and its graphic representation, the indifference curve. Starting from any combination or point, if the consumer is given an additional amount of one good, a certain amount of the other must be taken away if the consumer's level of satisfaction is to remain unchanged. The amount taken away is the minimum amount of the one good that the consumer is willing to part with in order to have an additional unit of the other good. It is just the amount that will leave the consumer feeling as well off as, but no better off than, before. *The rate at which the consumer is just willing to substitute good B for good A so as to leave his or her level of satisfaction unchanged is called the* **marginal rate of substitution**. For the consumer of Table A20.1, the marginal rates of substitution between the combinations *a* to *f* are shown in the third column. For example, between the combinations *a* and *b*, the consumer would be just willing to give up 1 unit of A in exchange for 3 units of B — a move from *b* to *a*. Or alternatively, the consumer would be just willing to give up 3 units of B in exchange for 1 unit of A — a move from *a* to *b*.

TABLE A20.1
A Consumer's Indifference Schedule for Two Goods, A and B

Combination	Indifference Schedule (Combinations of B and A)	Marginal Rate of Substitution Between B and A
a	10B, 2A	
		3/1 = 3.0
b	7B, 3A	
		2/1 = 2.0
c	5B, 4A	
		1/1 = 1.
d	4B, 5A	
		1/2 = .5
e	3B, 7A	
		1/3 = .3
f	2B, 10A	

Diminishing Marginal Rate of Substitution

Another important characteristic of the indifference schedule and the indifference curve is that the marginal rate of substitution between B and A gets smaller the larger is the amount of A the consumer has relative to the amount of B. For example, suppose the consumer initially has combination *a*. If the consumer is given one more unit of A, it is necessary to take away 3 units of B to maintain the same level of satisfaction. Then the consumer has combination *b*. Continuing in the same fashion from point *b* to *c*, *c* to *d*, *d* to *e*, and *e* to *f*, observe that to maintain the same level of satisfaction the amount of B that the consumer is willing to give up per additional amount of A becomes less and less. This characteristic of the behaviour of the marginal rate of substitution along an indifference curve is sometimes referred to as the **diminishing marginal rate of substitution**. It reflects the fact that the more of good B a consumer has *relative* to good A, the more of good B the consumer is willing to part with in order to get an additional unit of good A. It plays a role in indifference theory very similar to the role played by the law of diminishing marginal utility in utility theory.

The Consumer Has Many Indifference Curves

The indifference curve of Figure A20.1 represents only one of a family of indifference curves that characterise the particular consumer's feelings of satisfaction derived from consumption of the two goods A and B. All points on it represent combinations of the goods A and B that give the consumer the *same* level of satisfaction — a level of satisfaction that is but one among many possible levels of satisfaction. Each of the other possible levels of satisfaction also has an associated indifference curve.

This is illustrated in Figure A20.1. The indifference curve I_1 is exactly the same one as in Figure A20.1. We are talking about the same particular consumer. Assume the consumer is at point e on I_1, a combination consisting of 7 units of A and 3 units of B. Suppose the consumer was given 4 more units of B while still keeping 7 units of A. The consumer would then have combination h, consisting of the

FIGURE A20.1
A Consumer's Indifference Curve

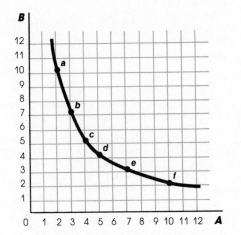

The consumer's indifference curve represents all possible combinations of the goods A and B that give the consumer equal satisfaction.

The points *a* through *f* are plotted from Table A20.1. The curve through these points is the indifference curve — the consumer is indifferent between the various combinations of A and B on it. In other words, each combination on the curve gives the same satisfaction as every other combination on the curve. Any point above and to the right of the curve is a preferred combination to any point on the curve. Any point on the curve is a preferred combination to any point below or to the left of the curve. Movement along the indifference curve requires the consumer to give up a certain amount of one good for every unit acquired of the other. This represents the rate at which the consumer is just willing to substitute good A for good B so as to leave his or her level of satisfaction unchanged — it is called the *marginal rate of substitution*. This rate diminishes with movement down the indifference curve, reflecting the fact that the consumer is willing to give up less B for an additional unit of A the smaller the quantity of B the consumer possesses relative to the quantity of A.

same amount of A as combination *e* but more B. Since at *h* the consumer has more of the one good and the same amount of the other as at *e*, the consumer must feel better off (or feel a higher level of satisfaction) at *h* than at *e*. Since the consumer experiences the same level of satisfaction at all points on I_1 as at *e*, it follows that the consumer feels a higher level of satisfaction at point *h* than at any point on the curve I_1.

Now suppose we again ask the consumer to tell us other combinations that give exactly the same level of satisfaction as that at point *h*. We would then be able to derive the indifference curve I_2 in exactly the same way that we derived the indifference curve I_1. Because the level of satisfaction associated with point *h* is greater than that associated with any point on I_1, it follows that any point on I_2 represents a higher level of satisfaction than any point on I_1.

Proceeding in this manner, it would be possible to derive an unlimited number of **indifference curves**, or the indifference map, for this particular consumer. *Each indifference curve represents a unique and different level of satisfaction. Therefore, they can never intersect with one another.* If they did, we would have the logical absurdity that the consumer experiences two different levels of satisfaction at the same point. *Any indifference curve represents a higher level of satisfaction than the curves that lie to the left and below it.*

In the example shown in Figure A20.2, I_2 represents a higher level of satisfaction than I_1. Note, however, that it is not necessary to measure something like utility to establish this. The consumer simply *prefers* combinations on I_2 to those on I_1, because the consumer feels better off on I_2 than on I_1. All that is involved is an ordering. Combinations on I_2 are ranked above those on I_1. No mention is made or need be made about a measure of *how much* better combinations on I_2 are than those on I_1.

If we chose another consumer and established that consumer's indifference

---

FIGURE A20.2
The Consumer's Indifference Map

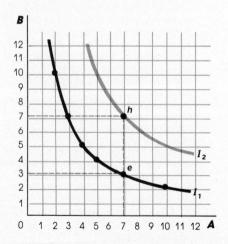

The consumer has an unlimited number of indifference curves, each of which represents a different level of satisfaction. These curves make up the consumer's indifference map. Two from among this unlimited number are shown here. All points on a particular indifference curve, such as I_1, represent alternative combinations of the goods A and B that give the consumer equal satisfaction. The farther out an indifference curve lies from the origin, the higher the level of satisfaction it represents. Hence *h* represents a higher level of satisfaction than I_1. For example, the consumer must feel better off at point *h* than at point *e* because combination *h* contains the same quantity of good A as combination *e*, but a greater quantity of good B.

map in the same way, we would find that it looks somewhat different from that for the consumer of Figures A20.1 and A20.2. As with fingerprints, no two consumers' tastes are perfectly identical.

THE BUDGET CONSTRAINT

The consumer's indifference curves reveal how he or she *feels* about having different quantities of the goods A and B. The question of what combinations of A and B the consumer can actually have is a wholly separate issue. Its answer depends entirely on the size of the consumer's budget and the prices of the goods A and B.

Suppose, for example, that the consumer has a budget of $50 and that the price of A is $10 per unit, while the price of B is $5 per unit. The budget constraint, or limit, that this puts on the consumer is depicted in Table A20.2 and in Figure A20.3, part a. If the consumer's entire budget of $50 is spent on A, 5 units of A can be purchased — line f in Table A20.2 and point f in Figure A20.3, part a. At the other extreme, if the consumer spends the entire $50 on B, 10 units of B can be purchased — line a in Table A20.2 and point a in Figure A20.3, part a. The consumer can, of course, spend the $50 so as to have some of both goods. For example, the consumer could purchase 8 units of B and 1 unit of A (line b and point b), or 6 units of B and 2 units of A (line c and point c), or 4 units of B and 3 units of A (line d and point d), or 2 units of B and 4 units of A (line e and point e). If the two goods can be purchased in fractions of a unit, then any combination of A and B lying along a straight line connecting these points can be purchased. This line is called the **budget constraint** or budget line.

The budget constraint is a straight line representing all possible combinations of goods that a consumer can obtain at given prices by spending a given size budget. Note that the slope of this line is just equal to the price p_A of the good on the horizontal axis divided by the price p_B of the good on the vertical axis (ignoring the negative sign):

$$\text{slope of budget constraint} = \frac{p_A}{p_B}$$

In the example of Figure A20.3, part a, this slope is calculated as

$$\frac{\$10}{\$5} = 2$$

If the price of good A decreased from $10 to $5, the slope of the budget constraint would then equal 1. The budget constraint would be pivoted counterclockwise about point a to the position depicted in Figure A20.3, part b, by the straight line connecting the points a and f'. Whatever combination of goods the consumer selected on the old budget constraint, he or she can now select combinations on the new budget constraint that contain more of both goods. For example, if previously the consumer selected point c, he or she can now select a combination anywhere between b' and c' on the new budget constraint.

If the consumer's budget doubled from $50 to $100, the budget constraint in Figure A20.3, part a, would shift outward to a position parallel to its initial position. It would connect the point at 10 on the horizontal axis to the point at 20 on the vertical axis. Similarly, in part b of the figure, the new budget constraint would connect the point at 20 on the horizontal

TABLE A20.2
Budget Constraint and Possible Combinations of A and B Purchased

Combination	P_A × Units of A	+ P_B × Units of B	= Budget Constraint
a	$10 × 0	+ $5 × 10	= $50
b	$10 × 1	+ $5 × 8	= $50
c	$10 × 2	+ $5 × 6	= $50
d	$10 × 3	+ $5 × 4	= $50
e	$10 × 4	+ $5 × 2	= $50
f	$10 × 5	+ $5 × 0	= $50

axis to the point at 20 on the vertical axis. In either case, the consumer can buy twice as much as previously.

In sum, *for a given size budget, decreases (increases) in the price of a good cause the budget constraint to pivot outward (inward) about the point on the axis of the good whose price has not changed.* A price decrease allows the consumer to buy more goods, a price increase fewer. *For given prices, a budget increase (decrease) causes the budget constraint to shift outward (inward) parallel to itself.* A budget increase (decrease) means the consumer can buy more (fewer) goods.

The Consumer's Optimum Combination

The consumer's objective is to purchase a combination of A and B that puts him or her on the highest possible indifference curve, given the size of his or her budget. By doing this, the consumer will achieve the highest possible level of satisfaction.

The consumer's indifference map reveals how he or she feels about various combinations of quantities of the goods A and B. It is a *subjective* matter reflecting the consumer's tastes. On the other hand, the consumer's budget constraint reflects the *objective* facts of the world that

impinge on the consumer's decisions — the amount of money available for expenditure and the prices of the goods. These constraints cannot be ignored — like them or not. They tell what is possible as opposed to what is desirable.

To reconcile the consumer's tastes and desire with what is possible, the consumer's budget constraint and indifference map must be brought together. In this way the consumer determines from among all the possible combinations of A and B the one that is most desirable in the sense that it maximises his or her feeling of satisfaction. How this is done is shown in Figure A20.4, which combines the consumer's indifference map with the budget constraint of Figure A20.3, part b. The price of both good A and good B is $5 per unit, and the consumer is assumed to have a budget of $50. Of the unlimited number of indifference curves that make up the consumer's indifference map, three are shown in Figure A20.4.

Of all the possible combinations of the two goods A and B along the consumer's budget constraint *bb*, which one will the consumer choose? For example, if either combination *c* or *d* were chosen, the consumer would experience the level of satisfaction associated with the indifference curve I_1. However, since the consumer's objective is to achieve the greatest level of satisfaction possible, neither of

FIGURE A20.3
The Budget Constraint

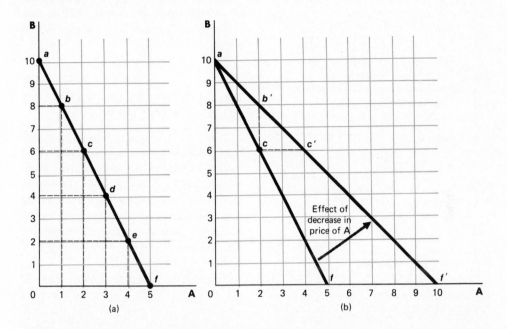

(a)

(b)

The budget constraint shows all the possible combinations of the goods A and B that the consumer may purchase with a given size budget and for given prices of A and B.

In part a the consumer is assumed to have a budget of $50. The price of A is assumed to be $10 per unit and the price of B is assumed to be $5 per unit. The points a through f represent the combinations of goods A and B listed in Table A20.2 that may be purchased with this budget at these prices. The slope of this line is just equal to the price of good A on the horizontal axis divided by the price of good B on the vertical axis (ignoring the minus sign). In this example, the slope equals 2.

In part b the effect on the budget constraint of a change in price of good A is shown. When the price of good A is reduced from $10 per unit to $5 per unit, the budget constraint pivots counterclockwise about point a from position af to position af'. Whatever combination of A and B was purchased before the price reduction, the consumer may purchase a combination containing more of both goods after the price reduction. For example, if combination c were purchased before, the consumer may now purchase any combination between b'c' on the new budget constraint af'.

An increase in the size of the consumer's budget causes the budget constraint to shift outward parallel to itself. For example, if the budget were doubled, from $50 to $100, the budget constraint in part a would shift out until it connected the horizontal axis at 10 units with the vertical axis at 20 units.

these combinations would be the optimum choice. The reason is that it is possible to get to a higher indifference curve. If combination e is chosen, the consumer will be on the highest possible indifference curve I_0, and thereby achieve the highest *possible* level of satisfaction. It is the highest *possible* given the budget constraint.

Note that the optimum combination e

FIGURE A20.4
The Consumer's Optimum Purchase
Combination

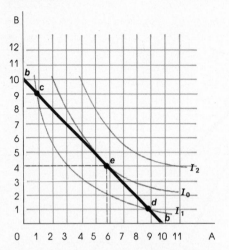

If the consumer has a budget of $50 and the price of both A and B is $5 per unit, the consumer can purchase any combination given by the budget constraint bb. For example, the consumer could spend the $50 to purchase combination c or d. The level of satisfaction associated with d is represented by the indifference curve I_1. The consumer can do better than this, however, by selecting the combination of 6 units of A and 4 units of B represented by point e. Point e lies on the highest indifference curve it is possible to reach by moving along bb. It is therefore the combination of goods A and B that gives the consumer the highest level of satisfaction allowed by his or her budget constraint.

is the point where bb and I_0 touch each other. This is known as the point of tangency. All indifference curves below I_0 have two points in common with the budget constraint bb. Only the highest possible indifference curve has only one point in common with it — the point of tangency. Any combination of A and B on an indifference curve above I_0, such as I_2, is unattainable given the budget constraint.

In sum, *the point of tangency of an indifference curve with the budget con-*

straint determines the optimum purchase combination. *It is optimum in that the consumer realises the highest possible level of satisfaction.* In Figure A20.4 this combination consists of 6 units of A and 4 units of B.

FROM INDIFFERENCE CURVES TO DEMAND CURVES

Figure A20.5 shows again the consumer's budget constraint bb and the two indifference curves I_0 and I_1 from the consumer's indifference map. If the consumer has a budget of $50 and the prices of A and B are each $5 per unit, the consumer will buy combination e consisting of 6 units of A and 4 units of B.

Suppose the price of A rises from $5 per unit to $10 per unit, while the price of B remains $5 per unit and the consumer's budget is still $50. The budget constraint would pivot clockwise from bb to bb '. The consumer is now constrained to purchase one of the possible combinations along bb '. That combination of A and B that maximises the consumer's satisfaction by putting him or her on the highest possible indifference curve is at point g. At g the consumer will purchase 6 units of B and 2 units of A. Hence the doubling of the price of A, with the price of B and the size of the consumer's budget staying the same, has caused the consumer to reduce his or her demand for A from 6 units to 2 units.

Suppose we plot the price of A (p_A) on the vertical axis and the quantity of A demanded (q_A) on the horizontal axis as in Figure A20.6. Given the price of B of $5 per unit and the consumer's budget of $50, if the price of A is $5 per unit, the quantity of A demanded is 6 units, point e in Figure A20.5. Corresponding to point *e* in Figure A20.5, we have point *e'* in Figure A20.6. If the price of A is increased to $10 per unit and the price of B and the consumer's budget remain the same, the quantity of A demanded decreases to 2 units, point *g* of Figure A20.5. Corresponding to point *g* of Figure A20.5, we have point *g'* in Figure A20.6. If we continued to vary the price of A while holding the price of B and the consumer's budget constant in Figure A20.5, we could derive the entire demand curve *dd* for good A in Figure A20.6.

Thus by the use of indifference curves, we can explain the existence of a downward-sloping demand curve. Unlike the utility theory approach, it is not

necessary to measure *how much* a consumer likes a certain quantity of a good. All that is required is that the consumer be able to tell which combinations of goods are regarded as equivalent and which combinations are preferred to others. The indifference curve approach thereby gets around the problem that utility cannot be measured. This problem is the major shortcoming of the utility theory approach in explaining why a

FIGURE A20.6
Derivation of a Demand Curve

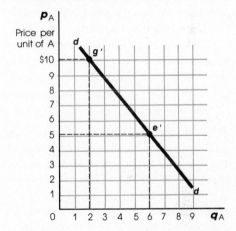

FIGURE A20.5
Effect of a Price Change

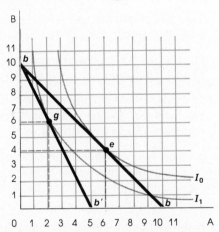

If the consumer has a budget of $50 and the prices of A and B are each $5 per unit, the consumer's optimum purchase combination is *e* (6 units of A and 4 units of B). If the price of A were to rise from $5 to $10 per unit, the budget line would pivot clockwise about point *b* from the position *bb* to *bb'*. The consumer's optimum purchase combination would then be *g* (2 units of A and 6 units of B). Conversely, if the price of A had fallen from $10 to $5 per unit, the quantity of A purchased would increase from 2 units to 6 units, while the quantity of 8 purchased would decrease from 6 units to 4 units.

The demand curve *dd* is derived from the points of tangency between the consumer indifference curves and budget constraints of Figure A20.5. The price per unit of good A is measured on the vertical axis and the number of units of good A on the horizontal axis. Given that the consumer has a budget of $50 and that the price of good B is $5 per unit, when the price of good A is $5 per unit, we see from point *e* in Figure A20.5 that the consumer demands 6 units of A. This is plotted here as point *e'*. If the price of good A is raised to $10 per unit, we see from point *g* in Figure A20.5 that the consumer demands 2 units of A. This is plotted here as point *g'*. By varying the price of A in this fashion, it is possible to derive the entire demand curve *dd* from the points of tangency between the budget lines and indifference curves in Figure A20.5.

demand curve slopes downward left to right.

SUMMARY

1. Indifference curves reflect the consumer's tastes or feelings about goods. They are therefore subjective. The size of the consumer's budget and the prices of goods are objective facts that determine the consumer's budget constraint or budget line.

2. By bringing the consumer's indifference map, which consists of all the consumer's indifference curves, together with the consumer's budget constraint, it is possible to determine the optimum purchase combination of goods. This combination is optimum in the sense that it is the one, from among all *possible* combinations, that gives the consumer the greatest satisfaction.

3. By varying the price of one good while holding the size of the consumer's budget and the price of the other good fixed, it is possible to derive the demand curve for a good from the tangency points of the consumer's indifference curves and budget constraints. Hence the existence of a downward-sloping demand curve can be explained without resorting to the measurement of utility — an exercise that is not practicable.

KEY TERMS AND CONCEPTS

budget constraint
diminishing marginal rate of substitution
indifference curve
indifference map
indifference schedule
marginal rate of substitution

QUESTIONS AND PROBLEMS

1. Draw one of your possible indifference curves between the following goods:

a. brand X salt and brand Y salt;

b. right-hand gloves and left-hand gloves;

c. red apples and yellow apples;

d. bread and water.

2. Suppose there is a change in the tastes of a consumer, one of whose indifference curves is shown in Figure A20.1. Suppose this consumer develops a stronger preference for good A relative to good B. How do you think this will change the indifference curve shown in Figure A20.1?

3. Consider again the consumer budget constraint shown in Figure A20.3, part a. Show how each of the following will affect the budget constraint:

a. The consumer's budget is reduced from $50 to $30.

b. The consumer's budget is increased from $50 to $80.

c. The price of B is increased from $5 per unit to $10 per unit.

d. The price of A is reduced from $10 per unit to $5 per unit and the consumers budget is reduced to $35.

4. In Figure A20.1, suppose the consumer's tastes change in such a way as to increase the consumer's preference for good B relative to good A.

a. How would this affect the optimum combination purchased by the consumer?

b. Using Figure A20.5, show how this would affect the position of the demand curve in Figure A20.6.

5. Suppose the consumer's budget were increased from $50 to $60. Using Figure A20.5, show how this would affect the position of the demand curve in Figure A20.6.

21

Applications of Demand and Supply

AFTER READING THIS CHAPTER YOU WILL BE ABLE TO:

1. Describe the problems of enforcing price ceilings and show how price ceilings affect resource allocation.

2. Explain how price supports are maintained and demonstrate their effect on resource allocation.

3. Explain what is meant by the terms Consumer Surplus and Producer Surplus and use them to measure the welfare effects of market changes.

4. Demonstrate the relationship between the concept of tax incidence and the elasticity of demand and supply.

5. Explain the concept of market externalities and the external, or spillover, costs and benefits they cause.

In the previous two chapters the fundamental concepts of demand and supply as market forces were developed. So too was one important tool economists use for measurement — elasticity. This chapter will show how these concepts can be used to examine a wide variety of modern economic issues. They are a valuable aid to our understanding of complex problems and sometimes in finding solutions to those problems. Among the problems and issues to be considered in this chapter are the effects on markets of government price controls and regulation. The effects of price ceilings and the setting of minimum prices are analysed as are other forms of direct control such as the use of quotas and licences. Taxes and subsidies have an important effect on consumers and producers and so too do world events such as international price changes and changes in the commercial policies of Australia. To analyse their effects more thoroughly this chapter introduces a welfare measure many economists find useful. Finally, the chapter introduces the notion that sometimes costs and benefits are also borne by people who do not directly buy and sell in a particular market.

DIRECT PRICE CONTROLS

One of the commonest ways in which governments intervene in the market place is by directly controlling the prices of goods and services. Price controls take many forms. They are introduced for a variety of reasons and maintained in a variety of ways. Sometimes the motive may be to protect the consumer, and the establishment of a price ceiling is a common way of doing this. They may be introduced during wartime or some other emergency to save scarce resources and direct them to necessary ends, or to make it possible for the poor to buy. Price controls may set a price floor, rather than a ceiling, designed to keep prices up, usually for the benefit of producers.

Price Ceilings

A maximum price or **price ceiling** when set by the government imposes a legally binding price that cannot be exceeded. When the maximum price is set below the equilibrium market price serious economic consequences may follow. You should understand these consequences because there is so much regulation in the Australian economy that the effects can be seen all around you. One common form of price ceiling that is used from time to time to help consumers is rent control. The motive for this can be explained. If rents are too high, only the richer people will be able to afford rented accommodation. Government can control rents by either setting maximum rents, or what amounts to much the same thing, legislating to stop them increasing. The consequences of setting a maximum rent

FIGURE 21.1
Effects of a ceiling on the rental housing market

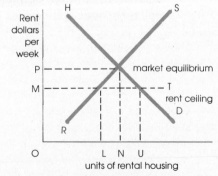

units of rental housing

below the market equilibrium price are shown in Figure 21.1. HD is the demand curve for rental housing and RS is the supply curve. If there were no ceiling rental would be $OP per week and the number of apartments rented out would be ON.

Suppose the state government decided that housing rents were too high and the poor were suffering. They react by setting a maximum rental level of $OM per week. This is less than the free market rate of $OP and is shown on the diagram by the line MT. The horizontal line means landlords are not permitted to charge a higher rent than $OM per week. We now have all the tools at our disposal to examine the likely consequences of the government's decision. Consumers are better able to pay the lower rents and the number of apartments they are prepared to take now rises to OU units. Unfortunately the lower rents have the opposite effect on landlords. The number of apartments they are prepared to make available for rent falls from ON to OL units. In this example rent control is a mixed blessing. Rents are lower, but because of this there is a smaller amount of housing available. If the aim was to help the poor, it has only partly succeeded. Some of the poor may get housing but the total housing stock available falls. How much of a housing market will subsequently develop in these circumstances will depend on two things. First, how different from market prices is the price ceiling set by the government? Second, how elastic are the demand and supply for rental accommodation? The more elastic they are (the flatter the curves, in this example) the more serious will the imbalance between demand and supply become for any given reduction in the price that can legally be charged.

There are two very important points to

be learned from this analysis. First, when you are thinking of the way government price controls are depicted in demand and supply diagrams you should think of them in terms of a horizontal price barrier. This tells us, in the case of a price ceiling, that no amount of the good can be sold legally above that price. Second, while price controls distort the market and change the price and the output bought and sold at that price, they do not remove the underlying forces of demand and supply. They simply limit their powers to operate. Sellers cannot be compelled to supply more at the maximum price than is indicated by the supply curve.

FIGURE 21.2
A Price Ceiling Causes a Shortage

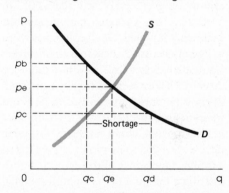

A freely working market with demand curve D and supply curve S determines an equilibrium price p_e, and quantity q_e. If a price ceiling of p_c is imposed on the market, suppliers are only willing to supply the quantity q_c while buyers demand the larger quantity q_d. Market forces are prevented from eliminating the resulting shortage because buying and selling at prices above the ceiling price is illegal and prohibited.

Price Ceilings Divert Resources

How do price ceilings divert resources? This is illustrated in Figure 21.2, which is a more general vision of Figure 21.1. If market forces were allowed to operate freely, the equilibrium price and quantity would be p_e and q_e, respectively. However, with the imposition of a price ceiling at p_c (which is below p_e), suppliers would only be willing to produce and supply a quantity of the good equal to q_c — for the reasons already discussed. Since q_c is less than q_e, fewer of the economy's resources will be devoted to producing this good. The resources that would have been used to produce the additional units of the good between q_c and q_e are now available for the production of other goods. During wartime the resources may be used for weapons, transport equipment and supplies to the armed forces.

However, we know that at the price ceiling of p_c, buyers will demand an amount q_d that is greater than the amount q_c actually supplied. Obviously, since there is less of the good available than buyers want, demands of all buyers cannot be satisfied. There is now a shortage equal to the difference between q_d and q_c. Since the rationing mechanism of a rising price is not allowed, some nonprice rationing device is needed to portion out the limited supply. One possibility would be to distribute the quantity q_c on a first-come-first-served basis. This would mean some of those, possibly many, who are willing to pay the ceiling price p_c would end up getting none of the good. Another possibility would be to let suppliers distribute the available quantity as they see fit. This would most likely favour the suppliers' close friends, family and long-time customers. The rest of those willing to pay the price p_c for the good would again go without.

Rationing with Ration Coupons

Since these kinds of solutions to the problem seem inequitable and unjust, the governments sometimes resort to the use of the **ration coupon**. Each coupon is a claim to a unit of the good. The government prints up just the amount of coupons that will lay claim to q_c units of the good and then distributes them among those who want to buy the good on the basis of so many per person. If the good were bacon, for example, a family of four would be entitled to a certain number of coupons, and a family of two could have half that amount. Hence all who want to buy the good at price p_c would be assured of getting some, though often not as much as they might want. They present their coupons to the supplier, pay the price p_c per unit of the good, and receive no more than the amount of the good their coupons allow.

Note that a price ceiling's effectiveness in cutting back on the quantity of a good produced and thereby releasing resources for use in a war effort, depends on the elasticity of the supply curve. The less elastic the supply curve is, the less effective a price ceiling will be in achieving this objective. Indeed, if the supply curve were perfectly inelastic (or vertical), the quantity supplied would not be reduced at all.

Although we have now discussed the need for rationing and coupons to overcome allocation problems with price controls we have not discussed the alternatives of direct quantitative controls, i.e. quotas. Quotas and licences, their merits and the problems they create are discussed later in the chapter.

Black Markets

So far, we have been looking at the way in which a system of price ceilings and ration coupons should work in theory.

How close it comes to this ideal in reality will depend on how vigorously the system is policed. The demand curve in Figure 21.2 tells us that there are many buyers who are willing to pay more than the ceiling price in order to get some of the good. Hence there are profits to be made by those suppliers who are willing to risk breaking the law by selling the good at prices above the ceiling price. Even if they don't expand output beyond q_c which they might well do, there is a great temptation to charge a price as high as p_b and reap large profits. A market where goods are traded at prices above their ceiling prices is known as a **black market**.

It should also be noted that some consumers may profit from the existence of rationing. There will typically be consumers who don't want any of a commodity at the ceiling price or as much of the commodity as their coupon allotments would entitle them to. On the other hand, there will be other consumers who would like to buy more than their coupon allotment of a commodity at or above the ceiling price. Those with unneeded coupons will sell them to those who want more of the commodity. This doesn't violate the spirit of a rationing system, however, because each consumer is at least given the option to have some of the commodity. It is when suppliers sell a commodity at a price above the ceiling price to individual buyers in amounts exceeding those buyers' coupon allotments that the spirit of the system is violated. Then other buyers will not be able to get all of the good that their coupon allotments entitle them to at the ceiling price.

Given the incentive provided by the above-normal profits from black market activity, a system of price ceilings without 'teeth', in the form of an adequate task force for enforcement, may end up being more fiction than fact. The large bureaucracy needed to administer the price ceilings and coupon-rationing system in many countries during World War II testifies to this. The ceilings often proved 'leaky', and black markets were not uncommon — a testimony to the predictability of human behaviour in economic matters.

Price floors

A government imposed **price support** has just the opposite effect to a price ceiling. A *floor price, price support* or *minimum price* imposes a lower level, or floor, below which a price is not allowed to fall. The most common reason for imposing such a minimum price is to bolster the income of suppliers *above* the level that would otherwise prevail in a freely operating market. In the past this has been one of the main reasons for government price support for Australian farmers. It remains extremely important in other countries which are concerned to protect domestic producers from imports. As we shall see protection of domestic agriculture takes a wide variety of forms throughout the world. Direct price controls are only one of the devices used to support farmers against imports.

One of the most familiar examples of a price floor in Australia is the determination of wage rates by the Commonwealth Conciliation and Arbitration Commission, the state industrial commissions and a variety of industrial tribunals. In such cases the minimum rate that employers may pay to workers is not determined by the government but by an independent body. The effects are similar. A binding determination is made that becomes a price floor beyond which employers cannot go. Of course, they can pay more. The effects of such a price floor are illustrated in Figure 21.3.

FIGURE 21.3
Price Supports Cause a Surplus

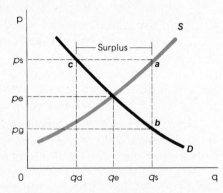

A freely working market with demand curve *D* and supply curve *S* determines an equilibrium price p_e and quantity q_e. However, if price is supported at the level p_s, buyers will demand the quantity q_d, while suppliers will supply the larger quantity q_s. The result will be the indicated surplus.

When the market forces created by buyers and sellers are allowed to operate freely, the equilibrium price p_e and quantity q_e will prevail. Suppose, however, that the government decides to establish a price support p_s above the equilibrium price p_e. At the price p_s buyers will demand the quantity q_{ab} corresponding to *c* on the demand curve *D*. However, sellers will supply a larger quantity q_s, corresponding to point *a* on the supply curve *S*. Hence supply will exceed demand, giving rise to excess output, or a surplus, equal to the horizontal distance between points *a* and *c* (also represented by the distance between q_s and q_d on the horizontal axis).

There is a major difference between the price floor analysis and the maximum price analysis conducted earlier. With a price ceiling, demand was unsatisfied and the system had to find some way of allocating resources between people who were prepared to pay the maximum price — and more. Here the problem is that not enough people are interested in paying the minimum price. There is an oversupply — it may be goods or it may be labour (unemployment) in the labour market.

In the case of agricultural markets often the challenge to government is to find ways by which the producer can sell the quantity he wants to supply at the minimum price. As we have seen simply setting a minimum price does not guarantee this. Consequently to achieve the desired goal legal price floors often need to be supplemented by some other action. This may take the form of buying and stockpiling or destroying the surplus to prevent it being unloaded on the market at prices lower than the floor price. The European Economic Community's Common Agricultural Policy has operated to maintain floor prices for many commodities such as grains, dairy products and wine and in so doing has resulted in the accumulation of vast commodity 'mountains' and 'lakes'. These surpluses have maintained farm prices and incomes, but at considerable cost to the EEC budget and ultimately, of course, to European consumers.

There are a number of ways in which the objective of achieving a minimum price for producers can be realised. Often the objective of supporting the prices is pursued not by means of a legally enforced minimum price. The Australian Wool Corporation has operated a reserve price scheme for wool for many years. Most of Australia's wool clip is sold at auction with international demand for wool having a strong influence on realised prices. The Corporation has claimed that

POLICY PERSPECTIVE

Deregulation of Housing Loan Interest Rates

For many years the Australian housing finance market has consisted of two parts. A regulated sector consisting principally of the savings banks provided a large part of first mortgage finance. However, a large and increasing share of home loans has come to be provided by what are known as non bank financial institutions (NBFI). The NBFI include permanent building societies, credit unions, finance companies and insurance companies, but the first of these has been by far the largest in providing housing finance.

One of the main ways in which the banks have been limited in the housing finance market is that the Federal Government has maintained an interest rate ceiling for loans. The principal reason for this interest rate ceiling for the savings banks was that past governments have seen the banks as a principal means of assisting Australians to become home owners and provided the banks a special place in the financial system to achieve this social objective. However, today the banks argue that interest rate ceilings merely limit the amount of housing finance they are able to provide and this in itself makes it more difficult for less affluent Australians to obtain housing loans from them. In contrast the building societies are under no such restriction and are able to charge the general market interest rate for funds they lend.

FIGURE P21.1

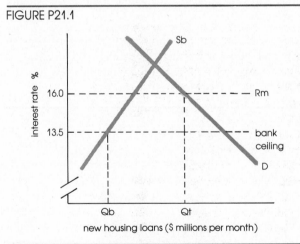

The diagram depicts in simple form the main features of the housing finance market as it operated in 1987. D is the demand curve for new housing loans. It tells us that the lower the interest rate on new housing loans the more home buyers in total will want to borrow. Sb is the banks' supply curve of housing funds. This tells us that the higher the rate of interest they are allowed to charge the more they have available for housing finance. The horizontal line Rm, which represents the general market rate of interest, tells us that NBFI's are able and willing to supply unlimited funds at that rate. By the mid-1980s Australia was experiencing high and increasing general interest rate levels. There was also a strong demand for housing and housing finance particularly in Sydney and Melbourne. The banks were not permitted to charge more than the ceiling of 13.5 per cent, a rate well below the prevailing general interest rate level. A consequence was that the banks were only able to meet a small part of the total demand. In the diagram the banks supplied $Qb million per month at 13.5 per cent while the NBFI's provided $(Qt-Qb) million at a higher interest rate. We have used 16 per cent as that rate for illustrative purposes. Many people, including the banks, called for the abolition of the interest rate ceiling that applied to bank loans. They argued it restricted the total supply of funds to the housing market and that free market forces would allow more people to buy homes. Opponents of deregulation arged that higher home interest rates would make it much more difficult for poorer people to buy homes. If the interest rate ceiling was lifted and applied to existing loans this would cause hardship among poorer people currently living in and buying their homes. The government found a compromise solution. It raised the interest rate ceiling from 13.5 per cent to 15.5 per cent on new housing loans but maintained the previous ceiling on old loans.

Questions

1. Reproduce the diagram. Analyse the effects of raising the interest rate ceiling on new loans from banks to 15.5 per cent. What effect would this have on the total amount of housing finance available to Australians? How would it affect the lending by the non bank financial institutions?

2. Given the analysis just completed, what advantages and disadvantages do you see for potential home buyers (rich and poor) in raising the ceiling? What effect, if any, do you think restricting the change to new home loans would have on the demand for housing in Australia?

---

its policy of buying at predetermined prices, stockpiling and selling again later has not only prevented very low prices, but has exerted an important psychological effect on buyers which has also helped to keep prices up. Other methods of supporting prices including direct initiatives such as restricting production by quotas and individual licences, payment of subsidies that produce a difference between the price the producer gets and the market price, and promotional measures that stimulate demand. The effects of these types of policies will be considered later in the chapter.

OTHER FORMS OF REGULATION

Quotas and Licences

As we have seen, price control does not always achieve the desired results by itself. It cannot ensure that producers will be able to sell all they want to at the specified price because demand is not sufficient. On many occasions quotas or limitations on the quantity produced are imposed to avoid the problem caused by surpluses. As we shall see this form of market regulation also poses problems.

FIGURE 21.4
Effects of Imposing a Production Quota

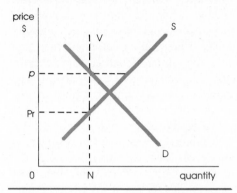

The effects of imposing a production quota are shown in Figure 21.4. In this example the objective is to maintain the price to producers at $OP per unit. To set a minimum price at that level would achieve that result, but would leave a production surplus. This problem is overcome if a production quota is set that limits supply to ON units. This is shown in Figure 21.4 by the vertical line NV. (It is illegal to supply more than ON units to the market whatever the price.) The result (if the quota is effective) is achieved without the need to determine a minimum price because demand is sufficient to ensure that a market price of $OP eventuates. It is important to appreciate that the quota will be effective only when the vertical line VN lies to the left of the intersection of the demand and supply curves as it does in Figure 21.4. However, even there it will not be effective at prices

less than Pr because producers will not be prepared to supply as much as the quota when the price falls below that level.

Why use quotas to reduce supply? Quite simply because they are more certain in their effects than other policy instruments. Other measures such as taxes affect supply indirectly, as we shall see, by increasing costs and shifting the producer's supply curve to the left. Unless government has very good knowledge of the producers' supply curve it cannot be certain that the desired reduction in supply will occur after a tax is levied, nor of the timing of that reduction. Mandatory controls on quantities are an entirely different matter. This aspect of certainty, particularly during times of crisis, is a reason why governments sometimes use quotas to restrict imports rather than import duties when facing balance of payments difficulties. Despite these advantages there are very considerable difficulties associated with the use of quotas. A major disadvantage is that not only do they prevent the market mechanism from working, but if employed for a long period, they deny policy makers the all important signals that the market mechanism provides. When Australia relaxed quantitative controls on imports in the early 1960s no one had a clear idea of what the true demand and supply for imports was. A second major problem is that quota systems are complex to administer and usually require the licensing of individual producers. If no provision exists for transferring these licences between producers and letting new producers into an industry, trade and innovation may be hampered. A secondary problem is that quotas can result in fortunate producers, or importers, with licences earning substantial profits. The licence holders, or if licences can be sold, the previous licence holders, enjoy the benefits of the restrictions rather than the community at large.

MEASURES OF WELFARE CHANGES

Two additional concepts many economists concerned with the welfare of buyers and sellers have found useful are **consumer surplus** and **producer surplus**. These are concepts that are used to provide a rough measure of the benefits or costs that consumers and producers respectively experience from changes to a particular market. They are sometimes added to obtain the net welfare effects when a market adjusts to a shock: price controls, a tax or quota restrictions.

Consumer surplus

Consumer surplus is the net benefit to a consumer defined as the difference between what the consumer is prepared to pay and the amount the consumer actually pays. It is reasoned that if a consumer obtains an article more cheaply than the price they were prepared to pay, they receive a benefit equal to the difference. This argument has been extended and related to the demand curve. In Chapter 4 it was said that the demand curve of the indidivual showed the maximum price an individual was prepared to pay for a given quantity. Figure 21.5 makes use of this definition of the demand curve to explain how consumer surplus can be measured.

FIGURE 21.5
Consumer Surplus

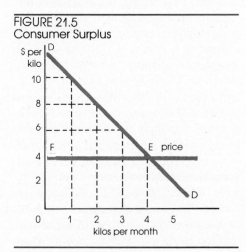

In Figure 21.5 the line DD represents an individual consumer's demand curve for cheese. It shows that the consumer would be prepared to pay $10 per kilo to obtain 1 kilogram of cheese. If the price were $8 per kilo the consumer would increase purchases from 1 kilo to 2 kilos. Suppose, as shown in Figure 21.5, the price was $4 per kilo. The consumer would now be prepared to increase the purchase to 4 kilos. The first 3 kilos have yielded a surplus ($10 — $4) = $6 on the first kilo + ($8 — $4 = $4) on the second kilo and ($6 — $4 = $2) on the third kilo: a total surplus of $12. If instead of the consumer buying cheese in units of a kilo it was perfectly divisible, consumer surplus could be depicted by the area DEF in Figure 21.5. That is the area between the demand curve and the horizontal line representing market price. Although this argument has been applied to the individual consumer it is usually extended to the market as a whole. The area under the demand curve, but above market price measures the surplus for consumers as a whole. This approach to the measurement of consumer benefits has caused some controversy when applied to the market as a whole and when the good in question is an important one. Nevertheless, despite the criticism many economists find the measure a useful indicator of consumer welfare.

Producer surplus

Producer surplus is the net benefit to a producer defined as the difference between what the producer requires to supply the good and the amount the producer actually receives. Like consumer surplus it is reasoned that if the producer obtains a higher price for an article than the price they needed to supply it, they receive a benefit equal to the difference. This idea can be expressed using the supply curve. In Figure 21.6 RS represents the supply

curve of a single cheese manufacturer. It shows the maximum quantity of cheese the firm is willing to supply at any given price or the minimum price it will require to supply any given quantity. The Figure shows that the producer is willing to accept $1 per kilo in return for supplying 500 kilos per month. If the price were $2 per kilo it would be willing to increase supplies to 1500 kilos per month, and so on. In fact, if the going market price is $4 per kilo all units sold receive that price. At that price the producer is willing to supply 3,500 kilos. The fact that he was prepared to sell much of that at less than $4 per kilo means he enjoys a surplus if he sells 3,500 at $4. This surplus is $4,500 if there are only finite increases in supply available to the producer. It is made up of 500 ($4 – $1) + 1000 ($4 – $2) + 1000 ($4 – $3). With complete divisibility producer surplus is measured by the shaded triangle MFR. In other words this is the area between the supply curve and the market price line.

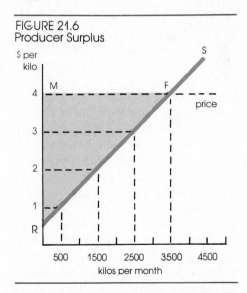

FIGURE 21.6
Producer Surplus

Like consumer surplus, the idea of producer surplus can be extended to all the producers in a market. Changes in market price alter the surplus going to producers as a whole. The area above the supply curve changes. We thus have a convenient measure of the welfare effects on producers to put alongside the measure of welfare effects on consumers. Normally economists are less interested in the absolute size of consumer and producer surplus than they are in the *net changes* following a particular event. In the following sections the welfare consequences of market and policy shocks will be analysed as well as the effects on price and output.

SALES AND EXCISE TAXES

Sales and excise taxes are levied on goods in the markets where they are bought and sold. **Sales taxes** apply to a broad range of goods, while **excise taxes** are levied on particular goods. Sales taxes are used extensively by governments as a source of revenue and are applied to a wide variety of goods (sometimes all goods) sold within the state. In Australia, excise taxes are imposed on specific goods such as tobacco and liquor by the federal government.

Sales taxes are typically calculated as a flat percentage of the retail price of a good. Excise taxes are sometimes calculated as a flat percentage of the retail price, and sometimes as a fixed amount of money per unit of the good sold. If a sales or excise tax is calculated as a flat percentage of price, it is called an **ad valorem tax**. If either is calculated as a fixed amount of money per unit of the good sold, it is called a **specific tax**. Hence we can have a specific sales tax or an ad valorem sales tax, and similarly a specific excise tax or an ad valorem excise tax. *Sales and excise taxes amount to the government's legal claim on a portion of the price paid for each unit of a good sold.* They may be thought of as driving a wedge between the price buyers pay for a unit of the good and the amount that suppliers receive for it. Because of this wedge, the price paid for the good by the buyer is higher and the amount received by the supplier is lower than is the case in the absence of the tax. The way in which the burden of these taxes is divided is called **tax incidence**: that is, what portion of the tax or wedge is paid by the buyer in the form of a higher price per unit, and what portion is paid by the supplier in the form of a lower revenue received per unit of the good sold.

Tax Incidence and Elasticity of Demand and Supply

Who bears the greater incidence or brunt of the tax? The answer to this question depends on the elasticity of the demand and supply curves.

Elasticity of Demand

Suppose the market supply and demand curves for red table wine are S and D_e in Figure 21.7, part a. Their intersection gives an equilibrium price of $20 per bottle and an equilibrium quantity of 5,300 bottles per month. Now what would happen if the government decided to impose a specific excise tax of $10 on each bottle of wine sold? Would the price of a bottle of wine rise from $20 to $30? The answer is no. Here's why.

Suppose the tax is collected from suppliers. Now in addition to the costs of producing a bottle of wine, the supplier must also pay the government $10 on each bottle produced. This effectively means that the cost of supplying a bottle of wine is now $10 more than before the tax was imposed.

Suppliers in part a of Figure 21.7 were willing to supply 5,300 bottles per month at a price of $20 per bottle before the tax was imposed. This $20 was just sufficient to compensate them for the cost of producing a bottle of wine. But now when suppliers have to pay a tax of $10 per bottle, they will have to receive a price of $30 per bottle in order to be willing to supply 5,300 bottles of wine per month — $20 in order to receive the same per unit price as before plus an additional $10 compensation for the tax they now pay. Similarly, whatever quantity of output we consider, suppliers must now receive $10

more per bottle for them still to be willing to supply that quantity after the imposition of the $10 tax. The supply curve is therefore shifted upward by $10 from its before-tax position S to its after-tax position S_a.

How does this affect the market equilibrium price and quantity of wine bought and sold? Given the supply curve, it depends on the elasticity of demand. In part a of Figure 21.7 demand is more elastic than in part b. Consider the case shown in part a. The new equilibrium point now occurs at the intersection of S_a and D_e. This means that the new equilibrium price is $22 per bottle and the new equilibrium quantity is 3,300 bottles

FIGURE 21.7
Demand Elasticity and the Incidence of an Excise Tax

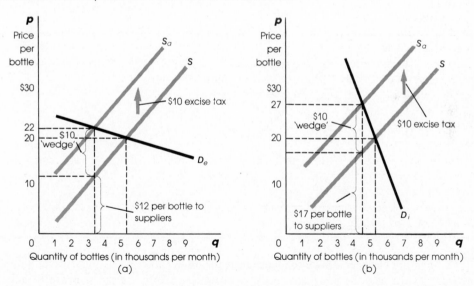

When demand is elastic, as in part a, the imposition of an excise tax forces the price to buyers up by less than it forces down the amount suppliers are able to keep after the government has been paid the tax. In part b, the supply curve is the same as in part a, but the demand curve is inelastic. The imposition of the same excise tax forces the price to buyers up by more than it forces down the amount suppliers are able to keep after tax payment. The incidence of the tax bears heaviest on suppliers when demand is elastic (part a) and heaviest on buyers when demand is inelastic (part b).

POLICY PERSPECTIVE

Can Excise Taxes Stop People from Smoking?

In Great Britain smoking is singled out as the biggest single casue of premature deaths, killing at least 50,000 Britons a year, mainly through heart disease and lung cancer. Since the mid-1960s the British health department has been putting out the statistics and alarming reports on the health risks of smoking. The government, as in Australia, has required warnings to be carried on cigarette packages and a ban on television advertising has operated. Despite this, cigarette consumption fell only gradually until 1981. In that year the government increased the excise tax on cigarettes by 30 per cent sending the price of a pack to the equivalent of $2.50. The British Treasury was then taking about 75 per cent of the retail price of a pack of cigarettes in excise tax. Britons were paying up to three times more than people in other European countries. After the tax was increased the tobacco companies reported the quantity of cigarettes they were selling had dropped by 10 per cent. *The Guardian* newspaper described it as 'the biggest and most abrupt change in national smoking habits since cigarettes were introduced at the turn of the century', and back up the tobacco companies' figures with survey estimates that 2 million out of Britain's 17 million adult smokers had given up.

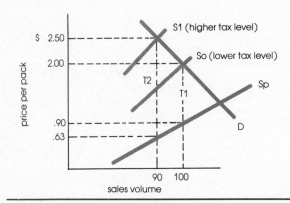

The diagram has been drawn to incorporate the information given above. In addition it supposes the average price of a pack of cigarettes before the tax increase to have been $2.00. It therefore includes part of an estimated British demand curve for cigarettes, the estimated producer's supply curve and the market supply curve at the old and new tax levels.

Questions

1. From the information provided do you consider the demand for cigarettes in Britain to be elastic or inelastic? (use the arc formula)

2. On whom did the incidence of the increase in excise tax fall primarily?

3. Reproduce the diagram and mark on it,
   (a) the net change in consumer surplus
   (b) the net change in producer surplus
   (c) the change in taxation revenue going to the government.

---

per month. The price paid by buyers has risen by only $2, from $20 to $22. Of this $22, $10 goes to the government to pay the excise tax. After this 'wedge' is paid, suppliers receive $12 per bottle — $8 less than previously. Therefore, the incidence or burden of this tax is such that buyers pay $2 of it per bottle and suppliers $8. The incidence of the tax bears heaviest on the suppliers.

What if demand were less elastic? In Figure 21.7, part b, the supply curve is the same as in Figure 21.7, part a, but the demand curve D_i is less elastic than the demand curve D_e in part a. The initial equilibrium price and quantity determined by the intersection of S and D_i is the same as before ($20 and 5,300 bottles per month). However, now when the government imposes the $10 excise tax, shifting the supply curve up to S_a, the new equilibrium price is $27 per bottle and the new equilibrium quantity is 4,600 bottles per month. In this instance the price paid by buyers has risen by $7 (from $20 to $27). Out of this $27, $10 once again goes to the government to pay the excise tax. This time, the wedge between the price paid per bottle by buyers and the amount received by suppliers leaves suppliers with $17 per bottle — $3 less than before the tax was imposed. Hence in this instance, where demand is less elastic, the incidence of the tax is such that buyers are burdened with $7 of it per bottle and suppliers with only $3. The incidence of the tax now bears heaviest on the buyers. In sum, the

example of Figure 21.7, parts a and b, illustrates the following fact about the tax incidence of an excise tax or a sales tax. In general, *given the elasticity of supply, the less elastic is demand the greater is the burden of the incidence of the tax on buyers and the smaller is the burden of the incidence on suppliers.*

Finally, note also that the greater the elasticity of demand (compare parts a and b of Figure 21.7), the larger is the reduction in the quantity of the goods produced and sold due to the imposition of the tax, given the elasticity of supply. Hence if the government's primary purpose is to raise revenue from such taxes, it should impose them on goods and services that have the most inelastic demands. For example, the total tax revenue obtained from the imposition of the $10 tax in Figure 21.7, part a, is $33,000 per month ($10 x 3,300 bottles per month). In Figure 21.5, part b, it is $46,000 per month ($10 x 4,600 bottles per month).

Not only can we discuss the incidence of a tax on producers and consumers but we can also use the notions of consumer surplus and producer surplus to provide a further measure of the effects of such a policy initiative. Initially in Figure 21.8 (both diagrams) consumer surplus is indicated by the area gbcf, while the producer surplus is measured by the area fcdh. After the tax is imposed consumer surplus falls to the area gba and producer surplus is reduced to edh. It can be seen that the relative areas are quite different in the two diagrams. In the first the loss of producer surplus is comparatively large. In the second it is consumer surplus that mainly suffers. Where the demand curve is relatively inelastic there is a relatively large reduction in consumer surplus. In addition the diagrams also measure the gains to the government in the form of tax revenue. It is the area *abde* in both cases. One approach to the welfare question allows us to compare the losses to producers and consumers with the gains to the government from tax revenue and to express the overall effect as a net loss or gain in national welfare. The greater part of the loss to producers and consumers goes to the government. But a careful examination of either diagram shows that

there is an area *bcd* which represents losses not covered by government revenue gains. This represents a net loss to society as a whole.

Elasticity of Supply

How does the elasticity of supply affect the way in which the incidence of the tax is distributed between buyers and suppliers? *Given demand, the less elastic is supply, the greater is the burden of the incidence of the tax on suppliers and the smaller is the burden of the incidence on buyers.* This is illustrated in Figure 21.8. The supply curve in Figure 21.8, part a, is more elastic than that in Figure 21.8, part b. Of the total excise tax of $10 per

FIGURE 21.8
Supply Elasticity and the Incidence of an Excise Tax

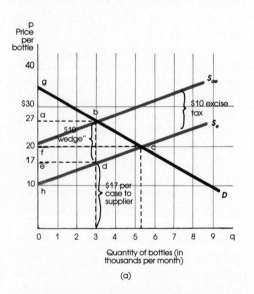

(a)

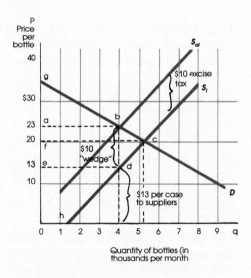

When supply is elastic, as in part a, the imposition of an excise tax forces the price to buyers up by more than it forces down the amount suppliers are able to keep after the government has been paid the tax. In part b, the demand curve is the same as in part a, but the supply curve is inelastic. The imposition of the same excise tax forces the price to buyers up by less than it forces down the amount suppliers are able to keep after the tax payment. The incidence of the tax bears heaviest on buyers when supply is elastic (part a) and heaviest on suppliers when supply is inelastic (part b).

bottle in Figure 21.6, part a, buyers pay $7 while suppliers pay only $3. However, in the case of the less elastic supply curve in Figure 21.8, part b, suppliers bear the heaviest incidence of the tax, paying $7 per bottle while buyers pay only $3.

CHECKPOINT 21.2
Australia has a downward-sloping demand curve and an upward-sloping domestic supply curve for many products. As a small country it faces a perfectly elastic supply of imports, which can be depicted on a demand and supply diagram as a horizontal line. Draw such a diagram and mark on it the market price in Australia. Draw it in such a way that the domestic Australian industry has about 25 per cent of the market and the balance comes from imports. Suppose the Government decides to impose a tariff on imports that raises their landed price. How will this affect the price to consumers, the quantity of domestic production and the quantity of imports? Mark these effects on your diagram and also mark the changes in consumer surplus, the change in producer surplus, the government revenue from the tariff and the change in foreign exchange payments.

Subsidies

The same analysis used to examine the effects of an excise tax in Figures 21.7 and 21.8 can be applied to a study of the effects of government subsidies. A **subsidy** can be thought of as the reverse of an excise or sales tax. While such taxes take money away from buyers and suppliers, a subsidy gives them money.

For example, suppose the government wanted to encourage wine production

because it would promote economic development and help alleviate poverty in certain parts of the country suited to grape growing. Let's assume that the market supply curve is initially S_a in Figure 21.7, part a, with the equilibrium price and quantity determined by its intersection with D_e. Now suppose the government decides to pay suppliers a subsidy of $10 per bottle. This effectively reduces suppliers' costs by $10 per bottle of wine. The supply curve is therefore shifted down by this amount from S_a to S. The price of a bottle of wine falls to $20 per bottle, and the quantity supplied and sold rises from 3,300 to 5,300 bottles per month, as determined by the intersection of S and D_e. *A subsidy typically has the effect of reducing price and increasing quantity supplied.* The extent of the price reduction and the quantity increase depends on the elasticity of the demand and supply curves. This can be seen by examining Figures 21.7 and 21.8.

Here also we can examine the wider welfare implications. A subsidy leads to an increase in consumer surplus and to an increase in producer surplus. In Figure 21.9 the net gain in consumer surplus is measured by the area *fcde*. The gain in producer surplus is the area *abcf*. Adding them together gives an approximate welfare gain of *abcde*. Against this must be offset the cost of providing the subsidy which is represented by the area *abde*. So here again the costs of providing support are greater than the benefits it provides to society. There is a net loss of *cbd* to society.

CHECKPOINT 21.3
Suppose the supply curve is perfectly elastic (that is, horizontal) and the demand curve is like any of those shown in Figures 21.7 and 21.8. If an

excise tax of $10 per bottle is now imposed, how will the incidence of this tax be distributed between buyers and sellers? Suppose the demand curve is perfectly elastic and the supply curve is like any of those shown in Figures 21.7 and 21.8. If an excise tax of $10 per bottle is imposed, how will the incidence of this tax be distributed between buyers and sellers? Suppose the demand curve is perfectly inelastic (that is, vertical) and the supply curve is like any of those shown in Figures 21.7 and 21.8. If an excise tax of $10 per bottle is imposed, how much will the price of a bottle of wine increase? Sometimes those who push for the imposition of excise taxes on liquor and tobacco do so because of a desire to reduce the consumption of these 'socially harmful' goods. For any given size of the excise tax imposed, how will the elasticity of demand affect the degree to which consumption of these goods will be reduced?

FIGURE 21.9
Welfare Effects of a Subsidy

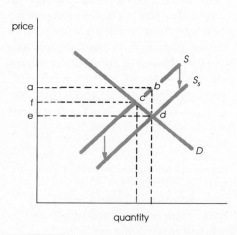

Externalities — External Costs and Benefits

We have already seen in Chapter 4 how the intersection of the demand and supply curves for a good determines the equilibrium price and quantity. This is shown in Figure 21.10. To the right of the intersection, the supply curve is above the demand curve. This means that if suppliers produced an amount q_1 that is larger than the equilibrium quantity q_e, buyers would not be willing to pay a price high enough to cover the costs of supplying the additional units of output from q_e to q_1. That is, buyers do not value the additional benefits, represented by the area aq_eq_1b under the demand curve over the units of output from q_e to q_1, as highly as the value of the resources needed to produce them. The value of these resources is measured by their opportunity cost as represented by the area aq_eq_1c under the supply curve over the units of output from q_e to q_1. Resources would be overallocated to this activity in the sense that the cost to society of producing the units of output from q_e to q_1 exceeds their value to society by an amount represented by the triangular area abc. Therefore it would be economically inefficient to produce the output beyond q_e.

On the other hand, if suppliers produced an amount q_2 that is less than the equilibrium quantity q_e, buyers would be willing to pay a price that is more than enough to cover the costs of supplying additional units of output beyond q_2. This is reflected by the fact that the demand curve is higher than the supply curve to the left of the intersection. Producing the smaller quantity of output q_2 would mean an underallocation of resources to this activity. This is so because buyers value the additional benefits from the extra units of output from q_2 to q_e (represented by

FIGURE 21.10
The Optimum Quantity of Output

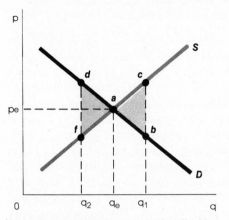

If suppliers produced an amount q_1 that is larger than the equilibrium quantity q_e, buyers would not be willing to pay a price high enough to cover the costs of supplying the additional units of output from q_e to q_1. To produce these extra units would be a waste of society's resources because buyers do not value the additional benefits as highly as the resources needed to produce them. Resources would be overallocated to this activity. If suppliers produced an amount q_2 that is less than the equilibrium quantity q_e, buyers would be willing to pay a price that is more than enough to cover the costs of supplying additional units of output from q_2 to q_e. To produce the smaller quantity of output q_2 would be an underallocation of resources to this activity. The optimum quantity is therefore q_e.

the area dq_2q_ea under the demand curve) more than the value of the resources needed to produce them. (Once again, the value of these resources is measured by their opportunity cost as represented by the area fq_2q_ea under the supply curve.) If suppliers produce no more than the quantity q_2, society forgoes the excess of the value of the benefits over the costs represented by the triangular area dfa. In sum, the equilibrium quantity q_e determined by the intersection of the demand and supply curves is the only one for which

buyers are just willing to pay a price p_e sufficient to cover the cost of the last unit produced. The value of the benefits of this last unit are just equal to the value of the resources needed to produce it. The equilibrium quantity q_e is therefore the optimum quantity.

However, what if all the costs associated with producing the good are not paid by the firms who supply it? For example, when air and water are polluted by the production process, society at large typically bears the cost of either cleaning it up or suffering the higher health care and other costs that it may lead to. In such cases these costs are not reflected in the market supply curve for the good.

Similarly, what if the benefits associated with a good extend to others besides the buyers of the good? In this case, the total benefits may not be fully reflected in the demand curve for that good. Consider for example, the purchase by farmers of fencing to keep their livestock from wandering. The fencing protects their investment in livestock, a private benefit that they derive directly. Society at large also benefits however. There is a reduction in safety hazards, such as livestock wandering onto highways, and a reduction in crop loss caused by livestock wandering onto other farmers' wheat and corn fields. However, the market demand curve for fencing reflects only the value of the private benefits to the buyers of fencing, in this case the owners of the livestock.

Costs and benefits that fall on others besides the buyers and sellers of a good are often called **externalities**, or *external costs* and *benefits*. Frequently they are also referred to as *spillovers, or neighbourhood effects, or external economies and diseconomies. All these terms refer to the fact that these costs and benefits fall on others besides the buyers and sellers* *directly involved in the transactions of the particular market for the good.*

External Costs

Suppose a particular industry pollutes the environment when it produces its product, but the cost of cleaning up the environment or suffering the consequences is borne by others. Since the firms in the industry do not have to pay the cleanup cost, this cost is not included in the market supply curve S shown in Figure 21.11. It is an external cost borne by others not directly involved in the purchase or sale of the product. Given the market demand for the product, represented by the demand curve D, the equilibrium quantity produced and sold would be q_n and the equilibrium price p_n.

However, what if the firms in the industry had to pay the cleanup costs associated with the production of each unit of output? These costs would be added in just like an excise tax along with the other production costs to give the market supply curve S_a, which includes all costs. Because of this, S_a lies above S. The equilibrium quantity produced and sold when firms pay all costs associated with production would be q_o, an amount smaller than q_n. The equilibrium price would be p_o, which is higher than p_n. The incidence of this added cost would be distributed between suppliers and buyers of the good in the same way as an excise tax, rather than falling on other parties who do not buy or sell the good.

Hence, when there are external costs associated with a good, costs not paid for by the buyers and suppliers of a good (sometimes called spillover costs), a greater quantity of output is produced and sold than is optimum. This is shown in Figure 21.11, where the supply curve S_a, which includes all costs, lies above the demand curve D for all units of the good from q_o to q_n. This means that the value of the benefits to buyers of this additional quantity of the good is less than the value of all the resources used to produce it by an amount represented by the triangular area abc.

In sum *when there are external costs — costs of production not borne by the immediate buyers and suppliers of a good — there is an overallocation of resources to the production of that good. Therefore more of it is produced and sold than is optimum.*

FIGURE 21.11
Externalities and the Allocation of Resources

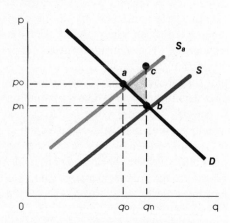

The presence of externalities in the form of spillover costs means the *market* supply curve S lies below the supply curve S_a, which includes all costs associated with production of the good. As a result, there is an overallocation of resources to the production of this good. Therefore the market equilibrium quantity q_n exceeds the optimum quantity q_o. Because buyers and suppliers don't pay all the costs of production, the market equilibrium price p_n is below the price p_o, which covers all costs.

External Benefits

The market demand curve for a good reflects the value of the benefits of that good that accrue directly to those who buy it. If the good also provides externalities in the form of benefits to others who do not buy the good, these spillover, or external, benefits are not reflected in the market demand curve. The market demand curve for fencing reflects the value of its benefits to the farmers who buy the fencing to protect their investment in their livestock. It does not reflect the benefits of this fencing to motorists who drive on highways adjacent to cattle fields or to farmers who raise crops next door to cattle farms. Similarly, those who buy health care to protect their own well-being also generate benefits for others. For example, they reduce the spread of contagious diseases.

Since the market demand curve for these kinds of goods and services does not reflect the value of these social, or spillover, benefits, it must lie below a demand curve that is drawn to include them. Figure 21.12 shows a hypothetical market demand curve D and supply curve S for flu shots. If the value of the spillover benefits to society at large from these shots is added on, we get the demand curve D_a, which includes the value of all benefits and therefore lies above D. The market equilibrium quantity of flu shots supplied and purchased is q_n (determined by the intersection of S and D). However, the existence of externalities in the form of social benefits means that this is less than the optimum quantity q_o (determined by the intersection of S and D_a). As a result, the demand curve D_a lies above the supply curve S for the additional flu shots from q_n to q_o. This means that the value of all the benefits to society from having these

additional flu shots is greater than the cost of supplying them by an amount represented by the triangular area adf.

In general *when there are external or spillover, benefits associated with a good too few resources are allocated to the production of that good and less of it is produced and sold than is optimum.*

FIGURE 21.12
Spillover Benefits and Resource Allocation

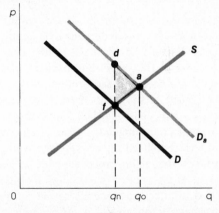

The presence of externalities in the form of spillover benefits means the market demand curve D lies below the demand curve D_a, which reflects all benefits associated with the consumption of a good. As a result, there is an underallocation of resources to the production of this good, so that the market equilibrium quantity q_n is less than the optimum quantity q_o.

CHECKPOINT 21.4
Suppose Senator Codswallop says that requiring pollution control equipment in a certain industry will result in costs that will be 'passed on' entirely to consumers. What must the senator be assuming (probably unknowingly) about the elasticity of supply and demand in that industry? If strict pollution control laws were imposed on an

industry, what combinations of supply and demand elasticities would result in severe reductions in employment in that industry?

Given your own impressions of the elasticity of demand for cigarettes, how do you think imposing an excise tax of $.20 per pack would affect the frequency of lung cancer?

SUMMARY

1. Government-imposed price ceilings result in an excess of demand over supply, or a shortage, at the legal ceiling price. Because of this, strict enforcement measures are needed if the product is not to be traded in the black market at prices above the ceiling price. Government-managed rationing schemes are often used to ensure that all buyers who are willing to pay the ceiling price are able to get some of the good. Price ceilings are often used to affect resource allocation during wartime. Rent control is an example of how peacetime price ceilings can have wide-ranging economic and social implications.

2. Government-imposed price supports result in an excess of supply over demand, or a surplus, at the support price. In order to support the price at a level above that of market equilibrium, the government must do one of the following: buy and store the surplus, impose limitations on production, pursue policies that promote demand, or pay producers the difference between the support price and the lower price that producers receive in the market. In the case of services, such as labour services, the government may make it illegal to buy or sell them at a price less than a certain minimum price. Such policies have been used to support

agricultural prices at various times.

3. Quotas have the advantage that they are a more certain means of restricting production than taxes and may be preferred during crises. They also have serious disadvantages. If used for long periods they obstruct market signals and trade stagnates. They are administratively complex and often involve individual licensing of producers. They can bring large profits to quota holders at the expense of consumers.

4. Consumer and producer surplus are expressed as the difference between the market price and the price consumers and producers respectively were willing to trade a particular quantity of good. They provide another welfare measure that is sometimes used to give an indication of the effects of a policy shock or other event on the market.

5. Sales and excise taxes are the government's legal claim on a portion of the price paid for a unit of a good. They affect the equilibrium price and quantity in the market where they are imposed. The more elastic is the demand for a good, the smaller is the portion of the tax paid by buyers and the larger the portion paid by suppliers — the tax incidence is shifted onto suppliers. The more elastic is the supply for a good, the smaller is the portion of the tax paid by suppliers and the larger the portion paid by buyers — the tax incidence is shifted onto buyers.

6. Whenever the production and purchase of a good gives rise to costs or benefits that fall on parties other than the immediate buyers and sellers of the good, external, or spillover, costs and benefits are said to exist. When there are external costs associated with the production of a good, a greater than optimum quantity of the good is produced.

KEY TERMS AND CONCEPTS

ad valorem tax
black market
consumer surplus
excise tax
externalities
parity
price ceiling
price support
producer surplus
ration coupon
rent control
sales tax
specific tax
subsidy
tariff
tax incidence

QUESTIONS AND PROBLEMS

1. If an effective price ceiling were imposed on butter, what would happen to the price of margarine?

2. Suppose that during a war price ceilings were imposed on certain consumer goods industries in order to shift workers away from the production of peacetime goods and into the production of war goods.

a. What would have to be true of supply elasticities in consumer goods industries to make this a very effective way of achieving this objective?

b. What sort of demand elasticity conditions would make such a policy easier to administer for those responsible for the enforcement and administration of a rationing scheme?

c. What would be the sort of supply-and-demand conditions that would cause

you as a policymaker to shy away from imposing price controls on certain industries to achieve your objective?

3. It has been observed that when rent controls are imposed, owners of apartment buildings often convert them to home units (apartments that are owned by the occupant rather than rented). Can you explain this phenomenon?

4. Some have observed that in a way it is fortunate that the demand for agricultural products is relatively inelastic. They point out that the cost to government (and hence the taxpayer) of trying to support agricultural prices might otherwise have been larger than it has been all these years. Can you explain what these observers have in mind?

5. The government has been concerned about the low price Australian companies have been receiving for coal exported to Japan. Recently it announced that it was considering imposing a minimum price condition on exports. What effect do you think such a proposal would be likely to have on the Australian trade?

6. Suppose an excise tax is levied on the output of television sets. What effect do you think this would have on the prices charged by film theatres and the prices of TV dinners?

7. In 1987, concerned with the effects of inflation, the president of the Tasmanian Housewives Association called for a 12-month freeze on supermarket grocery prices. What problems would you foresee as being likely to occur if the Tasmanian Government introduced such a freeze? What effect would it have had on small corner stores? Would similar results have followed if a freeze had been imposed by governments in New South Wales and Victoria?

8. A government could protect a domestic industry equally effectively by imposing a tariff on imports, or by paying local producers a subsidy. It can be shown that subsidies are in some ways better than tariffs. What differences do you think result from subsidies being applied instead of tariffs. Why is it that governments often choose to impose tariffs instead?

9. A number of arguments are put forward to support the restriction in the number of taxis allowed to operate in most cities and large towns. What arguments can you think of that might involve externalities? How valid do you think those arguments would be in Melbourne or Sydney?

22

The Firm and Its Costs of Production

AFTER READING THIS CHAPTER YOU WILL BE ABLE TO:

1. Define the three legal forms of the firm — the proprietorship, the partnership, and the company — and state the differences between them.

2. Define the nature of the firm's explicit and implicit costs and the distinction between short-run and long-run costs.

3. Formulate the law of diminishing returns and show how it affects the behaviour of variable costs as output changes.

4. Distinguish between fixed and variable costs and between total, average, and marginal costs.

5. Explain the relationship between the firm's short-run and long-run average total cost curves and how the shape of the latter is explained by economies and diseconomies of scale.

In the last two chapters we increased our understanding of the essential concepts of demand and supply and the ways in which they interact in a market. We analysed the overall effects on producers and consumers of various government policies and other stocks. However, to be able to understand how the market operates we need to know much more about the producers. This means studying the basic unit of organisation — the firm. This chapter deals with the ways in which a firm may be organised in Australia, the nature of production processes and, in particular, the costs of production they incur. In doing so it provides a framework we shall use in later chapters to explain how firms in different kinds of product and resource markets behave, both as sellers and as buyers. The world in which Australian businesses operate is complex and confusing. These businesses need to identify market needs, determine what to produce and how to reach the target markets they have identified. They need to be able to estimate their costs of production and to determine production strategies after taking into account this cost information.

THE FIRM

In Chapter 1, we said that a firm uses factors of production to produce goods that are sold. We need to expand on this definition here. *A firm is a business organisation that owns, rents, and operates equipment, hires labour and buys materials and energy inputs. It organises and coordinates the use of all these factors of production for the purpose of producing and marketing goods and services.*

The concept of a plant is related to a firm, but quite distinct. A plant is a facility where production takes place. A factory, a mine, a farm, a store — each of these is a plant — it has a specific geographical location. A firm may very easily own and operate more than one plant. BHP, a large Australian firm, has oil wells, steel works and other plants in each Australian state. Coles/Myer, David Jones and Woolworths have plants (retail stores) all over Australia. Firms that own several plants at the same stage of production, that do the same thing, are said to be horizontally integrated. On the other hand, a firm may own several plants each of which handles a different stage in the production process. Again BHP owns coal and iron deposits, bulk carriers, steel mills and fabricating plant. A firm that combines the various stages of production in this way is said to be vertically integrated.

Sometimes a firm has a wide diversity of interests with no apparent link between them. The firm may be a mining company such as CRA Ltd with interests in iron-ore, nickel, copper, coal and other minerals, or it may have even wider interests. Elders IXL have developed from a pastoral company to mining, brewing and many other activities. Western Australian corporations Bell Resources and Bond have also developed wide interests within Australian and overseas. The term firm covers the complete spectrum of business activity, from the small one man business to the large multinational corporation with an enormous payroll and diverse interests. They face different problems, but in many ways they face the same problems and are inspired by the same motives — survival and the desire to make profits.

Legal Forms of the Firm

So far, we have been concerned with the

firm in terms of what it does, how it is organised, what it produces and how big it is. But a firm is also a legal entity that operates subject to certain obligations and constraints under the law. Just what these are depends on the legal form the firm takes. There are three basic legal forms for a firm: the sole proprietorship, the partnership and the company.

The Sole Proprietorship

This is the simplest form of business organisation in Australia. As the name suggests there is a single owner who makes the decisions and bears the final responsibility for everything the firm does. *Australian income tax statistics* provide us with a great deal of information about the number of people who carry on business in this way and the industries they operate in.

In 1985-86 there were around 1 million sole proprietorships in Australia. The largest single category was primary production, followed by building and construction, finance and business services, wholesale and retail trades and entertainment, restaurants and hotels. Significantly two industry sectors where there were very few sole proprietorships were mining and manufacturing.

The reasons for this pattern are not hard to understand. Sole proprietorship is an excellent arrangement for a small scale business activity, precisely because it offers direct personal control and because it is relatively easy to set up. But if the business is in a form of activity that requires large amounts of investment capital it is likely to find raising these funds difficult. A second disadvantage of this form of business organisation is that the owner has unlimited liability. He or she is fully liable for the debts and obligations of the

enterprise. If the firm gets into financial difficulties and does not have adequate funds to pay these debts, the owner's personal property and funds may be seized by the firm's creditors (i.e. those to whom the firm owes money). Many new sole proprietorships are set up every year in Australia, but many fail to survive even a year. Often this is because the project was ill advised. Sometimes unfortunately the idea was a good one and the firm fails because of cash flow problems — unable to cope with the cash demands inherent in too rapid development. The third major disadvantage the sole proprietor faces is that if the business does grow he simply lacks the necessary knowledge, time and ability to manage the expanding operation successfully. It is common then, either for the firm to remain of a size the proprietor can handle comfortably, or alternatively to adopt a more suitable market form.

The Partnership

A partial solution to the problems of inadequate finance and limited management skills is to form a partnership. A **partnership** is formed whenever two or more individuals get together and agree to own and operate a business jointly. There are around 400,000 partnerships in Australia operating in the same general areas as sole proprietorships. Professionals such as doctors, solicitors, accountants, architects and consulting engineers find this is a useful form of organisation because it allows them to put together a team, often with different talents of specialisation. A successful professional partnership may well have better access to finance than a sole proprietorship.

There remains the important disadvantage that the partners each have unlimited liability. Like the sole proprietorship they are responsible for the firm's debts. In a way the disadvantage is more severe than for a sole proprietorship because any one partner is risking his or her personal assets on the management decisions of others. Trust and confidence in the other partners is an essential ingredient in a successful partnership. Another disadvantage of a partnership is that if a partner dies or leaves, the partnership arrangements must be dissolved and reorganised. This can interrupt the business operations of the firm for a time.

The Company

Unlike proprietorships and partnerships, a company has a legal identity separate and distinct from the people who own it. In contrast to proprietorships and partnerships, a company can, in the course of doing business, enter into all manner of contracts that are legal obligations of the company but not of its owners. The owners are therefore said to have **limited liability**. In essence this means that a company can be sued but not its owners. In the event of failure to meet its debts, pay its bills, or deliver goods and services it has contracted to produce, the limits of financial liability extend only to the assets of the company. They do not extend to the personal assets of its owners, those who own shares of stock in the company. A shareholder's financial liability is limited to only the amount of money that is invested in the firm through the purchase of shares.

In 1986 there were about 250,000 companies in Australia with total business receipts of $380 billion. There are two major types of company; **public companies** and **private companies**. Both have limited liability of their shareholders as explained above. **Public companies** raise

funds from the public by selling shares, have no restriction on the number of shareholders and need to meet strict accountability conditions such as the publication of an annual report. Stock exchanges commonly provide a market for the shares in these companies to change hands. **Private companies** cannot offer shares to the general public, cannot have more than 50 shareholders and need not publish an annual report. As one might expect the private company is often a more suitable form for a smaller enterprise that wishes to obtain access to adequate financial resources for its purposes while protecting the owner's personal assets. Of the 250,000 companies in Australia in 1986 only about 160,000 were public companies but they contributed about 70 per cent of business receipts from companies.

Advantages of the Public Company

The chief advantage of setting up a firm as a public company instead of as a proprietorship or partnership is that it makes it much easier to raise money for investment in the firm. Because their liability is limited, numerous investors, both large and small, are willing to invest their money in an incorporated firm. Such firms are therefore able to raise the large amounts of money needed to finance the large plants and complex production processes used in a highly industrialised economy. In exchange for their money, investors receive ownership shares, or stock, in the firm. These shares entitle them to vote for a board of directors who are responsible for the overall supervision of the firm and the hiring of its top-level managers. They are also entitled to share in the company's profits, which are called **dividends** when paid out. Profits not paid out, called **undistributed profits**, also belong to the shareholders. They are usually reinvested in the firm's operations.

Organised stock exchanges make it relatively easy for investors to acquire or sell shares in public companies. They can diversify risks by owning shares in several firms that are engaged in widely different businesses without having to become directly involved in the management of any of them. All of these considerations make it easier for investors to share in the monetary returns from enterprise without having to bear the risks and shoulder the management responsibilities associated with either a proprietorship or a partnership.

Because the shares in a public company can be easily bought and sold, change of ownership does not cause disruptions in operations the way it does in either a proprietorship or a partnership. This gives the public company a life of its own apart from its ownership. This continuity of existence makes long-range planning easier and also increases the ability of the incorporated firm to borrow money.

Disadvantages of the Public Company

Compared to a proprietorship or partnership, the shareholder in a public company often has little meaningful influence over the board of directors and management policy. Even though each share of stock entitles the owner to one vote, a large public company may have so many shares outstanding that most investors can't hope to own enough of them to have a significant voting bloc. As a result, ownership and control can become separated to a much larger extent than is typically possible in a partnership. In a proprietorship, of course, the two

functions are one and the same.

The main reason the principal forms of legal business organisation have been discussed at length is because of the cost implications they hold for businesses. As we have seen sole proprietorships are common in primary industry and services, partnerships are common in the professions and mining and manufacturing are dominated by large public companies. Although much of what will be said in this chapter about the firm's costs of production is common to sole proprietorships, partnerships and companies there are some significant differences that will emerge. They relate to the availability of finance and the predominant types of costs businesses meet.

Costs of the Firm

In Chapter 2 we saw that all costs are opportunity costs due to the fact that resources are scarce and have alternative uses. The production possibilities frontier shows that if resources are used to produce one good, they are not available to produce other goods. The economic cost of a good is therefore the alternative goods that must be foregone in order to produce it. This notion of cost is directly applicable to the individual firm.

The resources that a firm needs in order to produce its product have costs attached to them because they have alternative uses in the production of other products by other firms. Economists generally divide these costs into two groups, *explicit* costs and *implicit* costs. Added together, they make up the opportunity costs for the firm.

Explicit Costs

Some of the resources the firm needs must be purchased or hired from outside the firm and must be obtained by a direct monetary payment. Such resources include electricity, fuel, materials, labour, insurance and so forth. The payments that must be made for these resources are considered **explicit costs**. Take for example a typical family owned corner store or milk bar in any Australian town or suburb. Explicit costs would include property taxes, maintenance costs, payments to wholesalers for goods to be sold in the store and the salary of a shop assistant.

Implicit Costs

Some resources needed by the firm are actually owned by the firm itself. Such resources include the managerial skills and financial resources of the owners. In the case of managerial skills, the cost of such resources is the payments they could have received were they employed in their next best alternative. Similarly, the cost of financial resources is the return they would have received were they invested in their next best alternative. Since these resources are not obtained by direct monetary payments, their costs are considered to be **implicit costs**.

Returning once again to the corner store, let's assume that the family own the store outright, use their own funds to finance inventories and put 80 hours a week into running the store. The implicit cost of such resources would include the rent the family could receive if they leased the building to another firm, the interest or dividends their money could earn if invested elsewhere and the salaries they could earn if they were employed in another business. Sole proprietorships such as family farms, and partnerships such as firms of architects will have relatively high levels of implicit costs.

Large companies with a large employed workforce are likely to have relatively low implicit costs.

Accounting Profit, Economic Profit and Normal Profit

There are three distinct notions of profit, each of which is based on a different way of measuring the costs of the firm in relation to its revenues. These three types of profit are *accounting profit, economic profit, and normal profit.*

Accounting profit is determined by subtracting the firm's explicit costs from its total sales receipts. This notion of profit does not consider any implicit costs.

Economic profit is the difference between the total revenue obtained from the firm's sales and the opportunity costs of all the resources used by the firm. (As we have already seen, the opportunity costs of all the resources used by the firm are the total of all explicit and implicit costs.) If this calculation results in a value of zero, then these opportunity costs are just being covered by sales receipts. Since all resources are therefore receiving just the amount they could get in their best alternative uses, there is no incentive for any of them to move to another firm. If economic profit were zero for each and every corner store or milk bar, none would be going out of business.

What if our calculation of economic profit for the corner store resulted in a negative value? That is, what if the sum of explicit and implicit costs were larger than sales receipts? In this case, we would say that the business was operating at an economic loss. It would now be impossible for all the resources used in the corner store to be compensated by the full amount of their opportunity costs. *Negative economic profit, therefore, causes resources to move to alternative lines of productive activity where markets value their services enough to pay their opportunity costs.* If economic profit were negative for one or more firms for any length of time, we would see firms going out of business and resources leaving the industry.

On the other hand, what would happen if our calculation of economic profit resulted in a positive value? This would mean that sales receipts are more than adequate to cover the sum of explicit and implicit costs. In other words, sales receipts cover more than the opportunity cost of all resources used. *Positive economic profit, therefore, attracts resources away from other lines of productive activity into those where they can earn more than their opportunity cost.* If economic profit were positive for one or more firms for any length of time, we would see new firms opening up and resources moving into the industry.

The size of economic profit determines whether resources will be moving into or out of particular lines of productive activity. If economic profit is positive in a particular line of productive activity, resources will be drawn into that activity. If it is negative, they will tend to move out of that activity. If economic profit is zero, there will be no incentive for resources to move into or out of that activity. In this way, economic profit allocates resources among alternative productive activities in the economy.

Normal profit is what the firm is said to earn when economic profit is zero. In that case, all resources employed by the firm are just earning their opportunity costs. In particular *when the financial capital and the entrepreneurial skills used by the firm are being compensated just enough to keep them from leaving and going into*

some other line of productive activity, it is said that they are earning a normal profit. In the case of the corner store, the proprietors' entrepreneurial skills, their own funds invested in the business, and the building they own and use for the store are receiving a normal profit. That is, sales receipts are just sufficient to pay all explicit costs with enough left to just cover the implicit costs of entrepreneurial skills and financial capital.

Note that in this instance financial capital includes the proprietors' own funds put directly into the business, to purchase inventories, say, plus the money value of the building they own and use in the business. Whether these funds are tied up in inventories or in buildings, they constitute the financial capital required to run a corner store. The inventories and building necessary to do business are merely the physical capital counterpart to the financial capital. The proprietors did not need to use their own funds in this way. Instead, they could have rented the building from someone else and borrowed the funds necessary to acquire inventories. It makes no difference whether the proprietors provide the financial capital or whether they borrow and rent it from other parties. If the financial capital is not compensated at a rate of return equal to that which it could earn in its next best alternative, it will not be made available for use in the corner store.

When economic profit is positive, the entrepreneurial skills and financial capital used by the firm are earning more than a normal profit. Similarly when economic profit is negative, these resources are earning less than a normal profit.

This relationship between explicit and implicit costs, accounting, economic and normal profits is illustrated in Figure 22.1. It shows three representative firms. For

FIGURE 22.1
The Relationship Between Accounting and Economic Profits

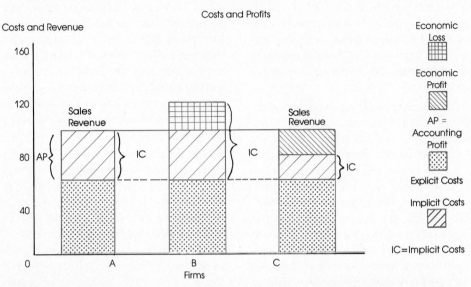

For each of the three firms the accounting profit (AP) is the same. It is the difference between sales revenue and explicit costs. Firm A makes 'normal' or zero economic profits because when implicit costs are added to the explicit costs they just equal sales revenue. Firm A is on the brink of leaving the industry. Firm B is in an even worse situation because it has higher implicit costs. Added to the explicit costs they produce an economic loss, which if not reversed will lead to the firm leaving the industry. Note this firm is nevertheless making an accounting profit just like Firm A. The reason it is making economic losses may be a reflection of the wages its proprietor could earn in another occupation and may have nothing to do with how good he is at the business he is in at the moment. Firm C is in the best position and making a positive economic (supernormal) profit because it has a very low level of implicit costs. The proprietor may deliberately undervalue his earning potential outside and hence have low implicit costs.

simplicity, the diagram has been drawn so that each firm has the same sales revenue and each has the same level of explicit costs. Their implicit costs differ.

The Short Run and the Long Run

In Chapter 20 we noted that in economic analysis it is frequently useful to make a distinction between the short run and the long run. *By the* **short run** *we typically mean a period of time short enough so that the amounts of at least one or more of the factors of production used by the firm cannot be changed.* In a barbershop

it takes little time, perhaps a week, to install another chair and find another barber to increase the production of haircuts. For a barbershop, therefore, the short run may be as little as a week. It may also take only a week or two to lease some space and get started in many small businesses. BHP, on the other hand, needs considerably more time to add another rolling mill or more blast furnaces and hire a work force to run them. The short run for BHP may be months or even years. Obviously, the actual length of time of the short run will depend on the kind of firm and industry we are talking about.

By the **long run** *we mean a period of time long enough so that the amounts of all factors of production used by the firm can be changed.* In other words, the long run is the amount of time it takes for a new firm to get started and operating or for an existing firm to shut down, dispose of its assets, and go out of business. For a barbershop the long run may be any time period longer than a week or two. For BHP it may be any time period longer than 2 or 3 years. The difference between the behaviour of the firm's costs in the short run and the long run is very significant in the analysis of the firm, as we shall see.

CHECKPOINT *22.1
Explain how it might be that relatively inefficient backyard egg producers can continue in business? Why is it that large egg farms seek to prevent these small producers from holding licences to sell eggs in competition? Is there a similar argument for preventing motorists from charging passengers in competition with taxis?

PRODUCTION AND COSTS IN THE SHORT RUN

In the short run, as we have just noted, some of the firm's factors of production are fixed. Therefore the firm's level of output during this period can be altered only by changing the quantities of the factors of production that are not fixed — the variable factors. We need to examine the way output typically changes when these variable factors change. This in turn will allow us to examine how the firm's costs vary when output is changed in the short run.

To simplify matters somewhat, we will analyse the output and costs of a firm that has only two factors of production — capital and labour. In the short run, we will assume that capital (plant and equipment) is the **fixed factor**. Labour (number of labourers) will be the **variable factor**. Our analysis would be more complicated if we considered a firm that had several fixed factors and several variable factors. Since the conclusions would be the same, however, we will choose the simpler case for analysis.

Let's suppose that our firm makes chairs. Given its fixed stock of capital, the firm can vary the quantity of chairs produced only by changing the quantity of labour it uses. The data on quantity produced and labourers employed are given in Table 22.1. From this table, we can see that the total quantity of chairs produced (column 2) gets larger as more labourers are employed (column 1). At first glance, we might be tempted to assume that the way to expand the quantity of output indefinitely is simply to keep adding more workers. A closer look will show us that this is not the case, however.

Law of Diminishing Returns

Let's begin by assuming that the firm's fixed capital stock is idle and no labour is employed — hence there is no output. Now consider how total output changes with the addition of each successive labourer. The increase in output per each additional labourer is called the **marginal product**. The employment of the first labourer (where none had been working before) increases total output from zero up to 1 chair (column 2). Thus the marginal product of the first labourer is 1 (column 3). Adding a second labourer increases total output by 2 chairs, from

1 up to 3 chairs (column 2). The marginal product of the second labourer therefore equals 2 (column 3). The marginal product continues to increase until 4 labourers have been hired, the marginal product of the fourth labourer being equal to 4 (column 3). Hence up through the employment of 4 labourers, the addition to total output attributable to each successive labourer gets larger and larger — in other words, the marginal product (column 3) increases as the first labourers are employed. This occurs because the plant and equipment are difficult to operate effectively with just a few labourers. As more are added, each is able to specialise at fewer tasks and the production process runs more smoothly.

However, once 4 labourers are employed, the marginal product of each successive labourer employed after that gets smaller. Total output continues to get larger (column 2), but by smaller and smaller amounts (column 3). For instance, while the fourth labourer has a marginal

product of 4, the fifth labourer's marginal product is 3, the sixth's is 2 and so on. Why is this so? As more labourers are added, but the fixed stock of capital remains the same, crowding becomes a problem. Some labourers are idle part of the time while waiting for others to finish using a piece of equipment. Eventually there is simply not enough equipment to go around. In the extreme, if enough labourers were crammed into the plant, production would be halted completely as movement became impossible.

In Figure 22.2, part a, the total quantity of chairs produced (Table 22.1, column 2) is plotted on the vertical axis. The number of labourers employed in the production process (Table 22.1, column 1) is plotted on the horizontal axis. This graph showing the relationship between the number of labourers employed and the total quantity of output produced, given the fixed quantity of capital, is the **short-run production function**. In Figure 22.2, part b, the marginal product (Table 22.1,

TABLE 22.1
Chair Production and the Law of Diminishing Returns

(1) Number of Labourers Used	(2) Total Quantity of Chairs Produced per Week	(3) Marginal Product (Change in Output of Chairs)	(4) Average Product
0	0		—
		+1	
1	1		1
		+2	
2	3		1.5
		+3	
3	6		2
		+4	
4	10		2.5
		+3	
5	13		2.6
		+2	
6	15		2.5
		+1.5	
7	16.5		2.3
		+1	
8	17.5		2.2
		+0.5	
9	18		2
		0	
10	18		1.8

column 3) is plotted on the vertical axis and, as in part a, the number of labourers is plotted on the horizontal axis. (Note that the marginal product data are plotted midway between the labour levels for which they are computed.) The marginal product graph clearly shows how the marginal product rises until 4 labourers are employed and then begins to decline as labourers are added beyond this point. Its shape illustrates the **law of diminishing returns**. *This law states that as more and more of a variable factor of production or input (such as labour), is used together with a fixed factor of production (such as capital), beyond some point the additional or marginal product attributable to each additional unit of the variable factor begins to fall.*

Comparison of parts a and b of Figure 22.2 clearly shows that total output is increasing as long as marginal product is positive. When marginal product falls to zero, total output reaches its peak. There are increasing returns when marginal product is rising, and diminishing returns when it is declining.

Another measure that also reflects the law of diminishing returns is **average product**, or output per labourer (Table 22.1, column 4). The average product equals total output (column 2) divided by the corresponding quantity of labour (column 1). Average product is also plotted in Figure 22.2, part b, along with marginal product. Note that as long as marginal product is greater than average product, average product must rise, and when marginal product is less than average product, average product must fall. It necessarily follows that the marginal product graph crosses the highest point on the average product graph (corresponding to 5 units of labour, part b of Figure 22.2). This is simply a property of

the mathematics of averages. If the additional, or marginal, product of one more labourer is greater than the average product of all previous labourers, then the additional labourer's contribution will raise average product. On the other hand, when the additional, or marginal, product of one more labourer is less than the average product, the additional labourer's contribution will cause average product to fall. The same principle causes the average height of the people in a room to be raised whenever an additional (marginal) person enters who is taller than the average of those already in the room. Similarly the average height is lowered whenever someone enters whose height is below the average.

Total Cost in the Short Run

Table 22.2 shows the chair firm's short-run cost schedule. That is, the table indicates the various measures of the firm's costs (columns 3, 4, and 6-9) that are associated with each level of output (column 2) and the corresponding input of labour (column 1). First consider the relationship between the total output of chairs (column 2) and total cost (column 5) and its two components, total fixed cost (column 3) and total variable cost (column 4).

Total Fixed Cost (TFC)

In the short run the firm is saddled with its **total fixed cost**, *the cost of its unchangeable, or fixed factors of production.* The property tax on its land and buildings, the interest payments on the money it borrowed to finance purchase of plant and equipment, and the opportunity cost of its own money invested in such facilities, measured as the return that money could earn if it were invested

FIGURE 22.2
The Law of Diminishing Returns

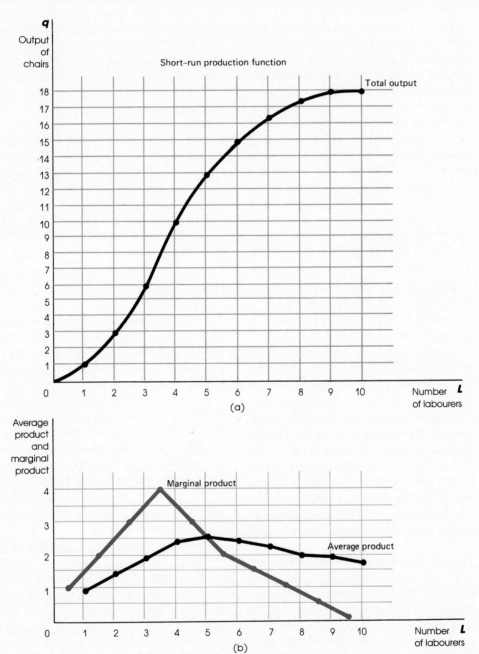

TABLE 22.2
Short-Run Cost Schedules for a Firm Producing Chairs (Hypothetical Data)

(1)	(2)	(3)	(4)	(5)	(6)	(7)	(8)	(9)
Number of Labourers (L)	Quantity of Output per week (Q)	Total Fixed Cost (TFC)	Total Variable Cost (TVC)	Total Cost (TC)	Average Fixed Cost (AFC)	Average Variable Cost (AVC)	Average Total Cost (ATC)	Marginal Cost (MC)
			$TVC = $ wage $\times$ L (wage = $50 per week)	$TC = $ TFC + TVC = (3) + (4)	$AFC = \dfrac{TFC}{Q} = \dfrac{(3)}{(2)}$	$AVC = \dfrac{TVC}{Q} = \dfrac{(4)}{(2)}$	$ATC = \dfrac{TC}{Q} = \dfrac{(5)}{(2)}$	$MC = \dfrac{\text{change in TC}}{\text{change in Q}} = \dfrac{\text{change in (5)}}{\text{change in (2)}}$
0	0	$50	$ 0	$ 50				
1	1	50	50	100	$50.00	$50.00	$100.00	$ 50.00
2	3	50	100	150	16.66	33.33	50.00	25.00
3	6	50	150	200	8.33	25.00	33.33	16.66
4	10	50	200	250	5.00	20.00	25.00	12.50
5	13	50	250	300	3.84	19.23	23.07	16.66
6	15	50	300	350	3.33	20.00	23.33	25.00
7	16.5	50	350	400	3.00	21.20	24.20	33.33
8	17.5	50	400	450	2.80	22.80	25.70	50.00
9	18	50	450	500	2.77	25.00	27.77	100.00

elsewhere, are all fixed costs in the short run. (Total fixed cost is often referred to as 'overhead'.) In the short run, total fixed cost is always the same no matter what level of output the firm produces — which is what is meant by the term 'fixed'.

Suppose that for the firm making chairs the total fixed cost attributable to its fixed factor, capital, amounts to $50 per week. This cost (column 3) is the same no matter what quantity of chairs is produced per week (column 2). It is plotted in Figure 22.3 to give the total fixed cost curve TFC.

Total Variable Cost (TVC)

The costs that the firm can vary in the short run by changing the quantity of the variable factors of production and hence the quantity of output produced make up the **total variable cost**. Payments for natural gas, fuels, electricity, materials and

Part a, based on the data from columns 1 and 2 of Table 22.1, shows how larger quantities of total output (vertical axis), can be produced by using larger quantities of labour, the variable input (horizontal axis), given a fixed amount of capital. As more labour is added, total output at first rises by ever larger amounts, up to 4 labourers, and then rises by ever diminishing amounts until it reaches a maximum at 9 labourers. Further additions of labour would actually reduce total output. This is further illustrated in part b (using the data of columns 3 and 4), where the graph of marginal product shows how the increase in total output associated with each additional labourer at first rises and then declines as more labour is used. Average product rises as long as marginal product exceeds it and declines when marginal product is below it. Hence marginal product intersects average product where the latter is a maximum.

FIGURE 22.3
Total Cost Equals Total Variable Cost Plus Total Fixed Cost

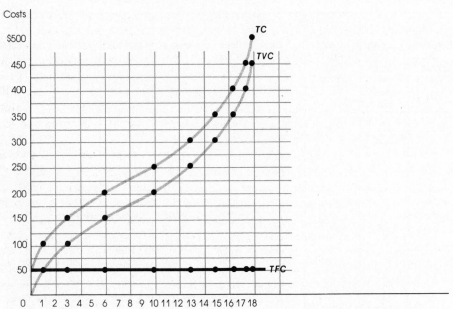

Total fixed cost (*TFC*) is the cost of the firm's fixed factors and is the same no matter what the level of production. Hence the *TFC* curve is horizontal. Total variable cost (*TVC*) is the cost of the firm's variable factors. This cost varies with the level of production and is zero at zero level of output. The shape of the *TVC* curve shows that variable cost rises at a decreasing rate up to some point and at an increasing rate beyond. This reflects the law of diminishing returns. The total cost (*TC*) is the sum of total variable cost and total fixed cost. The *TC* curve is therefore parallel to the *TVC* curve and lies above it by the amount of the total fixed cost. The points on the curves shown here are plotted from the data of Table 22.2.

labour are all variable costs.

In the case of the chair firm, the only variable cost is that due to the variable factor labour. Suppose each labourer is paid $50 per week. Multiplying the number of labourers (*L*) in column 1 by this wage therefore gives the *TVC* in column 4 associated with each quantity (*Q*) of chairs produced (column 2). The total variable cost is plotted in Figure 22.3 to give the total variable cost curve *TVC*.

Note that if the graph in Figure 22.2,

part a, is turned around so that the vertical axis measuring *Q* becomes the horizontal axis and the horizontal axis measuring *L* becomes the vertical axis, we get the *TVC* curve of Figure 22.3 by simply multiplying the number of labourers by their weekly wage of $50 per labourer. Hence we see that the *TVC* curve reflects the law of diminishing returns in that it first rises at a decreasing rate and then at an increasing rate as the production of chairs is increased.

Total Cost (TC)

The firm's **total cost** *is the sum of its total fixed cost and its total variable cost at any given level of output.* For the chair firm, total costs *TC* (column 5) are the sum of *TFC* (column 3) and *TVC* (column 4).

The total costs are plotted to give the *TC* curve of Figure 22.3. It is parallel to the *TVC* curve. For each output level *Q*, the associated point on the *TC* curve lies directly above the associated point on the *TVC* curve. The distance between these points is equal to the amount of the total fixed costs. This reflects the fact that because total fixed costs are constant, the variation in total costs is due entirely to the changes in total variable costs when the level of output is changed.

It can also be seen from Table 22.2 and Figure 22.3 that when output is zero, *TFC* and *TC* are one and the same. This simply reflects the fact that when nothing is produced, no labour is used and so there are no variable costs.

CHECKPOINT 22.2
How would the curves in Figure 22.3 be affected if total fixed cost was increased from $50 to $75? How would these curves be affected if wages rose from $50 to $75 per week? Show the effects of such changes graphically.

Average Cost in the Short Run

Now consider columns 6, 7, and 8 of Table 22.2. These columns represent average fixed cost, average variable cost, and average total cost.

Average Fixed Cost (AFC)

The **average fixed cost** at any given output level is calculated by dividing total fixed cost by that output level. In symbols this becomes

$$AFC = \frac{TFC}{Q}$$

This equation may also be interpreted as the firm's total fixed cost per unit of output produced. For the firm of Table 22.2, the *AFC* shown in column 6 is obtained by dividing the *TFC* of column 3 by the *Q* of column 2. Looking at column 6, we can see that *AFC* falls as *Q* is increased. This happens because *TFC* is the same no matter what the output level. Therefore the larger the output level, the more these overhead costs are spread out. This is clearly shown in Figure 22.4, where the *AFC* data of column 6 are plotted to give the *AFC* curve.

Now we can understand what is meant by a news item commenting on declining business profits with the statement: 'When a company's volume of sales for the year turns out to be lower than was budgeted, its fixed costs, which include such items as depreciation, interest, and overhead, must be spread over a smaller volume of sales. This cuts into the company's profits per unit of sales'. The lower the level of output, the larger is average, or per unit, fixed cost. Given the price at which a unit of output is sold, the larger is the portion of the price that must go to cover the per unit fixed costs. Hence the smaller is the portion of the price left over for profit.

Average Variable Cost (AVC)

The average variable cost at any given output level is calculated by dividing total

FIGURE 22.4
The Average and Marginal Cost Curves

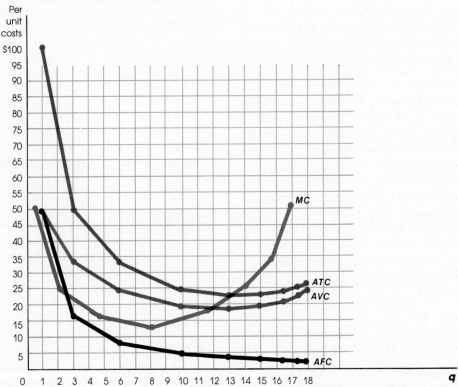

Average fixed cost (*AFC*) is equal to total fixed cost (*TFC*) divided by output (*Q*). The *AFC* curve here is plotted from the data in column 6 of Table 22.2. *AFC* falls as *Q* is increased because *TFC* is the same no matter what the output level. Hence the overhead costs are spread out.

Average variable cost (*AVC*) is equal to total variable cost (*TVC*) divided by output (*Q*). The *AVC* curve is plotted from the data in column 7 of Table 22.2. *AVC* first falls as *Q* increases and then rises, reflecting the law of diminishing returns.

Average total cost (*ATC*) is equal to total cost divided by output (*Q*). The *ATC* curve is plotted from the data in column 8 of Table 22.2. Since *ATC* equals *AFC* plus *AVC*, the *ATC* curve may be viewed as the sum of the *AFC* and the *AVC* curves. Hence at any output level the distance between the *ATC* curve and the *AVC* curve equals *AFC*.

Marginal cost (*MC*) is the change in total cost associated with the production of an additional unit of output (*Q*). Equivalently, marginal cost is the change in total variable cost associated with the production of an additional unit of output. The *MC* curve is plotted from the data in column 9 of Table 22.2. Its shape reflects the law of diminishing returns. The *MC* curve always crosses the *AVC* and *ATC* curves at their bottommost points.

variable cost by that output level. In symbols this becomes

$$AVC = \frac{TVC}{Q}$$

In Table 22.2 the *AVC* shown in column 7 is obtained by dividing the *TVC* of column 4 by the *Q* of column 2. The figures from column 7 are plotted in Figure 22.4 to give the *AVC* curve.

Notice that *AVC* at first falls as *Q* increases and then rises. This happens because the *AVC* data are derived from the *TVC* data, and since *TVC* reflects the law of diminishing returns so does *AVC*. When output falls to low enough levels, *AVC*, or average variable cost per unit, rises in the same manner as *AFC*, or average fixed cost per unit. This can be seen clearly in Figure 22.4.

Average Total Cost (ATC)

The **average total cost** at any given output level is obtained by simply dividing total cost by that output level:

$$ATC = \frac{TC}{Q}$$

However, since TC = TFC + TVC, we see that

$$ATC = \frac{TFC + TVC}{Q}$$

And knowing that

$$\frac{TFC}{Q} = AFC$$

and

$$\frac{TVC}{Q} = AVC$$

we can say that

$$ATC = AFC + AVC$$

The data for *ATC* are shown in column 8 of Table 22.2. At any output level, it can be seen that the figure in column 8 can be obtained by dividing the figure in column 5 by that in column 2, or alternatively by adding the figures in columns 6 and 7. The data in column 8 are plotted in Figure 22.4 to give the *ATC* curve. At any output level, the distance between the *ATC* curve and the *AVC* curve equals *AFC*.

Because *ATC* is the sum of *AFC* and *AVC*, the diagnosis given in the news item referred to above could be carried even further. Observe that as output falls to low enough levels, *ATC*, or average total cost per unit, rises as shown in Figure 22.4. Given the price per unit of output, this means a larger portion of the price is required to cover average total cost per unit. Hence a smaller portion is left for profit. The news item most likely means accounting profit when referring to 'profits per unit of sales'.

CHECKPOINT 22.3
Suppose total fixed cost falls by $10. Show how this will affect average fixed cost, average variable cost, and average total cost in Table 22.2 and Figure 22.4. Suppose the weekly wage of a labourer increases from $50 to $60 per week. Show how this will affect average fixed cost average variable cost and average total cost in Table 22.2 and Figure 22.4.

Marginal Cost in the Short Run

Marginal cost (*MC*) is one of the most important concepts in economics. *The addition or increment, to cost associated with producing one more unit of output is the* **marginal cost**. Since total cost changes with output only because total variable cost changes, marginal cost may be viewed equivalently as either the addition to total cost or the addition to total variable cost associated with the production of an additional unit of output. Therefore, we can say that

$$MC = \frac{\text{change in } TC}{\text{change in } Q} = \frac{\text{change in } TVC}{\text{change in } Q}$$

Marginal Cost and the Law of Diminishing Returns

Marginal cost for our hypothetical chair firm is given in column 9 of Table 22.2. Since labour is the only variable factor, *TC* and *TVC* change only because of the change in the employment of labour. Starting from a zero level of output, the marginal cost of the first chair produced is $50, which is just the change in *TVC* (column 4). It is also the change in *TC* (column 5) divided by one chair. The successive changes in total output *Q* (column 2) associated with the employment of each additional labourer (column 1) vary according to the law of diminishing returns, as indicated by the marginal product figures in column 3 of Table 22.1. (Note that columns 1 and 2 of Table 22.1 are the same as columns 1 and 2 of Table 22.2.) This is reflected in the data for *MC* (column 9 of Table 22.2), which is computed as the change in *TC* divided by the change in *Q* or the marginal product associated with the employment of each additional labourer.

Since the marginal product of labour *increases* up to the point where 4 labourers are employed, and since the increase in cost associated with each additional labourer is always the same ($50), marginal cost *decreases* over this range. However beyond this point, the marginal product of labour begins to *decrease* with the employment of each additional labourer. Again, since the increase in cost due to each additional labourer is always $50, marginal cost *increases* from this point on.

The marginal cost data of column 9 are plotted in Figure 22.4 to give the *MC* curve. (Note that the *MC* data are plotted midway between the output levels for which they are computed.) *The shape of the MC curve clearly reflects the fact that MC falls when the marginal product of the variable factor (labour) rises, and that MC rises when the marginal product of the variable factor falls.*

The Relationship Between Marginal and Average Cost

Looking at columns 7, 8, and 9 of Table 22.2, we can see that, starting from a zero level of output, *AVC* and *ATC* fall as output increases so long as *MC* is lower than *AVC* and *ATC*. This is true up to the point where 5 labourers are employed during 13 units of output. Beyond this point *MC* rises above *AVC* and *ATC*, and *AVC* and *ATC* then rise as output is increased. This relationship is reflected in Figure 22.4 by the fact that the *AVC* and *ATC* curves decline over the range where the *MC* curve is below them and increase over the range where the *MC* curve is above them. It follows from these observations that *the MC curve passes through the AVC and ATC curves at their minimum, or bottommost, points.*

POLICY PERSPECTIVE

The Australian Family Farm

The sole proprietorship and the partnership are a much more important form of business organisation in agriculture than in mining or manufacturing. Why is this so? Does it mean farming is inefficient? Can we expect the family farm to survive? In 1974 an Australian Government Green Paper on Australian rural industry discussed the special features of the family farm and its future prospects. Amongst the advantages that a family farm enjoyed over a company there were the following:

1. The family provides the bulk of labour and management requirements. A relatively simple decision making structure exists. There are intangible benefits to the owners who are prepared to work long hours and are often prepared to accept lower rewards than those to be gained working elsewhere. Unlike the company it does not have to achieve a rate of return on invested funds to satisfy its shareholders.
2. Much agricultural activity is better in small production units. Diseconomies occur when farms get too big. Family farms may therefore have a competitive edge over company farms.
3. The taxation structure has tended to favour the family farm in the past.

However the family farm also faces some serious difficulties.

(i) The family farm finds it more difficult to raise capital because it does not have the same access to the capital market as companies do. It often has an inadequate capital base and therefore cannot exploit technological developments or scale economies.
(ii) Its smallness often places it in a weak position in the market place, when selling produce to national supermarket chains or on international commodity markets. The family farm often lacks people with marketing expertise and will tend to be production oriented.

The Green Paper concluded that the family farm would probably continue to survive in Australia and that community attitudes were also in favour of it. It argued that this community support might provide a good enough reason for government to intervene particularly by improving the access of family farms to finance. It argued that such access would lead to a greater efficiency in resource use and thus to a more efficient agricultural industry.

Questions

1. Draw two diagrams representing the short-run average and marginal cost curves of a family farm and a company farm. The differences between these will reflect some of the advantages and disadvantages listed above. In particular you will need to take into account the following factors:
   (a) relative levels of explicit and implicit costs (the family farm will have low explicit costs compared with companies — what about implicit costs?)
   (b) relative levels of variable costs (treat implicit costs as one of the fixed costs)
   (c) relative length and position of the marginal cost curve.

2. With the help of the diagrams you have drawn discuss whether the family farm or the company farm would be in a better position in the short run to cope with rural depression.

3. Compare their relative ability to cope with
   (a) an increase in wage rates for employed farm labourers
   (b) an increase in interest rates on funds for machinery and equipment
   (c) an increase in demand for their produce.

The reason for this relationship between the marginal magnitude MC and the average magnitudes AVC and ATC is strictly mathematical, as we have already discussed. When the addition to total cost (the marginal cost) associated with the production of another unit of output is greater than ATC, ATC rises. Conversely, if the marginal cost of another unit is less than ATC, ATC will fall. Hence ATC declines as long as MC is below ATC. When MC is above ATC, ATC rises. Therefore, at the output level at which MC rises from below ATC to just above it, ATC ceases to decline and begins to rise. It follows therefore that ATC reaches its lowest point at the output level at which MC crosses ATC. Exactly the same argument applies to AVC. There is no such relationship between MC and AFC, however. This is so because AFC depends upon TFC, and since TFC is unaffected by changes in TVC, AFC declines continuously as output changes no matter what the behavior of MC.

The Significance of Marginal Cost for the Firm

The importance of marginal cost is that it tells the firm exactly how much it will cost to produce an additional unit of output. Conversely, it tells the firm the reduction in cost that will result if it reduces production by a unit of output.

Average variable and average total cost do not give this kind of information because they are based on the cost of *all* output produced.

As we shall see repeatedly in the next few chapters, the firm's output decision in the short run is always made at the margin. The answer to the question, 'Should we produce an additional unit of output?' will be found by comparing the cost of producing that additional unit (the marginal cost) with the additional revenue received from the sale of that unit.

CHECKPOINT 22.4
Notice that in Table 22.2, columns 7, 8, and 9, the change in average variable cost between successive output levels is always less than the change in the marginal cost. Notice also that the same is true of the change in average total cost only after the point at which 3 labourers are employed and 6 units of output are produced. Why is this so? If diminishing returns are larger than is the case in Table 22.2, how would the MC curve of Figure 22.4 be affected?

PRODUCTION AND COSTS IN THE LONG RUN

The long run in economic analysis is a period of time long enough for the firm to be able to change the quantities of all its factors of production. The firm has maximum flexibility to decide how to produce a good and the amount of the good. The term *production function* is used to describe the technical relationship between combinations of factors of production and final output. It is a useful idea to introduce at this stage because it helps to explain the distinction between the short period and the long period and the differing cost structures the firm has to face in each.

The notion of a production function can be explained most simply by considering our example of chair production and again supposing that only two factors of production, capital and labour, are used to make chairs. In the short period, the firm could only increase production of chairs by hiring more labour. Capital was fixed. The short run production function information was given in Figure 22.2 and Table 22.2 on pages 570 and 571. The long run production function is more complicated because both factors of production can be varied. Instead of the two columns of information in Table 22.2 (columns 1 and 2) we need to show what will be produced when various combinations of

two variable factors are employed. Such information is provided in Table 22.3.

Table 22.3 provides information about the number of chairs that the firm would be able to produce if it used different combinations of labour and capital. There are 36 possible combinations listed. Thus 4 units of labour and 1 unit of capital would produce 10 chairs in a week while 3 units of labour and 3 units of capital would produce 12 chairs. In the long period the firm can select any level of capital equipment and thus may choose any of the 36 combinations, whereas in the short run it is committed to a given level of capital equipment and can only achieve the production levels indicated by the appropriate column.

This information about the firm's production function can also be presented in diagrammatic form. This has been done in Figure 22.5. The quantities of factors used are measured on the axes of the diagram and each point inside the diagram represents a specific marked level of output. Points representing the same level of output have been joined together by lines, showing that these are alternative ways of producing the same level of output. Thus, for example 15 chairs can

TABLE 22.3
Long-Run Production Function Data for a Firm Producing Chairs (Hypothetical Data)

Units of Labour	Units of Capital						
	0	1*	2	3	4	5	6
0	0	0	0	0	0	0	0
1	0	1	3	5	6	7	8
2	0	3	6	8	11	13	15
3	0	6	10	12	15	18	21
4	0	10	13	15	18	22	26
5	0	13	15	18	19	24	29
6	0	15	17	16	21	26	30

*see table 22.2

FIGURE 22.5
Equal Product Curves or Isoquants

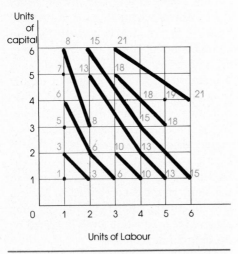

Units of Labour

FIGURE 22.6
Stylised Isoquant Map Showing Smooth Equal Product Curves

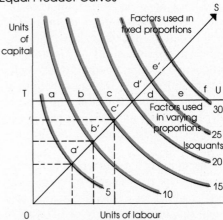

The equal product curves, or isoquants, show the various combinations of the factors capital and labour that can be used to produce a given level of output. In total they provide a picture of the production function. Notice each isoquant has a number (the level of output attached to it). Any point on any isoquant has coordinates and reading these off on the two axes gives the quantities of labour and capital used to produce that amount. The distance between isoquants can also tell us something about the production relationship. In Figure 22.6 each successive isoquant is 5 units of output more than the previous one, so the gap between them contains valuable information. The ray OS indicates capital and labour are being used in fixed proportions and the effects on output as the *scale of operations* increases. If a'=b'=c' etc. then we have constant returns to scale. If, however, a'<b'<c'<d' the firm would have decreasing returns to scale. The line TU allows us to see the effect of holding capital fixed and increasing labour; or varying the proportions of the factors employed. Here notice that on Figure 22.6 c<d<e<f indicating that increasingly large additions of labour are needed to raise production by 5 units. The law of diminishing returns is in operation.

be produced either by using 6 labour and 1 capital, 5 labour and 2 capital, 4 labour and 3 capital, 3 labour and 4 capital and 2 labour and 6 capital. It is sometimes possible to make very small adjustments to labour and capital used in production. Under such circumstances the same level of production can be achieved by making infinitely small replacements of one factor by the other. The line showing all combinations of factors that produce the same level of output is known as an *equal product curve* or *isoquant*. A stylised version of an isoquant map showing smooth equal product curves or contours is shown in Figure 22.6.

In the discussion about the short period the term *diminishing returns* was used to refer to the tendency of the marginal product of a factor to fall at some stage if used in ever increasing quantities with a fixed factor. Sometimes the 'law of diminishing returns' is referred to by an alternative title — the law of variable proportions — to emphasise that the diminishing marginal product is a consequence of one factor at least being in fixed

supply. The proportion in which the factors are used relative to one another must vary — hence the name, law of variable proportions. In the long period it is, of course, possible to change all factors. Where the use of the factors is increased, but they *continue to be employed in the same proportion to one another* we refer to the effect of this increased use of the factors as the *returns of scale*. Returns of scale may be increasing, constant or decreasing. Increasing returns to scale occur when an increase in the use of all factors in fixed proportions produces a more than proportionate increase in production. For example, in Table 22.3 when 1 unit of labour and 1 unit of capital are used only 1 chair is produced, but when 2 units of labour and 2 units of capital are used production rises to 6 chairs. At higher levels of production the imaginary chairmaking factory experiences constant returns to scale when labour and capital are used in a 1 to 1 relationship. We saw that 2 units of labour and 2 units of capital produced 6 chairs. Notice 3 units of each produces 12 chairs, 4 units of each produces 18 chairs, 5 units of each produces 24 chairs, and so on. Each additional unit of labour, when employed with an additional unit of capital produces another 6 chairs. After the initial application where increasing returns to scale applied, constant returns to scale took over.

In our discussion of the long period and the inherent flexibility the firm has, it is important to remember that we have only thought about technical relationships between factors of production and output. We have said nothing about the price of these factors and hence the firm's costs of production. If factor prices are known this technical information can readily be converted into cost information. Suppose the unit price of both labour and capital is $50. It is a simple matter to work out the total cost of producing 15 chairs, using the five alternative methods given in Table 22.3. Which do you think is the cheapest of the five methods? Suppose instead the price of capital was $100 per unit. How does this affect the cost of producing 15 chairs?

Changes in Plant Size

When all factors of production are variable, there is, of course, no longer a distinction between variable and fixed costs. In the long run the only relevant average cost concept is the long-run average total cost, because when all factors are variable, so are all costs. In order to understand average total cost in the long run, we must first look at how changes in plant size affect costs and output.

The firm can change the entire plant in the long run to meet its production needs. For any given output level there is an optimum-size plant — one that entails lower per unit production cost (or average total cost) than any other. Each possible plant size can be represented by its short-run *ATC* curve.

Let's see how different plant sizes and their short-run *ATC* curves are usually related to different output levels. Starting from a zero output level, larger and larger plant sizes typically have lower and lower *ATC* curves at successively higher output levels up to some point. Beyond a certain output level, however, successively larger plant sizes give rise to successively higher *ATC* curves. This is illustrated for three possible different plant sizes in Figure 22.7. The lowest point on the *ATC* curve for the smallest plant (Plant 1) occurs at 700 units of output. For the next largest plant (Plant 2), the lowest point on its *ATC* curve occurs at a larger level of output, 1,800 units, and is obviously lower than that of Plant 1. The lowest point on the *ATC* of the largest plant (Plant 3) occurs at 2,700 units of output and is clearly higher than that of Plant 2.

Points *a* and *b* of Figure 22.7 are of particular interest. If the firm produces less than 900 units of output, Plant 1 is the best plant size to use because it has the lowest per unit costs for output levels less than 900. This is clear from the fact that to the left of point *a* the *ATC* curve for Plant 1 lies below that for Plant 2. If the firm produces between 900 and 2,400 units of output, Plant 2 is the best plant size to use because it has the lowest per unit costs for this range of output. This is reflected in the fact that the *ATC* curve of Plant 2 lies below that of Plant 1 to the right of *a*, and below that of Plant 3 to the left of *b*. If the firm produces more than 2,400 units of output, Plant 3 is the best plant size to use because it has the lowest per unit costs for this range

of output. This is apparent from the fact that the *ATC* curve of Plant 3 lies below that of Plant 2 to the right of point *b*.

Long-Run Average Total Cost

The observations we have just made about the firm's selection of the optimum plant size to produce different output levels suggest the nature of the firm's long-run average total cost curve. *The long-run ATC curve, sometimes called the firm's planning curve, shows the lowest per unit cost at which it is possible to produce a given output when there is enough time for the firm to adjust its plant size.* In Figure 22.7 the long-run *ATC* curve consists of the segment of Plant 1's *ATC* curve up to point *a*, the segment of Plant 2's *ATC* curve between *a* and *b*, and the

FIGURE 22.7
Average Total Cost Curves for Three Possible Plant Sizes

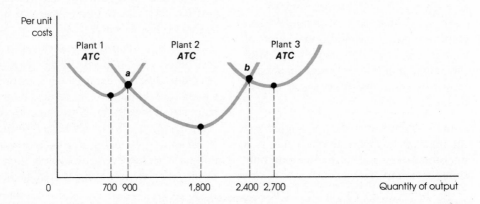

In the long run the firm can change the size of its plant. Starting from a zero output level, successively larger plants typically have lower and lower *ATC* curves up to some output level and then successively higher *ATC* curves beyond. The three representative *ATC* curves associated with the three successively larger plants shown here illustrate this.

Plant 1 is the best plant size for output levels less than 900 units because its *ATC* curve is the lowest to the left of point *a*. Plant 2 is the best plant size for output levels between 900 and 2,400 units because its *ATC* curve is the lowest between points *a* and *b*. Plant 3 is the best plant size for output levels greater than 2,400 units since its *ATC* curve is the lowest beyond point *b*.

If these are the only three possible plant sizes, the long-run *ATC* curve consists of the segment of Plant 1's *ATC* curve up to point *a*, the segment of Plant 2's *ATC* curve between points *a* and *b*, and the segment of Plant 3's *ATC* curve from point *b* on.

segment of the *ATC* curve for Plant 3 from point *b* on.

While only three possible plant sizes are shown in Figure 22.7, a firm may, in fact, have an almost unlimited number from which it may choose. The larger the number of possible plant sizes, the smaller will be the part of each plant's *ATC* curve used to make up the long-run *ATC* curve. This is illustrated in Figure 22.8. Here, two more possible plant sizes and their associated short-run *ATC*s have been added to the three shown in Figure 22.7. With the addition of *ATC* curves for Plants 4 and 5, it can be seen that the segments *a'a*, *aa''*, *b'b*, and *bb''* of the three original short-run *ATC* curves are no longer parts of the long-run *ATC* curve. They are replaced by the segments *a'a''* and *b'b''* of the *ATC* curves associated with the two additional possible plant sizes.

FIGURE 22.8
The Long-Run Average Total Cost Curve

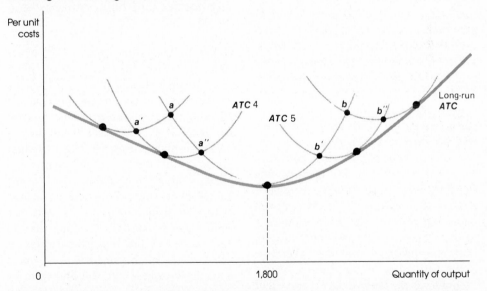

Two more possible plant sizes with short-run *ATC* curves *ATC* 4 and *ATC* 5 are shown here together with the short-run *ATC* curves for the three plant sizes shown in Figure 22.7. The segments of the plant *ATC* curves that now make up the long-run *ATC* curve are the segment of the smallest plant's *ATC* curve up to point *a'*, the segments *a'a''*, *a''b'*, *b'b''*, and the segment of the largest plant's *ATC* curve from *b''* on.

The segments *a'a*, *aa''*, *b'b*, and *bb''* of the three original short-run *ATC* curves are no longer part of the long-run *ATC* curve once we add the fourth and fifth plants. This illustrates that as more and more possible plant sizes are taken into account, the segments of their associated *ATC* curves that are part of the long-run *ATC* curve become smaller and smaller until they are no more than points. Hence given an unlimited number of possible plant sizes, the long-run *ATC* curve is made up of all the points of tangency with the unlimited number of short-run *ATC* curves.

Only the minimum point of the long-run *ATC* curve is tangent to the minimum point of the short-run *ATC* curve (at 1,800 units of output). Below 1,800 units, the long-run *ATC* curve is tangent to the short-run *ATC* curves along their declining portions, and above 1,800 units it is tangent along their rising portions.

As output increases, the firm realises economies of scale along the falling portion of the long-run *ATC* curve and diseconomies of scale along the rising portion.

As more and more possible plant sizes are considered, the segments of their associated *ATC* curves that are part of the long-run *ATC* curve become smaller and smaller. With an unlimited number of possible plant sizes, the long-run *ATC* curve is a smooth curve, made up of all the points of tangency with the unlimited number of short-run *ATC* curves. This curve appears as a heavy line in Figure 22.8. Only five of the unlimited number of short-run *ATC* curves that make up the long-run *ATC* curve are shown. Note that only the minimum point of the long-run *ATC* curve at 1,800 units of output is tangent to the minimum point of a short-run *ATC* curve. At output levels below 1,800 units, the points of tangency occur to the left of the minimum points on the short-run *ATC* curves. At output levels above 1,800 units, the tangency points occur to the right of the minimum points on the short-run *ATC* curves.

It is clear now why the long-run *ATC* curve is sometimes called the planning curve. At any output level the associated point on the long-run *ATC* curve is a point on a short-run *ATC* curve corresponding to that plant size that is the most efficient for producing that output level. Therefore if the firm plans to produce a certain output level, the long-run *ATC* curve tells it the best-size plant to construct. It is best in the sense that the planned output level may be produced at the lowest possible per unit cost.

CHECKPOINT 22.5
It has been said that a firm's long-run ATC curve really represents nothing more than a collection of blueprints. In what sense is this true? When a plant operates at a point to the left of the minimum point on its short-run ATC curve, it is said to be underutilised.

Assuming there are an unlimited number of plant sizes making up the long-run ATC curve of Figure 22.8, why is it always cheaper at any given output level less than 1,800 units to underutilise a larger plant than to overutilise a smaller one? Similarly why is it always cheaper at any given output level greater than 1,800 units to overutilise a smaller plant than to underutilise a larger one?

Economies and Diseconomies of Scale

Why do the short-run *ATC* curves associated with successively larger plant sizes become steadily lower up to some output level and then begin to rise, giving the long-run *ATC* curve the shape shown in Figure 22.8? The reason is *not* the law of diminishing returns, which assumes that some of the factors of production are fixed. That law only explains the U-shape of the short-run *ATC* curve associated with a particular plant size. It does not apply here because, in the long run, all factors are variable. Hence the reasons for the U-shape of the long-run *ATC* curve must lie elsewhere. We will find them by examining what economists call *economies* and *diseconomies* of scale.

Economies of Scale

Economies of scale are the decreases in the long-run average total cost of production that occur when the firm's plant size is increased, as represented by the declining portion of the long-run *ATC* curve. Economies of scale can occur for a number of reasons.

1. *Specialisation of factors of production.* In a small firm labour and equipment

must be used to perform a number of different tasks. It is more difficult for labour to become skilled at any one of them and thereby realise the gains in productivity and reductions in per unit costs that specialisation permits. In the same way, management functions cannot be as specialised in a smaller firm. Supervisors may have to devote time to the screening of job applicants, a task usually more efficiently handled by a personnel department in a larger firm. Executives may have to divide their attention between finance, accounting, and production operations — functions that could be handled more proficiently by departments specialising in each of these areas in a larger firm.

Similarly, machinery and equipment cannot be used as efficiently when they have to be switched back and forth between tasks. Moreover, in many types of production processes, the most efficient types of production facilities are practicable only at high levels of output. It is very expensive to build custom-made cars by hand, but it would be equally or more expensive to use the large Ford Motor Company's plant at Broadmeadows in Melbourne to build only 10 Ford Lasers per year. However, if the plant is used to build 40,000 cars per year of a similar type, the highly specialised assembly line and integrated techniques allow the cost per car to be reduced greatly.

2. *Volume discounts on the prices of materials and other inputs used in production.* Often the suppliers of raw materials, machinery, and other inputs will charge a lower price per unit for these items if a firm buys in large quantities. When a firm produces at high output levels, it needs a large volume of inputs and can take advantage of the associated price discounts to reduce its per unit costs.

3. *Economic use of by-products.* The production of many types of goods gives rise to by-products that also have economic value. Large-scale firms are often able to recycle 'waste' by-products that smaller-size firms simply have to throw away because it is not economical to do anything else with them. For example, a small sawmill may simply throw away sawdust and old wood scraps. A large timber-processing firm often finds the volume of these waste products large enough to make it economical to package sawdust and sell it as a sweeping compound for cleaning floors and hallways in large buildings. The wood scraps may be packaged, processed, and sold as kindling wood and artificial logs for home barbecues and fireplaces. In this way, the sale of by-products effectively reduces the per unit costs of producing timber in large volume. For the same reasons, large oil firms often produce a host of petroleum by-products, and meat-packing firms produce fertilisers, glue, leather, and other by-products of meat production.

4. *The growth of supporting facilities and services is encouraged by the firm's large scale of operation.* As a firm's scale of operations gets larger, it often becomes worthwhile for other firms and local governments to provide it with services. If a firm builds a large plant in a particular area, an improvement in highways and expanded transportation services may soon follow. Smaller suppliers, which find a large part of their sales going to the larger firm, may move closer to the larger firm to reduce transportation costs. All of these developments result in lower per unit costs for the large firm.

Diseconomies of Scale

Diseconomies of scale refer to the increasing long-run average total cost of produc-

---

POLICY PERSPECTIVE

Economies and Diseconomies of Scale and the Number of Firms in an Industry

The number of firms in an industry is an important determinant of the degree of competition that exists among firms in that industry, a major concern of competition policy which we will study in Chapter 27. In general, competition will be more intense if there are more firms, other things equal. The existence of economies and diseconomies of scale is an important determining factor of how many firms there are in an industry.

Consider the three different long-run *ATC* curves shown in Figure P22.1. In part a, economies of scale are relatively small and diseconomies of scale set in relatively quickly as output is increased. In part b, economies of scale are again quickly exhausted, but there is a considerable range of output over which the long-run *ATC* curve is flat before diseconomies of scale set in. In part c, economies of scale are realised over a much larger range of output before diseconomies of scale set in.

Given the consumer demand facing an industry, there is likely to be a greater number of smaller-sized firms in the industry if the typical firm's long-run *ATC* curve is like

---

FIGURE P22.1
Three Different Types of Long-Run Average Total Cost Curves

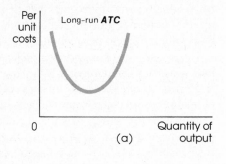

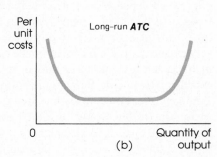

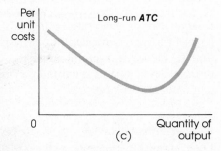

that of part a than if it is like that of either part b or part c. On the other hand, if the typical firm's long-run ATC is like that of part c, the industry is more likely to be composed of a smaller number of larger-sized firms. This is so because firms will not realise minimum per unit costs until they push production to relatively higher output levels. The inbetween case depicted in part b suggests the possibility of an industry composed of firms more varied in size, each of which realises similar levels of minimum per unit costs.

Question

1. If there were a decline in demand for an industry's product, which one of the long-run ATC curves in Figure P22.1 would probably entail the least number of firms having to go out of business? Why?

---

tion represented by the rising portion of the long-run ATC curve. When the firm produces at output levels greater than those corresponding to the minimum point on the long-run ATC curve, the upward pressure on per unit costs due to diseconomies of scale more than offsets the downward pressure resulting from economies of scale.

Diseconomies of scale are largely a result of the firm's growing so large that it becomes cumbersome to manage. Once the firm gets beyond a certain size, the problems of efficiently coordinating a large number of plants and diverse operations become more complex. Central management must communicate with many more areas of the firm and process more information in order to keep tabs on what's going on. This often means that more authority must be delegated to middle- and lower-management levels. The increased chances of misguided decisions, combined with central management's difficulty in monitoring all operations, may result in inefficiencies that cause the per unit costs of output to rise.

SUMMARY

1. The three primary legal forms of the

firm are the proprietorship, the partnership, and the corporation. While proprietorships and partnerships are more numerous, the corporation is the dominant form of large business enterprise. This is so mainly because it is the only legal form of business organisation that affords owners the protection of limited liability. This feature enhances the corporation's ability to raise capital.

2. Whether resources are owned directly by the firm or must be hired from outside, their cost is the money payment they could have received if employed in their next best alternative use. The firm's costs include explicit costs, which are the payments to resource suppliers outside the firm, and implicit costs, which equal the compensation that resources already owned by the firm could earn in alternative uses outside the firm. Implicit costs include a normal profit from the entrepreneurial skills and financial capital supplied by a firm's owners.

3. In the short run, some of a firm's factors of production, such as its plant, are fixed. Its level of output can be varied only by changing the quantities of its variable factors, such as its labour. In the long run, there is sufficient time for the firm to vary all its factors of production, including the size of its plant.

4. In the short run, the law of diminishing returns describes the changes in output that result as increasing amounts of a variable input are applied to a fixed input. It says that the additions to total output, called the marginal product, associated with the addition of each successive unit of the variable factor will begin to decline beyond some point.

5. Total fixed cost (*TFC*) includes all the firm's costs associated with the factors of production that are fixed in the short run. The firm is saddled with fixed cost no matter what level of output it produces. Total variable cost (*TVC*) includes all the firm's costs associated with the factors that are variable in the short run. Total variable cost changes with the level of the firm's output. At any output level the firm's total cost (*TC*) equals the sum of total fixed and total variable cost.

6. Average fixed cost (*AFC*) equals total fixed cost divided by the output level. It falls continuously as the output level is increased. Average variable cost (*AVC*) equals total variable cost divided by the output level. As output is increased, *AVC* first falls and then rises, reflecting the law of diminishing returns. Average total cost (*ATC*) equals the sum of average fixed cost and average variable cost. It falls and then rises as output increases.

7. Marginal cost (*MC*) is the increment, or addition, to total cost resulting from the production of an additional unit of output. As output increases, *MC* first falls and then rises, reflecting the law of diminishing returns. It cuts the *AVC* and *ATC* curves at their bottommost points.

8. Because all factors of production are variable in the long run, so are all costs.

When the firm has sufficient time to adjust the size of its plant, it will select the plant size that has the lowest short-run *ATC* curve at the desired output level. For this reason the long-run *ATC* curve is composed of segments of all the short-run *ATC* curves. It is sometimes called a planning curve.

9. The long-run *ATC* curve is U-shaped, its declining portion reflecting economies of scale and its rising portion reflecting diseconomies of scale. Economies of scale result from increased specialisation of the factors of production, price discounts on volume purchases of inputs, more economical use of byproducts and the growth of supporting firms and services. Diseconomies of scale result from the increased difficulty of managing large-scale operations once the firm has grown beyond a certain size.

10. Economies and diseconomies of scale play a major role in determining the size and number of firms in an industry. In general given the demand for an industry's product, the larger the economies of scale, the greater will be the size and the smaller the number of firms in an industry. Conversely, when economies of scale are few, in general the size of firms will be smaller and the number of firms will be larger in the industry.

KEY TERMS AND CONCEPTS

accounting profit
average fixed cost (*AFC*)
average product
average total cost (*ATC*)
average variable cost (*AVC*)
conglomerate
company
creditor
diseconomies of scale

dividends
economic cost
economic profit
economies of scale
explicit costs
firm
fixed factor
horizontally integrated
implicit costs
law of diminishing returns
limited liability
limited partner
long run
marginal cost
marginal product
normal profit
partnership
plant
short run
short-run production function
sole proprietorship
total cost (*TC*)
total fixed cost (*TFC*)
total variable cost (*TVC*)
undistributed profits
variable factor
vertically integrated

QUESTIONS AND PROBLEMS

1. Attempt to identify the main cost items of a long distance lorry driver, who was buying his own rig. What would be the possible effects on his costs and his economic profits if he developed severe arthritis and was unable to walk without pain? Could it conceivably lead to an increase in his economic profits?

2. Which of the following economic activities is likely to have a very high level of fixed costs in the short run,

a. a pop concert at the Sydney Entertainment Centre

b. a market stall selling fresh vegetables

c. a clothing manufacturer

d. the Southern Aurora passenger train

e. the Townsville Casino?

3. Rank the following firms according to the maximum length of calendar time you think would constitute the short run: retail shoe store, road construction company, real estate firm, shoeshine stand, nuclear power company, and oil refinery. Suppose the demand for the goods and services produced by these businesses were to increase tenfold. Rank the industries represented by each of these types of business according to the speed with which you think each would exhibit a complete supply response.

4. Describe how the law of diminishing returns works in each of the following situations, taking care to identify the product and classify the fixed and variable factors in each case: preparing for a final exam, insulating a house, looking for a parking spot within walking distance of a city store at 3:00 p.m. on a weekday, controlling crime in a big city, convincing somebody to give you a job, cleaning up the environment, protecting the population against nuclear attack, protecting yourself from heart attack, getting to the other side of town as fast as possible, discussing the weather, and increasing unemployment benefits to help unemployed people get by financially while looking for a job.

5. For each of the firms in problem 3, describe the nature of their fixed and variable costs. Is there any relationship between your cost description and how you ranked the firms in your answer to problem 3? Why?

6. Consider the fixed, variable, and total costs of an electric power company. How are its *TFC*, *TVC*, *TC*, *AFC*, *AVC*, *ATC*, and *MC* curves affected by the following changes:

a. an increase in interest rates;

b. an increase in wages;

c. a decrease in property taxes;

d. an increase in the price of coal, oil and nuclear fuel;

e. a decrease in the purity of the water it takes in for use in its boilers;

f. imposition of an excise tax on electricity sales collected by the government from the company;

g. a tax on plant size to cover the city's water cleanup costs;

h. passage of an antipollution law;

i. increase in premium rates for hazard insurance.

7. Because of technological progress, there have been considerable increases in economies of scale in farming in the past 50 years. How do you think this has affected population shifts between urban and rural areas, all other things remaining the same?

8. As an economist, what do you think would be the major pros and cons of merging the army, the navy, and the air force into *one* large military organisation?

9. Use the information given in Table 22.3 to construct a long-run average cost curve for the chair manufacturing firm. Take the unit price of labour as $50 and the unit price of capital as $100. Draw on the same diagram the three short-run average total cost curves corresponding to three plant sizes where capital is 1, 3 and 6 units respectively. What can you conclude about the relative costs of the three plants? Suppose the unit price of capital fell to $50. How would this affect the long period average cost curve and the three plant sizes under consideration?

10. Suppose that the firm had no choice about production technology. The only way it could produce chairs was by using 2 units of labour for every unit of capital. Suppose that every 2 units of labour and single unit of capital produced 4 chairs and that the price of units of labour and capital were $50 and $100 respectively. Draw the firm's isoquant map and mark in an expansion path from 2 to 20 chairs. Suppose it is currently producing 8 chairs each period. Draw in its likely short-run average and marginal cost curves. Draw also the long-run average and marginal cost curves.

SIX

Market Structure, Pricing and Government Regulation

23

Perfect Competition and Price Takers

AFTER READING THIS CHAPTER YOU WILL BE ABLE TO:

1. Define the concept of market structure and have a basis for classifying firms by market form.

2. Characterise the form of market organisation known as perfect competition.

3. State the relationship between the perfectly competitive firm's demand curve and the demand curve of the industry.

4. Show how cost and revenue considerations lead the perfectly competitive firm to decide whether or not to produce in the short run and, if so, how much to produce using the marginal cost-marginal revenue criterion.

5. Explain the long-run adjustment process in a perfectly competitive industry and the nature of the long-run industry supply curve.

6. List the reasons why a perfectly competitive world is considered to be an ideal of efficiency in the allocation of scarce resources to satisfy consumer wants.

7. Explain some of the criticisms of perfect competition.

Firms face different market challenges. Wheat farmers in Western Australia and woolgrowers in New South Wales face a completely different market situation from BHP, Telecom Australia or the appliance manufacturer Email Ltd. How does a firm function in a situation where it is one of many firms, where it is one of a few or maybe even has the entire market to itself? This chapter begins to provide the answer to these questions. Our very first task is to suggest that *it is important to be able to distinguish between types of markets so that we can better understand how firms behave in the real world.* How firms do behave depends on a number of considerations such as the number of buyers and sellers in a market and the similarity of their products in terms of consumers' demands. It also depends on the ease with which firms can enter and leave the industry and the nature of the restraints government may place on the firm's activities.

MARKET BEHAVIOUR AND MARKET FORMS

A basic classification of firms is between those that are **price takers** and those that are **price makers**. The names say it all. A price taker is a firm that cannot influence the market price. As far as pricing decisions are concerned it is in a straightjacket. It has to accept the going market price and then has to organise its production to maximise its economic profits or some other objective on the basis of the going or expected market price. A firm that is a price maker has more flexibility in determining its policies. It does have scope to set its own prices — maybe lots, maybe not much — how much will depend on a host of factors partic-

ularly real or expected competition and real or expected government action. This is probably the most important behavioural distinction of all between the way in which firms operate. It is one that we will continue to emphasise in the following chapters. A second important difference in the environment in which firms operate is in the degree of **uncertainty** they have about how a market will operate. Price takers may not know what the price will be next season but they do know that their decisions will not affect the market price. Some price makers have a clear belief that when they set a price they can anticipate how much they will be able to sell. They can therefore estimate their sales revenue with some confidence. But others operate under conditions of much greater uncertainty. They have rival firms breathing down their necks. What their share of the market will be if they increase their price is uncertain. Naturally, uncertainty affects how they behave.

So far we have classified firms according to whether they are able to set prices and how the degree of certainty affects the way they behave. There is a second and more conventional way of classifying firms. This is based on the number of firms competing in a market. For purposes of description and analysis economists identify four types of market structure:

perfect (or pure) competition
monopoly
monopolistic competition
oligopoly.

While each of these market types appears to be related primarily to the number of sellers, the underlying reason for the classification is that *it distinguishes between four different types of markets in which firms behave in different ways.* The number of firms in a market is by far the most important influence on how

TABLE 23.1
Principal Market Forms and Behavioural Characteristics

Market Form	Ability to Set Price for	Certainty About Rivals Reactions
Perfect Competition	Price Taker	
Monopoly	Price Maker	No Rivals
Monopolistic Competition	Price Maker	Certainty
Oligopoly	Price Maker	Uncertainty

they behave, but it is not the only one that determines market behaviour and market power as we shall see.

In this chapter we will focus on the economist's model of perfect competition and real world situations in which firms are price takers. In the following chapters we will consider the monopoly, monopolistic competition and oligopoly models and real world situations where firms are price makers and face varying degrees of uncertainty. Table 23.1 provides an overview of the four conventional market forms and their underlying behavioural characteristics.

We start in this chapter with perfect competition and the price taker for two reasons. First, in many respects economists consider this kind of market structure to be an ideal form of market organisation for providing goods and services to consumers as efficiently as possible. For this reason it is often used as a standard or norm against which other forms of market structure are compared, as we shall see in the next three chapters. Second, the Australian economy is a small economy open in many areas to overseas competition and selling its products on competitive world markets. So many Australian firms are effectively price takers that the study of perfect compe-

tition is the most logical and relevant place to start our study of Australian markets.

PERFECT COMPETITION IN THEORY AND REALITY

Perfect competition exists only if each firm, or seller, in a market or industry is a **price taker**. Each firm is unable to affect its price because its production of output is such a small portion of total industry supply — a mere 'drop in the bucket'. Hence the firm can change its level of production and sales without having any noticeable effect on the price of the good it sells. The firm is therefore a price taker because it must accept the sales price established in the market as given.

Four Market Characteristics That Promote Perfect Competition

What kind of characteristics of an industry or a market promote the existence of perfect competition? Basically there are four: (1) ease of entry into and exit from the industry by firms (2) all firms sell an identical product (3) there are many firms and (4) buyers are perfectly informed about the prices at which all market transactions take place. Strictly speaking the perfect competition model has a couple of other features that result in all firms having identical costs. Some economists prefer the term *pure competition* for a market with the four characteristics listed above. Others are happy to use the term *perfect competition* more loosely to distinguish this broad market form from *imperfect competition* meaning monopoly, monopolistic competition or oligopoly. It is in this looser sense we will use it in this chapter. Those four characteristics give us a market form that embodies the essential features of a competitive market and one that comes a little closer to reality than the strict model. Let's examine how each of these characteristics tends to promote the existence of perfect competition.

1. Ease of Entry into and Exit from the Industry by Firms

Firms and the resources they employ may easily enter and leave the industry. There are no significant financial, legal, technological, or other barriers to new firms entering the industry or existing firms leaving it. Low barriers to entry put pressure on firms in the industry to operate as efficiently as possible because otherwise new, more efficient firms can easily enter the industry and replace them.

2. All Firms Sell an Identical Product

The important thing here is that the product of one firm is considered by the buyer to be the same as that of any other firm. Therefore in the mind of the buyer, each firm's product is viewed as a perfect substitute for the product of any other firm in the market. This ensures that no

buyer has any economic incentive to pay any firm a higher price for the product than is charged by other firms.

An important implication of this product homogeneity in a perfectly competitive industry is that there is no incentive for firms to engage in nonprice competition. Nonprice competition is encouraged by differences in the products of different firms that can be exploited by advertising and other types of sales promotion. When no such differences exist and buyers know it, advertising by individual firms will yield them no market advantage over other firms.

3. There Are Many Firms

'Many firms' does not mean any specific number. Rather, there are enough firms so that any one firm's contribution to total industry supply is so small that whether a firm produces at full capacity or not at all, market price will not be noticeably affected.

4. Buyers Have Perfect Knowledge About Prices

When buyers have perfect knowledge about the prices at which transactions take place in the market, it is not possible for sellers to charge anyone more than the market price for the homogeneous product.

It is also assumed that there are many buyers and that not one of them is able to affect market price because each is such an insignificant part of the market. Therefore, like firms, buyers are also price takers.

Let's summarise how these four characteristics promote the existence of perfect competition, a market structure where each firm is a price taker. Because the firm's product is indistinguishable from that of any other firm in the market (characteristic 2), there is no incentive for buyers to pay a higher price for it than for that of any other firm. The existence of many other such firms (characteristic 3) and the easy entry of new firms (characteristic 1) ensures that any one firm's output is but a drop in the bucket. Because buyers are perfectly informed about the prices of all market transactions (characteristic 4), they will know if any firm tries to charge them a higher price than any other firm. Accordingly, no firm will be able to sell its product if it charges a price higher than the given price. Since a firm can effectively sell all it can produce at the given price, there is no reason for it to sell its output at a lower price.

Does Perfect Competition Exist?

By this time you may be scoffing at the notion that a perfectly competitive market exists. Your scepticism is understandable. It would be hard to find an industry that has a market structure *perfectly* exhibiting all four characteristics. However, there are industries or markets that come close and, more importantly, ones in which firms, or sellers, are price takers.

Competition in Agriculture

Agriculture in Australia provides good examples of such markets. There are many producers of the main crops and livestock. A survey was carried out in 1985 by the Bureau of Agricultural Economics with the help of the Australian Bureau of Statistics. The survey which excluded hobby farms and properties too small to be considered commercial indicated that

there were about 20,000 beef properties in Australia, 20,000 sheep properties, 26,000 mixed livestock and crops and 17,000 specialist wheat farms. Take any one of the those major types of rural activity. Even though there are some very large wheat growing properties and even bigger pastoral enterprises, it is clear that none of them would dominate the market. If we take the average farm we can see that it is likely to contribute less than one hundredth of one per cent to production. Certainly it seems reasonable to believe that whether or not one farm produces beef, or wool, or wheat or any crop, it will have no noticeable effect on production or on prices. For many agricultural products it is very difficult to tell the output of individual farmers apart. In the market one farmer's wheat is much the same as a second producer's wheat. These considerations (many farmers and a near homogeneous product) suggest perfect competition is a very useful starting point from which to examine the economics of agricultural industry in Australia.

These agricultural markets do have most of the characteristics of a perfectly competitive market. Even here, one characteristic, ease of entry and exit, is missing. When times are hard farmers don't sell their farms and leave the industry. Nor can they readily buy a farm and get back into production when things look good. Eventually, if prices and market conditions don't pick up farmers do give up. They sell up, are sold up by their creditors or if prospects are completely hopeless, just walk off their properties. Nevertheless, these agricultural markets do come close in some ways to the competitive model. In particular as we have stressed, the great majority of farmers are price takers and have to live with the prevailing prices.

A Standard for Market Structure

The concept of perfect competition provides a useful standard against which other market structures may be compared. Economists regard it as capturing the spirit of free enterprise and unbridled competition. In many respects it also exemplifies the most efficient way to allocate scarce resources among unlimited wants — a matter we will examine at the end of this chapter. In this way, perfect competition is an idealisation of several important notions in economics. Perfect competition also provides the simplest starting point for studying the nature of price and output determination by the firm, and the role that the cost concepts of the previous chapter play in this process.

Market Demand and the Firm's Demand in Perfect Competition

It is important to understand the relationship between the demand curve of the individual firm and the market or industry demand curve. It is also important to understand the relationship between total, average and marginal revenue for the perfectly competitive firm.

The Market Demand Curve and the Firm's Demand Curve

When we say that the perfectly competitive firm is a price taker, or that it cannot affect the price at which it sells its product, we are saying something about the shape of the demand curve as seen by the individual firm. Specifically we are saying that this demand curve is horizontal (perfectly elastic) at the level of the prevailing market price over the range of output that the firm can feasibly produce.

Such a demand curve looks like the one in Figure 23.1, part a. In this example we will assume that the firm's highest feasible output level is 1,200 units. The industry demand and supply curves for the entire competitive market are shown in Figure 23.1, part b. Their intersection determines the equilibrium market price p_e and equilibrium market quantity, which in this case is 1 million units of output.

The firm's demand curve is perfectly elastic for two reasons. First, its product is indistinguishable from that of any other firm in the industry. Hence if the firm were to raise its price above p_e, it would sell nothing since buyers can get the identical product at the price p_e from other firms. Second, since the individual firm's output capacity is but a drop in the bucket compared to that of the entire industry, the firm can effectively sell all it can produce at the market equilibrium price $p_e!$

Two important points are clearly illustrated in Figure 23.1, parts a and b. First, because the individual firm provides such a small fraction of the total industry output (about 1/1,000 in this example), it has no effect on the market-determined price p_e. The actions of all firms taken together, however, do affect market price and therefore the market demand curve D is downward sloping even though the individual firm's demand curve d is perfectly horizontal. Second, although price is *determined* by the interaction of all buyers and sellers in the market as represented in part b, this price p_e is essentially given to, and beyond the influence of, any individual firm as shown in part a. Again this simply reflects the fact that the individual firm's contribution to total output is a drop in the bucket as far as the whole market is concerned. Indeed the 1,200 units on the horizontal

FIGURE 23.1
Relationship Between a Competitive Firm's Demand Curve and the Competitive
Industry's Demand Curve

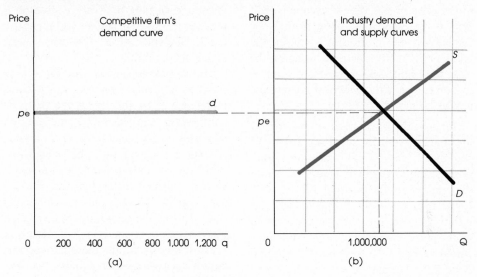

Because the industry demand curve *D* is downward sloping, the production of all firms taken together can affect the market price in part b. The market equilibrium price *pe is determined by the intersection of the market demand curve D* and market supply curve *S* representing the output of all firms — in this case 1,000,000 units. Because the individual competitive firm can only contribute a small fraction (about 1/1,000) to this total, its actions cannot affect price. Therefore, its demand curve is perfectly elastic, or horizontal at the market-determined price level *pe* as shown in part a. The horizontal axis in part a represents little more than a dot on the horizontal axis in part b.

axis of part a are hardly bigger than a dot on the horizontal axis of part b.

Total, Average, and Marginal Revenue of a Perfectly Competitive Firm

A demand curve may be looked at from two different viewpoints. On the one hand, it shows the quantity of a good that consumers will purchase per period of time at different prices. On the other, it shows the price, or revenue, per unit that a seller can receive for different quantities of output per period of time. We now want to consider the second interpretation from

the standpoint of the perfectly competitive firm.

Suppose the price given to the firm by the market is $10. Since the firm's level of production does not affect this price — it can sell any amount of output it produces — **total revenue** *equals quantity sold multiplied by the selling price* of $10 per unit. The relationship between total revenue and quantity sold for a given price of $10 per unit is shown by the total revenue curve *TR₁₀* in Figure 23.2, part a. For example, when 5 units (measured on the horizontal axis) are sold at a price of $10 per unit, total revenue (measured on the vertical axis) is $50. This is represented by point *a* on TR_{10}. If an additional unit is sold, making a total of 6, total revenue rises by an amount equal to the price of $10. Total revenue is then $60, as represented by point *b* on TR_{10}. Similarly if one more unit is sold at the given price of $10 per unit, bringing the total to 7 units, we move from point *b* to point *c* on TR_{10}, where total revenue is $70.

Suppose the price given to the firm by the market were to fall from $10 to $5 per unit. This would cause the total revenue curve to pivot clockwise about the origin from the position TR_{10} to TR_5. If the firm now sells 5 units of output, total revenue will be $25, as represented by the point *a'* on TR_5. The sale of 6 units would bring a total revenue of $30, point *b'* on TR_5. The sale of yet one more unit at the given price of $5 would bring total revenue to $35, point *c'* on TR_5.

Notice that the *TR* curves in Figure 23.2, part a, are straight lines — their slopes are unchanged, $10 per unit on TR_{10} and $5 per unit on TR_5, no matter what the output level. Because of this, starting from the origin, average revenue per unit sold is the same no matter what total quantity of output is sold. For example, at point *a* on TR_{10}, average revenue per unit sold equals the total revenue of $50 divided by 5 units, or $10 per unit. At point *b*, average revenue equals $60 divided by 6 units or, again, $10 per unit. Similarly at point *c*, $70 divided by 7 units gives an average revenue of $10 per unit. Hence *for a perfectly competitive firm average revenue is the same at all output levels.* **Average revenue** *is always equal to the price per unit of output.* For TR_{10} the average revenue AR, which equals price per unit (or $10), is plotted in part b. Hence, average revenue is represented by the perfectly competitive firm's demand

curve D_{10} when price equals $10 per unit. Similarly, for TR_5, the average revenue AR, which equals price per unit (or $5), is plotted in part b. Average revenue is represented by the perfectly competitive firm's demand curve TR_5 when price equals $5 per unit.

Marginal revenue *is the addition to total revenue resulting from the sale of one more unit of output.* Since the perfectly competitive firm sells each and every unit of output at the same price, the marginal revenue associated with the sale of one more unit of output is always the same. This is reflected in the fact that the *TR* curves in Figure 23.2, part a, are straight lines. Along TR_{10} each additional unit sold increases total revenue by $10. Hence at every level of output, marginal revenue equals average revenue equals price. We see, therefore, that if the marginal revenue of $10 per unit is plotted against output in part b, it is the same as the competitive firm's demand curve D_{10}. If price per unit were $5, then the marginal revenue curve would be the same as the demand curve D_5 at the level of $5 per unit in part b. *Note that AR = MR at all output levels only in perfect competition.* In each of the other three forms of market structure that we will discuss — monopoly, monopolistic competition and oligopoly — this is not true.

*CHECKPOINT *23.1*
Suppose the price of a competitive firm's product were to rise from $10 to $15. How would this affect its TR curve in Figure 23.2, part a, and the associated demand curve in part b? Explain your answer. Suppose that an industry starts out being perfectly competitive, but after a time buyers detect differences in quality between the product of each firm. Does this mean that each firm's

FIGURE 23.2
The Total Revenue Curve, Marginal Revenue Curve, and Demand Curve for a Perfectly
Competitive Firm

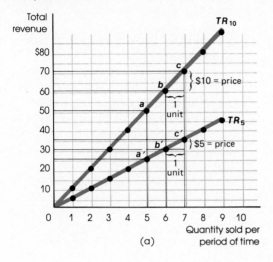

(a)

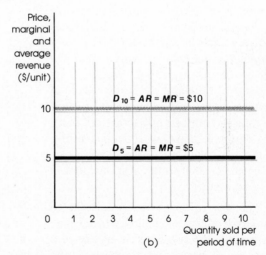

(b)

Because the perfectly competitive firm's level of production does not affect its price, it can sell any amount of output it produces for the same price. Total revenue, which is equal to the quantity sold multiplied by the selling price, therefore rises at a constant rate, equal to the price per unit, as the quantity of output sold is increased. This constant rise is represented by an upward-sloping straight-line total revenue curve. In part a, this curve would look like TR_{10} if price is $10 per unit or TR_5 if it is $5 per unit.

Since the price per unit sold is always the same no matter what quantity of output is sold, average revenue AR in part b, which is equal to total revenue divided by the number of units sold, equals price. It is therefore the same at all levels of output. It is also the same as the firm's demand curve D. Marginal revenue MR, which is equal to the change in total revenue resulting from the sale of one more unit of output, also equals price in part b. It is therefore equal to AR at all output levels in part b. Hence the perfectly competitive firm's demand curve is the same as its marginal revenue curve and is perfectly elastic (horizontal). When price is $10, the demand curve associated with TR_{10} in part a is D_{10} in part b. When price is $5, the demand curve associated with TR_5 in part a is D_5 in part b.

product becomes more, or less, of a substitute for that of every other firm? How will this affect each firm's demand curve?

* Answers to all Checkpoints can be found at the back of the text.

THE COMPETITIVE FIRM IN THE SHORT RUN

In the short run, the competitive firm's plant is fixed. It can only change the quantity of output it produces by changing its variable inputs, such as labour, materials, electricity, and other energy inputs. *We assume that the firm's objective is to use an amount of the variable inputs together with its fixed plant to produce and sell a quantity of output that will maximise its economic profit or, if necessary, minimise its losses.* If total revenue is greater than total cost (the sum of total variable cost plus total fixed cost), the firm will make an economic profit. If it is less, the firm will experience a loss. (Remember that total cost includes a normal profit.)

The way in which the firm seeks to maximise profits or minimise losses may be looked at in two ways. It may be seen either as a process of comparing total revenue and total cost or, equivalently, as a process of comparing marginal revenue with marginal cost. Both approaches will be explained here in order to demonstrate the relationship between them. However, economists typically rely on the marginal revenue-marginal cost approach. Both approaches may also be used to study the firm's behaviour in the context of the other three market struc-

tures as well — monopoly, monopolistic competition, and oligopoly.

Should the Firm Produce in the Short Run?

In the short run, the firm is saddled with its fixed costs regardless of whether it produces or not. If it produces nothing, variable costs will be zero, but it will suffer a loss equal to its fixed costs. Hence, the first question the firm has to answer is whether or not it can reduce the size of this loss, or better still make a profit, by employing variable factors to produce and sell some quantity of output. Simply put, *the firm's first question in the short run is whether to produce or not.*

The answer to this question depends on the following considerations. Variable costs are incurred only if the firm produces some quantity of output. Suppose the total revenue received from the sale of this output is greater than the total variable cost of producing it. In this case, the excess of total revenue over total variable cost will offset some or possibly all of the fixed cost. Hence, it pays the firm to produce something. Even if the excess doesn't fully offset the fixed cost, the loss realised by the firm if it produces something will be smaller than its loss, which is its fixed cost, if it produces nothing. Better still, if the firm's total revenue exceeds its total variable cost by an amount that is greater than its total fixed cost, it will earn an economic profit. In sum, *the firm should produce in the short run if the loss it incurs is less than its fixed cost or better still, if it can earn an economic profit.*

There are clearly three possible situations that may arise in the short run. (1) The firm's total revenue from the sale of its output exceeds its total cost, which is the sum of its total variable and total fixed cost, and it earns an economic profit by producing. (2) The firm's total revenue exceeds its total variable cost and thus offsets some of its total fixed cost as well. The loss incurred by producing is therefore less than the firm's total fixed cost, which is the loss if the firm remains idle. (3) The firm's total revenue is not sufficient to cover the total variable cost to which production gives rise. In this case, the loss (equal to total fixed cost) of remaining idle is less than the loss of producing (which is equal to total fixed cost plus the amount by which total variable cost exceeds total revenue).

In the first two cases, *where it pays the firm to produce, the second question the firm must answer is how much to produce.* In the third case, the firm obviously should not produce at all. In the first case, the firm will answer the question by choosing that output level that maximises economic profit. In the second case, the firm will answer by choosing that output level that minimises losses. This is also essentially the choice it makes in the third case, when it chooses an output level of zero. Assuming given cost data for a hypothetical perfectly competitive firm, we will now consider how the answer to the question of how much to produce is determined in each of these cases. In each case we will examine how the firm can answer the question from the viewpoint of total revenue and total cost, as well as from the viewpoint of marginal revenue and marginal cost.

Maximising Economic Profit

Table 23.2 contains the total, average, and marginal cost data, as well as the price, total revenue and marginal revenue data, for a hypothetical perfectly competitive firm that wants to maximise its economic profit. (All data in Table 23.2 are measured per some period of time, such as a month.)

Total Cost-Total Revenue Viewpoint

The firm's total cost data and its associated output levels appear in columns 1-4. The price p at which the firm can sell its output is always $9 per unit (column 8). The firm's total revenue TR (column 9) from sales at each output level is obtained by multiplying this price by output (column 1). Profit or loss (column 10) equals the difference between total revenue TR and total cost TC (column 4).

Examination of column 10 shows that the answer to the question as to whether the firm should produce or not is yes. If the firm remains idle (output level of zero), it will incur a loss of $10, the amount of its TFC (column 2). The table shows us it can do much better than this, however. Column 10 clearly shows that the firm can realise a maximum economic profit of $9. This figure is achieved by producing an output of 5 units. The answer to the second question of how much the firm should produce is therefore 5 units.

The reason for this answer is demonstrated graphically in Figure 23.3, part a. Given the price of $9 per unit, the total revenue curve TR_9 is obtained in exactly the same way that we obtained the TR curves in Figure 23.2. The Total cost curve TC is plotted from the data in columns 1 and 4 of Table 23.2. The total variable cost curve TVC is plotted from the data in columns 1 and 3. (This is exactly the same procedure we used to obtain the TC and TVC curves of Figure 22.2 in the previous chapter.) The shape of the TC and TVC curves reflects the law of diminishing returns. At each output level,

TABLE 23.2
Output, Revenue, and Costs of a Profit-Maximising, Perfectly Competitive Firm (Hypothetical Data)

	Total Costs			Average and Marginal Costs			Price and Revenues		
(1)	(2)	(3)	(4)	(5)	(6)	(7)	(8)	(9)	(10)
Quantity of Output (Q)	Total Fixed Cost (TFC)	Total Variable Cost (TVC)	Total Cost (TC)	Average Variable Cost (AVC)	Average Total Cost (ATC)	Marginal Cost (MC)	Price = Marginal Revenue	Total Revenue	Economic Profit (+) or Loss (−)
			(TFC) = TFC + TVC	AVC = TVC/Q	ATC = TC/Q	MC = $\frac{\text{change in TC}}{\text{change in Q}}$	p = MR	TR = p × Q	TR − TC
0	$10	$ 0	10					$ 0	$-10
						$ 6	$9		
1	10	6	16	$6.00	$16.00			9	− 7
						4	9		
2	10	10	20	5.00	10.00			18	− 2
						4	9		
3	10	14	24	4.66	8.00			27	+ 3
						5	9		
4	10	19	29	4.75	7.25			36	+ 7
						7	9		
5	10	26	36	5.20	7.20			45	+ 9
						11	9		
6	10	37	47	6.16	7.83			54	+ 7
						23	9		
7	10	60	70	8.57	10.00			63	− 7

the vertical distance between TR_9 and TC equals the loss or profit given in column 10 of Table 23.2.

At output levels of 1, 2 and 7 units the firm realises losses. This is reflected by the fact that the TC curve lies above TR_9. At about $2^1/3$ units of output the firm just breaks even (TR_9 equals TC). At output levels beyond this point the firm makes a profit because TR_9 lies above TC. Another breakeven point (a point at which total revenue TR equals total cost TC) occurs at about 6½ units of output, beyond which the firm again experiences losses. The maximum profit, equal to $9, is represented by the maximum vertical distance between TR_9 and TC, which occurs at 5 units of output.

Marginal Cost Marginal Revenue Viewpoint

An alternative way of viewing how the firm decides how much to produce is to consider the relationship between marginal cost and marginal revenue. As with the total cost-total revenue viewpoint, the marginal cost-marginal revenue viewpoint is applicable to all firms whether they are perfectly competitive, monopolists, monopolistically competitive, or oligopolists. The perfectly competitive firm is different from the others in one important respect, however. Only for the perfectly competitive firm is it true that price p always equals marginal revenue MR, as we have shown earlier in this chapter.

FIGURE 23.3
Maximising Profit in a Perfectly Competitive Firm

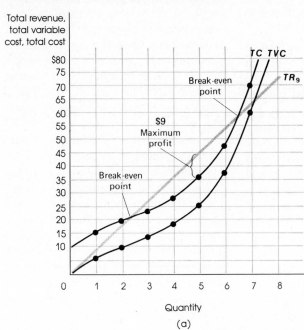

(a)

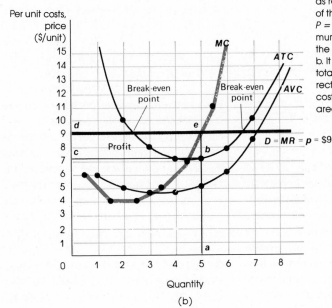

(b)

Assuming a price of $9, total revenue is plotted from the data in columns 1 and 9 of Table 23.2 to give the TR curve TR_9 in part a. The total cost data of column 4 and total variable cost data of column 3 are also plotted against output to give the TC and TVC curves. TR minus TC equals profit and is represented by the vertical distance between TR_9 and TC at any output level. The maximum distance between these two curves represents the maximum profit of $9, which occurs when 5 units of output are produced and sold.

For the perfectly competitive firm, marginal revenue MR always equals price p and is the firm's demand curve D at the level of the price of $9 per unit in part b. (These data come from column 8 of Table 23.2.) The AVC, ATC, and MC curves of part b are plotted from the average variable cost, average total cost, and marginal cost data of columns 5, 6 and 7 respectively in Table 23.2. The profit-maximising level of output occurs at 5 units, where MC = MR as represented by the intersection of the MC curve with the D = MR = P = $9 curve at point e. The maximum profit of $9 is represented by the rectangular area cbed in part b. It equals the difference between total revenue (represented by the rectangular area 0aed) and total cost (represented by the rectangular area 0abc).

The marginal cost-marginal revenue viewpoint assumes that the firm has already decided to produce.

How does the firm use this method to determine how much to produce? The firm must compare the *marginal cost* (the addition to total cost) associated with the production of one more unit of output with the marginal revenue (the addition to total revenue) received from the sale of that unit. If the marginal cost is less than the marginal revenue, the firm will 'make money' by producing and selling an additional unit of output because the increase in total revenue will exceed the increase in total cost. In the profit-maximising case, this excess of marginal revenue over marginal cost is an addition to total profit. The firm should continue to increase its production so long as the marginal revenue from each additional unit exceeds the marginal cost of producing that unit. If the marginal cost of producing an additional unit exceeds the marginal revenue from that unit, the production and sale of that unit will 'lose money'. In the profit-maximising case, this means that the additional unit will reduce total profit. It therefore 'does not pay' to produce it. Hence, the firm should produce output up to the point where the marginal revenue of an additional unit of output no longer exceeds its marginal cost.

Consider the hypothetical perfectly competitive firm of Table 23.2. Starting from a zero output level, when the firm increases production to the successively higher output levels of column 1, it incurs the associated marginal cost MC shown in column 7. The MC of column 7 falls at first and then rises as production is increased, which reflects the law of diminishing returns. The marginal revenue

MR (column 8) always equals the price of $9, for the reasons discussed earlier in connection with Figure 23.2. Note that MC is always less than MR up through the production of 5 units of output. However, if the firm produces a sixth unit of output, the associated MC will be $11. This is larger than the MR of $9 associated with the sale of the sixth unit. Hence, it will not pay the firm to produce more than 5 units of output. Similarly the firm will not maximise profit if it produces less than this amount. If it produces less, it will forgo the addition to profit associated with producing and selling additional units of output. Indeed, it can be seen from column 10 that the firm realises its maximum possible profit of $9 when it produces 5 units of output. This is the same result we obtained when we took the total cost-total revenue point of view.

The marginal cost-marginal revenue viewpoint is depicted graphically in Figure 23.3, part b. The MC curve is plotted from the data in column 7 of Table 23.2. The firm's demand curve D is perfectly elastic (horizontal) at the price $p = MR = $9, the data in column 8 of Table 23.2. That MC is less than MR up through the production and sale of 5 units of output is demonstrated by the fact that the MC curve lies below the MR curve, or demand curve D, up to this point. Beyond 5 units the MC curve lies above the demand curve D.

Comparison of the Two Viewpoints

We know from the total cost-total revenue graph in Figure 23.3, part a, that the firm realises its maximum economic profit of $9 at 5 units of output. This can also be seen in Figure 23.3, part b, by looking at the *ATC* curve, which is plotted from the average total cost data in column 6 of Table 23.2. At 5 units of output the average total cost per unit is $7.20, which is represented by the distance 0*c*, which equals *ab*. Total cost can then be computed as the 5 units multiplied by $7.20, which gives a total cost of $36. This is represented by the rectangular *area* 0*abc* in part b. (For comparison, remember that total cost is also represented by the vertical *distance* directly above 5 units up to the *TC* curve in part a.) The price per unit of $9 is represented by the distance 0*d*, which equals *ae*. Total revenue from the sale of 5 units of output equals 5 multiplied by $9, or $45. This is represented by the rectangular area 0*aed* in part b. (Remember that in part a, total revenue is represented by the vertical distance directly above 5 units up to the total revenue curve *TR*₉.) Since total economic profit equals total revenue minus total cost, it is represented by the difference between the areas of the rectangles 0*aed* and 0*abc*. Hence, the total economic profit of $9 is represented by the area of the rectangle *cbed* in part b. (Remember that in part a, total economic profit is represented by the vertical distance between *TR*₉ and *TC*.)

An alternative way of arriving at the total economic profit is to multiply the economic profit per unit by the number of units. Economic profit per unit is represented by the vertical distance *cd*, which equals *be,* in Figure 23.3, part b. It equals the average revenue per unit (which is the price *p*) minus the *ATC* per unit — $9 minus $7.20, or $1.80. Multiplying this by 5 gives the total profit of $9.

Note that the break-even points in Figure 23.3, part a, where the *TC* curve intersects the *TR*₉ curve, correspond to the points at which the *ATC* curve intersects the *D* curve at the same output levels in Figure 23.3, part b. At output levels in between these breakeven points the firm's economic profits are positive. This is shown in part b by the fact that average total cost per unit, as represented by the *ATC* curve, is less than average revenue per unit, as represented by the demand curve *D*. (Remember that average total cost, like total cost, includes an allowance for normal profit.) At output levels less than the lower break-even point and greater than the upper break-even point, the firm realises a loss. This is indicated by the fact that the *ATC* curve lies above the demand curve *D*.

We may summarise our results for the marginal cost-marginal revenue point of view as follows: *To maximise economic profit the firm should produce up to that level of output where marginal cost equals marginal revenue.* This is true whether the firm is perfectly competitive, a monopolist, monopolistically competitive, or an oligopolist, as we shall see in subsequent chapters. The perfectly competitive firm is a price taker and therefore price is the same as marginal revenue. Hence, the *perfectly competitive firm maximises profit by producing up to the point where marginal cost equals price.* For most sets of data, such as those in Table 23.2, there is typically no whole-number level of output at which marginal cost *MC* is exactly equal to marginal revenue *MR*. In that case, the firm should produce output up to the point where the *MR* associated with the last unit produced is greater than the *MC* associated with that unit.

TABLE 23.3
Output, Revenue, and Costs of a Loss-Minimising, Perfectly Competitive Firm (Hypothetical Data)

	Total Costs			Average and Marginal Costs			Price and Revenues		
(1)	(2)	(3)	(4)	(5)	(6)	(7)	(8)	(9)	(10)
Quantity of Output (Q)	Total Fixed Cost (TFC)	Total Variable Cost (TVC)	Total Cost (TC)	Average Variable Cost (AVC)	Average Total Cost (ATC)	Marginal Cost (MC)	Price = Marginal Revenue	Total Revenue	Profit (+) or Loss (–)
			TC = TFC + TVC	AVC = TVC/Q	ATC = TC/Q	MC = change in TC / change in Q	p = MR	TR = p × Q	TR – TC
0	$10	$0	$10	$0				$0	$–10
						$6	$6		
1	10	6	16	6.00	$16.00			6	–10
						4	6		
2	10	10	20	5.00	10.00			12	– 8
						4	6		
3	10	14	24	4.66	8.00			18	– 6
						5	6		
4	10	19	29	4.75	7.25			24	– 5
						7	6		
5	10	26	36	5.20	7.20			30	– 6
						11	6		
6	10	37	47	6.16	7.83			36	–11
						23	6		
7	10	60	70	8.57	10.00			42	–28

CHECKPOINT 23.2
Use the data in columns 1, 6 and 8 of Table 23.2 to convince yourself that profit is maximised at 5 units of output. Use these data to lightly sketch in the rectangular areas representing total profit in Figure 23.3, part b, for output levels of 3, 4, and 6 units. Can you see that the rectangular area representing total profit at 5 units of output is larger than any of these?

Minimising Loss — 'Hanging in There'

In this case the firm's total revenue is less than its total cost, but it exceeds its total variable cost and thus offsets some of its total fixed cost. Hence, the loss that results from producing is less than total fixed cost, which is the loss if the plant remains idle. The output and cost data from columns 1-7 of Table 23.2 are reproduced in columns 1-7 in Table 23.3. The firm is still perfectly competitive, but now it is assumed that the price given to the firm is $6 instead of $9. Therefore the revenue data in columns 8-10 of Table 23.3 are different from those in columns 8-10 of Table 23.2.

FIGURE 23.4
Minimising Loss in a Perfectly Competitive Firm

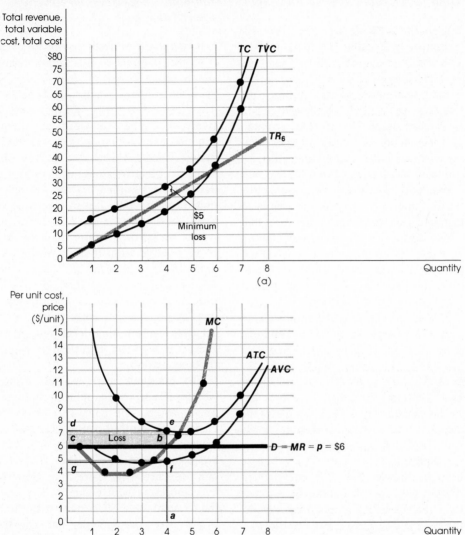

Assuming a price of $6, total revenue is plotted from the data in columns 1 and 9 of Table 23.3 to give the *TR* curve *TR₆* in part a. The *TC* and *TVC* curves are exactly the same as those in Figure 23.3. Here *TC* is greater than *TR* at all output levels, so that the firm experiences a loss represented by the vertical distance between *TC* and *TR₆* at any output level. The minimum distance between these two curves represents the minimum loss of $5, which occurs when 4 units of output are produced and sold.

The competitive firm's demand curve *D* is now at the level of the price of $6 per unit in part b. The *AVC*, *ATC* and *MC* curves of part b are exactly the same as those in part b of Figure 23.3. The loss-minimising level of output occurs at 4 units, where *MC* = *MR* as represented by the rectangular shaded area *cbed* in part b. It equals the difference between total revenue, represented by 0*abc*, and total cost, represented by 0*aed*. Total fixed cost is represented by *gfed*. The amount by which total revenue exceeds total variable cost, and thus offsets some of the fixed cost, is represented by *gfbc*.

Total Cost-Total Revenue Viewpoint

When price is $6 per unit, the firm's TR (column 9) is less than TC (column 4) at all levels of output (column 1). Therefore, the firm cannot avoid losses (column 10). If the firm were to produce nothing, the loss at a zero output level would be $10 — just the amount of its TFC (column 2). Examination of column 10 shows that the firm can do better than this by producing. In fact, if it produces and sells 4 units of output, it will minimise its loss to $5. Another way of seeing this is to compare columns 9 and 3 and note that TR exceeds TVC by its largest amount at 4 units of output. Hence, this output level provides the largest excess of TR over TVC to offset the TFC that the firm is saddled with in the short run.

This situation is depicted graphically in Figure 23.4, part a. TC and TVC are plotted from the data in columns 1, 3 and 4 of Table 23.3. They are, of course, exactly the same as the TC and TVC curves of Figure 23.3. However, the TR curve TR_6 is less steeply sloped than TR_9. This reflects the fact that total revenue rises more slowly with output when price is $6 per unit than when price is $9 per unit. The TC curve now lies above the TR curve TR_6, reflecting the fact that total cost exceeds total revenue at all output levels. Nonetheless, the TR_6 curve lies above the TVC curve at output levels from 2 to 5 units, so that producing at any of these output levels will always result in some excess of TR over TVC, which offsets some part of TFC. The vertical distance of TR_6 above TVC is a maximum at 4 units of output. At this level of output the vertical distance of TC above TR_6 is a minimum. It equals the minimum loss of $5.

Marginal Cost-Marginal Revenue Viewpoint

Looking at the perfectly competitive firm from the marginal cost-marginal revenue standpoint in the loss-minimising case, we focus on columns 7 and 8 of Table 23.3. These are the MC and MR data, respectively. For the first unit of output produced, the MR — equal price of $6 just covers MC, which is also $6. However, if the firm increases output, it finds that MC will be less than MR up through 4 units of production. If it were to produce 5 units of output, the MC of the fifth unit would be $7, or $1 more than the MR of $6 received from the sale of the fifth unit. Hence, the firm should produce neither more nor less than 4 units of output. If we look at column 10 again, we can see that this corresponds to the same loss-minimising level output we came up with by the total cost-total revenue method.

The marginal cost-marginal revenue viewpoint is depicted graphically in Figure 23.4, part b. The AVC, ATC and MC curves are plotted from the data in columns 5, 6 and 7 of Table 23.3. They are exactly the same as the AVC, ATC and MC curves of Figure 23.3. However, by comparison with Figure 23.3, part b, the demand curve D is now at the level of the lower price of $6 per unit. The MC curve intersects the $MR = D$ curve at point b. This corresponds to the loss-minimising output level of 4 units.

It should be noted that the loss-minimising level of output does not necessarily correspond to the lowest level of ATC (the lowest point on the ATC curve). ATC at the loss-minimising level of output of 4 units is $7.25 (Table 23.3, column 6). *ATC* at 5 units of output is in fact lower, \$7.20. Similarly, in the profit-maximising case, the profit-maximising level of output is typically not the one associated with the lowest level of *ATC*. For example, suppose price was \$12. By looking at column 7 of Table 23.3, we can see that the profit-maximising rule of producing up to the point where $p = MR = MC$ would lead the firm to produce 6 units of output. But by looking at column 6 we can see that this does not correspond to the lowest level of *ATC*.

Comparison of the Two Viewpoints

Total revenue can be calculated by multiplying the output of 4 units (the distance $0a$ in Figure 23.4, part b) by the price of \$6 (the distance $0c = ab$) to give a *TR* of \$24. This is represented by the rectangular area $0abc$ in Figure 23.4, part b. (This area corresponds to the vertical distance up to the TR_6 curve at 4 units of output in Figure 23.4, part a.) To get total cost, multiply 4 units of output by the *ATC* of \$7.25 (from Table 23.3, column 6), which is the distance $0d = ae$. The resulting *TC* of \$29 is represented by the rectangular area $0aed$ in Figure 23.4, part b. (This corresponds to the vertical distance up to the *TC* curve at 4 units of output in Figure 23.4, part a.) The firm's loss of \$5 is represented by the shaded rectangular area *cbed*, which is the difference between $0aed$ and $0abc$ in Figure 23.4, part b. (This area corresponds to the vertical distance between the *TC* curve and the TR_6 curve at 4 units of output in Figure 23.4, part a.)

The firm chooses to produce rather than shut down in the loss-minimising case because *TR* exceeds *TVC*, as represented by the vertical distance of the TR_6 curve above the *TVC* curve at 4 units of output in Figure 23.4, part a. *TVC* can be calculated by multiplying 4 units of output by the *AVC* of \$4.75 (from Table 23.3, column 5), the distance $0g = af$ in Figure 23.4, part b. This gives the *TVC* of \$19, which is represented by the rectangular area $0afg$. Therefore in Figure 23.4, part b, the amount by which *TR* exceeds *TVC* is represented by the difference between $0abc$ and $0afg$, which is the rectangular area *gfbc*. If the firm produces nothing, it incurs a loss equal to the total fixed cost. Since $TFC = TC - TVC$, this loss is represented by the difference between the rectangular areas $0aed$ and $0afg$. This difference is the rectangular area *gfed* in Figure 23.4, part b, which is equal to \$10. (This area corresponds to the vertical distance between the *TC* and *TVC* curves in Figure 23.4, part a.) Figure 23.4, part b, makes it clear that the loss, represented by *cbed*, that results when the firm produces 4 units of output, is less than the loss, represented by *gfed* (equal to *TFC*), that results if it remains idle. This is so because the amount by which total revenue *TR* exceeds total variable cost *TVC* offsets total fixed cost *TFC* (equal to *gfed*) by the amount *gfbc*.

In sum, *when the firm's total revenue is at least as great as total variable cost but not larger than total cost, it should produce up to that level of output where marginal cost equals marginal revenue in order to minimise its losses*. This is true whether the firm is perfectly competitive, a monopolist, monopolistically competitive, or an oligopolist. Since price equals marginal revenue in the case of the perfectly competitive firm, it should produce up to the point where price equals marginal cost when the object is to minimise losses.

Finally, summing up both cases, *as long as the firm has decided to produce, it will maximise profit or minimise loss by producing up to that output level where marginal cost equals marginal revenue. For the perfectly competitive firm this means producing up to the point where marginal cost equals price.*

CHECKPOINT 23.3
Use the data in columns 1, 6 and 8 of Table 23.3 (which assume that price

equals $6) to convince yourself that loss is minimised at 4 units of output. Use these data to lightly sketch in the rectangular areas representing loss in Figure 23.4, part b, for output levels of 2, 3 and 5 units. Can you see that the rectangular area representing total loss at 4 units of output is smaller than any of these? Also, use the data from columns 1, 5, and 8 to lightly sketch in the rectangular areas representing the excess of TR over TVC in Figure 23.4, part b, for output levels of 2, 3, 4, and 5 units. Can you see that the rectangular area representing this excess at 4 units of output is larger than any of these?

TABLE 23.4
Output, Revenue, and Costs of a Perfectly Competitive Firm in the Shutdown Case (Hypothetical Data)

	Total Costs			Average and Marginal Costs			Price and Revenues		
(1)	(2)	(3)	(4)	(5)	(6)	(7)	(8)	(9)	(10)
Quantity of Output (Q)	Total Fixed Cost (TFC)	Total Variable Cost (TVC)	Total Cost (TC)	Average Variable Cost (AVC)	Average Total Cost (ATC)	Marginal Cost (MC)	Price = Marginal Revenue	Total Revenue	Profit (+) or Loss (−)
			TC = TFC + TVC	AVC = TVC/Q	ATC = TC/Q	MC = change in TC / change in Q	p = MR	TR = p × Q	TR − TC
0	$10	$ 0	$10				$4	$ 0	$-10
						$ 6			
1	10	6	16	$6.00	$16.00		$4	4	-11
						4			
2	10	10	20	5.00	10.00		4	8	-12
						4			
3	10	14	24	4.66	8.00		4	12	-12
						5			
4	10	19	29	4.75	7.25		4	16	-13
						7			
5	10	26	36	5.20	7.20		4	20	-16
						11			
6	10	37	47	6.16	7.83		4	24	-23
						23			
7	10	60	70	8.57	10.00			28	-42

Deciding to Shut Down — Closing the Doors

When the firm's total revenue is not even large enough to cover its total variable cost, it will minimise its loss by producing nothing at all, Its loss will then equal its total fixed cost. Note that in the short run this does not mean that the firm goes out of business, but rather that it simply remains idle. (Of course, in the long run all factors are variable and therefore so are all costs. So if demand does not improve, the firm will go out of business.)

The shutdown case for a perfectly competitive firm is depicted in Table 23.4 and Figure 23.5. The cost data in columns 1-7 are the same as those in Tables 23.2 and 23.3. All the cost curves in Figure 23.5 are the same as in Figures 23.3 and 23.4. However, the firm can now only sell its output at a price of $4 per unit (column 8).

Total Cost-Total Revenue Viewpoint

By looking at column 10, we can see that the firm's loss is clearly minimised by producing nothing. This is represented in Figure 23.5, part a, by the fact that the TR curve TR_4 (plotted from the data in columns 1 and 9) now lies below the TVC curve at all levels of output above zero. The vertical distance between TVC and TR_4 at each output level represents the loss in addition to that due to the total fixed cost, which is represented by the vertical distance between TC and TVC. The sum of these two sources of loss at each output level is represented by the vertical distance between TC and TR_4, which equals the amounts shown in column 10 of Table 23.4.

Marginal Cost-Marginal Revenue Viewpoint

The data in columns 7 and 8 of Table 23.4 tell us that MC is greater than MR

at all levels of output, except 2 and 3 units of output, where $MC = MR$. However, for the first unit of output MC is greater than MR. This means that the firm would not cover its AVC per unit (column 5) even if it did produce 2 or 3 units of output. This is so because the average revenue per unit (column 8), which is its price (also equal to MR for the perfectly competitive firm), is less than AVC (column 5) at all levels of output. This is clearly demonstrated in Figure 23.5, part b, by the fact that the demand curve D lies below the AVC curve at all levels of output.

Summing up all three cases now, *if price exceeds average variable cost the perfectly competitive firm should produce that output level where MC = p in order to maximise profit or minimise loss. If price is less than average variable cost, it will minimise loss if it produces nothing.*

CHECKPOINT 23.4
For 4 units of output, sketch in the rectangle in Figure 23.5, part b, that corresponds to the vertical distance between the TVC and TR_4 curves in Figure 23.5, part a. What does this rectangle represent? Also for 4 units of output, sketch in the rectangle in Figure 23.5, part b, that corresponds to the vertical distance between the TC and TR_4 curves in Figure 23.5, part a. For 4 units of output, sketch in the rectangle that represents TFC.

The Firm's Marginal Cost and Short-Run Supply Curve

We have seen that the perfectly competitive firm maximises profit or minimises loss by adjusting its production to that level of output where marginal cost equals price. (This was shown in Figures 23.3, part

FIGURE 23.5
Shutdown Case, Perfectly Competitive Firm

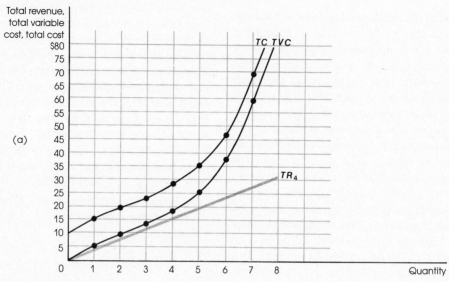

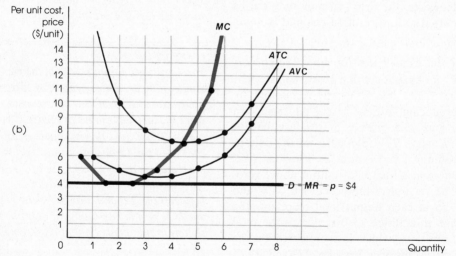

The cost curves in parts a and b are exactly the same as those in Figures 23.3 and 23.4. Assuming a price of $4, total revenue is plotted from the data in columns 1 and 9 of Table 23.4 to give the *TR* curve *TR₄* in part a. The vertical distance between the *TC* and *TVC* curves is the same at all output levels because it equals *TFC*. The distance by which the *TVC* curve lies above the *TR₄* curve at all output levels represents the additional loss the firm incurs if it produces. It can be seen that this additional loss is eliminated and the total loss minimised only when the firm produces nothing. The minimum loss will then be the *TFC* of $10.

This situation is represented in part b by the fact that the demand curve *D* is at the price level, or average revenue level, of $4, which is below the *AVC* curve at all output levels. Average revenue per unit is not sufficient to cover *AVC* per unit at any output level. The difference will represent a loss in addition to that due to *TFC* if the firm produces.

b, 23.4, part b and 23.5, part b.) In other words, as long as price is equal to or greater than average variable cost, the perfectly competitive firm adjusts output by moving along that part of its marginal cost curve that lies above its average variable cost curve. This part of that curve conforms precisely with the definition of a supply curve. As you may recall from our earlier definition of such a curve, a supply curve indicates the amount of a good a supplier is willing to provide per period of time to the market at different possible prices.

The relationship between the supply curve and the marginal cost curve for a hypothetical perfectly competitive firm is shown in Figure 23.6, part a. At a price of p_1, the firm is just able to cover its average variable cost. It therefore produces 60 units of output, the level of output at which its MC curve intersects its MR curve MR_1. MR_1, of course, is the same as its demand curve d_1 at the price level p_1. If price were to rise to p_2, the firm would increase its production to 73 units, the point at which its MC curve intersects $MR_2 = d_2$. And if price were to rise to p_3, MC would equal MR at the point where the MC curve intersects $MR_3 = d_3$. The firm would then produce 92 units of output.

In sum, *that part of the perfectly competitive firm's marginal cost curve that lies above its average variable cost curve is its short-run supply curve.*

The Industry Supply Curve

Suppose there are 1,000 firms like that in Figure 23.6, part a, which together make up the perfectly competitive industry. The industry supply curve S is the sum of all the individual firms' supply curves. These supply curves are the same as their marginal cost curves (E may be read 'sum of'), as shown in Figure 23.6, part b. For example, in Figure 23.6, part a, at a price of p_1, each individual firm supplies 60 units of output. Therefore, the total amount supplied by 1,000 such firms is 60,000 units at a price of p_1, as shown in Figure 23.6, part b. At a price of p_2, each individual firm supplies 73 units of output (Figure 23.6, part a). The total amount supplied by the industry is 1,000 times this amount or 73,000 units (Figure 23.6, part b). Finally, if price were p_3, each individual firm would supply 92 units (Figure 23.6, part a), and the total industry supply would be 92,000 units (Figure 23.6, part b).

We conclude that *at each price level the industry supply curve is constructed by summing the amounts each individual firm will supply, as indicated by its marginal cost curve above its AVC curve.* At a price below p_1, firms are not able to cover their average variable costs and therefore will produce nothing. Hence, the industry will supply nothing at a price below p_1, as indicated by the fact that the industry supply curve in Figure 23.6, part b, does not extend below this level.

Firm and Industry Equilibrium

We have seen in earlier chapters how market supply and demand interact to determine equilibrium price and quantity for an industry. Earlier in this chapter, when looking at Figure 23.1, we saw that in a perfectly competitive industry the perfectly competitive firm contributes such a small fraction of total industry supply that it cannot affect the market price. The competitive firm's demand curve is therefore perfectly elastic (horizontal). Putting these considerations

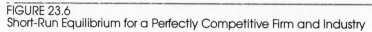

FIGURE 23.6
Short-Run Equilibrium for a Perfectly Competitive Firm and Industry

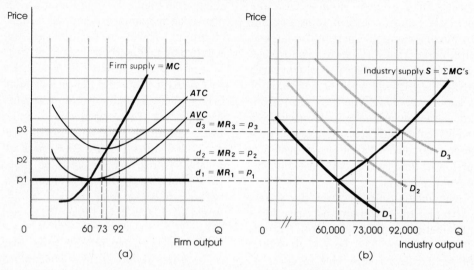

The perfectly competitive firm's supply curve is that part of its *MC* curve that lies above its *AVC* curve, as shown in part a. The industry supply curve *S* shown in part b is obtained by summing up the quantity of output that each firm will produce at each price in part a. Since there are 1,000 firms like the one shown in part a, industry supply at each price in part b is equal to 1,000 times the amount supplied by the typical firm in part a at each price. Three such prices, p_1, p_2, and p_3, and the associated output levels for an individual firm (part a) and the whole industry (part b) are shown here.

The intersection of the industry demand curve and supply curve in part b determines the equilibrium market price and output level. Since each firm supplies a fraction equal to 1/11,000 of this output, the firm cannot significantly affect market price. The firm's demand curve is therefore horizontal at the market-determined price. The position of the firm's demand curve corresponding to three different positions of the industry demand curve D_1, D_2, and D_3, (part b) is d_1, d_2, and d_3 (part a). The associated level of price is p_1, p_2, and p_3.

Because p_1 and p_2 lie below the firm's *ATC* curve, but at or above its *AVC* curve, the firm minimises losses by producing to the point where $MC = MR_1$ or MR_2 for each of these price levels. Since p_3 lies above the *ATC* curve, the firm maximises profit by producing to the point where $MC = MR_3$.

together with the perfectly competitive firm's cost curves and the industry supply curve, we can examine the relationship between the competitive industry equilibrium and the competitive firm equilibrium in the short run.

This relationship can be seen by examining the relationship between parts a and b of Figure 23.6. When the market demand for the industry's output is given

by the market demand curve D_1 in part b, its intersection with the industry supply curve S determines the equilibrium price level p_1 and industry output of 60,000 units. A typical firm (part a) in the industry therefore faces the horizontal demand curve d_1 at the price level p_1 and supplies 60 units of output. (These 60 units are equal to 1/1,000 of the industry total.) Since the firm is just covering its *AVC*

POLICY PERSPECTIVE

Why Agricultural Prices Fluctuate

Many agricultural products selling in Australia or on world markets are subject to severe price fluctuations. In the two year period 1984/85 to 1986/87 world wool prices showed an 80 per cent variation, sugar prices varied by 100 per cent and wheat a 50 per cent difference between the lowest and highest average prices. These in themselves are only averages and actual individual price variations were far greater. It is not uncommon for prices for some products to be three or four times as high in one season than another. Fruit and vegetables are good examples. Why is this so? How can we explain such events using the laws of demand and supply.

The first feature of Australian and most other agricultural markets is that demand and supply are highly inelastic. The result — small changes in demand or supply are sufficient to create proportionately large changes in price. Simply explaining price fluctuations with reference to inelastic demand and supply is not enough. The demand side is clear enough — the demand for nearly all food products is very inelastic. Most people will only buy a limited amount of food and would prefer to spend their income not on extra potatoes, bread or apples but on consumer durables, clothes, travel or entertainment. It may be a bit more difficult to understand the supply side, because an inelastic supply curve implies the producers will be prepared to supply the market at almost any price. In fact, in unregulated markets this is pretty much the case. Once a decision has been made to grow a crop and to harvest it there is little alternative but to send it to market. But if all farmers do send the product to market they will depress further the already low prices. If the crop has been grown the farmer has got a bit more choice about what to do. He can leave it to rot in the ground if he thinks the returns will not cover the harvesting, grading and transport costs. Supply is still highly inelastic but much less inelastic than if the crop is already picked. If he expects prices to be low before he plants, he has wider choice still. He may decide on an alternative use for his farmland. Clearly supply is less elastic. Even in the longer time period, when he has more flexibility in decision making supply is likely to be quite inelastic. As we have commented, the very nature of the family farm with its low explicit and average variable costs means that the individual farmer has an inelastic marginal cost curve and that prices will need to be very low before the farmer is forced off the land.

Question

1. Use the information given above to produce a set of diagrams showing how a sudden shock in the form of a fall in demand for a crop (say grapes for winemaking) would affect the market. You will need to show the effects on the individual farmer and the industry. You will also need to distinguish between short-run and longer-run effects of the fall in demand. If there is no further change in demand are grape prices likely to be higher or lower in the following season than immediately after the sudden fall in demand?

at this price (the demand curve d_1 is tangent to the AVC curve at its lowest point), if the industry demand curve were to shift to a position lower than D_1, firms would decide to produce nothing at all. On the other hand, if the industry demand curve shifted to D_2 in part b, the intersection of industry supply and industry demand would determine a price of p_2, and the industry would supply 73,000 units of output. The typical firm, part a, would now face a demand curve d_2. It still would not be able to cover its total costs because d_2 lies below the ATC curve. But it would minimise losses by producing to the point where marginal cost equals marginal revenue. This point is indicated by the intersection of its MC curve with its $d_2 = MR_2 = p_2$ curve at 73 units of output. Hence, in the short run, when the industry demand curve is at positions such as D_1 or D_2, firms in the industry are operating at a loss.

What happens if industry demand shifts outward to a position such as D_3 in part b? Equilibrium price is now p_3, and industry output is now 92,000 units. The typical firm's demand curve in part a would now be shifted up to the position d_3. To equate marginal cost and marginal revenue, the typical firm would increase output to 92 units. Since p_3 is above the ATC curve at this point, the firm would be maximising profit. Hence, with industry demand at D_3, firms in the industry are now realising profits instead of losses.

CHECKPOINT 23.5

Suppose there is a rise in the cost of raw materials used by the firms in the industry depicted in Figure 23.6. How would this affect the firm's cost curves in part a? How would it affect the industry supply curve in part b? If the industry demand curve were at D_1, what would happen to
firm and industry output? If the demand curve were D_3, what would happen to price? What would happen to firm and industry output?

THE COMPETITIVE FIRM AND INDUSTRY IN THE LONG RUN

In the long run, all factors of production are variable. It is possible for new firms to enter the industry and for existing firms to leave the industry or go out of business. What is the nature of this adjustment process and how does it determine the long-run industry supply curve?

Long-Run Adjustment

We will first examine the long-run adjustment process by considering what happens when there is an increase in industry demand. We will then look at what happens when there is a decrease in demand.

Demand Increases: Excess Profit Induces Firms to Enter Industry

Suppose initially that the demand and supply curves for the perfectly competitive industry are in the positions D_1 and S_1 as shown in Figure 23.7, part b. Their intersection determines the equilibrium price p_1 and equilibrium industry output of 80,000 units. Suppose there are initially 1,000 firms in the industry, each like that shown in Figure 23.7, part a. The firm's demand curve is d_1 at the price level p_1, which of course is also its marginal revenue MR_1. MC equals MR_1 at the point where the MC curve intersects the demand curve d_1. The desire to maximise profit will therefore lead each firm to produce 80 units of output. Notice that initially each firm is just earning a normal profit. This is so because at a price of p_1, each is just covering its average total cost, as represented by the tangency of its ATC curve with the demand curve d_1 in Figure 23.7, part a. (Remember that *ATC* includes a normal profit.)

Now suppose that there is an increase in industry demand as represented by the rightward shift in the industry demand curve from D_1 to D_2, as shown in Figure 23.7, part b. The supply curve S_1 is the short-run industry supply curve. It is therefore the sum of the 1,000 marginal cost curves of each firm (above AVC), such as *MC* in Figure 23.7, part a. Initially price rises to p_2 and industry output to 100,000 (the intersection of D_2 and S_1 in part b) because each firm in the industry expands output to 100 units, as deter-

FIGURE 23.7
Long-Run Adjustment of a Perfectly Competitive Firm and Industry to an Increase in Demand

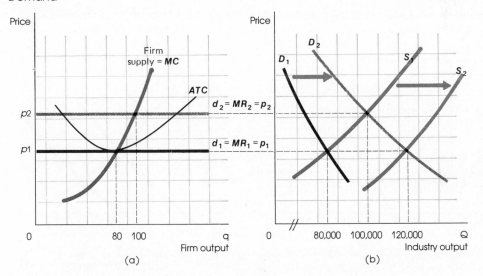

The initial equilibrium position of the perfectly competitive industry is determined by the intersection of the industry demand curve D_1 and short-run supply curve S_1 in part b. The associated equilibrium position of the representative firm is determined by the intersection of the firm's *MC* curve and its demand curve d_1. Initially each firm is just earning a normal profit because at price p_1, each is just covering its average total cost.

When the industry demand curve (shown in part b) shifts rightward to D_2, price initially rises from p_1 to p_2 as firms already in the industry respond by increasing output. An increase in output means each firm moves up along its *MC* curve to the point of intersection with its now higher demand curve d_2 (shown in part a). At this point, firms are making a profit in excess of normal profit. This attracts other firms into the industry, causing the industry supply curve shown in part b to shift rightward.

When enough firms have entered so that the short-run industry supply curve has shifted to S_2, price will return to p_1. A larger number of firms will now be in the industry in the new equilibrium, each earning a normal profit and facing a demand curve d_1, as in the original equilibrium position in part a.

mined by the intersection of its MC curve and its now higher demand curve d_2 (part a).

However, at the now higher price of p_2, each firm will be earning a profit per unit in excess of the normal profit. This excess is represented by the vertical distance between the demand curve d_2 and the ATC curve at 100 units of output. It will serve as a signal to other resource suppliers in the rest of the economy that above-normal profits can be earned by starting new firms and entering this industry.

As new firms enter the industry, the total number of firms like that in Figure 23.7, part a, increases. This increase causes the short-run industry supply curve in part b to shift rightward. *New firms will continue to enter the industry as long as excess profits exist, since in the long run all factors of production are variable.* As the short-run supply curve shifts rightward, its intersection with D_2 in part b will occur at lower and lower prices until it has reached the position S_2. At this point, price will have fallen back to the initial level p_1, and each firm's demand

FIGURE 23.8
Long-Run Adjustment of a Perfectly Competitive Firm and Industry to a Decrease in Demand

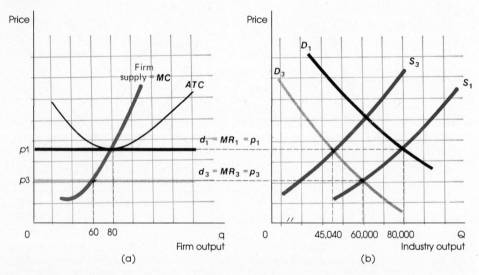

The perfectly competitive industry is initially in the equilibrium position determined by the intersection of the industry demand curve D_1 and the short-run industry supply curve S_1 in part b. The associated equilibrium position of the representative firm is determined by the intersection of the firm's MC curve and its demand curve d_1 in part a.

When the industry demand curve shifts leftward to D_3, part b, price initially falls from p_1 to p_3 as firms already in the industry respond by reducing output. This means they are moving down along their MC curves to the point of intersection of their now lower demand curves d_3, part a. At this point firms are incurring losses and some begin to go out of business. This causes the short-run industry supply curve in part b to shift leftward.

When enough firms have left so that the short-run industry supply curve has shifted to S_3, price will return to p_1. A smaller number of firms will now be in the industry in the new equilibrium, each again earning a normal profit and facing a demand curve d_1 as in the original equilibrium position in part a.

curve will once again be in the position d_1. Each firm will once again produce and sell 80 units of output, as shown in part a. Each firm will again just be earning a normal profit. However, there will now be 1,500 firms in the industry ($120,000 \div 80$ = 1,500) producing and selling a total of 120,000 units of output at the price p_1 (part b).

Demand Decreases: Losses Induce Firms to Exit

Suppose we start from the same initial equilibrium we did in Figure 23.7, only now, in Figure 23.8, we will assume that industry demand falls. This is represented by the leftward shift of the industry demand curve from D_1 to D_3, as shown in Figure 23.8, part b. The 1,000 firms in the industry each see this decline in demand as a fall in their demand curves from d_1 to d_3, in Figure 23.8, part a. The typical firm reduces output by moving down its marginal cost curve to reduce output from 80 units to 60 units. That is, it reduces output until marginal cost again equals marginal revenue at the point where the firm's MC curve intersects its demand curve $d_3 = MR_3 = p_3$. This lower level of output for each individual firm is reflected at the industry level by a fall in industry output from 80,000 to 60,000 units along the industry supply curve S_1, shown in part b.

Remember, however, that *in the long run all factors are variable and therefore so are all costs. Hence, unlike the short-run situation, if price is not high enough to cover average total cost, the firm will go out of business.* Since p_3 lies below the ATC curve in Figure 23.8, part a, the typical firm is now operating at a loss. Firms will therefore begin to leave the industry because the resources they use

can no longer earn their opportunity cost. These resources will move to other lines of activity in the economy where they can be paid their opportunity cost.

As firms leave the industry, the short-run industry supply curve will shift leftward until it reaches the position S_3. Here, price once again is p_1 at the intersection of D_3 and S_3 (Figure 23.8, part b), and industry output is 45,040 units. The typical firm in the industry will once again face a demand curve d_1. Marginal cost will equal marginal revenue at the point where the MC curve intersects the $d_1 = MR_1 = p_1$ curve at an output level of 80 units (part a). In the new equilibrium, firms are once again just covering their average total cost — that is, they are again earning a normal profit. There will now be 563 firms in the industry ($45,040 \div 80 = 563$) as compared to 1,000 before the fall in demand. Losses have caused 437 firms to go out of business in this industry.

Let us summarise these results. When a perfectly competitive industry is in long-run equilibrium, each firm is operating at the bottommost point on its ATC curve. This is the point of tangency with its horizontal demand curve. Hence, *when the perfectly competitive firm is in long-run equilibrium price equals marginal cost equals marginal revenue equals average total cost.* Each firm is just earning a normal profit. That is, economic profit is zero in long-run equilibrium. An increase in demand causes a rise in price, which leads to excess profits (above-normal profits). This attracts new firms into the industry, causing the short-run industry supply curve to shift rightward until price falls back to the level of minimum average total cost. Once again, each firm operates at the minimum point of its average total cost curve, just earning

FIGURE 23.9
Long-Run Supply Curves for a Perfectly Competitive Industry — Constant-, Increasing-, and Decreasing Cost Cases

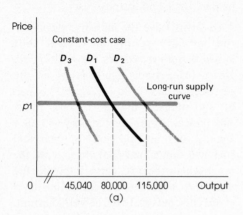
(a)

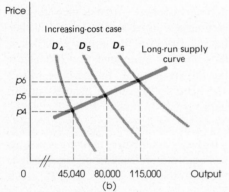
(b)

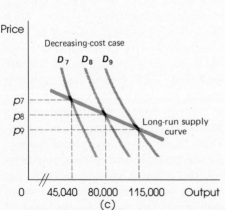
(c)

When the prices of inputs to the industry are constant (that is, unaffected by the level of the industry's production), the per unit costs of production, and hence the level of the ATC and MC curves of the firms in the industry, are the same at all levels of industry output in long-run equilibrium. Therefore, the long-run industry supply curve is perfectly elastic (horizontal) at the same long-run equilibrium price level no matter what the level of demand in the constant-cost case as shown in part a.

When the prices of inputs to the industry rise with increases in the level of the industry's production, the per unit costs of production, and hence the level of the ATC and MC curves, of the firms in the industry rise. Therefore, the long-run industry supply curve is upward sloping in the increasing-cost case as shown in part b.

When the prices of inputs to the industry fall with increases in the level of the industry's production, the per unit costs of production, and hence the level of the ATC and MC curves, of the firms in the industry fall. Therefore, the long-run industry supply curve is downward sloping in the decreasing-cost case as shown in part c.

a normal profit. A decrease in demand causes a fall in price and leads to losses. Firms, therefore, leave the industry, causing the short-run supply curve to shift leftward until price rises back to the level of minimum average total cost for the remaining firms in the industry. Each again is just earning a normal profit.

Long-Run Industry Supply Curve

The supply curves S_1, S_2, and S_3 in Figures 23.7 and 23.8 are short-run industry supply curves. Along any one of them, the number of firms in the industry is assumed constant, or fixed. For S_1 in Figures 23.7, part b, and 23.8, part b, there are 1,000 firms, for S_2 in Figure 23.7, part b, there are 1,500 firms and for S_3 in Figure 23.8, part b, there are 563. Since we have been considering the long-run adjustment, what is the *long-run* industry supply curve for a perfectly competitive industry? To answer this question, we must consider three distinct situations that may arise — one in which costs are constant, one in which costs are increasing, and one in which costs are decreasing.

The Constant-Cost Case

This is the case we have described in Figures 23.7 and 23.8. Throughout our analysis of the long-run adjustment process, we assumed that the prices of all the factors of production purchased by the firms in the industry remained unchanged, no matter what level of output was produced by the industry. This means that when new firms enter the industry or existing ones leave it, the ATC and MC curves of all firms in the industry remain at the same level — that shown in Figures 23.7, part a, and 23.8, part a.

We observed three different possible positions of the industry demand curve, D_1, D_2 and D_3 in Figures 23.7, part b, and 23.8, part b, each of which had an associated long-run industry equilibrium. Although the number of firms in the industry associated with each long-run equilibrium varied, the long-run equilibrium position of each firm in the industry was always the same. Namely, each produced 80 units of output at the lowest point on its ATC curve where its MC curve intersected its demand curve $d_1 = MR$, at the price level p_1 (Figures 23.7, part a, and 23.8, part a).

Suppose we considered all other possible positions of the industry demand curve D. In each case, after all adjustments are completed in the long run, there would be just enough firms in the industry so that total industry supply would equal industry demand at the price p_1. Therefore, the long-run industry supply curve for the perfectly competitive industry in the constant-cost case is just the horizontal line at the equilibrium price level p_1, as shown in Figure 23.9, part a. If you like, you may think of it as consisting of all the points formed by the intersections of all possible industry demand curves with the associated short-run industry supply curves, such as the intersections of D_1 and S_1, D_2 and S_2, and D_3 and S_3 in Figures 23.7, part b and 23.8, part b.

The Increasing-Cost Case

If the resources used by the competitive industry constitute a large enough portion of the total supply of such resources, their prices may rise as the competitive industry purchases more of them. This is particularly true if the supply of these resources is not easily increased. Conversely, when

---

POLICY PERSPECTIVE

Is Perfect Competition an Ideal? — The Pros and Cons

The concept of perfect competition has often been held up as an ideal or standard for judging other kinds of industry or market structures. Indeed, it might be said that the principal objective of trade practices policy (to be discussed in Chapter 27) is to see to it that the economy's various industries perform to the greatest possible extent according to standards exhibited by perfect competition. However, while perfect competition has many desirable economic attributes, it has shortcomings as well. We should sharpen our perspective by taking a look at both sides of the picture.

The Case for Perfect Competition

The economic case for perfect competition is largely based on the contention that it is the most efficient form of market structure for allocating resources to satisfy consumer wants. At another level, the concept of perfect competition has an appeal that is emphatically more political than economic. Like most issues in economics, these two types of appeal cannot, of course, be entirely separated. (In fact, for a great many years, the subject of economics was typically referred to as 'political economy'.) But for the purpose of understanding the issues here, we'll consider these two aspects separately.

Perfect Competition as an Efficient Allocator of Resources

What does it mean to say that perfect competition is the most efficient way for allocating resources to maximise consumer satisfaction? There are two basic points underlying this argument.

1. *When the perfectly competitive industry is in long-run equilibrium competition forces firms to use a technology that yields the lowest possible ATC curves and to operate at the lowest point on their ATC curves, and consumers pay a price equal to this minimum ATC.* Any firm that doesn't operate in this fashion will be forced out of business. This follows because the existence of many firms producing an identical product means that if any firm tries to charge a higher price, consumers will simply buy from its competitors — the firm will have zero sales. Therefore each firm is forced by competition to produce at the lowest point on its *ATC* curve if it wants to stay in business. Hence, the industry produces the good at the lowest possible per unit cost and distributes it to consumers at a price that just covers this cost. Because each firm must use the least-cost technology to survive, there is no way to improve on this situation given the prevailing state of technical know-how.

2. *In a perfectly competitive equilibrium (short run or long run), price equals marginal cost, and hence for the last unit of a good purchased consumers pay a price that just covers the cost of producing it.* Given that the industry demand curve is downward sloping, let's suppose that production is not pushed to the point where marginal cost equals price for good A. In other words, consumers are willing to pay a price for additional units of A that is greater than the cost of producing these units. The marginal

cost of the additional units of A is the opportunity cost of using the resources needed to produce them, that is, the value of the resources in some alternative use. The fact that consumers are willing to pay a price greater than this opportunity cost for the use of these resources in the production of A suggests that society values additional units of A more highly than the alternative goods that these resources could produce. Hence, if production of A is not pushed to the point where marginal cost equals the price of A, there will be an underallocation of resources to the production of A.

On the other hand, let's suppose that the production of A were pushed beyond the point where marginal cost equals price. Because marginal cost rises as output increases, the price received for the additional units will be less than their marginal cost. This would indicate that the value society places on these additional units is less than the opportunity cost of the resources needed to produce them, or society's valuation of alternative goods that could otherwise be produced with these resources. Hence, there is an overallocation of resources to the production of good A.

What are the implications for consumer satisfaction? When *all* industries in an economy are in a perfectly competitive equilibrium, each will produce just that quantity of its product so that price will equal marginal cost. Therefore, *in a perfectly competitive equilibrium, there will be no misallocation of resources between the production of different goods, and consumer satisfaction will be as large as possible.* Why is this so? If production of good A were pushed beyond the quantity at which $p = MC$, so that the marginal cost of the additional units exceeded their price, society would have to relinquish some amount of alternative goods that it values more highly than the additional units of A. Consumer satisfaction would thus be reduced. To produce an amount of A less than the quantity where $p = MC$, so that p is greater than MC, means society is forgoing an amount of A that it values more than the alternative goods these resources are producing elsewhere. Again, consumer satisfaction is less than it might be.

Finally, because there is ease of entry to and exit of firms from perfectly competitive industries, a perfectly competitive economy will quickly reallocate resources to meet changing consumer preferences or supply conditions. This will serve to preserve allocative efficiency over time.

The Political Appeal of Perfect Competition

The notion of an economy characterised by perfectly competitive markets has a special appeal for those who view concentration of power in a few hands as dangerous. Anyone who believes that power groups, whether governmental or private, pose a potential threat to individual rights and personal freedom finds much to recommend in the perfectly competitive world.

Markets composed of many buyers and sellers, not one of which is large enough to have a significant impact on price and output, lead to about as much diffusion of power as one could imagine. The forces of keen competition that characterise such markets put a premium on performance. For example, firms that discriminate among workers on grounds other than their ability to perform a job will find themselves at a competitive disadvantage vis-a-vis firms who hire workers solely on the basis of ability. Indeed, they will soon be out of business. When consumer demands shift, resources will move quickly to those production activities that will satisfy them. Resources will be efficiently allocated to society's needs without being compelled by any force other than the impersonal signals of the market — the 'invisible hand' of the marketplace, as Adam Smith called it.

Criticisms of Perfect Competition

Perfect competition is not without its critics. The most common criticisms levelled against it are that (1) it provides little incentive for innovation, (2) it does not capture spillover costs and benefits, (3) it leads to a lack of product variety, and (4) the accompanying distribution of income may be 'inequitable'. All of these charges raise doubts about whether perfect competition is the best form of market organisation for maximising consumer satisfaction.

Let's look at these criticisms individually.

Perfect Competition Provides Little Incentive for Innovation

In a perfectly competitive world, information about technology is readily available to all. In an agricultural market, for example, it would be hard for a farmer to keep a newly developed production technique a secret from competitors for long. As a result, a firm cannot expect to gain much competitive advantage over other firms by developing new technology. The higher than normal profits that the firm might realise would be short lived as other firms quickly adopted the new technique and once again competed on an equal footing. Therefore, with little prospect of reaping much gain from technological innovation, there is little incentive for a perfectly competitive firm to devote much effort to such activity.

Since technological innovation is considered essential to the dynamics of economic growth (measured as the rate of increase of output per capita), it is often argued that a perfectly competitive world is lacking in this respect. The existence of *patent laws* that give inventors the legal right to exclusive use of their inventions for a stipulated period of time is in large part justified by this consideration. Of course, the existence of perfect competition is precluded in industries where there are patents held by certain firms, as we will see in subsequent chapters.

Perfect Competition Fails to Capture Spillover Costs and Benefits

We discussed spillover costs and benefits in Chapter 21 (you may need to go back and review these concepts at this point). Clearly when spillover costs exist, such as water and air pollution, the firm's marginal cost curve does not include them. Producing to the point where marginal cost equals price will therefore mean producing some goods that, in fact, cost more than the value society places on them. In this case, it can no longer be argued that the existence of perfectly competitive markets leads to the maximisation of consumer satisfaction. The same argument holds when there are spillover benefits such as those associated with keeping one's automobile in safe working condition or those associated with the purchase of flu shots.

Perfect Competition Leads to a Lack of Product Variety

This criticism of perfect competition alleges that because a perfectly competitive firm produces a product indistinguishable from that of the other firms in the industry, there may be a dull sameness about a perfectly competitive world. While this may be true, economists are generally not in favour of solving this problem through attempts to create distinctions between the products of different firms when in fact no real difference exists. For example, there is no difference between beet sugar and cane sugar despite advertising to the contrary. Such advertising uses resources that could be used in other activities, with the result that the products advertised cost the consumer more than necessary. This is not to say that all advertising in a perfectly competitive market is a waste of resources. 'Drink milk for good health' is an ad that may well be informative and increase the sales of all milk products, unlike an ad that says, 'Sunny Farm's milk is more wholesome than any other'.

The Distribution of Income Associated with Perfect Competition May Be Inequitable

A perfectly competitive world provides for an efficient allocation of resources, *given* the existing distribution of wealth or income among members of the economy. If that distribution were different, the allocation of resources provided by the perfectly competitive markets would be different as well — though still efficient by the criterion that price would equal marginal cost in each and every market. However, society's opinions about an equitable distribution of income are a separate consideration from that of the efficient allocation of resources. *The 'fairness' of a particular income distribution is a normative issue — disputes over this cannot be settled by an appeal to facts alone.* Hence, one may have no quarrel with the efficiency with which resources are allocated in a perfectly competitive world (price equals marginal cost in each market). However, it is at the same time possible for one to feel that the prevailing distribution of income is 'unfair'. If Jones feeds his dog steak while Brown cannot even afford to feed his children beans, many observers may feel that this reflects an inequitable distribution of income. We will examine the subject of income distribution in greater detail in Chapter 31.

Question

1. Copyright laws, patents on inventions and protection for the breeders of new plant varieties are features of modern society designed to protect those who innovate. Since, to some extent such legal restraints prevent a competitive market from operating should we conclude,

(a) these types of legal protection are undesirable, or
(b) perfect competition is undesirable?

What approach to this problem would you suggest to the Federal Government when considering patents for drug companies?

the competitive industry reduces its level of production, and therefore buys fewer of these resources, their prices may fall. For each individual firm in the industry, such as that in Figure 23.8, part a, a rise in the prices of its inputs, and hence its unit costs, will be reflected in an upward shift in its ATC and MC curves. Conversely, a decline in input prices, and hence unit costs, will be reflected in a downward shift in the ATC and MC curves.

Suppose we were to consider successively higher levels of industry demand, for example, as represented by the industry demand curve shifting rightward to positions such as D_4, D_5, and D_6 in Figure 23.9, part b. When the demand curve shifts from D_4 to D_5, new firms will enter the industry in response to the above-normal profits that are initially realised. As new firms enter, these excess profits will now be eliminated in two ways. First, as we have already seen, excess profits will be reduced by the fall in price that takes place during the adjustment process because of the expanding level of industry output. Second, excess profits will be further reduced by the upward shift of the typical firm's ATC and MC curves, which results from the rise in the price of inputs as industry expansion increases the demand for them. Once the excess profits have been eliminated by these two effects, the industry will be in a new long-run equilibrium position producing a larger output with more firms. Each will again be operating at the minimum point on its ATC curve, but now the typical firm's ATC curve will be higher than before. Hence, the larger long-run equilibrium level of industry output is supplied at a higher price.

Suppose the industry demand curve shifts rightward again. After the adjustment process has worked itself out once

more, there will be an even larger level of long-run equilibrium output supplied at a yet higher price. Hence, the long-run perfectly competitive industry supply curve is upward sloping in the increasing-cost case, as shown in Figure 23.9, part b. As a result, the long-run equilibrium price associated with the successively larger levels of demand represented by D_4, D_5, and D_6 is successively higher — p_4, p_5, and p_6 respectively — at output levels of 45,040, 80,000, and 115,000 units.

The Decreasing-Cost Case

It is also possible as a perfectly competitive industry increases output that the prices it pays for inputs, and hence its per unit costs of production, may decline. This could occur, for example, if some of the industries supplying the inputs to the perfectly competitive industry experienced economies of scale as they produced larger quantities of the inputs. The resulting lower costs of producing these inputs might then be passed along to the perfectly competitive industry in the form of lower input prices. Then the long-run supply curve of the perfectly competitive industry would be downward sloping, as shown in Figure 23.9, part c. For the successively larger demands D_7, D_8, and D_9, the long-run equilibrium prices are the successively lower p_7, p_8, and p_9.

An example of a decreasing-cost industry might be the development of agriculture in a typical frontier area in nineteenth-century America. As the farming industry got larger in such a region, a more extensive railway network could be supported. The resulting economies of transporting a larger volume of agricultural commodities to market, as well as supplies to farmers, would lower the per unit costs of agricultural production.

CHECKPOINT 23.6
What does the notion of opportunity cost have to do with long-run equilibrium in a perfectly competitive industry? What does it mean when we say that firms are just earning a normal profit in long-run competitive equilibrium?

PRICE TAKERS AND MARKET POWER

At the very start of this chapter we distinguished between price takers and price makers. Later, when discussing the features of perfect competition it was said that in perfect competition all firms are price takers. It is the principal fact of life competitive firms have to live with. It is very important to realise that very many of the firms that are price takers do not look at first glance as if they fit markets where the four characteristics of perfect competition apply. This section deals with them.

The giant mining companies operating in Australia certainly don't look as if they meet the characteristics of perfect competition. There are very few producing each mineral and they don't enter or leave this capital intensive industry easily. But they do sell similar products and buyers certainly have an excellent knowledge about prices — world prices. Mount Isa Mines Ltd (MIM) is the country's largest copper producer and a large producer by world standards but its prices are determined on competitive world markets. The same is true for CRA Ltd and North Broken Hill. The first lesson then is that the market may be much larger than just Australia. *Many Australian mining companies are price takers on world markets and their task is to select the level of output that equates marginal cost with the ruling world price.* Even if the company is selling in Australia the world price is likely to prevail if there are no import duties. It may not be able to set a price that is different from the prevailing world price because of overseas competition.

The two important aspects of being a price taker are first, that the firm has to take the going price and second, it can sell its entire output and larger output levels, without affecting the market price. For Australian firms selling commodities determined on world markets, this is usually the case — even for the mining giants. Average revenue = marginal revenue = price. Such firms are said to *lack market power*. But other firms also lack market power without the advantages of the price taker. *Fear of potential competition* or *the threat of government intervention* may also prevent a firm from setting a price, or at least from setting a price higher than the competitive price. They are worse off than the genuine price taker only in the sense that they cannot produce and sell unlimited quantities without depressing their prices. They can't get higher prices, but if they overproduce or misjudge the market they may have to take a lower price to sell their entire output.

CHECKPOINT 23.7
Large mining companies have a completely different form of business organisation than the family farms that predominate in agriculture. How then would you explain why there are equally large fluctuations in mineral prices and prices of some major agricultural commodities?

SUMMARY

1. To enable understanding of how firms behave it is necessary to classify them. One important distinction is between price takers and price makers. An alternative common classification is into four market forms; perfect competition, monopoly, monopolistic competition and oligopoly.

2. In the short run, the perfectly competitive firm must decide whether or not to produce, and if it does decide to produce, how much. This decision process may be viewed from the standpoint of comparing total revenue and total cost or from that of comparing marginal revenue and marginal cost. The firm will produce as long as total revenue exceeds total variable cost or, equivalently, as long as price per unit exceeds average variable cost.

3. If the firm decides to produce, it will maximise profits by producing that quantity of output at which total revenue exceeds total cost by the greatest amount. If total cost exceeds total revenue but total revenue exceeds total variable cost, the firm will minimise losses by producing that output level where total revenue exceeds total variable cost by the maximum amount.

4. From the marginal cost-marginal revenue point of view, the firm will be able to maximise profit, or minimise loss, by producing to the point where marginal cost equals marginal revenue. Following this rule, it will maximise profit whenever price exceeds average total cost, or minimise loss whenever price is less than average total cost but greater than average variable cost. When price is less than average variable cost, the firm will shut down.

5. The segment of the perfectly competitive firm's marginal cost curve that lies above the average variable cost curve is the firm's short-run supply curve. Summing the supply curves of all firms gives the short-run industry supply curve.

6. In long-run equilibrium, a perfectly competitive firm receives a price just equal to its minimum average total cost, the lowest point on its ATC curve, so that it just earns a normal profit (economic profit is zero). The existence of greater than normal profit (an economic profit) would attract new firms into the industry, increasing industry supply until competition has forced price to the minimum average total cost level. Conversely, economic losses would lead firms to leave the industry, decreasing industry supply until price has risen to the minimum average total cost level. This long-run adjustment process implies that the long-run industry supply curve is horizontal in the constant-cost case, upward sloping in the increasing-cost case, and downward sloping in the decreasing-cost case.

7. It may be argued that an economy consisting entirely of perfectly competitive markets leads to a maximisation of consumer satisfaction. This follows because in long-run equilibrium, competition forces firms to produce with the least-cost technology available, at the lowest possible average per unit cost, and sell to consumers at a price that just covers this cost. In addition, price equals marginal cost, so that consumers pay a price that just covers the cost of the last unit of each kind of good produced. Because of the ease of entry and exit of firms to and from industries, a perfectly competitive economy will quickly reallocate resources to meet changing consumer preferences or reflect changing supply conditions. Hence, resources are always efficiently allocated in accordance with consumers' tastes.

8. There are several reservations about whether perfect competition will ensure maximum consumer satisfaction. It is felt that perfect competition provides little incentive for technological innovation, spillover costs and benefits are not captured, there is a lack of product variety, and income distribution may not be 'equitable'.

KEY TERMS AND CONCEPTS

average revenue
break-even point
marginal revenue
market power
market structure
price maker
price taker
total revenue

QUESTIONS AND PROBLEMS

1. Rank the following industries according to how closely they approximate a perfectly competitive industry — that is, judge them according to the four characteristics of a perfectly competitive industry: car manufacturing, coal mining, hair dressing, dry cleaning, residential construction, wallpapering, soft drinks, airlines, orange growing, stereo manufacturing, retail shoe stores, and television set manufacturing.

2. The following industries have some characteristics of a perfectly competitive industry but lack others. In each case, determine what perfectly competitive characteristics they have and what ones they seem to be lacking: petroleum refining, shoeshining, steel production, hairdressing, medical care, sewage disposal, portrait painting, and cattle farming. Which, if any, would you think of the

individual producers might be price takers?

3. Suppose a perfectly competitive industry is in short-run equilibrium. Suppose the industry demand curve shifts rightward. Thinking in terms of Figure 23.1, what difference does the elasticity of the industry demand curve make to the individual firm?

4. Suppose the costs of the individual firms in a competitive industry are identical. They are those given in columns 1-7 of Table 23.2. Suppose you are told that the industry is in short-run equilibrium with total industry production and sales equal to 2,200 units at a price of $8 per unit.

a. How many firms are there in the industry?

b. Are they making a profit or are they operating at a loss? What is the amount of the profit or loss per unit?

c. How will each firm adjust if price falls to $4.60? Why?

d. Given your answer to part a, derive the points on the industry supply curve corresponding to each of the following prices: $6, $8, $12, and $23.

5. Will the short-run equilibrium position stipulated for the firm in Table 23.3 be consistent with a long-run equilibrium position for the perfectly competitive industry made up of such firms? Why or why not?

6. Consider the short-run equilibrium position of the firm in Table 23.4.

a. Describe the process of long-run adjustment that this implies for the perfectly competitive industry made up of such firms initially in such positions.

b. What would the long-run equilibrium price be in this industry?

c. Suppose the industry demand curve is downward sloping starting from a price level of $6.80 on the vertical axis. Would this affect your answer to part b? What would be the long-run equilibrium level of output for the industry, given this industry demand curve?

7. One of the concerns sometimes expressed is that competitive industries do not provide sufficient incentive for technological innovation. Use the competitive model with its four characteristics to demonstrate that there are still potential gains to be had for the innovative firm. Consider both the short run and the long run effects.

24

Monopoly and Monopoly Power

AFTER READING THIS CHAPTER YOU WILL BE ABLE TO:

1. Explain the characteristics of the form of market organisation known as monopoly and what is meant by monopoly power.

2. Define the conditions that make a monopoly possible.

3. Explain the relationship between a downward-sloping demand curve and its associated marginal revenue curve.

4. Demonstrate how the monopolist's profit-maximising price and output levels are determined by equating marginal cost and marginal revenue.

5. Give the reasons why monopoly is considered inefficient as an allocator of resources, inequitable as a distributor of income, and controversial as a promoter of innovation and technological change.

6. Explain the nature of natural monopoly and public utility regulation.

7. List the conditions necessary for price discrimination and the reasons why it pays firms to discriminate.

Monopoly is commonly defined as a form of market structure in which the entire market for a good or service is supplied by a single seller, or firm. In our classification of market structures it lies at the opposite end of the spectrum from perfect competition. Whereas perfect competition was characterised by many sellers facing vigorous competition from other firms, monopoly exists where there is total dominance by a single firm. But what, in practice, is a monopolist? It may be the single firm in a major industry serving a large national market. Or it may be the local taxi in an outback town or the vendor selling pies at a football match. Sometimes things are not clear cut. It may be difficult to decide what constitutes the industry or what we mean by a market. Another formal definition is that *a monopolist is the single supplier of a good or service for which there is no close substitute.* The importance of this definition is that it focuses on the power the monopoly has in the market. If there are no close substitutes the firm has greater opportunity to follow an independent pricing policy and set its prices than if there is direct competition from producers of close substitutes. Monopolists are price makers whereas in perfect competition the firms were price takers.

A second important definition is **monopoly power**. *A firm is said to have monopoly power if it is able to set prices, as if it were the only firm in a market with no close substitutes.* As the definition suggests, it is possible for a firm to exert monopoly power without being the only firm in a particular market. How can this be? A firm may be so large that it is able to dominate a market completely. Other small firms pose no threat and do not compete with it. It is an effective monopolist in these circumstances and is able

to behave as if it were the only firm.

A market may be supplied by a small number of firms. Normally we call this market form *oligopoly* and it will be discussed in the following chapter. However, if the firms get together to fix prices or share the market between them they effectively behave in a very similar way to a monopolist. They are exercising market power. For simplicity, much of our discussion in this chapter is going to treat a monopoly as if it was a single firm supplying a market. We are going to take it that the firm has no close substitute and that it does possess effective monopoly power which it can use to set prices.

This chapter is concerned with three main questions:

1. How do firms come to get monopoly power and keep it?

2. How can a firm with monopoly power maximise profits?

3. How desirable, or undesirable is monopoly as a market form compared with perfect competition?

There is a widely held view that monopoly may well be undesirable because it lacks those very characteristics of perfect competition that make competition appear to be an ideal state of affairs, and perfect competition an ideal market form. In most western industrial countries it has been recognised that monopolies can work against the interests of consumers and reduce economic welfare. We shall see later that whilst monopoly as such is not illegal in Australia the Commonwealth Government and the state governments have taken action to remove many trade practices regarded as anticompetitive.

WHAT MAKES A MONOPOLY?

There are four conditions that can give rise to a situation in which one seller or firm is able to exercise monopoly power. These are:
1. the firm's exclusive ownership of a unique resource,
2. the existence of economies of scale,
3. the legal granting of a monopoly by the government,
4. an agreement between firms.

Exclusive Ownership of a Unique Resource

A seller or a firm that has exclusive ownership of a unique resource may have monopoly power. The ownership may be a physical resource such as a rare mineral deposit. It may have unique strategic geographical qualities such as a site for a bridge or a port facility. Or it may be some special human skill. Uri Geller has been able to command huge fees in oil exploration because of his ability to indicate potential oil rich locations by flying over them. Red Adair is the acknowledged world expert at fighting oil well fires and blow outs. De Beers, the South African mining giant has effective monopoly power in the international diamond market. Not only is it the largest producer, but it maintains its power by managing its enormous stocks of gems and maintaining control over the marketing of diamonds. New producers invariably decide to market through De Beers who effectively determine world prices.

Economies of Scale

We saw in Chapter 22 that on occasions the technology of production is such that firms may enjoy economies of scale. Big *is* sometimes beautiful. The long-run average cost curve of a firm may fall over almost the entire range of output for which there is demand. In such circumstances it is possible for an individual firm to have a **natural monopoly**. *A natural monopoly exists where a firm is able to take advantage of economies of scale and to produce for the entire market at a price which new and potential rival firms cannot match.* The established firm is able to keep rivals out and to maintain its monopoly position. The size of the market is an important influence on whether natural monopoly exists. Very many productive activities exhibit economies of scale at low output levels. The smaller a market, the more likely will it be that a single firm is able to gain an unassailable cost advantage and supply the entire market.

Government-Granted Monopoly

Being able to maintain monopoly power depends often on there being artificial barriers that prevent competition from arising to challenge the position of the monopolist. One of the most secure types of artificial barrier that protects monopolists is when their position is legally sanctioned by the government. Two of the main ways in which government creates monopolies are:
1. through patents, copyrights and licences, and
2. through public utilities and the establishment of marketing boards.

Patents, Copyrights and Licences

As we noted in the discussion on the merits of perfect competition in the previous chapter, there is a strong case for encouraging those responsible for technological progress or innovation. Without such protection much of the incentive would disappear. If new ideas could be readily copied and used by all, everyone would attempt to take a 'free ride' on the inventor's back. Patents provide inventors with an exclusive right to use their ideas for a specified time. They confer monopoly power on the inventor. It has been felt that society generally benefits from such arrangements. Similarly, the government also grants copyrights to writers and to composers. It gives them exclusive legal control over the production and reproduction of their work for a given period of time. Without the protection of the copyright laws it is doubtful whether many authors and publishers would be persuaded to produce textbooks.

State and federal government grant licences in many areas of economic activity. Licences to operate legal gambling casinos and radio and television stations in Australia have been highly sought after and have conferred varying degrees of monopoly power on successful applicants. Not all licensing arrangements lead to the establishment of a monopoly, but they do have the effect of limiting the number of producers in the area.

Public Utilities and Marketing Boards

Many economic services in Australia are provided by government-run monopolies. Telephones, the postal service, electricity and public transport are but four common examples. Telecom, Australia Post, and various state electricity commissions, rail and metropolitan transport authorities are all protected from competition by acts of parliament. Why? There are various economic and social reasons. Uppermost is the idea that these are important services society needs and that a free market

system would not provide them in a satisfactory form and at a satisfactory price. Can you imagine four or five electricity companies supplying power to your street, or a single electricity company that decided to use its monopoly power to increase charges sharply? Two features of most public utilities are that they are required to provide services of a minimum standard and that their charges are subject to government approval. They cannot operate as freely as a privately owned monopoly.

Agricultural marketing boards are another form of monopoly created by government legislation. Their purpose is quite different from public utilities. Normally, their objective is to provide farmers with more market power and higher returns than they could achieve under competitive conditions. Marketing arrangements differ widely in Australia. Dairy authorities set (or recommend) milk prices in much the same way that another monopoly, the state electricity commission does.

Agreement Between Firms

The last means of establishing an effective monopoly is when the existing firms in an industry agree not to compete. A **cartel** is the name given to a group of independent firms that act as a monopoly. A cartel may achieve this market power by agreeing on measures like a common price, setting market shares for each producer or dividing markets into sub markets that each will serve exclusively. Restrictive trade practices of this nature are not always enduring, but as long as they last they have many of the same features of single firm monopoly. In Australia, the Trade Practices Commission has responsibilities to examine and, if necessary, prosecute firms that make agreements considered not to be in the public interest. In 1987 it took the view that a proposed agreement by the three shipping companies carrying freight across Bass Strait to operate a combined service was anticompetitive and that it would lead to their exercising monopoly power. In itself an agreement between the existing firms in an industry to combine to form a cartel is not sufficient to give them lasting monopoly power. Whether they achieve this depends first on the stability of the cartel. Will they continue to agree on price and output or how to divide the market? Second, will other firms be attracted to the industry as competitors if they exercise their monopoly power? The experience of the OPEC countries illustrates both problems. After an outstanding early period when the members were able to achieve massive real price increases for oil there developed considerable subsequent disagreement about pricing policy and members' production levels. Difficulties were accentuated because a number of producers such as the United Kingdom refused to join and followed an independent competitive policy.

The more difficult it is for firms to enter an industry, the more scope there is for cartel type agreements to give existing firms monopoly power. The very existence of a cartel may increase the difficulties of entry particuarly if the cartel members are able to put pressure on the suppliers of materials new firms would require to start business. A new newspaper may find it difficult to obtain supplies of newsprint, or a new airline may find that existing airlines work to prevent it obtaining landing rights or terminal facilities.

Barriers to Competition
We have seen that the fundamental reason why firms come to have monopoly power is that there are barriers to competition. In Chapter 23, ease of entry was identified as one of the characteristics of perfect competition. In this section 'what makes a monopoly?', lack of ready access to resources, economies of scale and limited market demand, government restrictions and restrictive trade practices, have been identified as the main types of barriers to entry.

Fear on the part of a single supplier that an existing barrier will disappear will affect the way it operates. Setting high prices and making high profits may encourage other firms to seek and develop alternative supplies of essential resources. There will be a limit to the price a natural monopolist will be able to charge. If he charges too much, another firm with high establishment costs may be tempted to enter the market. A government-conferred monopoly may have the least to fear from the entry of other firms as long as it receives the protection of the law, but it usually has to justify its pricing policies to the government and its powers are thus limited. Knowledge that many trade practices are regarded by government in Australian as anticompetitive acts as a powerful deterrent to firms using such methods to prevent competition from developing.

CHECKPOINT 24.1*
BHP is the only producer of steel in Australia. Does that mean it is a monopoly? Does it have monopoly power? How would you decide whether it did?
Recently Tony Hocking went to the San Diego Zoo. Improbably — it poured with rain. The kiosk at the entrance sold umbrellas. Did it have a monopoly?

*Answers to all Checkpoints can be found at the back of the text.

HOW DOES A FIRM WITH MONOPOLY POWER SET ITS PRICE?

How does a monopolist, or, more importantly, a firm with monopoly power decide what price to charge? What output should it produce? In fact, it turns out that the answer to either one of these questions necessarily gives the answer to the other. In this discussion, we will assume that potential rivals are kept out of the market and that the monopolist is not governed by any regulatory commission.

Demand and Marginal Revenue for a Monopolist

We saw in the previous chapter that a firm in a perfect competitive industry cannot affect the price at which it sells its output. It can, however, sell as little or as much as it wants at the same, given price. As a result, it is a price taker, and therefore its demand curve is perfectly horizontal. By contrast, if a firm has monopoly power, the demand curve for its product slopes downwards from left to right and the firm can change the price by varying the amount of its product that it delivers to the market. It should be emphasised that is not a characteristic unique to a monopoly. Whatever the market structure of an industry, so long as an individual firm in that industry can affect price by changing its level of output, that firm faces a downward-sloping demand curve. Later, we shall see that this is true of firms in monopolistically competitive as well as oligopolistic industries. In fact, it is only the firm in a perfectly competitive market that faces a perfectly horizontal demand curve. So bear in mind that the following discussion of a downward-sloping demand curve and

its associated marginal revenue curve also applies to firms in other market contexts besides monopoly.

Table 24.1 contains hypothetical data on demand and revenue for a monopolist. Observe that the monopolist can sell a larger quantity Q of output (column 1) only by charging a lower price p, or average revenue AR, per unit (column 2). Total revenue TR (column 3) equals the price p (column 2) multiplied by the quantity Q (column 1). Starting from a zero output level, total revenue TR

TABLE 24.1
Demand and Revenue Data for a
Monopolist (Hypothetical Data)

(1) Quantity of Output (Q)	(2) Price = Average Revenue	(3) Total Revenue (TR)	(4) Marginal Revenue (MR)
	$p = AR$	$TR = p \times Q$	
0	$13	$ 0	
			$ 12
1	12	12	
			10
2	11	22	
			8
3	10	30	
			6
4	9	36	
			4
5	8	40	
			2
6	7	42	
			0
7	6	42	
			-2
8	5	40	
			-4
9	4	36	
			-6
10	3	30	
			-8
11	2	22	
			-10
12	1	12	
			-12
13	0	0	

(column 3) initially gets larger as price is lowered. It reaches a maximum when 6 units of output are sold at a price of $7, or when 7 units are sold at a price of $6, and declines thereafter. This merely reflects a characteristic of a downward-sloping demand curve, which we have already discussed.

Marginal Revenue Declines for a Monopolist

At this point, however, we note a very important difference between a firm with monopoly power and a perfectly competitive firm. Remember, a perfectly competitive firm can sell each additional unit of output at the same price because its demand curve is perfectly horizontal. Hence, the marginal revenue (equal to the change in total revenue) associated with the sale of one more unit of output is always equal to price for a perfectly competitive firm. Since price doesn't change, neither does marginal revenue. This is not true for a monopolist because a monopolist's demand curve is downward sloping. *In order to sell an additional unit of output the monopolist must lower price. And the monopolist not only must accept a lower price for an additional unit sold but for all the units sold — units that otherwise could have been sold at a higher price.*

This means that for a monopolist marginal revenue is less than price at every level of output, except when it produces a total output of only one unit. The reason is that when price is lowered to sell an additional unit of output, the resulting change in total revenue equals the sum of two parts, one a plus and the other a minus. One part is the *increase* in total revenue equal to the price received for the additional unit sold. The other part equals

the *decrease* in total revenue due to the reduction in price on all other units that was necessary in order to sell the additional unit. Thus, *for a monopolist marginal revenue (the change in total revenue) equals the price of the additional unit less the amount of the price reduction on the other units multiplied by the quantity of the other units. Therefore, marginal revenue is less than price at every level of output, except the first unit. And it follows from this that, since price declines as output increases (because the demand curve is downward sloping), marginal revenue must also decline as output increases.*

These relationships between price, total revenue, and marginal revenue are illustrated in Table 24.1. Only for the first unit of output sold is it true that price (column 2) equals marginal revenue (column 4), in this case $12. To sell two units, price must be lowered to $11. Not only is the second unit sold for $11, but now so is the first. Otherwise the first unit could have been sold for $12 — if the monopolist had been satisfied to sell just one unit. Therefore, to sell two units of output, the monopolist has to give up $1 on the first unit, while getting an additional $11 from the sale of the second. The change (increase) in total revenue is therefore $10 ($11 minus $1), the marginal revenue shown in column 4. The marginal revenue of $10 is the increase in total revenue from $12 to $22 (column 3) resulting from the sale of the second unit of output. If the monopolist wanted to sell 3 units, price would have to be lowered to $10 per unit. This means that the first two units would have to be sold at $10 per unit as well, instead of the $11 per unit received when only 2 units were sold. The marginal revenue would be equal to the $10 received from the sale of the third unit less $1 per unit given up on each of the first two units, or $8. You should now be able to convince yourself of the validity of the marginal revenue data in Table 24.1. Note that when output exceeds 7 units, marginal revenue becomes negative. Negative marginal revenue is associated with the range over which increases in total output lead to decreases in total revenue.

Relationship Between the Total Revenue, Demand, and Marginal Revenue Curves

The data from Table 24.1 are plotted in Figure 24.1. For each output level in column 1, the associated price is plotted to give the demand curve D in parts b and c. (Demand curves are not necessarily straight lines — we use them for simplicity.) Total revenue (Table 24.1, column 3) is plotted in part a to give the TR curve.

Comparison of parts a and b clearly shows that total revenue TR for the monopolist reaches its maximum at 6 units of output with a price of $7 per unit. Observe that if price is reduced from $7 to $6 (part b), the quantity of output sold increases from 6 to 7 units, but TR remains unchanged at $42 (part a). Why is this so? Part b shows us that when price is lowered from $7 to $6, there is a loss in TR of $6 ($1 per unit on the first 6 units). This loss is represented by the shaded horizontal rectangle. However, this loss is just offset by the gain in TR of $6, realised from the sale of the seventh unit. This is represented by the vertical shaded rectangle. Putting it another way, we can say that the marginal revenue MR (the change in total revenue TR) associated with the sale of the seventh unit of output is zero. The marginal revenue information

from column 4 is plotted on part c of Figure 24.1. Note that the points on the marginal revenue curve are plotted exactly half way between successive output levels. This is to emphasise that marginal revenue is measuring the change in total revenue as the result of selling an extra unit of output. In part c it can be seen that the consequence of selling the 7th unit of output is to leave sales revenue at the same level as when six units were sold. Marginal revenue is zero.

Note in part a that at levels of sales less than 6 units TR can always be increased by lowering price (part b) and selling an additional unit. Therefore, marginal revenue is always positive up to the sale of the seventh unit. This means that the MR curve in part c lies above the horizontal axis at all output levels less than 7 units. Furthermore, starting from a zero level of output, note that TR (part a) rises less and less steeply as price is lowered and the number of units sold is increased (part b). This is reflected in the fact that the MR curve (part c) is downward sloping left to right.

Observe that only when one unit of output is sold is it true that marginal revenue equals total revenue, or $12. The marginal revenue MR from producing the first unit must be equal also to the price of that unit — $12. When more units of output are sold their price is greater than the marginal revenue that is added. The demand curve lies above the marginal revenue curve. Note also that when sales are increased beyond the 7th unit the MR curve lies below the horizontal axis. This reflects the fact that the sale of each additional unit beyond this level *decreases* total revenue — MR is negative. Note also that when marginal revenue is negative a reduction in sales *increases* total revenue.

FIGURE 24.1
Relationship Between the Total Revenue Curve, the Demand Curve, and the Marginal
Revenue Curve

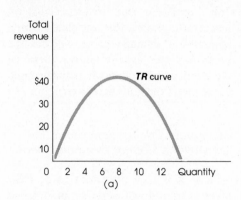

(a)

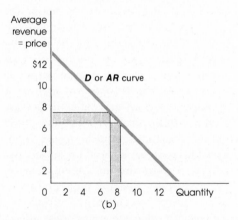

(b)

The total revenue curve *TR* in part a is plotted from the data in columns 1 and 3 of Table 24.1. The demand *D*, or average revenue *AR*, curve in parts b and c is plotted from the data in columns 1 and 2 of Table 24.1. The marginal revenue curve *MR* in part c is plotted from the data in columns 1 and 4 of Table 24.1

Because the *TR* curve rises at a decreasing rate up to 6 units of output in part a, the *MR* curve is downward sloping and lies above the horizontal axis up to 7 units of output in part c. It crosses the axis at this point, reflecting the fact there is no change in total revenue (part a) resulting from the sale of the seventh unit of output. This is also represented by the fact that the horizontal shaded rectangle in part b, representing the loss in total revenue on the first 6 units, is just equal to the vertical shaded rectangle, representing the gain in total revenue from the sale of the seventh unit. Because the *TR* curve falls at an increasing rate beyond 7 units of output in part a, the *MR* curve is downward sloping and lies below the horizontal axis beyond 7 units in part c.

The *MR* curve always lies below the demand curve *D* after the first unit of output, part c. This is so because the marginal revenue from the sale of an additional unit of output is less than the price received for that unit by the amount of the sum of the price cuts on all previous units sold.

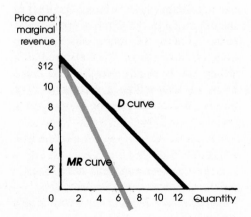

Relationship Between Demand and Marginal Revenue Curves: Further Comments

For purposes of illustrating the basic relationship between total revenue, demand, and marginal revenue, we have used rather small numbers when talking about quantity in Table 24.1 and Figure 24.1. However, it would be more realistic in general to assume that we are dealing with much larger quantities of output. This changes the scale on the horizontal, or quantity, axis so that the number of units is so large that the distance equal to one unit is no larger than a dot. This explains why the demand curve and the marginal revenue curve meet at the same point on the vertical axis. It is because we cannot distinguish the first unit of output, though we attempted to do so in Figure 24.1.

There is another relationship to be noted at this stage. For any downward-sloping, straight-line demand curve it will then be true that at any price level, the horizontal distance between the vertical axis and the marginal revenue curve will be exactly half the distance to the demand curve. Note that this means the marginal revenue curve will cross the horizontal axis exactly halfway between the origin and the point where the demand curve crosses the horizontal axis.

One way to see why this is so is to recall our discussion of elasticity in Chapter 20. There we observed in Figure 20.5 that a straight-line demand curve is unit elastic exactly at its midpoint. Corresponding to this point on the demand curve, we also observed that total revenue is a maximum. In other words, just to the left of this point, marginal revenue is positive, while just to the right of it, marginal revenue is negative. Therefore, exactly at that point marginal revenue is zero. Hence, where

total revenue is a maximum, the marginal revenue curve cuts the horizontal axis. This can be seen by comparing parts a and c of Figure 24.1. It follows that the marginal revenue curve associated with a straight-line demand curve will cut the horizontal axis exactly halfway between the origin and the point where the demand curve meets the horizontal axis.

Monopoly Pricing Policy and the Downward Sloping Demand Curve

Finally, it is very important to be clear about what a downward-sloping demand curve does and does not say about the pricing policy of the firm with monopoly power. Contrary to the usual belief of the person in the street, it *does not say* that the monopolist can sell a given output at any price desired. It *does not say* that a monopolist can set price at some desired level and *independently* decide how much output to sell at that price, or vice versa. This fallacy is just a variation on the first fallacy. The downward-sloping demand curve does say that the monopolist can affect price by changing output or, equivalently, that the monopolist affects sales by changing price. But the level of one automatically determines the level of the other due to the shape of the demand curve. Hence, the monopolist's pricing policy is not free of the constraint that selling more means accepting a lower price, or that selling a certain level of output means charging no more than a certain price level.

CHECKPOINT 24.2
Use the numbers from Table 24.1 to demonstrate the relationship between the elasticity of the demand curve in Figure 24.1, parts b and c, and its associated marginal revenue curve. (You may find it

helpful to review briefly the concept of elasticity in Chapter 20.)

Bringing Together Costs and Revenues

In order to see how a profit-maximising monopolist determines what output level to produce and what price to charge, we must bring the cost side of the picture together with the demand and marginal revenue side. To make it easier to compare the profit-maximising behaviour of the monopolist with that of the perfectly competitive firm discussed in the previous chapter, we will assume that the monopolist's costs, shown in Table 24.2, are the same as those we looked at in Table 23.3. For each output level in column 1 of Table 24.2, the monopolist's average total cost, total cost, and marginal cost data are

shown in columns 5, 6, and 7, respectively. Columns 2, 3, and 4 repeat the revenue data from columns 2, 3, and 4 of Table 24.1.

The Total Revenue-Total Cost Viewpoint

The monopolist's procedure for choosing that output and price level that maximise profit may be viewed from the standpoint of total revenue *TR* and total cost *TC*. Subtracting *TC* (column 6) from *TR* (column 3) at each level of output (column 1), we get the profit or loss (column 8) associated with producing and selling that output at the price given in column 2. Column 8 tells us that the monopolist realises a maximum profit, which equals $7, when 4 units of output are produced (column 1) and sold at a price of $9 (column 2).

TABLE 24.2
Output, Revenue, and Costs of a Monopolist (Hypothetical Data)

(1) Quantity of Output (Q)	(2) Price = Average Revenue	(3) Total Revenue	(4) Marginal Revenue (MR)	(5) Average Total Cost (ATC)	(6) Total Cost (TC)	(7) Marginal Cost (MC)	(8) Profit (+) or Loss (−)
	$p = AR$	$TR = p \times Q$					$TR - TC =$ $(3) - (6)$
0	$13	$ 0			$10		$-10
			$12			$ 6	
1	12	12		$16.00	16		− 4
			10			4	
2	11	22		10.00	20		2
			8			4	
3	10	30		8.00	24		6
			6			5	
4	9	36		7.25	29		7
			4			7	
5	8	40		7.20	36		4
			2			11	
6	7	42		7.83	47		− 5
			0			23	
7	6	42		10.00	70		−28

This is shown graphically in Figure 24.2, part a. The *TC* curve is plotted from the total cost data (column 6) of Table 24.2 and the *TR* curve is plotted from the total revenue data (column 3). The maximum vertical distance by which the *TR* curve exceeds the *TC* curve occurs at 4 units of output. This distance equals the maximum profit of $7.

The Marginal Revenue = Marginal Cost Viewpoint

The marginal revenue = marginal cost point of view is by far the commonest approach to viewing the determination of that output and price that maximise the monopolist's profit. The basic principle behind this method is exactly the same as that described in the case of the perfectly competitive firm. The monopolist also continues to expand output as long as the marginal cost of producing an additional unit is less than the marginal revenue associated with its sale. The monopolist will produce up to that output level where the marginal cost of the last unit produced is just covered by, or is equal to, its marginal revenue.

Note, however, that the case of the monopolist differs from that of the perfect competitor in two respects. First, marginal revenue for the monopolist is always less than that price (except for the first unit). For the perfectly competitive firm, marginal revenue always equals price. Second, marginal revenue for the monopolist falls as output is increased. For the perfectly competitive firm marginal revenue is the same at all levels of output because price is the same at all levels.

Compare the marginal revenue data (column 4) of Table 24.2 with the marginal cost data (column 7). Observe that *MR* exceeds level *MC* at all output levels up

to 4 units. If a fifth unit is produced, however, its *MR* of $4 is less than its *MC* of $7. Therefore, according to the marginal cost-marginal revenue principle, profit will be at a maximum, which equals $7 (column 8), when 4 units of output are produced and sold at a price of $9 (column 2). This is, of course, the same answer we found from the total cost-total revenue point of view.

The marginal cost-marginal revenue point of view is shown graphically in part b of Figure 24.2. The *ATC* and *MC* curves are plotted from the data in columns 5 and 7 of Table 24.2. (Note that the points on the marginal revenue and marginal cost curves are plotted exactly halfway between successive output levels.) The demand curve and its associated *MR* curve are plotted from the data in columns 2 and 4 of Table 24.2.

That it pays the firm to increase output up through and including 4 units is indicated by the fact that the *MR* curve lies above the *MC* curve up to that point. Beyond 4 units of output, the *MC* curve lies above the *MR* curve, indicating that marginal cost exceeds marginal revenue. Hence, the monopolist maximises profit by producing and selling 4 units of output at a price of $9 per unit. The profit-maximising price is the point on the demand curve that lies directly above the intersection of the *MC* and *MR* curves. We have labelled this point *c*. The profit-maximising output level of 4 units is the point on the horizontal axis that lies directly below the intersection of the *MC* and *MR* curves.

The vertical distance *ad* = *bc*, which equals $1.75, is the average profit per unit, so that 4 units times $1.75 gives the total profit of $7, represented by the shaded rectangular area *abcd*. Note that according to Table 24.2, the average profit per

FIGURE 24.2
The Relationship Between Revenues and Costs for a Monopolist

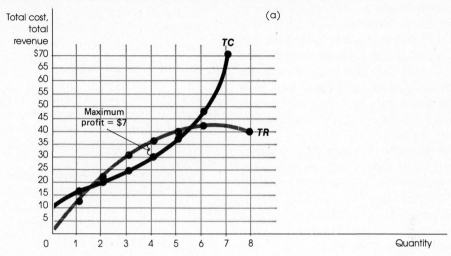

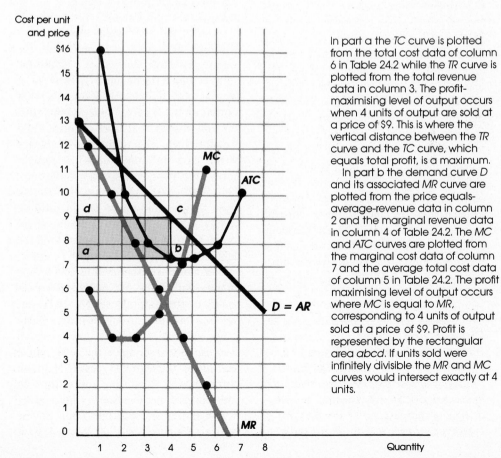

In part a the *TC* curve is plotted from the total cost data of column 6 in Table 24.2 while the *TR* curve is plotted from the total revenue data in column 3. The profit-maximising level of output occurs when 4 units of output are sold at a price of $9. This is where the vertical distance between the *TR* curve and the *TC* curve, which equals total profit, is a maximum.

In part b the demand curve *D* and its associated *MR* curve are plotted from the price equals-average-revenue data in column 2 and the marginal revenue data in column 4 of Table 24.2. The *MC* and *ATC* curves are plotted from the marginal cost data of column 7 and the average total cost data of column 5 in Table 24.2. The profit maximising level of output occurs where *MC* is equal to *MR*, corresponding to 4 units of output sold at a price of $9. Profit is represented by the rectangular area *abcd*. If units sold were infinitely divisible the *MR* and *MC* curves would intersect exactly at 4 units.

unit at 3 units of output is $2, the difference between a price of $10 per unit (column 2) and an ATC of $8 per unit (column 5). However, total profit for 3 units of output at a price of $10 per unit is only $6 (3 units times an average profit per unit of $2). This illustrates the fact that the level of output that maximises total profit does not necessarily correspond to the one that maximises average profit per unit.

Suppose the firm with the cost curves depicted in Figure 24.2 were perfectly competitive instead of a monopolist. Let us assume that its perfectly elastic (horizontal) demand curve is at a level of $9 — that is, as a price taker it is given a price of $9. Then by the $MC = MR = p$ rule we discussed in the previous chapter, it would maximise profit by producing 5 units of output. This is one more unit than would be produced by the monopolist at the same price of $9. The reason for this difference, given that the two firms have identical cost curves, is that marginal revenue equals price is constant at $9 for all levels of output for the perfectly competitive firm but not for the monopolist. For the monopolist, price, and therefore marginal revenue, falls as output increases. Therefore, at a price of $9 marginal revenue is lower for the monopolist than it is for the perfectly competitive firm. This reflects the fact that the monopolist's marginal revenue takes into account the reduced price on all prior units sold.

CHECKPOINT 24.3
If the monopolist shown in Figure 24.2 maximised profit by producing 7 units of output and selling them at the equilibrium price of $6, what would have to be true of marginal cost? Would you ever expect to see a monopolist sell at an equilibrium price in the inelastic portion of the demand curve? Why or why not?

Losses and Small Profits

Probably the most common image brought to mind by the term *monopoly* is that of a firm making large, even 'rip-off', profits. This isn't necessarily the case, however.

Consider the monopolist depicted in part a of Figure 24.3. Marginal cost equals marginal revenue at the output level Q_n, as indicated by the intersection of the MC and MR curves at that point. Producing this level of output and selling it at the price p_n, the monopolist's total revenue is equal to the rectangular area OQ_nbp_n. However, this area also represents the monopolist's total cost, since b is also the point at which the demand curve D is just tangent to the ATC curve. Remember that a point on the ATC curve represents total per unit cost at that level of output and therefore includes a normal profit. Hence in this case the monopolist just earns a normal profit, and economic profit is zero. This is the best the monopolist can do given the demand curve D. To produce at any other output level would entail losses, since at any other output level the demand curve D lies below the ATC curve.

Consider the monopolist in part b. The intersection of the MC and MR curves occurs at the output level Q_l. However, this is a loss-minimising position. There is no way the monopolist can cover all costs in this case, since the ATC curve lies above the demand curve D at all output levels. Producing the output Q_l and selling it at the price p_l, the monopolist incurs a loss per unit equal to the vertical distance ab. The total loss is represented by the shaded rectangular area. The monopolist is only willing to operate at a loss like this in the short run, and then only so long as it is possible to cover average variable cost. Note that in the case depicted in part b, p_1, lies above the AVC curve at the output level Q_1.

The monopolist depicted in Figure 24.2, in contrast to those of Figure 24.3, is earning more than a normal profit. The positive economic profit earned is represented by the shaded rectangular area $abcd$ in part b of Figure 24.2. The basic distinction between earning positive economic profit in a monopoly situation and earning it under perfect competition is that such a profit will attract new firms into the perfectly competitive industry in the long run but not into the monopoly industry. Output will be expanded in the competitive industry and rivalry among firms will cause price to fall until economic profit for each and every firm is driven to zero. In the case of the monopoly, however, barriers to competition prevent this from happening. The monopoly is therefore in the position, provided costs are low enough and demand high enough, to earn positive economic profit — in this case called monopoly profit — almost indefinitely.

Why do we say 'almost indefinitely'? Even a monopolist is not protected from long-run advances in technology or changes in consumer demand that may weaken its advantage. The development of the internal combustion engine brought the decline of many activities and industries that catered for the horse as a means of transport or power. Electric power similarly brought an end to activities that were based on more expensive, less efficient and dirtier power sources. With the new technology monopoly power for some disappeared. Research and changing technology, and the discovery of new resources and supplies can all lead to the weakening of a monopoly market. Paradoxically, such progress can also lead to a firm that offers the old products and the old technology acquiring monopoly power. It may find a niche in the market. That is it may discover a separate market segment just large enough for it to supply. Thatching cottages in England is one example. Most people want slate or tiles and the technology delivers these at an acceptable price. A few people with very old cottages are quite prepared to pay the high price demanded by thatchers.

The Marginal Cost Curve Is Not a Supply Curve for the Monopolist

We observed in the previous chapter that in the short run the part of the perfectly competitive firm's marginal cost curve MC that lies above its average variable cost curve AVC constitutes its supply curve. That is, at each possible price above the minimum point of the AVC curve, the MC curve tells us the quantity of output that the perfectly competitive firm is willing to produce. A supply curve is a unique relationship between price and output. At any given price there is one, and only one, quantity of output that the firm is willing to supply. Conversely, at any given output level, there is one and only one price that makes the firm willing to supply that output level.

In the case of a monopolist, or any other firm that faces a downward-sloping demand curve, there is no such unique relationship between price and quantity. This is illustrated in Figure 24.4. Suppose the demand curve is D_1, with the associated marginal revenue curve MR_1. The intersection of the MC curve and the MR_1 curve dictates that in order to maximise

FIGURE 24.3
Monopoly Equilibrium Without Economic Profit

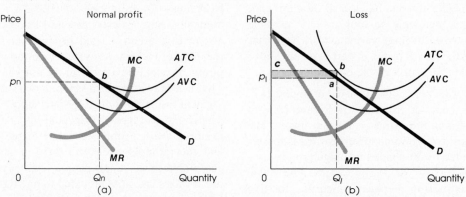

The monopolist in part a is earning a normal profit — a zero economic profit. Producing the output Q_n where marginal cost equals marginal revenue, total revenue, represented by the rectangular area OQ_nbp_n, is just equal to total cost. The equilibrium price p_n is just equal to total cost per unit, including a normal profit, since the demand curve D is just tangent (point b) to the ATC curve at that price.

The monopolist in part b is operating at a loss — a negative economic profit. The intersection of the MC and MR curves dictates the production of Q_l units of output to be sold at the price p_1. This is a loss-minimising position, with the total loss represented by the shaded rectangle. Given that the demand curve D lies below the ATC curve at all output levels, this is the best the monopolist can do. Even though there is a per unit loss equal to ab, the monopolist is willing to operate at this position in the short run because the price p_1 is above the AVC curve — average variable cost is more than covered.

profit the monopolist should produce the output level Q and sell it at the price p_1. If the demand curve were D_2, with the associated marginal revenue MR_2, the intersection of MC and MR_2 would still occur at the same place as that of MC and MR_1. The same quantity Q of output would be produced, but it would be sold at the lower price p_2. Obviously it is possible for the same level of output to be sold at different prices, depending on the shape of the demand curve.

In fact, it is possible to construct an unlimited number of demand curves, each with an associated MR curve that intersects the same point on the MC curve. Hence, there are an unlimited number of prices at which a given level of output may be sold, depending on which demand curve actually prevails.

It is also true that at any given price it is possible for there to be an unlimited number of equilibrium output levels. You can convince yourself of this by constructing a graph. Plot two different demand curves shaped so that their associated MR curves intersect a given MC curve at two different points, so that each dictates a different output level to be sold at the same price.

CHECKPOINT 24.4
How would an increase in fixed costs affect the equilibrium price and output levels in Figure 24.3? How would such an increase affect economic profit? If the monopolist had to pay a licence fee to the state to operate and the fee were doubled, how would that affect the

FIGURE 24.4
A Firm with a Downward-Sloping Demand Curve Has No Unique Supply Curve

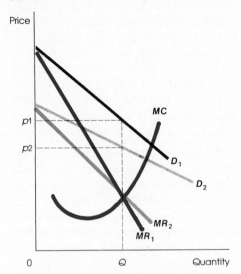

Two possible demand curves, D_1 and D_2, shaped such that their associated MR curves, MR_1 and MR_2, intersect the firm's MC curve at the same point, are shown here. If the prevailing demand curve is D_1, the profit-maximising firm will produce the output Q and sell it at price p_1. However, if the prevailing demand curve is D_2, the profit-maximising firm will produce the same output but sell it at the lower price p_2. It is possible for an unlimited number of such demand curves with associated MR curves to intersect the MC curve at the same point. Hence, a given output level may be sold at an unlimited number of possible prices, depending on the shape of the particular demand curve.

You should sketch two different demand curves and their associated MR curves in such a way as to convince yourself that it is also true that there are an unlimited number of possible output levels that may be sold at the same price.

short-run equilibrium price and output combination of the monopolist? Suppose that, without a decrease in costs, a monopolist is observed to produce and sell a certain output level at a lower price than previously was charged.

What would you say to someone who claims that the monopolist must no longer be acting as a profit maximiser? Suppose the government imposes a price ceiling on a monopolist's product. How might this affect output?

IS MONOPOLY UNDESIRABLE?

So far we have examined the conditions that produce monopoly and monopoly power. We have also discussed the principles a monopolist who wishes to maximise profits will follow when determining what to charge or deciding how much to produce. This section turns to a crucial question. Is monopoly an undesirable market form? How does it compare with perfect competition?

In our study of perfect competition in the previous chapter, we focused on certain questions that are relevant to any market structure. How efficiently does it allocate resources? What sort of incentives does it provide for innovation and technological change? What implications does it have for income distribution? All these questions can be asked about monopoly as well. Since, as we noted in the previous chapter, perfect competition is regarded as a useful standard for market structure, it will be helpful to compare the answers for monopoly with those for perfect competition.

Throughout this section we are going to take it for granted that the monopolist behaves like the textbook monopolist described in this chapter. The firm has monopoly power and sets its price, or determines its output to maximise profits. It equates marginal cost with marginal revenue. The outcome of this behaviour compared with the outcome of perfect competition depends to a large extent on the underlying reasons why the monopoly exists. In addition, in comparing the effects of monopoly and competition it is necessary to make a distinction between the immediate effects and the longer term dynamic effects on the industry. These will be considered separately.

Resource Allocation

Imagine a competitive industry becomes a monopoly overnight. The commonest ways in which this happens is if a marketing board takes over the selling of an agricultural product, or if there is an agreement between the firms in an industry to form a cartel. The Organisation of Petroleum Exporting Countries (OPEC) did just that in 1973. The effects of such an action are shown in Figure 24.5. Part a of Figure 24.5 represents a perfectly competitive industry. Part b, the lower diagram, is the same industry after the firms have reached agreement to act as a monopolist. In both parts the demand is identical and shown by the line D. In part a, the supply surve S is the sum of the marginal cost curves of the individual firms. Also in part a of Figure 24.5 the equilibrium price p_c and market-clearing output Q_c are determined by the intersection of the demand and supply curves. In part b the marginal cost curve MC is identical to the supply curve in part a. It still represents the marginal cost curves of the firms that have come together to form the monopoly. The crucial difference between monopoly and competition lies in the fact that the monopolist is a price maker. It has a marginal revenue curve and it can set marginal revenue equal to price. The result can be seen at a glance. The monopoly price is p_m compared with p_c under perfect competition. The monop-

olist's output is Q_m compared with Q_c under perfect competition. *We see therefore that, under these conditions, when the industry is a monopoly, consumers pay a higher price for the product and receive less of it than under perfect competition.* The words *under these conditions* have been included above to sound a warning about taking it for granted that monopoly will always lead to a higher price and a lower output than competition. Often it does, but not always, as we shall see later.

But first, why do economists regard the outcome of a higher price and lower output, that can often come from monopoly, as undesirable? Economists say there is an inefficient allocation of resources where there are consumers who are willing to pay a price that covers the marginal cost of producing more of the good, but who will not be able to have more at those prices. Under perfect competition, output is produced up to that point, Q_c, where the price, p_c, paid for the last unit produced is just equal to the cost of producing that last unit. In other words, price per unit is equal to marginal cost. *In a perfectly competitive market, each and every consumer who is willing to pay a price sufficient to cover the marginal cost of producing the good will have some of the good.*

By contrast, if the market is organised as a monopoly, the portion of the demand curve D over the range Q_m to Q_c lies above the MC curve. Hence, there are consumers who are willing to pay a price for the units of output from Q_m to Q_c that exceeds the marginal cost of producing them, but are unable to do so because the monopolist will not produce and sell them at such a price. *Whenever there is a monopoly, there will be consumers who are willing to pay a price that equals the marginal cost of producing the good but who will*

FIGURE 24.5
Effect of Monopolising a Competitive Industry

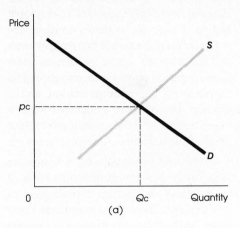

(a)

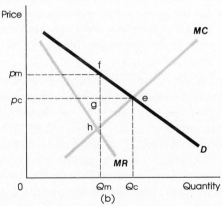

(b)

The supply curve *S* and demand curve *D* for a perfectly competitive industry are shown in part a. They determine an equilibrium price *pc* and quantity *Qc*.

In part b it is assumed that a single firm takes over all the firms in the competitive industry of part a without affecting costs and becomes a monopoly. The *MC* curve of the monopolist of part b is therefore the same as the supply curve *S* of part a. The profit-maximising monopolist uses the *MR* curve associated with *D*, together with the *MC* curve, to decide to produce the lower output *Qm* to be sold at the higher price *pm*.

Under perfect competition, every consumer who is willing to pay a price that covers the marginal cost of producing the good will have some of it. If the market is monopolised, the part of the demand curve over the range from *Qm* to *Qc* will lie above the *MC* curve. Thus, there will be consumers willing to pay a price that covers the marginal cost of producing the good who will not be able to get any at that price.

not be able to have any of the good at that price.

By looking at Figure 24.5 you can also see the effects on consumers and the producers using the measures, consumers and producers surplus. Part b shows there has been a clear net loss in consumers' surplus as a result of the monopoly being established. It is the area under the demand curve, *e, f, pm, pc*. The producers' surplus has increased, though the result is not so clear. There is a gain to producers of the area *g, f, pm, pc*, but a loss of the triangle *efh*. They gain from a higher price,

but lose somewhat from selling a smaller quantity. You can see from inspection that the gain outweighs the losses.

We learned in Chapter 21 that a rough measure of net gains or losses could be obtained by adding the effects of a change in producers and consumers surpluses. Again it must be stressed this is a rough measure and that there are difficult problems when it comes to making welfare comparisons between individuals and groups. However, the result of taking into account the net effects on both consumers surplus and producers surplus is a net loss to society equal to the area *efh* in Figure 24.5. The other changes may be regarded as a transfer from consumers to producers.

Market Structure and Industry Cost

The comparison between monopoly and perfect competition was made by considering the effects of many producers deciding to band together overnight to exercise monopoly power. The reasons this example was used was so that we could take it for granted that the formation of the monopoly would have no effects on the cost structure of the industry. Often it does have cost implications and we need to take those into consideration before arriving at final conclusions about the effects of monopoly.

Suppose now we consider the effects of the firms in an industry combining to form a single firm. It may well be that certain kinds of organisational and technological efficiencies are realised. If so, the monopolist's MC curve in part b of Figure 24.5 will not be the same as the perfectly competitive industry supply curve S in part a.

This is illustrated in Figure 24.6. When the industry is perfectly competitive, equilibrium price p_c and quantity Q_c are determined by the intersection of the industry supply curve S and the industry demand curve D. Suppose that when all the perfectly competitive firms are combined together to form a monopoly, the increased efficiencies of operation result in a lowering of the per unit costs of production. Hence, the monopolist's marginal cost curve MC lies below the perfectly competitive industry's supply curve S. If the per unit cost reductions resulting from monopolisation of the industry are great enough, the monopo-

list's equilibrium price p_m may be lower than p_c and its equilibrium output Q_m greater than Q_c (corresponding to the intersection of MC and MR), as shown in Figure 24.6. If, on the other hand, the per unit cost reduction is not great enough to cause the MC curve to intersect MR to the right of point b, corresponding to output level Q_c, monopolisation of the industry will result in a higher price and lower output level than would exist under perfect competition.

Given that monopolising the industry may lower per unit production costs, it is entirely possible that consumers may be able to purchase more output at a lower price (as in Figure 24.6) than is the case when the industry is perfectly competitive. This is a question that can only be answered by examining the facts for a particular industry.

Where a monopolist does enjoy substantial cost advantages over competitive firms this can often be attributed to economies of scale. We identified scale economies earlier as the condition that could lead to a firm gaining monopoly power through natural monopoly. This also then raises the critical question, is natural monopoly desirable? It can be answered in part with reference to Figure 24.6. We will suppose that although S represents the short run industry supply curve if many firms existed, powerful scale economies have resulted in one firm becoming entrenched with the short run marginal cost curve MC. As we saw above consumers do get a better deal under monopoly than under competition. They get a lower price. They get a larger quantity. Can we conclude natural monopoly is desirable? Not quite! While it is true consumers are better off than under competition they, and society, could be still better off if a system could be devised that achieved the cost advantages of the monopoly without allowing the monopolist to exercise monopoly power. The most efficient solution would be for the price under monopoly to be $p_{c'}$ and the output $Q_{c'}$. Unfortunately there is no incentive for the natural monopolist, or indeed any monopolist to produce at the point where the marginal cost curve and the demand curve intersect. And this, as we shall see later, is one of the strong arguments for *allowing natural monopolies to exist, but regulating them in the public interest*. It explains why many natural monopolies are public utilities in Australia.

CHECKPOINT 24.5

Study Figure 24.6 carefully and reproduce it. Mark on the diagram the changes to consumer and producer surplus that would occur if the price was established at $p_{c'}$ instead of p_m. What is the net effect of the changes? Why would the monopolist not lower the price to $p_{c'}$ voluntarily?

Incentives for Innovation

In the previous chapter we saw that a perfectly competitive firm must use the most efficient available technology to compete effectively with the multitude of other firms in the industry. But using the best *available* technology is not the same thing as product innovation and development of new, more efficient production techniques. The incentive for a perfectly competitive firm to innovate is small because the prospect of reaping above-normal profits from such activity for any length of time is slight. Firms in the industry can all too readily adopt the innovations of others, thereby quickly eliminating any competitive advantage

otherwise realised by the innovating firm. As evidence that perfect competition does not promote innovation, it might be said that much agricultural research in Australia is carried out by state departments of agriculture and the agricultural departments of universities and colleges. Industry bodies such as the Australian Meat and Livestock Corporation provide research funds. Others involved in research include the chemical industry and the farm machinery industry. Relatively little seems to be initiated by the multitude of farms that make agriculture so closely resemble perfect competition.

For a monopoly, the situation would seem to be almost the reverse. Since there are no competing firms in the industry, the monopolist, unlike the competitive firm, is not forced by the existence of many rivals to use the most efficient available technology. This is not to say that it isn't in the monopolist's best interest to do so — lower costs mean larger monopoly profits. As well for the more dynamic activity of product innovation and the development of new production techniques there would seem to be just the incentive for the monopolist that is lacking for the perfectly competitive firm — the prospect of above-normal profit for a prolonged, possibly indefinite period of time. In addition, the existence of such profit provides the monopolist with a source of funds to finance technological change and product innovation, a source unavailable to the perfectly competitive firm.

It is sometimes argued, however, that because the monopolist doesn't face the strong competitive threat of rival firms, there is a tendency to stand pat and simply reap the profits from the existing situation. In fact, it has been argued that it is in a monopolist's best interest to protect the existing monopoly situation from the threat of new products and technological change introduced by potential rivals. Therefore, the monopolist may buy up and stockpile patents, effectively putting a stop to technological changes and product innovation.

In sum, there is a wide variety of opinion on the pros and cons of monopoly as a market structure that either promotes or inhibits the advancement of product change and production technology. The thrust of public policy, at least that of competition policy, leans toward the view that monopoly most likely inhibits innovation.

Income Distribution

Most economists believe that the existence of unregulated, profit-maximising monopoly contributes to income inequality. In long-run equilibrium under perfect competition a great many firms earn a normal profit and the payments to productive factors, including labour, are just sufficient to cover their opportunity costs. By contrast, monopoly gives rise to a much greater concentration of economic power. Therefore, the potential exists for above-normal, even extraordinary, profit for a prolonged or even indefinite period of time. Hence, the owners of a monopoly are potentially in a position to earn much more than their time and financial capital could earn in the next best alternative use.

If the monopoly is a company, the shareholders reap the above-normal, or monopoly, profits. Some economists argue that since shareholders tend to be from middle- to upper-income brackets to begin with, monopoly profit distributed to stockholders only tends to widen the gap between them and those who belong to lower-income groups.

We hasten to emphasise that the issue of income inequality, and whether a particular income distribution is 'good' or 'bad', typically generates controversy and deeply felt opinions. It is a normative issue and differences of opinion on the subject are rarely settled by an appeal to facts.

REGULATION OF NATURAL MONOPOLY: PUBLIC UTILITIES

We have already pointed out that where natural monopolies exist, public policy has sought to ensure that the consumer benefits from the low per unit costs of production by regulating the price the monopolist can charge. This has resulted in the creation of public utilities. Public utilities are regulated natural monopolies that provide such products as electricity, gas, telephone service, water and sewage treatment, and certain kinds of transportation. How in principle should regulators decide what price a public utility should be allowed to charge?

Difficulty with Marginal Cost Pricing

The picture of the natural monopoly presented in Figure 24.6 left out the monopolist's average cost curve and in so doing ignored a complicating feature of the analysis. This defect must now be remedied. The cost and demand curves for a natural monopoly are depicted in Figure 24.7. The firm's average total cost curve ATC and its marginal cost curve MC fall throughout the range of output covered by the market demand curve D. Of course, as long as the ATC curve is falling, the MC curve must lie below it. (If you can't remember why, reread the

POLICY PERSPECTIVE

Bass Strait Shipping

In 1987 the three shipping companies running freight services across Bass Strait from the Australian mainland to Tasmania applied to the Trade Practices Commission for authorisation to establish a Joint Venture for the provision of joint coastal shipping services. The three companies were the Australian Shipping Commission, Union Steamship Company of Australia Pty Ltd and William Hollyman and Sons Pty Ltd. Under the proposal the three companies planned to set common freight rates and pool revenue and expenses on an agreed basis. They argued that the Bass Strait trade had become extremely volatile with increased competition coming from two new carriers, Brambles Ltd and the TT Line operated by Transport Tasmania. The three companies claimed that the proposed arrangement would make their service more efficient and cost effective. Subsequently they argued that if it were considered by the Commission to be anti-competitive it had sufficient benefits for the public to outweigh any adverse effects of a reduction in competition.

In its draft determination the Trade Practices Commission found that the proposed arrangement would indeed substantially lessen competition. While it accepted there were efficiency gains from the proposed arrangement it did not accept that they were sufficiently great 'to tip the balance in favour of authorisation'. In coming to this preliminary conclusion the Commission noted the independent operators Brambles and TT Line were comparatively small, could not offer the same range of services as the proposed Joint Venture and that a clause in the proposed agreement made it possible for the other operators to join the three companies in the Joint Venture.

Questions

1. Whether an agreement between firms is likely to produce a reduction in the competitive conditions in a market will depend on how the market is defined and what constitutes competition. Suppose you were appointed by the three companies to argue that competition would continue after the arrangement came into operation. How would you define the market in which you were operating and how would you argue that competition would not be diminished?

2. Suppose instead you work for the Trade Practices Commission. Draw a demand and supply diagram that explains your conclusions. The agreement would reduce costs, but would nevertheless not be in the public consumers' interests.

---

section on marginal and average cost in Chapter 22.)

We have seen before that the most efficient allocation of resources — that which maximises consumer satisfaction — occurs when output is produced up to the point where price equals marginal cost. It is most efficient in the sense that output is produced up to the point where the price paid for the last unit produced just covers the cost of producing it. For the natural monopolist of Figure 24.7, this occurs where the *MC* curve intersects the *D* curve at point b to determine the price *pc* and output level *Qc*.

This is a much larger output and lower price than the monopolist would choose if left unregulated and allowed to max-imise profit. The unregulated, profit-maximising monopolist would produce the amount *Qm* to be sold at a price *pm* as determined by the intersection of the *MC* and *MR* curves. Monopoly profit would equal the rectangular area *efgh*. However, if regulators force the monop-olist to produce the amount *Qc* to be sold at the price *pc*, the monopolist will operate at a loss because the average total cost per unit of output sold will be greater than the price per unit sold by the amount *bc*. The total loss incurred by the monopolist is represented by the rectangle *abcd*. If regulators insist on a marginal-cost-equals-price solution, it will be necessary to somehow subsidise, or pay the monop-olist back, by this amount. Otherwise, the firm will go out of business.

Average Cost Pricing

Although economists argue strongly on efficiency grounds for governments and commissions that run public utilities to follow the marginal cost pricing rule they are seldom successful. More often they follow the **average cost pricing rule**. This practice of seeking a **fair return** to the enterprise is something of a compromise between the profit-maximising price-output combination chosen by the unreg-ulated monopolist and the marginal-cost-equals-price solution. It is a compromise in the sense that the resulting price and output levels under a fair-return solution will lie somewhere between these two extremes. Hence, the consumer still realises benefits from the lower per unit

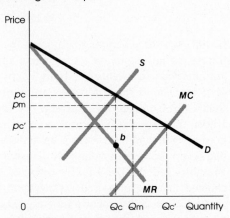

FIGURE 24.6
Monopolisation May Lead to Lower Price and Higher Output

It is possible that monopolisation of a per-fectly competitive industry will lower per unit costs of production.

The perfectly competitive industry's supply curve *S* and demand curve *D* determine equilibrium output *Qc* and price *pc*. If mono-polisation of the industry results in a suffi-ciently large reduction in per unit production costs, the monopolist's marginal cost curve may assume a position such as *MC*. Given *MC* and the marginal revenue curve *MR*, the monopolist in this case will charge a lower price, *pm* and produce a larger output, *Qm* than occurs when the industry is perfectly competitive.

Note, however, that with lower per unit costs, it is still possible to improve on the profit-maximising monopolist's price and output combination. A price-equals-marginal-cost solution would provide consumers with the yet lower price *pc'* and greater output *Qc'*.

costs resulting from the economies of scale of the natural monopoly, while the monopolist is allowed to charge a price sufficient to cover all costs of production including a normal profit, or a fair return on capital.

The fair-return or average cost pricing solution is given by the intersection of the *ATC* curve with the demand curve *D*. In Figure 24.7, this determines that the output

FIGURE 24.7
Fair-Return and Marginal Cost Pricing for a Public Utility

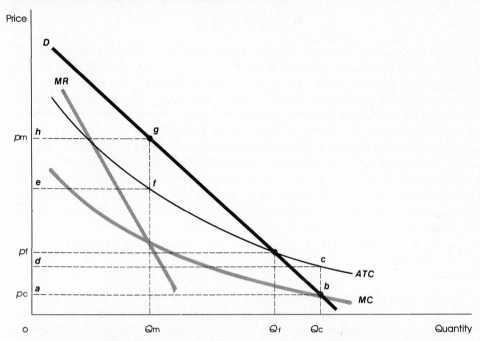

A natural monopoly has continuously declining *ATC* and *MC* curves over the entire range of output covered by the market demand curve *D*. In the absence of any regulatory constraints, the profit-maximising monopolist would produce an output Q_m and sell it at a price p_m as determined by the intersection of the *MC* and *MR* curves.

If the natural monopoly is turned into a public utility, its price and output policy is subject to regulation by a utility commission. If the commission enforces a marginal-cost-equals-price rule, the utility will have to produce an output Q_c *to be sold at a price p_f* as determined by the intersection of the *MC* and *D* curves at point *b*. However, in that case the monopolist will operate at a loss represented by the rectangle *abcd*. The monopolist will go out of business unless this loss is made up for by a government subsidy.

If the commission enforces a fair-return or average cost pricing rule, the utility will produce an output Q_f to be sold at a price p_f as determined by the intersection of the *ATC* and *D* curves. In this case, the monopolist will receive a price just sufficient to cover all costs, including a normal profit. In this sense, the monopolist earns a fair return on capital.

Q_f will be produced and sold at the price p_f. The price p_f received for each unit sold is just sufficient to cover the average total cost per unit, including a normal profit, or fair return on capital. (Remember that a normal profit is included in the average total cost curve.)

Recall that in long-run competitive equilibrium, price also equals average total cost. While the average cost pricing solution is similar to the perfectly competitive outcome in this respect, it differs in that price does not equal marginal cost as in perfect competition. As a result, there will still be consumers who would be willing to pay a price that is greater than marginal cost for additional units of output, but these units will not be

---

POLICY PERSPECTIVE

The Egg Industry

Egg production is one economic activity where there are substantial economies of scale. Of course a backyard producer who fails to take account of their own labour, who produces eggs as a hobby will also be able to compete. But apart from this, large battery chook farms seem to have big cost advantages over small and medium commercial egg producers. In some Australian states the government has regulated the egg marketing industry partly to provide price and income stability for producers, but partly to protect small and medium egg producers from the very large producers. The form this regulation may take, for example, is to require anyone with more than say 24 laying hens to have a licence, to place a quota on the number of hens a producer may own and also to set the price of eggs with reference to costs of production. Producers may sell their licences and the quotas that go with them, but must first obtain the permission of the regulatory authority (the Egg Board) to prevent large producers buying up the small producers.

Questions

1. Suppose an Egg Board estimates production costs and discovers each producer has indeed a falling long-run average cost curve. Suppose also it issues 1000 licences, sets production quotas and egg prices so that all eggs are sold and the producers all make normal profits. Reproduce the situation on a diagram.

2. Suppose the Egg Board decides on a modest amount of deregulation. It agrees to allow licences to be bought and sold freely, but not to change either total output or the price of eggs. What will happen?

3. Suppose, instead, the government abolishes the Egg Board. What effect will this have on the industry?

---

produced. This is represented in Figure 24.7 by the fact that the demand curve D lies above the MC curve over the range of output from Q_f to Q_c.

MONOPOLY AND PRICE DISCRIMINATION

We have seen why a monopolist may be able to earn more than normal profit. Under certain conditions a monopolist may be able to practise price discrimina-tion and thereby realise even greater profit. **Price discrimination** *is possible whenever the same good or service can be sold at different prices for reasons not associated with cost.* We should emphasise that price discrimination can also be practised by firms that are not monop-olists. However, a monopoly firm is often in a better position to engage in price discrimination by virtue of the fact that it is the only supplier of a particular product.

Price discrimination is fairly common

in our economy. For example, airlines and movie theatres charge different prices for children and adults, doctors often charge different patients different fees for the same kind of operation, and utility companies charge different rates for businesses and residences. Why? Because it is more profitable to do so. Let's explore some of the reasons as well as the conditions that make price discrimination possible.

The Ingredients for Price Discrimination

The following conditions contribute to a firm's opportunities to engage in price discrimination.

1. *Resale not possible.* The firm must be able to prevent one buyer from selling any of its product to another buyer, or the nature of the firm's product must be such that it is not resalable. For example, it would be almost impossible to charge different prices for bread to different customers. Imagine the grocer charging Jones $1 per loaf and Smith $.75 per loaf. Then Jones could simply have Smith buy enough bread for both of them at $.75 per loaf. However, if a doctor charges Jones more than Smith for an appendectomy, there is nothing Jones can do about it. Jones cannot buy Smith's appendix operation. Obviously, whether a good can be sold from one buyer to another depends on the nature of the good. Services typically cannot be resold. I cannot buy your haircut and you cannot buy my dental work.

2. *Segmentation of the market.* It must be possible for the firm to segment the market by classifying buyers into separate, identifiable groups. For instance, it is relatively easy to charge one price for adults and another for children. Similarly, Telecom is able to charge different rates for phone calls during peak period business hours, after hours and at weekends. Airlines charge different fares and segment their markets to appeal to businessmen, tourists and groups. often a monopolist can charge a different price in different states, or different countries. Sometimes it is possible to segment a market by charging a different rate according to how many units of the good or service are sold. A multi-storey car park may charge 40 cents an hour for the first three hours and perhaps 60 cents an hour for each subsequent hour. Alternatively the rate may fall.

3. *Monopoly control.* If there is only one supplier of a good or service, it is easier for that supplier to engage in price discrimination. Buyers charged discriminatory prices by the monopolist cannot turn to an alternative supplier who might sell to them at a lower price.

4. *Differing demand elasticities.* Different buyers have different degrees of willingness to buy a good. Since people are usually as unique in their tastes and preferences for goods as they are in their fingerprints, the shapes of their individual demand curves for a particular good are typically different. Assume individual A's demand curve for a good is inelastic and individual B's demand curve is elastic. From our discussion of elasticity (Chapter 20), we know that we will get more sales revenue from A by charging A a high price and more sales revenue from B by charging B a low price. Assuming the good cannot be resold, it clearly pays to charge A and B different prices for the good — to price discriminate between them. Wherever a market can be segmented according to differing demand elasticities, price discrimination will generate larger total sales revenue than if the good is sold at the same price to all.

FIGURE 24.8
A Price-Discriminating Monopolist

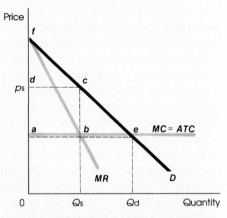

The monopolist depicted here is assumed to have constant marginal cost *MC* equal to average total cost *ATC*. If the monopolist charges the same price for all units sold profits are maximised by producing *Qs* and selling it at the price *ps* as determined by the intersection of the *MC* and *MR* curves at point *b*. Monopoly profit is then the rectangular area *abcd*.

If the monopolist is able to price discriminate by charging the maximum price buyers are willing to pay for each additional unit sold the demand curve *D* is also the marginal revenue curve. The monopolist would then maximise profit by producing the output *Qd*, determined by the intersection of the *MC* and *D* curve at point *e*. The monopolist's profit is then the triangular area *aef*, which is clearly larger than the rectangle *abcd*.

A Price-Discrimination Monopolist: Maximising Profit

Assume that a firm is a monopolist, is able to identify different buyers according to the price they are willing to pay for its product, and is able to prevent resale of its product.

Examination of the monopolist's downward-sloping demand curve suggests that more profit can be made if the monopolist is able to charge each buyer the full amount he or she is willing to pay, rather than charging all buyers the same price. To see why, in the simplest way, suppose the monopolist has a constant marginal cost equal to average total cost. That is, the $MC = ATC$ curve is represented by a horizontal line as shown in Figure 24.8. Now if the monopolist charges a single price for all output produced, that profit-maximising price would be p_s and the quantity sold Q_s, as determined by the intersection of the MR and MC curves at point b. The monopoly profit is thus represented by the rectangular area *abcd*.

Alternatively, suppose that the monopolist is able to charge each buyer of the good the maximum price that each is willing to pay for the good. That is, assume that all the conditions necessary for price discrimination, as discussed before, are satisfied. The maximum price that each and every buyer is willing to pay for the good is therefore represented by all the points on the demand curve D. For example, if the monopolist charges the single price p_s, all the buyers represented by the demand curve over the range from f to c are getting the good at a price below that which they would be willing to pay for it (except for the last unit sold at point c). If instead the monopolist were to charge each and every buyer just what each is willing to pay for the good, the monopolist would make the added profit represented by the area *dcf*.

Carrying this further, if the monopolist charges for each additional unit sold the maximum price that buyers are willing to pay, the addition to total revenue will always be equal to the price received for the last unit. There now will be no offsetting reduction in total revenue as before when charging a single price for all units, which requires reducing the price on all previous units in order to sell an additional unit. Thus, selling each unit for the maximum price buyers are willing to pay means that the demand curve D will also be the marginal revenue curve MR. The monopolist will therefore expand output to Q_d, the point where the MC curve intersects the demand curve D at point e — the point at which marginal cost equals marginal revenue. The total profit is now represented by the triangular area aef. This is clearly larger than the rectangle $abcd$, the profit earned when the monopolist does not discriminate but rather charges the same price p, for all units sold.

If Telecom were not subject to public regulation it is conceivable that it could take price discrimination to the ultimate and practise perfect price discrimination. It could behave like the monopolist in Figure 24.8. How? By studying each customer's pattern of use it could get a pretty good idea of how much each would be prepared to pay for phone calls. Substitutes are hard to come by. It would be very inconvenient to go next door because their charge was cheaper, particularly if 'next door' is five miles down the road.

CHECKPOINT 24.6
Suppose all buyers have identical demand curves for a good that is not resaleable. If you are the monopoly producer of the good, would it pay to price discriminate? Why or why not?

SUMMARY

1. Monopoly is a form of market structure where there is a single producer or seller of a good for which there are no close substitutes.

2. For a firm to have monopoly power there must be large, in effect insurmountable, barriers to competition from potential firms seeking entry to the industry. Such barriers may take a number of different forms, such as exclusive ownership of a unique resource; economies of scale possibly even large enough to create a natural monopoly; and government-sanctioned protection in the form of patents, licences, copyrights, and franchises. Restrictive trade practices also give firms monopoly power and can also create barriers to entry. No barrier, with the possible exception of those that are government sanctioned, is as insurmountable in the long run as it is in the short run.

3. The monopolist's demand curve slopes downward and lies above the marginal revenue curve, unlike that of a perfectly competitive firm, whose demand curve is horizontal and the same as the marginal revenue curve. The profit-maximising monopolist produces that output and sells at that price at which marginal cost equals marginal revenue. This does not mean that the monopolist always makes an above-normal or positive economic profit, however. If costs are high enough or demand falls, a monopolist may even operate at a loss in the short run. Unlike a perfectly competitive firm, the monopolist's marginal cost curve is not always identical with its supply curve.

4. Compared to a perfectly competitive firm with the same costs, a monopolist will always produce less and sell at a higher price.

5. Because an unregulated monopolist's profit-maximising price always lies above marginal cost, there are always consumers who are willing to buy additional units at a price greater than the marginal cost of producing them. However, because the monopolist restricts output, these consumers cannot have these additional units. Compared to a perfectly competitive market, where demand is satisfied for all who are willing to pay a price that covers marginal cost, monopoly results in an inefficient allocation of resources.

6. While many economists agree that monopoly tends to contribute to income inequality, there is far less agreement on whether it promotes or inhibits product innovation and technological advancement. Some argue that the existence or potential of large profit, protected by barriers to competition, provides a great incentive to innovation and the use of improved production methods. Others argue that barriers to competition and the consequent lack of rivals causes the monopolist to be lethargic and disposed to preserve the status quo.

7. Where natural monopolies exist, as in the provision of utility services, franchises are often granted to monopolists in exchange for submitting to public regulation, thereby creating a public utility. Either marginal cost pricing or average cost pricing (fair-return) regulations may then be imposed on the utility in order to pass the low per unit cost benefits on to consumers.

8. Where a monopolist can conveniently classify buyers and effectively prevent resale of output, it is possible to price discriminate by selling a good or service at different prices to different buyers. Because different buyers almost always exhibit different degrees of willingness to buy a product, price discrimination is usually more profitable than selling the product at the same price to all.

KEY TERMS AND CONCEPTS

average cost pricing
barrier to competition
cartel
copyright
fair return
marginal cost pricing
monopoly
monopoly power
natural monopoly
patent
price discrimination
public utility
rate base

QUESTIONS AND PROBLEMS

1. What is the nature and source of monopoly power in each of the following cases: the Australian Medical Association, Apple Computers, the Sydney Harbour Bridge, James Bond, the Victorian Dairy Authority, Greg Norman, Wrigley's chewing gum?

2. It is often said that in a spectrum of competitive characteristics, monopoly and perfect competition are the extreme opposites. Arrange the following industries according to where you feel they fall on that spectrum: electrical appliance manufacturers, automobile manufacturers, electric power production, dry cleaners, airlines, taxicab services, automotive repair services, film theatres, steel production, newspapers, canned goods, and professional football.

3. If you were a monopolist, in what portion of your demand curve would you set price — the elastic or the inelastic? Why?

4. If we observed a monopolist who always set price at that point on the demand curve where the elasticity is 1, what might we conclude about the monopolist's variable costs? If this monopolist's fixed costs were cut in half, how would this be reflected in the monopolist's price and output behaviour?

5. Is normal profit part of monopoly profit?

6. Suppose the government levies a tax on a monopolist equal to 50 per cent of all profit in excess of normal profit. How would this affect the profit-maximising monopolist's choice of price and output combination? Why? How would the price and output combination be affected if such a tax were increased to 75 per cent?

7. If all of a monopolist's profit in excess of normal profit were taxed away, would it improve the monopolist's performance as an allocator of resources? Why or why not? Do you think such a tax could be used to reduce income inequality? How?

8. Suppose a natural monopoly is regulated by a government appointed commission which follows average-cost pricing policies. However, it then finds it difficult to keep costs down.
a. Show how this problem would be reflected in the natural monopoly's average and marginal cost curves over time.
b. In view of your answer to part a, at which point might it be wiser to drop enforcement of average cost pricing?

Instead you would simply allow the utility to set price like a profit-maximising monopolist, and then tax away the monopoly profit, redistributing it to consumers in proportion to the quantity each buys from the utility? Demonstrate your answer graphically.

9. For each of the following goods or services, tell why you think price discrimination is or is not possible and why: motel accommodation, wedding dresses, haircuts, taxi fares, doctors' consultations, new cars, antiques, Sony television sets.

10. Suppose a monopolist is told by a marketing consultant that price discrimination is possible for his product, but that to achieve it he will need to spend a large sum of money on an advertising campaign. How might the monopolist go about deciding whether price discrimination was worthwhile? Draw a diagram to show the effect of implementing such a campaign on his output and his profits compared with selling to a single market at a monopoly price.

11. Ansett and Australian Airlines both charge different air fares for First or Business Class, Economy Class, and Standy-By passengers. What differences would you expect there to be in the elasticity of demand for each type of fare? What methods do the airlines use to segment their market?

25

Monopolistic Competition and Product Differentiation

AFTER READING THIS CHAPTER YOU WILL BE ABLE TO:

1. Define the characteristics of a monopolistically competitive market.

2. Demonstrate how a monopolistically competitive industry adjusts in the long run to eliminate short-run profits or losses.

3. Discuss the efficiency of resource allocation under monopolistic competition as compared to perfect competition and understand the significance of product differentiation for this comparison.

4. Explain the role of nonprice competition in the form of advertising and the economic arguments for and against it.

5. Evaluate the incentives for innovation and technological change under monopolistic competition.

In the last two chapters we have examined two types of market behaviour. The first, in Chapter 23, was where the firms were price takers. The second, in Chapter 24, was of price makers who had monopoly power. In this chapter we are concerned with an intermediate type of behaviour — where non-price competition is crucial. Monopolistic competition is the name given to the market form that best fits this type of behaviour.

A monopolistically competitive industry is one in which there are many firms, as in perfect competition, but each of them produces a product that is slightly different from that produced by its competitors. Some of the best examples of monopolistic competition are found not in industries that produce goods, but in those that supply services. Examples include all sorts of shops: milk bars, pharmacies, restaurants, pubs and service stations. On a spectrum of types of industry structure with perfect competition at one extreme and monopoly at the other, monopolistic competition may be thought of as the one that comes closest to perfect competition. As in the previous two chapters we are mainly concerned with explaining the behaviour and the business policies of firms that fall into this category. As we shall see, the distinguishing feature is that they have only limited scope to engage in price making and need to find nonprice means of increasing their profits.

CHARACTERISTICS OF MONOPOLISTIC COMPETITION

Four general characteristics distinguish **monopolistic competition** from other forms of market structure: (1) there are a very large number of firms; (2) each firm's product is slightly different from the others in the industry, so that each firm has a slightly downward-sloping demand curve; (3) there is freedom of entry to and exit from the industry; and (4) the firms engage in nonprice competition.

1. *Large number of firms.* The number of firms that make up a monopolistically competitive industry may be about the same as that in a perfectly competitive industry. As a result, none of them is large enough to dominate the market. In the Hong Kong clothing industry there are countless firms making shirts and dresses. No firm could possibly dominate the market or be large and powerful enough to set its prices for basic lines in a way that a firm with effective monopoly power can, there are too many other firms looking for the consumer's dollar. The competition is just too fierce. While a large number of firms is one of the main characteristic features of monopolistic competition you should not think that the existence of a very large number of firms is essential for firms to behave as monopolistic competitors. What is essential is that there are enough firms for there to be strong competition between the firms. Each firm is so small that it has a small share of the total market and that changes in its output have no noticeable effect on the sales of other firms in the industry.

2. *Product differentiation.* The second important feature of a monopolistically competitive market is that the firms do not produce identical products. One firm's product or service differs from that of its rivals. The variation may lie in the type of service that is offered in the case of retail stores, or in quality or packaging in the case of a tangible product. The distinction may be created and preserved by the firm 'branding' its products. It

promotes its name, or the name of the product so that consumers recognise the brand and develop brand loyalty. Trade marks are another device that firms use to differentiate their products. A perfectly competitive firm's product will be identical to products of other firms in the industry as we saw in Chapter 23. The demand for the firm's product is perfectly elastic. At the other extreme we defined a monopolist as a firm that was the sole producer of a good or service for which there are no close substitutes. The monopolistic competitor faces competition from *close but not perfect substitutes*. Demand for the individual firm's product is highly elastic, but not perfectly elastic.

The implications of this are so important that it needs further explanation. If the firms produced exactly the same product, the relatively large number of firms would ensure that the demand curve was a horizontal straight line. Because they produce differentiated products, the firm's demand curve slopes downwards. Why is this so? Consider the likely reaction of consumers to the business decisions of first, a perfectly competitive firm, and second, a monopolistically competitive firm. We know the competitive firm has no power to charge anything but the going market price. Charge more — it will sell nothing at all. In monopolistic competition things are different. There is no such thing as the market price, because firms are not selling an identical product. Nevertheless differences in prices between firms will reflect the values consumers have placed on them, which recognise differences in quality, standard of service and so on. Now, if one firm decides to increase its price it is likely to lose sales to its competitors. They provide close substitutes and the word quickly gets round. But, unlike perfect competition,

the firm does not lose all customers. This is because some customers do not see the other firm's products as alternatives even though they are now relatively cheaper. Brand loyalty means the firm keeps some customers. The higher it pushes its price, the more customers it loses.

Suppose, instead, it decided to cut its price. The reverse happens. It gains sales as the word goes round. But again, unlike perfect competition, it cannot sell unlimited quantities at a lower price — or capture the entire market, which is what is implied by a horizontal demand curve. Customers of other firms remain faithful, brand loyalty works against the firm when it is cutting price, just as it worked for it when it raised price. Because demand is highly, but not perfectly, elastic, the demand curve of the monopolistically competitive firm is conventionally shown as sloping gently down from left to right. Remember, in practice you cannot assume anything about elasticity of demand by looking at the negative slope of a demand curve without reference to the scales on the axes. We follow the convention that the gentle slope represents elastic demand here, simply because it would be more misleading not to do so.

Because the monopolistically competitive firm's demand curve is downward sloping, the firm uses the associated marginal revenue curve to select its optimum price and output level in the same fashion as a monopolist. This is the 'monopolistic' aspect of monopolistic competition. 'Competition' results from characteristics 1 and 3.

3. *Freedom of entry and exit.* In a monopolistically competitive industry firms have the same kind of freedom to enter into and exit from the industry as they do in a perfectly competitive industry. We will explore in greater detail how this

characteristic makes for keen competition among firms. For the moment, note that it ensures that in the long run no monopolistically competitive firm is able to make a greater than normal profit. Freedom of entry and exit means that there are no barriers to competition in a monopolistically competitive industry.

4. *Existence of nonprice competition.* Since each firm produces a similar but somewhat different product from every other firm in the industry, there is an incentive for each firm to play up the difference in its product in order to boost its sales. This is known as **nonprice competition** and takes many forms. 'Service with a smile', or, 'If we forget to clean your windshield, you get a full tank free' are common examples. Hairdressing salons may compete with one another by having background music, better magazine selections, and fancy interior decorating. Anything that may serve to distinguish a firm's product from that of its competitors in this way might be tried — so long as the firm feels that the cost of such promotional activity is more than made up for by the resulting increase in sales. Advertising in local newspapers, shoppers' guides, and other media outlets is common. You only have to drive down a typical main street in any suburb or country town to observe fancy signs beckoning you to come in and try this or buy that.

This type of competition is common among monopolistically competitive firms. By contrast, there is no incentive for this activity in a perfectly competitive industry because one firm's product is indistinguishable from any other's.

CHECKPOINT *25.1
Consider the following activities. Which of them have some or all of the four

characteristics of monopolistic competition?
  secondhand car yards
  boutiques
  real estate and rental accommodation
  dressmaking
  hotel and motel accommodation
By way of review, explain why the slope of a demand curve is a reflection of the existence of substitutes.

*Answers to all Checkpoints can be found at the back of the text.

EQUILIBRIUM IN A MONOPOLISTICALLY COMPETITIVE INDUSTRY

Examination of the above characteristics clearly indicates that the most important difference between monopolistic competition and perfect competition is product differentiation. It is this factor that causes the monopolistically competitive firm's demand curve to be slightly downward sloping, and it is this factor that gives rise to nonprice competition.

In terms of the concept of elasticity, the less product differentiation there is between firms in the industry the more elastic will be the individual firm's demand curve. This follows from our earlier study of the determinants of demand. The more a firm's product is similar to that of other firms in the industry, the more willing consumers will be to switch to that firm's product if it lowers its price, and away from that firm's product if it raises its price. Thus the greater the degree of similarity, and therefore substitutability, between a firm's product and those of its competitors, the greater will be the change in its sales resulting from any given change in price.

FIGURE 25.1
Equilibrium for a Monopolistically Competitive Firm

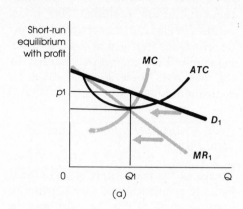

Short-run equilibrium with profit

(a)

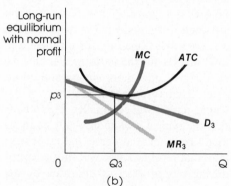

Long-run equilibrium with normal profit

(b)

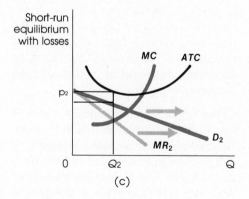

Short-run equilibrium with losses

(c)

The monopolistically competitive firm in part a is in short-run equilibrium, producing output Q_1, and selling it at p_1, as determined by the intersection of the MC and MR curves. It is earning a profit equal to the shaded area. Assuming it is representative of the many firms in the industry, the above-normal profits will attract new firms into the industry in the long run, causing each firm's demand curve to shift leftward. This process will continue until above-normal profits are eliminated and each firm in the industry is in a long-run equilibrium position like that shown in part b.

Alternatively, suppose firms in the industry are realising losses, equal to the shaded area for the representative firm in part c. Some firms will leave the industry, and those that remain will have a larger share of the market, as represented by the rightward shift in each of their demand curves. This process will continue until the remaining firms are just making a normal profit, as represented by the long-run equilibrium position shown in part b.

Since the monopolistically competitive firm is able to affect its level of sales by changing its price, it is in this respect similar to a monopoly. It knows that in

order to sell an additional unit of output it must lower price, not only on the additional unit, but on all previous units as well. Therefore, like the monopolist but unlike the perfect competitor, at any output level price is always greater than marginal revenue for the monopolistically competitive firm. This is reflected in the fact that the monopolistically competitive firm's demand curve lies above its associated marginal revenue curve, just exactly as in the case of the monopolist.

Short-Run Equilibrium

The short-run equilibrium position of a monopolistically competitive firm looks just like that of a monopolist. Of course, the difference is that there are many firms in the monopolistically competitive industry, rather than just one, as in a monopoly.

One such firm is shown in Figure 25.1. Two possible short-run equilibrium positions are shown in parts a and c. Whatever the position of the firm's demand curve and its associated marginal revenue curve, the firm adjusts price and output so that marginal cost equals marginal revenue. This is determined by the intersection of the MC and MR curves (assuming it can cover its average variable costs). In part a, the firm's demand curve D_1 is such that it produces Q_1 to be sold at the price p_1. The resulting profit is represented by the shaded area. In part c, demand for the firm's product is weak, and so the entire demand curve D_2 lies below its ATC curve. Assuming it can cover average variable cost, the best the firm can do is produce Q_2, sell it at the price p_2, and minimise its losses, which are represented by the shaded area.

Adjustment to Long-Run Equilibrium

For a monopolist, part a of Figure 25.1 could represent a long-run equilibrium

position. However, for a monopolistically competitive firm, it can only be a short-run equilibrium position. This is so because, unlike the monopoly situation, there is free entry of new firms into the monopolistically competitive industry in the long run. There are no barriers to competition.

Above-Normal Profits — Entry of New Firms

If each of the many firms in a monopolistically competitive industry is realising above-normal profits like the one in Figure 25.1, part a, new firms will be attracted to the industry in the long run. As more firms open up for business, the total market for the industry will have to be divided up among more and more firms. Therefore, each firm's share of the whole market will get smaller. This means that the typical monopolistically competitive firm's demand curve and associated marginal revenue curve will shift leftward during this process, as indicated by the arrows in part a. New firms will continue to enter the industry as long as above-normal economic profits exist. Hence, the demand curves of firms already in the industry will continue to shift leftward until the above-normal profits of each have been eliminated.

The typical monopolistically competitive firm will finally be in the long-run equilibrium position shown in part b. It will produce output Q_3 and sell it at price p_3 as determined by the intersection of MC and MR_3 The price p_3 will just be equal to the average total cost per unit, as indicated by the fact that the demand curve D_3 will be tangent to the ATC curve at this point. The typical firm's total revenue will just equal its total cost, including a normal profit. There will be no incentive for any new firms to enter the industry.

Why is it that in long-run equilibrium the monopolistically competitive firm's demand curve D_3 is tangent to ATC at just that output level Q_3 where $MC = MR$? Note that for any output level greater than Q_3 the price received per unit would be less than the average total cost per unit, as represented by the fact that the demand curve D_3 lies below the ATC curve. The same is true for any output level less than Q_3. Only at output level Q_3 does price just cover average total cost per unit. Given the demand curve D_3 and associated marginal revenue curve MR_3, the best the firm can do is produce and sell Q_3 at price p_3. (It is best in the sense that it is the only output level where the firm does not realise a loss.) Hence it must be the output level corresponding to the point where marginal cost equals marginal revenue, as represented by the intersection of MC and MR. At any output level greater than Q_3, marginal cost exceeds marginal revenue, represented by the fact that the MC curve lies above the MR curve. Therefore it does not pay for the firm to produce output beyond Q_3. For any output level less than Q_3, marginal revenue exceeds marginal cost — the MC curve lies below the MR curve. Hence, it pays for the firm to expand output up to the level Q_3.

Losses — Exit of Existing Firms

Alternatively, suppose each of the many firms in the monopolistically competitive industry is realising losses, such as the typical firm shown in Figure 25.1, part c. In the long run, if a firm continues to realise losses like this, it will be forced out of business. Therefore, firms will leave the industry. As this process continues, the share of the market left for each of the firms remaining in the industry will grow. Their demand curves and associated marginal revenue curves will shift rightward, as indicated by the arrows in part c. This process will continue until enough firms have left the industry so that those remaining are just able to cover costs, including a normal profit. The industry will then be in long-run equilibrium, with the typical firm again in the equilibrium position depicted in part b.

CHECKPOINT 25.2
One of the features of the Australian clothing industry is the use it makes of 'outworkers — people who make garments in their own homes and are paid for each piece they complete. Recently such workers have gained increases in the abysmally low rates they received, but employers complained it would wreck the clothing industry. Use graphs like parts b and c of Figure 25.1 to analyse the likely effects of such wage increases. Make sure you explain how the individual Australian firm would be affected and the effects on the local industry in the face of overseas competition.

ECONOMIC EFFECTS OF MONOPOLISTIC COMPETITION

We can evaluate the economic effects of monopolistic competition by answering some of the same questions we considered in analysing perfect competition and monopoly. How efficiently does monopolistic competition allocate scarce resources to fill consumer wants? What are the pros and cons on the economic effects of advertising, that often controversial form of nonprice competition? How much does monopolistic competition promote innovation and technological advancement? What about the effects of such a market structure on income distribution?

Efficiency of Resource Allocation

It is often claimed that monopolistic competition is inefficient because it results in too many firms in an industry, each operating with excess capacity and selling output at a price that exceeds marginal cost.[1] This is illustrated by the monopolistically competitive firm shown in Figure 25.2.

Monopolistic Competition Versus Perfect Competition

Because of the downward-sloping demand curve and free entry into the industry, the market forces the typical firm to produce Q_1 and sell it at the price p_1. This corresponds to point a, at which the downward-sloping portion of the ATC curve is tangent to the demand curve D. Attracted by above-normal profits, so many firms have entered the industry that the typical firm has excess capacity. If the typical firm were able to use this idle capacity, it could produce the larger output Q_2, corresponding to the lowest possible average total cost per unit. In sum, *the normal profit, long-run equilibrium position of a monopolistically competitive firm occurs at an output level less than that at which average total cost is a minimum.* It is often argued that

---

[1] By convention, we say that a firm is operating at capacity when it is at the lowest point on its ATC curve. When the firm is operating on the downward-sloping portion of the ATC curve, at a point to the left of the lowest point, we say that the firm has excess capacity. When the firm is operating on the upward-sloping portion of the ATC curve, at a point to the right of the lowest point, we say that it is overutilising its capacity.

consumers' needs could be satisfied at a lower cost with fewer firms if somehow each firm could be forced to operate at the larger output level. This is the level at which average total costs are lowest, and corresponds to the minimum point on the ATC curve. There would be fewer corner stores, hairdressers and service stations, and each would be more fully utilised.

There are other implications of monopolistic competition that are closely related to the excess capacity issue. In long-run equilibrium, the monopolistically competitive firm produces the output Q_1 and sells it at the price p_1 in Figure 25.2. If you look to the right of this point, you will see that there is a range of the demand curve that lies above the marginal cost curve. This means that *under monopolistic competition there are consumers willing to pay a price for the product that exceeds the marginal cost of producing it but who are unable to buy it at such a price.* This follows from the fact that *for a monopolistically competitive firm the long-run equilibrium price is above marginal cost.*

Suppose the cost curves shown in Figure 25.2 were those of a typical firm in a perfectly competitive industry. In long-run equilibrium the perfectly competitive firm would produce the output Q_2 and sell it at the price p_2. Price would equal MC as well as the minimum level of ATC. Why? Because, as we saw in Chapter 23, the perfectly competitive firm's demand curve is perfectly horizontal. This means that the demand curve and the marginal revenue curve are one and the same. Moreover, in long-run equilibrium the perfectly competitive firm's demand curve is tangent to the ATC curve at its bottommost point. The firm produces the output level corresponding to this point because here price equals marginal cost. It is also the output level where the firm produces at the lowest possible level of average total cost.

In terms of Figure 25.2, the perfectly competitive firm would produce output right up to the point where the marginal cost of the last unit produced is just covered by the price consumers are willing to pay for it. Here p_2 equals MC equals the lowest possible level of ATC. Consumers would pay a price for the good that just covers the lowest possible average total cost of producing it. By contrast, the monopolistically competitive firm produces the smaller output level Q_1 and sells it at the higher price p_1. This price is higher than marginal cost and higher than the lowest possible level of average total cost (the bottommost point on the ATC curve).

If the perfectly competitive long-run equilibrium position is taken as the ideal of economic efficiency (for the reasons discussed in Chapter 23), then monopolistic competition falls short of this standard.

Implications of Product Differentiation for Economic Efficiency

In the above comparison with perfect competition, monopolistic competition appears to be a less desirable market form than perfect competition. But let's carry the comparison a bit further. After all, under monopolistic competition, it is true that in long-run equilibrium no more than a normal profit is earned — just as in perfect competition. But in addition, it can be argued that monopolistic competition offers the consumer more product variety in the forms of quality, service, information, and other aspects of nonprice competition.

Are the added costs of the product variety and production at less than full capacity necessarily 'bad'? The fact that consumers are willing to pay for product differentiation suggests that they think it is a benefit. If consumers want variety, who are economists to say that this is 'inefficient and undesirable'? If it were decreed that the garment industry should produce only one standard outfit of

FIGURE 25.2
Efficiency and Equilibrium in Monopolistic Competition

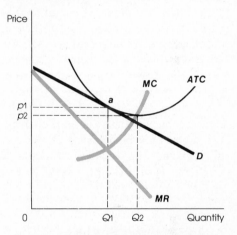

In long-run equilibrium, the monopolistically competitive firm is forced to operate at a point along the declining portion of its ATC curve. We have labelled such a point a. At this point the firm is producing Q_1, to be sold at a price p_1. Hence, average total cost per unit is above minimum ATC. If the resulting idle or excess capacity were used, the output level Q_2 could be produced at minimum ATC.

Over a range to the right of Q_1, the demand curve D lies above the MC curve. This means there are consumers willing to pay a price greater than marginal cost to have some of the product, but who are unable to get it.

If a perfectly competitive firm had the same cost curves, in long-run equilibrium it would produce the output Q_2 and sell it at the price p_2. By comparison to the monopolistically competitive firm, price for the perfectly competitive firm is lower and output higher. Moreover, price equals MC, which equals the minimum ATC.

clothes in order to ensure that price equals *MC* equals minimum *ATC*, the dreary sameness of everyone's appearance would be dull indeed. In a society where consumers prefer variety over sameness and are willing to pay the extra cost to have it, it is simply a value judgment (a normative statement) to say that 'product differentiation is less desirable than product homogeneity'. Comparisons between sameness and variety are like comparisons between apples and oranges. They are different goods.

In order to make the claim that monopolistic competition is inefficient, one must have a standard for comparison, an alternative that is 'better'. But can monopolistic competition really be compared with the alternative of perfect competition and marginal cost pricing? Perfect competition may be more efficient, but it can only be achieved at the cost of reducing the variety of available products. Is it therefore 'better'? Any answer is open to debate.

Middlemen and Product Differentiation

We have said that the place where monopolist competition is found most frequently is in the service industries such as the retail industry. Customers choose where to shop not just in terms of prices, but nonprice factors such as quality of the goods, standard of service, convenience, parking and after sales service. This brings us to a fact of life that we have ignored so far in this book. Retail shops, supermarkets, department stores, chemists, service stations are middlemen. They play an important part in the distribution chain between the producers or manufacturers of goods and the consumer. So the choice that confronts the shopper is the result of the separate business decisions often of manufacturers and shopkeepers. Go into a branch of your local supermarket and look at the cans on the shelves. Some lines carry the brandnames of the manufacturer, while others carry the brandname of the store — Fabulous, or Farmland. Some goods are even distinguished by simply a uniform coloured package, or a name such as 'plain wrap'. This last category of goods are known as *generics* — no-name or unbranded products. The aim behind such generic products is to offer consumers products without an established brand name, at an attractive price.

How then do we explain the effects of middlemen and the existence of both manufacturer and retailer branding in terms of our economic theory of monopolistic competition and product differentiation? It comes down to relative market power of manufacturers and stores and what is sometimes called the battle of the brands. As we have seen successful branding gives a firm a limited monopoly, and if for some reason entry is not too easy, branding also brings the opportunity for profits. It has spinoffs too. The Heinz name for baby food helps sell Heinz soups. So firms seek to establish and maintain the differentiated product. But so too do the retailers. If a store can establish its own brandname instead of a manufacturer it enjoys the limited monopoly power the branding confers. Manufacturers then simply agree to provide the product packaged to the seller's specifications. The lion's share of the profits go to the store and not to the producer — and the spillover is that customers look for the store's brandname on a range of products.

Figure 25.3 shows the difference it can make to a producer and to a middleman or retailer depending on who gets to do

FIGURE 25.3
Middlemen and Producers' Profits
Depend on Who Does the Branding

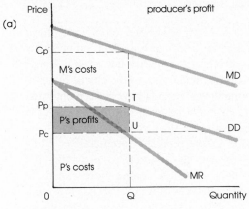

(a)

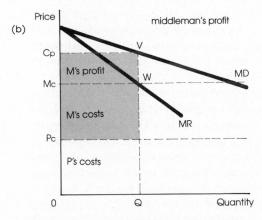

(b)

the branding. In part a the producer brands the goods. In part b the retail store does the branding. For simplicity, we assume that consumer demand is the same in both parts. Unlike other Figures we need to take into account both the costs of the manufacturer and the final seller — the store. MD is the market demand curve in both part a and part b. For simplicity producers' and middlemen's average costs are assumed to be constant. In part a it is the producer who does the branding and has the limited monopoly power. The average revenue and marginal

revenue he faces is obtained by subtracting the middleman's distribution costs from the market demand curve. He then equates MR with P_c (producer's costs = AC = MC) and produces OQ. This is sold to final consumers by the retailer for C_p per unit. The retailer (middleman) just covers costs, but the producer makes a profit of P_cP_pTU. In contrast, in part b the branding and limited monopoly power lies with the middleman who reimburses the producer his costs, P_c. He then equates MR with MC (middleman's costs = AC = MC) and sells OQ to the consumer at the same price C_p. On this occasion it is the middleman who takes the profits, shown by the area P_cC_pVW.

The Pros and Cons of Advertising

If the monopolistically competitive firm is able to differentiate its product from that of its competitors in the right way, it may be able to gain a competitive advantage. Successful product differentiation amounts to tailoring the product to best suit consumer demands. Nonprice competition in the form of advertising serves this goal to the extent that it informs the consumer about differences between products. However, advertising may go beyond the simple conveying of facts when it attempts to tailor consumer demands to goods, rather than simply making consumers aware of the nature of a product. (Much of what we will say here about advertising also applies to oligopolistic market structures, the subject of the next chapter.)

There is a grey area in all this, of course. It is often difficult to distinguish informative advertising from that which simply urges consumers to buy for reasons only superficially related to the product, or even on the basis of claims that may be

POLICY PERSPECTIVE

The Battle of the Brands

In the last decade large supermarket chains such as Coles-Myer and Woolworths have taken a very large share of the total retail trade for many lines of branded food products and grocery items. Each of these chains has promoted not one but several house brandnames including generic packages. Some of the advantages to the chains in being able to sell their own brands rather than manufacturers' brands have been mentioned in the text. They include both the opportunity to make larger profits at the expense of the manufacturers and food processing firms who lose their power as monopolistic competitors when required to produce and pack to the retailer's specifications. They also give the retail chain an opportunity to segment the market, by providing the cheap no-name generics and in-house brands as a substitute to the more expensive brand products. We now know quite a lot about the chances of retailer brands replacing manufacturers' brands. In one sense the retailer is in a strong position. After all he makes the final decision about what his stores will sell. He controls the allocation of shelf space to lines and brands and he also controls store promotions. Having said that, we must recognise that stores don't have absolute power over their customers. They are in the business of stocking what customers will buy at prices and at a speed that will return them profits.

Much of the attraction of store brands and generics lies in their price advantage over branded goods. Against that branded goods are usually advertised on the basis of being high quality products. Store brands are more likely to succeed if the consumer can be convinced about their product quality, or if quality is not of critical importance. During economic recession there is also likely to be a swing to cheaper substitutes and generics have an advantage then. For the middleman a number of other signs point to success. If there are many producers and no one manufacturer's brand is dominant, or if manufacturers are charging high prices the opportunity for introducing the store brand to the product may be there. Before making the decision it would be necessary to ensure the store could find a regular source of supply.

Questions

1. Visit the nearest large supermarket and identify six types of packaged groceries for which the store is carrying both manufacturers' brands and store or 'no-name' brands. In addition, identify six lines where there is no store brand available. What reasons might there be for the existence of store brand competition in some cases but not in others?

2. Consider products from the store you might be likely to use at home. Which products would you be prepared to purchase in the plain wrap or store brand and which would you require in the manufacturer's brand? What reasons can you give for your choice?

entirely false. Sometimes the difference between real information and pure hype is pretty obvious. What can a black panther have to do with the road holding qualities of a motor car tyre? Do you really believe a certain breakfast cereal would make a hole in your kitchen table?

Since any form of advertising costs something, the question is whether the benefits justify the use of scarce resources in this kind of activity. Is it worth it? This issue is as much debated as it is unsettled.

Is Advertising Informative?

To the extent that advertising provides consumers with knowledge about product prices, quality, alternatives (substitutes), and where particular products can be purchased, it can save the consumer the costs of searching and shopping. Newspaper advertising, particularly classified ads, and shoppers' guides appear to serve this end well. On the other hand, television and radio often provide relatively noninformative types of advertising pitched along lines such as you will be more of a man if you buy this or more of a woman if you buy that. The 'hidden persuaders' of this type of advertising often bear little relation to the realities of the product.

It has been argued that the prohibition of advertising by some trade groups is a practice intended to reduce information that would promote competition and lead to lower product prices. In recent years there has been a relaxation in restrictions on advertising on a range of products from spectacles to condoms. There is still resistance to advertising by the medical and legal professions in Australia. Such advertising is claimed to be unethical or likely to lead to a reduction in essential standards. Those in favour of removing restrictions on this type of advertising

claim the major purpose however is to restrict competition. It has also resulted in more advertising by lawyers, providing the public with greater information about the fees charged for different legal services. Such advertising is informative and very likely promotes competition among sellers that results in lower prices to consumers.

Can Advertising Reduce the Costs of Goods?

It is sometimes argued that by increasing sales and therefore revenue, advertising allows firms to introduce new products at lower costs to consumers. This argument is illustrated in Figure 25.4.

Suppose that in the absence of advertising the monopolistically competitive firm has average total cost represented by the ATC curve. Given the demand curve D_1, the long-run equilibrium occurs at point a, where output Q_1 is produced and sold at price p_1.

Now suppose the firm advertises. Let's say that advertising costs push the ATC curve upward to the position ATC'. If the advertising is effective, it should result in increased demand for the firm's product, represented by a rightward shift in the demand curve. If the demand curve shifts to a position such as D_2, then in the new long-run equilibrium the firm will operate at point b, producing output Q_2 and selling it at price p_2. This price, which is equal to average total cost, will indeed be lower. The lower price is due to the production of the larger output Q_2, which allows the firm to realise some economies of scale. But what if advertising causes the demand curve to shift rightward to a position such as D_3? The new long-run equilibrium will occur at point c. Although a larger output Q_3 is produced, price p_3, which is equal to average total cost, is now higher than initially.

In sum, while it is possible that advertising can lead to reduced costs of production and lower product price, it is obviously possible for just the opposite to happen. Furthermore, the monopolistically competitive firm typically advertises with the intent of making the firm's product more distinguishable or different

FIGURE 25.4
The Effect of Advertising on the Monopolistically Competitive Firm

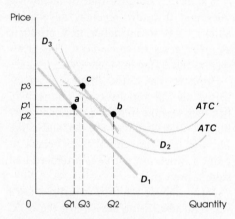

Before making any expenditures on advertising, the monopolistically competitive firm's average total cost curve is *ATC*. Its long-run equilibrium position is at point *a*, the point of tangency with its demand curve *D₁*, where it produces output *Q₁* and sells it at price *p₁*.

The cost of advertising causes the *ATC* curve to shift upward to the position *ATC'*. If the effect of advertising increases consumer demand for the firm's product in such a way as to shift the demand curve outward to *D₂*, the new long-run equilibrium position is at point *b*. In that case the firm will produce *Q₂* and sell it at the lower price *p₂*. However, if the demand curve is shifted outward to *D₃*, the new long-run equilibrium will be at point *c*. Output will then be *Q₃* and price will rise to *p₃*.

Either outcome is possible. But since advertising tends to increase product differentiation, product substitutability will likely decrease. This will result in the somewhat steeper demand curve. Hence, point *c* may be the more likely outcome — advertising gives rise to the higher price *p₃*.

from those of other firms in the industry. This will decrease the degree of substitutability between its product and those of other firms. Therefore, the demand curve will become less elastic, or more steeply sloped, like D_3 rather than D_2. This makes it less likely that advertising will lead to a lower price.

Is Advertising Wasteful?

Advertising that is informative can certainly improve a firm's competitive position. However, much advertising aimed at improving the firm's competitive position is not informative. It merely claims brand X to be superior to brands Y and Z on the basis of doubtful allegations and meaningless comparison tests. In order to defend their market shares, brands Y and Z respond in kind with similar advertising campaigns.

As a result of such competitive advertising efforts, the total market for the industry's product may hardly increase at all. Even the market shares of the individual firms may remain unchanged because their efforts merely offset one another. But the *ATC* curves of each will be higher, reflecting the increased advertising costs. A typical participant in such a competitive advertising 'war' may simply end up in a position such as point *c* instead of point *a* in Figure 25.4. Some firms may be producing a little more, others a little less. In the end, all that seems certain is that consumers will be paying higher prices for the industry's output to cover the costs of competitive advertising, which may have very little 'hard' information content.

However, this may be an unduly harsh judgment. It may be that to the extent that this type of advertising persuades consumers to try different brands, they will be exposed to the 'true facts' of each firm's product through their own sampling activity. 'Try it, you'll like it' may, at least, result in a 'try it and see'. Such advertising may result in the acquiring of hard information after all.

Excluding store catalogues, the print media — newspapers and magazines and direct mail — account for about 55 per cent of advertising in Australia. In general this method of advertising aims at providing information. Television 30 per cent, radio 8 per cent and outdoor advertising with 6 per cent place more emphasis on persuasion.

How Significant Is Advertising in Monopolistic Competition?

It should be recalled at this point that in long-run equilibrium the monopolistically competitive firm can only earn a normal profit, just like a perfectly competitive firm. And this is true no matter what form of nonprice competition the firm may engage in. Nonprice competition, such as advertising, can only result in above-normal profits in the short run. We have seen how the competitive force of free entry leads to an adjustment process that eliminates them in the long run. The fact that competitive advantage obtained through expenditures on advertising is fleeting no doubt puts a limit on just how much of this activity is 'worth it' to the monopolistically competitive firm. Your barber probably advertises little — perhaps no more than an occasional ad in the neighborhood paper. The same is true of service stations, dry cleaners, florists, and car washes.

Much of what we have said about advertising applies equally, perhaps even more so to oligopolistic market structures — the subject of the next chapter.

CHECKPOINT 25.3
What reasons can you think of for regulating the advertising of goods and services? Is it necessary or desirable to have controls on any particular form of advertising? Should the control of advertising be by a government organisation or is it better left to an individual industry to control the advertising of the member firms?

Innovation and Technical Change

Does monopolistic competition provide much incentive for innovation and change? Remember that in a perfectly competitive market free entry of new firms makes it difficult for any firm to reap above-normal profits for any length of time. Any above-normal profit earned by the perfectly competitive firm as a result of innovation is eliminated by rivals who quickly copy and adopt the new development, thereby keeping themselves on the same competitive footing with the original innovator. Long-run equilibrium entails nothing more than a normal profit. Since a monopolistically competitive industry is also characterised by free entry and a normal profit in long-run equilibrium, it might be expected that the incentive to innovate is no greater than in perfect competition.

On the other hand, it is possible that product differentiation provides an added spur for monopolistically competitive firms to innovate. Nonprice competition may stimulate product development aimed at further distinguishing the firm's product from those of other firms in the industry. If nothing else, a firm may gain some additional, above-normal profits in the short run through such activity. Here again, however, because such profits are short-lived, the incentive to innovate is definitely limited. For this reason, some economists argue that in monopolistically competitive industries, product innovation and technological change is more cosmetic than real. Since cosmetic change is cheaper, the development of more eye-catching packaging techniques may substitute for substantive product improvement. Given the prospect of additional short-run profit but nothing more, such changes may appear to be 'worth it,' while the greater expense of real innovation does not.

Some evidence suggests that this is the case. The construction industry is made up of a large number of independent contractors and might well be characterised as monopolistically competitive. Compared to other areas of the economy, the technology of constructing residential housing does not appear to progress very rapidly. (Some might argue that union work rules and outdated building codes have had more to do with unchanging techniques in residential construction than the market structure has.) True, more power tools and motorised equipment are used today. But these were developed by other industries more oligopolistic in structure — the automotive, heavy machinery, and electrical equipment industries.

SUMMARY

1. Monopolistic competition is very similar to perfect competition in that it is a market structure with many firms and an absence of financial, legal, or other barriers to entry into or exit from the industry. It differs from perfect competition in that each firm in a monopolistically competitive industry produces a slightly different variation of the same product. Product differentiation means each firm's product is a close but not perfect substitute for that of every other firm. This is reflected in the fact that each firm's demand curve is slightly downward sloping.

2. Because of its downward-sloping demand curve, a monopolistically competitive firm makes its price and output decisions in a manner that appears the same as for a monopolist. It produces where marginal cost equals marginal revenue and sells at a price above that at which marginal cost equals marginal revenue. However, because of low barriers to competition, the entry and exit of firms to and from the industry allows them to earn only a normal profit in the long run.

3. Compared to perfect competition, monopolistic competition is considered inefficient because in long-run equilibrium price exceeds minimum average total cost of production as well as marginal cost. Hence, consumers are not getting the product at the lowest price permitted by cost conditions, and there are consumers who are willing to pay a price greater than the marginal cost of the product but who are unable to have any of it. However, these alleged shortcomings of monopolistic competition may be offset by the benefits of product differentiation.

4. Consumers frequently buy from middlemen (stores) rather than producers. Many stores operate under conditions close to monopolistic competition and engage in nonprice competition including quality of service. Large stores have taken over some product differentiation also and seek to increase their profits by branding.

5. Product differentiation is the primary means by which monopolistically competitive firms engage in nonprice competition. An important but controversial form of nonprice competition is advertising. To the extent that advertising provides consumers with hard information about prices, factual characteristics of products, and where they can be purchased, it provides them with benefits in the form of reduced search and shopping costs. To the extent that it misleads consumers by distorting facts or making false claims, it only confuses them, wastes resources, and leads to higher product prices.

6. Under monopolistic competition innovation and technological advancement are limited by the fact that the above-normal profits that may reward such activity are limited to the short run. Furthermore, nonprice competition may lead to innovation in the form of product differentiation that is more cosmetic than substantive.

KEY TERMS AND CONCEPTS

branding
generics
middlemen
monopolistic competition
nonprice competition
product differentiation
surplus capacity

QUESTIONS AND PROBLEMS

1. Do you think a monopolistically competitive industry is composed of many firms selling slightly differentiated products at the same price, or each at slightly different prices? Why? Do you think the cost curves of all the firms must necessarily be identical?

2. Rank the following products according to the degree to which they may be truly differentiated, as opposed to 'artificially' differentiated through advertising and packaging: toothpaste, sugar, clothing, gum, aspirin, coffee.

3. Suppose the government forced all monopolistically competitive firms to set price equal to marginal cost. What sort of difficulty would this create in long-run equilibrium? What would you suggest the government do if it insists on enforcing such a policy? (Figure 25.2 will help you to answer this question.)

4. Do you think advertising makes the long-run equilibrium position of monopolistically competitive firms more, or less, like that of perfectly competitive firms? Why?

5. Rank the following goods according to the degree to which you think their advertising is informative: heavy machinery (advertised in trade journals), perfume, used cars, cigarettes, apartments, new cars, clothing, dairy products, dogs, patent medicine. Give reasons for the rankings you select.

26

Oligopoly and Market Concentration

AFTER READING THIS CHAPTER YOU WILL BE ABLE TO:

1. List and explain the characteristics of an oligopoly market.

2. Explain the concept of industrial concentration.

3. Evaluate the current evidence on the occurrence and extent of oligopoly characteristics in Australian industry.

4. Explain how mutual interdependence among oligopolistic firms can lead to price rigidity in oligopolistic industries and to collusive behaviour among oligopolistic firms.

5. List the conditions that affect the possibilities for collusive behaviour.

6. Assess the evidence on the efficiency of oligopolistic industries, their impact on technological change and innovation, and the relationship of these considerations to the degree of industrial concentration.

A large part of our economy is made up of industries that are dominated by a few large firms. An industry of this type is called an **oligopoly**, a word of Greek origin that loosely translated means 'few sellers'. Another term **duopoly** is used to refer to a market dominated by only two sellers. Duopoly is in effect merely one type of oligopoly. In terms of sheer volume of economic activity, oligopolistic industries are usually considered the most representative form of market organisation in Australia.

Our analysis of oligopoly will complete our examination of types of market structures. If we were to order these structures along a spectrum according to their similarities with one another, they would line up as follows: perfect competition, monopolistic competition, oligopoly, and monopoly. Oligopoly is like monopolistic competition in that there are several firms typically (but not always) producing a differentiated product. It is like monopoly in that there are barriers to entry of new firms to the industry. The existence of a small number of firms has a very distinctive effect on the firms' behaviour. The most important consequence is that they cannot ignore the behaviour of other large firms in the industry. If they cannot be sure about their rivals' policies it is very difficult to devise simple profit making rules of the type we applied to the monopolist and to firms operating under conditions of perfect and monopolistic competition. Often the response to such uncertainty is for the firms in an oligopolistic industry to collude; to form a cartel or agree on common policies of one sort or another. We studied that type of behaviour in Chapter 24. While such agreements may be unstable or illegal they are fundamentally no different from monopoly. This chapter is concerned with the fundamental nature of the uncertainty problem facing an oligopolist and the various solutions to that problem, other than collusion. The essential features of oligopoly can lead to a wide range of outcomes for the individual oligopolist. They range from intense competition and normal or close to normal profits to clear market leadership and profits akin to those of a monopolist. For these reasons you should bear in mind that oligopoly is the most complicated and varied form of market organisation that we will study.

Oligopolies may be divided into two major types. Those that produce undifferentiated, or homogeneous, products are often called perfect or **undifferentiated oligopolies**. One firm's product is no different from that of the other firms in the industry. The metals industries, producers of aluminium, steel, and copper, are examples. A manufacturer who uses one of these metals usually orders by exactly specifying characteristics such as tensile strength and carbon content. There is little, if any, room for product differentiation. Oligopolies that produce differentiated products, so-called imperfect or **differentiated oligopolies**, are more numerous. These include the electrical appliance, motor vehicles, and aircraft industries, among many others. Some oligopolies, such as the petroleum industry, often produce identical products but attempt to differentiate them through advertising. But since all petrols are characterised by lead content, octane rating, and other such specified traits, there is little room for true product differentiation.

CHARACTERISTICS OF OLIGOPOLY

Figure 26.1 sets out the three principal characteristics of oligopoly and four of the commonest outcomes of this market form. The three common characteristics present in all oligopolistic markets, though to different degrees, are:

(1) substantial barriers to entry,
(2) few dominant firms, and
(3) recognised mutual interdependence.

The diagram also shows four of the most common solutions firms have selected when operating initially in an oligopolistic market to resolve the uncertainty problem. These are:

(1) outright price competition,
(2) price rigidity with firms turning to nonprice competition,
(3) one firm becoming accepted as price leader in the market, or,
(4) strong incentives for firms to collude, form cartels or merge.

Thus this market form can lead to very widely differing solutions, ranging from akin to competition to monopoly. We have already defined oligopoly as a market dominated by a few large firms and this identifying characteristic calls for little comment at this stage. Later we will examine measures of market concentration economists have developed in their

efforts to ascertain whether oligopoly exists. *Barriers to entry* are the reason why a market comes to be dominated by a few firms. The principal barriers to entry are similar to those observed with monopoly. They include economies of scale, cost differences and a variety of other barriers including government regulation and restrictive trade practices by existing firms. Economies of scale are often so large relative to the size of the total market that it only takes a few firms to supply the whole market. In the case of a natural monopoly, we saw that one firm could supply the entire market because its long-run average total cost curve declined over the entire range of output covered by the market demand curve. An oligopolistic industry is a less extreme form of this situation.

This is illustrated in Figure 26.2, where D represents the industry demand curve for an undifferentiated oligopoly. Given this industry demand curve, the individual firm with the long-run average total cost curve ATC realises sizeable economies of scale. This is represented by the fact that its ATC curve reaches its minimum point

FIGURE 26.1
Characteristics and Outcomes of Oligopoly

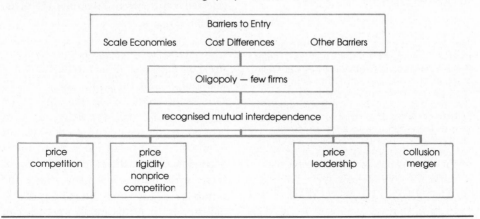

at output level q, which is a sizeable share of the total quantity Q demanded at the industry-wide price p. Hence, at a price that just covers per unit costs when firms are operating most efficiently, total market demand will only support a small number of such firms.

At the current time there are five automotive manufacturers in Australia: Ford, GMH, Mitsubishi, AMI (Toyota) and Nissan. It is generally agreed that five are too many. For all to survive, high levels of protection from imports are required. Various plans have been devised to reduce the number of producers and reduce the levels of protection. For example the Button Plan (after the Minister for Manufacturing Industry in the Hawke Government) was designed to reduce the number of manufacturers from 5 to 3 so that each could enjoy economies of scale and become more competitive. There is little doubt that even further economies could be attained if the number of firms were reduced to two and if the number of models and types of engines were cut.

Few Dominant Firms

One of the characteristics of oligopoly is that there are few dominant firms. The *concentration ratio* is often used to test for the existence of oligopoly. This measures the extent to which a few firms dominate the industry. Other types of evidence include whether prices appear to be rigid or flexible and finally whether there is activity towards merger within an industry. One of the commonest concentration ratios used by economists to measure the extent to which a few firms dominate an industry is the sales ratio. *The sales ratio for a given industry is computed on the percentage of total industry sales accounted for by the largest four, or eight (in terms of sales) firms in the industry.* Concentration ratios for selected industries in Australia are given in Table 26.1.

Recognised interdependence among firms of the effects of their individual price and output decisions on one another's sales is the characteristic that causes the oligopolist his real problems. Just as economies of scale lead to fewness of dominant firms in an industry, so interdependence is a direct consequence of there being only a few firms. Since the number of firms in an oligopolistic industry is typically small, no firm can

FIGURE 26.2
Economies of Scale Can Lead to Oligopoly

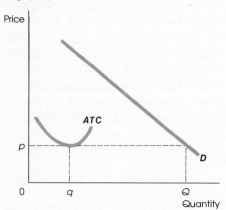

The demand curve D represents the total market demand for the output of an undifferentiated oligopolistic industry. The typical firm in the industry realises significant economies of scale, as represented by the long, downward-sloping portion of its ATC curve. When it operates at its minimum per unit cost level of production, it produces an output level q that is a sizeable portion of the quantity demanded by the total market. At a price p that would just cover per unit costs when firms are operating most efficiently, total market demand is Q and only a few such firms can be supported by the market.

TABLE 26.1
Sales Ratios of Selected Australian Industries 1982-83

| | percentage of industry sales | |
	4 largest	8 largest
Footwear	43	54
Log sawmilling	17	29
Furniture	11	16
Paper bags	62	84
Publishing	37	50
Chemical fertilisers	81	98
Paints	66	79
Petroleum refining	85	100
Clay bricks	55	76
Cement	82	100
Steel pipes and tubes	92	95
Motor vehicles	84	95
Ships	66	77
Boats	16	27
Photographic goods	97	99
Radio & TV receivers	58	84
Rubber tyres	79	89
Jewellery	15	25

Source: Australian Bureau of Statistics, *Census of Manufacturing Establishments and Electricity and Gas Establishments; Industry Concentration Statistics 1982-83*, Cat. No. 8207.0, Canberra, 1985.

make pricing decisions without thinking about how the other firms in the industry will react. Take the extreme form of oligopoly — duopoly. There are only two sellers. If one seller raises his price, how much he sells at that new price will be directly affected by whether the other duopolist retaliates by increasing his price, or engaging in some form of nonprice competition. If the duopolist doesn't know how the rival firm will respond *he doesn't know what his average and marginal revenue curves* are and he cannot therefore determine price by setting marginal revenue equal to marginal cost. He faces a fundamental *uncertainty* problem, because he doesn't know what the demand curve for his product is. Previously we have defined a firm's demand curve as

showing the quantity of its product that it could sell at various prices other things being equal. This definition was useful when talking about a monopolist since the demand curve for the firm was the demand curve of the industry. For the perfect competitor, or the monopolistic competitor, it was also fine because the individual firm was so small that its price decisions had no effect on other firms. For the oligopolist the quantity that it will sell at any given price is directly affected by the prices charged by the other firms in the industry. And the prices charged by the other firms in the industry will be directly affected by the pricing decisions of this firm. How the firms in an oligopolistic industry can best deal with this interdependence and the uncertainty it creates is the major theme in this chapter.

Much of the discussion about oligopoly will refer to the special form — duopoly. It is easier in some ways to understand the oligopoly problem when referring to only two firms. Second, the fewer the number of large firms the more significant are the consequences of their actions for one another. Third, we can show that whilst duopoly only involves one more firm than monopoly the market outcome in terms of price and output may be very different depending on how the two firms behave. Because barriers to entry are so crucial to the existence of oligopoly, we will examine them in greater detail in the next section. After that we will examine in greater depth the question of certainty and the various solutions to the oligopoly problem.

BARRIERS TO ENTRY IN OLIGOPOLY

Substantial barriers to entry of new firms into oligopolistic industries can take many forms. Among the most important are economies of scale, cost differences, product recognition, and product complexity and proliferation.

Economies of Scale

Economies of scale can be a serious barrier to entry into an oligopolistic industry. This is illustrated in Figure 26.3. Suppose a firm already in the industry has a demand curve that looks like D_e in part a. Since a potential new firm would be unfamiliar to consumers in the industry at first, let us say that its demand curve would look

like D_1 in part b. But let's suppose that both the new firm and the old firm have the same average total costs, represented by ATC. In order to make a go of it, the new firm would have to charge a price no lower than p_1 and produce an output no greater than q_1, part b. If it tried to produce more, it would have to sell it at a price lower than par unit production costs, as represented by the fact that D_1 lies below ATC to the right of q_1. If the new firm did so, it would incur losses.

If the new firm enters, the firm already in the industry knows that its share of the total market will be diminished. Its demand curve D_e, part a, would therefore

---

FIGURE 26.3
Economies of Scale as a Barrier to Entry
in Oligopoly

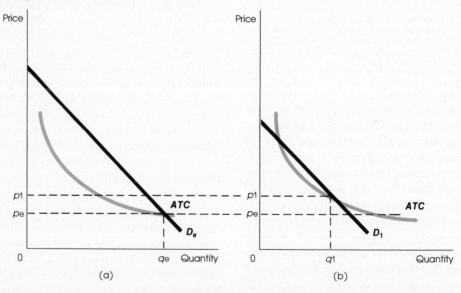

(a)   (b)

An established firm in the industry has a demand curve D_e, part a. It has an average total cost curve ATC, which declines over a large range of output, reflecting the presence of substantial economies of scale. Suppose a potential entrant to the industry can expect to have the same costs and therefore the same ATC curve, but it also expects to have a much lower level of demand, represented by the demand curve D_1, part b. If the established firm sets price anywhere below p_1 but above p_e, it can still cover costs and make an above-normal profit. However, because D_1 lies below ATC in this price range, the new firm would incur losses and is therefore discouraged from entering the industry.

shift leftward. To keep the new firm out, the existing firm can take advantage of its economies of scale by charging a price below p_l. In fact, the existing firm can still make a profit at any price below p_l so long as it doesn't charge a price below p_e and produce more than q_e. Though the existing firm might be able to maximise its profits for a time by charging a price above p_l, it might feel that such gains would not be worth it given the likely loss in market share to a new entrant attracted by the large profits. By pricing below p_l, the existing firm effectively discourages the new firm from entering the industry.

Suppose that there were no economies of scale beyond q_l, and that instead the ATC curve either became horizontal or began to rise. Then the firm already in the industry would not be able to charge a price below p_l without incurring a loss. It would therefore not be able to charge a price low enough to keep out the potential new entrant.

Cost Differences

A potential new entrant into an industry may not have the same ATC curve as a firm already in the industry. Even putting aside economies of scale, the costs of production for a new entrant may well be higher than those of established firms for a host of reasons.

Existing firms can have lower costs because of know-how gathered from long experience in the industry. Their management organisations have had time to 'shake down' into more coordinated and effective units. Their labour forces may be more experienced and production problems may be fewer. Established firms often can get better credit terms from bankers and suppliers. They also may have patents on production processes that

reduce costs. Some new firms may be able to overcome these barriers eventually, but this takes time. As a result, these barriers can discourage the entry of many potential rivals.

A simple example of the potential entrant's problem is shown in Figure 26.4. The potential entrant's ATC curve, represented by ATC_n, is higher at all levels of output than that of an existing firm, represented by ATC_e. For simplicity, we will suppose that the new firm's demand curve can be just like that of an established firm, once it gets going. This curve is represented by D_e. If the established firm didn't have to worry about a possible reduction in its market share as a result of the new entry, it might well charge a price such as p_l and produce q_l in order to maximise profits. However, the threat of a potential new entrant leads it to never charge a price greater than or equal to p_L. At any price lower than p_L the potential new entrant is not able to cover per unit costs and is therefore discouraged from entering the industry. The established firm, on the other hand, can still earn a profit at a price below p_L. This is represented by the fact that the demand curve D_e still lies above ATC_e to the right of q_L.

The price p_L is often called a **limit price** because if an established firm never charges a price greater than or equal to p_L, the entry of new firms to the industry will be limited.

In sum, *when a potential new firm is at a disadvantage relative to established firms because of economies of scale, cost differences, or both, existing firms can turn these disadvantages into barriers to entry by keeping product price low enough. Yet this price may still be high enough to ensure existing firms more than a normal profit.*

FIGURE 26.4
Cost Differences as a Barrier to Entry in
Oligopoly

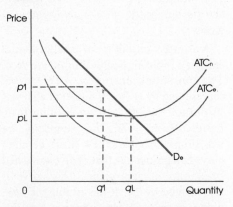

An established firm's *ATC* curve, *ATCe* is lower
than that of a potential new entrant, represented by *ATCn*. The established firm can
effectively discourage entry of the new firm by
setting price below the limit price *pL*. This is
because the new entrant would have to
operate at a loss while the established firm
could still cover costs and earn an above-
normal profit, as represented by the fact that
De lies below *ATCn* and above *ATCe* over a
range to the right of *qL*. Were it not for the
threat of entry, the established firm might
make a larger profit by setting price at *p1* and
selling *q1*.

Other Barriers to Entry

In oligopolistic industries, capital requirements, control of input supplies, government regulation, product recognition,
product complexity, and product proliferation often constitute formidable barriers to entry. The cost of overcoming
these barriers can cause the *ATC* of a
potential new entrant to be higher than
that of an established firm.

Capital Requirements

To operate a firm at its most efficient size
in an oligopolistic industry can require
many millions, even billions, of dollars of
capital. A potential entrant into the
airline, motor vehicle, chemical or electrical appliance industries, to name but
a few, needs large amounts of capital.
Such capital requirements are a substantial barrier to entry.

Control of Input Supplies

When existing firms in an industry control
important inputs to the production
process, potential new firms may face an
almost insurmountable barrier to entry.
For example, for many years in Tasmania,
newspapers seeking to establish themselves found a perennial problem in being
able to obtain supplies of newsprint.

Government Regulation of Entry

Government (state, local, or federal)
sometimes regulates entry into various
industries by granting exclusive franchises
and by requiring and issuing licences.
Until recently the government's Two
Airline Policy effectively ensured that only
Ansett and Australian Airlines could
operate in competition over much of the
Australian domestic network. Restrictions
on the importation of suitable planes
similarly restricted competition on domestic air freight services. Government
restriction also controls entry into radio
and television broadcasting and into
banking. Until the partial deregulation of
the Australian banking system four large
banks dominated everyday banking
business. There are numerous other such
examples where the force of law is a
barrier to entry.

Product Recognition

A potential new firm typically must
introduce its product into a market where

the products of existing firms are already well known and established in the minds of consumers. To overcome this 'new kid on the block' problem usually requires a sizeable advertising campaign. The cost of this campaign may well be higher than the cost of advertising that is needed to maintain the market positions of already established firms.

Product Complexity

Closely related to the problem of product recognition is that of product complexity. For products such as motor cars, television sets, refrigerators, stereo equipment, and many others, the very complexity of the item requires that consumers have more information about the product than that provided by mere recognition if they are going to be convinced to buy. Product complexity often extends to such areas as the availability and quality of product service. For example, one of the major hurdles that must be bridged by a new entrant to the motor vehicle industry is the establishment of an extensive dealer network through which major service and other product problems can be handled.

Product Proliferation

Product proliferation has proved to be an effective barrier to new entrants in a number of oligopolistic industries. Ford makes the Falcon, Fairlane, Laser, Telstar and Meteor, GMH makes the Commodore, Camira, Gemini and Astra, Mitsubishi produce Magna, Sigma and Colt and so on. When the range within each of these models is considered the choice provided to the Australian motorist from Australian made cars is enormous.

Why is this? One reason may well be that product proliferation helps each of the Big Three to preserve its respective share of the motor market from the inroads of rivals and the entry of new firms into the industry. A potential entrant is not confronted with the prospect of competing with just one kind of car, but many. If the new entrant successfully takes sales away from the Nissan Pintara these sales will only represent a small fraction of the entire motor vehicle market. It certainly would not allow a new entrant to achieve the economies of scale enjoyed by Ford or GMH. The motor vehicle industry world wide learned an important lesson by observing a fundamental mistake made by Henry Ford in the 1920s. Ford lost its leadership in the United States industry which it had come to dominate after introducing the Model T. Ford's obsession with the assembly line and a homogeneous product was reflected in his quip, 'they can have any colour they like as long as it is black'. GM rightly grasped a basic principle of marketing — to succeed in a tough world you should aim to give customers what they want. They did so by introducing a greater variety of models and colours.

PRICE AND OUTPUT BEHAVIOUR

It has been emphasised that the oligopolist faces a more difficult problem than a monopolist or a competitive firm because of its interdependence on rival firms. We said earlier that the consequence of this is that the oligopolist may not know for certain what his average revenue and marginal revenue curve are. If this is the case he cannot follow the normal profit maximising rule of setting marginal revenue equal to marginal cost. This section explores in more detail the four

CHECKPOINT *26.1

Every time the motor vehicle industry changes models, which is every couple of years or so, plants must be equipped with new tools in order to deal with new body styling and mechanical changes. This retooling is very costly. Some estimates suggest that production costs might be reduced 20 to 30 percent if the industry did not change models. Hence, it would seem firms could enjoy larger profits if they refrained from model changes. So why do you think there are model changes? If Ford, GMH, Toyota, Mitsubishi and Nissan collude in an agreement not to change models wouldn't each be better off?

*Answers to all Checkpoints can be found at the back of the text.

common outcomes or 'solutions' to his problem that were set out in Figure 26.1. Each of these outcomes depends to a large extent both on the assumptions an oligopolist makes about his rivals' behaviour and, of course, on whether those assumptions if put to the test, turn out to be correct.

Price Competition and Price Wars

The simplest solution is if the oligopolist decides that he will be able to increase profits by lowering his price below those of his rivals. he is likely to do this in one of two situations. First, he may be convinced that if he lowers his price his rivals will not drop their prices. Under these circumstances, he may well face an elastic average revenue curve and his sales revenue will increase and his market share will rise. Depending on his costs the

strategy will lead to an increase in profits. Provided he can be sure that his rivals are not going to respond, he has no problem. It pays him to cut the price to the point where marginal revenue equals marginal cost. This outcome is possible, but not very likely. It is far more likely that the other firm or firms in the industry will match the firm's price cuts and the result will be a **price war**. The overall effects of such a price war are uncertain and the firm's average revenue curve is necessarily less elastic than when the rivals do not cut their prices. It may well be inelastic, so the result of the price cutting war is to reduce sales revenue and profits. A French economist writing in the 19th century believed that the most likely consequence of oligopoly was price competition that resulted in the firms charging a competitive price and earning only normal profits.

The second reason firms engage in price competition is if they believe that they have a cost advantage over their rivals. A price war may have the effect of driving one or more of the firms out of business and if reentry costs are high this may enable the successful firm to achieve monopoly power. In the short run, limited production facilities may prevent a firm from pushing its attempts to cut prices and put others out of business. Once the price cutting firm has reached full capacity and cannot supply all who want to buy at that price, the remaining firms can, at least temporarily, ignore the price cutter. They have, in effect, a separate market to themselves. Price wars tend to be short lived, when they lead to lower profits. Petrol is a case in point. From time-to-time a price war breaks out among petrol resellers, backed by the oil companies who supply them. After a time when motorists enjoy substantially lower petrol prices the prices go up again. As if by magic, all resellers raise their prices within a few hours. The reasons for such wars seem to be the attempts by independent owners to gain market share at the expense of oil company leased service stations, or vice versa.

CHECKPOINT 26.2

Petrol stations within a city usually charge the same price for petrol. Explain why this is so? On the other hand it is common to find the price of petrol on main routes outside cities cheaper than in the city. What logic could there be behind such a policy? Why is it that city suppliers don't lower their prices to match the country outlets?

Price Rigidity and Nonprice Competition

Competitive price cutting is only favoured under specific circumstances by oligopolists. Normally, their knowledge about their own cost structure and their beliefs about how their rivals will react are sufficient to convince them that price cutting is either doomed to failure or too risky to try. They search for an alternative strategy. This strategy takes into account the likely reactions of rivals, but as we have seen their ability to predict is limited at best. The following is a more formal presentation of the interdependence problem described earlier.

The Firm's Demand Curve and Rival Reaction

Figure 26.5, part a, shows an oligopolist's demand curve D_n based on the assumption that there is no reaction from rivals when the firm changes price. D_r is the oligopolist's demand curve based on the assumption that rivals will react to any price change initiated by the firm. Suppose that initially price is p_1, so that the firm is at point b on its demand curve. If the firm reduces price to p_2 and rivals do not react by reducing their prices, the relevant demand curve is D_n, and the firm will sell an output level given by the point c'. Its increase in sales will be made up in part of purchases by customers who switch to it and away from other firms in the industry. The rest of its sales increase will be due to the substitutability of its product for similar products of other industries that are now relatively more expensive.

If instead other firms in the industry react by cutting their prices, the relevant demand curve will be D_r and the firm will move to point c as price is reduced from p_1 to p_2. The firm experiences a smaller increase in sales, reflecting the fact that its rivals in the industry have matched its price cut and therefore have not lost any customers to it. Nonetheless, the firm does experience some increase in sales, as do the other firms in the industry, because the industry's product is now cheaper relative to the substitute products of other industries. By the same line of reasoning, if the firm had reduced price to p_3 and the other firms in the industry hadn't reacted, the firm would have moved to point d' on demand curve D_n. On the other hand, if the other firms match the price cut, the firm's sales will increase less as it moves to point d on D_r.

Let's go the other way. Suppose the firm were to raise price from p_1 to p_0. If the other firms in the industry don't raise their prices, the firm will lose customers to them and will be at point a' on D_n. However, if the other firms in the industry also raise price, the firm will end up at point a on

D_r and will not lose customers to them. Its loss in sales, which is now less, will only be to other industries that produce substitute products.

The Kinked Demand Curve

Given that a firm in an oligopolistic industry is initially at a position such as point b in Figure 26.5, part a, it is only reasonable to assume that its demand curve for price *decreases* will be D_r. This is the curve that assumes that rivals will react and match any price cuts in order to avoid losing customers to the initiator of the price cut. What about a price **increase** to a level above p_1? Rivals might well refrain from reacting to any price

---

FIGURE 26.5
Rivals' Reaction to Price Change and the Kinked Demand Curve

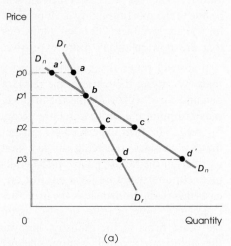

(a)

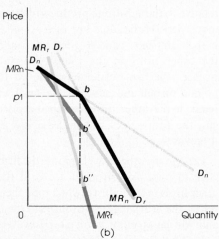

(b)

In part a, D_n is the firm's demand curve when rivals in the industry do not react to its price changes but keep their own prices unchanged. D_r is the firm's demand curve drawn on the assumption that rivals match any price change the firm makes.

Starting from an initial position such as point b, if the firm lowers its price from p_1 to p_2 it will end up at c' on D_n if other firms do not react by lowering their prices. If other firms do react by matching the price cut, the firm will not be able to induce customers away from rivals and its increase in sales, therefore, will be less putting it at point c on D_r. Similarly, if the firm raises its price from p_1 to p_0 and rivals raise theirs as well, the firm will end up at point a on D_r. However, if rivals do not raise prices, the firm will lose customers to rivals and end up at point a' on D_n.

The demand curves D_r and D_n of part a are reproduced in part b. If it is assumed that rivals will match any price cut that the firm initiates, but they refrain from matching any price increase, then the relevant parts of the firm's demand gives the kinked demand curve represented by the highlighted part of D_n above point b and the highlighted part of D_r below point b. The marginal revenue curve associated with D_r is MR_n, and the relevant part of MR_n associated with that part of the kinked demand curve above point b is the highlighted part of MR_n above point b'. The marginal revenue curve associated with D_r is MR_r and the relevant part of MR_r associated with that part of the kinked demand curve below point b is the highlighted part below point b''. Thus the marginal revenue curve associated with the kinked demand curve has a gap, or vertical segment, from b' to b''.

increase the firm initiates. The firm will then lose customers to its rivals in the industry because its product becomes more expensive relative to theirs. Therefore, starting from the initial position at point b, price level p_1, the relevant demand curve for any price increase will be D_n.

The demand curves D_r and D_n are reproduced in Figure 26.5, part b, with the relevant parts highlighted. It is clear that if the firm is initially at point b, its demand curve is the kinked demand curve formed by the highlighted parts of D_r and D_n, with the kink occurring at point b. MR_n is the marginal revenue curve associated with D_n. The part of the marginal revenue curve associated with the highlighted part of D_n is the highlighted part of MR_n extending down to b'. Similarly, MR_r is the marginal revenue curve associated with D_r. The part associated with the relevant section of D_r is the highlighted part of MR_r starting at point b'' and extending downward. Hence, the marginal revenue curve associated with the kinked demand curve has a gap, or a vertical segment, extending from b' to b'' (indicated by the dark broken line) and lying directly below the kink in the demand curve at point b.

The kinked demand curve offers some possible insights as to why prices in oligopolistic industries appear to be slow to change, or 'sticky'. If the existing price is p_1, the firm may be reluctant to lower price because its rivals will follow suit and resulting gain in its sales will be modest. In fact, it is entirely possible that the segment of its kinked demand curve below point b is inelastic. In that case any cut in price to a level below p_1 would result in a fall in total sales revenue and any profit the firm might be making. (Note that in this case the point b'' would be at or below the horizontal axis. Why?)

Remember, although we can draw the kinked demand curve and talk as if the firm knows its shape exactly, in reality the firm may be quite uncertain as to the curve's exact shape because it may be uncertain about the extent of rivals' reactions. Cutting price below the existing level is 'chancy' given that the segment below point b may in fact turn out to be inelastic. Why run the risk of 'upsetting the applecart' by possibly starting a price war that could be disastrous, especially if demand is inelastic below point b.

For similar reasons the firm is reluctant to increase price to a level above p_1. The segment of the kinked demand curve above point b is elastic, as indicated by the fact that the associated marginal revenue curve above point b' lies well above the horizontal axis. Hence, if the firm raises price but rivals do not follow suit (the kinked demand curve above point b is based on the assumption that they will not), the firm will lose sales to rivals, and total revenue and any profit it may be making will fall.

The other reason why price may be 'sticky' at the level p_1 has to do with the gap, or vertical segment, of the marginal revenue curve from b' to b''. Let's assume that the firm arrived at the price p_1 by equating marginal cost with marginal revenue, and that its marginal cost curve is MC_0, as shown in Figure 26.6. Suppose production costs rise, so that the marginal cost curve shifts upward. Unless costs rise enough to shift the marginal cost curve up above the position MC_2, the firm will have no incentive to change price or output. Similarly, if production costs fall so that the MC curve shifts downward, the firm will have no incentive to change price or output unless the MC curve falls to a position below MC_1. As long as the MC curve lies in the gap in the MR curve, between *b'* and *b"*, the firm will not change its level of production or its selling price.

The kinked demand curve provides one possible explanation of why firms in an oligopolistic industry are reluctant to change an established price.

The desire to avoid price wars is often characterised by price stickiness or rigidity, but firms do compete in other ways — by nonprice competition. This nonprice competition usually relies heavily on advertising and product differentiation.The competitive advantage that a firm may realise through these activities may not easily be matched by rivals as is a price cut. Take the motor vehicle industry as an example again. Competition is pursued effectively by getting the right concept, the right mode, the right features and 'selling' the package to the market. Ford's success in the Australian market in recent years and Holden's decline has been due in no small measure to effective nonprice competition.

Leaders and Followers

Price rigidity with or without nonprice competition is a solution to the oligopoly problem than can readily be understood — at least in the short term. One difficulty with it is that it starts from the assumption that there is a going price for the firm's product and then explains why the firm is reluctant to increase or reduce price. It does not explain how that price came to be established in the first place. Second, in these days of rising costs and rising prices a solution that comes up with rigid prices is either of very limited value or not likely to appear very realistic. To make a case for price rigidity as being likely at such times it would be necessary to redefine price in real rather than nominal terms. Such a discussion is way beyond

the scope of this book and would be a very difficult one for many businessmen to understand. So the practical feature of modern Australia is that oligopolists find themselves faced with rising costs and have to find some way of continuing to make profits, usually by increasing prices.

One common outcome is that one firm comes to be accepted as the pace setter, or market leader. Without any agreement between the firms, the rest watch what one firm does and react accordingly. When it raises its price, they follow shortly afterwards. For this type of arrangement to work the leader needs to have a pretty good idea that the others will react by following his lead. He is therefore able to make his pricing and output decisions with a high degree of certainty. If the others react as he expected, the outcome will be more likely to be as he expected and there will be no pressure on the market leader to make further price adjustments until a new set of circumstances arise.

Collusion and the Tendency to Merge

It is only a short step in practice between price leaders and followers to collusion between firms. It is extremely difficult to determine whether firms are colluding and engaging in anticompetitive behaviour or whether they are acting independently and sensibly, from their point of view, following the market lead of one firm. In one sense it does not make much difference whether there is collusion or market leadership — what is important from the consumer's point of view is the price output decision that is finally made and the extent to whch it differs from the competitive solution, or robs the consumer of the advantages of economies of scale or freedom of choice.

As we saw in Chapter 24, collusion gives the firms in an industry effective monopoly power, without necessarily realising the economies of scale that may come with monopoly. This section demonstrates how the oligopolist can expect to benefit from collusion.

Why Collusion Pays

Consider a duopoly in which both firms have identical costs of production and

FIGURE 26.6
Price Rigidity and the Kinked Demand Curve

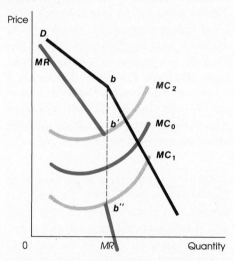

An oligopolistic firm is producing output and selling it at the price associated with point *b*. Its kinked demand curve is *D*, its associated marginal revenue curve is *MR*, and its marginal cost curve is *MC₀*. If production costs increase, the firm will have no reason to change price or output level as long as the increase is not large enough to push the *MC* curve above *MC₂*. On the other hand, if costs decrease, the firm will still have no reason to change price or output level as long as the decrease is not large enough to push the *MC* curve below *MC₁*. The existence of the vertical segment of the marginal revenue curve associated with the kinked demand curve therefore provides one explanation for price rigidity in oligopoly.

both produce exactly the same product. To make matters even easier, we will assume that marginal cost is the same at all levels of production and that it always equals average total cost. All these assumptions are shown in Figure 26.7. Parts a and b represent the individual firms, and part c represents the entire industry.

Total industry demand is represented by the demand curve D_m. Its associated marginal revenue curve is MR_m, as shown in part c. Since each firm produces exactly the same product, it is reasonable to assume that when each charges the same price, each will have exactly half of the total industry demand given by the demand curve D_m. This is shown in parts a and b of Figure 26.7, where the total industry demand curve D_m is shown for comparison with each firm's demand curve D_f. At any price note that D_f lies halfway between the vertical axis and the total market demand curve D_m. Hence, at any price the sum of the quantities demanded from each firm equals the total industry demand. For example, at the price p_4 the quantity demanded from firm X is q_4 and the equivalent quantity, q_4, is demanded from firm Y. The sum of these two quantities, or 2 times p_4, equals the total quantity demanded from the industry at the price p_4 — the quantity Q_4 shown in part c.

CHECKPOINT 26.3
What would cause a firm to move price to a level above the kink in the demand curve, even though the demand curve is elastic above this point and a price rise results in a fall in total revenue? Under what conditions would the firm never reduce price below the level of the kink, no matter what happened to costs?

Also note the following. Recall that at any given price the marginal revenue curve always lies exactly halfway between the vertical axis and the straight-line demand curve. Hence, each firm's demand curve D_f, parts a and b, is in exactly the same position as MR_m, the marginal revenue curve associated with the industry demand curve D_m in part c. The marginal revenue curves associated with each firm's demand curve D_f are shown as MR_f, parts a and b.

Suppose initially that each firm is charging the price p_1. This is the price that corresponds to the point where $MC = MR_f$ for each firm, as represented by the intersection of the MC and MR_f curves in parts a and b of Figure 26.7. At this price each firm produces and sells q_1. The sum of their outputs, $2q_1$, equals total industry output Q_1, as shown in part c. Note that this result is exactly the same as it would be if both firms colluded to act like a monopoly, or if both firms had in fact merged to form a monopoly firm. In the latter case the intersection of the curve $MC = ATC$ with MR_m determines the profit-maximising output Q_1 and price p_1 in part c. Here the monopoly profit equals the shaded rectangle $abcd$. Producing output q_1 and charging the price p_1 is the best that each firm can do, subject to the existence of the other selling at the same price. Each realises a profit equal to that represented by the rectangular areas $abcd$ in parts a and b, which added together equal the shaded rectangle $abcd$ in part c.

However, if the firms are not colluding in any way, either may be tempted to undercut the price of the other and take the whole market. That is, when one cuts price below that charged by the other, the price-cutting firm's demand curve becomes the industry demand curve D_m. Suppose firm X tries this by cutting price to p_2. Since the firms produce an identical product, firm Y, still charging p_1, loses all its customers to firm X, which now supplies the entire market the quantity Q_2. For the moment, firm X is making a larger profit than it was initially since the gain in profit, represented by the larger shaded rectangular area, exceeds the loss in profit, represented by the smaller shaded rectangular area in part a of Figure 26.7. Indeed, this was firm X's motive for cutting price. Firm Y now has no sales at all. Consequently, it reacts by cutting price to p_3, thereby undercutting firm X's price of p_2. Total industry sales Q_3 now go entirely to firm Y, and firm X's sales fall to zero. Firm X now reacts by cutting its price to p_4, and firm Y must do likewise if it is not to lose all its sales. However, neither can cut price below this level because at p_4 both firms are just covering all costs including a normal profit.

At this point the price war is over, each firm selling q_4, or half the total market sales of Q_4 (which is equal to $2q_4$). Each firm is now just making a normal profit. Each is worse off than before the price war started because at the initial price p_1, each was making a profit (in excess of normal profit) represented by the rectangle $abcd$ in parts a and b. The outcome of the competitive price war is a marginal-cost-equals-price solution, just like that in perfect competition. Consumers are better off, but each firm considers itself worse off. At this point the firms may sit down together at a 'peace table' and mutually agree not to get involved in any more 'shoot-outs' with each other. Both can see that it is in their own best interest to collude and jointly maximise profits by agreeing to keep price at p_1. In effect they agree to split total market sales of Q_1, with q_1 going to each. The moral of the story? Collusion pays, price wars don't.

If price leadership is not considered satisfactory and collusion doesn't work for some reason — maybe its illegal — there may be a tendency for the firms in the industry to merge into a single legal entity. There is often therefore a tendency towards monopolisation. In Australia, although the dangers of such mergers are well recognised there has been far less government opposition to monopolisation than in the United States. Partly this is a function of the size of the Australian market. As we have seen the government has encouraged Australian motor vehicle manufacturers to find ways of reducing the number of manufacturers. Joint ventures between the existing manufacturers has been seen as the most sensible way of achieving the goal of reducing the major manufacturers to three by 1990.

CHECKPOINT 26.4
Is it necessary for both, or just one, of the firms in Figure 26.7 to misjudge the likely reactions of the other in order for events to lead them to the price level p_4?

FIGURE 26.7
The Incentive to Collude in an Oligopolistic Industry with Two Firms

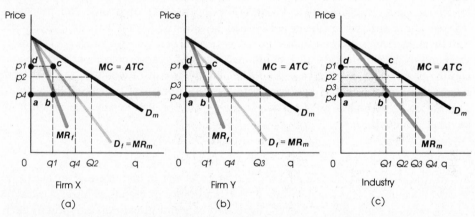

The two oligopolistic firms, X and Y, produce an undifferentiated product and have identical production costs with marginal cost *MC* and average total cost *ATC* equal to each other and the same at all levels of output, as indicated by the horizontal *MC = ATC* curves. Total industry demand is given by the demand curve Dm with its associated marginal revenue curve MRm in part c. Each firm's demand curve Df in parts a and b is the same as the MRm curve.

If each oligopolist charges a price p_1 and sells an output q_1, they split the total market sales Q_1, and each earns a maximum possible profit (represented by the rectangular area *abcd*, parts a and b) equal to half the shaded rectangle *abcd* in part c. In effect if they collude to maintain price at p_1, they act as if they were a monopoly firm producing output Q_1, and setting price p_1, where *MC* intersects MRm to give the maximum monopoly profit represented by the shaded rectangle abcd in part c.

Instead of colluding, suppose firm X cuts price to p_2 and takes all market sales equal to Q_2. As a result, firm Y loses all its sales and therefore reacts by cutting price to p_3, whereupon it takes all market sales, equal to Q_3, and firm X loses all its sales. This process of price cutting continues until price is driven down to p_4, where it just covers all costs of each firm including a normal profit and each firm produces and sells q_4. The price war is over, and each firm is worse off than when price was initially p_1. It obviously pays for the firms to collude and jointly maximise profit by charging the price p_1, splitting industry sales of Q_1 so that q_1 is sold by each.

POLICY PERSPECTIVE

Reorganising the Motor Vehicle Industry

The plan to rationalise the Australian Motor Vehicle Industry was designed to reduce the number of manufacturers by 1992 from 5 to 3 and to reduce the number of models from 12 to 5. Initially, there was considerable speculation about which of the 5 manufacturers and which major models would disappear. Senator Button's plan for the industry was given teeth by the Automotive Industry Authority and the threat to remove protection from imports for those models that did not achieve specified sales levels of 40,000 or more a year.

In the event the plan produced serious negotiations between the five (General Motors Holden, Ford, Nissan, AMI Toyota and Mitsubishi). Elements in the emerging solution were the merger of Holden and Toyota's local operations, a closer relationship between Ford and Nissan, the removal of some models and the renaming of others. Not only are engines and chassis, but also names, likely to be exchanged. Thus a model sold under a familiar name may have the same engine as another currently well known model and use the chassis of a third. While the number of brands and models is reduced under such arrangments, old brand loyalties and confidence is likely to die with them. Variety is lost and so too the illusory and ill defined superiority the consumer attributes to their preferred make and model. The gains come from economies of scale and the prospect of cheaper cars. Another consequence of rationalisation apart from the reduction in choice may be the reduction in the number of franchised dealerships. The Button Plan makes no provision for who will sell and service the products of the three groupings.

Questions

1. To what extent are these changes likely to be in the public interest? In particular what conclusions can you draw about the importance of brands as far as Australian consumers are concerned? Does the increasing concentration mean that price is likely to become more or less important in the future?

2. What might be the consequences for dealers and ultimately for consumers as dealers face the effects of a reduction in the number of manufacturers?

3. What effect would you expect these changes to have on the demand for imported motor vehicles?

OTHER BUSINESS OBJECTIVES

The entire discussion about market behaviour has been based on the assumption that firms seek to maximise profits. For a great many, not only is profit maximisation desired and aimed for, it is essential for survival. The marginal firm will soon go out of business if it does not attempt to maximise profits. Increasingly, the firm that does not maximise profits is an easy prey for firms seeking to takeover those that are not realising their profit potential. Australian subsidiaries of foreign companies understand only too well the importance of profit performance and keeping the parent company happy. So, all in all, the profit maximisation assumption we have adopted has served us well. However, the real world of business is not that simple. Writers in recent years have suggested the simple profit maximisation hypothesis does need to be qualified in a number of ways. One of the most obvious is that short term profitability may not be the same thing as long term profits. A firm may decide against short term profit maximising decisions if it believes this will threaten long term profitability. We have already mentioned that a firm with apparent monopoly power in the short run will need to consider carefully how strong are the barriers to entry of competitors or how real the threats of government intervention.

A firm in a protected secure position may choose to maximise something other than profits. The more complex the structure of the company, the more likely are the objectives of divisions, or individual managers likely to influence decision making. It may place emphasis on growth of sales revenue, or market share or salary and life style package for its executives. If it is in a powerful and protected position in the market place it may believe it can enjoy the luxury of inefficiency. In oligopoly, we have seen that uncertainty about rivals' reactions makes profit maximising decision making quite difficult on occasions. Hardly surprisingly, there may be a temptation to choose other objectives rather than profits around which to develop the corporate policies.

MARKET FORMS AND MARKET POWER — A SUMMARY

The last four chapters have discussed the four principal conventional market forms used to analyse business behaviour in Australia — perfect competition, monopoly, monopolistic competition and oligopoly. On every possible occasion it has been stressed that while these market forms are usually described in terms of the number of firms currently operating in the industry, it is the way in which they behave and the reasons for this behaviour that are of more importance.

Figure 26.8 draws together the relationship between conventional market forms and business behaviour. It makes the fundamental distinction between price takers and price makers, relates them to conventional market forms, explains the main influences on their behaviour and identifies their common characteristics.

ECONOMIC EFFECTS OF OLIGOPOLY AND INDUSTRIAL CONCENTRATION

How well does oligopoly allocate scarce resources to unlimited wants? The criteria we have used to try to answer this question for the market structures discussed in previous chapters are relevant here as well. Because oligopolistic industries account for such a large share of the economy's output and typically represent large concentrations of economic power, economists have spent a good deal of effort trying to determine how well oligopoly measures up by these criteria. We will try to summarise some of these findings and their implications in the next few pages.

FIGURE 26.8
Business and Market Form

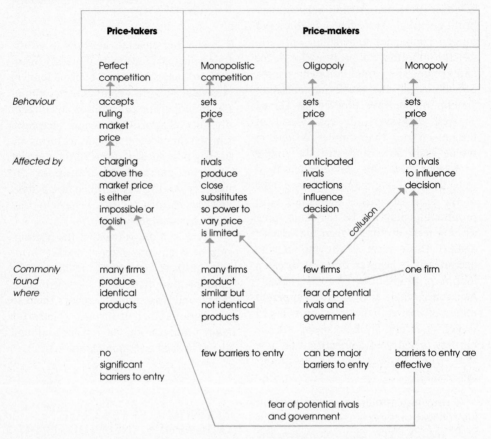

	Price-takers	Price-makers		
	Perfect competition	Monopolistic competition	Oligopoly	Monopoly
Behaviour	accepts ruling market price	sets price	sets price	sets price
Affected by	charging above the market price is either impossible or foolish	rivals produce close substitutes so power to vary price is limited	anticipated rivals reactions influence decision	no rivals to influence decision
Commonly found where	many firms produce identical products	many firms product similar but not identical products	few firms / fear of potential rivals and government	one firm
	no significant barriers to entry	few barriers to entry	can be major barriers to entry	barriers to entry are effective
			fear of potential rivals and government	

collusion

Note: This is based on a diagram in A. Hocking *Investigating Economics* and developed with permission from Longman Cheshire, 1980.

Efficiency

Clearly oligopolies do not produce at that level of output for which marginal cost equals price. Even if an oligopoly had exactly the same cost curves as a perfectly competitive firm producing the same product, nothing ensures that it would produce at the minimum point on the *ATC* curve as the perfectly competitive firm would. If it does not produce that level of output at which per unit costs are lowest, it would not be efficient by this criterion.

This comparison is largely a fiction, however, because of the significant role that economies of scale play in oligopoly. These economies make it unreasonable to suppose that if an oligopolistic industry were reorganised to be perfectly competitive, the resulting perfectly competitive firms would have the same cost curves

POLICY PERSPECTIVE

Keeping an Eye on Pantyhose

As we have seen, the Australian clothing industry comes close in many of its activities to monopolistic competition. The Prices Surveillance Authority reported in October 1987 that in general competitive conditions prevailed in the clothing industry. It based its conclusions on the evidence of

(1) competition among local manufacturers

(2) competition between local manufacturers and imports — it is expected this competition will increase

(3) competition between local manufacturers and mass merchandisers with the latter sourcing house brands from Australia and overseas

(4) competition among retailers.

Clothing Industry Concentration — Selected Activities

ASIC Industry	4 larges firms percentage of industry turnover
Hosiery	58
Cardigans and Pullovers	28
Women's outerwear	13
Men's trousers, shorts	57
Foundation garments	76
Headwear	15

Source: Prices Surveillance Authority Inquiry in Relation to the Retail Price of Clothing Report No. 15, October 1987, Table 7.

While the PSA was generally happy about the degree of competition in the industry it noted that the supply of pantyhose could be an exception to this. This is not obvious from the table above because the category hosiery also includes socks and stockings. Two firms, Australian Consolidated Hosiery and Kolotex, dominate the industry on the manufacturing side; imports are relatively small. Only 7.5 per cent of pantyhose were imported in 1985 compared with 30 to 40 per cent of other women's clothing. In addition the capital intensive nature of production creates a barrier to entry. The PSA also noted that retail prices for pantyhose had risen at a faster rate than many other types in the preceding year.

The Authority decided that pantyhose prices should be monitored in more detail and proposed to invite the two major manufacturers to regular consultations to provide information about market conditions and operating costs.

Questions

1. Suppose you were a member of the Prices Surveillance Authority reviewing the above information. What would you see as the influences most likely to prevent a rapid increase in the price of pantyhose in Australia?

2. Do you think Australian women have cause to be concerned? What would your feeling be if Kolotex and Australian Consolidated Hosiery were to merge?

---

as the oligopolist. Suppose the motor vehicle industry was composed of small competitive firms. Hundreds of small plants would make the components and assemble vehicles that are produced by five main producers in Australia today. And of course, none woud be able to realise the economies of scale that are achieved by Ford, and the other dominant firms that presently make up the industry. Therefore, per unit costs of production would be higher under perfect competition, even though each firm would be operating at the minimum point on its *ATC* curve.

But now we have to ask the following question: Do firms in oligopolistic industries tend to be just large enough to take advantage of economies of scale so that per unit production costs are at a minimum, or do they tend to be so large that inefficiencies in production and distribution are encountered?

Research on this question tends to suggest that most firms in the industries studied are larger than the need to realise economies of scale would warrant. It appears that economies of scale are realised in the plant in manufacturing and that multiplant operation seldom lowers costs further. Large manufacturers typically have large plants and many plants, not all of optimum scale. Large manufacturers tend to grow past the point of maximum efficiency and encounter rising per unit costs of production and distribution. The largest multiplant firms realise economies in borrowing funds, purchas-

ing supplies, and advertising, rather than in production and distribution. Overall, however, concentration ratios in most industries studied seem considerably higher than economies of scale would justify.[1]

Technological Change and Innovation

Does oligopoly encourage technological change and innovation? Some economists would say 'most definitely'. They argue that oligopoly may well be the most progressive of all types of market structure because it comes closest to the 'ideal' combination of the carrot of profits and the stick of competition.

The possibility of above-normal profits, protected by substantial barriers to entry, provides an incentive for innovation as well as a ready source of funds to finance innovative activity. In this respect, oligopoly is much the same as monopoly. However, in an oligopolistic industry the existence of rival firms, coupled with a reluctance to engage in price competition, creates unusually heavy pressures to engage in nonprice competition. Such competition takes the form of product development and innovation to spur sales, and advances in production techniques to lower production costs. It is argued that

[1] F.M. Scherer, A. Beckenstein, E. Kaufer, and R.J. Murphy, *The Economics of Multiplant Operation* (Cambridge, Mass.: Harvard University Press, 1975), p. 339.

since firms are wary of price competition as a means of capturing a larger share of the market and increasing profits, there is more emphasis on technological change and innovation. The competitive advantages that a firm may realise through these activities are not as easily or quickly matched by rivals as is a price cut.

In sum, it may be argued that technological change and innovation are encouraged in an oligopoly because of the existence of potentially high profits, as in monopoly. However, unlike monopoly, in an oligopoly technological change and innovation are also stimulated by the competitive pressures created by rival firms. Similarly, it may be argued that technological change and innovation in oligopoly benefit from the competitive pressures created by rival firms as in perfect and monopolistic competition, but unlike these forms of market structure oligopoly does not suffer from a lack of profit incentive.

The preceding paragraph sums up briefly the arguments of some economists in support of oligopoly as the form of market structure most favourable to technological progress and innovation. However, other economists argue that to the extent oligopolistic industries are characterised by collusive arrangements of one kind or another, a 'live-and-let-live' mentality may develop. As a result, they claim, there is less progressive and innovative behaviour than the existence of several 'apparently' competitive rivals would seem to suggest. It may be that collusive behaviour among oligopolistic firms results in a sort of shared-monopoly situation. In that case the implications for innovation and technological change are much more like those of monopoly than those of an oligopoly characterised by the existence of vigorous competition. What does the evidence suggest?

The Evidence[2]

It does not appear that invention has been particularly dependent on the activities of large firms. Studies to date suggest that inventive efforts, inventive output, and the efficiency of inventive efforts (measured, say, by the inventive output per dollar of research and development expenditure) tend to increase with firm size only among small- to medium-sized firms. Beyond that, no further gains from size are evident and, if anything, losses are more likely than gains. A study of case histories for 70 major twentieth-century inventions found only one-third of them came out of the research laboratories of companies.[3] More than half were due to individuals working on their own. However, over the course of the twentieth century the relative importance of individual inventors seems to be shrinking.

What about the process of turning new inventions into mass-produced products? Here it would seem that costs of engineering, testing, tooling, and marketing, along with the inherent risks of bringing a new product to market, would tend to favour the larger firm. However, researchers find that innovative activity typically rises with size only from small- to medium-sized firms. Beyond that, larger firm size does not generally seem to be associated with greater innovative zeal.

A cross section of industry studies shows that some innovations do require

2 This section draws from D.F. Greer, *Industrial Organization and Public Policy* (New York: Macmillan, 1984), Chapter 9.
3 J. Jewkes, D. Sawers, R. Stillerman, *The Sources of Invention,* 2nd ed. (New York: Norton, 1969), p. 28.

financial resources that exceed those of small firms in some industries. A distinguished researcher on this issue sums up the evidence: 'All things considered, the most favourable industrial environment for rapid technological progress would appear to be a firm size distribution which includes a preponderance of companies with sales below $500 million, pressed on one side by a horde of small technologically oriented enterprises bubbling over with bright new ideas and on the other by a few larger corporations with the capacity to undertake exceptionally ambitious developments'.[4]

Is there any relationship between market structure and the speed with which a new technique developed by one firm is adopted by others in an industry? The evidence on this seems consistent with the theory advanced by economists that imitation is stimulated more by a less concentrated market structure.[5]

What about the effects of market structure on economic growth? It seems that invention, innovation, and imitation play a large role in economic growth. Here the evidence seems to suggest that large size and concentration are associated with higher growth in labour productivity up to very high levels of concentration, beyond which just the opposite seems to be the case.[6]

To sum up, studies suggest that for a large portion of invention and innovation, high concentration ratios and obstructive barriers to entry seem to stifle progress. At the other extreme, very low concentration ratios and high firm turnover in

an industry do not appear conducive to technological progress either. Intermediate market structures, tending to the competitive side of the spectrum, seem best. The exception might be for productivity growth.

Profits, Advertising and Concentration

Economic theory suggests that oligopoly is likely to give rise to above-normal profits, particularly when firms engage in collusion. There are several aspects to this issue and a certain amount of evidence to support this theory. In our analysis of monopolistic competition in Chapter 25, we discussed the pros and cons of advertising. We pointed out (and you might wish to reread that section at this time) that advertising may play an even larger role in oligopoly than in monopolistic competition. In oligopolistic industries advertising may well contribute to excess (above-normal) profits because it stimulates product differentiation and proliferation. As we said in Chapter 25, product differentiation and proliferation can be formidable barriers to entry and thereby help exclude potential competitors from an industry. This makes it easier for established firms to charge higher prices and realise monopolistic profits.

On balance, studies of this issue seem to suggest that the ratio of advertising expenditures to sales is highest in those industries where concentration ratios are neither extremely high nor especially low, but somewhere in the middle or upper-middle region.[7] One of the most consistent findings reported by different studies is that: 'The higher the advertising/sales ratio was in an industry, the higher industry (or in some cases, firm) profits

[4] F.M. Scherer, *Industrial Market Structure and Economic Performance*, 2nd ed. (Chicago: Rand McNally, 1980), p. 422.
[5] Edwin Mansfield, *Industrial Research and Development* (New York: Norton, 1968), Chapter 7.
[6] Greer, *Industrial Organization*, p. 529.

[7] Scherer, *Industrial Market Structure*, p. 390.

tended to be'.[8] In addition, numerous studies find that in industries where concentration ratios are high, profit rates tend to be relatively high as well.[9]

An Evaluation of Oligopoly

Looking at the great variety of industries that have pronounced oligopoly characteristics, all observers might agree on one point. Namely, all could cite a few oligopolistic industries to support the claim that oligopoly is an ideal combination of the carrot of profit, which provides incentive, and the stick of competition, which enforces efficiency. At the same time one could point to a few oligopolistic industries that bear a disturbing resemblance to an unregulated monopoly situation — a shared monopoly. Where the latter situation occurs, or where there are strong overtones of it, economists raise the same kind of concerns about the efficiency of resource allocation, technological progress, income distribution, and the concentration of economic power that we have discussed in the case of unregulated monopoly.

The evidence does suggest that generally in those industries where concentration ratios are high, profit rates (measured as either the ratio of after-tax profit to sales, or to the market value of the firms' common stock) tend to be somewhat higher as well. It also suggests that for most industries studied, concentration ratios seem higher than can be justified by economies of scale. This finding implies the existence of production and distribution inefficiencies.

With regard to invention and innovation, the evidence that has been gathered so far generally does not support the

[8] Ibid., p. 391.
[9] Ibid., Chapter 9.

contention that high industrial concentration and very large firm size provide a definite increase in benefits in this direction.

Advertising outlays tend to be large in increasingly concentrated consumer goods industries and also to bear a distinct relationship to above-average profits in those industries. Much of the money goes for television advertising, which has a dubious information value. (According to a recent survey, about 46 per cent of the public thinks television commercials are misleading; only 28 per cent feels that way about newspaper and other printed ads.)

It should be emphasised that this somewhat negative appraisal is not a blanket evaluation of all oligopolistic industries. Rather it is directed at those that appear to fall into the grey area in which the complex of oligopolistic characteristics becomes more noticeably shaded by overtones of monopoly.

CHECKPOINT 26.5
The evidence cited above suggests that in industries where concentration ratios are high, profit rates tend to be relatively high as well. How would the implications you might draw from this conclusion be affected by information about the degree to which the identity of the four largest firms in such an industry changes over time? If an industry was found to have a concentration ratio that could be justified by economies of scale, what do you think its profit rate would be like compared to that associated with a finding that the concentration ratio was larger than could be justified by economies of scale? Why? Would the nature of an industry's product have an effect on the implications you might draw from a finding that its advertising outlays are large and its concentration ratio is high?

*Why? Use the information in Table 26.1
on concentration ratios as a test of your
beliefs.*

SUMMARY

1. An oligopoly is an industry dominated
by a few large firms. The market share
of each is large enough that its actions
cause reactions among the others. The
competitive behaviour of each firm reflects
its awareness of this situation.

2. The occurrence of oligopoly depends
heavily on economies of scale and
substantial barriers to entry. The solution
to the oligopolist's problem is likely to
be one of the following — price competition, price rigidity and nonprice competition, being a price leader or follower
and collusion or the tendency to merge.

3. Price wars are seldom a long-term
solution. They are most often undertaken
because one firm wrongly estimates a
rival's reaction or because a firm believes
it has a cost advantage and can drive
others out of business.

4. The kinked demand curve and its
associated discontinued marginal revenue
curve is one possible explanation for price
rigidity in oligopolistic industries where
there is no collusion. An explanation
producing sticky nominal prices does not
seem realistic when money costs are rising.

5. Firms have a strong incentive to reduce
uncertainty about rivals' reactions. They
may almost subconsciously adopt the
practice of following a market leader.
There will be even stronger profit incentives to collude so as to maximise profits
for all. Much collusive activity is illegal
in Australia. Mergers meet with some
scrutiny, but greater concentration rates

are encouraged by government in some
instances.

6. Given the reluctance of firms to engage
in price competition, oligopolistic firms
rely heavily on product differentiation,
product proliferation and advertising. It
takes rivals more time and it is more
difficult for them to match efforts along
these lines than it does to match price cuts.

7. Concentration ratios, which measure
the share of total industry sales contributed by the large firms indicate oligopoly
is prevalent in Australia, although market
power of such firms depends on the degree
of existing or potential foreign competition. Evidence suggests that merger and
acquisition is a significant cause of
increasing industrial concentration.

8. Not all firms seek to maximise profits,
though there are often powerful incentives
to do so. Firms may seek to maximise
other goals such as sales, the net worth
of shareholders' funds, growth of the firm
or even the standard of living of the
decision makers. Inattention to profits is
likely to make the firm more vulnerable
in the long run, particuarly if other firms
currently identify the opportunities being
lost.

9. Some economists contend that oligopoly provides an ideal combination of the
opportunity for profit, which gives
incentive to innovation, and the existence
of competition, which encourages efficiency. However, evidence suggests that
concentration ratios are higher in some
industries than can be justified by economies of scale, and that high industrial
concentration and large firm size are not
consistently related to inventive and
innovative activity. There also tends to be
a positive relationship between industrial
concentration and the amount of adver-

tising, a large part of which is of dubious information content.

KEY TERMS AND CONCEPTS

collusion
duopoly
interdependence
kinked demand curve
nonprice competition
oligopoly
price follower
price leader
price rigidity
price war
rivals' reactions
uncertainty

QUESTIONS AND PROBLEMS

1. In what ways is oligopoly similar to monopolistic competition? Most people would describe both the Australian domestic airline industry and the international route to the west coast of the USA as oligopolistic markets. What similarities and differences are there between these markets? How have the 'solutions' of operators differed in recent years?

2. Two firms dominate an industry and there are strong barriers to entry. They sell an indentical product and charge the same price — $10 per unit. Each firm has a monthly sales revenue of $100,000. However, they face different cost structures. Firm A has fixed costs of $20,000 and variable costs of $60,000, while Firm B has fixed costs of $50,000 and variable costs of $55,000. In both cases average variable costs are constant. What possible strategies might Firm B consider to improve profitability? How do you think Firm A would react? Should the manage-

ment of Firm A be content with the original situation?

3. Suppose the two firms have additional information about their market. They have discovered that the market demand for the product is such that every increase in its price by $1 will lead to consumers reducing purchases from the two firms combined by 2,000 units per month. Each time the price is reduced by $1, combined sales increase by 2,000 units. Suppose that Firm A has a maximum plant capacity of 22,000 units per month and Firm B has a maximum plant capacity of 60,000 units per month. The firms are fiercely competitive. What alternative strategies should each consider in the light of their market knowledge and plant capacity. Will both, or only one survive the competition?

4. Suppose the management of Firm A suggested the two firms meet to consider either collusion or merger. Would either of these suggestions have any attraction for Firm B given the limits to demand and plant capacity in Question 3? What do you think is the sensible strategy for Firm B, a price war, price rigidity, collusion or merger?

5. Using the diagram depicting the oligopolistic firm of Figure 26.6, demonstrate the likely effects if the firm steps up its advertising. Demonstrate the likely effects if the firm's rivals step up their advertising.

6. Rank the following industries according to how difficult you think it would be for the firms in them to collude:
tyre manufacturers
motor vehicle manufacturers
TV networks selling advertising space
textbook publishers.
   In each case be careful to take into account all the characteristics of oligopoly

mentioned in this chapter as well as the nature of the product, and give the reasons for your ranking.

7. It is sometimes claimed that collusive price behaviour actually stimulates technological change and innovation. What arguments are there, both for and against this claim?

8. Small shopkeepers, fearful that the large supermarket chains will crush them if there is no restriction on shopping hours at all, sometimes argue in this way, 'We can only afford to stay open because we have the market to ourselves for part of the weekend. Consumers would also lose out because the supermarkets and large stores would have to pay high wages to open and prices would rise'. Expose the fundamental fallacy in their argument.

27

Government Regulation and Policy

AFTER READING THIS CHAPTER YOU WILL BE ABLE TO:

1. Explain why market outcomes may not be optimal due to the existence of public goods, externalities, imperfect information, and nonmarket goals.

2. Explain why it is important to assess the trade-offs between the benefits and costs of government regulation.

3. Show how benefit-cost analysis can be used to determine the optimal amount of government regulation.

4. Explain why the total elimination of pollution is not necessarily optimal and describe the government's role in environmental protection.

5. Describe and evaluate government efforts in regulating working conditions, product safety, and consumer advertising and labelling.

6. Understand the arguments for and against privatisation of government owned enterprises.

The Australian economy is a government-regulated market — one in which the questions of what and how much to produce, how to organise production, and for whom to produce are answered by a mixture of government regulation and control in some areas of the economy, coupled with a reliance on private enterprise and free markets in other areas. We have already examined government intervention in areas of the economy where monopoly, oligopoly, and collusion have threatened to diminish competition — a problem that has been attacked through trade practices and price surveillance legislation and government regulation (often controversial) of some markets. We have also seen how government has attempted to provide a minimum standard of living for all citizens through social security, minimum-wage legislation, and various welfare programs. All such forms of government intervention give recognition to the fact that some outcomes of pure market, laissez faire capitalism are undesirable — that indeed government intervention is sometimes necessary to improve on the results.

In this chapter we extend our analysis of the ways in which freely operating markets may not give satisfactory results. We will consider whether or not government regulation can be expected to improve matters and whether the costs of regulation are justified by the potential benefits. We will then examine the kinds of government regulation that attempt to correct shortcomings of the market mechanism. In particular, we will consider government regulation to protect the environment and to promote better working conditions, product safety, and consumer protection. Finally, we will examine in more detail the arguments for

privatisation of government owned enterprises.

SHORTCOMINGS OF THE MARKET

We may identify four major problem areas for the market. First, markets cannot be depended on to provide certain products (such as national defence and lighthouses), called *public goods*. Second, markets do not always capture the full costs and benefits associated with the production of a particular good or service — these are the so-called *external* or *spillover* costs and benefits. Third, while markets convey information about prices, they sometimes suffer from a lack of other kinds of *information* — for example, information about the possible hazards of a complex product such as a new drug. Finally, some goals such as an equitable income distribution or equal employment opportunities often cannot be achieved through the market mechanism; these are the so-called *nonmarket goals*. Let us consider each of these market shortcomings in turn.

Public Goods

We briefly introduced the concept of a public good in Chapter 3. Here we will elaborate on this concept by distinguishing between a pure public good and a near-public good.

Pure Public Goods

A **pure public good** *is a good that cannot be provided to one person without being provided to others. That is, it is impossible to prevent joint consumption.* The beacon from a lighthouse is an example. If one ship in the vicinity can see the beacon, so can others. Suppose a shipping company were to buy and operate a lighthouse. There is no way it could exclude other shipping companies' ships from benefiting from the beacon, even though they contributed nothing to the purchase of the lighthouse. The other shipping companies would be so-called *free riders. A* **free rider** *is anyone who receives the benefits from a good or service without having to pay for it.*

Markets will fail to supply pure public goods precisely because of the free-rider problem. Since anyone can have all the benefits provided by a pure public good without paying, no one will pay for it. Therefore private producers will have no incentive to produce it. Hence despite the fact that a pure public good yields valuable benefits to society, the market mechanism will not provide such a good. Pure public goods must be provided by the government and paid for with tax money or with revenues from the sale of government bonds.[1]

In sum, a pure public good is *not* subject to the **exclusion principle.** *Any good whose benefits accrue only to those who purchase it is said to be subject to the exclusion principle.* Those who do not pay for the good are excluded from its benefits. If you buy a car, your neighbour is excluded from its benefits, unless you choose to allow him or her to use it.

What are some other examples of pure public goods? Our legal system is one. Laws that protect you also protect me, but neither of us would be willing to finance the system alone. Another example is national defence. Even if I am on welfare and pay no income taxes, our

national defence system protects me as much as any multimillionaire who pays hundreds of thousands of dollars in income taxes. Neither I nor the multimillionaire would have any incentive to pay voluntarily for national defence, and, since it is provided, we are both free riders. (If it were not provided, neither of us individually could really make a significant contribution to it anyway, even though we both may value national defense highly.) The quality of the air we breathe is also a pure public good. If it is clean and free of pollutants for one, it is so for all. If many pay taxes to finance the costs of antipollution efforts, those who don't pay taxes share equally in the benefits as well — they are free riders.

If the legal system, national defence, and environmental protection were not provided by government, they would not be provided at all. For why should any individual producer of these services provide them, knowing that it is not possible to charge free riders for consuming the benefits — and why should any individual pay if he or she can be a free rider? In short, since no one would voluntarily pay for these services, no private producer would find it profitable to provide them. Yet they are important to our society, and so government is authorised to provide them.

Near-Public Goods

Near-public goods a*re goods that are consumed jointly, though it is possible to exclude nonpaying customers.* Pure public goods are consumed jointly too, but it is *not* possible to exclude anyone from consuming them. Examples of near-public goods are athletic events, plays, movies, television and radio broadcasts, parks, and toll bridges. Government provision

[1] Note that the government may simply contract with private firms to have the good produced.

of pure public goods is necessary because of the free-rider problem. However, near-public goods are subject to the exclusion principle. Hence it is feasible for them to be provided by private producers responding to market demand.

In our economy we see near-public goods provided both publicly and privately. ABC radio and television, and SBS television, are funded by the government, while at the same time private firms operate radio and TV stations all over Australia in competition. There are government owned national parks that compete in some degree with privately owned outdoor leisure resorts. There are also publicly funded and private museums and art galleries.

Since near-public goods may be produced privately, why should the government ever produce them? Critics of government provision argue that since consumers get the good at a zero price, there is no way of knowing how much of it to provide. Is the cost of providing more of the good covered by what consumers would be willing to pay if they had to? This question suggests that government provision may result in either over- or underproduction of near-public goods. Society may end up devoting too many or too few resources to such goods, which is economically inefficient in either event. Hence, the case for government provision of near-public goods is not as persuasive as the case for government provision of pure public goods.

Externalities

We previously discussed externalities in Chapter 21. Here we will briefly review the concept to provide a basis for our discussion of government regulation.

Recall that **externalities** *are any costs or benefits that fall on others besides the buyers and sellers of a particular good or service.* Externalities are often referred to as *external costs or benefits, spillovers, neighbourhood effects, or external economies and diseconomies.*

There are numerous examples of external costs. Nonsmokers trapped in a meeting room with smokers cannot avoid inhaling some of the smoke. The health hazard of the smoke is an external cost to the nonsmoker. Similarly, residents in the vicinity of a steel mill bear an external cost when smoke from the mill corrodes the paint on their houses, pollutes the air they breathe, and stunts the growth of the surrounding plant life. If residents feel they must move, then they bear an external cost in the form of moving expenses. When Aunt Ethel uses her power tools they may cause static interference on her neighbour's television. The static is an external cost borne by the neighbour. Some electronic heating machines used to make plywood and plastic goods can cause serious interference with frequencies used by airport flight-control towers. The resulting reduction in air passenger safety, possibly leading to airline crashes, is an external cost borne by airlines and their passengers.

Examples of external benefits are not hard to find either. You may invest considerable time and money caring for your garden. Your neighbour reaps the external benefit of viewing a beautiful lawn and garden without spending a cent. If you buy a flu shot, you protect yourself from sickness, an obvious benefit to you. However, others get an external benefit because they are less likely to catch the flu from you. Similarly, if you spend money maintaining the brakes on your car, you bestow an external benefit on other drivers because your car is now less likely to run into them. A pure public good is an extreme example of a good that provides external benefits to parties not directly involved in the purchase or sale of the good. A shipping company may pay you to provide a lighthouse beacon. But nonpaying shippers receive an external benefit because they can use the beacon free of charge — they are free riders, as are all recipients of external benefits.

Society's Loss Due to External Costs

Recall our discussion of external costs in Chapter 21. There we considered an industry (any industry) that pollutes the environment while producing its product. The cost of cleaning up or suffering the consequences is an external cost borne by others. Hence this cost is not included in the industry or market supply curve S shown in Figure 27.1. Given the market demand curve D, the equilibrium quantity produced and sold without regard for this external cost is q_n and the equilibrium price is p_n.

Suppose the firms in the industry had to pay some or all of the environmental cleanup costs associated with the production of each unit of output. These costs would be added to the firms' other production costs to give the market supply curve S_a, which includes all costs and hence lies above S. The equilibrium quantity produced and sold would now be q_0, an amount smaller than q_n. The equilibrium price would be p_0, which is higher than p_n. In this new equilibrium, the cost of pollution would be borne entirely by the buyers and sellers of the product — it is no longer borne by nonconsenting third parties.

The new equilibrium is optimal from society's standpoint; the old equilibrium

is not. Why? Because the external costs associated with a good — costs not borne by the buyers and sellers of the good — foster the production of additional units of output that are not valued as much as the cost of producing them. This can be seen in Figure 27.1 from the fact that the supply curve S_a (which includes all costs) lies above the demand curve D for all units of the good from q_0 to q_n. The dollar value of the total benefits to buyers of this additional quantity $q_n - q_0$ of the good is represented by the area $q_0 q_n bc$. The cost, or dollar value, of the resources used to produce these additional units is represented by the area $q_0 q_n dc$. The dollar amount by which the costs of the additional units exceed their benefits is represented by the area cbd. This is society's loss due to external costs (spillover costs).

This loss is a consequence of the fact that output q_n exceeds the optimal output level q_0 — resources are overallocated to the production of this good. The price per unit of the good p_n fails to cover the costs of producing the good. Society's loss due to external costs is the result of a market shortcoming — namely, a failure to prevent some of the costs of the good from being borne by nonconsenting third parties.

Society's Loss Due to Missed Opportunities: External Benefits

In our discussion of external benefits in Chapter 21 we saw that if a good provides benefits to others who do not buy the good, these spillover, or external, benefits are not reflected in the market demand curve. For example, the market demand curve for flu shots reflects the value of their benefits to the people who buy them to prevent themselves from contracting the

FIGURE 27.1
Society's Loss Due to External Costs

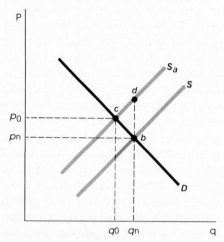

The presence of external costs means that the actual market supply curve S lies below the supply curve S_a that includes all costs associated with production of the good. The external (or spillover) costs lead to the production of additional units of the good (equal to $q_n - q_0$) that are not valued as much as the cost of producing them. The dollar amount of this excess of costs over value equals the area cbd; it represents society's loss due to external costs when the amount q_n is produced.

flu. It does not reflect the benefits of the flu shots to those who don't buy them, but who are nonetheless better off due to the reduction in the spread of a contagious disease.

Since the market demand curve for goods and services providing external benefits does not reflect the full value of these benefits, it must lie below a demand curve that is drawn to include them. Figure 27.2 shows a hypothetical demand curve D and supply curve S for flu shots. The market equilibrium quantity of flu shots supplied and purchased is q_n, and the equilibrium price is p_n. If the value of the external (or spillover) benefits to society at large from these flu shots were added on to D, we would get the demand curve D_a. Since D_a includes the value of all benefits, it lies above D. The equilibrium quantity produced and sold would now be q_0, an amount larger than q_n, and the equilibrium price would be p_0, which is higher than p_n.

Why is the new equilibrium, q_0 and p_0, optimal from society's standpoint? Because when external benefits are associated with a good-benefits that accrue to others who don't pay for it — the market will not produce enough of the good. When only q_n units of the good are produced, society forgoes a quantity of goods ($q_0 - q_n$) that it values more than the cost of producing them. This can be seen in Figure 27.2 from the fact that the demand curve D_a (which includes the value of all benefits) lies above the supply curve S between output quantities q_n and q_0. The dollar value of the benefits to society of the additional quantity $q_0 - q_n$ of the good is represented by the area $q_n q_0 h k$. The cost of the resources used to produce these additional units is represented by the area $q_n q_0 h e$. The dollar amount by which the total benefits of these additional units exceed their cost is represented by the area ehk. This represents society's loss due to the missed opportunity of not having the additional output from q_n to q_0 — a loss caused by the failure of the market to capture external benefits.

The loss reflects the fact that output q_n falls short of the optimal output level q_0. Resources are underallocated to the production of this good because the price per unit of the good p_n fails to reflect the full value of the good.

In summary, *where there are external costs, the market mechanism tends to encourage overproduction, the provision of goods whose costs exceed the value of their benefits. Where there are external* benefits, *the market mechanism gives rise to underproduction, the failure to provide goods even though the value of their benefits exceeds their costs.*

How can the external costs that arise in the markets for certain kinds of goods be internalised to those markets? That is, how can we ensure that such costs are borne by the buyers and sellers directly involved in the transactions in those markets, rather than by others? Similarly, what might be done to encourage a greater production of goods that have external benefits? We cannot give an exhaustive account of all the possible proposals for

FIGURE 27.2
External Benefits: Society's Loss Due to Missed Opportunities

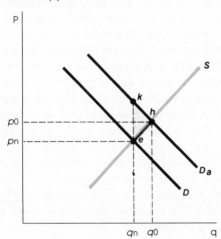

The presence of external benefits means that the market demand curve *D* lies below the demand curve *Da* that includes the value of all benefits associated with the good.
Because of the external (or spillover) benefits, the market fails to produce additional units of the good (the quantity $q_0 - q_n$) that are valued more than the cost of producing them. The dollar amount of this excess of benefits over costs equals the area *ehk*; it represents society's loss because the market produces less than the optimal amount of the good.

dealing with these questions. However, the following are often used or suggested by policymakers.

Policy and External Costs

Policies must be devised to make the suppliers and buyers in the market, rather then third parties who are not the immediate buyers and sellers of the good, bear the external costs. Corrective policy must somehow internalise these costs in the market where they occur. When the externalities associated with a good are external, or spillover, benefits, policies are needed that will encourage the production of a quantity of the good more in line with a demand that takes account of the value of all its benefits to society.

One way to deal with external costs is to pass laws that make them illegal. For example, a state or municipal government might pass laws against dumping untreated industrial wastes in rivers or pouring toxic smoke or particulate matter into the air. If the laws are backed up by sufficiently stiff fines and court actions against offenders, producing firms will take it on themselves to incur directly the costs of installing waste treatment and smoke abatement equipment as part of their production facilities. This means that the market supply curves in industries where there are external costs would shift upward as in Figure 21.11. The firms or suppliers in those industries are forced to pay those costs directly. The incidence of these additional costs would be distributed among the buyers and suppliers in proportions determined by the elasticities of demand and supply just as in the case of an excise tax.

Laws against external costs may not always be easy to enforce, however. Detection of offenders and a determination of the extent of their violation of the law can be difficult. Many different firms using a number of different production processes typically add to air pollution over a metropolitan area. Simply checking the air quality rarely gives a clear picture of who contributed what and how much to the situation. The condition of the water in rivers downstream from these areas raises the same kinds of problems for detection. How often do you read or hear of oil spills and oil slicks where the source is unknown? There may be many smokers but none willing to step forward and lay claim to the cigar and cigarette butts, especially when a fine is to be levied.

In such situations, it may be easier and more effective to simply levy excise taxes on those goods the production of which is known to give rise to spillover costs. This effectively shifts the market supply curves for these goods upward as in Figures 21.7 and 21.8. The tax revenues collected in this fashion can then be used by the government to finance cleanup operations such as waste treatment plants. In any event, such taxes have the effect of making the buyers and sellers in those markets bear the cleanup costs, while at the same time adjusting output so that it is closer to the optimum level.

Policy and External Benefits

How might the government encourage an increase in the production of those goods that give rise to external benefits? That is, how can it encourage the market depicted in Figure 21.12 to increase output from q_n to q_o? One way is to increase demand by giving buyers purchasing power in a form that can only be used to buy the particular good.

Another way the government might increase the output of a good would be simply to pay a per unit subsidy to suppliers (the reverse of an excise tax). This would shift the supply curve downward and increase output in the manner already discussed above in connection with subsidies.

Imperfect Information

The market mechanism may fail to provide adequate information. Information is an economic good; it has value. When consumers have to acquire this information they incur *search costs*. Consumers spend time and money seeking information about products — how good is the product, how safe, what are the alternatives, how much does the product cost in one store as compared to another? Sometimes the information desired is prohibitively expensive or perhaps unavailable at any price. For example, a new drug may have side effects that are as yet unknown. Buyers must always make decisions to varying degrees on the basis of imperfect information. To what extent is there a conflict between producer and consumer interests where product information is concerned? To what extent is product information a public good? To what extent is the lack of perfect information fit cause for government market intervention?

Conflict Between Consumer and Producer Interests

A buyer who purchases a product repeatedly will become quite familiar with its characteristics by trial and error. Foods, beverages, clothing, haircuts, restaurant meals, and dry cleaning are all examples of goods and services whose producers are very dependent on repeat sales if they are to stay in business. Producers have a considerable incentive to ensure consumer satisfaction, because consumers will become fairly well informed about their products in a short period of time. If brand A soap causes a skin rash or brand B toothpaste tastes bitter, sales will drop off fairly rapidly. However, even repeat-purchase items can have characteristics that consumers may not learn about on their own. For example, it is typically not in the producer's best self-interest to inform consumers about possible health hazards associated with long-run use of a product. Cigarette companies were certainly not pleased when the federal government forced them to print health-hazard warnings on cigarette packets. There is, then, often a disparity between what consumers would like to know about a product and what producers want them to know.

Products that are only purchased infrequently, or that are too complex for the typical consumer to evaluate knowledgeably tend to allow greater scope for conflict between consumer and producer interest. Suppose you hire a contractor to build a house. Suppose 10 years later you discover that faulty foundations are cracking, giving rise to basement flooding during heavy rains. The contractor may have long since become wealthy building subdivisions of homes like yours. The market's failure to provide information that protects home buyers from such calamities is one reason most local governments establish building codes. Drugs provide another good example of product complexity that is beyond the information-gathering ability of the consumer. Imperfect information concerning these products has given rise to significant government regulation. And sometimes the cost of gathering informa-

tion is so high that the use of standards set by government regulatory agencies may be a cheap substitute for other, expensive information.

At its worst, the conflict between consumer and producer interests can lead to producer attempts to deceive consumers deliberately. Such deception may take the form of false advertising claims and misleading labelling of products. Subtle manipulation of demand through advertising that appeals to the consumer's ego or emotions is common. Deceptive advertising and labelling amount to attempts to misinform the consumer. Over the years increasing government regulation has been used in an attempt to curb such practices. At the same time, a good deal of government activity has been devoted to the provision of additional product information.

Is Product Information a Near-Public Good?

As we already noted, information is an economic good. There is a market for it. Sellers spend money on advertising to spread information about their wares in trade journals, in newspapers, and on radio and television. Consumers spend money to get information from shoppers' guides, newspapers, and magazines. (Recall our discussion of the information content of advertising in Chapters 25 and 26.) There are private organisations that specialise in selling information to consumers.

One example is *Choice*, a magazine that contains reports on the results of its own testing of hundreds of products and recommends best buys. The Australian Consumers Association provides *Choice* to its members as part of their subscription and to avoid any conflict of interest does not accept commercial advertising. Despite providing a service for its members, the Consumers Association in publishing *Choice* provides a near-public good. Anybody can read a copy in a public library for nothing. Obviously many people could read a single copy, yet the publisher would receive only the purchase price of that one copy. The publishers of such information are unable to capture the full value of the service provided, because they cannot keep those who don't pay for the information from getting it.

In short, the external benefits from *Choice* are probably considerable. As we saw in Figure 27.2, this means that the market produces less of this information than is optimal from society's standpoint. Hence, it may be argued that government action is appropriate to provide additional product information. Indeed, as will be discussed below, there has been a good deal of government activity in this area.

Nonmarket Goals

Certain of the goals and values of any society are either ill-served or not served at all by the marketplace. For instance, markets do not keep people from harming themselves and each other in ways that society considers unacceptable. Also, freely working markets will reward some and penalise others to extremes that may conflict with society's sense of fairness and justice.

Protecting Individuals from Themselves and Others

Markets are capable of providing many kinds of goods and services that society at large considers harmful to the buyer. The government may declare the production and sale of such products illegal or limit their distribution in some way. For example many drugs can be obtained only on a doctor's prescription to prevent abuse. Wearing seat belts is compulsory, licences are required to drive motor vehicles on public roads and restrictions exist on the ownership and use of firearms. Examples of such restrictions that limit our freedom of choice and action abound. Often there is considerable public debate about whether government is acting oppressively when it introduces such restrictions on personal freedom. Watchdog groups exist to protect our civil liberties and often new proposals for restriction run into fierce opposition. The Australia Card was proposed by the Hawke Labor Government, principally as a means of reducing tax evasion. However a campaign against the proposal in 1987 arguing that it constituted a serious invasion of privacy gained momentum and led to the proposal being abandoned. Attempts to introduce tougher gun laws in 1988 faced similar opposition.

In part the reason for restrictions is to protect people from one another. Of course, this is a major reason why governments and the rule of law exist in the first place. The market system may be based on the free actions of buyers and sellers reacting to market signals but there need to be some basic and enforceable rules of the game. Cheating and fraud, standover tactics and unfair pressure on buyers or sellers would make a mockery of the notion that an unregulated market worked in everybody's interests.

For many years there have been laws restricting the hours children can work and laws requiring compulsory schooling. That safety conditions and limitations on working hours are also built into many industrial awards is also a reflection that an unregulated market can produce undesirable effects. Government intervention to prevent exploitation and unfairness in Australia goes quite a lot further today than it did a few years ago. Antidiscrimination and equal opportunities legislation has done much to raise the status of women, minority groups and the disabled. While in one sense such regulation interferes with the market solution it is also society's response to market shortcomings.

Income Redistribution

Freely working markets will reward some and penalise others. Those who are hardworking, able, and lucky may live handsomely by the market. Most people have little sympathy for the able-bodied but lazy whom the market treats sternly. But the impersonal forces of the market are indifferent to the disabled, the handicapped, and others beset by misfortune beyond their control. Society generally takes the attitude that, in such cases, private charitable organisations, government policies, or both should be used to redistribute income from the more fortunate to the less fortunate. (We will examine a number of policies with this goal in Chapter 31, where we will focus on the problems of poverty.)

Some argue that antipoverty efforts are a public good. When you give money to private charity to help alleviate poverty, you bestow external benefits on nongivers. That is, the benefits that stem from poverty reduction (a decline in disease, slums, and so forth) accrue to society at large. Hence each would-be giver is tempted to be a free rider — let the other person do the giving. As illustrated in Figure 27.2, whenever there are external benefits associated with a good, there will

be underproduction of the good — in this case, antipoverty efforts.

GOVERNMENT REGULATION: A RESPONSE TO MARKET SHORTCOMINGS

When markets perform inadequately in the ways we have discussed, should government regulations be used in an attempt to attain perfection, or are there trade-offs between the reduction of shortcomings and its costs? How do we know how much government regulation is needed? And what about the possibility that government regulation will make matters worse? We now turn to these questions. In addition we will also briefly examine four areas of government regulation: protection of the environment, working conditions, product safety, and consumer protection — the last through regulations aimed at preventing deceptive advertising and labelling.

How Much Government Regulation Is Appropriate?

How do we know how much government regulation is needed to correct the undesirable consequences of market shortcomings? Attempts to answer this question are a source of continual, often heated debate among politicians, policymakers, and citizens and special interests affected by regulation. The kind of regulation called for can vary greatly from one type of market shortcoming to another. But in all cases, in determining the appropriate amount of regulation, we must recognise that there is a trade-off between the benefits and costs of regulation. Moreover, we should be aware that any regulation can have perverse effects, outcomes quite the opposite of those intended.

Trade-offs Between the Costs and Benefits of Regulation

Economics is a study of trade-offs. To have more of one thing we have to give up a certain amount of something else. The cost (or opportunity cost) of having more of one thing is the value of the other things that must be given up. *Intelligent decisions about the appropriate amount of regulation require recognition of the fact that regulation has a cost too, and that there is a trade-off between the costs and benefits of regulation.*

Consider government regulation to promote safety. Some argue that it is impossible to put a dollar value on human suffering or human life. However, any decision concerning the imposition of safety regulations unavoidably makes such a valuation. For example, the imposition of maximum speed limits on all roads rather than just in cities and towns was, of course, based on the argument that such restrictions would save lives. Speed kills. The judgment is that the saving of those lives (along with any fuel savings) is more valuable than the time that is lost through slower travel. On the other hand those who advocate unlimited or higher speed limits particularly on main highways imply that the time saved is worth more than the reduction in life and suffering and loss of life that results from the fewer traffic accidents at the lower speed.

If human life were priceless, people would not travel in aeroplanes, work on skyscrapers, build bridges, drive motorcycles, mine coal, or go to war. The question, then, is not whether or not a value can be placed on human life; when society sets any policy or takes any action, it implicitly decides on such a value. The only question is whether that value is acceptable. Most modern vehicles can achieve speeds of 140 kph. But society values life too highly to accept 140 kph as the speed limit, even on the best roads in Australia.

CHECKPOINT *27.1
Motorists long complained about a road through the mountains in one of the eastern states. It was narrow and winding and when stuck behind a truck a motorist would find the journey extremely slow. The state Minister for Transport defended the decision not to replace the road with a modern highway by saying that it was the safest road in the state — people had to drive slowly and there were therefore few accidents. How would you counter that argument? What factors do you think the state should have taken into consideration in deciding whether to replace the road?

On some freeways there is a minimum speed limt as well as a maximum. What justification can there be for minimum speed limits?

* Answers to all checkpoints are given at the end of the book.

Regulation and Perverse Results

It has been said that the road to hell is paved with good intentions. Sometimes, regulations that are motivated by the best of intentions can actually make matters worse.

For example, most people would agree on the desirability of some minimum level of qualifications for doctors and health care facilities. Regulations in most states stipulate that many medical services may be provided only by a licensed physician. Nurses and paramedics could provide some of these services equally well, but regulations prevent them from doing so. Such regulations tend to restrict the supply of medical care and thus drive up its price. The result is that people who otherwise would seek professional care now resort to home remedies: bandages instead of stitches, over-the-counter medicines instead of more effective prescription drugs, birth at home instead of in hospitals. Thus, as regulation aimed at improving the quality of health care drives up its price, the consumption of professional medical services (and perhaps the overall quality of health care) declines.

Benefit-Cost Analysis

The optimal amount of regulation should be determined in the way we determine the optimal amount of any other good or service. That is, *regulation should be extended up to the point where the dollar value of the last unit of benefit just equals the cost of obtaining it*. A determination of the optimal amount of regulation according to this principle requires a benefit-cost analysis. We will illustrate how benefit-cost analysis can be used to determine the appropriate amount of regulation for environmental protection.

Environmental Protection

Environmental pollution is a scourge of industrialised societies. It plagues capitalist, socialist, and communist countries alike. It is an inevitable consequence of economic growth, the increase in the output of goods and services per capita.

Industrialisation and increased production of goods and services also mean increased production of 'bads' and 'disservices': noxious waste products that pollute air and waterways; junkyards, slag heaps, smokestacks, derricks, and mining and industrial sites that spoil the landscape; and urban and suburban congestion and noise that cause tension and stress.

The costs imposed on society by these bads and disservices take the form of health and property damage and, generally, an impaired quality of life. Moreover, these costs are external, or spillover, costs — they are borne by parties other than the producers and buyers of the goods whose production causes them. These costs cannot be eliminated, but they can be shifted to the parties who cause them. This is done by internalising such costs to the markets where they occur.

For example, suppose the residents in the vicinity of a steel mill incur property damage and health-care costs as a consequence of air pollution caused by the mill. If the steel mill is required to purchase equipment that eliminates its emission of air pollutants, then the cost of the pollution is shifted to those directly involved in the production and sale of steel. Those who buy and use steel now pay all the costs of producing steel; none of the cost is imposed on people living near the steel mill. The supply curve of steel is shifted leftward as discussed in connection with Figure 27.1. Those who buy steel now pay a higher price, which includes the cost of pollution. (For a discussion of how this cost is distributed between buyers and sellers, see Chapter 21.)

Environmental pollution occurs because clean air and clean rivers, lakes and oceans are public goods. It is impossible to keep the air or water clean for some in a region and not for others. The exclusion principle does not apply.

A firm that *voluntarily* invested in equipment to reduce the amount of pollutants emitted from its smokestacks would not be able to charge for this service. Why? Because those who won't pay will have clean air just the same as those who do. Everyone has an incentive to be a free rider and 'let the other guy pay'. If the firm charged a higher price for its product to cover the cost of its antipollution efforts, it would lose sales to competitors who did not incur such costs and who therefore could charge lower prices. Environmental protection thus seems to require government regu-

lation. The tough questions are, How much and in what form?

How Much Pollution Control: Benefits Versus Costs

Regulation, like any 'product,' provides certain benefits and gives rise to certain costs. These benefits and costs vary as the amount of regulation varies. A **benefit-cost analysis** is an examination of the benefits and costs associated with differing levels of output (here the output is regulation) to determine the most effective level according to some criterion.

To illustrate, let's consider a hypothetical benefit-cost analysis of pollution

TABLE 27.1
Benefit-Cost Analysis for Pollution Control (Hypothetical Data)

	(1) Annual Units of Pollution (Thousands)	(2) Annual Pollution Damage (Thousands of Dollars)	(3) Marginal Benefit of 10,000 Units of Added Pollution Reduction (Thousands of Dollars)	(4) Annual Total Costs of Pollution Reduction (Thousands of Dollars)	(5) Marginal Cost of 10,000 Additional Units of Pollution Reduction (Thousands of Dollars)	(6) Total Benefits Equal Total Reduction in Pollution Damage (Thousands of Dollars)	(7) Net Gain Equals (6) Minus (4) (Thousands of Dollars)
1.	100	$1,000		$0		$0	$0
			$100		$10		
2.	90	900		10		100	90
			150		15		
3.	80	750		25		250	225
			175		25		
4.	70	575		50		425	375
			115		40		
5.	60	460		90		540	450
			110		60		
6.	50	350		150		650	500
			100		85		
7.	40	250		235		750	515
			90		120		
8.	30	160		355		840	485
			80		200		
9.	20	80		555		920	365
			45		350		
10.	10	35		905		965	60
			35		500		
11.	0	0		1,405		1,000	-405

control in a particular region, as illustrated in Table 27.1. Suppose that as a by-product of its production process, a large company is polluting the air, giving rise to external, or spillover, costs. In the absence of government regulation requiring the company to control its pollution, suppose the company's smokestacks annually emit 100,000 units of pollutant (row 1, column 1 of Table 27.1), causing external costs equal to $1 million of damage (external costs) to the surrounding area (row 1, column 2 of Table 27.1). The government decides to take action to regulate this pollution. Should government regulators force the company to stop polluting entirely, or should they require only that some portion of the pollutant be removed from smokestack emissions?

The answer is that *regulators should require the company to remove pollutants from smokestack emissions up to the point where the marginal cost of pollution reduction equals the marginal benefit of pollution reduction.*

Suppose the company is required to reduce pollution from 100,000 to 90,000 units (column 1, rows 1 and 2). Pollution damage would be reduced from $1 million to $900,000 (column 2, rows 1 and 2), so that the marginal benefit of pollution reduction is $100,000 (column 3). The total cost to the company of reducing pollution this much is $10,000 (column 4, row 2), which is also the marginal cost (column 5) since the company starts from a level of zero pollution expenditures. Total benefits from pollution reduction amount to $100,000 (column 6, row 2). This amount of pollution reduction is clearly worthwhile since the marginal benefit of $100,000 (column 3) certainly exceeds the marginal cost of $10,000 (column 5). In fact, examination of columns 3 and 5 indicates that the marginal benefits of

increasing pollution reduction continue to exceed the marginal cost of such reduction until pollution has been reduced to a level of 40,000 units (column 1, row 7). Reducing pollution from 50,000 to 40,000 units gives rise to marginal benefits of $100,000, which exceeds the marginal cost of $85,000 associated with reducing pollution by another 10,000 units.

It would not be worthwhile to force the company to reduce pollution to 30,000 units (column 1, row 8). Why? Because the required additional, or marginal, cost of $120,000 (column 5) would exceed the additional, or marginal, benefit of $90,000 (column 3). This would amount to an overallocation of resources to pollution control.

In sum, *the marginal benefit-marginal cost rule implies that pollution control should be expanded as long as marginal benefits* (column 3) *exceed marginal costs* (column 5). According to this criterion, the most effective amount of control is at, or as close as possible to, that point where marginal benefits equal marginal costs. Note that *this rule maximises the excess of total benefits over total costs* (column 7); *that is, it provides the greatest net gain from pollution control* (equal to $515,000, column 7, row 7). In our example, government pollution regulations should require that the company not emit more than 40,000 units of pollution annually.

Three important observations should be made at this point.

1. The Optimal Level of Control. The total elimination of pollution is not necessarily optimal. We know it is not optimal to reduce speed limits to the point where there are no traffic accidents. The benefit-cost analysis of our pollution control problem (Table 27.1) shows why it is not optimal to eliminate pollution completely. The total annual cost of reducing pollution to zero is $1,405,000 (column 4, row 11). The total benefits resulting from the complete elimination of pollution damage equal $1 million (column 6, row 11). The net gain is *minus* $405 thousand (column 7, row 11), a loss! In other words, the cost of completely eliminating pollution exceeds the value of the benefits — it isn't worth it. Complete elimination of pollution would be optimal only if the marginal cost of pollution reduction were always less than the marginal benefits. While this is not true for our example in Table 27.1, it could be the case for certain kinds of pollution problems. In any event, a benefit-cost analysis is necessary to determine the optimal amount of pollution control. More generally, *a benefit-cost analysis is required to determine the optimal amount of any form of government regulation.*

2. Enforcing Pollution Control. With the benefit-cost data of Table 27.1, government regulators could calculate the optimal pollution level as we have. They could use either of the two approaches to the problem we discussed earlier in the chapter, direct control or the use of the tax system to achieve a market solution. We will discuss two specific options commonly tried (a) adoption of legislated standards, or (b) the levying of pollution emission taxes.

(a) *Legislated standards.* The government could pass laws empowering government regulators to establish minimum allowable levels of pollution. For instance, regulators could declare it illegal for the company of Table 27.1 to emit pollutants in excess of 40,000 units per year (row 7). If the law were backed by sufficiently stiff fines and possible court action, the company could be compelled to incur the $235,000 cost of abiding by the 40,000 units per year pollution limit.

(b) *Pollution emission taxes.* The government could also achieve the optimal pollution level by placing a tax on pollution. For example, if the government levies a pollution tax of $90,000 for each 10,000 units of pollutants, the company in Table 27.1 would have an incentive to keep pollution down to the optimal level of 40,000 units. To see why, note that the marginal cost of reducing pollution by another 10,000 units is less than $90,000 (column 5, rows 1-7) all the way to the point where pollution has been reduced to a level of 40,000 units. To this point it is cheaper for the company to pay the cost of reducing pollution than to pay the pollution tax. However, the company will find it cheaper to pay the pollution tax on the remaining 40,000 units of pollution. Why? Because the marginal cost of eliminating each successive 10,000 units of pollution once the pollution level has been reduced to 40,000 units is always greater than the $90,000 tax per 10,000 units of pollution. (That is, the last four entries in column 5 are all greater than $90,000.)

You would find it instructive at this point to answer questions 4 and 5 at the end of this chapter.

3. Problems of Measurement. In our discussion to this point, we have assumed that government regulators know the dollar value of the pollution damage associated with each level of pollution. It also has been assumed that they can measure the quantity and nature of the pollution as well as the benefits and costs of preventing it. In other words, we have assumed that the government regulators known all the data in Table 27.1. In reality this is rarely the case. Deciding what is the optimal level of pollution regulation is therefore very difficult in practice. Nonetheless, *a benefit-cost analysis forces the analyst to ask the right questions and to seek the information needed for wise decision making.*

CHECKPOINT 27.2
In the benefit-cost analysis example of Table 27.1, suppose the marginal cost of pollution reduction were $70,000 higher at every level — that is, assume every entry in column 5 is larger by $70,000. What would be the optimal level of pollution?

Working Conditions

Can the market effectively deal with problems of occupational health and safety? Those who say yes argue as follows. Workers will take hazardous jobs only if they are offered higher wages to compensate for the increased risk of injury. Employers will reduce work hazards if it costs less than paying higher wages. On the other hand, if paying higher wages is cheaper than reducing hazards, then workers will be compensated for the hazards.

Those who disagree with this argument claim there are factors that hamper the labour market's ability to deal effectively with problems of occupational health and safety. They argue that often there is inadequate information on the relationship between job conditions and health and safety hazards. For example, the effects of many health risks, such as exposure to cancer-causing substances, may not show up for years, or such hazards may not be known during the term of employment. Unsafe or unhealthy

working conditions also may give rise to external costs — costs borne by parties other than the employer and employee. For instance, workers exposed to certain substances subsequently may have children with birth defects attributable to this exposure — the children are the injured third parties. Imperfect information and the presence of external costs will tend to inhibit workers from demanding wages adequate to compensate for health and safety hazards. Therefore employers will not have adequate incentive to incur the costs of reducing work hazards, and consequently there will be an underallocation of resources to the maintenance of health and safety in the workplace. It can be argued that these considerations make a case for government regulation of occupational health and safety.

Product Safety

Government regulation of product safety is based on the contention that many products are too complex for consumers to make informed purchase decisions. Moreover, as we observed earlier, information is like a near-public good in that the market tends to produce less than the optimal amount of information. Product complexity, together with inadequate market provision of information, may lead consumers to underestimate the hazards associated with certain products.

The legal position of the consumer relative to that of the seller has changed substantially during the last century. That position has shifted from one of *caveat emptor*, 'let the buyer beware', to one of *caveat vendor*, 'let the seller beware'. Under the doctrine of *caveat emptor*, buyers bore responsibility for the consequences of their purchase decisions. They could not claim damages from sellers for faulty products. Gradually, legal rules of fraud evolved that allowed buyers to recover damages if they could prove that sellers had misrepresented their products. In addition, negligence rules evolved that held the seller responsible for the costs of injuries caused by product defects that the seller either knew about or should have known about. Recent years have seen a dramatic upsurge in product liability actions against sellers. Judges and juries are increasingly deciding that sellers are responsible for the goods they market.

Paralleling the emergence of the doctrine of *caveat vendor* has been an expansion of government regulation to ensure product safety. The Australian states each have a Product Safety Committee or branch of its consumer protection agency and there is also considerable consultation between the states and the federal government to remove harmful products from sale. The federal government has powers to restrict the import of hazardous products. Drugs are subject to close investigation by the Drug Evaluation Committee of the National Health and Medical Research Council before being approved. Federal, state and local government health authorities have complementary roles in enforcing standards.

Consumer Protection

Government measures to protect Australian consumers go well beyond questions of health and safety as we have already noted. Much of the discussion in Chapters 23 to 26 has been about the merits of competition and the disadvantages to consumers and society as a whole of restrictive trade practices such as collusion and cartel activity. We noted in Chapter 24 that while economies of scale led to

natural monopoly with potential benefits, it has often been necessary for the government to take over or regulate such natural monopolies to prevent the benefits flowing largely to the producer, rather than the consumer. The work of federal bodies such as the Trade Practices Commission and the Prices Surveillance Authority has a direct bearing on the relative benefits producers and consumers receive from the market. Their existence too, is an indication that there is a widely held view in our society that specific rules and procedures are required in our society for the market to work in the public and in the consumers' interests. As mentioned earlier all states have a ministry of consumer affairs or its equivalent and a bureau or office with the responsibility of ensuring consumers' interest are not ignored. It would be tedious to describe the many and complex ways in which governments in Australia work to protect consumer interests these days. Consumer pressure groups generally feel government does not do enough, while business and commerce tends to the view that consumers are overprotected. The business response often is that government regulation to protect the consumer stops the market from working properly and imposes higher costs on producers which are ultimately passed on to consumers.

One aspect of consumer protection that must be mentioned is the development in the states whereby consumers can obtain redress of grievances. Sometimes, after a transaction the consumer is dissatisfied and the supplier is not prepared to recognise the consumer's complaint. The goods may be faulty, the producer may refuse to honour a commitment about price, warranty conditions may not be adhered to or the consumer may feel the supplier exerted undue pressure in making

POLICY PERSPECTIVE

Consumer Protection — The United Nations Guidelines on Consumer Protection

In 1985 the General Assembly of the United Nations adopted a set of guidelines for consumer protection. The general subjects identified were:
(a) the protection of consumers from hazards to their health and safety;
(b) the promotion and protection of the economic interest of consumers;
(c) access of consumers to adequate information to enable them to make informed choices according to individual wishes and needs;
(d) consumer education;
(e) availability of effective consumer redress;
(f) freedom to form consumer and other relevant groups or organisations and the opportunity for such groups to present their views in decision-making processes affecting them.

In addition to these general principles the guidelines contained quite specific statements on the various matters covered. These included the need for national safety and quality standards conforming where possible to internationally accepted standards, international transmission of information relating to banned products and restriction on import of such products.

One of the purposes of developing such a set of guidelines was that it would be a minimum set of objectives thought to be particularly useful for developing countries. The Australian National Consumer Affairs Advisory Council reported in 1986 that consumer policy in Australia largely met the guidelines and that while the aim might have been to assist developing countries, the guidelines also provided a useful framework against which the policies of advanced countries could be evaluated.

Questions

1. Why is it that developing countries are more likely to find it difficult to accept the UN Guidelines on consumer protection than is Australia?

2. Occasionally firms are criticised by the international consumer movement for exporting products that fail to reach the minimum standards specified for sale in their own country. Alternatively it is still possible to sell Australian beef in Australia with higher pesticide residues than are acceptable in the United States. Suppose you were a firm that followed these business practices. How would you answer your critics?

a sale. Each state has a system for investigating complaints and a high proportion of such complaints are resolved every year — not always in the consumer's favour, for consumers can be wrong on occasions. Cheap informal tribunals or courts operate in each state to hear small claims, while of course consumers have recourse to the courts where larger amounts are involved. It is sometimes argued that such consumer protection machinery is not needed, and that the market will sort out the good reliable firms from the dishonest, uncooperative or unfair trader. It is said the consumers should find out about goods before they buy, learn by their mistakes and adjust their consumption patterns and by doing so 'vote for the good guys'. This argument has been rejected in Australia for the following reasons:

(1) many goods are complex and we cannot find out all we know about them before purchase,

(2) many goods are purchased infrequently, or maybe only once in a lifetime; they therefore may involve large sums of money and there may not be the opportunity to learn by experience,

(3) where goods or services are not homogeneous each new purchase involves obtaining new information,

(4) why should consumers have to learn by their mistakes?

(5) it is likely to be cheaper from society's point of view to have a system that combines redress provisions and statutory obligations on suppliers than to place onerous search costs on consumers to determine the validity of suppliers' claims.

CHECKPOINT 27.3
Compared to regulations for product safety, do you think regulation of deceptive advertising serves to enhance or restrict consumer choice?

Privatisation

Much of the discussion in this chapter has been about the circumstances in which government should regulate a market to overcome market shortcomings. It has been noted that there are arguments for and against such regulation. It invariably imposes costs as well as benefits. Some people believe there is much unnecessary regulation in the Australian economy and that these costs outweigh the benefits. Arguments for deregulation are largely the opposite of those for regulation.

A somewhat different debate that has gathered momentum in Australia in recent years has been whether there are benefits to be had from **privatisation** as distinct from deregulation. A number of Australia's largest business enterprises are government owned and controlled. Some such as Telecom have a monopoly over major telecommunication services, while others such as Qantas, the Commonwealth Bank and Australian Airlines compete with privately owned enterprises. Privatisation involves the selling of such enterprises to the public. There are a number of powerful arguments for privatisation. First, it is claimed that where the enterprise needs large amounts of investment capital, it is more likely to obtain this as a private enterprise organisation than if it has to meet government guidelines. Qantas and Australian Airlines have argued that lack of investment capital has reduced their capacity to compete for business. Similarly, it is argued that political control prevents some state owned enterprises from making the 'best' decisions. Some claim, of course, that the management structure and rewards of private enterprise produce efficiency while state run enterprises are inefficient.

On the other hand there is strong opposition to privatisation. A large part of the Australian Labor Party is philosophically opposed to selling off 'national assets'. It is argued that where the enterprise holds a monopoly, such as Telecom or Australia Post government should continue to own it to prevent exploitation. A similar argument is one that recognises that government continues to use its ownership of major enterprises to achieve social objectives. It can impose a pricing structure that assists particular groups such as people living in rural areas, the poor and home buyers. Where a government-owned enterprise is competing satisfactorily — the Commonwealth Bank — why should it be sold to the private sector? It is also argued that such enterprises should not be sold to achieve windfall gains. Just as there is no simple answer to the question, is deregulation a good thing? so it is with privatisation. The case for selling Australian Airlines is likely to be quite different from the case for selling off Telecom. Leaving aside the question of principle, the costs and benefits (social as well as economic) are likely to be quite different.

CHECKPOINT 27.4
Is privatisation an economic or a political subject? To what extent is it possible to separate the arguments? How is it that some members of the Australian Labor Party such as Mr Hawke see merit in privatisation when much of the party is opposed?

SUMMARY

1. The market mechanism has several problem areas: it does not provide pure public goods, it gives rise to external costs and benefits in providing certain goods, it provides inadequate amounts of certain kinds of information, and its results are incompatible with some of society's goals. Government intervention, in the form of regulation, may be used in an attempt to correct such faults.

2. Government provision of pure public goods, such as national defence, is necessary because such goods are not subject to the exclusion principle. Near-public goods are jointly consumed, like pure public goods, but they are subject to the exclusion principle and hence they will be provided by the market.

3. Whenever external costs are associated with the market for a good, society suffers a loss because too much of the good is produced. Whenever there are external benefits, a loss occurs because too little of the good is produced. In either case government regulation may be used to achieve the optimal output level.

4. Imperfect information is usually a problem in the purchase and sale of products that are not purchased repeatedly or that are complex. The market probably provides less product information than is optimal because such information is like a near-public good.

5. Society has goals and values that are sometimes at odds with market outcomes. Government may ban products that markets will provide but that society deems harmful to those who would buy them. Government regulation is also used to prevent people from exploiting one another in ways society considers unacceptable. And the government plays an ever increasing role in the redistribution of income to modify the income distribution otherwise provided by market outcomes.

6. Any determination of the appropriate amount of government regulation must recognise that there is a trade-off between the costs and benefits of regulation, and that it is possible for regulation to make matters worse rather than better. Benefit-cost analysis is a useful tool for determining the optimal amount of regulation.

7. Environmental pollution imposes external, or spillover, costs, because clean air and clean rivers, lakes, and oceans are public goods. Benefit-cost analysis suggests that total elimination of pollution is usually not optimal. Legislated standards and pollution emission taxes can be used to regulate the amount of pollution and internalise its costs to the markets that cause it.

8. Imperfect information about job hazards and the presence of external costs in the labour market suggest that there is an underallocation of resources to maintaining health and safety in the workplace. Government regulation of working conditions also extends to the enforcement of minimum-wage laws and child-labour laws and to the elimination of discriminatory hiring practices.

9. In addition to government measures to protect consumers from hazardous goods and unfair trade practices there are powerful arguments to justify mechanisms to provide redress for grievances.

10. The debate on the merits of privatisation is complex. Widely differing views prevail as they do on the merits of deregulation. While general principles may be considered, the strength of the arguments for deregulation or privatisation are likely to depend on the particular circumstances in each case.

KEY TERMS AND CONCEPTS

benefit-cost analysis
exclusion principle
externalities
free rider

near-public good
privatisation
pure public good

QUESTIONS AND PROBLEMS

1. What is the distinction between a pure public good and a near-public good? Classify each of the following as either a pure public good, a near-public good, or neither: a movie, a radio program, a symphony concert, a clean ocean, a haircut, a cable television program, a quiet neighbourhood, a football game, a clean lake, a keg of beer, the spectrum of radio waves, international relations.

2. It has been observed that community owned property (such as a public park, roadside, or stadium) tends to be more littered with wastepaper and empty bottles than private property (such as people's yards and driveways). How would you relate this observation to each of the following concepts: public good, external costs, the free-rider problem? Suggest some product regulations that might reduce this litter. Illustrate the nature of the problem for bottled beverages in terms of either Figure 27.1 or 27.2, indicating how you would measure the size of the external costs on such a graph and the effect of regulations to eliminate the external costs.

3. Why does the market provide less product information than is optimal? Do you think that information in general is likely to be underproduced or overproduced?

4. Suppose the total amount of pollution damage in Table 27.1 were $1 million greater at every level of pollution (that is, add $1 million to each entry in column 2). A public outcry about the problem leads the local government to hire you as an economic consultant to advise them what to do. Assume that prior to the $1 million jump in pollution damage the government already taxed pollution emissions at the rate of $90,000 per 10,000 units of pollutants. What would you advise the government to do now? Is it possible for pollution damage to get worse even though you always follow an optimal environmental protection strategy?

5. Suppose there are two firms in a neighbourhood, each emitting 5 units of pollutants in the absence of regulation. Suppose their marginal costs of eliminating each unit of pollution are as shown in the following table.

	Emissions Without Regulation	Marginal Cost of Eliminating Each Successive Unit of Pollution				
		1st	2nd	3rd	4th	5th
Firm A	5	$100	200	300	400	500
Firm B	5	$200	400	600	800	1,000

Assume regulators wish to reduce neighbourhood pollution by a total of 6 units. You are called in as a consultant and asked whether they should set a maximum emission limit of 2 units of pollution per firm or, alternatively, use a pollution emission tax to accomplish their goal. What would you tell them, and why? What does this indicate about the relative merits of maximum emission standards and pollution emission taxes as tools for pollution control?

6. Suppose a plant has a number of safety hazards. How should the plant manager allocate available resources to eliminate these hazards? That is, how should the manager decide the amount of resources to allocate to each problem area?

7. Discuss the merits of the following consumer protection measures, compulsory ingredient labelling of foods, date marking on frozen chickens, a ban on cheap imported cotton dresses, a ban on fireworks, mandatory installation standards for woodburning heaters, prevention of supermarkets from selling medicine, registration of home builders and tradesmen. In each case weigh up the benefits and likely costs to consumers of the policy.

8. Choose two of Australia Post, the Commonwealth Bank and the ABC and draw up a list of the advantages and disadvantages of privatisation of each organisation. Which would you sell off first if you had to — and why?

SEVEN

Price Determination of Economic Resources

28

Production and the Demand for Productive Resources

AFTER READING THIS CHAPTER YOU WILL BE ABLE TO:

1. Explain why the demand for a productive factor is a derived demand.

2. Summarise the marginal productivity theory of factor demand.

3. Understand the interrelationship between resources and product markets and see how a shock in one affects the other also.

4. List and explain the determinants of the elasticity of a factor demand curve.

5. Delineate the causes of shifts in a factor demand curve.

6. Set forth the principles underlying the firm's determination of the optimum combination of several productive factors that it uses.

Up to now we have focused on the way prices are determined in the markets for the goods and services produced by firms, the markets where households are on the demand side and businesses on the supply side. We have said little about the determination of the prices of the economic resources, or factors of production, that the firm must use to produce these goods and services, the markets where firms are on the demand side and households on the supply side. The prices of such economic resources as land, labour, capital (plant and equipment), energy, and raw materials are matters of major significance. In this chapter we will look at some of the basic considerations that enter into the determination of these prices.

WHY RESOURCE PRICING IS IMPORTANT

Resource pricing is important basically for two reasons. First, it determines how the economy's limited supply of economic resources is allocated to the various production activities necessary to produce the multitude of goods and services that society wants. Second, it determines how income earned from productive activities is distributed among the citizens of the economy.

Allocation of Economic Resources to Productive Activities

Resource prices are the signalling devices that direct resources to the different industries, firms, and governmental activities that constitute the economy's productive capacity. If the wages paid to machinists in the motor vehicle industry

rise relative to those paid to machinists in the aircraft industry, this type of labour resource will tend to move away from aircraft production and into vehicle production. If the price of land for residential use rises relative to that for agricultural use, the rate at which farmland is converted into suburbs will tend to increase. If the rate of return on financial capital invested in physical capital (plant and equipment) in the computer industry rises relative to the rate earned in the steel industry, the rate of new physical capital formation in the computer industry will tend to rise relative to that in the steel industry. If the wages paid to government employees rise relative to those paid to workers in the private sector, labour will tend to flow into the government sector and away from the private sector.

Determination of Income Distribution

All productive resources in our economy are owned by somebody. The owners sell the services of their resources and the payments received in exchange constitute their incomes. There are two variables that make up this exchange: the quantity of resource services sold, and the price at which a unit of the service is sold. A labourer's income depends on the number of labour hours sold and the price (or wage rate) of a labour hour. A landlord's income depends on the number of hectares of land or square metres of floor space rented out and the rental rate per unit. The income that a stockholder in a corporation receives depends on the number of shares owned and the dividends and capital gains earned per share.

Whether we are talking about labourers, landlords, or stockholders, it is obvious that the prices received per unit of the resource service sold enter into the determination of the income they receive. This income in turn determines the share of the economy's output of goods and services that each of them may purchase. Given the implications for the welfare of different groups in the economy that follow from this, it is little wonder that the determination of resource prices is frequently a matter of considerable controversy. What is a 'just' wage or a 'fair' return? Questions such as these go to the heart of the often emotional issue of income distribution, a subject fraught with normative judgments. We will delve more deeply into various aspects of the roles of labour unions, business, and government, and explore other institutional characteristics of this subject over the course of the three following chapters.

Our discussion in this chapter is concerned with the analysis of factor demand from the viewpoint of the firm. We will be concerned with how it works rather than with the normative questions of its implications for the distribution of income among different groups in the economy, a subject to be taken up in a subsequent chapter. The demand for economic resources, or factors of production, is really just a special application of the general principles of demand with which you are already familiar.

FACTOR DEMAND IS A DERIVED DEMAND

The basic characteristic of factor demand is that it is a **derived demand**. *This means that the demand for any productive factor ultimately depends upon, or derives from, the demand for the final product or products that the factor is used to produce.*

The demand for steelworkers derives from the demand for steel. The demand for steel derives from the demand for the many products that contain steel. The demand for farmland derives from the demand for agricultural products, as does the demand for farm machinery and other capital equipment needed in agricultural production. The demand for high-technology space scientists and engineers is derived from the demand for space vehicles and their support facilities. Examples of derived demand are almost endless.

The importance of the fact that demand in the factor market is a derived demand cannot be over emphasised. The business decisions the firm makes in hiring resources are completely tied in with what is happening in the product market. We will always refer to the nature of the product market and specify both the demand and supply conditions prevailing there when we discuss business behaviour in the factor market.

The demand for any particular productive factor may well derive from its use in the production of several different products. The more narrowly we define a productive factor, the fewer the products its demand will be derived from. Labour is used in the production of all goods. Barbers are used only in the production of haircuts. Similarly, drill presses are a general category of capital equipment needed in many production processes, but only certain types of presses are used to produce wristwatches. The complexity of explaining *the* derived demand for a productive factor will therefore depend on how broadly or narrowly we define that factor.

MARGINAL PRODUCTIVITY THEORY OF FACTOR DEMAND

The nature of the demand for a productive factor can be made more precise by determining the productive factor's specific contribution to the making of the final product. Common sense suggests that the larger the contribution the factor makes to the output of a product, the greater will be the demand for the factor. The **marginal productivity theory of factor demand** provides an explanation of why this is so.

To understand the basis of this theory let us consider a firm that operates under perfect competition in the *product market*. Notice it is necessary to specify the precise conditions that will operate in both the *product market* and the *factor market*. The firm is a price taker in the product market. As we have seen this means the firm can sell as little or as much as it wants at the given market price because it provides an insignificant proportion of total supply. Hence if it varies its output it has no effect on the price of the product. We also assume that the firm (like the firm we discussed in Chapter 22) uses a fixed factor — say capital — and one variable factor of production — say labour. In other words the quantity of one factor is fixed and the other variable. It was these assumptions that led us in Chapter 21 to the familiar U shaped average cost curve and rising marginal cost curve.

Now we want to consider demand in a resource market and to use those assumptions. First, however, we need to make another assumption — this time about the market for the variable resource — labour. We will assume that the market for this factor is also perfectly competitive, meaning that the individual firm can buy as much of the variable factor as it wants to at a given price. In other words, the firm's purchases of the variable factor represents such a small fraction of the total supply of the factor that the firm cannot affect the factor's market price.

In summary, we are assuming the firm is a price taker in both the product and the resource markets. Three things are of critical importance:
(a) the product price which the firm must take as given
(b) the factor price which the firm must take as given, and
(c) the marginal physical product of the variable factor.

Marginal Revenue Product

Suppose the firm has a certain quantity of the fixed factor. Table 28.1 illustrates the way in which the quantity of the variable factor F contributes to the production of the firm's final product and therefore to the revenue the firm realises from the sale of that product.

As more of the factor F is used (column 1), the quantity of output of final product Q increases (column 2). The increase in total output associated with the addition of one more unit of the factor F to the production process is the **marginal physical product** MPP (column 3). Columns 2 and 3 of Table 28.1 measure total output and marginal physical product in terms of physical units, such as the number of bushels of wheat or the quantity of widgets. Because of the law of diminishing returns, the MPP decreases as more and more of the factor F is added and used together with the given quantity of the fixed factor. The relationship between the quantity of the factor F and the total quantity of output of final product Q (column 2) is the short-run production function, a concept that we looked at in Chapter 22. Figure 28.1, part a, plots the data in columns 1 and 2 of Table 28.1 on a graph. The relationship between the factor F and the marginal physical product MPP is illustrated in

TABLE 28.1
Relationship Between Productive Factor and Marginal Revenue Product, Assuming Perfect Competition in Both Factor and Product Markets

(1) Quantity of Productive Factor (F)	(2) Total Output of Final Product (Q)	(3) Marginal Physical Product (MPP)	(4) Price of Product (p)	(5) Total Revenue (TR)	(6) Marginal Revenue Product (MRP)
		$MPP = \dfrac{\text{change in } Q}{\text{unit change in } F}$		$TR = p \times Q$	$MRP = \dfrac{\text{change in } TR}{\text{unit change in } F}$
0	0			$0	
		12			$120
1	12		$10	120	
		10			100
2	22		10	220	
		8			80
3	30		10	300	
		6			60
4	36		10	360	
		4			40
5	40		10	400	
		2			20
6	42		10	420	
		1			10
7	43		10	430	

Figure 28.1, part b, using the data in columns 1 and 3 of Table 28.1. (Note that the marginal physical product data are plotted midway between the integers on the horizontal axis. This is so because they represent the changes in total output and total revenue respectively from one unit of the factor to the next.)

In order to arrive at the relationship between the quantity of the factor F and the sales revenue it helps to produce, it is necessary to multiply the output of column 2 by the price at which it is sold. Since the firm sells its product in a perfectly competitive market, this price is the same no matter what the output level. Assuming that the price p is $10 (column 4), total revenue TR, which equals $p \times Q$ (column 4 times column 2), is given in column 5. The increase in total revenue associated with each 1-unit increase in the variable factor F is called the marginal revenue product MRP. This figure is given in column 6. It may be computed either by determining the difference between the successive total revenue figures in column 5 or by multiplying the MPP of column 3, which is the addition to total output Q by the price p of column 4. The marginal revenue product curve MRP is plotted in part c of Figure 28.1 from the data in column 6 of Table 28.1. Note that it mirrors the MPP curve of part b. This is so because MRP may be obtained by multiplying the given final market price p (which does not change with the firm's output under perfect competition) by MPP.

FIGURE 28.1
Relationship Between Short-Run Production Function, Marginal Physical Product, and Marginal Revenue Product, Assuming Perfect Competition in Both Factor and Product Markets

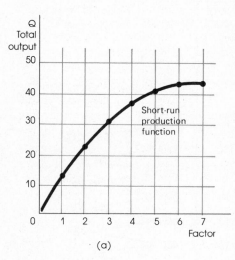

(a)

Part a shows the perfectly competitive firm's short-run production function plotted from the data in columns 1 and 2 of Table 28.1. The law of diminishing returns is reflected in the fact that the curve rises less and less as more and more of the variable factor is added to the production process and used together with the given quantity of the fixed factor.

Part b is a graph of the marginal physical product, the increase in total output attributable to each additional unit of the variable factor. It is plotted from the data in columns 1 and 3 of Table 28.1. Its downward slope reflects the law of diminishing returns.

Part c is a graph of the marginal revenue product, the increase in total revenue attributable to each additional unit of the variable factor, plotted from the data in columns 1 and 6 of Table 28.1. It is an image of the MPP curve of part b because MRP may be obtained by multiplying the given final market price p (equal $10 in this case) by MPP.

The marginal curves of part b and c are plotted at the midpoints of the integers on the horizontal axes. This is because they represent the change in total output and total revenue respectively from one unit of the factor to the next.

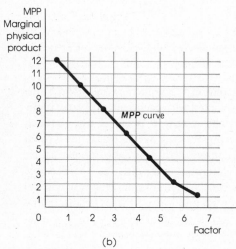

(b)

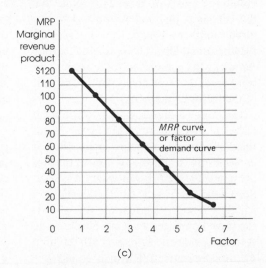

(c)

Determining the Quantity of a Factor to Employ

How does the firm decide how much of the variable factor to employ? The principle that is used to answer this question is very similar to the marginal-cost-equals-marginal-revenue rule used to decide how much output to produce.

Employ the Factor Until MCF = MRP

In Chapter 22, we found the question, How much output should be produced? was answered as follows: Produce that level of output at which *the marginal cost of the last unit produced is just equal to the marginal revenue obtained from the sale of that last unit*. The answer to the question, How much of the variable factor should be employed? is really just a slight variation on the answer to the question, How much output should be produced? This is not surprising if we remember that when the firm produces its optimum output level (the one that maximises profit), it must of necessity use a certain amount of the variable factor to produce it. This amount is the answer to the question, How much of the variable factor should be employed? In short, we may view the firm's profit-maximising level of activity either from the vantage point of input or from the vantage point of output.

From the vantage point of input (how much of the variable factor should be employed?) — *the firm should employ the variable factor up to the point at which the marginal cost of the factor MCF is just equal to the marginal revenue product MRP*. In other words, it should employ the variable factor up to the point at which the cost of the last unit of that factor employed is just equal to the additional revenue realised from the sale of the additional output produced by that last unit of the factor.

This may be illustrated by use of the data in Table 28.1. Suppose the price of the factor, its per unit cost to the firm, is $50. Since the firm is a price taker in the factor market, it must pay $50 per unit of the factor no matter how much or how little of the factor it buys — the firm's *MCF* equals $50 at every level of output. At this price the firm will employ 4 units of the factor. Why is this so? Because the *MRP* (column 6) exceeds *MCF* (equal $50) for every unit of the factor up through 4 units, and falls below it for every additional unit of the factor beyond 4 units. Each additional unit of the factor employed up through the fourth adds more to total revenue than it costs to purchase the factor. Hence, it is profitable for the firm to employ each of these units of the factor. For instance, the addition of the fourth unit of the factor increases total revenue by $60. The marginal cost of the factor *MCF* is $50, which is less than the marginal revenue product *MRP* of $60 (column 6). The firm realises $10 profit. However, if the firm were to add a fifth unit of the factor, the *MCF* of $50 would exceed the *MRP* of $40 realised from the sale of the fifth unit. Hence, the firm would lose $10 on the production and sale of the additional output realised from the employment of the fifth unit of the factor. Similarly, the firm would lose money on each additional unit of the factor employed beyond the fifth. Thus, the firm should employ no more or less than 4 units of the variable factor.

Factor Demand Curve is MRP Curve

The *MRP* curve of part c of Figure 28.1 is reproduced in Figure 28.2. According to the data in column 6 of Table 28.1, the first unit of the factor F has an MRP of $120. If the price of 1 unit of F is less than this, the firm will hire the factor. The MRP of a second unit of the factor is $100. If the price of the factor is $110, say, then the firm will hire 1 unit but not a second. On the other hand, if the price of 1 unit of the factor is $90, the firm will hire 2 units of F. We can continue this line of reasoning by considering successively lower prices for the factor. Assuming that the factor is divisible into fractional units (so many hours, minutes, and seconds of labour services, for example), the result will be the smooth MRP curve that in effect constitutes the firm's demand curve D_F for the factor. It tells us how much will be demanded at each possible price of the factor.

For example, if the price of the factor is $50 and the firm can buy as much as it wants of the factor at that price, the MCF of the factor is $50 at every level of output. The supply curve of the factor is then S_F as shown in Figure 28.2. The firm will employ 4 units of the factor as determined by the intersection of S_F and D_F, the point where $MCF = MRP$.

Variable Product Price and Factor Demand

So far we have analysed the firm's demand for a variable factor of production assuming that it sells its product in a perfectly competitive market. Therefore the price at which it sells each unit of output is the same no matter how much the firm produces. Marginal revenue product for each additional unit of the variable factor is obtained by multiplying the marginal physical product by the given product price. Since $MRP = MPP \times p$, the only reason the factor demand, or

MRP, curve of Figure 28.1, part c, and Figure 28.2 slopes downward is that MPP falls, reflecting the law of diminishing returns. (The fall in MPP is shown in column 3 of Table 28.1 and in Figure 28.1, part b.) However, if the firm is a price maker in the product market we can no longer take the product price as given and this affects its demand curve for the variable factor. Suppose the firm in question is a monopolist in the product

FIGURE 28.2
Marginal Revenue Product Curve Is the Firm's Demand Curve for a Productive Factor

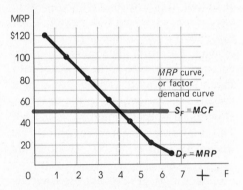

The marginal revenue product curve MRP shown here is the same as that shown in part c of Figure 28.1. Since the price of a productive factor is the marginal cost of the factor MCF to the firm, and since the firm will purchase the factor up to the point where $MCF = MRP$, the curve tells us how much of the factor the firm will demand at each price. Therefore, the MRP curve is the firm's factor demand curve D_F.

If the firm can purchase as much as it wants of the factor at a price of $50, the marginal cost of the factor, or MCF, to the firm is $50 and the supply curve of the factor to the firm is S_F. The firm will purchase 4 units of the factor, as determined by the intersection of D_F and S_F, the point where $MRP = MCF$.

Since $MRP = MPP \times p$, the factor demand curve D_F will be steeper, or less elastic, the more rapidly MPP declines as the firm expands its output by using more of the factor.

market — the price at which it sells its product would vary with the quantity of output it produces. That is, the demand curve for the firm's product would slope downward, reflecting the fact that the price p the firm receives for its product falls as more of that product is supplied to the market. Hence both MPP and p fall as the firm increases output.

The combined effect of the fall in both MPP and p on total revenue and marginal revenue product is illustrated in Table 28.2. The firm is the same as that in Table 28.1 so that columns 1, 2 and 3 remain unchanged. However, it is now assumed that the demand curve for the firm's product is downward sloping, so that the firm must accept a lower price in order to sell larger quantities of its product, as indicated in column 4 of Table 28.2.

Because of this, total revenue and marginal revenue product (columns 5 and 6) fall more rapidly in Table 28.2 than is the case in columns 5 and 6 of Table 28.1.

Using the data in column 6 of Table 28.2, the marginal revenue product curve, which is the same as the firm's factor demand curve for the variable factor, is plotted as D_F' in Figure 28.3. The D_F curve from Figure 28.2 is reproduced in Figure 28.3 for comparison.

Clearly the factor demand curve D_F' lies to the left of D_F and is more steeply sloped. This is so because D_F' reflects the decline in the price of the firm's product *in addition to* the decline in MPP when more of the factor is used to increase the imperfectly competitive firm's output. The result, as can be seen in Figure 28.3, is that at any price of the factor the

TABLE 28.2
Relationship Between Productive Factor and Marginal Revenue Product, Assuming Imperfect Competition in Product Market and Perfect Competition in Factor Market

(1)	(2)	(3)	(4)	(5)	(6)
Quantity of Productive Factor (F)	Total Output of Final Product (Q)	Marginal Physical Product (MPP)	Price of Product (p)	Total Revenue (TR)	Marginal Revenue Product (MRP)
		$MPP = \dfrac{\text{change in Q}}{\text{unit change in F}}$		$TR = p \times Q$	$MRP = \dfrac{\text{change in TR}}{\text{unit change in F}}$
0	0		$10	$0	
		12			$108
1	12		9	108	
		10			68
2	22		8	176	
		8			34
3	30		7	210	
		6			6
4	36		6	216	
		4			-16
5	40		5	200	
		2			-32
6	42		4	168	
		1			-39
7	43		3	129	

imperfectly competitive firm will demand less of the factor than the perfectly competitive firm, all other things remaining the same. For example, at a factor price of $50, the imperfectly competitive firm will demand 2 units of the factor, while the perfectly competitive firm will demand 4 units.

Finally, note that the less elastic is the demand curve for an imperfectly competitive firm's product, the more rapid is the decline in product price as the firm increases output. Therefore, the less elastic the demand curve for the firm's product, the less elastic will be the factor demand curve.

Market Demand Curve for a Factor

Recall we get a market demand curve for a product by summing all the individual demand curves for the good. Unfortunately, things are not quite so simple in the factor market when the industry is made up of price takers. We cannot add each firm's marginal revenue product curve to get that industry's demand for the factor. The reason for this is that although the individual competitive firm is a price taker in the product market, all the firms in the industry as a whole are not. When they sell more output, price drops, just as it does for a monopolist, reflecting the downward sloping market demand for the product.

Figure 28.4 can be used to demonstrate why the sum of the marginal revenue product curves of the firms is not the market demand curve for the variable factor. The figure depicts both the factor market (top diagrams) and the produce market (bottom diagrams). Both markets are shown because understanding of their interrelationship is necessary to appreciate the nature of the derived market demand curve for the factor. Part a of the factor and product market diagrams depicts the situation facing the individual firm, while part b represents the industry as a whole. Figure 28.4 demonstrates these relationships by examining the effects of an

---

FIGURE 28.3
The Factor Demand Curves of an Imperfectly Competitive Firm and a Competitive Firm Compared

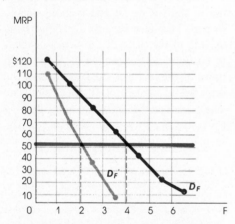

The factor demand curve of the perfectly competitive firm of Table 28.1 and Figures 28.1 and 28.2 is shown again as D_F. The factor demand curve D_F' of the imperfectly competitive firm of Table 28.2 is plotted from the data of column 6. The two firms are the same in all respects except that the demand curve for the final product of the imperfectly competitive firm is downward sloping and that of the perfectly competitive firm is horizontal.

The factor demand curve D_F of the perfectly competitive firm is downward sloping only because MPP falls as more of the variable factor is used, a reflection of the law of diminishing returns. The factor demand curve D_F' of the imperfectly competitive firm lies to the left of D_F and is more steeply sloped because in addition to the fall in MPP, the price of the firm's product falls as more of the factor is used to produce more output. The less elastic the demand curve for the firm's product, the more rapid will be the fall in price, and therefore the steeper, or less elastic, will be the factor demand curve.

increase in the price of the variable factor. We will assume for convenience that neither the firm nor the industry has any control over the factor price. Before the factor price increase occurs the situation is as follows. In the product market (bottom diagram) the industry is in equilibrium at A. Demand D equals Supply S_0. The product price is P_0 and Q_0 is produced and sold by the industry. The individual firm (bottom diagram, part a) equates MC_0 with price and produces G_0. In the factor market (top diagram) the factor price is FC_0, the individual firm (part a) equates MRP_0 and FC_0 and hires l_0 of the variable factor. In the resource market as a whole (part b) the firms are hiring L_0.

Now for the effects of an increase in the factor price. It rises from FC_0 to FC_1 and this is shown on the top diagram by a vertical movement in the factor price line. But the effects on the product market cannot be ignored and these are shown on the bottom diagram. The increase in the factor price increases the firm's costs. In part a, MC_0 is displaced by MC_1. It also moves the industry's supply curve to the left in part b. S_1 replaces S_0. The effect of these cost increases and the fall in supply is a new product market equilibrium; point B in part b. The product price has risen from P_0 to P_1 and the quantity sold has fallen from Q_0 to Q_1. The factor market is affected in two ways. First, as we have seen, the factor price rise was the shock that disturbed the initial equilibrium. But second, any increase in the product price raises the marginal revenue product curve because marginal physical product is multiplied by a higher product price. In the new equilibrium position MRP_0 is replaced by MRP_1 in the factor market, part a. This shows that at FC_1 the firm will now buy l_1 equating

FC_1 with MRP_1. The industry will demand L_1 (part b). The line ID can be regarded as the industry demand curve for the factor. *It shows the quantity of the factor the industry will demand at each factor price and it fully takes into account changes in the product price as the product's market price changes.* Notice, this curve is less elastic than the sum of the individual MRP_0 curves.

Two things have emerged from this section. First, you have learned that the demand curve for a factor in a competitive market is not obtained simply by summing individual marginal revenue product curves. Second, and more important, you have explored the interrelationship between the product and factor markets, which exists irrespective of whether a firm is a price maker or a price taker in either or both markets.

CHECKPOINT 28.1*
Show that you understand fully how the demand for a variable factor is derived by explaining how the firm will respond to changes in the price of that factor by varying the quantity of the factor demanded.

* Answers to all Checkpoints can be found at the back of the text.

SHIFTS IN THE DEMAND CURVE FOR A FACTOR

Up to this point we have only considered movements along a factor demand curve. What causes shifts in the position of a factor demand curve? There are essentially four major reasons for the curve to shift: (1) changes in the demand for the final product, (2) changes in the quantities of other productive factors, (3) technological improvements, and (4) changes in the prices of other factors. Let's consider each in turn.

Changes in the Demand for the Final Product

If there is an increase in demand for the final product that the factor helps produce, firms will need to use more of the productive factor in order to increase production of the final product to meet this demand. This will cause the demand curve for such a factor to shift rightward. Similarly, a decrease in demand for the final product will ultimately result in a leftward shift of the factor demand curve. As demand for the final product decreases, firms will produce less and therefore use smaller amounts of the productive factor. Looking back to Table 28.1, suppose there is an increase in demand for the final product that causes product price p to rise from $10 to $15 in column 4. If you redo the calculations, you will find that for each quantity of the productive factor in column 1, the *MRP* in column 6 will now be larger. Consequently, the factor demand curve in Figure 28.1, part c, and Figure 28.2 will be shifted rightward.

Changes in the Quantities of Other Productive Factors

If the amounts of other productive factors used by a firm are increased while the quantity of one factor remains the same, the marginal productivity of the unchanged factor will increase. For example, suppose we give one labourer half a hectare of land and some seed but no capital equipment such as a shovel or a hoe. He or she then produces a certain quantity of output. The labourer's productivity will rise considerably if he or she is provided with some capital equipment; it will rise even more if another half hectare of land is added. If the labourer is given more capital equipment in the form of

a tractor and plough plus another 100 hectares of land, the labourer's productivity will rise still higher. In terms of Table 28.1, if the firm were to get more of the factor that was assumed to be fixed, the *MPP* (column 3) of the variable factor would be larger for every amount of that factor shown in column 1. This would mean that the factor demand curve of Figure 28.1, part c, and Figure 28.2 would be shifted rightward.

Technological Improvements in Productive Factors

If there is an increase in the productivity of some factors due to technological changes specific to those factors, the productivity of other factors used in conjunction with those factors will be increased as well. For example, if a timbercutter's handsaw is replaced by a power saw, the timbercutter's productivity will increase. Of course, the timbercutter's productivity may be increased even more by added education in the art of timbercutting. In sum, the *MPP* of a factor may rise either because of improvements in other factors or because of improvements in the factor itself. If the *MPP* figures in column 3 of Table 28.1 are increased, the *MRP* figures of column 6 will also be increased. As a result, the factor demand curve of Figure 28.1, part c, and Figure 28.2 will be shifted rightward.

Changes in the Prices of Other Factors

We have already noted that there is a certain amount of substitutability among the productive factors used in most production processes. We also know from our study of demand curves that if the

FIGURE 28.4
Effects on Factor and Product Markets of an Increase in the Price of a Variable Factor of Production under Competition

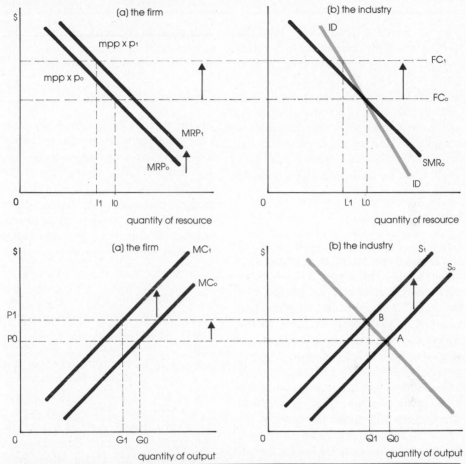

The two top diagrams represent the resource market. The bottom two the product market. The two left hand diagrams (a) represent the individual firm while the right hand (b) diagrams depict the market for the resource and the product. The individual firm and the industry's demand curves for the factor are derived from the produce market demand. The two sets of diagrams are included to show this relationship and also to show why the market demand for the factor is not the sum of the marginal revenue product curves of the individual firms. Initially the market price for the product is P_0 and Q_0 is produced and sold. (A on bottom diagram b.) This individual firm is producing G_0 (bottom diagram a) and equating marginal cost with the market price P_0. In the factor market, that same firm is equating MRP ($=$ MPP $\times$ P_0) with FC_0 and hiring I_0 (top diagram a). The total resources market is hiring L at that price (top diagram b). SMRP is the sum of the individual firms MRP curves. When the price of the factor rises to FC_1 (top diagrams) this immediately increases each firm's production costs and moves the industry supply curve to the left (bottom diagrams). The new equilibrium in the product market is shown by B and the new product price is P_1 with the market selling Q_1. The individual firm equates MC with price and produces G_1.

The top diagrams show how the factor market has been affected. There are two effects for the firm. The price of the factor has increased, but so too has its MRP curve because the price of the product has increased — in equilibrium — from P_0 to P_1. The new curve, MRP_1 = MPP $\times$ P_1. At the new factor price the industry hires L₁ and the individual firm I₁. The line ID can therefore be regarded as the true demand curve of the industry for the variable factor, since it shows what quantity the industry will demand at each factor price level. Note the industry demand curve is less elastic than the sum of the original MRP curve.

price or prices of goods *other* than the one for which the demand curve is drawn change, then the demand curve for that good will shift. We learned that the direction of the shift in the demand curve will depend on whether the other good whose price changes is a substitute or a complement for the good for which the demand curve is drawn. Similar principles apply when we consider a factor demand curve.

Substitute Factors

Given the demand curve for a factor F, let's suppose that the price of a substitute factor S falls. The effect on the demand curve for factor F must be broken into two parts. *First*, because the substitute factor S is now cheaper relative to the factor F, there will be a tendency to substitute factor S for factor F in the production process. This happens because firms desire to produce their output in the least costly manner. This **substitution effect** alone will reduce the demand for factor F and thereby cause factor F's demand curve to shift leftward. *Second*, the reduction in the price of factor S means that the cost of producing the final product whose production requires the use of factors F and S is now lower. This means the supply curve of the final product will be shifted rightward. Hence, there will be an increase in the production of the final product, which will require the use of more of both factors F and S. This **output effect** alone will shift factor F's demand curve to the right. Since the output effect and the substitution effect push factor F's demand curve in opposite directions, the final position of the factor demand curve

after a fall in the price of S will depend on which effect is larger. This can only be established on a case-by-case basis.

Complementary Factors

Just as there is complementarity among some final products, such as between coffee and sugar or ham and eggs, there is complementarity among some factors of production. These are called, logically enough, **complementary factors** of production. Two factors are complements in production if an increase in the amount of one of them used in production requires an increase in the use of the other one as well. Conversely, a decrease in the use of one factor will lead to a decrease in use of the other. For example, to produce freight transportation service in a city requires trucks (capital) and drivers (labour). If the price of trucks falls, it will be cheaper to provide freight service. It can be sold at a lower price and more of it will be used. The demand curve for the factor trucks will therefore shift rightward. Since each truck needs a driver, a complementary factor, the demand curve for drivers will also shift rightward. In the case of complementary factors there is only an output effect, since complementary factors are not substitutes for one another and so cannot be used in place of one another.

ELASTICITY OF FACTOR DEMAND

The elasticity of the derived demand curve for a particular productive factor is determined by the nature of the demand for the final product produced with the aid of the factor, as well as by the nature of the production process and costs associated with producing the final product.

CHECKPOINT 28.2
Use the same analytical framework employed in Figure 28.4 to analyse (a) an increase in demand for the final product, (b) a technological improvement increasing the productivity of the variable factor. Check your conclusions against those in the text on pages 748 and 749.

Determinants of the Elasticity of Factor Demand

When we consider the effect of a change in the price of a productive factor, we want to know how much the quantity demanded of that factor will change as a result of the change in its price. That is, we want to know the shape of the derived demand curve. This requires an examination of four links between the demand curve for the productive factor and the demand curve for the final product it helps produce. These links are four of the basic determinants of the shape of the derived demand curve for the productive factor. These determinants are (1) the elasticity of the demand curve for the final product, (2) the ratio of the cost of the productive factor to the total cost of producing the final product, (3) the degree of substitutability of the productive factors used to produce the final product, and (4) the rate of decline in marginal physical product *MPP* that occurs as the firm expands its output by using more of the factor. We will consider each determinant separately.

1. Elasticity of Final Product Demand

Suppose the price of a productive factor is reduced. The price of that factor is a cost to the firms that use the factor to produce a final product. Hence, the reduction in the factor's price means that the cost of producing the final product will be reduced as well. This in turn will lead to a fall in the price of the final product. Consequently there will be an increase in the quantity of the final product demanded. The extent of that increase will depend upon the elasticity of the demand curve for the final product. The more elastic the demand, the greater the increase will be. The larger the increase in the quantity demanded, the larger quantity of the final product that will be produced. The larger the quantity of the product produced, the larger will be the increase in the quantity of the inputs needed to produce it. In sum, *the greater the elasticity of the demand curve for the final product, the more elastic will be the derived demand curve for a factor used to produce it, all other things remaining the same.*

2. Ratio of Factor Cost to Total Cost

The meaning of this determinant will become clear if we consider a case in which only one productive factor is used to produce a final product. If the price of this productive factor is reduced by 50 per cent, the cost of producing the product will also be reduced by 50 per cent, since that cost is exactly the same as the cost of the productive factor. Alternatively, let us suppose that the cost of this one productive factor accounts for only 2 per cent of the cost of producing the final product, with the cost of other productive factors accounting for the remaining 98 per cent of the total cost of production. A 50 per cent reduction in the price of this one productive factor will result in only a 1 per cent reduction (50 per cent of 2 per cent) in the cost of producing the final product. Given the shape of the demand curve for the final product, the resulting decrease in the price of the good that results from the reduction in the cost of production will be greater in the first case than in the second. It follows, then, that the increase in production of the final product that results in the first case will be greater than in the second. Consequently, the increase in the demand for the productive factor will be greater as well. In general, *the larger the ratio of the cost of a productive factor to the total cost of producing the final product the greater will be the elasticity of the derived demand curve for the productive factor, all other things remaining the same.*

3. Degree of Factor Substitution

The production of most products typically involves the use of several different productive factors. However, it is often true that there are a number of different combinations of these productive factors that might be used to produce a given amount of a product. A thousand cubic metres of wheat may be grown by use of a number of different combinations of land, labour, and capital equipment. Many labour hours can be combined with a modest amount of capital equipment (such as hoes and sickles) and a certain amount of land. Alternatively, a few labour hours may be combined with more sophisticated capital equipment (such as tractors, combines, and harvesters) and a different amount of land. Generally, if we reduce the amount of one productive

factor, we must increase the amounts of one or more of the other productive factors in order to be able to produce the same amount of a product. In other words, there is a certain amount of substitutability between factors used in any production process.

The particular combination of productive factors used to produce a given quantity of a product will depend on the prices of the factors. If the price of one factor falls, it becomes cheaper relative to other productive factors and the firm will tend to use more of it in place of other productive factors. The degree to which this will take place will depend on the degree of substitutability between factors, and this varies with the kind of product produced. For example, the degree of substitutability between labour and capital equipment in the production of wheat is greater than that between these two factors in the production of hothouse orchids. The degree of substitutability between steel and aluminium is greater in the production of beer cans than it is in motor vehicles and greater in either of these than spaceships. In general, *the greater the degree of substitutability of a factor for other factors in the production of a final product, the greater will be the elasticity of the derived demand curve for the productive factor, all other things remaining the same.* That is, the greater the degree of substitutability of a factor for other factors, the larger will be the increase in the quantity demanded of that factor in response to a given reduction in its price.

4. Rate of Decline in Marginal Physical Product MPP

Finally, note that since $MRP = MPP \times p$, the elasticity of the MRP curve (see

Figure 28.2), or factor demand curve D_F, also depends on how much the marginal physical product MPP of the variable factor declines as output is increased by using more of the factor. If MPP tends to decline rapidly, then the factor demand curve will decline rapidly, and if MPP tends to decline slowly, the factor demand curve will decline slowly. In sum, *the MRP curve, or factor demand curve, will be less elastic the more rapidly MPP declines as the firm expands its output by using more of the factor, and it will tend to be more elastic the less rapidly MPP declines.*

Summary of Determinants of Elasticity of Factor Demand

In summary, the elasticity of the derived demand curve for a productive factor depends upon the following:

1. *The elasticity of the demand curve for the final product.* The greater the elasticity of the demand curve for the final product, the greater the elasticity of the factor demand curve.

2. *The ratio of the cost of the productive factor to the total cost of producing the final product.* The larger the ratio of the cost of the productive factor to the total cost of producing the final product, the greater the elasticity of the factor demand curve.

3. *The degree of substitutability of the factor for other factors in the production of the final product.* The greater the degree of substitutability, the greater the elasticity of the factor demand curve.

4. *The rate at which marginal physical product MPP declines as the firm expands its output by using more of the factor.* The slower the decline in MPP, the greater the elasticity of the factor demand curve.

CHECKPOINT 28.3
Describe what you think the demand curve for rubber looks like in terms of the first three basic determinants listed above that link it to the final products in which it is used. Take care to think about the likely relative importance of these final products in terms of the proportion of total rubber output that each uses. List five examples of factor inputs that you think would have very inelastic demand curves, and in each case explain your selection in terms of the first three basic determinants that link it to the goods in which it is used. Which do you think has a more elastic demand curve, farm tractors or Ford farm tractors? In general, do you think anything can be said about the relationship between the breadth of the definition of a factor and its elasticity of demand?

OPTIMUM USE OF SEVERAL FACTORS

Our discussion up to this point has assumed that there is only one variable factor of production. In reality a firm typically uses several variable factors of production. How in principle does a firm decide how much of each of these factors to employ? In other words, what determines the optimum (or best) combination of inputs of factors to use in the production process? The answer may be arrived at by two closely related methods: the least-cost combination and the maximum-profit combination. For simplicity we will assume that there are two variable factors of production, both of which are sold in perfectly competitive markets. The analysis, however, readily extends to cases where there are several factors.

The Least-Cost Combination of Factors

In previous chapters whenever we have used the concept of a cost curve, it has always been *assumed* that at any output level the corresponding point on the cost curve represents the least possible cost at which that output level can be produced. But how does the firm select that particular combination of factors that minimises the cost of producing a given output level? Or in other words, for any given output level, how much of each of the factors should the firm employ if it wants to produce that output level at the least possible cost? The answer can best be understood by going right back to the ideas of the production function and isoquants developed in Chapter 22. Recall

FIGURE 28.5
Least Cost Combinations of Factors
Given Factor Prices

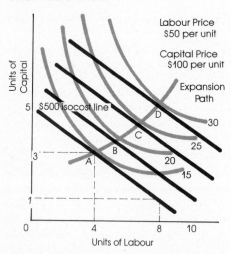

ABCD is the least cost method of increasing production in the long run. Points of tangency A, B, C, D all obey the rule

$$\frac{MPP_{LAB}}{Price_{LAB}} = \frac{MPP_{CAPITAL}}{Price_{CAPITAL}}$$

that an isoquant, or equal product curve, told us the various combinations of factors that could be combined to produce the same output level. We can now use that notion to work out the cheapest way of producing a given output level. Figure 28.5 is an **isoquant map**. Earlier we called it a pictorial representation of a production function. In addition to the isoquants, numbered to show levels of production obtained by using the quantities of resources marked on the axes, notice the diagonal line. *This diagonal line represents the combinations of factors that can be bought for a given amount of money.* Sometimes it is called in isocost line.

How is the isocost line determined? If the prices of the two factors are known and are not affected by the amount of each the firm buys, the slope of the isocost line shows the *relative* prices of the factors. In Figure 28.5 the price of labour is $50 per unit and the price of capital is $100 per unit. Thus $500 can be used by the firm to buy various combinations of factors ranging from 10 units of labour and no capital, 8 units of labour and 1 capital, to no labour and 5 units of capital at the other extreme. It is these combinations that have been plotted in Figure 28.5. This information about what combinations of factors can be purchased for $500, together with the information contained in the isoquants holds the key to determining the least cost way of producing a given output. In Figure 28.5 point A represents the least cost way of producing 15 units of the good. It is the point (of tangency) between the isocost line and the isoquant. A moment looking at the Figure will show why this is so. At point A the firm uses 4 units of labour and 3 units of capital (total cost $500) to produce 15 units of output. There are many other ways of producing 15 units of output, but they all involve combinations of resources that use more than $500 worth of resources. All points on the 15 isoquant lie above and to the right of the $500 isocost line. Figure 28.5 extends the argument. It presents a series of isocost lines and joins up the points where each isocost line is tangential to an isoquant. This line A-B-C-D is called an *expansion path* because it shows the combinations of factors that a firm should use in the long period if it wanted to increase production using least cost methods.

One important feature of an isoquant must now be discussed. *The slope of an isoquant measures the relative marginal physical products of the factors of production.* To understand this think of a movement around an isoquant such as from A to A′ in Figure 28.6 as consisting of two parts. First hold capital fixed and increase labour employed by one unit. Production would increase and the amount would be the marginal product of labour. We are now above the 15 isoquant and have to consider the second part of the movement — to A′. Now we hold labour constant and reduce capital sufficiently to maintain production at 15 units. Dividing the fall in production by the reduction in capital used gives us a similar measure for the marginal product of capital. In Figure 28.6 the firm substituted 1 unit of labour for ½ unit of capital moving from A to A′. The marginal product of capital was twice the marginal product of labour.

The slope of the isocost line is also important. It measures, as we saw earlier, the relative prices of the factors of production. The two pieces of information can be used to develop an important rule for the least combination of factors. *A firm produces a given level of output as cheaply as possible when the relative*

factor prices are equal to the relative marginal physical products of the factors, or

$$\frac{\text{Price of Labour}}{\text{Price of Capital}} = \frac{\text{Marginal Product of Labour}}{\text{Marginal Product of Capital}}$$

This can be rewritten as

$$\frac{\text{MPP of Labour}}{\text{Price of Labour}} = \frac{\text{MPP of Capital}}{\text{Price of Capital}} = \frac{\text{MPP of other factor}}{\text{Price of other factor}}$$

To convince yourself of this, take another example using only capital and labour. Suppose a firm is producing a given level of output with a quantity of capital and a quantity of labour such that

$$\frac{MPP \text{ of capital}}{\text{price of capital}} = \frac{60 \text{ units of output}}{\$10}$$

and

$$\frac{MPP \text{ of labour}}{\text{price of labour}} = \frac{30 \text{ units of output}}{\$10}$$

With the price of a unit of labour and the price of a unit of capital each being $10, the firm could produce more output for the *same* total cost by spending $10 less on labour and $10 more on capital. The cutback of 1 unit of labour would reduce total output by 30 units, while the increase of 1 unit of capital would increase total output by 60 units. Hence, by simply shifting $10 away from expenditure on labour and toward expenditure on capital, there will be a net increase in total output of 30 units.

As long as there is a difference between the marginal physical product of capital MPP_c per dollar and the marginal physical product of labour MPP_L per dollar, the firm can always increase the total output produced for a given total dollar expenditure by reallocating this expenditure away from the factor with the lower

FIGURE 28.6
Marginal Physical Products and the
Isoquant

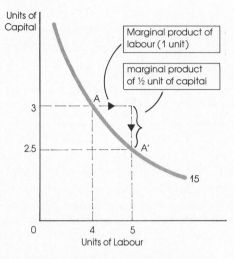

Capital is twice as productive as labour
between A and A' since twice as much capital (1 unit) is needed to substitute for the loss
of ½ a unit of capital. The slope of the isoquant measures the ratio of (the relative)
marginal physical products of the factors of
production.

MPP per dollar and toward that one with
the higher MPP per dollar. As the
quantity of labour is reduced and capital
increased, we would move up along
labour's downward-sloping MPP_L curve
while moving down capital's downward-
sloping MPP_c curve. In our example we
would continue to reduce the quantity of
labour used and increase the quantity of
capital until

$$\frac{MPP_L}{p_L} = \frac{MPP_c}{p_c} \quad (1)$$

(p_L and p_c are respectively the price of
a unit of labour and capital.) Once a
combination of capital and labour is
employed such that this equality holds,
it is not possible to increase total output

further by reallocating the given total
expenditure between the two factors. At
this point the maximum possible output
is being produced given the total dollar
expenditure on factors. Stated the other
way around, but equivalently, the quantity
of output is being produced with the least
costly combination of factors whenever
the equality in Equation 1 holds.

Any given output level that a firm might
choose to produce typically can be
produced with a variety of different
possible combinations of factors. However, only that combination which satisfies
the equality in Equation 1 allows the firm
to produce the given output level at the
least possible cost. If the quantities of both
the factors of capital and labour are
variable, it follows that whenever we say
that a firm is producing and selling that
level of output that *maximises* profit, we
are implicitly assuming that the equality
in Equation 1 holds. If this were not true,
it would mean there exists a less costly
combination of the factors that could be
used to produce that output level, in which
case profit could be made larger.

The Maximum-Profit Combination of Factors

Looking at the employment of two or
more factors of production from the
standpoint of the maximum-profit combination is really just a straightforward
extension of the marginal revenue product
principle that we have already examined
in the case of one variable factor.

Recall that so long as the cost of an
additional unit of the factor (the marginal
factor cost) is less than the addition to
total revenue (the marginal revenue
product) resulting from the sale of the
additional product produced with the help
of that unit, the firm will be able to

increase profit by using more of the factor to increase output. The firm will expand output until a point is reached at which the marginal factor cost of using one more unit of the factor is equal to the marginal revenue product realised from the sale of the additional output produced with the aid of that unit. If the factor were labour and it cost the firm p_L per unit, the firm would hire labour up to the point where this price was equal to the marginal revenue product of labour MRP_L, or $p_L = MRP_L$.

The same principle applies if there are two or more variable factors of production. If the firm is a price taker in the market for these factors (it can't affect the prices of these factors), it will be able to increase its profit as long as the MRP of any factor still exceeds the price of that factor. If the firm has two factors, capital and labour, it will maximise profit by employing that quantity of each factor such that

$$p_L = MRP_L$$

and

$$p_c = MRP_c$$

Note that these two expressions may be rewritten as

$$\frac{MRP_L}{p_L} = 1$$

and

$$\frac{MRP_c}{p_c} = 1$$

or

$$\frac{MRP_L}{p_L} = \frac{MRP_c}{p_c} = 1 \quad (2)$$

Relationship Between Least-Cost and Maximum-Profit Approaches

How is the least-cost combination of factors viewpoint, expressed by Equation 1, related to the maximum-profit combination of factors viewpoint, expressed by Equation 2? Recall that the marginal revenue product of a factor equals its marginal physical product multiplied by the price p of the product that it helps to produce. That is, we know that $MRP_L = p \times MPP_L$ and $MRP_c = p \times MPP_c$. Hence, if we multiply both sides of Equation 1 by p we get

$$\frac{MRP_L}{p_L} = \frac{MRP_c}{p_c} \quad (3)$$

This looks very much like Equation 2 *except that* this equality can hold even if the ratio of the marginal revenue products of the factors to their factor prices does not equal 1, as is required by the maximum-profit combination of factors point of view expressed in Equation 2. In other words, if the equality in Equation 2 holds, then the equality in Equation 1 must hold as well, but if the equality in Equation 1 holds, it does not necessarily mean that the equality in Equation 2 holds.

What is the meaning of this distinction? Recall that when both labour and capital are factors that the firm can vary in its production process, the equality in Equation 1 must be satisfied at all points along the firm's cost curve. This is so because each point on the cost curve represents the least possible cost for which the associated output level can be produced. However, it is entirely possible for the firm to produce and sell a quantity of output that does not maximise profit according to the marginal-cost-equals-

---

POLICY PERSPECTIVE

Will Robots Replace Workers?

During the 1980s a strange new word became more commonplace in our vocabulary — 'robotics', a new field dealing with the technology and use of robots in all sorts of practical applications. No longer a science-fiction fantasy, robots are beginning to replace workers in a wide variety of manufacturing operations. They promise greater automation of the office as well. It is becoming so apparent that robots will take over an increasing share of the American workload that both labour leaders and their rank and file are concerned about job losses due to robots.

Why hire robots? There are lots of reasons. A robot doesn't have good or bad days — only perfect days. Robots don't belong to unions. A robot does the same task over and over again without mistakes. A robot will work all night without complaint. A robot doesn't require a salary, fringe benefits, or pension. Robots don't go on vacation and they don't call in sick. A robot never talks back or asks for a rise.

The Economics of Robots

About half the robots used in the United States, Japan and Europe are employed in the motor vehicle industry. This is not surprising given the levels of wages in this industry and the pressure to contain costs as firms seek to increase their share of the domestic and international markets for motor vehicles. In US manufacturing, General Motors alone plans to have more than 14,000 robots in place by 1990.

When rising wage demands make it more and more difficult to run a manufacturing plant at a profit, robots are increasingly seen as an alternative. Reports suggest that typically an industrial robot purchased for $50,000 can be paid for and operated for about $6 per hour, compared to an average minimum cost in excess of $20 for a human worker. It is not hard to see why it has been predicted that by the year 2,000, 45 million factory and office jobs could be affected by automation in some way. Robots simply seem to be a sensible alternative to human workers from a 'bottom-line' standpoint.

Displaced Workers and Fears of Unemployment

The prospect of robots replacing millions of humans in the workplace worries a lot of people. Even the most profit-minded management is concerned that greater efficiency might not mean much if millions of people are thrown out of work by robot technology. There is particular concern that unskilled workers, who have traditionally worked on the lowest rung of American industry, will be lost in the shuffle as businesses rush to buy robots to increase efficiency and match the competition.

There is an old and familiar ring to all this however. The history of rising living standards is one of technological change eliminating certain kinds of jobs while creating new ones, and improving labour productivity in the process. Candlemakers were replaced by makers of kerosene lamps, who in turn were replaced by electricians. Blacksmiths and carriage makers were replaced by auto workers. One farmer today can produce the equivalent of what 50 produced at the turn of the century. The other 49 are now working in other sectors of the economy which, in fact, were able to develop and expand precisely because labour was released from the farm. Automation of manufacturing assembly lines and the office place has been going on for decades — machines replacing labourers. The advent of robots is just a continuation of that process. They too are just another kind of capital, a new type of machine. Their development is no more ominous for jobs and employment than the development of the steam shovel for ditch digging, the printing press for reproducing manuscripts, or the automatic cash teller for dispensing money.

Questions

1. How does the development of robots affect the marginal physical product of capital? Illustrate your answer in a graph.

2. Are robots likely to affect the marginal physical product of labour and, if so, how? Are robots likely to affect labour productivity, defined as the average product of labour? If so, why?

---

marginal-revenue criterion that we studied in previous chapters. Nonetheless, it can still be producing that quantity of output at the least possible cost. That is, the equality in Equation 1 will be satisfied and so will the equality in Equation 3, which is simply obtained by multiplying both sides of Equation 1 by the product price p. However, the ratio of the marginal revenue product of each factor to its respective price will not equal 1. The equality in Equation 2 is satisfied *only* if the firm is also producing and selling that level of output that maximises profit.

Example of Distinction Between Least-Cost and Maximum-Profit Approaches

In sum, the equality in Equation 2 says that in order to maximise profit, the firm should use that least-cost combination of productive factors such that the marginal revenue product per dollar spent on each factor equals 1. For example, suppose p_L

and p_c each equal $1 and that a firm is producing a level of output such that $MRP_L = MRP_c = \$5$. The equality in Equations 1 and 3 is satisfied — the firm is producing output at the least possible cost. However, Equation 2 is clearly not satisfied. The firm is not maximising profit. Since the firm can buy an additional unit of each factor at $1 apiece, and since the MRP of each factor exceeds its price by $4 ($5 — $1), the firm can increase profit by hiring more of the factors and increasing its level of output and sales. It should continue to hire capital and labour until the MRP of each falls to $1. At that point, the equality in Equation 2 will be satisfied and the firm will produce and sell that quantity of output that maximises profit.

SUMMARY

1. There are two basic reasons why resource pricing is important: (1) it determines how the economy's limited

supply of productive resources, or factors, is allocated to the various production activities necessary to produce the multitude of goods and services society wants, and (2) it is a major determinant of how income earned from productive activities is distributed among the economy's citizens.

2. The demand for a productive factor ultimately derives from the demand for the final product or products that it helps to make.

3. The marginal productivity theory of factor demand says that when a firm is a price taker in a factor market, it will hire the factor up to the point at which the price of the factor just equals its marginal revenue product. Because of this, the marginal revenue product curve of the factor constitutes the firm's demand curve for the factor.

4. Because of the law of diminishing returns, the marginal physical product of a factor falls as additional units of it are used. Consequently, the marginal revenue product curve, or factor demand curve, is downward sloping for this reason alone if the firm is a price taker in the product market. However, if the firm's product demand curve is also downward sloping, the factor demand curve will be downward sloping not only because of the decline in marginal physical product with the use of additional units of the factor but also because of the decline in product price.

5. The factor demand curves of individual firms can be summed to obtain the market demand curve for a factor. However, when doing so, it should be recognised that it is not realistic to assume that the price of the product the factor helps produce remains constant when we change factor

price and thereby move along the factor demand curve.

6. Shifts in a factor demand curve are caused by (1) changes in demand for the final product; (2) changes in the quantities of other productive factors; (3) technological improvements in the factor for which the factor demand curve is drawn or in the other factors with which it is combined in the production process, or both; and (4) changes in the prices of other factors.

7. If two factors X and Y are substitutes in production and there is a change in the price of X, there will be a substitution and an output effect, each of which pushes the factor demand curve for Y in a direction opposite to the other. The ultimate direction of the shift depends on which effect dominates. On the other hand, if X and Y are complements in production and the price of X rises (falls), then the factor demand curve for Y will shift leftward (rightward) since there is only an output effect among complementary factors.

8. The elasticity of a factor demand curve depends on (1) the elasticity of the demand curve for the final product, (2) the ratio of the cost of the productive factor to the total cost of producing the final product, (3) the degree of substitutability of the productive factor for other productive factors used to produce the final product, and (4) the rate at which the marginal physical product declines as the firm expands output by using more of the factor.

9. To produce any given level of output, the firm's least-cost combination of productive factors is determined by employing that quantity of each such that the marginal physical product per dollar spent on each factor is the same for every factor.

10. To produce that level of output that maximises profit, the firm should use that least-cost combination of productive factors such that the marginal revenue product per dollar spent on each factor equals 1.

KEY TERMS AND CONCEPTS

complementary factors
derived demand
expansion path
isocost line
marginal physical product
marginal productivity theory of factor demand
marginal revenue product
output effect
substitution effect

QUESTIONS AND PROBLEMS

1. Specify how each of the following would affect the demand curve for a productive factor X that is used in the production of a product Y. Where there is uncertainty, explain why.

a. an increase in the demand for Y;

b. a decrease in the number of substitute products for Y;

c. a change in production technology that has the effect of reducing the amount of X used relative to other factors;

d. a technological improvement in one of the other factors that is used with X in the production process;

e. a fall in the price of one of the other factors that is used with X in the production process;

f. a decrease in the price of X;

g. a natural disaster that destroys some of the other factors used with X in the production process.

2. 'The major cause of youth unemployment in Australia is not recession, nor is it because they don't want to work. It's simply because the legal minimum wage for juniors has been raised too much'. Use the marginal productivity theory of factor demand and a good clear diagram to examine this statement.

3. How is the derivation of the demand curve for a factor by a firm that is a price maker in the product market similar to the derivation of the market demand curve for a factor?

4. Sometimes it is argued that the way to help poor people is to educate and train them in ways that will increase their productivity. Assuming a perfectly competitive industry, how might this point of view be refuted or reinforced by the marginal productivity theory of factor demand? (Remember that while each firm in the industry is a price taker in the labour market, this does not rule out the possibility that the supply curve of labour to the industry may be upward sloping — even though to the individual firm it appears horizontal as in Figure 28.2.) In assessing this point of view, what difference does it make whether the supply curve of labour to the industry is horizontal or upward sloping?

5. Consider the production and sale of cars. Suppose that the price of each of the following items falls by 5 per cent: safety glass, copper, aluminium, steel, rubber, synthetic fibre, plastic, and wood.

a. Rank the items according to the degrees of impact that you think the 5 per cent price reduction in each has on the price of cars. Explain the reasoning underlying your ranking.

b. Rank the items according to their degree of substitutability in the production of cars. Explain your ranking.

c. Rank the items according to the elasticity of the motor vehicle industry's demand curve for each of them, and explain the reasons underlying your ranking.

6. Explain why it is possible for a firm to use a least-cost combination of factors and yet still not maximise profit.

7. Consider a firm that uses only two factors capital and labour to produce a good. The firm experiences constant returns to scale and the information available on the alternative ways of producing 100 units of output is as follows,

---
Alternative Methods of Producing
100 Units

Capital	Labour
10	20
8	24
6	30
4	38
2	48

The price of labour is $10 per unit and the price of capital is $30 per unit.

a. Draw an isoquant map for the output

values 100, 200, 300, 400 and 500.

b. Draw isocost lines and an expansion path showing the cheapest way of producing any given output.

c. What would the be cheapest way of producing 300 unit of output if the units cost of labour doubled?

8. Suppose a firm uses labour and capital to produce furniture. Suddenly there is a major technological breakthrough and new power tools are developed that are much more productive than the handtools previously used.

a. Draw an original isoquant map and then a new one showing the effect of the firm's production function of this new technology.

b. The firm now has a choice between the old technology and the new technology. But suppose the new tools are much more expensive than the old tools. Is it possible the firm might not find it worthwhile to use the new technology? How would you analyse the effects of both a change in technology and a sharp increase in the price of tools (capital) using the isoquant and isocost line diagram? *Hint:* The firm now has a choice between the old technology (old isoquant map — old factor prices) and new technology (new isoquant map — new factor prices) so draw two diagrams.

29

Wage Determination, Labour Market Structure and Unions

AFTER READING THIS CHAPTER YOU WILL BE ABLE TO:

1. Understand the special characteristics of labour markets.

2. Identify the determinants of supply in a free labour market.

3. Explain the role of market structure in the determination of wage and employment levels in a labour market.

4. Describe the institutional framework of Australian labour markets including compulsory unionism and the Arbitration Commission.

5. Distinguish between money wages and real wages.

6. Summarise the reasons why wages differ between workers and across occupations.

In the last chapter we examined the marginal productivity theory of factor demand. We saw that it provides a convenient starting point for thinking about the demand for labour. However, there is much more to be explained about the nature of wage determination in today's labour markets. The existence of large unions confronting large companies to hammer out agreements on wages, fringe benefits, working conditions, hiring, layoffs, grievance procedures, and management-versus-union prerogatives tends to conjure up images of war games more often than the cut-and-dried inter-action of supply and demand curves.

For most households wages and salaries are the primary source of income. They are therefore a major determinant of most people's aspiration for a decent standard of living, or perhaps even a claim on 'the good life'. They are the payment to our most important resource — people, or what economists often refer to as human capital. Little wonder that real-world wage determination has often been accompan-ied by hostile confrontations and even violence.

In this chapter we will look more deeply into the nature of wage determination, and in particular the role played by unions, employers' organisations, federal and state governments and the arbitration commis-sion and similar institutions that have fashioned the current methods of wage determination.

CHARACTERISTICS OF LABOUR MARKETS

In the discussion of the firm's costs and the demand for factors of production we have usually taken labour to be a variable factor in the short run and have used capital or land as the fixed factor and then demonstrated the effects on a firm's costs, or its demand for the variable factor when diminishing returns set in. This was a simplification in many respects. First, a firm will employ many types of resources, including many different types of labour, different types of capital equipment and a variety of natural resources. Real life production functions are much more complex than our two factor one good model. Even defining what we mean by labour is a difficult job. We have already used the term *human capital* in this chapter to indicate that people are not just strength and muscle power. Their ability to do a specific job depends on the skills, knowledge, attitudes and habits they have acquired. Society through its education system, its social and legal systems and its health care system invests a consider-able proportion of gross domestic product in developing this human capital.

But labour is people. It is different from other factors of production because of this. It is true that other factors, capital equipment and resources, are owned by people just as people own the ability to work. But labour is different because it has to be delivered personally. The worker has to give his or her time to the job — even if they work at home or conduct business on the telephone. Working conditions are important to the worker and jobs that offer no personal satisfaction often prove to be a depressing experience. Because people have feelings working or not working has both a positive and a negative effect. At the extreme wages need to be sufficiently high in the long run so that workers do not die of starvation. In the 19th century the so-called *iron law of wages* was fashionable. This suggested that the supply of labour would be such in the long run that wages would tend to the subsistence level. If wages rose above that level in the short run the population would increase and wage rates would fall again. No one believes in the iron law of wages today in the advanced industrial countries. For a variety of reasons wage levels are well above subsistence level for the great majority of workers. In poor countries, however, it is a different matter and extreme poverty, actual and disguised unemployment and too high rates of population increase provide a daunting prospect for families trying to escape from grinding poverty.

Even in advanced countries most workers have a *reservation wage* below which they cannot or are not prepared to work. It may, in the last analysis, be starvation wages, or more likely the opportunity cost of working in a particular occupation. When there is no 'next best' job to go to the choice may be between working or taking some form of social security benefit. While governments discourage such a choice between working and 'bludging' in our society for full time single adults, they continue to provide such a choice for married couples who are attracted by being one income families. It has been said that the employer views labour in a completely different light from the employee who supplies the labour. To the employer what is important is the productivity of labour — the factor of production — and the marginal revenue product deriving from employing additional units of labour. To the worker, it is the selling or hiring of personal services. Karl Marx in *Kapital* distinguished between labour and labour power, reserving the latter for the service the employee sells to the employer.

The Individual's Supply Curve

The willingness of the individual to work in a particular job will be influenced by many factors including the wage rate, the number of hours worked, working conditions and other available employment opportunities. Figure 29.1 shows a supply curve that expresses the willingness of an individual to work in a particular occupation.

Figure 29.1 shows a possible relationship between alternative hourly rates of pay and the number of hours a worker is willing to work in a week. This individual supply curve of labour slopes upwards from left to right for part of its length, from B to A. The curves suggests that higher rates of pay are necessary to induce the worker to work longer hours. Conventionally, this is the theory behind

FIGURE 29.1
Possible Labour Supply Curve of an Individual May be Backward Bending at Higher Wage Rates

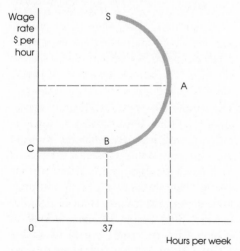

While higher wage rates may induce a worker to work longer hours, the point may come (A on the supply curve) beyond which the worker prefers to work fewer hours and to substitute leisure for work.
Below point B the worker is not prepared to work at all in this occupation.

overtime and penalty pay rates. Workers need added inducement to work longer than a standard week of say 37 hours. Two other features of Figure 29.1 call for comment. The first is that the worker is unwilling to work for less than a wage of $C per hour. In the diagram the supply curve is horizontal between C and B indicating that at an hourly rate of $C the worker is prepared to work any length of time per week up to 37 hours. Alternatively the supply curve might rise continuously from C indicating willingness to work longer hours as the rate rose. The second feature of Figure 29.1 is that beyond point A the supply curve bends backwards. The worker responds to higher rates of pay by working fewer hours. He prefers to substitute leisure for work and finds the higher rate of pay per hour is able to compensate for the smaller number of hours worked. Such a relationship has been observed in jobs that require work in a dirty or unhealthy environment.

CHECKPOINT *29.1
What significance do you think the elasticity of the individual's supply curve might have on their willingness to work at high rates of pay?

*Answers to all checkpoints are given at the back of the text.

The Market Supply Curve

Adding together the number of hours all workers are prepared to offer a particular skill at each rate of pay gives a market supply curve for that type of labour. From the employer's point of view the number of hours that he can obtain rather than the number of people he employs is likely to be the relevant feature of labour supply.

Hence we shall continue to measure the quantity of labour supplied in terms of hours of work rather than people employed. The supply curve of a particular type of labour is likely to slope upwards from left to right. This indicates that the higher the rate of pay, the more hours of work that will be offered by workers as a whole. The supply curve is far less likely to bend back on itself than the individual worker's supply curve simply because while an individual worker may trade off increased leisure for higher wages, the higher rates of pay are likely to encourage other workers to choose to enter the market. This is not always the case, however. Increasing the rates of pay of British coalminers after the Second World War led to a noticeable increase in absenteeism and refusal to work Saturday shifts. On the other hand paying high wage rates encourages people to work on oil rigs and in isolated areas for mining companies.

THE DETERMINANTS OF SUPPLY

The supply curve of a particular type of labour skill has been defined as showing the relationship between the wage rate and the number of hours workers are prepared to offer. The wage rate is therefore one of the determinants of labour supply. Other determinants are, (1) social attitudes to work and leisure (2) the number of people with the necessary skills in the population and (3) wages and conditions in other labour markets. Changes in any of these other 3 determinants will cause *a shift in the supply curve for labour* while a change in the wage rate produces *a movement along the supply curve.* We continue to distinguish between them by referring to movements of the curve as *changes in supply* and movements along the curve as *changes in the quantity supplied.*

A change in social attitudes to work and leisure may lead to an increase or to a reduction in supply of a particular skill. In Figure 29.2 the supply curve moves to the right because of an increase in the willingness of people to work. Nurses who are married may decide to return to the labour force and in the last three decades there has been a complete shift in Australian attitudes to married women working. Alternatively, there may be a reaction against work. For some years there has been a trend to earlier retirement and also to fractional time employment. In the former people decide they would sooner retire at an earlier age so that they can enjoy a longer period of active retirement. In the latter case people opt

to work fewer than the standard number of hours to enjoy leisure or attend to pressing tasks. Similarly, changes in relative wage rates may cause a movement in the supply curve for a particular skill. A rise in wage rates in another labour market to which workers can transfer is likely to produce a fall in the supply of labour in the first market. It is probable that the rise in wages in other occupations is an important reason why the supply of domestic servants has declined.

Increases in the population offer a larger base from which a larger number of people with necessary skills can be obtained. Skilled migrants or education and training programs are likely to increase the supply of labour. The elasticity of supply of labour is of crucial importance. As you would expect labour supply is less elastic in the short run than in the longer period. In the short run employers cannot normally obtain large increases in the supply of labour by hiring more workers (though this will depend on whether there is a large unemployment pool). They obtain more labour by using their existing workforce more intensively — through overtime work and payments. Industries or firms that require specialist skills may find that special training programs or international recruitment are necessary and on a national level obtaining the right amount of labour may take months or even years.

FIGURE 29.2
An Increase in the Supply of Labour

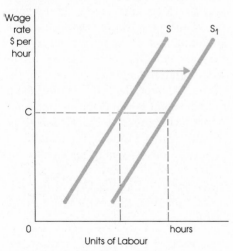

A change in one of the determinants of supply other than the wage rate causes a shift in the supply curve. Here supply increases as a result of an increased willingness to work, perhaps by married women.

CHECKPOINT 29.2
Draw short-run and long-run supply curves for a market for labour skill. Explain their shape and the relationship between wages and the quantity of labour supplied shown by each curve.

MARKET STRUCTURE AND WAGE DETERMINATION

In previous chapters, we have seen how the equilibrium quantity and price of a final product depend on the structure of the market in which it is bought and sold. Similarly, the wage rate and the quantity of labour services bought and sold in a particular labour market also depend on market structure. We will now consider several important types of labour market structure and the significant role played by unions in some of them.

Wages and Competitive Markets

In a perfectly competitive labour market, there are so many labourers competing with one another for jobs that no one of them individually is able to affect the wage that he or she receives. The same is true on the buyers' side of this market. There are so many employers that each represents but a small fraction of the entire market. So small in fact that no one of them can affect, by their individual hiring and firing decisions, the wage that must be paid for labour services. In aggregate, however, employers in such a labour market will have to pay a higher wage if they want to increase the quantity of labour they hire.

As long as workers have alternative employment opportunities, it will be necessary to pay a wage high enough to induce them away from their next best employment opportunity in some other area of the economy. As more workers are hired, employers can only compete for those with other employment opportunities by paying them a higher wage.

Figure 29.3 depicts equilibrium in a perfectly competitive labour market (part b) and the associated equilibrium position of a typical firm hiring labour in that market (part a). This figure might be the market for fruitpickers in South Australia, for example. The market demand curve D_m in part b is the sum of the individual firms' demand curves for labour, such as d_f in part a. These demand curves are the marginal revenue product curves MRP for labour for each firm. The demand curve d_f is a factor demand curve like those studied in the previous chapter (D_F in Figure 28.2, for example). The market supply curve S_m in part b is upward sloping, reflecting the fact that if all firms want to hire more labour in this market, they will have to pay a higher wage. The market equilibrium money wage w_0 is determined by the intersection of the market demand and supply curves, D_m and S_m respectively, in part b.

The supply curve of labour for the individual firm (part a) is perfectly horizontal at the money wage rate w_0. This reflects the fact that the individual firm cannot influence the wage no matter how little or how much labour it hires. Because of this, the supply curve of labour for the individual firm is the same as the marginal cost of labour MCL for the firm. (Each additional unit of labour service adds its price per unit, the wage rate w_0, to the firm's total costs.) As we saw in the previous chapter, the firm will hire labour up to the point at which the marginal cost of that factor equals its marginal revenue product. In this instance, the quantity of labour L_f is determined by the intersection of MCL and d_f in part a. This amount represents but a tiny fraction of the total amount hired, L_M, in the entire market, part b.

Unions and Wages in Competitive Markets

The labourers in the perfectly competitive labour market we have just described compete with one another for jobs, and

FIGURE 29.3
A Perfectly Competitive Labour Market

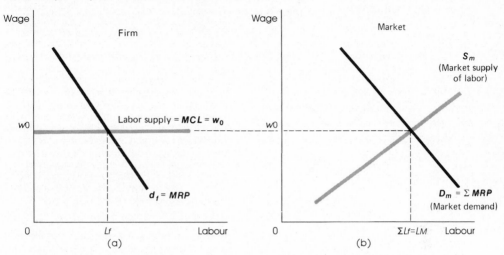

In a perfectly competitive labour market, there are many firms and labourers, each one consti-
tuting such a small fraction of the total that none can affect the wage rate by its individual
actions alone. The supply curve of labour to the typical firm (part a) is therefore horizontal (or
perfectly elastic) at the money wage w_0. This wage is determined by the intersection of the
market demand curve for labour D_m and the market supply curve of labour S_m in part b.

According to the marginal productivity theory of factor demand, the typical firm hires the
quantity of labour L_f (part a) determined by the point where the marginal cost of labour MCL
equals its marginal revenue product MRP.

The market supply curve of labour S_m (part b) is upward sloping because if the aggregate of
all firms buying labour in this market want more labour, they must bid it away from its alternative
employment in other areas of the economy. The market demand curve D_m (part b) is the aggregate of all the individual firm demand curves for labour, $d_f = MRP$ — that is, $D_m = MRP$. The total
amount of labour services bought and sold in the labour market shown here is L_M.

The labour market for fruitpickers in South Australia is an example of the type of labour market
depicted here.

each deals directly with his or her
employer on all matters concerning the
terms of employment. Suppose, instead,
that the labourers band together to form
a union. *A* **union** *is an organisation that
all labourers agree will represent them
collectively in bargaining with employers
over wages and other terms of employment.* Labourers agree to this arrangement because in unity there is strength.
It is still assumed that there are a large
number of employers on the buyers' side

of the market, all competing with one
another in the hiring of labour.

The usual objective of the union, but
typically not the only one, is to put labour
in a stronger bargaining position in order
to secure higher wages for its members.
There are basically three different ways
for a union to do this: restrict the supply
of labour, impose a wage above the
equilibrium wage, and support policies
that promote increased demand for
labour.

FIGURE 29.4
The Effect of Craft Unions on Wages and Employment

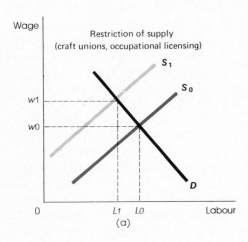

(a)

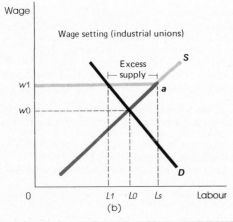

(b)

Craft unions directly restrict the supply of skilled labour by controlling apprenticeship programs and limiting union membership. As shown in part a, this effectively shifts the supply curve leftward from S_0 to a position such as S_1, causing employment to fall from L_0 to L_1 and wages to rise from w_0 to w_1. Many occupations, such as law and medicine, have licensing requirements, which also have the effect of shifting the supply curve leftward and raising wages. Child-labour laws, immigration quotas, compulsory retirement at a certain age, and a shorter workweek also have this effect on the general labour supply.

In contrast to craft unions, industrial unions attempt to organise all the hourly paid workers, skilled and unskilled, in a given industry. As shown in part b, the union then uses the resulting bargaining power to set the wage rate at a level such as w_1, which is above the equilibrium wage rate w_0 that would otherwise prevail in a perfectly competitive labour market. Because the demand curve D is downward sloping and the supply curve S is upward sloping, the amount of labour demanded and employed is L_d, while the amount supplied is L_s. There is thus an excess supply, or quantity, of unemployed union members, represented by the difference between L_s and L_d. The supply curve of labour to the industry is effectively w_1aS.

Restriction of Supply: Craft Unions, Occupational Licencing

In certain occupations that require the development of special skills, training in a craft, or extensive education before one can 'do the job', it is possible to restrict the supply of labour and thereby increase wages. This is much more difficult in labour markets for unskilled labour because, by comparison, lower educational and skill requirements allow a great

many more workers to enter the market to compete for jobs.

For example, workers in the skilled trades, such as bricklayers, electricians, and printers, have often banded together to form **craft unions**. By controlling the length of apprenticeship programs and restricting membership (which is often necessary to get into such programs), unions are able to control the supply of skilled labour in these trades. The more effectively they can do this, the easier it is to force employers to agree to hire only union members. This in turn further strengthens the craft union's ability to restrict the labour supply. The effect of this on the wage rate and the level of employment in such a trade is shown in Figure 29.4, part a. Before formation of the craft union, the equilibrium wage is w_0 and the equilibrium level of employment is L_0, as determined by the intersection of the labour demand curve D and supply curve S_0. When the craft union is formed and operating effectively, less labour will be supplied at every wage rate. This causes the supply curve to shift leftward from S_0 to S_1. The new equilibrium wage is now increased to w_1 and the level of employment is reduced from L_0 to L_1.

To work in a number of occupations and professions, it is necessary to have a licence — no licence, no job. The medical and legal professions are examples. To practise medicine in Australia it is not only necessary to study for six years for the medical degree, it is also necessary to meet the stringent ethical and professional standards imposed by the Australian Medical Association. Many other professional and trade organisations restrict the right to practise to those who they deem to have met standards they deem necessary. They include lawyers, accountants, airline pilots, electricians and plumbers. While the need for training and the restriction of the right to practise is defended in the public interest, it is nonetheless true that they restrict entry, restrict supply and tend therefore to push up the wages of the practitioners.

Wage Setting: Industrial Unions

Industrial unions, unlike craft unions, do not restrict their membership to only those workers in a particular trade. On the contrary, they attempt to organise all the hourly paid labourers, skilled and unskilled, in a given industry. Indeed, given the easy substitutability of readily available nonunion semiskilled and unskilled labour, it would be foolish for the union to restrict membership. In effect, by maximising the size of its membership and getting complete control of the labour supply needed by the industry, an industrial union forces firms in the industry to bargain exclusively with the union over wages and other conditions of employment. Firms unwilling to reach mutually agreeable terms with the union face the threat of being closed down by a walkout or **strike** — the loss of their labour supply — at least until one or the other side gives in.

Armed with this kind of bargaining power, an industrial union is able to set wages above the level that would otherwise prevail in a perfectly competitive labour market. This situation is illustrated in Figure 29.4, part b. Without the union, the equilibrium wage would be w_0 and the quantity of labour bought and sold would be L_0, corresponding to the intersection of the demand curve D and the supply curve S. Using its bargaining power, the union is able to push the wage up to w_1. Because the demand curve is downward sloping and the supply curve is upward sloping, the quantity of labour demanded falls to L_d while the quantity of labour supplied increases to L_s. This gives rise to an excess supply of labour, which is represented by the distance from L_d to L_s. These are workers who would like to have jobs in the industry at this wage but can't — they are involuntarily unemployed.

Obviously, *the higher the union pushes the wage, the larger will be the pool of*

*unemployed workers among its member-
ship. This fact limits the union's ability
to push up the wage rate.* A large pool
of unhappy, unemployed members may
lead to defection within the ranks and
threaten the very solidarity on which
union bargaining strength is based. The
more inelastic (steeply sloped) the demand
and supply curves, the smaller the rise in
such unemployment as the wage is pushed
up. Thus there will be less of an unemployment constraint on the union's ability
to push up the wage.

With the wage rate at w_1, the supply
curve of labour to the industry is represented by w_1aS. The industry can hire as
much labour as it wants up to the quantity
L_s. If it wants more than this, it will have
to raise the wage, as indicated by the
upward-sloping portion of the curve aS.

While both the craft union and the
industrial union reduce the level of
employment as a result of their efforts to
raise members' wages, their methods
differ. *The craft union pursues policies
aimed at directly restricting the supply of
labour. This is represented by the fact that
the craft union causes the supply curve
to be shifted leftward (Figure 29.4, part
a), which then leads to a rise in the wage
rate. By comparison, the industrial union
uses its bargaining power directly to set
the wage rate higher (Figure 29.4, part
b), which then leads to a fall in
employment.*

Monopsony: The Monopoly Employer

*A **monopsony** is a market structure in
which one buyer purchases a good or
service from many sellers.* It may be
thought of as the opposite of a monopoly,
in which one supplier sells to many buyers.
A labour market in which one employer,

the monopsonist, confronts a nonunio-
nised group of labourers competing with
one another for jobs, may be characterised
as a monopsony. It is not so common
these days in Australia, but in the past
mine workers in remote areas often found
themselves working in a company town.
The mining company was in a powerful
position to determine conditions of work,
at least in the short term. It was a
monopsonist. These days company towns
still exist; a mine, a dockyard, an abattoir
or a factory may be the only source of
employment in the district and the firm
is in a powerful position. Just how
powerful depends on the effectiveness of
the workers to form a union and defend
their interests.

Table 29.2 and its graphical representation in Figure 29.5 illustrate how wages
and employment are determined in a
monopsony labour market. Being the only
buyer of labour services in the market,
the monopsonist firm must pay a higher
and higher wage to employ more and more
labour. This is indicated in columns 1 and
2 of Table 29.2, and depicted by the supply
curve S in Figure 29.5. The higher wage,
or average cost of labour, must be paid
not only to the last unit of labour hired
but to all those units of labour already
employed as well. If this were not done,
previously employed labourers would
become unhappy, quit, and have to be
rehired at the higher wage paid the last
worker employed. (This is very similar to
the way a monopolist who wants to sell
an extra unit of output in the product
market must be willing to take a lower
price not only on the extra unit sold but
on all previous units as well.) Therefore,
the additional, or marginal, cost of hiring
one more unit of labour is the sum of
the wage paid to the additional labourer
plus the increase in the wage that must

be paid to all previously employed labourers, multiplied by the number of such labourers. Equivalently, the marginal cost of labour MCL (column 4) is simply the increase in the total cost of labour TCL (column 3) due to the employment of one more unit of labour. Figure 29.5 shows clearly that MCL rises faster than the wage rate, which is governed by the supply curve S.

How much labour will the monopsonist hire? According to the marginal productivity theory of factor demands the firm will hire labour up to the point at which the marginal cost of the factor equals its marginal revenue product. That is, it will hire labour up to the point at which MCL = MRP. Columns 4 and 5 of Table 29.2 tell us that this point is reached when 4 units of labour are hired. At that point, the marginal cost of labour and its marginal revenue product both equal $9. This corresponds to the point at which the MCL and MRP curves in Figure 29.5 intersect. Here the monopsonist will pay

labour a wage w_m of $6, the amount necessary, according to the supply curve S (and columns 1 and 2 of Table 29.2), to induce 4 units of labour to offer their services. Note by comparison that if the labour market were perfectly competitive, the equilibrium level of employment would be 5 units of labour at a competitive wage rate w_c of $7, as given in columns 1, 2 and 5 of Table 29.2 and as represented by the intersection of S and MRP in Figure 29.5.

In summary, *when labourers compete with one another for jobs offered by a monopsonist employer, the resulting equilibrium wage and level of employment will be lower than would be the case if the particular labour market were perfectly competitive.*

Finally, it should be noted that while the monopsonist firm is a monopoly buyer in the labour market, it may be selling its product in any kind of market structure, ranging over the entire spectrum from perfect competition to monopoly.

TABLE 29.2
Wage and Employment Determination in a Monopsony Labour Market

(1)	(2)	(3)	(4)	(5)
Number of Units of Labour Service (L)	Wage Rate = Average Cost of Unit of Labour Service or Supply Price of Labour (w)	Total Cost of Labour (TCL)	Marginal Cost of Labour (MCL)	Marginal Revenue Product of Labour (MRP)
1	$3	$ 3	$3	$15
2	4	8	5	13
3	5	15	7	11
4	6	24	9	9
5	7	35	11	7
6	8	48	13	5

FIGURE 29.5
Wage and Employment Determination in a Monopsony Labour Market

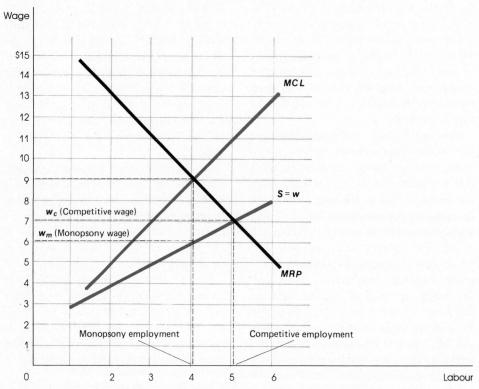

The monopsonist's demand curve for labour is the marginal revenue product curve MRP plotted from the data in column 5 of Table 29.2. The supply curve of labour S is plotted from the data in column 2, while the marginal cost of labour curve MCL is plotted from the data in column 4.

The MCL curve lies above the S curve, reflecting the fact that to hire an additional labour unit, the monopsonist must pay a higher wage not only for the additional unit but for all previously hired units of labour as well. The monopsony firm hires the factor labour up to the point at which its marginal cost equals its marginal revenue product, MCL = MRP = $9, as determined by the intersection of the MCL and MRP curves. The monopsonist thus hires 4 units of labour at a wage w_m of $6 per unit of labour.

By contrast, if the labour market were perfectly competitive, the equilibrium wage w_c would be $7 and the quantity of labour hired would be 5 units, as determined by the intersection of the MRP and S curves. Clearly the monopsonist pays a lower wage and hires less labour.

Bilateral Monopoly

So far, we have considered a labour market in which the supply of labour is controlled by an industrial union and a monopoly seller of labour and the demand for labour consists of many employers

(firms) competing with one another in the hiring of labour. In that case, we saw that the wage is set by the union as shown in Figure 29.4, part b. At the other extreme, we have considered the case of a monopoly buyer of labour services, a monopsonist, and labourers who are not unionised but instead compete with one another for jobs. These labourers receive the monopsony wage as shown in Figure 29.5.

But what happens when there is monopoly power on both sides of the market — that is, when there is a **bilateral monopoly**? Suppose a large industrial union represents the labour force in the sale of labour to a monopsonist. The monopsonist, or monopoly buyer of labour, may be one large firm or several firms acting in a collusive, oligopoly fashion in the hiring of labour services.

In order to characterise such a situation, we combine the analysis of the industrial union shown in Figure 29.5, part b, with that of the monopsonist shown in Figure 29.5. This is illustrated in Figure 29.6. Given a labour supply curve S and the associated marginal cost of labour curve MCL, the monopsonist would like to hire L_0 units of labour service at a wage of w_m. On the other hand, the industrial union would like to set the wage at w_u when L_0 units of labour services are sold. The union may wish to set the wage higher than this but then, of course, the employer will hire less than L_0 units of labour service.

There is obviously a discrepancy between the desired wage objective of the union and that of the monopsonist when L_0 units of labour service are employed. This discrepancy is equal to the difference, or gap, between w_u and w_m. When 'push comes to shove' and the monopoly hiring power of the employer is set against the monopoly selling power of the union, what mutually agreeable wage level in this gap will finally prevail? The bargaining power of the union typically depends on the willingness and financial ability of its membership to endure the hardship of a strike. Similarly, the bargaining power of

the employer depends on the willingness to incur the loss of business that will result from a shutdown. The greater the bargaining power of the union relative to that of the employer, the closer we would expect the ultimate wage settlement to be to w_u. Conversely, the greater the bargaining power of the employer relative to that of the union, the closer we would expect the ultimate wage settlement to be to w_m.

If the union prevails completely on the issue of wages, the supply curve of labour is w_uaS. If the employer prevails completely, it is w_mcS. Indeed, it is possible for the relative bargaining power of the two sides to be such that the wage settlement occurs at w_c with an amount of labour employed equal to L_c. This is the same outcome as would result in a perfectly competitive labour market! The supply curve of labour would then be w_cbS. In sum, the level of the ultimate wage settlement depends on the bargaining power of the union relative to that of the employer, and this varies from one industry and time to the next.

In general, *in a bilateral monopoly labour market, at the level of employment corresponding to the intersection of MCL and MRP, the wage level mutually agreeable to the monopoly employer and monopoly union will lie somewhere between the most desired wage w_u of the union and the most desired wage w_m of the employer.*

============================

CHECKPOINT 29.3
What difference does it make in the position of the MRP curve in Figure 29.5 whether the monopsonist is a monopolist or a perfect competitor in the product market? In a news item it was reported that union leaders in the construction industry were going to push for higher wages despite the reces-

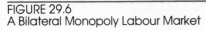

FIGURE 29.6
A Bilateral Monopoly Labour Market

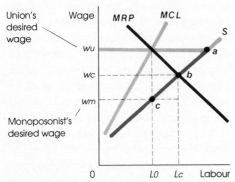

A situation in which there is a monopsonist on the employer side of the labour market and an industrial union on the seller's side may be represented by combining the analysis of the industrial union in Figure 29.4, part b, with that of the monopsony in Figure 29.5, as shown here.

The monopsonist would like to hire L_o units of labour service at a wage of w_m. The industrial union would like to set the wage at w_u when L_o units of labour service are sold. The wage that will be mutually agreeable to both sides will lie somewhere between w_u and w_m, depending on the relative bargaining power of the industrial union versus that of the monopsonist. The greater the strength of the monopsonist relative to that of the union, the closer the wage will be to w_m. Conversely, the greater the strength of the union relative to that of the monopsonist, the closer the wage will be to w_u.

If the union prevails completely, the supply curve of labour is $w_u a S$, while if the monopsonist prevails completely, it is $w_m c S$. Indeed, it is possible that their relative bargaining power might be such that the equilibrium wage is w_c and employment level L_c, the same as the perfectly competitive outcome. The supply curve of labour is then $w_c b S$.

sion in the industry. Using a diagram like that in Figure 29.4, part b, for the industrial union analysis, show why the union leaders' objective is more difficult to achieve during a recession than during more normal times. In recent years there has been a large reduction in the

number of trade unions in Australia as industrial unions replace craft unions. Explain why such moves may well be in the best interest of the labour movement.

AUSTRALIA'S ARBITRATION SYSTEM

Arbitration and Conciliation

The most distinctive feature of wage determination in Australia is the central position of **arbitration** and the institutions that are involed in arbitration procedures. Arbitration is a system in which an independent third party makes a decision about conflicting claims which is binding on both parties. Thus arbitration in industrial relations matters usually involves employers and union representatives and an independent commission, court or tribunal which hands down a decision with which *both sides must comply.* The questions considered may include wage rates, special allowances, holidays, hours and conditions of work; in short all matters that affect the interests of workers and the supply of labour to employers. The distinction is sometimes made between *compulsory arbitration* and *voluntary arbitration.* Compulsory arbitration takes place within a legal framework and needs only one of the two sides to ask the arbitrator to act. A union may press a series of claims for higher wages and better conditions and under a compulsory arbitration arrangement the arbitrator will make a decision whether the employer likes it or not. Voluntary arbitration requires both employers and employees to agree to arbitration procedures being used. But once they both agree to go to arbitration they are also agreeing to accept the decision, whatever it may be. *Conciliation* also involves the assistance of a third party to solve industrial disputes, but the opinions of the conciliator are not binding on the employers and unions involved.

The formal analysis of the economic effects of arbitration is similar to the effects of the imposition of a legal market price discussed in Chapter 21. Most arbitration decisions affecting wage rates specify a minimum wage that must be paid to employees. On occasions arbitration decisions also effectively prohibit employers from paying more than the determined rate. This occurs particularly when the decision has been made within the context of a national wages policy and where the arbitration system is designed to preserve relative wage rates for employees in a range of industries. When arbitration is used to determine wage rates to resolve disputes the decision of the arbitrator is imposed on the market forces as a horizontal line. This, as we saw earlier, does not mean that the forces of demand and supply have no influence. The marginal revenue product of labour still affects how much labour employers will be prepared to hire. The higher the award wage the smaller the amount of labour likely to be employed, other things being equal. Similarly, the lower the award wage, the smaller the quantity of labour likely to be offered. If the wage rate set by the arbitration system is too high supply will exceed demand and unemployment will result. Too low a wage rate will mean that employers cannot get enough labour and there will be a tendency for wages to rise.

A distinction should be made between the wage rate which is the price of labour, often expressed at so much per hour, or per standard working week, and the

worker's *wages* or *earnings*; the sum of money the workers earns in a specified period. To the worker it is the amount earned that is likely to be of paramount importance. Overaward payments and overtime may bring earnings greater than multiplying the award wage rate by the number of hours in a standard working week. Thus even if the award wage is prescribed by arbitration decisions there are many ways including special overtime that allow workers to earn more and to supply more labour and allow employers to pay more than standard wage rates.

The Commonwealth Conciliation and Arbitration Commission

There are many institutions in Australia involved in arbitration, but the Commonwealth Conciliation and Arbitration Commission (The Arbitration Commission) is by far the most imporant. Not only does its jurisdiction extend over a large percentage of the Australian labour force, but it has an important influence on national wages policy. While state industrial commissions and individual industry tribunals are independent they pay considerable attention to the decisions of the Arbitration Commission and their decisions are generally consistent with those of the Commission. Over the last twenty years governments, unions and employers have seen the role of the Commission as one of not only finding solutions to industrial disputes, but determining both the relative rewards to workers in different occupations, and the general level of rewards to labour in Australia. National wages policy is concerned with the determination of wage levels and consequence of changes in wage levels on national economic objectives.

So far we have been concerned with

microeconomics rather than macro-economics. We have not been interested in the general effects on the economy of the actions of firms, consumers or workers. Similarly we have used partial equilibrium analysis and have looked at an industry, or a market form in isolation.

FIGURE 29.7
Possible Effects on Product and Factor Markets of an Increase in Money Incomes and Wages

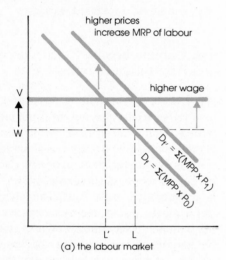

(a) the labour market

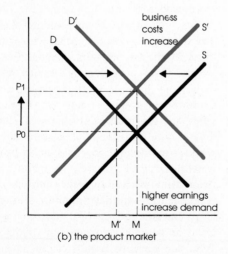

(b) the product market

Part a represents the factor market and part b a product market. The labour sold in the factor market imposes costs on the firm in the product market but we suppose the earnings generate demand for the product itself. An increase in wages (part a) increases costs (part b) moving the supply curve to the right. Higher wages increase demand for the product (part a) and price increases. The product price increase raises the marginal revenue product of labour allowing businesses to hire as much labour after the wage increase.

For the remainder of this chapter, and again in Chapter 31, we will widen our scope. It makes no sense to examine the Australian labour market by pretending it is isolated from product markets. It is equally stupid to ignore the severe inflation which Australians have had to live with since 1973. Australian consumers have faced rapidly increasing prices, businesses have faced higher costs of imported materials, higher wage bills and higher interest rates on borrowed funds. Workers have attempted to gain higher wages.

LABOUR MARKETS, WAGES AND INFLATION

This is not the place to examine the causes of the severe inflation that Australia has experienced in the last twenty years. A number of explanations have been put forward. In most of these wages and business costs have some part to play in the story. To some people wages costs are often a major cause of inflation, to others they are a link in the chain that prevents inflation being controlled. Successive governments have accepted that general levels of wages do have a bearing on the rate of inflation either through the effects on business costs or through the demand for goods and services generated by higher money incomes.

Figure 29.7 is drawn to show the interrelationship between wage costs and demand for goods. It makes a simplifying assumption, that labour is used in a single product market and the earnings of workers are spent on that good. Part a of Figure 29.7 represents the labour market and part b, the market for the good. Initially the wage is $w per hour and the industry hires L units of labour. The industry (part b) produces M units of the good for $P_0 per unit. Suppose now the workers demand or are awarded a rise. The wage increases to $v per hour. The higher wage increases costs to businesses and the industry supply curve moves to the left. Were this the only effect (as we normally assume in microeconomics) the results would be clear. The product price would rise and consumers would buy less. In the factor market the sequel is that businesses would hire less labour. In fact, we have taken the story one stage further by suggesting that workers will spend their higher wages on the product. If this happens in the way set out in the diagram product demand increases (the demand curve shifts to the right in part b) and the industry's demand for labour increases because the firm's marginal revenue product curve has moved to the right (higher product price × MPP). The eventual result is a higher money wage, but the same level of employment, and a higher product price but no change in the quantity produced. Figure 29.7 therefore depicts a situation in which no real change has occurred — gains to workers are illusory and we have inflation.

Of course, the real world is more complicated. Labour is used in many industries. It constitutes a varying proportion of total costs. When money wages rise they do not lead to even increases in demand of the type shown in Figure 29.7. The figure could easily be redrawn to show that the industry produced less after the wage increase and employment fell. But for much of the time taking the economy as a whole increases in money wages without accompanying increases in productivity are unlikely to produce increases in living standards. Much of Australian wages policy since 1973 has been based on attempts to find ways of protecting workers' living standards during inflation without awarding wage increases that would perpetuate or accentuate the rate of price increase.

Productivity Increases

Increases in money wages obtained by restricting supply, by direct bargaining or through arbitration may either lead to less employment or contribute to inflation when producers' supply curves shift to the left. One way in which labour can gain increases in wages is through an increase in productivity. This is illustrated in Figure 29.8. If the demand curve for labour can be shifted from D_0 to D_1, the equilibrium wage and level of employment will rise from w_0 and L_0 to w_1 and L_1, respectively.

How can unions cause the demand curve for their labour services to shift rightward? The marginal productivity theory of labour demand tells us that anything that increases labour productivity will cause the demand curve to shift rightward. Australian workers have been made increasingly aware that higher wages depend in many cases on achieving increases in productivity. There is now recognition that to pursue successful wage claims in bargaining with employers and in arbitration it may be necessary to demonstrate such increases in productivity have been achieved.

Another way to increase labour demand in specific industries is to put tariffs and import quotas on imported goods that compete with domestically produced goods, thereby, directly or indirectly, raising the prices of the foreign goods. This tends to increase the demand for domestically produced goods, which are substituted for the now more expensive or less readily available imported goods. The derived demand for the labour used to produce the domestic goods is thereby increased. Because of this it is not surprising that labour unions frequently join with employers to support tariff legislation that protects their industry from import competition.

FIGURE 29.8
Increased Labour Demand Leads to
Higher Wages and Increased
Employment

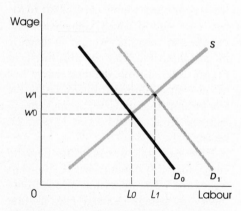

If unions can somehow increase the demand for their labour services, they can have the best of both worlds — higher wages and more employment. A shift in the demand curve for labour from D_0 to D_1 results in an increase in the wage from w_0 to w_1 and a rise in employment from L_0 to L_1.

The marginal productivity theory of labour demand tells us that when unions promote policies that increase labour productivity, a rightward shift in the labour demand curve will take place. Tariffs and import quotas will also have this effect.

Money Wages Versus Real Wages

It is very important in any discussion of wages always to keep in mind the distinction between money wages and real wages. *The **money wage** is simply the size of the wage measured in dollars and cents. The **real wage** is the size of the wage measured in terms of the quantity of goods that can be purchased with it.* The real wage is a more meaningful measure of workers' wage because it indicates the standard of living that the wage makes available to the workers in terms of purchasing power.

For example, suppose you were offered a job paying a money wage of $20 per hour. Sounds pretty tempting, doesn't it? However, suppose you find out that the price of a loaf of bread has risen to $10, a pair of shoes to $400, and a litre of petrol to $2. Similar price increases have also taken place for a host of other commodities. You would probably decide that an hourly money wage of $20 is not much of a real wage — it simply doesn't allow you to buy very much. Almost unconsciously we tend to think of a dollar in terms of what it will buy. In other words, we think of its real value, measured in terms of the goods it enables us to have. We do the same thing when quoted a money wage. That is, we convert it to a real wage by envisaging the quantities of various goods that it will buy.

Converting a Money Wage to a Real wage

How do we convert a money wage to a real wage? Let's take a simple example. Suppose the only good in the economy is bread. Also, suppose your money wage is $6 per hour and that the price of bread if $1 per loaf. Since the real wage is the size of the wage measured in terms of the quantity of goods that can be purchased, your real wage must be 6 loaves of bread. It is the money wage of $6 divided by the price of a loaf of bread, which is $1. Suppose that next year the price of a loaf of bread rises to $2 per loaf. If the money wage remains at $6 per hour, the real wage must fall to 3 loaves of bread per hour, or $6 divided by $2. Since the money wage of $6 only buys half as many loaves as previously, the real wage has been halved.

In reality there are many goods in our economy. So when economists want to convert a money wage to a real wage, they usually divide the money wage by an index of the general price level such as the Consumer Price Index. The index of the general price level is constructed in such a way as to measure the cost of the 'basket' of goods purchased by a 'typical', or 'representative', household. The real wage obtained in this fashion is a measure of the money wage's purchasing power in terms of such a basket of goods.

Real Wages and Productivity

In the last chapter we saw how the demand for a factor such as labour depends on its productivity. In particular, the marginal productivity theory of factory demand tells us that if a firm purchases labour services in a perfectly competitive market (the firm can buy as many labour hours as it wants at the given wage rate) it will hire labour up to the point where the marginal revenue product MRP of labour equals its money wage w. Recall also that the MRP of labour is equal to the marginal physical product of labour MPP multiplied by the price p of the product that the labour is used to produce. This may be written

$$w = p \times MPP = MRP \qquad (1)$$

Equivalently, by dividing both sides of the equation by p, this may be expressed as

$$\frac{w}{p} = MPP \qquad (2)$$

The left side of Equation 2 is the real wage, which is the money wage w divided by the price p. Note that since p is the price of a unit of the firm's product, $w \div p$ is the real wage in that it measures the compensation of labour in terms of the number of units of the firm's product.

We know from the last chapter that technological progress and an increase in other factors used in combination with labour lead to increases in labour productivity. This in turn is reflected in increases in MPP and rightward shifts in the demand curve for less labour. From Equation 2 we can see that such increases in MPP mean that labour's real wage, $w \div p$, will rise when labour productivity increases. This suggests that the rise in the real wage is likely to reflect the growth in demand for labour due to the growth in labour productivity. Of course the supply of labour in Australia has been growing over the years and we know from supply and demand analysis that this factor in isolation would tend to push money wages and real wages down.[1] But real wages have been rising and the conclusion we come to is that the growth in labour productivity has been great enough to cause the demand for labour to grow at a faster rate than the supply

[1] You may convince yourself of this by turning back to Figure 28.2. The marginal cost of the factor MCF in that figure shifts down along D_F. Given the price level p, from Figure 28.1, part b, we can see that this means that the MPP of labour falls. From Equation 2, this means that the real wage, $w \div p$, falls.

of labour. This is illustrated in Figure 29.9. Note carefully that Figure 29.9 uses the real wage and not the money wage on the y axis.

In the last chapter we noted increases in labour productivity, or the *MPP* of labour, may be due to a number of factors. The most obvious is increased years of schooling and job specific training; so-called investment in human capital that improves labour productivity directly. In addition, labour productivity increases when labour is combined with new capital equipment embodying the latest advances in technology and scientific knowhow. Output per labour hour on the farm increased greatly when the tractor, with its much greater pulling power, replaced the horse. Somewhat less obvious at first though, but nonetheless of great importance to the growth of labour productivity, are the improvements in economic organisation and other institutionanal arrangements in our society. The improvement

FIGURE 29.9
Effect of Growth in Labour Supply and Demand on Real Wages

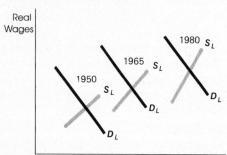

The increase in productivity in Australia has caused the demand for labour to increase at a faster rate than the increase in the supply of labour. Hence, over time the demand curve for labour has shifted farther rightward then the supply curve, thereby causing the real wage to rise.

of traffic flows through and around metropolitan areas makes the transport of goods to markets and labour to jobs easier, thereby contributing to increased productivity. Effectively enforced trade practices legislation laws may well promote the quest for more efficient operation of firms trying to get a competitive edge on rivals. Similarly, the more competitive environment may provide greater incentive to develop and adopt more productive technologies.

Does Technological Progress Create Unemployment and Make Labour Worse Off?

One thing is clear. It is very difficult to disentangle, identify, and separate out the individual sources of growth in labour productivity. With this in mind it is interesting to consider the common allegation that new machines and technology eliminate jobs and create unemployment, thereby making labour worse off. It is true that this kind of progress may well eliminate certain jobs and cause certain workers to seek other employment. But this is typically, though not always, a short-run adjustment process. In the long run, new machines and technology increase labour productivity and thus increase output per labour hour and make possible an increase in real wages. The jobs eliminated release a certain amount of labour and make it available to produce more goods and services previously unavailable. Hence, for a given size of the economy's labour force, it is possible to produce a larger total output. Over the long run it is this process that allows the real wage of all workers to rise and thereby results in an increase in the general standard of living.

POLICY PERSPECTIVE

The Two Tier Wage System

In 1987 the Commonwealth Conciliation and Arbitration Commission announced a new approach to wage determination; a mixture of arbitration and collective bargaining. For the previous 15 years the Arbitration Commission had attempted to implement wages policies aimed at settling industrial disputes by taking into account the needs of workers and the ability of industry to pay against a background of moderate to severe inflation. In that period the Commission varied its principles, guidelines and its decisions. One approach was full indexation. This involved granting increases in wage rates under its jurisdiction equal to the rate of increase of the Consumer Price Index. Such an approach provided workers with real income protection and maintained relativities between workers in different occupations. However, it was criticised as perpetuating inflation and also failing to recognise underlying changes in demand and supply forces in product and labour markets.

A number of variants were tried over the years. *Partial indexation* gave across the board wage rate increases but the rate of increase was less than the rate of increase of the CPI. While this has an element of fairness to all and provided the possibility for winding down inflation it effectively led to a reduction in everyone's real wages and like full indexation ignored market forces. *Plateau indexation* was an arrangement that gave full indexation to workers on lower wages, but smaller percentage increases to workers above a certain level. This approach had the advantage that it protected the poor and made possible an attack on wage cost induced inflation. It destroyed relativities between different jobs and thus again ignored market forces. The two tier wage system introduced in 1987 was an attempt to meet some of these problems. The first tier consisting of an award of $10 per week to all workers under the Commission's jurisdiction was related to the increase in the CPI and the Commission's estimate of the needs of poorer workers in relation to the CPI. It certainly fell far short of full indexation for most workers and was, of course, a considerably smaller percentage increase for those on higher wage rates. The Commission also announced that it would approve second tier increases of 4 per cent to workers in occupations which were able to negotiate successfully with employers on the basis of productivity gains. In short they were requiring that any more than the basic $10 increase only be paid if it was unlikely to have adverse inflationary consequences. In setting the formal procedures the Commission also effectively deferred the date at which any negotiated and approved wage rate increases could be paid for until 1988. By 1988, government and unions were searching for an alternative to the two-tier system, with unions claiming that it did not provide sufficient protection of living standards.

Questions

1. What effect do you think the introduction of this system would be likely to have on the levels of employment in an industry where labour productivity was not increasing and in another where labour productivity had increased by 4 per cent?

Examine the effects on each after the first stage and also the second stage and take it that workers in the second industry eventually receive the increase.

2. Suppose you were a worker in an industry that was showing a 4 per cent growth in labour productivity. What would you prefer — to receive a wage rate increase in line with the growth of the CPI or your industry's productivity? What are the relative effects likely to be on employment of the two methods of changing money wage rates?

For example, even if all of India's labour force were fully employed, the total output of the Indian economy would be minuscule compared to that of the United States. Because labour productivity in India is low, so are real wages. The low productivity is due to a number of factors: a generally high rate of illiteracy and poor health due to low investment in human capital (in the form of education, job training, and medical care), an insufficient quantity of modern physical capital (machines, paved highways, and so forth) to complement the labour force and make is possible to engage in modern production activities, and, of course, political and cultural institutions that are often not conducive to a change in these conditions. Yet if India's labour force were fully employed, this would amount to several hundred million jobs! This example points out that jobs are not the source of an economy's wealth. Rather it is the high productivity and the high real wages that high productivity makes possible. It is differences in productivity that explain the differences in real wages between nations.

CHECKPOINT 29.4
There was considerable opposition in Australia to the introduction of one person operated buses. Transport authorities claimed it would cut costs and increase the productivity of labour.
Show how workers could (a) lose, or (b)

gain, as a result of the one person system.

Why Wages Differ

Why do wages differ from one occupation to another and between individuals in the same occupation? Doesn't it seem unfair that some professional athletes are paid several hundred thousand dollars a year for playing a game while a coal miner makes but a small fraction of that sum for performing a dangerous, grimy job providing an essential source of energy for the economy?

These differences can be explained in terms of supply and demand. Hardly anyone can play golf as well as Greg Norman or play tennis like Pat Cash. The supply of that kind of talent is extremely limited and the public's demand to see it displayed is large. While the demand for coal and consequently the derived demand for coal miners is also large, many people possess the ability and willingness to be coal miners. In short, the difference in wages between great professional athletes and coal miners is due to the difference between the size of the supply *relative* to the demand for the services provided in each of these occupations; the supply of great professional athletes *relative* to the demand for their services in producing coal.

But what are the factors underlying such differences in demand relative to supply in various labour markets both within and across occupations? Perhaps the best way to identify these factors is to envisage the nature of an economy in which there are no wage differences.

Suppose all members of the labour force were exactly alike in ability, skills, and educational background. Each worker could therefore do any job as well as any other worker, whether it were brain surgery, plumbing, professional football or violin playing, or collecting garbage. If in addition each labourer were completely indifferent as to choice of job or occupation, the wage would be the same for each and every labourer in a competitive economy. For example, if the wage were higher in one occupation relative to that prevailing in the others, labourers would tend to move into that occupation and out of the others. Then the increased supply of labour to that occupation would push its wage rate down and the decreased supply to the others would push theirs up until a uniform wage prevailed once again. Conversely, if the wage in one occupation were lower than that prevailing in others, workers would move from that occupation and into the others until the wage difference was similarly eliminated. Of course, the elimination of wage differences requires that labour be perfectly mobile. If members of the labour force are *not* perfectly mobile, are not indifferent as to job preference, and are not exactly alike in ability, skills and education background, wage differences will exist between occupations, between workers in the same occupation, and between geographic locations. We will now look at each of these factors in turn.

Labour Mobility

One has only to look at the persistently high unemployment rates and low wages in parts of rural Australia to see that low wages and a lack of jobs do not necessarily cause labour to move. Family ties, old friends, a sense of 'roots', the costs of searching for a new job,the costs of moving, ignorance about alternatives, and a fear of the unfamiliar are all factors that may inhibit labour mobility. These factors do not mean, however, that labour is immobile 'at any price'. They lead to labour immobility only when the alternatives to the status quo as perceived by a worker are not felt to be worth the cost of change. Often these factors contribute more significantly to immobility among older workers. Given that their working-life horizon is shorter than that of younger workers, they have less chance to recoup the costs of searching out and moving to a new job. This is even more the case when costs of retraining and acquiring new skills are required in order to successfully make such a move.

Labour immobility can also foster high wages. For example, there are institutional constraints on labour mobility that tend to keep wages high in some occupations. Law, medicine, dentistry, and a number of other occupations require participants to be licensed before they may legally practice their trade in a given state or locality. Those already licensed typically exercise firm control over the local licensing board. Obviously they are not eager to issue more licences that would permit an influx of practitioners from other areas of the country and thereby push their wages down.

Of course, in addition to all these considerations there is the fact that demand for different kinds of labour in different parts of the economy is always changing. Indeed, the resulting differences in wage rates between occupations and regions are signals that tell the labour force where more lucrative opportunities exist and when local ones may be drying up. In a dynamic economy where this allocation mechanism is at work, we would naturally expect to see wage differences for this reason alone. Since labour is not perfectly mobile, it takes time for it to move in response to these signals.

Another factor that impedes labour mobility is discrimination by race and sex despite such discrimination being illegal. This takes many forms, from an employer not being willing to hire a member of a particular minority group or sex to the erection of barriers to the training and education necessary to gain admittance to a particular occupation.

Job Preference and Nonpecuniary Considerations

Even if each labourer were exactly like every other labourer in ability, skills, and educational background, there might be considerable variation in how much each enjoys, or does not enjoy, doing a particular job. Hence, two equally able workers might have to be offered considerably different wages in order to induce them to take a given job.

For example a great many people feel the death penalty is an unconscionable punishment for the state to impose, no matter what the crime. Yet states of the USA where the death penalty exists have no trouble finding executioners when they pay them $200 per execution. It takes no special training or talent to turn the gas valves or throw the electrical switch. What wage would it take for you to be willing to do this job? Some of you may say there is no wage that could induce you to it. Others of you may feel it would require a lot more than $200. Though reluctant

to admit it, a few might pay (accept a negative wage) to be given the job depending on the nature of the particular case. In a technical sense all are equally able to do the job, but because of the great differences in feelings about doing it, the necessary wage may vary greatly from one potential executioner to the next.

Many jobs in the economy may differ in the wages they pay in part because of the so-called nonpecuniary advantages or disadvantages associated with them. Working conditions, the degree of danger associated with doing the job, the location, and even the degree of pride or humiliation one may feel in having a particular kind of job are all nonpecuniary considerations. *The* **nonpecuniary considerations** *surrounding a job are the characteristics associated with it that will cause labour to require either a higher or a lower wage, depending on whether the particular characteristics make the job either less or more attractive.* Welders who work on skyscrapers get higher wages than welders who work at the ground level. The difference is necessary as compensation for the greater danger associated with working at such heights.

Ability, Skills and Education

The marginal productivity theory of factor demand tells us that the greater the productivity of a factor such as labour, the greater will be the demand for it. Labour's productivity can be enhanced by vocational training, formal education, on-the-job experience, improved health care, and any form of investment in human capital. Of course, such factors as innate ability and motivation play a large role in determining just how much productivity can be improved by education and specialised training. Very few of us will ever play tennis like Pat Cash, or be scientists like Einstein or Marie Curie, no matter how much training and education we receive.

In general, the greater one's productivity in any given occupation, the greater will be one's earnings. The more skilled house painter, the more motivated sales person, and the more competent manager all have an edge over their less capable coworkers. Their greater productivity will typically mean that the demand for their services is larger. If you can do a job more efficiently and quickly than the next person, your output per unit of time is greater and you can expect to earn more. A barber who can give more haircuts per hour than other barbers will usually earn a higher wage. Unusual talent or skills will not necessarily result in higher wages, however. Again, it depends on the relationship between supply and demand. The supply of blacksmiths is less today than a hundred years ago, but so is the demand for their services. Thus, wages are not particularly high for the few that remain.

CHECKPOINT 29.5
Rank the following jobs according to your preference for them, assuming each pays an hourly wage of $10 per hour: postman, policeman, night watchperson, garbage collector, waiter. If the night watchperson's job pays $10 per hour, what hourly wage would each of the other jobs have to pay for you to feel indifferent as to which job you take? (The necessary wage of each will typically be different from that of every other). Now have a friend answer these questions and compare answers. If I wanted to fill one garbage collector's job and one waiter's job, what would be the minimum hourly wage I would have to

offer to pay for each of these two jobs if I want to get each of you to fill one of them? Explain what factors determined which one of you took which job.

SUMMARY

1. The labour market has special characteristics. It is delivered personally. Employers are interested in the labour power they can hire and the number of hours work they can obtain. Conditions and wage levels are critical to workers because of their personal involvement. There is likely to be a reservation wage below which the individual prefers to leave the workforce and at higher wage rates the individual's supply curve may bend backwards.

2. The determinants of the market supply of labour include the price of labour, social attitudes to work and leisure, the number of people with requisite skills and wages and conditions in other labour markets.

3. The structure of a labour market is as important to an explanation of wage determination as the structure of a product market is to explaining price determination. In a perfectly competitive labour market, a large number of employers compete with one another to hire labour from among a large number of workers competing with one another for jobs. The intersection of demand and supply curves for labour determines the equilibrium wage rate and quantity of labour employed. If workers organise a union in such a market they can push the wage level above the equilibrium level, but employment will be reduced.

4. A craft union is an organisation of skilled workers in a particular craft or trade. It raises competitive wages by controlling the supply of labour. An industrial union is an organisation that attempts to encompass and represent all workers, skilled and unskilled, in a given industry. It uses its bargaining power to set the wage rate higher than the competitive level. It is limited in its ability to do this by the unemployment that this causes among its membership. The main bargaining weapon of a union is the strike.

5. A monopsony labour market is one in which there is a monopoly buyer of labour services confronting unorganised workers competing with one another for jobs. Because the monopsonist must bid up wages to hire additional labourers and pay the higher wage to all workers employed, the marginal cost of labour curve will lie above the labour supply curve. When the monopsonist hires labour up to the point at which the marginal cost of labour equals its marginal revenue product, less labour will be employed at a lower wage than would be the case if the structure of the market were perfectly competitive.

6. When a monopsonistic employer buys labour services from a union that is a monopoly supplier of labour, the structure of the labour market is that of a bilateral monopoly. The level of the wage that prevails in such a market depends on the bargaining strength of the union relative to that of the employer. No more definite statement can be made about the effect of such a market structure on wages and labour supply.

7. The most distinctive feature of the labour markets in Australia is the use made of arbitration and the role of the Commonwealth Conciliation and Arbitration Commision. When the Commission determines wage rates or conditions its effect on the labour market is akin to the imposition of a minimum price in the product market. In 1987 the Commission introduced a mixed system of arbitration and collective bargaining as its contribution to a national wages policy.

8. Much wage determination in Australia in recent years has taken place against a background of unacceptably high inflation levels. The pressure from unions has been to maintain real wages by ensuring nominal wage rates rise at least at the same rate as prices, if possible by anticipating increases in costs of living. Counter arguments have been that this makes inflation worse and then means need to be found of breaking the inflation cycle. Australian workers have become increasingly aware that higher real wages depend on achieving and demonstrating productivity gains.

9. Since 1985 the Commonwealth Government has sought to reduce real wages in an attempt to increase Australia's competitiveness on world markets. It has been seen as a necessary complement to the substantial depreciation of the Australian dollar between 1985 and 1987.

KEY TERMS AND CONCEPTS

arbitration
bilateral monopoly
collective bargaining
compulsory unionism
conciliation
craft union
earnings
industrial union
job preference
labour mobility
mediation
minimum wage
money wage
monopsony

nominal wage
real wage
reservation wage
strike
union

QUESTIONS AND PROBLEMS

1. In 1987 the Australian Government made substantial reductions in the rate of personal income tax payable by most wage and salary earners. This effectively increased their disposable incomes. What effect, if any, would you expect this policy initiative to have had on the supply curve of labour in any particular market? Draw well labelled diagrams and use them in your explanation.

2. A concern is that when monopoly replaces competition in the product market prices rise and output falls. What would you expect the effect to be on the demand for and employment of labour? Would it make any difference if the monopolist was a competitor or a monopsonist in the factor market?

3. What sort of problems would you expect a firm that was operating in an oligopolistic product market to have when deciding how much labour to hire? Check back to Chapter 26 to recall the oligopolist's problem.

4. It is argued by many employers and individual workers that membership of a trade union should not be compulsory. Some workers are prepared to give an amount equal to the union subscription to charity. Apart from the moral issue what benefits could such workers hope to gain by not joining the union? Why is the proposed course of action often not acceptable to the unions?

5. The Liberal and National Country Parties in opposition have advocated a freer labour market in Australia with much greater emphasis on collective bargaining. They believe that across the board decisions of the Arbitration Commission have had undesirable effects on business profits and the economy. Can we take it that this support for collective bargaining is based on the view that the majority of unions would be in a weak bargaining position in face to face negotiations? What do you see as the merits of collective bargaining compared with arbitration?

6. Discuss the merits of industrywide unions compared with craft unions from the point of view of both employers and employees.

7. Consider separately the likely effects on a competitive labour market of the following events:

a. reduction in the standard working week to 35 hours (without loss of earnings);

b. removal of the 17.5 per cent holiday leave loading (annual wage bonus paid to workers).

8. The index of the consumer price index is constructed in such a way that it measures the cost of the 'basket' of goods purchased by a typical, or representative, household. Suppose two workers are paid the same money wage, and suppose this money wage rises by the same per cent as the general price level year in and year out. Why might you expect that the real wages of each of these workers are, in fact, changing at different rates.

9. Explain why the level of *real* wages is a reflection of labour productivity. How do you think each of the following would affect real wages?

a. passage of a law allowing taxpayers an income tax deduction for expenditures on schooling and vocational training;

b. raising restrictions on immigration quotas;

c. increasing the size of the reward paid workers who have their suggestions, which they place in the employee suggestion box, chosen for adoption by the plant;

d. increasing the tax on oil;

e. passage of laws restricting the use of coal.

30

Rent, Interest and Capital

AFTER READING THIS CHAPTER YOU WILL BE ABLE TO:

1. Define the concept of economic rent.

2. Explain how economic rent can be viewed as both a cost and a surplus.

3. Explain how capital may be viewed as a roundabout process of production.

4. Explain the meaning of the net productivity of capital and its relation to the rate of return on capital.

5. State the relationship between saving, capital formation and interest rate determination.

6. Give the reasons why there are many different interest rates, and explain their role in resource allocation and the important distinction between real and nominal interest rates.

The wages of labour, which we looked at in the previous chapter, constitute by far the largest source of income in our economy. They amount to about 80 per cent of total income when we consider not only the wages of hourly and salaried workers, but also that form of labour income earned in the professions (by doctors, lawyers, etc.) and by the proprietors and partners in the many forms of unincorporated businesses. In this chapter we will examine two other main sources of income — rent and interest.

No doubt, the terms rent and interest are already familiar to you from everyday conversation. In this chapter, however, we will see how the economic concept of rent applies to the pricing of all resources, not just land and buildings. The theory of interest rate determination and its relation to the concept of capital is a complex subject. We will touch only on some of its more elementary aspects here.

ECONOMIC RENT

For most people the term rent brings to mind the monthly payment due on their apartment or the payment made to Avis or Hertz for the use of a car. Although we think of rent as a simple payment, we can easily see that it covers a host of costs. The rent on an apartment goes to pay property taxes, insurance, heat, maintenance, and other costs connected with the apartment building. Car rental payments go toward all the costs associated with operating a car rental business.

In economics the term rent, or economic rent, has a much more definite meaning than that often associated with the term in everyday usage. **Economic rent** *is any amount of payment a resource receives in excess of its supply price when there*

is market equilibrium. The supply price of any resource is the price that the resource must be paid in order to cover its opportunity cost. In other words, it is the price the resource must receive in order to keep it from going into its next best alternative use. If a buyer is willing to pay the supply price, the resource will be supplied to that buyer. The qualifier 'when there is market equilibrium' is necessary because resources will often receive *temporarily* higher payments while markets are adjusting to shifts in demand and supply curves.

Economists first developed the concept of economic rent in connection with the nature of the payments received by landlords for the use of their land. Subsequently, it came to be recognised that other factors and resources also receive economic rent. First we will illustrate the meaning of economic rent in the case of land, and then we will examine its meaning more generally for any resource.

Land

The most prominent characteristic of land is that there is a fixed supply of it. It is true that in some parts of the world it has been possible to reclaim land from the ocean, such as in the Netherlands, and it is also true that its fertility can be depleted by some crops, such as cotton. Aside from these qualifications, *it is an essential characteristic of land that its supply is fixed and exhaustible.* In economic terms, the supply curve of land is vertical, or perfectly inelastic.

Economic Rent and Land

Economists first used the term economic rent to refer to the payments for the use of land. In early nineteenth-century England the price of corn (the term used to refer to all grains at that time) rose to such levels that it became a matter of heated public debate as to what to do about it.

On one side were those who claimed that it was the fault of the landowners. It was argued that they charged farmers such high rents for the use of their land that the farmers in turn had to charge a high price for corn in order to cover these costs. Proponents of this point of view proposed that the government should control the amount of rent that landlords could charge farmers. Central to their position was the belief that high rents *caused* high corn prices.

On the other side of the debate were those who claimed just the opposite — high corn prices *caused* high rents. Perhaps the most lucid proponent of this position was David Ricardo, the renowned English classical economist. Ricardo's analysis is illustrated in Figure 30.1. Essentially, he argued that the supply of land available for growing corn was fixed, say at the amount Q and that it had no other use except the growing of corn. In modern economic terms its supply curve S was perfectly inelastic, or vertical. As with any factor of production, the demand for the land is a derived demand. In this case, the demand curve D is derived from the demand for corn, the final product that the land produces. It was argued that as a result of the Napoleonic Wars, there was a shortage of corn and therefore the price of corn was high. Farmers thus found it very profitable to produce corn. In competing with one another to obtain the use of the fixed supply of cornland, they bid up its price, or rent.

In modern economic terms we know

that the price of the final product determines the position of the derived demand curve for a factor of production (as we discussed in Chapter 28). Hence, the higher the price of corn, the higher the position of the derived demand curve D for land in Figure 30.1. The price, or rent, p_0 per acre paid by farmers to landlords for the use of their land, is determined by the intersection of D and S.

But what did Ricardo mean when he claimed that high corn prices caused high rents? Essentially, Ricardo assumed that the land had no other use, that it was simply there and the quantity of it available was completely unresponsive to any change in the price, or rent, paid for its use. Landlords simply rented their land to the highest bidder, and they would certainly rather earn something from it than let it lie idle. If the demand curve fell to a position such as D_1 in Figure 30.1, landlords would be offered nothing for the use of their land — its price, or rent, would be zero — yet the amount supplied would still be the same, Q. If the price, or rent, was p_a and the demand curve was D, there would be an excess demand for land equal to the distance a. In their attempts to obtain land, farmers would bid the rent up to p_0 as landlords rented it out to the highest bidder. If on the other hand rent per acre was p_b and the demand curve was still D, there would be an excess supply of land equal to the distance b. Rather than leave this land idle and therefore earning nothing, landlords in competition with one another to rent their land out would lower rent to p_0. In short, land receives whatever rent the demand for it dictates. The price of corn determines ('causes') the position of the derived demand curve for land, and landlords react — accordingly. The landlords' role is passive. *Hence, Ricardo claimed the price, or rent, of cornland was high because the price of corn was high, not the other way around.* Advocates of this point of view argued that the solution to the problem of high corn prices was not to control landlords but rather to lower restrictions on the import of foreign corn. This would increase the supply of corn and lower its price, thereby lowering the demand for cornland and reducing its rent.

Ricardo's analysis generally came to be accepted by economists as correct. It gave rise to the concept of economic rent. Economic rent, once again, is defined as the surplus, or amount of payment to a factor over and above its supply price, or opportunity cost, when there is market equilibrium. In the case of Ricardo's cornland in Figure 30.1, the economic rent per acre is p_0, the entire rent, or price, paid for the use of an acre of cornland. This is so because the cornland is presumed to have no other use (its supply price is zero) and therefore can be kept in the activity of corn production even at a zero rent. The total economic rent received by cornland is equal to the rectangular area $0Qcp_0$.

Taxing Land's Economic Rent

Land's economic rent has struck many, both economists and laypeople alike, as an 'unearned surplus'. When population and incomes grow, the demand for the fixed quantity of land increases. The good fortune of landowners is to sit back and effortlessly watch the economic rents they receive grow accordingly as the demand curve for their land shifts rightward. How many times have you heard of someone who bought a corner lot on some sleepy country crossroads 20 years ago that is

now worth a small fortune as commercial property on a busy suburban intersection? It has always appeared to many that

FIGURE 30.1
Economic Rent for Cornland

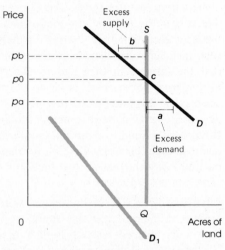

When there is a fixed supply Q of a factor or resource such as cornland, its supply curve S is perfectly inelastic (vertical). Since the demand for corn is a derived demand, the position of the demand curve for cornland depends on the price of corn. If the price of corn is high, the demand curve for cornland is D and the rent per acre of cornland is p_0, which is determined by the intersection of D and S. On the other hand, if the price of corn is low enough so that the demand curve for cornland is D_1, landlords will receive a zero rent per acre for their land.

Since the cornland is assumed to have no other use, landlords passively accept whatever rent demand dictates, renting their land to the farmers who bid highest for it (however little this might be) rather than leaving it idle and earning nothing. For this reason Ricardo argued that high corn prices cause high rent.

This argument gave rise to the concept of economic rent, which is defined as the surplus, or amount of payment a factor or resource receives in excess of its supply price, or opportunity cost, when there is market equilibrium. Since cornland has no other use, its supply price is zero and the rent, or price, received per acre, p_0, is its economic rent. The total economic rent received by cornland is represented by the rectangular area $0Qcp_0$.

economic rent is more a product of good fortune than the fruits of 'honest' work. It is little wonder that land rents should have become a ready target for taxation.

In the latter half of the nineteenth century, Henry George, a printer with a penchant for economics, gathered a large following of supporters behind his **single-tax movement**. Running on this platform, he was almost elected mayor of New York in 1886. The main objective of George's movement was to finance government by taxing away the 'unearned increment' that landowners receive as economic rent on their land. George and his followers argued that in a growing economy, particularly in urban areas, these economic rents were an ever growing 'surplus' obtained by landowners without effort. To them it seemed only just that government should be financed by taxing away this surplus — that economic rent rather than the wages of the working person should bear the burden of taxation. Since the land was there as the bounty of nature, George argued that these economic rents rightfully belonged to the public and should be used for public purposes. This position was forcefully advanced in his popular book *Progress and Poverty* (1879).

Aside from its compelling appeal to the public's sense of justice, *a single tax on land has another advantage over most other forms of taxation — it is neutral in its effects on production incentives and resource allocation*. We know, for example, from our discussion of excise and sales taxes in Chapter 21, that taxes typically affect the prices and the quantities bought and sold of the goods and services on which they are levied. The reason this does not happen when a single tax is levied on the economic rent of land is illustrated in Figure 30.2.

The supply of land Q, being fixed, is inelastic, as indicated by the vertical supply curve S. This, together with the demand for the use of land, represented by the demand curve D, determines an economic rent received by landowners equal to p_0. Now suppose the government levies a tax amounting to 50 per cent of the economic rent received on all land. In other words, 50 per cent of any rent payment made for the use of a piece of land must go to the government. This tax is just like the sales or excise taxes we studied in Chapter 21. In particular, recall that when the supply curve is perfectly inelastic, as in Figure 30.2, the entire burden of the tax is borne by the supplier — in this case the landowner.

The position of the demand curve D and its intersection at point a with the supply curve S are unaffected by this tax. It thus follows that the price, or rent, p_0 paid for the use of a unit of land remains the same as before the imposition of the tax. However, after the government has taxed away 50 per cent, the portion actually received by the landowner per unit of land is p_n — the rent net of (or minus) tax. This is represented by the intersection of the net demand curve D_n, with the supply curve S at b. The net demand curve D_n is the one effectively facing the landowners after the government has taken its cut out of the economic rent. Any point on the demand curve D_n lies one-half the distance below the point vertically above it on D, a reflection of the 50 per cent tax.

In sum, *the full burden of the tax falls entirely on the landowners and there is nothing they can do about it*, despite the fact they don't like it. The quantity of land is fixed and they must take whatever is given to them by demand. *Since the quantity of the land Q and the rent paid for it p_0 are the same as before the tax,*

*there is no distortion of resource alloca-
tion. This is true because if the rent p_0
paid by farmers or other users is
unchanged it means that the tax does not
affect the prices and quantities of any
products that use land as a factor of
production.* This would be true whether

the tax is 10 per cent, 75 per cent, or any
other per cent.

Difficulties with a Land Tax

Taxing the economic rent earned by land
appeals to many in theory, but it is difficult
to carry out in practice. The problem is
that rent payments cover the costs of other
things in addition to the land itself, as
we noted at the outset of our discussion
of economic rent. For example, how do
you separate out that part of the actual
rent payment for agricultural land that is
made because the land is more productive
due to investment in land clearing,
drainage canals, and other such
productivity-increasing activities? Indiscriminate taxation of land rents would
discourage landowners from spending
money to make such improvements,
because unlike the land itself, the supply
of such activities is dependent upon the
return they bring in. To the extent such
indiscriminate taxation of actual rent
payments applies to the portion that goes
to pay for other factors besides the land
itself, production incentives and resource
allocation will be disturbed.

The same problem arises when we
consider rent payments made on urban
and suburban properties. A part of such
payments covers the services of the
buildings and facilities that stand on the
land. How do you separate this part from
the part that is the economic rent for the
land? Is it really possible to do so? Rent
payments cover the costs of the building
and a host of other factors that have to
be sorted out to get at the economic rent
attributable to the land. To the extent that
attempts to tax the economic rent of land
in urban and suburban areas also apply
to the rent for the buildings on this land,
the construction of new buildings and the

FIGURE 30.2
Landowners Bear the Entire Burden of a
Tax on Land's Economic Rent

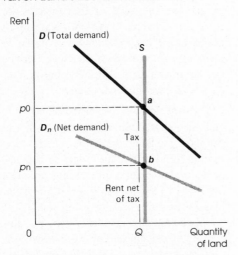

Suppose the economic rent on land is initially
p_0, as determined by the intersection of the
demand curve D and the perfectly inelastic
supply curve of land S. If the government
levies a 50 per cent tax on economic rent, D
and S are unchanged and so is the rent p_0
paid by farmers and other land users. However, landowners now only receive half of this
rent after the government takes its cut. From
the landowners' viewpoint, the demand curve
for land is effectively D_n, which is the demand
after tax, or net demand. The economic rent
p_n received by the landowners corresponds to
the intersection of D_n and S at b.

Because the supply of land is fixed, landowners bear the full burden of the tax. Since
the rent p_0 paid by land users remains unaffected by the tax, the prices and quantities of
products that use land as a factor of production (corn, for example) are similarly unaffected. Hence, a single tax on land is neutral
in its effects on production incentives and
resource allocation.

maintenance of existing ones will be retarded. Again, production incentives and resource allocation will be disturbed.

Economic Rent on Other Factors

The concept of economic rent first arose in connection with land. The supply of land was usually assumed to be unchangeable and to have but one use, such as corn growing. Given these assumptions, the supply curve of land is vertical. It is more realistic, however, to recognise that a given piece of land typically has more than one use. For example, farmland can be converted to residential and urban use. The greater the demand for housing, the larger the portion of available farmland that is converted to such use. Hence, the supply curve for land for residential use is upward sloping, left to right, rather than vertical. Because they have alternative uses this is true of most resources that are used as factors of production. When a factor's supply curve is upward sloping, part of the payment to the factor is economic rent and part is the factor's supply price.

This is illustrated for the factor labour in Figure 30.3, part a. Labour is a factor whose supply is responsive to price, as reflected by the fact that its supply curve is upward sloping, left to right. In the perfectly competitive labour market of Figure 30.3, part a, the intersection of the labour demand curve D and supply curve

---

FIGURE 30.3
Economic Rent Results When Factor Owners Differ in Willingness to Supply Them

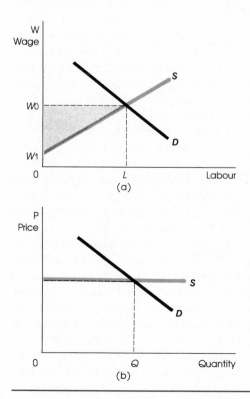

In a perfectly competitive labour market (part a), labourers differ in their willingness to supply labour and therefore have different supply prices. The upward-sloping supply curve reflects this fact. The equilibrium wage and level of employment in such a market are w_0 and L respectively, determined by the intersection of the demand curve D and supply curve S. The supply price of the last labourer hired is just equal to the market wage w_0, so that this last labourer earns no economic rent. However, the supply price of the first labourer hired is w_1, so that in market equilibrium the first labourer earns an economic rent equal to the difference between w_0 and w_1. The supply price of each succeeding labourer is higher, but below the market-determined wage w_0 that each receives, Hence, each earns economic rent (except the last labourer hired). The total economic rent earned by labour in this market is represented by the shaded area. There are many factors of production besides labour that have such supply curves and therefore earn economic rent.

If, unlike the situation in part a, all owners of a factor have the same supply price, no economic rent will be earned. In that case the supply curve of the factor is horizontal, or perfectly elastic, as shown in part b.

POLICY PERSPECTIVE

Subsidised Job Training Versus Labour's Economic Rent

In the early days of the motor vehicle industry, Henry Ford foresaw that the growing industry would need a large and increasing supply of skilled labour — tool- and die makers, layout designers, and so forth. One way to get more labour into these trades would be simply to allow the increasing demand for such services to raise wages — that is, let the usual market forces of supply and demand solve the problem. Another way would be to subsidise training in these areas and thereby increase the supply of skilled workers. Ford tried the latter route and opened the Ford Trade School.

FIGURE P30.1
Employers' Costs Versus Labour's Economic Rent

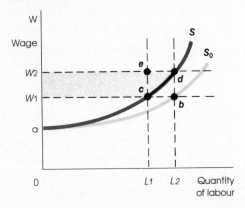

The Alternatives Compared

The two alternatives just mentioned have different implications for employer costs and skilled labour's wages. The difference turns on the issue of economic rent. This is illustrated in Figure P30.1. Suppose the objective is to increase the quantity of skilled labour from L_1 to L_2. Given the supply curve S for skilled labour, this could be done by raising the wage from w_1 to w_2, a movement from point c to point d on S. Note that this results in a considerable increase in the economic rent paid labour, which is represented by the shaded area w_1cdw_2. Note also that a large part of this increase in economic rent has to be paid to the quantity of skilled labour L_1 that was already willing to work at the previous wage of w_1. This part of the economic rent increase is represented by the shaded area to the left of the vertical hatched line between points c and e — that is, the area w_1cew_2.

Now let's look at the other alternative — subsidising the training of skilled labour, as Henry Ford did by setting up the Ford Trade School. This subsidy has the effect of increasing the quantity of skilled labour that is available at any wage level, as represented by the rightward shift of the supply curve from S to S_0. This means that the required increased supply of labour L_2 can now be had at the same wage w_1 as before.

Compare the costs of the two alternative ways of increasing the quantity of labour from L_1 to L_2. It can be seen that increasing the labour supply simply by raising the wage from w_1 to w_2 along supply curve S means that the employer will have to pay more in total wages than if the employer subsidises the training of workers. The additional amount of total wages is represented by the rectangular area w_1bdw_2, the largest portion being the additional economic rent represented by the shaded area w_1cdw_2. Remember that this market is the demand and supply of labour services per some unit of time, such as a month or year. If the additional amount of total wages per unit of time is greater than the costs per that same unit of time of subsidising the operation of the trade school, it will be cheaper for the employer to obtain L_2 labourers by operating the trade school rather than paying a higher wage w_2. If the reverse is true, it will be cheaper for the employer to simply pay the higher wage.

Choosing the Best Alternative

Obviously, the best alternative from the employer's standpoint depends on the elasticity of the labour supply curve. The more inelastic it is, the greater will be the increase in total wages and in labour's economic rent if the payment of a higher-wage alternative is followed. Hence, the greater the likelihood that it is better for the employer to take the subsidisation of the trade school approach. Organised labour, such as craft unions, always prefer the higher-wage alternative because it gives labour higher wages and therefore higher economic rents.

Henry Ford operated the Ford Trade School through the 1930s. Then, with the great surge in the labour union movement after 1935, organised labour in the motor vehicle industry recognised what the school was costing them in terms of lower wages, in particular their forgone economic rents. Labour pressure led to the closing of the school.

Policy Implications

The same type of issue is still very much alive today. Policymakers often advocate various sorts of government-subsidised job-training programs to deal with high unemployment among teenagers and other hard-core unemployment problem areas in the economy. One can understand why union members might have mixed feelings about such programs. One can also see why big business often seems eager to cooperate with and lend support to these programs.

Questions

1. How would you explain the fact that there are many fellowships and scholarships available for graduate students in physics, chemistry, and other basic scientific disciplines, while there are comparatively very few available for medical students?

2. Why do you think some economists favour high death duties?

S determines the equilibrium wage w_0 and level of employment L. In equilibrium each and every labourer is paid the wage w_0. However, only for the last labourer employed is w_0 just the amount necessary to induce that labourer to work in this line of activity instead of some other. That is, w_0 just equals the last labourer's supply price, represented by the point at which the supply curve S is intersected by the demand curve D. The supply price of each labourer hired prior to the last one is represented by a point on the supply curve to the left of this intersection.

For example, the supply price of the first labourer employed is w_1, the point at which the supply curve meets the vertical axis. In equilibrium, the first labourer's economic rent is represented by the difference between w_0, the wage actually received, and w_1 the labourer's supply price. The supply price of each successive labourer hired after the first is progressively higher, as represented by the upward-sloping supply curve. Consequently, the economic rent received by each successive labourer becomes progressively less until the last labourer hired receives a zero economic rent. The total economic rent received by labour in this market is represented by the shaded area. Other factors with upward-sloping supply curves also receive economic rent that is represented in this manner.

There are many factors of production that have upward-sloping supply curves because owners differ in their willingness to supply the factor. Therefore part of the price received for these factors by their owners is economic rent. No economic rent will be earned only if all owners of a factor have the same supply price. In that case the supply curve of the factor is horizontal, or perfectly elastic, as shown in Figure 30.3, part b.

Economic Rent as Cost and Surplus

Whether we are talking about resources with perfectly inelastic supply curves, such as any type of land that has only one use, or those with upward-sloping supply curves, such as labour, the nature of economic rent depends on whether you are a buyer or seller. If you are a farmer renting land to grow corn, the economic rent you must pay is a cost of production as far as you are concerned. Similarly, if you are a firm hiring labour, that part of the wages you pay that is economic rent is still a cost to you. From the standpoint of the owner of the productive factor, the economic rent is an excess above supply price, the price at which the owner would be willing to supply the factor anyway. From the owner's vantage point, economic rent is 'gravy' — a surplus above that needed to engage the factor in the particular line of productive activity.

Explicit and Implicit Economic Rent

In Chapter 22 we made a distinction between explicit and implicit costs. (You might want to look back over that section at this point.) That distinction is also relevant for economic rent. Landowners might use their land themselves rather than rent it out, as is the case with farmers who farm their own land. Such farmers would be kidding themselves as to how well they are doing if their calculations didn't include the cost of using their own land — that is, its implicit cost, or rent. The implicit rent equals the economic rent the farmers would receive if they were to rent the land out to someone else.

Similarly, an owner who personally manages his or her business would make the same kind of mistake if the wages he or she could make managing someone else's business weren't included as costs. Moreover, the owner should not calculate the opportunity cost of these services as the price for which he or she would be willing to work somewhere else — his or her supply price. Rather, the cost should be calculated as the wage the market would pay for this work. It may well be that this market wage is greater than the owner's supply price. To use the supply price rather than the market wage would leave out the economic rent the owner could earn and therefore understate his or her opportunity costs.

CHECKPOINT *30.1
It is sometimes said that movie stars and great professional athletes earn large economic rents. Explain this observation. As a proportion of their earnings, how do you think the economic rents earned by top Australian business executives compare with those of movie stars and great professional athletes? Why? If the American economic theorist Henry George were alive today, what do you think his position would be on the taxation of economic rent of individuals with unique or unusual skills? Comparing landowners and such individuals, what do you think would be a 'just' position?

*Answers to all Checkpoints can be found at the back of the text.

INTEREST AND CAPITAL

When you borrow money, maybe to buy a car or house, or simply to make ends meet until the next pay packet or wage cheque, you must pay a special price called **interest** for the use of such funds. This aspect of interest is quite familiar to most people. What is not so obvious is the intimate relationship between interest and capital. In Chapter 1 we observed that businesses need capital — plant, equipment, inventories — to produce goods and services, and that they need money, or financial capital, to purchase this productive factor. It is the productivity of the capital that allows businesses to pay the interest necessary to obtain this money.

Why There Is Capital

Recall that capital, or capital goods, are all man-made goods used in production, or goods used to produce other goods. Factories, trucks, drill presses, and computers are but a few examples. The economy has limited resources and therefore can only produce so much output per period of time. Thus if a portion of that output is to take the form of new capital goods, the economy will have to forgo a certain amount of goods that could otherwise be produced for current consumption. We know this from our discussion of the production possibilities frontier in Chapter 2. Moreover, if society is to be persuaded to sacrifice some current consumption goods in order to produce capital goods, it must perceive some gain or return from doing so.

Capital Productivity and Roundaboutness

The gain from the production of capital goods today essentially derives from the fact that it will make possible a greater production of goods (of all types) tomorrow than would be otherwise possible without those capital goods. Ranking in importance with the invention of the wheel was the realisation that the most direct way of producing goods was not necessarily the most efficient.

Stone Age people discovered that it was usually more productive to take some time off from hunting game and tilling a plot of ground with bare hands or sticks and use this time to fashion stone hatchets and crude stone hoes to use in these activities. The first hunting and growing season they did this they had less game and food to consume than usual because of the hunting and crop-tending time lost to toolmaking. But in the next season, aided by their new tools, they were able to kill more game and grow more food than before when they were hunting and producing only with the aid of sticks. This is a simple example of a roundabout process of production. *A **roundabout** process involves taking time and effort away from the direct production of goods for current consumption and instead producing capital goods that will provide a larger subsequent production of goods than would be otherwise possible.*

Just as in a Stone Age economy, modern economies, whether centrally planned like that of the Soviet Union or more market-oriented like that of the United States, use the same principle of roundaboutness to increase their productivity. By devoting a portion of this year's production to the formation of capital goods instead of consumption goods, the total output of the economy in future years will be larger than if those capital goods were not produced this year. The current sacrifice of consumption to produce capital is rewarded by the gain in future production that it makes possible. The larger the prospective gain, the more willing society is to sacrifice current consumption to this end.

Net Productivity of Capital and its Rate of Return

The expenditure for a new unit of capital is typically referred to as **investment** in capital, or simply investment. You may think of capital as an investment in a roundabout process. How do we calculate the net productivity of capital and its rate of return?

First, since capital is only one of the factors of production, we need to know the portion of the total dollar value of the sales of the final product attributable to it. By deducting the costs of the other factors of production (including allowance for a normal profit) from total sales, we obtain the dollar receipts of capital. The sum of these receipts over the life of a capital good minus (or net of) the cost of the capital good is a dollar measure of its net productivity. If this calculation doesn't yield a positive dollar value, there is no net productivity. If net productivity is positive, we are usually interested in determining whether the net productivity is large enough to justify investment in the capital good.

In order to do this, we determine the ratio of the dollar measure of the capital good's net productivity to the cost of the capital good and express it as a percentage per year, or **rate of return**. We may then say that *the **net productivity of capital** is the annual percentage rate of return that can be earned by investing in it.*

For example, in a large, bustling city a taxi might last a year (after that it becomes scrap). Suppose you buy a taxi for $8,000, employ a taxidriver for $11,000 per year, spend $7,000 on petrol, $2,000 on maintenance, $1,000 on insurance, $1,000 for a licence, and $1,000 in taxes. Also suppose you take $1,000 per year as a normal profit compensating you for your management services and the entrepreneurial risks of running your taxi business. Suppose total receipts from taxi fares for the year come to $32,800. Total costs exclusive of the cost of the taxi, which is a capital investment of $8,000, are $24,000. Subtracting this from total receipts leaves $8,800, which is what is left to cover the cost of the taxi. Subtracting the cost of the cab ($8,000) from $8,800 leaves $800. That $800 is attributable to the productivity of the capital good, the taxi. The net productivity, or rate of return, on this capital good is therefore $800 ÷ $8,000, which equals .10, or 10 per cent.

As we noted earlier, you must pay interest in order to borrow money. Since the interest on borrowed money must be paid with money, interest is expressed as a percentage rate just like the rate of return on capital. What market interest rate would you be willing to pay to borrow the money to buy the $8,000 taxi and start your own taxi business? Certainly not more than 10 per cent, because a higher interest rate than this would exceed the rate of return on your investment in the taxi and you would realise a loss. Any lower interest rate would allow you to realise a profit. Rather than borrow the money you might choose to use your own money. But the decision as to whether to invest or not would be no different. You would not be willing to invest your own money in the taxi if the market interest rate exceeded 10 per cent. Why? Because the opportunity cost of doing so exceeds the net productivity, or rate of return, on the taxi. You would be better off lending your money out to someone else at the higher interest rate.

The Demand for Capital

The demand for capital derives from its net productivity in the production of goods. Like the demand for any factor of production, it is a derived demand.

Recall that the demand curve for labour is its marginal revenue product curve. Similarly, the demand curve for capital may be thought of as its marginal revenue product curve expressed in percentage terms, or what we have called its net productivity.

This is illustrated in Figure 30.4, where for simplicity it is assumed that there is only one kind of capital. The demand curve D is made up of the points representing the net productivity of capital (vertical axis) associated with each additional unit of capital (horizontal axis). The first unit of capital has a net productivity of 14 per cent. (The scale on the horizontal axis is such that one unit of capital is no larger than a point.) If the interest rate is higher than this, it will not pay to invest in this unit of capital. Note that each additional unit of capital has a lower net productivity than the previous unit — hence the demand curve is downward sloping. This reflects the fact that the law of diminishing returns applies to capital just as it does to other productive factors, such as labour. Given the fixed amounts of all other factors, the net productivity of each additional unit of capital decreases as the total quantity of capital is increased.

If the market interest rate is 10 per cent, for example, it pays to invest in capital, or undertake those roundabout processes that have a net productivity greater than 10 per cent. Once the economy has created the capital that has a net productivity of 13 per cent, it will move on to invest in capital that has a net productivity of 12 per cent, and so on until it has exploited all those opportunities to create capital that have a net productivity, or rate of return, greater than 10 per cent per year. Therefore at an interest rate of 10 per cent, the stock of capital demanded will equal

K_0. If the market interest rate were 6 per cent, the economy would desire to invest in all those capital projects with a rate

of return greater than 6 per cent, and the stock of capital demanded would equal K_1.

FIGURE 30.4
The Demand for Capital Depends on Its
Net Productivity

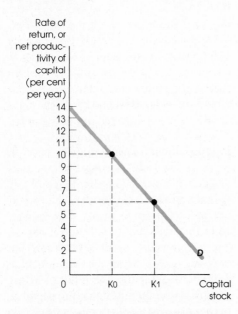

The demand for capital, like that for any other productive factor, is a derived demand.

Its demand curve *D* may be thought of as its marginal revenue product curve expressed in percentage terms, or what we have called its net productivity. The demand curve *D* is made up of the points representing the net productivity of capital (vertical axis) associated with each additional unit of capital (horizontal axis).

As shown here, the first unit of capital produced has a net productivity of 14 per cent. Because of diminishing returns, each additional unit of capital has a lower net productivity than the previous one, as reflected in the fact that *D* is downward sloping. If the market interest rate is 10 per cent, it will pay to invest only in those capital projects that have a net productivity, or rate of return, greater than 10 per cent. Hence, the stock of capital demanded will equal K_0. If the market interest rate is 6 per cent, it will pay to invest in all those capital projects with a rate of return in excess of 6 per cent, and therefore the total demand for capital will equal K_1.

Interest and Saving

We have seen that to produce capital goods it is necessary to give up a certain amount of current consumption. Only by doing so can a portion of this period's total production take the form of capital goods. The sacrifice of current consumption to the roundabout process of capital formation must be made up for by the prospect of a future gain in order to make the sacrifice worthwhile.

Economists call this sacrifice of current consumption **saving.** *For the economy as a whole, saving is defined as not consuming all of this period's production of output.* It is the extent of saving, or refraining from current consumption, on the part of the individual members of the economy that determines the amount of total saving. This total saving is the amount of this period's total production that can be devoted to the output of capital goods, as opposed to goods for current consumption.

People save part of their incomes for many reasons — to provide for old age, to buy a home or a car, to give their children a college education, and so on. The attainment of these goals is the reward they expect for the sacrifice of current consumption that saving requires. Another very tangible reward is the interest they can earn on their saving. Whatever the other reasons for saving, the higher the interest rate received, the larger the reward for saving, and therefore the more people will be induced to save part of their incomes.

The relationship between the interest rate and the total amount of saving (or refraining from current consumption) for the whole economy is illustrated in Figure 30.5. The saving curve S gives the relationship between the interest rate (vertical axis) and the economy's total saving per year, or the dollar amount of that part of the economy's total annual output that may take the form of capital goods. The higher the interest rate, the larger the amount each individual will want to devote to saving and hence the greater the total amount of saving. As a result, the saving curve is upward sloping. For example, at an interest rate of 4 per

---

FIGURE 30.5
The Relationship Between the Interest Rate and Saving

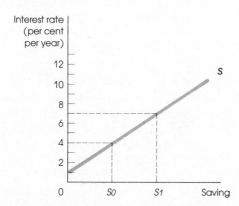

Saving is defined as refraining from current consumption. To this extent, it entails a sacrifice.
   Among the possible rewards of saving is the rate of interest that can be earned. The higher the interest rate, the larger this form of reward and the greater is the incentive to save. The upward-sloping saving curve S reflects this fact. The higher the interest rate (vertical axis), the larger the economy's level of saving per year (horizontal axis). The level of saving is also the dollar amount of that part of the economy's total annual output that may be used to obtain capital goods. At an annual interest rate of 4 per cent, the total amount of saving would equal S_0, while at the higher interest rate of 7 per cent, total saving would be the larger amount S_1.

---

cent, the total amount of saving would equal S_0, while at the higher interest rate of 7 per cent, saving would be the larger amount S_1.

Interest Rate Determination

We are now in a position to lay out the basics of the traditional theory of interest rate determination. This is illustrated in Figure 30.6. Part a shows the economy's net productivity, or demand curve for capital, like that shown in Figure 30.4. Part b shows the economy's saving curve, like that shown in Figure 30.5.

   It should be emphasised that it is the stock of capital that is measured (in units of capital) along the horizontal axis in part a of Figure 30.6. It takes time, often many years, for an economy to accumulate a sizeable capital stock. Suppose the economy's capital stock is K_0, the endowment from many years of accumulation that is represented by the perfectly inelastic (vertical) stock supply curve k_0. This curve intersects D at a, and the net productivity, or rate of return, on the last unit of this capital stock is therefore 10 per cent. Hence, if the economy saves, that is, refrains from consuming, a part of this year's total production of output (a flow measured as so many dollars of output per year) so that this part may take the form of investment in new capital goods, the rate of return on these new capital goods will not be greater than 10 per cent. Investors in new capital stock will therefore be willing to pay an interest rate up to 10 per cent to induce people to lend them their savings so that the investors can buy newly produced capital goods.

   But point a on D represents a short-run equilibrium. Let us see why. At an interest rate of 10 per cent, people will be induced to save an amount totalling

S_0 dollars per year, as shown in part b of Figure 30.6. Remember that the horizontal axis of part b measures *flow*, the dollar flow of saving out of this year's dollar flow of output. Lent out to investors it becomes the dollar flow of investment, or expenditure on new capital goods, produced in the current year. The new units of capital produced in the current year and purchased with this money are then added to the stock of capital K_0. (Assume for simplicity that there is no depreciation, or wearing out, of the existing capital stock, so that new capital isn't used for replacement of old.) Hence, over time the stock of capital will grow and the vertical stock supply curve in part a will move rightward. Its resulting intersection with the capital stock demand curve D at lower and lower points down

FIGURE 30.6
The Determination of the Interest Rate

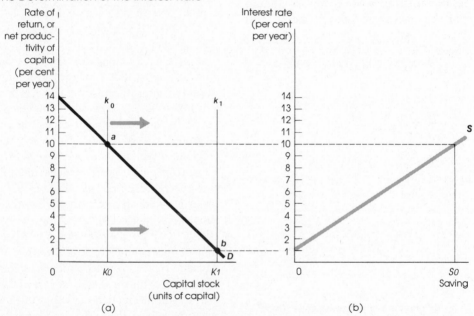

(a)   (b)

The net productivity, or demand, for capital curve D in part a is the same as in Figure 30.4. The saving curve S in part b is the same as in Figure 30.5.

Given the economy's stock of capital, which has been accumulated over time, the vertical stock supply curve of capital k_0 intersects D at point a, where the rate of return on capital, and therefore the interest rate, is 10 per cent. At this interest rate the economy is willing to save (refrain from consuming) S_0 dollars worth of the economy's annual production of output. Lent out to investors, this becomes the dollar flow of investment, or expenditure, on new capital goods produced in the current year. Point a on D is therefore only a short-run equilibrium position because this new capital formation will increase the size of the capital stock. This is represented by the rightward shift of the vertical stock, supply curve of capital (part a).

As long as the interest rate is high enough to induce saving, capital formation will continue. This will eventually drive down the rate of return on capital, and hence the interest rate, to the point where saving becomes zero. This occurs with a capital stock of K_1, where the supply curve k_1 intersects D at b (part a) to determine an interest rate of 1 per cent. At this point saving becomes zero (part b), and investment in capital formation ceases. This is the point of long-run equilibrium.

along D means that the rate of return on capital, and therefore the interest rate, will fall.

As the interest rate becomes progressively lower, it is clear from part b that the amount of saving that makes new additions to the capital stock possible will also decline. Finally, when the capital stock has grown to the size K_1, so that the vertical stock supply curve of capital k_1 intersects D at b, the rate of return on capital and the interest rate will be 1 per cent. The flow of saving will be zero (part b) and new capital formation will cease. The economy will consume its entire annual production of output, and nothing will be devoted to capital formation. Point b on D (part a) therefore corresponds to its long-run equilibrium position.

In sum, *the existing stock of capital together with the net productivity or demand curve for capital determines the interest rate, which in turn determines the amount of saving. The amount of saving is the amount of total output produced that is not devoted to current consumption and that is therefore available for the production of new capital goods, which increase the size of the capital stock. The long-run equilibrium interest rate is that interest rate at which saving becomes zero and new capital formation therefore ceases.*

Why We Never See Long-Run Equilibrium

To reach long-run equilibrium, we must move down the demand curve D and realise diminishing returns because all other things are assumed constant. In reality, of course, the other things, such as technology and population, do not remain unchanged. New inventions and technological progress cause the net productivity of capital to increase. This causes the demand curve D for capital to shift rightward. We know from our discussion in Chapter 28 that when the supply of one factor of production increases, the marginal productivity of other factors is increased. Therefore increases in the labour supply resulting from population growth also increase the net productivity of capital and, likewise, cause the demand curve D to shift rightward. In a dynamic, growing economy the demand curve for capital will be continually shifted rightward as a result of such ongoing changes. Consequently, the rate of return on capital, and hence the interest rate, never falls to the extent necessary to reach the long-run equilibrium position.

In our discussion of the demand curve D in Figure 30.6, part a, it was implicitly assumed that the net productivity, and hence the rate of return on capital, is known to investors in capital with certainty. This is, of course, not true in reality. Any assessment of the net productivity of capital goods or roundabout processes undertaken today can at best only be based on educated guesses about the demand for the goods that they will produce in the future. Given this, the demand curve for capital is subject to changes in such guesses, and changes in events will lead to a continual revision of these guesses. Shifts in business optimism about the future, which often occur rapidly, cause sporadic movement in the demand curve D and therefore its intersection with the vertical stock supply curve of capital. The interest rate will move about accordingly.

Historically, the saving habits of the economy have been much more stable than investor willingness to undertake new capital formation. This is not surprising given that saving is a decision made about the disposition of income already in hand (how much of it to save and how much to spend on current consumption), while investment in new capital is based to a much greater extent on guesses about events yet to happen. Nonetheless, the saving curve in part b of Figure 30.6 can shift around and thereby affect the rate of capital formation. This in turn will affect the amount of change in the interest rate over time.

Consumption Loans

From time to time some people want to spend more than their total income on current consumption. To do so, they may borrow from others in the economy who save a part of their income. In this case the amount of such borrowed funds that the borrower spends on current consumption is just equal to the amount the lender must refrain from spending on current consumption in order to make the loan. What one consumes, the other doesn't. The aggregate, or sum, of all such consumption loans in the economy therefore does not affect the amount of total expenditure on current consumption. Hence, it does not affect the position of the economy's saving curve in Figure 30.6, part b. At any interest rate above 1 per cent, total saving is positive. This means that the total amount saved by those not spending all their incomes exceeds the total amount spent by individuals on current consumption in excess of their incomes.

Why There Are So Many Different Interest Rates

Up to now we have talked about 'the' interest rate. Economists find this conve-nient in order to spell out the basic elements of the traditional theory of capital formation. However, a casual observer of the financial pages of any newspaper or the behaviour of the numerous financial institutions in our economy knows that there are, in fact, many different interest rates. These rates correspond to the many different debt instruments issued by borrowers to lenders. *These* **debt instruments** *are the written contracts between borrower and lender specifying the terms of a loan such as its expiration or maturity date, its size, and the rights of the borrower and lender under the agreements.* Bonds, bank deposits, commercial paper, ordinary and preference shares, credit union shares, and mortgages are all examples of debt instruments. Interest rates on debt instru-ments differ because of differences in risk, length of loan, marketability of the loan, and the structure of financial markets.

Risk essentially depends on the likeli-hood that the borrower will default on (be unable to pay back) the loan. The greater this likelihood, the larger the interest rate that will have to be paid to induce lenders to make the loan. A small company in a highly competitive space age technology industry will typically have to pay a higher interest rate to borrow money than GMH does because there is a higher risk of the small company defaulting on its loan.

Loan length, or maturity, refers to the duration of time until the loan must be repaid. Naturally the greater the length of time over which the money is borrowed, the greater the possibility that the lender may run into financial difficulty some-where down the road. Therefore, the interest rate is usually higher on longer-term loans to compensate the lender for this risk.

Marketability, or the liquidity of a loan, refers to the ease with which the lender may sell the debt instrument to someone else before the loan matures. If you write me an IOU for a gambling debt, I will probably be able to sell it to someone else only if I am willing to take considerably less for it than the amount owed. By comparison, the market for a Telecom bond is much more extensive and well developed. The chances of selling it for what I paid for it are much greater. Interest rates on less marketable debt instruments tend to be higher, all other things remaining the same, to compensate the lender for their lower marketability.

Financial market structure plays much the same role in determining the level of interest rates as product market structure considerations play in determining the price level of goods. A monopoly lender is in a better position to charge a higher interest rate than many lenders competing with one another to make loans.

Interest Rates and Resource Allocation

The existence of many different interest rates on the many different kinds of debt instruments in the economy serves the same kind of resource allocation function as does the existence of many different prices on the many different kinds of goods the economy produces. There is in reality a large variety of capital investment projects, ranging from building dams and ships to starting up a corner grocery store. Capital projects differ in their riskiness and life expectancy, as well as their size. Shifts in the demand for the products that capital goods help produce will cause changes in the capital goods' relative net productivity and thus in the interest rates they can pay to attract financial capital.

For example, during the last 50 years the increased demand for airline passenger service relative to that for railway passenger service increased the net productivity of capital used in the former industry relative to that used in the latter. The interest rates that could be paid to attract financial capital into the building of aeroplanes and airports thus rose relative to those that could be paid to finance railways, carriages, and stations. Consequently, the rate of capital formation in the airline industry rose relative to that in the railway passenger industry.

The problem of capital allocation has to be solved by every economy. Centrally planned economies like that of the Soviet Union must resort to some sort of interest rate structure to do this just as do market-oriented economies like that of the United States. The institutional structure surrounding the determination of interest rates, and even the terminology used, differs, reflecting the differences in political and ideological orientation between the two countries.

Nominal and Real Interest Rates

Suppose there is no inflation occurring in the economy. (Inflation is defined as an ongoing increase in the general price level at some percentage rate per year.) Suppose also that lenders are lending money at an interest rate of 5 per cent, based on the expectation that there will continue to be no inflation. A lender just willing to lend out $1 worth of purchasing power today is induced to do so by the promise of getting back $1.05 worth of purchasing power tomorrow, or 5 per cent more purchasing power than originally loaned. In terms of goods, or 'real' terms, the lender will be able to obtain 5 per cent more goods tomorrow than today. The annual percentage rate of increase in the lender's purchasing power on money loaned is the **real interest rate**.

Now suppose for some reason lenders come to expect a rate of inflation of 4 per cent per year. They no longer will be willing to lend at an interest rate of 5 per cent, but will now charge an interest rate of 9 per cent. Why? Because the dollars they lend out today will be worth 4 per cent less in terms of their purchasing power in a year — 4 per cent less in real terms. Hence, lenders must charge an additional 4 per cent in interest to ensure that they still get back 5 per cent more purchasing power than they originally loaned. In short, in order to continue to realise an increase in purchasing power, or a real rate of interest, of 5 per cent, it is necessary to charge a nominal rate of interest of 9 per cent. *The* **nominal interest rate** *equals the real interest rate plus the rate of anticipated inflation.*

In our example, when the anticipated rate of inflation was zero, the real interest rate and the nominal interest rates were the same, 5 per cent. Only when the anticipated rate of inflation equals zero is it true that the nominal interest rate and the real interest rate are equal. The quoted interest rates we observe in financial markets are nominal interest rates. To arrive at the real interest rate, it is necessary to subtract the anticipated rate of inflation from these nominal interest rates. However, as a practical matter, it is difficult to measure accurately the public's anticipated rate of inflation.

The Government and Interest Rates

The government can affect interest rates in many ways. Two major avenues of influence are the federal government's fiscal and monetary policy actions.

Fiscal policy affects interest rates through government expenditure and tax policies. For example, if government expenditures exceed tax revenues, then the Treasury must issue government bonds to finance the deficit. Government bonds must compete for financial capital alongside private debt instruments and will cause interest rates to rise, other things remaining the same.

Monetary policy, as implemented by the Reserve Bank of Australia, affects the amount of money available to accommodate loan demand. If the Reserve Bank limits expansion of the money supply, interest rates will tend to rise, at least in the short run, as borrowers' demand for loans grows relative to the rate of growth in the availability of lendable funds through the banking system. On the other hand, if the Reserve Bank increases the availability of funds more rapidly than the rate of growth of loan demand, interest rates will tend to fall, in the short run at least. In the long run, if the Reserve Bank continues to expand the nation's money supply at such a rate, prices are likely to rise correspondingly and cause the public to anticipate an ongoing inflation. As we discussed above, this means that nominal interest rates will rise relative to the real interest rate as lenders attempt to protect themselves against the erosion of the purchasing power of the dollars they lend out.

CHECKPOINT 30.2
How is a college education a roundabout process? How would you measure the net productivity, or rate of return, of such an investment in human capital? If for some reason people became less willing to save, how would this affect the saving curve in Figure 30.6, part b? How

would this affect the long-run equilibrium stock of capital? Why? Suppose there is a sharp increase in the rate of population growth. How will this affect the position of the demand curve for capital in Figure 30.6, part a, and the long-run equilibrium stock of capital?

SUMMARY

1. Economic rent is any amount of payment a factor, or resource, receives in excess of its supply price when there is market equilibrium.

2. Because land is basically in fixed supply and available whether or not it receives payment, any economic rent received by land may be considered a surplus. Taking this point of view, in the late nineteenth century the American Henry George initiated the single-tax movement, which advocated taxing the economic rent on land to finance government. In theory such a tax would not affect resource allocation. However, in practice it is difficult to distinguish that part of economic rent attributable to land from that earned by buildings and other capital improvements on the land.

3. Any productive factor — not just land — may earn economic rent. The economic rents of productive factors are a surplus to the economy as a whole, but they are costs to firms and others who must pay to use them.

4. When factors are used by their owners, their economic rents are implicit. Implicit economic rent is equal to the explicit economic rent that could be received by a factor if its owner hired it out to its next best alternative use.

5. Interest is the price, expressed as a percentage rate, that must be paid for the use of borrowed funds.

6. When an economy saves, it refrains from consuming a portion of its current output. This allows it to undertake roundabout production processes by devoting that portion to the formation of capital goods. The gain from capital formation is the net productivity of capital, measured as the annual percentage rate of return that can be earned by investing in it.

7. Capital's demand curve may be expressed in percentage terms. Plotted on a graph, the stock of capital demanded is measured on the horizontal axis and its annual percentage rate of return on the vertical axis. Any point on the demand curve represents that market interest rate at which it just pays to invest in the associated stock of capital.

8. One of the rewards of saving, among others, is the interest people can earn by lending their savings. Hence the higher the interest rate, the more people will be induced to save.

9. The existing stock of capital together with the demand curve for capital determines the interest rate, which in turn determines the amount of saving in the economy and hence the rate of new capital formation. The long-run equilibrium interest rate, where saving becomes zero and new capital formation ceases, is never attained because of continual technological change and population growth. Uncertainty, which plays a large role in the assessment of capital's net productivity, and changes in saving habits may also cause the interest rate to fluctuate.

10. A certain amount of lending takes the form of consumption loans. Summing across all borrowers and lenders this nets out, so that the economy's total saving at any interest rate is the amount available for capital formation.

11. In our economy there is a variety of interest rates because there are many kinds of loans differing in risk, maturity, marketability, and the structure of the financial market in which the loan is made. These interest rates play the same kind of role in the allocation of resources as do prices in goods markets. Inflation's erosion of the purchasing power of money leads to a distinction between nominal and real interest rates.

12. The federal government affects interest rates through monetary and fiscal policy. State governments affect interest rates by issuing of bonds to finance public works.

KEY TERMS AND CONCEPTS

    debt instrument
    economic rent
    financial market structure
    interest
    investment
    loan length
    marketability
    net productivity of capital
    nominal interest rate
    rate of return
    real interest rate
    risk
    roundabout process
    saving
    single-tax movement

QUESTIONS AND PROBLEMS

1. Using the marginal productivity theory of factor demand, explain why some pieces of land receive higher economic rents than others.

2. Why is it often said that the economic rent of land is demand determined, unlike the economic rent of other productive factors? In what way does the levying of a tax on the economic rent of land have different implications for resource allocation than the levying of a tax on the economic rent of other kinds of productive factors?

3. It has been argued that if the economic rent of land is an 'unearned surplus' that should be taxed, then so is the economic rent received by anyone who owns an unusual natural talent, such as a great singing voice or an above-average IQ. If land is a gift of nature, then so are such unusual abilities, and if land's economic rent should be taxed, it is only just that the economic rent of these abilities should also be taxed. Would you agree with this position? What difficulties might hamper the implementation of such a policy?

4. Suppose you own some grapevines, and it costs you $20 to turn this year's grapes into grape juice. Suppose that after 1 year you can sell the juice as wine for $22. Assuming there are no other costs, what is the net productivity, or rate of return, on this roundabout process?

5. Some observers have maintained that many underdeveloped countries are held back by their low levels of saving. What do you think is the rationale for this point of view?

6. What is the relationship between the economy's willingness to sacrifice current consumption, the net productivity of capital, interest, and saving?

7. In the mid-1970s inflation in Australia was running at an annual rate of between 15 and 20 per cent. For a time there was a marked increase in the proportion of disposable incomes people saved rather than spent. Often these savings earned a negative real rate of interest. Critically examine their behaviour. In what ways was it similar to the increase in savings with banks that followed the stock market crash in 1987?

8. How would you rank the following loans according to their riskiness; a Telecom Bond maturing in 1999, a 25 year mortgage loan on a harbourside residence in Sydney, a personal loan to a student and a 10 year bond issued by the Government of Israel?

31

Income Distribution, Poverty and Welfare Policy

AFTER READING THIS CHAPTER YOU WILL BE ABLE TO:

1. Explain the concept of income distribution and show how income inequality is measured.

2. Summarise some of the major determinants of income inequality.

3. Explain the measurement, description, and basic causes of poverty.

4. Explain how poverty may be attacked through the labour market and by use of an income tax transfer system.

5. Recognise that policies which redistribute income also affect both factor and product markets.

Few issues generate more heated discussion and controversy than those related to income distribution, poverty, and welfare policy. These issues go to the very heart of the questions, For whom is the economy's output produced? What is a 'just distribution' of income?

The kind of social order we call 'capitalism', constructed on the basis of a market economy, was from its beginnings hostile to any political or 'social' definition of distributive justice. Its basic premise is that a 'fair' distribution of income is determined by the productive input of individuals to the economy — 'productive' as determined by the marketplace. Specific talents, character traits, and just plain luck enter into the determination of such productivity. Capitalism holds that this market-based distribution of income creates economic incentives that encourage the production of goods and services. Such production provides society's material standard of living, which is not necessarily shared equally by all. And, this system may shape society in ways not everyone likes. Historically, market-oriented capitalistic societies have been reluctant to concede to any authority the right to overrule the determination of income distribution provided by the marketplace.

By contrast, noncapitalist societies historically have adhered to a very different notion of distributive justice. For them, it is based on the individual's contribution to the society, not merely to the *economy*. Economic rewards are 'socially' justified, as distinct from economically justified. For example, in the Middle Ages the activities of the Church and the clergy were deemed to have a social significance and value that justified compelling ordinary people to provide their economic support. Similarly, the

Communist party in the Soviet Union today does not have to defend its budget on economic grounds. The value of its contribution to the society as a whole is beyond question.

In today's world there are no pure forms of market capitalism, nor are there any noncapitalistic societies that do not allow some capitalistic, free-market practices to exist. All noncapitalistic societies recognise to one degree or another the need for differences in rewards, based on individual skills, as a spur to economic activity. Likewise, all capitalistic, market-oriented societies recognise to one degree or another that if the marketplace were the sole judge of the individual's claim to a piece of the economic pie, cruel hardships would befall some.

What can be said about these different concepts of a 'good' society and the principles of 'fairness' in income distribution by which they operate? In the abstract, the question of which principle of distribution is 'better' is a normative issue. It cannot be settled by a mere appeal to facts. A society's judgment about this issue will depend on such things as its traditions, attitudes, social conventions, and history. It is pointless to argue that a society 'should' be capitalist or socialist, if the vast majority of its people will not be bound by the different kinds of discipline that each of these systems requires in order to work.

This book has concentrated on the microeconomics of a market system. In particular much has been said about how perfectly competitive markets for goods and resources lead to optimal allocations of resources. How do such claims square the the problem of poverty and achieving an 'ideal' distribution of income? Is there a conflict between measures designed to remove poverty and an economic system operating to its full productive potential? In this chapter we will examine the measurement and determinants of income distribution and the way in which income is distributed in Australia. We will also examine the consequences for markets and the economic system of attempts to change the distribution of income and end by asking whether there is a best attainable distribution for Australia.

INCOME DISTRIBUTION

There are many possible ways to look at the distribution of income. Whichever way we choose, however, it is always the case that all the economy's income is ultimately received by households. This happens because households are the ultimate owners and suppliers of all resources (land, labour, and capital) used to produce the economy's output. Another fact that should be kept in mind in any analysis of income distribution is that reported income data usually do not include all the income that households receive. Unearned income (such as gifts and favours), income received in kind such as occurs in a barter transaction (I give you a load of firewood in exchange for your cutting my lawn during the summer), and cash transactions for goods and services are all examples of income that may go unreported to tax collectors and census takers, our main sources of income data.

Keeping these limitations in mind, we will now look at the two commonest ways of analysing income distribution. These are the functional distribution of income approach and the size distribution of income, or personal distribution of income, approach.

The Functional Distribution of Income

In preceding chapters we have examined the determinants of wages, rent, interest, and profits — the earnings of the factors of production labour, land, and capital. Since all income derives from the sale of factors of production, economists have long been interested in the distribution of income among the owners of these factors — that is, the distribution of income according to the function performed by the income receiver. *The* **functional distribution of income** *approach to the analysis of income distribution characterises the way income is distributed according to the function performed by the income receiver.* Rent payments are the money income received by property owners, wages are the money income received by labour, and interest and profits compensate those who provide financial capital and own businesses (either incorporated or unincorporated).

Labour, landowners, and capitalists were the three major social classes in the eyes of nineteenth-century economists such as David Ricardo and Karl Marx. The relatively clear distinctions between these classes perceived in the nineteenth century are considerably more blurred today. It is now common for any given individual to receive income from ownership of at least two, and possibly all three, of these factors. For example, the rise of the company as the dominant form of business organisation has made it possible for large numbers of the labour force to be capitalists through ownership of shares in companies and the receipts of dividend income.

A simple functional distinction is between that part of the value of the production of goods and services that goes to households in the form of wages and salaries and the balance of rewards which can be thought of as going to other factors (capital and land). The term *wages share* is used to refer to the proportion of

FIGURE 31.1
Wages Share as a Percentage of Gross Domestic Product at Factor Cost in Australia
1971–72 to 1986-87

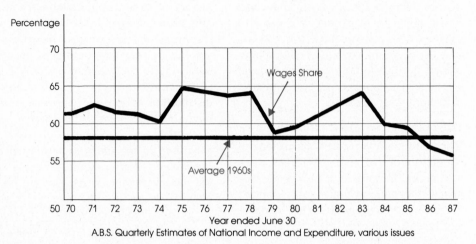

A.B.S. Quarterly Estimates of National Income and Expenditure, various issues

Employers claim that wages share in Australia is too high. A larger proportion going to business in profits is said to be necessary to promote investment and stimulate the economy.

production distributed to wage earners. Formally it is defined as

$$\text{Wages Share} = \frac{\text{the aggregate of wages and salaries}}{\text{gross domestic product at factor cost}^1} \times 100$$

Figure 31.1 shows how the wages share has varied in Australia since 1970-71 and how it compares with the average level in the 1960s. The wages share rose sharply in the early 1970s from 58 per cent of GDP at factor cost to around 65 per cent before declining again. In the early 1980s the wages share again rose sharply, during a period of accelerated inflation and government encouragement of collective bargaining. Since 1983 there has been a steady fall in wages share and an increase

in the share of GDP going to businesses as profits.

The question of what should be the right share of production going to wage earners was the subject of intense debate in Australia in the 1960s and 1970s and is still implicitly of concern to employers and employees. Employers' representatives appearing before the Arbitration Commission have argued that awards that effectively increase the share of production going to wages reduce the share going to profits and that without profitability Australian industry loses the incentives it needs to invest and expand production. Ultimately, without an adequate return on capital the economy as a whole suffers. The Hawke Labor Government from 1985 viewed with concern Australia's declining competitiveness on world markets. The very substantial depreciation of the Australian dollar, referred to in Chapter 5, was a reflection of the worsening position. The depreciation was expected

---

[1] gross domestic product at factor cost measures the total value of goods and services produced by an economy and specifically excludes distortions to the true value of production by excluding government taxes on or subsidies to businesses.

to do much to restore competitiveness and provide an environment in which Australian industry would restructure and expand. As part of the readjustment process government argued that Australians were living beyond their means and that real wages must fall. Along with this a fall in wages share was to be expected. The concept of wages share has its limitations when considering income distribution and welfare. Rationally one would think that workers would be more interested in the real wage level they received (their capacity to buy goods and services) than the share of total production they were receiving. However, to many people a sense of 'fairness' and relative rewards is even more important. They would sooner have a low absolute standard of living but one that was high relative to others, instead of a higher absolute standard of living that was low relative to other people.

CHECKPOINT *31.1
Suppose you were told that the Australian economy was growing and that

wages share was declining. What, if anything could you conclude about real wage levels? Under what circumstances might the wages share be rising but real wages falling?

*Answers to all checkpoints are found at the end of the text.

The Size Distribution of Income

The size distribution of income *approach to the analysis of income distribution ranks all income units in the economy according to the size of the income they receive regardless of the sources (wages, interest or profits) of their income.* An income unit is a group of people who live together and form a single spending unit. It therefore, for our purposes, includes married couple income units, one parent income units and one person income units. Since people live in families and households and their living standards depend on the family or household income it makes much more sense to examine

TABLE 31.1
Income Distribution by Income Unit in Australia, 1986

Gross Annual Income Deciles	Upper Income Boundary $	Average Income of Income Units $	Share of Total Income	Average Earned Income of Income Units $
top 10 per cent	n.a.	60,740	28.4%	50,610
2nd 10 per cent	41,400	36,410	17.0%	33,460
3rd 10 per cent	32,388	29,050	13.5%	26,130
4th 10 per cent	26,021	23,500	11.0%	21,000
5th 10 per cent	21,000	18,950	8.9%	16,210
6th 10 per cent	16,918	15,030	7.0%	11,940
7th 10 per cent	13,079	11,460	5.4%	6,120
8th 10 per cent	9,952	8,790	4.1%	2,560
9th 10 per cent	7,470	6,130	2.9%	1,270
bottom 10 per cent	5,304	3,390	1.8%	660

Source: Australian Bureau of Statistics, Canberra, *1986 Income Distribution Survey Australian Preliminary Results,*December 1987, Ref. 6545.0 Table 1.

Australia's income distribution this way than by looking at the incomes of individuals separately. It may then be asked what percentage of income is earned by income units in different income brackets. For example, what percentage of total income goes to income units earning less than $10,000 per year, or $200 per week? Alternatively we may ask what percentage of total income is earned by the lowest 20 per cent of all income units, and so on. Table 31.1 provides information about the distribution of income in Australia to income units in 1986 from the 1986 Income Distribution Survey conducted by the Australian Bureau of Statistics.

Table 31.1 shows that the bottom 10 per cent (decile) of Australian income units had an average income in 1986 of less than 55,300 while their average income was less than $4,000. The next lowest 10 per cent had an income of less than $7,500 and the third lowest decile (making a total of 30 per cent of all income units) received less than $10,000. At the other end of the scale the average income of the top 10 per cent was over $60,000. Table 31.1 also provides information about the percentage of the total income earned by each 10 per cent of income units. Column 4 shows that over 45 per cent of income went to 20 per cent of income units. In stark contrast the bottom 20 per cent of income units obtained only 4.7 per cent.

The Lorenz Diagram

A convenient way to represent the degree of inequality in the size distribution of income is to construct a **Lorenz diagram**. This is illustrated in Figure 31.2.

The lengths of the horizontal and vertical axes are the same in the Lorenz diagram, and the units of measurement along each are percentages. The percent of total families in the economy is measured along the horizontal axis, and the percent of the economy's total income is measured along the vertical axis. Suppose income were distributed equally among all families. This would mean, for example, that 20 per cent of all families would receive 20 per cent of the economy's total income as represented by point a. Forty per cent would receive 40 per cent of total income as represented by point b, and so on. Hence, if each family received exactly the same income as every other, this would be represented by a straight diagonal line passing through points a, b, c, and d connecting the corners of the square Lorenz diagram.

Because the straight diagonal line represents perfect equality of income distribution, it provides a benchmark against which to compare the degree of inequality in the actual size distribution of income. Using the data in Table 31.1 for Australian income units in 1986 the curve (called the Lorenz curve) has been constructed.

This curve, which represents the size distribution of income in Australia, passes through the points a', b', c' and d'. Point a' indicates that the lowest 20 per cent of income units received under 5 per cent of the economy's total income. Point b' records the information that the bottom 40 per cent received 14.2 per cent. Points c' and d' record similar information for the bottom 60 per cent and 80 per cent respectively. The greater the degree of inequality in the size distribution of income, the more the Lorenz curve will be bowed towards the lower right hand corner of the Lorenz diagram.

CHECKPOINT 31.2
If we look at the size income distribution

FIGURE 31.2
Measuring Income Inequality Using a Lorenz Diagram, Australia 1986

Cumulative percentage of income

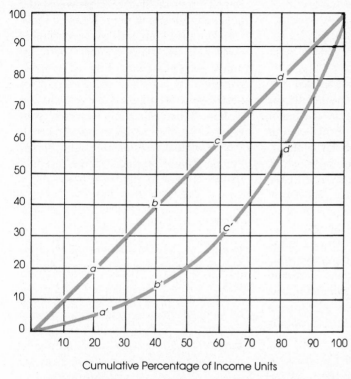

Cumulative Percentage of Income Units

In the Lorenz diagram shown here the percentage of total income units in the economy is measured along the horizontal axis and the percentage of the economy's total income is measured on the vertical axis. If total income were divided equally among all income units, 20 per cent of all income units would receive 20 per cent of total income as represented by point a. Forty per cent would receive 40 per cent of total income as represented by point b, and so on. Hence the straight diagonal line in a Lorenz diagram corresponds to perfect equality in the size distribution of income. The greater the degree of inequality in the size distribution of income, the more bowed the Lorenz curve will be toward the right-hand corner of the diagram. For example, the Lorenz curve based on the data given in Table 31.1 for Australia for 1986 passes through the points, a', b', c', and d'.

among full time workers in Australia in 1986 for males and females we get the following information.

income	males %	females %
bottom 20	8.5	9.3
2nd 20	14.9	15.9
3rd 20	18.5	18.4
4th 20	22.9	22.9
top 20	35.2	33.0

Draw a Lorenz diagram to show the difference in income distribution between male and female workers. Explain why we cannot conclude anything about whether female workers are close to receiving equal pay from this information.

Determinants of Income Inequality

What causes an unequal distribution of income? In many respects an answer to this question is as complex as an answer to the question, Why do people have different tastes and behaviour patterns? Some of the primary factors economists cite as explanations of income inequality are differences in the productivity of labour, market structure, the distribution of wealth, differences in earning power with age, the tax structure, and sheer luck. Let's consider each of these.

Marginal Productivity and Factor Demand

In Chapters 28 and 29 we examined how wages are determined according to the marginal productivity theory of factor demand. We saw that, other things remaining the same, the greater a labourer's productivity, the higher the wage the labourer is likely to receive, and hence the higher the labourer's income. (Don't forget that a labourer can be anyone from a floor sweeper to the managing director of a giant company.) It follows that those things that determine a labourer's productivity are therefore important determinants of the size of a labourer's income. They are also important to any explanation of differences in income among labourers.

As we noted in our earlier discussions, natural abilities, character traits, education, and job training are all important determinants of a labourer's productivity. Therefore, we would expect different endowments of these factors among individuals to lead to differences in income. Natural ability certainly makes it possible for Barbra Streisand to earn a larger income than the typical member of the local choir. Character traits referred to by terms such as 'work ethic', 'grit', and 'stickability' are difficult to measure but no doubt are very important.

Data indicate that there is a definite positive relationship between the amount of education a person has had and their earning power. It does not follow of course, that more education is a guarantee of a higher income any more than it is

a guarantee of getting a job. There are many graduates who cannot find well-paid work in the area they have trained for. But in times of high unemployment the better educated tend to get jobs and those with less education and fewer marketable skills find the going harder. There are many exceptions to this of course. Australia abounds with success stories of businessmen who have made it to the top without formal education. Nevertheless *in general* the information is consistent with the notion that investment in education or human capital increases labour productivity and leads to higher earnings.

Market Structure

In our previous discussions of the four basic forms of market structure — perfect competition, monopoly, monopolistic competition, and oligopoly — we touched on some of their implications for income distribution. We noted that economists generally believe that monopoly and oligopoly, with their accompanying excess, or above-normal, profits, lead to a less equal distribution of income than do market structures more aptly characterised as monopolistically or perfectly competitive. We also observed that the evidence suggests that profits tend to be higher in those industries where concentration is higher.

In our study of labour markets in Chapter 29, we saw how the level of the wages depends on market structure. In particular, if there are many firms competing with one another to purchase labour services from a large union, the wage level will be higher than if both sides of the market are perfectly competitive. The wage level will also be higher if the labour market is perfectly competitive than if there is a monopsony purchasing labour services from a large body of unorganised labourers competing with one another for jobs. Clearly the structure of labour markets will have an effect on the relative distribution of income between employers and employees.

Professional organisations, such as the Australian Medical Association and craft unions, that seek higher wages by restricting the supply of labour in their respective fields, also have an effect on income distribution. The existence of these groups tends to increase the incomes of those accepted into their ranks relative to the incomes of those who are excluded. Licensing requirements, which restrict entry to many occupations, have a similar effect.

The Distribution of Wealth

Wealth includes holdings of cash, bank balances, shares, bonds, promissory notes and mortgages, life insurance and capital assets of one form or another. With the exception of cash, all of these types of wealth typically generate income, called property income for their owners. The 1986 Survey of Income Distribution in Australia distinguished between the average income unit income and the average income unit *earned* income. The information is reproduced in Table 31.1. For the top 10 per cent of income units average income was over $60,000 in the year, but average earned income was only $50,000. In contrast, for the majority of middle income groups in Australia property or wealth income made very little contribution. Average earned income was close to average income. A big difference appeared again at lower levels between average income and average earned incomes for the lowest 30 per cent of income units. While this might appear

strange, at first sight, it reflects the fact that many of these income units are either aged persons depending on property income and pensions, or other groups relying largely on social security payments to overcome poverty. The distribution of wealth has an effect on the distribution of income. Clearly the greater the inequality in the distribution of wealth, the greater are likely to be differences in the distribution of income as a whole.

Differences in Earning Power with Age

Figure 31.3 provides information about the number of Australians in each earned income decile in 1986. Three age groups, 15-24 years, 35-44 and 55-64 have been selected. They represent those entering the labour force, those in the middle of their working lives and those about to leave the labour force.

It is apparent from the group that age does have an important bearing on the earning power and hence on the distribution of income in Australia. As you would expect the 15-24 year olds figure prominently in the bottom half of earned income decile. While advancement is often rapid early in a person's working life it seldom brings an earned income necessary to put them in the upper deciles. Check those earnings levels from Table 31.1. At the other end there are those from 55-64 who are in their last 10 years in the labour force. Notice that there are about the same number in each decile. The middle age group, from 35-44 years, presents a very different picture. While numbers are evenly distributed among the lowest six deciles they then increase progresssively with the largest number being found in the top 10 per cent of income earners.

FIGURE 31.3
Number of People in Each Earned Income Decile, by Age Group, Australia 1986

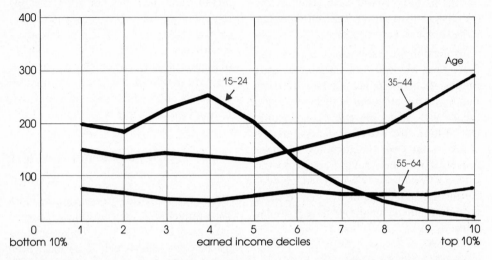

number of persons ('000)

Figure 31.3 shows how many people in each age group were in every 10 per cent of those with *earned* incomes. The largest numbers of 15–24-year-olds were in the bottom 4 declines (bottom 40 per cent). 55–64-year-olds were evenly spread through the declines. 35–44-year-olds were most numerous in the top 20 per cent.

CHECKPOINT 31.3
Examine Figure 31.3 and Table 31.1 carefully. What, if anything, can you say about the income level an individual is likely to achieve at different stages in their working life? Can you safely conclude from the evidence that it is likely to rise and then fall again as they near retirement?

Tax Structure

On a par with the weather, people probably complain about few things more than taxes. Year in and year out there always seem to be some politicians seeking votes with promises to close tax 'loopholes', perfectly legal aspects of the tax laws that seem to give special tax breaks to those in the highest income brackets. Many believe that such breaks tend to make it easier for those who are rich to stay rich.

It is often argued that under our present tax structure those in middle-income brackets who aspire to climb the economic ladder by work, saving, and capital accumulation have a tough time because too much of their income is taxed away. Indeed, as their incomes rise, a larger and larger per cent is taken because of our marginally progressive income tax rates. On the other hand, it is often argued that families living off the income earned from inherited wealth are the beneficiaries of lenient inheritance and gift taxes. Our discussion of the evidence on the distribution of wealth in Australia seems to lend strength to this point of view. To the extent that these criticisms are valid, our tax structure may well contribute to an unequal distribution of income.

In short, one question will continue to be heatedly debated among economists and laypersons alike: 'Are our tax laws such that it is too easy to stay rich and too difficult to get rich?'

Preferences, Luck and Opportunity

Suppose everyone were born with identical talents and abilities and given equal access to training and education. It would still be true that income would differ among individuals. Although all would be equally capable of being poets and folksingers, those who preferred to be poets might well find their incomes lower than that of those who prefer being folksingers. For better or worse, society's demand for poets might be slight relative to the supply, while the demand for folksingers might be great relative to the supply. For the most part, differences in preferences will lead to differences in income, all other things being equal.

Good or bad luck, being at 'the right place at the right time' or 'the wrong place at the wrong time', is also a source of differences in income. Similarly, opportunity or a lack of it has the same effect, a subject we will consider in more depth later in this chapter when we look at the problem of poverty.

CHECKPOINT 31.4
Using Lorenz curves, show how a marginally progressive tax structure (one that taxes each successive dollar of income at a higher rate than the previous one) would affect the distribution of after-tax income as compared to the distribution of before-tax income. What effect do you think the 'baby boom' of the late 1940s and 1950s would have on the Lorenz curves of income distribution for 1970, 1980, 1990, and 2000?

THE ECONOMICS OF POVERTY

What is poverty? Is it definable? What are its causes?

What is Poverty?

In general, a person is considered to live in **poverty** *if his or her income and other means of support are insufficient to provide for basic needs as defined according to some social norm.* Obviously different societies, and different people and groups within the same society, may disagree as to what constitutes 'basic needs'. In many underdeveloped countries of the world, tens of millions of people exist on a per capita income of less than $100 per year. (Income data for underdeveloped countries can be misleading, however, because in such countries much trade is carried on by barter and therefore escapes official money measures of economic activity.) In such countries a person with an annual income of $5,600 per year generally would be considered rich. In Australia a single working person with no dependents would have been considered to be on the poverty line in 1983 according to the calculations of the University of Melbourne's Institute of Applied economic and Social Research. Poverty is relative to what a society considers a 'decent standard of living'.

A family's needs depend on its size, the age of its members, and the state of its members' health. A family consisting of a married couple with the head in the workforce was estimated to be below the poverty line in the September Quarter of 1983 if it earned less than $145.90 per week. This compares with $109.10 for the single person and $234.40 for a couple with three children. Families without a head in the workforce were estimated to require lower amounts to stay above the poverty line. The Institute needs to update these poverty line estimates continually to take into account increases in the cost of living. Of course such poverty lines are only guesses. They cannot take into account the differing material needs of Australians and any such estimate is arbitrary and open to debate. Though imperfect the estimates do at least provide a focus for attention, particularly when living costs are increasing and there is a perceived need to reduce real wages in Australia. Such lines draw attention to the fact that apparently sound economic policies may have serious effects on the poor.

Aside from the aged, the infirm, and those who are by nature dependent (such as children), poverty is often much more than a simple shortage of money. Mere numbers do not tell the complete story. Poverty is also a human condition, as distinct from a statistical condition. When considering the statistics of poverty, bear in mind that there is a social dimension to poverty that cold numbers cannot completely convey. The poverty population, particularly in our cities, is often demoralised, as evidenced by higher rates of crime, juvenile delinquency, drug addiction, unwanted teenage pregnancy, and alcoholism.

Identifying the Poor

Identifying the poor is a difficult task and poverty lines certainly help. On most estimates between 10 and 20 per cent of Australian income units can be considered as either very poor or rather poor. We saw from Table 31.1 that the average gross annual income of the lowest 10 per cent of income units in 1986 was less than $4,000 (well above the poverty line). The next 10 per cent all earned less than $7,500 and the average was $6,000. Many of these income units were also on or below the poverty line. Table 31.2 examines these bottom 20 per cent of Australian income units in more detail. It shows us the size of the income unit, where income came from and the work record of the head of the household.

Note first the types of income units that predominated in the bottom and next lowest 10 per cent. Single person units accounted for 85 per cent and 75 per cent respectively. Less numerous were one parent families, but these accounted for 8 per cent of the second decile. Notice also that in only about 10 per cent of these income units did the head of the household have full time work for the whole year and for two thirds of the units the head did not work in the year. This low participation rate is reflected in the sources of income. Wages and salaries were the principal income source for only 17 per cent of the units while over 70 per cent relied mainly on government pensions and benefits.

Causes of Poverty

As you might expect, many of the factors we have already cited as causes of inequality in the distribution of income are also important causes of poverty. A lack of natural abilities, training, education, and opportunity, as well as labour markets that restrict entry, all come

TABLE 31.2
Australia's Lowest Twenty Per cent of Income Units 1986

	Gross Annual Income Decile	
	Lowest 10% %	Second Decile %
Proportion of income units with income unit type being:		
With dependent child	5.5	2.5
Without dependent children and husband aged (a):		
15-44 years	0.5	0.4
45 years and over	5.1	2.7
One-parent units	4.6	8.0
One-parent units — Male	35.5	29.9
Female	48.9	56.4
Total	**100.0**	**100.0**
Proportion of income units with principal source of gross income being:		
Wages or salary	17.2	17.0
Own business, trade or profession	2.9	2.7
Other private income	8.8	3.6
Government pensions and benefits	71.2	76.7
Total	**100.0**	**100.0**
Proportion of income units with labour force participation being (b):		
Full-year, full-time	11.6	8.8
Full-year, part-time	3.2	4.0
Part-year, full-time	11.8	11.7
Part-year, part-time	7.6	5.6
No weeks worked	65.8	70.0
Total	**100.0**	**100.0**

(a) At time of interview
(b) Participation relates to husband in married couple income unit, parent in one-
     parent income unit and person in one-person income unit.

Source: Australian Bureau of Statistics, Canberra, *1986 Income Distribution Survey Australia Preliminary Results,*
        December 1987, Ref. 6545.0, Table 1.

immediately to mind. Several other factors should be noted, including poverty itself, lack of political influence, and discrimination.

Poverty As a Cause of Poverty

Poverty has been likened to a vicious circle. It tends to perpetuate itself from one generation of a family to the next.

Because a family is poor, it suffers from a lack of dental and medical care, adequate nutrition, and other amenities important to childhood development. A poverty-line income typically cannot provide sufficient fruit, vegetables, meat, and clothing or proper housing conditions. Newspapers, magazines, books, and other sources of cultural and educational enrichment are luxury items that must usually be forgone. All these conditions impair the ability of children in such families to perform in school and keep up with their more prosperous contemporaries. Discouraged in school, and often finding little encouragement in the home to pursue educational endeavours, these children drop out of school or attend only in a perfunctory manner, gaining little from the educational system. They are destined to have job opportunities no better than those of their parents. In short, because they are poor, they are ill-educated. Because they are ill-educated, the job market offers little opportunity for economic improvement. Because of this, they grow up to be poor and form below-poverty-line families of their own. The vicious circle is complete.

Serious students of the poverty problem find the evidence on the circle of poverty disheartening. The odds on poverty families breaking out of this circle appear to be about one in five.

ATTACKING POVERTY: WAYS AND MEANS

One proposal that involves attacking poverty is through the labour market. A number of lines of attack have been followed. These include economic policy measures designed to increase the level of economic activity, antidiscrimination measures and minimum wage policies.

Increasing Economic Activity

An increasing level of economic activity offers the possibility of reducing poverty and of carrying more income units above the poverty line. An increased demand for goods and services means an increased demand for labour, more employment and higher wages. As we have seen, unemployment remains one of the principal apparent causes of poverty in Australia today. Discussion of the policies Australian governments can implement in an effort

to raise the level of economic activity are outside the scope of this book. However, it should be mentioned that such measures help not only the poor, when successful, but all groups. Those particularly concerned with the alleviation of poverty sometimes argue that poverty requires special policies to ensure that the poor receive assistance and basic help at all times. During chronic unemployment the people in the bottom 10 per cent are usually the last to feel the benefit.

Antidiscrimination and Job Training

A second approach to the poverty problem through the labour market is to improve the job prospects of the poor through antidiscrimination measures. These were mentioned in Chapter 29. Similarly, job training programs provide the poor with improved opportunities in the labour market. These are aimed at helping the young and unemployed develop the job skills they need to increase their employability. These programs also aim at improving the job skills of older workers who are below the poverty line even when fully employed because they lack the skills to hold any but low-paying jobs.

The Rationale for Job-Training Programs

The basic rationale behind this approach is that by increasing workers' skills, their productivity and hence their earning power is increased. This is illustrated in Figure 31.4. Recall from Chapter 28 that the marginal physical product of labour MPP, together with the price p of the final product that labour helps to produce, determines the position of the marginal revenue product (MRP) or demand curve for labour, $D = p + MPP$. (You may want to review these concepts in Chapter 28 at this point.) Given the existing state of labour productivity, along with the price of the final product, suppose the demand curve for labour in the labour market of Figure 31.4 is D (which is equal to MRP). This, together with the labour supply curve S, determines the equilibrium wage w_0 and level of employment L_0. A training program that increases labour's productivity, and hence its MPP, causes the demand curve for labour to shift rightward to a position such as D_1 (which is

FIGURE 31.4
Increased Labour Productivity Leads to Increased Labour Demand and Higher Wages

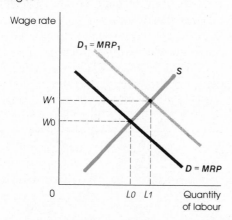

The demand curve D for labour is its marginal revenue product curve MRP. Recall that $MRP = p \times MPP$, or the price p of the final product labour helps to produce times the marginal physical product of labour MPP. The basic intent of the job-training approach to reducing poverty is to increase labour productivity, or MPP, by increasing workers' skills. In the labour market shown here, this causes the labour demand curve D (which equals MRP) to shift rightward to D_1 (which equals MRP_1). Given the supply curve of labour S, this results in an increase in employment from L_0 to L_1 and an increase in the wage rate from w_0 to w_1.

equal to MRP_1). As a result, workers now receive a higher wage w_1 and in addition a larger number of workers, L_1, are employed. There is no question about the increase in employment. And along with this increase, workers will receive a higher wage because they are more productive and therefore have more market value in the production process, not because of a statute requiring that they receive a higher wage.

The Minimum Wage Approach

The third approach, used extensively in Australia and going back eighty years has been for the Arbitration Commission to set minimum and basic wages based on needs. The argument for a minimum wage has been generally accepted in the Australian community. Analysis of the effects of imposing a minimum wage is precisely the same as that used in Chapter 29 where we considered the effects of arbitration on the labour market. If you are unsure of the details of that analysis and the effects on employment both in competitive and monopsonistic markets check back. In both cases it is possible that setting a minimum wage too high will lead to an increase in unemployment. This then is a major problem in fighting poverty through minimum wage levels. It can raise the income of those who are able to find work, but it does nothing for the unemployed and may even increase their number. Certainly, many people believe that raising juniors' wages has had a marked effect on youth unemployment.

Social Security and Taxation

The second broad attack on poverty is through social security payments and the

---

POLICY PERSPECTIVE

Negative Income Tax — How to Redistribute Income with a Minimum of Fuss

One solution to the problem of our piecemeal social security system that has been proposed is the idea of having a negative income tax. A **negative income tax** *is taxation in reverse on any income that is less than a certain statutory level. If a household's earned income falls below the statutory level, the government gives the household a subsidy, or negative income tax, equal to a certain fraction of the difference between the statutory income level and the income earned by the household.*

Example of the Negative Income Tax

One form of negative income tax that has received widespread attention in Australia was that proposed by the Commission of Inquiry into Poverty that reported to the Commonwealth Government in 1974. The Report proposed that the Commonwealth Government should guarantee all income units a guaranteed minimum income that would notionally be paid to all by the government. In addition the government would tax all earned income at a constant marginal tax rate, of say 40 per cent. The following tables uses hypothetical data to show how the scheme might work.

TABLE P31.1
Negative Income Tax — A Hypothetical Example

(1)	(2)	(3)	(4)	(5)
Private Income ($)	Tax on Private Income $ (1) × .4	Retained Private Income $ (1) –(2)	Minimum Income ($)	Disposable Income ($) (3) + (4)
0	0	0	4,000	4,000
2,000	800	1,200	4,000	5,200
4,000	1,600	2,400	4,000	6,400
6,000	2,400	3,600	4,000	7,600
8,000	3,200	4,800	4,000	8,800
10,000	4,000	6,000	4,000	10,000
12,000	4,800	7,200	4,000	11,200
14,000	5,600	8,400	4,000	12,400
16,000	6,400	9,600	4,000	13,600

Column (1) in the table represents different levels of private income and all taxpayers are taxed on that private income at a rate of 40 cents in the dollar (column 2), leaving retained private income (column 3). Their total disposable income (column 5) consists of this amount plus the government's notional payment in each of $4,000 (column

4). The term notional is used to indicate that for the majority of taxpayers this will simply offset tax due on private income. Thus, in our hypothetical example someone with a private income of $12,000 has a notional tax bill of $4,800 less $4,000 guaranteed income payment and has an *actual net tax bill* of $800. The $4,000 is an offsetting credit. Someone with an income of $10,000 pays no tax because the tax on private income is exactly offset by the minimum income payment. However, another person with a private income of $6,000 has a notional tax bill of $2,400, but the guaranteed income payment more than offsets this bill leaving a *negative income tax bill* of $1,600. Finally, the person with no private income receives the entire guaranteed income of $4,000 as a negative income tax.

A negative income tax scheme of this type has much to recommend it. It produces a simple all embracing social welfare system which would have a single scale of benefits. The single rate of income tax on private incomes would overcome the objections that progressive income tax systems discourage effort. Despite this, ingeniously, the incorporation of a guaranteed minimum income means the system remains a progressive one. This is so because of the net tax payable increases at higher income levels as a proportion of income. The system also strongly suggests redistribution is taking place because the payments to those below $10,000, in our example, are being supported by the positive tax receipts from those with private incomes above $10,000.

Such a scheme has not been implemented in Australia. Much opposition comes from those who are opposed to the notion of flat rate taxes, failing to appreciate that any system can still be progressive for the reason given above. Opposition is also to be found among those who cannot accept the idea of a minimum guaranteed payment to all, irrespective of their individual needs. To others there are practical problems involved in implementation including the definition of appropriate income units and the determination of both an appropriate guaranteed minimum payment level and an acceptable flat tax rate.

Questions

1. Either construct a table or draw a graph illustrating a negative income tax scheme. Your scheme should tax private income at 25 cents in the dollar and it should guarantee any family (of four people say) a minimum income of $8,000.

2. Does it seem reasonable to say that a family is not poor if its income is above this poverty line? How does your response affect the argument that a negative income tax may subsidise the wrong people?

---

progressive taxation structure. Take taxation first. The Australian income tax system requries income earners to pay tax at increasing marginal tax rates. This progressive system works to reduce the inequality in the distribution of income by reducing high taxable incomes by a greater proportion than lower incomes. Very low income earners pay no income tax at all and their taxable income is equal to their disposable income. While the progressive income tax system reduces the inequality between taxpayers, it does nothing to eliminate poverty — it simply takes more from the affluent. But of course it does provide the federal government with revenue, a major part of which is used to finance its social security program.

Australia has a variety of social security programs designed to alleviate poverty. These include aged, single parent and handicapped persons' pensions and unemployment benefits. There has always been a lively debate on what level Australia should pay social service benefits, particularly to the unemployed. All would agree that there is a need for balance between providing support at a level designed to remove abject poverty and ensuring that support does not deter the poor from seeking to escape from poverty. While there is agreement on that principle, Australians are far from agreed about what that level of support should be, who should qualify for support and how long they should receive it for. There is also concern that the social security system has been put together in a piecemeal fashion and that the treatment of different categories of poor in different ways is not only unfair and inconsistent, but expensive to administer.

OPTIMAL RESOURCE ALLOCATION AND THE DISTRIBUTION OF INCOME

This section is concerned with the effects on production and the allocation of resources that may follow from government policies that aim to change the distribution of income or attack poverty directly through the labour market or taxes and subsidies. It makes use of what we learned in previous chapters about ideal market situations and the effects of policy shocks on market equilibrium and on welfare.

Competitive Markets and Optimal Allocations

We have noted that generally speaking perfectly competitive markets are believed to work more in the public interest than imperfect competition or government regulated markets. In previous chapters we have noted some of the optimising principles that consumers and producers need to follow if they are to maximise satisfaction or profits. We saw in Chapter 20 that consumers maximise utility if they set the ratio of marginal utility to the price equal for every single good. No switch in consumption can increase total utility. In Chapter 22 we noted that producers minimise long run costs for any given output if they set the ratio of the marginal physical product to the price of any factor equal to the ratio for any

FIGURE 31.5
An Optimal Allocation of Resources for an Economy — 2 Good Model

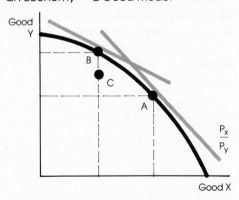

The economy produces at A, the point of tangency between the production possibilities curve and the relative price line. Relative prices reflect opportunity costs and the demand for the two goods. Point B and C do not represent an optimal allocation of resources. Although point B is on the production frontier the rate of substitution does not reflect relative prices and the demand of society for the two goods.

other factor of production. Under perfect competition the firm also maximises profits by setting marginal cost equal to price and in the long run earns normal (zero economic) profits. Under these conditions, and in the absence of deterrents to technological progress or natural monopoly, competition leads to greater output and lower prices than the alternatives. Put another way, perfectly competitive markets mean that if the conditions for maximisation are followed a country has the opportunity of operating on its production possibilities frontier. Such a situation is shown in Figure 31.5.

As we saw in Chapter 2 the production possibilities curve shows the technically efficient combinations of goods an economy can produce. Points A and B are both technically efficient, while C, lying inside the frontier, is not. However, despite A and B both being technically efficient, only A represents an *optimal allocation* of national resources. This is so because at A the rate of substitution in production (measuring opportunity cost) is equal to the relative price ratio of the goods — determined by the relative demand consumers have for the goods.

The Policy Problem

These optimum allocation principles are frequently used to argue that free unregulated markets produce the best of all worlds and that a laissez faire system produces an optimal allocation of resources — one that is in the public interest. This argument is then extended to say that government policies that attack poverty or attempt to achieve a redistribution of income say through taxes or subsidies, or intervention in the labour market, distort markets and carry an economy away from this optimal allocation of resources. There

is some truth in such arguments. It is true, as we have seen, that government intervention distorts markets. In Chapter 6 we saw how taxes and subsidies produced net welfare losses to society using producer and consumer surpluses as welfare measures.

It is not true, however, that there will be a unique optimal allocation of resources for a society, despite the appearance of this given in Figure 31.5. The key to understanding this lies in the relative prices of the two goods which we said were determined by demand. Demand itself reflects the existing distribution of income. *There can, in fact, be a different optimal allocation of resources for every distribution of income.* Thus B, and not A, would be the optimal allocation point for a distribution of income that made good Y relatively expensive because of stronger demand for it. Thus provided nothing impairs the efficient operation of markets a society has a number of potential optimum solutions reflecting different relative price valuations and different income distributions. Unfortunately, this conclusion still doesn't solve the problem. It is extremely difficult for a government to determine an approriate distribution of income and introduce policies that attack poverty or change the distribution of income in a desirable way when the cost is a reduction in total production and a loss of efficiency.

The Social Conclusion

The arguments against government intervention are not as powerful as they might appear. They are three fold. First, a change in the distribution of income will, as we have seen affect demand for goods and change relative prices so that the old optimum is no longer relevant anyway. Second, and very important, we do not operate in an economic system where perfectly competitive markets are the rule, so we are most unlikely to be operating on the technically defined production possibilities curve in the first place. Where perfect competition does not prevail government intervention to attack poverty may improve production levels rather than make them worse. In the absence of perfect competition it may lead to a second best solution. Thirdly, and decisively, there are many occasions when it may be considered desirable to trade off technical efficiency and maximum production levels so as the meet the needs of the poor. A redistribution of income may be considered essential even though government can find no practical way of maintaining production on the possibilities frontier, or at its previous levels. It will effectively be taking more from the 'haves' than it gives to the 'have nots'.

Needless to say there is often considerable controversy when governments seek to redistribute income and it is hardly surprising therefore that governments and economists pay considerable attention to technological change and economic growth as a means of reducing poverty and achieving increasing living standards for all.

SUMMARY

1. The distribution of income in an economy goes to the heart of the question, For whom is the economy's output produced? One important measure of this distribution is the functional distribution of income, which shows how the economy's total income is divided between wages, rents, interest, and profits. Another is the size distribution of income, which shows how total income is divided between individual households, the ultimate recipients of all factor income.

2. The basic determinants of the observed inequality in the distribution of income are (a) the differences between individuals in ability, education, training, and motivation; (b) the various market structures of the many different markets in our economy; (c) the distribution of wealth among individual households; (d) the age distribution of the population; (e) the economy's tax structure; and (f) differences between individual job preferences, luck, and opportunities.

3. Identifying who are the poor is a difficult task. On most estimates between 10 and 20 per cent of Australian income units are considered either very poor or rather poor. One person and one parent units comprise the bulk of the bottom 20 per cent. The head of the income unit did not work at all in over two thirds of these cases and for over 70 per cent, government pensions and benefits were the main source of income.

4. Poverty can be attacked in a number of ways, apart from social service payments to the needy. An indirect method that offers hope for the unemployed are policies designed to increase the general level of economic activity and to stimulate demand for labour. Unfortunately such policies are uncertain in their effects, slow to act and they help those most in need last, if at all.

5. Antidiscrimination measures are designed to assist specific groups such as women, migrants and juniors. While such measures have been effective, particularly in changing Australian attitudes, wages policy designed to provide equal pay for equal work may have made it more difficult for some to find work.

6. Minimum-wage legislation has established statutory minimum-wage levels. While providing higher wages for some workers, others may be forced into unemployment by this approach, which raises doubts about its overall effectiveness in combating poverty. The job-training approach attempts to increase the employability and wages of poor people by improving their productivity and labour skills. While this approach has experienced modest success and shows promise, it has proved costly.

7. Income tax transfer schemes attempt to combat poverty by taxing higher-income groups and transferring the proceeds to lower-income groups. Under one such proposal, the negative income tax, the government pays households with incomes below some statutory level an amount equal to some percentage of the difference between the statutory level and the household's earned income. While this approach may be an economically efficient way to fight poverty, some argue that simply handing money to poor people does not come to grips with the social pathology of poverty.

8. There is no unique optimal allocation of resources for a market economy though competitive conditions if met may lead to an allocation that is optimal for a particular distribution of income. Unfortunately, although attempts to change the distribution of income by government policies, such as taxes, subsidies and benefits may succeed they often do not produce an optimal allocation of resources.

9. Arguments that the government should intervene in the economy to change the distribution of income and to attack poverty are based on the view that perfectly competitive conditions do not prevail in Australian markets anyway and that second, our social conscience demands improvements in the living standards of the poor even if overall production of goods and services were to be reduced somewhat.

KEY TERMS AND CONCEPTS

functional distribution of income
job-training programs
Lorenz diagram
minimum-wage law
negative income tax
poverty
progressive income tax
size distribution of income

QUESTIONS AND PROBLEMS

1. It has been said that if perfect equality in the distribution of income could be enforced, possibly by means of some kind of redistributive tax scheme, individuals would unavoidably be treated unequally. In what ways might this be so?

2. In the early days of the Russian Revolution, one much-publicised dictum of Communist party ideology held that income distribution would be determined according to the dictum 'from each according to his ability, to each according to his need'. How are workers' 'needs' and 'abilities' reflected in a perfectly competitive labour market? How well might the objective of the dictum be achieved in an economy where factors are employed in accordance with the marginal productivity theory of factor demand?

3. Harriet Martineau, a nineteenth-century English writer, once hypothesised that if the government redistributed income in the morning to achieve perfect income equality, by nightfall the rich would once again be back in their comfortable beds and the poor asleep under the bridges. What factors would Martineau most likely stress as the important determinants of income inequality?

4. Suppose you constructed the Lorenz curves representing income distribution in *each* of the following occupational groups: primary school teachers, gamblers, lawyers, business proprietors, and boxers. How do you think the curves would look relative to one another and why?

5. In recent years a number of important social changes have taken place in Australia. These include antidiscrimination and affirmative action legislation and the introduction of the principle of equal pay for work of equal value. Women, migrants, aboriginals, the disabled and young people have all been affected in one way or another. Discuss in class the possible effects on the labour market of such government imposed or legal changes. Are they, on balance, likely to be in the public interest? If so, in what ways?

6. Historically, the aged have typically had to depend on the young for their support. It was fairly traditional for older people to live with their children, often largely dependent on their offsprings' sense of duty and parental respect. As originally conceived, the social security system could be said to lessen that dependence to some extent. Today some critics of the social security system say that the old are again becoming dependent on the younger generation for financial support. What is the basis of this contention, and in what sense is it correct?

7. What effects do you think minimum-wage laws would have on employment in each of the following: apple orchards, clothing workers in Melbourne, and dry-cleaning businesses?

8. Some argue that minimum-wage laws have effects that are the same as if the age limit on child-labour laws was increased. Why is this so and how might job-training programs get around this problem despite the presence of minimum-wage laws? Illustrate your answer graphically.

9. In what way would the size of the negative tax rate affect the incentive of those receiving a negative income tax to seek work?

EIGHT

International Economics

32

The Gains from Trade and Barriers to Trade

AFTER READING THIS CHAPTER YOU WILL BE ABLE TO:

1. Explain why nations can have a larger total output if they each specialise according to comparative advantage and trade.

2. Describe the nature of the barriers to trade nations often erect to protect domestic industry from foreign competition.

3. Describe briefly the trends in Australian trade policy since the 1930s.

In Chapter 27 we looked at some of the overall quantitative dimensions of world trade, as well as the basic pattern of Australian trade with other countries. Additionally we saw the way that trade affects the determination of total income, output and employment. We now consider why nations trade with one another. What is the basis of trade? We also look at why countries erect trade barriers — that is, why governments protect some domestic producers from the competition of foreign trade.

THE BASIS FOR TRADE: SPECIALISATION AND COMPARATIVE ADVANTAGE

In general, trade occurs because nations have different resource endowments and technological capabilities. Because of these differences, each nation can gain by specialising in those products that it produces relatively efficiently and by trading for those it produces inefficiently or cannot produce at all. In short, international trade allows nations to increase the productivity of their resources through specialisation, and thereby, to realise a higher standard of living than is possible in the absence of trade.

This general description of why nations trade sounds reasonable enough. However, to understand why it is correct requires an examination of the role of specialisation and the important principle of comparative advantage. In essence, it is the principle of comparative advantage that makes it worthwhile for nations to specialise and trade.

In order to illustrate this principle and see why it leads to specialisation and trade, let's consider the following *hypothetical* example. Suppose there are only two

countries in the world economy, Australia and New Zealand. And suppose that each can produce both wheat and timber but with differing degrees of efficiency. The production possibilities frontier for each country is shown in Figure 32.1, parts a and b. (Recall from Chapter 2 that each point on a production possibilities frontier represents a maximum output combination for an economy whose available resources are fully employed.) Tonnes of timber are measured on the vertical axis and tonnes of wheat on the horizontal.

Notice that each frontier is a straight line instead of a curve, as was the production possibilities frontier discussed in Chapter 2. The frontiers here are straight lines because we are assuming that costs are constant. Along a straight-line frontier, a nation must give up the same amount of production of one good in order to produce an additional unit of the other, no matter which point on the frontier is considered. In other words, we are assuming that the law of increasing costs (see Chapter 2), which causes the frontier to be curved, does not apply here. The assumption of constant costs makes our discussion simpler but still allows us to illustrate the principle of comparative advantage.

Comparative Advantage: Differences in Opportunity Costs

As we can see, the production possibilities frontiers of the two nations differ. Observe that at any point on New Zealand's production possibilities frontier (part a), it is necessary to sacrifice 2 tonnes of timber in order to have 1 more tonne of wheat. For New Zealand, 1 tonne of wheat, therefore, has an opportunity cost of 2 tonnes of timber. Put the other way around, 1 tonne of timber has an opportunity cost of ½ tonne of wheat. For Australia (part b), 1 tonne of timber must be given up to have 1 more tonne of wheat. Hence for Australia, the opportunity cost of 1 tonne of wheat is 1 tonne of timber, or the opportunity cost of 1 tonne of timber is 1 tonne of wheat. We can see from this that the opportunity cost of wheat is higher for New Zealand than for

Australia. While it costs New Zealand 2 tonnes of timber for each tonne of wheat, it costs Australia only 1. Conversely the opportunity cost of timber is higher for Australia than for New Zealand. It costs Australia 1 tonne of wheat for each tonne of timber, while it costs New Zealand only ½ tonne of wheat for each tonne of timber.

In short we can say that New Zealand

FIGURE 32.1
Production Possibilities Frontiers for New Zealand and Australia (hypothetical data)

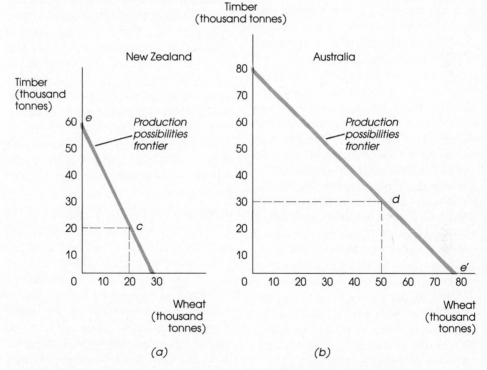

Each nation can produce both timber and wheat. The production possibilities frontiers are straight lines because costs are constant — that is, the same amount of production of one good must be given up in order to produce an additional unit of the other, no matter which point on the frontier is considered.

The slope of New Zealand's production possibilities frontier (part a) indicates that 1 tonne of wheat has an opportunity cost of 2 tonnes of timber, or put the other way round, 1 tonne of timber has an opportunity cost of 1/2 tonne of wheat. The slope of the Australian production possibilities frontier (part b) indicates that the opportunity cost of 1 tonne of wheat is 1 tonne of timber. Since the opportunity cost of wheat is lower for Australia than for New Zealand, Australia has a comparative advantage in producing wheat. On the other hand, since the opportunity cost of timber is lower for New Zealand than for Australia, New Zealand has a comparative advantage in producing timber.

has a *comparative advantage* (compared to Australia) in producing timber. Australia has a *comparative advantage* (compared to New Zealand) in growing wheat. The difference in opportunity costs between the two nations reflects differences in their resource endowments, climates, and technological know-how.

Inefficiency of Self-sufficiency — Efficiency of Specialisation

As long as there is no trade between New Zealand and Australia, each is isolated and must be self-sufficient. Each country is limited to choices along its own production possibilities frontier. Suppose New Zealand chooses to produce the output combination represented by point *c* on its production possibilities frontier (Figure 32.1, part a), a combination consisting of 20 thousand tonnes of timber and 20 thousand tonnes of wheat. Suppose also that the output combination Australia chooses to produce is represented by point *d* on its production possibilities frontier (Figure 32.1, part b), 50 thousand tonnes of timber and 30 thousand tonnes of wheat.[1] Total 'world' output is therefore 50 thousand tonnes of timber (the sum of 20 thousand tonnes in New Zealand and 30 thousand tonnes in Australia) and 70 thousand tonnes of wheat (the sum of 20 thousand tonnes in New Zealand and 50 thousand tonnes in Australia).

Figure 32.1 shows us that the world economy is not producing efficiently when each nation is isolated and self-sufficient, even though each nation is on its production possibilities frontier. Why do we

say this? Suppose each nation specialised in the production of that product in which it has a comparative advantage. New Zealand would produce only timber, corresponding to point *e* (part a), and Australia would produce only wheat, point *e'* (part b). Total world output would then consist of 60 thousand tonnes of timber (New Zealand) and 80 thousand tonnes of wheat (Australia). By specialising according to comparative advantage, total world output is greater by 10 thousand tonnes of timber and 10 thousand tonnes of wheat as compared to what it is when each nation produces some of both products at points *c* and *d*. This example illustrates the principle of comparative advantage. *The principle of* **comparative advantage** *states that total world output is greatest when each good is produced by that nation having the lower opportunity cost of producing the good — that is, by that nation having the comparative advantage in the production of the good.*

When New Zealand produces 1 tonne of wheat, the opportunity cost is 2 tonnes of timber. It is clearly an inefficient use of the world's resources for New Zealand to produce wheat when Australia can produce it at an opportunity cost of only 1 tonne of timber per tonne of wheat. Similarly it is an inefficient use of world resources for Australia to produce timber at an opportunity cost of 1 tonne of wheat per tonne of timber when New Zealand can produce a tonne of timber at an opportunity cost of only ½ a tonne of wheat. If New Zealand produces wheat, the world must give up more timber than is necessary to have wheat. And if Australia produces timber, the world gives up more wheat than is necessary to have timber. *The allocation of world resources is most efficient when each nation*

---

[1] Presumably each country's choice of output combination is made through its pricing system, as described in Chapter 2.

ECONOMIC THINKERS

David Ricardo — 1771–1823

David Ricardo was born in London, the son of a merchant-stockbroker. At 14 (after a very brief commercial education in Holland), he entered his father's business, but for family reasons left the firm at 19 and went out on his own with borrowed funds. He was an immediate success, and in a decade he had amassed a fortune of some £2 million (an immense amount by the standards of the day). He retired from trade and in 1814 purchased a country estate and a seat in Parliament. Sensitive about his lack of education, Ricardo hesitated to put his views on paper, but began to do so in 1815. Despite stylistic shortcomings, Ricardo made major advances in the science of economics, and his contribution might well have been greater had he not died only 8 years later.

One of Ricardo's most significant contributions was his theory of rent, which he approached by putting forth the theory of diminishing returns. He observed that successive applications of inputs to a productive process resulted in lower additional returns to output. That is, in agriculture, for example, more intensive use of manpower, fertiliser, and other inputs yielded larger output, but the increases were successively smaller than those at earlier stages of production. Thus, a point might be reached where output would reach an absolute level and, in fact, decline as more inputs were applied. For a fixed resource such as land, it would be necessary over time to cultivate lands that were increasingly less productive in order to satisfy the pressing needs of increased population. As the demand for increased output rose, rent would rise (or increase) on that land of higher quality.

Ricardo was also the first to set forth the theory of comparative advantage in international trade in formal terms. According to this law, he argued, England would be better off if it imported food and exported manufactured goods. As a result, he was a supporter of the repeal of the tariff on grain as a method of lowering prices and thereby stimulating trade.

FOR FURTHER READING

St. Clair, Oswald. *A Key to Ricardo.* New York: Kelley & Millman, 1957.
Sraffa, Piero. *The Works and Correspondence of David Ricardo*, Vols. 1-9. London: Cambridge University Press, 1951-1955.

---

specialises according to comparative advantage.

Since total world output of both goods is greatest when each nation specialises according to comparative advantage, clearly there can be more of both goods for both nations if each specialises and engages in trade instead of remaining isolated and self-sufficient. Let's see what particular conditions will motivate Australia and New Zealand to specialise and trade.

Terms of Trade

Consider again the output combinations chosen by New Zealand and Australia when each is self sufficient, represented by points c and d respectively on Figure 32.1. Note that New Zealand must forego the production of 40 thousand tonnes of timber in order to produce 20 thousand tonnes of wheat associated with point c, since each tonne of wheat costs 2 tonnes of timber. Australia must forego producing 30 thousand tonnes of wheat in order to produce 30 thousand tonnes of timber — each tonne of timber costs 1 tonne of wheat. If New Zealand could get 1 tonne of wheat by giving up *less* than 2 tonnes of timber, and if Australia could get 1 tonne of timber by giving up *less* than 1 tonne of wheat, each would be eager to do so.

Is this possible? Yes, because of the difference in opportunity costs between the two nations. Let us suppose that New Zealand offers to pay Australia 1½ tonnes of timber for each 1 tonne of wheat it is willing to sell. For New Zealand this is cheaper than the 2 tonnes of timber that must be foregone for 1 tonne of wheat

if New Zealand remains self-sufficient. For Australia such a trade would mean that timber could be obtained at a cost of $2/3$ of a tonne of wheat for each 1 tonne of timber. This is certainly cheaper than the 1 tonne of wheat per 1 tonne of timber it costs Australia if it tries to be self-sufficient. Therefore, Australia agrees to New Zealand's offer. The *terms of trade*, the ratio of exchange between timber and wheat at which both nations agree to trade, would therefore be 1½ tonnes of timber per 1 tonne of wheat or, equivalently, ⅔ tonne of wheat per 1 tonne of timber.

Specialisation and Trade

Having established the terms of trade, New Zealand now specialises according to its comparative advantage in producing timber. It produces 60 thousand tonnes of timber, which is the maximum it can produce on its production possibilities frontier. Australia now specialises according to its comparative advantage in growing wheat, producing 80 thousand tonnes, the maximum it can produce on its frontier. Though each nation specialises in production of one good, each nation's citizens want to consume both goods. This

---

Each nation can have more of both goods if each specialises according to its comparative advantage and trades with the other.

When each nation is isolated and self-sufficient, each is forced to choose an output combination on its production possibilities frontier. For example, New Zealand may choose to produce 20 thousand tonnes of wheat and 20 thousand tonnes of timber (point c), and Australia may choose to produce 50 thousand tonnes of wheat and 30 thousand tonnes of timber (point c').

Alternatively if each nation specialises according to its comparative advantage, New Zealand would produce 60 thousand tonnes of timber (point e) and Australia 80 thousand tonnes of wheat (point e'). Then each nation could export some of its specialty in exchange for some of the other nation's specialty at terms of trade represented by the slope of the trading possibilities frontier. Such trade would move New Zealand down its trading possibilities frontier from point e to a point such as d, 24 thousand tonnes of wheat and 24 thousand tonnes of timber. Australia moves up its trading possibilities frontier from point e' to a point such as d', 56 thousand tonnes of wheat and 36 thousand tonnes of timber. Each nation is able to have more of both goods. The gains from trade for New Zealand amount to 4 thousand tonnes of wheat and 4 thousand tonnes of timber (point d compared to point c), and for Australia they amount to 6 thousand tonnes of wheat and 6 thousand tonnes of timber (point d' compared to point c').

FIGURE 32.2
Trading Possibilities Frontiers and the Gains from Trade (Hypothetical Data)

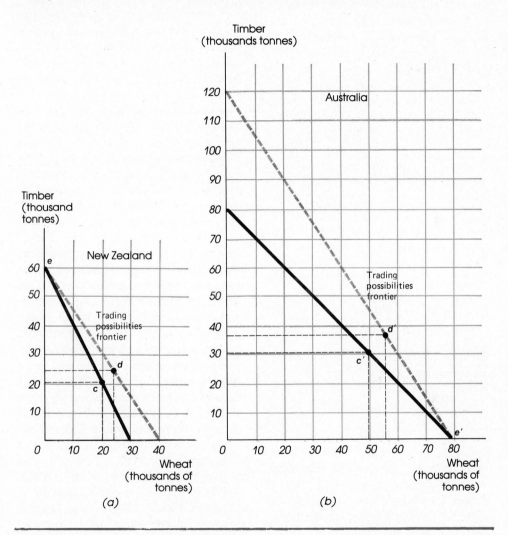

(a)

(b)

is possible, of course, because the nations can exchange goods at the agreed-upon terms of trade. This is shown in Figure 32.2, in which each nation's production possibilities frontier (exactly the same as in Figure 32.1) is shown along with its **trading possibilities frontier**. The trading possibilities frontier shows the choices that are open to a nation if it specialises in

the product in which it has a comparative advantage and trades (exports) its specialty for the other product in which it has a comparative disadvantage.

When New Zealand produces 60 thousand tonnes of timber, point *e* in part a, it can trade (export) this timber to Australia. Given the agreed-upon terms of trade of 1½ tonnes of timber per 1 tonne of wheat, New Zealand can trade with Australia to get (import) 1 tonne of wheat for every 1½ tonnes of timber it exports to Australia. Starting from point *e*, such trade is represented by movement down the trading possibilities frontier as New Zealand gives up 1½ tonnes of timber for every 1 tonne of wheat it gets. This is obviously better than the ratio of exchange along the production possibilities frontier that requires New Zealand to give up 2 tonnes of timber for each 1 tonne of wheat it gets. Similarly, Australia produces 80 thousand tonnes of wheat, corresponding to point *e'* in part a. It can then move up the trading possibilities frontier by exporting 1 tonne of wheat for every 1½ tonnes of timber it imports from New Zealand. Again, this beats the ratio of exchange along the production possibilities frontier that requires Australia to give up 1 tonne of wheat for every 1 tonne of timber it gets.

In sum, the terms-of-trade ratio of exchange along the trading possibilities frontier is better than the self-sufficiency ratio of exchange along each nation's production possibilities frontier. Hence, New Zealand can get *more* than 1 tonne of wheat for 2 tonnes of timber if it specialises in timber and trades for wheat with Australia. On this two-way street, Australia can get *more* than 1 tonne of timber for every 1 tonne of wheat if it specialises in wheat and trades for timber with New Zealand.

The Gains from Trade

Earlier we noted that if each nation specialised according to comparative advantage, total world output would be larger than if each produced some of both goods. Now we can see how trade makes this possible by allowing the citizens of each nation to consume more of both

goods despite the fact that each nation produces only one of them.

Starting from point *e* (Figure 32.2, part a), New Zealand specialises in the production of timber (60 thousand tonnes), which it trades to Australia for wheat. Starting at point *e'* (part b), Australia specialises in the production of wheat (80 thousand tonnes) which it trades to New Zealand for timber. Given the mutually agreed-upon terms of trade of 1½ tonnes of timber per 1 tonne of wheat, suppose New Zealand exports 36 thousand tonnes of its timber to Australia in exchange for imports of 24 thousand tonnes of wheat. This gives New Zealand a combination of 24 thousand tonnes of timber and 24 thousand tonnes of wheat represented by point *d* on its trading possibilities frontier. Compared with the self-sufficient combination of 20 thousand tonnes of timber and 20 thousand tonnes of wheat, represented by point *c* on its production possibilities frontier, New Zealand is now able to have more of *both* goods. The 4 thousand more tonnes of timber and 4 thousand more tonnes of wheat represent the gains of trade to New Zealand. Similarly, Australia exports 24 thousand tonnes of its wheat to New Zealand in exchange for imports of 36 thousand tonnes of timber from New Zealand. Australia thus has a combination of 36 thousand tonnes of timber and 56 thousand tonnes of wheat, point *d'* on its trading possibilities frontier. This is clearly superior to the self-sufficient combination of 30 thousand tonnes of timber and 50 thousand tonnes of wheat, point *c'* on its production possibilities frontier. The gains from trade for Australia amount to 6 thousand more tonnes of timber and 6 thousand more tonnes of wheat.

We noted earlier that if each nation specialised according to comparative advantage, total world output would be larger than if each produced the output combinations represented by points c and c' in Figure 32.2. Specifically, we noted that specialisation would increase total world output by 10 thousand tonnes of timber and 10 thousand tonnes of wheat. Given the terms of trade (1½ tonnes of timber to 1 tonne of wheat), we now see how trade distributes this additional output — 4 thousand tonnes of timber and 4 thousand tonnes of wheat to New Zealand and 6 thousand tonnes of timber and 6 thousand tonnes of wheat to Australia. *Because of specialisation and trade, there is an efficient allocation of world resources in production. Each good is produced by the nation that can produce the good at the lower cost. Consequently, each nation is able to have more of both goods.*

Finally, it should be noted that Australia is more productive than New Zealand in an absolute sense. The production possibilities frontiers in Figure 32.2 (or 32.1) show that Australia can produce any combination of wheat and timber that New Zealand can *plus* more of both goods. This highlights the fundamental point that the incentive to specialise and trade stems from the fact that New Zealand and Australia have different opportunity costs in the production of wheat and timber. For New Zealand the opportunity cost of producing wheat is greater than that for Australia while for Australia the opportunity cost of producing timber is greater than that for New Zealand. If the opportunity costs for New Zealand and Australia were the same, there would be no incentive to trade. However, because nations all differ in resource endowments, climate, size, and technological capabilities, it is little wonder that there is so much specialisation and trade in the world.

CHECKPOINT 32.1
Suppose there are two pioneers in the wilderness. Each builds a home and each chops wood and grows wheat. Construct an illustration showing why it would benefit both to trade with each other.

*Answers to all Checkpoints can be found at the back of the text.

Some Qualifications

So far in our discussion, we have simply assumed a particular ratio of exchange as the terms of trade. But what in fact determines the terms of trade? We have also assumed constant costs throughout our discussion, so that the production possibilities frontier is a straight line. It is more realistic to assume increasing costs — that the production possibilities frontier is curved, bowed outward from the origin. How does this affect the analysis? Let's consider each issue in turn.

Determining the Terms of Trade

We have been assuming that the terms-of-trade ratio of exchange between New Zealand and Australia is 1½ tonnes of timber per 1 tonne of wheat. However, in our hypothetical example both New Zealand and Australia would find trade beneficial at terms of trade lying anywhere between 2 tonnes of timber per tonne of wheat, the ratio of exchange along New Zealand's production possibilities frontier, and 1 tonne of timber per tonne of wheat, the ratio of exchange along Australia's production possibilities frontier. Any terms-of-trade ratio of exchange lying in this range allows each nation to obtain a good at a lower cost through trade than it costs to produce the good domestically.

The terms-of-trade exchange ratio within this range at which trade will actually take place depends on world supply-and-demand conditions for the two goods. If world demand for timber is strong relative to timber supply and the demand for wheat is weak relative to wheat supply, the price of timber will be high and the price of wheat low. The terms of trade will be closer to the 1 tonne of timber per 1 tonne of wheat limit which is more favourable to New Zealand than Australia. If world demand-and-supply conditions are the opposite, the price of timber will be low and that of wheat high. Then the terms of trade will be closer to 2 tonnes of timber per 1 tonne of wheat which is more favourable to Australia. In any event, the terms of trade are determined competitively by consumers and producers in the two countries (not by their governments).

Increasing Costs

Suppose each nation's production possibilities frontier is curved so that it bows out from the origin. That is, each nation is faced with increasing costs as it expands production of the good in which it has a comparative advantage. Suppose New Zealand is initially at the point on its production possibilities frontier at which the cost ratio is 2 tonnes of timber for 1 tonne of wheat, and Australia is initially at a point on its frontier where the cost ratio is 1 tonne of timber for 1 tonne of wheat.

Now suppose they begin to specialise and trade. As New Zealand expands its production of timber, the cost of producing it increases. That is, it will have to give up more than 1 tonne of wheat to produce 2 tonnes of timber. Similarly, as Australia expands production of wheat, increasing cost will require it to give up

more than 1 tonne of timber to produce 1 tonne of wheat. Hence, the cost ratio for New Zealand goes from 2 tonnes of timber for 1 tonne of wheat, to $1\frac{7}{8}$ tonnes for 1 tonne to $1\frac{3}{4}$ tonnes for 1 tonne and so forth as it expands the production of timber. The cost ratio for Australia goes from 1 tonne of timber for 1 tonne of wheat to $1\frac{1}{8}$ tonne for 1 tonne to $1\frac{1}{4}$ tonne for 1 tonne and so forth as it expands the production of wheat. The cost ratios of the two nations are now getting closer to each other.

At some point, after each nation has expanded the production of its specialty far enough, the cost ratios may become equal. At that point the basis for trade — a difference in opportunity costs between the two nations — will have been eliminated. Furthermore, at that point it is likely that each nation still produces both goods. New Zealand may still produce some wheat along with its timber, and Australia some timber along with its wheat. *Hence, when there are increasing costs, specialisation will not be as complete, nor the volume of trade as large, as is the case when costs are constant.*

The Argument for Free Trade

We now have seen how specialisation and trade lead to an efficient allocation of world resources. They make it possible for each nation to have more of all goods than is possible in the absence of specialisation and trade. While we have illustrated these points using only two nations and two goods, advanced treatments of the subject show that these conclusions hold for a multination, multiproduct world as well. Hence, it may seem odd that there are so many instances in which there is outright opposition to trade with foreign nations. The rest of this chapter will focus on the barriers to trade that nations often erect as a matter of policy. We will examine critically the most often heard arguments in favour of restricting trade. But before considering these matters, we should state the argument for free trade from a somewhat different, yet compelling perspective.

When each nation specialises in production according to its comparative advantage and trades with other nations, each nation is able to move out beyond its individual production possibilities frontier. The effect of specialisation and trade is therefore the same as if each nation had gained more technological knowledge, more resources, or both. That is, the effect is the same as if each nation experienced an outward shift in its production possibilities frontier (such as we discussed in Chapter 2). It is possible for each nation to have more of all goods, thereby lessening the problem of scarcity.

CHECKPOINT 32.2
List examples which illustrate the role of the principle of comparative advantage in explaining trade between the Australian states. Queenslanders and Western Australians sometimes complain that their exports to New South Wales and Victoria are far less than their imports from these states. How can such a situation occur on a continuing basis?

BARRIERS TO TRADE AND ARGUMENTS FOR PROTECTION

The argument for free trade based on the principle of comparative advantage is one of the most solid cornerstones of economic analysis. No other issue seems to command such unanimous agreement among economists as the case for free trade.

However, for a variety of reasons different groups in any economy are always prevailing on government to erect barriers to trade — that is, they want protection from the competition of foreign trade. We will first examine some of the commonest barriers and then consider the merits of some of the commonest arguments for protection.

Barriers to Trade

Tariffs and quotas are the main weapons in the arsenal of protectionism. More recently, so-called antidumping legislation has also been used as a barrier to foreign imports.

Tariffs

A tariff (or duty) *is a tax on imports, most often calculated as a per cent of the price charged for the good by the foreign supplier.* For example, if the price of a tonne of imported steel were $100, a 10 per cent tariff would require the domestic purchaser to pay an additional $10 per tonne. This effectively raises the price of imported steel to $110 per tonne. A tariff may obviously be used as a source of revenue for the government. However, a more common purpose of tariffs is protection against foreign competition. By raising the prices of imported goods relative to the prices of domestically produced goods, tariffs encourage domestic consumers to buy domestic rather than foreign products.

For example, suppose Japanese steel companies can produce steel at a lower cost than Australia's only producer, BHP, with the result that the price of imported Japanese steel is $100 per tonne while the price of domestically produced steel is $102 per tonne. Domestic buyers will import the lower-priced Japanese steel. Sales of BHP will suffer. Consequently, suppose domestic producers, both company officials and trade unions prevail on the Australian government to place a 10 per cent tariff on imported steel. This raises the price of imported steel to $110 per tonne, a price $8 higher than a tonne of domestic steel. Domestic steel users now switch from importing Japanese steel to buying the cheaper domestic steel. Steel imports decline while sales and employment in the domestic steel industry rise. Recognise, however, that while domestic steel producers are better off, the rest of the nation's citizens will have to pay higher prices for all products containing steel.

Of course, tariffs need not completely eliminate imports. *As long as tariffs are not larger than the difference in production costs between domestic and foreign producers, tariffs will not completely eliminate imports.* In our example, suppose Japanese steel producers would just be able to cover costs as long as they receive a minimum of $92.73 per tonne. Suppose BHP cannot afford to sell steel at a price less than $102 per tonne. With a 10 per cent tariff, Japanese producers would just be able to remain competitive with the Australian producer. Japanese steel unloaded at Australian ports at a price of $92.73 would be taxed 10 per cent by the tariff, or $9.27 (.1 × $92.73), thus costing Australian importers $102 per tonne ($92.73 paid to Japanese producers plus $9.27 in tariff revenue paid to the government). However, if the tariff were greater than 10 per cent, imports of Japanese steel would cease because Japanese producers would suffer losses if they sold their steel at less than $92.73. And this price plus a tariff *greater* than 10 per cent would increase the price of imported Japanese steel to domestic buyers above the price of domestic steel of $102, making Japanese steel noncompetitive.

Finally, it should be noted that the use of a tariff as a source of tax revenue runs counter to the use of a tariff for protection. A tariff generates tax revenues only to the extent that there are purchases of imported goods on which tariffs can be collected. In general, to the extent tariffs successfully serve protectionist objectives by cutting back imports, the tax revenues from tariffs are also reduced. A tariff so high as to effectively block out all imports, giving complete protection from foreign competition, would generate no tax revenue at all.

Import Quotas

Import quotas *limit imports by specifying the maximum amount of a foreign-produced good that will be permitted into the country over a specified period of time (per year, for example).* Import quotas are a very effective tool of protection, unlike a tariff whose effect on the volume of imports can be hard to predict. After legislating a certain level of tariffs on a particular good, a class of goods, or even an across-the-board tariff on all goods, protectionists may find that imports are not limited to anywhere near the extent they had hoped for. Import quotas remove such uncertainty. Those favouring protection simply specify in the import quota legislation the exact quantity of a particular good that may be imported over a specified period of time. An import quota on Japanese steel, for example, might limit imports of such steel to 1 million tonnes per year.

Antidumping Laws

Domestic producers of particular products often argue that they are unfairly victimised by competing foreign imports that are 'dumped' in domestic markets. Dumping refers to a situation where the prices of an imported good are not only lower than those paid for the domestically produced equivalent good but also lower than the foreign supplier's cost of production. For example, if a car imported from Japan sold for $20,000 in the Australian market, as opposed to $21,000 for its Australian competition, but it cost $22,000 to produce in Japan, dumping would have occurred.

Antidumping laws usually set a minimum price on an imported good. If the import enters the country at a price below that minimum, the law triggers a government investigation of possible dumping. Should it conclude that dumping is taking place, the imported good is not allowed to be sold at a price below the minimum, or 'trigger', price. In Australia antidumping action has been the responsibility of the Customs Service. Reviewing the operation of the Customs Tariff (Anti-Dumping) Act of 1975, Professor Fred Gruen noted in 1986 that Australia has made more use of anti-dumping action than other countries. In 1985 Australia had a greater number of anti-dumping duties in place than Canada, the European Economic Community or the United States. Indeed Gruen held the view that overzealous use of anti-dumping legislation may affect the opportunities of Australian companies to open new export markets.

Difficulty of Detection. When domestic producers of any product cry 'dumping', there is always reason to suspect they are simply campaigning for protectionist measures to shelter them from foreign competition. It may well be that foreign producers are not charging prices below their costs of production, but are simply more efficient than domestic producers. That is, foreign producers can charge prices that cover their costs but yet are still below the costs of domestic producers. In that case domestic consumers reap the benefit of lower prices for imported products that cost more when produced at home. Domestic producers' claims of dumping simply amount to 'crying wolf' in that case. Furthermore, it is hard to establish whether or not foreign producers are selling their goods at prices below their costs. It is difficult if not impossible for an outsider to determine just what foreign producers' costs are. And just such information is necessary to determine whether dumping exists.

Export Subsidies and Dumping. Nonetheless, there are circumstances under which dumping can occur and indeed does amount to 'unfair' competition with domestic producers. In many nations it is not uncommon for the government to provide an **export subsidy**, or payment, to export industries to cover part of their costs of production. For example, suppose a government pays steel producers $10 for every tonne of steel they export. If it costs the steel producers $90 to produce a tonne of steel, the $10 subsidy from the government effectively reduces their cost to $80 per tonne. Without the subsidy the steel producers could not sell steel abroad for less than $90 a tonne. With the subsidy they can sell exported steel for as little as $80 a tonne. Domestic steel producers in the nations importing this subsidised steel may be more efficient than the foreign producers. Let's say they can produce steel at a cost of $85 per tonne. However, they will not be able to compete with the subsidised imported steel priced at $80 per tonne. Domestic producers in a nation importing the subsidised steel have a legitimate complaint that imported steel is being dumped in their market.

Note that though foreign trade may increase as a result of export subsidies, it is not the kind of trade that gives rise to the world gains from trade due to specialisation according to comparative advantage. In our example, the subsidised steel imports are in fact more costly to produce than the unsubsidised domestic steel. That is, the nation in which the subsidised steel is produced in fact has a comparative disadvantage in steel production relative to the nation importing the subsidised steel.

Protecting Employment and Jobs

One of the most common protectionist arguments is that importing foreign goods amounts to 'exporting jobs'. It is claimed that buying foreign goods instead of domestic goods creates jobs for foreign labour that would otherwise go to domestic labour. It is charged that domestic unemployment will increase as a result. The merits of this argument depend on whether it is made with reference to the short run or the long run.

The Short Run: Adjustment Problems

There is indeed truth to this argument in the short run. Recall again our hypothetical example of trade between New Zealand and Australia. When each was isolated and self-sufficient, each had a timber industry and a farming industry growing wheat. However, when the two nations began to trade, New Zealand's farmers could no longer compete with the wheat imported from Australia. All resources previously devoted to farming, including labour, had to be shifted into

New Zealand's specialty industry, timber production. Similarly, in Australia timber products could no longer compete with imported New Zealand timber. Labour and other resources in the timber industry had to shift into Australia's specialty.

The gains from trade *after* these shifts have occurred are clear. However, the transitional period of readjustment and reallocation of resources within each country could be painful and costly to many citizens. Workers experienced and trained in farming in New Zealand and in timber production in Australia would no longer have a market for their skills. With their old jobs eliminated, many would need retraining to gain employment in their country's expanding specialty industry. Many would have to uproot their families and move to new locations, leaving old friends and severing familiar community ties. While both nations would realise the material gains from trade in the long run, it is understandable that those threatened with loss of job and an uncomfortable and personally costly transition might well support protectionist measures.

Public policy in a number of nations recognises that changing trade patterns typically impose transition costs on affected industries and workers. In Australia adjustment assistance is sometimes provided to workers in firms that suffer from increased imports resulting from government actions, such as tariffs and quotas, that lower trade barriers. Workers may be eligible for lengthened periods of unemployment compensation, retraining programs, and allowances to cover costs of moving to other jobs and other assistance.

The reasoning behind a policy of transitional adjustment assistance is this: The removal of trade barriers leads to increased trade. Since the whole nation realises gains from increased trade, some of these gains can be used to compensate those citizens who suffer losses during the period of adjustment. *Quite aside from any issue of 'fairness', it may not be politically feasible to lower trade barriers unless those injured by such a move are compensated As long as not all of the gains from trade are needed to compensate (or possibly bribe) the injured parties, the gains left over after compensation payments still make it worthwhile to lower barriers to trade.*

The Long Run

Is there any reason why workers whose jobs have been eliminated by import competition should remain permanently unemployed? No, not as long as the economy is operating near capacity. Workers displaced by import competition will have a more difficult time making a transition to other jobs if the economy is in a recession and unemployment is high. Adjustment assistance cannot overcome a lack of alternative jobs. However, in the long run, if the economy is operating near full employment, workers displaced by foreign competition will become employed in other areas of the economy. Hence, if the argument prevails that protection from foreign competition is needed to protect domestic jobs and avoid unemployment, in the long run the nation will end up forgoing the gains from trade. *Unemployment that results from increased foreign competition should only be transitional. Any long-run unemployment problem should be blamed on fiscal and monetary policy and other domestic policies for dealing with unemployment, not on a policy of free trade.*

Protection from Cheap Foreign Labour

Another popular argument for protection is that we must protect domestic industries from competition from cheap foreign labour. This argument appeals to the labour vote in particular because they view cheap foreign labour as a threat to their standard of living as well as to their jobs. The argument does not stand up, however. Let's see why.

Suppose two countries have exactly the same size labour force, but one's production possibilities frontier looks like that in part a of Figure 32.1, and the other's looks like that in part b. The labour force of part b is absolutely more productive because it can produce more of both goods. Hence, compared to the country of part a, the country of part b can pay its labourers more in both industries. Or, put the other way around, labour in the country of part a is cheaper than that of the country in part b.

But absolute differences in productivity are not the basis of trade — differences in opportunity costs are. Hence, despite the fact that labour in part b is more expensive than labour in part a, it pays for both countries to trade, as shown in Figure 32.2. Moreover, note that despite the fact that labour is cheaper in part a, it would cost the country in part b more to import wheat from part a than to produce it itself. And despite the fact that labour is more expensive in part b, it still costs less for the country in part a to import wheat from the country in part b than to produce it itself. Yes, it is true that the country in part b imports wheat from part a *and* that labour is cheaper in part a than part b. But cheaper labour in part a is not the reason why part b imports timber from part a. It does so because the opportunity cost of producing timber in part a (2 tonnes of timber for each tonne of wheat sacrificed) is lower than it is in part b (only 1 tonne of timber for each tonne of wheat sacrificed).

To clinch the point, suppose the cheap labour argument prevails and insurmountable tariff barriers are erected between the two countries so that trade ceases. In each country some labour that previously worked in the industry in which the country specialised according to comparative advantage would now have to work in the less efficient industry. Real wages (the quantity of goods that can be purchased with a given money wage) would *fall* in both countries because each now has *less* output. In terms of Figure 32.2 each country is now on its production possibilities frontier at points such as c and c', rather than on their trading possibilities frontiers at points such as d and d'. Living standards in both countries are reduced.

Protection for Particular Industries

Industries faced with competition from foreign imports naturally have a special interest in erecting barriers to such competition. A news item reports of warnings by Australian cement producers 'that cut-rate imports of foreign cement "dumped" on Australian shores mean fewer jobs and, in the long run, a weaker Australian cement industry'. We should be suspicious of such statements, of course. Any industry seeking protection either can't operate efficiently enough to meet the market test of foreign competition or simply wants a larger share of the domestic market and a chance to milk it by charging higher prices. In either case consumers will have to pay higher prices for the industry's products if protectionist measures are enacted into law.

The protected industry and associated special interest groups stand to gain a lot from such legislation. Hence, they organise lobbies and campaigns to pressure the government for tariffs, quotas, and other protective barriers. The rest of the nation's citizens are often not aware of the losses that trade restrictions imply for them. The forces that might oppose such legislation are often nonexistent, disinterested, or too disorganised to offset the industry and special interest groups who favour it. The problem is that protection provides relatively large gains to a few, while freer trade helps everybody a little.

But are there circumstances that might warrant protection for a special industry because it is in the best interest of everybody? Yes, some convincing arguments have been made for protecting industries important to national defence. There is also the so-called infant-industry argument.

The National Defence Argument

Certain industries are indispensable to any war effort — steel, transportation equipment, aircraft, mining of strategic materials, textiles, and so forth. Even though a nation may not have a comparative advantage in the production of any of these products, it may be difficult or impossible to import them when war disrupts world trade. In that case, protective tariffs and quotas may be justified to enable these industries to survive on domestic soil during peacetime. Defence considerations override the usual economic arguments. The difficulty is that many industries seek special protection in peacetime by arguing that they would be indispensable during wartime. Whether in fact they would be or not, the argument provides another vehicle for gaining protection from foreign competition.

POLICY PERSPECTIVE

The Changing Fortunes of the Australian Steel Industry

Australian steel production is dominated by one company, Broken Hill Proprietary Limited (BHP). Until the early 1980s the local product competed effectively against imports in the domestic market. As a result of a major economic recession at that time coupled with escalating labour costs and poor worker productivity, BHP's steel division incurred heavy losses. Furthermore, pressure grew among Australian consumers to increase imports of steel from countries such as South Korea and Japan.

To bolster its position BHP approached the Federal government seeking import quotas on steel and requesting tax incentives to invest in new plant and equipment. Not surprisingly the trade unions involved supported the BHP submission. Equally unsurprising was the strong opposition expressed by downstream steel users. In reporting to the government the Industries Assistance Commission argued against any assistance. After considerable further negotiation on the matter with the interested parties, the government announced a Steel Industry Plan to run for five years from the beginning of 1984 until the end of 1988.

Under the plan, the Australian government agreed to pay bounties of up to $71.6 million per year for the production and domestic sale of certain steel products. Furthermore these agreements would be reviewed whenever the local industry's market share in any of eight designated steel product categories fell below 80 per cent or rose above 90 per cent during any three month period. For its part BHP agreed to continued operation of its 3 integrated steel plants (at Newcastle, Port Kembla and Whyalla). It would invest $800 million in new plant and equipment during the first 4 years of the plan, provide job security to current workers if the plan was successful, and agreed to a government appointed Steel Industry Authority monitoring steel prices. The trade unions in the industry agreed to restraining wage demands and to adherence to established grievance settlement procedures. Together with BHP they also agreed to target a productivity level of 250 tonnes per employee per annum at the major steel works initially, with subsequent increases above the national productivity trend rate.

During its first years of operation the Steel Plan appears to have worked very well. There has been a significant increase in labour productivity. The price of steel increased less quickly than the Consumer Price Index, and exports of Australian steel rose. There were negligible labour retrenchments. In 1987 BHP commented publicly however that progress in changing work practices to enhance productivity had been slow.

Questions

1. Why would a program such as the Steel Industry Plan be preferable to introducing import quotas on a continuing basis? What other industry plans have recently been introduced in Australia?

2. Why might a recovery of the world economy make it easier for governments to resist domestic pressure for protectionist measures?

Protection and Trade Policy — The Two-Way Street

International trade is a two-way street.It requires that nations import as well as export. However, the history of trade policy among nations clearly indicates that their eagerness to export is not matched by a similar zeal for imports. While domestic producers welcome exports as a way of expanding their markets, they often view imports as a competitive threat to be stopped if at all possible. While policymakers frequently welcome exports as a way of increasing total income and employment, they may often be concerned about the fact that imports have the opposite effect (recall our analysis of Figure 12.4). Add to these considerations the often emotional, alarmist-type arguments for protection we have previously examined, and the basis for a nation's bias in favour of exports and against imports is readily apparent.

Unfortunately, if every nation indulges this bias in the long run, international trade must cease. Why? Because every nation's exports must be another nation's imports. For example, if Australia doesn't buy goods from other nations (imports), then other nations can't earn dollars to buy goods from Australia (exports). Thus, if a nation raises tariffs, quotas, and other barriers to imports, that nation's export industries will eventually decline. Labour and other resources will have to be reallocated from the nation's shrinking export industries to its expanding industries that produce domestic goods protected by increased trade barriers. Hence, barriers to imports shift resources away from those industries in which the nation is so efficient as to have a comparative advantage. The gains from trade are lost and the nation's standard of living is diminished. If every nation cuts imports, then every nation's exports must eventually decline as well. Everyone loses the gains from trade.

Tariffs of Retaliation

The process of shrinking world trade just described could begin with one nation's attempts to cut back its imports. Others might then retaliate by erecting their own barriers to imports. This has been an all too common occurrence in the history of world trade. During the Great Depression the Australian government increased tariffs to help to reduce imports. (There was, however, agreement at the so-called Ottawa Conference in 1932 that countries of the British Empire should give trade preferences to one another.) If Australian exports had remained the same, the reduction in imports caused by these tariffs would have increased net exports. This would have had an expansionary impact on total income and employment in Australia (recall our discussion in Figure 12.4). Of course, the levels of income and employment in other nations were adversely affected since a reduction in Australian imports meant a reduction

FIGURE P32.1
Average Effective Rates of Assistance to Australian Manufacturing 1969-1987

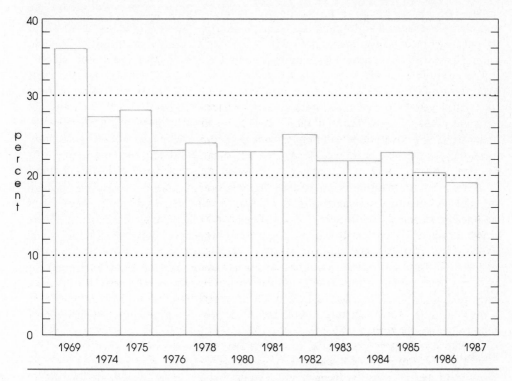

in their exports. Hence, other nations raised trade barriers in retaliation, and Australian exports also declined. Overall, the resulting contraction of world trade aggravated the decline in income and employment in many nations, making the Great Depression even worse.

Reducing Trade Barriers

Australian tariff levels remained high during World War II. After the war our manufacturing sector developed behind this continuing tariff wall. By contrast, government assistance to agriculture was quite low. In the late 1960s, particularly following criticism by the Committee of Economic Enquiry (the Vernon Committee) in 1965, Australian government thinking on the advisability of high tariff levels began to change. The Tariff Board which had previously supported protection for manufacturing began to advocate lower trade barriers. This view has continued until the present day. The Industries Assistance Commission, which replaced the Tariff Board as the main government agency advising the government on all forms of industry assistance, has often drawn criticism from vested interest groups because of its support of reducing trade barriers.

Recent Developments

Since 1970, government assistance to Australian agriculture has remained at quite low levels. The higher levels of protection for manufacturing have fallen slowly and considerable structural adjustment has taken place. Those secondary industries in which the effective rate of protection has been highest have faced considerable pressure. Notable among these have been the textiles, clothing and footwear industries, and motor vehicles.

The average effective rate of assistance provided by government to the total manufacturing sector stood at 19 per cent (see Figure P32.1). Average effective rates for textiles were 68 per cent, for clothing and footwear 176 per cent, and for transport equipment 46 per cent. Each of these areas are currently party to 'industry plans' under which the government will only provide assistance where evidence of significantly increased productivity is shown. A parallel, but slightly different, situation applies to the steel industry which is the subject of the other policy perspective in this chapter.

These recent developments in Australia have occurred against a world background of relatively free trade in manufactures but high protectionism in agriculture, particularly among the European nations and Japan. Even the United States has recently joined this bandwagon — partly in response to growing imbalances between its imports and exports and partly to compete on world markets with highly subsidised European exports of wheat and other agricultural products. More than 90 countries around the world are signatories to the General Agreement on Tariffs and Trade (GATT) which aims to support freer international trade. During the 1980s, however, there have been signs that protection is increasing. As in the 1930s periods of recession and uncertainty tend to undermine trade.

Questions

1. When a nation raises tariffs or imposes other restrictions on imports in an attempt to reduce domestic unemployment, it is said to be engaging in a 'beggar-thy-neighbour' policy — literally, to make beggars of other nations. Explain why.

2. What effect would an 'across-the-board' tariff cut be likely to have on Australian industry? How would it affect those industries protected by import quota regulations?

Indeed, the Australian steel industry could make a compelling case for protection on these grounds.

The Infant-Industry Argument

It is sometimes argued that certain industries would develop into strong competitors in world markets if only they had a chance to get started. Unfortunately, so goes the argument, without protection from the competition of their already established counterparts in other countries, these infant industries never survive to the point where they can go head-to-head with foreign competition.

There may be some merit to this argument. However, the problem lies in correctly identifying those so-called infant industries that are destined, with the aid of temporary protective measures, to mature into productive enterprises in which the nation will definitely have a comparative advantage in a world of free trade. For example, how is it to be decided when maturity has arrived and protection can be removed? Will it eventually become the case that protective measures have simply spawned a mature special interest that is more efficient at maintaining continued protection for itself than it is at producing goods? In the meantime the nation loses in two ways. First, it forgoes the gains from trade available with the purchase of more efficiently produced foreign goods. Second, domestic resources tied up in the protected industry are not available for employment in more efficient industries elsewhere in the economy.

The Diversification-for-Stability Argument

An economy can be highly specialised in a few products and depend to a large extent on its exports of these products for its ability to import the diversity of other goods it needs. Many nations fit this description. Brazil depends heavily on its coffee bean exports, New Zealand on exports of dairy products, and Saudi Arabia on its exported oil. Such nations often suffer from the risks inherent in having too many of their eggs in one basket. If world demand for their particular specialty fluctuates widely, real GDP and employment can be very unstable.

It is often argued that such nations could reduce this instability by diversifying their economies — that is, by encouraging the development of a variety of industries producing largely unrelated products. To do this, it is argued, many of these industries would have to be protected from foreign competition by tariffs, import quotas, and other barriers. Otherwise, they would not be able to compete because of their relative inefficiency compared to their foreign counter-

parts. The main issue here is that there presumably is a trade-off between the gains from trade due to specialisation according to comparative advantage on the one hand, and economic stability on the other. Some nations, like some people, prefer to have a higher *average* income level even though it means greater year-to-year income variability, rather than a lower average income with less year-to-year variability. The diversification-for-stability-through-protection argument obviously leans toward the lower average income, lower variability point of view.

CHECKPOINT 32.3
Explain why a reduction in tariffs would force Australian firms to become more efficient. Would reduced protection automatically wipe out entire industries, as some people believe?

SUMMARY

1. The basis for international trade lies in the fact that nations differ in their resource endowments and technological capabilities.

2. Differing resource endowments and technological capabilities typically make the opportunity cost of producing any given good different between nations. Because of this, nations that specialise according to comparative advantage and engage in trade can have a larger total output than is possible if they remain self-sufficient and isolated.

3. The terms of trade determine how the larger world output made possible by specialisation and trade is distributed among nations. And the terms of trade between any two traded goods depend on world supply-and-demand conditions for the two goods. Increasing costs diminish the extent of specialisation and trade relative to what it would be if costs were constant.

4. The argument for free trade is based on the fact that when nations specialise according to comparative advantage and trade, there is a more efficient allocation of resources. The resulting increase in world output lessens the problem of scarcity and makes possible a higher standard of living.

5. Nations often erect barriers to trade in the form of tariffs, import quotas, and antidumping laws. These measures effectively reduce the quantity of imports and allow domestic producers to sell more at higher prices. To the extent such barriers block trade, there is a less efficient allocation of world resources and a reduced level of total world output.

6. Most of the arguments for protection are flawed. However, short-run adjustment problems resulting from a reduction of trade barriers can cause real hardship for those in affected industries, possibly justifying short-run adjustment assistance. In the long run the economy must operate near capacity so that the full gains from trade may be realised. Protection may be justified where national defence considerations are concerned.

KEY TERMS AND CONCEPTS

comparative advantage
dumping
export subsidy
import quotas
tariff (or duty)

terms of trade
trading possibilities frontier

QUESTIONS AND PROBLEMS

1. Why is it that a doctor hires a secretary even though the doctor may be a better typist than the secretary?

2. Suppose there are two nations, and that one is able to produce two goods, X and Y, and the other is able to produce only good X. Is there likely to be trade between these two nations? Why or why not? If you think they would trade, what do you think would be the terms of trade?

3. Is it conceivable that trade between New Zealand and Australia in Figure 32.2 could lead each nation to have more of one good and less of the other — that is, say, as compared to the combinations c and c' that they have when there is no trade? If so, why is each still better off with trade than without it?

4. Suppose one nation (such as Australia) has a lot of land relative to the size of its population and another nation (such as Japan) has a large population relative to the amount of its land. Suppose also that these two nations have similar levels of technological know-how. What do you think might be the pattern of trade between these two nations? If, on the other hand, the nation with the higher land-to-labour ratio also had a much higher level of technological know-how, how might this change your answer? Why?

5. It is sometimes argued that tariffs can force foreign exporters to provide their goods to us at a lower price. Can you explain why this is true?

6. One argument for protection runs as follows: 'If I buy a car from Japan, Japan has the money and I have the car. But if I buy a car in Australia, Australia has the money and I have the car'. Explain why you do or do not think this is a valid argument for putting a stiff tariff on imported cars.

33

Balance of Payments, Exchange Rates, and the International Financial System

AFTER READING THIS CHAPTER, YOU WILL BE ABLE TO:

1. Explain the balance of payments concept and describe the major components of the balance of payments account.

2. Describe a balance of payments deficit and a balance of payments surplus.

3. Explain how flexible exchange rates eliminate balance of payments deficits and surpluses.

4. Describe how balance of payments adjustments are made under a system of fixed exchange rates.

5. Give the major arguments in the debate over a flexible versus a fixed exchange rate.

6. Explain how a gold standard works.

7. Describe the Bretton Woods system and why it has been replaced by a mixed system of flexible exchange rates and managed floats.

8. Appreciate the evolution of Australia's exchange rate system.

In the previous chapter we focused on the real aspects of international trade. That is, we looked at the way in which nations can have a larger quantity of goods, or more real output, by specialising according to comparative advantage and trading with one another. But international trade also has a monetary aspect because goods are exchanged for money and each nation has its own unique money. For example, when Australians buy goods from Great Britain, they must pay for them with British money, or pounds sterling. Similarly, British citizens must pay for Australian goods with dollars. In short, every movement of goods and services between nations requires a financial transaction[1]. The flow of goods and services in one direction requires a flow of money in the other.

In this chapter we will examine how the international financial system may be organised to handle the financial transactions that accompany international trade. This requires that we become familiar with such concepts as the balance of payments, exchange rates and their determinants, and 'official intervention operations'. We also will examine why gold has often played an important role in international trade in the past, and how and why the present system of international financial arrangements evolved.

EXCHANGE AND THE BALANCE OF PAYMENTS

When Australians import goods and services from other nations, they must pay for these imports with foreign currencies, often called foreign exchange. For exam-

ple, West German marks must be paid for goods produced in West Germany, French francs for goods produced in France, Japanese yen for goods from Japan, and British pounds for goods from Great Britain. Similarly, when Australians export goods to other nations, Australian suppliers want to be paid with dollars. Whatever the country, domestic producers selling goods abroad want to receive payment in domestic currency because that is what they must use to pay wages and all other factors employed in production. Australian workers don't want to be paid in French francs, nor do French workers want to be paid in dollars.

The fundamental point is this. If a nation wants to buy goods and services (imports) from other nations, it must somehow obtain the foreign currencies needed to make payment for these imports. Broadly speaking, the only way it can do this is to export some of of its own goods and services to other nations and thereby earn the foreign currencies that it needs to pay for its imports. That is, to make payments for imports, a nation must use the payments received from exports – exports must finance imports. Hence, a nation's payments to other nations must be equal to, or balanced by, the payments received from other nations. It is in this sense that there is a balance of payments.

While basically correct, this is a very simplified description of how nations obtain foreign currency. The nature of the balance of payments and the way it is calculated is also considerably more involved in reality. We need to look at currency exchange and the balance of payments in more detail.

---

[1] The only apparent exception to this is barter trade. Here nations exchange commodities for one another without financial transactions occurring. Such trade occurs in some primitive societies. It has also been practised between many of the socialist countries. Even Australia has been involved in barter trade in its recent dealings with Eastern European nations.

[2] We assume that trade is occurring with the Federal Republic of Germany (West Germany).

Currency Exchange

Suppose an Australian firm wishes to buy a German machine.[2] The German manufacturer ultimately will want to receive German marks from the sale of the machine. The Australian firm can go to its bank, buy the amount of marks needed to pay for the machine, and send them to the German manufacturer. (The bank typically will charge the Australian firm a small fee for obtaining and providing the marks in exchange for dollars.) Alternatively, the Australian firm may pay the German manufacturer in dollars. The German manufacturer will then take the dollars to its own bank, where it will exchange them for marks. Either way, dollars are exchanged for marks.

The exchange rate *is the price of foreign currency. It is the amount of one currency that must be paid to obtain 1 unit of another currency.* Suppose, in our example, that the exchange rate between Australian dollars and German marks is $.50 for 1 mark. Equivalently, it may be said that 2 marks can be exchanged for $1. Suppose the price of the German machine is 100,000 marks. This means that the Australian firm will have to give its bank $50,000 to obtain the 100,000 marks needed to pay the German manufacturer. Alternatively, the Australian firm may give the German manufacturer $50,000. In that case, the German manufacturer will take the $50,000 to its own bank and exchange it for 100,000 marks. Either way the Australian firm pays $50,000 for the machine and the German manufacturer ultimately receives 100,000 marks.

[2] We assume that trade is occurring with the Federal Republic of Germany (West Germany).

Our example illustrates that *trade between nations requires the exchange of one nation's currency for that of another.* The Australian purchase of a German machine gives rise to a supply of dollars and a demand for marks. Similarly, a German purchase of an Australian product would give rise to a supply of marks and a demand for dollars. Hence, *international trade gives rise to the international supply and demand for national currencies, or a* **foreign exchange market.** *The exchange rates between different currencies are determined in the foreign exchange market.* We will investigate how foreign exchange rates are determined and what these rates mean for the balance of payments later in this chapter. First, however, we must become more familiar with the balance of payments concept.

Balance of Payments

The term **balance of payments** *means just what it says: a nation's total payments to other nations must be equal to, or balanced by, the total payments received from other nations.* When Australians supply dollars in foreign exchange markets, they are demanding foreign currencies in order to make payments to other nations. The currencies Australians receive in exchange for their dollars are supplied by foreigners who demand dollars in order to make payments to Australia. Every dollar sold must be bought, and every dollar bought must be sold. Hence, Australian payments to other nations must be matched exactly by payments from other nations to Australia.

We have already seen how nations keep national income accounts in order to measure domestic economic activity (Chapter 7). Similarly, nations also keep balance of payments accounts in order to keep track of their economic transactions with other nations. *A nation's* **balance of payments account** *records all the payments that it makes to other nations, as well as all the payments that it receives from other nations during the course of a year.* The total volume of payments made to other nations is exactly equal to the total volume of payments received from other nations.

The balance of payments account breaks down the nation's payments to other nations into the following categories: the amount spent on foreign goods; the amount spent on foreign services; the amount loaned to foreign businesses, households, and governments; and the amount invested abroad. Similarly, the account breaks down the payments received from other nations to show the amount of foreign purchases of the nation's goods; the amount of foreign purchases of the nation's services; the amount of foreign lending to the nation's businesses, households, and government; and the amount of foreign investment in the nation. While the total volume of a nation's payments to other nations must always equal the total volume of payments received from other nations, individual categories in the balance of payments accounts need not and typically do not balance. For example, in any given year Australians may export a larger dollar volume of goods than they import or buy more services from foreigners than are sold to foreigners.

The balance of payments account for Australia during the 1986–87 financial year is shown in Table 33.1. International transactions that give rise to payments to other nations are recorded as debit items (designated by a minus sign) in the balance of payments account. Such transactions

supply dollars to the foreign exchange market and create a demand for foreign currency because Australians must sell dollars to obtain foreign currency. The import of a good is an example of a debit item. (Recall our example of an Australian business importing a German machine, which gave rise to a supply of dollars and a demand for marks.) Transactions that give rise to payments to Australia from other nations are recorded credit items in the balance of payments account. Such transactions supply foreign currency to the foreign exchange market and create a demand for dollars because foreigners must sell their currency to obtain dollars. The export of a good is an example of a credit item.

The credit and debit items in the balance of payments account are broadly divided into a current account and a capital account.

The Current Account

The balance of payments on current account includes all payments received during the current period for the export of goods and services and all payments made during the current period for the import of goods and services. Additionally it includes income from foreign investment in Australia, and from Australian investment abroad, as well as unrequited transfers abroad and to Australia.

Imports and Exports of Goods — Visibles. The largest portion of the current account is represented by merchandise imports and exports in row 1 of Table 33.1. These are the imports and exports of goods — the so-called visible items such as steel, wheat, wool, iron ore, television sets, cars, and all the other objects that can be seen and felt. In 1986–87 Australia imported

TABLE 33.1
Australia's Balance of Payments, 1986-87

Debits (−)		Credits		Balance	
Australian Payments to Other Nations ($ million)		Australian Receipts from Other Nations ($ million)		($ million)	
Current Account					
(1) Merchandise imports	−37,293	Merchandise exports	$35,377	Balance on merchandise trade	−1,916
(2) Services	−10,142	Services	7,233	Net services	−2,909
(3) Imports of goods and services	−47,445	Exports of goods and services	42,610	Balance on goods and services	−$4,825
(4) Income from Foreign Investment in Australia	−12,595	Income of Australian Investment abroad	2,509	Net Income	−10,086
(5) Unrequited transfers abroad	−1,693	Unrequited transfers to Australia	3,041	Net unrequited transfers	1,348
(6)	−$61,723		48,160	Balance on Current Account	−13,563
Capital Account					
Foreign Investment in Australia		Australian Investment abroad			
(7) General govt.	3,868	General govt.	−416	General govt.	3,452
(8) Reserve Bank	−3,394	Reserve Bank	18	Reserve Bank	−3,376
(9) Non-official	21,613	Non-official	−8,975	Non-official	12,638
(10)				Balance on Capital Account	12,714
(11)				Balancing Item	849

SOURCE: *ABS Balance of Payments Australia* June Quarter, 1987.
(Catalogue No: 5302.0).

$37,293 million of such merchandise and exported $35,377 million. The difference between merchandise exports and merchandise imports is called the balance on merchandise trade. *When merchandise exports exceed imports a nation has a balance on merchandise trade surplus. When imports exceed exports, it has a balance on merchandise trade deficit.*

In 1986–87 Australia had a balance on merchandise trade deficit of $1,916 million ($35,377 million of exports minus $37,293 million of imports). As noted before, there is no particular reason why individual categories of a nation's balance of payments should in fact balance. However, when a nation has an overall balance on merchandise deficit, it is often said to have an unfavourable balance of trade. The balance is unfavourable in the sense that the nation is earning less from its merchandise exports than it is spending on its merchandise imports — exports of goods do not entirely finance imports of goods. However, it is not clear that it is unfavourable for a nation to get more goods from other nations than it gives in return. Besides, other categories in a nation's balance of payments will necessarily offset a balance of trade deficit because overall the balance of payments must balance. Similar observations may be made about a so-called favourable balance of trade, a balance on merchandise surplus.

Imports and Exports of Services — Invisibles. The import and export of services, or so called invisibles, is another sizeable component of the current account. For example, Australians pay for tickets to fly on foreign airlines and pay foreign shippers to carry cargo. They also buy meals and pay for hotel rooms when travelling abroad and pay premiums for insurance provided by foreign insurance companies. All of these transactions are examples of imports of services. Like the payments for imported goods, payments for imported services give rise to a supply of dollars in the foreign exchange market and a demand for foreign currencies because foreigners want to be paid in their own currencies. Similarly, Australians also export services to foreigners. Like the export of goods, the export of services gives rise to a supply of foreign currencies in the foreign exchange market and a demand for dollars.

In the Australian Balance of Payments accounting framework the sum of the balance on merchandise trade and net services is known as the balance on goods and services. In 1986–87, the ABS estimated this to be a deficit of $4,825 million (i.e. a deficit of $1,916 million in the Balance on Merchandise Trade and a net services deficit of $2,909 million).

Income from Foreign Investments. Like services, income from foreign investment in Australia is another invisible item on the current account. Such income consists of the payment of interest and dividends on Australian bonds (both government

and private) and stocks held by foreigners, as well as the income earned by foreign-owned businesses on Australian soil. It can be thought of as payment for the import of the services of the financial capital provided by foreigners to Australian government and industry. Such payments give rise to a supply of dollars and a demand for foreign currencies in the foreign exchange market. Similarly, receipts of income on Australian assets abroad represent payments received by Australians (government, firms, and households) for the services of capital exported to other nations. These payments to Australians give rise to a supply of foreign currencies and a demand for dollars in the foreign exchange market.

Table 33.1, row 4, indicates that income from foreign investment in Australia in 1986–87 ($12,595 million) substantially exceeded income received by Australians from their overseas investments ($2,509 million).

Unrequited Transfers. Unrequited transfers represent payments made to another nation for which nothing is received in exchange. Private unrequited transfers are gifts given by Australians to foreigners. Government unrequited transfers consist of foreign aid. It is a convention of balance of payments accounting that such gifts are recorded as credit items under merchandise exports, just as if goods had been sold abroad. A balancing entry is made under unrequited transfers.

As can be seen from Row 5 of Table 33.1 net transfers were in surplus by $1,348 million for Australia for 1986–87. A significant contribution to this was made by migrants' transfers which accounted for $1,657 million.

Balance on Current Account. Row 6 shows that the total of the debit items on current account $61,723 million was greater than the sum of credit items $48,160 million in 1986–87. In other words, the total payments made by Australia to other nations on current account was greater than the total payments made by other nations to Australia. On current account Australia supplied more dollars to the foreign exchange market than other nations demanded. Or equivalently, Australia demanded more foreign currency (to pay other nations) than other nations supplied (to get dollars to pay Australia). In short, on current account, payments received from other nations were less than sufficient to finance Australian payments to other nations. The deficit on current account amounted to $13,563 million for the 1986–87 financial year. This was 5.1 per cent of GDP. It is worth noting that Australia's Balance on Current Account during much of its history of white settlement has been in deficit. Since 1945 there has been a surplus only once.

The Capital Account

There is no reason why there has to be a balance of payments on current account any more than there is a reason why merchandise imports should exactly equal merchandise exports. The current account is itself just a part of the balance of payments. Overall, however, the balance of payments must balance. Since the balance of payments is divided into the current account and the capital account, it follows that *if there is a deficit on current account, there must be a compensating surplus on capital account. Likewise, if there is a surplus on current account, there must be a compensating deficit on capital account.*

For example, if there is an excess of payments over receipts on current account (a deficit), then there must be a matching excess of receipts over payments on capital account (a surplus). That is, if more foreign currency is spent (in payments to other nations) than is earned (in payments from other nations) on current account, the difference must come from an excess of foreign currency earned over foreign currency spent on capital account. Alternatively, an excess of receipts over payments on current account (a surplus) must be matched by an excess of payments over receipts on capital account (a deficit). In that case, less foreign currency is spent than is earned on current account, and the surplus matches the deficit on capital account, where more foreign currency is spent than is earned.

Since the balance of payments is divided into the current account and the capital account, the capital account includes all international transactions not included in the current account. Specifically, the capital account includes all purchases and sales of assets, or what is termed *capital*. It is traditionally broken up into an official government sector's transactions and non-official private sector transactions.

Government Imports and Exports of Capital. These consist mostly of loans to or from other governments; changes in government holdings of official international reserve assets such as foreign currencies, gold, and reserves with the International Monetary Fund called Special Drawing Rights or SDRs (which we will discuss later); and changes in liquid claims on official reserve assets.

Loans to other governments are debit items on the government's capital account because they represent payments to other nations for the import of their IOUs, just like lending on the private capital account. Such lending gives rise to a supply of dollars and a demand for foreign currency in the foreign exchange market. Similarly, foreign governments make loans to the Australian government. These are recorded as credit items on the government's capital account because they represent payments received from other nations in exchange for the export of the Australian government's IOUs (such as Australian government bonds and Treasury bills). Such transactions create a supply of foreign currency and a demand for dollars in the foreign exchange market.

The government capital account transactions in official reserve assets and liquid claims on official reserve assets play an accommodating role in the balance of payments. They adjust to satisfy the requirement that overall the balance of payments must balance. Therefore, they adjust because the total amount of foreign currency needed to make all payments to other nations must necessarily equal the total amount of foreign currency earned from all payments received from other nations.

In 1986–87, foreign investment in Australia in the area of general government amounted to $3,868 million. This was offset only partially by Australian government investment abroad of $416 million. During the year, however, the Reserve Bank of Australia disposed of foreign reserves worth $3,396 million.

Private Imports and Exports of Capital. When Australian businesses and households invest and lend abroad (to foreign businesses, households, and governments), they receive IOUs from foreigners in the form of stocks, bonds, and other debt claims and titles of ownership. Such investments and loans are entered as debit items in the capital account. They represent an increase in Australian ownership of foreign assets. For example, in 1986–

87 Australian households and businesses invested and loaned $8,975 million dollars abroad (Table 33.1, row 9). Why are such transactions recorded as a debit item, just like a merchandise import? There are two basic reasons. First, these transactions represent a payment to other nations. Second, they give rise to a supply of dollars in the foreign exchange market and a demand for the foreign currencies Australians need in order to pay for foreign stocks and bonds. Moreover, you can think of Australians importing share certificates and bonds, just like they import merchandise. Both types of payment represent the acquisition of a claim of ownership or property right from a foreign nation.

Similarly, foreign businesses and households also invest and make loans in Australia (to Australian businesses, households, and governments) for which they receive Australian shares and bonds. These represent an increase in foreign ownership of Australian assets and are entered as credit items in the capital account. Such transactions give rise to a supply of foreign currencies in the foreign exchange market and a demand for dollars needed by foreigners to make payment for their investments and loans in Australia. In exchange Australia may be thought of as exporting share certificates and bonds — that is, exporting property rights and ownership claims. Such transactions amounted to $21,613 million in 1986–87 (Table 33.1, row 9).

For much of the postwar period the majority of Australia's net capital inflow has taken the form of investment in shares. This balance changed in the early 1980s as Australian companies began importing much more capital through borrowing overseas. In 1985–86, for example, equity foreign investment in Australian companies was about $1,500m while debt investment stood at nearly $8,000m.

In 1986–87 Australia had a surplus on its private capital account equal to $12,638 million (Table 33.1, row 9). This surplus on the private capital account added to the deficit on current account (row 6) amounted to a deficit of $925 million. This deficit was clearly funded by the government and Reserve Bank financial activities which we discussed above.

Overall Balance. One other item that does complicate the issue a little is the so-called balancing item. Because of errors in data collection and the government's inability to keep track of virtually all Australian transactions with other nations, there is often a situation where the debits and credits sides of the Balance of Payments accounts do not balance with one another. In 1986–87 for instance the deficit on current account was $13,563 million. The recorded Balance on Capital Account was $12,714 million. A Balancing Item of $849 million was necessary.

---

*CHECKPOINT *33.1*

Explain how you would classify the following international transactions on the balance of payments account and why each is a credit or a debit item: an Australian resident on holiday in Malaysia gets a haircut; you give a birthday present to a cousin in Canada; you buy a Volkswagen and finance payments on it with a loan made to you by an Australian bank (instead, suppose you finance it with a loan made to you by Volkswagen); and the government buys French francs and finances the purchase with a liquid claim.

*Answers to all Checkpoints can be found at the back of the text.

EXCHANGE RATES AND BALANCE OF PAYMENTS ADJUSTMENTS

The size of balance of payments deficits and surpluses, as well as the adjustment process for their elimination, depends on the role that exchange rates are allowed to play in international transactions. At one extreme, exchange rates between national currencies can be freely determined by the forces of supply and demand in the foreign exchange market. At the other extreme, exchange rates can be rigidly fixed by government intervention in the foreign exchange market. We will now examine each of these extremes.

Flexible Exchange Rates

When exchange rates between national currencies are freely determined by supply and demand in the foreign exchange market, they are said to be **flexible (or floating) exchange rates**. They are free to change in response to shifts in supply and demand.

Currency Depreciation and Appreciation

When the exchange rate between dollars and a foreign currency increases, the foreign currency gets more expensive in terms of dollars — it takes more dollars or cents to buy a unit of foreign currency. Since this is the same thing as saying that a dollar will buy less foreign currency, we say that the value of the dollar has *depreciated* relative to the foreign currency. **Currency depreciation** *means that now more units of a nation's currency will be required to buy a unit of foreign currency.*

Conversely, if the exchange rate

between dollars and a foreign currency decreases, it takes fewer dollars or cents to buy a unit of foreign currency. Since a dollar will now buy more foreign currency, the value of the dollar is said to have *appreciated* relative to the foreign currency. **Currency appreciation** *means that now fewer units of a nation's currency are required to buy a unit of a foreign currency.*

Note that *an appreciation in the value of one nation's currency is necessarily a depreciation in another's.* For example, suppose the rate of exchange between dollars and French francs is initially $1 per franc. Suppose the value of the dollar appreciates relative to the franc. For instance, say the rate of exchange decreases to $.50 per franc. It now takes half as many dollars to buy a franc. For French citizens this means the rate of exchange has risen from 1 franc per dollar to 2 francs per dollar. In other words, the value of the franc has depreciated relative to the dollar. It now takes twice as many francs to buy a dollar.

Exchange Rates and the Price of Foreign Goods

Exchange rates allow citizens in one country to translate the prices of foreign goods and services into units of their own currency. Suppose $1 exchanges for 4 French francs on the foreign exchange market. If the price of a French-made car is 20,000 francs, its price in dollars is $5,000, or 20,000 multiplied by .25. Similarly, if the price of a tonne of Australian wheat is $30, its price in francs is 120 francs, or 30 multiplied by 4.

Changes in exchange rates alter the prices of foreign goods to domestic buyers and the prices of domestic goods to foreign buyers. Suppose in the above example that

the dollar depreciates, so that $1 will now only exchange for 3 francs on the foreign exchange market. Now the French-made car selling for 20,000 francs will be more expensive for an Australian. It will cost $6,666 (.33 × 20,000). On the other hand, a tonne of Australian wheat selling for $30 will be less expensive to a French citizen because the depreciation of the dollar means an appreciation of the franc. The tonne of wheat will now cost a French

---

FIGURE 33.1
Determination of the Equilibrium Level of a Flexible Exchange Rate

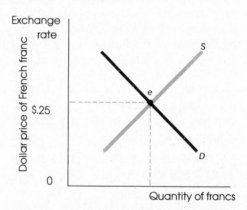

Underlying the demand curve *D* for French francs is the desire of Australians to exchange dollars for francs needed to buy French goods and services and to acquire French assets. Similarly, behind the supply curve *S* for francs is the desire of French citizens to exchange francs for dollars needed to buy Australian goods and services and to acquire Australian assets.

The equilibrium level of the exchange rate is $.25 per franc, determined by the intersection of the demand curve *D* and supply curve *S* at point *e*. If the exchange rate is less than $.25 per franc, the demand for francs in the foreign exchange market will exceed the supply and the rate will be bid up. If the exchange rate is greater than $.25 per franc, the supply of francs in the foreign exchange market will exceed the demand and the rate will be bid down.

buyer 90 francs (3 × 30).

Free-Market Determination of the Exchange Rate

In Chapter 4 we saw how supply and demand work in a freely operating market (one in which the government does not intervene) to determine the price of a good. The exchange rate is just the price of one currency stated in terms of another. And the determination of the equilibrium level of a flexible, or floating, exchange rate is determined by supply and demand just like the price of wheat or haircuts.

For example, suppose Australia and France are the only two trading countries in the world. And suppose that the exchange rate between dollars and French francs is determined by supply and demand in the foreign exchange market as shown in Figure 33.1. (Our example uses hypothetical data.) The vertical axis measures the exchange rate, the price of a franc in terms of dollars. The horizontal axis measures the quantity of francs. The equilibrium level of the exchange rate is $.25 per franc, which corresponds to the intersection of the supply curve S and the demand curve D at point e.

The demand curve D shows the quantity of francs demanded by Australians at each possible level of the exchange rate. It comes from the desire on the part of Australians to exchange dollars for francs. The francs are needed to buy French goods and services and to pay interest and dividends on French loans and investments in Australia. They are also needed to make unrequited transfers such as gifts and foreign aid grants, and to pay for the Australian acquisition (by government, businesses, and private citizens) of French assets. In short, the demand curve D represents the Australian demand for

francs needed to make payments to France — all the transactions with France that enter as debit items on the Australian balance of payments account.

The supply curve S shows the quantity of francs supplied by French citizens at each possible level of the exchange rate. Underlying it is the desire of the French to exchange francs for dollars needed to pay for Australian goods and services and for the French acquisition of Australian assets. These payments are represented by all the credit items on the Australian balance of payments account.

The supply and demand curves have the usual slopes. If the exchange rate were below the equilibrium level, the quantity of francs demanded would exceed the quantity supplied, and the exchange rate (the price of a franc) would be bid up. If the exchange rate were above the equilibrium level, the quantity of francs supplied would exceed the quantity demanded, and the rate would be bid down. At the equilibrium exchange rate, there is no tendency for the rate to change because the quantity of francs demanded is just equal to the quantity supplied.

Flexible Exchange Rates and the Balance of Payments

The argument for flexible exchange rates is that they automatically adjust to eliminate balance of payments surpluses and deficits. Let's see how this happens.

The equilibrium in the foreign exchange market of Figure 33.1 (represented by the intersection of D and S at point e) is reproduced in Figure 33.2. In equilibrium there is no balance of payments deficit or surplus as we have defined these concepts. That is, there are no government capital account transactions in official reserves and liquid claims between the two

FIGURE 33.2
Adjustment of a Flexible Exchange Rate
to Eliminate a Balance of Payments
Deficit

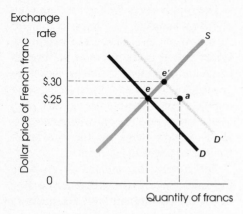

An increase in Australian imports of French
goods will cause the demand curve for francs
to shift from D to D' because Australians now
need more francs to make payments to
France. At the initial exchange rate of $.25 per
franc, Australia will have a balance of payments deficit. With a flexible exchange rate
the excess demand for francs, equal to the
distance between points e and a, will cause
the rate to be bid up. The rise in the
exchange rate will make French goods more
expensive to Australians and Australian goods
cheaper for French citizens. Therefore, Australian imports of French goods will decline and
French imports of Australian goods will rise.
This adjustment will continue until the
exchange rate has risen to the new equilibrium level of $.30 per franc (corresponding to
the intersection of S and D' at point e'). At this
point, the Australian balance of payments
deficit will be eliminated.

nations. Moreover, the total of all other
Australian payments to France is exactly
equal to the total of all payments received
by Australia from France.

Now suppose Australians step up their
imports of French goods (say because
more Australians develop a taste for
French wines and other French goods).
Total payments to France will now exceed

total payments received from France.
Australian demand for francs needed to
make these payments will increase, as
represented by the rightward shift in the
demand curve for francs from D to D'
in Figure 33.2. At the initial exchange rate
of $.25 per franc, there will now be a
shortage of francs. Equivalently, we can
say there will be an excess demand for
francs equal to the distance between points
e and a. Australia will now have a balance
of payments deficit.

How will a flexible exchange rate
eliminate this deficit? The excess demand
for francs will cause the exchange rate,
the dollar price of francs, to be bid up.
But this will alter the prices of *all* French
goods to Australians and the prices of all
Australian goods to French citizens in the
way we discussed earlier. Since Australians will now have to pay more for francs,
the prices of French goods will now be
higher when translated into dollars.
Therefore, as the exchange rate is bid up,
French goods will become more expensive
for Australian buyers, and Australian
imports will tend to decline. This decline
is represented by a move from point *a*
toward point *e'* along *D'* in Figure 33.2

But a rise in the dollar price of francs
is the same thing as a fall in the franc
price of dollars. (The dollar depreciates
relative to the franc, and the franc
appreciates relative to the dollar.) French
citizens will now find that they don't have
to pay as much for dollars. The prices
of Australian goods will therefore be lower
when translated into francs. Since Australian goods are now less expensive for
French citizens, French imports will tend
to increase. This increase is represented
by a move from point *e* toward point *e'*
along *S* in Figure 33.2.

Hence, as the exchange rate rises to the
new equilibrium position corresponding

to *e'*, an exchange rate of $.30 per franc, Australian imports from France decline while Australian exports to France increase. The result will be to eliminate the balance of payments deficit in Australia. In sum, *when exchange rates are flexible, or freely determined by supply and demand, balance of payments deficits and surpluses will be quickly eliminated. Indeed it is often argued that foreign exchange markets adjust so quickly that there would be no deficits or surpluses if governments didn't interfere.* (Later in this chapter we will see how governments interfere with the mechanism.)

Factors Affecting Flexible Exchange Rates

We have just seen how a change in one nation's demand for the products of another can affect the exchange rate. Other factors can also cause shifts in supply and demand in foreign exchange markets and, hence, changes in flexible, or floating, exchange rates. Two of the more important factors in supply and demand are differences in rates of inflation between nations and changes in the level of interest rates in one nation relative to the interest rates in others.

Differences in Rates of Inflation

Assume again that the equilibrium exchange rate between dollars and francs is $.25 per franc, determined by the intersection of *D* and *S* at point *e* in Figure 33.3. Now suppose the general price level in Australia (the prices of all Australian products) rises relative to the general price level in France (due to an expansionary Australian fiscal and monetary policy, say). As a result, French goods become less expensive relative to Australian

goods, *given the exchange rate of $.25 per franc*. Hence, Australians increase their demand for imports from France, thereby causing their demand for francs to increase, as indicated by the rightward shift in the demand curve for francs from *D* to *D'*. At the same time, the rise in the Australian price level causes French citizens to reduce their demand for Australian goods. This results in a reduction of their supply of francs (their demand for dollars), indicated by a leftward shift of the supply curve of francs from *S* to *S'*.

At the initial exchange rate of $.25 per franc, there is now an excess demand for francs equal to the distance between points *a* and *b*. This excess demand will cause the exchange rate to be bid up from $.25 per franc to $.35 per franc, corresponding to the intersection of *S'* and *D'* at point *f*, in Figure 33.3. The Australian demand for French imports will be cut back and the French demand for Australian goods will increase in exactly the manner already described in connection with Figure 33.2. In short, the rise in the general price level of Australian goods relative to French goods causes a depreciation of the dollar relative to the franc in the foreign exchange market.

Our hypothetical example illustrates a general observation about exchange rate movements in the real world. *Given a sufficient length of time, the exchange rate between the nations' currencies will tend to adjust to reflect changes in their price levels, all other things remaining the same.* Of course, all other things typically do not remain the same. Hence, it is usually difficult to observe real-world adjustments that are as clear-cut as our hypothetical example.

The process of exchange rate adjustment due to differential changes in national price levels operates continuously when two nations experience different rates of inflation. *If two nations are each experiencing the same rate of inflation the relation between their general price levels remains the same. The exchange rate between their currencies will therefore remain unchanged all other things remaining the same. However, if a nation's rate of inflation is greater than that of a trading partner, the nation with the higher inflation rate will experience an increase in its exchange rate — a depreciation of its currency — all other things remaining the same.* For instance, in our example of Australia and France, suppose the Australian price level continued to rise relative to that of France. Then the rate of exchange between the dollar and the franc would continue to rise. The dollar would continue to depreciate relative to the franc.

FIGURE 33.3
Differential Changes in the Price Levels of Two Nations Cause the Exchange Rate to Change

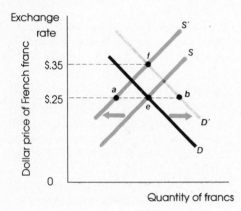

The rise in the general price level of Australian goods relative to French goods causes a depreciation of the dollar relative to the franc in the foreign exchange market.

When the general price level in Australia rises relative to the general price level in France, French goods become less expensive relative to Australian goods. Hence, at the initial exchange rate of $.25 per franc Australian demand for French imports increases and French citizens reduce their demand for Australian goods. The demand curve for francs therefore shifts rightward from D to D' and the supply curve for francs shifts leftward from S to S'. The resulting excess demand for francs (equal to the distance between points a and b) causes the exchange rate to be bid up to $.35 per franc. This depreciation of the dollar relative to the franc cuts back the Australian demand for French imports and increases French demand for Australian goods in exactly the manner described in connection with Figure 33.2.

Changes in Interest Rates

In our discussion of the capital account of the balance of payments, we observed that money is loaned and borrowed across national borders. Some of these funds are moved around the globe almost continually in search of those highly liquid financial assets (such as short-term government bonds and commercial paper) that pay the highest interest rates. When the interest rates prevailing in one country change relative to those prevailing in another, funds tend to flow toward that country where interest rates are now highest, all other things remaining the same.

For example, suppose the interest rate on Australian Treasury bills is 7 per cent, the same as that on comparable short-term French government bonds. If the interest rate on Treasury bills suddenly drops to 6.5 per cent (due to Reserve Bank open market purchases, say), short-term French government bonds paying 7 per cent interest will look relatively more attractive to Australian investors. They will therefore increase their demand for francs in order to buy more French bonds.

FIGURE 33.4
Fixed Exchange Rates: Balance of Payments Deficits and Surpluses

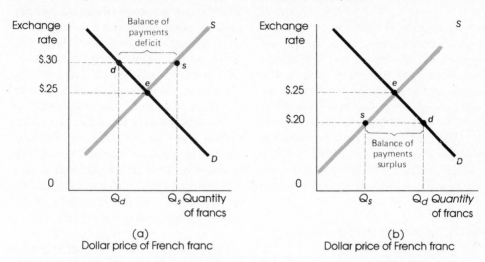

(a)
Dollar price of French franc

(b)
Dollar price of French franc

The equilibrium level of the exchange rate between dollars and francs would be $.25 per franc (the intersection at point e of the supply and demand curves for francs) if the forces of supply and demand were allowed to operate freely.

However, suppose the French government wants to fix, or peg, the exchange rate above the equilibrium level at $.30 per franc, as shown in part a. Then it will have a balance of payments deficit equal to the excess supply of francs, represented by the distance between points d and s. In order to maintain the exchange rate at $.30 per franc, the French government will have to buy up the excess supply of francs using dollars out of its holdings of official reserves.

Alternatively, suppose the French government wants to fix the exchange rate below the equilibrium level at $.20 per franc, as shown in part b. Then it will have a balance of payments surplus equal to the excess demand for francs, represented by the distance between points s and d. In order to maintain the exchange rate at $.20 per franc, the French government will have to supply the foreign exchange market with a quantity of francs equal to the excess demand.

The demand curve for francs will shift rightward, just as in Figure 33.3. Similarly, French investors will reduce the supply of francs since Treasury bills will also be relatively less attractive to them. Hence, the supply curve for francs will shift leftward, again as in Figure 33.3. The result will be a rise in the exchange rate of dollars for francs, a depreciation of the dollar relative to the franc.

Since funds can be quickly transferred between countries, changes in the relative levels of interest rates between countries are a primary cause of day-to-day changes in flexible, or floating exchange rates.

CHECKPOINT 33.2
When one currency depreciates, why does another necessarily appreciate? In what sense is the supply curve in Figure 33.1 a demand curve for dollars, and the demand curve a supply curve of dollars? What would happen to the exchange rate of dollars for pounds sterling if Australian authorities started to pursue a more expansionary monetary policy, all other things remaining the same? Why? What do you think would happen to the exchange rate of dollars for pounds sterling if British authorities started to pursue a more restrictive fiscal policy, all other things remaining the same? Why?

Fixed Exchange Rates and the Balance of Payments

Governments have often chosen to fix, or 'peg', exchange rates, which is just the opposite of allowing the forces of supply and demand to determine rates in the foreign exchange market freely. *In order to fix the exchange rate at a level above or below the equilibrium level determined by supply and demand, governments must continually intervene in the foreign exchange market.* Let's see why this is so, and how governments must intervene.

Fixing the Rate Above Equilibrium

Consider the supply and demand for francs in Figure 33.4, part a. If the exchange rate were flexible, or floating, it would be equal to the equilibrium rate of $.25 per franc, as determined by the intersection of the demand curve D and supply curve S at point e. However, suppose the French government wants to fix, or peg, the exchange rate at $.30 per franc. At this price the quantity of francs demanded by Australians in order to make payments to France equals Q_d, corresponding to point d on D. The quantity of francs supplied by French citizens in order to get dollars to make payments to Australia equals Q_s, corresponding to point s on S. The quantity of francs supplied exceeds the quantity demanded — payments by France to Australia are greater than payments by Australia to France. Therefore, France has a balance of payments deficit represented by the distance between points d and s (also equal to Q_s minus Q_d).

But what will keep market forces from bidding the exchange rate down to the equilibrium level at point e? The French government must buy up the excess supply of francs (equal to the distance between d and s) at a price of $.30 per franc using dollars out of its holdings of official reserve assets (foreign currencies, gold, and SDRs). The French government will be able to continue fixing the exchange rate above the equilibrium level only as long as it has reserves of dollars. Once the reserves run out, the exchange will fall to the equilibrium level of $.25 per franc. When the price of a currency (the exchange rate) is pegged above the equilibrium level that would prevail in a free market, the currency is often said to be overvalued. In this case the franc is overvalued relative to the dollar.

Fixing the Rate Below Equilibrium

Now consider the opposite case, in which the exchange rate is fixed below the equilibrium level — the franc is under-valued relative to the dollar. For example, suppose the French government wants to peg the exchange rate at $.20 per franc, as illustrated in Figure 33.4, part b. In this case the quantity of francs demanded by Australians Q_d (corresponding to point d on D) exceeds the quantity supplied by French citizens Q_s (corresponding to point s on S). Payments by France to Australia are now less than payments by Australia to France. France now has a balance of payments surplus equal to the distance between points s and d.

How will the French government keep the excess demand for francs from bidding up the exchange rate to the equilibrium level at paint e? It will have to supply the foreign exchange market with a quantity of francs equal to the excess demand (the distance between points s and d). In exchange for these francs the French government will acquire dollars, which will increase its holdings of official reserves.

Policy Implications of Fixed Exchange Rates

It is generally easier for a government to keep its currency undervalued (the exchange rate is pegged below the equilibrium level) than to keep it overvalued (the exchange rate is pegged above the equilibrium level). As we have seen, a government must draw down its reserves of foreign currencies in order to keep its currency overvalued. Obviously, it can't do this indefinitely, or it will run out of such reserves. It may be able to borrow more from other nations, but again not indefinitely. By contrast, in order to keep its currency undervalued, a government only has to supply its own currency to the foreign exchange market. And, as discussed in previous chapters, a government has unlimited capacity to do this.

Overvalued Versus Undervalued Currencies

Clearly, it is easier to keep currencies undervalued than to keep them overvalued. What are the policy implications of this fact? Suppose all nations are trading under a system of flexible exchange rates, so that there are no balance of payments deficits or surpluses. Now suppose they all agree to fix exchange rates at currently prevailing levels. As time passes supply and demand curves in foreign exchange markets inevitably shift due to changing trade patterns and differing economic developments within each nation. Since exchange rates are fixed, some nations end up with overvalued currencies and balance of payments deficits while others have undervalued currencies and balance of payments surpluses.

Nations with overvalued currencies and payments deficits must do something to correct their situation or they will run out of official reserves. By contrast, those with undervalued currencies and payments surpluses are not under this pressure — they need only keep supplying their own currency to the foreign exchange market. Hence, to eliminate its payments deficits and preserve its reserve holdings, a nation with an overvalued currency is often forced to allow its currency to depreciate. In a world of fixed exchange rates, this is called a **currency devaluation** — the exchange rate is now fixed at a lower level. Of course, the problem could also be cured if nations with undervalued currencies allowed their currencies to appreciate, called a **currency revaluation** in a world of fixed exchange rates. Obviously, if one currency is overvalued, another must be undervalued. But the pressure on the nation with the overvalued currency to devalue is simply greater than that on the nation with the undervalued currency to revalue.

Bias Toward Contractionary Fiscal and Monetary Policy

Unfortunately, devaluing a nation's overvalued currency is not a politically popular thing for the government in office to do. It is often seen as a sign of a weakening economy and a loss of international stature. Similarly, a nation with an undervalued currency faces political obstacles to revaluation because sales abroad by its export industries benefit when its currency is underpriced in the foreign exchange market.

But the nation with the overvalued currency and the balance of payments deficit must do something to avoid running out of official reserves. One possibility is to pursue a contractionary fiscal and monetary policy, thereby curbing total demand. As we saw in

Chapter 11, this also will tend to reduce the nation's demand for imports. And a reduction in imports will help to reduce its balance of payments deficit. Unfortunately, however, curbing total demand will also increase the nation's unemployment rate and reduce its total output. Its domestic policy goals will have to be sacrificed to its international policy goal of reducing its payments deficit.

Of course, another possibility for the nation with an undervalued currency and payments surplus is to pursue an expansionary fiscal and monetary policy. Such a nation's total demand would rise, causing an increase in its imports from the nations with overvalued currencies and payments deficits. Unfortunately, this might cause unacceptable inflationary pressures in the expanding nation. Such a nation is likely to be very reluctant to sacrifice its own domestic price stability for the sake of reducing another nation's balance of payments deficit, especially since this will reduce its own payments surplus as well. Consequently, the burden usually falls on the nation with the overvalued currency (the one running out of official reserves) to pursue contractionary fiscal and monetary policy in order to reduce its payments deficit. Hence, *many critics of a fixed exchange rate system contend that it is biased toward enforcing contractionary fiscal and monetary policies on nations with overvalued currencies and chronic balance of payments deficits. As a result, they claim, worldwide unemployment rates are higher and worldwide output levels lower under such a system.*

Finally, what if a nation with an overvalued currency and a payments deficit is neither willing to devalue nor to curb total demand with restrictive fiscal and monetary policy? Such a nation may simply erect tariff, and other trade barriers

to curb its imports. In that event everybody loses, as we saw in the previous chapter.

Flexible Versus Fixed Exchange Rates

Which is to be preferred, a system of flexible exchange rates or a system of fixed exchange rates?

Fiscal and Monetary Policy Considerations

Under a system of fixed exchange rates nations will run balance of payments deficits and surpluses because exchange rates cannot automatically adjust to equalise supply and demand in the foreign exchange markets. As we have just seen, nations with chronic balance of payments deficits may have to sacrifice high employment in order to reduce their payments deficits. Hence, critics argue that fixed exchange rates interfere with a nation's freedom to use fiscal and monetary policy to pursue domestic policy goals. These same critics often advocate flexible exchange rates because they automatically eliminate balance of payments problems, thus freeing fiscal and monetary policy to focus strictly on domestic objectives. However, some advocates of fixed exchange rates argue just the opposite. They claim that the fear of running large balance of payments deficits serves as a check on governments that might otherwise pursue excessively expansionary fiscal and monetary policies that cause inflation.

Stability and Uncertainty

Critics contend that flexible exchange rates inhibit international trade because of the uncertainty about their future levels. For example, suppose an Australian importer puts in an order to purchase woollen sweaters from a Scottish woollen mill. Suppose that the current exchange rate is $2 per pound sterling, and that a woollen sweater costs £20, or $40. At this price the Australian importer feels that the Scottish sweaters will be very competitive with Australian-made sweaters that sell in shops for $45. However, suppose that the sweaters are delivered to the Australian importer 3 months after the order is placed, and that in the meantime the exchange rate has increased to $2.50 per pound. The Scottish woollen mill agreed to sell the sweaters for £20 each to the importer. But in dollars it will now cost $50 per sweater ($2.50 × 20), a price that is no longer competitive with Australian-made sweaters selling for $45.

Advocates of flexible exchange rates argue that it is possible to hedge against the risks of changing exchange rates by entering into futures contracts. For instance, at the time the Australian importer placed the order for the sweaters, a futures contract could have been obtained that guaranteed delivery of pounds to the wholesaler at a rate of $2 per pound 3 months hence. Whatever happens to the exchange rate between dollars and pounds in the meantime, the wholesaler will be assured of getting pounds at $2 per pound when it comes time to pay for the sweaters. Who will enter into the futures contract agreeing to supply pounds to the wholesaler at this rate of exchange? Someone needing dollars 3 months hence who wants to be sure they can be obtained with pounds at a rate of $2 per pound. That someone might be an English firm that has ordered goods from an Australian firm to be delivered and paid for in 3 months.

While acknowledging the protection that hedging can offer, some critics still claim that flexible exchange rates can fluctuate wildly due to speculation — for example, the purchase of pounds at $2 per pound on the gamble that the rate will rise say to $2.25 per pound, yielding the speculator a profit of $.25 per pound. To the contrary, advocates of flexible exchange rates respond that speculative activity will tend to stabilise exchange rate fluctuations. They claim that speculators must buy currencies when they are low priced and sell them when they are high priced if they are to make money. Hence, it is argued that speculators will tend to push the price of an undervalued currency up and the price of an overvalued currency down, thus serving to limit exchange rate fluctuations.

It is often argued that fixed exchange rates invite destabilising speculation even more than flexible exchange rates. Suppose a currency is overvalued, such as the franc in Figure 33.4, part a. And suppose word spreads that the French government is running out of the dollar reserves needed to fix the price of francs above the equilibrium level and finance its payments deficit. Anticipating a devaluation of the franc, holders of francs will rush to the foreign exchange market to get rid of their francs before the price of francs drops. This will shift the supply curve of francs rightward, making the excess supply even larger. With a larger payments deficit and reserves now declining faster, actual devaluation may be unavoidable.

CHECKPOINT 33.3

Describe what a government must do in order to fix an exchange rate. Why are balance of payments deficits and surpluses inevitable under fixed exchange rates? If a nation's currency was over-

valued and it decided to tighten its monetary policy, what would happen to its official reserve holdings? Why?

THE INTERNATIONAL FINANCIAL SYSTEM: POLICIES AND PROBLEMS

The international financial system consists of the framework of arrangements under which nations finance international trade. These arrangements influence whether exchange rates will be fixed, flexible (or floating), or some combination of fixed and flexible, often called the *managed float*. The arrangements also influence the way balance of payments adjustments take place and the way nations finance balance of payments deficits. We will now examine the principal ways in which the international financial system has been organised during the twentieth century. First we will briefly consider the gold standard, which prevailed during the late nineteenth and early twentieth centuries. We will then examine the Bretton Woods system, which governed international transactions from 1944 to 1971, and finally the mixed system that prevails today.

The Gold Standard

For about 50 years prior to World War II, the international financial system was predominantly on a gold standard. Following the example of Britain, Australia used the Gold Standard for most of this period. During World War I from 1914–18 we abandoned its use, but during the 1920s we utilised it once more.

Gold and a Fixed Exchange Rate

Under a **gold standard** gold serves as each nation's money. Each nation defines its monetary unit in terms of so many ounces of gold. The use of this common unit of value automatically fixes the rate of exchange between different currencies. For example, suppose Australia defines a dollar as equal to $1/30$ of an ounce of gold. This means the Australian Treasury would pay \$1 for every $1/30$ ounce of gold to anyone who wants to sell gold to it or give $1/30$ of an ounce of gold for every dollar of its currency to anyone who wants to buy gold. Australian currency (coins and paper money) would be redeemable in gold. Suppose Great Britain defines its monetary unit, the pound sovereign, as equal to $5/30$ of an ounce of gold. The British Treasury would redeem its currency at the rate of $5/30$ of an ounce of gold for every pound sovereign (called a pound for short). What would be the international rate of exchange between dollars and pounds?

Obviously it would be fixed at \$5 per pound. People who wanted pounds to buy British goods would never pay more than \$5 per pound. Why? Simply because they could always go to the Australian Treasury and get $5/30$ of an ounce of gold for \$5, then ship the gold to Great Britain, where they could exchange it at the British Treasury for a British pound. (For simplicity, we will ignore shipping costs.) Similarly, it would not be possible to buy a pound for less than \$5. Why? Because no one would sell a pound for less than this when they could exchange it at the British Treasury for $5/30$ of an ounce of gold and then ship the gold to Australia, where it could be exchanged at the Australian Treasury for \$5.

The Gold Flow Adjustment Mechanism

Now that we see why the exchange rate

was rigidly fixed under a gold standard, let's see how balance of payments adjustments took place under such a system.

Clearly, if Australia imported more from Great Britain than it exported, Australia would have to pay the difference by shipping gold to Great Britain. What would eliminate the Australian balance of payment deficit and Great Britain's balance of payments surplus to ensure that Australia wouldn't eventually lose all its gold to Great Britain?

When Australia ran a payments deficit, the nation's money supply, its gold stock, would decrease while that of its trading partner, Great Britain, would increase. Every time an Australian bought British goods, dollars (Australian currency) would be turned in to the Australian Treasury in exchange for gold. The gold would then be shipped to Great Britain and exchanged at the British Treasury for the pounds needed to pay British exporters. Similarly, every time a British citizen bought Australian goods, pounds (British currency) would be turned in to the British Treasury in exchange for gold. The gold would then be shipped to Australia and exchanged at the Australian Treasury for the dollars needed to pay Australian exporters. If Australians bought more from the British than the British bought from Australians, more gold would be flowing out of Australia than was flowing into it. The reverse would be true of Great Britain — more gold would be flowing in than out. Hence, Great Britain's money supply would increase while that of Australia would decrease.

Now recall the effect of money supply changes on an economy, as discussed in previous chapters. If Great Britain's money supply was increasing, this change in the money supply would increase its total demand and income. Its price level

would tend to rise and its interest rates to fall. As prices of its goods rose, they would become more expensive for Australians and lead to a reduction of Australian imports from Britain. Similarly, the fall in British interest rates would make British securities less attractive, so that Australian purchases (imports) of such securities would decline. At the same time, the rise in Britain's total demand and income would tend to stimulate its imports — its purchases of Australian goods and services. All of these factors would amount to a reduction in Australian payments to Britain and an increase in British payments to Australia. All these factors would work together to reduce the Australian balance of payments deficit and decrease Great Britain's payments surplus.

Consider what would be happening in Australia at the same time. The Australian money supply would be decreasing, reducing its total demand and income. This would put downward pressure on its price level. The reduction in its money supply would also tend to push Australian interest rates up. To the extent Australian prices fell, British citizens would find Australian goods cheaper and would therefore buy more of them. Similarly, higher interest rates would lead British citizens to step up their purchases of Australian securities. Finally, the reduction in total demand and income would tend to reduce Australian imports of British goods. Again, all these factors would contribute to an increase in Britain's payments to Australia and a reduction in Australian payments to Britain.

In short, the Australian balance of payments deficit and the British payments surplus would automatically set in motion forces that would reduce Australia's payments deficit and Britain's payments surplus. And, as long as an Australian payments deficit and a British payments surplus exist, these forces would continue to operate until both the deficit and the surplus were eliminated. At that point, the flow of gold to Australia from Britain would exactly equal the flow of gold from Australia to Britain. Balance of payments equilibrium would be restored.

To summarise, *under a gold standard nations with balance of payments deficits would lose gold to nations with balance of payments surpluses. The increase in the money supplies of the surplus nations would tend to push up their price levels, reduce their interest rates, and increase their imports from deficit nations. The decrease in the money supplies of the deficit nations would tend to reduce their price levels, increase their interest rates, and reduce their imports from surplus nations. This process would continue until balance of payments equilibrium in all nations was restored.*

Shortcomings of the Gold Standard

The major difficulty with a gold standard is that balance of payments adjustments operate through interest rate, output, employment, and price level adjustments in each nation. Deficit nations may have to suffer recession and high rates of unemployment, while surplus nations experience unanticipated inflation with all the gains and losses that this bestows arbitrarily on different citizens. In short, domestic goals, such as the maintenance of high employment and output, as well as price stability, are completely at the mercy of the balance of payments adjustment process. Most economists feel that this amounts to letting the tail wag the dog.

Moreover, gold discoveries, which can happen at any time, can cause haphazard increases in money supplies and inflation. Conversely, a lack of gold discoveries can result in money supply growth lagging behind worldwide economic growth. Consequently, tightening money supply conditions may trigger recessions and put a damper on economic growth.

Demise of the Gold Standard

The Great Depression of the 1930s was the undoing of the gold standard. Many nations, faced with high unemployment, resorted to protectionist measures, imposing import tariffs and quotas and exchange controls (regulations that make it difficult to exchange domestic for foreign currency). Through such measures each hoped to stimulate sagging output and employment at home by maintaining exports and reducing imports. Clearly, this was no more possible than for each participant in a footrace to run faster than everyone else. In percentage terms, world trade fell even more than world output.

As the worldwide depression deepened, nation after nation had cause to fear that if its economy began to recover while those of its trading partners remained depressed, its imports would increase while its exports remained low. Under a gold standard such a nation would lose gold, and the resulting contraction of its money supply would drag its economy back into depression. This consideration, combined with the desire to stimulate exports, led nations to devalue their currencies in terms of gold throughout the 1930s. The resolve to keep the rates of exchange between national monetary units and ounces of gold permanently fixed (and hence permanently fix rates of exchange between currencies) — the essence of an orthodox gold standard — had been broken. This state of affairs persisted until the end of World War II.

The Bretton Woods System

In 1944 the industrial nations of the world sent representatives to the small town of Bretton Woods, New Hampshire in the United States of America, to establish a new international financial system for international trade. They set up a system of fixed exchange rates with the dollar serving as the key currency. That is, the United States agreed to buy and sell gold at $35 per ounce, while the other nations agreed to buy and sell dollars so as to fix their exchange rates at agreed-upon levels. Hence, all currencies were indirectly tied to gold. For example, someone holding marks could exchange them for dollars at a fixed exchange rate and then exchange the dollars for gold in the United States.

The agreements seemed a logical way to set up the new system for two reasons. First, the United States had the most gold reserves. Second, the war-ravaged economies of Europe viewed the dollar as soundly backed by the productive capacity of the American economy. Other nations such as Australia held a similar view. The **Bretton Woods system** (sometimes called the *gold exchange system*) clearly reflected a widespread belief that international trade would function better under a fixed exchange rate system than under one of flexible rates. It also reflected an age-old belief that money should be backed by a precious metal such as gold.

Establishment of the International Monetary Fund (IMF)

Recall from our earlier discussion of fixed exchange rates that if a nation's currency is fixed above the free-market equilibrium level, it will lose holdings of official reserves. When these are gone, it simply has to devalue its currency. The International Monetary Fund (IMF) was established to deal with this problem, as well as to supervise and manage the new system in general. Member nations were required to contribute funds to the IMF. Then to bolster its ability to keep exchange rates fixed, the IMF was given the authority to lend these funds to member nations running out of reserves. For example, if the British government used up its dollar reserves purchasing pounds to fix the dollar price of pounds above the free-market equilibrium level, the IMF would lend Britain dollars to continue its support operations. The situation should be temporary, and Britain eventually should earn enough dollars in world trade to repay the IMF. A nation would be allowed to devalue relative to the dollar only if its currency were chronically overvalued, so that it continually ran a balance of payments deficit.

Problems with the Bretton Woods System

We have already examined some of the major problems that plague a fixed exchange rate system. All of these troubled the Bretton Woods system until its demise in 1971. Nations often had to compromise their domestic policy goals out of concern for balance of payments considerations. The burden of adjustment usually fell on the nations with overvalued currencies and balance of payments deficits. They often had to pursue more restrictive fiscal and monetary policies to curb total demand and income in order to reduce their imports. Deficit nations also had to devalue their currencies more often than surplus nations revalued. Deficit nations were the ones borrowing from the IMF and 'allegedly' the source of difficulty. In addition, as it became more apparent that a currency would have to be devalued, the day of reckoning was hastened by those selling the currency to beat the fall in the exchange rate. Was a world of such sudden readjustments really more conducive to international trade than a world of flexible exchange rates? Was the uncertainty surrounding such abrupt adjustments really less than the uncertainty that would exist under flexible exchange rates? These questions were often raised.

The End of the Bretton Woods System

As the postwar period unfolded into the 1960s, the fixed levels of exchange rates established after World War II became increasingly out of line with the levels that would give balance of payments equilibrium in most countries. Fixed exchange rate levels established when the Japanese and European economies were still suffering from the ravages of war became increasingly unrealistic as these nations recovered and became more competitive internationally. As a result, during the 1960s the dollar became increasingly overvalued and the United States ran chronic and growing balance of payments deficits. At the same time countries such as Germany and Japan ran chronic balance of payments surpluses as their currencies were increasingly undervalued. They found themselves continually accepting dollar claims (IOUs) from the United States. In the meantime the United States lost more than half of its gold stock. More and more foreigners became nervous about holding overvalued dollars and forced the United States to honour its commitment to exchange gold for dollars at $35 per ounce.

What could be done? The dollar, the key currency of the system, was overvalued. The United States was not willing to sacrifice domestic policy goals, such as high employment, to reduce its payments deficit. Countries with undervalued currencies often found it difficult to revalue (increase the dollar price of their currencies) because their politically powerful export industries would lose sales as their goods became more expensive to foreign customers. Finally, in 1971 the United States government announced that it would no longer buy and sell gold. The link between gold and the dollar was broken and the era of the Bretton Woods system was over.

Flexible Exchange Rates and Managed Floats

Despite initial attempts by the industrial nations to restore fixed exchange rates in late 1971, the international financial system has become a mixture of flexible exchange rates and managed floats. Some nations have allowed their exchange rates to float freely. Many others operate a **managed float**, a system whereby exchange rates are largely allowed to float but are subject to occasional government intervention. For example, a nation with an overvalued currency may from time to time use its holdings of foreign reserves to buy its own currency, thus easing its rate of depreciation. Such a managed exchange rate policy is sometimes termed a *dirty float*. In the spirit of Bretton Woods, some countries still attempt to peg their exchange rate more or less to the dollar.

Between 1971 and 1983 Australia followed a managed exchange rate policy. This took a number of forms but invariably it involved the Reserve Bank intervening in the market to stabilise the

POLICY PERSPECTIVE

Does the J Curve Apply in Australia?

If a country devalues its currency this makes its exports cheaper to foreigners and imports are more expensive. Providing that inflation remains under control, balance of payments deficit problems will often subside. This is especially so as long as demand for the country's exports is reasonably elastic and its demand for imports is similarly elastic. A problem may arise in the short run, however, when the exchange rate falls. It takes foreigners some time to recognise the situation and buy more of our country's exports. Local exporters and producers of import-competing goods will also take time to increase their output and sales. This may lead to an initial worsening of a deficit on current account but eventually the situation will improve. A 'J curve' may result when one plots the current account balance against time on a graph, see Figure P33.1.

FIGURE P33.1
The J-Curve Effect

Current
Account
Balance
as
Percentage
of
GDP

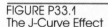

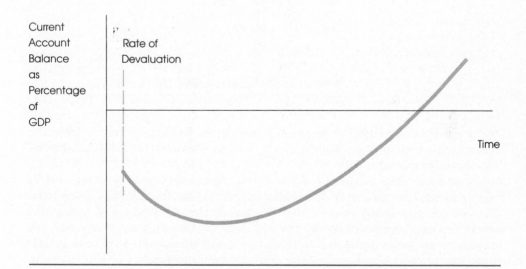

During the first months of 1985, the Australian dollar depreciated dramatically against the currencies of its major trading partners. The trade-weighted index of the Australian dollar against the currencies of its major trading partners, which stood at 80.8 in January 1985 (May 1970 = 100), fell to 64.2 in April 1985 — a drop of more than 20 per cent. It fell again in mid-1986, plunging from 60.7 in May 1986 to 49.3 in July 1987, a further drop of almost 20 per cent.

As can be seen from Figure P33.2 Australia's current account deficit initially increased as a percentage of Gross Domestic Product. While it was 5.3 per cent of GDP in

FIGURE P33.2
Balance on Current Account as Per Cent of GDP — Australia 1985–1987

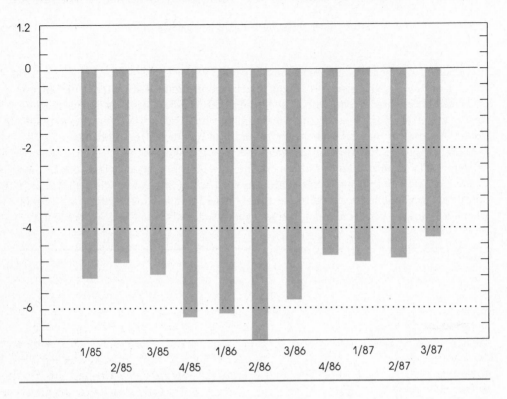

the March quarter of 1985, it rose to 6.8 per cent in the June quarter of 1986. For the next five quarters it gradually declined reaching a level of about 4.1 per cent for the September quarter of 1987.

Casual observation suggests that the J-curve effect seems to be at work. Yet its emergence has been quite slow. It has been impeded by factors such as declining terms of trade for agricultural commodities (affected by the subsidisation of agricultural production and export activity by the EEC and USA), and a run down domestic manufacturing sector during the 1970s so that it has been unable to expand quickly enough to provide substitutes for now expensive imported inputs and final products. A further insight into the J-curve is gained by considering the movement of exports and imports of goods and services during the 1985–87 period. Between the June quarter, 1985 and the September quarter, 1987 the value of Australia's rural exports rose by 3.9 per cent (after allowance for the effects of inflation). Non rural exports rose by 7.8 per cent. Over the same period total imports fell by 1.8 per cent.

Questions

1. When would the J-curve effect occur most quickly after a country devalued its currency? What factors might prevent a J-curve from emerging at all?

2. Why is the J-curve a short-run phenomenon? What would you expect to happen to the balance on current account in a country such as Australia over a longer time period (say 100 years)?

value of the Australian dollar in terms of other currencies. In December 1983 Australia decided that the dollar should float. Since that time our exchange rate has been much more volatile, and also its value has fallen against the currencies of most of our trading partners. Even since 1983 it is apparent that the Reserve Bank intervenes in the market from time to time trying to reduce wild swings in the value of the Australian dollar.

The Declining Role of Gold

What has happened to the role of gold in the international financial system? In 1968, before the link between gold and the dollar was broken, the IMF created a paper substitute called **Special Drawing Rights (SDRs)**. SDRs serve as an official reserve in addition to gold and currency holdings. SDRs are really special accounts at the IMF that can be swapped among member nations in exchange for currencies. Since this is exactly what nations used to do with gold, the SDRs are popularly dubbed 'paper gold'. Unlike gold, however, the IMF can create SDRs whenever it feels more official reserves are needed to meet the financial needs of expanding world trade. In this sense the creation of SDRs to expand official reserves in the world economy is much like a central bank's creation of member bank reserves in a national economy. Since the elimination of the fixed rate of exchange between the dollar and gold in 1971, gold has become more like any other metal bought and sold in world markets. In

recent years both the US Treasury and the IMF have attempted to de-emphasise the importance of gold as money by selling some of their gold holdings.

Adjustment in the New Environment

The 1970s were turbulent years for the world economy. Oil prices quadrupled from 1973 to 1974 and abruptly rose again with the revolution in Iran in 1979. During 1974 and 1975 industrial nations experienced the severest recession since the Great Depression of the 1930s. Inflation emerged as a major problem for a number of nations such as the United States and Australia. And differences in domestic inflation rates between major industrial powers changed over the decade of the 1970s. All these factors required continual readjustment of exchange rates. Many economists feel that the more rigid exchange rate structure of the Bretton Woods system would never have survived these stresses and that the mixture of managed floats and flexible exchange rates has probably served the world economy better.

CHECKPOINT 33.4

Some economists argue that the Bretton Woods system imposed a certain amount of fiscal and monetary discipline on governments that was missing in the world economy of the 1970s and early 1980s. What do they mean?

POLICY PERSPECTIVE

How Could the US Dollar Be So Strong When the Trade Deficit Was So Large?

Since 1981 the United States has experienced a sharp decline in both its current account balance and its balance of trade, or equivalently, a large increase in its current account deficit and its balance of trade deficit, as shown in Figure P33.3. Both the trade and current account deficits exceeded $100 billion by 1985.

Over this same period of time the dollar appreciated steadily against a weighted average of other major currencies until by 1985 its value in terms of these currencies, or the nominal exchange rate, had increased roughly 65 per cent, as shown in Figure P33.4. Even after adjusting for the lower rate of inflation in the United States, the dollar's real value in terms of the average of these other currencies, the real exchange rate, had increased about 60 per cent (see Figure P33.4). In short, relative to 1980, by 1985 the dollar bought 60 per cent more in foreign markets than it did at home.

FIGURE P33.3
Balances on Trade and Current Account

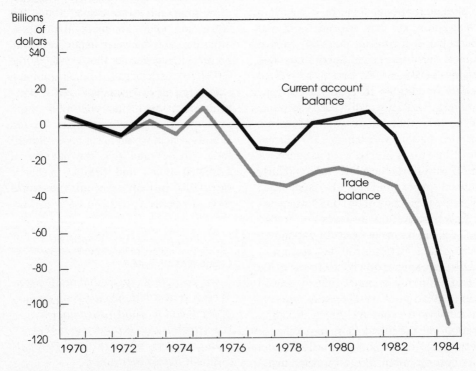

SOURCE: U.S. Department of Commerce.

The Puzzle

Traditionally, an imbalance between exports and imports that produced large current account deficits in an industrialised nation has been regarded as a sign of economic weakness and a reason to expect that nation's currency to depreciate. The traditional view would argue that as US imports get ever larger relative to exports (increasing the current account deficit) the demand for foreign currency by Americans would go up relative to the supply and the dollar would depreciate, as in Figure 33.4 for example.

However, since the dollar was appreciating as the current account deficit increased over the 1980-1985 period, the supply of foreign currency must have been increasing relative to the demand for it — the supply curve of foreign currency was shifting rightward faster than the demand curve. The appreciating dollar made US exports more expensive to foreigners while at the same time it made imports less expensive to Americans. This dampened foreign demand for US exports and increased US demand for imports. Hence it must have been the appreciation of the dollar that *caused* the current account deficit to increase.

The Role of the Capital Account

But what caused the appreciation of the dollar, or equivalently, what caused the supply of foreign currency to increase relative to the demand for it? Recall that corresponding to the current account deficit there must be a matching capital account surplus. Foreigners must invest and lend more in the United States than Americans are investing and lending abroad. The increase in foreigners' desire to lend and invest in the United States by buying dollar securities (American bonds, stocks, and other debt claims and titles of ownership) caused the United States's capital account surplus to increase during the 1980-1985 period. This increased the supply of foreign currency (the demand for dollars) relative to demand for foreign currency (the supply of dollars) and caused the dollar to appreciate, which in turn caused the increase in the current account deficit.

Why Foreign Demand for Dollar Securities Increased

Economists have generally identified four basic reasons why dollar securities became relatively more attractive investments than foreign assets during the 1980-1985 period.

1. *Higher real interest rates in the United States.* Starting in late 1979 US monetary policy tightened significantly, causing a sharp increase in nominal interest rates and a subsequent fall in actual and expected inflation. Consequently US real interest rates moved strongly upward, with a brief interruption in mid-1980, and peaked in 1982. Though they fell somewhat after that, they still remained at relatively high levels. There was also a rise in real interest rates abroad, but because it was less pronounced a positive gap existed between US and foreign real interest rates during most of the 1980-1985 period, as indicated in Figure P33.4. In addition, the Federal Reserve System's commitment to pursuing an inflationary policy continued to reduce the perceived risk of future inflation. This, together with the positive real interest rate gap, increased the attractiveness of dollar securities.

FIGURE P33.4
Nominal and Real Exchange Rates and Expected Real Interest Differential

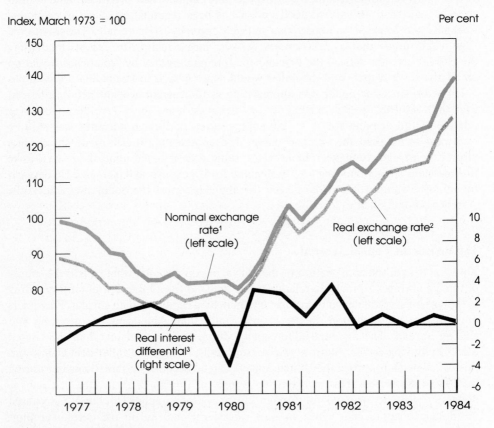

Index, March 1973 = 100   Per cent

¹ Multilateral trade-weighted dollar.
² Nominal exchange rate adjusted by relative consumer prices.
³ US interest rate (3-month) minus trade-weighted average interest rate (also 3-month) for six industrial countries adjusted by corresponding OECD inflation forecasts.

SOURCE: *Economic Report of the President*, 1985, p. 104.

2. *Higher after-tax rates of return on US investments after 1981.* The Economic
Recovery and Tax Act of 1981, together with the reduced rate of inflation, substantially
reduced the effective tax rate on income earned on investments in plant and equipment.
This increased the after-tax real rate of return on business investment in the United
States and was reflected in higher real rates of return on dollar-dominated assets generally.
At the same time, Europe's sluggish economic performance and high wage rates squeezed
pre-tax profitability in Europe to levels that appear to have been well below those
in the United States. Taken together, these developments also tended to make dollar
securities more attractive relative to foreign securities.

3. *The US government budget deficit.* Many economists argue that a principal cause
of the high real rate of return on dollar securities has been, and will continue to

be, the large federal government budget deficits. The budget deficit constitutes a large portion of the demand for funds provided by the net savings generated in the US economy by households, businesses, pension funds, and state and local governments. The real rate of interest has had to rise to balance the supply and demand for these funds by dampening private investment and by attracting a capital inflow from abroad, as reflected in the balance of payments surplus on the capital account. During the 1980–1985 period the expanded US budget deficit was accompanied by a monetary policy that curbed inflation. The increased budget deficits accompanied by a generally sound monetary policy brought the expected inflation rate down while raising the real interest rate.

4. *The strength of the US economy.* The three factors listed above do not account for all of the increased attractiveness of dollar securities to foreigners. The fact that the dollar has appreciated steadily, while the real interest rate gap in favour of the dollar has narrowed since 1982, suggests other factors also contributed to the increased demand for dollar securities. The robust US economic recovery from the 1982 recession (relative to the sluggish performance of the European economies), the sharp reduction of the US inflation rate, and the increased after-tax profitability of US businesses all contributed to more favourable apparent longer-run prospects for the US economy. All of these developments combined probably prompted additional demand for dollar securities based on confidence in the growing strength of the US economy relative to many of the other industrialised economies.

Questions

1. Explain why it is claimed that the behaviour of the US capital account, rather than that of the current account, caused the appreciation of the dollar during the 1980–1985 period.

2. Explain why foreigners found dollar securities so attractive during the 1980–1985 period.

SUMMARY

1. International trade has a monetary aspect because trade between nations requires the exchange of one nation's currency for that of another. A nation's exports of goods, services, and financial obligations (IOUs) give rise to a demand for its currency and a supply of foreign currencies in the foreign exchange market. A nation's imports of goods, services, and financial obligations give rise to a supply of its currency and a demand for foreign currencies in the foreign exchange market.

2. A nation's balance of payments is an accounting statement that itemises its total payments to other nations and the total payments it receives from other nations. This statement reflects the fact that total payments to other nations must be equal to (or balanced by) total payments received from other nations.

3. A nation has a balance of payments deficit when its government must draw on its official reserves, issue liquid claims (to other nations) on these reserves, or both, to finance an excess of payments to cover payments from other nations. A balance of payments surplus occurs when payments received exceed payments to

other nations, so that the government receives official reserves and liquid claims from other nations to finance the difference.

4. The forces of supply and demand automatically adjust flexible, or floating, exchange rates to eliminate balance of payments deficits and surpluses. They do this by changing the relative attractiveness of goods, services, and assets between nations. Flexible exchange rates tend to adjust to reflect differential rates of inflation and changes in relative interest rate levels between nations.

5. Exchange rates can be fixed, or pegged, only if governments intervene in foreign exchange markets to buy and sell currencies. Fixed exchange rates give rise to balance of payments deficits and surpluses. Under fixed exchange rates deficits can be eliminated either by currency devaluation or by pursuing a restrictive fiscal and monetary policy to curb total demand and income. Conversely, surpluses can be eliminated either by revaluation or by an expansionary fiscal and monetary policy. Devaluation and revaluation are often resisted because of political considerations.

6. Critics contend that in practice a fixed exchange rate system tends to be biased toward forcing contractionary fiscal and monetary policies on nations with overvalued currencies. Advocates of fixed exchange rates argue that the uncertainty about future levels of flexible exchange rates tends to put a damper on international trade. Advocates of flexible exchange rates respond that it is possible to hedge against much of this uncertainty by entering into futures contracts. Moreover, they note, fixed exchange rates are not immune to uncertainty — namely, uncertainty about currencies that are

likely to be devalued to eliminate chronic balance of payments deficits.

7. The gold standard has provided a system of fixed exchange rates in the past. However, balance of payments adjustments under this system often require severe changes in employment, income, and prices, thus sacrificing domestic policy objectives to balance of payments equilibrium.

8. The Bretton Woods system provided the financial framework for international trade from 1944 to 1971. Under this system nations fixed their exchange rates in terms of the dollar, the key currency, which was convertible into gold at a fixed rate of exchange maintained by the United States. The International Monetary System (IMF) was established to supervise the system, to lend official reserves to nations with temporary payments deficits, and to decide when exchange rate adjustments were needed to correct chronic payments deficits. The system eventually foundered in 1971 due to chronic and rising US payments deficits that led to growing concern about the dollar's continued convertibility into gold.

9. Since the demise of the Bretton Wood system, the international financial system has been a mixture of flexible exchange rates, managed floats, and continued attempts to fix some exchange rates in terms of the dollar.

KEY TERMS AND CONCEPTS

balance of payments
balance of payments account
balance of payments deficit
balance of payments surplus
balance on merchandise trade
balance on capital account
balance on current account

balance on goods and services
Bretton Woods system
currency appreciation
currency depreciation
currency devaluation
currency revaluation
exchange rate
flexible (or floating) exchange rate
foreign exchange market
gold standard
managed float
Special Drawing Rights (SDRs)

QUESTIONS AND PROBLEMS

1. When a nation has a balance of payments deficit, would you say it is exporting or importing official reserves and liquid claims? Why?

2. Tell whether each of the following generates a demand for foreign currency (any currency other than dollars) or a supply of foreign currency on foreign exchange markets.

a. A German firm builds a manufacturing plant in Victoria.

b. A British firm transfers a million dollars from its bank account in a major Australian bank to its bank account in a major British bank.

c. The Australian government makes a foreign aid grant to Papua-New Guinea.

d. An Australian firm transports goods from Sydney to Perth on a Liberian freighter.

e. Belgium has a balance of payments deficit in its transactions with Australia.

f. An Australian's French government bond matures.

3. Suppose you observe the following exchange rates: 5 French francs exchange for $1, 4 German marks exchange for $1, and 3 French francs exchange for 2 German marks.

a. Can you think of a way to make money out of this situation?

b. What would you expect to happen if exchange rates were flexible?

c. What would you expect to happen if exchange rates were fixed at these levels?

4. How would a nation's exchange rate likely be affected by each of the following, all other things remaining the same?

a. The nation's trading partners start to pursue relatively more expansionary monetary policies.

b. The nation increases its imports.

c. The nation experiences a decline in the growth of productivity relative to that of its trading partners, thus weakening its competitive position in the world economy.

d. The nation cuts its income taxes.

e. The nation has a recession.

f. The nation steps up its advertising about its tourist attractions.

5. Suppose Great Britain and the United States were the only two trading nations in the world. Suppose also that the exchange rate between pounds and dollars is fixed so that pounds are overvalued in terms of dollars. Furthermore, suppose Britain decides to let its currency float but the United States wants to keep the dollar pegged. Will Britain lose dollar reserves? What will the United States get for its efforts? Which country gets the 'better deal' out of this situation and why?

6. Explain why exchange rates are fixed under a gold standard and describe how balance of payments adjustments take place. Explain why you never hear about balance of payments adjustment problems between Western Australia and New South Wales, Tasmania and Victoria or between any other Australian states. How does balance of payments adjustment take place between the states? How has balance of payments adjustment occurred between working class neighbourhoods and middle class suburbia?

7. Compare and contrast a gold standard with the Bretton Woods system. Given that both operate under a system of fixed exchange rates, why could there be persistent balance of payments deficits and surpluses under the Bretton Woods system but not under a gold standard?

34

Comparative Economic Systems

AFTER READING THIS CHAPTER YOU WILL BE ABLE TO:

1. List the four basic features of any economic system.

2. Describe capitalism, market socialism, and planned socialism in terms of their four basic features.

3. Outline the ideological differences among the three main variants of socialism: Communism, social democracy, and third world socialism.

4. Summarise the performance of socialist countries with regard to economic performance, liberty and individual freedom, quality of life, and equality.

5. Outline socialism's basic criticisms of capitalism and capitalism's responses to these criticisms.

6. Describe and contrast the economic systems of China and Yugoslavia as examples of planned and market socialism.

There is a wide variety of ways of organising an economy to answer the basic questions of what and how much to produce, how to organise production, and for whom to produce. In this book we have focused almost exclusively on the mixed capitalist economy, where households and firms rely largely on markets to answer these questions, assisted by government intervention when it is considered necessary to improve upon the results. Australia, Britain, New Zealand, the United States, West Germany, Japan, and Canada are good examples of such economies.

But what about the rest of the world? The economic systems of many countries differ markedly from the mixed capitalist economies with which we are familiar. Moreover, these countries deal with the basic economic problem of scarcity — and the questions it poses — in a way that often reflects a quite different vision of the relationship between the individual and society. The various economic systems thus to a large extent reflect different political ideologies. A comparison of the relative merits of differing economic systems cannot avoid an examination of differing political ideologies.

In this chapter we will examine other types of economic systems and compare them with the mixed capitalist economy already more familiar to us. We will begin by considering the basic features that describe any economic system. This will be of help in our examination of the major classifications of economic systems. We will then consider the ways in which particular political ideologies and types of economic systems tend to be related. Finally, to illustrate how socialist systems have worked in practice, we will look briefly at the economies of China and Yugoslavia.

Before we begin, a word of caution is in order. Any attempt to classify the economic systems of different countries into broad categories, such as 'communistic' or 'socialistic' or 'capitalistic', is bound to hide a great variety of differences between them. Such broad classifications are meant to identify economic systems only insofar as they may share, or not share, certain basic characteristics. However, countries may differ in a variety of ways not revealed by simple labels: property may be owned privately or by the state; decision making may be in the hands of a few or of many; decisions may be coordinated by the market or by a plan; incentives may be material, moral, or due to threats of force. These and other possible variations should be kept in mind when the economic systems of different countries are compared — even those that might be classified under the same broad label.

DEFINING AND COMPARING ECONOMIC SYSTEMS

Most people would agree that the United States has a capitalistic economy and the Soviet Union a socialistic economy. But what do these labels mean? What do they say about the operation of an economic system? To find out, we will look at four basic features of economic systems and use them to develop some broad categories of systems. Later, we will see that these categories are more in the nature of idealisations than descriptions of actual economic systems.

Basic Features of Economic Systems

When we speak of a country's economy, we mean its particular form of organisation for the production, distribution, and consumption of goods and services by its citizens. We often refer to an economy as an *economic system* when we want to focus on its organisational features. Quite generally, an **economic system** *consists of the institutions, rules, and decision-making processes that a country uses to organise and allocate its scarce resources to produce and distribute goods and services*. A complete description of a country's economic system would require an understanding of the ways in which its institutions, organisations, laws, rules, values, traditions, beliefs, and basic political ideology affect economic behaviour and outcomes.

Obviously, each country's economic system may differ from that of every other country in a number of ways. But do all economic systems have certain basic features that allow them to be classified into only two or three broad categories of systems? Does it make sense to speak of an economic system as being 'capitalistic' or 'socialistic'? We all know it is common practice to simplify in this way — in the news media and in casual and even learned discussions. It is, in fact, also reasonable. Economists often focus on four features of a country's economic system. Based on these four features, the country may be classified as representative of a basic type of economic system. These features are:

1. the decision-making process;
2. the mechanism for providing information and coordinating activities;
3. property rights; and
4. incentives to performance.

Some economists argue that there are other important features, such as a country's level of economic development.

There is certainly room for debate. Nonetheless, it is generally recognised that the four features just listed are crucial to any description of an economic system. Moreover, the details of these four features often differ considerably from one country to another; the differences provide a basis for comparing the economic systems of various countries. In addition, similarities of features are useful in classifying economic systems according to broadly defined types, such as capitalistic or socialistic. Let us examine each feature more closely.

Decision-Making Process: Centralised or Decentralised

Perhaps the most important characteristic of an economic system's decision-making process is its degree of centralisation or decentralisation. *Decision making is said to be centralised to the extent that the authority to make decisions is concentrated in the hands of a few at the upper levels of an economic system's organisational structure. Decision making is decentralised to the extent that such authority is spread among many at the lower levels of the organisational structure.*

Centralised economic decision making is characteristic of command, or planned, economic systems, in which government planning boards dictate how to organise production, what and how much to produce, and for whom. China and the Soviet Union and its East bloc satellites provide examples, to varying degrees, of centralised economic decision making. On the other hand, decentralised decision making is characteristic of economic systems in which decisions are made primarily by individual households and firms interacting through a network of markets, with limited government direction and interference. Australia, New Zealand, the United States, Japan, Canada, and the Western European countries provide examples of decentralised economic decision making.

Of course, the extent to which decision making is centralised or decentralised can vary widely. The decision-making process is completely (perfectly) centralised if decision-making authority rests solely in a single command unit that issues orders to all lower units in the economy. In less extreme cases some decision-making authority is granted to subunits at different levels within the economy. As more decision-making authority is granted to lower economic units, the economy tends more toward decentralisation. Finally, if all decision-making authority rests with the lowest subunits in the economic structure (with individual households and firms, say), independent of higher levels of authority, the decision-making process is completely decentralised. This is the other end of the spectrum from complete centralisation. In sum, *an economic system can be characterised as centralised or decentralised according to the extent to which decision-making authority is distributed among the various units, subunits, and levels of the system's organisational structure.*

Mechanism for Providing Information and Coordination: Plan or Market

In today's world, the two commonest mechanisms for providing information and coordinating decisions in economic systems are the plan and the market.

An economic *plan*, designed by a central planning board, is used in so-called **planned economies** to inform, direct, and coordinate the economic activities of subunits such as firms. Details may vary, but generally in a planned economy economic activity is guided by instructions devised by higher units and handed down to lower units in the organisational structure. A variety of incentives may be used to encourage or compel the subunits to operate according to instructions derived from the plan. Economies that are popularly called planned can in fact vary considerably. For example, the Soviet Union and Yugoslavia are planned economies. Yet planning is more centralised in the Soviet Union. Yugoslavia relies to a significant extent on a combination of planning and market mechanisms.

The *market* mechanism, the interaction of demand and supply on prices, provides information signals that direct subunits to make resource allocation decisions in a **market economy**. A network of markets thereby coordinates the activities of different decision-making units in the system. For example, households earn income by providing land, labour, and capital to the system, and with this income they generate demand in the market-place to which firms respond in pursuit of profit. In other words, the subunits — firms and households — work through and respond to the market.

A central issue in the comparison of economic systems is the relative merits of the planning versus the market mechanism. The contrast is apparent in that a planned economy allocates resources through the instructions of planners, thereby replacing the market's role as an allocator of resources. It is commonly argued that in a market economy there is **consumer sovereignty**, which is exercised by consumer 'votes' in the market-place. That is, the basic decisions about what to produce (which products and services) and how much are dominated by consumers. By contrast, planners' preferences dominate in a planned economy, since the important decisions about what and how much to produce are made by planners.

In fact, complete consumer sovereignty in the market economy and complete planner dominance in the planned economy are extremes not typically observed in reality. Planners often feel compelled to consider consumer preferences (say for more TV sets as opposed to more tanks) at least to some degree, perhaps for political reasons or to promote morale or provide incentives. And in market economies, advertising and the market power of large corporations tend to reduce the degree to which consumer sovereignty actually dictates resource allocation. Moreover, in market economies governments typically have considerable influence over the mix of goods and services actually produced. For example, in Australia, federal, state, and local government expenditures account for roughly 40 per cent of total spending in the economy.

Property Rights: Who Owns What?

The nature of property ownership arrangements has traditionally been the main feature used to classify economic systems.

The popular image of socialism, and even more so of Communism, is that the state or government owns the means of production: land, raw materials, and capital. Socialists often argue that since the state represents its citizens, the people 'collectively' own the means of production through the state. In the Soviet Union the government does indeed own all the principal means of production: factories, railways, airlines, raw materials, and so forth. But even the Soviet Union allows

citizens some limited ownership of the means of production in areas such as agriculture, retail trade, and housing.

At the other extreme, the popular view of capitalism holds that citizens, individually and collectively (through partnerships and corporations), own the means of production. Yet even in the capitalistic Australia, where private ownership is dominant, government owns the postal service, the railways, bus services, and airlines, some banks, power production facilities, public schools and universities, highways, libraries, national parks, bridges, fire and police protection equipment, numerous public buildings, and the means for waging war.

Ownership patterns will differ from one economic system to another. For example, Great Britain does not have as much government ownership of industry as the Soviet Union, but it does have more than the United States. However, the most important point is that differences in ownership rights affect economic outcomes in complex ways. For instance, Soviet agricultural productivity is lower than that of Australia. It is often argued that this is because Soviet farm workers have less incentive to work state-owned collective farms to meet state quotas, than Australian farmers have to work their own farms to make a profit for themselves. Differences in ownership lead to differences in decision making, incentives, motivation, and goals, and these lead to differences in outcomes, such as the distribution of income.

Incentives: Material or Moral

Another important feature of an economic system is the nature of the rewards and incentives that motivate people to work in the system. Capitalistic, market-oriented societies rely mainly on the monetary or material incentives provided by wages and profits. Such a system of *material incentives* promotes desirable behaviour by giving a larger claim over material goods to those who perform better than others.

Socialist societies rely more on *moral incentives*, which promote desirable behaviour by appealing to the citizen's sense of responsibility to society. For example, a worker may be awarded a medal in the name of the state for outstanding performance on the job. Note that moral incentives, unlike monetary incentives, do not provide more productive citizens with greater command over material goods.

Nowadays the authorities in most socialistic economic systems seem to recognise that material incentives are needed, that people will not respond to moral incentives alone. The early idealism of the Communist Revolution in Russia held that the state would take 'from each according to his ability' and give 'to each according to his needs'. But experience has taught that the hardworking and able are typically not willing to settle for the same rewards received by people of lesser motivation and talent. Attempts to reward all workers equally tend to dampen the motivation of the more able and potentially harder-working members of society.

Classifications of Economic Systems

The four basic features may be used to distinguish a few broad classifications of economic systems. Suppose we consider three: capitalism, planned socialism, and market socialism. It is important to realise in this discussion that there is no general agreement on three as the appropriate number of classifications. For example, it might be argued that the classification 'capitalism' could be further subdivided according to the extent of the role played by government.

Table 34.1 shows how our three classifications of economic systems are distinguished by particular combinations of the four features. Elaborating on the table, we may define these economic systems as follows.

Capitalism. Decision making is decentralised and is done by households and firms. The market mechanism provides information for decision making and coordinates economic activities. Perhaps the most frequently cited characteristic of capitalism is private ownership of the factors of production. Material incentives such as wages and profits are the primary incentives.

Market socialism. Decision-making authority is mainly decentralised, with information and coordination provided largely by the market mechanism. Ownership of land and capital resides principally with the state. Economic units are motivated to achieve goals by both material and moral incentives.

Planned socialism. Decision-making authority is mainly centralised and economic activities are coordinated by a central plan. The factors of production are owned by the state. Economic units are motivated to achieve planned goals by both material and moral incentives.

No real-world economic system fits any one of these definitions exactly. The definitions merely describe what might be considered the most important characteristics of three generally recognised types of economic systems. We will consider real-world examples of planned socialism and market socialism later in this chapter.

TABLE 34.1
A Classification of Economic Systems

	Decision-Making Process	Information and Coordination Mechanism	Property Rights	Incentives
Capitalism	Decentralised	Market	Mainly private	Mainly material
Market Socialism	Mainly decentralised	Mainly market	State or collective ownership or both	Material and moral
Planned Socialism	Mainly centralised	Mainly plan	Mainly state ownership	Material and moral

*CHECKPOINT *34.1*

Do you think there is any relationship between an economic system's property rights arrangements and its system of incentives? Explain.

*Answers to all Checkpoints can be found at the back of the text.

SOCIALISM: VARIATIONS, RECORD, AND CAPITALIST RIVALRY

We noted at the outset that any economic system is, to a large extent, a reflection of a political ideology. Let's turn now to a consideration of the ideology of socialism, its general record of economic performance, and the pros and cons of the socialist and capitalist points of view.

There is no universal model of socialism. Socialism is an ideology that has been adopted in one form or another by a variety of countries ranging from Western-style democracies to repressive Communist dictatorships, from constitutional republics to hereditary monarchies. Despite this diversity, socialists of whatever stripe share several beliefs. One is the conviction that if the means of production

remain under the complete control of private owners, workers will be exploited. It was Karl Marx (1818–1883) who originally made the accusation that capitalism turned labour into a commodity and thus exploited and dehumanised workers while enriching bourgeois owners. Another socialist principle is egalitarianism, the notion that all should share equally in the fruits of production. A closely related socialist belief is that people live for society, or, in a more extreme form, that the individual exists to serve the state — as opposed to the more capitalistic idea that the state exists to serve the individual.

We will briefly consider the main political forms of socialism in today's world, the overall experience of countries living under socialism, and the most often heard socialist criticisms of capitalism.

Socialism in Today's World

Although it may take on many forms, socialism in today's world is recognisable in three main political varieties: Communism, social democracy, and third world socialism. We emphasise that these are *political* classifications, as distinct from the two *economic* classifications of socialism — market socialism and planned

---

ECONOMIC THINKERS

Karl Marx — 1818-1883

Karl Marx combined his abilities as a philosopher, sociologist, historian, economist, and professional revolutionary to become the chief founder of revolutionary Communism. His criticisms of capitalism and prophecies of its downfall have inspired socialist movements and Communist revolutions throughout the world. Marx and his lifelong benefactor and collaborator Friedrich Engels published the *Communist Manifesto* in 1848, the most succinct statement of Marxist ideas, as well as the best-known declaration of the principles of the international Communist movement.

Marx's most complete and celebrated work is *Das Kapital,* the first volume of which was published in 1867; the second and third volumes were edited and published posthumously by Engels. In *Das Kapital* Marx described and analysed what he considered to be the historically inevitable transition from capitalism to socialism. According to Marx, society's beliefs, laws, and ideologies reflect and are shaped by the material conditions of life and the material interests of different classes. Marx argued that the production process under capitalism inevitably gives rise to a division of labour that results in two classes — a ruling class, the capitalists who own the means of production, and an oppressed class, the workers who are exploited by the capitalists. Indeed, Marx claimed that all history could be viewed as a struggle between the ruling and the working classes. Capitalism would be but one stage in that conflict.

Marx argued that private ownership of the means of production under capitalism was the heart of the class conflict. Moreover, he claimed that capitalism would experience severe periods of depression and inflation that, coupled with an increasing class consciousness among workers, would lead to capitalism's collapse. The collapse would take place when the *proletariat* (working class) revolted against the *bourgeoisie* (owners of the means of production, the capitalists). Then, Marx claimed, man would be truly free. The means of production would be publicly owned by the whole community, and there would be a classless society. Even the government, formerly used to oppress the working class, would become unnecessary and 'wither away'. In the new classless, Communist society, individuals would contribute 'according to their ability' and take 'according to their needs'.

Many of Marx's prophecies have not come to pass. Communist revolutions have not occurred in the advanced capitalist societies, as Marx predicted, but rather in countries with less developed economies such as Russia (1917) and China (1949). Moreover, in advanced capitalist countries the distinction between the owners of the means of production and the working class has become less sharp as the growth of the modern corporation has opened business ownership to masses of small investors. In addition, increased upward and downward social and economic mobility in Western economies has lessened class consciousness. Finally, in the most advanced Communist countries, such as the Soviet Union, the government shows no signs of 'withering away', nor can it be said that these societies are classless. Perhaps Marx's most enduring contribution is his perception of society as a process of continual change, an ongoing struggle for power between competing groups motivated by their particular material interests in the production process.

FOR FURTHER READING

Balinsky, Alexander. *Marx's Economics: Origins and Development.* Lexington, Mass.: Heath, 1970.
Heilbroner, Robert L. *Marxism: For and Against.* New York: Norton, 1980.

socialism. Any one of the three political varieties of socialism may have an economic system that is either market socialism or planned socialism. For example, China and Yugoslavia are both classified politically as Communist countries. Yet the economic system of China generally would be classified as planned socialism, while that of Yugoslavia typically would be classified as market socialism.

Communism

Sometimes called Marxism-Leninism, Communism is the form of socialism governing the Soviet Union and its East bloc satellites, as well as Albania, Cambodia, China, Cuba, Laos, Mongolia, North Korea, Vietnam, and Yugoslavia. Communism is the most totalitarian form of socialism. With a religious zeal, its adherents preach the necessity of class warfare. It calls for a dictatorship of the proletariat (the working class) and the concentration of near total power in a tightly structured party that supposedly represents the revolutionary masses. Communism's ultimate goal is a classless society in which there is no private property and the means of production are owned by the state.

Social Democracy

Social democracy is the most liberal and flexible form of socialism. At various times in the postwar era, social democrats have controlled the governments of Austria, Belgium, Britain, Denmark, Finland, Luxembourg, the Netherlands, Norway, Portugal, and Sweden, to name some European examples. The Australian Labor Party governments also espouse social democratic ideals. Social democracy involves the belief in gradual, peaceful means of reaching socialist goals, and it accepts a multiparty political system. Hence, social democrats have concentrated on removing what they regard as the hardships created by capitalist economies (such as unemployment and 'unjust' wage and salary differences). They are less interested than Communists in restructuring societies according to some utopian blueprint. States ruled by social democrats are generally mixed economies, combining state ownership or direction of key industries with elements of free-enterprise competition and the market mechanism.

Third World Socialism

The term *third world socialism* refers to the variety of socialist regimes that exist among the underdeveloped countries of the world. These include such different systems as the Islamic socialism of Algeria and Libya, the Baathist socialism of Syria and Iraq, and the communalism of tribal Africa. Despite the differences among third world socialist countries, they have several things in common. First, although these countries call themselves socialist, their beliefs may be rooted more in nationalism than in the tenets of traditional Marxism. Second, they reject capitalism, identifying it with imperialism and exploitation, largely because of their experience with the colonialism of capitalist countries. Third, they tend to discourage investment by foreign firms and pursue policies aimed at decreasing the economic role of private property.

The Socialist Experience

What has been the overall experience of countries living under socialism? We can only summarise it briefly here, focusing on such issues as economic performance, the extent of liberty and respect for individual freedom, the general quality of life, and the extent to which socialist countries have achieved the equality of the classless society.

Economic Performance

All socialist countries try to inject order into their economies through government controls or by use of central planning. All reject what they consider the wasteful disorder of the capitalist marketplace. Socialists believe that controls and central planning will give rise to increased output, a more equitable distribution of goods, and a greater concentration of resources in socially useful production.

Communist States. Communist states can point to many significant achievements, which they attribute to their Five-Year Plans and all-embracing command of industry and agriculture. The Soviet Union has made dramatic economic gains, transforming itself in 7 decades from a war-shattered economy in the earliest stages of industrialisation into a military superpower that produces more steel, crude oil, and manganese than the United States. The Chinese Communists seem to be on a similar growth path, and appear to have banished the recurring famines that once plagued that country's vast population.

However, Communist economic systems face serious difficulties. Communist countries claim to have abolished unemployment, but it appears they have succeeded only in hiding it in the form of underemployment — in heavily overstaffed offices and factories, for example, where workers seldom can be sacked for failing to produce, or where workers cannot be kept fully occupied with productive work. Often bureaucratic controls reduce efficiency and leave managers little leeway for innovation. Consumer goods are chronically scarce and typically shoddy. Rumours that a shop is about to receive a shipment of shoes, fresh fruit, or fish often cause long lines to form in Moscow, Warsaw, Prague, Havana, and other Communist cities. Communist countries claim to be immune to inflation. But in fact inflation is merely hidden because wages, prices, and even the kinds of goods available are set by the state. For example, while the 'official' price of a good can remain stable for years, the product may not be available except on the black market, where it sells at a much higher price.

One of the most troublesome problems in Communist countries is lagging agricultural output. Critics argue that agricultural productivity suffers because state ownership of farmland deadens the initiative of farm workers. Hence, despite heavy investment in farm machinery and irrigation systems, food productivity remains low.

In recent years, with the accession of Mr Gorbachev to leadership in the Soviet Union, there have been significant attempts made to change parts of the USSR's economic system to improve its performance. Similar initiatives have been undertaken in most socialist economies, following the Soviet example.

Yugoslavia is the least rigidly controlled economy in Eastern Europe, and it seems to have the fewest economic problems among Communist states. Yugoslav enterprises out-perform the state-owned plants of most other Communist countries. Many observers argue that this is because Yugoslav planning and management have been decentralised. In addition, hard work and quality output have been rewarded with wage increases and generous bonuses.

Social Democracies. Social democrats have mostly come to power in industrially advanced and politically democratic nations. Therefore their efforts to change existing systems — by nationalising industries, for example — have been cautious. Traditionally social democrats have pressed toward their goal of greater income equality by levying steep progressive taxes on income (up to 98 per cent in Britain, 72 per cent in the Netherlands, and 85 per cent in Sweden) and on capital gains, profits, and inheritances. The tax revenues have been used to provide a host of cradle-to-grave benefits, such as nationalised health care. This practice amounts to taking income from those with higher incomes and redistributing it in the form of goods and services to the rest of the citizenry.

However, there are increasing fears that these heavy taxes have begun to discour-age initiative, innovation, and enterprise by reducing the material rewards from work. This shows up in several ways: increased worker absenteeism; the emigration of skilled professionals (such as doctors and engineers), managers, and entrepreneurs to countries with lower tax rates; and increased tax evasion through the use of barter, which leaves no record for snooping tax collectors. In recent years many social democratic governments have introduced taxation reform and other measures to attack these developments. The policies of the Hawke Labor Government in Australia, and the Lange Labour Government in New Zealand provide ample evidence of this.

Social democrats have also weakened some of the traditional rights of property ownership. For example, British and Dutch laws have made it increasingly difficult for management to dismiss workers.

Third World Socialists. Many third world countries have turned to socialism as much from necessity as ideology. Since few of their citizens were able to develop managerial and entrepreneurial skills under colonialism, central planning and socialism often seemed the only way to solve their economic problems once they became independent.

Most third world socialist countries have placed centralised controls on their economies and have nationalised manufacturing, mining, and agriculture. But due to poor management and, often, corruption, the results frequently have been disappointing. While socialist regimes may have aided economic growth in some instances, high population growth rates have made it difficult to increase living standards.

Liberty and Individual Freedom

Socialists have routinely accused capitalism of wage slavery, and of worker exploitation and alienation. They have long claimed that socialism will end these and other forms of repression. However, aside from social democracy, the historical record suggests just the opposite.

Instead of greater liberty, Communism and third world socialism have invariably led to authoritarian one-party and even one-man rule. The Soviet constitution guarantees freedom of speech, but it is in practice not guaranteed at all. Serious critics of the regime are harassed, imprisoned, exiled, and even threatened with execution. Workers' strikes are not allowed. All organs of information and communication are rigidly controlled and used for the purposes of the state. How do Communists justify such human rights violations? They usually argue that the situation is only temporary, that once true Communism is established the dictatorship of the proletariat will disappear and the individual will be truly free. Among some third world socialist countries, the record on liberty and respect for individual freedom is no better than that of Communist countries.

In contrast, the social-democratic governments of Western Europe and elsewhere have consistently shown respect for parliamentary processes and human rights. Nevertheless, certain developments in social democracies pose potentially worrisome threats to liberties. Expanding bureaucracies, spawned by ambitious economic and social programs, threaten to become much larger than those in nonsocialist states. Large bureaucracies represent large concentrations of power that can and often do restrict individual freedom and enterprise. Critics of social-

ism argue that it is surely more than coincidence that the only functioning democracies are the capitalist or mixed-economy countries, while, except for the social democracies, authoritarianism is a fact of life in every socialist country.

General Quality of Life

State-provided social services are a hallmark of socialist regimes. Elaborate programs for improving health care and expanding educational facilities are typically top-priority items in socialist countries. Consequently, in most socialist states, infant mortality has dropped dramatically, life expectancy has risen, and illiteracy has been greatly reduced.

In China, the mass training of doctors, nurses, and paramedics and the establishment of rural health centres have nearly eliminated cholera, plague, and other diseases that had periodically ravaged the population for centuries. When Fidel Castro came to power in Cuba in 1959, nearly one-quarter of the population could not read or write. Since then, illiteracy has been reduced to less than 4 per cent by compulsory primary education and an ambitious school construction program.

The essential human services provided by Communist states often match and sometimes top those of Western democracies. Illness seldom imposes heavy financial burdens on patients. Eastern European states offer free education, though the Communist parties have considerable control over who is admitted to the universities.

The social democracies have provided an extensive array of social services, often referred to collectively as the welfare state. For example, Swedish citizens are given annual allowances for each child, free tuition through university, free hospital care, sick pay equal to 90 per cent of working wages, and a substantial retirement pension. The British Labour party has passed laws that provide maternity allowances, free family planning services, retirement pensions, income supplements, and health care that includes treatment for alcoholism and drug addiction. However, critics of the British health-care system point out that treatment is impersonal and that there are often long waits for admission to hospitals. In Australia, family allowances are available for most children. Education has been free. Medical service, subject to payment of a levy on income, is freely available. Unemployment benefits, old age and other pensions also provide a social security 'safety net'. Yet poverty still exists among a small percentage of our population.

In Communist states, central planning commissions, not consumers, decide what will be produced and how much. As a result, desired consumer goods and services are often scarce. Central planning and government controls give rise to economic inefficiencies that cause bottlenecks in production and shortages of most consumer goods. These difficulties contribute to the corruption, black marketeering, bribery, and theft that are reported to be a considerable problem in Communist states. For example, bribery is a recognised way of avoiding a prolonged wait in buying a car. While medical care is supposed to be free, demand so exceeds supply in some Communist states that it is often necessary to bribe doctors or hospital administrators just to get a bed.

Equality or a New Elite?

A cornerstone of socialist ideology is that capitalism gives rise to an unjust gulf between rich and poor, between the privileged and the downtrodden. Socialism makes a moral commitment to egalitarianism. Has the commitment been realised?

Communism seems to have spawned a kind of class distinction of its own. The new privileged class in Communist states consists of party officials, managers of state enterprises, ranking bureaucrats, and superstars from sports and the arts. This new class receives larger monetary rewards than other citizens. However, because Communist states are often short of certain kinds of goods, the comfortable life-style of the new class depends less on money than on their privileged access to scarce goods and services. In the Soviet Union, various grades of party officials have access to special stores selling imported and otherwise scarce goods at very low prices. Average Soviet citizens never see such a selection of goods in the stores where they must shop. Even supposedly classless China is not exempt from the new elitism. High-ranking Chinese officials have access to special shops, and their children have access to special schools.

Social democracies have pursued egalitarianism by using taxes to redistribute income and wealth. As we have already noted, the tax revenues from inheritance taxes and steeply progressive personal income taxes are used to provide all manner of medical, educational, and other social services to the general citizenry of social democracies.

Socialist Criticisms of Capitalism and the Capitalist Response

Debates over the relative merits of socialism and capitalism are often more emotional than informative. Here we will briefly outline some of socialism's main criticisms of capitalism, along with responses from the capitalist point of view.

Inequalities of Wealth and Income

Socialist critics of capitalism charge that it creates severe inequalities of wealth and extravagantly rewards success.

Capitalism's defenders respond that the inequality of wealth under the free-enterprise system is the unavoidable result of the rewards that must be offered to encourage hard work, risk taking, and genius. They are quick to argue that the equality of results desired by socialist reformers tends to discourage initiative and produce a stagnant society and that, in fact, there is inequality in socialist countries as well. Winston Churchill once put it this way: 'The inherent vice of capitalism is the unequal sharing of blessings; the inherent virtue of socialism is the equal sharing of miseries'.

Capitalist societies have acknowledged some socialist criticism, particularly that large differences in income can be a cause of serious social tensions. Progressive income taxes and social welfare programs are capitalism's way of providing some levelling of income. On the issue of income distribution, capitalism's defenders are quick to point out that Marx's predictions were off the mark. Marx predicted that capitalists would push workers deeper into poverty. But in fact capitalism has lifted the vast majority of workers into the middle class. Moreover, trade unions have given workers an effective counterforce to management power.

Instability of Capitalist Economies

Communism claims that capitalism requires periodic depressions in order to keep workers poor and on the defensive.

The business cycle has always plagued capitalism. However, some defenders of capitalism (such as Joseph Schumpeter) have argued that recessions are often beneficial because they purge the system of excesses, poor products, and mismanaged companies. Moreover, such slumps have been less severe since World War II. In addition, unemployment benefits have greatly reduced the hardship of those thrown out of work.

Assumptions About Human Nature

Socialists have argued that the uncertainty of the marketplace and the social flux associated with capitalism, coupled with the drive for profit, cause people to be overly competitive, warped, and aggressive.

Defenders of capitalism respond that while socialism assumes that people are cooperative and instinctively look out for one another, capitalism has never had any such illusions about human nature. Adam Smith argued that each individual is motivated strongly and primarily by what is in his or her best self-interest. Defenders of capitalism argue that the economic success of capitalist countries lies precisely in the way such an economic system harnesses the self-interest of the individual to promote the general good of all. Advocates of capitalism argue that socialism blunts the powerful force of individual self-interest by stressing equality of reward regardless of performance and by eliminating the private ownership of the means of production.

The Mix of Goods in Capitalist Economies

Critics have charged that a capitalistic market system tends to value wasteful private consumption more than needed public services.

Capitalists respond that the types of goods produced by any economic system raise the fundamental question of who is to direct and dominate whom. Defenders of capitalism argue that the market system provides the most democratic answers. By voting in the marketplace, consumers decide what should be produced, rather than having government planners dictate what society should produce. Nevertheless, even the most capitalistic governments tamper with the market mechanism to some extent, if only to regulate the money supply, set tariffs and import duties, and levy taxes. However, while socialists see the state as the main engine of social change, capitalists view such interference as an unfortunate but necessary compromise with an ideal. But capitalism has had to recognise, to some extent, the demands for social justice advanced by socialism.

Capitalism's Ultimate Defence

Advocates of capitalism argue that its ultimate justification is that it permits and promotes freedom. How? By reserving ownership of the means of production for the private citizen, not the state. Defenders of capitalism argue that freedom is not possible without economic freedom. In the words of Hilaire Belloc, English poet and essayist, 'The control of the production of wealth is the control of human life itself'. According to the defenders of capitalism, history suggests that the more the state attempts to control society, for whatever desirable end, the greater are the ultimate restrictions on individual freedom.

A Spectrum of Real-World Economic Systems

We have noted before that any classification of economic systems, such as that in Table 34.1, is an oversimplification. Nonetheless, most economists agree that real-world economic systems can be characterised as lying along a spectrum between pure, market economy capitalism at one extreme and pure, centrally planned socialism at the other. At any rate, any debate over the pros and cons of capitalism versus socialism that tries to look at the evidence must necessarily construct such a spectrum.

An example is provided in Figure 34.1. The countries indicated are listed along the spectrum according to the degree to which their economic systems tend to be more like one of the extremes — pure, market economy capitalism on the left or pure, centrally planned socialism on the right. Listed beside each country is a number indicating its rank among all countries in the world according to a measure of the country's economic and social conditions.

CHECKPOINT 34.2
What are the main differences between Communism and social democracy?

TWO SOCIALIST COUNTRIES: CHINA AND YUGOSLAVIA

We will now look briefly at two socialist economies: that of China, which is an example of planned socialism, and that of Yugoslavia, an example of market socialism. Politically, these two countries adhere to Communism. The economic system of each will be characterised in terms of the four basic features that we examined at the outset of this chapter: the decision-making process, information and coordination mechanism, property rights, and incentives.

China and Planned Socialism

When the Chinese Communist party came to power in 1949, China was an underdeveloped country with a population about 100 times larger than that of Australia, and a land mass only slightly greater than ours. There was significant population pressure on arable land and other resources. Per capita income was low. Starting with a predominantly rural, peasant economy, the Chinese Commu-

nists have used planned socialism to achieve a substantial degree of economic growth and development.

Rapid industrialisation has been the primary objective of the Chinese Communist regime since the founding of the People's Republic of China by Mao Tsetung in 1949. However, this objective has been pursued jointly with other goals, such as the reeducation of the populace to increase social consciousness and the subordination of the self to the group, the achievement of a more equal distribution of income, and the provision of some guaranteed minimum standard of living for the individual. These social goals have often conflicted with the main goal, rapid industrialisation. And from time to time this conflict has resulted in abrupt shifts

FIGURE 34.1
A Spectrum of Economic Systems and a World Ranking of Selected Countries by Economic and Social Conditions

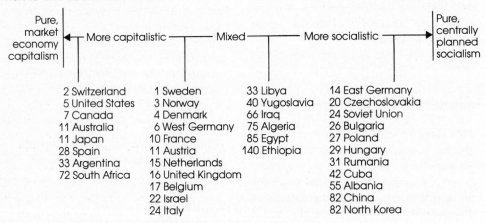

Pure, market economy capitalism	←— More capitalistic ——	Mixed ——	—— More socialistic —→	Pure, centrally planned socialism
	2 Switzerland	1 Sweden	33 Libya	14 East Germany
	5 United States	3 Norway	40 Yugoslavia	20 Czechoslovakia
	7 Canada	4 Denmark	66 Iraq	24 Soviet Union
	11 Australia	6 West Germany	75 Algeria	26 Bulgaria
	11 Japan	10 France	85 Egypt	27 Poland
	28 Spain	11 Austria	140 Ethiopia	29 Hungary
	33 Argentina	15 Netherlands		31 Rumania
	72 South Africa	16 United Kingdom		42 Cuba
		17 Belgium		55 Albania
		22 Israel		82 China
		24 Italy		82 North Korea

The countries shown here are listed along a spectrum according to the degree to which their economic systems tend to be more like pure, market economy capitalism at the one extreme or pure, centrally planned socialism at the other.

The number beside each country indicates its rank among all countries in the world according to a measure of the country's economic and social conditions. Rank is based on average ranks for gross national product per capita, education (encompassing public expenditures per capita, school-age population per teacher, percent school-age population in school, percent women in total university employment, and literacy rate), and health (encompassing public expenditures per capita, population per physician, population per hospital bed, infant mortality rate, and life expectancy).

SOURCE: Ruth Leger Sivard, World Military and Social Expenditures, World Priorities, Inc., Leesburg, Va., 1980.

in policy when it was deemed important to shore up progress toward the social goals — usually following periods of sustained progress toward industrialisation.

Decision-Making Process

Up until October 1984 all major industrial enterprises in China were under central control. In the autumn of 1984 the Chinese Communist party's Central Committee approved a landmark economic plan aimed at a gradual abandonment of Soviet-style central planning. Over the next several years, more than a million state enterprises and factories are to be cut loose from government planning and protection and will rise or fall on their own economic merit. It is still too early to tell how this bold move toward market socialism will actually work, or how quickly it will be implemented. But much of Chinese industry was already decentralised, with control resting with authorities at the provincial and local levels. And the setting of prices was already largely decentralised to the provincial level. In the past both central and provincial authorities have allocated the most important producer goods, such as capital equipment.

The Chinese Communist party plays a large role in the decision-making process throughout the economic system and has often intervened directly in management. But the party's Central Committee communique of October 1984 states that: 'From now on government departments at various levels will, in principle, not manage or operate enterprises directly'. In sum, while the overall system seems basically a command system, there is a fair degree of freedom of action at local levels, coupled with some officially sanctioned use of the market mechanism.

The Soviet system of planned socialism served as the original model for the Chinese Communists. While there is considerable similarity between the organisational and administrative structures of the two countries, the differences suggest that there is more flexibility of organisation and administration in China. In addition, small-scale firms, often using primitive techniques and the large supply of unskilled labour, are much commoner in China than in the Soviet Union. Moreover, in China there seems to be relatively greater freedom of action at local levels and more legal use of the market mechanism. The economic plan approved in 1984 indicates that China will move even further away from the Soviet model of planned socialism.

Information and Coordination Mechanism

The primary information and coordination mechanism in China has been the national economic plan. The Chinese planning structure, initiated in the early 1950s, was patterned after the Soviet model. Experience has led to subsequent modifications. The enterprise is the basic unit of production activity. A dual party-state administrative structure generates and implements a 5-year plan to guide both agricultural and industrial production. Plans are initially formulated by the State Planning Commission. The commission communicates with regional and enterprise officials through an industrial ministry system to arrive ultimately at a final working plan. Then after approval by the State Council (the highest administrative body, directed by the premier), the plan becomes law.

The process of generating a workable

plan is complicated. The State Planning Commission specifies output targets — a list of goods and services to be produced during the plan period. Based on knowledge of the quantities of inputs (land, labour, and capital) required to produce a unit of output, the commission assigns inputs to the production of the various output targets. Obviously, the commission would like to produce as much as possible, but production is limited by the availability of inputs. If sufficient inputs are not available for a particular output target, then either the output target must be reduced or additional inputs must be allocated to that target. When all factor input allocations have been made, there must be an aggregate input balance for the whole economy, termed a *material balance*. That is, the sum of the amounts of all factor inputs needed to produce all output targets must equal the sum of all available factor inputs.

Using both central direction and local information, a material balance eventually is reached. There are difficulties in this process, however. Inevitably, the complexity of the process, coupled with the usual unforeseeable 'breakdowns' of any production activity, gives rise to imbalances and shortages, poor quality, and deviations of results from targets.

Property Rights

State ownership of the means of production predominates in China. The transfer of ownership of economic units began almost immediately after the Chinese Communists seized control in 1949. During the land reform of 1950, the holdings of landlords and some of the holdings of the rich peasants were seized. Some land was distributed to landless labourers and poorer peasants. However,

most of the land was used to establish large collective farms, or communes, owned by the state. The communes each comprised an average of almost 5,000 households. For capital as well, private ownership was largely replaced by state ownership. By 1956, ownership and control in industry, finance, agriculture, and various other production sectors rested with the government.

In 1978 China did an about-face on agricultural policy and began dismantling collectivised farming, restoring family farms and villages, and introducing production and free-market incentives to a rural population of 800 million. Production soared. The policy's success spawned the economic plan of 1984 aimed at applying some of the same types of reforms to the industrial sectors of the economy.

Incentives

While the Soviet Union has served as a model for the Chinese Communists, the Chinese have tended to put more stress on moral incentives as opposed to material incentives. Indeed, ideological fervour has generally been more characteristic of the Chinese experience than of the Soviet. The Chinese have emphasised that the pursuit of social aims should accompany industrial progress. Chief among these aims is the development of a socially conscious citizenry guided by concern for the common good rather than for material possessions.

Yet material incentives do play a role in the Chinese economy, and inequality in the distribution of income does exist. Evidence suggests that there may be as much inequality of income in China as in the Soviet Union. Moreover, among the economic policy changes approved by the party's Central Committee in the bold initiative of 1984 was an expressed intent to tolerate larger income differentials and an endorsement of the idea that some people must be allowed to accumulate wealth and improve their standard of living before others.

Moral incentives in China take the form of ideological indoctrination and close administrative, even coercive, control. Such means are used to stimulate job performance as well as to transfer labour among firms, industries, and regions of the country.

On the income-equalising side, most medical and educational services are free. In addition, China has an extensive social security system that provides a floor under every citizen's standard of living. Finally, compared to other Communist countries, the quality, variety, and availability of consumer goods in China is generally quite good.

Yugoslavia and Market Socialism

A Communist regime led by Tito took control of Yugoslavia after World War II, accomplishing this feat without the assistance of the Soviet Union. From the end of the war until 1949, the Yugoslavs patterned their economy after the Soviet example of planned socialism. However, as a consequence of a falling out between Tito and Stalin in 1948, Yugoslavs undertook a critical reevaluation of their economic system. They concluded that it neglected consumer needs and was inefficient and overcentralised, and that the individual worker had no sense of meaningful involvement in the production process. Moreover, the collectivisation of agriculture (the creation of state-owned farms) hampered agricultural productivity and was unpopular with farm workers.

These shortcomings led the Yugoslavs to remodel their economic system along the lines of market socialism. Since 1950 their system has combined management by workers with a relatively high degree of decentralisation and reliance on the market mechanism.

Decision-Making Process

Self-management of enterprises (firms) by workers is probably the most distinctive feature of the Yugoslav economic system. Worker self-management is based on the idea that workers (including white-collar employees) will run an enterprise well, even though they do not own it. In fact, they do have a financial interest in the enterprise, insofar as their wages are tied to its financial success or failure.

Within the individual enterprise, the highest governing body is the workers' council, which is elected by and responsible to all the enterprise's employees. The workers' council is responsible for the hiring (and firing) of an enterprise director, who runs the enterprise on a day-to-day basis. In addition, the workers' council has long-range policymaking responsibilities, such as setting wage rate differentials and establishing smaller decisionmaking units within the enterprise.

The enterprise is related to the rest of the economy much more by means of the market mechanism than by a Soviet-style command hierarchy. The enterprise director and workers' council develop an operating plan that determines what the enterprise will produce and, to a limited extent, the selling price. State control over prices has increased in recent years.

The state has maintained substantial control over the flow of bank loans to enterprises. The central banking system influences the flow of credit to coincide with regional or national objectives. In some instances the state uses rules to allocate enterprise income between investment and wages. This reflects state concern that worker-managed firms might allocate too much income to wages and not enough to investment in plant and equipment, which would retard Yugoslavia's economic growth.

The Yugoslav Communist party does not have the kind of centralised power of the Communist parties in China, the Soviet Union, and elsewhere in Eastern Europe. However, it is an important force in decision making, since many managers are party members. The trade unions that exist in Yugoslavia are also closely associated with the party. At the plant level they tend to handle worker grievances rather than wage bargaining with individual enterprises. On the national level they have on occasion fought for an increase in the portion of national income going to private consumption. From time to time there are strikes by workers against their own managements. Sometimes whole enterprises strike against the central authorities when there is discontent with the government's setting of taxes, control of prices, or management of investment funds, all of which affect the fortunes of the labour-managed enterprises.

Information and Coordination Mechanism

Compared to the planned socialism of China or the Soviet Union, Yugoslavia has a relatively weak planning apparatus. Planned socialist economies impose compulsory plans from above. By contrast, under the market socialism of Yugoslavia, national plans originate with the enterprises — they are constructed 'from the ground up'. Enterprises declare their targets to planners, who aggregate these targets into a national plan. In 1976 a social-planning law was passed, requiring enterprises to draw up long-term plans committing themselves to output, wage, price, and investment targets. Enterprises that fail to meet the targets of their own plans are subject to fines, although there is some doubt about the actual significance of such penalties. Investment is the one area of the Yugoslav economy for which there is any significant centralised planning. Here the government exercises considerable influence over the flow of investment funds among the republics and provinces of Yugoslavia. Overall, however, the production and distribution of output is primarily a decentralised process consistent with the model of market socialism.

The extent to which markets have been allowed to operate free of government interference has varied over time. Until 1970, most enterprises set their own production schedules and selling prices. Exceptions were the product prices set by monopolists and near monopolists, which were negotiated with government authorities; ceiling prices on certain 'strategic' goods, which were set by government; price supports on some agricultural products; and periodic price freezes on some or all goods. In the late 1960s, some 40 per cent of prices were subject to some form of direct price control. However, since the mid-1970s this figure has risen to about 80 per cent.

Since 1971 there has been more state control in the Yugoslav economic system. Much of this control represents a response to higher unemployment, increased inflation, and balance of payments problems — the same difficulties facing many capitalist economies. Nonetheless, worker self-management remains dominant, economic decisions still are made largely at the enterprise level, and planning is still done at the enterprise level.

Property Rights

In Yugoslavia property rights reside mostly with the state. However, private ownership predominates in agriculture, where about 85 percent of arable land is in private hands. The only restriction on private farms is that they are not allowed to be larger than 24.7 acres. Outside of agriculture, there is private ownership in small-scale production and trade, although a private employer may employ no more than five persons (excepting family members). The assets of all other Yugoslav enterprises are held in trust for society by the workers who manage the enterprises. In other words, these assets are state owned.

Incentives

Market socialism places much greater emphasis on material incentives than does planned socialism, where moral incentives are more important. In Yugoslavia a minimum annual wage is guaranteed to the workers in worker-managed enterprises. Wages in excess of the minimum may be paid if the enterprise performs well. Obviously, this provides workers with an incentive to operate the enterprise so as to maximise net income — the difference between revenues from sales and the costs of production. If an enterprise does not earn enough net income to cover the guaranteed minimum wages, then the workers are paid out of a reserve fund maintained for this purpose. If an enterprise's reserve fund is inadequate, the state must subsidise the minimum-wage payment.

Subject to limits set by law, each enterprise's workers' council determines the wage differentials that are to exist within their enterprise. These differentials are used to reward special employee contributions to the success of the enterprise. Because some enterprises are more successful than others, it is common for workers doing the same task in different enterprises to earn different wages. (Nevertheless, some evidence suggests that wage differentials are smaller in Yugoslavia than in most Western European countries.) Given such differentials, and given the freedom of worker mobility in Yugoslavia, workers obviously have an incentive to make their job choices based on the earning prospects of different enterprises. This enhances the efficiency of the Yugoslav economy, because labour tends to be allocated to those productive activities that use it most effectively.

Individual enterprises make their decisions about outputs, inputs, technology, and investments largely in response to the market incentives provided by prices. In turn, the activities of all enterprises are interrelated and coordinated primarily by the market mechanism. The market mechanism is not allowed to work unchecked, however. Under capitalism, continued losses by a firm usually put it out of business. In Yugoslavia, failing enterprises are typically kept afloat with help from local authorities and the banks. Moreover, Yugoslav authorities do not particularly encourage price competition. Antitrust-type laws are weak, and enterprises are allowed to collude through the formation of business associations.

The force of moral incentives and persuasion is represented by government officials and the Communist party. Although the Communist party in Yugoslavia does not have the centralised power of the parties in other Communist countries, it does have an important role in the Yugoslav economic system.

CHECKPOINT 34.3
Compare and contrast the economic systems of China and Yugoslavia in terms of the four criteria listed in Table 22.1.

SUMMARY

1. An economic system consists of the institutions, rules, and decision-making used to organise and allocate scarce resources to produce and distribute goods and services. Each country's economic system may differ from that of every other in a number of ways.

2. There are four basic features to any economic system: the process by which decisions are made, the mechanism for providing information and coordinating activities, the nature of property rights, and the types of incentives used to motivate performance. The details of these features may be used to compare and classify economic systems. One useful classification scheme identifies the following economic systems: capitalism, market socialism, and planned socialism.

3. Under capitalism, decision making is decentralised among households and firms; the market mechanism determines prices, which provide economic information and coordinate economic activity; the means of production are privately owned; and incentives are mainly material — prices and wages. Under market socialism, decision making is mainly decentralised, information and coordination are provided mainly by the market mechanism, assets are owned mainly by the state, and incentives are both material and moral. Under planned socialism, decision making is mainly centralised, information and coordination are provided mainly by plan, assets are predominantly owned by the state, and incentives are mainly moral.

4. There are three basic political variants of socialism in today's world: Communism, social democracy, and third world socialism. Communism, the most totalitarian form of socialism, advocates class warfare, dictatorship by the proletariat, and the achievement of a classless society with state ownership of the means of production. Social democracy advocates gradual, peaceful means of reaching socialist goals in the context of a multiparty political system. Third world socialism consists mainly of a variety of socialist regimes among the underdeveloped countries; these tend to be nationalistic, to identify capitalism with imperialism, to subordinate the role of private property, and to discourage investment by foreign firms.

5. Communist regimes have made some dramatic economic gains, industrialising relatively backward economies and achieving notable economic growth. However, they tend to suffer from cumbersome bureaucracies, chronically scarce and shoddy consumer goods, lagging agricultural output, and bureaucratic controls that stifle efficiency and innovation. Social democracy, typically found in industrially advanced states, tends to concentrate on nationalising existing industries and income redistribution through the levying of heavy taxes to finance elaborate social welfare programs. There is concern in social democracies that heavy taxation is discouraging initiative, innovation, and enterprise.

Economic performance among third world socialist countries has been disappointing for the most part.

6. Communist and third world socialist regimes have shown little regard for liberty and individual freedom. Social democracies have consistently shown respect for individual freedom, although many see a potential threat in the growing concentration of power in large government bureaucracies.

7. The general quality of life, measured by such standards as availability of health care, educational opportunity, and cradle-to-grave social services, is impressive in most Communist and social-democratic countries. However, there are deficiencies as regards the general availability, variety, and quality of consumer goods in Communist countries.

8. Although socialist ideology advocates egalitarianism, Communist states have spawned an elite class of party officials, managers, ranking bureaucrats, and superstars in sports and the arts. This privileged class has access to otherwise scarce goods and services. Social democracies have promoted egalitarianism by redistributing income through taxation and the provision of all kinds of social services.

9. Socialism charges capitalism with creating inequalities of wealth and income; capitalism's defence is that this is the inevitable result of the rewards necessary to encourage enterprise and a dynamic economy. Communism charges that capitalism needs depressions to keep workers in line; capitalism responds that such episodes have been less severe since World War II, and that unemployment benefits have reduced the hardship of the unemployed. Socialism charges that capitalism makes people overly competitive and aggressive; capitalism responds that people are naturally motivated by self-interest and that capitalism's strength lies in the harnessing of such self-interest to promote the good of all. Socialism charges that capitalism promotes wasteful private consumption while shortchanging needed public services; capitalism responds that it provides more democratic answers to the question of the proper mix by allowing consumers to decide this question rather than planners. Capitalism's ultimate defence to all charges is that it best promotes freedom.

10. China has used planned socialism to achieve a substantial degree of economic growth and development. China's economic system is basically a command system, combined with a degree of freedom of action at local levels and some (officially permitted) use of the market mechanism. A national economic plan is the primary information and coordinating mechanism in China. State ownership of the means of production predominates. Moral incentives are heavily stressed through ideological indoctrination, administrative control, and even coercion. Material incentives are also used, particularly in agriculture.

11. Yugoslav market socialism is an attempt to improve on shortcomings in the Soviet model of planned socialism. A keystone of the Yugoslav system is the self-management of enterprises by workers. The enterprises are related to the rest of the economy by the market mechanism. A national plan is constructed by aggregating individual enterprise plans, but except for investment planning, there is little centralised planning. Except for agriculture and small enterprises, all property is held in trust for society by the workers who manage the enterprises. Material incentives in the form of wages and prices play a large role in Yugoslavia, although price controls, lax enforcement of antitrust-type laws, and government support of failing enterprises somewhat dampen competition and modify market forces.

KEY TERMS AND CONCEPTS

consumer sovereignty
economic system
market economy
planned economy

QUESTIONS AND PROBLEMS

1. What are the main differences between a capitalistic economic system and a socialistic economic system?

2. Socialism is often criticised for focusing too much on equality of results, such as a more equal distribution of income. It has been argued that equality of opportunity is more important for economic performance, and that there is a conflict between equality of results and equality of opportunity. Explain why you either agree or disagree with this point of view.

3. Do you think there is any relationship between an economic system's decision-making arrangements and the nature of its information and coordinating mechanism? Explain.

4. Some have claimed that socialism is a society based on cooperation instead of competition. What do you think an advocate of capitalism would say about the relationship between cooperation and competition?

5. Explain the nature of the relationship, if any, between an economic system's information and coordination mechanism and the nature of its system of incentives.

6. Yugoslav authorities have been concerned that the worker-managed enterprise might be too oriented to the short run. What is there about the incentive structure within such an enterprise that might justify this concern, and what are the implications for the economic performance of the Yugoslav economy?

7. Why is the concept of material balance important to the information and coordination mechanism used in China? What is the equivalent concept in a capitalistic economic system?

Hints and Answers to Checkpoints

CHAPTER 1

Checkpoint 1.1
There is considerable leeway on what might be counted as correct in response to this question. Some statements in the news item have both positive and normative elements. What should be emphasised are the (potentially, at least) *verifiable* nature of the positive statements in the paragraph and the value-judgment nature of the normative statements. The use of 'loaded language' as a prop for a shortage of factual statements should be noted.

Checkpoint 1.2
The long queues could be shortened — that is, the quantity of petrol demanded could be reduced — if the price increased.

Checkpoint 1.3
If the demand in the other state is less sensitive to changes in price, then the graph of its demand would be more vertical than the demand curve illustrated in Figure 1.3. This would show that a change in price would induce a smaller change in quantity demanded in the less sensitive state. Hence, the state whose demand is illustrated in Figure 1.3 would experience the greatest reduction in the quantity of electricity demanded, given an equal price change in the two states.

Checkpoint 1.4
Some examples of cause-and-effect confusion might include:

> *People looking at the night sky for a longer time will see more shooting stars than people who look for a shorter time. But this does not mean that looking at the sky longer causes more shooting stars.*

> *Ships can often be seen preparing to sail before high tide. But this does not mean that preparing to sail causes high tide.*

A football game crowd illustrates the fallacy of composition in this way: If one person stands up to watch the game, he or she will be able to see the game better. But this certainly does not remain true if everyone stands up.

CHAPTER 2

Checkpoint 2.1
The opportunity cost to Paddy of choosing combination *d* instead of combination

c in Figure 2.1 is what Paddy must give up to move from combination *c* to combination *d*, that is, 10 sacks of potatoes. Similarly, the opportunity cost of choosing *b* instead of d is what must be given up to move from *d* to *b*, namely, 10 tonnes of wood. The opportunity cost of choosing *d* instead of *b* is the 20 sacks of potatoes that must be forgone in order to move from *b* to *d*.

Checkpoint 2.2
The cost of moving from *d* to *c* is 20,000 scrubbers, the cost of moving from *c* to *b* is 30,000 scrubbers, and the cost of moving from *d* to *a* is 100,000 scrubbers. Figure 2.2 can be used to illustrate the law of increasing costs as follows: The move from *e* to *d* gains 20 million bundles of other goods (including food) at a cost of 10,000 scrubbers, the move from *d* to *c* gains 20 million bundles at a cost of 20,000 scrubbers, the move from *c* to *b* gains 20 million bundles at a cost of 30,000 scrubbers, and the move from *b* to *a* gains 20 million bundles at a cost of 50,000 scrubbers. In each step, the 20 million bundles of other goods gained has a greater opportunity cost in terms of scrubbers, thus illustrating the law of increasing costs.

Checkpoint 2.3
The questions of what to produce and for whom to produce are of a normative nature because they cannot be answered strictly by an appeal to the facts.

Checkpoint 2.4
A pure market economy would select a point on the production possibilities frontier without any government intervention, using only the price signals generated in the marketplace to determine what quantity of scrubbers and bundles would be produced and purchased. If the public desired a different quantity of scrubbers

than was currently being produced, its desires would cause changes in demand for scrubbers relative to other goods, and hence would cause changes in relative prices, profits, and production of scrubbers and bundles of other goods. In a command economy, the point on the production possibilities frontier would be mandated from above, with quotas for scrubbers being assigned from a central authority in the same manner as quotas for all other goods.

For both types of economies, greater industrial development would allow greater indulgence in the 'luxury' of scrubbers. Less developed economies would probably consider food, shelter, and producer goods (capital goods) necessary to survival and development rather than scrubbers.

CHAPTER 3

Checkpoint 3.1
A coincidence of wants is lacking here. If trade were to be carried on at all, one of the people would have to accept an unwanted good, and later trade for the wanted good. For example, since C wants fish and has wheat, C can travel to A's island, trade wheat for corn, and then travel to B's island and trade the corn for the fish C desires. Substantial transport time and costs are involved, even if C knows in advance what the supplies and wants of the other people are. If A, B, and C used money, C could travel to A's island and sell his wheat for money and then transport only the money to B's island to buy fish. Coincidence of wants would no longer necessitate someone transporting goods they did not want.

Checkpoint 3.2
Gompers meant that a business that cannot operate at a profit is not operating

efficiently. Since it wastes resources, it will eventually be driven out of business. The resulting loss of jobs will hurt working people. Also, a firm that is not able to operate at a profit cannot attract the investment capital necessary for growth and the creation of new jobs. While Marx saw capitalists' profits as a surplus value stolen from the working class, Gompers saw profits as a reward for wise management and entrepreneurship and as a return to attract financial capital.

Checkpoint 3.3

The government's power to enforce contracts contributes to the development of markets by making the process of exchanging goods and services less risky. Government's power to enforce gives all parties to a contract added assurance of its fulfillment.

The postal service is not a public good because the exclusion principle applies: only those who pay for the service can have it. Furthermore, there is a private market incentive for providing such service. Several courier services currently operate in Australia.

The military draft may be thought of as a transfer of income from those who are drafted to those outside the military services, because the draftees are paid at less than the free-market wage for military labour services (if military wages were determined in a free market, there would be no shortage of military labour and the draft would be unnecessary). Also, since the draft did not discriminate in terms of wealth or income (at least in the absence of corruption), persons who would not enter military service even at the free-market wage were forced to serve. This too constitutes a redistribution of income.

In contrast to government agencies, private businesses that don't operate very efficiently are forced out of business by experiencing losses.

CHAPTER 4

Checkpoint 4.1

1. The demand for oranges would probably increase (demand curve shifts to the right) because oranges are a substitute for bananas.
2. Demand would increase (complementary goods).
3. Motorists switched from increasingly expensive to operate 6 cylinder cars to 4 cylinder cars. Strictly demand theory assumes the goods are homogeneous and not broad categories such as 'cars'. When there are several categories within a broad class (meat, vegetables etc.) they will not be prefect substitutes for one another and may have quite different cross elasticities.
4. An increase in demand was observed a few years ago as people rushed to stock up to beat the expected price rise.

Checkpoint 4.2

1. The supply curve moves to the left.
2. The productivity of an important factor of production (cows) has increased milk supplies and the price of manufacturing milk is likely to fall. Costs to cheese producers fall and the supply curve moves to the right.
3. If the price of butter increases because of say increase in demand, butter becomes relatively more attractive to the manufacturer. Other things being equal there will be a tendency to produce more butter (increase in quantity supplied) and to reduce the amount of cheese the maker will produce at any given price (a fall in supply). The supply curve of cheese moves to the left.
4. Land use is likely to change if the alternative use offers a higher return to the owner than existing use. Thus a farmer will use land to produce crops or run

animals that offer the greatest return. A petfood manufacturer or a manufacturer of dairy products is likely to be able to offer a farmer a higher return for the sale of land for a factory than the farmer could gain from crops. However the amount the factory would need to offer for the land will be related to how much the farmer could hope to earn from alternative (normal) uses. Hence other things being equal, poor quality land would come cheaper to the factory even though fertility is irrelevant to the factory. Of course, nature of the site, transport, access and other features are likely to determine the factory's choice of site and willingness to buy the required land.

Checkpoint 4.3
1. Both demand and supply move to the right. Dealers offer a 'temporary' price reduction on supply. They hope demand will increase (move to the right) for the moment, as buyers respond in the expectation that lower prices will be temporary. If buyers believe it is not temporary, but permanent the demand curve does not shift and the new equilibrium occurs at a lower price on the original demand curve.
2. Increase in both demand and supply. More cheese is sold with indeterminate effects on price.
3. Manufacturing costs rise and the firm's supply curve moves to the left. In the simple market we have used expect an increase in cheese prices and a reduction in quantity sold.
4. If shoes are a normal good the demand for shoes will increase as consumers' incomes increase, other things being equal. If we observe sales are falling then plainly other things are not equal. A fall in supply, (shift in the supply curve to the left) brought about by, say, an increase in manufacturing costs could offset the

increase in demand and lead to the observed result.

CHAPTER 5

Checkpoint 5.1
The operation of public enterprises means that government now produces certain goods and services. This is represented in the flow diagram of Figure 5.3 by the addition of a flow channel connecting government with the flow channel where goods and services are exchanged for money payments. Like the business sector, government is producing and selling goods and services to households, and also to the business sector.

Checkpoint 5.2
The sales commissions are included in GDP because although the goods being sold are not considered final goods produced in the current period, the service of selling represents current productive activity.

An increase in the proportion of working wives increases GDP. This is because housekeeping and child-rearing services performed by housewives are not included in GDP. When housewives move into the labour market and take paying jobs, their work activity is measured and included in GDP.

A sample table for bread could look like Table A.1.

Checkpoint 5.3
The calculation procedure is the same as that in Table 5.2, except that the price index would be computed by dividing by $3, which is the price in year 2. The resulting real GDP figures would be year 1, $2,985; year 2, $3,300; year 3, $3,623; year 4, $3,999; and year 5, $4,397.

A given year's real GDP will be larger than its nominal GDP if it comes before

TABLE A.1

	Production Stage	Product	Sale Price of Product		Cost of Intermediate Product		Value Added (Wages, Interest, Rent, Profit)
Firm 1	Wheat farm	Wheat	$.30	—	$.00	=	$.30
Firm 2	Flour mill	Flour	.40	—	.30	=	.10
Firm 3	Baker	Bread	.65	—	.40	=	.25
Firm 4	Grocery store	Retailing service	.75	—	.65	=	.10
							$.75 (Final sale price = sum of value added)

the base year, and its real GDP will be smaller than its nominal GDP if it comes after the base year. This means that nominal GDP is 'inflated' to arrive at real GDP before the base year, and it is 'deflated' to arrive at real GDP after the base year.

Checkpoint 5.4

Movement along a demand curve for an individual good corresponds to a change in the price of that good, the price of all other goods assumed constant. By contrast, movement along the economy's aggregate demand curve corresponds to a change in the economy's price level, an average of the prices of all the goods and services that make up total output.

The aggregate demand curve has a negative slope because a higher price reduces the purchasing power of fixed-dollar assets, thereby reducing the purchasing power of consumer wealth, and causes consumers to cut back on the quantity of goods and services they demand.

CHAPTER 6

Checkpoint 6.1

A visual inspection of Figure 6.1, part a, gives the impression that the expansion phases of business cycles are a great deal longer than the recession phases because

of the effect of economic growth. This impression is lessened in Figure 6.1, part b, which shows variations around the growth trend. The monthly seasonal adjustment factors for textbook sales would have to account for large seasonal bulges in sales in the beginning months of each semester, declining dramatically until the beginning of the next semester.

Checkpoint 6.2

(1) From a high to low degree of price reduction, they probably ranked: agricultural commodities, food products, leather, cement, textile products, petroleum, iron and steel, automobile tyres, motor vehicles, and agricultural implements. (2) From a high to low degree of output reduction, they ranked the same way as in (1).

Checkpoint 6.3

Based on Figure 6.4, parts b and c, the unemployment rate that is associated with achieving potential GDP is 4½ to 5 per cent.

Checkpoint 6.4

An unanticipated deflation would redistribute wealth from debtors to creditors, because creditors would be paid back dollars that would buy more than the dollars they originally lent. Since debtors have not anticipated the fall in the general price level, they will not have protected themselves against the fact that their borrowings will have to be paid back with more purchasing power (dollars that buy more) than the purchasing power they originally borrowed. Had borrowers anticipated the deflation, they would have entered into the loan agreement at a lower interest rate than the one they in fact contracted for. It would have been lower by the amount of the rate of deflation. In this way borrowers would take account of the fact that they would have to pay back more valuable dollars than the ones they borrowed.

An unanticipated deflation would redistribute wealth from non-fixed-income groups to fixed-income groups. The fixed-income group would earn the same number of dollars, but these dollars would buy more as the price level fell. The non-fixed-income group would find their incomes falling right along with the general price level. Hence they would lose purchasing power relative to the fixed-income group.

Deflation essentially gives you money by giving each dollar you have more purchasing power.

The abrupt and dramatic increase in the rate of inflation in 1973 and 1974 may well have increased uncertainty about what the future rate of inflation would be. Fear of the consequences of unanticipated inflation may have made businesses and households more cautious about entering into loan agreements to finance investment and consumption spending. Hence further expansion in these expenditures was retarded, thus contributing to the recession.

CHAPTER 7

Checkpoint 7.1
Inventories accumulate when consumers do not buy as much as businesses expect them to at the time production plans were being made. This is not as desirable as increases in consumer expenditures because unanticipated increases in inventories mean goods are accumulating faster than they are being sold, and this will very likely lead to a cutback in production, output, and employment.

Checkpoint 7.2
The double taxation of company profits tends to make retained earnings larger relative to the size of dividends. The owners of the company, the shareholders, could avoid the double taxation of their profits if the company held the after-tax profit in the form of retained earnings rather than paying it out in dividends which would then be subject to income tax.

Checkpoint 7.3
(a) National turnover
= GDP + Imports
= $192,276m + $30,764m
= **$223,040 million**

(b) Gross domestic product at factor cost
= GDP — (Indirect taxes —
Subsidies)
= $192,276m — ($25,660m —
$3,247m)
= **$169,863m**

(c) Domestic factor incomes = GDP at factor cost — Depreciation allowances
= $169,863m — $30,653m
= **$139,210m**

(4) Gross national expenditure
= National turnover — Exports
= $223,040m — $28,010m
= **$195,030m**

CHAPTER 8

Checkpoint 8.1

The increase in the economy's aggregate demand would cause increases in demand in the many markets making up the economy. This would lead to price increases in these markets. Attempting to increase output in response, firms would increase their demand for labour. Since there is already full employment, wages would be bid up. Equilibrium would be restored with wages and prices at a higher level.

If the investment curve in Figure 8.1 shifts leftward and the interest rate for some reason cannot fall below i_e, then the savings-investment equality will break down and aggregate demand will fall (since the declining investment demand is a part of aggregate demand). The drop in the economy's aggregate demand will cause a leftward shift in the demand curves in the many markets making up the economy. Price and output will fall in these markets, and employers will be forced to lay off workers. This unemployment will cause wages to fall because unemployed labour will bid wages down in their attempts to find jobs. As long as the interest rate cannot fall below i_e, to equate saving and investment, wages and prices will continue to fall.

Checkpoint 8.2

On Crusoe's island all saving and investment plans were made in one man's head. Hence, planned saving necessarily equalled planned investment. There could be no unemployment problem, since Crusoe was both the demander and supplier of all labour, and the quantity supplied and demanded must always have been equal. Say's Law describes such an economy perfectly, since supply (the quantity that Crusoe was *willing* and able

to supply) did in fact create its own demand (the quantity that Crusoe was willing and *able* to demand). In modern industrialised economies, supply does not necessarily create its own demand because the leakage caused by saving may not be matched by the injection of investment, since savers and investors are typically different people.

Checkpoint 8.3

If interest rates decline, as the forecasters predict, then consumers will be encouraged to borrow more to finance consumption expenditures. Hence the consumption function will shift upward and the savings function will shift downward. In other words, when one of the 'other things assumed constant' as we move along a fixed consumption function or saving function changes — in this case the interest rate — it causes these functions to shift.

Checkpoint 8.4

An increase in the prices of new capital goods will cause the investment schedule to shift downward because the expected profit per dollar will be less. If wage contracts were successfully negotiated without strikes, this would reduce the uncertainty associated with future production and would make producers more willing to invest. This would in turn shift the investment schedule upward.

Checkpoint 8.5

Examining the fourth row of Table 8.3, we can explain the various columns as follows. Based on past experience and expectations of the future, businesses expect total spending over the next period to occur at an annual rate of $80 billion (column 1). They produce $80 billion in goods and services and in the process generate exactly $80 billion in income (column 2). At this income level, consumer demand plus business demand gives a total expenditure of $90 billion (column 3). Since this dollar expenditure for goods is larger than the dollar value of goods actually produced in this period, business is forced to sell $10 billion out of inventories (column 4). Since sales have been larger than expected, businesses increase their expectation of sales for the next period and increase production accordingly. This makes total income rise (column 5).

CHAPTER 9

Checkpoint 9.1

Investment (realised) is always equal to saving because what consumers don't buy, businesses do buy — either as part of planned investment (at income levels below the equilibrium level) or as 'purchases' to add to inventories (at income levels above the equilibrium level). Why is it sometimes said that 'this is obvious because that part of output that is not consumed must go somewhere'? Because total output not consumed by households must either end up in business inventories or be purchased by businesses.

Checkpoint 9.2

In Figure 9.2, part a, the attempt by consumers to save less shifts their savings function downward, say from S_1 to S_0, but the resulting increase in total income leaves saving (the quantity actually saved) unchanged. In part b of the figure the downward shift in the saving function, from S_1 to S_0, actually results in an increase in the quantity saved.

As savers try to rebuild their savings, they will shift up their savings function and shift their consumption function downward. This will result in a decline in total output and income and will possibly result in layoffs for car workers and steelworkers.

Checkpoint 9.3

In order for the APC and the MPC to be equal at all levels of disposable income, the consumption function must be a straight line through the origin. In this case the APS and the MPS would also be equal at all levels of disposable income, and the saving function would be a straight line through the origin. The APC would increase and the MPC would remain unchanged if the consumption function shifted upward in parallel fashion.

Checkpoint 9.4

If there was a $20 billion upward shift in the consumption function, the total expenditure curve in Figure 9.4, part a, would shift upward by $20 billion (note that this would look just like the shift in total expenditure caused by the $20 billion upward shift in the investment function). The equilibrium level of total income

TABLE A.2 (figures in $billion)

Expenditure Round	Change in Income and Output	Change in Consumption	Change in Saving
First round	$10.00	$8.00	$2.00
Second round	8.00	6.40	1.60
Third round	6.40	5.12	1.28
Fourth round	5.12	4.10	1.02
Fifth round	4.10	3.28	0.82
Rest of rounds	16.38	13.10	3.28
Totals	$50.00	$40.00	$10.00

would increase to $140 billion. In part b of the figure, the saving function would shift downward by $20 billion, intersecting I_0 at the new equilibrium level of $140 billion.

If the MPS is $1/5$ then the MPC is $4/5$, as shown in Table A.2.
Note that the shift in consumption is downward, so that all these changes are *decreases*. Graphically, the consumption function shifts downward by $10 billion and the saving function shifts upward by $10 billion. The final change in total output is a decrease of $50 billion. The slope of the consumption function (and the total demand schedule) is $4/5$, and the slope of the saving function is $1/5$.

The word *savings* is being used in the news item to refer to consumers' accumulated savings balances, which have been drawn on to enable consumers to 'spend so heavily'. In terms of a diagram like Figure 9.4, the upward shift of the consumption function has resulted in the increased total spending, partly by a shift and partly by being 'farther out' on the consumption function.

CHAPTER 10

Checkpoint 10.1
The $10 billion increase in government spending will raise total spending by $10 billion, which will increase equilibrium by $40 billion ($10 billion × 4, the multiplier) if it occurs by itself. The $10 billion increase in taxes will shift consumption down by $7.5 billion (= MPC × $10 billion) which will tend to decrease equilibrium income by $30 billion. The net effect will be an increase in equilibrium income of $10 billion. Viewed on the injections-and-leakages side, the $10 billion increase in government spending will shift the $I + G$ line up by $10 billion, which tends to

increase equilibrium income by $40 billion. The tax increase of $10 billion will have two effects: (1) it will shift savings downward by $2.5 billion (= MPS × $10 billion) and (2) it will shift the $S + T$ line up by the $10 billion increase in taxes (this shift will occur in the $S + T$ line, which includes the newly shifted saving function). These two effects on the S and T schedules will tend to decrease equilibrium income by $30 billion. The overall effect will therefore be an increase in equilibrium of $10 billion.

When the government takes a certain amount of income ΔT away from households in taxes, it spends all of it. If the money had been left in the hands of the households (not taxed away from them), the households would have spent only part of it. The part they would have spent would equal (MPC × ΔT). The net effect on total income equals $\Delta T(1/MPS)$ — $(\Delta T)(MPC)(1/MPS)$, or $\Delta T(1/MPS)$ $(1 - MPC)$. But since $1 - MPC = MPS$, this reduces to ΔT, which equals ΔG. Hence the balanced budget multiplier equals 1 no matter what the value of MPS or MPC.

Checkpoint 10.2
With a lump-sum tax, as is depicted in Figure 10.4, part a, taxes do not change with changes in GDP, so that increases or decreases in investment will have no effect on the state of balance of the budget.

With a proportional tax (Figure 10.4, part b), when investment increases and GDP increases (the economy is 'heating up'), the tax revenues collected will increase. Since government spending is invariant, the budget will be pushed toward surplus. When investment decreases, tax revenues will decrease and the budget will be pushed toward deficit.

With a progressive tax (Figure 10.4, part c), the tax changes resulting from investment changes will be in the same directions as in the proportional tax case, but the magnitude of the changes toward surplus or toward deficit will be greater.

The automatic stabilisation effect works by making the budget tend more toward surplus when the economy is 'heating up' and by making the budget tend more toward deficit when the economy is 'cooling off'.

Checkpoint 10.3

From 1971 to 1975 the actual level of GDP was fairly close to the level of potential GDP, and the cyclically adjusted budget concept seemed to work fairly well. Between 1975-76 and 1979-80 cyclically adjusted deficits did little to close the gap between actual and potential GDP. With surpluses after 1980-81 the GDP widened even further.

The effect of a cyclically adjusted deficit will be greater if the deficit is financed by printing money than it will be if it is financed by issuing bonds. If the cyclically adjusted budget is becoming less effective, this could be due in part to increased bond financing.

If a cyclically adjusted budget surplus is eliminated by holding funds from a budget surplus idle, the contractionary effect on GDP will be greater than if the funds are used to retire debt. However, if the cyclically adjusted budget is in surplus, the actual budget may not be in surplus. It is only when the actual budget is in surplus that funds can be held idle or used to retire debt, and the actual budget has not been in surplus since the 1930s in Australia — except very recently.

Checkpoint 10.4

Since half of the citizens would be holding the debt and receiving the interest payments on it, as the debt gets larger half of the citizens (the non-debt-holding citizens) would find themselves giving an ever larger share of their incomes in taxes to finance interest payments to the other half of the citizens holding debt. At some point the interest payments on the debt would involve such a large transfer of income from those without debt holdings to those holding the debt that political unrest would become serious. Certainly the government would be considered bankrupt when the interest payments became so large that the half of the population with no bonds was being taxed at 100 percent of their income to make interest payments to the other half of the population. No doubt there would be a tax rebellion (refusal to pay taxes) before this point was reached.

CHAPTER 11
Checkpoint 11.1

Changes in the price level change the purchasing power of consumers' fixed-dollar assets, hence the purchasing power of consumer wealth, thereby causing shifts in the total expenditure schedule that change the equilibrium level of real GDP. The inverse relationship between the price level and real GDP traced out in this fashion is the AD curve.

For a given price level, any exogenous expenditure or tax rate change will cause the total expenditure schedule to shift and the equilibrium level of real GDP to change. Given the price level, the change in real GDP certainly can't be represented by movement along an AD curve. Therefore it must be represented by a shift in the AD curve.

From Chapter 10 we know that a $10 billion increase in government expenditures financed by a $10 billion increase in lump-sum taxes gives rise to a balanced budget multiplier equal to one. Therefore, for any given price level, real GDP will increase by $10 billion. Hence the AD curve will shift rightward by $10 billion at each and every price level.

Checkpoint 11.2

A decline in the price of imported oil would reduce the cost of energy which in turn would lower firms' costs of producing goods and services throughout the economy. Firms therefore will be willing to produce any level of output at a lower product price than was the case before the decline in the price of imported oil. Hence the AS curve would shift downward.

Checkpoint 11.3

If the AS curve were more steeply sloped to the right of point e_0 in part b of Figure 11.6, then the price level would rise more and real GDP would rise less. The total expenditure schedule in part a of Figure 11.6 would shift downward from E_1' to a position below E_1 so that the new equilibrium level of real GDP would be less than y_1.

In order for there to be no change in real GDP as a result of the simultaneous demand-pull and cost-push inflation, the leftward shift in the AS curve and the rightward shift in the AD curve would have to be such that the intersection of the two curves continued to lie directly above the initial level of real GDP prevailing before the shifts occurred.

Checkpoint 11.4

A strictly demand-side, or Keynesian, point of view would only recognise the leftward shift in the AD curve caused by an increase in marginal tax rates. The position of the AS curve would remain unchanged. However, the supply-side effects of the increase in marginal tax rates would tend to discourage work effort and reduce after-tax rates of return, thereby causing the AS curve to shift upward and leftward. Recognition of the leftward shift in the AS curve would mean that real GDP would fall further than is the case when only the leftward shift in the AD curve is taken into account. According to a strictly demand-side point of view, the price level would fall or remain unchanged (the latter if the demand curve shift occurred along the horizontal range of the AS curve). Taking account of supply-side effects, the price level could rise or fall depending on the relative sizes of the leftward shifts in the AD and AS curves, and their initial positions prior to the increase in the marginal tax rates.

Closing all tax loopholes most likely would increase the tax revenues collected for any given tax rate. Hence the Laffer curve in Figure 11.10 would be bowed further outward to the right.

CHAPTER 12

Checkpoint 12.1

Up until the 1950s Britain was our major export destination and had been so since the beginning of white settlement. Japan, the USA, New Zealand, China and Korea are now larger markets than Britain. Between the 1950s and 1981/82 Britain's share of our total exports fell from nearly 40 per cent to less than 4 per cent.

In 1981/82 Asia received 56 per cent of our exports. Britain's share of our exports has declined as a result of factors such as:

- its membership of the European Community;
- its indifferent economic performance;
- the strong economic growth of Japan, the ASEAN nations and other geographically closer economies.

Checkpoint 12.2

I tend to buy about 80-90 per cent

Australian goods on a typical supermarket visit. Among imported goods New Zealand produce e.g. cheese, tinned goods etc. makes up the highest percentage from other countries. By contrast most of the electrical appliances in our house are imported — the refrigerator, stereo system, clock radio, portable radio, and vacuum cleaner are all examples of this. This is a significant percentage since my usual aim is to buy local goods wherever a choice exists with the imported article. Our television, washer and drier are all Australian made.

In most Australian states at least about half of resource developments or mining is devoted to export.

Checkpoint 12.3

If the economy's citizens decide to reduce the volume of goods and services then buy from abroad no matter what the level of GDP, then imports will decrease at all levels of GDP. This means that the $S + T + Imports$ line will shift downward, increasing the equilibrium level of GDP.

Although the leakages from imports exceed injections from exports, $140 billion is indeed the equilibrium value of GDP, because the total injections ($G + I + Exports$ are equal to the total leakages ($S + T + Imports$) at that point. This means that the injections from $I + G$ alone must exceed the leakages from $S + T$ alone by the same amount that leakages from imports exceed injections from exports.

The effect of positive (negative) net exports on the economy is similar to the effect of a government budget deficit (surplus) because they add to (subtract from) total spending and hence increase (decrease) equilibrium GDP through the multiplier effect. But note that the multiplier is different in an economy with imports and exports from the multiplier

in an economy without them, because imports change the slope of the injections function.

CHAPTER 13

Checkpoint 13.1

The one that is easiest to carry. If aluminium has a higher value per pound, $10 worth of aluminium would be lighter to carry around. On the other hand, steel might be less bulky.

From high to low liquidity, the items would be ranked as follows: a $10 bill, a demand deposit, a Master Card credit card, a $100 bill, a savings deposit, a 90-day Treasury bill, a stamp collection, a block of land in a suburb.

From high to low usefulness as a store of value, assuming a 10 per cent rate of inflation: a block in a suburb, a stamp collection, a 90-day Treasury bill, a savings deposit, a $10 bill, a $100 bill, a demand deposit, a Master card credit.

The statement 'money is acceptable because it is acceptable' means that what gives money its value as a medium of exchange is the willingness of people to accept it in exchange for goods and services.

From Figure 13.1, it would appear that a dollar bill has not been a very good store of value, since a 1987 dollar bill would have bought $1/9$ of the market basket that the same amount of money would have bought in 1950. (This ratio is obviously somewhat simplistic, since it abstracts from changes in the quality of goods and all the other problems associated with the measurement of price level over such a long period of time.)

Checkpoint 13.2

A bank note might be said to be an IOU because it is a piece of paper testifying to the bank's willingness to pay the bearer a given quantity of money that the bearer has deposited in the bank.

When currency is convertible into gold, there must be enough gold to redeem the currency. This means that the rate of growth of the supply of currency is limited to the rate of growth of the gold supply.

If people were to become less trusting of the soundness of banks, then they would be more likely to withdraw their money. Consequently banks would feel compelled to keep more reserves in their vaults. This would reduce their ability to create deposits through the making of loans. And this would reduce the upper limit to the economy's money supply.

If bankers were to become more cautious, then they would be less willing to make loans, and this would reduce the amount of IOUs on their balance sheets. If they made fewer loans for a given level of reserves, then the money supply would be smaller. This would make money conditions 'tighter', and in the aggregate, people would spend less on goods and services.

Checkpoint 13.3

The Reserve Bank makes the money supply more elastic because it is able to create reserves at a rate commensurate with growth in the level of economic activity.

The Reserve Bank is sometimes referred to as the lender of last resort, because authorised short term money market dealers can borrow reserves from the Reserve Bank if they find themselves in a credit squeeze.

CHAPTER 14

Checkpoint 14.1

The commercial banks held larger excess reserves from 1933 to 1940 because many banks experienced difficulties when panics led depositors to withdraw their deposits in the 1929-1932 period, the early years of the Great Depression. Wary of such surges of withdrawals, banks kept a large quantity of excess reserves on hand.

Checkpoint 14.2

The resulting table is shown as Table A.3.

If a bank decided to hold all its excess reserves and make no new loans, it would stop the expansion process completely at that point. If at any point a depositor receiving one of the new loans took the entire value of his or her new loan out in cash, this would also put a stop to the expansion process.

If a bank's willingness to lend increases, the bank will keep fewer excess reserves as cautionary balances, and it will become more 'loaned up'. This will increase the money supply.

With a required reserve ratio of .25, the maximum effect of a $100 cash withdrawal is a decrease in the money supply of $400 (= $100 × [1/.25]). The withdrawal will have a minimum effect if the bank was holding excess reserves, since it can pay out the cash without calling in any of its investments. In that case, M1 will be unaffected, because the only demand deposit effect will be a decrease in your balance by $100, and this will be countered by the increase in the cash component of M1 by $100.

Checkpoint 14.3

An increase in money demand accompanied by a decrease in the money supply would have the greatest effect on the interest rate. This can be easily demonstrated by graphs similar to Figures 14.4 and 14.5. If people were to revise their notions of a normal level of the interest rate upward, the money demand curve would shift upward and money demand would be greater at every level of the

TABLE A.3

Bank	New Reserves and Demand Deposits	Excess Reserves Equal to the Amount Bank Can Lend, Equal to the New Money Created	Required Reserves
A	$1,000	$ 750	$ 250
B	750	563	188
C	563	422	141
D	422	316	105
E	316	237	79
F	237	178	59
G	178	133	44
H	133	100	33
All remaining banks	401	301	100
	$4,000	$3,000	$1,000

interest rate — that is, money demand would increase. If people were to become more uncertain about their jobs, then they would tend to hold higher precautionary balances. This means that they would hold larger money balances at any given interest rate, and hence money demand would increase.

CHAPTER 15

Checkpoint 15.1
If the investment demand curve in part b of Figure 15.2 was made steeper, then the interest rate decrease resulting from the increase in money supply from M_0 to M_1 would cause investment spending to increase by less than before. If the money demand curve in part a of Figure 15.2 became steeper, then the shift in money supply from M_0 to M_1 would result in a larger decrease in the interest rate and hence a larger increase in investment spending. If money demand were more sensitive to a change in total income, then the increase in total income resulting from the money supply change in Figure 15.3 would be smaller than before. This is because the shift in money demand resulting from the change in total income

tends to counteract the investment increase that results from the initial interest rate drop associated with movement along the money demand curve.

Checkpoint 15.2
Stated by itself, the equation of exchange is true by definition. But if it is postulated that the velocity of money is inherently stable, then the equation of exchange becomes a theory linking changes in the money supply to changes in money GDP.

If the money demand curve becomes flat at some low level of the interest rate, then when the money supply is increased into the flat range, further increases in the money supply cause no changes in the interest rate, investment, or money GDP. If the money supply increases and there is no change in money GDP, then velocity must decrease in order for the equation of exchange to remain balanced.

CHAPTER 16

Checkpoint 16.1
The crucial point in this question is to realise that small multipliers can be offset by large policy doses to achieve the desired end. Thus, those arguing for high multipliers must base their argument on the

basis that the government may be politically constrained from applying large policy doses. For example, the government may have difficulty getting through Parliament large tax changes or big cuts in government spending. Similarly, large changes in the money supply may unsettle financial markets and hence be counterproductive. For these reasons it may be preferable to have big multipliers.

However, the case for small multipliers is equally strong — if not stronger. The argument here is that if a government errs in its policy (for example, mistimes a policy dose) then large multipliers will amplify the disturbance, giving a much worse result than if the economy had small multipliers. Government policy changes need not be the only relevant changes. Other shocks to the system as changes in exports or foreign investment would also have an amplified effect on an economy with high multipliers. Thus one may well argue that smaller multipliers are 'safer', giving rise to more dampened business cycles.

Checkpoint 16.2

If there was a prolonged decrease in the price level, and there was an anticipated deflation, the money interest rate would be less than the real interest rate by an amount equal to the anticipated rate of deflation. Since borrowers would be paying back dollars that are worth more than the dollars they borrowed, they would demand compensation for this in the form of a lower money interest rate.

The nominal interest rate shown in Figure P16.1, tends to move with the rate of inflation shown in Figure P16.2, because the anticipated rate of inflation is part of the money interest rate (money interest rate = real interest rate + anticipated rate of inflation).

CHAPTER 17

Checkpoint 17.1

If the Phillips curve were to rotate anticlockwise, then unemployment could be reduced with a smaller increase in inflation. If the economy could have a zero per cent rate of inflation with 9 per cent unemployment, then the Phillips curve would intersect the horizontal axis at 9 per cent unemployment. It would also be twisted clockwise. If the Phillips curve represents a true menu of choices, then the choice of a point on the curve is a normative one, since it cannot be decided by an appeal to facts.

Checkpoint 17.2

Short-run Phillips curves might well be shaped like those in Figure 17.4 based on the evidence for the years from 1962 through 1969, and 1976 through 1982 (see Figure 17.3). However, other years are not as suggestive of this shape.

Checkpoint 17.3

The pattern of the data in Figure 17.2 suggests that the average level of the unemployment rate has increased over time. Certainly one possible explanation is the changing nature of the labour force we have discussed above. Another possibility is that there has been an increase in the natural rate of unemployment caused by the increasing variability of inflation, as hypothesised by Milton Friedman. Of course, both types of phenomena could jointly contribute to the apparent upward drift in the average level of the unemployment rate.

CHAPTER 18

Checkpoint 18.1

Wage and price controls can be said to operate 'artificially' because they do not allow the market price-setting mechanism to determine price. Although prices can be held below those that would equate supply and demand (as illustrated in Figure 18.1) if there is a large enough enforcement effort, such controls do not eliminate the underlying demand and supply curves or prevent them from shifting while the controls are in effect. As soon as the controls are lifted, price will rise to the level that equates supply and demand, and this could be termed a 'price explosion'.

Checkpoint 18.2

The index of real unit labour costs is meant to take into account the following:

(a) the growth in total labour costs involved in producing goods and services;

(b) the growth in productivity per hour worked. All other things being equal, a faster growth in productivity reduces the costs of production; and

(c) the rate of increase in business prices. Again, assuming all other factors remain unchanged, higher business prices increase profitability so that they must be taken into consideration in arriving at an index which measures real unit labour costs.

Comparing Figure 18.5 with Figure P17.2 clearly shows that both the unemployment rate and the overhang tended to develop at the same time, starting in 1974. Restrictionists use this correlation to argue that the wages explosion of 1974 and 1981–82 were the cause of the high unemployment rates during this period. That is, real unit labour costs increased so much that they rendered part of firms existing and potential output unprofitable to produce. This is a strong and persuasive argument. However, expansionists point out that despite the fact that the Accord has whittled away the real wage overhang, unemployment has not fallen back to pre-overhang rates. This, to them, suggests that other factors, such as the low level of demand as a result of slower economic growth, have been more important in discouraging output growth than the increase in real unit labour costs.

CHAPTER 19

Checkpoint 19.1

The rule of 72 tells us that the rate of growth for the time period 1950 to 1981 is approximately 2.3 per cent (= 72/31 years).

If the rate of growth of productivity is 1.5 per cent and the 'safe growth ceiling' is 3 per cent, then the combined growth projected for the other three factors (population, per cent of population in the labour force, and number of hours worked per labourer) must not exceed 1.5 per cent.

Checkpoint 19.2

Technically, an increase in any factor while other factors are held constant brings about diminishing returns for the increased factor. Historically, however, technical change and investment in human capital have tended to be the major sources of economic growth. This phenomenon would seem to suggest that technical change and investment in human capital are bound less by the law of diminishing returns than are the other factors. Hence, technical change and investment in human capital probably will have a larger impact on long-run growth than will increases in other factors of production.

CHAPTER 20

Checkpoint 20.1

Using the arc formula the elasticity is

$$\frac{10,000}{(20,000+30,000)} \Big/ \frac{2}{(18+16)} = 3.40$$

As we move down the demand curve from left to right, we observe the elasticity of demand declines (in absolute value). If the M.C.G. is filled to its 100,000-seat capacity and total revenue is at its maximum, then we could be at the unit elastic point on a demand curve that is to the right of the illustrated demand curve. However, it is also possible that the demand curve is so far to the right that the unit elastic point on the demand curve lies to the right of the 100,000-seat capacity point on the horizontal axis. In that case the point on the demand curve lying directly above the 100,000-seat capacity would be in the elastic range of the demand curve. The maximum *possible* revenue would still be obtained by charging a ticket price corresponding to that point on the demand curve — still a sellout. The point lying above the 100,000-seat capacity could not be in the inelastic range of the demand curve. If it were, the unit elastic point would lie to the left of the 100,000-seat capacity, and revenue maximisation would require setting the ticket price higher (at the unit elastic point) and not filling the M.C.G.

Checkpoint 20.2
Supply elasticities are positive and demand elasticities are negative because supply curves are direct (positive-slope) relationships and demand curves are inverse (negative-slope) relationships.

Checkpoint 20.3
If the marginal utility per dollar of X is greater than the marginal utility per dollar of Z, then this would mean that if the consumer took a dollar away from expenditure on Z and spent it on X instead, there would be a gain in total utility. This is so because the loss in utility from consuming a dollar's worth less of Z would be more than offset by the gain in utility from consuming an additional

dollar's worth of X. This reallocation of expenditure would also mean that the marginal utility of X per dollar would decrease while that of Z would increase. We know this from the law of diminishing marginal utility. As long as the marginal utility of Z per dollar is less than that of X, the consumer's total utility can be increased by shifting expenditure away from Z and toward X. Because of the law of diminishing marginal utility, we know that eventually the marginal utility of Z per dollar would be brought into equality with the marginal utility of X per dollar.

If we begin from a point where the consumer is maximising utility, and only the price of Z rises, then we will have a situation where the marginal utility per dollar spent on Z is less than the marginal utility per dollar spent on X, which is exactly the situation in the foregoing paragraph. And as before, the law of diminishing marginal utility will cause the consumer to shift expenditure away from Z and toward X. Thus we have shown that an increase in the price of Z results in a decreased demand for it, which is a description of a demand curve that slopes downward to the right.

CHAPTER 21

Checkpoint 21.1
The diagram has been drawn to depict a realistic situation in which separate measures have eliminated supply from the rest of the world and insulated the European market. ED and ES are European demand and supply respectively. First the EEC sets a guaranteed minimum price for agricultural products and agrees to buy surpluses at that price. Consumers buy OC but producers supply OP leaving the EEC with a mountain or lake that is increasing by CP every period. It is also paying for the surplus at the guaranteed

minimum price GP.

If the EEC imposes a quota on production this superimposes the vertical line Q on the diagram. If it continues to maintain the guaranteed minimum price consumer prices are unchanged and the only effects are to reduce surplus production and the cost of the program to the community, apart from reduction in farm incomes because of the reduction in unwanted production.

If the EEC sells its surpluses on world markets this will increase world supply and reduce the world price. If European surpluses are large and the quantity sold is unrelated to the price the supply curve moves to the right (parallel to the old one) by a large amount. With demand inelastic the effect of prices can be catastrophic for Australian and New Zealand butter producers selling on the oversupplied world market.

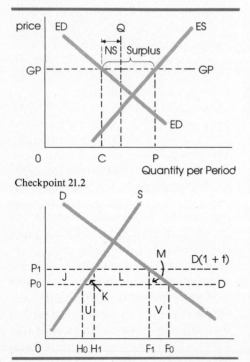

Checkpoint 21.2

Checkpoint 21.2

(a) Initially the import price P_0 is the market price. Australian producers supply $0H_0$ and imports make up the balance H_0F_0.

(b) The tariff raises the landed price to P_1 and again this becomes the market price because Australian producers are unable to satisfy the entire market at that price or a lower one. Home production increases to $0H_1$ whilst imports are reduced to H_1F_1. Consumer surplus falls by the marked areas $JKL + M$, but these losses are partly offset by the increase in domestic producers' surplus J and government tariff revenue L (a net loss of $K + M$). $U + V$ (the reduction in the quantity of imports $\times$ P_0) measures the reduction in the import bill valued in Australian currency.

Checkpoint 21.3

With a perfectly elastic supply curve, the entire incidence of the $10 excise tax falls on buyers. With a perfectly elastic demand curve, the entire incidence of the $10 excise tax falls on sellers. If the demand curve is perfectly inelastic, then the selling price will increase by the entire amount of the tax and the entire incidence of the tax will fall on the buyer. For any given size of excise tax, the more elastic the demand curve, the greater will be the reduction in quantity consumed.

Checkpoint 21.4

The senator must be implicitly assuming that the supply for this product is perfectly elastic or that the demand for this product is perfectly inelastic.

If strict pollution control laws were imposed on an industry, employment and output would fall more the greater were the elasticities of both supply and demand.

Since the demand for cigarettes seems to be quite inelastic, a $.20 tax per pack would probably not change the quantity consumed very much and hence would have little effect on the frequency of lung cancer.

CHAPTER 22

Checkpoint 22.1
Backyard egg producers almost invariably fail to cost their labour. When they sell their surpluses they tend therefore to price so as to meet only the costs of feed and add perhaps a notional profit margin. During the spring flush surpluses are considerable and by unloading them backyard producers create a serious reduction in demand for commercial producers. The argument against allowing private motorists to carry fare paying passengers is similar in one sense. A typical argument is that such competition would be unfair because private motorists would gain a short run cost advantage by not pricing labour appropriately. Safety considerations and stability have been the two principal arguments for regulation of the taxi industry in Australia. To many economists these arguments are not all that convincing, believing that often such regulation is a device for allowing existing firms to make supernormal profits. Why is it that taxi licences often change hands for large sums of money? Surely it is a reflection of the profitability of business.

Checkpoint 22.2
If total fixed cost increased from $50 to $75, then the fixed cost line (*TFC*) would shift upward by $25, and the total cost curve would also shift upward by $25. The total variable curve would remain unchanged.

If wages rose from $50 to $75, then the *TC* and *TVC* curves would both pivot counterclockwise about their intercepts. The *TFC* curve would remain unchanged.

Checkpoint 22.3
If fixed cost fell by $10, then average fixed cost would shift downward by $10 at 1 unit of output, by $5 at 2 units of output, and so on. Average total cost would shift downward in the same manner. Average variable cost would remain unchanged.

TABLE A.1

	OUTPUT	AVC	ATC
1	1	$60.00	$110.00
2	3	40.00	56.67
3	6	30.00	38.33
4	10	24.00	29.00
5	13	23.08	26.92
6	15	24.00	27.33
7	16.5	25.45	28.48
8	17.5	27.43	30.28
9	18	30.00	32.78

If weekly wages increase from $50 to $60, average fixed cost will not be affected, but average variable cost and average total cost will both increase, and the curves will shift upward. The new *AVC* and *ATC* columns are shown in Table A.1.

Checkpoint 22.4
The change in average total cost includes the change in average fixed cost, which falls more rapidly than marginal cost over the first six units of output. If diminishing returns are larger than is the case in Table 22.2, then the slope of the marginal cost curve would be greater to the right of its lowest point.

Checkpoint 22.5
The long-run *ATC* curve represents a collection of blueprints, because each point on it corresponds to a different plant — a different-size plant. In the long run a business can choose from a number of different sizes of plants in the planning stage. Hence the long-run *ATC* is a collection of blueprints. Selection of a plant size corresponds to the selection of a particular blueprint.

Underutilising a larger plant when production is below 1,800 units and overutilising a smaller plant when production is over 1,800 units is necessary if the firm is to produce a given output level at the lowest possible per unit cost in the long run — that is, if it is to operate on its long-run *ATC* curve.

CHAPTER 23

Checkpoint 23.1
The total revenue curve (Figure 23.1 (a)) becomes steeper, still originating at 0 of course. In part b the demand curve shifts up and is horizontal AR=MR=$15. Initially the demand curve is horizontal because the firm's product cannot be successfully distinguished from those of other firms. If buyers detect differences demand is likely to be less than perfectly elastic, a less than perfect substitute and the demand curve will slope downwards from left to right. See Chapter 25.

Checkpoint 23.2
Table 23.2 makes it clear that the difference between average revenue and average cost is greatest at 5 units produced and sold.

Figure 23.3, part b, was designed so that the number of profit squares shaded at 5 units of output is greater than the number shaded at 3, 4, or 6 units of output. At 5 units of output, approximately 10 squares are shaded, while at 3, 4, and 6 units of output, approximately 3, 8, and 6 squares respectively are shaded.

Checkpoint 23.3
Figure 23.4, part b, was designed so that the number of loss squares shaded at 4 units would be at a minimum. At 4 units of output, approximately 4 loss squares are shaded, while at 2, 3, and 5 units of output, approximately 8, 6, and 5 squares respectively are shaded.

Figure 23.4, part b, shows that the shaded area of the excess of total revenue over TVC is 5 squares at 4 units (1.25×4), while the excess is 2, 4(= 1.34×3), and 4(= $.80 \times 5$) squares at 2, 3, and 5 units respectively.

Checkpoint 23.4
The shaded area would represent the loss associated with producing 4 units of output as opposed to just shutting down.

The area corresponding to the vertical distance between the TC and TR_4 curves would be the area between $4 and $7.25 out to 4 units of output. The area representing TFC would be the area between $7.25 and $4.75 out to 4 units of output.

Checkpoint 23.5
An increase in the cost of raw materials would shift the MC, AVC, and ATC curves upward. This would shift the industry supply curve upward. If demand curve D_1 represented the industry demand, then the firms would decide to produce nothing at all, and firm and industry output would fall to zero. If the demand curve were D_3, then the equilibrium price would increase, and firm and industry output would decline.

Checkpoint 23.6
When a perfectly competitive industry is in long-run equilibrium, all factors employed by the industry are earning just what they could earn in alternative endeavors. Hence all factors are compensated by an amount that just equals their opportunity cost. If firms are just earning a normal profit in long-run competitive equilibrium, then the financial capital and entrepreneurial skill employed by the firms are earning an amount just equal to their opportunity cost.

Checkpoint 23.7
Mining companies sell their product on world markets and their product is also homogeneous. Seldom is a company sufficiently large to be able to set its own price without reference to world market conditions. Demand for most mining products is derived demand. They are used as raw materials in secondary industry and demand tends to reflect changes in market conditions for those products. Demand tends therefore to be relatively inelastic

contributing to price fluctuations. Supply also tends to be highly inelastic in the short run because mining has high development (fixed) costs and relatively low variable costs.

CHAPTER 24

Checkpoint 24.1

BHP is the only steel producer for many products but it cannot be said to have complete effective monopoly power because imported steel products act as a continual check on pricing policies. Only if there were effective import restrictions on steel would BHP be able to exercise effective monopoly power. Even then it would be conscious that exercising that power might be folly in the long run if it led to its customers' Australian manufacturing and construction industries ceasing to be competitive.

The kiosk certainly had a monopoly. It was get wet or buy. Happily the kiosk charged a resonable price and saved the day for many people.

Checkpoint 24.2

The relationship may be most easily demonstrated in an area around the maximum point. Between 6 and 7 units of output, marginal revenue is zero and total revenue is at a maximum ($42). The (midpoint) elasticity of demand at this point is $1.0 = (1/6.5)/(1/6.5)$. At 1 unit of output less, between 5 and 6 units of output, total revenue is $41 and marginal revenue is $2. The elasticity is $1.37 = (1/5.5)/(1/7.5)$. At a point where output is one unit more than at the revenue-maximising point (between 7 and 8 units), total revenue is $41, marginal revenue is -$2, and the elasticity of demand is .73 $= (1/7.5)/(1/5.5)$. This shows that where demand is inelastic, marginal revenue is negative, and where demand is elastic, marginal revenue is positive.

Checkpoint 24.3

Given the monopolist pictured in Figure 24.2, if profit was being maximised at an output of 7 units and a price of $6, then the marginal cost would have to be 0. This is because marginal revenue and marginal cost are always equal when profits are being maximised, and marginal revenue at 7 units is 0.

You would never expect a monopolist to sell at an equilibrium price in the inelastic portion of the demand curve, because marginal revenue in this region is negative and the marginal revenue and marginal cost equality would necessitate a negative marginal cost.

Checkpoint 24.4

An increase in fixed costs in Figure 24.3 would move *ATC* upward (increasing losses) but would not affect equilibrium price and output levels, since these are the loss-minimising levels regardless of the level of fixed costs (variable costs determine loss-minimising levels of price and output). The increase in fixed costs would increase negative economic profit (losses). Doubling a licence fee paid to the state would constitute an increase in fixed cost and hence would not change price and output levels. If a monopolist changes price without changing output, then it could be in response to a change in demand (and hence marginal revenue). The demand curve could change position in such a way that the marginal revenue curve still intersects the marginal cost curve at the same point. If the government imposes an effective price ceiling, this could cause output to increase, since this would make the monopolist's effective demand curve horizontal, just like the perfect competitor's. The intersection of the marginal cost and marginal revenue curves would occur farther to the right of the original intersection.

Checkpoint 24.5

The consumer surplus is increased by the shaded are J + K but producers gain L but lose J. Thus whilst there is an overall gain of K + L producers will be worse off if, as appears, the loss to them of J is greater than the gain of L.

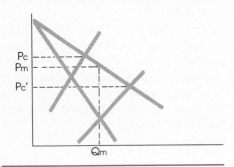

Checkpoint 24.6

If all buyers have identical demand curves, then all buyers have identical demand elasticities, and the profit-maximising monopolist will charge the same price to all of them.

CHAPTER 25

Checkpoint 25.1

All have at least some of the characteristics of monopolistic competition. All offer a differentiated product for example, and to a greater or lesser extent engage in nonprice competition. We cannot say anything about the number of firms or freedom of entry and exit since this will vary from one city to another. Recall that a perfectly competitive firm is a price taker, its demand curve is perfectly elastic and the products of other firms are identical. The higher the degree of product differentiation the less elastic will be the demand for the firm's product and the less perfect the substitute brands.

Checkpoint 25.2

The increase in wage raises the average and marginal cost curves to the individual firms in Figure 25.2, parts b and c. With no change in demand in the short run both firms would make losses even after setting marginal cost equal to marginal revenue. If the industry faced no import competition we would expect some firms to leave the industry and for there to be a long term increase in demand for the products of the remainder — restoring the normal profits tangency position. The fear of the local industry was that imports would increase and that a very severe contraction of the local industry would occur. The actual consequences depend on how strong is the degree of substitution between local and imported garments.

Checkpoint 25.3

Many people believe that advertising should not be deceptive or misleading. Claims that are patently absurd and made with no intention of being taken as true are generally regarded as acceptable. Professional organisations such as doctors often take the view that the advertising of their services is not in the public interest — though there remains the suspicion that this stems from a desire to restrict the flow of information and competition. Many people believe television advertising should be controlled. Thus restrictions are placed on tobacco advertising. Until recently the amount of advertising allowed on commercial television was subject to controls because of the concern that programs would be swamped.

It is hard to justify restricting some advertising to particular media forms and not others.

Whether the control of advertising should be by the government or by an industry or by the advertising industry itself can only be decided after assessing what society regards as acceptable. In general there is much to be said for industry self regulation when it is effective.

CHAPTER 26

Checkpoint 26.1

The constant model changes constitute part of a policy directed at increasing product proliferation and product complexity. This helps each of the car makers to keep the others off balance and serves as a very substantial barrier to the entry of new producers. The existing car manufacturers are quite experienced at maintaining a fairly constant stream of new and changed models. This means that a new entrant into the market must not only be able to produce cars but to produce them while constantly changing styles in order to sell to a public that has grown used to such changes. It is not at all clear that under such circumstances it would be better for the four car makers to collude in order to stop such model changes. It is even possible that the overall industry demand is being increased by this behaviour, in which case ending the constant model changes would be detrimental to the sales of all four firms.

Checkpoint 26.2

It makes good sense for petrol resellers outside the city to charge a lower price than those in the city. They effectively segment the market between people who travel into the city and those who travel only in the city and gain a larger share of the market by doing so. With lower prices they persuade those who travel along the highways and into the city to buy from them. Nevertheless it is not worthwhile for the great majority of motorists who travel only in the city to drive out for lower prices. Because of this there is no pressure on city service stations

to drop their prices. If on the other hand petrol stations along a highway are close together, charging a lower price in the country may spread into the city as each service station must compete with its nearest neighbours.

Checkpoint 26.3

A firm could move price to a level above the kink in the demand curve if its marginal cost curve shifted upward until it intersected the marginal revenue curve at a point to the left of the kink.

The firm would never reduce price below the kink if the demand were inelastic to the right of the kink — that is, when marginal revenue is negative to the right of the kink.

Checkpoint 26.4

It is only necessary for one of the firms in Figure 26.7 to misjudge the likely reactions of the other in order for events to lead them to the price level p_4.

Checkpoint 26.5

A finding that there was very little change in the identity of the top four firms in an industry characterised by high concentration and high profits would strengthen the implication that through overt or covert collusion, the top firms were acting as a joint monopoly and reaping monopoly profits. If the top four firms were subject to frequent turnover, however, it would be much more difficult to draw such a conclusion.

If an industry is more concentrated than is justified by economies of scale, then it would experience higher costs per unit than if its concentration were more in accord with available scale economies. The too-concentrated industry would experience a lower profit rate than if its concentration ratio were more in line with available scale economies.

In an industry where both advertising outlays and concentration are high, one would be tempted to draw the conclusion that the high advertising outlays are responsible for the high concentration. But the nature of the product would certainly have a bearing on this conclusion.

CHAPTER 27

Checkpoint 27.1

The problem with the argument is that it considers only one aspect of the costs and benefits of a road system. Poor and dangerous roads may induce great care and freeways may lead to more acccidents and higher costs. But the benefits from the freeways come from time saving and other economic benefits which will almost certainly outweigh the losses to society from road accidents. Minimum speed limits are imposed to produce both time savings and the resultant benefits but more particularly they often make for safer freeway driving since a single slow driver can provide an unexpected hazard.

Checkpoint 27.2

If the marginal cost of pollution reduction were increased by $70,000 at every level of pollution reduction shown in Table 27.1, the optimal level pollution would be 60,000 units. If pollution were reduced below this level, the marginal benefit from pollution reduction (column 3) would be less than the marginal cost (column 5).

Checkpoint 27.3

There is no unambigously correct answer to this question. However, it might be argued that because regulations for product safety prevent or slow down the introduction of new medical drugs to the markplace, such regulations are more restrictive of consumer choice. Regulation of deceptive advertising is less likely to restrict the introduction of products to the marketplace because its aim is to regulate what is claimed about products rather than to prevent the sale of them altogether.

Checkpoint 27.4

Both. There are strong political and social opinions on the subject and it is the traditional view of the Australian Labor Party that public ownership of important monopolies and essential services is desirable. Much of the recent privatisation debate has been about perceived economic benefits from privatisation and it is these benefits that have attracted the attention or Mr Hawke and his treasurer, Paul Keating.

CHAPTER 28

Checkpoint 28.1

The explanation will consist of a demonstration that the demand curve for a variable is derived by multiplying the marginal physical product by the price of the final product. The second important feature is to show that the short run profit maximising condition is to hire that quantity of the factor for which marginal revenue product = price of the factor, thus establishing a point on the demand curve. Changes in the price of the factor then produce different profit maximising outputs, leaving us with the marginal revenue product curve as the firm's demand curve for the factor.

Checkpoint 28.2

(a) The increase in demand for the product can be analysed by tracing the following consequences of the initial shock (that is, the rightwards shift of the demand curve in the industry section of the product market diagram). These are,

i) an increase in the price of the product to the firm

ii) an increase in demand for the variable factor which is available to the industry at a fixed price.

The firms produce more of the product and receive more for it. They pay no more for the variable factor but hire more labour.

(b) Follow a similar course of analysis, but on this occasion the shock is produced by an increase in demand for the variable factor because the marginal physical product of that factor has risen. The firm's costs are reduced and the industry's supply curve moves to the right. The increase in demand for the factor has no effect on the price of the variable factor to the firms in the industry, but unit costs fall because of the increase in productivity.

Checkpoint 28.3

The tyre and tube industry is by far the largest user of rubber, and rubber cost is a large proportion of final cost of tyres, implying a larger elasticity for the rubber demand curve of the tyre industry. Rubber is not very easily substituted for in tyre production, tending to decrease the rubber demand elasticity. The demand for tyres is probably inelastic, and so the tyre industry's demand for rubber will tend to be inelastic. Industrial hoses, belts, and tubes use rubber and probably have an inelastic demand for rubber for the same reasons. The footwear industry uses rubber, but because it can be fairly easily substituted for in many applications, the footwear demand for rubber is probably more elastic than that of the tyre or hose industries. Using 'armchair averaging', it would probably be correct to say that the rubber demand, overall, is fairly inelastic.

Some inelastically demanded factor inputs (and their elasticity-determining factors) might be diesel fuel (the transportation industry's product demand is

fairly inelastic, substitution of other input factors is difficult and limited, and fuel is a fairly large proportion of total transport cost), transistors (the electronics industry has a fairly inelastic product demand, substitution of other factors is difficult, and the transistor cost is a small part of total product cost), nails (although demand for wood construction might be fairly elastic, substituting for nails in the production process is difficult, and nails are a small part of the cost of the final product), crude oil (although its cost is a large part of the cost of the final products, it is difficult to substitute for, and the demand for products using crude oil seems to be quite inelastic), and fertiliser (the demand for products using it is inelastic, fertiliser is usually a fairly small cost relative to the final product cost, and it is quite difficult to substitute for).

The demand for Ford tractors is more elastic than the demand for tractors in general. The broader the definition of a factor, the more inelastic its demand is likely to be.

CHAPTER 29

Checkpoint 29.1

An elasticity of supply coefficient of -1 (backward bending supply curve) is critical, since an increase in the wage rate coupled with the same proportional reduction in hours worked will leave total earnings the same. If supply is backward bending and inelastic total earnings rise.

Checkpoint 29.2

The short run supply curve will be steeper than the long run supply curve indicating that it is less elastic. Thus if an industry wishes to hire more labour it will have to pay more in the short run to obtain a given quantity than in the long run. A given increase in wages is likely to attract a larger number of people in the long run than the short run. The converse is also true. A fall in wages is likely to result in fewer people leaving the occupation in the short run than in the long run.

Checkpoint 29.3

As pointed out in Chapter 28, the monopolist and the perfect competitor have different demand curves for labour. The *MRP* curve would have a steeper slope for the monopolist — see Figure 28.3 in Chapter 28.

During a recession, the demand for labour will decline. This could be modelled in Figure 29.5 by shifting the demand curve to the left. This will further increase the excess supply at the union wage, which makes it difficult for the union to push for wage increases.

Checkpoint 29.4

Demand for bus transportation is inelastic and most transport authorities make losses and are subsidised. One person buses offer a substantial opportunity to reduce labour costs and hence operating costs because labour productivity is doubled. Hence a likely outcome is a reduction in the number of people hired, because there is not sufficient demand for bus services even at lower fares to support the existing workforce. Hence workers expect to lose notwithstanding the increase in productivity. The more elastic demand, the more they are likely to gain in terms of employment.

Given the strong likelihood of reduced employment it is hardly surprising that unions have vigorously sought increased wages and conditions for their members to reward them for the increased productivity. Greater productivity means normally greater capacity to pay. In the case of buses and trains higher wage payments

to retained workers reduce the impact that improved technology makes on loss reduction policies.

Checkpoint 29.5

The purpose of this question is to illustrate the fact that more unpleasant jobs will have to have a higher wage rate in order to induce someone to take them.

CHAPTER 30

Checkpoint 30.1

Film stars and great professional athletes earn large economic rents because they typically do not have alternative employment opportunities that are nearly as lucrative. As a proportion of earnings, the economic rents earned by top business executives are most likely considerably smaller than those of film stars and great athletes because business executives have more lucrative alternatives, such as other top management positions.

To be consistent, Henry George would probably argue that the economic rents earned by individuals with unique skills should be taxed in the same way as economic rent on land.

A just position might recognise that gifted individuals must still work hard to develop their talents. As with the development of land, it is difficult to determine what is truly economic rent and what is the result of an individual's efforts to develop his or her innate abilities.

Checkpoint 30.2

A college education is a roundabout process because an individual typically gives up 4 years of full-time wages in order to acquire education and skills that will enable him or her subsequently to make higher wages than otherwise would be possible. One way to measure the rate of return on this investment would be to compare the lifetime earnings of college-educated and non-college-educated people and see what difference in earnings per year the 4-year college investment has made.

If people became less willing to save, the saving curve in Figure 30.6, part b, would shift to the left. This would decrease the long-run equilibrium stock of capital because the saving curve would intercept the vertical axis at a higher interest rate — that is, the long-run equilibrium interest rate would be higher, and therefore the long-run equilibrium capital stock would be less.

An increase in the rate of population growth would increase the rate of growth of the labour force and hence increase the potential productivity of capital. This would shift the demand for capital to the right and increase the long-run equilibrium stock of capital.

CHAPTER 31

Checkpoint 31.1
No firm conclusion can be drawn about real wage levels. It is quite possible that if the economy is growing rapidly the greater production of goods and services will provide labour and capital owners with greater rewards. If production of goods and services is declining, during recession, wages share may become greater even though real wages fall. In both cases it has been taken that the size of the labour force is unchanged. Obviously, per capita real wage levels can vary independently of aggregate real wage payments and the wages shares.

Checkpoint 31.2
The Lorenz curves should be drawn on the same diagram. The curve for the females sags further from the diagonal indicating a somewhat less equal distribution of income. We cannot conclude anything about whether women are getting close to receiving equal pay because the table tells us nothing about the levels of earnings. In fact the average (mean) income of women employees was $17,500 compared with $22,800 for men.

Checkpoint 31.3
It is reasonable to conclude that an individual's income will rise after entering the labour force, gaining work skills and benefiting from promotion. However, we conclude this using the data provided and our prior knowledge of how work is rewarded. It would be dangerous to conclude people earn less as they near retirement though some may do so. A few may be demoted, but others may opt for part-time work. Figure 31.3 provides information about numbers of people in different age groups at a single date. It does not map the income path of an individual over their working life. Nevertheless the great majority of people reach their income earning maximum in their thirties or early forties and then level off.

Checkpoint 31.4
A marginally progressive tax structure should make the distribution of after-tax income more equal than the distribution of before-tax income.

The 'baby boom' people began entering the work force in the late 1960s and have increased their experience and earning power with the passage of time. So one would expect the Lorenz curves for successive decades to show increasing income equality, other things being equal.

CHAPTER 32

Checkpoint 32.1

Although the pioneers probably would be subject to increasing costs and hence would have nonlinear production possibility frontiers, this problem is illustrated most simply with linear production possibilities frontiers like those used in the text's New Zealand and Australia example (Figure 32.1). If the two pioneers have differing abilities in the production of wood and wheat, then their production possibilities frontiers would have different slopes, reflecting different opportunity costs. Comparative advantage would lead to specialisation and trade, giving rise to trading possibilities frontiers for the two pioneers that lie above the two production possibilities frontiers. This would allow each pioneer to have more of both goods than they would have in the absence of specialisation and trade.

Checkpoint 32.2

Although Tasmania could produce sugar (from sugar beets) and Queensland can grow apples, climatic differences give rise to a comparative advantage for Queensland in sugar production and for Tasmanian apples — hence there is a specialisation in trade. Similarly Victoria is the centre of dairy production in Australia, whereas South Australia specialises in wine. Three states — Victoria, New South Wales and South Australia — are the centres of Australian manufacturing. Because of its favourable climate, Queensland attracts more tourists. Western Australia dominates in gold and iron ore production as a result of its geological form. You should be able to list a number of similar examples.

Both Queensland and Western Australia have export surpluses to the outside world (because of major mining activity).

Part of this surplus will be used to import commodities and services from New South Wales and Victoria.

Checkpoint 32.3

A reduction in tariffs would make imports cheaper to domestic consumers. Local firms would have to reduce prices and probably costs to maintain their market share. Those firms unable to do this might face closure. In confronting competition however they may be forced to add new capital intensive technology to maintain a competitive position. Firms which reacted in this positive way may find themselves internationally competitive for the first time. In such circumstances industries would change and their employment levels may even grow.

CHAPTER 33

Checkpoint 33.1

The Malaysian haircut is paid for with an Australian payment to Malaysia and hence is a debit on the current account. The birthday present is a private unrequited transfer and by convention is entered as a credit item on the current account. A balancing debit entry is made under unrequited transfers. If you finance the Volkswagen domestically, then Volkswagen is paid 'cash' for the car, and this constitutes an Australian payment to Germany and is a merchandise import debit on the current account. If you buy the car and finance it with Volkswagen, then Volkswagen is 'buying' your IOU for the amount of the purchase price, and this is a credit on the private capital account. As you pay off the loan, your payments will be debits on the private capital account. When the government buys French francs and finances the purchase with a liquid claim, this will be recorded as a credit item on the government's capital account because it is a payment received from France in exchange for the export of the Australian government's IOU.

Checkpoint 33.2

When one currency depreciates, it takes more of that currency to buy a unit of foreign currency. But of course this means that it takes less of the foreign currency to buy a unit of the first currency, and hence the foreign currency has appreciated.

The supply curve in Figure 33.1 is a demand curve for dollars in the sense that it is a schedule showing the quantity of francs that the French are willing and able to supply in exchange for dollars, which is the same thing as the quantity of dollars that the French are willing and able to purchase in exchange for francs. The demand curve in Figure 33.1 is a supply curve for dollars in the sense that it is a schedule showing the quantity of francs that Australians are willing and able to purchase in exchange for dollars, which is the same thing as the quantity of dollars that Australians are willing and able to supply in exchange for francs.

An Australian expansionary monetary policy will, *ceteris paribus*, increase the exchange rate of dollars for pounds (that is, it will take more dollars to buy a pound). This is because an expansionary monetary policy will increase money GDP in Australia and increase the demand for British imports. This will increase the demand for British currency to pay for these imports and will hence drive the equilibrium exchange rate upward when the demand curve for pounds shifts rightward.

A more restrictive British fiscal policy will, *ceteris paribus*, increase the exchange rate of dollars for pounds (that is, it will take more dollars to buy a pound). This

is because a restrictive British fiscal policy will decrease GDP in Britain and decrease British demand for Australian exports. This will decrease the supply of British pounds in the foreign exchange market, since fewer pounds are needed to be exchanged for Australian dollars to pay for Australian goods. The supply curve for British pounds will decrease (shift leftward), and the equilibrium exchange rate of dollars for pounds will increase.

Checkpoint 33.3

If a government wants to fix an exchange rate, it must be prepared to use its reserves to buy up the excess supply of currency at the fixed rate when the fixed rate is above the equilibrium and to supply the foreign market with currency equal to the excess demand when the fixed rate is below the equilibrium rate (this will increase its official reserves).

Balance of payments deficits and surpluses are inevitable under fixed exchange rates since as time passes, supply and demand curves in foreign exchange markets inevitably shift because of changing trade patterns and differing economic developments within each nation. Only occasionally will the equilibrium rate and the fixed rate happen to be equal — the rest of the time balance of payments deficits and surpluses will occur as the government has to intervene to maintain the fixed rate.

If a nation's currency was overvalued, then the fixed rate of exchange would be above the equilibrium rate and the nation would have to buy up the excess supply of currency continually at the fixed rate. This would continually draw down its official reserves. If the nation were to tighten its monetary policy, then its money GDP would decline and its demand for imports of foreign goods would decline. This would decrease the supply of its currency in foreign exchange markets and hence decrease the excess supply. This would decrease the drain on the nation's official reserves.

Checkpoint 33.4

Since one of the costs of inflation to a nation is a depreciation of its currency relative to that of nations with less inflation, nations that had easy monetary and fiscal policies would experience an increased balance of payments deficit. This is because the Bretton Woods system required a member nation to use its official reserves to prevent devaluation of its currency. Hence fiscal and monetary policies that encouraged inflation would cost a nation increased drains on its official reserves, and this would 'impose a certain amount of fiscal and monetary discipline on governments', since they could not allow their official reserves to be drained continuously.

CHAPTER 34

Checkpoint 34.1

It seems to be characteristic of human behaviour, at least in Western cultures, that the right to acquire and own property provides a strong incentive for people to work hard to achieve that end. Soviet experience with agricultural productivity on communes (large farms owned by the state) versus that on small plots that peasants are allowed to own individually appears to indicate that there is greater productivity where peasants own their own land. Both observation of human nature and evidence such as the Soviet experience suggest that property rights arrangements bear a close relationship to the system of incentives in an economy.

Checkpoint 34.2

You should be able to answer this checkpoint by going over a previous section of this chapter ('Socialism: Variations, Record, and Capitalist Rivalry') and using that material to compare and contrast Communism and social democracy.

Checkpoint 34.3

You should be able to answer this checkpoint by going over a previous section of this chapter ('Two Socialist Countries: China and Yugoslavia') and using that material to compare and contrast the economic systems of China and Yugoslavia. It would be useful to organise your answer in terms of the four features listed in Table 34.1.

Glossary

A

absolute energy reserves The world's total stocks of energy reserves, equal to the sum of proven reserves plus unproven reserves.

accelerationist view Holds that there is no stable long-run Phillips curve trade-off between the inflation rate and the unemployment rate, and that persistent attempts to stimulate aggregate to reduce the unemployment rate below the natural rate will cause an ever-increasing rate of inflation.

accelerator principle The relationship between changes in level of retail sales and the level of investment expenditures.

accounting profit Profit obtained by subtracting the firm's explicit costs from its total sales receipts. Does not consider any imputed costs.

ad valorem tax Sales tax or excise tax calculated as a flat percentage of the sales price of a good.

aggregate demand curv (AD) Shows the inverse relationship between the economy's total demand for output and the price level of that output.

aggregate supply curve (AS) Shows the amount of total output the economy's businesses will supply at different price levels.

antidumping law Law that sets a minimum price on an imported good such that if the import enters the country at a price below the minimum, the law triggers a government investigation of possible dumping.

arbitration Process for settling labour-management disputes: an impartial third party, whose decision is binding on both parties, acts as a judge.

arc elasticity Method of calculating the coefficient of elasticity in which the averages of the two quantities and the two prices are used as base points when computing the percentage changes in quantity and price.

authorised dealers Short-term money market dealers who have a special relationship with the Reserve Bank of Australia. They borrow money from people and firms wishing to keep it at call, and invest it in appropriate secure assets.

automatic stabilisers Built-in features of the economy that operate continuously without human intervention to smooth out the peaks and troughs of business cycles.

average cost pricing Setting the price on the basis of the average cost of production.

average fixed cost (AFC) Cost determined by dividing total fixed cost by the number of units of output.

average product Total output divided by the number of labourers required to produce that output.

average propensity to consume (APC) The fraction or proportion of total income that is consumed.

average propensity to save (APS) The fraction or proportion of total income that is saved.

average revenue Total revenue divided by the number of units sold.

average total cost (ATC) Cost determined by dividing total cost by the number of units of output.

average variable cost (AVC) Cost determined by dividing total variable cost by the number of units of output.

award rates of pay   Wage levels which are accepted in a formal bargaining agreement between employers' groups, unions and the Arbitration Commission.

B

balance of payments   A nation's total payments to other nations must be equal to, or balanced by, the total payments received from other nations.

balance of payments account   Record of all the payments made by a nation to other nations, as well as all the payments that it received from other nations during the course of a year.

balance of payments deficit   The excess of a nation's payments to other nations over the payments received from other nations, exclusive of government capital account transactions in official reserve assets; means that the government is reducing its holdings of official reserve assets or that the liquid claims of foreign governments against these reserves are increasing, or both.

balance of payments surplus   Excess of payments received from other nations over the payments made to them, exclusive of government capital account transactions in official reserves and liquid claims; means that the government is increasing its holdings of official reserves or its holdings of liquid claims on the official reserve assets held by foreign governments, or both.

balance on capital account   The difference between a country's sale and purchase of assets to the outside world during the current period.

balance on current account   The difference between payments received during the current period for the export of goods and services and payments made during the current period for the import of goods and services.

balance on merchandise trade   The difference between merchandise exports and merchandise imports.

balanced budget multiplier   The ratio of the amount of change in GDP to the change in government spending financed entirely by an increase in taxes; indicates that a simultaneous increase, or decrease, in government expenditures and taxes of a matched or balanced amount will result in an increase, or decrease, in GDP of the same amount.

balanced budget   A budget in which total expenditures equal total tax revenues.

bank note   Paper money issued by a commercial bank.

barrier to competition   Any circumstance that makes it difficult for a new firm to enter an industry. Examples are the exclusive ownership of a unique resource; economies of scale; and government-sanctioned protection in the form of patents, licences, copyrights, and franchises.

barter economy   Trading goods directly for goods.

basic wage   The concept of a fair and reasonable minimum wage introduced by the Australian Arbitration Court in 1907.

benefit-cost analysis   An examination of the benefits and costs associated with any government program; is based on the principle that any program should be carried on to the point at which the last dollar spent (the last dollar of cost) on the program just yields a dollar's worth of benefit.

bilateral monopoly   Market structure in which there is monopoly power on both the buyer's and the seller's side of the market.

black market   Market in which goods are traded (illegally) at prices above a government-imposed ceiling.

bracket creep   A process whereby inflation pushes people into higher marginal tax brackets as their nominal income rises due to inflation, even when their real income remains unchanged; it causes the proportion of their personal income paid in taxes to increase.

branding   Providing a product with distinguishing characteristics and marks so that it can be distinguished from others in the market place by consumers.

break-even point   Point at which the quantity of output produced by a firm is such that total revenue just equals total cost or, equivalently, where average revenue (price) equals average total cost.

Bretton Woods system   System of fixed exchange rates in which only the dollar was directly convertible into gold at a fixed rate of exchange; all other currencies were indirectly convertible into gold by virtue of their convertibility into the dollar. Also called the *gold exchange system*.

broad money   M3 plus borrowings from private sector by non-bank financial institutions less the latter's holdings of currency and bank deposits.

budget constraint   Straight line representing all possible combinations of goods that a consumer can purchase at given prices by spending a given-size budget. Also called *budget line.*

budget deficit   Expenditures are greater than tax revenues.

budget surplus   Expenditures are less than tax revenues.

building societies   Thrift institutions whose funds come predominantly by borrowing from members. These funds are lent primarily for the purchase of housing. Building societies are controlled by state legislation.

business cycles   The somewhat irregular but recurrent pattern of fluctuations in economic activity.

business fluctuations   Recurring phenomena of increasing and decreasing unemployment associated with decreasing and increasing output. Also called *business cycles.*

C

capital consumption allowance   See *capital depreciation.*

capital deepening   An increase in the stock of capital (machines, tools, buildings, highways, dams, and so forth) relative to the quantities of all other resources, including labour.

capital depreciation   The wearing out of capital, often measured by its decline in value. Also called *capital consumption allowance.*

capital gains taxes   Taxes levied on any gain one realises from selling an asset at a price greater than the original purchase price.

capitalism   Form of economic organisation in which the means of production are privately owned and operated for profit and where freely operating markets coordinate the activities of consumers, businesses and all suppliers of resources.

cartel   A group of firms that collude to set prices or share markets.

certificate of deposit (CD)   Special type of time deposit that depositor agrees not to withdraw for a specified period of time, usually 3 months or more.

ceteris paribus   Latin expression for 'all other things remaining the same.'

closed economy   An economy that does not trade with other nations.

coefficient of elasticity   Number obtained by dividing the percentage change in quantity by the percentage change in price.

coincidence of wants   The possibility of barter between two individuals that occurs when each has a good that the other wants.

collective bargaining   Process by which labour and management negotiate mutually acceptable wages and other conditions of employment.

collusion   Agreement by firms in an industry on pricing or other policies that substantially reduce competition between them in some way.

command economy   An economy in which the government answers the questions of how to organise production, what and how much to produce, and for whom to produce.

commercial bank   Bank that can create money in the form of a demand deposit (cheque account) by extending credit in the form of loans to businesses and households.

commodity composition of trade   The composition of a country's exports and imports by type of commodity.

company   Firm that has a legal identity separate and distinct from the people who own it.

comparative advantage   Theory holds that total world output is greatest when each good is produced by that nation which has the lower opportunity cost of producing the good — the nation is said to have a comparative advantage in that good.

complementary good   A good that tends to be used jointly with another good.

conglomerate   A firm that produces a wide variety of goods and services for a number of largely unrelated markets.

consumer price index (CPI)   A commonly used and widely publicised measure of the general level of prices in the economy, constructed as a weighted average of the prices of a market basket of goods and services purchased by a typical urban worker's family.

consumer sovereignty   The condition that exists when the basic decisions about what to produce (which products and services) and how much to produce are dominated by consumers acting individually or as households.

consumer surplus   The net benefit to customers of being able to buy units of a good more cheaply than the amount they were willing to pay.

consumption function   The relationship between the level of disposable income and the level of planned consumption.

copyright   Exclusive right granted to composers and writers that gives them legal control over the production and reproduction of their work for a certain period of time.

cost-push inflation   Inflation that occurs when suppliers of factors of production increase the prices at which they are willing to sell them.

craft union   A union of skilled workers trained in a particular trade or craft.

credit unions   Thrift institutions controlled by state legislation which operate predominantly by lending to and borrowing from members. Loans are for a variety of purposes and membership is often limited.

creditor   A person or organisation to whom money is owed.

crowding out   The reduction in investment spending that can occur as a consequence of an expansionary fiscal policy.

currency appreciation   A rise in the free-market value of a currency in terms of other currencies, with the result that fewer units of a currency will be required to buy a unit of a foreign currency.

currency depreciation   A fall in the free-market value of a currency in terms of other currencies; means that more units of a currency will be required to buy a unit of a foreign currency.

currency devaluation   A lowering of the level at which the price of a currency is fixed in terms of other currencies.

currency revaluation   A rise in the level at which the price of a currency is fixed in terms of other currencies.

cyclically adjusted budget   Equals the difference between the actual level of government spending and the level of tax revenue that would be collected if the economy were operating at a high-employment level of GDP.

D

debt instrument   Written contract between borrower and lender specifying the terms of the loan.

deduction   Reasoning from generalisations to particular conclusions; going from theory to prediction.

deflation   A general fall in prices that causes the value of a dollar measured in terms of its purchasing power to rise.

demand (current) deposit   A deposit from which funds may be withdrawn on demand and from which funds may be transferred to another party by means of a cheque.

demand curve   Graphic representation of the law of demand.

demand schedule   Numerical tabulation of the quantitative relationship between quantity demanded and price.

demand-pull inflation   Inflation that occurs because the economy's total demand for goods and services exceeds its capacity to supply them.

deposit multiplier   Assuming banks are fully loaned up, the multiplier is the reciprocal of the required reserve ratio.

depository institution   A financial institution that can create money in the form of a chequeable deposit (cheque account) by extending credit in the form of loans to businesses and/or households.

depreciation allowance   Funds set aside for the replacement of worn-out capital equipment.

depression   An unusually severe recession.

derived demand   Term used to characterise the demand for a productive factor because that demand is dependent upon, or derives from, the demand for the final product that the factor is used to produce.

differentiated oligopoly   Oligopoly in which each firm produces a product that is somewhat different from that produced by the other firms. Also called an *imperfect oligopoly*.

diminishing marginal rate of substitution   Characteristic of the behaviour of the marginal rate of substitution along an indifference curve, reflecting the fact that the more of good B a consumer has *relative* to good A, the more of good B the consumer is willing to part with in order to get an additional unit of good A.

direct relationship   Relationship between variables in which the value of each changes in the same way (both decrease or both increase).

diseconomies of scale Increasing long-run average total cost of production that results when a firm grows so large that it becomes cumbersome to manage.

disembodied technical change Change that takes the form of new procedures or techniques for producing goods and services.

disposable income (*DI*) Personal income minus personal taxes.

dividends Share of a firm's profits paid out to stockholders.

domestic factor incomes (*DFI*) That part of the value added by factors of production which accrues as income to their suppliers after allowing for consumption of fixed capital.

dumping Selling a product in a foreign market at a price below the cost of producing the product.

E

economic problem How to use scarce resources to best fulfill society's unlimited wants.

economic system The institutions, rules and decision-making processes used to organise and allocate a nation's scarce resources to produce and distribute goods and services to its citizens.

economic cost The alternative goods that must be forgone in order to produce a particular good. Also called *opportunity cost.*

economic efficiency Using available resources to obtain the maximum possible output.

economic growth An outward shift in the production possibilities frontier caused by an increase in available resources and technological know-how.

economic policy Proposed method of dealing with a problem or problems posed by economic reality that is arrived at through the use of economic theory and analysis.

economic profit Difference between the total revenue obtained for the firm's sales and the opportunity costs of all resources used by the firm.

economic theory A statement about the behaviour of economic phenomena, often referred to as a law, principle, or model.

economics 1. A social science concerned with the study of economies and the relationships among economies. 2. A social science concerned with the allocation of scarce resources between competing and insatiable ends.

economies of scale Decrease in the long-run average total cost of production that occurs when a firm's plant size is increased.

economy A particular system of organisation for the production, distribution, and consumption of all things people use to obtain a standard of living.

elastic demand Coefficient of elasticity is greater than 1.

elastic supply Coefficient of elasticity is greater than 1.

elasticity of demand Degree of responsiveness of quantity demanded to a change in price.

elasticity of supply Degree of responsiveness of quantity supplied to a change in price.

embodied technical change Technological change that is embedded in the form of the capital good itself.

equation of exchange A relationship between the economy's money supply M, the money supply's velocity of circulation V, its price level p, and total real output Q: states that the total amount spent, $M \times V$, on final goods and services equals the total value of final goods and services produced, $p \times Q$ — that is, $M \times V = p \times Q$.

equilibrium income level The level of total income that will be sustained once it is achieved. At equilibrium, the total income earned from production of the economy's total output corresponds to a level of total spending or demand just sufficient to purchase that total output.

equilibrium price Price at which market equilibrium is achieved.

equilibrium quantity Quantity of the good supplied and demanded at the point of market equilibrium.

equity The difference between a firm's total assets and its total liabilities.

escalator clause Clause in a labour contract that indexes wages to inflation by stipulating that wages must be periodically adjusted upward to keep pace with the rising cost of living.

excess reserves Total reserves minus required reserves.

exchange rate The price of foreign currency, or the amount of one currency that must be paid to obtain 1 unit of another currency.

excise tax   A tax levied on the sale of a particular good.

exclusion principle   Distinguishing characteristic of private goods, the benefits of which, unlike those of public goods, accrue only to those who purchase them.

expansion path   Shows the least cost combination of factors of production a firm will hire to increase production in the long run when factor prices are fixed.

expansion   The upswing of a business cycle.

expansionists   A term used by the authors of the *State of Play* series to describe economists in Australia who believe in a macroeconomic policy stance which assists or permits the economy to grow.

expected rate of return   The amount of money a firm expects to earn per year on funds invested in a capital good, expressed as a percent of the funds invested.

explicit costs   Direct monetary payments made by a firm to purchase or hire resources from outside the firm.

export subsidy   Government payments to an export industry to cover part of the industry's cost of production.

exports   The goods and services a nation produces and sells to other nations.

externalities   Costs or benefits related to a good or service that fall on others besides buyers and sellers of that particular good or service. Also called *spillovers, neighborhood effects, external costs or benefits, spillover costs or benefits, or external economies or diseconomies.*

F

factors of production   The inputs (land, labour, and capital) necessary to carry on production. Also called *economic resources.*

fair return   Pricing rule under which the price of a good is determined by the intersection of the average total cost curve with the demand curve.

fallacy of composition   Error in reasoning that assumes that what is true for the part is true for the whole.

fallacy of division   Error in reasoning that assumes that what is true for the whole is true for its individual parts.

fallacy of false cause   Error in reasoning that assumes one event is the cause of another event simply because it precedes the second event in time.

fiat money   Money that is declared by the government to be legal tender — it is neither backed by nor convertible into gold or any other precious metal.

financial intermediary   A business that acts as an intermediary by taking the funds of lenders and making them available to borrowers, receiving the difference between the interest it charges borrowers and the interest it pays lenders as payment for providing this service.

financial markets   Markets that take the funds of savers and lend them to borrowers.

firm   A business organisation that owns, rents, and operates equipment, hires labour, and buys materials and energy inputs. The firm organises and coordinates the use of all these factors of production for the purpose of producing and marketing goods and services.

fiscal drag   The tendency for leakages from the economy to rise when an economy is just coming out of a recession. This acts as a drag on economic recovery.

fiscal policy   Government's efforts to use its spending, taxing, and debt-issuing authority to smooth out the business cycle and maintain full employment without inflation.

fixed factor   Factor of production that cannot be changed in the short run.

fixed-dollar assets   Any kind of asset that guarantees a repayment of the initial dollar amount invested plus some stipulated rate of interest.

flexible (or floating) exchange rate   Exchange rate freely determined by supply and demand in the foreign exchange market without government intervention.

flow   A quantity per unit of time.

foreign exchange market   Market in which exchange rates between different currencies are determined.

fractional reserve banking   Managing a bank so that the amount of reserves on hand is equal to only a fraction of the amount of deposits.

free rider   Anyone who receives benefits from a good or service without having to pay for them.

fringe benefits tax   A tax introduced by the Hawke Labor Government on benefits associated with employment which previously had been tax free.

functional distribution of income   Method of characterising the way income is distributed according to the function performed by the income receiver.

G

GDP gap Potential GDP minus actual GDP which is equal to the value of goods and services not produced because there is unemployment.

general equilibrium analysis Analysis of the adjustments a change in one market will cause in each and every other market.

generics Brandfree or unbranded products offering cheapness and minimum package design.

gold standard A monetary system in which nations fix the rates of exchange between their currencies and gold and, hence, the exchange rates between their currencies.

government budget An itemised account of government expenditures and revenues over some period of time.

gross domestic product (GDP) The market value of all final goods and services produced in an economy during a given time period (usually a year).

gross domestic product at factor cost GDP Less indirect taxes plus subsidies.

gross national expenditure The sum of C, I and G.

gross private investment The total expenditures by business firms on new capital.

H

high-employment budget Difference between the actual level of government spending and the level of tax revenue that would be collected if the economy were at a high-employment level of GDP.

horizontal merger Merger between two firms selling the same, or very similar, products in the same market.

horizontally integrated Term used to describe a firm that owns several plants, each of which performs the same functions.

household disposable income (DI) HI less direct taxes, fees, fines, consumer debt interest and unrequited transfers to overseas.

household income (HI) Total income which a country's residents receive in a given period. It consists of wages, salaries and supplements, income from unincorpor-

ated enterprises, personal transfer payments and some transfers from overseas.

I

ideology Doctrine, opinion, or way of thinking.

implicit costs Costs of resources actually owned by the firm itself. These costs are the payments such resources could have received were they employed in their next best alternative.

import quotas Limitation on imports that specifies the maximum amount of a foreign-produced good that will be permitted into the country over a specified period of time.

imports The goods and services a nation purchases from other nations.

income effect A decrease in the price of a good allows the consumer to buy more of it even though the consumer's money income remains the same.

indexing Method of keeping the purchasing power of wages, taxes, and fixed-dollar, or nominal, assets constant by adjusting their dollar-denominated values to the change in the general price level.

indifference curve A graphical representation of an indifference schedule — the consumer gets the same level of satisfaction at any point along the curve.

indifference map All of an individual's indifference curves taken together.

indifference schedule A listing of all possible combinations of goods that give a consumer the same level of satisfaction.

indirect taxes Sales and excise taxes and business property taxes.

induction Reasoning from particular facts and observations to generalisations.

industrial union A union that seeks to organise all hourly paid workers, skilled and unskilled in a given industry.

inelastic demand Coefficient of elasticity is less than 1.

inelastic supply Coefficient of elasticity is less than 1.

inferior good A good that people typically want more of at lower income levels and less of at higher income levels.

inflation A rise in the general level of prices of all goods and services; this rise causes the purchasing power of a dollar to fall.

inside lags The time between when economic policy action is needed and when it is undertaken by government.

interdependence The quantity demanded for the product of one firm depends on the price it charges and the pricing policies of its rivals.

interest rate, or interest The price of borrowing money, or the price received for lending money, expressed as a percentage.

inventory A stock of unsold goods.

inverse relationship Relationship between variables in which the value of one increases as the value of the other decreases.

investment Expenditure on capital formation. Investment is a roundabout means of increasing production by diverting resources from the direct production of consumption goods to the production of capital goods.

involuntary unemployment Occurs when workers willing to work at current wage rates are unable to find jobs.

isocost line A line showing different bundles of goods that can be produced for the same cost or a line showing different combinations of factors of production that can be purchased for the same cost.

isoquant A line showing different combinations of factors that can be combined to produce a given quantity of a product (equal product curve).

isoquant map All of a firm's isoquants taken together. A simple graphical representation of a two factor production function.

J

job-training   programs Government-subsidised efforts aimed at improving work skills among the poor. Also called *manpower* programs.

K

kinked demand curve In Oligopoly firms sometimes believe they face a demand curve that is kinked at the current price, because they think rivals will react differently if they raise their price or lower it. Commonly the kink leads to a price stickiness.

L

labour contract Binding agreement between labour and management stipulating the terms of employment and the wages to be paid labour.

labour force All persons over the age of 15 who are employed, plus all those actively looking for work.

Laffer curve Shows a relationship between the marginal tax rate and the amount of tax revenue the government receives. In particular, starting from a zero marginal tax rate, tax revenues rise as the rate is increased up to some point beyond which further increases in the marginal tax rate cause tax revenue to decline.

laissez faire ('let [people] do [as they choose]') The belief that people should be allowed to conduct their economic affairs without interference from the government.

law of demand Theory that the lower the price of a good, the greater will be the demand for it and, conversely, the higher the price, the smaller will be the demand.

law of diminishing marginal utility Given the consumer's tastes, the marginal utility associated with the consumption of any good over a given period of time eventually begins to fall as more and more of the good is consumed.

law of diminishing returns As more and more of a variable factor of production is used together with a fixed factor of production, beyond some point the marginal product attributable to each additional unit of the variable factor begins to decrease.

law of increasing costs The cost per additional good obtained, measured in terms of the good sacrificed, rises due to the different productivity of resources when used in different production processes.

law of supply Theory that suppliers will supply larger quantities of a good at higher prices than they will at lower prices.

LGS convention An agreement between the Reserve Bank of Australia and the trading banks under which each trading bank agreed to conduct its affairs so that its LGS ratio did not fall below an agreed minimum percentage. This agreement began in 1956 and was discontinued in 1985.

licence Right granted, usually by a state, to practice certain professions or to produce certain goods.

limit price   The lowest price at which a new firm can enter an industry and just cover average total cost. Existing firms in the industry with lower average total costs can set price below the limit price level and discourage new entrants.

limited liability   Characteristic of a corporation that makes it attractive to investors (the owners) in that financial liability extends only to the assets of the corporation, not to personal assets of the investors.

liquidity   The degree to which any form of wealth is readily convertible into other goods and services; money is the most liquid form of wealth.

loan length   The duration of time until a loan must be repaid. Also called *maturity*.

long run   Period of time long enough so that the quantity of all factors used to produce a particular good can be changed.

Lorenz diagram   Method of illustrating the extent to which actual income distribution deviates from a perfectly equal distribution of income.

M

M1   Money defined as the sum of currency and deposits in cheque accounts at trading banks.

M2   Money defined as M1 plus all other deposits with trading banks.

M3   Money defined as M2 plus deposits with savings banks.

macroeconomics   Branch of economic analysis that focuses on the workings of the whole economy or large sectors of it.

managed float   Exchange rates subject to freemarket forces modified by government intervention, but without any formal commitment to fix rates at specified levels. Also called *dirty float*.

manpower programs   Job-training programs aimed at developing the job skills of the young and hard-core unemployed in order to increase their employability.

marginal cost   Change in total cost resulting from a unit change in output.

marginal cost pricing   Setting the price so that it is equal to the cost of producing the last unit of output.

marginal physical product   Increase in total revenue associated with each one-unit increase in a variable productive factor.

marginal product   Increase in total output that results from the addition of a unit of a variable factor of production.

marginal productivity theory of factor demand   Theory that states that a profit-maximising firm will increase its use of a productive factor up to the point where the factor's marginal revenue product equals the factor's price.

marginal propensity to consume (*MPC*)   The fraction or proportion of any change in income that is consumed — equals the slope of the consumption function.

marginal propensity to save (*MPS*)   Fraction or proportion of any change in income that is saved — equals the slope of the saving function.

marginal rate of substitution   Rate at which the consumer is just willing to substitute one good for the other along an indifference curve.

marginal revenue   Change in total revenue resulting from the sale of one more unit of output.

marginal revenue product   Increase in total revenue associated with each 1 unit increase in a variable productive factor.

marginal tax rate   Indicates how much of an additional dollar of income, the marginal or last dollar earned, must be paid in taxes.

marginal utility   The change in total utility that occurs with the consumption of an additional unit of a good.

market   An area or focus within which buyers and sellers of a particular good or service are in such close communication that the price of the good tends to be the same. It need not be confined to a specific geographical location.

market demand curve   The sum of all the individual demand curves for a good.

market economy   An economy in which the interaction of demand and supply on prices — the market mechanism — provides the information upon which firms and households make resource allocation decisions.

market equilibrium   Equilibrium established at the price where the quantity of the good buyers demand and purchase is just equal to the quantity suppliers supply and sell.

market period Period of time so short that none of the factors of production used to produce a particular good can be changed.

market structure Characteristics of market organisation, such as the number of buyers and sellers, the similarity of their product, and the ease of entry or exit from the industry.

marketability Ease with which a lender may sell a debt instrument to someone else before the loan must be repaid in full. Also called *liquidity*.

mediation Nonbinding advisory process for settling labour-management disputes in which an impartial third party attempts to reconcile differences.

merchant banks Money market corporations which raise most of their funds in the short-term market. They then undertake a wide variety of financing of business loans as well as investing in government bonds.

microeconomics Branch of economic analysis that focuses on individual units or individual markets in the economy.

middlemen Intermediate traders who stand between the producer and the consumer and perform a function in the marketing of the product.

minimum-wage law Law that makes it illegal for employers to pay workers a wage below a certain statutory level that is often called the minimum wage.

mixed economy An economy in which what, how, and for whom to produce goods are determined partly by the operation of free markets and partly by government intervention.

monetarism A school of thought that believes money is the main causal factor determining the level of economic activity.

money Anything that is generally acceptable in trade as a medium of exchange and that also serves as a unit of account and a store of value.

money GDP GDP measured in current prices or dollars.

money interest rate The interest rate calculated in terms of units of money, not purchasing power over goods.

money wage Price per unit of labour services measured in dollars and cents.

monopolistic competition Industry or market structure where there is easy entry and exit, and in which there are many firms, each of which produces a product that is slightly different from that of the others.

monopoly Form of market structure in which the entire market for a good or service is supplied by a single seller or firm.

monopoly power The capacity to act like a monopolist and to be an effective price maker even though there may be other firms in the industry.

monopsony Market structure in which one buyer purchases a good or service from many sellers.

multiplier The number of times by which the change in total income exceeds the size of the expenditure change that brought it about.

N

national disposable income (*NDI*) National income less net transfers to overseas.

national income (*NI*) The income received by a country's residents. It is GDP less net income paid overseas less depreciation allowances.

national turnover of goods and services The total annual flow of goods and services in the economy, free of duplication. It is equal to GDP plus imports of GNE plus exports.

nationalised industry An industry owned by the government.

natural monopoly Industry in which the economies of scale make it possible for an established firm effectively to prevent rivals from entering the industry.

natural rate of unemployment The existence of frictional unemployment and a certain amount of structural unemployment constitutes a natural rate of unemployment towards which the economy automatically gravitates in the absence of other disturbances.

near money Assets that are like money except that they can't be used as a medium of exchange, though they are readily convertible into currency or demand deposits.

near-public good A good that is consumed jointly, though it is possible to exclude nonpaying customers — a movie is an example.

negative income tax Tax plan through which households with incomes below a statutory level receive a subsidy from the government equal to some fraction of the difference between the statutory income level and their earned income.

net domestic product (*NDP*) The dollar value of GDP less the consumption of fixed capital (depreciation).

net exports The difference between the dollar value of the goods produced and sold to foreigners and the dollar value of the goods foreigners produce and sell to us.

net private investment The increase (decrease) in the economy's capital stock.

net productivity of capital The annual percentage rage of return that can be earned by investing in capital.

net worth See *equity*.

new classical view Holds that systematic monetary and fiscal policy efforts to affect real variables in the economy, such as total output (real GDP) and the unemployment rate, will be ineffective because people can predict and anticipate such systematic actions according to rational expectations theory.

nominal interest rate The real interest rate plus the anticipated rate of inflation.

nonprice competition Competition among firms for sales by means other than price cutting such as by advertising and product differentiation.

normal good A good that people typically want more of as their income rises.

normal profit Payments to financial capital and entrepreneurial skill that are just sufficient to keep them employed in a particular productive activity – that is, to keep them from leaving and going into some other productive activity.

normative statement A statement of what should or ought to be that cannot be supported or refuted by facts alone; a value judgment or opinion.

O

oligopoly A market dominated by a few sellers.

open economy An economy that trades with other nations.

open market operations The Reserve Bank's buying and selling of government securities in the open market in which such securities are traded.

opportunity cost The cost of a unit of a good measured in terms of the other goods that must be forgone in order to obtain it.

optimal allocation Resources are allocated in a technically efficient way and so as to maximise welfare for any given distribution of income.

output effect When the price of a factor falls (rises), the costs of production fall (rise), leading to a rise (fall) in the output of final product and a consequent increase (decrease) in the use of all factors.

outside lags The time between when economic policy action is taken and when the economy feels its major impact.

P

paradox of thrift If each household tries to save more, all households may end up saving and earning less.

partial equilibrium analysis Analysis of a change in one market and its consequences for that market, and possibly a few others. All other markets are assumed to remain unchanged.

partnership A firm owned and operated jointly by two or more individuals who are liable for its debts.

patent Exclusive right granted to the inventor to market a product for a certain period of time.

pattern of trade The flows of a country's exports to and imports from other countries.

peak The uppermost point in the upswing (expansion) of a business cycle.

per capita GDP An economy's GDP divided by the size of its population.

perfectly elastic Quantity of good demanded changed by an unlimited amount in response to a change in price.

perfectly inelastic Quantity of good demanded does not change at all in response to change in price.

Phillips curve An alleged relationship between the rate of inflation and the rate of unemployment suggesting that they tend to move in opposite directions to each other.

planned economy An economy in which an economic plan, designed by a central planning board, is used to inform, direct, and coordinate the activities of subunits such as firms.

plant A facility in which production takes place.

positive statement A statement of what is, was, or will be that can be verified or refuted by looking at the facts.

potential GDP What GDP would be if the economy were 'fully' employed.

poverty State in which an individual's or family's income and other means of support are insufficient to provide for basic needs.

precautionary demand The demand for money to cover unforeseen events or emergencies that require immediate expenditures.

predatory behaviour Actions by one firm directly intended to eliminate a rival firm.

predatory pricing Practice whereby a large firm, operating in many markets, can afford to sell at prices below costs in some markets until smaller competitors in those markets are driven out of business.

price ceiling Government-imposed upper limit on price.

price discrimination Selling the same good or service at different prices to different buyers.

price follower A firm that decides to base its pricing decision on those of the market leader rather than initiating changes itself.

price index Ratio of current prices to prices in some base year.

price leader A firm that is recognised by others in the industry as the one that will initiate price changes.

price maker A firm with the power to determine the price it will charge rather than one that has to accept the ruling market price.

price support Government guarantee to suppliers that they will receive a specific price for a good even if the market will not pay this price.

price taker A firm that must accept the sales price of its product as given by the market and beyond its control.

price The exchange value of a good in terms of other goods, most often expressed as the amount of money people will pay for a unit of the good.

Prime Assets Ratio (*PAR*) Each trading bank subject to the Banking Act undertakes to hold not less than 12 per cent of its Australian dollar assets in prime assets. These 'prime assets' include notes and coins, some balances with the Reserve Bank, Treasury Notes and other Commonwealth Government securities, and loans to authorised short-term money market dealers.

private final consumption expenditure Household expenditures on goods and services.

producer surplus The net benefit a producer obtains by obtaining a higher price for any unit than the additional cost incurred in producing that unit.

production possibilities frontier A curve representing the maximum possible output combinations of goods for a fully employed economy.

productivity The efficiency with which each labour hour combines with the capital stock and the existing state of technology to produce output — often measured as output per labour hour.

progressive tax A tax that takes a *larger* percentage out of high income that it does out of a low income.

proportional tax A tax that takes the same percentage of income no matter what the income level.

proprietors' income Income earned by the owners of unincorporated businesses.

proven energy reserves The quantities of oil, natural gas, and coal that producers are almost certain they can bring out of the ground given current energy prices and the state of mining and drilling technology.

public assistance programs Government programs aimed at providing help to dependent families, the sick, the handicapped, and the aged — those who for reasons largely beyond their control cannot work.

public debt The accumulation of all past deficits, less surpluses, of the government sector.

public goods Goods that will not be produced in private markets because there is no way for the producer to keep those who don't pay for the goods from using them — for example, a lighthouse beacon.

public sector borrowing requirement The deficit of a country's government sector during a given period.

public utility Natural monopoly whose operation, including the setting of prices, is regulated by a government agency.

pure market economy An economy in which what, how, and for whom to produce goods is determined entirely by the operation of markets.

pure public good A good that cannot be provided to one person without being provided to others — national defence is an example.

Q

quantity theory of money Asserts that velocity, v, in the equation of exchange, $M \times V = p \times Q$ is stable and not just whatever number is necessary to make the equation true; therefore, changes in the money supply M are asserted to cause proportional changes in money GDP, $p \times Q$.

R

rate base Allowable capital cost used in determining the prices that may be charged by a public utility.

rate of return Ratio of the dollar measure of a capital good's net productivity to the cost of the capital good expressed as a percentage per year.

ration coupon Coupon issued by government entitling an individual or household to buy a certain number of units of a good.

rational expectations theory Holds that people form their expectations about the future course of economic activity (wages, prices, employment, and so forth) on the basis of their knowledge, experience, and understanding of how the economy works (including the effects of systematic monetary and fiscal policy) and on all relevant economic data and information, and that they do not persist in making systematic mistakes when predicting future events.

real GDP GDP measured in terms of prices at which final goods and services are sold in some base year. Changes in real GDP are due only to changes in the quantity of final goods and services, not changes in price.

real interest rate The interest rate adjusted for inflation and contrasted with the nominal interest rate that makes no such allowance for rising prices.

real wage Price per unit of labour services measured in terms of the quantity of goods that can be purchased — often measured as the money wage divided by an index of the general price level.

realised investment Intended investment minus any unintended inventory reduction or plus any unintended inventory addition.

recession A contraction, or slowing down, in the growth of economic activity.

regressive tax A tax that takes a smaller percentage out of a high income than it does out of a low income.

rent control Government-imposed price ceiling on the rent a tenant may be charged.

required reserve ratio The ratio of required reserves to the total amount of demand deposits.

required reserves Reserves that a bank is legally required to hold against demand deposits – equal to the required reserve ratio multiplied by the amount of demand deposits.

reserves Cash held in the bank's vault and the deposits of the bank at the Reserve Bank of Australia.

resource misallocation See *underemployment.*

restrictionists A term used by the authors of the *State of Play* series to describe economists in Australia who believe that economic policy should fight inflation first, and avoid growth which may lead to a balance of payments crisis. Once inflation is overcome, the economy will be much more competitive and growth oriented.

restrictive licence Agreement under which the holder of a patent allows others to sell the product or use the process under restricted conditions (price limitations, quantity limitations, and so forth) stipulated in the licence.

retained earnings Money saved by businesses out of sales revenue.

risk Lack of complete information but the capacity exists to estimate the likelihood of each outcome occurring.

rival's reaction The price or nonprice responses to change in an oligopolist's policies.

roundabout process   Taking time and effort away from the direct production of goods for current consumption and using that time to produce capital goods that will ultimately make possible a larger subsequent production of goods than otherwise possible.

S

sales tax   A tax levied on the sale of any of a broad classification of goods.

saving function   The relationship between the level of disposable income and the level of planned saving.

saving   Refraining from current consumption.

savings bank   A thrift institution which accepts deposits from households in interest-bearing accounts. These are used to finance loans for housing and other activities. These banks are subject to the provisions of the Banking Act.

Say's Law   Supply creates its own demand.

scarce   Existing in a limited amount relative to wants.

scientific method   Ongoing cycle of induction from observation to theory, followed by deduction from theory to prediction, and explanation and checking of predictions and explanations against new facts to see if theory is verified, refuted, or needs to be modified.

seasonal variation   Regular patterns in economic data associated with custom and weather over the course of the year.

short run   Period of time short enough so that the quantity of one or more factors of production used to produce a particular good cannt be changed.

short-run production function   Relationship between the amount of a variable factor of production used and the total quantity of output produced.

single-tax movement   Late nineteenth-century movement, led by Henry George, to finance government by taxing the economic rent on land.

size distribution of income   The ranking of all families in the economy according to the size of the income received by each, lowest to highest, regardless of the source of their income.

slope of the demand curve   Change in price over some range of the curve divided by the change in quantity demanded over that same range.

social security system   A form of social insurance and public assistance to aid the old, the disabled, the sick, the unemployed, and families financially crippled by the death of the breadwinner.

social security tax   Tax on wages and salaries (shared equally by employee and employer) used to finance social security benefits.

sole proprietorship   A firm with a single owner who makes all decisions and bears full responsibility for everything the firm does.

Special Drawing Rights (*SDRs*)   Special accounts that the International Monetary Fund *(IMF)* creates for member nations, to be used as an official reserve to finance balance of payments deficits.

specialisation of labour   System of production in which each worker performs only one task for which he or she is specifically trained.

specific tax   Sales tax or excise tax calculated as a fixed amount of money per unit of good sold.

speculative demand   The demand for money that arises from the anticipation that bond prices are more likely to fall than to rise.

SRD ratio   This percentage ratio is set by the Reserve Bank, and may be varied from time to time as an instrument of monetary policy.

stagflation   The existence of high rates of inflation and unemployment at the same time.

Statutory Reserve Deposits *(SRD)*   Each trading bank is required to keep a specified percentage of its deposits in a low interest-bearing account at the Reserve Bank for security purposes.

subsidies   Payments to firms to undertake production of particular commodities or services.

subsistence living level   The minimum standard of living necessary to keep the population from declining — the death rate just equals the birthrate.

substitute good   A good that can be used in place of another good because it fulfills similar needs or desires.

supply curve Graphic representation of the law of supply.

supply schedule Numerical tabulation of the quantitative relationship between quantity supplied and price.

T

tariff A tax, normally on imports. A specific tariff is a tax of a fixed amount per unit irrespective of the value of the product. An *ad valorem* tariff is a fixed percentage of the value of a product.

tax incidence Distribution of the burden of a tax between the buyer and the seller.

technology The production method used to combine resources of all kinds, including labour, to produce goods and services.

terms of trade The ratio of exchange between an exported and an imported good.

time deposit A deposit at a trading bank that earns a fixed rate of interest and must be held a stipulated amount of time. Early withdrawal of funds is penalised, often by a loss of or a reduction in the interest rate earned.

token coins Coins that contain an amount of metal (or other material) that is worth much less than the face value of the coin.

total cost The sum of the firms total variable cost and total fixed cost at a given output level; the sum of the opportunity costs of the inputs used to produce that output.

total fixed cost *(TFC)* Cost of the unchangeable, or fixed, factors of production in the short run.

total revenue Quantity of the good sold multiplied by the price per unit.

total variable cost *(TVC)* Costs that the firm can vary in the short run by changing the quantity of the variable factors of production and, hence, the quantity of output produced.

total wage A wage rate which includes a 'basic wage' element and a skills margin.

trade credit Credit extended by one business to another business, allowing the latter to buy goods from the former without making immediate full payment by cheque or with currency. Serves as short-term medium of exchange though it is not a store of value like money.

trade weighted index An index of the value of a country's currency in terms of the currencies of its major trading partners.

trade-off The amount of one thing that a person (country) is willing to give up to obtain a specified quantity of another desired objective, quantity of a good, etc.

trading bank A financial institution which provides cheque account facilities and accepts deposits on the one hand, and loans money and provides overdraft facilities to its customers on the other. Trading banks can create money (and destroy it).

trading possibilities frontier Graphical representation of the choices that a nation has by specialising in the product in which it has a comparative advantage and trading (exporting) its specialty for the product in which it has a comparative disadvantage.

transactions costs The costs associated with converting one asset into another asset — brokerage fees, telephone expense, time and effort, advertising cost, and so on.

transactions demand Demand for money for its use as a medium of exchange to transact the purchase and sale of goods and services.

transfer payments Payments characterised by the fact that the recipient is neither expected nor required to provide any contribution to GDP in return.

Treasury bill A short-term government bond that matures 13 weeks after the day issued.

trough The lower turning point of a business cycle.

U

unanticipated inflation The amount of inflation that occurs that is unexpected.

uncertainty Lack of complete information and an inability to calculate the probability of an event occuring.

underemployment A condition in which available resources are employed in tasks for which other resources are better suited or in which the best available technology is not used in a production process. Also called *resource misallocation*.

undifferentiated oligopoly Oligopoly in which each firm produces the same product. Also called a *perfect oligopoly*.

undistributed profits Profits not paid out to shareholders (but still belonging to them). Undistributed profits are usually reinvested in the firm's operations.

unemployment A condition in which available factors of production are idle; in reference to labour, unemployment is said to exist whenever workers are actively looking for a job but are unable to find one.

unemployment benefits Payments to workers who are involuntarily unemployed (they want work but can't find a job).

union An organisation of workers that represents them collectively in bargaining with employers over wages and other terms of employment.

unit elastic Coefficient of elasticity equals 1. Also called *unitary elasticity*.

utility The service or satisfaction a good yields to the consumer.

V

value added The difference at each stage of production between what the firm sells its product for and what it pays for all the materials it purchases to make the product.

variable-dollar asset An asset that has no guaranteed fixed-dollar value.

velocity The number of times a typical dollar of the money stock must go around the circular flow of money exchanged for final goods and services during a year.

W

wage Price per unit of labour services.

wage-price controls Government-specified rate of increase in wages and prices that it is illegal for business and labour to exceed — compliance is mandatory.

wage-price guidelines Government-specified rate of increase in wages and prices that business and labour are requested not to exceed — compliance is voluntary.

wage-price spiral A process by which wage rises induce price rises which bring further wage rises and price rises. The process may continue unabated unless restrictive government policies are introduced.

wages drift The extend to which actual wages paid exceed award rates of pay.

Index